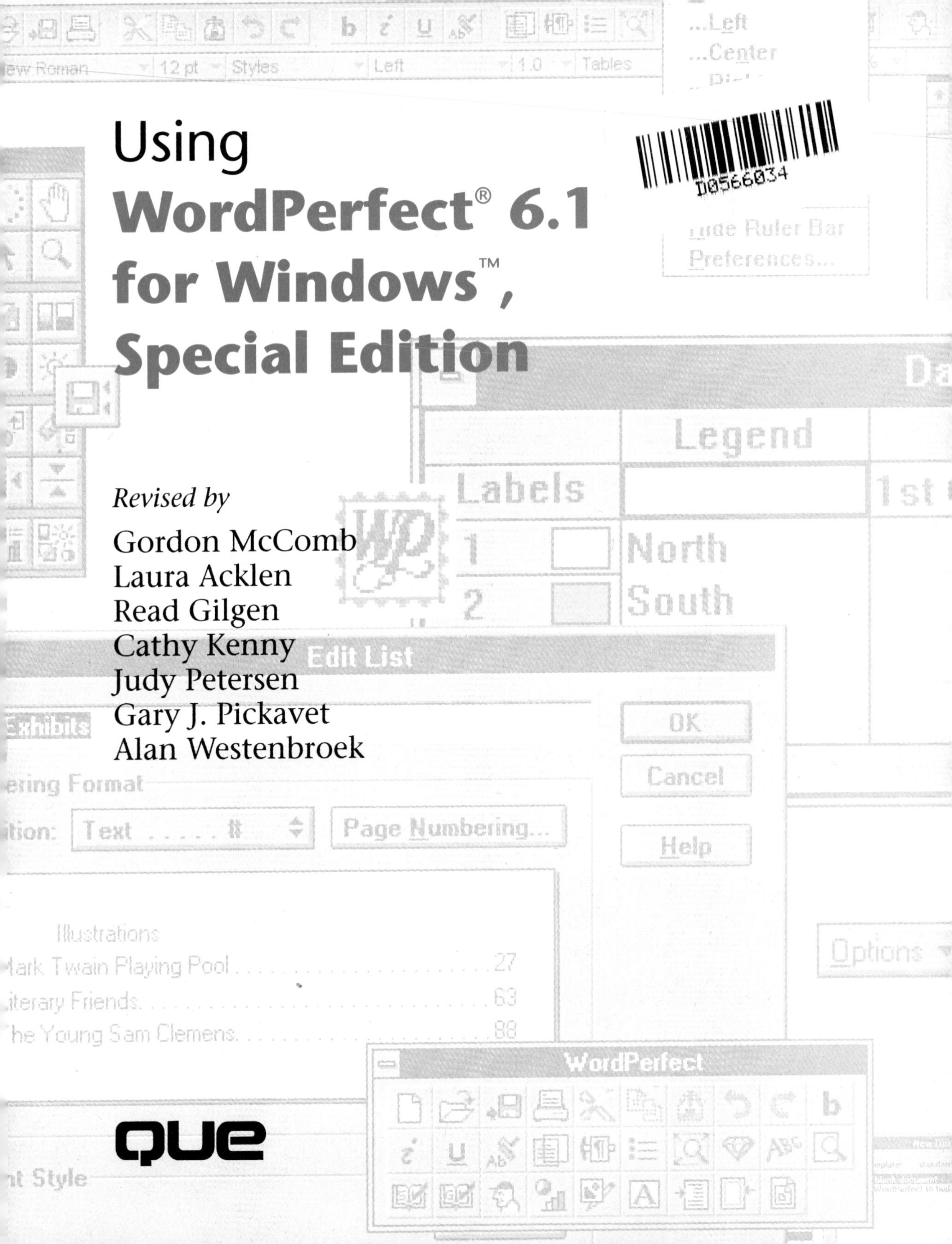

Using WordPerfect® 6.1 for Windows™, Special Edition

Revised by

Gordon McComb
Laura Acklen
Read Gilgen
Cathy Kenny
Judy Petersen
Gary J. Pickavet
Alan Westenbroek

QUE

Using WordPerfect 6.1 for Windows, Special Edition

Library of Congress Catalog No.: 94-69629

ISBN: 0-7897-0083-2

97 96 95 10 9 8

Interpretation of the printing code: the rightmost double-digit number is the year of the book's printing; the rightmost single-digit number, the number of the book's printing. For example, a printing code of 94-1 shows that the first printing of the book occurred in 1994.

Using WordPerfect 6.1 for Windows, Special Edition, is based on WordPerfect 6.1 for Windows.

Screen reproductions in this book were created with Collage Complete from Inner Media, Inc., Hollis, NH.

Publisher: David P. Ewing

Associate Publisher: Don Roche, Jr.

Associate Publisher—Operations: Corinne Walls

Managing Editor: Michael Cunningham

Credits

Publishing Manager
Nancy Stevenson

Acquisitions Editors
Deborah F. Abshier
Jenny L. Watson

Product Directors
Kathie-Jo Arnoff
Joyce J. Nielsen

Technical Editors
Mitch Milam
N. Christine Pichereau
Linda Hefferin
Joyce J. Nielsen

Production Editor
Lori A. Lyons

Editors
Lynn Northrup
Julie A. McNamee
Geneil Breeze
Charles K. Bowles
Lisa M. Gebken
Diana R. Moore
Nicole L. Rodandello
Maureen Schneeberger

Technical Specialist
Cari Ohm

Acquisitions Coordinator
Tracy M. Williams

Operations Coordinator
Patricia J. Brooks

Editorial Assistant
Jill Pursell

Book Designer
Paula Carroll

Cover Designer
Dan Armstrong

Production Team
Stephen Adams
Claudia Bell
Stephen Carlin
Maxine Dillingham
Chad Dressler
Karen L. Gregor
Aren Howell
Bob LaRoche
Elizabeth Lewis
Steph Mineart
Kaylene Riemen
Clair Schweinler
Mike Thomas
Tina Trettin
Donna Winter
Jody York

Indexer
Rebecca Mayfield

Composed in *Stone* and *MCPdigital* by Que Corporation

About the Authors

Gordon McComb is a WordPerfect specialist and consultant and the author of *WordPerfect 5.1 Macros and Templates,* which won *PC Magazine*'s Editors' Choice Award. He is also the author of Que's *I Hate Windows* and a contributing author of *Using WordPerfect Version 6 for DOS,* Special Edition, and *Using WordPerfect Version 6 for Windows,* Special Edition.

Laura Acklen is an independent author and instructor located in Austin, Texas. She has been training and supporting computer users in DOS and Windows products since 1986. Laura has written over 15 student manuals and instructor guides for the national training company, Productivity Point International. She is the author of Que's *WordPerfect 6.0 SureSteps* and co-author of *Oops! WordPerfect...What To Do When Things Go Wrong.* She is also a contributing author of *Using WordPerfect Version 6 for Windows,* Special Edition, and the revision author for *Windows QuickStart, 3.11 Edition.* Her most recent writing project is Que's *First Look at Windows 95.*

Eric Baatz has held a variety of managerial and programming jobs in the New England computer industry during the last 17 years. He has most recently been writing UNIX applications that deal with words and speech recognition. He was a contributing author of Que's *Using WordPerfect for Windows,* Special Edition; *Using MS-DOS 6,* Special Edition; *Using WordPerfect Version 6 for DOS,* Special Edition; and *Using WordPerfect Version 6 for Windows,* Special Edition.

George Beinhorn is a writer, editor, and commercial photographer. He serves as a document design consultant for business clients and may be reached through Que Corporation. He is a contributing author of *Using WordPerfect Version 6 for Windows,* Special Edition; the author of Que's *Using Professional Write Plus for Windows, Look Your Best with WordPerfect for Windows, Look Your Best with WordPerfect 5.1, Word for Windows Hot Tips, Upgrading to WordPerfect 6;* and is the revision author of *Using Q&A,* 4th Edition. He writes the "Pro Tips" word processing column and is a contributing author for *PC Computing* magazine.

Judy Felfe is the owner of Felfe Consultants, a personal computer training company in Houston, Texas. Judy has been a WordPerfect Certified Instructor since 1988. She has coauthored WordPerfect 6.0 DOS and WordPerfect 6.0 Windows books for Que Corporation.

Pat Freeland is a Design-Verification Engineer with Lotus Development Corporation and a former public-school teacher and software trainer. He has written articles for *PC World Lotus Edition* and written or contributed to several books on using computer software, including Que's *1-2-3 Release 4 for Windows QuickStart* and *Using WordPerfect Version 6 for Windows*, Special Edition. He lives with his wife, two children, and two dogs in Hingham, Massachusetts, near Boston.

Read Gilgen is Director of Learning Support Services at the University of Wisconsin, Madison. He holds a Ph.D. in Latin American Literature. His professional interests include support of higher education, especially foreign language education. He has taught and written extensively on DOS and WordPerfect. He is author of Que's *WordPerfect for Windows Hot Tips*, and contributing author to Que's *Using WordPerfect Version 6 for Windows*, Special Edition, and a frequent contributor to *WordPerfect for Windows* Magazine.

Rick Hellewell is a microcomputer specialist for the city of Sacramento. At home, he is the resident "computer guru," working as a part-time consultant. His wife, Pam, and three children, Christine, Jason, and Stacy, know that they can find him in the home office staring at his computer for hours at a time. Rick is a contributing author of *Using WordPerfect Version 6 for DOS*, Special Edition, and *Using WordPerfect Version 6 for Windows*, Special Edition.

Cathy Kenny is an associate technical editor for *PC World Lotus Edition*. Before joining *PC World*, Kenny produced training materials for a microcomputer training company in Boston. She has also served as technical editor on more than 100 books for Que and Howard W. Sams.

Mitch Milam is the president of Milam Enterprises, a Dallas-based consulting firm specializing in WordPerfect Corporation products. He has written articles that feature WordPerfect for *The WordPerfectionist* and *Law Office Computing* and has acted as technical editor on several books published by Que. Mitch has been active in the WordPerfect community since 1988.

Gordon Nelder-Adams is the WordPerfect expert for the Sacramento PC Users Group and a computing assistant at the University of California, Davis. He is the leader of the WordPerfect Special Interest Group for both organizations. Gordon has used WordPerfect extensively since Version 4 and has been a beta tester for many WordPerfect products. He was a contributing author of Que's *Using WordPerfect Version 6 for Windows*, Special Edition, and *Using WordPerfect Version 6 for DOS*, Special Edition.

Judy Petersen provides software training and support privately and through a retail facility. In her own business, Judy is a lawyer, computer software consultant, and trainer for businesses and individuals in the Tallahassee area. She is a contributing author of Que's *Using WordPerfect Version 6 for Windows*, Special Edition; *Using WordPerfect Version 6 for DOS*, Special Edition; *Killer WordPerfect 6 Utilities*; *Upgrading to Windows 3.1*; *Killer Windows Utilities*; and *Using PC Tools for Windows*, Special Edition. She also was a revision author for *Using PC Tools 8*, Special Edition. She recently was the revision author of *Que's Computer User's Dictionary*, 5th Edition.

Gary J. Pickavet is the Assistant Superintendent for Business and Data Processing Services for the Santa Barbara County Education Office. His wife Marilyn, daughter Debbie, and son Gary Jr. know his Que projects are truly family projects. Gary has used WordPerfect extensively since version 3.0. As an author, he contributed to the Que books *Using WordPerfect Version 6 for Windows; Using WordPerfect Version 6 for DOS*, Special Edition; *Upgrading to Windows 3.1*, and *Killer Windows Utilities*. He has also served as technical editor for several books for Que.

Susan Plumley owns and operates Humble Opinions, a consulting firm that offers training in popular software programs and network installation and maintenance. Sue is the author of nine Que books, including *Crystal Clear DOS*, *Crystal Clear Word 6*, and *Microsoft Office Quick Reference;* and coauthor of ten additional books, including *Using WordPerfect Version 6 for DOS*, Special Edition; *Using OS/2 2.1*, Special Edition; and *Using Microsoft Office*, Special Edition.

Anthony W. Rairden is the principal in Rairden Associates, a strategic marketing consulting firm based in Nashville, Tennessee. He also has provided computer systems consulting for many of his marketing consulting clients. A microcomputer user since 1980, he is a longtime WordPerfect user with extensive experience using and beta-testing WordPerfect Corporation products.

Steven M. Schafer is a publishing manager at Que Corporation. He has a wealth of WordPerfect knowledge and was formerly the editor of the international newsletter *The WordPerfectionist*. He was also a contributing author for *Using WordPerfect Version 6 for DOS*, Special Edition; and *Using WordPerfect Version 6 for Windows*, Special Edition.

C. Brian Scott is the managing shareholder of the Portland, Oregon law firm of Danner, Scott & Martin P.C. A user of WordPerfect since version 4.0, he has used WordPerfect to create several law practice applications and innumerable forms. He was a contributing author of Que's *WordPerfect Tips, Tricks,* *and Traps*, 2nd Edition; *Using WordPerfect 5.1*, Special Edition; *WordPerfect 5.1 Tips, Tricks, and Traps*, 3rd Edition; *Using WordPerfect Version 6 for DOS*, Special Edition; and *Using WordPerfect Version 6 for Windows*, Special Edition.

Alan Westenbroek is a teacher and researcher for Datastorm Technologies, Inc., a communications software company in Columbia, MO. He also consults and lectures on communications and spends all his free time surfing the Internet and writing books about surfing the Internet.

Rick Winter is a Senior Partner at PRW Computer Services. He is President of Information Systems Trainers, a nonprofit organization of trainers in the Denver Metro area. Rick has trained over 2,600 adults on personal computers. Rick is a contributing author for Que's *Using Microsoft Office*, Special Edition; *Using Excel Version 5 for Windows*, Special Edition; *Using WordPerfect Version 6 for Windows*, Special Edition; and *Using PC Tools 8*. Rick won the Rocky Mountain Chapter Society for Technical Communication's Distinguished Award for his work on Que's *Excel for Windows SureSteps*. Rick has also written course manuals for Lotus 1-2-3, WordPerfect, Windows, Word, Excel, and Q&A.

Trademark Acknowledgments

Contents at a Glance

Basic Tasks

Automating Your Work

Specialized Procedures

Professional Output

Large Documents

Becoming an Expert User

Appendixes 1089

Appendixes

Contents

III Specialized Procedures 467

14 Working with Text Columns 469

15 Organizing Documents with Outlining 493

19 Assembling Documents with Merge and Sort 623

IV Professional Output 667

20 Using Fonts and Special Characters 669

22 Using WP Draw and TextArt 735

VI Becoming an Expert User 953

28 Advanced File Management 955

29 Advanced Macro Techniques 991

VII Appendixes 1089

A Installing and Setting Up WordPerfect 6.1 for Windows 1091

B Making the Transition to WordPerfect 6.1 for Windows 1113

Introduction

Using WordPerfect 6.1 for Windows, Special Edition, is a collaboration of a number of WordPerfect and Windows experts. It provides extensive coverage of all WordPerfect's features and combines tutorial steps with reference information. The authors have made this book unique among books about WordPerfect for Windows because this book is a collaboration in the best sense of the word.

Why a collaboration? When you need to accomplish a complex and difficult job on a tight schedule, an excellent strategy is to pull together a team of experts, each one specializing in a particular aspect of the overall discipline. The resulting product in a collaborative effort can be superior to even the best efforts of any individual contributor. This collaborative book on WordPerfect 6.1 for Windows pools the knowledge of a range of WordPerfect experts—all experts in particular areas or applications.

As software companies adapt their programs to work with graphical user interfaces (GUIs) and as word processors become increasingly complex, powerful, feature-laden, and useful to a diversity of users, the need for in-depth expertise across a range of experience becomes clear. This kind of coverage is unavailable in a single-author book. Only a team of experts can adequately cover a program as advanced, complex, and versatile as WordPerfect 6.1 for Windows.

WordPerfect 6.1 for Windows Enhancements

WordPerfect 6.1 for Windows is the newest version of WordPerfect's Windows product since Version 6.0 was released in 1993. This version brings many new features and enhancements that promise to make WordPerfect 6.1 for Windows the most versatile and powerful Windows word processor.

If you were a WordPerfect 5.2 for Windows user, the principal added features and enhancements in Version 6.1 enable you to do the following:

- Run the Tutorial for an introduction to the basics of WordPerfect for Windows.
- Create and expand Abbreviations for frequently used words and phrases.
- Assemble a variety of graphs (for example, pie or bar) with the Chart feature.
- Use the Coaches feature in the Help system for a step-by-step guide to complete a task.
- Delay the action of certain codes for a specified number of pages with Delay Codes.
- Choose from additional document summary fields (a total of 51) to customize the summary information.
- Fax documents from within WordPerfect for Windows.
- Insert floating cells (single table cells with full spreadsheet capabilities) anywhere in a document.
- Create hidden text to be displayed only when necessary.
- Insert hypertext links to jump to different sections of the document or to another document.
- Select from two new interface bars—power bars and feature bars—and an enhanced status bar and new Toolbars.
- Search through files with an improved QuickFinder program and automate the update of index files with the new Kickoff program.
- Edit document text as well as headers, footers, footnotes, and page numbers with Page Mode.
- Copy fonts, font attributes, and paragraph styles from one section of text to another with QuickFormat.
- Double-click codes to quickly access the appropriate dialog box where changes can be made.
- Access QuickMenus by clicking the right mouse button in different areas of the document window.

- Record and attach sound clips to a document.
- Create mini-spreadsheets with over 100 predefined spreadsheet functions in tables.
- Automatically print pages in booklet format with Subdivide Pages.
- Create and use "boilerplate" documents with the Template feature.
- Assign special effects (color, shapes, shadowing) to text with TextArt.
- Create and edit graphics images with WP Draw, a scaled-down version of WordPerfect Presentations.
- Automatically insert typographically correct *smart quotes* (curly quotes) when you press the " (quote) key.

If you were a WordPerfect 6.0 for Windows user, you'll find many additional features that make version 6.1 a snap to use:

- Quicker access to features with an easier-to-use streamlined interface, along with an improved Power Bar and Toolbar. (In versions 5.2 and 6.0 of WordPerfect, Toolbars were called Button Bars.)
- Insert drop caps effortlessly at the beginning of paragraphs.
- Choose from among several dozen premade table formats using WordPerfect's Table Expert.
- Create instant letters using the Letter Expert, which consists of over two dozen "fill-in-the-blank" business letters.
- Create and edit graphics "in place" using Windows OLE 2.0 technology. By "in place," you no longer need to switch between WordPerfect and a separate graphics program—everything is done in the WordPerfect document!
- Undo up to 300 of the most recent editing steps you've made.
- Reformat documents automatically so that the text better fits within a defined number of pages. WordPerfect does all the work!
- Build custom dialog boxes in macros with the Macro Dialog Editor.
- Quickly switch from a competing word processor (such as Microsoft Word) using the Upgrade Advisor.

Who Should Use This Book?

WordPerfect for Windows is based to some degree on the best-selling WordPerfect for DOS. If you have never used any version of WordPerfect, this book's complete coverage of program features and its mix of step-by-step procedures with reference information, real-world examples, and clear instructions can help you master WordPerfect quickly.

If you're upgrading from WordPerfect 5.2 or 6.0 for Windows, this book can help you make the transition to the newest version of WordPerfect for Windows. Appendix B, "Making the Transition to WordPerfect 6.1 for Windows," addresses the costs of upgrading, improvements to existing features, new features, changes in menus, and the enhancements made when Novell (formerly known as WordPerfect Corporation) released WordPerfect for Windows, Version 5.2. Experienced WordPerfect users will appreciate the tips, notes, cautions, Power Bar, and Toolbar ideas in each chapter.

Note

To ensure your success with WordPerfect 6.1 for Windows, you should have a basic understanding of Windows 3.1. This book assumes that you are familiar with Windows. As you learn about WordPerfect in Chapter 1, "Getting Started," you also learn about Windows. If you are new to Windows, however, you might want to consult any of the following books published by Que Corporation for information on Windows basic operation: *Easy Windows for Version 3.1*; *Windows VisiRef*, 3.11 Edition; or *Using Windows 3.11*, Special Edition.

How To Use This Book

Using WordPerfect 6.1 for Windows, Special Edition, is designed to complement the reference manual and workbook that come with WordPerfect. Beginners will find the step-by-step information in this book helpful; experienced users will appreciate the comprehensive coverage and expert advice. After you become proficient with WordPerfect 6.1 for Windows, you can use this book as a desktop reference.

Each chapter in this book focuses on a particular WordPerfect operation or set of operations. Overall, the book begins by showing you the steps typical of any document's creation (such as entering text, checking spelling and grammar, and printing) and leads you to more specialized topics (such as macros, styles, equations, and integrating text and graphics). *Using*

WordPerfect 6.1 for Windows, Special Edition, distills the real-world experience of many WordPerfect experts, making this book workplace-based and task-oriented.

The tips included in the book's margins either point out information often overlooked in the documentation or help you use WordPerfect more efficiently. You will find many of these tips useful or pertinent as you become more comfortable with the software. Cautions alert you to potential problems you should avoid. In *Using WordPerfect 6.1 for Windows*, Special Edition, figure captions do far more than merely label a screen illustration, such as "The Font Dialog Box." They have been designed to provide enough explanation and description to allow some readers to look at the illustration, read the caption, skim the text, and complete a task without having to read an entire section.

If you run into trouble, check for the special Troubleshooting sections found throughout the book. These sections highlight many of the more common problems that can occur when using specific features of WordPerfect, and what to do about them. See Appendix C, "Index of Common Problems," for a compilation of the topics found in the troubleshooting sections.

How This Book Is Organized

This book is organized to follow the natural flow of learning how to use WordPerfect 6.1 for Windows. *Using WordPerfect 6.1 for Windows*, Special Edition, is divided into seven parts:

Part I: Basic Tasks

Part II: Automating Your Work

Part III: Specialized Procedures

Part IV: Professional Output

Part V: Large Documents

Part VI: Becoming an Expert User

Part VII: Appendixes

Part I introduces you to WordPerfect 6.1 for Windows and explains how to use WordPerfect to accomplish a range of basic word processing tasks as you complete the cycle of document preparation: planning, creating, editing, formatting, printing, and checking the spelling and grammar of documents. In Part I, you also learn how easy it is to insert graphic images into WordPerfect.

Part II shows you how to take advantage of a number of WordPerfect features to streamline your work. You see how to change default program settings, use styles to automate document formatting, use templates to create forms, use macros to automate repetitive tasks, and use the innovative Toolbar to place frequently used commands and macros on buttons for instant access.

Part III covers more specialized word processing techniques, such as working with text columns, creating tables, organizing documents with collapsible outlining, creating and modifying charts, importing data and working with other programs, and generating mass mailings with merge and sort.

Part IV focuses on high-quality printed output and WordPerfect's capabilities as a desktop publishing system. This part of the book begins with a look at using fonts and special characters. It takes you through customizing graphics lines, borders, and boxes and editing graphic images. You also will learn how to use the WP Draw and TextArt applets to create graphics images. Part IV includes a brief primer on page layout, choosing fonts, using color, and advanced printing techniques. This section wraps up with using the Equation Editor for scientific or mathematical publications.

Part V is especially useful to those who must work with large documents. You see how to annotate documents with footnotes and endnotes, as well as with document reference tools such as tables of contents, lists, indexes, tables of authority, and cross-references.

Part VI is designed for users who want to gain more expertise with WordPerfect. This section begins with advanced file management techniques using QuickFinder and QuickList; discusses advanced macro commands; provides additional coverage of the tables feature, particularly the spreadsheet capabilities; and concludes with an explanation and demonstration of the user of hypertext links and sound clips to create interactive business documents.

Appendix A covers installation, program setup, and WordPerfect's start-up options. Appendix B, designed for WordPerfect 5.2 for Windows users, covers enhancements and new features added to WordPerfect 6.1 for Windows.

Appendix C serves as an index to the common problems you may encounter while using WordPerfect and lists where in the book you can find solutions to these problems.

Where To Find Help

If you find yourself stymied on a particular point, WordPerfect's built-in Help feature may answer your questions. Help is explained in Chapter 1. In addition, you can turn to this book or WordPerfect's manual and workbook for help.

Should all else fail, Novell provides toll-free telephone support. Call the appropriate number in the following list to receive assistance.

Customer Support, 7 a.m. to 6 p.m. (MST) M-F:

Features	(800) 228-1029 (801) 228-9907
Graphics/Tables/Equations	(800) 228-6013 (801) 228-9907
Installation	(800) 228-6076 (801) 228-9907
Macros/Merge/Labels	(800) 228-1032 (801) 228-9907
Laser/PostScript Printers	(800) 228-1023 (801) 228-9907
Printers other than Laser or PostScript	(800) 228-1017 (801) 228-9907
Networks	(800) 228-6066 (801) 228-9907
FAX Support	(801) 222-4377
After Hours Support	(801) 228-9010
After Hours Schedule (MST):	
Monday	2:00 a.m. to 7:00 a.m. (after midnight on Sunday)
Monday - Thursday	6:00 p.m. to 7:00 a.m.
Friday	6:00 p.m. to 10:00 p.m.
Saturday	8:00 a.m. to 4:00 p.m.
Sunday	Not available

Novell maintains an electronic bulletin board service, which is also a source of information and assistance:

IBM 1200/2400 baud (24 hours)	(801) 225-4414
IBM 9600 baud (24 hours)	(801) 224-4444
Voice Only	(801) 228-9904

Additional on-line help for WordPerfect for Windows is available through an electronic forum on CompuServe Information Service (CIS). WPUSERS is managed by Support Group Inc., an independent group not affiliated with WordPerfect Corporation. There is also a WPFILES forum exclusively used for WordPerfect files, such as current printer drivers, video drivers, and utilities.

For up-to-date information on WordPerfect 6.1 for Windows, read *WordPerfect for Windows Magazine*, an excellent monthly magazine filled with tips, feature articles on WordPerfect, product information, answers to all types of problems, a disk of the month, and other timely and useful information of interest to WordPerfect users. The magazine is available at many magazine newsracks and bookstores; or you can subscribe to *WordPerfect for Windows Magazine* at the following address:

WordPerfect for Windows Magazine
MS-3232
1555 N. Technology Way
Orem, UT 84057-2399
(801) 228-9626

The WPMAG forum on CompuServe provides technical support for articles that appear in *WordPerfect Magazine* and *WordPerfect for Windows Magazine.*

Conventions Used in This Book

The conventions used in this book have been established to help you learn to use the program quickly and easily. Instructions in this book emphasize use of the mouse to access commands, make choices in dialog boxes, and so forth. WordPerfect enables you to use both the keyboard and the mouse to select menu and dialog box items: you can press a letter (or number) or you can select an item by clicking it with the mouse. The letter or number you press appears in boldface: Choose **P**rint. If you use a mouse with WordPerfect, you place the mouse pointer on the relevant menu or dialog box item and click the left mouse button to make your selection. Instructions for navigating in WordPerfect for Windows appear in Chapters 1 and 2.

The following examples show typical command sequences (note that a semicolon is used to set off the alternate function-key interface):

> Choose **E**dit, **G**o To; or press Ctrl+G.
>
> Choose Fo**r**mat, **F**ont; or press F9. Then choose **B**old.

Uppercase letters are used to distinguish file names, macro names, and merge commands, such as HLINE.WCM. In most cases, the keys on the keyboard are represented as they appear on your keyboard (for example, J, Enter, Tab, Ctrl, Ins, and Backspace). For keystrokes separated by plus signs, such as Speller (Ctrl+F1), hold down the first key (Ctrl in this example) and press the second key (F1 in this example) to invoke the command. When a series of keys is separated by commas, press and release each key in sequence. For example, to move to the beginning of the line before any hidden codes, press Home twice (Home, Home).

WordPerfect also provides a Power Bar and various Toolbars for your convenience. By clicking a button from either the Power Bar or one of the Toolbars, you can execute a command or access a dialog box. Chapters in this book often contain Toolbar button icons in the margins, like the one shown here, indicating which button you can click to perform the task at hand.

Text you are asked to type is shown in **boldface**. On-screen messages and WordPerfect hidden codes are shown in monospaced font: `[Left Tab]`. Special words or phrases defined for the first time appear in *italic* type.

Part I

Basic Tasks

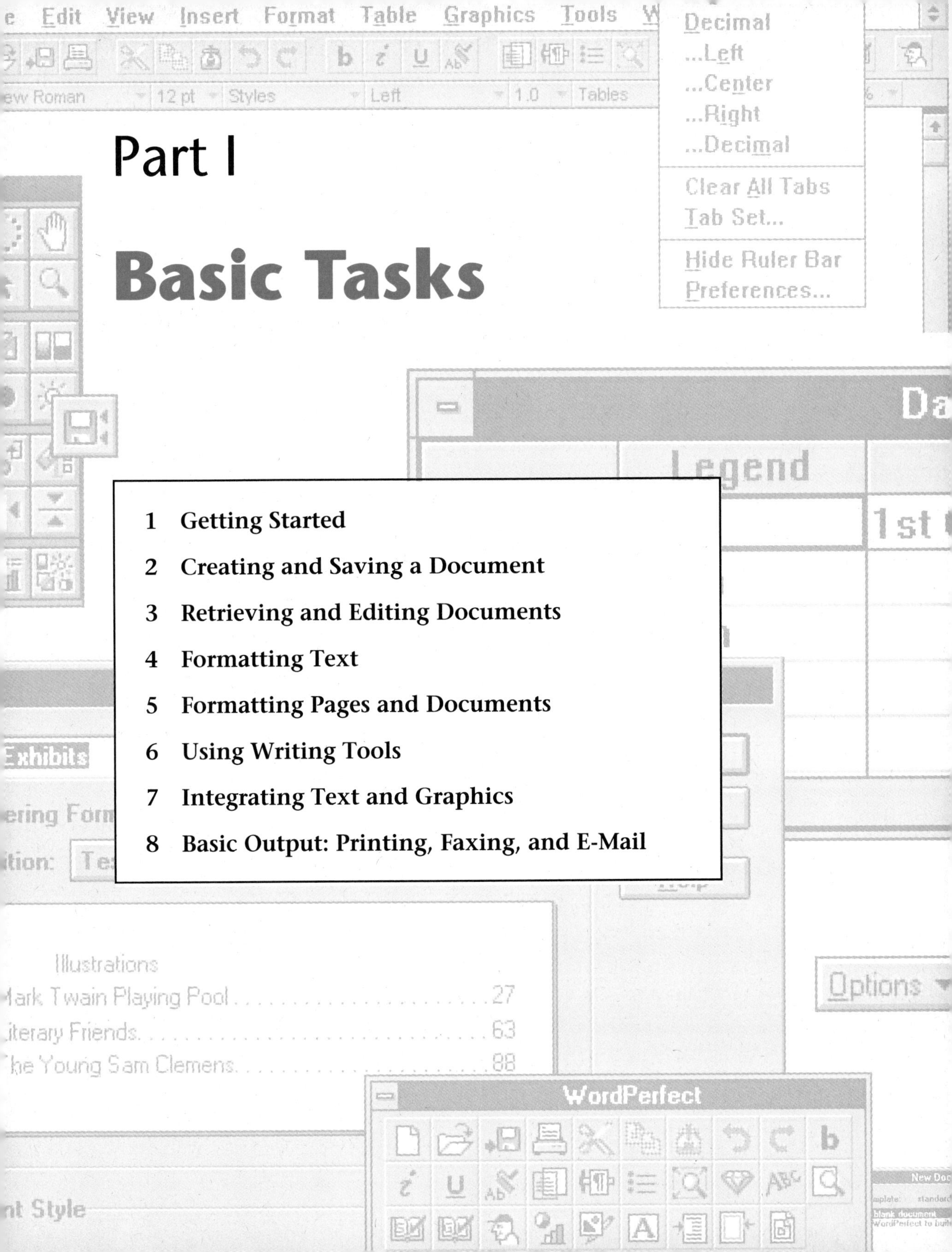

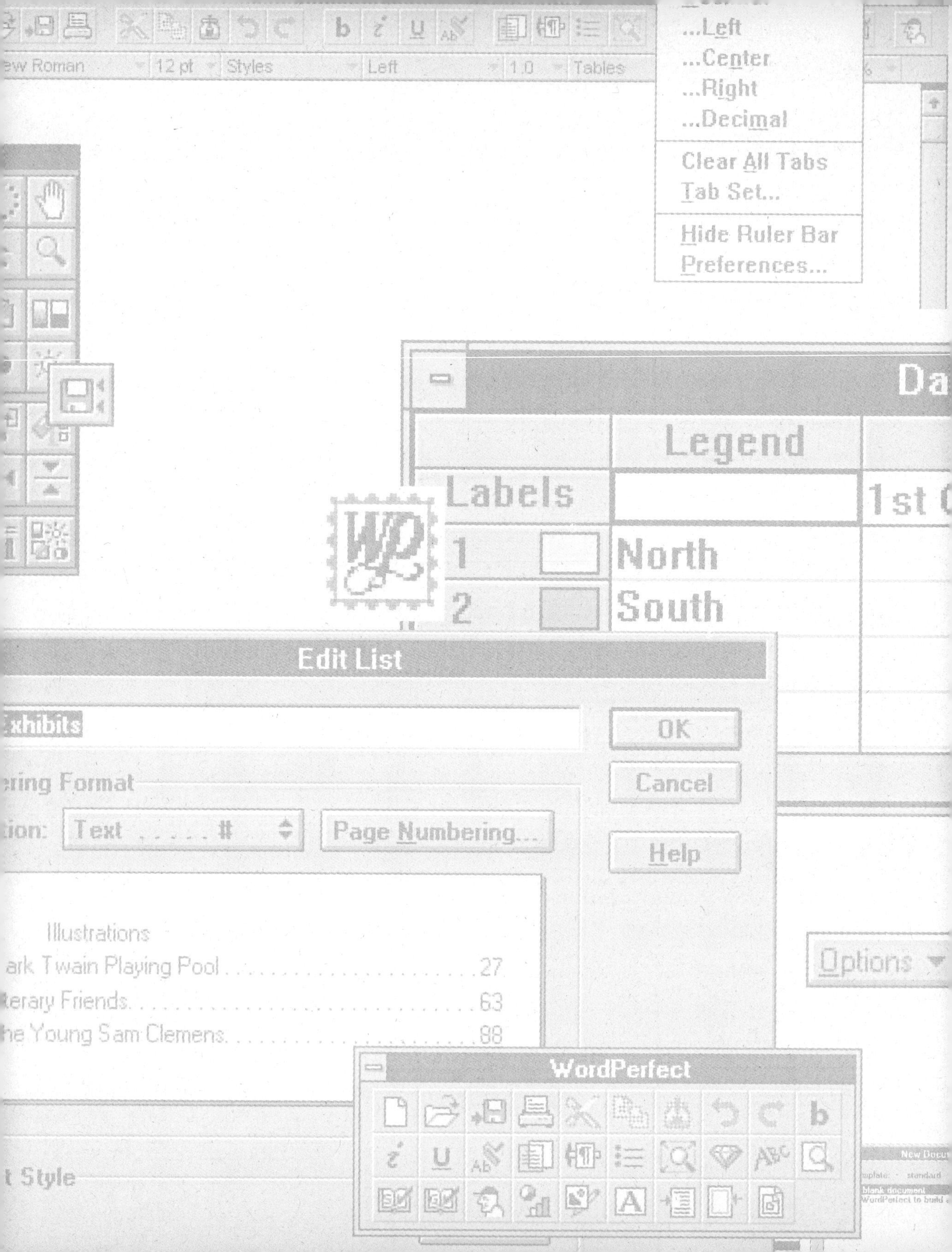

...Left
...Center
...Right
...Decimal
Clear All Tabs
Tab Set...
Hide Ruler Bar
Preferences...
Legend
Labels
1st
1
North
2
South
Edit List
OK
Cancel
Help
Page Numbering...
Illustrations
ark Twain Playing Pool 27
terary Friends. 63
he Young Sam Clemens. 88
Options
WordPerfect

Chapter 1

Getting Started

by Steve Schafer and Judy Petersen

WordPerfect 6.1 for Windows is a powerful word processing program containing many powerful tools; the program is, however, easy to use. WordPerfect can handle any word processing task, from a simple letter to a complex desktop-publishing document such as a newsletter or a book.

This chapter is designed to introduce you to WordPerfect 6.1 for Windows and its various interfaces. If you are familiar with previous versions of WordPerfect for Windows, you also should read Appendix B, "Making the Transition to WordPerfect 6.1 for Windows."

This chapter covers the following topics:

- Starting and exiting WordPerfect
- Using the keyboard and the mouse
- Understanding the editing screen
- Using dialog boxes
- Working with multiple documents
- Using Help

Starting and Exiting WordPerfect

Before learning how to be productive with WordPerfect for Windows, you must learn how to start and exit the program. WordPerfect 6.1 for Windows must be run from within Windows. If you are not in Windows, type **win** at the DOS prompt and press Enter to start Windows. Windows starts and displays the Program Manager window, similar to that shown in figure 1.1.

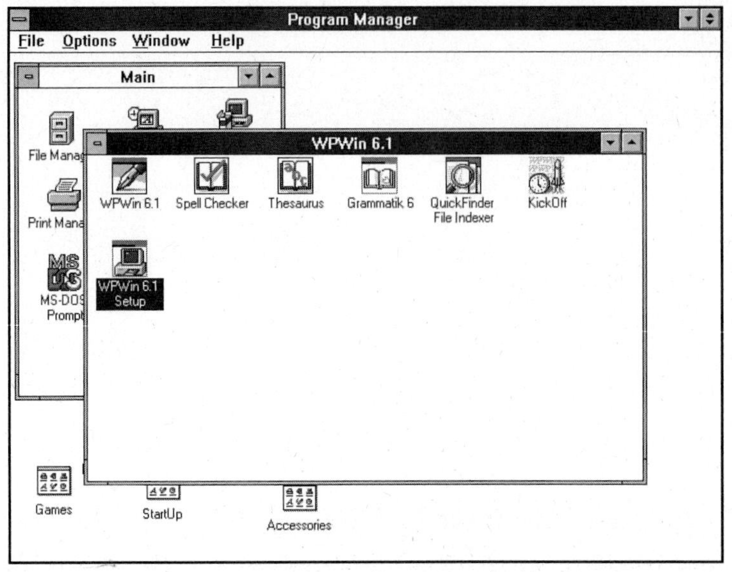

Fig. 1.1
The WPWin 6.1 program group contains the WordPerfect 6.1 for Windows program icon and other icons.

Note

WordPerfect 6.1 for Windows requires Windows 3.1, which must be running in Enhanced mode. For a full list of system requirements, see Appendix A.

If you followed the instructions in Appendix A, "Installing and Setting Up WordPerfect 6.1 for Windows," the WordPerfect for Windows icon is in the WPWin 6.1 program group.

If necessary, double-click the WPWin 6.1 program group to open the group window and see the icon. Figure 1.1 shows the Program Manager with the WPWin 6.1 program group open.

To start WordPerfect 6.1 for Windows, double-click its icon in the WPWin 6.1 group; Windows starts WordPerfect. A copyright screen appears briefly before the QuickStart Coach appears, announcing `Welcome to WordPerfect 6.1 for Windows`. For now, press Tab to select the Skip this Coach button and press Enter, or click the button with the mouse. WordPerfect displays its main editing screen (see fig. 1.2).

Tip
To quickly close WordPerfect or any other Windows application, press Alt+F4.

To exit WordPerfect for Windows, click the mouse pointer on the word **F**ile in the pull-down menu bar; or press Alt+F. Either method opens the **F**ile menu, as shown in figure 1.3. Then click the mouse pointer on the E**x**it command in the **F**ile menu; or press X.

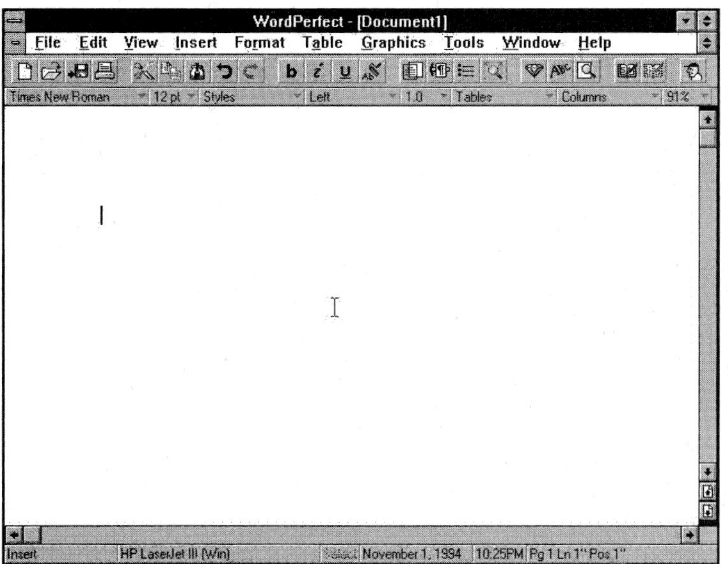

Fig. 1.2
The WordPerfect 6.1 for Windows main editing screen.

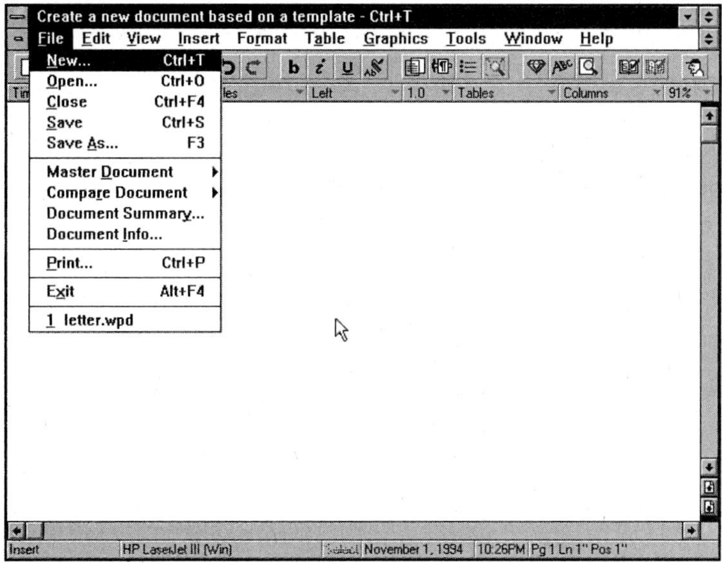

Fig. 1.3
The WordPerfect 6.1 for Windows **F**ile menu.

If you have not saved the current document, WordPerfect displays a dialog box similar to the one shown in figure 1.4. If you choose **Y**es, WordPerfect asks for a file name under which to save the document before exiting. If you choose **N**o, WordPerfect exits without saving the document. Choosing Cancel stops the exit operation, and you return to your document.

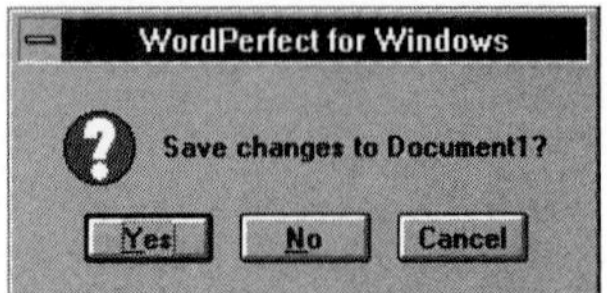

Fig. 1.4
The WordPerfect confirmation dialog box for saving changes.

Using the WordPerfect 6.1 for Windows Interface

This section explains the basics of using the keyboard and mouse to control WordPerfect. More detailed instructions on how to use specific WordPerfect features are provided in later chapters.

Using the Keyboard

WordPerfect uses *mnemonics* (clues to jog your memory about which keystrokes to use) for most of its options. To access the pull-down menus, you must press and hold the Alt key as you press the menu's mnemonic. To access the **F**ile menu, for example, you press Alt+F. To choose an option or command, simply press the mnemonic letter in its description. To choose **O**pen from the **F**ile menu, for example (after the File menu is open), you press O.

Note

Mnemonics for all options and commands are underlined on-screen but are shown in boldface in this book. The F in **F**ile, for example, is underlined on-screen but represented here by boldface type.

WordPerfect also enables you to use the arrow keys to navigate through the pull-down menus and the Tab and Shift+Tab keys to move around in dialog boxes. In menus, a highlight bar appears on the selected item. In dialog boxes, a dotted line outlines the selected item. After you highlight a menu item, you press Enter to choose, or execute, that command. The key, or keys, used to choose selected items in dialog boxes differ by the object selected. See the later section, "Using Dialog Boxes," for more information about how to work with dialog boxes.

WordPerfect 6.1 for Windows also uses the Ctrl key and function keys as shortcut keys to access dialog boxes directly. To open a document, for example, you can either open the **F**ile menu (or press Alt+F) and then choose **O**pen (or press O), which takes you to the Open File dialog box; or you can press Ctrl+O to bypass the menu system and directly access the Open

Document dialog box. Similarly, you can press F3 to directly access the Save As dialog box instead of choosing **F**ile, Save **A**s.

Note

Shortcut keys appear on the pull-down menus next to the items these keys operate. Ctrl+O, for example, appears next to the **O**pen command on the **F**ile menu.

Using the Mouse

Depending on the manufacturer, a mouse can have two or three buttons. By default, the left button is the primary mouse button, and the right is the secondary button.

Tip

If you prefer another button as your primary mouse button, you can make this change through the Mouse option of the Windows Control Panel.

The *mouse pointer* is an arrow or I-beam that moves around the screen as you move the mouse across the desktop or mouse pad. You use the mouse pointer to "point" at on-screen items.

WordPerfect's features are activated and controlled using either the mouse or the keyboard. By using a mouse, actions that otherwise take numerous keystrokes or complex keystroke combinations can be accomplished simply by moving the mouse pointer to a menu choice and pressing a mouse button.

Using the mouse, however, also removes your hand from the keyboard. You may, therefore, find yourself using keyboard commands to format text as you enter it, but switching to the mouse to format existing text.

The three basic mouse operations are clicking, double-clicking, and dragging, as described in the following paragraphs:

- *Clicking*. Quickly pressing and releasing the primary mouse button while the pointer is on a menu option, a button, or another selection to activate that item. Clicking the name of a menu causes that menu to appear on-screen, for example, and clicking the Toolbar's Speller button starts WordPerfect's spell-checker feature. Clicking is used to execute a command or an option or to relocate the insertion point in the text. (The insertion point is the thin bar that marks your current position in the text.)

- *Double-clicking*. Quickly pressing and releasing the primary mouse button twice while the pointer is on a menu option, a button, or another selection. Double-clicking is primarily used to simultaneously select an item and execute an action. You can double-click a graphic, for example, to access the Edit Graphics Box for that graphic.

- *Dragging*. Positioning the mouse where you want to start and then holding down the primary mouse button while you move the mouse across your desk or mouse pad. Within a document, you can drag to select blocks of text or to move graphics or other objects. As you drag the object, its position on-screen changes or a dotted line appears to show your progress.

You can use the mouse to move the insertion point from one place in your document to another. Place the mouse pointer in the location where you want the insertion point, and then click. The insertion point moves to the specified location. Using this mouse technique to move from one part of a document to another often is much quicker than using the arrow keys.

Used in combination with certain keyboard keys, the mouse is particularly helpful for moving quickly through a lengthy document. Use the scroll bars or the PgDn and PgUp keys to move from page to page. After you reach the page you want to edit, move the mouse pointer to the word you want to change, and click. The insertion point moves instantly to the specified location.

Note

The mouse pointer assumes different shapes on-screen, depending on its particular task. If you use the mouse to position a graphic box, for example, the pointer becomes a four-headed arrow.

Understanding the Editing Screen

With its default settings, the WordPerfect 6.1 for Windows editing screen offers many tools to help with word processing tasks. Many of its screen elements, however, can be customized to further enhance your productivity. Figure 1.2 shows the WordPerfect editing screen in its default state. Figure 1.5 shows the WordPerfect editing screen with many of its graphical tools active.

In the following sections, you learn the basics about each element shown in figure 1.5. In following chapters, you learn in detail how to use these elements most effectively.

Note

For more information on customizing the screen, see Chapter 9, "Customizing WordPerfect."

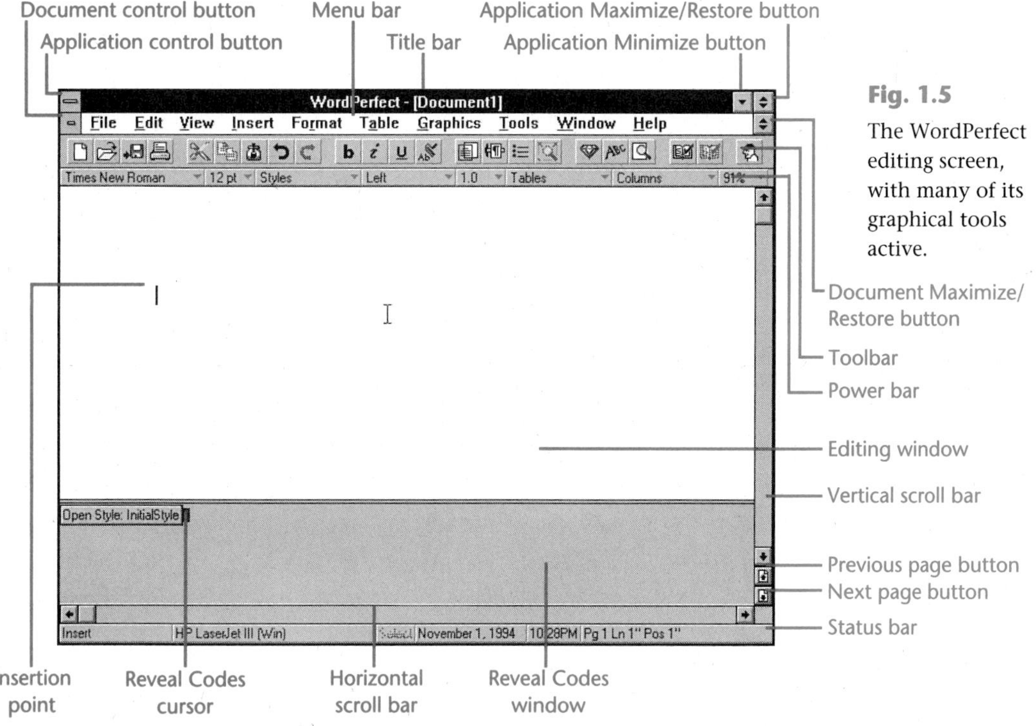

Fig. 1.5
The WordPerfect editing screen, with many of its graphical tools active.

Windows Controls

Because WordPerfect 6.1 for Windows is a fully capable Windows application, it operates in a window. This window is called an application window. All WordPerfect operations occur within this window. The WordPerfect application window includes all the controls offered by other Windows programs. Figure 1.5 shows the various control buttons available on the WordPerfect 6.1 window. These include the Maximize/Restore button, the Minimize button, and the Application Control button. The following sections explain each button in detail.

Maximize/Restore and Minimize Buttons

The button in the upper-right corner of the window is known as the Maximize/Restore button. This button functions as a toggle. Click it once, and it maximizes the WordPerfect window, expanding the window to occupy the entire screen. If the window is already full-screen, clicking the button returns the window to its former smaller size.

To the left of the Maximize/Restore button is the Minimize button. Clicking this button reduces the window to a small icon on the Windows desktop.

To restore the minimized window, select the icon by using the keyboard or mouse and then press Alt+space bar, or click the icon once and choose **R**estore from the Application Control menu.

> **Note**
>
> The Maximize/Restore and Minimize buttons can be used only with a mouse. To use the Maximize, Restore, and Minimize functions with a keyboard requires using the Application Control menu, described in the following section.

Application Control Menu

In the upper-left corner of the application window is the Application Control button. This button is marked with a long horizontal bar, much like a dash. To access the Application Control menu, click this button or press Alt+space bar.

The control menu enables you to Ma**x**imize, Mi**n**imize, or **R**estore the application window. If the application is not full-screen, you also can choose **M**ove or **S**ize. After choosing either option, you can use the arrow keys to move the application window around the screen or to resize the window.

Choosing S**w**itch To (or pressing Ctrl+Esc) accesses the Windows Task List dialog box. This Windows dialog box enables you to switch to another active application, close an active application, or arrange applications and icons on-screen. You also can close the application window (and exit WordPerfect) by choosing **C**lose.

> **Note**
>
> To move or size the window using the mouse, simply drag the application's title bar to move the window to a new location on-screen or drag the appropriate border to resize the window. You can also drag one of the corners of the application's border to resize it horizontally and vertically at the same time. A dotted line shows your progress. Release the mouse button to drop the window or border at its new location.

To move the window, open the Application Control menu and choose **M**ove. Press the arrow key that corresponds to the direction you want to move the window. As you press the arrows, a dotted line shows you the motion of the window. Press Enter to drop the window at its new location.

To resize the window, open the Application Control menu and choose **S**ize. Press an arrow key to move the pointer to the corresponding side of the window and then use the arrows to move that side. Pressing the left-arrow key, for example, moves the pointer to the left border of the window; pressing the left- or right-arrow key then moves the border left or right. A dotted line shows your progress. Pressing the Enter key stops the sizing process, leaving the window at its new size. Pressing Esc aborts the sizing process, leaving the window at its original size.

Document Controls

Each document you work with in WordPerfect 6.1 for Windows is contained in a *document window*. If you work with only one document, the document window is usually maximized; that is, the document window takes up the entire WordPerfect editing window. Each document window has its own frame, title bar, Minimize button, Maximize/Restore button, and Control button.

If a document is maximized in the editing window, its title bar and frame are the same as those of the application window. If a document window is sized to be smaller than the application window, its border and title bar are separate from those of the application. A minimized application becomes an icon in the WordPerfect for Windows application window.

The Document Control menu (see fig. 1.6) operates much like the Application Control menu and contains many of the same menu options. Notable differences include the use of Ctrl+F4 as the shortcut key for **C**lose (instead of Alt+F4) and the inclusion of a Nex**t** command. The Nex**t** command switches to the next open document in WordPerfect.

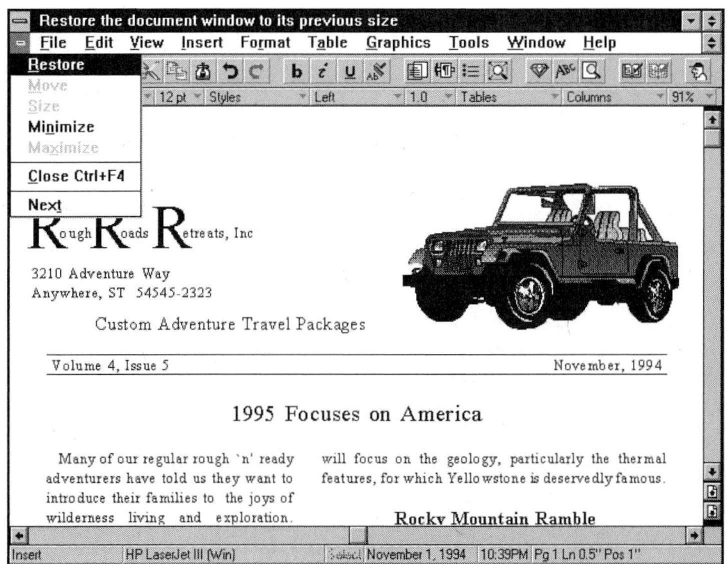

Fig. 1.6
The Document Control menu.

You can open the Document Control menu by clicking the mouse pointer on the Document Control button, or by pressing Alt+- (Alt and hyphen).

For more information about the document controls and on editing multiple documents in WordPerfect for Windows, see the later section "Working with Multiple Documents."

The WordPerfect Title Bar

The WordPerfect window title bar (refer to fig. 1.5) serves several purposes. Its primary purpose is to identify the WordPerfect application window. It also acts as an information resource—displaying the current document's name (if the document is maximized) and identification information for other graphical tools.

If you position the mouse pointer on any of the buttons in the Toolbar, for example, the text in the title bar changes to reflect that button's function (see fig. 1.7). The title bar also provides information on pull-down menu choices, buttons in the Power Bar, items on the status line, and the Previous and Next Page buttons.

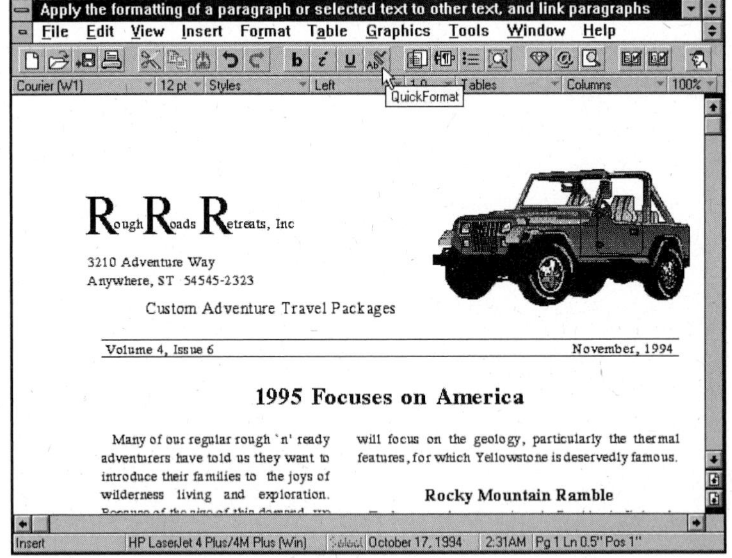

Fig. 1.7
The title bar shows you textual information about elements on the WordPerfect screen. If you place the mouse pointer over a button and pause briefly, the button name appears.

Note

When you position the mouse pointer on a button in the Toolbar or Power Bar and pause briefly, a text box containing the name of the button is displayed at the base of the pointer.

The Pull-Down Menus

The pull-down menu bar always appears at the top of the screen. You can access all of WordPerfect's features by using these menus.

To activate one of the menus, press and hold the Alt key while pressing the menu's mnemonic. Pressing Alt+F, for example, activates the **F**ile menu. You also can use the mouse to move the mouse pointer to the menu you want and then click the mouse button to activate the menu.

Pressing and releasing the Alt key also activates the pull-down menus, highlighting the Document Control menu. You can then use the arrow keys and the Enter key to choose the appropriate menu. This method displays a menu's main features on the title bar while that menu is highlighted. Watch the text in the title bar for information on each menu item as you navigate through the pull-down menus.

Take time now to open WordPerfect's menus one at a time and notice the commands contained in each menu. Although you cannot expect to memorize the location of every command, notice that each menu contains a logically grouped set of commands. After you understand the logic behind the grouping of commands in the WordPerfect menus, you can speed through all your writing, editing, and document-formatting tasks.

Note

You can fully customize WordPerfect 6.1 for Windows menus to rearrange items as you prefer—or even to add entirely new menu items. See Chapter 9, "Customizing WordPerfect," for more information.

QuickMenus

You can use WordPerfect's QuickMenus to help speed customizing the interface and formatting text. QuickMenus are pop-up menus that appear after you click the right (or secondary) mouse button while the mouse pointer is at a particular location on-screen. If you press the right mouse button while the mouse pointer is in a document margin, for example, the QuickMenu shown in figure 1.8 appears.

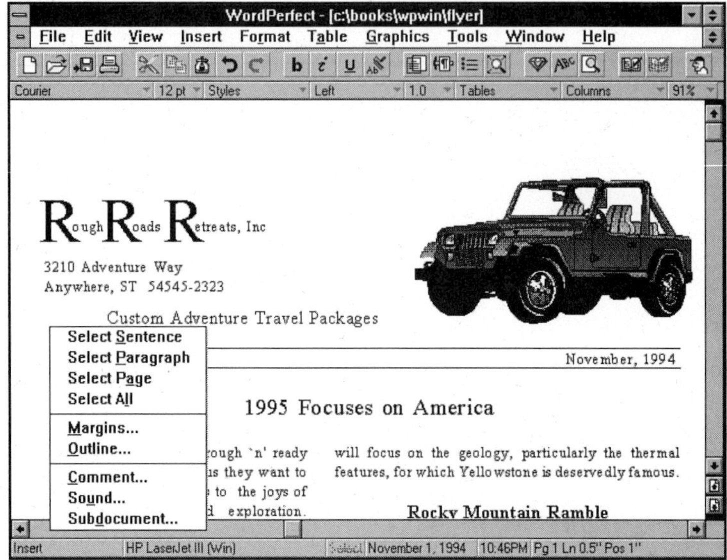

Fig. 1.8
Click in the left or right margin to access a QuickMenu that includes commands to select text, change margins, insert a comment, sound or subdocument, or change to Outline mode.

Try pressing the right mouse button while the mouse pointer is on the following elements:

- Between the left or right margin and the edge of the page
- Between the top or bottom margin and the edge of the page
- Document text
- A table
- A graphic figure or line, sound clip, or OLE object
- The Toolbar, Power Bar, status bar, Ruler Bar, or scroll bar

Tip
To see more document text when both the Power Bar and Ruler are active, choose the left or right on-screen position for the Toolbar.

The Toolbar

By default, the Toolbar appears at the top of the screen between the Power Bar and the pull-down menus. You also can display the Toolbar on the left, right, or bottom of the screen, or in a floating palette that you can position anywhere on-screen. To change the Toolbar's position, choose **E**dit, Pr**e**ferences, **T**oolbar, **O**ptions, and then choose **L**eft, **R**ight, T**o**p, **B**ottom, or P**a**lette.

While the mouse pointer is on any of the Toolbar buttons, that button's function is described on the WordPerfect title bar and a box appears containing the name of the button. To use any of the buttons, position the insertion point in the document where you want to use the feature, and click the appropriate button.

Tip

To quickly move the Toolbar, place the mouse pointer between, above, or below the buttons until the mouse pointer becomes a hand; then drag the Toolbar to a new location onscreen.

WordPerfect provides many Toolbars, each one geared toward a different set of features. You can use one Toolbar for tables, for example, another for text formatting, one for commonly used macros, and a fourth for cross-referencing functions. Each Toolbar can also be customized; you can add any feature, command, or macro to the bar as a button. Choose **E**dit, Pr**e**ferences, **T**oolbar, select the Toolbar you want to customize, and then choose **E**dit to open the Toolbar Editor.

Note

You must use the mouse to access the Toolbar.

Finally, you can hide (or redisplay) the Toolbar by choosing **V**iew, **T**oolbar.

For more information on the Toolbar, see Chapter 13, "Working with Toolbars."

The Power Bar

The Power Bar consists of several buttons that give you quick access to commonly used text layout and formatting features. If active, the Power Bar appears near the top of the screen (refer to fig. 1.5).

Using the Power Bar, you can instantly access frequently used text functions, such as a list of font faces or sizes, with a single click of the mouse button. The Power Bar enables you to work quickly without needing to hunt through menus or remember obscure keystroke combinations to accomplish basic tasks.

You can choose to display or hide the Power Bar by choosing **V**iew, P**o**wer Bar. You also can add or delete buttons to fit your needs.

Note

You must use the mouse to access the Power Bar.

When the mouse pointer is on any of the Power Bar buttons, its function is described in the title bar and the button name is displayed. To use any of the buttons, position the insertion point in the document where you want to use the feature, and then click the appropriate button.

The Power Bar can also be customized; you can add any feature, command, or macro. Choose **E**dit, Pr**e**ferences, P**o**wer Bar to customize the appearance of the Power Bar or choose **E**dit to open the Toolbar Editor-Power Bar dialog box where you can add and remove buttons.

You can add buttons for your most commonly accessed feature's to the Power Bar. For more information on the Power Bar, see Chapter 13, "Working with Toolbars."

The Status Bar

The Status Bar appears along the bottom of the WordPerfect window. It informs you of the status of many WordPerfect for Windows features. By default, the status bar displays the following information:

- Whether Insert or Typeover mode is active, or the status of such features as columns, tables, macros, merge, and paragraph styles
- The current printer
- Whether any text or code is selected
- The current date and time
- The current page, vertical, and horizontal position of the insertion point

The status bar can be configured to show additional—or less—information, as desired. You can move and size any of the items displayed on the status bar as needed. Items that can be added include the current alignment character, the Caps Lock, Num Lock and Scroll Lock state, the active keyboard definition, and whether Outline is on or off.

In addition to showing information, most items on the status bar act as buttons that can be double-clicked to access related features. Position the mouse pointer on any item, and look at the title bar for information on how to use that item.

Note

You must use the mouse to use the status bar items as buttons.

You can choose to display or hide the status Bar by choosing **V**iew, St**a**tus Bar. Add or remove buttons on the status Bar and customize its appearance by choosing **E**dit, Pr**e**ferences, St**a**tus Bar.

The Ruler Bar

If active, the Ruler Bar appears below the Power Bar at the top of the screen (refer to fig. 1.5). The Ruler Bar consists of a ruler with the default measurements (either inches, centimeters, millimeters, points, or WordPerfect units) and displays markers for all tabs. Each tab stop is represented by a marker that also shows what type of tab is set at that position. You choose to display or hide the Ruler by choosing **V**iew, **R**uler Bar.

The top of the ruler shows the current left and right margins, and small triangles indicate the current paragraph indentations. If the insertion point is currently in a column or table, this area also shows the margins for the columns or cells.

You can use the mouse to move tabs or margins on the Ruler Bar. Drag the tab marker or margin bar to a new location. To remove a tab stop, drag its marker off the ruler. To add a tab, click the mouse pointer on the ruler where you want to add the tab, and then click the right mouse button on the tab stop to access the Ruler's QuickMenu and choose the type of tab. For more information on tabs and margins, see Chapter 4, "Formatting Text."

The Scroll Bars

The scroll bars enable you to move quickly through a document that is too long or too wide to fit on-screen. The vertical scroll bar moves up and down through the document, while the horizontal bar moves right and left.
To enable the scroll bars or display them only when needed, choose **E**dit, Pr**e**ferences, **D**isplay, and then choose either **V**ertical or Horizo**n**tal.

To use a scroll bar, place the mouse pointer on the scroll arrow that points in the direction you want to move, and click the mouse button. (Scroll arrows are located at the top and bottom of the vertical scroll bar and at either end of the horizontal scroll bar.) Hold down the mouse button on a scroll arrow, and you continue to scroll through the document until you release the mouse button. To move quickly from one part of the document to another—for example, to move from the top to the bottom—place the mouse pointer on the scroll box, and then drag the box up or down.

You also can click anywhere in the gray area between the scroll box and the arrows to move a screen forward or backward (using the vertical scroll bar) or left or right (using the horizontal scroll bar). Use the scroll bar QuickMenu to access the Go To and Bookmark features.

Note

You must use the mouse to use the scroll bars.

Previous and Next Page Buttons

At the bottom of the vertical scroll bar lie two small buttons with a graphic of a page on each of their faces. The top button moves the display one page backward in a document; the bottom button moves it one page forward.

Caution

Like the scroll bars, Previous/Next Page buttons do not move the insertion point; they only change the part of the document displayed on-screen.

Note

Previous/Next Page buttons are displayed only if the vertical scroll bar is displayed.

Feature Bars

Various features in WordPerfect have their own Feature Bars. (These are bars that contain buttons representing common commands used with that feature.) The Feature Bars appear on-screen if you use that feature. If you work in Outline mode, for example, the Outline Feature Bar appears on-screen, as shown in figure 1.9.

You can use the mouse with the Feature Bars to quickly make changes while using various features. WordPerfect includes Feature Bars for the following features:

- Caption
- Comment
- Cross-Reference
- Delay Codes
- Footnote/Endnote
- Graphics Box

- Header/Footer
- Hypertext
- Index
- List
- Macro Edit
- Merge
- Outline
- Sound
- Table Formula
- Table of Authorities
- Table of Authorities Full Form
- Table of Contents
- Template
- Text Box
- Watermark

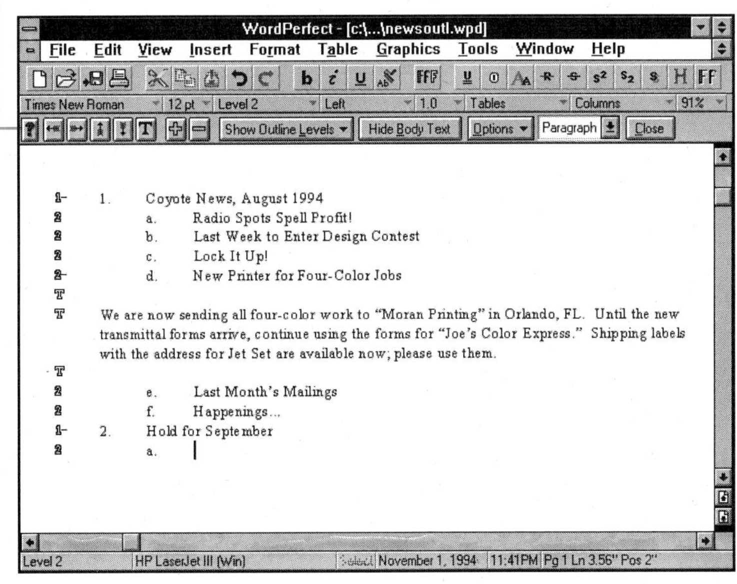

Fig. 1.9
The Outline Feature Bar is activated if you work in Outline mode.

Each Feature Bar is discussed in the chapter in which its specific feature is covered.

View Modes

WordPerfect has three View modes that provide different views of your document. These views are all WYSIWYG (What You See Is What You Get) views, but each displays different elements than its counterparts. You change modes by opening the **V**iew menu and choosing **D**raft, **P**age, or T**w**o Page, as appropriate.

In Draft and Page modes, you also can control the Zoom—that is, how much of and the size at which the document is displayed.

Draft Mode

Draft mode displays your document text close to how it will look when it is printed, but does not show headers, footers, watermarks, and other page formatting features on-screen. Because of this, you can usually work faster in Draft mode. You do, however, sacrifice a certain amount of WYSIWYG (What You See Is What You Get).

Page Mode

By default, WordPerfect displays your document in Page mode, its full WYSIWYG mode. While in Page mode, you can see all aspects of a page, including such elements as headers, footers, and watermarks.

Note

The amount of the page displayed on-screen in Page mode is governed in part by the current Zoom ratio. See the later section "Zoom" for more information.

Because WordPerfect displays all screen elements in this mode, working in Page mode can be significantly slower than working in Draft mode.

Two Page Mode

The third view WordPerfect 6.1 for Windows offers is Two Page mode. This mode displays two pages side by side on the editing screen, as shown in figure 1.10.

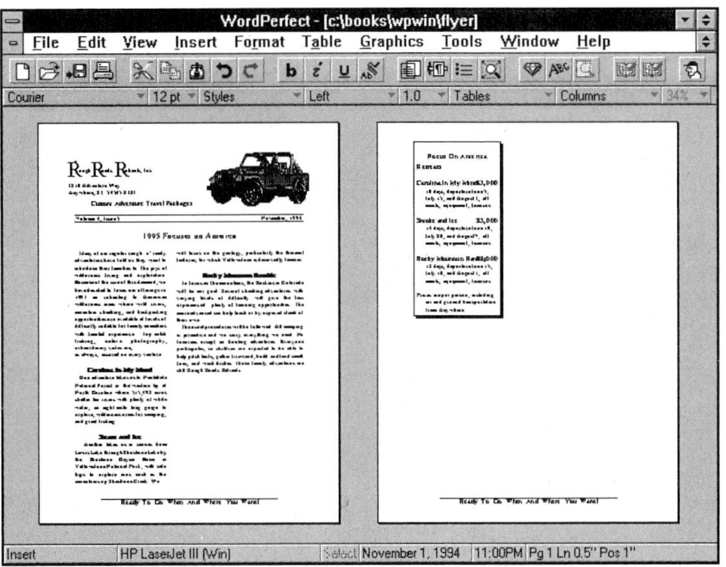

Fig. 1.10 WordPerfect's Two Page mode. Two Page mode is particularly helpful when you want to check the layout of facing pages.

Although you can edit in this mode, you may find it impractical to do so on a textual level. Two Page mode does present the best view of the page as a whole, however, and header, footer, or graphic placements can be fine-tuned at this level.

> **Note**
>
> Two Page mode does not enable you to choose the Zoom ratio; this mode always displays two pages on-screen, as shown in figure 1.10.

Zoom

In Draft or Page mode, you can control the zoom ratio of the document—that is, the size in which the document appears on-screen in relation to its size when printed. You can choose a value between 25 percent and 400 percent by choosing **V**iew, **Z**oom and then choosing the zoom ratio you want from the Zoom dialog box, as shown in figure 1.11.

> **Note**
>
> Remember that you cannot use Zoom while in Two Page mode.

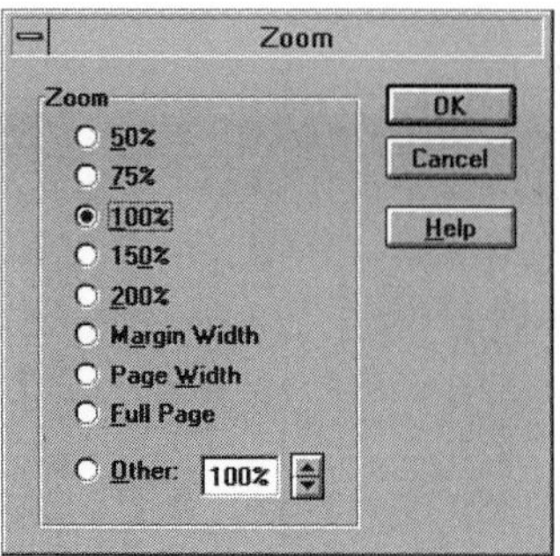

Fig. 1.11
The Zoom dialog box allows you to customize the size of the document on-screen in relation to its size when printed.

WordPerfect also supports three zoom values determined by the document's page and margin size instead of by a percentage:

- *M**a**rgin Width.* Zooms the document so that you can see all the text and graphics between the left and right margins.
- *Page **W**idth.* Displays the entire document between the left and right edges of the page.
- ***F**ull Page.* Shows the complete current page on-screen.

Instead of picking one of the dialog box's preset percentages, you also can set your own value between 25 and 400 percent by choosing **O**ther.

Hide Bars

To display another full-page view, choose **V**iew, **H**ide Bars; or press Alt+Shift+F5. This feature affects all the various editing bars (Ruler, Button, Power, pull-down menu, and so on), as well as the title bar, but not the Feature Bars. After you choose **H**ide Bars, WordPerfect zooms the editing window to full-screen size and displays only the document and any active Feature Bars. A document with Hide Bars active is shown in figure 1.12.

Note

This view is governed by the current zoom ratio. If ZOOM is set to 100 percent, for example, the document is shown at 100 percent when you hide the bars.

To redisplay the hidden bars, press Esc or Alt+Shift+F5.

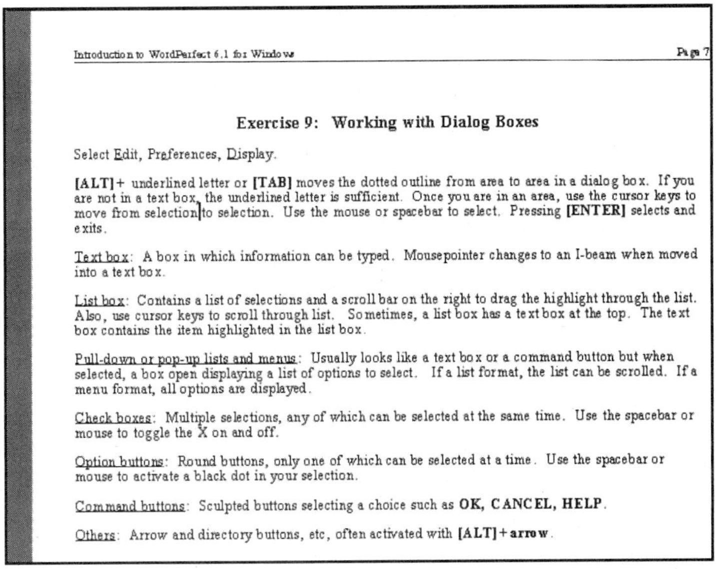

Introduction to WordPerfect 6.1 for Windows Page 7

Exercise 9: Working with Dialog Boxes

Select Edit, Preferences, Display.

[ALT]+ underlined letter or **[TAB]** moves the dotted outline from area to area in a dialog box. If you are not in a text box, the underlined letter is sufficient. Once you are in an area, use the cursor keys to move from selection to selection. Use the mouse or spacebar to select. Pressing **[ENTER]** selects and exits.

Text box: A box in which information can be typed. Mousepointer changes to an I-beam when moved into a text box.

List box: Contains a list of selections and a scroll bar on the right to drag the highlight through the list. Also, use cursor keys to scroll through list. Sometimes, a list box has a text box at the top. The text box contains the item highlighted in the list box.

Pull-down or pop-up lists and menus: Usually looks like a text box or a command button but when selected, a box open displaying a list of options to select. If a list format, the list can be scrolled. If a menu format, all options are displayed.

Check boxes: Multiple selections, any of which can be selected at the same time. Use the spacebar or mouse to toggle the X on and off.

Option buttons: Round buttons, only one of which can be selected at a time. Use the spacebar or mouse to activate a black dot in your selection.

Command buttons: Sculpted buttons selecting a choice such as **OK, CANCEL, HELP**.

Others: Arrow and directory buttons, etc, often activated with **[ALT]+arrow**.

Fig. 1.12
The WordPerfect editing screen with the Hide Bars feature active. The shaded area shown here—indicating the binding offset—and other document format elements continue to display.

I

Basic Tasks

Troubleshooting

When I use the scroll bars to move through a document and press a cursor key to move to a specific line, the display jumps back to where I began scrolling. What am I doing wrong?

The scroll bars change the part of the document displayed, but do not move the insertion point. To move to a new location in the document, use the scroll bars to go to that location, then use the mouse to click where you want the insertion point to appear on-screen.

Why does pressing Alt plus the mnemonic for a button on a feature bar not access the button?

To select feature bar buttons using the keyboard, press Alt+Shift plus the mnemonic.

Using Dialog Boxes

If you choose a menu option that requires additional information before WordPerfect can execute the command, a dialog box appears. The dialog box enables you to provide any additional information needed by WordPerfect to execute the command. The names of menu options that access dialog boxes end in ellipses (...). Because the **F**ile **O**pen command ends in an ellipsis, for example, you know that a dialog box appears after you choose this command.

> **Note**
>
> Some command buttons in dialog boxes open additional dialog boxes. The label on these buttons ends in an ellipsis (see fig. 1.13).

Some dialog boxes require you to choose an option box or button or to type any necessary information. Other dialog boxes offer choices in drop-down or pop-up lists. Each of these items is known as a dialog box control. Many dialog boxes require the manipulation of several different controls and options. Figure 1.13 shows the Font dialog box, which presents several different types of choices.

The various dialog box controls and how to use them are discussed in the following sections.

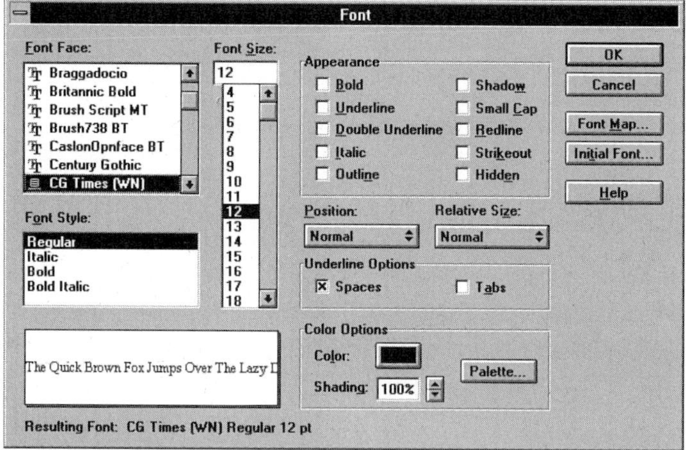

Fig. 1.13
The Font dialog box shows several different dialog controls, including lists, pop-up lists, check boxes, and command buttons.

Moving Around in a Dialog Box

You can move from section to section in dialog boxes simply by clicking the part of the dialog box in which you need to work. If you prefer using the keyboard, simply press the Alt key and the mnemonic for the option you want to change or the area in which you want to work. To select **B**old in the Font dialog box, for example, click the word **B**old (or the check box next to it), or press Alt+B (refer to fig. 1.13).

Alternatively, you can use Tab and Shift+Tab to move among the available options in the dialog box. After an item is selected (signified by the dotted line surrounding that item or an active highlight bar in lists), the keystroke to activate or change that item varies depending on the control's type. See the following sections about each specific dialog box element for information on how to control that element.

Note

In Windows terms, a highlighted control is said to have the focus. That is, the next action, command, or keystroke affects that object.

Understanding Dialog Box Elements

WordPerfect for Windows dialog boxes use several different controls. Each control is discussed individually in the following sections.

Understanding Buttons

Every dialog box in WordPerfect for Windows 6.1 has at least one button: OK or **C**lose. Either button closes the dialog box and affects the changes you make in the box. Most dialog boxes also have a Cancel button. You use the Cancel button to leave the dialog box without executing the changes you made.

Note

Some confirmation dialog boxes do not have an OK or **C**lose button. Instead they have **Y**es, **N**o, and Cancel buttons.

Many other buttons also are available, as shown in the Font dialog box (refer to fig. 1.13). Typically, if you choose a dialog box button with an ellipsis, another dialog box appears. Choosing Ini**t**ial Font from the Font dialog box, for example, accesses the Document Initial Font dialog box. After you leave the Document Initial Font dialog box, you return to the Font dialog box.

To choose a button, click that button, or use the keyboard to move to the button and then press Enter. If the button has a mnemonic, or if a function key is listed on the button, you can use the mnemonic or function key to activate the button.

Understanding Text Boxes

One of the most common dialog controls is the text box. The Find and Replace Text dialog box shown in figure 1.14, for example, contains two text boxes. You select each box by using the mouse or keyboard, and then you type information in the provided space.

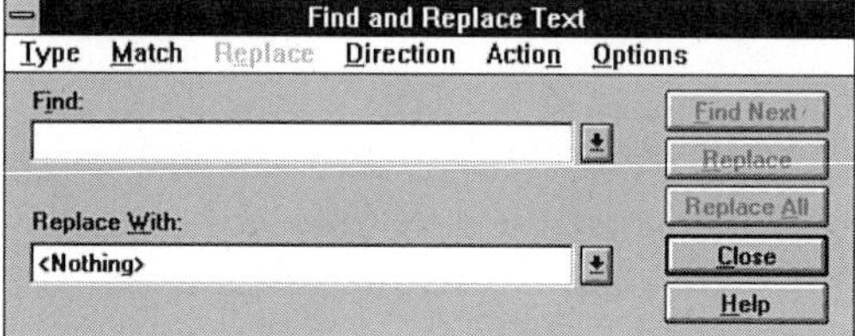

Fig. 1.14
The Find and Replace Text dialog box contains two text boxes: F**i**nd and Replace **W**ith.

After you press Enter or move away from the text box, WordPerfect evaluates your entry and displays the applicable text in the box. If you type **1 1/3** as the measure for the left margin in the Margins text box, for example, WordPerfect displays 1.33.

> **Note**
>
> Most text boxes do not accept invalid information. If you type a letter instead of a number in the Left Margin box, for example, WordPerfect responds with the Windows default beep to inform you that a letter is invalid in this text box.

If you move to a text box that already contains text, WordPerfect selects that text. To replace the text, begin typing. The current entry is deleted and replaced with what you type. To edit an existing entry, use the arrow keys or the mouse to position the insertion point in the text where you want to make a change.

Most text boxes containing numeric values in WordPerfect 6.1 for Windows use increment and decrement arrows to change the current value by a set amount. The Number of Columns text box in the Columns dialog box, for example, displays a set of increment and decrement arrows beside it (refer to the Shading text box in fig. 1.13). Clicking the up arrow increases the value in the text box by 1. Clicking the down arrow decreases the value by 1.

Understanding Check Boxes

Check boxes enable you to choose more than one of the offered choices. An X in a check box indicates that the option is active. In the Font dialog box, for example, you can choose several text appearance attributes (refer to fig. 1.13).

To make your text bold, italic, and small caps, for example, choose the check box next to each item. Clicking the option name or its box, or using the keyboard to choose the option, alternately displays or clears the X in the check box. You can choose as many or as few of the check boxes as you want. Check boxes act independently of each other.

Note

When a check box has the focus, pressing the space bar alternately puts an X in and clears the box.

Understanding Radio Buttons

Radio buttons (sometimes referred to as option buttons), appear as small round dots in the dialog box and always occur in groups. Their operation is similar to that of check boxes, except that you may select only one of these options. In the Columns dialog box, for example, you can choose **N**ewspaper as the Type of column, but you cannot choose **P**arallel at the same time (see fig. 1.15). After you choose a radio button, the circle is filled in to indicate that the button is selected.

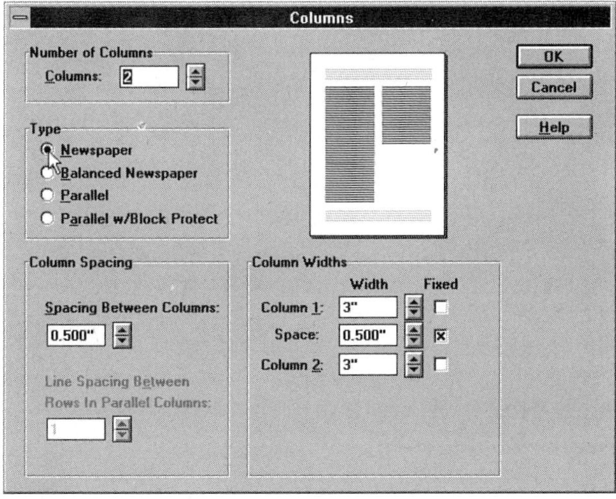

Fig. 1.15
The Columns dialog box contains several radio buttons used to select the type of columns you want to define.

Radio buttons also are used to control the contents of some dialog boxes. Selecting a different radio button changes the contents of the dialog box accordingly. Such dialog boxes are used primarily to set up features or functions within WordPerfect.

Understanding Lookup Buttons

WordPerfect for Windows also uses several special buttons to help you input values. These buttons take you to another dialog box or open up a special selection list to help you enter values into text boxes. These buttons are placed next to the text boxes to which they apply; a graphic representing the button's function appears on its face.

Figures 1.16 and 1.17 show some of the lookup buttons that may appear in certain dialog boxes.

The contents of some dialog boxes vary depending on the option(s) chosen. These dialog boxes are used primarily to set up features or functions within WordPerfect.

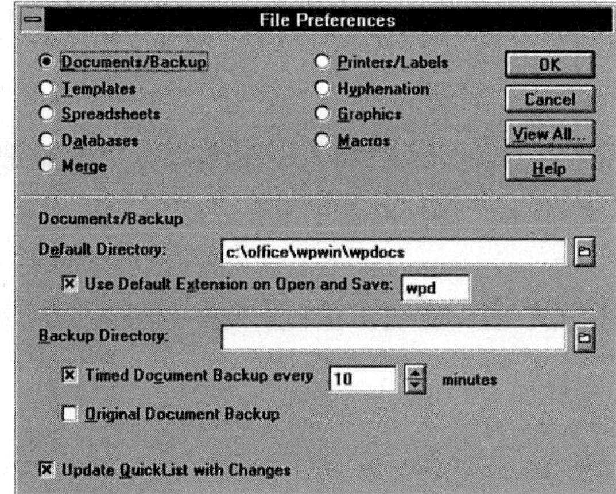

Fig. 1.16 The small buttons with a file folder on them in the File Preferences dialog box open the Select Directory dialog box.

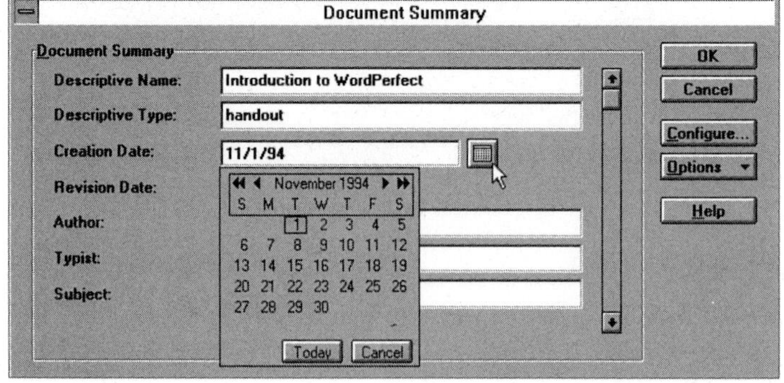

Fig. 1.17 Selecting the small calendar graphic next to the Creation Date text box in the Document Summary dialog box opens a small calendar dialog box from which you can select a date.

Understanding Selection Lists

If you can choose only from a specific list of textual choices for one option, a list of all the valid choices is usually provided. Such lists are known as *List Boxes*. The Font dialog box, for example, has three such lists: **F**ont Face, F**o**nt Style, and Font **S**ize (refer to fig. 1.13).

To change the font face in the Font dialog box, first choose **F**ont Face to select the Font Face list, and then choose from among the choices provided.

You can select an item from a list by clicking the item or by using the arrow keys to highlight the option you want; you do not need to press Enter to select items in a normal list. After making a selection, the list remains open.

Some lists are contained in drop-down lists. Usually these lists relate to options in which the current value is important, but constantly seeing all the various values that option may contain is not as important. The Save As dialog box, for example, contains two such drop-down lists: Dri**v**es and Save File as **T**ype (see fig. 1.18). Pressing the list's mnemonic and then pressing the down arrow, or clicking on the downward-pointing arrow next to the list, opens that list, as shown in figure 1.19.

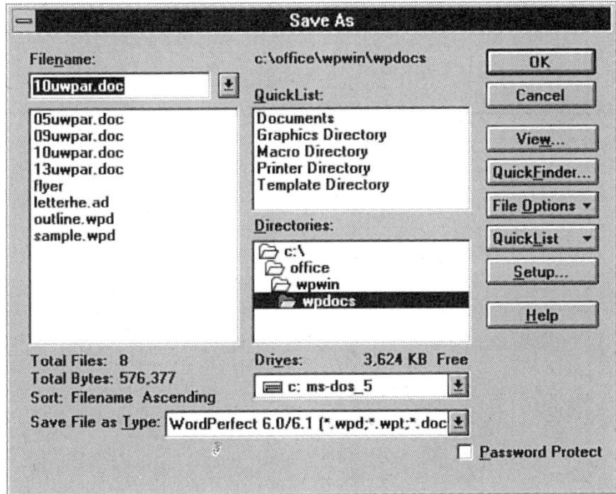

Fig. 1.18
The Save As dialog box, containing two list boxes and two drop-down lists.

After the list is open, you can select an item by double-clicking that item or by using the arrow keys to highlight the option you want and pressing Enter. After you make your choice, the list closes.

Some text boxes may feature a combination of text box and selection list, such as the File**n**ame text box in the Save As dialog box (refer to fig. 1.18). These text boxes differ from the standard drop-down list, because you can either type in new text or select an option from the supplied items.

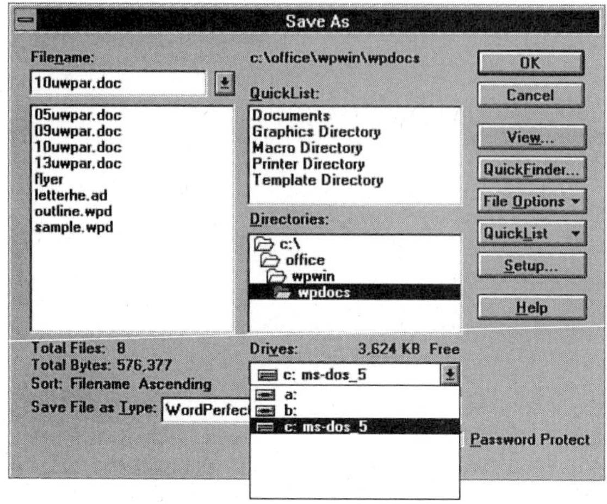

Fig. 1.19
The Drives drop-down list, shown open with the current drive selected.

Understanding Pop-up Lists

One other type of list that WordPerfect offers is the *pop-up list*. Examples of pop-up lists include the G**e**nerated By, and Print **Q**uality lists in the Print dialog box (see fig. 1.20). Pop-up lists resemble buttons with upward- and downward-pointing arrows on the right side of the button's face. The currently selected item also usually appears on the button's face, to the left.

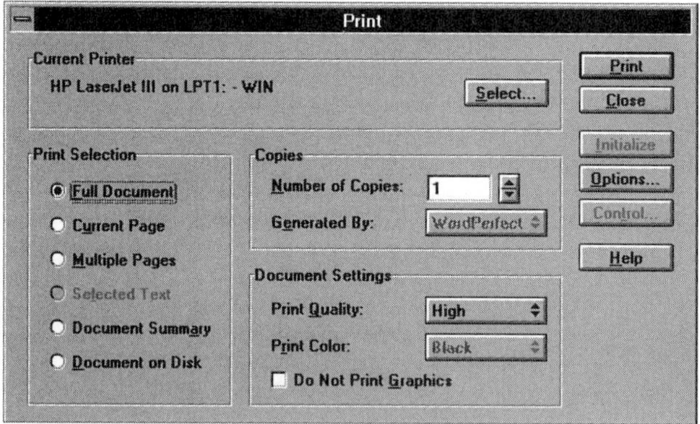

Fig. 1.20
The Print dialog box contains several pop-up lists, including the G**e**nerated By and the Print **Q**uality lists.

Note

Some pop-up lists are marked with only a down arrow or triangle and display the name of the feature rather than the currently selected value. The **O**ptions button on the Outline bar, for example, expands into a list of options that lead to dialog boxes that help you configure the current outline.

After it is selected, the button expands into a list of items from which you can choose. Choosing Print **Q**uality, for example, opens the pop-up list from which you can choose **H**igh, **M**edium, or **D**raft (see fig. 1.21). After you choose an item, that option reverts to its original button-like state.

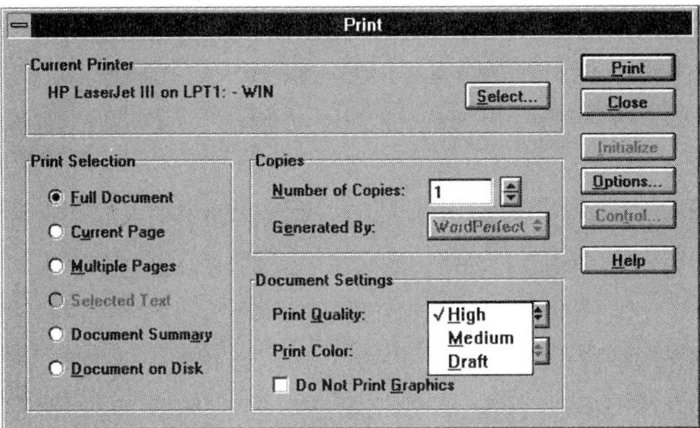

Fig. 1.21
Selecting Print **Q**uality expands the pop-up list so that you can choose an item.

Example-type pop-up lists display graphic representations of your choices. The Column Border dialog box in figure 1.22, for example, contains two example pop-ups—**B**order Style and **F**ill Style—represented by square buttons. The graphic lists usually are accompanied by lists of equivalent options in text form.

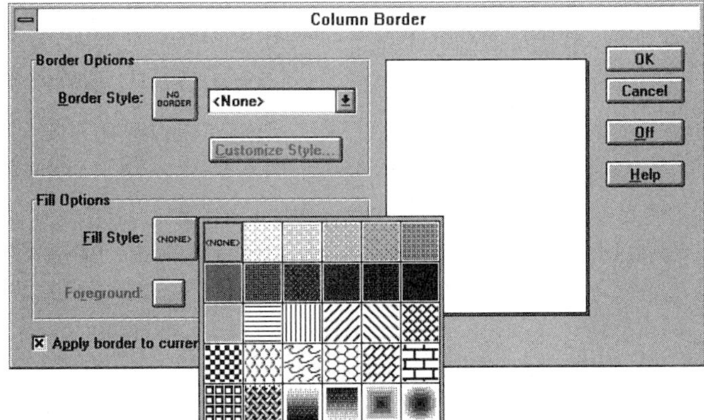

Fig. 1.22
The Column Border dialog box, which contains two example pop-up lists: **B**order Style and **F**ill Style (shown open). Drop-down lists beside each example type list allow you to choose the same options by their name if you want.

Using the keyboard, press Tab to move the selection to the button and then press the space bar, or click the button with the mouse. After the button is activated, a box showing the graphic equivalent of the various acceptable values appears, with the current value outlined in red (refer to fig. 1.12).

Use the mouse to click the desired value, or use the arrow keys to move to your choice and press Enter. After you make a selection, the button reverts to its former state, displaying the currently selected option on its face.

Troubleshooting

When I am using features for the first time, I often end up opening the wrong dialog box. Can I close a dialog box quickly using the keyboard?

Yes. Just press the Esc key.

Understanding What You Don't See

WordPerfect 6.1 for Windows, like its DOS predecessors, operates on a clean screen principle. Many formatting codes are inserted while you work on a WordPerfect document, but they do not appear in the editing document.

Likewise, spaces, tabs, and hard returns (from pressing Enter in a document) are not displayed in the document text. Occasionally, however, knowing where the formatting codes, spaces, tabs, and hard returns occur in text is helpful. WordPerfect 6.1 for Windows, therefore, does offer options for displaying these elements.

Reveal Codes

WordPerfect inserts hidden codes into your document for almost everything it does. These hidden codes may seem complex at first, but you cannot afford to ignore them. These codes indicate margin settings, tabs, carriage returns, indents, and much additional information about how your document appears in the editing window.

Hidden codes also contain information about headers, footers, font changes, document comments, and nonprinting notes. Other hidden codes turn certain features on and off. Such codes occur in pairs and show you exactly where the feature is active in the text.

To see the hidden codes in a document, choose **V**iew, Reveal **C**odes; or press Alt+F3. Repeat the procedure to turn off Reveal Codes. Figure 1.23 shows the Reveal Codes window.

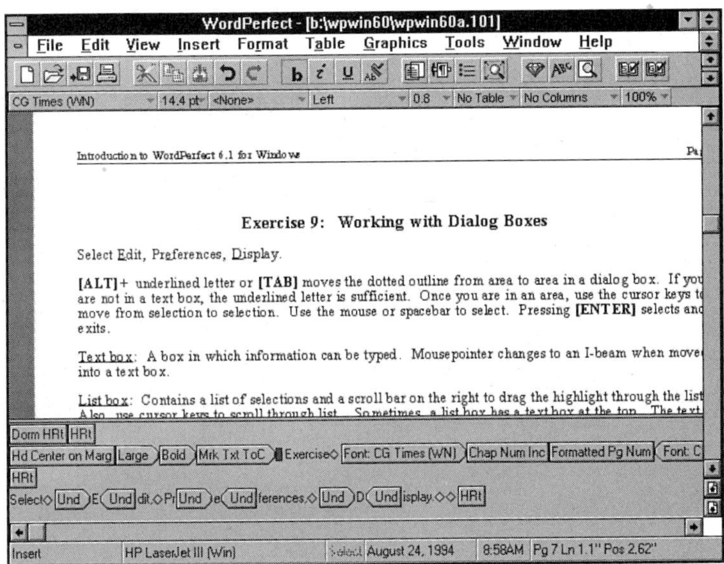

Fig. 1.23
The Reveal Codes window shows you the codes that WordPerfect uses to format your text.

If Reveal Codes is active, the document window is split between the editing screen and the Reveal Codes window. A cursor (highlighted block) in the Reveal Codes window shows where the insertion point is in regard to the text and surrounding codes.

Show Spaces, Tabs, and Hard Returns

Along with the formatting codes displayed in the Reveal Codes window, you can choose to show graphic representations of spaces, tabs, hard returns, and more in your document text. Figure 1.24 shows a document displaying spaces, tabs, and hard returns.

Choose **E**dit, Pr**e**ferences, **D**isplay, **S**how ¶, and then select the items you want to display or hide.

In addition to the preceding three elements, you also can choose to display **I**ndents, S**o**ft Hyphens, and C**e**nter, **F**lush Right, **A**dvance, and Ce**n**ter Page codes.

Fig. 1.24
WordPerfect 6.1 for Windows can show you where spaces, tabs, and hard returns occur in the text.

Templates

Templates play an important role in WordPerfect 6.1 for Windows. Templates primarily act as a boilerplate document construction tool, enabling you to build a document from preformatted text. Templates, however, can do much more.

Templates act as containers for WordPerfect tasks. They also can hold Styles, Macros, Abbreviations, Toolbars, Menus, and Keyboard definitions. By using Templates, you can make sure that the tools you need for a specific task are close at hand. You can create a Newsletter template, for example, that contains Newsletter Styles, Macros, Toolbars, and Menus. By accessing the Newsletter template, you activate all these specific tools for use on the Newsletter.

WordPerfect uses a special template named Standard to define the standard tools available to all templates you create. This Template is used as the default to create new documents after you first start WordPerfect.

More information on templates can be found in Chapter 11, "Using Templates."

Working with Multiple Documents

WordPerfect enables you to open as many as nine documents at a time—memory permitting. This capability gives you an exceptional amount of freedom in exchanging information between documents. With several documents open, for example, you can move quickly from one document to the next, copying parts of each to create a new document.

WordPerfect loads each document into a document window. The document can be displayed as a full screen, in a window, or minimized (refer to the earlier section "Document Controls"). You can move these windows around the screen, and you can open and close each window without affecting the others. By displaying documents in these ways, WordPerfect enables you to accomplish the following tasks:

- Remove a document almost completely from the screen by minimizing it to an icon.
- Move a document window from one location to another.
- Overlap document windows so that you can switch between them by clicking one or the other.
- Position two or more documents side by side so that you can compare files or cut and paste data from one to the other.

Arranging Documents On-Screen

The most common way to work in a WordPerfect document is to maximize its window to occupy the entire editing area. Maximizing the window provides the best view of the entire document. You also can reduce, or minimize, the document window so that it uses only part of the main WordPerfect screen. You minimize a document by clicking the Minimize button or by choosing Mi**n**imize from the Document Control menu. You can return the document to its original size by clicking the Maximize button or by choosing Ma**x**imize from the Document Control menu.

As mentioned in the earlier section "Application Control Menu," you can size and position the window by using the mouse or the keyboard.

Switching between Documents

Tip
You also can click the document you want to make active if you can see any part of its border on-screen.

Although you can have up to nine documents open at one time, only one document can be active at a time. You can make changes only to the active document. A document must be active before you can close or save it.

The active document's title bar is displayed in a color different than the color of the title bars in inactive documents. To work on a document, you first must make it active. To make a document active, choose **W**indow, and press the number corresponding to the document you want active. You can quickly switch to the next document by choosing Nex**t** from the Document Control menu.

Tiling or Cascading Documents

To help you arrange multiple documents so that you can switch more easily from one to another, WordPerfect enables you to tile or cascade your document windows. Tiling windows gives each window the same amount of screen space without overlapping (see fig. 1.25). Cascading windows overlaps the windows but leaves each title bar showing (see fig. 1.26). To tile or cascade windows, choose **W**indow, **T**ile Horizontal or Tile **V**ertical; or **W**indow, **C**ascade, respectively.

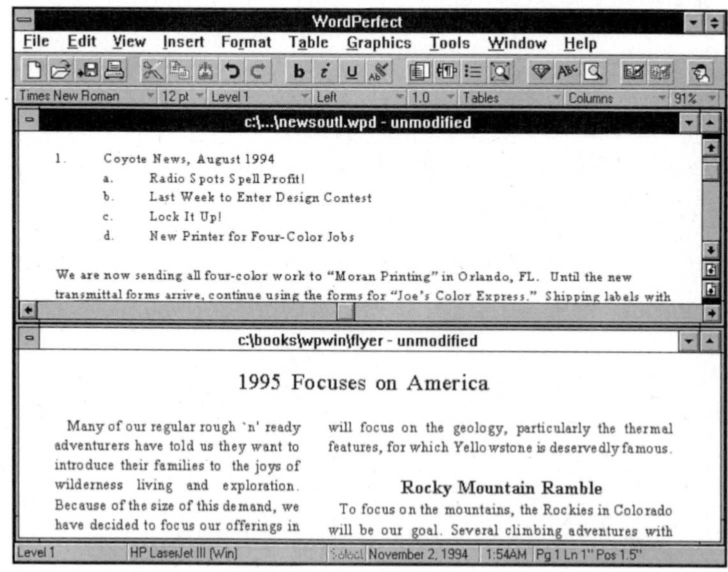

Fig. 1.25
Two documents tiled horizontally in the editing window. Tiling is useful if you want to compare two documents or if your work requires that both documents remain visible.

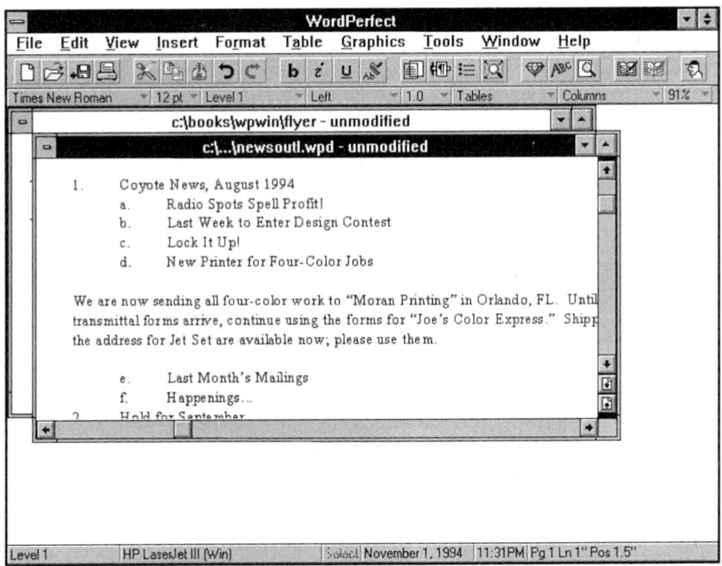

Fig. 1.26
Two documents cascaded in the editing window. Cascading is useful if you need access to multiple documents but want to see as much of the active document as possible.

Using Help

WordPerfect's Help system provides quick, easy access to a large body of explanatory information on WordPerfect, including an automated tutor that can walk you through such operations as italicizing, boldfacing, or underlining text or creating a table of contents. Except to perform highly technical operations, you may only rarely need to refer to the program's manual; the information available from Help is usually sufficient.

Help anticipates your questions about the program and understands that you may not know the correct terminology to use as you look for answers in an index. For step-by-step instructions on printing a document, for example, you simply choose **H**elp, **H**ow Do I, and then choose Print Documents.

WordPerfect's Coaches offer automated procedures in which WordPerfect instructs you step by step on how to perform an operation. The Coach tells you when to select text, what to do next, how to complete the operation, and how to save your changes. Coaches walk you through the task in your current document. Consequently, after you complete the task, you have not merely been taught the operation but have actually performed the task in your document.

You can access Help from virtually anywhere in the program, either through the **H**elp menu, as shown in figure 1.27, or by pressing F1 (Help). Help is especially useful if you are in the middle of an operation and do not know exactly how to complete it. Whether you are in a dialog box or adding special formatting to a section of text, you can press F1 to access *context-sensitive help*—that is, help that pertains directly to the current task.

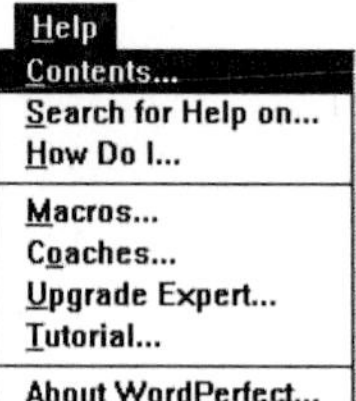

Fig. 1.27
The WordPerfect **H**elp menu enables you to select from several common Help features.

You also can obtain help on a specific element on-screen by pressing Shift+F1. The mouse pointer turns into a pointer with a question mark balloon. Position the pointer on the button or other element with which you want help, and click. The Help system displays help specific to that element.

Help is actually a separate application, run in a separate window from WordPerfect. Help has its own Maximize/Restore, Minimize, and Control Menu buttons and border. You can treat it as any other Windows application, keeping it active so that you can instantly switch to it, or tiling the Help and WordPerfect windows on the desktop so that you can read the Help text as you work.

The Help Menu

WordPerfect's **H**elp menu contains eight different options that provide different levels and functions of help. The Help menu includes the following items:

- *Contents*. This option lists a handful of common help topics, many of which are available from the main Help menu (see fig. 1.28). Those that are not are explained in the following table.

Item	Function
How Do I	Provides a separate window where you can select a specific task with which you want help.
Examples	Provides pictures of documents you can create, and explains how to perform the illustrated task.

Item	Function
Search	Enables you to search for specific help topics by using keywords.
Additional Help	Information about what is new, keystrokes, help with printing, glossary, additional products, and accessing customer support.
Macros	Displays help specific for Macros (the same as choosing **M**acros from the **H**elp menu).
Using Help	Provides more information on using the Help system.

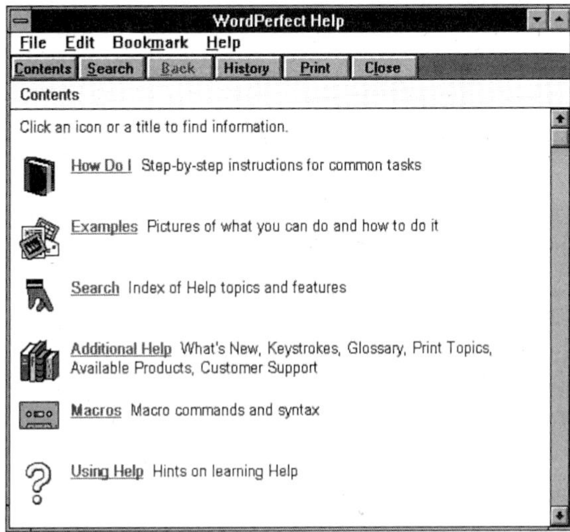

Fig. 1.28
The Help Contents screen enables you to select from several specific Help topics. Click the topic you want or press the Tab key to move the highlight bar to the topic and press Enter.

- ***S**earch for Help On.* Opens a dialog box that enables you to search for help by entering keywords. You can then list the various topics that contain or relate to the keywords and finally pick the topic to display. Figure 1.29 shows the Search dialog box used in Help.
- ***H**ow Do I.* Provides information on all WordPerfect functions in common, easily understood terminology. If a task is possible, How Do I can tell you how to do it without the frustration of searching through the manual (or the Help Index) for a feature the name of which you do not know.
- ***M**acros.* Provides help on WordPerfect's extensive Macro Language. To use this option, you must have WordPerfect's On-line Macro Help

file installed. See Appendix A, "Installing and Setting Up WordPerfect 6.1 for Windows," for more information on installation.

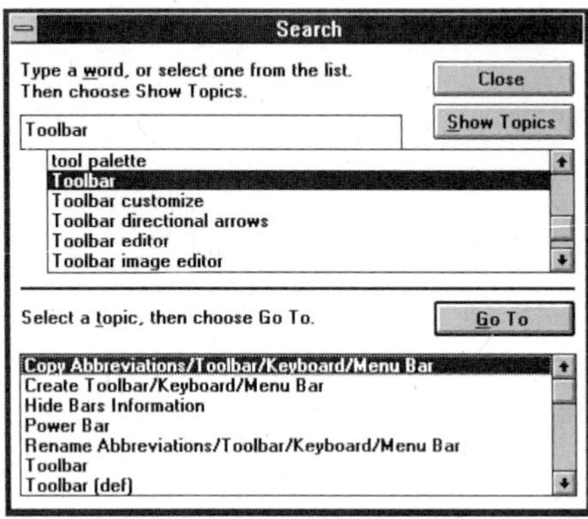

Fig. 1.29
The Search dialog box used in the WordPerfect 6.1 for Windows Help system. In this case, all the various Help topics under Toolbar are displayed.

- ***Co**aches.* Provides a list of automated procedures designed to help you learn a task while you perform it.
- ***U**pgrade Expert.* Provides information about WordPerfect features as compared to other word processing applications. Choose your old program in the upper list box, then choose a feature from your former program to see a display of the corresponding WordPerfect menu command, what the feature does, and a graphic illustration. Using the buttons at the bottom of the window, you can obtain even more Help on how to use the feature in WordPerfect.
- ***T**utorial.* Runs the WordPerfect Tutorial program, which teaches you the basics of using WordPerfect 6.1 for Windows. The program walks you through several lessons designed to make you knowledgeable about basic WordPerfect operations. The WordPerfect Tutorial can help you learn about the basics of WordPerfect 6.1 for Windows.
- ***A**bout WordPerfect.* Provides information on WordPerfect and the current operating environment. You can use this feature to see your registration number when calling WordPerfect Customer Support.

Meet the Coaches

When you first start WordPerfect, you are greeted by a QuickStart Coach that offers to tell you great news for WordPerfect 6.1 users, how to use time-saving features, and how to get more help (see fig. 1.30).

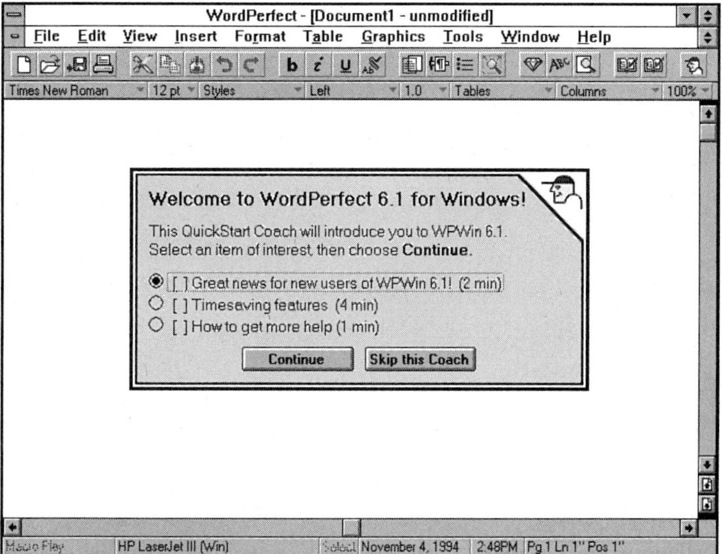

Fig. 1.30
Use the option buttons in the QuickStart Coach to run several tutorials that introduce you to WordPerfect 6.1 for Windows, several special features, and how to get more Help.

Additional Coaches are available to help you use several dozen of Word-Perfects most popular features. Choose C**o**aches from the WordPerfect **H**elp menu to see a list of the features that have Coaches. Select one to run an interactive Coach that provides information screens explaining each step in detail; with hands pointing to the buttons or commands you need to select. When you have completed a Coach, you have also completed using the feature in the current document.

Tip
The QuickStart Coach is included on the list of Coaches if you want to run it again in the future.

Help's Jump Terms, Glossary Terms, and Hints

Throughout the Help system are *jump terms*, usually displayed in green with a solid underline, and *glossary terms*, which appear in green with a dotted underline. Notice the many underlined items in figure 1.31, which shows a Help selection. The underlined terms `Toolbar Customize` and `Toolbar Image Editor` are jump terms; `Toolbars` and `Keyboard Script` have dashes under the letters and are glossary terms. You can use the jump terms to jump to another related Help topic. Use the glossary terms to access a definition of terms and an explanation of how they relate to WordPerfect.

To select a jump term or glossary term, double-click the term, or use Tab and Shift+Tab to highlight the term and then press Enter. After you select a jump term, WordPerfect takes you to the Help text for that term; from there, you can return to the origin of your jump by choosing the **B**ack button at the top of the screen. After you select a glossary term, a small pop-up box appears, offering a definition of the selected term. Click outside the box or press Enter to close the box.

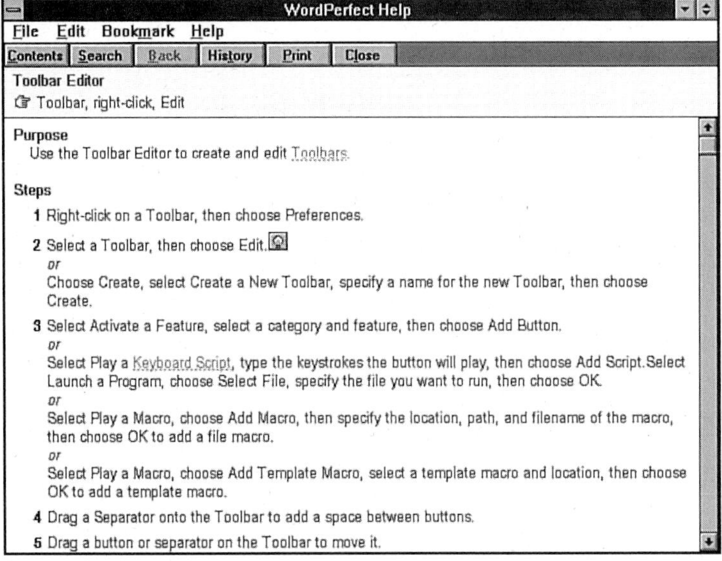

Fig. 1.31
The Toolbar Editor Help screen, showing jump terms and glossary terms.

Note

The contents of Help are part of the WordPerfect program. The Help features, such as the pull-down menus, buttons, and items such as hint buttons, are provided by Microsoft Windows. The text of this and the next few sections describe the features available if you use Windows 3.1. If you upgrade your version of Windows in the future, the menus, buttons, and icons may be slightly different. If you then need additional help, check the manual provided with the new Windows program.

The Help system also contains hints. A hint is represented as a small button with a light bulb on its face (see fig. 1.29). Choosing these buttons with the keyboard or mouse displays a small box containing a hint relating to the current topic, as shown in figure 1.32. To close the Hint box, click the mouse outside the box or press Enter.

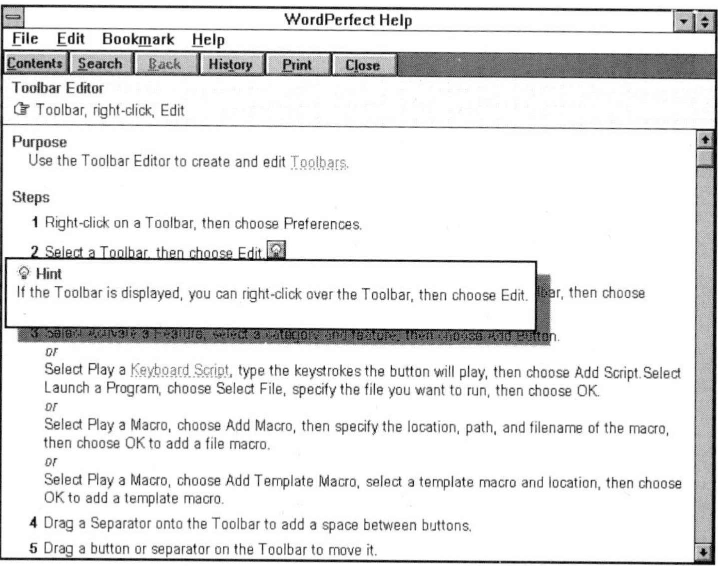

Fig. 1.32
A hint activated in the Toolbar Editor topic.

Navigating the Help System

Along with the jump terms and glossary terms, you can use the buttons at the top of the Help screen to access information. These buttons, which appear on all Help screens, provide rapid movement from one part of the Help system to another. The following list briefly describes each help button and its use:

- ***Contents***. Returns to the contents screen.
- ***Search***. Enables you to find help by specifying a word describing a feature or function and then selecting a specific topic to display.
- ***Back***. Returns to the previous Help screen.
- ***History***. Displays a dialog box listing all the topics accessed. You can select any previous topic and jump to it by double-clicking its entry or by using the arrows to highlight it and pressing Enter.
- ***Print***. Prints the currently displayed Help topic in its entirety.
- ***Close***. Closes the Help application.

You can use the arrow keys to move from one jump term or glossary term to the next. Use the PgUp and PgDn keys to move from one page of Help information to the next.

The Help Pull-Down Menus

Help also has four pull-down menus containing additional functions and options. The menus and their functions are described in the following:

- ***F**ile*. Enables you to **O**pen another Help file, **P**rint the current topic, set up the printer (P**r**int Setup), and E**x**it Help.
- ***E**dit*. Enables you to **C**opy part or all of a Help topic to the Windows clipboard or to **A**nnotate a topic with comments of your own.
- *Book**m**ark*. Enables you to **D**efine bookmarks in the Help system to help find a particular topic at a later time.
- ***H**elp*. Enables you to obtain more information on **H**ow to Use Help, set the Help window so that it is Always on **T**op of other windows, and obtain additional information about the Help system (**A**bout Help).

For more information on the Help system, choose **H**elp, **H**ow to Use Help from any Help screen.

Troubleshooting

How can I use Help to learn the steps for a task when Help disappears every time I click in my document?

Try using the Coach feature found on the WordPerfect **H**elp menu. Select the task you want to apply from the list of coaches and execute each step in the Coach. The Coach remains visible as you work in your document. When you have completed the task, the changes remain in your document. If you want to refer to another Help feature while working in your document, choose Always on **T**op from the **H**elp menu and then resize the Help window so it does not block your work.

I found a helpful topic that I want to see again but cannot remember its title or how I originally found it. How can I find it now?

If you have not exited Help since you displayed the topic, choose the His**t**ory button to see a list of every topic you have opened while in any Windows application. Scroll through the list to find the topic you want.

How can I keep Help open while I am working in several programs?

You can minimize the Help program or just click the window in the background. Then, press F1 for Help or use Alt+Tab to cycle to Help when you need it again.

From Here...

This chapter has given you an overview of WordPerfect 6.1 for Windows. The rest of the book goes into greater detail on specific features and tasks, expanding on the information in this chapter.

For information relating to the features in this chapter, consider reviewing these chapters:

- Chapter 2, "Creating and Saving a Document." This chapter teaches you about entering text, moving around the document, printing, saving your work, and exiting WordPerfect.
- Chapter 9, "Customizing WordPerfect." In this chapter you learn how to use all the customizing features available in WordPerfect, including creating toolbars, customizing the power bar, and changing the on-screen display.

Chapter 2

Creating and Saving a Document

by Gary Pickavet

In Chapter 1, you learned how to start WordPerfect and were introduced to the major features in WordPerfect 6.1 for Windows. You learned about the WordPerfect environment and its graphical user interface. You also learned how to use the Help system to quickly obtain information about a feature. You are now ready to learn how to use WordPerfect to create basic documents.

This chapter provides basic information on how to use WordPerfect to compose documents and safely save them to disk, and how to print documents.

In this chapter, you learn how to:

- Use built-in settings to control the way WordPerfect works
- Enter text, insert blank lines, use Typeover, and insert additional text
- Move the insertion point through the document by using the mouse and keyboard
- Print a single page or an entire on-screen document
- Save a document to disk
- Exit WordPerfect

Understanding WordPerfect's Built-in Settings

Even before you start typing, WordPerfect is at work for you. Many features, such as line spacing, tabs, margins, and fonts, are set at initial (or *default*) values when you start the program. For example, all margins are set at one inch, and the line spacing is set at single space. The paper size is assumed to be 8 1/2-by-11-inch letter with a portrait orientation (printing left to right across the shorter side of the page). Because WordPerfect starts with these default settings, you don't have to make any formatting decisions to start entering text. In subsequent chapters—especially those chapters devoted to formatting, printing, and desktop publishing—you learn how to override the default settings, alter the look of your documents, and create new templates where you can store custom settings to be applied to only certain documents.

Table 2.1 lists a few of WordPerfect's many default settings. Other defaults are covered where appropriate in chapters throughout this book. In addition, WordPerfect enables you to change default settings to suit your needs.

Table 2.1 Examples of WordPerfect's Built-in Initial Settings

Setting	Default Value
Margins	1-inch top, bottom, left, and right
Line spacing	Single-spaced
Page numbering	None
Justification	Left
Automatic timed backup of files	Automatically backs up files every 10 minutes
Hyphenation	Off
Paper size	Letter-size paper (8 1/2 inches by 11 inches)
Tabs	Every 1/2 inch

Entering Text in WordPerfect

When WordPerfect first starts, it displays a clean editing screen and several graphical tools to help you with your primary task: writing your document. These helpful tools—the Toolbar , the Power Bar, and the status bar—are described in Chapter 1, "Getting Started." These graphical tools enable you to quickly perform WordPerfect commands or start WordPerfect tools such as the writing tools or the WordPerfect TextArt, Draw, and Chart applications. The status bar provides you with a variety of useful information and also enables you to perform actions such as inserting the current date and time, or displaying the Go To dialog box. As detailed in Chapter 1, all these bars can be extensively modified to enable you to operate at peak efficiency.

If any of the bars are displayed on-screen and you find them distracting, you can turn them off, freeing even more screen space for text. These bars are turned on and off by making selections from the **V**iew pull-down menu. To turn off the Power Bar, for example, choose **V**iew. Then choose P**o**wer Bar to turn off the Power Bar. To turn off ALL bars, including the vertical and horizontal scroll bars, choose **V**iew, **H**ide Bars; or press Alt+Shift+F5. To bring the bars back, press Esc or again press Alt+Shift+F5; or choose **V**iew, **H**ide Bars. The bars reappear.

Think of the WordPerfect editing window as a piece of paper you have just rolled into a typewriter, ready to receive your thoughts. Unlike using a typewriter, using WordPerfect frees you from having to be concerned with the final product of your work when you start typing. You can first devote your energy and time to getting your thoughts down, and then go through the document adding formatting commands for each page and for your text. Formatting of text and pages is covered in Chapters 4, "Formatting Text," and 5, "Formatting Pages and Documents."

As you type documents into WordPerfect, remember these VERY important word processing rules:

- Do not stop typing text or press Enter at the end of each line. Let WordPerfect wrap the text for you. With a typewriter, you must press Return at the end of each line. With WordPerfect, you press Enter only when you want to end a paragraph or insert blank lines in the document. If WordPerfect cannot fit a word on a line, the program inserts a hidden code called a *soft return* into the document. This code ends the line and wraps the word to the next line. This feature is often called *word-wrap*.

  When you let WordPerfect wrap words and determine the end of each line, exciting things happen. If you change the size of the font you are using, WordPerfect automatically reformats the text so that each line still extends from the left to the right margin. WordPerfect moves words between lines as necessary so that each line is still full. WordPerfect also reformats your text when you add or delete text in a paragraph, moving words down a line or up a line as necessary.

- Do not indent lines by inserting spaces with the space bar. Always use the Tab key when you want to indent only the first line of a paragraph, or the Indent key (F7) to indent all the lines in the current paragraph.

  Text can be monospaced or spaced proportionally. With monospaced text, every letter, number, space, or any other character is represented by the same amount of space (for example, the letter *m* takes up the same space as the letter *i*). Most printers (especially laser printers) print proportionally, which means that smaller letters (like *i*) are printed in less space than wider letters or numbers (like *m*). Spaces on a proportional printer take up very little space. The Tab and Indent keys move the insertion point to an exact line position, making it possible to line up text neatly in a document.

Entering Blank Lines

Within a paragraph, you don't press the Enter key at the end of each line; instead, you let WordPerfect end each line and move words to the next line if they don't fit on the current line. WordPerfect places a hidden soft return formatting code in the document.

To end a paragraph or insert one or more blank lines, you press the Enter key. Pressing Enter causes the program to insert a hidden hard return formatting code at the place where you pressed Enter, and moves the insertion point to the next line. Pressing Enter twice ends the paragraph and places a blank line into the document. Each time you press Enter, WordPerfect places another hard return code into the document and creates a new line.

Chapter 3, "Retrieving and Editing Documents," describes a method of viewing WordPerfect's hidden codes. This feature is called the Reveal Codes window. Even without using the Reveal Codes feature, you can have WordPerfect show you where the hard returns are located in a document—right in the editing window. To view the location of hard returns, and also graphics symbols to represent spaces, tabs, and other formatting codes in the document window, choose **V**iew, **S**how ¶; or press Ctrl+Shift+F3. WordPerfect shows the hard returns in the editing window as a paragraph symbol. Follow the same steps to turn this feature off and hide the paragraph symbols.

Creating a Sample Letter

To illustrate the concepts introduced up to this point, and to get you accustomed to entering text, this section asks you to create a sample letter. Over the course of this chapter, you will complete the letter.

Start WordPerfect as described in the "Starting and Exiting WordPerfect" section in Chapter 1, then type the text in the following paragraph. Don't worry if you make a mistake; just use the Backspace key to erase the mistake and then retype the text. Don't forget to indent the first line of each paragraph by pressing Tab, not by using the space bar. Do not press Enter at the end of each line. Just keep typing and let WordPerfect wrap words as necessary. Press Enter twice at the end of each paragraph to end the paragraph and insert a blank line.

> **Thank you for the recent gift you sent me for my birthday. The rhinoceros earrings were perfect. Right after I received them, I attended a reception at the Holly Zoo. The earrings were the hit of the reception. I can't tell you how many people came up to me and commented on how unusual they thought the earrings were.**

(Press Enter twice.)

> **I'm looking forward to seeing you over your spring break. I received the note you sent telling me about your arrival at our airport on April 5th at 9 a.m. My nephew Gary and my niece Debbie will also be visiting that week. Remember how much fun we had when we all got together last summer? I have planned several events to keep you all busy for the week. I can't wait to see you! We have so much to catch up on.**

(Press Enter twice.)

> **Sincerely,**

(Press Enter five times to insert four blank lines for your signature.)

> **Marilyn Boyd**

Figure 2.1 shows the sample letter to this point, with the appropriate spacing. Soft returns are placed in a document by WordPerfect at the end of each line. Hard returns are line breaks that you insert to create additional white space in the document—for example, between paragraphs.

Moving through the Document

After you have entered text for a while, you may need to move the insertion point to a different place in the document to insert or delete text. WordPerfect provides a variety of methods for you to move to a different place in your text. You can move the insertion point by using the keyboard or the mouse.

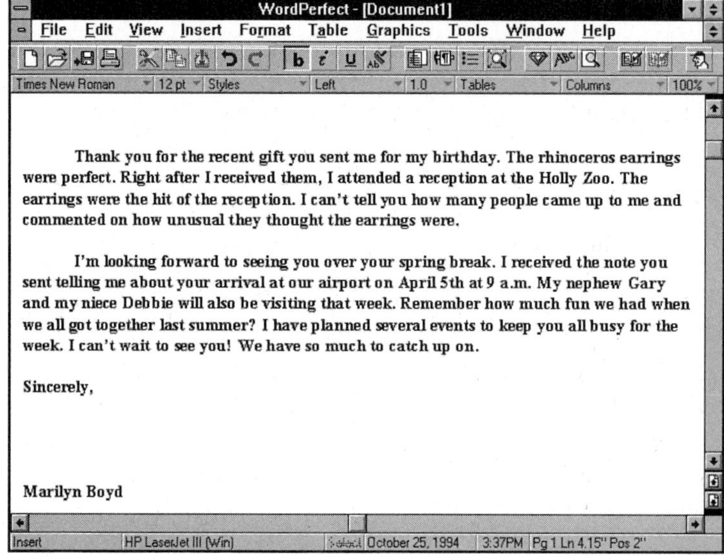

Fig. 2.1
A sample letter demonstrating soft and hard returns.

The insertion point can be moved as little as one character at a time or in major increments throughout the document. You can also use scroll bars that enable you to move the insertion point quickly, using a mouse.

◀ See "Understanding the Editing Screen," p. 18

If you are not familiar with the basic parts of the WordPerfect screen, see Chapter 1 for details.

Moving with the Mouse

You can use the mouse to move the insertion point quickly to a new location on the current screen or to move through the document. To move the insertion point only a very short distance, it's probably faster to use the keyboard insertion point-movement keys (described in the next section).

To move the insertion point quickly to a different location on the current screen, follow these steps:

1. Move the mouse pointer to the location on-screen where you want to move the insertion point. (While in the document, the mouse pointer looks like a tall, thin capital letter I, called the I-beam pointer.)

2. Click the left mouse button. The insertion point moves to the desired location.

Note

WordPerfect has a Left-Handed Mouse feature that enables you to switch the left and right button functions. This feature is helpful if you are left handed and prefer to use the right mouse button as the primary button. For more information on swapping the mouse button functions, see Chapter 9, "Customizing WordPerfect."

Using the scroll bars, you can scroll through the document. The scroll bars normally are shown only when a document extends beyond the boundaries of the screen (although you can set a display preference so that they are always displayed).

The following text covers using the vertical scroll bar to scroll a document from top to bottom. The steps for using the horizontal scroll bar to scroll the document from left to right are similar. To scroll a document with the scroll bars, use these methods:

Tip
When you use the mouse to scroll through a document, the insertion point does not move until you stop scrolling. To move the insertion point, move the mouse pointer into the document editing screen, and click the left mouse button.

- You can scroll a document one line at a time by clicking on the scroll arrow that points in the desired direction at the end of the scroll bar. A new line of text moves onto the screen and a line of text at the opposite side of the screen scrolls off the screen. The text that scrolls off is not lost; WordPerfect keeps track of the entire document. To scroll text continuously, click a scroll arrow and hold down the mouse button.

- With the scroll bar, you can scroll a document one screen at a time. If you click on the scroll bar between the scroll box (the gray square box shown on the scroll bar between the scroll arrow boxes) and the scroll arrow (but not on them), the next screen of the document appears and the current screen of text scrolls off the screen.

- Use the scroll box to scroll to any place in a document. The location of the scroll box on the scroll bar shows you the relative position of the current screen in relation to the entire document. If the scroll box is near the top of the scroll bar, you are near the beginning of the document. To scroll the document quickly to another location in the document, drag the scroll box to the position you want. When you release the mouse button, that portion of the document appears. If you drag the scroll box to the bottom of the scroll bar, for example, the end of the document appears on-screen.

- At the bottom of the vertical scroll bar, you see a pair of icons that each look like a page—one with an up arrow (called the Previous Page button) and one with a down arrow (called the Next Page button). If you click on the Previous Page or Next Page icon, the document is positioned at the top of the current page (if you click on the up arrow) or the top of the next page (if you click on the down arrow).

▶ See "The Status Bar," p. 340

- You can also use the Status Bar Preferences option to display the page number on the status bar at the bottom of the screen. When you choose Page in the Status Bar Items box as a Status Bar Preferences option, the page number appears, and an icon of a book is displayed with left and right arrows on the book's pages. Click on the left arrow to go to the top of the previous page. Click on the right arrow to go to the top of the next page. Unlike the scroll bars, which do not move the insertion point in the document, choosing the book icon moves the insertion point and places it at the top of the page after the page is displayed on-screen. For information about adding the Page item to the status bar, see Chapter 9.

Moving with the Keyboard

Most keyboards in recent years have separate insertion point-movement keys and a ten-key number pad. With some keyboards, you use the number pad to move the insertion point. If you must use the number pad for insertion point movement, you can temporarily turn off the Num Lock feature so that when you press an insertion point-movement key (for example, the 4 key doubles as the ← key), a number is not printed. If you turn off Num Lock and want to enter a number with the number pad, hold down the Shift key and the number is displayed instead of the insertion point being moved.

The WordPerfect directional keys are Home, End, Page Up, Page Down, up arrow, down arrow, left arrow, and right arrow. As you can see in table 2.2, you can use these keys alone or in combination with other control keys (such as the Alt and Ctrl keys) to move quickly and easily throughout the document. When you move through the document by using the keyboard directional keys, the insertion point moves too.

Note

Table 2.2 is based on the assumption that you are using the default WordPerfect for Windows 6.1 keyboard.

Table 2.2 Moving the Insertion Point with the Keyboard

Movement	Key
One character left	←
One character right	→
One word left	Ctrl+←
One word right	Ctrl+→
One line up	↑
One line down	↓
Beginning of the preceding paragraph	Ctrl+↑
Beginning of the following paragraph	Ctrl+↓
Beginning of the current line (after codes)	Home
Beginning of the current line (before codes)	Home, Home
End of the current line	End
Top of the editing screen	PgUp
Bottom of the editing screen	PgDn
First line of preceding page	Alt+PgUp
First line of following page	Alt+PgDn
Top of the document	Ctrl+Home
Bottom of the document	Ctrl+End

Tip
You can add a Go To button to the Power Bar or Toolbar, or double-click on the Combined Position box (the one that displays the page number, line, and position) on the status bar to display the Go To dialog box.

Moving the Insertion Point with Go To

WordPerfect's Go To command enables you to quickly move to a specific location in a document. You can choose Go To from the menus or from the keyboard.

To use the Go To feature, follow these steps:

1. Choose **E**dit, **G**o To; or press Ctrl+G. The Go To dialog box appears (see fig. 2.2). This dialog box gives you options to move the insertion point to a specific position, page number, bookmark, table, or cell/range.

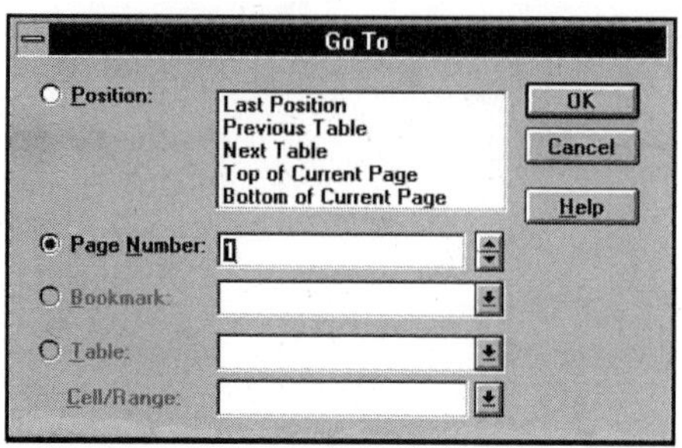

Fig. 2.2
The Go To dialog box enables you to quickly move to a specific location in a document.

2. Move the insertion point to the desired location by choosing from the following options:

   Position—Last Position. Returns the insertion point to its position before the last major move (for example, after doing Ctrl+Home).

   Position—Previous Table. Moves to the top of the table prior to the current location of the insertion point.

   Position—Next Table. Moves to the top of the table following the current location of the insertion point.

   Position—Top of Current Page. Moves to the top of the current page.

   Position—Bottom of Current Page. Moves to the bottom of the current page.

   Page Number (this is the option WordPerfect offers as the default). Moves to a specific page number in the document. Type the desired page number or use the up and down arrows to scroll the page number.

▶ See "Selecting Text," p. 103

If you have highlighted selected text in your document, several other options are listed in the **P**osition list box. These additional options are:

Position—Beginning of Selection. Moves the insertion point to the beginning of the selected text. The text is deselected.

Position—End of Selection. Moves the insertion point to the end of the selected text. The text is deselected.

Position—Reselect Text. This option reselects the text that was selected when either the Beginning of Selection or End of Selection options are used.

After you have selected and then deselected a portion of your document, the following additional option is available:

Position—Reselect Last Selection. Re-highlights the portion of a document that was last selected.

In certain situations, other actions are also available in the Go To dialog box:

Bookmark. Moves to the location of the selected bookmark. This choice is not available if the document has no bookmarks set. Type the bookmark name or choose the drop-down list arrow to display a list of bookmark names from which to choose.

Table. Moves to the selected table. This choice is available if a document contains one or more tables. Type the table name or choose the drop-down list arrow to display a list of table names from which to choose.

Cell/Range. Moves to the cell or range within the selected table. Type the cell or range name or choose the drop-down list arrow to display a list of names from which to choose.

Completing the Sample Letter

Now that you have learned the various methods with which to move the insertion point and scroll your document, you are ready to finish the sample letter by following these steps:

1. Press Ctrl+Home to move the insertion point to the top of the first paragraph of the letter.

2. Press Enter twice.

3. Press Ctrl+Home to again move the insertion point to the top of the document.

4. To enter today's date, choose **I**nsert, **D**ate, Date **T**ext; or press Ctrl+D; or double-click the date on the status bar at the bottom of the WordPerfect window.

   WordPerfect inserts the current date, based on your computer's internal clock. If the date and time are incorrect, use the DOS DATE and TIME commands to correct them as needed.

5. Press Enter twice.

6. Type the following name and address. Don't forget to press Enter at the end of each line to insert a hard return and move to the next line.

    Ms. Kelly Jeffers
    1234 El Camino Real
    Holly, CA 12345

7. Press Enter twice and type the following salutation:

    Dear Kelly,

Your screen now shows the completed sample letter (see fig. 2.3).

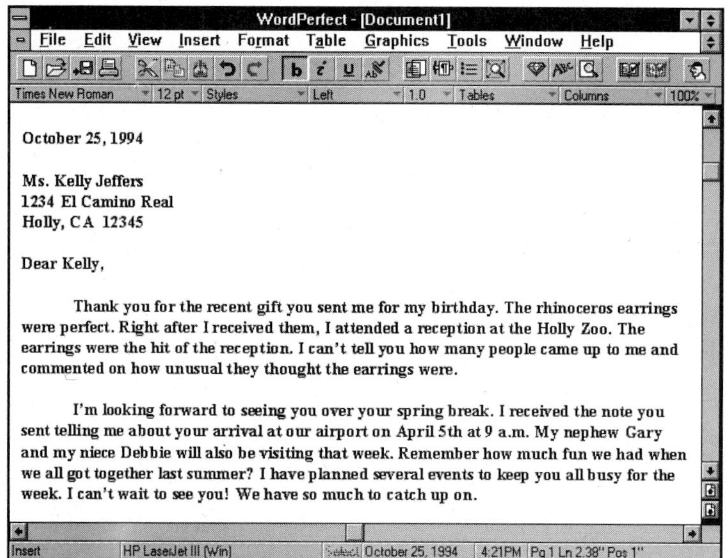

Fig. 2.3
The completed sample letter.

Adding Text within a Document

One of the most powerful features of word processing is its ability to move or add text anywhere in a document. With a typewriter, adding text in the middle of a document requires retyping one or more pages. With WordPerfect, you simply move the insertion point to the location in the document where you want to add the text, and type. WordPerfect takes care of adjusting line breaks and page breaks.

Suppose that you want to add a sentence in the second paragraph of the sample letter used in this chapter. To do so, follow these steps:

1. Use the mouse or insertion point-movement keys to move the insertion point to the word *I* at the beginning of the next-to-last sentence of the second paragraph.

2. Type the following:

 Don't forget to bring your bathing suit.

As you type the new text, existing letters are moved to the right, making room for the new text.

Using Typeover

If you don't want to add new text but just want to type over existing text, you can use the Typeover feature. To turn the Typeover mode on and off, press the Insert key on the keyboard or double-click the General Status display box on the status bar at the bottom left of the screen. When Typeover mode is on, `Typeover` is displayed in the General Status box on the status bar at the bottom left of the screen. Instead of moving text to the right to make room for the new text, what you type replaces existing text. When Typeover is off and Insert mode is on, `Insert` is displayed.

▶ See "Inserting and Overwriting Text," p. 90

Tip
If a style is in use at the location of the insertion point, its name is shown in the General Status field and the Insert/Typeover status is not shown.

Typeover mode is useful when making character-for-character replacements, such as changing a misspelled word (for example, changing the word *teh* to *the*).

Using Cancel (Esc)

To cancel a function-key command or to back out of a menu, use Cancel (Esc).

You can also use Esc to redisplay the various bars (for example, the menu bar, Power Bar, and status bar) after you have chosen the **H**ide Bars option on the **V**iew pull-down menu.

▶ See "The Status Bar," p. 340

Now that you have composed your document, you may want to print it. In the next section, you learn how to print an on-screen document on your printer.

Printing an On-Screen Document

You do not have to save your document before you print it (although saving your document before printing is a good idea in case a problem occurs while you are printing that causes your machine to crash).

► See "Selecting and Configuring Your Printer," p. 305

Although in this section you will be printing only an on-screen document, with WordPerfect you have much flexibility when printing. A document does not have to be on-screen to print. WordPerfect can also print documents directly from disk. (Refer to Chapter 8, "Basic Output: Printing, Faxing, and E-mail," for more detailed information on printing.) The steps listed in this section are the most basic for printing an on-screen document.

Note

The steps that follow assume that you have already installed and selected either a Windows or WordPerfect printer driver, as described in Chapter 8.

To print the on-screen document, follow these steps:

1. Decide whether you want to print one page or the entire document. To print just one page, make sure that the insertion point is located somewhere on the desired page.

2. Choose **F**ile, **P**rint; or press F5; or press Ctrl+P; or click the Print icon on the Toolbar. The Print dialog box appears (see fig. 2.4).

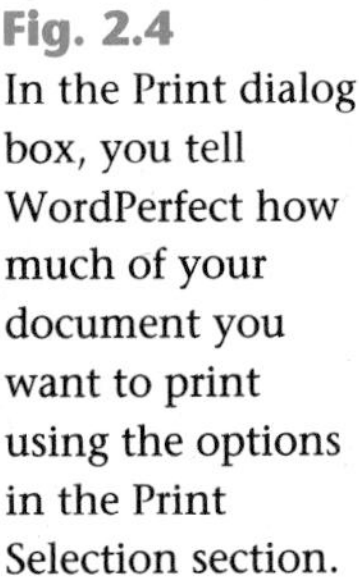

Fig. 2.4
In the Print dialog box, you tell WordPerfect how much of your document you want to print using the options in the Print Selection section.

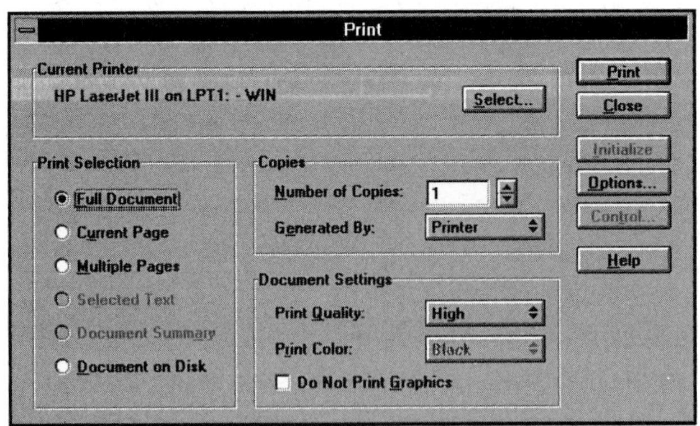

Note

If the printer shown in the Current Printer text box at the top of the Print dialog box is not the printer you will be using, use **S**elect to select the correct printer before continuing. For information on selecting printers, see Chapter 8.

3. Because the sample letter is less than one page, leave the default setting at **F**ull Document. For a document that is more than one page, choose C**u**rrent Page to print just one page.

4. Choose **P**rint to print the desired selection. You return to the document.

WordPerfect displays the message `Preparing Document For Printing` on-screen as it prepares to print. If the printer is configured and connected properly, printing begins almost immediately.

Figure 2.5 shows the printed sample letter.

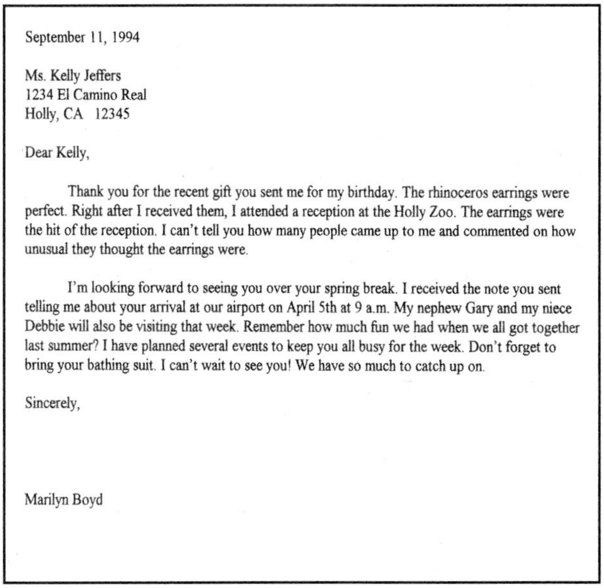

September 11, 1994

Ms. Kelly Jeffers
1234 El Camino Real
Holly, CA 12345

Dear Kelly,

Thank you for the recent gift you sent me for my birthday. The rhinoceros earrings were perfect. Right after I received them, I attended a reception at the Holly Zoo. The earrings were the hit of the reception. I can't tell you how many people came up to me and commented on how unusual they thought the earrings were.

I'm looking forward to seeing you over your spring break. I received the note you sent telling me about your arrival at our airport on April 5th at 9 a.m. My nephew Gary and my niece Debbie will also be visiting that week. Remember how much fun we had when we all got together last summer? I have planned several events to keep you all busy for the week. Don't forget to bring your bathing suit. I can't wait to see you! We have so much to catch up on.

Sincerely,

Marilyn Boyd

Fig. 2.5
The printed sample letter.

You do not have to wait until the document is printed to continue working in WordPerfect. WordPerfect and Windows print documents in the background, so you can continue your work on the same or a new document while the printing occurs.

Note

Your document doesn't have to be on-screen to print. You can print a document stored on disk (either a floppy or hard disk) directly from the disk. You can also print selected pages from a document rather than the entire document or a single page. Chapter 8 explores the various print options.

Now that you have composed and printed your document, you may want to save it safely to disk for future use. In the next section, you learn how to save an on-screen document to a disk.

Troubleshooting

I forgot to turn on my printer. Even after I turned on the printer, my document still won't print.

You are probably using the Windows Print Manager. If so, when you print a document, it is copied to your hard disk drive for printing by the Print Manager. This enables you to continue working in a Windows application very quickly while printing occurs in the background. Although WordPerfect has a separate print process that works similar to the Windows Print Manager, most people have the Print Manager turned on so it is used with their other Windows applications.

When an error occurs with your printer (like not turning it on), the Windows Print Manager notes the error and stops trying to print. Correcting the problem does not restart the Print Manager. In fact, as you continue to select Print in your Windows applications, the print jobs continue to back up rather than print.

To fix this problem, switch to the Windows Print Manager. Press the Alt key and hold it down while pressing Tab until a box that says Print Manager appears on your screen. Release the keys and the Print Manager appears. The word `Error!` appears in the Status column next to your printer. Highlight the printer, and then select **P**rinter, **R**esume Printer. The stalled job and the jobs following it will print.

Saving a Document to Disk

You often want to keep on disk a copy of the documents you create. If you don't want to save your new document (or changes to an existing document), simply exit WordPerfect without saving. WordPerfect gives you several methods of saving a document as a file on disk.

With the **F**ile **S**ave or **F**ile Save **A**s command, you save a copy of the on-screen document to disk. When you use **F**ile **S**ave or **F**ile Save **A**s, the document remains on-screen for additional work.

If you have not saved the on-screen document or have made changes since the last time you saved the document, when you use the **F**ile **C**lose (Ctrl+F4) or **F**ile E**x**it command (Alt+F4), a dialog box appears that asks whether you want to save the on-screen document. Choose Cancel to return to the on-screen document. If you answer No, the document is not saved. If you previously chose **F**ile **C**lose, the current document window closes and you remain in WordPerfect. If you previously chose **F**ile E**x**it, WordPerfect closes and you return to the Windows Program Manager.

Note

When you close a document, you are telling WordPerfect that you are finished with the on-screen document but don't want to exit WordPerfect. To close a document, choose **F**ile, **C**lose; or press Ctrl+F4. A dialog box appears and asks whether you want to save the on-screen document. After you indicate whether you want to save the document, the text is cleared. You are now ready to continue with your next project.

The first time you save a document, WordPerfect prompts you for a file name to assign to your document. The file name must meet normal DOS conventions. The file name consists of a primary file name (which can be from one to eight characters) and an optional extension (which can be from one to three characters). If you choose to enter a suffix, the primary file name and suffix must be separated by a period. The file name cannot contain spaces or certain DOS reserved characters (such as ? or *).

Within a directory, file names must be unique. For example, if you are working in a directory named LETTERS, and have saved a file called KIMBER, you cannot save a *different* file also called KIMBER in that same directory unless you replace the older file with the newer file. However, you can have a file named KIMBER in the directory named LETTERS and also in a directory named PETS. Although both files are named KIMBER, they can both exist because they are stored in different directories. Think of them as stored in two different folders. Although DOS limits the number of characters in file names, it is a good practice to make the file name as meaningful as you can for the subject it contains. For a letter to your father, for example, you can use the file name DAD.LTR. Letters to other family members may be MARILYN.LTR, DEBBIE.LTR, GARY.LTR, and so on.

Tip

If you do not enter a file extension, WordPerfect adds the extension WPD by default. You can customize WordPerfect to use a different default file extension, or to not add a file extension at all.

Entire chapters in books are written on file management and how to name directories and files within the directories. In the end, only you can decide on what is a meaningful system for *your* use. The best advice is to keep your system logical and think it through before you start saving files. Then, always organize and save your files in accordance with the system you have chosen to use.

To save the sample letter, follow these steps:

1. With the sample letter on-screen, choose **F**ile, Save **A**s; or press F3. The Save As dialog box appears (see fig. 2.6).

   The insertion point is placed in the File**n**ame text box, where you can give the document a name. The characters *.* are displayed in the File**n**ame text box and must be replaced with a valid file name. These highlighted characters are replaced when you type a character.

▶ See "Customizing File Preferences," p. 329

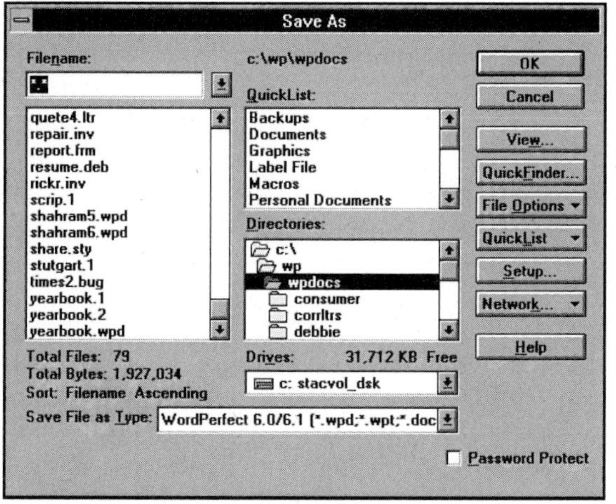

Fig. 2.6
The Save As dialog box contains useful information and a variety of option buttons. It also displays the file format that is used to save the file.

2. To save the file to a drive or directory different from the current drive and directory—shown above the **Q**uickList list box—enter the full path name.

   You can type the new path name in the File**n**ame text box, or you can use the mouse or Tab and arrow keys to highlight a directory in the **D**irectories list or a drive in the Dri**v**es text box. If you type a drive and directory in the File**n**ame text box instead of actually selecting another drive or directory, the default drive and directory do not change, but the file is saved to the alternate drive and directory as shown in the File**n**ame text box.

The Save As dialog box provides you with several options. These options include the File **O**ptions and **S**etup buttons. The **S**etup button displays the Open/Save As Setup dialog box and enables you to change a variety of options that affect the display of files, directories, and file formats in the file Open and Save As dialog boxes. The File **O**ptions button enables you to perform a variety of file and directory functions normally done at the DOS prompt. The Quick**L**ist button enables you to display the QuickList list box and use the QuickList feature to build shortcut paths to your files and directories. The **S**etup, File **O**ptions, and Quick**L**ist functions are explained in detail in Chapter 28, "Advanced File Management."

▶ See "Setting Up the File List Display," p. 963

▶ See "Using the QuickList Feature," p. 978

A Vie**w** button is also provided. If you aren't sure of the contents of a file listed in the File**n**ame list box, highlight the file and choose Vie**w** to run the WordPerfect file Viewer. For more information about using the Viewer, see Chapter 3.

3. Type **SAMPLE.LET** as a file name for the sample letter in the File**n**ame text box of the Save As dialog box.
4. Choose OK or press Enter to save the sample letter.

The default WordPerfect document window name (for example, Document1) displayed on the title bar at the top of the document editing window is replaced by the file name and directory you specify for the document.

To tell WordPerfect the directory you want as the default when you save and open files, follow these steps:

1. Choose **E**dit, Pr**e**ferences. The Preferences dialog box appears.
2. Choose **F**ile. The File Preferences dialog box appears, displaying the options for the **D**ocuments/Backup choice.
3. Choose D**e**fault Directory and type the desired path in the text box. You can also click the File Browse button to the right of the text box for help with locating the desired directory.
4. To save your change, choose OK and **C**lose until you return to the document. The selected directory will now be used as the beginning point for file open and save functions.

After you save your file, subsequent saving of the document is even easier. After making subsequent changes to the document, you don't have to type the document name again unless you want to change its name. After you save the document on-screen and give it a name, WordPerfect remembers the name.

To save an already named on-screen document, choose **F**ile, **S**ave; or press Ctrl+S. The file is saved with the same name you assigned previously. Because you have already assigned the document a file name, WordPerfect saves the file without stopping to display the Save As dialog box.

► See "Opening a File," p. 84

As the file is being saved, the mouse pointer changes to an hourglass, showing that WordPerfect is saving the file.

You can tell WordPerfect where you want your documents stored as the default or normal location. This location will be used when you open or save files, unless you change it.

Saving a Document with a Different Name or File Format

Unless you specify otherwise, WordPerfect assumes that you want to save files in WordPerfect 6.0/6.1 format. WordPerfect enables you to save files in a variety of other file formats as well, including prior WordPerfect formats. WordPerfect 5.1 cannot read WordPerfect 6.x files unless you have upgraded to WordPerfect 5.1+. So, if you are giving a file to someone who does not have WordPerfect 6.x or 5.1+, you need to save a copy of your file in WordPerfect 5.1 format. WordPerfect also includes many other common file formats, such as various versions of Microsoft Word, MultiMate, and WordStar.

You also may want to save a file under a different name, to a different directory, or to a different disk drive. If you plan to give a copy of a file to someone else, for example, you may want to save the file onto a floppy disk.

When you want to save an existing file under a different name or in a different format, follow these steps:

1. Choose **F**ile, Save **A**s; or press F3. The Save As dialog box appears with the file name shown in the File**n**ame text box and WordPerfect 6.0/6.1 as the file format in the Save File as **T**ype text box. The insertion point appears in the File**n**ame text box.

2. If you want to save the document with a different file name, type a different file name in the File**n**ame text box. Because the file name is highlighted, typing a character causes the existing entry to disappear. To change only a small part of the existing information, move to the point where you want to make the change by using the arrow keys or the mouse. Then use the Delete key and type new characters as necessary to complete your changes to the information in the File**n**ame text box. Use the **D**irectories and Dri**v**es list boxes if you want to save the file to a different directory or drive.

3. To save the file with a different file format, choose Save File as **T**ype. A drop-down list is displayed that shows other file formats (see fig. 2.7). Many file formats are available from which you can select, both for WordPerfect Corporation and other word processing programs. In the figure, WordPerfect 6.0/6.1 format is highlighted. Use the scroll bar or keyboard arrow keys to move to the desired file format. Double-click your choice or press Enter to select it.

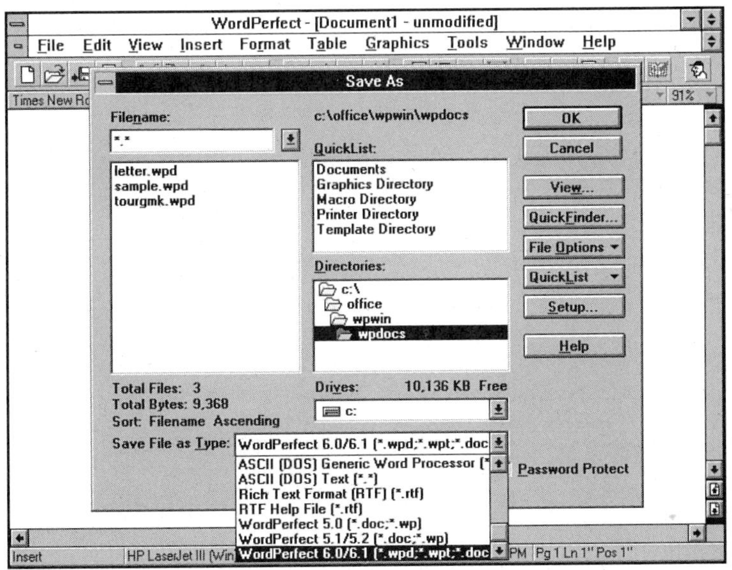

Fig. 2.7
The Save As dialog box with the Save File as **T**ype drop-down list of file format options for saving text.

4. When you have the file name, drive, directory, and file type information the way you want it, choose OK or press Enter to save the file.

Note

You can display a list of the ten most recently saved files. While in the File**n**ame text box, click the drop-down list button or press the down arrow key to display the drop-down list of recently saved files. To select a file name, double-click the file name, or highlight the file name and press Enter.

► See "Moving Files," p. 957

► See "Renaming Files," p. 957

► See "Deleting Files," p. 958

Troubleshooting

I accidentally saved my file with the wrong name (or to the wrong place). What should I do now?

WordPerfect is extremely well prepared for these kinds of mistakes! Unlike many other programs, WordPerfect enables you to fix problems like this from within WordPerfect. If you've saved the document to the wrong name, simply rename it. If you've saved the document to the wrong location, you can move it.

First, close the document you've saved with the wrong name or location following the instructions in the section "Closing Documents" that follows.

To access the WordPerfect file management commands, choose **F**ile and then choose either **O**pen or Save **A**s. Use File**n**ame, **D**irectories, and Dri**v**es to highlight the file you want to manipulate; then choose File **O**ptions.

Choose **M**ove or **R**ename as appropriate. If you've saved the file with both the wrong and right name, choose **D**elete to delete the incorrectly saved document.

Choose Cancel to close the Open or Save As dialog box and return to the editing screen.

Closing Documents

When you are finished editing or composing a document, you can close the document and continue editing or composing other documents in WordPerfect. To stay in WordPerfect but close the document you are working on, do the following:

1. Choose **F**ile, **C**lose; or press Ctrl+F4. If you have modified the document during the current editing session, a dialog box similar to the one shown in figure 2.8 appears and asks whether you want to save the on-screen document. If the document has already been assigned a name, the file name and directory are shown. If this document is new and

hasn't been saved, the file name appears as Document1. (Or, if the document is an untitled document from a document editing window other than 1, the number after the word Document is the same as the document editing window in which you are working.)

If you have not modified the document, WordPerfect does not display a message dialog box—it simply closes the document.

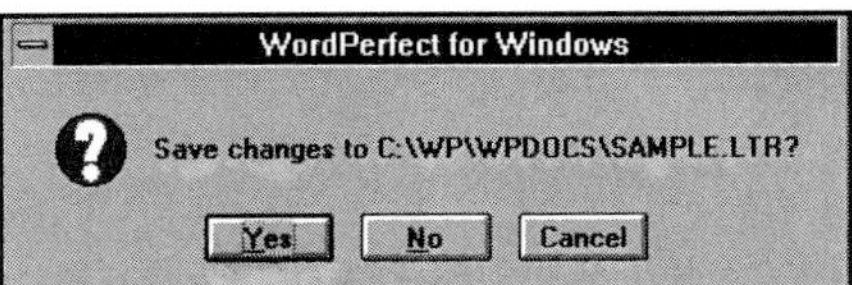

Fig. 2.8
The WordPerfect dialog box with the `Save changes to <filename>` message.

2. Choose **Y**es to save the file, **N**o to clear the screen without saving the document, or Cancel (Esc) to change your mind and return to the on-screen document.

If you close the last open document, you can continue the WordPerfect session in a new document window. If the document you close is not the last open document, you are switched to one of the current open documents, which you can edit.

Note

WordPerfect has a Close All feature that can be added to the Toolbar or Power Bar. It can also be found on the Utilities Toolbar provided by WordPerfect. When you add the icon and then use this feature, all open document windows are closed. A convenient Close All Documents dialog box appears. This dialog box has an x in the Save check box for each modified document. It enables you to indicate whether or not you want to save each file, and to enter the file name you want used for each saved file.

▶ See "Switching between Toolbars," p. 451

▶ See "Customizing a Toolbar," p. 455

▶ See "Customizing the Power Bar," p. 462

Opening New Document Windows

WordPerfect enables you to have up to nine document editing windows open at the same time. To open a new document, follow these steps:

1. Choose **F**ile, **N**ew; press Ctrl+T; or click the New Document Toolbar icon. The New Document dialog box appears (see fig. 2.9). By default, this dialog box highlights the Create a Blank Document choice in the Main group. This creates a new blank document based on the default

standard template. WordPerfect has created and provides a variety of templates for your use, or you can create your own templates. From this dialog box you can also view or edit templates.

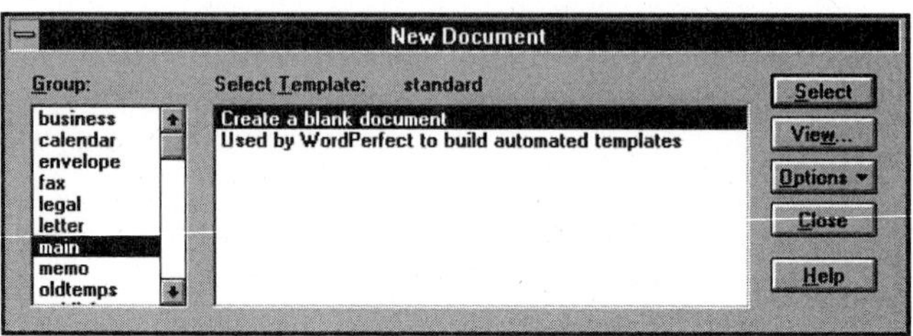

Fig. 2.9
Make selections from the New Document dialog box to create a new document based on a variety of templates.

2. To begin a new document based on the standard template, in the **G**roup entry box, choose main.

▶ See "Using the Templates Provided with WordPerfect for Windows," p. 394

3. In the Select **T**emplate list box, highlight Create a Blank Document. "Standard" is displayed above the Select **T**emplate list box to tell you that the new document will be based on WordPerfect's standard document.

4. Choose **S**elect or press Enter. A new blank editing screen appears and you are ready to begin composing your document.

Tip
You can create a new document based on the default template without displaying the New Document dialog box by pressing Ctrl+N. A new document is immediately displayed.

To begin a new document using the settings from a template other than the standard template, choose the desired template. WordPerfect has created a variety of templates that enable you to quickly create professional looking letters and memos, fax cover sheets, business cards, resumes, and even term papers.

Exiting WordPerfect

To exit WordPerfect, optionally saving any open files, follow these steps:

1. Choose **F**ile, E**x**it; or press Alt+F4. WordPerfect prompts you to indicate whether you want to save each open document.

2. Respond **Y**es if you want WordPerfect to save the file and exit to Windows, **N**o to exit immediately to Windows without saving the file, or Cancel to return to the document without saving the file or exiting WordPerfect. If you have more than one document window open, you are prompted to save each modified document, and then WordPerfect exits to Windows.

If you have made no changes to any open document windows, WordPerfect exits immediately to Windows.

From Here...

In this chapter, you learned how to compose a document in WordPerfect. You saw that with WordPerfect, you can concentrate your effort on getting your thoughts typed without regard to format or exact accuracy; unlike using a typewriter, using WordPerfect enables you to easily edit your documents. You learned some fundamental word processing rules to remember while you are entering text into WordPerfect.

After composing, you learned how to print and save the on-screen document to disk. Finally, you learned how to close each document, how to open a new document, and how to exit WordPerfect when you finish using the program.

For more information, refer to the following chapters:

- Chapter 1, "Getting Started," shows you how to work with the WordPerfect graphical user interface and understand the purpose of the various on-screen controls and tools.
- Chapter 3, "Retrieving and Editing Documents," shows you how to retrieve a previously saved document and modify it until the document expresses your ideas the way you want them conveyed.
- Chapter 8, "Basic Output: Printing, Faxing, and E-mail," leads you through the steps necessary to print a document and control the print jobs. You also learn how to transmit a document from your computer to someone else using a fax machine or electronic mail.
- Chapter 11, "Using Templates," shows you how to quickly produce a variety of professional documents, signs, calendars, and even business cards using templates.

Chapter 3

Retrieving and Editing Documents

by Gary Pickavet

In this chapter, you learn how to retrieve a previously saved document from disk and edit it. If you are new to word processing, this chapter acquaints you with electronic editing. When using a typewriter, editing a document entails retyping one or more pages—even to make a very small change. With WordPerfect's electronic editing features, you can make changes and print corrected pages quickly and easily. After you become accustomed to Word-Perfect's editing features, you may wonder how you got along without them!

Preparing a document from beginning to end involves at least three essential steps: creating, editing, and formatting. Chapter 2 covered creating a document. In the next chapter, you learn about WordPerfect's powerful formatting commands. But between creating a document and formatting its appearance, you need to edit the document to make sure it says what you want, the way you want to say it.

In this chapter, you learn how to:

- Open and edit an existing document
- Retrieve an existing document into an open document
- Use the Reveal Codes window to view hidden codes
- Use the Select function to select text and graphics
- Move or copy text and graphics

- Save a portion of a document to disk
- Find and replace text and codes
- Move information between windows and Windows applications
- Use Undo, Redo, and Undo/Redo History to set the number of Undo/Redo levels

Opening and Retrieving Files

Chapter 2, "Creating and Saving a Document," discusses how to save a file to disk. Normally, you save a file because you want to work on it or refer to it later. For example, you may be composing a document and want to stop for the day. You can save the document, and then reopen it the next day to continue working.

WordPerfect has two commands that copy a document from disk to your screen: **F**ile, **O**pen and **I**nsert, F**i**le.

The **F**ile, **O**pen command copies a previously saved document from disk to a blank editing screen, called the *document window*. The document retains its initial settings, such as margins, justification, font, and file name. If you are already composing a document in a document window, WordPerfect opens another blank window for the file you are opening. The newly opened document becomes the active document editing window.

The **I**nsert, F**i**le command copies a previously saved document from disk into the current on-screen document at the insertion point. In other words, this command is used to retrieve a previously created document that is already stored on disk and insert it within another document.

Opening a File

Although you can revise a document created during a current WordPerfect session, often you will want to open and edit an existing, previously saved document. For example, you may have a sales report for the prior quarter on disk that you want to use as a starting point for the current quarterly report. To do this, you open the prior quarterly report file, make the necessary changes, and save the revised report (most likely with a new file name).
To open a file previously saved to disk, follow these steps:

1. Choose **F**ile, **O**pen; or press Ctrl+O. The Open File dialog box appears (see fig. 3.1).

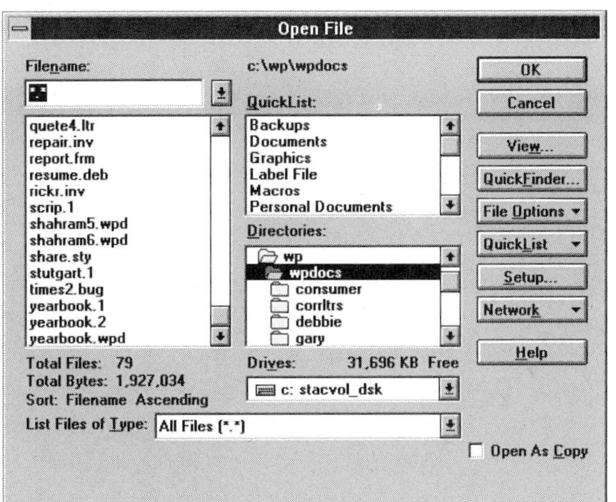

Fig. 3.1
The Open File dialog box gives you several options, including the capability to display a list of the last ten files opened.

Note

WordPerfect keeps track of the last four files you have opened. When you choose **F**ile, the names of these files are displayed at the bottom of the File pull-down menu. If the file you want to open is listed, highlight it and press Enter; or click the file name.

2. After the dialog box opens, you may choose from several actions to open a file:

   - If the file you want to open is in the current default directory, you can type the file name in the File**n**ame text box (for example, SAMPLE.LET). Then click OK, or press Enter.

     Alternatively, scroll the list of files in the File**n**ame list box until the desired file name is highlighted. Double-click the file name, or press Enter.

   - If the file you want to open is one of the last ten files opened, you can choose the file from the File**n**ame drop-down list. This list shows the ten most recently opened files. Click the drop-down list button or press the down-arrow key to display the drop-down list of recently opened files. Double-click the file name, or highlight the file name and press Enter.

- WordPerfect provides several filters so you can restrict the files listed in the File**n**ame list box. The default is to list All Files (*.*). To change the filter and restrict the files listed, choose List Files of **T**ype. Click the drop-down list button or press the down-arrow key to display the drop-down list of file type filters. These filters replace the asterisks in the file extension with letters so files of only that type are listed. For example, when you select Documents (*.doc), WordPerfect replaces the *.* characters in the File**n**ame text box with `*.doc`. Now, only files on disk that end with the extension doc will be displayed in the File**n**ame list box. Double-click the filter, or highlight the filter and press Enter. WordPerfect lists only the files that qualify in the File**n**ame list box. (See Chapter 18, "Importing Data and Working with Other Programs," for more information about other file formats.)

- If the document is on a disk or in a directory other than the current one, you can type the complete path (drive, directories, and file name) in the File**n**ame text box—for example, **C:\WPWIN\WPDOCS\1STQTR.RPT**.

  If you don't remember the location of the file you want to open, or don't want to type the complete path, you can use the Dri**v**es and/or **D**irectories list boxes to move between disk drives (including floppy drives) and directories.

- If you are unsure of the contents of a file listed in the File**n**ame list box, highlight the file name and choose Vie**w** to run the WordPerfect file Viewer (see fig. 3.2). If WordPerfect cannot view the file (the Viewer cannot convert files created by some programs), a message is displayed. Some document elements, such as headers and footers, are not displayed by the Viewer.

You also can use the Viewer to listen to sound files. When you view a sound file, standard tape player buttons—play, stop, fast forward, and rewind—are displayed on-screen, enabling you to stop and start the playing of the sound. In addition, on-screen buttons are provided for Reset (move to the beginning of the sound file) and End (move to the end of the sound file.)

The file format is displayed on a status bar at the bottom-left corner of the Viewer window. You can scroll through the document being viewed by using the scroll bars or other scrolling techniques described in Chapter 2, "Creating and Saving a Document."

After you select the Viewer window and change the focus to that window (the title bar changes colors), you can use Find (F2) to locate characters—a word or phrase in the viewed document. (For more information about Find, see the section "Using Find and Replace" later in this chapter.)

You can copy one or more lines from the viewed document to the Windows Clipboard to be pasted into WordPerfect or another Windows application. To copy lines to the Windows Clipboard, move the mouse pointer to the first line to be included. Drag the mouse, and the lines of text are selected. Press Ctrl+C to copy the text, or press the right mouse button to display the QuickMenu and choose Copy to C**l**ipboard. (For more information about moving text, see the section "Transferring Selected Text to Another Location" later in this chapter.)

Press F9 to change the font used to display the viewed document and press F5 to print the viewed file. Close the Viewer by clicking the Viewer's control menu box and then choosing **C**lose; or press Alt+F4.

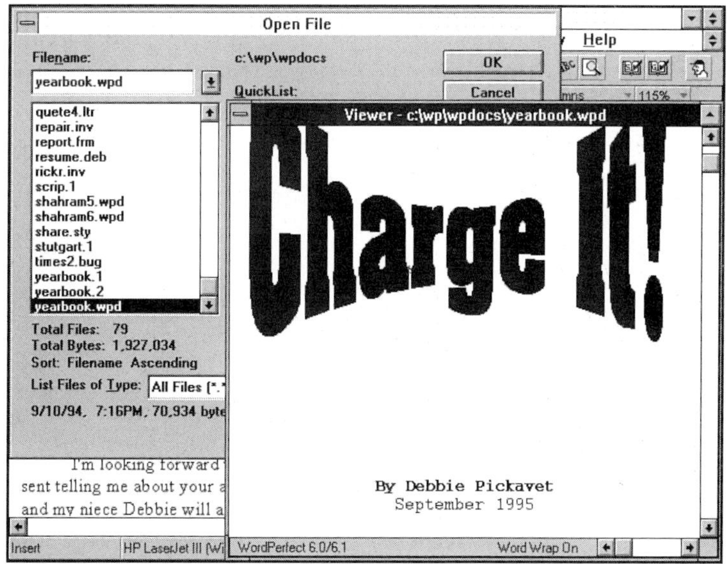

Fig. 3.2
The Viewer enables you to look at a document without opening it into a document editing window. As with any window, you can resize the Viewer window to see more of the viewed document.

Troubleshooting

I selected a file to view and instead of displaying the file, I see the message `No Viewer Available` *on my screen.*

If you see the `No Viewer Available` message, the conversion file you need was probably not installed during installation. You can quickly install additional conversion files after WordPerfect's initial installation.

▶ See "Understanding the Conversion Process," p. 591

The Open File dialog box also provides the following option buttons that enable you to look for text in files, perform DOS functions on files or directories, or change how files are listed in the Open File dialog box:

- ***S**etup*. Displays the Open/Save As Setup dialog box, in which you can change a variety of options that affect the display of files and directories in the Open and Save As dialog boxes.
- *File **O**ptions*. Enables you to perform a variety of file and directory functions normally performed at the DOS prompt.
- *Quick**L**ist*. Enables you to display the QuickList list box and use the QuickList feature to build shortcut paths to your files and directories.
- *Quick**F**inder*. Helps you find files with certain names or certain text within the file on your hard disk.
- *Open as **C**opy*. Enables you to open a file as a Read-Only copy to ensure that you don't accidentally save the modified document over the original document.

The **S**etup, File **O**ptions, Quick**L**ist, Quick**F**inder, and Open as **C**opy functions are explained in detail in Chapter 28, "Advanced File Management."

Using Insert File to Combine Files

You can retrieve a document from disk into the current on-screen document. When you use **I**nsert F**i**le, WordPerfect copies the requested file from disk into the current on-screen document at the location of the insertion point. WordPerfect ignores the retrieved file's initial codes and file name and instead uses the initial codes and file name of the on-screen document. Any formatting codes applied to the text that aren't contained in the document's "initial codes" are inserted into the on-screen document with the inserted document text. If you have already named the on-screen document, that name is used when you save the new combined file.

When you copy the contents of a saved document into the on-screen document, the file on disk is not modified when you save the on-screen document. For example, suppose that you are working on an annual report, named ANNUAL.RPT, on-screen. On disk you have a file called NORTH.REG with the sales figures from the Northern region. You can copy NORTH.REG into the ANNUAL.RPT document by using **I**nsert F**i**le. When you save the revised file ANNUAL.RPT, the original NORTH.REG file is not modified.

Save your current document before inserting another document into it. That way, if you don't like the results of the file combination, you can simply close the file without saving it, and then reopen the original document and try again.

To insert a document into the current document, follow these steps:

1. Move the insertion point in the on-screen document to the location where you want to place the document you are inserting.

2. Choose **I**nsert, F**i**le. The Insert File dialog box appears. This dialog box looks similar to the Open File dialog box (refer to fig. 3.1), except that Insert File has an **I**nsert button instead of an OK button.

3. If the file you want to retrieve is in the current default directory, type the file name in the File**n**ame text box (for example, **SAMPLE.LET**).

   If the document is on a disk or in a directory other than the current directory, you must type the complete path (drive, directories, and file name) in the File**n**ame text box (for example, **C:\WPWIN\WPDOCS\1STQTR.RPT**).

   If you don't remember the file name or location of the file you want to insert, you can use the information detailed in step 2 in the preceding section, "Opening a File."

4. Click **I**nsert or press Enter. WordPerfect displays the confirmation message `Insert file into current document?` Choose **Y**es to have WordPerfect copy the file into the current on-screen document at the insertion point's location. Choose **N**o to cancel.

▶ See "Finding Files," p. 965

▶ See "Using the File Options to Perform File Management Functions," p. 956

▶ See "Using the QuickList Feature," p. 978

▶ See "Using the QuickFinder File Indexer," p. 980

Revising and Editing Text

The amount of revision each document requires varies greatly. Some people find when they review their documents that very few changes are needed. Others find that a great deal of fine-tuning is required to make the document say just what they want, in just the way they want it said. In some cases, other people review a document, with the author responsible for incorporating the changes into his or her document file. Whatever the reason for editing, WordPerfect enables you to make changes quickly and easily.

Inserting and Overwriting Text

With a standard typewriter, you cannot insert text into a document without retyping an entire page. Electronic editing with a word processor such as WordPerfect enables you to make corrections quickly to a single character, a word, a sentence, or entire pages and paragraphs. You simply make the change and reprint any pages that need reprinting.

By default, WordPerfect inserts new text that you type at the location of the insertion point. As you type, existing text after the insertion point is pushed ahead (moves to the right) to make room for the new text. Words move down to new lines as necessary, and pages are reformatted to adjust for the added text.

Note

To toggle Typeover mode on and off, press the Insert key or double-click the General Status display box on the status bar at the bottom left corner of the screen. If a style is in use at the location of the insertion point, its name is shown in the General Status field, and the Insert/Typeover status is not shown. You can add an Insert Mode item to the status bar that displays Ins when in Insert mode and Typ when in Typeover mode. For more information about adding the Insert Mode status bar item to the status bar, see Chapter 9, "Customizing WordPerfect."

If you want to type over (replace) existing text, you can use the Typeover feature. The Insert key on your keyboard turns Typeover mode on and off. When Typeover mode is on, `Typeover` is displayed on the status bar at the bottom of the screen. The text that you type replaces existing text instead of pushing it to the right. Typeover mode is useful for making one-for-one replacements, such as changing a misspelled word (for example, changing the word *teh* to *the*).

Deleting Text

WordPerfect makes deleting text easy. You can delete a single character, or entire words, sentences, paragraphs, or pages with only a few keystrokes. If you accidentally delete text, you can restore that text with WordPerfect's Undelete and Undo features, covered in the section "Restoring Deleted Text" later in this chapter.

Deleting a Single Character

To delete a single character in WordPerfect, use one of these methods:

- Press the Backspace key to delete the character to the left of the insertion point. Use this method while entering text to delete a typing mistake immediately.

- Press the Del key to delete the character to the right of the insertion point.

- Press the space bar or another character while in Typeover mode to replace the character to the right of the insertion point.

After using each deletion method, determine which method works best for you in each editing situation you encounter.

Holding down the Backspace or Del key repeats the action, deleting several characters quickly. Using this method, however, often results in deleting more characters than you intend. This requires you to retype accidentally deleted text or to restore all deleted text using Undo or Undelete, and then repeat the deletion. If you need to delete more than a few characters, use one of the deletion techniques described in the following sections.

Deleting Words and Lines

To delete a word, place the insertion point anywhere in the word and press Ctrl+Backspace. The word and any spaces or punctuation (up to the next word) are deleted.

To delete text from the insertion point to the end of the current line, press Ctrl+Del. If the line ends with a soft return code (SRt), the text on the next and subsequent lines is reformatted after the deletion occurs. When the line ends with a hard return code (HRt), the command does not delete the code and the text on lines following the hard return code does not change.

To delete an entire line of text in which the insertion point is located anywhere, press Home to move the insertion point to the beginning of the line; then press Ctrl+Del to delete the line.

Deleting Other Selections of Text

In addition to the various methods described in the preceding sections, WordPerfect offers another method of deleting a portion of your document. With the Select function, you can select any portion of your document and delete it. This method of deleting text is described in detail in the section "Deleting and Undeleting a Selection" later in this chapter.

Restoring Deleted Text

While editing your document, you may accidentally delete text or graphics. If you accidentally delete a few characters or a word, retyping the deleted text is relatively simple, but accidentally deleting larger portions can be very frustrating. WordPerfect offers two useful features to recover and restore deleted text and graphics: Undelete and Undo.

The Undo feature reverses many editing actions, including restoring deleted text and graphics. Undelete is designed for the purpose of restoring deleted text and graphics. Each time you delete something, WordPerfect remembers the deletion and stores the deleted material in case you want to restore it to the document. In fact, WordPerfect remembers the last three deletions made during your current editing session. Because WordPerfect only stores the last three deletions, use the Undelete feature as soon as possible after you make the deletion. To restore deleted material with Undelete, follow these steps:

1. Position the insertion point where you want the deleted material to be restored.

2. Choose **E**dit, U**n**delete; or press Ctrl+Shift+Z.

   A selection of highlighted text appears on the editing screen, displaying the most recently deleted material, and the Undelete dialog box appears (see fig. 3.3).

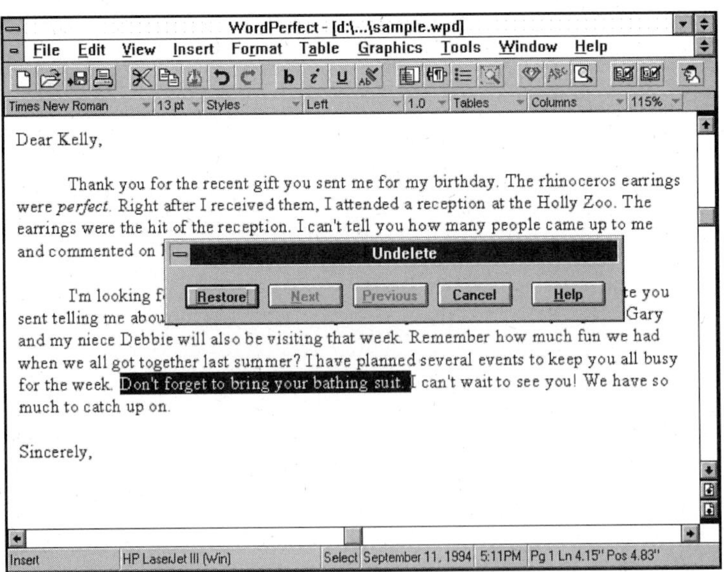

Fig. 3.3
A highlighted block showing deleted text to be restored. WordPerfect remembers the last three deletions and enables you to view and then restore them as desired.

3. Choose **R**estore if the highlighted text is what you want to restore. Choose **N**ext or **P**revious to examine the other choices of previously deleted text. When the text that you want restored appears on-screen, choose **R**estore. If none of the choices are appropriate or you change your mind, choose Cancel.

WordPerfect offers another method for restoring deleted text. Undo reverses up to the last 300 editing actions. When you Undo a deletion, the result is similar to what happens when you restore a deletion with Undelete. Undo, however, restores text at the location from which it was deleted, regardless of the insertion point's location. If you delete a word and then move the insertion point anywhere else in the document, Undo returns to the place of deletion and then restores the word.

The next section covers the Undo feature in detail.

Using WordPerfect's Undo and Redo Features

The WordPerfect Undo feature enables you to do much more than simply restore deleted text; it can reverse up to the last 300 editing actions. Likewise, the Redo feature enables you to redo undone editing actions. By default, WordPerfect remembers the last ten editing actions unless you increase it. Likewise, the Redo/Undo history is saved with your document unless you tell WordPerfect to do otherwise.

An editing action can be as simple as deleting a word or applying a bold attribute to text. Or, an editing action can be not so simple—like accidentally changing the word *the* to *them* in an entire document. In this case, you can't simply use Find and Replace to change the word *them* back to *the*—the word *them* likely is used properly many places in your document, and those occurrences shouldn't be changed. With WordPerfect's Undo feature, you can reverse both simple and complex editing actions.

Although most editing actions can be undone, some actions such as saving a document, adjusting the reveal codes window, or changing the zoom settings cannot be undone.

To undo the most recent editing action, choose **E**dit, **U**ndo; or press Ctrl+Z; or click the Undo icon on the Toolbar. The editing action is undone.

As you undo one or more steps, the editing actions are added to the Redo list. If the undone editing action is not what you intended, choose **E**dit, **R**edo; or press Ctrl+Shift+R; or click the Redo icon on the Toolbar. The undone editing action is reversed.

If you want to undo or redo more than the last editing action, use the Undo/Redo History feature to select the actions to undo or redo.

To undo or redo more than the most recent editing change, follow these steps:

1. Choose **E**dit, Undo/Redo **H**istory. The Undo/Redo History dialog box appears (see fig. 3.4). Editing actions that can be undone are shown in the U**n**do list on the left half of the screen. Undone editing actions that can now be redone are shown in the Re**d**o list on the right half of the screen. The list of actions is displayed with the most recent editing actions at the top and the least recent actions at the bottom.

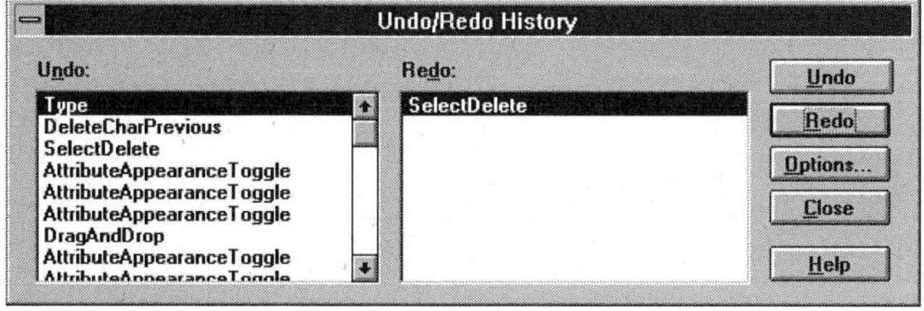

Fig. 3.4
The Undo/Redo History dialog box has two list boxes.

2. In the U**n**do list, choose one or more editing actions to be undone or, if you want to redo actions that have been undone, choose from actions listed in the Re**d**o box. When you choose an action below the top item in the Re**d**o or U**n**do lists, all actions from the selected action to the top of the list also are selected.

Tip
As you undo editing actions, they are moved to the Re**d**o list. After you return to your document and perform another editing action, the actions listed in the Re**d**o list are deleted and cannot be redone.

WordPerfect normally saves the last ten editing actions to be undone. To increase this to a larger number, follow these steps:

1. Choose **E**dit, Undo/Redo **H**istory. The Undo/Redo History dialog box appears.

2. Choose **O**ptions. The Undo/Redo Options dialog box appears.

3. Choose **N**umber of Undo/Redo Items: and either type a new value or use the increment/decrement arrows to change the value.

4. Click OK and Close to save the changes and return to your document. Changes made in the Undo/Redo Options dialog box remain in effect until you change them again.

When you save your document, WordPerfect normally saves the undo/redo items with the document. This enables you to reverse editing actions even if you save your document and then open it for editing at a later time.

Saving undo/redo items with your document however, makes the file size larger when it is stored on disk. The higher the number of undo/redo items, the more space the file takes.

If you don't want WordPerfect to save the undo/redo items with your document, follow the preceding steps to display the Undo/Redo Options dialog box. Choose **S**ave Undo/Redo Items With Document to uncheck the option. Unless you turn the option back on, undo/redo items no longer are saved with your current and future documents.

Understanding WordPerfect's Hidden Codes

When you choose a command such as Underline, you see the results of the action on-screen (text will be underlined), but you don't see the hidden codes placed in your document that tell WordPerfect to begin and end underlining. By hiding the codes, WordPerfect keeps the document window uncluttered.

To make certain formatting changes or to make sure that the hidden codes are in the right place, you must display the codes. WordPerfect provides a method called the Reveal Codes window to display hidden codes and make electronic editing easier. WordPerfect uses various hidden codes to control the display of your document. When you are typing text and reach the end of the line, for example, WordPerfect moves text that does not fit on that line to the next line and places a hidden soft return code (`[SRt]`) at the end of the line to indicate that text was wrapped because the line crossed the right margin. Pressing Enter to end a line rather than allowing WordPerfect to wrap text causes WordPerfect to place a hidden hard return code (`[HRt]`) in your document.

Tip
Do not stop typing or press Enter at the end of each line. Let WordPerfect wrap the text for you.

Some codes, such as those that set margins, are single codes placed in your document wherever you choose to set the value of the feature. Text attribute codes, such as bold and underline, are placed into your document in pairs indicating where an attribute is turned on and where it is turned off.

Among the features of WordPerfect 6.1 are revertible codes. When you select text and change its formatting—for example, if you change the font size—WordPerfect places a code at the beginning of the selection to change the formatting and another code at the end of the selection to return the formatting to how it was before the change. These codes are called revertible codes and point at each other when viewed in the Reveal Codes window.

In WordPerfect 5.1, when the Reveal Codes window is closed and you move the cursor through your text, the cursor pauses one keystroke when you encounter a hidden formatting code. This makes it possible to delete the code. If you deleted the text within the codes, just the formatted character is deleted. A warning message appears when you attempt to delete a hidden code at the beginning or end of the text to which the code applies. If you delete the code, the text formatted with the code's attribute becomes unformatted.

By default, WordPerfect 6.1 does not provide a warning when you delete formatted text or stop on the hidden formatting code when you move the insertion point over it. The hidden formatting codes are deleted after you delete all of the text formatted with the attribute.

You can have WordPerfect 6.1 emulate the WordPerfect 5.1 cursor movements, including the warning when codes might be deleted. To turn this option on and off, follow these steps:

1. Choose **E**dit, Pr**e**ferences. The Preferences dialog box appears.
2. Choose **E**nvironment. The Environment Preferences dialog box appears.
3. Choose **C**onfirm Deletion of Codes, Stop Insertion Point at Hidden Codes.

Working with Reveal Codes

Although you don't need to memorize all WordPerfect's hidden codes, knowing more about the codes can help you understand how WordPerfect controls and displays text. At times, your screen does not look the way you want it to, and you can't figure out why. Using the Reveal **C**odes command to open the Reveal Codes window may provide a quick answer. In addition, when you need to delete a code, such as bold or underline, it is often easiest to do so by using the Reveal Codes window. When you open the Reveal Codes window, WordPerfect splits the screen, showing the document window in the upper three-quarters and the same text with the hidden codes revealed in the lower quarter (see fig. 3.5). You can change the size of the Reveal Codes window as described in the sections "Changing the Size of the Current Reveal Codes Window" and "Changing the Default Size of the Reveal Codes Window" later in this chapter.

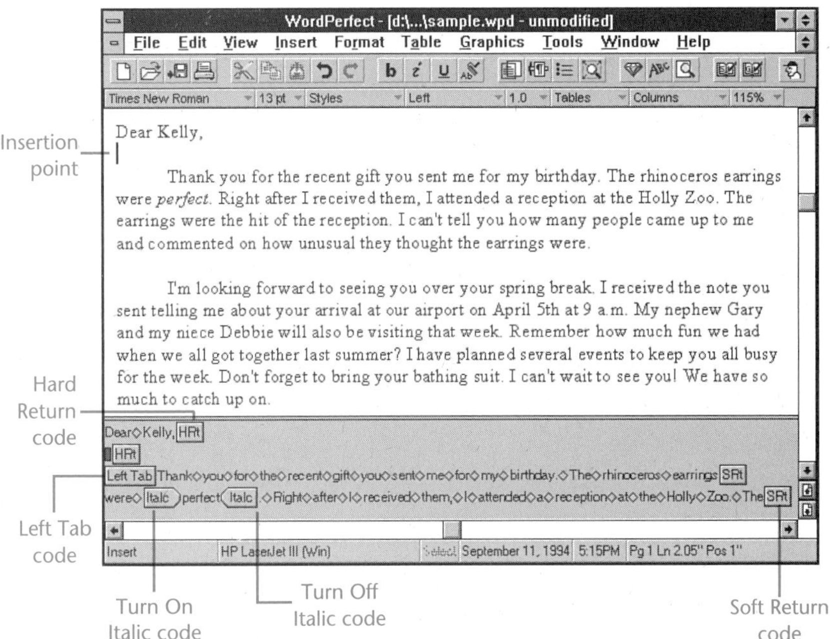

Fig. 3.5
A typical Reveal Codes display. WordPerfect automatically places the soft return code [SRt] at the end of a line when it breaks the line and wraps to the next line.

WordPerfect Corporation ships WordPerfect with the Reveal Codes window closed. You need to experiment by working with documents with the Reveal Codes window open and closed to determine which way you prefer it.

You can open the Reveal Codes window several ways to see your document's hidden codes. Choose the method that works best for you from the following list:

- Choose **V**iew, Reveal **C**odes; or press Alt+F3.
- Move the mouse pointer to the heavy black line at the top or bottom of the vertical scroll bar at the right of your screen. The mouse pointer changes to a double-headed arrow. Press and hold the left mouse button. The Reveal Codes dividing line appears horizontally across the document window (see fig. 3.6). Drag the dividing line to the point where the screen is split in the proportion you want; then release the mouse button.

- Move the mouse pointer into the document editing screen and not in the header or footer area of the document. Press the right mouse button to display the QuickMenu. Choose Re**v**eal Codes.

Unless you exit WordPerfect or change the size of the Reveal Codes window, it remains as you set it. The default size of the Reveal Codes window can be changed for all future documents by using the Display Preferences dialog box. For more information, see the section "Changing the Default Size of the Reveal Codes Window" later in this chapter.

As you move through your document using the mouse or keyboard, the Reveal Codes cursor moves through the Reveal Codes window.

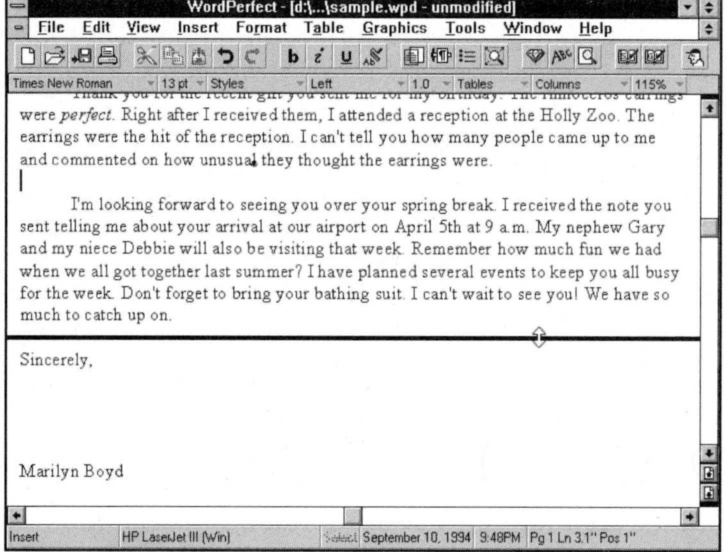

Fig. 3.6
The mouse pointer changes to a double-headed arrow and a dividing line appears, enabling you to quickly set the size of the Reveal Codes window.

Closing the Reveal Codes Window

You can close the Reveal Codes window and redisplay the entire document window several ways. From the following list, choose the one that works best for you:

- Choose **V**iew, Reveal **C**odes; or press Alt+F3.
- Move the mouse pointer to the Reveal Codes window and click the right mouse button. A QuickMenu appears. Choose **H**ide Reveal Codes.

- Move the mouse pointer to the dividing line at the top of the Reveal Codes window. The mouse pointer changes to a double-headed arrow (refer to fig. 3.6). Press and hold the left mouse button. Drag the dividing line to the bottom of the screen and release the mouse button.

After you hide the Reveal Codes window, notice that small, thick black bars reappear at the top and bottom of the vertical scroll bar.

Editing in the Reveal Codes Window

WordPerfect codes appear as sculptured icons. Among the codes shown earlier in figure 3.5 are hard return (`[HRt]`), tab indent (`[Left Tab]`), soft return (`[SRt]`), and the codes that turn on and off the italic attribute (`[Italc]`). Notice that attribute codes always appear in pairs; the code that turns on the feature points to the right and the code that turns off the feature points to the left.

Being able to see the hidden codes enables you to edit many things in WordPerfect quickly. For example, if you have a section of text that is currently bold and underlined, but you only want it underlined, you simply delete the bold code. This can be done in several ways:

- Place the insertion point just before either of the `[Bold]` codes in the Reveal Codes window and press Del.
- Place the insertion point immediately after either of the `[Bold]` codes and press Backspace.
- Move the mouse pointer to either of the `[Bold]` codes in the Reveal Codes window. Drag the code out of the Reveal Codes window and release the mouse button.

The text is no longer bold, but is still underlined. If you delete either the beginning or ending code, its paired code is also deleted, removing the attribute completely.

You can also quickly edit the value of a code, such as a margin code. For example, suppose that a code in your document sets the left margin to 1 1/2 inches. To quickly change the margin to 2 inches, locate and double-click on the `[Lft Mar"]` code in the Reveal Codes window. The Margins dialog box appears, allowing you to change the value of the margins; in the example, you change the left margin to 2.00 and choose OK.

Note

You may notice that each new document you create starts with an `[Open Style: InitialStyle]` code. The document's Initial Style is where you can place codes that you want to apply to the entire document. Formatting codes you place within your document text will take precedence over the formatting codes you place in the Initial Codes Style. You cannot delete this code, but you can modify its formatting codes by changing the Initial Codes Style settings. For information about creating and changing a document's Initial Codes Style, see Chapter 5, "Formatting Pages and Documents."

▶ See "Creating the Initial Codes Style," p. 207

▶ See "Creating Styles," p. 362

Working with a document with the Reveal Codes window open is a good way to become familiar with many of the codes WordPerfect places in a document to control its display and printing.

Changing the Size of the Current Reveal Codes Window

The Reveal Codes window can be distracting at times. For example, when you initially compose a document, you may want to see as much of your text on-screen as possible. You may find that you don't like to leave the Reveal Codes window open because it takes up too much of the screen (on most monitors, it takes up about one-fourth). If so, you can change the size of the Reveal Codes window. You can do so for just the current editing session, or you can change the size for future editing sessions as well.

To quickly change the size of the Reveal Codes window for just the current editing session, move the mouse pointer onto the dividing line at the top of the Reveal Codes window. The mouse pointer changes to a double-headed arrow (refer to fig. 3.6). Press and hold down the left mouse button, and drag the dividing line of the Reveal Codes window up or down until the location of the line you are moving is positioned where you now want the top of the Reveal Codes window. Release the mouse button, and the Reveal Codes and document windows are resized accordingly.

You can also change the size of the Reveal Codes window for all future documents. This is described later in the section "Changing the Default Size of the Reveal Codes Window."

Customizing Reveal Codes to Meet Your Needs

WordPerfect enables you to change a variety of options to customize Reveal Codes to fit your preferences. The various options are described later in this section.

Experiment with different settings until you find ones that you prefer. To open the Display Preferences dialog box and display the Reveal Codes section, follow these steps:

1. Choose **E**dit, Pr**e**ferences. The Preferences dialog box appears.
2. Choose **D**isplay. The Display Preferences dialog box appears.
3. Choose Reveal **C**odes. The bottom of the Display Preferences dialog box changes to show the Reveal Codes options (see fig. 3.7).

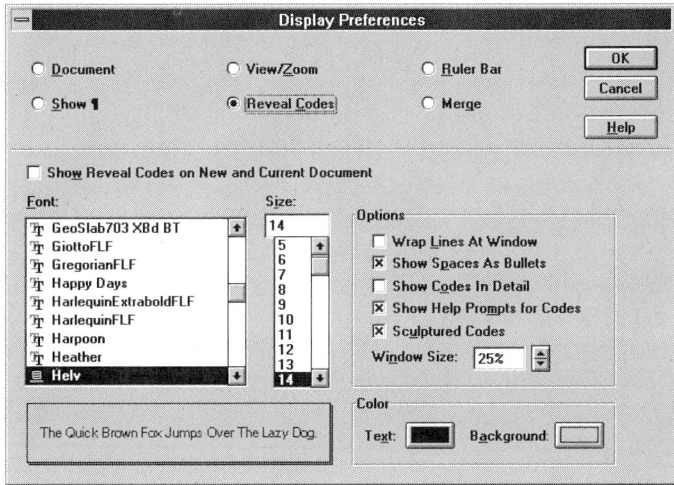

Fig. 3.7
The Display Preferences dialog box shows the Reveal **C**odes options. This dialog box allows you to change many options that affect how the WordPerfect Reveal Codes feature works.

4. Change the Reveal **C**odes preferences as needed. The options are described in later sections.
5. Choose OK and then Close to return to the document window.

Automatically Displaying the Reveal Codes Window

When you first install WordPerfect, the Reveal Codes window is set by default to be hidden. This means that when you start WordPerfect or open a new document, the Reveal Codes window is not displayed.

To automatically show the Reveal Codes window for all future editing sessions and new documents, choose Sho**w** Reveal Codes on New and Current Document.

Tip
You can also reach the Reveal **C**odes options by moving the mouse pointer to the Reveal Codes window, then clicking the right mouse button.

Changing the Default Reveal Codes Font, Typeface, and Size

To change the font used in the Reveal Codes window, choose **F**ont. Then choose a font from the font list.

To change the point size of the font, choose S**i**ze. Type the desired point size in the text box or choose a size from the S**i**ze list box.

A sample of the highlighted font is displayed in the box at the bottom-left corner of the Display Preferences dialog box.

Displaying Reveal Codes in Detail

WordPerfect abbreviates some text-formatting codes that contain much information. For example, if you have set a top margin of 0.5", the abbreviated code will show `[Top Mar]`. If you want WordPerfect to display all codes as expanded with their values, choose Show C**o**des in Detail. Now, when you look at the top margin code in the reveal codes window, the code appears as `[Top Mar: 0.50"]`.

Changing the Default Size of the Reveal Codes Window

To change the number of lines that display in the Reveal Codes window when you display it for future documents, choose Wi**n**dow Size. Then change the percentage by typing the desired value in the text box or by clicking the increment/decrement arrows. For all new documents, when you open the reveal codes window, the size will be as you have entered. To change the size of the reveal codes window for the current document, see the earlier section "Changing the Size of the Current Reveal Codes Window" in this chapter.

Changing the Default Colors of the Reveal Codes Window

WordPerfect enables you to select alternate colors to the default gray background with black text for the Reveal Codes window.

To change the colors of the Reveal Codes window, choose Te**x**t or B**a**ckground as desired. A palette of colors is displayed. Choose the desired color by using the mouse or the keyboard arrow keys to move the box that indicates the color to the section of the displayed palette with the color you desire. Press Enter to select the color. You return to the Display Preferences dialog box and the new Reveal Codes window colors are shown in the sample box at the bottom left corner of the Display Preferences dialog box.

Changing Other Reveal Codes Preferences

In addition to those listed in the preceding sections, several other preferences can be set in the Reveal **C**odes section of the Display Preferences dialog box. The other choices and their effects are as follows:

- *Wrap **L**ines At Window*. Choose this option to cause WordPerfect to wrap lines in the reveal codes window at code breaks so the lines don't run off the right side of the screen.

- *Show Spaces As Bullets.* Choose this option to represent each space in your document as a diamond-shaped bullet in the Reveal Codes window. This enables you to see the exact number of spaces between characters.

- *Show Help Prompts for Codes.* Choose this option to have WordPerfect display a help prompt for the code on the program title bar when you place the mouse pointer on the code.

- *Sculptured Codes.* Choose this option to display the WordPerfect formatting codes as pleasing sculptured icons, with a three-dimensional look, rather than as flat, two-dimensional icons.

Selecting Text

One of WordPerfect's powerful electronic editing tools is the capability to use the mouse or keyboard to select a portion of the document. This allows you to perform a variety of functions on only the selected portion of a document. Why work with selections? Often, you want to change the appearance of the document or the arrangement of your thoughts; selection enables you to do so quickly.

A selection can be as small as one character or as large as the entire document. You define what to include in the selection and then choose a WordPerfect function to perform on it.

In addition to applying the common functions described in this chapter to a selection, you can use the selection process with specialized WordPerfect functions, such as Tables (see Chapter 16, "Working with Tables"), the Speller (see Chapter 6, "Using Writing Tools"), and Index (see Chapter 26, "Assembling Document References").

Highlighting a Selection

You must make a selection before any operation can be performed on it. WordPerfect indicates a selection by displaying it highlighted on-screen and displaying `Select` on the status bar at the bottom of the screen (see fig. 3.8). The highlighted text shows exactly which portion of your document will change when you choose a function. Graphics and their captions, however, are not highlighted when included in a selection; only text is highlighted. For example, notice in figure 3.8 that the period is not highlighted (and therefore is not selected), so any action you perform on the highlighted text does not affect the period. You can make selections by using either the mouse or the keyboard. Experiment and choose the method you find most comfortable.

Tip

Choose **V**iew, Reveal **C**odes; or press Alt+F3 to open the window that shows hidden formatting codes.

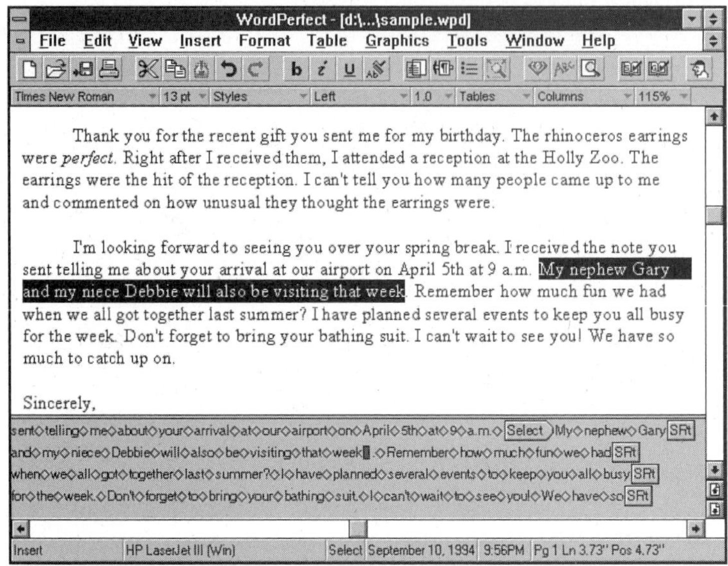

Fig. 3.8
An example of highlighted text showing a selection.

> **Note**
>
> Often you want your selection to include formatting codes. When you make a selection, the code `[Select]` appears in the Reveal Codes screen indicating where your selection starts (refer to fig. 3.8). Make sure that the formatting codes you want to include in the selection are between `[Select]` and the end of the selection (shown by the Reveal Codes cursor).

Using the Mouse to Highlight a Selection

If you have used a mouse with other programs, you should feel right at home with WordPerfect for Windows. The mouse techniques are similar to techniques in other Windows applications and those for Macintosh computers.

In WordPerfect, selecting a portion of your document with the mouse is quick and easy, as in the following steps:

1. Move the mouse pointer to the left side of the first character you want included in the selection. (In the document window, the mouse pointer looks like a tall, thin capital letter *I* and is called the *I-beam pointer*.)

2. Click the left mouse button to move the insertion point to the location of the I-beam pointer. This action anchors your selection at that location. The insertion point is displayed on the left side of the first character to be included in the selection.

Note

If the Reveal Codes window is open at the bottom of the screen, the Reveal Codes cursor represents the insertion point's current location.

3. Hold down the left mouse button and move the mouse pointer to the end of the area you want to select. This process is often referred to as *dragging*. As you select text, it is highlighted on-screen. Release the mouse button when you have everything highlighted that you want to include in the selection.

Note

Keep the left mouse button pressed while dragging the mouse pointer to highlight a selection. If you let go of the mouse button, you can still continue the selection process. Press and hold the Shift key; then press the left mouse button again. Let go of the Shift key but continue to hold the left mouse button, and resume selecting. Or, you can change the size of the selection by holding down the Shift key and using the insertion point-movement keys. Pressing the left mouse button again without holding down the Shift key cancels the current selection and moves the insertion point to the I-beam's location. Likewise, using an insertion point-movement key without holding the Shift key cancels the current selection and moves the insertion point according to the key pressed.

Clicking on an object outside the document editing window—for instance, on the vertical scroll bar—will not cancel the selection.

To highlight a selection that extends beyond the portion of the document currently displayed on-screen, continue holding down the mouse button and move the mouse pointer beyond the document window in the direction you want to move. WordPerfect scrolls the document, highlighting text as it scrolls, until you bring the mouse pointer back into the document window. When the desired ending location of the selection appears on-screen, move the mouse pointer to that location and release the mouse button.

To speed your editing, by default WordPerfect highlights full words as you drag the mouse. If you want to highlight less than a full word, hold down the Shift key and use the keyboard arrow keys to highlight one character at a time. If you highlight a selection of words using the mouse and want to expand or reduce the selection one character at a time, also hold down the Shift key and use the keyboard arrow keys.

If you find that highlighting full words is cumbersome and does not work well with the type of editing you do, you can turn off this feature. WordPerfect then selects by character rather than by words. To change the way WordPerfect selects text as you drag the mouse, follow these steps:

1. Choose **E**dit, Pr**e**ferences. The Preferences dialog box appears.

2. Choose **E**nvironment. The Environment Preferences dialog box appears.

3. Choose Automatically **S**elect Words to remove the X from this check box.

You can also use the Find command to extend a selection to a specific word or phrase in your document. See the discussion of the Extend Selection option in the "Understanding Find and Replace Options" section later in this chapter for more information.

If, after you have highlighted a selection, you change your mind about the *amount* of text to select, press Shift while you click the mouse pointer at a new location. The highlighted text area enlarges if you click farther from the anchor point, or reduces if you click closer to the anchor point.

Note

Besides dragging to highlight a selection, you can position the mouse pointer and click to anchor the insertion point where you want the selection to begin. Then move the mouse pointer to the desired ending location of the selection. Press and hold the Shift key and click the left mouse button. This action highlights the selection from the anchored location to the current location of the insertion point. This method is especially useful when highlighting large sections of text.

Caution

Pressing a keyboard character while a selection is highlighted will automatically delete the selected text and replace it with the character you type. This is a good shortcut for replacing text and saves you the trouble of deleting first. However, a letter hit unintentionally can be a problem. To remove the unwanted text and bring back the accidentally deleted text, immediately choose **E**dit, **U**ndo; or press Ctrl+Z.

WordPerfect provides two ways to quickly select a sentence, a paragraph, a page, or an entire document. You can use these methods by selecting from either of the following:

- From the pull-down menus, choose **E**dit, Se**l**ect. Then choose **S**entence, P**a**ragraph, or **P**age; to select the entire document, choose A**l**l.

- Move the mouse pointer to the area between the left margin of your document (before the text begins) and the left side of the screen. When the mouse pointer is moved into this area, the shape of the mouse pointer changes to an arrow pointing up and to the right. (If the arrow points up and to the left, you are not in the correct area.) Press the right mouse button, and a QuickMenu appears. Choose Select **S**entence, Select **P**aragraph, or Select P**a**ge; to select the entire document, choose Select A**l**l.

WordPerfect also provides several mouse shortcuts you can use when highlighting selections. These methods are shown in table 3.1. Using these shortcuts saves time when you want to highlight entire words, sentences, or paragraphs.

Table 3.1 Other Mouse Selection Methods

Selection Action	Result
Double-click	Selects a word
Triple-click	Selects a sentence
Quadruple-click	Selects a paragraph
Shift-click	Selects from the insertion point to the location of the mouse pointer

Troubleshooting

I'm left-handed and I find using the primary and secondary mouse buttons difficult in WordPerfect.

Although WordPerfect doesn't provide an easy way to fix this problem, Windows does. You can switch the button assignments so the primary button is the right button instead of the left button, enabling you to use the index finger on your left hand for the primary button.

To reverse the button assignments for a Microsoft mouse (other mouse control panels work in a similar way), first activate the main program group in the Windows program manager. Double-click the Control Panel icon, and then double-click the Mouse icon. A dialog box appears on which you can control the mouse settings. Choose **S**wap Left/Right Buttons. Then choose OK to close the Mouse dialog box.

Using the Keyboard to Highlight a Selection

You can highlight a selection from the keyboard without using a mouse by following these steps:

1. Move the insertion point to the first character you want to include in the selection.
2. Press Shift+right arrow or Shift+left arrow, depending on the direction in which you want to select.
3. While holding down the Shift key, use the insertion point-movement keys (right arrow, left arrow, up arrow, PgDn, Ctrl+End, and so on) to move to the end of the text you want to select. The common insertion point-movement keys are shown in table 2.2 in Chapter 2, "Creating and Saving a Document."

You can also turn on Select with the Select function key command. The primary difference between using the Select function key command and using a Shift+insertion point movement key combination is that with the former, you don't need to hold down the Shift key while you use insertion point-movement keys to move to the end of the selection.

To use the Select function key command to select text, follow these steps:

1. Move the insertion point to the first character you want to include in the selection.
2. Press Select (F8). `Select` is displayed on the status bar at the bottom of the screen. (If the Reveal Codes window is open at the bottom of the screen, the `[Select]` code is displayed at the anchor point for the selection.)
3. Use the insertion point-movement keys as needed to move to the end of the information you want to select. As text is selected, it is highlighted on-screen.

Canceling a Highlighted Selection

After highlighting a selection, you may change your mind and want to cancel it. You can cancel the selection by doing any of the following:

- Click the mouse anywhere in the document window (without holding down the Shift key).
- Move the insertion point with an insertion point-movement key, such as the right-arrow key. (If you started the selection by pressing Select

(F8), this will not cancel the selection because the direction keys are being used to change the selection area.)

- Press Select (F8).

Transferring Selected Text to Another Location

After you highlight a selection, you are ready to perform a WordPerfect operation on that portion of your document. This section deals with using Select to move portions of text between locations in a document or between documents. Other sections of this chapter deal with performing other commands on a selection.

As you work with documents, you will find information that you want to move or copy to another location. WordPerfect uses the Cu**t**, **C**opy, and Appen**d** commands to transfer information to the Windows Clipboard. Then you can use the **P**aste command to place the information elsewhere in the current document or in other Windows applications. The current Clipboard information remains unchanged until the next Cut, Copy, or Append operation is performed. If unchanged, the information remains on the Clipboard for the entire Windows session. To view the contents of the Clipboard, use the Windows Clipboard. See your Windows manual for more information about the Clipboard and the Clipboard Viewer application. When you exit Windows, any information on the Clipboard is erased.

If you use WordPerfect's drag-and-drop editing feature, described later in the "Drag-and-Drop Editing" section, the text and codes that you move or copy are not passed through the Windows Clipboard; you manipulate them directly on-screen from one location to another, using the mouse.

Beginning with Version 6.1, WordPerfect introduces a feature called *intelligent* cut and paste. When you cut or paste text, spaces are added or deleted where appropriate.

Moving or Copying a Selection

When you finish typing a document, you often find text that you want to place elsewhere in the document. You can move or copy this text easily with WordPerfect's Cut and Paste functions.

◄ See "Moving the Insertion Point with Go To," p. 65

To move or copy a selection, follow these steps:

1. Select the information (text and/or graphics) that you want to copy.

2. To *move* a selection, choose **E**dit, Cu**t**; or press Ctrl+X.

To *copy* a selection, choose **E**dit, **C**opy; or press Ctrl+C.

3. Move the insertion point to where you want to place the selection.

4. Choose **E**dit, **P**aste; or press Ctrl+V. Alternatively, you can click the right mouse button to display a QuickMenu, and then choose **P**aste.

Tip

After selecting the information, click the right mouse button to display a QuickMenu. Choose **C**ut or C**o**py as desired.

Drag-and-Drop Editing

WordPerfect's *drag-and-drop* editing feature enables you to visually relocate text and graphics within a document. This technique is more efficient than using Cut and Paste if you are moving or copying the material only a short distance within the same document.

To use the mouse to "pick up" and move or copy a portion of a document, follow these steps:

1. Select what you want to move, and then place the mouse pointer anywhere within the highlighted area.

2. Hold down the left mouse button. To *move* the selected block, drag the item to its new location and "drop" it into place by releasing the mouse button when the insertion point on the modified mouse pointer is where you want the block. To *copy* the highlighted selection, hold down the Ctrl key while dragging the selection to the new location, and then "drop" the copy into place by releasing the mouse button.

Note

You can change from a Cut and Paste to a Copy and Paste by pressing the Ctrl key before you let go of the left mouse button. If you have started a Copy and Paste and want to instead Cut and Paste, release the Ctrl key before you release the left mouse button. Notice, however, that the mouse pointer icon changes to indicate that you have changed the type of drag-and-drop procedure.

When you press the mouse button to begin dragging your selected item, the shape of the mouse pointer changes to indicate that the drag-and-drop function is occurring, and the insertion point travels with the mouse pointer. The mouse pointer has different icons attached to it to indicate whether the drag-and-drop procedure is a move or a copy. The move procedure has a dotted shadow; the copy procedure has a dotted shadow and a plus (+) sign to the right of the mouse pointer arrow.

Appending a Selection

To append a selection to the existing text in the Clipboard, follow these steps:

1. Select the information (text and/or graphics) that you want to append.
2. Choose **E**dit, Appen**d**.

You can now paste the original information plus the newly added information to the location of your choice. The **P**aste command is described in the earlier section, "Moving or Copying a Selection."

> **Note**
>
> After you cut or copy a selection to the Clipboard, you can add additional selections of information with the Append function. Because WordPerfect offers no Appen**d** command shortcut keys, consider adding the Appen**d** command to the Power Bar or Toolbar.

Moving Selected Information between WordPerfect Windows

Moving information between WordPerfect windows is as easy as moving information within a document. For information about arranging documents on-screen and switching between documents, see Chapter 1, "Getting Started."

To move information between open documents, follow these steps:

1. Open into separate document windows the documents between which you want to move information.
2. Switch to the document from which you want to copy or move information.
3. Select the objects (text and/or graphics) that you want to copy or move.
4. Use the desired Cu**t**, **C**opy, or Appen**d** command, described in the "Transferring Selected Text to Another Location" section earlier in this chapter.
5. Switch to the document into which you want to paste the information. Then move the insertion point to where you want to paste the information.
6. Use the **P**aste command, described in the "Transferring Selected Text to Another Location" section earlier in this chapter, to retrieve the cut,

copied, or appended information from the Clipboard. WordPerfect inserts the information in the document at the insertion point's location.

7. As appropriate, save any modified documents.

You also can use WordPerfect's *drag-and-drop* editing feature to copy or move information between WordPerfect documents. To do so, follow these steps:

1. Open into separate document windows the documents between which you want to move information.

2. You must be able to see on your screen all the WordPerfect documents you want to copy or move information between. Choose **W**indow, **T**ile Horizontal. Your open documents will all be visible on your screen. Move and resize the windows as necessary. For more information about moving a resizing document editing windows, see "Understanding the Editing Screen" in Chapter 1.

3. Using the scroll bars, position the documents in each document editing window so that the information you want to move and the location you want to move it to are both visible on-screen.

4. Using the techniques described earlier in the section "Drag-and-Drop Editing," highlight the information you want to copy or move. Then, drag the information moving the mouse pointer from the sending document to the receiving document. When you release the mouse button, the information is placed into the receiving document.

Transferring Selected Information to Other Windows Applications

When you choose Cu**t** or **C**opy in WordPerfect, the information is transferred to the Windows Clipboard, replacing any previous selection. Appended information is added to any existing selection on the Windows Clipboard. This information is available in other Windows applications that use the Clipboard. Likewise, information cut or copied to the Clipboard in other Windows applications is available to be pasted into WordPerfect. Information that you cut or copy onto the Clipboard stays there until you clear the Clipboard by using the Windows Clipboard Viewer application, cut or copy another piece of information onto the Clipboard, or exit Windows. To view the contents of the Clipboard, use the Windows Clipboard Viewer application. See your Windows manual for more information about the Clipboard and the Clipboard Viewer application.

Working with Rectangular Selections

In WordPerfect, a selection is not limited to continuous text. You can also select text within a defined rectangle. Figure 3.9 shows an example of a rectangular selection.

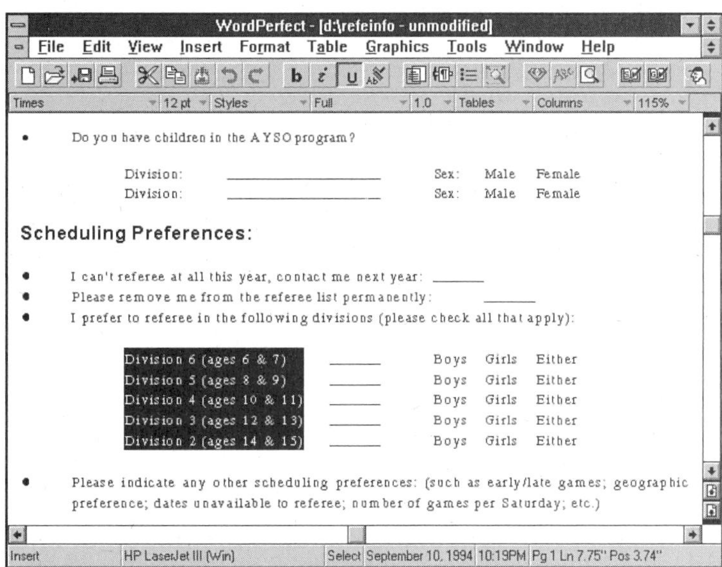

Fig. 3.9
A highlighted rectangular selection.

To highlight a rectangular selection of text, follow these steps:

1. Move the insertion point to the beginning or ending corner of the rectangle you want to select.

2. Move the mouse pointer to the opposite corner and press Shift+click; or press and hold down the left mouse button at the insertion point, drag the mouse pointer to the opposite corner, and then release the mouse button.

> **Note**
>
> At first it appears as if more text is being selected than you want, but after you perform the following step, the highlighted area shrinks to the intended rectangle size, as shown earlier in figure 3.9.

3. Choose **E**dit, Se**l**ect. Then select **R**ectangle. The highlight shrinks to just the rectangle.

You can now cut, copy, or delete the rectangular selection. To place the rectangle in a different location, choose **E**dit, Cu**t** or **E**dit, **C**opy; then move the insertion point to the desired location and choose **E**dit, **P**aste.

Caution

If you are going to delete or cut the rectangle, make sure that each line ends in a hard return to ensure that the selection is removed without disturbing other text on the page.

Deleting and Undeleting a Selection

Tip

You cannot retrieve a deleted selection by using the **P**aste command. Also, you can undelete only the last three deletions.

You can delete a selection by highlighting the selection and pressing either the Backspace or Del key. To restore a deleted selection, see the "Restoring Deleted Text" section earlier in this chapter.

Saving a Selection to a File

With the selection feature, you can save a portion of your document to be retrieved into another document later or to be retrieved into a non-Windows application that does not have access to the Windows Clipboard.

To save a selection to a file, follow these steps:

1. Highlight the selection you want to save as a separate file.
2. Choose **F**ile, Save **A**s; or press F3. The Save dialog box appears, asking whether you want to save the entire file or your selection.
3. Make sure the **S**elected Text option is selected and choose OK. The Save As dialog box appears.
4. If you want to save the file in a directory other than the current directory shown, choose the drive and directory to which you want the file saved.
5. Type a file name in the File**n**ame text box.

Note

You can display a list of the ten most recently saved files. While in the File**n**ame text box, click the drop-down list button or press the down-arrow key to display the drop-down list of recently saved files. To select a file name, double-click the file name, or highlight the file name and press Enter.

6. Choose OK to save the selection as a file and return to your document.

Tip
You can move selections between WordPerfect documents or to other Windows applications immediately by using the **C**ut (or **C**opy) and **P**aste commands.

Enhancing Text by Using Block Selections

WordPerfect provides a wide variety of enhancements to change the appearance of your text in the Font dialog box. To access the Font dialog box, choose Fo**r**mat, **F**ont; or press F9. Included on the list of enhancements are **B**old, **I**talic, **U**nderline, **D**ouble Underline, **R**edline, and Stri**k**eout. If you have a color printer, you can even change text color. See Chapter 4, "Formatting Text," and Chapter 20, "Using Fonts and Special Characters," for details about these and more text enhancements.

Sometimes you may want to enhance an entire selection of text. To do so, select the text you want to enhance. Then apply an attribute by choosing it from the Font dialog box or, when applicable, by pressing the attribute's shortcut key or key combination.

To apply Bold to a selection, for example, use one of these methods:

- Choose Fo**r**mat, **F**ont; or press F9. Then choose **B**old.
- Press Ctrl+B.
- Choose the Bold button on the Toolbar.

b

WordPerfect applies the attribute to the selected text and places hidden codes that show where the attribute has been turned on and off.

WordPerfect comes with several ready-made Toolbars. For more information about Toolbars and the Power Bar, see Chapter 13, "Working with Toolbars."

Note

WordPerfect leaves the selection highlighted after each attribute is applied. Therefore, you can apply several attributes to a selection before you deselect the text. You can also apply several attributes to a selection at once by using the Font dialog box. Choose Fo**r**mat, **F**ont; or press F9. Then make the desired attribute selections and choose OK to return to your document.

Converting the Case of a Selection

You can use case to emphasize a point in your document. If you use a printer that doesn't support certain enhancements, you may want to use uppercase letters for emphasis. Or you may find that you have used uppercase letters for a heading in your document and prefer to use a different font with only the first letter of each word an uppercase letter.

You don't need to delete and retype text to change the case. WordPerfect's Con**v**ert Case command changes selected text to lowercase, uppercase, or initial caps (where the first letter of each word is uppercase). Notice that when you switch a selection from uppercase to lowercase, certain letters remain capitalized, such as the letter *I* (when occurring by itself) or any character that begins a sentence.

To change the case of a selection, follow these steps:

1. Highlight a selection whose case you want to change.
2. Choose **E**dit, Con**v**ert Case.
3. Choose **L**owercase to convert the selection to lowercase, **U**ppercase to convert the selection to uppercase, or **I**nitial Capitals to convert the first letter of each word and single letters to capitals.

The selection remains highlighted so that you can apply additional WordPerfect commands.

You can add a Toolbar button called Case Toggle to the Toolbar. Each time this button is selected, WordPerfect converts the case (one conversion at a time) from Uppercase to Lowercase and then to Uppercase again. You can also add Toolbar buttons for the commands **L**owercase, **U**ppercase, and **I**nitial Capitals. For more information about Toolbars and the Power Bar, see Chapter 13, "Working with Toolbars."

Using Find and Replace

The **F**ind and Replace command enables you to locate text or hidden codes quickly and replace them if desired. A variety of powerful options is available, enabling you to find and replace character strings, whole words, phrases, codes (all or ones with specific values), and fonts and attributes. You can even find and replace word forms. The larger your document, the more efficient you can become by using this command.

Suppose that you are working on an orientation document for new employees in your company. You have changed health insurance carriers and want to change the section of the document that deals with Health Benefits. When you retrieve the document, the insertion point is on page 1. Using Find, you can quickly locate the words *Health Benefits*, and begin your editing there.

Or suppose that you discover that your boss's name is misspelled throughout the document! You can use **F**ind and Replace to fix that problem in seconds.

You can use **F**ind and Replace with the Select feature. When you use **F**ind and Replace on a selected portion of your document, the operation is performed only within the selection.

Finding Words and Phrases

Finding a piece of text in a document by visually scanning the document can be very time-consuming and is subject to error. The WordPerfect Find feature, however, accomplishes this task quickly and accurately.

You can begin a search from anywhere in your document. To find all occurrences of the text you are looking for, move the insertion point to the beginning or end of the document before starting the search. Or you can set options so that WordPerfect always begins a search at the top of the document or wraps a search at the end of the document in order to search the complete document before returning to the starting location.

You can search your document from top to bottom, or bottom to top. To find a word or phrase in your document, position the insertion point where you want to begin looking and follow these steps:

1. Choose **E**dit, **F**ind and Replace; or press F2. The Find and Replace Text dialog box appears (see fig. 3.10).

Fig. 3.10
The Find and Replace Text dialog box includes a variety of pull-down menus that enable you to perform a search more precisely.

2. Type the text you want to find (up to 80 characters) in the F**i**nd text box. This text is called a *search string*.

3. Choose **F**ind to search from the location of the insertion point toward the end of the document.

   You also can search from the location of the insertion point toward the beginning of the document. To do so, from the Find and Replace Text dialog box, choose **D**irection and then **B**ackward.

   WordPerfect enables you to start the search from a location other than the insertion point and to search the entire document even if you are not at the beginning or end of the document.

To have WordPerfect move to the beginning of the document before it begins searching, choose **O**ptions, **B**egin Find at Top of Document.

To have WordPerfect wrap when it gets to the beginning or end of the document and return to the location of the insertion point, thus searching the entire document, choose **O**ptions, **W**rap at Beg./End of Document.

When WordPerfect finds the first occurrence of the search string, the program highlights the string. If the word or phrase does not exist in the entire search area, a Find and Replace dialog box displays the search string and the message `Not found`. Click OK or press Enter to acknowledge the message and close the dialog box.

To find the next occurrence after the insertion point, again choose **F**ind; or if you've closed the Find and Replace Text dialog box, press Shift+F2. To find the next occurrence *before* the insertion point, choose **D**irection, **B**ackward, and then **F**ind; or if you've closed the Find and Replace Text dialog box, press Alt+F2. WordPerfect remembers the search string, so you do not need to retype it.

WordPerfect provides a *Find History* drop-down list that lists the search items you've previously looked for. To display the drop-down list of find items, click the drop-down list button or press the down-arrow key. Choose the desired find item (if necessary, use the scroll bar to display the item).

Unless you specify otherwise, WordPerfect searches in several sections of your document, including headers, footers, comments, graphics box captions, and text boxes. You can choose an option in the Find and Replace Text dialog box to prevent this extended find, as explained in the section, "Understanding Find and Replace Options," later in this chapter.

Choosing Search Criteria

Unless you use wild-card characters as described in the next paragraph or the word forms option described later in this chapter, WordPerfect looks for an exact match to the search string. Unless you've specified otherwise, the search is not case-sensitive. For example, searching for **gateway** or **Gateway** or **GATEWAY** finds *gateway, Gateway,* and *GATEWAY.*

Wild-card characters can assist in your search. You use the wild cards `[? (One Char)]` and `[* (Many Char)]` to represent unknown characters in your search. The `[? (One Char)]` code represents any single character. The `[* (Many Char)]` code represents two or more characters. For example, searching for **ca[?(One Char)]** finds *cat, cab,* and *car*. Searching for **w[*(Many Char)]fall** finds *waterfall*, but **w[?(One Char)]fall** does not.

You cannot insert wild-card characters by typing them from the keyboard. You must use the Codes option from the Find Text or Find and Replace Text dialog box. You choose the wild-card codes the same way you do any formatting code. For more information about the Codes option, see the section "Finding and Replacing Formatting Codes" later in this chapter.

You can set options from the Find dialog box to fine-tune the way Find works. For example, you can choose options for case-sensitive searching and searching for whole words only. See the section, "Understanding Find and Replace Options" later in this chapter for more information.

Finding and Replacing Words and Phrases

In addition to finding text, WordPerfect can replace the found text with different text. Or by typing nothing into the Replace With text box, you can delete the search string where it occurs in your document. For example, in a lengthy document, you may want to replace the word *waterfall* with *fountain* wherever it occurs. WordPerfect's Replace feature makes this change easy.

Caution

Although a Replace function can be undone, save your document just before doing a search and replace. Then, if something unexpected happens and you cannot undo the undesired replacements, you can simply retrieve the saved file from disk and try again with different find and replace strings.

To find and replace text, follow these steps:

1. Choose **E**dit, **F**ind and Replace; or press F2. The Find and Replace Text dialog box appears (refer to fig. 3.10).

2. Type the text to search for (up to 80 characters) in the F**i**nd text box. This text is the search string.

   Note

   WordPerfect automatically places the last search and replace strings in the F**i**nd and the Replace **W**ith text boxes. In addition, you can click on the drop-down list arrow (or press Alt+down arrow while in the text box) and a history list appears showing prior items used for Find and Replace actions.

3. Press Tab to move the insertion point to the Replace **W**ith text box. Type the text you want to put in place of the search string. If you just want to remove the search string from your document when found, do

Tip

To insert WordPerfect characters in the F**i**nd or Replace **W**ith text entry boxes, press Ctrl+W to display the WordPerfect Characters dialog box. Select the desired character and choose Insert **a**nd Close.

not enter anything in the Replace **W**ith text box and, if necessary, delete anything in the text box. (If you delete the replacement item, WordPerfect inserts the item <Nothing> to indicate you are replacing the found item with nothing, thereby deleting the found item.)

4. Choose **F**ind to locate the next occurrence of the search string. You can then choose **R**eplace to replace the found text with the contents of your Replace **W**ith text box and locate the next occurrence, or choose **F**ind to skip this replacement and locate the next occurrence of the search string.

Tip

To quickly copy text or codes from the F**i**nd text entry box to the Replace **W**ith text box, highlight the desired text and codes in the F**i**nd text box, and press Ctrl+Insert. Move the insertion point to the Replace **W**ith text box and press Shift+Insert to paste the copied information.

At any point, you can also choose Replace **A**ll, and WordPerfect immediately replaces all occurrences of the search string with the contents of the Replace **W**ith text box.

When WordPerfect does not find an occurrence of the search string, a Find and Replace dialog box appears stating that the search string is `Not Found`. Choose OK to continue.

Understanding Find and Replace Options

WordPerfect provides many options to fine-tune your search to find exactly what you want as quickly as possible. For example, you can choose the direction to search and choose what action should be taken when the end of the document is reached. You can also fine-tune replacement actions, like limiting the number of items to find and replace. These options are found on pull-down menus in the Find Text dialog box.

Choose **T**ype to select from the following options:

- *Te**x**t*. This normal search mode enables you to search for individual characters, words, or phrases.

- ***W**ord Forms*. Choose this option to find any form of the word you are looking for. For example, entering **threw** finds *threw*, *throw*, and *throwing*. For more information see "Finding and Replacing Word Forms" later in this chapter.

- ***S**pecific Codes*. Choose this option to search for WordPerfect formatting codes of a certain value. For more information, see the section, "Finding and Replacing Formatting Codes" later in this chapter.

While in the F**i**nd text box, choose **M**atch to select from the following find options:

- ***W**hole Word.* Choose this option to find the text you enter only if it is not part of other text. For example, with a normal WordPerfect Find, searching for **fall** finds both *fall* and *waterfall.* With this option checked, Find locates only *fall.*

- ***C**ase.* Choose this option to have WordPerfect match lower- and uppercase letters exactly. With this option checked, for example, **gateway** finds only *gateway*, and **Gateway** finds only *Gateway.*

- ***F**ont.* Choose this option to display the Match Font dialog box. In this dialog box, specify various fonts, font sizes, and text attributes. When you make a selection here, WordPerfect only finds the search string you enter if it is in the font, font size, and attributes you have selected.

- *C**o**des.* Choose this option to find WordPerfect formatting codes. For more information, see the section "Finding and Replacing Formatting Codes" later in this chapter.

While in the Replace **W**ith text box, choose R**e**place to select from the following replace options:

- ***C**ase.* Normally, when you enter a lowercase replacement string, WordPerfect uses the first character capitalization of the word being replaced. To force WordPerfect to use the case of the replacement string entered, choose this option. The word Case Sensitive appears below the Replace **W**ith text box.

- ***F**ont.* Choose this option to display the Replace Font dialog box. From this dialog box, you can choose a font, font style, and font attribute to be applied to the text when replaced.

- *C**o**des.* This option works the same as the codes option listed earlier under the **M**atch menu.

Note

Not all the codes listed in the Codes list box from the **M**atch menu are available in the Codes list box from the R**e**place menu. For example, you can search for a general `[Lft Mar]` code, regardless of its value. But it makes no sense to replace a code with a nonspecific `[Lft Mar]` code. The replacement needs to have a specific value (for example, two inches, so you need to use the Specific Codes option to choose a replacement code).

Choose **D**irection to select from the following options:

- ***F****orward.* Choose this option to search the document from the starting point toward the end of the document.
- ***B****ackward.* Choose this option to search the document from the starting point toward the beginning of the document.

Choose Actio**n** to select from the following options:

- ***S****elect Match.* Choose this option, and WordPerfect highlights the search string when it is found. This enables you to immediately perform WordPerfect operations on the selected text. This option is the default that WordPerfect selects each time you start WordPerfect.
- *Position* ***B****efore.* Choose this option to have WordPerfect position the insertion point immediately before the first item of the search string if it is found.
- *Position* ***A****fter.* Choose this option to have WordPerfect position the insertion point immediately after the last item of the search string if it is found.
- ***E****xtend Selection.* Choose this option to extend a text selection from the location of the insertion point to a specific word, phrase, or code. For example, to select text from the insertion point through the phrase *pay raises,* open the Find and Replace Text dialog box and choose Actio**n**, **E**xtend Selection. Type **pay raises** in the text box and choose **F**ind Next. The portion of your document from the insertion point up to and including *pay raises* is highlighted.

Choose **O**ptions to select from the following options (**B**egin Find at Top of Document and **W**rap at Beg./End of Document are covered in the section "Finding Words and Phrases" earlier in this chapter):

- ***L****imit Find Within Selection.* This option causes the find to be performed only on the selection you made in the document prior to performing the find.
- ***I****nclude Headers, Footers, etc. in Find.* Choose this option to search for words, phrases, or codes in places other than regular body text. These areas include headers, footers, text boxes, watermarks, footnotes, endnotes, comments, graphics box captions, equations, and tables of authorities full form.

- *Limit **N**umber of Changes*. Choose this option to limit the number of times a word, phrase, or code is replaced. Choosing this option causes the Limit Number of Changes dialog box, in which you enter the limit number, to appear.

Finding and Replacing Word Forms

In addition to finding specific words, you can use WordPerfect's Word Form option to find all the forms of a word. For example, you can search for the word *threw* and the words *threw, throw,* and *throwing* are all found. WordPerfect selects all the tenses of the root word, for example past and present tense, but does not find other parts of speech (verb, noun, and so on). For example, if you look for the word *run*, you would find *ran* and *running,* but not the noun *runner*.

The real power of working with word forms is apparent when finding and replacing text. Try the following example:

1. Type the following:

   Shahram said "I think Debbie is going to the store soon." Gary, realizing the mistake, said "No, she went to the store an hour ago and has already returned."

2. Press Ctrl+Home to move the insertion point to the top of the document.

3. Choose **E**dit, **F**ind and Replace; or press F2. The Find and Replace Text dialog box appears.

4. Choose **T**ype, **W**ord Forms.

5. Type **go** in the F**i**nd text box. Type **run** in the Replace **W**ith text box.

6. Choose Replace **A**ll.

7. Choose **C**lose to return to your document. The text now reads:

   Shahram said, "I think Debbie is running to the store soon." Gary, realizing the mistake, said "No, she ran to the store an hour ago and has already returned."

   Don't forget to deselect **W**ord Forms if you will be doing subsequent normal searches.

Note

If you choose Replace **A**ll and several word forms exist for the replacement word, a Word Form dialog box appears. Choose the desired replacement in the Word **F**orms list box and then choose **R**eplace to replace this occurrence of the word and locate the next. Choose **U**se Always to use the selected word form for all subsequent replacements, or **S**kip to not replace this occurrence of the found word and locate the next.

As you can see, finding and replacing text based on word forms can be a very powerful editing tool.

Finding and Replacing Formatting Codes

WordPerfect enables you to find or find and replace formatting codes. For example, if you want to find where you set the tabs in your document, you can search for the `[Tab Set]` code. You can search also for specific codes of a certain value. Instead of searching for all `[Lft Mar]` codes, for example, you can search for locations where the left margin is set to 2 inches (`[Lft Mar:2"]`). Additionally, you can change the 2-inch margin to 3 inches by finding and replacing the appropriate hidden codes.

To find and replace hidden codes, you follow the general steps described in the preceding sections for finding and replacing text—except that you do not type text in the F**i**nd and Replace **W**ith text boxes.

To find a code regardless of its value, follow these steps:

1. Choose **E**dit, **F**ind and Replace; or press F2. The Find and Replace Text dialog box appears (refer to fig. 3.10).

2. Choose **M**atch, C**o**des. The Codes dialog box appears (see fig. 3.11).

3. Use the scroll arrows to scroll through the list until you highlight the code you want to find, or type the characters of the code. To search for the `[Tab Set]` code, for example, type **Tab S**. As you type the characters, the highlight bar moves closer to your selection.

4. When the desired code is highlighted, choose **I**nsert. WordPerfect inserts the code in the F**i**nd text box of the Find and Replace Text dialog box. If you have no other codes to select, choose Close. Then continue with the same steps that you use to find text.

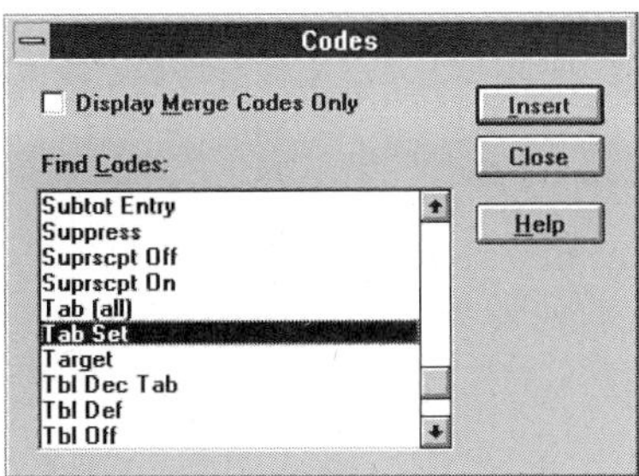

Fig. 3.11
The Codes dialog box showing `Tab Set` selected using the highlight bar.

To find a code with a specific value, follow these steps:

1. With the Find and Replace Text dialog box open, choose **T**ype, **S**pecific Codes. The Specific Codes dialog box appears.

2. Use the scroll arrows to scroll the list until you highlight the code you want to find, or type the characters of the code.

3. When the desired code is highlighted, choose OK. A Find and Replace dialog box specific to the selected code appears (see fig. 3.12).

4. Enter the value of the code that you want to find in the Find box (1.5 in this example) or use the increment/decrement arrows. Continue with the same steps used to find text.

Fig. 3.12
The Find and Replace Left Margin dialog box enables you to enter the value of the left margin code you want to find.

To replace codes with specific values, open the Find and Replace Text dialog box (choose **E**dit, **F**ind and Replace; or press F2), and then follow steps 1 through 4 in the preceding instructions. In step 4, however, type the value to be found and the value to be used as the replacement. Figure 3.12 shows an example of finding one or more left margin codes of 1.5 inches and replacing them with left margin codes of 3 inches. If you want to find codes with a specific value and delete them, choose Replace with **N**othing.

Note

Not all the codes listed in the Find Codes list box are available in the Replace Codes list box. For example, you can search for a general `[Lft Mar]` code, regardless of its value. But it makes no sense to replace a code with a nonspecific `[Lft Mar]` code. The replacement needs to have a specific value (for example, 2 inches, so you need to use the Specific Codes option to choose a replacement code).

Likewise, not all codes appear in the Specific Codes dialog box because many codes—such as bold and underline—do not have variable values.

From Here...

Using WordPerfect's powerful electronic editing commands to revise your document helps to ensure that your documents express your ideas the way you intend. In this chapter, you learned how easy it is to modify a document.

To learn more about working with documents in WordPerfect, refer to these chapters:

- Chapter 4, "Formatting Text," shows you how to take the documents you've used to express your ideas and apply formatting to text to make the documents readable and visually appealing.
- Chapter 5, "Formatting Pages and Documents," shows you how to change the layout of the lines, paragraphs, and pages of your documents to encourage readers to delve into the documents.
- Chapter 6, "Using Writing Tools," teaches you about the tools provided to check and correct the spelling and grammar of your documents and to help you select the right words to express your thoughts. You also learn how QuickCorrect can fix your spelling errors and correct punctuation as you type.
- Chapter 7, "Integrating Text and Graphics," shows you how to use graphics elements such as lines, borders, and boxes to break up a full page of text and create documents that captivate the reader's attention.
- Chapter 8, "Basic Output: Printing, Faxing, and E-mail," leads you through the steps necessary to print a document and control print jobs. You also learn how to transmit a document from your computer to someone else using a fax machine or electronic mail.

Chapter 4

Formatting Text

4

by George Beinhorn and Cathy Kenny

WordPerfect's text-formatting features help make documents readable and visually inviting. *Formatting* refers to the way you enhance text and other page elements on the printed page. For example, you can alter the appearance of text by changing the font, line spacing, margins, paragraph spacing, justification, and many other options.

Chapter 5, "Formatting Pages and Documents," describes options for formatting pages. To learn how to apply WordPerfect's font appearance and size controls, see Chapter 20, "Using Fonts and Special Characters."

In this chapter, you learn to do the following tasks:

- Change default formatting settings
- Use the Power Bar, Toolbar, and Ruler Bar to perform formatting tasks quickly
- Use "smart" Auto Code Placement
- Set margins and tabs
- Use indents and back tab
- Control justification
- Control hyphenation

Using WordPerfect's Text-Formatting Tools

WordPerfect sets ready-to-use defaults for formatting text when you install the program. If you prefer other formatting options, you can change the defaults or override them temporarily, as described in the next section, "WordPerfect's Default Text Format Settings," and in corresponding sections on formatting throughout this chapter.

The sections that follow describe various ways to access WordPerfect's text-formatting tools. The most basic way to choose text-formatting commands is with the Format menu. However, you can also format text quickly with the mouse. For example, you can click a button on the Toolbar to indent text or format paragraphs with bullets. A special button called QuickFormat lets you quickly apply fonts and attributes (boldface, italic, and more) or paragraph styles that you've used elsewhere in a document.

With the Power Bar, you can click buttons to change fonts, set tabs, justification, line spacing, and perform other common formatting functions. You can create customized Power Bars and Toolbars to use the mouse to access the commands you use most frequently. You can switch between Toolbars to perform specialized tasks, such as formatting tables or equations. WordPerfect comes with several ready-made Toolbars. For more information about Toolbars and the Power Bar, see Chapter 13, "Working with Toolbars."

WordPerfect's Default Text Format Settings

When you first install WordPerfect, the following defaults take effect for formatting text: one-inch margins at top, bottom, left, and right sides of the page; single-line spacing; and left justification. Depending on the currently selected printer you installed under Windows, WordPerfect chooses a default font—usually a common font such as Courier 10 pitch or Times New Roman Regular 12 point. The currently active font is shown at the left end of the Power Bar at the top of the screen.

Tip
To use formatting commands effectively, you should know how to turn on and work in the Reveal Codes screen, as described in Chapter 3. To turn Reveal Codes on and off, choose **V**iew, Re**v**eal **C**odes; or press Alt+F3.

When you change a default setting, it remains in effect for all new documents you create. If you change a setting "manually," as described in the various sections of this chapter, the manual setting overrides the default, and remains in effect for the current document only. To learn how to change defaults, see Chapter 9, "Customizing WordPerfect."

You can also insert formatting commands with the Document Initial Style feature, which is described in Chapter 5, "Formatting Pages and Documents," and in Chapter 10, "Using Styles." This feature "hides" codes so they don't clutter up the Reveal Codes window. You use this feature primarily for codes that remain in effect throughout a document. To create document initial codes, choose Fo**r**mat, **D**ocument, Initial Codes **S**tyle. You can override a formatting code contained in a Document Initial Style at any time by inserting a manual formatting command.

The Format Menu

Text-formatting commands are located on the Format menu. You can also choose many text-formatting commands with the Toolbar, Power Bar, and Ruler Bar, as described in corresponding sections of this chapter.

The Format menu provides the following text-formatting commands:

Fo**r**mat, **F**ont
Fo**r**mat, **L**ine
Fo**r**mat, P**a**ragraph
Fo**r**mat, **D**ocument
Fo**r**mat, **M**argins; or Ctrl+F8
Fo**r**mat, **J**ustification
Fo**r**mat, **Q**uickFormat

▶ See "Customizing the Display," p. 317

▶ See "Creating the Initial Codes Style," p. 207

▶ See "Using Styles," p. 375

The Toolbar, Power Bar, and Ruler Bar

You can change text-formatting settings quickly with the mouse by clicking the Toolbar, Power Bar, and Ruler Bar. The specific steps to perform these operations are described in corresponding sections of this chapter. This section gives basic instructions for using the bars.

Tip
To display the Ruler Bar, choose **V**iew, **R**uler Bar or press Alt+Shift+F3.

Figure 4.1 shows the default Toolbar, Power Bar, and Ruler Bar, with text-formatting buttons labeled.

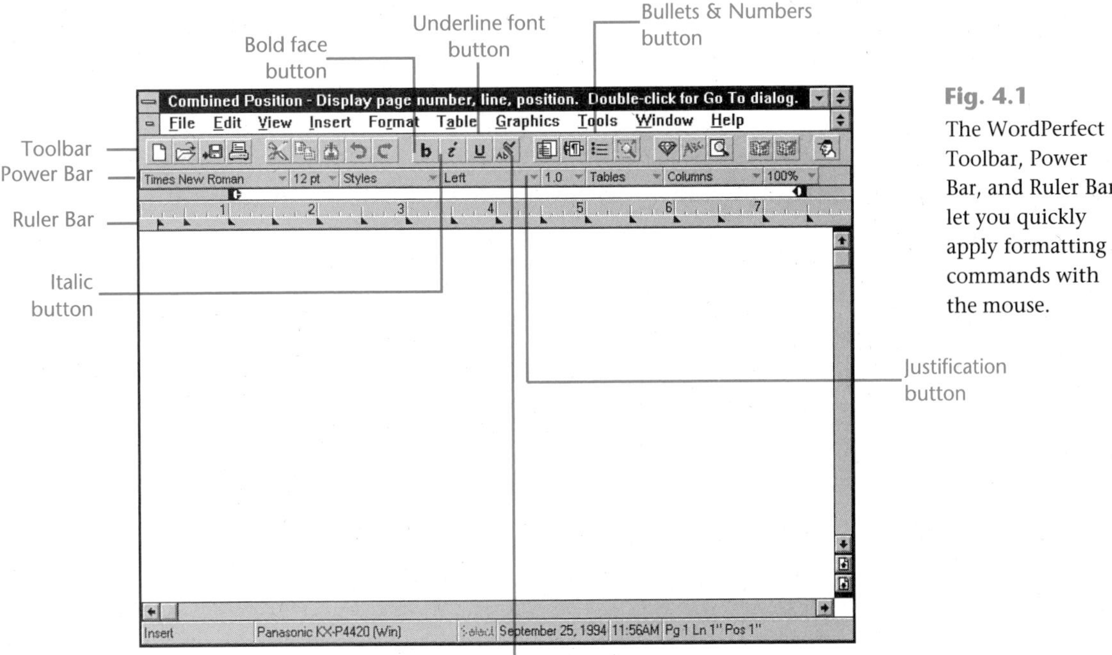

Fig. 4.1
The WordPerfect Toolbar, Power Bar, and Ruler Bar let you quickly apply formatting commands with the mouse.

To learn how to display or hide the various bars, refer to Chapter 1, "Getting Started."

QuickFormat

Notice that the Toolbar includes a button labeled QuickFormat. The QuickFormat command lets you quickly copy font, attribute, and/or paragraph style formatting from formatted text to other paragraphs or blocks of selected text. For details on using QuickFormat, see the section "Formatting Text with QuickFormat" later in this chapter.

Auto Code Placement

When you choose formatting commands, WordPerfect places hidden codes in the document. To view or hide hidden codes, choose **V**iew, Reveal **C**odes (Alt+F3). For more information on using Reveal Codes, see Chapter 3, "Retrieving and Editing Documents."

WordPerfect automatically repositions certain codes, regardless of where you enter them in a document. This feature is called *Auto Code Placement.* As an example, Auto Code Placement moves codes that affect an entire paragraph, such as left and right margins and justification, to the beginning of the paragraph. Formatting commands that affect an entire page are moved to the top of the page, even if you enter a command in the middle of the page. When you need to find a hidden code, Auto Code Placement ensures that the code is at the top of the document, page, or paragraph.

Formatting Characters

◄ See "Understanding WordPerfect's Hidden Codes," p. 95

You use WordPerfect's character formatting options to turn on character appearance attributes, such as boldface, italic, small caps, and underlining, and to change character size.

You can display any appearance attribute on-screen, but your printer may not be able to print all character attributes. To find out what your printer can do, retrieve and print the PRINTST.WPD file found in the WordPerfect shared code directory (normally C:\OFFICE\SHARED\WPC20).

Changing Character Appearance and Size

You can change character appearance and size attributes with the Font dialog box by following these steps:

1. Select existing text if you want to apply new character attributes to the text; or position the cursor if you want to apply attributes to new text only.

2. Choose Format, **F**ont; or press F9. The Font dialog box appears (see fig. 4.2). Clicking the Font button on the Toolbar also displays the Font dialog box.

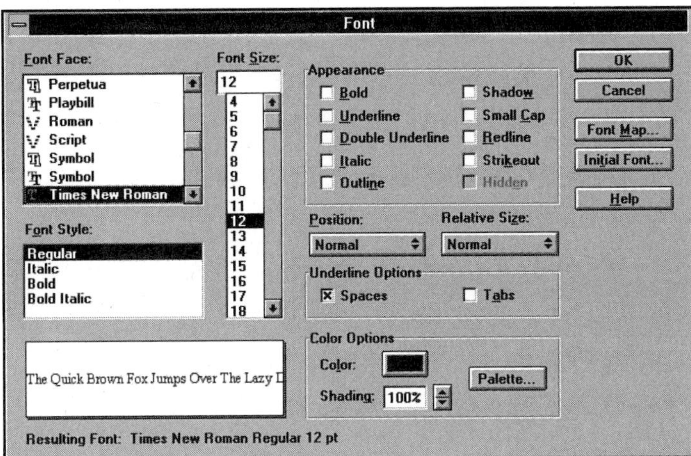

Fig. 4.2
In the Font dialog box, choose Microsoft Windows TrueType fonts or fonts that are supplied with your printer. You can also choose soft fonts that you've installed on your system.

3. Choose options from the **F**ont Face, Font **S**ize, F**o**nt Style, Appearance, **P**osition, Relative Size, Underline Options, and Color Options sections of the dialog box.

   As you make selections, your changes are reflected in the sample window in the lower left corner of the dialog box.

4. Choose OK or press Enter to return to the document screen.

The following list describes the Font dialog box options:

- ***F**ont Face.* Changes the font for selected or new text. Use the arrow keys or mouse to choose a font from the list. Or double-click a font name to select it and return to the document screen. With text selected, WordPerfect encloses the selected text in opening and closing font codes. With no text selected, WordPerfect applies the new font from the insertion point forward, until it encounters another font code.

- *Font **S**ize.* Changes the size of selected or new text. Choose Font **S**ize and use the arrow keys or mouse to choose a font size from the list; or type a font size in the Font **S**ize text box.

- *F**o**nt Style.* Displays style options available for the font selected in the **F**ont Face list. When you choose a font appearance option from the list and then choose OK (or double-click the appearance option),

WordPerfect inserts a `Font: [font name]` hidden code in the document. This code changes the font appearance from the insertion point forward. With text selected, WordPerfect encloses the selected text between opening and closing font codes. Use this option when you want to change the font and character attributes without having the font overridden if you later insert a font code before the insertion point.

You can choose font appearance options with check boxes in the Appearance section of the dialog box, as described in the next list item. When you use this method, WordPerfect encloses selected text in font attribute codes—for example, bold and italic opening and closing codes. Use this method to enclose new text in opening and closing codes. To change the font from the insertion point forward without inserting a closing code, choose F**o**nt Style. Using the check boxes to change the appearance attributes retains the attributes, but allows the font to change if you insert a new font code before the insertion point.

- *Appearance.* Choose check boxes from this section to apply attributes to new or selected text. As described in the preceding paragraph, WordPerfect encloses the new or selected text in the corresponding character attribute codes.

  The Appearance options are **B**old, **U**nderline, **D**ouble Underline, **I**talic, Outli**ne**, Shado**w**, Small **C**ap, **R**edline, Stri**k**eout, and Hidd**en**. When you choose one or more attributes, the sample window in the lower left corner of the dialog box reflects your changes.

Note

You can apply the most frequently used character appearance attributes to selected or new text with the following keyboard shortcuts:

Attribute	Keyboard shortcut
Bold	Ctrl+B
Italic	Ctrl+I
Underline	Ctrl+U

To return to normal type after applying an attribute, press the right-arrow key to move past the closing attribute code.

Note that Hidd**e**n is grayed unless text is selected. You must select text before you can format it as hidden. Hidden text is hidden on-screen by default, and is not printed. To turn on the on-screen display of hidden text, choose **E**dit, Pr**e**ferences and double-click the **D**isplay icon. Then select **D**ocument, choose Hidd**e**n Text, click OK and then Close. To display hidden text for the current document only, choose **V**iew Hidden Te**x**t.

- ***P**osition.* Choose this option, and then choose Su**p**erscript or Su**b**script to format selected or new text as superscript or subscript characters. WordPerfect formats superscript and subscript text in characters 60% as large as the current font.

- *Relative Si**z**e.* Choose this option to quickly change font size to one of several standard sizes. Table 4.1 shows the default size attributes:

Table 4.1 Size Attributes

Font size attribute	Default size ratio
Fine	60%
Small	80%
Normal	100%
Large	120%
Very Large	150%
E**x**tra Large	200%

To change the default font size attribute ratios, choose **E**dit, Pr**e**ferences, and double-click the P**r**int icon. Type a new percent ratio for each attribute, and then choose OK, **C**lose to return to the document screen. Use this method to change the size ratio for subscript and superscript characters as well.

- *Underline Options.* Choose Spaces to have WordPerfect underline spaces inserted with the space bar when underlining is turned on. Choose T**a**bs to have WordPerfect underline spaces inserted with the Tab key when underlining is turned on.

- *Color Options.* If your printer supports color, you can choose the color that WordPerfect uses to print selected or new characters. Choose Co**l**or

Tip

Click the Bold, Italic, and Underline tools in the Toolbar to apply the attribute to new or selected text.

Tip
The Shading option is useful for creating artistic effects with large display type—for example, to print a newsletter banner heading with 40% gray shaded letters.

and select the desired color. Choose Shading and choose a level of gray shading (from 0% to 100%).

Choose Palette to define a new color with the Define Color Printing Palette dialog box. For a complete discussion of using the Define Color Printing Palette dialog box, see Chapter 8, "Basic Output: Printing, Faxing, and E-Mail."

Changing Character Attributes with the Power Bar

You can change the following character attributes quickly by using buttons on the Power Bar:

▶ See "Printing Documents with Graphics," p. 299

- *Font.* To change the font, click the Font Face button to drop down a list of available fonts; then click the desired font. If no text is selected, WordPerfect inserts a font code and changes the font until it encounters another font code. With text selected, WordPerfect encloses the selected text in opening and closing font codes. The status line displays the name of the current font.

- *Font size.* Click one of the Font Size buttons, and then click a size on the drop-down list. If no text is selected, WordPerfect inserts a font size code and changes the font until it encounters another font code. With text selected, WordPerfect encloses the selected text in opening and closing font size codes.

- *Styles.* Click the Styles button and select a style to apply to selected or new text. WordPerfect inserts the Style opening and closing style codes, using the style name.

Formatting Lines and Paragraphs

▶ See "Examining the Toolbar and Power Bar icons," p. 452

You access WordPerfect's line and paragraph formatting commands through the Format menu (see figs. 4.3 and 4.4). You can also insert most formatting codes with the mouse by using the Toolbar, Power Bar, and Ruler Bar. The sections that follow give menu and mouse alternatives for choosing formatting commands.

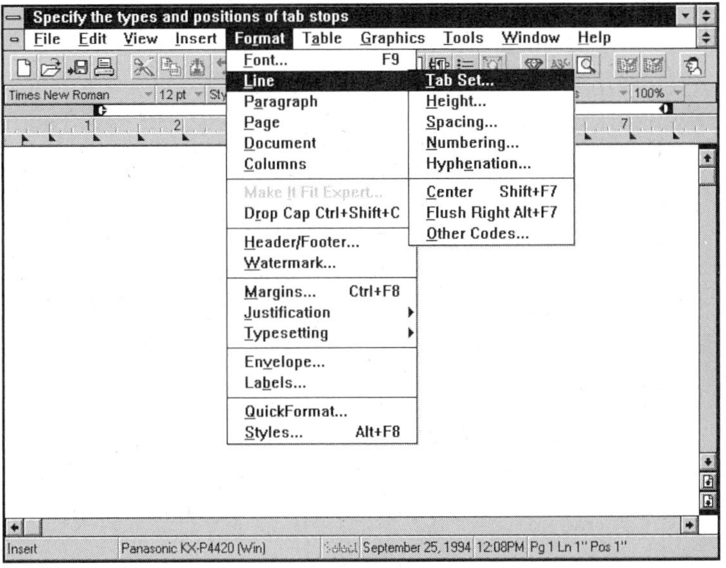

Fig. 4.3
The Format and Line menus contain the commands used to format lines in your document

Note

WordPerfect uses the Fo**r**mat **L**ine **O**ther Codes command to access several features not very obviously associated with lines: hard tab codes, dot leaders, and hard spaces.

Controlling Line Spacing and Line Height

When you first install WordPerfect, it sets line spacing to single-spacing, and automatically sets the line height to match the currently selected font. Margins are set to one inch on all four sides of the page. You can change these defaults, as described in Chapter 9, "Customizing WordPerfect." Or you can adjust line spacing and line height for part of a document or for the whole document, as described in the following sections. You can also insert formatting codes with Document Initial Style, as described earlier in the section "WordPerfect's Default Text Format Settings," and in Chapter 10, "Using Styles."

► See "Initial Style," p. 360

You can change the line spacing or line height for existing text by first selecting the text, and then choosing formatting commands. Or you can insert a line spacing or line height code and then begin typing with the new settings in effect. If you apply formatting codes to selected text, WordPerfect inserts a code to restore the preceding value at the end of the selected block. For example, if you change the line height for selected lines, WordPerfect inserts a code at the end of the selected block, returning line height to its previous value.

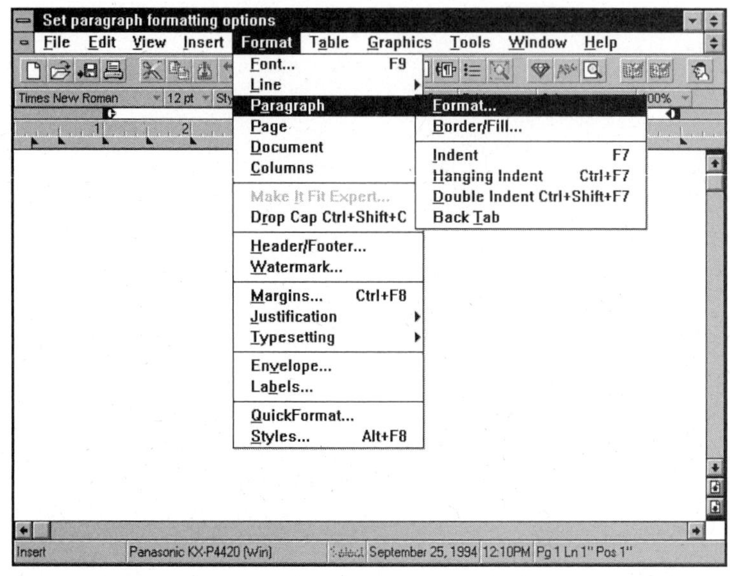

Fig. 4.4
The Format Paragraph menu provides commands for changing the appearance of paragraphs on a page.

Tip
The powerful Border/Fill option on the Paragraph menu provides a much easier method for placing text in boxes than creating and sizing a WordPerfect graphics text box.

Line Spacing

If you change line height or line spacing with no text selected, WordPerfect places the code at the beginning of the current paragraph. The code affects text that follows the code until you insert another code.

Notice that line spacing and line height are different functions in WordPerfect. With the **L**ine **S**pacing command, you can set the space between lines in fractions and multiples of the spacing that WordPerfect automatically selects for the currently active font. Line spacing is described in this section.

With the **L**ine **H**eight command, you can set the spacing of lines much more precisely. Line Height is described in the next section.

To change line spacing, follow these steps:

1. Position the insertion point where you want the change to take effect and choose Fo**r**mat, **L**ine, **S**pacing. The Line Spacing dialog box appears (see fig. 4.5).

2. Type a number in the **S**pacing text box, or click the increment and decrement arrows to change spacing in increments of 0.1 line.

By typing a number in the **S**pacing box, you can set spacing in increments of a hundredth of a line. You cannot specify line spacing in inches, centimeters, points, and so on. The basic line spacing value (1.0 in the **S**pacing box) depends on the current font.

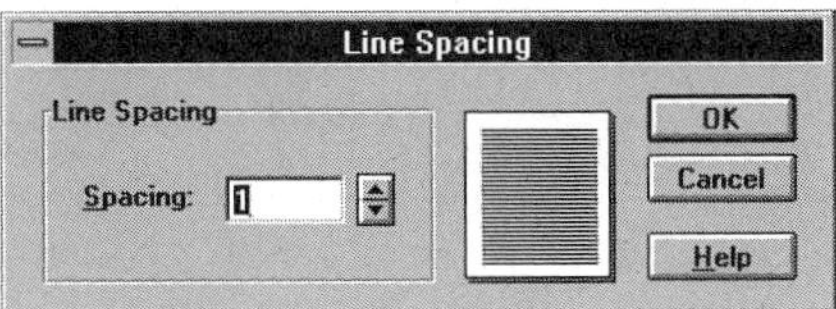

Fig. 4.5
If you are familiar with typesetting conventions, you can specify line spacing in points by typing the exact desired spacing in the **S**pacing text box followed by the letter **p**.

3. Choose OK or press Enter to return to the document window.

WordPerfect inserts the appropriate line spacing code.

Line Height

WordPerfect automatically chooses a line height that the program designers considered to be readable for the currently active font. If you use several type sizes on the same line, WordPerfect sets the line height for the largest font on the line. This is shown in figure 4.6.

You can override WordPerfect's automatic line height settings. This is very useful for precise placement of lines in desktop-published documents. If no text is selected, your line height choices take effect from the insertion point forward. If text is selected, they affect only the blocked text.

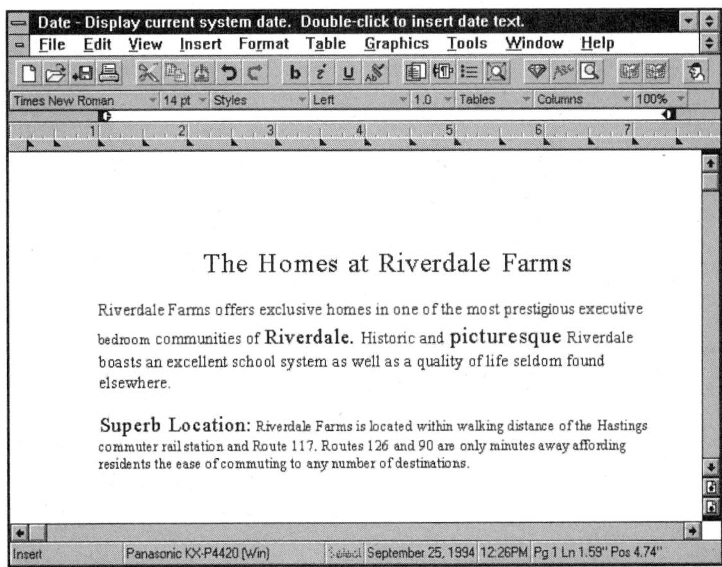

Fig. 4.6
The effects of WordPerfect's automatic line height choices. The default line heights work fine for most text, but for very long lines or large type, you may need to increase line height to keep text readable.

To change line height, follow these steps:

1. Choose Format, **L**ine, **H**eight. The Line Height dialog box appears (see fig. 4.7).

2. Choose **F**ixed, and type a measurement for line height, or click the increment/decrement arrows to change the setting. Insert the appropriate symbol after the number to specify the measurement in inches ("), points (p), or centimeters (cm or c).

3. Choose OK.

   WordPerfect inserts the line height code and returns to the document screen.

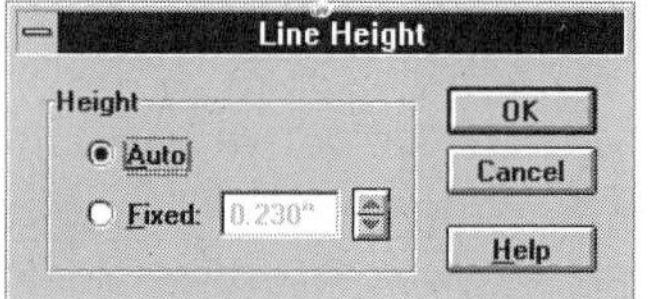

Fig. 4.7
Use the Line Height dialog box to set the spacing between lines exactly or to turn on WordPerfect's automatic line spacing.

You can fine-tune line height further by choosing Format, **T**ypesetting, **W**ord/Letter Spacing and making changes to the Adjust **L**eading setting. For complete information, see Chapter 23, "Desktop Publishing with WordPerfect."

You can also change line height with the QuickFormat feature or with a paragraph style.

Setting Margins

► See "Using Styles," p. 375

WordPerfect measures margin settings from the edges of the page. When you choose a different paper size, the margins remain the same. When you change to a different font, the margins also remain the same. Margins are measured in inches, unless you change the setting in Preferences.

To set margins, follow these steps:

1. Select text to which you want to apply margin settings. Or, to apply settings to the current and subsequent pages, proceed to step 2.

2. Choose Format, **M**argins; or press Ctrl+F8. Or, click the top of the Ruler Bar with the right mouse button. Then choose **M**argins from the resulting QuickMenu. The Margins dialog box appears (see fig. 4.8).

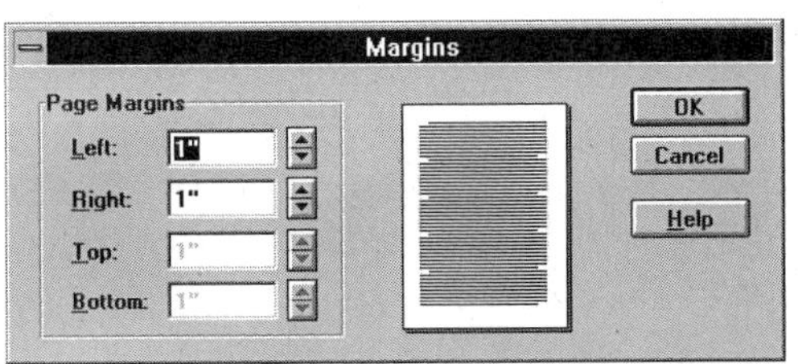

Fig. 4.8
Change the Margin settings in the current document using the Margins dialog box.

3. Type new margin settings in the dialog box or click the increment/decrement arrows to change the settings.

4. Click OK to return to the document screen.

WordPerfect inserts the new margin settings in the document. Notice that WordPerfect inserts two separate codes for Left/Right and Top/Bottom margins.

You can also change margins with the QuickFormat feature, or with a paragraph style. For details, see the "Formatting Text with QuickFormat" section later in this chapter.

Tip
To specify wide margins for binding left- and right-facing pages, choose Fo**r**mat, **P**age, B**i**nding/Duplex, and specify a binding width for the **L**eft, **R**ight, **T**op, or **B**ottom margin.

Note

WordPerfect automatically sets the margins for headers and footers that are in effect for the document at the point where you insert the header or footer code. You can set separate margins for headers and footers by inserting margin codes in the header or footer editing window. To find out how to create headers and footers, see Chapter 5, "Formatting Pages and Documents."

Tip
You can change the margins quickly with the Ruler Bar. Just drag the line margin markers on the bar.

Using Indent and Back Tab

You can indent one or more paragraphs to emphasize the text, format a long quotation, or create subordinate levels. You can use the **I**ndent command to indent text quickly, without changing the margins. Several related commands—**D**ouble Indent, Back **T**ab, and **H**anging Indent—let you change margins temporarily.

► See "Selecting Paper Size and Type," p. 186

► See "Using Styles," p. 375

Indent and Double Indent

To indent a paragraph to the first tab stop from the left margin, move the insertion point to the beginning of the paragraph and choose Fo**r**mat, P**a**ragraph, **I**ndent; or press F7. You can use multiple indents to indent the margin to the corresponding tab stops.

To indent both left and right margins, move the insertion point to the start of the paragraph and choose Fo**r**mat, P**a**ragraph, **D**ouble Indent; or press Ctrl+Shift+F7.

To indent several paragraphs at once, first select the paragraphs, and then follow the steps for indenting or double-indenting a single paragraph. Figure 4.9 shows the effect of various indenting options.

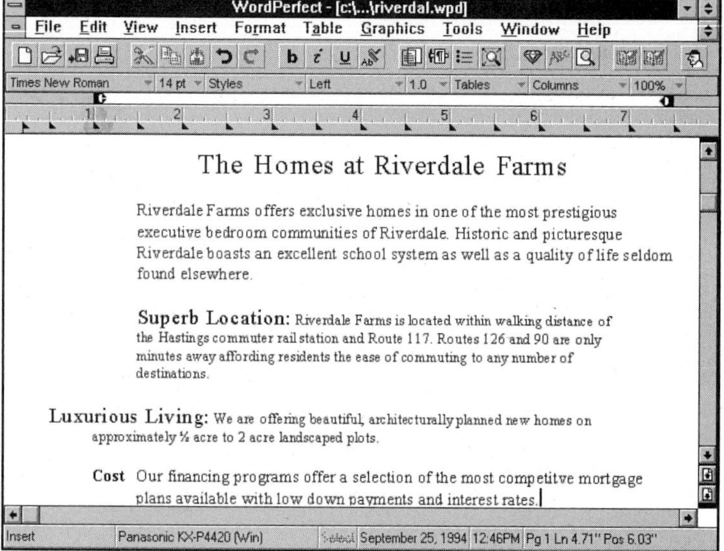

Fig. 4.9
The effect of indenting, double-indenting, back tab, and hanging indent. When you apply these commands "manually," they override any paragraph style settings for text indents.

To learn how to set tabs, see the section "Setting and Using Tabs" later in this chapter.

> **Caution**
>
> Don't try to create indents or tabs with the space bar and Enter key. You may get satisfactory results on-screen and even in a printout, but you won't be able to edit the text without adjusting the text with the space bar and Tab key.

Back Tab

To begin the first line of a paragraph to the left of the current left margin, choose Fo**r**mat, P**a**ragraph, Back **T**ab; or press Shift+Tab (refer to fig. 4.9).

You can release the margin only as far to the left as your printer can print.

Hanging Indent

To create a hanging indent, choose Fo**r**mat, P**a**ragraph, **H**anging Indent; or press Ctrl+F7.

This command inserts separate Left Indent and Back Tab codes. To delete a hanging indent, you must delete both codes.

You can also create a hanging indent by pressing F7 (Indent), Shift+Tab.

Setting and Using Tabs

Unlike indents, which affect all text until a hard return is encountered, tabs position text only in the current line (unless Outlining is turned on). To learn more about outlining, see Chapter 15, "Organizing Documents with Outlining".

Tabs are used primarily to indent the first line of a paragraph, to organize data in tabular columns, and to set tab stops for indents and tabs.

Tip
Don't use Tab when you want to indent an entire paragraph. Instead, use the **I**ndent, **H**anging Indent, **D**ouble Indent, and Back **T**ab commands.

Types of Tabs

WordPerfect has four types of tabs:

- *Left Align.* Text flows from the tab setting to the right; this alignment is commonly used for ordinary text.
- *Center.* Text centers at the tab stop and extends to right and left from the tab stop.
- *Right Align.* Text flows from the tab stop to the left.
- *Decimal Align.* Text flows from the tab stop to the left until you type the alignment character. After you type the alignment character, text flows to the right from the tab stop. This type of tab is used most commonly to align columns of numbers around decimal points. The default alignment character is a period (or decimal point).

You can use dot leaders with tabs so that a line of dots connects tab stops. Dot leaders are useful when the space between tabular columns is wide and the reader's eye needs help to associate elements across the gap.

You can create dot leaders with all four types of WordPerfect tab settings: Left, Center, Right, and Decimal. In each case, when you press Tab, WordPerfect moves the insertion point to the next tab setting on the Ruler, filling the space from the previous tab setting with dot leader characters.

The default tab settings are left-aligned, every 1/2 inch for 14 inches, from -1 inch to 13 inches.

Note

Tabs are measured from the left margin, not the left edge of the page. When you create text in columns, tabs are also measured from the left margin of each column, not the left edge of the current page.

Setting Tabs on the Ruler Bar

You can quickly set tabs with the Ruler Bar. To move a tab on the ruler, drag it to the new location. As you drag the tab marker, a vertical dotted line extends down through the text, indicating where the tab will be placed. To place the tab, release the mouse button.

To insert a new left tab with the Ruler Bar, click in the Tab area of the Ruler, beneath the numbered ruler scale. To remove a tab with the Ruler Bar, drag it onto another tab mark, or drag it below the ruler. Dragging a tab mark onto another tab marker replaces the "bottom" tab. If you change your mind about moving or deleting a tab while dragging the tab marker, move the mouse cursor above the Ruler bar until the tab marker snaps back to its original position.

To restore default tab settings to the Ruler Bar, choose Fo**r**mat, **L**ine, **T**ab Set, **D**efault, OK.

As you drag a tab mark with the mouse, the status bar shows the position of the tab in 1/16-inch increments. This makes it easier to place tabs at precise intervals. You can place tabs at even more precise intervals of one pixel by holding down the Shift key while you drag a tab marker. When you drag a tab marker, the status line indicates tab settings in hundredths of an inch. You can turn off the 1/16-inch increments permanently by following the procedure given in the next section.

Customizing the Ruler Display

You can set options that determine how WordPerfect displays the Ruler Bar.

To change the Ruler Bar options, follow these steps:

1. Choose **E**dit, Pr**e**ferences, and double-click the **D**isplay icon. Or, click the right mouse button above the tab line, and then choose **P**references from the resulting QuickMenu.

2. In the Display dialog box, select **R**uler Bar. WordPerfect displays the Display Preferences dialog box with Ruler options selected (see fig. 4.10).

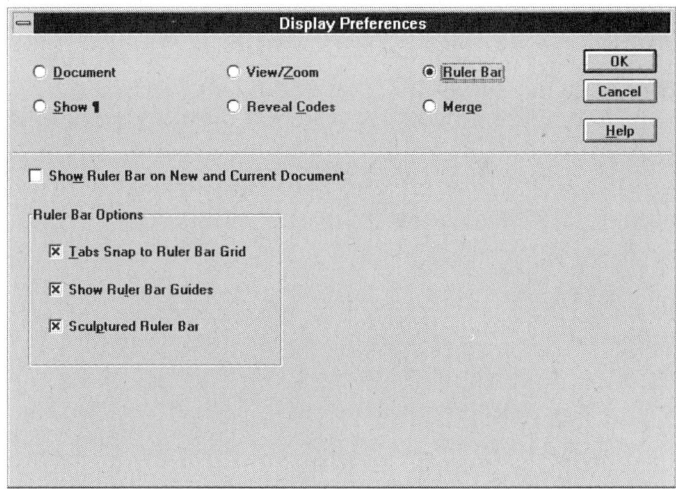

Fig. 4.10
To set WordPerfect to display the Ruler Bar in all new documents, choose **R**uler Bar in the Display Preferences dialog box, and mark Sho**w** Ruler Bar on New and Current Document.

3. Choose Ruler display options; then choose OK, **C**lose to return to the document screen.

Tip
You can also display the Display Preferences dialog box by double-clicking the Ruler Bar above the tab scale.

The following list describes the Ruler display options:

- *Sho**w** Ruler Bar on New and Current Document.* Selecting this check box turns on the ruler by default for each new WordPerfect document. It also turns on the ruler for the document currently displayed on-screen.

- ***T**abs Snap to Ruler Bar Grid.* Displaying the Ruler activates grid lines at 1/16 inch, 1/5 centimeter, or the equivalent interval for the unit of measure you choose. With this check box selected, when you move or place a tab, the tab snaps to the grid line nearest your placement. Deselecting this option allows you to place a tab anywhere on the ruler. WordPerfect will not snap the tab setting to the closest grid line.

- *Show Ru**l**er Bar Guides.* When you use the Ruler to position tabs, by default a dotted vertical line extends from the bottom of the tab to the bottom of the screen as you use the mouse to move the tab along the Ruler. To turn this feature off, deselect the check box.

- *Scul**p**tured Ruler Bar.* Selecting this check box displays the ruler with gray shading and a "sculptured" look, similar to the Toolbar and Power Bar. To view the effect of selecting or deselecting this option, choose OK; then drag the Preferences dialog box off the Ruler Bar.

Tip
To override the grid setting while placing a tab with the Ruler grid active, hold down the Shift key while you place the tab.

Setting Tabs from the Tab Set Dialog Box

The Tab Set dialog box enables you to set tabs precisely and to specify tab options that are not available with the Ruler Bar. To display the Tab Set dialog box, choose Format, **L**ine, and then choose **T**ab Set. Or, click the right mouse button in the Ruler Bar above the ruler line, and then choose **T**ab Set from the resulting QuickMenu. WordPerfect displays the Tab Set dialog box (see fig. 4.11).

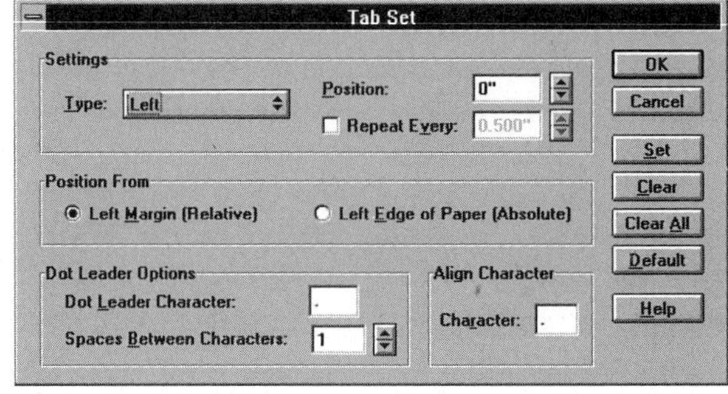

Fig. 4.11
Use the Tab Set dialog box to position tabs in precise increments as small as 1/1000 inch.

Tip
You can also open the Tab Set dialog box by double-clicking any tab mark.

With the Tab Set dialog box, you can position tabs from 0 inches to 54 1/2 inches.

To set a tab with the Tab Set dialog box, follow these steps:

1. Choose **T**ype and select a type from the list: Left, Center, Right, Decimal, Dot Left, Dot Center, Dot Right, or Dot Decimal.

2. Choose **P**osition and type or scroll to a position in inches (") or centimeters (c or cm).

   You can set a position from -1 inch to 40 inches, but WordPerfect won't insert tabs on or beyond the left edge of the currently selected paper size.

3. To insert tab marks across the ruler at even intervals, choose Repeat E**v**ery and type or scroll to an interval setting.

   You can specify tab intervals from 0.100 inch to 10 inches.

4. To position tabs from the left margin, choose Left **M**argin (Relative). Or choose Left **E**dge of Paper (Absolute) to measure tabs from the left side of the page.

If you use columns in a document, choose Left **M**argin (Relative) to create uniform paragraph indents throughout the columns. Tabs will be measured from the left margin of each column. If you change the left or right margins, the tabs shift with the new margins.

5. To insert dot leaders, choose Dot **L**eader Character and type a character for the dot leaders.

6. To adjust the space between dot leaders, choose Spaces **B**etween Characters and type or scroll to a new number.

7. To change the align character for decimal tabs, choose Cha**r**acter and type the new character.

8. Choose **S**et to insert the new tab.

   WordPerfect inserts a new tab mark in the Ruler bar.

9. Repeat steps 2-8 for each new tab that you want to set.

10. Choose OK to return to the document.

To clear all tab marks from the Ruler Bar, choose Clear **A**ll from the Tab Set dialog box. To clear a single tab, choose **P**osition and type the tab's position; then choose **C**lear. To restore WordPerfect's default tab settings, choose **D**efault.

You can set a maximum of 40 tabs. When you insert evenly spaced tabs, WordPerfect uses all the remaining available tabs.

Setting Tabs with the QuickMenu

You can also set tabs by selecting the type of tab you want to create from the QuickMenu. To display the QuickMenu, right-click the lower half of the ruler bar (see fig. 4.12.) Then, select the type of tab you want to set.

Inserting Hard Tabs

When you define new tab settings, WordPerfect reformats the text from that point forward in your document. If you replace a left tab mark with a center tab mark, for example, all the left tab marks at that tab stop become center tabs from that point forward. To restore the preceding tab settings, you must either delete the new tab set code or create a new tab setting with the former tab placement.

You can prevent tabs from changing when you redefine tab settings by using Hard Tabs. Hard Tabs remain constant, even if you later insert a new tab definition above the Hard Tab position.

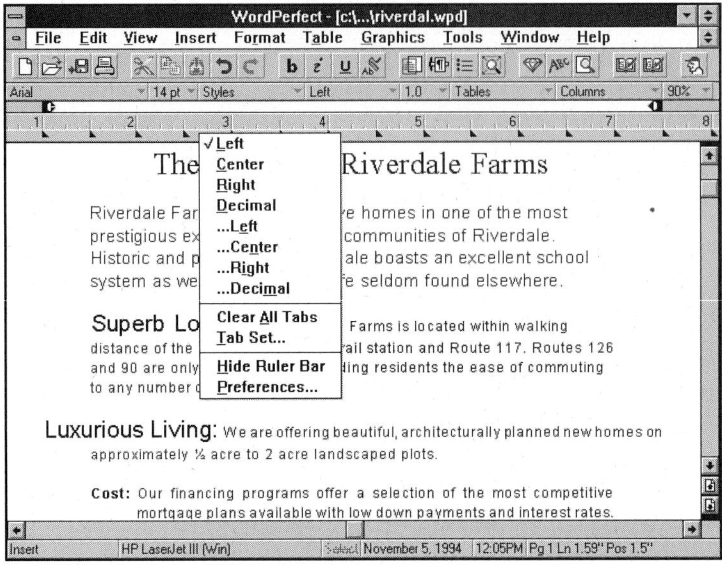

Fig. 4.12
Use the Tab QuickMenu to quickly set tabs.

To insert a Hard Tab, follow these steps:

1. Choose Format, **L**ine.
2. Choose **O**ther Codes. The Other Codes dialog box appears (see fig. 4.13).

Other Codes

Hard Tab Codes:
- Left [Hd Left Tab]
- Center [Hd Center Tab]
- Right [Hd Right Tab]
- Decimal [Hd Dec Tab]

Hard Tab Codes with Dot Leaders:
- Left [...Hd Left Tab]
- Center [...Hd Center Tab]
- Right [...Hd Right Tab]
- Decimal [...Hd Dec Tab]

Insert
Cancel
Help

Hyphenation Codes:
- Hyphen [- Hyphen]
- Hyphen Character -
- Soft Hyphen [- Soft Hyphen]
- Hyphenation Soft Return [HyphSRt]
- Cancel Hyphenation of Word [Cancel Hyph]

Other Codes:
- Hard Space [HSpace]
- End Centering/Alignment [END Cntr/Align]
- Thousands Separator: ,

Fig. 4.13
Use the Other Codes dialog box to insert Hard Tabs in your document.

3. Choose a Hard Tab Code, and then choose **I**nsert to return to the document.

Changing the Decimal Align Character

Decimal tabs are used most often to align columns of numbers at the decimal point. When you press Tab to move to a decimal tab and begin typing, WordPerfect inserts the text to the left until you type the decimal align character, and then inserts any further characters to the right.

You can change the decimal align character. For example, colons are often used in descriptive lists, and in some foreign countries, numbers are formatted with commas as the decimal character, instead of periods.

To change the decimal align character, follow these steps:

1. Choose Fo**r**mat, **L**ine, **T**ab Set. The Tab Set dialog box appears.

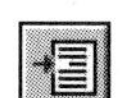

2. In the Cha**r**acter text box, type a new decimal align character; then choose OK to return to the document.

Centering and Flush Right

You can format text centered or flush-right. Flush-right text begins at the right margin and extends "backward" to the left. Centering and flush-right apply to just one line of text at a time; you must insert a new centering or flush-right code at the beginning of each line. Pressing Enter cancels centering or flush-right formatting.

You can also use the justification function to tell WordPerfect to continue to format text centered or flush-right even though you press Enter to start a new line. Justification is discussed in the later section, "Using Justification."

To create centered or flush-right text, follow these steps:

1. Position the insertion point at the left end of the line where you want to begin typing centered text, or at the left end of a line of existing text.

2. Choose Fo**r**mat, **L**ine, **C**enter; or press Shift+F7.

   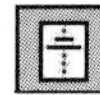

   or

   Choose Fo**r**mat, **L**ine, **F**lush Right; or press Alt+F7.

   If you insert the code at the left end of a line of existing text, WordPerfect centers the text or formats it flush-right.

3. Type new text and press Enter to turn off centering or flush-right.

You can align text flush-right or centered using the QuickMenu. First, position the cursor at the line you want to format and then click the right mouse button anywhere on the document screen. Select **C**enter or Flush **R**ight from the resulting QuickMenu.

> **Note**
>
> You can combine left, center, and flush-right formatting on the same line. For example, to type your name at the left margin, a report title centered, and the date flush-right at the right margin, type the flush-left text, press Shift+F7 and type the centered title; then press Alt+F7 and enter the flush-right date.

If you choose center or flush-right commands with text selected, WordPerfect inserts a `[Just: Center]` or `[Just: Right]` code at the beginning of the block and inserts the appropriate "restore justification" code after the `[HRt]` code at the end of the text. For example, WordPerfect inserts a `[Just: Left]` code when the text reverts to left justification. The lines of the selected text are formatted centered or flush-right.

Formatting Text with QuickFormat

QuickFormat lets you quickly copy fonts and attributes (boldface, italic, and more) or paragraph styles that you've already applied elsewhere in a document. The QuickFormat feature allows you to copy the formatting of a paragraph to another paragraph or to selected text. To copy formatting with QuickFormat, follow these steps:

1. Move the insertion point into a paragraph that has the format you want to copy; or select the text whose formatting you want to copy.

2. Choose Fo**r**mat, **Q**uickFormat.

   Alternatively, click the right mouse button in the document text window and choose **Q**uickFormat from the QuickMenu. WordPerfect displays the QuickFormat dialog box (see fig. 4.14).

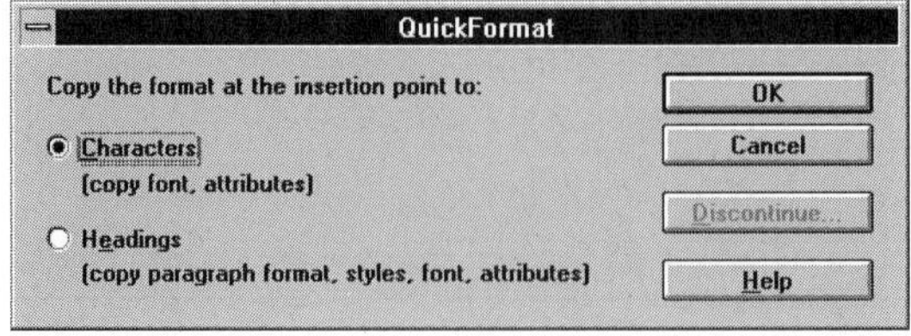

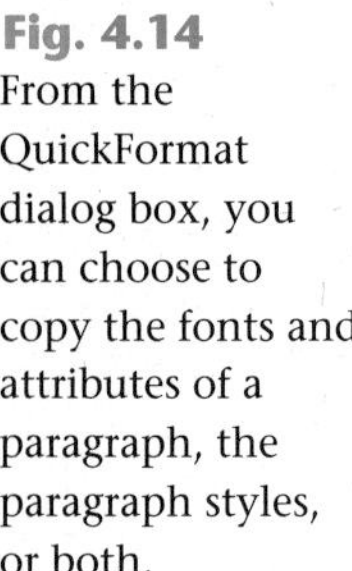
Fig. 4.14 From the QuickFormat dialog box, you can choose to copy the fonts and attributes of a paragraph, the paragraph styles, or both.

3. In the QuickFormat dialog box, choose **C**haracters to copy only the fonts and attributes of the paragraph that contains the insertion point; or choose H**e**adings to copy the paragraph styles, fonts, and attributes.

4. Choose OK.

   The cursor becomes a paint brush.

5. Drag the paint brush over the text you want to reformat.

6. Choose Fo**r**mat, **Q**uickFormat again to reformat the selected text.

   Alternatively, click the right mouse button in the document text window, and choose **Q**uickFormat from the QuickMenu.

QuickFormat remains in effect until you choose **Q**uickFormat again from the Fo**r**mat menu or the QuickMenu. When you need to copy paragraph formatting repeatedly, leave QuickFormat turned on. For example, if you are not using styles, you can copy formatting to all the paragraph headings in a document by turning QuickFormat on and selecting each heading and choosing **Q**uickFormat from the Fo**r**mat menu or the QuickMenu.

Customizing Formatting Options

WordPerfect can display symbols on-screen to indicate the position of tabs, spaces, and other formatting features. To turn on these display options, follow these steps:

1. Choose **E**dit, Pr**e**ferences.

2. Double-click the **D**isplay icon and select **S**how ¶.

   The Display Preferences dialog box appears with the **S**how preferences displayed (see fig. 4.15).

3. To turn on display of formatting symbols, choose the check box titled Sho**w** Symbols on New and Current Document.

4. Choose check boxes for the desired symbols under Symbols To Display; then choose OK, **C**lose to return to the document screen.

The options under Symbols To Display include S**p**ace, Hard Ret**ur**n, **T**ab, **I**ndent, C**e**nter, **F**lush Right, S**o**ft Hyphen, **A**dvance, and Ce**n**ter Page.

Table 4.2 lists the symbols that WordPerfect displays in the document window for each of these formatting options.

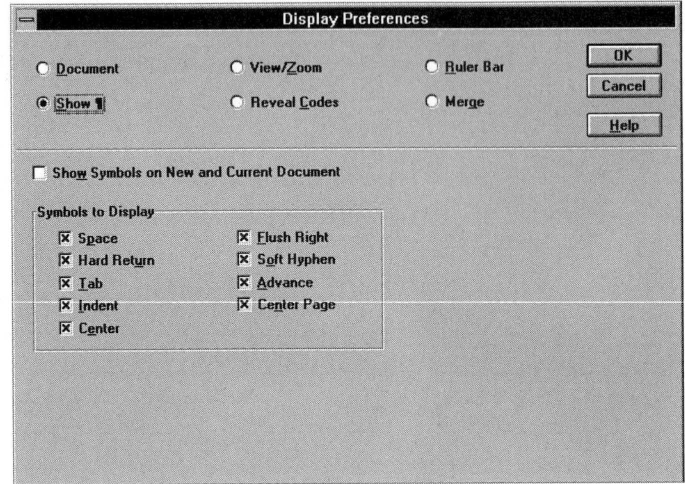

Fig. 4.15
The Show preferences screen in the Display Preferences dialog box enables you to turn on the display of formatting symbols.

Table 4.2 Formatting Symbols

Formatting command	Symbol
Space	Small square
Hard return	Paragraph symbol
Tab	Right arrow
Indent	Asterisk
Center	Two-headed arrow
Flush right	(No symbol)
Soft hyphen	Grayed hyphen
Advance	Bold two-headed arrow
Center page	Page graphic symbol

Tip
Choose **V**iew, **S**how or press Ctrl+Shift+F3 to toggle the display of these formatting characters.

These symbols are displayed in both Draft and Page views.

Using Justification

► See "Customizing the Display," p. 317

Justification aligns text on the left margin, right margin, both margins, or centered between the margins. These effects are shown in figure 4.16.

Full justification adjusts the word and letter spacing to format text flush with the left and right margins. This gives text a formal look. To apply full justification, choose Fo**r**mat, **J**ustification, **F**ull; or press Ctrl+J.

Left justification, the default in WordPerfect, is also called *flush left* or *ragged right.* Left justification aligns text with the left margin and leaves the right margin uneven. Left justification, used in most of this book, is considered to be slightly easier to read but less formal than full justification. To apply left justification, choose Fo**r**mat, **J**ustification, **L**eft; or press Ctrl+L.

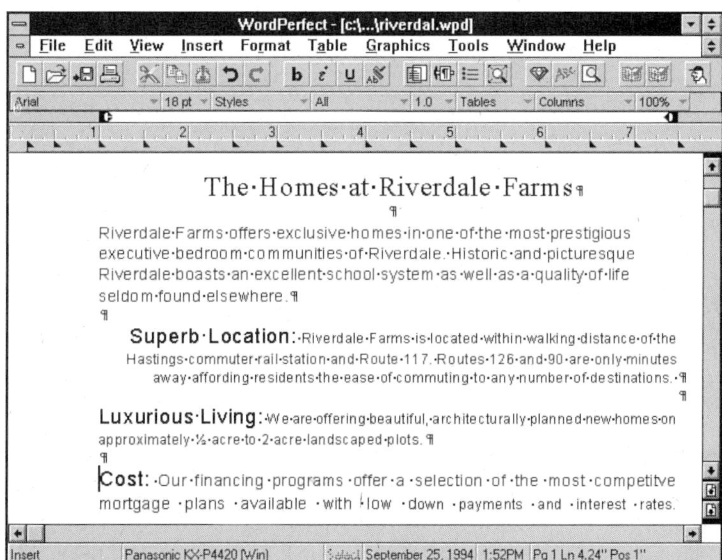

Fig. 4.16
Justification affects text alignment until you turn it off or insert a new justification code. When you press Enter and type a new line, WordPerfect applies the same justification that was in effect on the preceding line.

Right justification, sometimes called *ragged left* or *flush right,* aligns text on the right margin. Right justification is harder to read than left or full justification, and should be used sparingly. It is sometimes used in letterheads. To apply right justification, choose Fo**r**mat, **J**ustification, **R**ight; or press Ctrl+R.

Center justification centers each line between the left and right margins. To apply center justification, choose Fo**r**mat, **J**ustification, C**e**nter; or press Ctrl+E.

Justify all. When you choose full justification, WordPerfect does not justify lines at the ends of paragraphs that do not extend to the right margin. *Justify*

all forces WordPerfect to justify these lines. If a line contains just a few words, WordPerfect justifies the text by increasing the space between words and letters. Some graphic designers use this effect to create a special effect; for example, a company's name may be force-justified between the margins at the top of a letterhead. To apply forced justification, choose Fo**r**mat, **J**ustify, **A**ll. There is no quick keystroke for this code.

Tip
When using justified or flush-left text, be sure to hyphenate the text to improve the word and letter spacing.

When you apply justification with text selected, WordPerfect justifies the block of text and retains the previous text alignment for text following the selected block.

You can also use the Power Bar to apply justification to lines of text in your document. To do so, click the Justification button in the Power Bar (refer to fig. 4.1), and select the justification setting from the resulting list.

Using Hyphenation

► See "Considering Types of Styles," p. 358

► See "Designing Successful Publications," p. 774

The Hyphenation feature splits words that extend beyond the right margin instead of moving them to the next line. Hyphenation can improve the appearance of documents by preventing large spaces at the ends of lines in left-justified text, or between words and letters in full-justified text. WordPerfect can automate hyphenation for you, or you can insert hyphens manually. You can also override WordPerfect's placement of automatic hyphens.

Splitting Words with Hyphens

You can split words with four different kinds of hyphens, each of which serves a different purpose:

- *Hard hyphen.* This inserts a visible hyphen in a word: for example, "hard-won victories." WordPerfect hyphenates the word if the part after the hyphen extends beyond the hyphenation zone. (The hyphenation zone is explained later in this chapter, in the section "Setting the Hyphenation Zone.") You insert a hard hyphen by pressing the hyphen key on the top row of the keyboard or the minus key on the numeric keypad. The hidden code is `[-Hyphen]`.

- *Soft hyphen.* This inserts an invisible hyphen that becomes visible if the word is split at the end of a line. Inserting a soft hyphen lets you tell WordPerfect where to hyphenate words that may not be included in its hyphenation dictionary. You insert a soft hyphen by pressing Ctrl+Shift+hyphen, or by choosing it from the Other Codes dialog box. (Choose Fo**r**mat, **L**ine, **O**ther Codes.) The hidden code is `[- Soft Hyphen]`.

- *Hyphenation soft return.* This splits a word without a hyphen if a split is required at the end of a line. You insert a hyphenation soft return from the Other Codes dialog box. (Choose Fo**r**mat, **L**ine, **O**ther Codes.) The hidden code is [HyphSRt].

- *Deletable soft return.* This splits a word that won't fit between the left and right margins—for example, in a very narrow column. The hidden code is [DSRt].

Preventing Hyphenation

You may want to prevent WordPerfect from splitting certain words, such as company or product names (DuPont, WordPerfect) or long, hyphenated proper names (Santos-Dumas). WordPerfect has three codes that prevent words from splitting at the end of a line:

- *Cancel hyphenation of word.* This tells WordPerfect to move the entire word to the next line. You insert this code at the beginning of a word, from the Other Codes dialog box. The hidden code is [Cancel Hyph].

- *Hyphen character.* This is a short dash that is ignored during hyphenation—for example, in negative numbers and in subtraction problems. To insert a hyphen character, press the minus key on the numeric keypad, or press Ctrl+hyphen (on the top row of the keyboard). Pressing the hyphen character on the top row of the keyboard inserts a [- Hyphen] code, which is *not* ignored during hyphenation. You can also insert a hyphen character from the Other Codes dialog box. The hidden code is a hyphen (-).

- *Hard space.* This prints as a space but keeps two words together. You enter a hard space from the Other Codes dialog box. The hidden code is [HSpace].

Using Automatic Hyphenation

WordPerfect's default mode is Hyphenation Off; words are wrapped to the next line rather than hyphenated. Of course, you can hyphenate words manually, as described earlier under "Splitting Words with Hyphens."

To turn on hyphenation in a document, follow these steps:

1. Choose Fo**r**mat, **L**ine, Hyph**e**nation. The Line Hyphenation dialog box appears (see fig. 4.17).

2. Choose Hyphenation **O**n; then choose OK.

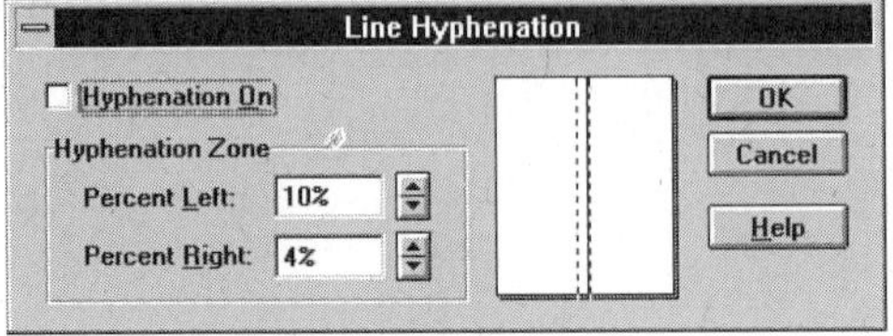

Fig. 4.17
Setting a wide hyphenation zone results in more informal, ragged-looking text.

WordPerfect places the `[Hyph: On]` code at the insertion point, where it affects all text that follows it.

Tip
Left-justified lines look best with the hyphenation zone set to the default 10% Percent **L**eft and 4% Percent **R**ight hyphenation zone settings or larger values.

To turn on hyphenation for the entire document, go to the top of the document (Ctrl+Home, Ctrl+Home) and follow the preceding steps. You can also turn on hyphenation in a Document Initial Style. To learn how to use a Document Initial Style, see Chapter 5, "Formatting Pages and Documents," and Chapter 10, "Using Styles."

When you turn hyphenation on for one document, WordPerfect automatically turns hyphenation on for subsequent documents until you turn it off again.

Setting the Hyphenation Zone

The Hyphenation Zone determines whether WordPerfect wraps a word to the next line or hyphenates it. By adjusting the hyphenation zone, you can affect whether justified or nonjustified text looks "loose" or "tight."

The hyphenation zone is composed of two areas, on either side of the right margin. Each hyphenation zone is set to a percentage of the distance between the left and right margins. You set the hyphenation zone in the Line Hyphenation dialog box (refer to fig. 4.17).

In order for WordPerfect to hyphenate a word, the word must span the entire hyphenation zone, crossing the left and right boundaries. The larger the hyphenation zone, the fewer words WordPerfect hyphenates; the smaller the hyphenation zone, the more words WordPerfect hyphenates.

To set the hyphenation zone, choose Fo**r**mat, **L**ine, Hyph**e**nation, set values for Percent **L**eft and Percent **R**ight, and choose OK.

Choosing a Hyphenation Point

When WordPerfect hyphenates a word, it consults a dictionary file, WP{WP}US.LEX, which contains hyphenation instructions for approximately 115,000 words. If the word is in the dictionary, WordPerfect inserts a soft hyphen at the break point nearest the right margin, and splits the word at that point.

If WordPerfect doesn't find the word in its dictionary, it displays the Position Hyphen dialog box and asks you to indicate where you want to put the hyphen.

The word is displayed with a hyphen initially positioned at the right margin. Use the mouse or arrow keys to place the hyphen where you want to divide the word. You can position the word break only within the hyphenation zone. After selecting a break point, you can split the word in the following ways:

- To split the word with a hyphen, choose **I**nsert Hyphen. WordPerfect inserts a soft hyphen at the break point and splits the word with a visible hyphen.

- To split the word or phrase without a hyphen, choose Hyph**e**nation SRt. WordPerfect inserts a hyphenation soft return code `[Hyph SRt]` at the break point and splits the word without a hyphen.

  If you later edit the text and move a word hyphenated with a soft hyphen or a hyphenation soft return away from the hyphenation zone, WordPerfect rejoins the word automatically.

- To break the word or phrase into two distinct elements separated by an ordinary space, choose I**n**sert Space. No hidden code is inserted. The elements subsequently function as if you had typed them as two distinct words.

  The I**n**sert Space option may be most useful when you insert text that abuts another word, and the combined words push across the hyphenation zone. With hyphenation on, WordPerfect treats the inserted text and adjoining word as a single word requiring hyphenation. You cannot continue until you choose one of the options in the Position Hyphen dialog box. By choosing I**n**sert Space, you put a space between elements that will probably end up separated by a space anyway. If the natural break point isn't visible in the window, choose S**u**spend Hyphenation.

- To keep the word intact, with no break, choose Ignore **W**ord. WordPerfect inserts a `[Cancel Hyph]` code before the word and wraps the word to the next line.

  While scrolling through a document, you may not want to stop to hyphenate words. WordPerfect includes an option to stop hyphenation temporarily.

Removing Hyphenation from a Document

▶ See "Customizing the Writing Tools," p. 349

Hyphenation codes that WordPerfect inserts remain embedded in the hyphenated words even after you turn off hyphenation. If a word containing an embedded hyphenation code spans the hyphenation zone, the code takes effect even if hyphenation is turned off. (The deletable soft return is an exception. WordPerfect removes this code if the conditions that forced its insertion are resolved—for example, if you set wider margins.)

You can remove the hyphenation codes from a document manually or automatically. To remove the codes manually, turn on Reveal Codes and delete them individually. To remove the codes all at once, you can use the **E**dit **F**ind and Replace command to replace the codes with nothing, as in the following steps:

1. Press Ctrl+Home, Ctrl+Home to move to the beginning of the document.
2. Choose **E**dit, **F**ind and Replace; or press F2. The Find and Replace Text dialog box appears.
3. Choose **M**atch, C**o**des. The Codes dialog box appears (see fig. 4.18).
4. Choose -Soft Hyphen, **I**nsert, Close.

   WordPerfect places a `[- Soft Hyphen]` code in the F**i**nd box.
5. Choose Replace **A**ll.

   WordPerfect replaces all soft hyphens with nothing.
6. Choose **C**lose to return to the editing screen.

You can also delete any Hyphenation Soft Return codes. Repeat the preceding steps, but choose Hyph SRt rather than - Soft Hyphen in step 4.

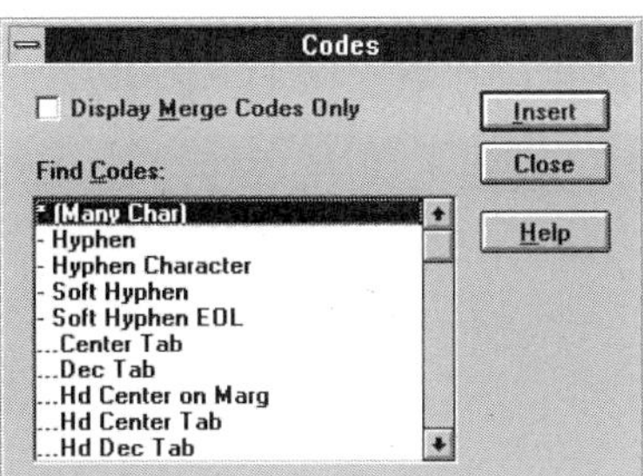

Fig. 4.18
The Find Codes list box in the Codes dialog box contains many useful codes that you can replace.

You can set several defaults that affect the way hyphenation works. These are described in the sections that follow. For specific steps on how to choose these options, see Chapter 9, "Customizing WordPerfect."

Modifying the Hyphenation Decision Resources

If you frequently use words WordPerfect can't hyphenate, or that it hyphenates in a manner you think is wrong, you can add your words and hyphenation point preferences to the hyphenation dictionary that WordPerfect consults, whether you use the External or Internal Hyphenation option.

◀ See "Using Find and Replace," p. 116

If you use external hyphenation, WordPerfect's SPELL.EXE utility provides several ways to add words and their hyphenation points to the dictionaries. To override WordPerfect's hyphenation of a word already in the dictionary, delete the word and reenter it with your preferred hyphenation. For more information, see Chapter 6, "Using Writing Tools."

Tip
To scroll quickly to the desired item in the Codes dialog box, begin typing the item. WordPerfect jumps to the entry. This "speed scroll" feature is built into all WordPerfect's scrollable list boxes.

If you use internal hyphenation, you can use WordPerfect's HYPHEN.EXE utility to create and edit a hyphenation exception dictionary, WP{WP}US.HYD (or another language equivalent). The first time you use the utility, WordPerfect asks if you want to create the file. Choose **Y**es.

WordPerfect creates the file and presents you with HYPHEN.EXE's self-explanatory main menu. The procedures for using HYPHEN.EXE are similar to those detailed in Chapter 6 for using SPELL.EXE on the main dictionary file.

Customizing the Hyphenation Prompt

The hyphenation options available in Environment Preferences establish how much input you can have in hyphenation decisions.

▶ See "Customizing the Writing Tools," p. 349

To set hyphenation prompt options, follow these steps:

1. Choose **E**dit, Pr**e**ferences.

2. Double-click the **E**nvironment icon. The Environment Preferences dialog box appears.

3. Choose Hyphenation **P**rompt and choose an option from the drop-down list.

4. Choose OK, **C**lose to return to the document screen.

The following list describes the Hyphenation Prompt options:

- ***A**lways.* WordPerfect prompts you to decide where to place the hyphen in every word that requires hyphenation.

- ***N**ever.* If the word cannot be found in the dictionary, or the dictionary indicates that no hyphenation for the word exists, or the rule-set doesn't indicate a logical place for hyphenation, the word wraps to the next line.

- ***W**hen Required.* The word is hyphenated according to the dictionary or the internal rule-set. If the word cannot be found or the rule-set cannot effect a decision, WordPerfect prompts you for a hyphenation point. **W**hen Required is the default.

If you choose **N**ever for the Hyphenation **P**rompt option, WordPerfect hyphenates fewer words, resulting in a more ragged right margin with left justification turned on, or more white space with full justification. If you choose **W**hen Required (the default), the internal rule-set asks for hyphenation confirmation more often than the external dictionary would.

From Here...

In this chapter, you explored WordPerfect's broad range of text-formatting capabilities. Refer to the following chapters for additional information:

- Chapter 5, "Formatting Pages and Documents," shows you how to change the appearance of the elements on a page.

- Chapter 7, "Integrating Text and Graphics," introduces you to the art of inserting and managing graphics in a document.

- Chapter 8, "Basic Output: Printing, Faxing, and E-Mail," shows you the ins and outs of printing in WordPerfect.
- Chapter 10, "Using Styles," teaches you how to create and assign styles on a document.
- Chapter 20, "Using Fonts and Special Characters," shows you how to get more specialized text formatting using fonts and characters from WordPerfect's character sets.
- Chapter 23, "Desktop Publishing with WordPerfect," teaches you how to take advantage of the desktop publishing capabilities of WordPerfect to enhance your printed product.

Chapter 5

Formatting Pages and Documents

by Judy Petersen

The variety of formatting features in today's word processing programs makes it possible for the simplest documents to have a professional appearance. The longer the document, the more important are features that enhance readability and organization, such as page numbering, headers, and footers.

A number of WordPerfect features are available to control page layout. Many are features that have previously been available only with more complex and specialized desktop publishing software. You can use these features to encourage readers to delve into a document and to guide readers through the document after catching their interest.

You need to make decisions about the layout of a document at many levels, including the layout of individual lines of text, paragraphs, entire pages, and for the document as a whole. WordPerfect for Windows groups these formatting commands in the Format pull-down menu. This chapter focuses on the features that format pages and documents.

All the features discussed in this chapter place hidden formatting codes in your text. Refer to Chapter 3, "Retrieving and Editing Documents," for more information about hidden codes. These codes provide special information on how to display your text on-screen or how to print the various formatting effects on the page or in your document.

This chapter includes the following topics:

- Centering text on a page and keeping text together
- Designing, creating, and editing headers and footers

- Numbering pages
- Creating, editing, and using paper definitions for documents, labels, and envelopes
- Modifying font, redline, and other initial settings
- Creating a database of document summaries

Note

When formatting a document, consider displaying the Page Toolbar where many of the frequently used page format commands are only a click away. Click on the current Toolbar with the right mouse button to display a menu of available Toolbars or choose the Page Toolbar using the **T**oolbar option in the Pr**e**ferences menu.

Instructions for customizing Toolbars and the Power Bar are in Chapter 13, "Working with Toolbars."

◄ See "Using WordPerfect's Text-Formatting Tools," p. 127

◄ See "Understanding WordPerfect's Hidden Codes," p. 95

► See "Reveal Codes Display," p. 323

Using Delay Codes

Documents longer than one page often require formatting changes after the first page. You may not want headers and footers to begin until after introductory material such as the table of contents and preface. When printing documents on letterhead, you may want to change to second sheets of letterhead after the first page. These and many other format changes can be applied beginning at a specific page in a document by including the codes in a Delay code at the beginning of the document. When you create Delay codes, you specify the number of pages to skip before the format changes take effect. The Delay code appears as `[Delay: #]`.

If you change page formatting when the cursor is on the page where you want the change to begin, WordPerfect inserts the codes in a `[Delay codes: *codes*]` code for you.

The # in the Delay code is the number of pages to skip to locate the associated `[Delay Codes]` code. If a Delay code appears as `[Delay: 16]`, for example, the `[Delay Codes]` that contains your formatting choices appears at the top of the 17th page (page 1 plus skip 16 = 17).

If you decide to add more formatting to a page that already has a Delay code, the additional formatting choices you make are added to the single Delay code.

You can manually insert any open code as a Delay code using the Delay Codes command. Open codes are single codes such as page numbering, font, justification, and margins. You can't include paired codes, such as bold and italics, or text in a Delay code; these codes and any text you attempt to include will be dropped when you close the Define Delay Codes screen.

Note

This chapter provides you with the actual code text that WordPerfect inserts in your document when you choose a format, although an abbreviated version of the code is displayed unless you choose to display codes in detail as described in the reveal codes section in Chapter 9, "Customizing WordPerfect."

To create a Delay code, follow these steps:

1. Choose Fo**r**mat, **P**age. The Page Format dialog box appears.
2. Choose **D**elay Codes; then, in the text box, enter the number of pages to skip.
3. Choose OK to open the Define Delayed Codes editing screen, containing a feature bar (see fig. 5.1).

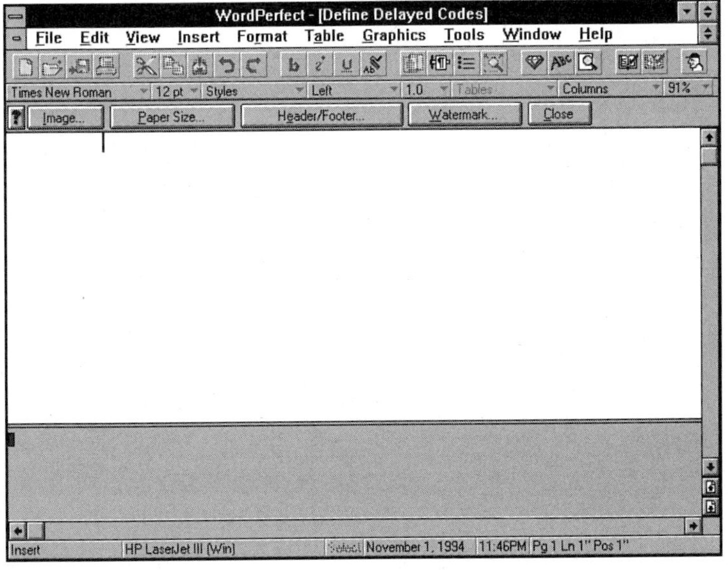

Fig. 5.1
The feature bar on the Define Delayed Codes editing screen includes several command buttons you can use to insert **P**aper Size, H**e**ader/Footer, and other codes when creating Delay codes.

4. Use any regular WordPerfect commands to create the hidden format codes you want applied to the specified page.

5. Use the command buttons on the feature bar to create headers and footers, a watermark or image, or change paper size. Choose the button with a question mark to obtain help or change feature bars.

6. Choose **C**lose to return to your document.

The cursor can be anywhere in the document when you create the Delay code. Take into account the current page when you enter the total number of pages to skip. If, for example, your cursor is on the 10th page when you set up a Delay code, and you request a delay of 15 pages to place codes on page 25, the Delay code placed at the beginning of the document is `[Delay: 24]` (first page plus 24 more). WordPerfect calculates the number of pages to skip based on physical pages rather than page numbers. (Refer to the "Physical and Logical Pages" section later in this chapter for information about physical and logical pages.)

Creating Separate Pages

WordPerfect automatically divides your document into pages based on the formatting choices you have made. These automatic page breaks are called soft page breaks. When you access Reveal Codes, each page of text ends with an `[SPg]` code. If the soft page break falls on the location of a hard return, the hard return code is saved and the new code appears as `[HRt-SPg]`.

A soft page break often occurs at a blank line, such as when a break falls on the hard return between paragraphs. To prevent this blank line from being carried to the top of the next page, but retain it should later editing move the page break location elsewhere, WordPerfect inserts a dormant hard return `[Dorm HRt]` to save the blank line.

Because it is often necessary to cause a page to break at a specific location or prevent page breaks from dividing text that should be kept together, WordPerfect offers ways to control where pages are divided, as described in the following sections and the later section "Keeping Text Together."

Inserting Page Breaks

As you edit a document, adding and deleting text and changing formats, WordPerfect recalculates the soft page break locations. To ensure that a page breaks at a specific location, regardless of format changes, use the Page Break feature. Use a page break to end a specific document section and to ensure that the new section starts on the next page. Page breaks also are appropriate to end a cover page, a preface, a chapter, an appendix, or a table of contents.

To insert a page break, place the cursor at the exact location where you want the page to break. Then choose **I**nsert, **P**age Break; or press Ctrl+Enter. A hard page break code in the Reveal Codes window appears as [HPg]. The only way to override this page break is to delete it.

Forcing New Pages

Beginning chapters or sections on the right side of facing pages gives a professional appearance to complex documents. The simple way to make sure that this occurs is to insert a page break at the beginning of a chapter or section and then force an odd page number. Forcing an odd page number ensures this right-side placement regardless of later text insertions or deletions.

Forcing a new page is another way to cause a page to break at a specific location. You can force a new page as well as force an odd or even page number.

To use the Force Page command, follow these steps.

1. Choose Fo**r**mat, **P**age, **F**orce Page. The Force Page dialog box opens (see fig. 5.2).

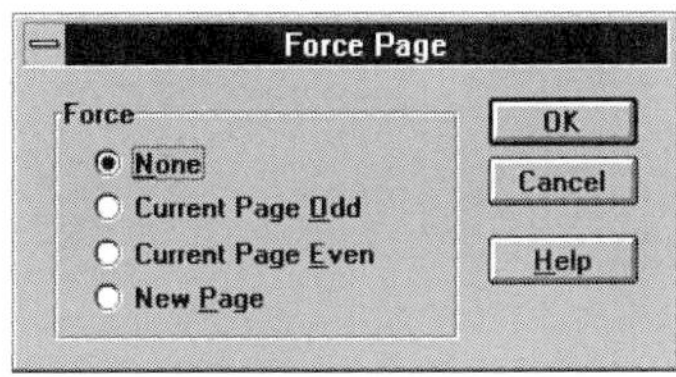

Fig. 5.2
In the Force Page dialog box, you can choose to force a new page or to force an odd or even page number for the current page.

2. From the options in the dialog box, choose New **P**age to start a new page at the beginning of the current paragraph. Alternatively, choose Current Page **O**dd or Current Page **E**ven to force the page number to change accordingly.

3. Choose OK or press Enter to return to your document.

If you chose to force a new page, WordPerfect inserts a [Force: New] code in your document at the beginning of the current paragraph. As with hard page breaks, later editing may move the new page to an unacceptable location. To cancel the code, locate and then delete it in the Reveal Codes window.

When you force an odd or an even page number, WordPerfect places a [Force: Odd] or [Force: Even] code at the top of the current page. If the code changes the current page number, WordPerfect adds a blank page by inserting a [THPg] (Temporary Hard Page Break) code before the Force code.

Page formatting—such as headers, footers, and page numbering—is continued on the blank page.

Tip
To center text properly on a page, the text should not start or end with extra hard returns unless you want to use the resulting blank lines to place the text slightly off-center.

Centering Pages

Centering a page between the top and bottom margins is a quick way to position a small amount of text that stands alone on a page. Centering a page repositions the material in relation to the top and bottom margins only.

You also can quickly center several sequential pages of a document by using the Center command. This feature is helpful, for example, with documents that begin with several individual pages of brief, introductory material.

To center text on the page, follow these steps:

1. Choose Fo**r**mat, **P**age, **C**enter. The Center Page(s) dialog box opens (see fig. 5.3).

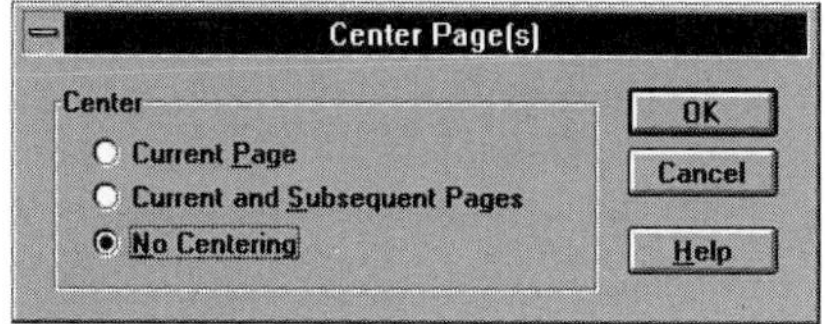

Fig. 5.3
Choose whether to center a single page, center multiple pages, or turn centering off in the Center Page(s) dialog box.

2. In the Center Page(s) dialog box, choose one of the following options:

   - Current **P**age to center only the page where the cursor is located
   - Current and **S**ubsequent Pages to begin centering all pages beginning at the current cursor location
   - **N**o Centering to end centering of Current and Subsequent Pages

3. Choose OK or press Enter to return to your document.

Tip
Use Center Page to quickly place a short note on letterhead stationary, or for title or cover pages, acknowledgments, and prefaces.

The single code `[Cntr Cur Pg: On]` appears in the Reveal Codes window to center the current page. The code for centering the current and subsequent pages is `[Cntr Pgs: On]`. The text displays centered on the page in Page mode, but does not appear centered when you are using Draft mode.

To center a single page of text in a document longer than one page, it is important to indicate the beginning and the end of the text to be centered. Insert a page break at the end of the centered text if it is the first page of your document. Place a page break at the beginning and the end of the text to be centered if the text is in the middle of a document. (Refer to the "Inserting Page Breaks" section earlier in this chapter for instructions on inserting page breaks.)

To cancel centering of a page, delete the code in the Reveal Codes window. To end centering of subsequent pages, place the cursor where you want to end centering and choose **N**o Centering in the Center Page(s) dialog box.

◀ See "Using Justification," p. 151

Keeping Text Together

The capability of word processing software to automate the layout of typed text may well be the most common impetus for purchasing a personal computer. To enhance the capabilities of automated layout, WordPerfect uses standard formatting rules for document layout, controlling the way that automated layout divides pages. You can use the Block Protect, Conditional End of Page, and Widow/Orphan protection commands to prevent problems such as section names that dangle at the bottom of a page and page breaks that occur in the middle of a list or table. The following sections cover these commands.

Block Protect

The Block Protect feature places codes at the beginning and end of a section of text that you want to keep together on the same page. As you edit the protected text, the block expands or shrinks to accommodate your changes.

When WordPerfect encounters a Block Protect code, the program determines whether the entire block of text fits in the space remaining on the present page. If the block doesn't fit, the program inserts a soft page break above the block, which then begins the next page. Block Protect is particularly useful for keeping a list, a table, a figure and the text that describes it, or a series of numbered paragraphs on the same page.

To protect a block of text, follow these steps:

1. Highlight the block of text you want to protect.
2. Choose Fo**r**mat, **P**age, **K**eep Text Together. The Keep Text Together dialog box opens (see fig. 5.4).

3. Choose **K**eep selected text together on the same page so an X appears in the check box.
4. Choose OK or press Enter to return to your document.

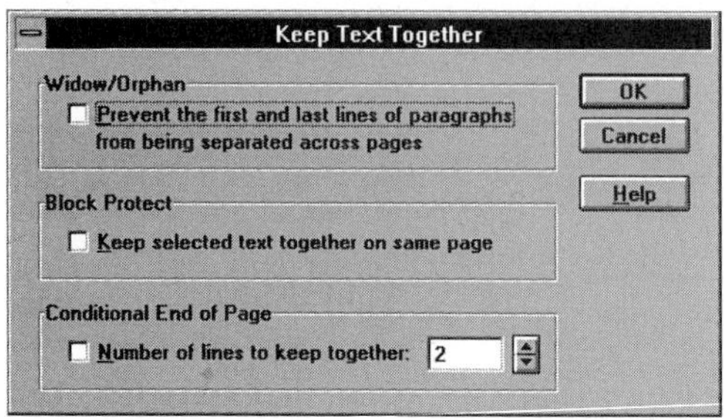

Fig. 5.4
In the Keep Text Together dialog box, you can choose to protect a block of text, turn on Widow/Orphan protection, or specify a number of lines to keep together following titles or headings.

The paired code that appears in the Reveal Codes window at the beginning and end of the selected text is `[Block Pro]`. You can remove the protection by deleting either code.

Note

Block Protect is designed to protect a page or less of text. If you add text to a protected block so that the amount of protected text exceeds one page, WordPerfect ignores the Block Protect codes and inserts a soft page break where needed. However, the codes remain around the text. Removing enough text restores the protection. If the text you want to protect contains more than a page of text, try using a smaller font or changing the line spacing to slightly less than 1.

Conditional End of Page

The Conditional End of Page feature acts to protect a specific number of lines rather than specific text. Use Conditional End of Page to ensure that titles, headings, and subheadings are not left dangling alone at the bottom of a page.

To insert a Conditional End of Page, move the cursor to the beginning of the text you want to protect and follow these steps:

1. Choose Fo**r**mat, **P**age, **K**eep Text Together. The Keep Text Together dialog box opens.

2. Choose **N**umber of Lines to Keep Together so an X appears in the check box.

3. In the adjacent text box, enter the number of lines to keep together.

4. Choose OK or press Enter to return to your document.

Note

When using Conditional End of Page to keep headings together with some of the text that follows, be sure to count the lines between the heading and text and any intervening subheading, as well as enough lines of text. If you triple-space after headings and double-space after subheadings, specify six to eight lines to protect a heading and text, and eight to ten lines for a heading, subheading, and the text that follows.

The single code `[Condl EOP: #]` appears at the beginning of the protected text in the Reveal Codes window, where # is the number of lines you have chosen to include. You can override a Conditional End of Page by inserting a page break within the lines the command protects.

Prevent Widows and Orphans

A heading or subheading dangling at the bottom of a page is not the only time lines appear to be stranded. A single line of a paragraph appearing by itself on the bottom of a page is called an *orphan*. A *widow* is a line from the end of a paragraph that is pushed to the top of the next page.

To place Widow/Orphan protection in a document, follow these steps:

1. Place the cursor where you want protection to begin, or use Ctrl+Home to move to the beginning of the document.

2. Choose Fo**r**mat, **P**age, **K**eep Text Together. The Keep Text Together dialog box opens.

3. Choose **P**revent The First And Last Lines Of Paragraphs From Being Separated Across Pages so that an X appears in its check box.

4. Choose OK or press Enter to return to your document.

Tip

Widow/Orphan protection is used most often to protect an entire document. If you use it regularly, consider including it in a template you create for your preferred document format.

The code that appears in the Reveal Codes window is `[Wid/Orph: On]`.

When Widow and Orphan protection is on, a soft page break cannot be inserted between the first two or last two lines of a paragraph. The two protected lines remain at the bottom of the page or, if located at the end of the paragraph, move to the top of the next page, leaving blank lines at the bottom of the preceding page. Two- and three-line paragraphs move in their entirety.

Working with Facing Pages

WordPerfect provides several commands designed for setting up documents with facing pages. You can place headers and footers on even or odd pages only, offset the printed pages to allow for binding, alternate page-numbering schemes, and force odd or even page numbers.

As you work with commands that place features on odd or even pages, it is easy to confuse odd and even, left and right pages so that you end up superimposing text you mean to place on alternating pages. When choosing an odd or even placement option, try visualizing a printed document bound on the left edge (like this book). When the document is placed on your desk, the top page of the closed document is the first page. When you turn the first page, facing pages are displayed. The second, or even, numbered page is on the left and the third, or odd, numbered page is on the right.

Physical and Logical Pages

Physical pages are the sides of the actual sheets of paper. *Logical* pages refer to the sides relative to the numbering system used in the document. For example, imagine a book in which the first 10 pages of introductory materials have Roman numerals. Those 10 physical pages are logical pages i-x, and the next physical page (11) is logical page 1.

When you work with labels, on the other hand, you may have an 8 1/2-by-11-inch sheet covered with 12 labels, for example. The sheet is one physical page, but WordPerfect treats the labels as 12 different logical pages.

When creating Delay codes, for example, the number of pages you specify when setting up a code are the physical pages to skip. The placement of features that you set up to appear on odd or even pages, such as forcing pages or headers and footers, is based on the logical page number. Refer to the earlier section "Using Delay Codes" and the later section "Using Headers and Footers" for more information.

Tip
Use a larger left margin to create a binding offset for documents that you print on only one side of the page.

Binding Offset

Binding offset refers to a space allowance on the edge of the pages for bound documents so they still have well-proportioned margins. When you set a binding offset, pages print so that the text on even pages moves the specified amount to the left and the text on odd pages text moves the same amount to the right.

To create a binding offset, follow these steps:

1. Move the cursor to where you want a binding offset to begin.
2. Choose Fo**r**mat, **P**age, B**i**nding/Duplex. The Binding/Duplexing Options dialog box appears (see fig. 5.5).

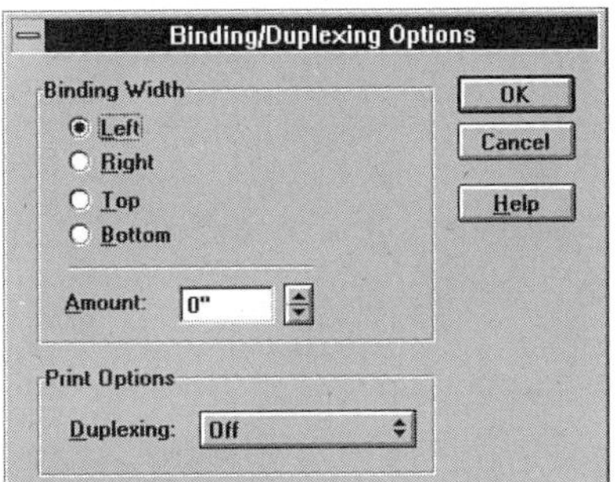

Fig. 5.5
In the Binding/Duplexing Options dialog box, you choose which edge of the document will be bound, the offset amount, and whether to use duplex printing.

3. Choose whether to apply the binding offset to the **L**eft, **R**ight, **T**op, or **B**ottom edge of the document.
4. In the **A**mount text box, enter the text offset amount you want.
5. Choose OK or press Enter to return to the document.

The code `[Binding Width: Left; 0.250"]` is inserted in the document if you plan to bind the document on the left edge and want the text offset 0.25 inches.

Double-Sided Printing

If your printer is capable of printing on both sides of the page, you can set up WordPerfect to automate double-sided, or duplex, printing. The duplex printing command is available in the Binding Options dialog box.

To set up duplex printing, follow these steps:

▶ See "Printing Specific Document Pages," p. 295

▶ See "Printing Odd or Even Numbered Pages," p. 297

1. In the Binding/Duplexing Options dialog box, choose **D**uplexing to open the adjacent pop-up menu.
2. Choose From **L**ong Edge or From **S**hort Edge. Documents are bound on the long edge for *portrait* or upright orientation. Short edge is used with *landscape* or sideways orientation.
3. Choose OK or press Enter to return to your document.

Your printer does not need to be able to duplex print to have a document printed on both sides of the paper. Instead, create a binding offset, headers, footers, and page number placement consistent with a facing pages layout. Print the document on one side of the page and then use a copy machine to make double-sided copies.

Alternatively, the Print feature enables you to print only even or only odd pages and reverse order printing so that you can print on the front and back of the page. Refer to Chapter 8, "Basic Output: Printing, Faxing, and E-mail," for instructions.

Using Headers and Footers

Headers and footers are blocks of text that appear at the top or bottom of a page. They can include graphics, page numbers, the section title, or any other information about the document. Headers and footers improve the appearance of your work and can provide organization information at the same time.

WordPerfect enables you to use two headers and two footers on each page, and they can be different on every page. They can appear on only even or odd pages, and you can suppress them where they would conflict with letterhead or figure placement.

Headers and footers start at the edge of the margin and print into the main text area with a blank line added to separate them from the main text. They can be as long as one page, although that size is not often useful. The headers and footers appear on the WordPerfect screen when you are using Page mode.

Creating a Header or Footer

You can create different headers and footers on any page in your document, although they are typically created at the beginning of the document. You may want to create new headers and footers at the beginning of each new chapter.

If you create a header or footer A or B, and one with the same letter is already in effect, the former header or footer is replaced beginning at that page where the next header or footer A or B is created. Headers and footers appear on the page the way they are designed. Designating one as A or B does not determine the order in which each appears on the printed page.

When you create a header or footer, WordPerfect displays a document editing screen with a features bar with command buttons you use to insert page numbers or graphics lines, and to choose the pages where you want the header or footer to appear. All default settings are applied to a new header or footer, including the default margins, font typeface, and size and tabs. To help you apply formatting appropriate for the current document, the WordPerfect formatting commands and menus are available.

All the instructions that follow refer to Header A, but are the same as the steps for Header B, or Footer A or B. To create a new header, follow these steps:

1. Choose Fo**r**mat, **H**eader/Footer to open the Headers/Footers dialog box.

2. Choose whether to create Header **A**, Header **B**, **F**ooter A, or F**o**oter B, and then choose **C**reate to open the appropriate editing screen. The Feature Bar from the header and footer editing screen is shown in figure 5.6.

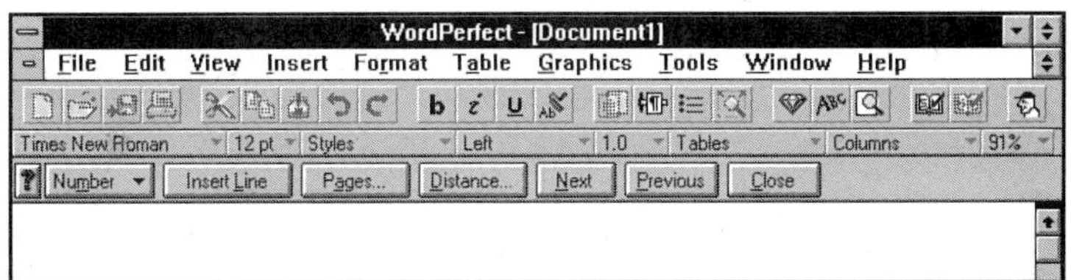

Fig. 5.6
The Header Editor includes a Feature Bar of commands to insert page numbers, add graphics lines, move to the next or preceding header, and close the Editor.

3. In the Header editing screen, insert any formatting codes you want. Features that are not available for use in a header or footer are grayed on the menus. Make sure you change the default document settings in the header where appropriate. Do not end a header with a hard return unless you want an extra blank line between the header and the body of the document.

4. By default, the header appears on every page. To change this placement, choose P**a**ges from the feature bar to open the Pages dialog box. Then choose **O**dd Pages if the header is to appear only on odd pages, and **E**ven Pages if you want it only on even pages.

   To include page numbering in the header, refer to the "Using Page Numbers in Headers and Footers" section that follows.

5. Choose **C**lose or click on the document portion of the screen to return to your document.

Tip
Use **I**nsert, F**i**le to retrieve boilerplate text saved as a file into a header or footer.

The following code, for example, appears in the Reveal Codes window:

```
[Header A:  Every page, [code]text[code]text..]
```

Up to three lines of text, including all codes, displays.

Tip
While in the header or footer editing screen, right-click the background to display a QuickMenu with several commands, including **P**aste, Spe**l**l Check, **F**ont, **C**enter, Flush **R**ight, and **I**ndent.

If you place two headers on the same page, the headers print in the same location at the top of the page. The same is true for two footers printing at the bottom of the page. Use formatting commands to design headers and footers so the text they contain does not overlap a second header or footer. Try aligning text in one header on the left margin and use flush right to align text on the left margin in the second header. You can also center some of the text, or place text on alternating lines.

Editing Headers and Footers

You can edit headers and footers as easily as the main body of a document. You can begin the editing process at any point in the document where the header or footer you want to edit is in effect.

To quickly edit a header or footer using the mouse in Page view, click on the header or footer text and make the desired changes. WordPerfect activates Editing mode, but the editing window does not display. Use the commands available on the menu bar, shortcut keystrokes, or the Button and Power Bars.

You cannot perform some tasks, such as adding a page number, by editing the header or footer on the page. As when creating a header or footer, certain menu commands and button faces are grayed while you are in Editing mode. In particular, some of the commands available on the header or footer Feature Bar are not available.

To edit a header or footer using the editing screen, follow these steps:

1. Choose Fo**r**mat, **H**eader/Footer.
2. Choose the header or footer you want to edit, and then choose **E**dit to display the Header editing window with the text you entered.
3. Enter any changes, making selections from the feature bar as needed.
4. Choose **C**lose from the Feature Bar to return to your document, or click on any part of the document portion of the screen.

Tip
You can display the Reveal Codes window while in the header/footer window. Use it to locate, insert, and delete codes.

Using Page Numbers in Headers and Footers

When you are working in a header or footer editing window, you can include a page number code by placing the cursor where you want the page number to appear and choosing the Number button from the feature bar.

Page numbers are often enhanced with text so they read "Page 24" or "- 24 -," for example. To include text with the page number, type the text you want before the page number, insert the page number, and then type any text you want to follow the page number.

When creating a header or footer, all commands on the Format Page menu, including Numbering, are grayed, limiting you to using only the Arabic page-numbering style. You can, however, use four types (normal, secondary, chapter, and volume) of numbering. (Refer to the section "Choosing a Numbering Style" later in this chapter.)

There are four ways to remove or override a header or footer. You can delete it in the Reveal Codes window or replace it by creating another header or footer with the same letter later in the document. You can suppress a header or footer on any one page by using the procedure in the next section. Or if the header or footer is not to appear again, you can discontinue it as explained in the later section "Discontinuing Headers and Footers."

Suppressing Headers and Footers

You usually create headers and footers on the first page of a document. However, because headers are often inappropriate when printed on the first page, especially if you use letterhead or chapter headings, and page number footers often start on the second page, you can suppress the printing of headers and footers on a page. You can also suppress headers and footers at the beginnings of chapters or elsewhere in a document where you don't want them to appear.

To suppress the header you created in the first section, place the cursor on the page where you want to suppress the header and follow these steps:

1. Choose Fo**r**mat, **P**age, **Su**ppress. The Suppress dialog box appears.

2. Choose H**e**ader A.
3. Choose OK or press Enter to return to the document.

The suppress code appears as `[Suppress: Header A]` in the Reveal Codes window. When you suppress the printing of a header or footer on one page, it continues to be printed on the following pages. If the header or footer contains a page number, the correct page numbering sequence is maintained.

Discontinuing Headers and Footers

To replace a header or footer, you simply create a new one and assign it the same letter as the existing one. You can use this method, for example, to have a different header in each chapter.

Discontinuing a header/footer is necessary when you do not want it to print again and another one does not replace it. To discontinue a header in the index of a report, for example, follow these steps:

1. Choose Fo**r**mat, **H**eader/Footer.

2. Choose Header **A** and then choose **D**iscontinue.

3. Choose OK or press Enter to return to the document.

Using Other Features with Headers and Footers

Headers and footers have an interesting hybrid status in a document. Some WordPerfect features can be used to good advantage in headers and footers; others require an extra step. The following sections describe a few features you may find useful.

Graphics

► See "Using Graphics Lines," p. 264

► See "Using Graphics Boxes," p. 275

The full range of graphics commands are available from the header or footer window. Choose all or any one or more of the following to enhance your header/footer.

- *Graphics lines.* You can use the Insert **L**ine button on the feature bar to place horizontal or vertical lines of any length, thickness, and shading into your header or footer. Center a short horizontal line above a page number in a footer or a full-width line to set a header off from the main text. Refer to the instructions in Chapter 7, "Integrating Text and Graphics."

- *Graphics boxes.* You can use any of the box styles available in the Graphics menu in a header or footer. You can import and link part of a spreadsheet, use any of the WPG figures that come with WordPerfect, or import other graphics. Many of the WPG figures can be used effectively in a two-line footer if you size the figure carefully. Specific instructions for using graphics are given in Chapter 7, "Integrating Text and Graphics."

- *Original drawings and charts.* Use the Draw and Chart utilities available in the Graphics menu to create a drawing or chart to include in a header or footer.

Spell Check

The Spell Check feature checks headers and footers if you choose to check the entire document, or if you check a page and a header or footer code is on that page. Refer to Chapter 6, "Using Writing Tools," for instructions on how to use Spell Check.

Search and Replace

Both the Search and the Replace features automatically search and replace in headers and footers. To include headers and footers created at the beginning of the document, press Ctrl+Home twice to place the cursor before any codes at the top of the document.

If you don't return to the beginning of your document before searching, you can search or replace backwards to find any headers and footers you may have missed. Refer to Chapter 3, "Retrieving and Editing Documents," for instructions on using Search and Replace.

Cut, Copy, and Paste

You can cut or copy text or a graphic from a document window or from another header or footer, and then paste the text or graphic into the current header/footer editing window. The reverse is as simple. You can cut or copy the contents of a header or footer in one document and paste the contents into the header/footer window in another document. Click with the right mouse button on the background to display the QuickMenu containing the Paste command. Instructions for selecting text and using Cut, Copy, and Paste are in Chapter 3, "Retrieving and Editing Documents."

Numbering Pages

WordPerfect has the capability of numbering pages automatically, even for complex documents where multiple chapters, introductions, and appendixes use different numbering schemes. You can number chapters individually, and opening and closing sections can have different numbering styles, for example.

The page number prints in the top or bottom line of the text area. WordPerfect inserts a blank line to separate the number from the rest of the text. If you use the default 1-inch top and bottom margins for 8 1/2-by-11-inch paper and a Courier 10-cpi (characters per inch) font, the text area contains 54 lines. Adding page numbers decreases the number of lines to 52.

In Page mode, page numbers appear where you place them on the page. This makes it easy to immediately preview the page number layout, font, and accompanying text.

Choosing a position for page numbers is all that is necessary to turn on page numbering.

Choosing a Page Number Position

There are eight preset page number positions, including two that place numbers at alternating positions on facing pages. You select the position you want from the **P**osition pop-up menu in the Page Numbering dialog box.

You can place numbers at the left, center, or right of the top or bottom of the page, and you can alternate page numbers on the outside top or bottom of facing pages, as in a book. The code inserted at the beginning of the page is `[Pg Num Pos: location]`, which you can see in the Reveal Codes window. Selecting a page number position also turns on page numbering.

To select a position for page numbers, follow these steps:

1. Choose Fo**r**mat, **P**age, **N**umbering. The Page Numbering dialog box shown in figure 5.7 opens.

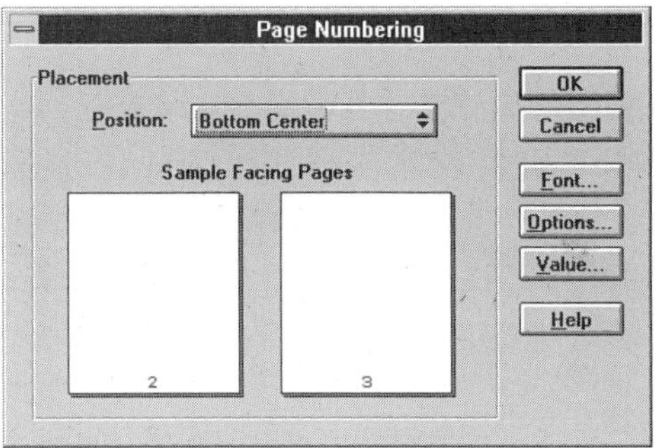

Fig. 5.7
After you choose the page number position in the Page Numbering dialog box, the selection is previewed in the Sample Facing Pages.

2. Choose **P**ositions, and then choose one of the following positions from the Positions pop-up list:

Top **L**eft	**B**ottom Left
Top **C**enter	B**o**ttom Center
Top **R**ight	Bo**t**tom Right
Alternating Top	Alt**e**rnating Bottom

3. Choose OK or press Enter to save the changes and return to your document.

You access all page-numbering options through the Page Numbering dialog box. Although the options are discussed here in separate sections, you can choose all the options you want before finally closing the Page Numbering dialog box.

Using Text with Page Numbers

You do not have to use a header or footer in order to place text with a page number. You can number appendixes—for example, A-1, A-2, B-1, B-2, B-3, and so on. Reference manuals often give the section name before the page number. Page numbers are more obvious when placed with text such as - Page ## -.

Tip
Use alternating numbering when you print text and staple the document in the upper corner. If the page is numbered in the upper-right corner, the number on the back of the page is under the staple.

You can place up to 42 characters around a page number, including ASCII or WordPerfect characters. These special characters may require more space than standard characters.

To include text with a page number, follow these steps:

1. In the Page Numbering dialog box, choose **O**ptions to open the Page Numbering Options dialog box (see fig. 5.8).

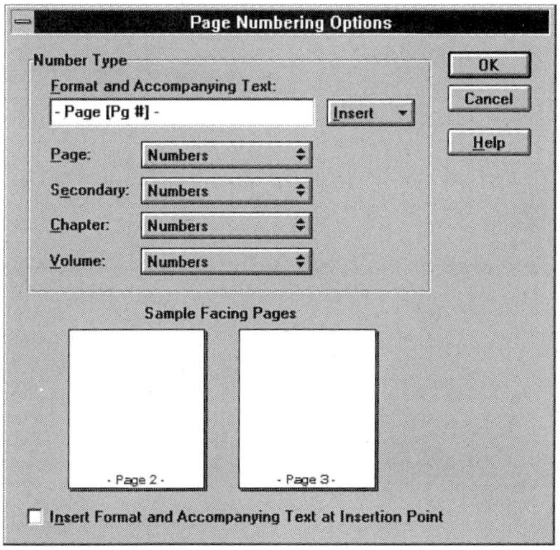

Fig. 5.8
Choose a page number type and whether to use numbers, letters, or Roman numerals, and create accompanying text in the Page Numbering Options dialog box. This figure illustrates the accompanying text in the Sample Facing Pages diagram.

2. Choose **F**ormat and Accompanying Text, or move the mouse pointer over the adjacent text box so it changes to an I-beam, and then click the I-beam into place. Type the text to appear on either or both sides of the page number code.

Text can precede and follow the page number code, as shown in figure 5.8. Do not delete the number code if you want text before and after the number. If you delete it, place the cursor where you want the code, choose **I**nsert, and choose the type of numbering code. WordPerfect inserts the code at the cursor location. Click with the right mouse button on the text box to display a QuickMenu that includes the Speller command.

3. Choose OK or press Enter to return to the Page Numbering dialog box.

The code appears as `[Pg Num Fmt: format]` in the Reveal Codes window. To change the text in another section of your document, repeat the steps listed in this section.

Caution

As you change Accompanying Text or Numbering Type at several points in your document, proofread the rest of the settings in the dialog box carefully. Your previous settings display when you reopen the Page Numbering box. As you move from numbering chapters to numbering appendixes, you may need to change more than one option.

Choosing a Numbering Type

Four page-numbering schemes are available with WordPerfect for Windows. In addition to standard page numbering, you can have another set of page numbers called *secondary numbers*. Journals and newsletters sometimes use two sets of numbers—one that numbers every page consecutively throughout the year, another that numbers the pages in individual issues. You can set up both regular and secondary page numbers in a document and start each with a different number. Either type of page numbers is increased, or incremented, automatically from page to page.

Chapter and volume numbering are also available. These numbering schemes differ from regular and secondary numbering in that you must instruct WordPerfect when chapter and volume number should change, or increment. You can use chapter and volume numbers to number multiple documents and the sections in each document. Use these with journals and newsletters to number the volume and issue.

To use standard page numbering, it is only necessary to choose a position for the numbering. To use secondary, chapter, or volume numbering or to use more than one numbering type, place the cursor on the page where you want the numbering to begin and follow these steps:

1. From the Page Numbering dialog box, choose **O**ptions to open the Page Numbering Options dialog box.

2. Choose **F**ormat and Accompanying Text or move the mouse pointer over the adjacent text box and click the I-beam into place. The text box initially contains the code `[Pg #]` for the current page number. Delete the code if you do not want regular page numbering.

3. To use or add another numbering type, move the cursor in the text box to where you want the additional number type to display in relation to the regular page number.

4. Choose **I**nsert to open a pop-up list of page-numbering types. Choose the type you want included in the page number format to insert the appropriate code in the text box:

Page Number	`[Pg #]`
Secondary Number	`[SPg #]`
Chapter Number	`[Chp #]`
Volume Number	`[Vol #]`

5. Repeat steps 3 and 4 to add additional page-numbering types.

6. Type any text before, after, and between codes that you want to include with the page numbering.

7. Choose OK or press Enter to return to the Page Numbering dialog box.

In the document, WordPerfect replaces the code with the text and the type(s) of numbering you have chosen. Using more than one numbering type with accompanying text, you can number pages to read Chapter 1, Page 1, or Appendix C, Page II, for example. The style used for the page numbers is also set up in the Page Numbering Options dialog box.

Using Page X of Y

A button is available in WordPerfect 6.1 that enables you to set up page numbering that reads `Page X of Y`. The numbering can be placed in any of the standard page numbering positions.

To use this feature, you must first add the Page X of Y button to the Toolbar. It is included in the list of features on the Format menu in the Toolbar Editor. After it is added, follow these steps:

1. Click the Page X of Y button on the Toolbar.
2. In the Page X of Y Macro dialog box, choose **P**osition and select one of the positions in the pop-up list.
3. Choose **F**ormat and select the one of the following appearance options for the numbering from the pop-up list:

   Page X of Y

   Page X of Y Pages

   Page X/Y

   X of Y

4. If you are ready to print the document, select Print **D**ocument so an X appears in the check box.
5. Choose OK.
6. A box opens, reminding you to replay the macro if you edit the document. Choose Close.

Tip
To remind yourself to update numbering before printing, insert a comment using **I**nsert, Co**m**ment at the beginning of your document where it's visible every time you retrieve the document.

Because the total number of pages is not known until you finish the document, add this numbering format when you are ready to print. If the document is a draft and subject to more editing, be sure to set up Page X of Y numbering again just before you print.

Choosing a Numbering Style

▶ See "Customizing a Toolbar," p. 455

You can number introductory pages, the body, and closing sections of a document differently with the five page-numbering styles available in WordPerfect for Windows. In addition to Arabic numerals (1, 2, 3), you can use upper- and lowercase Roman numerals (I, II, III and i, ii, iii), or upper- and lowercase letters (A, B, C or a, b, c).

To set or change the page-numbering style, move to the page where the style should begin and follow these steps:

1. From the Page Numbering dialog box, choose **O**ptions to display the Page Numbering Options dialog box.

2. Choose **P**age, **Se**condary, **C**hapter, or **V**olume to open pop-up lists of available numbering styles.

3. Choose one of the following numbering styles:

   Numbers

   Lowercase Letter

   Uppercase Letter

   L**o**wercase Roman

   U**p**percase Roman

4. Choose OK or press Enter to return to the Page Numbering dialog box.

Changing the Current Page Number

Occasionally you need to begin page numbering other than at page 1, or begin numbering again at 1 later in your document. When introductory, main body, and closing sections use different numbering styles, each section usually starts with page 1.

To change the number on the current page, follow these steps:

1. In the Page Numbering dialog box, choose **V**alue to open the Numbering Value dialog box (see fig. 5.9).

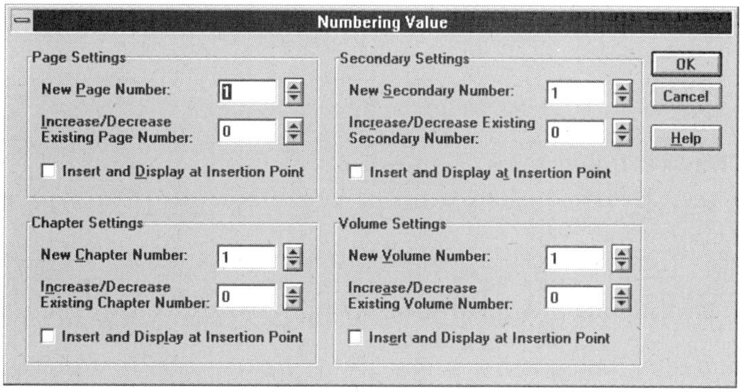

Fig. 5.9
In the Numbering Value dialog box, set new page numbers, increment chapter and volume numbers, or insert a number at the cursor location.

2. Choose New **P**age Number (or New **S**econdary, **C**hapter, or **V**olume Number). Enter in the adjacent text box the new number to appear on the current page.

Tip
Use New **P**age Number to return to number 1 at the beginning of a preface, an appendix, or an index.

3. Choose OK or press Enter to save your changes and return to the Page Numbering dialog box.

When you specify a new number in your document, WordPerfect does not adjust the number you provide if you later edit the document to add or remove text.

Incrementing Page Numbers

Although WordPerfect increments page and secondary numbers automatically, you can increment them when you want numbers to increase (or decrease) by a specific amount. As you edit the document to add or remove text, WordPerfect automatically adjusts the page numbering and any increments you have inserted.

The program does not automatically increment chapter and volume number types; rather, you must notify WordPerfect when and how much to change the current number. For instance, if your number format is "Appendix [Chp #], Page [Pg #]", then at the beginning of each appendix after the first one, you must instruct WordPerfect to increment the chapter number.

To increase or decrease the numbering on the current page, move the cursor to where you want the number to change, such as the beginning of the chapter or volume, and follow these steps:

1. From the Page Numbering dialog box, choose **V**alue to open the Numbering Value dialog box.
2. Choose I**n**crease/Decrease Existing Chapter Number (or Page, Secondary, or Volume Number) and enter in the adjacent text box the amount by which to increase or decrease the number. Use a hyphen in front of the number to indicate an amount to decrease.
3. Choose OK or press Enter to save the changes and return to the Page Numbering dialog box.

Regardless of the numbering type you are using, enter the new number as an Arabic numeral. The numbering style specified in the Page Numbering Options dialog box determines how the number appears in the document.

Inserting a Page Number

▶ See "Inserting Page Numbering Codes," p. 943

In addition to using the eight page-number placement options available, you can place a number anywhere else on a page. You can place a number in a specific location to avoid a header or footer, or in the text where you want to refer to the current page, chapter, or volume number.

Only the number in the number type(s) currently in use (Arabic or Roman numerals or letters) appears at the cursor location. You can enter appropriate text before and after the number directly in the document. To insert a regular or secondary page, chapter, or volume number, place the cursor where you want the number to appear and follow these steps:

1. In the Page Numbering dialog box, choose **V**alue to display the Numbering Value dialog box.
2. Choose Insert and **D**isplay at Insertion Point so an X appears in the adjacent check box.
3. Choose OK or press Enter to return to the Page Numbering dialog box.

If you want to include formatting and text with the number, follow these steps:

1. In the Page Numbering dialog box, choose **O**ptions to display the Page Numbering Options dialog box.
2. Set up the type and style options and any text for the page number that you want to insert.
3. Choose I**n**sert Format and Accompanying Text at Insertion Point so an X appears in the adjacent check box.
4. Choose OK or press Enter to return to the Page Numbering dialog box.

Suppressing Page Numbering

The first page of a document does not usually have a page number. On other pages, the page number may interfere with the way a graphic or table is positioned on the page. When this occurs, you can suppress the page number on that page so the number does not appear in the printed version, but still maintain the numbering of subsequent pages in proper order.

To suppress numbering on the current page, follow these steps:

1. Choose Fo**r**mat, **P**age, S**u**ppress. The Suppress dialog box opens.

2. Choose **P**age Numbering. An X appears in the adjacent check box.

   If centering the number at the bottom of the page solves the placement difficulty, choose Print Page **N**umber at Bottom Center on Current Page.

3. Choose OK or press Enter to close the dialog box and return to the document.

The Suppress code displays as `[Suppress: Page Num]` in the Reveal Codes window. You can suppress page numbering on any page and as often as necessary.

Troubleshooting

When I use Chapter Number to number the sections of my document and later rearrange the order of the sections, the section numbers do not change to reflect the new order.

You probably created each new section number by typing it in the New Chapter Number text box. After you begin numbering using Chapter or Volume numbers, increase the number in the Numbering Value dialog box by typing **1** in the I**n**crease/ Decrease Existing Chapter Number text box before inserting the number.

I set up page numbering with accompanying text at the bottom of every page. Then I created the first chapter title using Chapter Numbering and accompanying text. When I choose the Insert Format and Accompanying Text at Insertion Point command, my page numbering changes to look like chapter numbering.

You can use more than one type of page numbering in a *single* page numbering code. For additional numbers, you must type the accompanying text in the document. To include a chapter number in chapter headings, for example, create the heading in the document; place the insertion point where you want the number to display; choose Fo**r**mat, **P**age, **N**umbering, and **V**alue; and choose Insert and Disp**l**ay at the Insertion Point in the Chapter Settings section of the Numbering Value dialog box.

Selecting Paper Size and Type

The paper size and type options available by default in WordPerfect depend on the printer you have selected. You can create other sizes and types, such as custom stationery or 5 1/2-by-8 1/2-inch invoices. A specific paper size and type is called a *paper definition*. The paper definitions you can create are limited only by the demands of your task and the capabilities of your printer.

The default paper definition selected in the U. S. version of WordPerfect for Windows is Standard 8 1/2-by-11-inch continuous paper. This is the default even if no printers have been installed. You can choose any other paper definition. The paper definition you choose also manages the print job.

Choosing a Different Paper Size

In addition to the Standard 8 1/2-by-11-inch paper definition, most printers have several additional paper definitions available, such as Legal 8 1/2-by-14-

inch continuous and Monarch envelopes. Before you choose a different paper size, select the printer you want to use so that the available paper definitions appear in the Paper Size dialog box. Choose a printer in the Select Printer dialog box (accessed through the File menu).

After you choose a different paper definition, WordPerfect inserts a paper size/type code such as `[Paper Sz/Typ: 8.50" x 14", Portrait]`. You can change the definition at any point in your document by choosing another definition.

To change the current paper definition, follow these steps:

1. Choose Fo**r**mat, **P**age, Paper **S**ize. The Paper Size dialog box appears (see fig. 5.10).

   The name of the current printer and whether it's a WordPerfect (WP) or a Windows driver (WIN) is shown at the top of the dialog box, and the custom details for the highlighted paper size display at the bottom of the box.

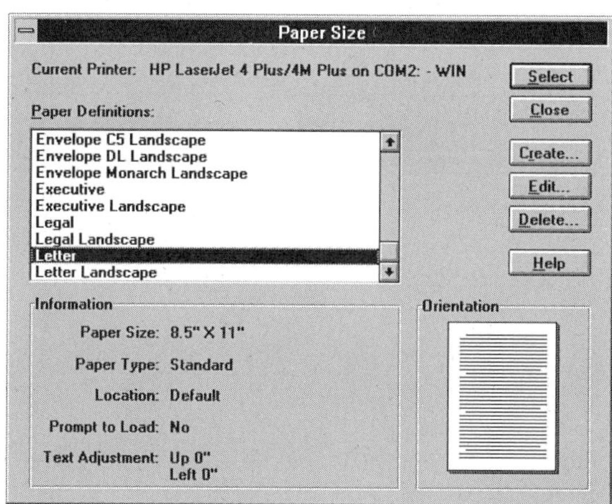

Fig. 5.10
The Paper Size dialog box provides the paper definitions for the active printer, information about custom details, and a diagram of the paper definition currently highlighted.

2. Highlight the paper definition you want to use and choose **S**elect to return to your document.

The versatility of the newest printers on the market means that the list of available paper definitions usually exceeds the number that can display at the same time in the Paper Definitions list box. Use the scroll bar to display more printers. To quickly display the name you want in the list box, type the first few letters of the paper name to move the highlight bar to the paper definition you want. As you type, the highlight bar moves to the paper definition name that begins with the letters you type.

Creating Custom Paper Definitions

Your printer may offer a greater variety of print options than the available paper definitions provide. Standard letter-size paper definitions are usually available only with portrait and landscape orientation definitions, both with a "continuous" paper location. You may want to manually feed special letter-size paper for some jobs, or place letterhead in one paper tray and second sheets of your letterhead in a second tray. Each paper location requires a separate paper definition. If you cannot find the definition you want in the list provided, you can create definitions for your personal print jobs.

Creating New Paper Definitions

When you want a custom paper definition, create a new definition rather than edit a definition provided by WordPerfect because the changes you make overwrite the original definition. If necessary, you can use Edit later to fine-tune paper definitions you have created.

To create a new paper definition, follow these steps:

1. From the Paper Size dialog box, choose C**r**eate. The Create Paper Size dialog box appears (see fig. 5.11).

2. Type a unique name for the definition in the **P**aper Name text box. You can click with the right mouse button on the text box to display a QuickMenu that includes the Speller command.

3. Choose the options you want for the paper definition you are creating, as described later in the "Customizing Paper Size" section.

4. Choose OK or press Enter to add the definition to the list in the Paper Size dialog box.

5. To use the new definition in the current document, double-click on the definition, or move the highlight bar to the definition, and then press Enter or choose **C**lose.

You do not need to use the new definition immediately. The paper definition you have created is added to the **P**aper Definitions list box where you can choose it later when you need it.

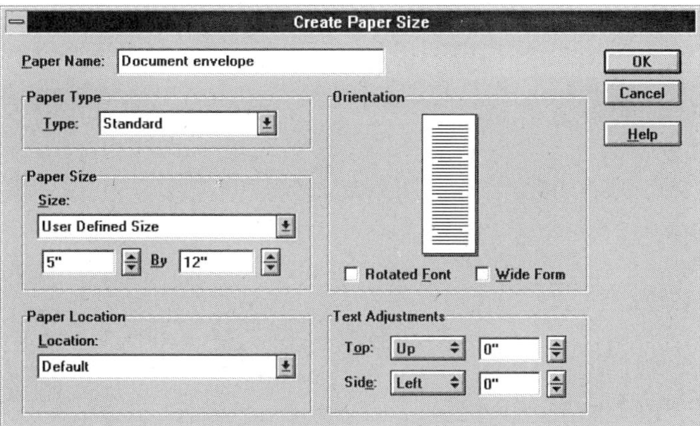

Fig. 5.11
As you choose paper-size options in the Create Paper Size dialog box, the diagram of the paper definition reflects your choices. Here a special document envelope is being created, but the font orientation has not yet been changed.

Note

The paper definition you create is added to the definitions for the current printer driver. When you select another printer driver, the paper size you have created is not available. You must create, or edit, the paper definition for every printer driver you want to use with the new paper definition.

Editing and Deleting Paper Definitions

To edit a paper definition, follow the steps for creating a new definition, except instead of choosing **C**reate, highlight the paper definition you want to change and choose **E**dit. The Edit Paper Size dialog box initially includes all the choices you made when you created the definition. The options available in the dialog box are described in the following section, "Customizing Paper Size."

If you edit a paper definition, WordPerfect does not incorporate the changes you make in documents created earlier using that definition. Nor do the changes affect earlier portions of the document that use the original paper definition. If the document in the active window uses the paper definition you are editing, you must select the definition after editing it to replace the original code. Place the cursor where you want the edited definition to take effect before following the steps to insert the edited definition code in the document. To replace the original definition with the edited definition, place the cursor on either side of the original code.

When you find that you no longer use a paper definition, remove it from the Paper Definitions list by highlighting it in the Paper Size dialog box and choosing **D**elete.

Customizing Paper Size

When you are creating or editing a paper-size/type definition, the following options are available in the Create Paper Size and Edit Paper Size dialog boxes. The Edit Paper Size and the Create Paper Size dialog boxes both provide the same options for customizing paper definitions (refer to fig. 5.11).

> **Caution**
>
> Pressing Enter while in the Create Paper Size or Edit Paper Size dialog box closes the box. Do not press Enter when making choices until you have customized all the options you want to change.

- *Paper Name.* Provide a name for the paper definition you are creating or edit the current name. Because this name distinguishes one paper definition from another, be as clear and descriptive as possible. Type the name in the text box provided and press Tab or choose another option to continue.

- *Paper Type.* Choose **T**ype to display the drop-down list. Make your choice from among the popular types in the list, such as Standard, Bond, Cardstock, and Glossy Film; or choose Other.

- *Paper Size.* When you are specifying a paper size, initially width displays in the first text box and height in the text box on the right for portrait orientation. If the width you specify is greater than the height, the text boxes reverse so the entry in the first box becomes the height.

  Choose **S**ize to display the drop-down list. Make your choice from the sizes available for the active printer. If you do not find the size you want, choose User Defined Size and enter the height and width in the text boxes.

- *Paper Location.* Paper Location describes how the paper feeds to the printer. Use Manual Feed if you want to hand feed letterhead stationery. Specify Continuous if your printer uses tractor-feed, or a single paper cassette. If your printer can pull paper from several cassettes or sheet feeder bins, the bins or trays are included in the drop-down list. If you later add a sheet feeder, choose **F**ile, **P**rint, **S**elect, **O**ptions, **S**etup to customize the printer installation. The new sheet feeder options then appear in the Paper **S**ource list.

  Choose **L**ocation to display the drop-down list and choose the location from the list provided.

- *Prompt to Load Paper.* If you choose P**r**ompt to Load Paper, displayed immediately under Paper Location if a WordPerfect printer driver is active, WordPerfect emits a beep when a the print job is sent to the printer. Go To the Windows Print Manager where a dialog box displays `Load Paper: Paper Type`. Refer to Chapter 8, "Basic Output: Printing, Faxing, and E-mail," for information on handling print jobs and print messages.

  Choose **P**rompt to Load Paper to place an X in the adjacent check box.

- *Orientation.* You can choose to use a rotated font and to print using a wide form. When you use either a regular (portrait) or rotated (landscape) font, the short edge of the paper feeds first. If necessary, you can opt to feed the long edge of the paper first by choosing **W**ide Form.

- *Text Adjustments.* Using the options available in Text Adjustments, you can reposition the text on the page if the text does not print on the page according to the margins you set. This printing difficulty is not visible in the document window, so any adjustments you set must be tested by printing a page of text.

  Choose T**o**p and specify a distance to adjust **U**p or **D**own, or Sid**e** to specify a distance to adjust the text to the **L**eft or **R**ight.

Using the All Others Definition

All Others is a generic paper definition available for all printers. You can create a document to be printed on a variety of printers that don't have your customized paper definition available, such as when a document is made available to others on a network or distributed on a floppy disk. An All Others paper definition is available with all printer drivers.

To choose the All Others paper definition, highlight All Others in the **P**aper Definitions list in the Paper Size dialog box, and then choose **S**elect to open the Select All Others Paper Size dialog box. Choose a paper type and size, and set up the orientation you require.

You also use the All Others paper definition when you want to insert a customized definition in a single document without creating a new definition. WordPerfect incorporates the type and size information you provide in the paper size/type code, and the All Others definition returns to the default settings.

To customize the All Others paper definition, highlight All Others in the **P**aper Definitions list box in the Paper Size dialog box. Then choose **E**dit to open the Edit Paper Size All Others dialog box, and change the width, text adjustment, and other options, as necessary.

When you edit the All Others definition, the changes you make in the Edit Paper Size All Others dialog box display when you next choose **E**dit.

Each of the options available for selecting and editing the All Others paper definition is described in the earlier section "Customizing Paper Size."

Considering Other Paper Size Factors

► See "Selecting and Configuring Your Printer," p. 305

► See "Printer Fonts and Graphic Fonts," p. 671

If you routinely use a paper size other than Standard 8 1/2 by 11 inches, you can replace the default definition for all new documents by including your preferred definition in the Standard template. Refer to Chapter 11, "Using Templates," for instructions on creating and editing templates.

If you have a printer with multiple paper trays, or bins, a frequent print job layout is to specify the bin containing letterhead for the first page of a document, and a second bin containing second sheets for the rest of the document. Choose the letterhead paper definition to begin the document; then create a Delay code with a one-page delay to cause WordPerfect to pull paper from the second bin for the remainder of the letter.

Use a slightly different technique if your printer has only one paper tray. Place the second sheets in the paper tray and a single page of letterhead in the manual or bypass feed location. When the document prints, the printer pulls the first page from the bypass location and remaining pages from the paper tray. No special paper definition is needed.

Changing paper definitions automatically changes the position of soft page breaks in your document. Review your document before printing to be sure that text is still placed on the pages the way you want.

Troubleshooting

I can't find a paper size definition that I know I have used before and that my printer can handle. Where did it go?

Paper size definitions are part of the printer driver for each printer you have installed. If you created the definition yourself, the new paper size is available only with the printer selected at the time you created the definition. The printer with that definition is probably not selected at the moment. Select the appropriate printer or refer to Chapter 8, "Basic Output: Printing, Faxing, and E-Mail," for instructions to select another printer.

Using the Make It Fit Expert Feature

New to WordPerfect 6.1 for Windows is the Make It Fit Expert command, which you can use to have WordPerfect reformat your document so that it fills the number of pages you specify. If the signature block at the end of your letter is at the top of the next page or the newsletter is just a bit too short this month, Make It Fit Expert is the quick solution. Experienced word processors have traditionally changed the font size and reduced or increased line height minute amounts to adjust document length, but this process often necessitates change after change until the desired result is achieved. Make It Fit Expert saves you the tedious process of adjusting and readjusting line height, font size, and margins to achieve just the right fit.

To have WordPerfect find the best fit for your document, follow these steps:

1. Choose Format, Make It Fit Expert to open the Make It Fit Expert dialog box (see fig. 5.12).

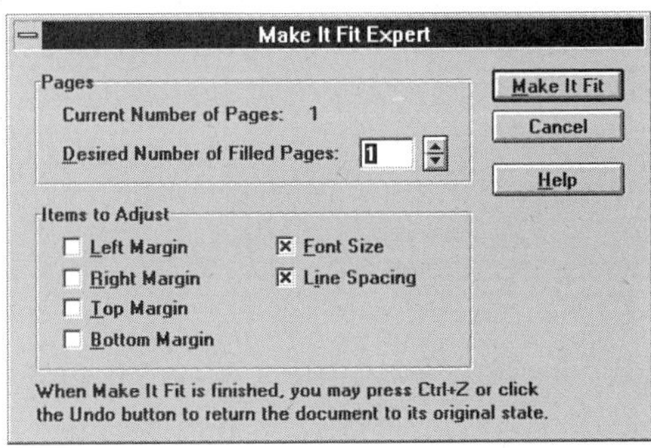

Fig. 5.12
The Make It Fit Expert dialog box offers several ways to adjust a document to achieve a specific page count.

2. In the Desired Number of Filled Pages text box, type the number of pages you want the document to fill.

3. Indicate the formatting changes you want WordPerfect to use to achieve the desired fit by choosing one or more of these options:

Left Margin	Bottom Margin
Right Margin	Font Size
Top Margin	Line Spacing

4. Choose the Make It Fit button to reformat the document.

Caution

Check your entire document very carefully immediately after using the Make It Fit Expert feature to see if the results are satisfactory. If the changes WordPerfect makes do not produce the desired appearance, choose Undo to remove the formatting.

Working with Labels

WordPerfect 6.1 for Windows includes approximately 130 definitions for standard labels that are readily available at office supply stores. The definitions are stored in a file named WP_WP_US.LAB, which displays at the bottom of the Labels dialog box as the default file. Included in this definition are several popular brand names with identifying label numbers for most of the labels available on the market. The types range from various styles of address labels to file folder, floppy disk, and name badge labels. Check on the label package for the label name and number. Open the Labels dialog box, choose the matching label definition, and you are ready to go!

Choosing a Label Definition

To choose a label definition, follow these steps:

1. Choose Fo**r**mat, La**b**els to open the Labels dialog box (see fig. 5.13).

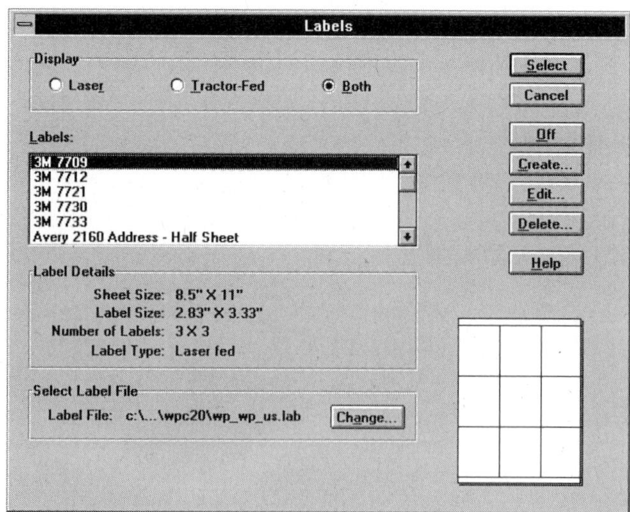

Fig. 5.13
The Labels dialog box displays the current label's file name, a list of available label definitions, and the custom label details for the highlighted label definition.

2. Move the highlight bar to the label definition you want to use and choose **S**elect.

The list of labels is lengthy. It is easy to make the list more manageable and target the labels you can use. Choose **T**ractor-Fed or Lase**r** to display only laser labels or only tractor-fed labels.

Using Labels

The labels arranged on a full page or a continuous-feed roll are individual logical pages, as described in the "Physical and Logical Pages" section earlier in this chapter. After you choose the label definition you want to use, begin typing the label information on-screen. When you complete a label, insert a page break by pressing Ctrl+Enter to move to the next label.

Tip

Begin typing the name of the label to open a search text box and move the highlight bar to the first label beginning with the letters you type.

Because a label is a document page, only a single label displays in Page mode. When you complete the first label and press Ctrl+Enter, a second, blank label appears on the page. You can use all the usual format commands. The following suggestions may help you get started:

- When typing several separate lines of text, press Enter at the end of each line.
- When typing a long entry rather than separate lines, the text word-wraps within the label.
- You can use the Center Current Page or Center Pages command to place the text in the middle of the label.
- Remember that labels are pages. Use Go To to quickly move to a specific label. Choose **E**dit, **G**o To, or press Ctrl+G; then type the label number.
- You can change fonts, apply bold and underline, insert graphics images, center or right justify the text, and create page or paragraph borders, to name a few possibilities.
- You can include labels in a document. Position the cursor where you want the labels and choose the appropriate label definition. To continue with your regular-text document after the labels are typed, open the Labels dialog box and choose Labels **O**ff to reinstate the original paper definition.

Creating Custom Label Definitions

When you want to create a new labels definition, WordPerfect displays a Create Labels dialog box in which you can specify the size of the page, the size of the labels, all four label margins, and more. To create a new label definition, follow these steps:

1. From the Labels dialog box, choose **C**reate. The Create Labels dialog box opens (see fig. 5.14).

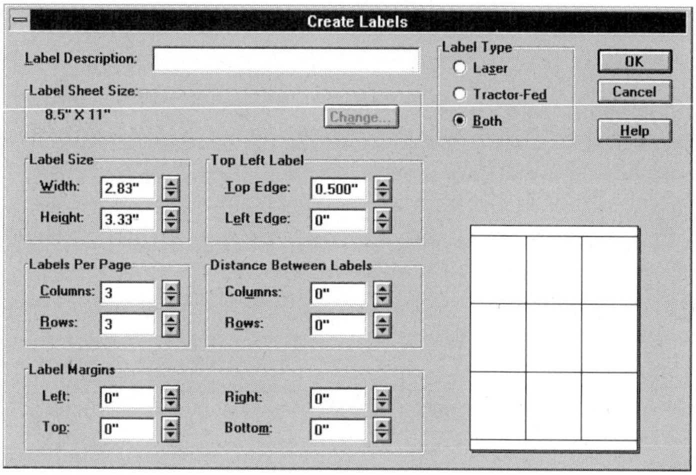

Fig. 5.14
Using the Create Labels dialog box, you can customize every aspect of the label spacing with precision. Watch the diagram in the lower-right corner of the dialog box to preview the results of the choices you make.

2. Provide the necessary information in the array of text boxes to set up the label definition for your print job. Refer to the later section, "Understanding Label Customizing Options," for information about the available options.

3. Choose OK or press Enter to add the definition to the list in the Labels dialog box.

4. To use the new label definition immediately, highlight it and choose **S**elect.

   To exit without selecting a definition, choose **C**lose or Cancel.

If you use the new label definition and find it needs some adjusting, you can edit the definition to incorporate needed changes.

Editing and Deleting Label Definitions

Because the labels available with WordPerfect all bear the name and number of commercially available labels, it is better not to edit those definitions. Instead, create a definition as described in the preceding section and give it a name that clearly identifies your personal product. Then edit the definition you have created as needed.

To edit a label definition, follow these steps:

1. From the Labels dialog box, move the highlight bar to the label definition you want to edit and choose **E**dit.

2. Enter in the various text boxes the information needed to edit the label definition to suit the needs of your print job. Refer to the next section, "Understanding Label Customizing Options," for information about available options.

3. Choose OK to return to the Labels dialog box. Choose the new label definition to use it immediately, or choose Cancel to return to your document.

If you create label definitions that you no longer need, you can delete them. To delete a label definition, highlight in the Labels dialog box the label definition you want to delete and choose **D**elete.

Understanding Label Customizing Options

The Create Labels and Edit Labels dialog boxes offer a variety of options you can customize:

- *Label Description.* Assign the label definition a descriptive name. The name you enter appears in the list box after you save the definition. You can click the right mouse button on the **L**abel Description text box to display the QuickMenu and choose the Speller to check the spelling of the entry.

- *Label Sheet Size.* For laser printers, paper size is usually 8 1/2 by 11 inches. Enter the dimensions of the entire physical page of labels as the label sheet size when working with labels to be printed with a laser printer. Tractor-fed labels are set up by WordPerfect with one row of labels to a page, whether the row contains one or several labels. This arrangement works well, and you should emulate it when designing your own label definitions.

  When you choose Ch**a**nge to choose a different label sheet size, a Define Sheet Size box appears listing the various paper sizes available with WordPerfect. Move the highlight to the size you want to use and choose **S**elect, or choose **C**reate to open the Create Paper Size dialog box in which you can enter a width and height for your custom paper size. The Create Paper Size dialog box is the same as that described in the earlier section "Selecting Paper Size and Type."

Caution

As you design or edit the sheet of labels, remember that the active printer probably has a small nonprinting area at the edges. Design your labels to allow for this or include text adjustments as described later in this section, or the labels may not print as you planned.

- *Label Size.* Enter the **W**idth and Hei**g**ht of the individual labels. Do not include the space, if any, between labels.
- *Labels Per Page.* Indicate the number of labels in the **C**olumns and **R**ows on a page.
- *Top Left Label.* Labels may be arranged on a page so that a border remains on all four edges of the page. To adjust for this, specify the location of the top-left corner of the first label. Enter the measurement from the edge of the sheet of labels to the **T**op Edge and the L**e**ft Edge of the label in the top-left corner.
- *Distance Between Labels.* Specify any distance between R**o**ws and between Col**u**mns of labels. The default is 0.
- *Label Margins.* Indicate the Le**f**t, R**i**ght, To**p**, and Botto**m** margins for the labels. The default is 0.

Caution

If you do not specify margins and a distance between labels, you run the risk of having text on adjacent labels actually touching, or the text may overlap the edge of adjacent label if the sheet of labels does not feed perfectly.

- *Label Type.* Indicate whether the labels are designed to print as La**s**er or Tractor-Fe**d** labels. If you can print the labels either way, choose **B**oth.

Several customizing options are available to provide instructions to the printer. By choosing to change the Label Sheet Size, you can choose **C**reate in the Define Sheet Size dialog box to open the Create Paper Size dialog box, enabling you to customize the following settings:

- *Paper Location.* From the **L**ocation drop-down list, choose Manual Feed if you want to hand-feed sheets of labels, or choose the cassette or bin containing the labels.

- *Prompt to Load Paper* (displayed for WordPerfect printer drivers). Choose Prompt to Load Paper to cause WordPerfect to halt a print job and beep. Go to the Windows Print Manager for a reminder dialog box telling you which paper type to load.

- *Rotated Font.* Choose Rotated **F**ont to have text printed sideways on the labels. To set up a page of labels where the width of the page exceeds the height, choose **W**ide Form.

- *Text Adjustments.* If the text does not print correctly on the label even though the settings are all correct, choose T**o**p and specify a distance to adjust **U**p or **D**own, or Sid**e** to specify a distance to adjust the text to the **L**eft or **R**ight.

The dialog box displayed when you choose **C**reate is the standard Create Paper Size dialog box. The printer adjustments and other features of the dialog box are discussed in greater detail in an earlier section, "Customizing Paper Size."

The label definitions you create or edit are saved in the current label file, either the default WP_WP_US.LAB file or a label file that you create. The program saves the printer information in the WordPerfect PRS file for the current printer or in the Windows WPCSET.WCS file. If you want to print your custom labels on another system, you must have the custom LAB file, and the PRS or WPCSET.WCS file on the other system must be updated with the custom printing information.

Creating Custom Label Files

Rather than hunting through a lengthy list of labels to find your custom creations, you can create a personal label file. Retrieve the file when you want to create a new label definition, and WordPerfect adds the new definition to your file. To create a labels file, follow these steps:

1. From the Labels dialog box, choose Ch**a**nge to open the Label File dialog box (see fig. 5.15).

2. Choose C**u**rrent Dir to change the directory location for the label files. Enter a new directory. To use the Select Directory dialog box to browse for the desired directory, click on the File button at the end of the text box or press Alt+down arrow.

3. Choose **C**reate to display the Create Label File dialog box. Type a description of the label file in the **D**escription text box. Type a file name

of up to eight characters in the **F**ilename text box. (WordPerfect supplies the extension LAB when you choose OK or press Enter.)

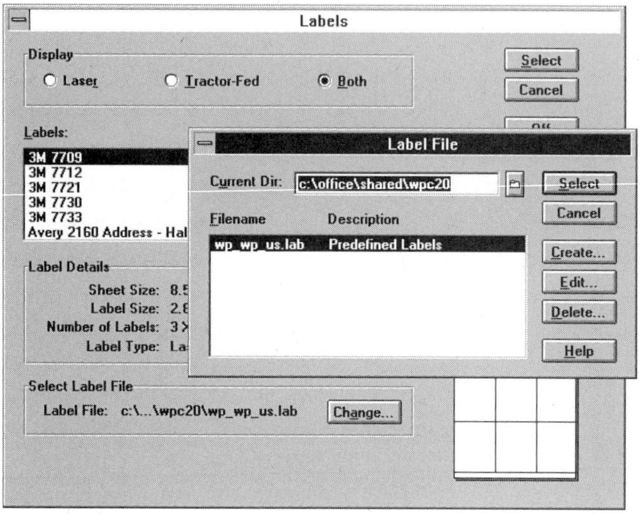

Fig. 5.15
The Label File dialog box provides commands for creating and editing label files, and lists the existing label files.

4. Choose OK or press Enter to return to the Label File dialog box.
5. Choose **S**elect to open the label file.

When you first select a file you have created, no labels are included in the Labels list box. As you create new label definitions, WordPerfect adds the label definition to the list box for the current label file.

You can change either the description or the file name of the label file. Choose **E**dit to open the Edit Label File dialog box where you can edit the file name and description.

If you have created label files and saved them in directories other than the default directory, choose C**u**rrent Dir and type the directory name in the text box. The default directory for label files is \office\shared\wpc20.

When you no longer need a label file that you created, choose **D**elete to remove the file.

Tip
To quickly highlight the file you want, type the first letter of the file name to open a text box and move to the first file that begins with that letter.

Using Subdivide Page

With the Subdivide Page command, you can subdivide a page into evenly spaced columns and rows. WordPerfect treats the full page as a physical page and the subdivided pages as separate, logical pages. For example, the program numbers each subdivision when you turn on page numbering.

As with labels, when you type on subdivided pages, pressing Ctrl+Enter to insert a hard page break moves the cursor to the next subdivision. The text you type word-wraps within the subdivided page and onto the next subdivision if you enter enough text but do not insert a page break.

To subdivide a page into columns and rows of pages, follow these steps:

1. Choose Fo**r**mat, **P**age, Subdi**v**ide Page. The Subdivide Page dialog box opens (see fig. 5.16).

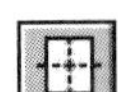

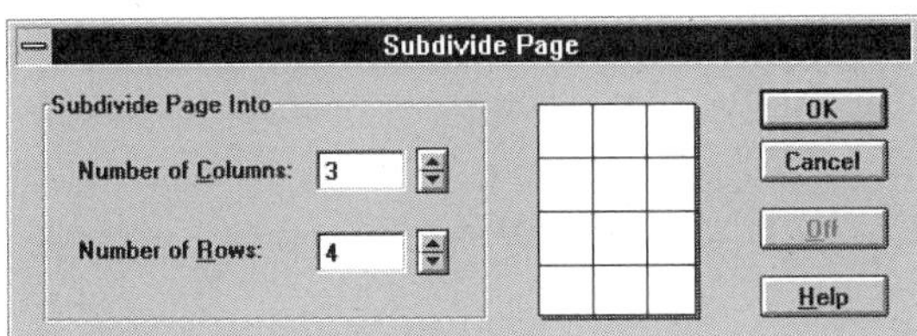

Fig. 5.16
As you enter the number of columns and rows in the Subdivide Page dialog box (here 3 by 4), you can preview the results in the page graphic.

2. Enter the number of columns and rows in the text boxes adjacent to Number of **C**olumns and the Number of **R**ows, or click on the arrows to increase or decrease the number displayed in each text box.

3. Choose OK or press Enter to return to your document.

When you choose Subdivide Page, WordPerfect uses the current margins for each page. Change the margins you want to use if you have more than a few subdivisions. To illustrate, two columns of subdivided pages use four inches of the page width and height for margins if you do not change the default one-inch margins.

All subsequent pages in your document are subdivided. You may want to subdivide only a single page in your document. To return to full-size pages, move the cursor to the page where you want to restore the original paper size and follow the steps to subdivide pages and choose **O**ff to turn Subdivide Page off.

Working with Envelopes

WordPerfect 6.1 for Windows includes an envelope form that automatically addresses envelopes using the return address you specify and the mailing address in your letter. If you use a standard business letter format where the mailing address is on the left, WordPerfect inserts the mailing address in the envelope form for you.

Addressing an Envelope

To fill in the mailing address, selection criteria are used to determine what text to select. WordPerfect first checks to determine whether text is currently blocked. If not, WordPerfect looks on the first page of the document for three to six lines of text where each line ends with a hard return and the last line is followed by two hard returns. If more than one block of text on the first page meets these criteria, the last block is selected. Using standard business letter formats, this ensures that a return address is ignored in favor of the mailing address that follows. Finally, a nonhard end-of-line code, such as the soft return used for word-wrapped text, terminates the search.

To address an envelope after typing a letter, follow these steps:

1. Choose Fo**r**mat, En**v**elope to open the Envelope dialog box (see fig. 5.17).

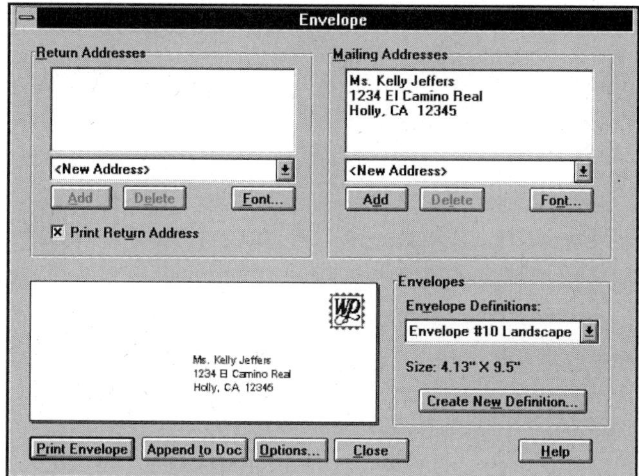

Fig. 5.17
The Envelope dialog box with the mailing address and ZIP code retrieved by WordPerfect.

2. Choose En**v**elope Definitions to open a drop-down list of envelope definitions. Choose the envelope size you want to use.

3. Choose **R**eturn Addresses to place the cursor in the text box, and type the return address.

   To change the typeface or size of the font used in the return address, choose **F**ont to open the Font dialog box, now titled Return Address

Font. Refer to Chapter 4, "Formatting Text," and Chapter 20, "Using Fonts and Special Characters," for instructions on choosing options in this dialog box.

After you begin typing a return address, the **A**dd command button becomes available. To have WordPerfect save the current return address so you can use it in future envelopes, choose **A**dd. The program uses the first line of the return address as the name of the saved return address. Once you have saved an address, you can choose it from the drop-down list under the Return Addresses window. If you no longer need to save an address, choose it from the drop-down list and choose D**e**lete.

4. To enter or edit a mailing address, choose **M**ailing Addresses and type the mailing address or edit the available text. Choose Add if you want to save the mailing address to use in the future.

   If a mailing address was included in your document and the document used one of the standard business letter formats, WordPerfect extracts the mailing address from the letter and displays it in the Mailing Addresses window automatically. You can edit the address, perhaps adding an ATTN: line or other details.

   As with the return address, you can change the typeface or size of the font used in the return address by choosing Fo**n**t to open the Font dialog box, now titled Mailing Address Font. Again, refer to Chapter 4, "Formatting Text," and Chapter 20, "Using Fonts and Special Characters," for instructions on working in this dialog box.

5. To add the envelope to your document, choose Append **t**o Doc. If you are ready to print the envelope, choose **P**rint Envelope. Otherwise, choose Close.

Tip

To check the spelling of either address, click the background of the Mailing Address or Return Address text box, and choose Speller from the QuickMenu that is displayed.

Note

The envelope uses the current document font to format text. You can use a different font or another size, run a macro, or apply other formatting to the mailing address and return address text. Using a larger font size for the mailing address makes the address easier to read, and the resulting overall envelope appearance is very attractive.

When you do not use a standard business format or you have several mailing addresses in a letter, block the desired address text before opening the Envelope form to have WordPerfect use the blocked text as the mailing address.

If you have several mailing addresses, create several envelopes by selecting each address in turn. Then print the envelope immediately or append each to the document so all the envelopes print when the document is printed.

Creating New Envelope Definitions

The envelopes available in the Envelope Definitions drop-down list are the default envelopes for the current printer, plus any envelope definitions you have created for the current printer. Whether you want to create a new envelope definition or edit an existing definition, the now familiar Create Paper Size or Edit Paper Size dialog box displays with a new title. For detailed instructions for entering information and making choices using the commands available in the Paper Size dialog box, see the earlier section "Customizing Paper Size."

Setting Envelope Options

In addition to the customizing options described earlier, the position of the return and mailing addresses, whether WordPerfect prints a U.S. POSTNET bar code on the envelope, and where the bar code is printed can be customized by choosing **O**ptions in the Envelope dialog box (see fig. 5.18).

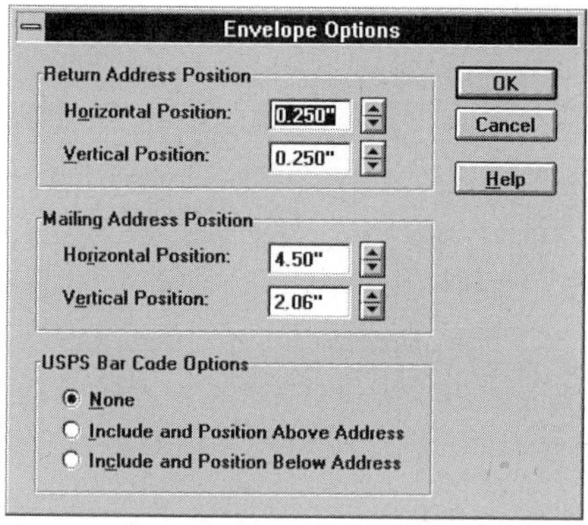

Fig. 5.18
In the Envelope Options dialog box, indicate where the mailing and return addresses should be, as measured from the edge of the envelope, and whether to include a POSTNET bar code on the envelope.

To change the position of the return or mailing address, choose the appropriate Horizontal Position or Vertical Position and enter a new value, measured from the edge of the envelope for both the return address and the mailing address.

To have the ZIP code printed on the envelope in the form of a bar code that can be scanned at the Post Office for automated mail sorting, choose whether to include a U.S. POSTNET Bar Code. Choose whether to position the bar code above the address or below the address so that an X appears in the appropriate check box. WordPerfect uses the 5-digit, 9-digit, or 11-digit ZIP code if one is included at the end of the last line of the mailing address. When you are done, choose OK to return to the Envelope dialog box.

Any changes you make in the Envelope Options dialog box are saved with the current envelope definition. The next time you choose the definitions, the options you entered display in the Envelope Options dialog box as the defaults.

Editing and Deleting Envelope Definitions

To edit or delete any of the envelope definitions you have created, you must use the Fo**r**mat, **P**age, Paper **S**ize command. The name of the envelope definition you created is in the **P**aper Definitions list box. Move the highlight bar to your choice and choose **E**dit. The Edit Paper Size dialog box displays. Refer to the instructions for editing and deleting paper definitions in the "Editing and Deleting Paper Definitions" section earlier in this chapter.

Using Advance To Place Text

The Advance command enables you to place text on the page at a precise location. Frequently used to start letters with a first-page-only allowance for letterhead, Advance can also be the solution for filling in preprinted forms when no typewriter is available. Advance enables you to ignore line height changes that occur when larger or smaller font sizes are selected.

Advance has two positioning schemes. You can use it to place text a measured distance—up, down, left, or right—from where WordPerfect inserts the Advance code. If you edit the preceding text, the position of the code shifts and the effect of the Advance adjusts accordingly.

With the second positioning method, you specify a specific distance from the top or the left edge of the page. This method results in absolute placement of the text, regardless of the final location of the Advance code.

To use Advance to place text at a specific location, follow these steps:

1. Place the cursor immediately before the text to be advanced.

2. Choose Fo**r**mat, **T**ypesetting.

3. Choose **A**dvance. The Advance dialog box appears (see fig. 5.19).

4. Choose a Horizontal Position option. The Hori**z**ontal Distance text box becomes available.

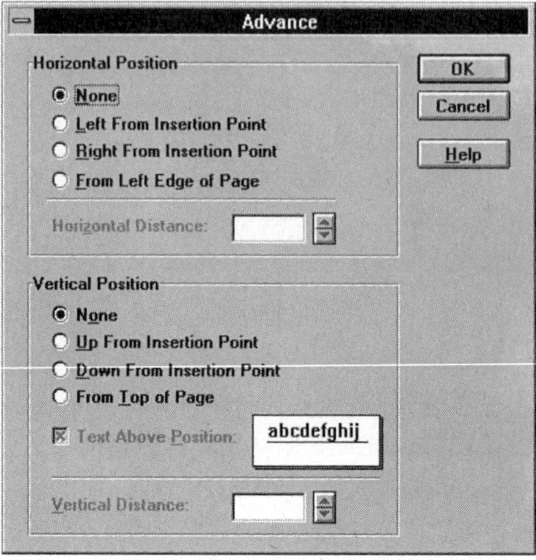

Fig. 5.19
Choose a Vertical Position or Horizontal Position in the Advance dialog box, and enter the distance in the corresponding text box.

5. Type the distance to move the text left or right from the insertion point, or from the left edge of the page.
6. Choose a Vertical Position option. The **V**ertical Distance text box becomes available.
7. Type the distance to move the text up or down from the insertion point, or from the top edge of the page.
8. Choose OK or press Enter to save the changes and return to your document.

Only one direction of movement is included in an Advance code, although you can specify both directions while in the Advance dialog box so that WordPerfect inserts both codes in your document at the same time.

To use Advance only to allow for letterhead on the first page of a document, enter a measurement down or from the top of the page to indicate where the document should start. If you are using Advance to fill in the blanks in a form, however, you will discover that Advance codes that advance text from the top of the page do not result in the text being printed on the form according to the measurements you have entered. This is because the measurement indicates where to place the top of the text. When you choose From **T**op of Page, the Text Above **P**osition check box becomes active. When an X is in the check box, WordPerfect places the bottom of the text line at the position you entered in the **V**ertical Distance text box.

Setting the Initial Font

You can change the initial font used in your document at any time and from any location in your document. Using the Initial **F**ont command to change the font in a document also changes the initial font for text in headers, footers, footnotes, and endnotes.

▶ See "Adding Fonts for Your Printer," p. 310

To change the initial font used in the active document, follow these steps:

1. Choose Fo**r**mat, **D**ocument, Initial **F**ont. The Document Initial Font dialog box opens.
2. Choose the name of the font you want from the **F**ont Face list box.
3. Choose the font size from the Font **S**ize list box or type a number for the size in the text box at the top of the list box.
4. From the F**o**nt Style list box, choose whether you want the font to be Regular, Bold, Bold Italic, or Italic type.
5. Check in the preview screen at the bottom of the dialog box to be sure the type appears as you want. Choose OK or press Enter to save the changes and return to your document.

This command is particularly useful if you have not yet changed fonts in your document. If you have, the initial font change takes effect at the beginning of your document and continues until it encounters a code for a different font name or size.

You also can change the document initial font from the Font menu. Refer to Chapter 20, "Using Fonts and Special Characters," for more about this feature and a full discussion of fonts and how they affect the appearance of your document.

Creating the Initial Codes Style

You can set up a document's initial codes without those codes appearing in the Reveal Codes window by including the codes in the `[Open Style: InitialStyle]` code that appears at the beginning of every document. If you include the codes in the `[Open Style: InitialStyle]` code in the Standard template, the codes you set up are thereafter used initially in every document you create. If you choose codes using Fo**r**mat, **D**ocument, Initial Codes **S**tyle, the codes you set up are used initially in the current document only. Also, if

▶ See "Using System Styles," p. 378

you choose Fo**r**mat, **D**ocument, Initial Codes **S**tyle, the codes you set up take precedence over those in the Standard template.

Initial codes can be very useful tools if many of your documents use similar codes to format the entire document. You can include Widow/Orphan protection, full justification, page-numbering position, and text to accompany the page number as initial codes, and every new document then begins that way. Using Fo**r**mat, **D**ocument, Initial Codes **S**tyle enables you to add or delete a few codes for more specialized documents, such as changing the page numbering position or adding a header. These changes affect only the current document.

Setting initial codes for a document involves creating a style called `[InitialStyle]`. Because this is a system style, few of the options in the Styles Editor are available, simplifying the task if you are unfamiliar with WordPerfect's Styles feature. You can change the descriptive name of the style, close the display of the Reveal Codes window, and choose the codes you want included in the `[InitialStyle]`. If you have included codes in the Initial Style in the Standard template, those codes display in the Styles Editor, and you can edit, rearrange, or delete them as appropriate.

To add codes to the `[Open Style: InitialStyle]` code for your document, follow these steps:

1. Choose Fo**r**mat, **D**ocument, Initial Codes **S**tyle to open the Styles Editor shown in figure 5.20.

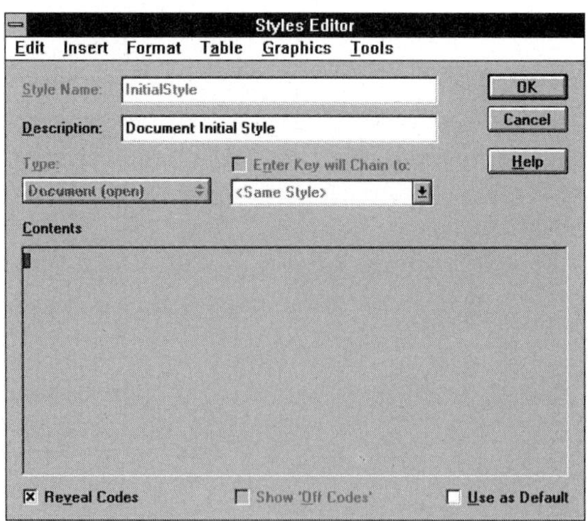

Fig. 5.20
The Styles Editor opens with a rectangular cursor in the **C**ontents window. A limited menu bar is available for choosing commands to insert codes and to edit the codes.

2. Use the menu bar at the top of the dialog box and keystrokes to choose commands to insert codes for the features you want initially in your document. The codes created appear in the Contents window.

3. Choose OK to save your changes and return to the document.

If you want to change the codes you have selected, follow the same steps to open the Styles Editor and make the changes you want. Any codes you insert later in your document take precedence over any contained in the `[Open Style: InitialStyle]`.

To provide a different description for the `[InitialStyle]` code, choose **D**escription and edit the current description to meet your needs. If you do not want to see the resulting codes as they are inserted, choose Re**v**eal Codes to remove the X from the check box and close the Reveal Codes display.

Setting Up the Redline Method

Redline and Strikeout are special fonts that allow you to edit documents while in WordPerfect by noting suggested additions (Redline) and deletions (Strikeout).

If you have a color monitor, redlined text appears red on-screen. Strikeout shows as a horizontal line (a hyphen) drawn through stricken text with either monitor.

You choose **R**edline and Stri**k**eout from the Fo**r**mat, **F**ont menu. Using these fonts as editing tools is discussed further in Chapter 20, "Using Fonts and Special Characters," but the printed appearance of these fonts is an important consideration for formatting documents.

To customize the Redline method to specify how redlined text appears when printed, follow these steps:

1. Choose Fo**r**mat, **D**ocument, **R**edline Method.

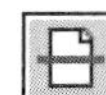

2. Choose one of the following four methods for marking Redlined text:

   - ***P**rinter Dependent.* Prints a shaded background with most printers.
   - *Mark **L**eft Margin.* Places a vertical bar (|) in the left margin area alongside your text.
   - *Mark **A**lternating Margins.* Places the vertical bar on either margin, alternating left and right.

- *Mark **R**ight Margin.* Places a vertical bar in the right margin area alongside your text.

3. If you elect to mark text in the margins, the Redline **C**haracter box becomes active. If you want to use a character other than the vertical bar, delete the bar and type in another character. If you want to use a Word-Perfect character, press Ctrl+W to access the WordPerfect Characters dialog box. Choose the appropriate Character **S**et, and then choose Cha**r**acters and the one you want to use. Finally, choose Insert **a**nd Close. Chapter 20, "Using Fonts and Special Characters," provides more information on using the WordPerfect characters.
4. Choose OK or press Enter to return to the document.

Choosing a different Redline method does not change the on-screen display. Because it only affects the way the text appears when you print, you may change the method as often as you want. Your final selection takes precedence over previous selections.

If you are satisfied with the printing results, you can choose **U**se as Default in the Redline dialog box to change the Redline method for all future documents.

Using Document Summaries

Creating a document summary enables you to maintain a database about your documents from which you can obtain information without retrieving individual documents. You can store a substantial amount of information in the document summary. In addition to document creation and revision dates, which WordPerfect automatically fills in, text boxes are available for eight separate pieces of information about your document and you can configure the summary to add more (see fig. 5.21).

The following list describes the text boxes in the Document Summary dialog box:

- *Descriptive Name.* This option enables you to enter a name for your document longer than the eight characters plus three-character extension you can use in DOS file-naming conventions.
- *Descriptive Type.* This option enables you to enter a category to classify your documents into categories such as Letter, Proposal, or Payroll Report.

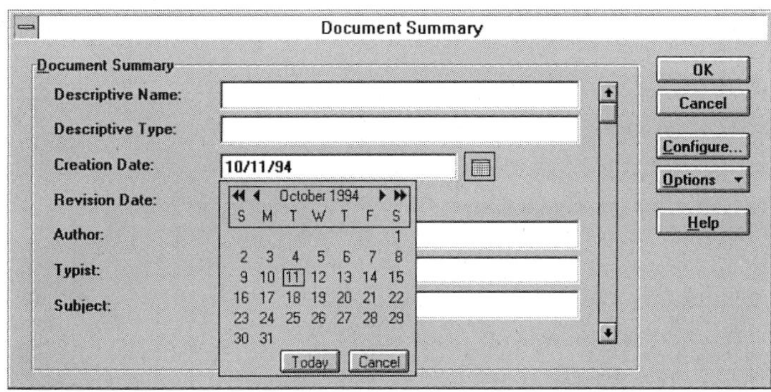

Fig. 5.21
The fields initially displayed in the Document Summary dialog box depend on whether you specify using descriptive names in the Preferences menu.

- *Creation Date.* WordPerfect fills in the Creation Date box when you create your document. You can change this information in the following format, using forward slashes or hyphens in the date and "a" or "p" following the time:

  08/07/1995 10:25a

  8-7-99 04:13p

  Choose the button at the end of the text box with the calendar icon on its face to open a calendar in which you can choose a creation date (refer to fig. 5.21). Click on the double arrows to change from year to year or on the single arrows to change from month to month; use the arrow keys to move from day to day and week to week; and use PgUp and PgDn to change from month to month. Press Enter or click on the desired date to enter it in the text box.

- *Revision Date.* WordPerfect updates the Revision Date every time you save your document. You cannot enter information in this field.

Caution

The program obtains the Creation Date and Revision Date from the current date and time available in your computer. Check the system date and time frequently to make sure they are correct.

- *Author.* This option enables you to enter text such as the author's name, job title, address, or other information. When you choose to extract information, WordPerfect inserts the contents of this text box from your last document summary here. Refer to the "Extract Information from Document" section later in this chapter for more information.

- *Typist.* This option enables you to enter text including the typist's name, job title, extension number, or other information. If you choose to extract information, the program inserts the contents of this text box from your last document summary here. Again, refer to the later section "Extract Information from Document."

- *Subject.* You can enter up to 250 characters about the subject matter of your document in the Subject text box. When you choose to extract information, WordPerfect inserts approximately 250 characters following the default subject text. Refer to the "Extract Information from Document" section later in this chapter for more information.

- *Account.* You can enter up to 160 characters of any information you want in the Account text box. This box provides an additional area for any descriptive information you want to add.

  Use the Account text box to identify a client, customer, or job that may not be apparent in the document summary. You can record an account number, court case number, or case style. This can be a particularly useful box if you regularly prepare routine correspondence to the same individuals about the same subjects on behalf of a different client or job.

- *Keywords.* Through the Advanced Search feature in File Manager, WordPerfect can search document summaries for keywords. Use the Keywords text box to enter highly descriptive information about the document that can be useful for a speedy word search.

- *Abstract.* The Abstract text box accepts up to 400 characters of text to describe your document. When you choose to extract information, WordPerfect inserts the first 400 characters (approximately) of your document here. Refer to the later section "Extract Information From Document" for more information on this feature. If the document is a letter, the text inserted includes the recipient's name, address, salutation, and opening paragraph, without hard returns. You can edit freely in the Abstract box, but Copy, Cut, Paste, and Undelete are not available.

  Consider listing here the names and descriptions of macros, styles, and other features you have saved in the document summary.

> **Note**
>
> Using the QuickFinder, click on the arrow at the end of the **S**earch For text box and choose **D**ocument Components from the pop-up list that displays. You can now choose to search in the **S**ummary Only or specify some or all of the Summary F**i**elds to search for keywords, an author's name, or case number. Refer to Chapter 28, "Advanced File Management," for more information on conducting searches using the QuickFinder.

Using the text boxes in the Document Summary dialog box, create a document summary by following these steps:

1. Choose **F**ile, Document Summar**y** to open the Document Summary dialog box.

2. Type the information you want included in the text boxes.
3. Choose OK or press Enter to save the summary and return to your document.

Tip

To check the spelling of an entry, click on the background of the text box containing the entry to display the QuickMenu, and choose Speller.

Creating a Summary on Save/Exit

You can have WordPerfect prompt you to fill in the document summary each time you save or exit your document. The program then displays the Document Summary dialog box for you to fill in, although you can choose Cancel to skip doing so. The summary box continues to display each time you save or exit until you fill it in.

To be prompted to complete the summary, follow these steps:

1. Choose **E**dit, Pr**e**ferences, **S**ummary to open the Document Summary Preferences dialog box.

2. Choose **C**reate Summary on Save/Exit to place an X in the adjacent check box.
3. Choose OK or press Enter; then choose Close to return to your document.

If you decide you no longer want document summaries, follow the same steps, choosing **C**reate Summary on Save/Exit to turn the feature off.

Using Document Summary Options

Several options are available that delete, save, or extract information for you, or print the summary. These options are found on the menu displayed by choosing the **O**ptions button from the Document Summary box.

Tip
If you do not want to create a document summary for every document, yet you create one fairly often, consider adding Document Summary to the Toolbar so you have the option handy, but are not confronted with the dialog box every time you save or exit.

Print Summary

To print the document summary you have created, choose **P**rint Summary.

Delete Summary from Document

The only way to remove a document summary after it is created is to delete it by choosing **D**elete Summary From Document. You cannot restore a summary after you have deleted it; you must create a new summary for that document. If you have chosen to be prompted to complete a summary, the prompt resumes the next time you save or exit.

Extract Information from Document

If you choose **E**xtract Information From Document, WordPerfect performs all the following tasks for you:

- Retrieves into their respective text boxes the Author and Typist entries from the last document summary you saved.
- Retrieves approximately 250 characters of text following the Subject text. WordPerfect searches your document for text that identifies the subject of the document and places the text in the Subject box. The default text for the search is RE:. You can change this text if you use other words in your documents to introduce the subject. (Refer to Chapter 9, "Customizing WordPerfect," for instructions to complete this task.)
- Retrieves approximately 800 characters of text at the beginning of the document into the Abstract box. You may want to edit the text included in the Abstract box, because in a letter, for example, this feature extracts the recipient's name and address, the salutation, and a repeat of the subject with the first words of the letter's body.

Save Summary as New Document

You can save document summaries as separate files by choosing **S**ave Summary As New Document. The regular Save As box appears, prompting you to type in a file name. The saved file contains the text box label and contents for each entry.

If you enter a file name that already exists, an Overwrite/Append dialog box warns that a file of that name already exists. Choose **O**verwrite if you want to replace the existing file; choose **A**ppend if you want to add the text to the end of the existing file. If you choose to append, WordPerfect adds a hard return to the end of the existing file before appending the new text.

Customizing the Document Summary Fields

You may want to include information in document summaries other than the fields provided in the default configuration. To change the fields in the Document Summary dialog box, follow these steps:

1. From the Document Summary dialog box, choose **C**onfigure. The Document Summary Configuration dialog box opens (see fig. 5.22).

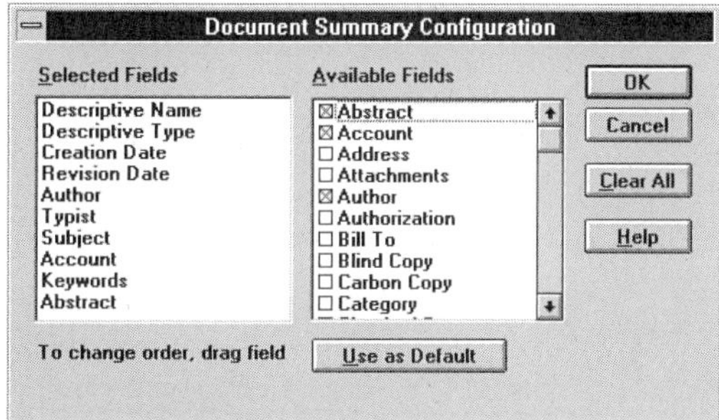

Fig. 5.22
The Document Summary Configuration dialog box enables you to choose the items of information about your documents to track.

2. Scroll through the **A**vailable Fields list box and choose any fields you want to add to the **S**elected Fields list box; an X appears in the adjacent check box. To remove a field, choose it so that the X disappears from the check box.

3. In the **S**elected Fields list box, drag field names to a new location in the list to change the order in which the fields appear in the Document Summary dialog box.

4. If it is easier to create your preferred list of fields from scratch, choose **C**lear All to deselect all fields, leaving the **S**elected Fields list box empty.

5. Choose OK to return to the Document Summary dialog box.

▶ See "Customizing Document Summaries," p. 337

▶ See "Using Quick-Finder To Search for Files," p. 967

The changes you make using **S**elected Fields apply to the summary for the current document. Choose **U**se as Default if you want to use your design for all future document summaries.

From Here...

This chapter focused on a number of WordPerfect features that provide the kind of layout details that are usually available only from professional typesetters. You have learned how to keep text together on a page in a variety of ways, how to set margins, center text on a page, and select paper sizes and types.

You have also learned how to enhance your document by designing, creating, and editing headers and footers and by numbering pages in simple and complex multipart documents.

Finally, this chapter explained the benefits of creating a database of document summaries, and you learned about the kinds of information that can be included in those summaries.

For information relating to the features in this chapter, consider reviewing these chapters:

- Chapter 8, "Basic Output: Printing, Faxing, and E-Mail," shows you how to choose and configure printers for specific jobs, set printer fonts and print selected pages and document summaries.

- Chapter 10, "Using Styles," teaches you how to create styles you can use to quickly format documents and help standardize the appearance of your work.

- Chapter 27, "Working with Large and Multi-Part Documents," describes how to include page numbering, headers and footers, and other document formatting in complex documents.

Chapter 6

Using Writing Tools

by Laura Acklen

Writing thoughtful and original material is enough of a challenge without having to worry about incorrect spelling or grammar. Thanks to WordPerfect, you no longer need to juggle a dictionary, thesaurus, and grammatical style book while you type at the keyboard. WordPerfect has these three tools (along with a few other useful features) built into the program to increase your efficiency and accuracy when you write.

WordPerfect's Spell Check points out misspelled words, duplicate words, and irregular capitalization. The Thesaurus provides lists of synonyms and antonyms from which you can select replacements for frequently used words. Grammatik proofreads your document for grammatical accuracy and offers suggestions for improving the readability of the material. Although these three useful tools can find many typos and grammatical errors, they do not replace proofreading. After you use these tools, always review your writing carefully to catch any missed errors.

WordPerfect's other helpful writing tools include Document Information, Languages, QuickCorrect, SmartQuotes, Comments, Hidden Text, Abbreviations, and Insert File Name. Document Information provides statistics about your document, such as the number and average length of words and sentences. The Language feature is used to indicate different languages being used in a document. QuickCorrect automatically replaces spelling errors and typos while you type. The SmartQuotes feature replaces the regular single and double straight quotes with typeset-quality paired quotes. You can use Comments in a document to annotate certain passages without printing or interfering with pagination. You can use Hidden Text in a document and then turn the display of that text on and off. Abbreviations can replace frequently used phrases or complex words; you later can expand the abbreviated words into their full and proper form. Finally, Insert File Name enables you to insert the document file name anywhere in the document, including headers and footers, for documentation purposes. Your printed documents then carry a reminder of the file name under which they are stored for your future reference.

In this chapter, you learn how to:

- Use Spell Check
- Expand Spell Check's capabilities
- Use Grammatik
- Use QuickCorrect to correct your typing errors
- Use SmartQuotes to replace regular quotation marks with typeset-quality quotation marks
- Compile a list of statistics about the document with Document Information
- Use the Language feature
- Use Document Comments
- Insert Hidden Text
- Use Abbreviations for complex or frequently used phrases
- Use Insert File Name

If you want to experiment with the writing tools and you don't have any text to work with, type in the following text, complete with the spelling errors and bad grammar:

> **Thank you so very much for your kind lettr about you stay with us at the Kalamar Inn from JUly 3rd thrugh July 13th. I hope you don't mind, but I possted the lettr in the locker room so the the other staff members could see it. YOur praise is very much apprecated from everyone here and we are all very happy that you enjoyed you're stay. THe entire staff looks forward to your return naxt yeare.**

Using Spell Check

Even the best spellers and typists can benefit from Spell Check's capability to locate typos, misspellings, and duplicate words. The longer the document you are typing, the greater are your chances of making mistakes.

You can use two different types of dictionaries with WordPerfect: main and supplementary. Spell Check's own *main* dictionary, which is included with the program, contains over 100,000 words. Additional language modules available from WordPerfect and other industry-specific dictionaries (such as legal, medical, or scientific) can be purchased and used with the Spell Check main dictionary to provide the most accurate spell check possible. You can chain up to nine WordPerfect-compatible main dictionaries with Spell Check's main dictionary to spell check a document.

You use *supplementary* dictionaries in conjunction with the main dictionaries. There are two supplementary dictionaries included with the Spell Check program: the Document Dictionary and the default dictionary, called WTSPELUS.SUP on a stand-alone system; and on a network, WTXXXXXX.SUP where XXXXXX represents the user initials and the language code. The Document Dictionary affects only the document to which it is attached; WordPerfect saves this dictionary with the document and the dictionary does not affect any other document. Within the Document Dictionary, for example, you can add specific terms found in a given document so Spell Check doesn't stop on those words.

The default supplemental dictionary, on the other hand, affects all documents. For example, you may add your company name, company address, client names and addresses, and so on. You can use up to eight characters to name new supplementary dictionaries (WordPerfect suggests using a SUP extension). Up to ten supplementary dictionaries can be used together with the main dictionaries to spell check a document.

Tip

You can use the QuickMenu to bring up the Spell Checker dialog box. Point in the document editing window and click the right mouse button to display the QuickMenu. Choose Spell Check. Or, if you prefer, you can press Ctrl+F1 to begin Spell Check.

Starting Spell Check

Before you start Spell Check, save your document. Because Spell Check is a separate Windows program, WordPerfect runs Spell Check for you and, when Spell Check has finished, it switches back to the document. During this operation, the computer is very vulnerable to system problems. Develop the habit of saving your work before switching to other programs, such as Spell Check, Thesaurus, or the QuickFinder File Indexer program.

To start Spell Check and spell check the on-screen document, click the Spell Check button on the Toolbar or choose **T**ools, **S**pell Check. The Spell Checker dialog box appears (see fig. 6.1) and Spell Check starts proofing the document for mistakes. At its default setting, Spell Check runs through the entire document. Other options for this setting are covered in the later section "Customizing Spell Check."

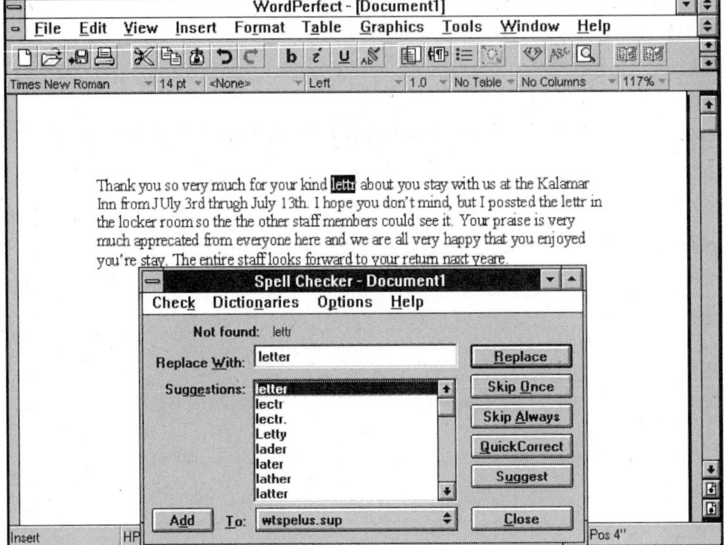

Fig. 6.1
A misspelled word can be replaced with one of the suggested replacement words or manually edited to correct the spelling.

Spell Checking the Document

Spell Check begins spell checking the document when you open the Spell Checker dialog box. The Spell Check program compares each word in your document with the words in the main and supplemental dictionaries. When the program finds a word that doesn't match an entry in the dictionaries, Spell Check stops, highlights the word, and gives several options to handle the word. When you are finished with that word, Spell Check resumes checking the document.

Note

You can minimize, rather than close, Spell Check by clicking the Minimize button (the downward-pointing triangle at the top right-hand corner) in the Spell Checker dialog box. This capability offers three advantages: Spell Check is available faster because the program is already loaded; you don't have to reset any of the options you specified; if you told Spell Check to make certain replacements (for example, to replace the misspelled word *lettr* with *letter*), Spell Check remembers and performs those replacements automatically during subsequent spell checks.

Using Suggested Replacement Words

When Spell Check stops on a word that is not in the dictionaries, it highlights the word and searches the dictionaries for similar words. Spell Check then offers these words as suggested replacements for the misspelled word. If you choose one of the suggested words, WordPerfect performs the replacement and resumes spell checking the document.

In the sample text, Spell Check stops on the word *lettr*, as shown in figure 6.1. Spell Check highlights the word on-screen. A `Not Found` message appears at the top of the Spell Checker dialog box with the questionable word displayed beside it. A list of suggested words appears in the Suggestions list box.

To replace the misspelled word, select the word (which moves the word into the Replace **W**ith text box), and choose **R**eplace. For the sample text, *letter* is the first suggestion in the list and is already selected, so choose the **R**eplace option to replace *lettr* with *letter* in the text. Notice that as you continue to spell check the document, Spell Check automatically corrects the second occurrence of *lettr* (in the second sentence). This is the Auto Replace feature, which is turned on by default. For more information about Auto Replace, see the section titled "Customizing Spell Check" later in this section.

Tip
If you prefer, you can double-click a suggested word to use it as a replacement.

Handling Correctly Spelled Words

Although Spell Check's dictionary is extensive, it is not exhaustive. The dictionary does not include all the surnames, street names, and technical jargon, for example, that you may use in a document. WordPerfect's dictionary does include many common proper names and common terms from various professions. The names Heather and Benjamin are in the dictionary, for example, but the name Maia isn't.

In the sample text, Spell Check stops on the word *Kalamar*, which is spelled correctly, and gives you several options. You can choose Skip **O**nce to tell WordPerfect to skip the word this time but to stop on future occurrences of the word. If you want the program to skip all future occurrences of the word, choose Skip **A**lways. WordPerfect saves the word in a temporary area, and Spell Check does not stop on the word again in this spell checking session. This temporary area is erased when Spell Check is closed, so if you start Spell Check again and spell check the document, Spell Check stops on the word. In the sample text, choose Skip **A**lways to skip the word *Kalamar*, even if it appears again in the document.

If you frequently use a correctly spelled word that is not included in the WordPerfect main dictionary, you can add the word to one of the supplementary dictionaries. For instructions on making this addition, see the sections "Adding Words to the Document Dictionary" and "Adding Words to a Supplementary Dictionary" later in this chapter.

Correcting Irregular Capitalization

In addition to checking for the correct spelling of a word, the Spell Check program also checks for irregular capitalization. This type of error occurs when the upper-and lowercase letters are combined in a way that doesn't make sense to Spell Check. The words *THe* and *REaDy*, for example, have irregular capitalization. This type of error can occur if you don't release the Shift key fast enough after capitalizing the first letter of a word.

In the sample text, Spell Check stops on the word `JUly`, and displays the message `Capitalization` in the Spell Checker dialog box, as shown in figure 6.2.

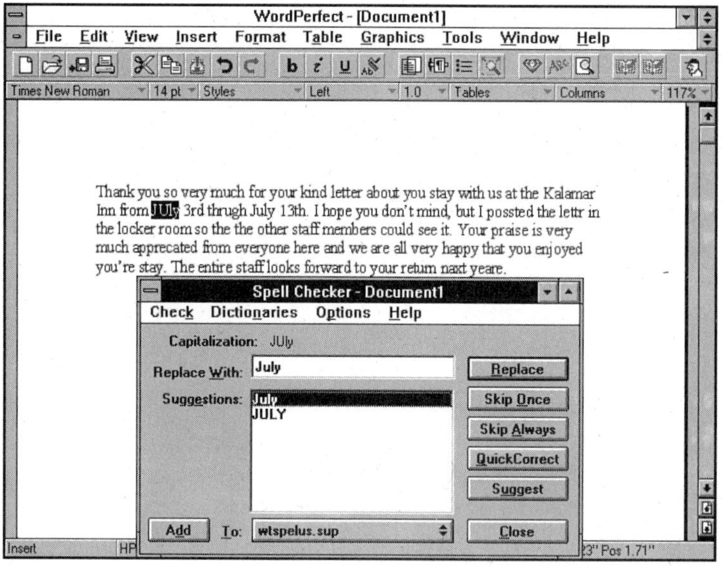

Fig. 6.2
If the word is in a WordPerfect dictionary, Spell Check displays the word in upper-, lower-, and mixed-case in the Suggestions box and enables you to select one of the suggestions.

Tip
If the word is not in the dictionary, you must manually type the replacement in the Replace **W**ith text box, and choose **R**eplace.

Sometimes irregular capitalization is necessary and correct. For example, McDonald and USAir are all words with correct, though irregular, capitalization. Choose Skip **O**nce or Skip **A**lways as necessary.

The word in the sample text, *JUly*, is in the main dictionary, so Spell Check offers *July* and *JULY* as suggestions. July is first in the list, so it is already selected and present in the Replace **W**ith text box. Choose **R**eplace to replace the incorrectly capitalized word with the correctly capitalized word.

Skipping Words with Numbers

In certain types of documents, word and number combinations are common (for example, W4 form or 10-dollar bill). Spell Check stops on such words, because they rarely are included in the program's dictionaries. You can choose Skip **O**nce or Skip **A**lways, depending on your preference, or you can turn off the option to check words with numbers by choosing Words with **N**umbers in the O**p**tions menu.

> **Caution**
>
> Be sure to proofread the document carefully after the spell check if you have Spell Check ignore words with numbers, because Spell Check cannot catch typos in those words.

Eliminating Double Words

Another; important task Spell Check performs is checking your document for duplicate words. A common duplication that proofreaders often miss is *the the*—the proofreader sees the first *the*, but not the second *the*. Spell Check does not delete the second occurrence of a word automatically, because in some phrases duplicate words are grammatically correct.

When Spell Check finds duplicate words, it stops, highlights both words in the document, and displays the message `Duplicate words` in the Spell Checker dialog box (see fig. 6.3). A single occurrence of the word appears in the Sug**ge**stions window and in the Replace **W**ith text box. To delete the second occurrence of the word, choose **R**eplace; otherwise, choose Skip **O**nce or Skip **A**lways. In the sample text, choose **R**eplace to correct the duplicate words.

Editing a Misspelled Word

Sometimes Spell Check stops on a word but does not offer any suggested replacements. This situation occurs if the word is not in the dictionaries, or if the word is so poorly spelled that Spell Check cannot offer any suggestions. When Spell Check stops on such a word, you can correct the spelling in one of two ways:

- Type the correctly spelled word in the Replace **W**ith text box and choose **R**eplace.
- Click the mouse pointer on the misspelled word in the document. Edit the word using the standard editing techniques. After correcting the word, click the Spell Check window (to make it active again) and

choose **R**esume. Spell Check rechecks the edited word for accuracy; if the word still isn't found in the dictionaries, Spell Check stops and highlights the word again. When the word has been replaced with a word found in the dictionaries, or has been added to a supplemental dictionary, Spell Check resumes spell checking the document.

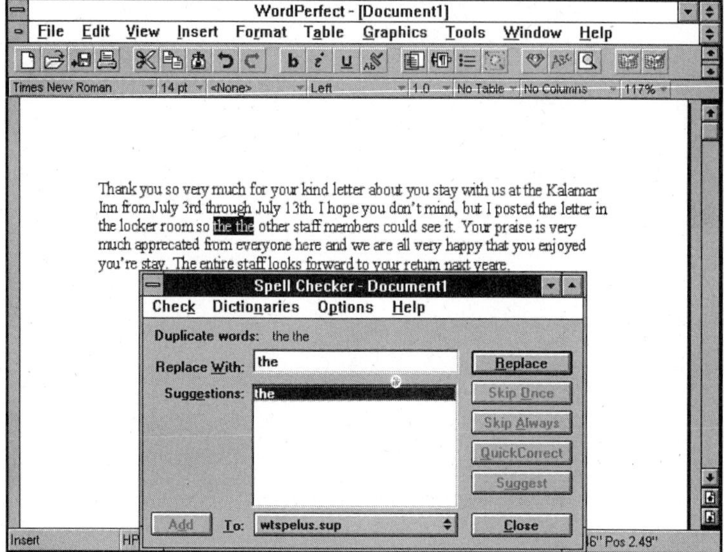

Fig. 6.3
Although Spell Check makes it easy to correct duplicate words, you should do so with caution. In some cases, duplicate words are necessary and grammatically correct.

> **Note**
>
> If you edit a word using either of the above methods, Spell Check automatically replaces any subsequent occurrences of the misspelled word with your chosen replacement.

Adding Words to a Supplementary Dictionary

Correctly spelled words can be added to the supplemental dictionaries with the A**d**d option. Subsequent spell checks will not stop on the added words unless they are spelled incorrectly. The dictionary displayed in the **T**o pop-up list is the one to which words are added during a spell check.

The default supplemental dictionary file is created when the program is installed. On a stand-alone system, the file name is WTSPELUS.SUP; on a network, the file name includes user initials or some other identifier to differentiate it from other users' supplemental dictionary files, and the language code.

To add words to the default dictionary, choose A**d**d when Spell Check stops on a word. For example, you can add your name, company name, company address, and other terms that might be common to your documents.

WordPerfect enables you to create separate supplementary dictionaries for different projects. There is no limit to the number of supplemental dictionaries you can create. Up to ten supplemental dictionaries can be linked to spell check a given document. To add words to another supplemental dictionary, select the dictionary in the **T**o pop-up list. For more information on using supplemental dictionaries, see the later section, "Creating and Editing Supplementary Dictionaries."

Adding Words to the Document Dictionary

The Document Dictionary is a supplemental dictionary that is automatically attached to every document. This dictionary is saved as a part of the document, and is therefore used only with that document. You should add those words that are only found in this document—for example, technical terms, jargon, or abbreviations.

Words can be edited and deleted from the Document Dictionary as necessary. For more information on using supplementary dictionaries, see the later section, "Creating and Editing Supplementary Dictionaries."

Caution

If you insert a file into a document, that file's Document Dictionary file is lost. The Document Dictionary file for the original document remains in effect.

Adding Words to the QuickCorrect Dictionary

The QuickCorrect dictionary is used to automatically correct typos and spelling errors while you type. If you wish, you can add a misspelled word and the correct spelling to the QuickCorrect dictionary while running Spell Check. To add a misspelled word and the correct spelling, wait until Spell Check stops on the misspelled word, and then place the correct spelling in the Replace **W**ith text box and choose **Q**uickCorrect. The next time you type the misspelled word, QuickCorrect locates the word in the QuickCorrect dictionary and substitutes the correctly spelled word automatically. To turn off this option, see the section titled "Customizing Spell Check" later in this section. For more information on the QuickCorrect feature, see the section "Using QuickCorrect" later in the chapter.

Finishing the Spell Check

When Spell Check finishes checking the specified text, a Spell Checker message dialog box appears with the message `Spell check completed. Close Spell Checker?` Choose **Y**es to close Spell Check and return to your document. If you want to be able to quickly access Spell Check for another function, choose **N**o.

Tip
Always save your document after running Spell Check to save any changes you made during the spell checking process.

To cancel a spell check before completion, press Esc or choose **C**lose. If you press Esc, you cancel the spell check, but the Spell Checker dialog box remains open. You can make any necessary changes to the Spell Check options, then resume the Spell Check. If you choose **C**lose, the Spell Check program closes, and the dialog box disappears from the screen.

Looking Up a Word

As you type a document, you can check the spelling of a word by looking it up in Spell Check. You can type the word phonetically (the way it sounds), or you can type the letters you know are right and use wild cards for the unknown letters.

To look up a word in Spell Check, begin typing the word in the Replace **W**ith text box. As you type, Spell Check displays a list of possibilities. If you type the phonetic spelling of a word in the Replace **W**ith text box and then choose S**u**ggest, Spell Check performs a phonetic lookup, and then displays a list of suggestions, as shown in figure 6.4.

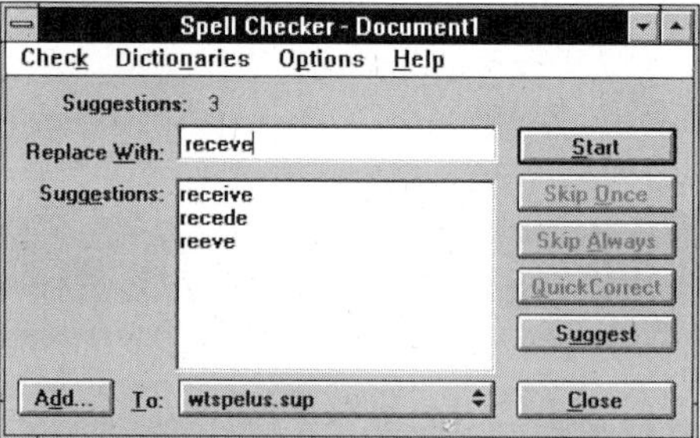

Fig. 6.4
A phonetic lookup on the text "receve" locates the correct spelling of the word receive.

> **Note**
>
> If you are running Spell Check as a stand-alone Windows program outside of WordPerfect, the Replace **W**ith option is changed to the **W**ord option; further, some of the menu options are dimmed to indicate the options are unavailable.

As you type the word in question, you can use wild-card characters for the letters you are unsure of. The asterisk (*) wild-card character represents an unspecified number of characters in a word; for example, if you type **water***, Spell Check suggests *water, water-repellant, water-resistant, waterbed,* and so on. A question mark (?) wild-card character represents a single character in a word; for example, typing **c?p** returns *C.P.A., C.P.R.,* and *cap* (see fig. 6.5). Choosing S**u**ggest narrows down the list even further. The wild-card characters are helpful if you know only portions of the word you need to look up.

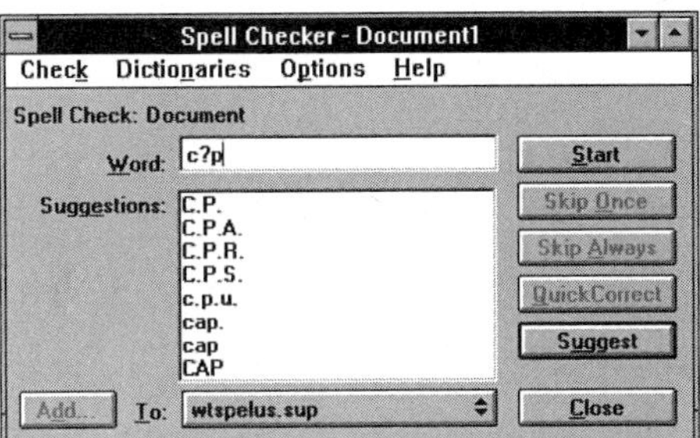

Fig. 6.5
You can use either or both types of wild cards in a word pattern to broaden the list of words.

> **Note**
>
> After looking up suggested words, Spell Check displays the number of suggestions at the top of the dialog box.

Customizing Spell Check

Before starting a spell check, you can change some of Spell Check's options to customize Spell Check for the session. You can specify what portion of the document is to be checked, which dictionaries Spell Check is to use, and what types of errors you want Spell Check to find. This section describes how to set the options to meet your needs.

Specifying What to Check

Spell Check enables you to run a spell check on a portion of a document; this feature saves time when you don't need to check the entire document. After you start Spell Check, you can specify which portion of the document you want to check. The Check menu in the Spell Checker dialog box has a list of nine different areas that you can specify within a document. By default, this option is set to Document, meaning Spell Check checks the entire document. If you have selected a block of text, Spell Check automatically switches to the Selected Text setting.

To specify the portion of the document to be spell checked, choose Chec**k**. A menu appears with your choices, as shown in figure 6.6.

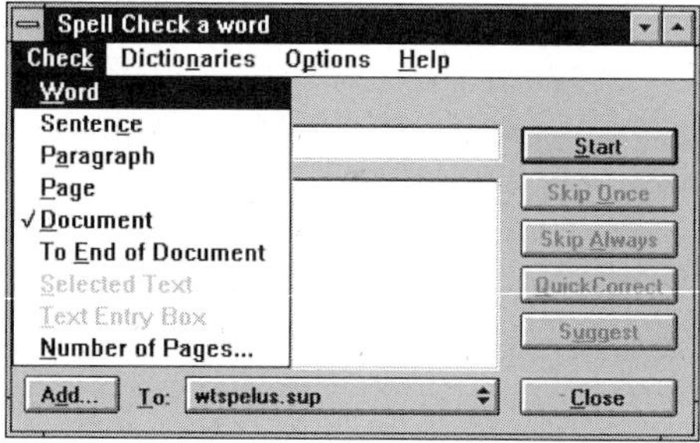

Fig. 6.6 Spell Check can be configured to spell check a specific portion of the document instead of spell checking the entire document.

The options on the Chec**k** menu provide a great deal of flexibility in determining the extent of your document's spell check. The options are as follows:

- ***W**ord.* Checks the word where the insertion point is located.
- *Senten**c**e.* Checks the sentence where the insertion point is located.
- *P**a**ragraph.* Checks the paragraph where the insertion point is located.
- ***P**age.* Checks the current page.
- ***D**ocument.* Checks the entire document and substructures, including headers, footers, captions, and so on. (This is the default Chec**k** menu setting.)
- *To **E**nd of Document.* Checks from the insertion point forward to the end of the document.
- ***S**elected Text.* Checks the selected (highlighted) text.
- ***T**ext Entry Box.* Checks text in the text entry field of a dialog box. For example, you can use this option to check the spelling of words you have entered as text for a Comment or the Abstract field in the Document Summary dialog box. See the later section, "Using Document Comments," for more information.
- ***N**umber of Pages.* Checks a specified number of pages from the current page forward.

Selecting Different Dictionaries

The Dictio**n**aries menu item gives you access to the Main Dictionaries and Supplementary Dictionaries dialog boxes. The Main Dictionaries dialog box is used to specify which main dictionary files you want to use with Spell Check. The Supplemental Dictionaries dialog box is used to create, add, edit, and delete supplemental dictionary files. See the next section, "Working with Main and Supplementary Dictionaries," for more information.

You can customize Spell Check with the selections on the O**p**tions menu. Your changes remain in effect until you close Spell Check. Choose O**p**tions to display the menu of options, as shown in figure 6.7.

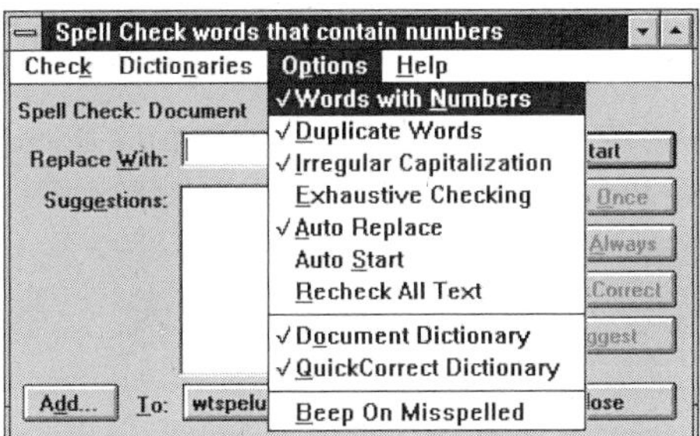

Fig. 6.7
You can turn off certain elements in Spell Check and change other settings in the Options menu.

In the O**p**tions menu, the items with a check mark next to them are currently selected (turned on). You can turn a selection off (and back on again) by choosing the item. You use the options as follows:

- If the Words with **N**umbers option is selected, Spell Check stops on all words that contain numbers and flags them as errors. If your document contains a lot of word/number combinations, you may want to turn off this option.

- The **D**uplicate Words option looks for two duplicate words in sequence and suggests that you replace them with a single occurrence of the word.

- The **I**rregular Capitalization option looks for capital letters inside a lowercase word and alerts you to the error.

- If your document is in a language other than English-US, English-UK, or Canadian-English, you can turn on and off **E**xhaustive Checking. Exhaustive Checking tells Spell Check to search for all possible suggestions in languages where limited suggestions are usually displayed.

- The **A**uto Replace option automatically makes any replacements you define in the supplementary dictionaries. Further, if you replace a misspelled word during the spell check, Spell Check automatically replaces other occurrences of the misspelled word with your replacement word.
- The Auto **S**tart option automatically starts Spell Check when you activate Spell Check.
- When you spell check only a portion of a document, Spell Check keeps track of which sections have been checked and which have not, so the next time you run Spell Check, only the unchecked areas will be spell checked. The **R**echeck All Text option checks the entire document each time you run Spell Check, regardless of what was checked in the previous session.
- You can disable the Document Dictionary for a document by choosing D**o**cument Dictionary. The Document Dictionary is a supplementary dictionary that is saved with a particular document, so it only affects that document.
- The **Q**uickCorrect Dictionary option will disable the QuickCorrect dictionary.
- If you want Spell Check to beep at you when it finds a spelling error, choose **B**eep On Misspelled.

Working with Main and Supplementary Dictionaries

As stated earlier, you use two types of dictionaries in WordPerfect: main and supplementary. Spell Check includes a main dictionary and two supplementary dictionaries. Additional main dictionaries can be purchased and used with Spell Check's main dictionary. An unlimited number of supplemental dictionaries can be created and used in conjunction with the main dictionaries. Main dictionaries must be created and edited *outside* of the WordPerfect program; supplemental dictionaries are created and edited from *within* the WordPerfect program.

Note

A SPELL utility program is available from WordPerfect that enables you to edit Spell Check's main dictionary file. You can locate and remove words that you never use to speed up spell checking. You also can create new main dictionaries and add words to those dictionaries. The SPELL utility is not included with WordPerfect 6.1 for Windows, but you can purchase the utility from WordPerfect Corporation.

Using Additional Main Dictionaries

The Spell Check main dictionary (named WT60EN.MOR for the English-U.S. version) contains over 100,000 common words. A variety of industry-specific dictionaries (such as legal, medical, and pharmaceutical) and non-English language dictionaries are available for use with WordPerfect's Spell Check program. When you install a new main dictionary, you can insert the name of the file on the Main Dictionary list. This action defines a new dictionary for use with the Spell Check's main dictionary, so Spell Check uses the two together. The process of defining and using a new dictionary in conjunction with the existing Spell Check main dictionary is called *chaining*. You can chain up to ten main dictionaries to spell check a document.

To add a main dictionary to the list, follow these steps:

1. From the Spell Checker dialog box, choose Dictio**n**aries.

2. Choose **M**ain, **A**dd to display the Select Main Dictionary dialog box, as shown in figure 6.8.

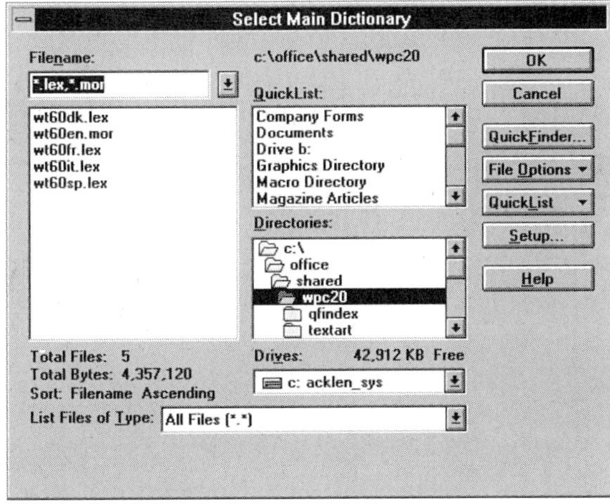

Fig. 6.8
Main dictionaries already contain a collection of words and must be created and edited outside of the WordPerfect program. Use the Select Main Dictionary dialog box to browse for and select another main dictionary file.

3. You can browse through the Dri**v**es, **D**irectories, and File**n**ame lists to locate the additional main dictionary file.

4. Select the dictionary file and choose OK.

After you close the Select Main Dictionary dialog box, the name of the new dictionary file you selected appears in the Dictionaries in Search Order list box. The order of the dictionaries in the list (or chain) determines the order in which Spell Check uses them during a spell check. You can delete and reinsert file names in the list to change the order in which Spell Check uses the files. When you delete a dictionary name from the chain, the file itself is not deleted, only the name on the list.

Note

You can greatly reduce the time it takes to spell check a document by optimizing the order of the dictionary files. During a spell check, the Spell Check program compares each word in the document with the words in the dictionary files associated with the document.

When Spell Check locates the word in a dictionary file, it stops searching for that word and moves on to the next one. Therefore, you should place the dictionary file that contains the words you use the most at the top of the list and the file that contains words you use the least at the bottom of the list.

Creating and Editing Supplementary Dictionaries

You can create additional supplementary dictionaries and add them to the list of supplementary dictionary files in the **T**o pop-up list. During a spell check, you can add words to any of the supplemental dictionaries on the list. In addition to adding words to skip, you can also set up automatic replacements and suggested alternatives for certain words.

Creating New Supplemental Dictionaries

There is no limit (other than disk space) to the number of supplemental dictionaries you can create for your projects. You can chain up to ten supplemental dictionaries (including the Document Dictionary) to spell check a document.

To create a new supplementary dictionary file, follow these steps:

1. Choose Dictio**n**aries from the Spell Checker dialog box.
2. Choose **S**upplementary, C**r**eate. The Select/Create Supplementary Dictionary dialog box appears, as shown in figure 6.9.
3. The insertion point is in the File**n**ame text box where you can type a name for the new supplementary dictionary file. You can use a maximum of eight characters for the name.

Note

WordPerfect suggests using a SUP extension to identify the file as a supplemental dictionary file.

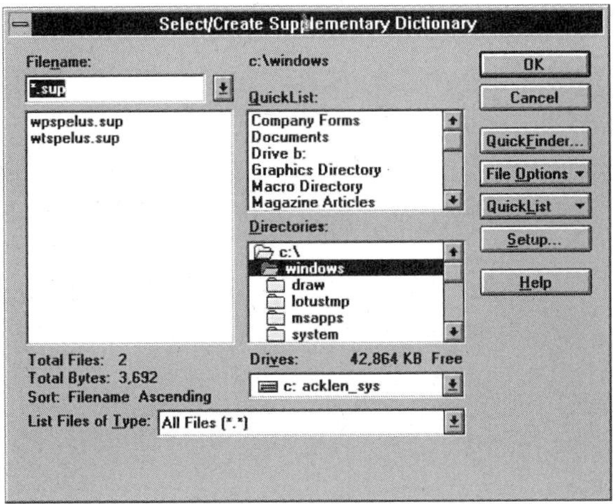

Fig. 6.9
A new supplemental dictionary must be created and named before you can begin adding words to it.

4. If the dictionary file you specify has not been created yet, Spell Check displays a message box stating the supplementary dictionary file is not found and asks if you want to create it.

5. Choose **Y**es to create the new supplementary dictionary.

   The name of the new dictionary file now appears in the Dictionaries in Search **O**rder list box. The order of the dictionaries in the list (or chain) determines the order in which Spell Check uses them during a spell check. You can delete and reinsert file names in the list to change the order in which Spell Check uses the files. When you delete a dictionary name from the chain, the file itself is not deleted—only the name on the list.

6. Choose **C**lose to exit the Supplemental Dictionary dialog box and return to Spell Check.

◀ See "Selecting Text," p. 103

◀ See "Using Hyphenation," p. 152

◀ See "Using Document Summaries," p. 210

After you close the Select/Create Supplementary Dictionary dialog box, the new supplementary dictionary appears on the **T**o pop-up list. Select **T**o to open the pop-up list where you can select the new supplemental dictionary. You can now add words to the new dictionary during a spell check by choosing A**d**d. When the dictionary is used again, Spell Check will not stop on the words you added unless they are misspelled in the document.

Editing Supplemental Dictionaries

You can edit the supplementary dictionaries and add additional words to skip. You can define words that you want Spell Check to use for automatic replacements for other words within the document. Perhaps you incorrectly type **hte**, for example, instead of **the**; Spell Check can refer to the supplementary dictionary and automatically correct this error whenever it encounters the misspelling in your document. In addition, you can assign alternative words for certain words that may be found in the document. For example, firms can establish standards for terminology in their documentation. These standard terms can be listed as alternatives to other terms that might be used. An explanation can be included to explain why the standard terms should be used.

Follow these steps to edit a supplemental dictionary file:

1. Choose Dictio**n**aries from the Spell Checker dialog box.
2. Choose **S**upplementary, highlight a dictionary file; then choose **E**dit. Choose **A**dd to display the Add Word/Phrase dialog box (see fig. 6.10).

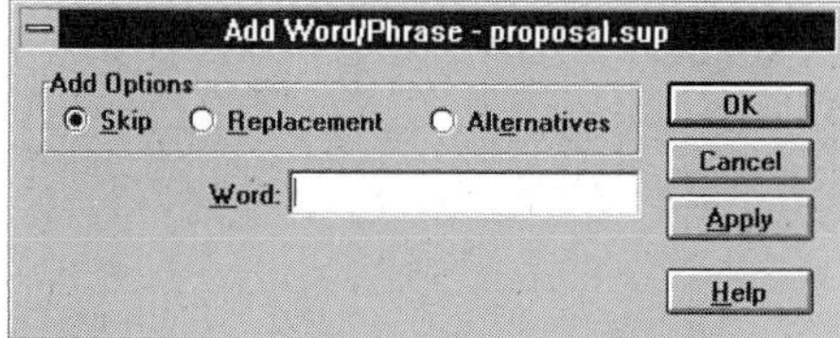

Fig. 6.10
You can design the supplemental dictionary files to do some of your spell checking without any user intervention.

The Add Word/Phrase dialog box offers the following options:

- To add words that you want to skip (unless the word is spelled incorrectly), choose **S**kip and type the word in the **W**ord text box.
- To add words to automatically replace other words, choose **R**eplacement. The **W**ord text box changes to the Key **W**ord text box, and the Rep**l**acement text box is added (see fig. 6.11). Type the word to replace in the Key **W**ord text box. Type the replacement word in the Rep**l**acement text box.

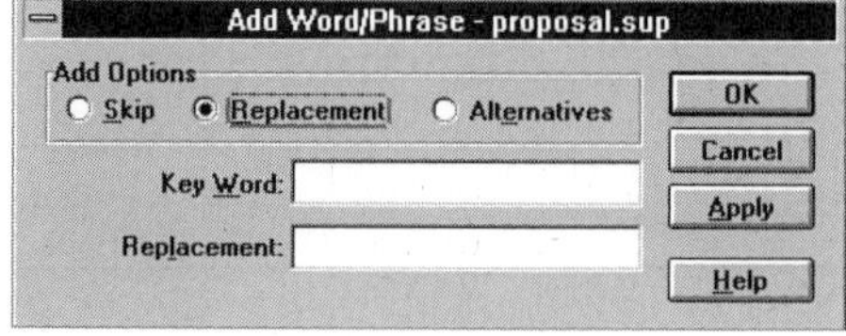

Fig. 6.11
If you habitually misspell certain words, you can specify those words and the correctly spelled replacements in the supplemental dictionary.

- To add a list of alternative words for a particular word, choose Alter**n**atives. The Add Word/Phrase dialog box expands to include an A**l**ternative, a Lis**t** of Alternatives, and a Co**m**ment text box (see fig. 6.12). Type the word for which you want to offer alternatives in the Key **W**ord text box. Type the primary alternative word in the A**l**ternative text box. If you want to suggest more than one alternative, type the alternatives in the Lis**t** of Alternatives. If you like, you can add a comment to display along with the alternative words; to do so, type the comment in the Co**m**ment text box.

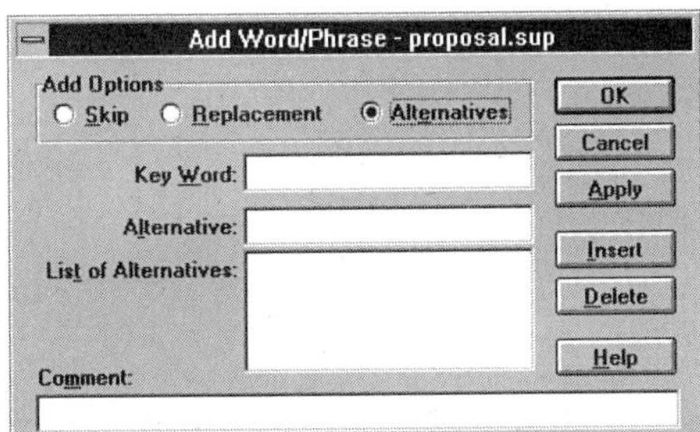

Fig. 6.12
Companies can use the Alternatives option to enforce standards for terms used in documentation—for example, discouraging the use of sexist terms in personnel policy and procedure manuals.

Troubleshooting

I accidentally added a misspelled word to my supplementary dictionary.

All of the supplementary dictionaries can be edited from within the WordPerfect program. The supplementary dictionaries, including the Document Dictionary, can be edited through the Dictio**n**aries menu. Choose Dictio**n**aries, **S**upplementary, select the dictionary file that contains the misspelled word, and then choose **E**dit. Highlight the misspelled word in the Key **W**ords text box and choose **D**elete. Choose Close three times to return to your document.

I accidentally added a misspelled word to the QuickCorrect dictionary.

Since QuickCorrect is a separate feature, you need to use the QuickCorrect dialog box to delete the misspelled word. Choose **T**ools, **Q**uickCorrect to display the QuickCorrect dialog box. Highlight the misspelled word and choose **D**elete Entry. Choose **C**lose to return to your document.

I have a misspelled word in my document, but the Spell Check program doesn't stop on it.

Believe it or not, it may be a valid word in the dictionary. However, you can have Spell Check suggest replacement words if you select the word, and then start Spell Check. You may have to choose S**u**ggest if you don't see the correct word right away.

Using Grammatik

A spell checker is a useful tool for catching typos and misspelled words, but Spell Check cannot recognize a typo that happens to be a word found in the dictionaries. Spell Check sees no error, for example, if you mistakenly type *their* for *there*, or *trial* instead of *trail*. Grammatik is a built-in grammar checker that checks your document for correct grammar, style, punctuation, and word usage, and thus catches many of the errors that pass by the Spell Check.

Similar to any of the writing tools in this chapter, Grammatik can't replace a human editor. Grammatik does not understand poetic or literary license or the intentional bending of rules to make a point. It cannot listen to a sentence to hear how it sounds. Grammatik doesn't find every error, and may even stop on correct phrases. If you set Grammatik to check a document in the Formal Memo or Letter writing style, for example, Grammatik alerts you to every sentence over 35 words. You may not want (or need) to shorten every sentence over 35 words. Long sentences can be difficult to read and understand, however, so this Grammatik feature offers you the opportunity to shorten the sentences when appropriate. Grammatik points out areas in your writing that you can consider changing to improve readability.

Running Grammatik

Before you start Grammatik, save your document. Therefore, if you decide not to keep any changes made by Grammatik, you have a copy of your original document.

To start Grammatik, click the Grammatik button on the Toolbar or choose **T**ools, **G**rammatik. The Grammatik dialog box appears, as shown in figure 6.13, and Grammatik starts checking the document for errors. By default, Grammatik is set to perform a Quick Check on the entire document for grammar, mechanics, style, and spelling errors with a general writing style of standard formality. Later in this chapter, you learn how to change these settings.

The rules by which Grammatik checks your document are organized into *Rule Classes*. Grammatik recognizes 66 different Rule Classes for the Checking Styles. Rule Classes have been established for grammatical style errors such as Sentence Variety, Passive Voice, Split Infinitive, Double Negative, Incomplete Sentence, Run-On Sentence Ellipsis, Split Words, and Unbalanced Parentheses and Brackets.

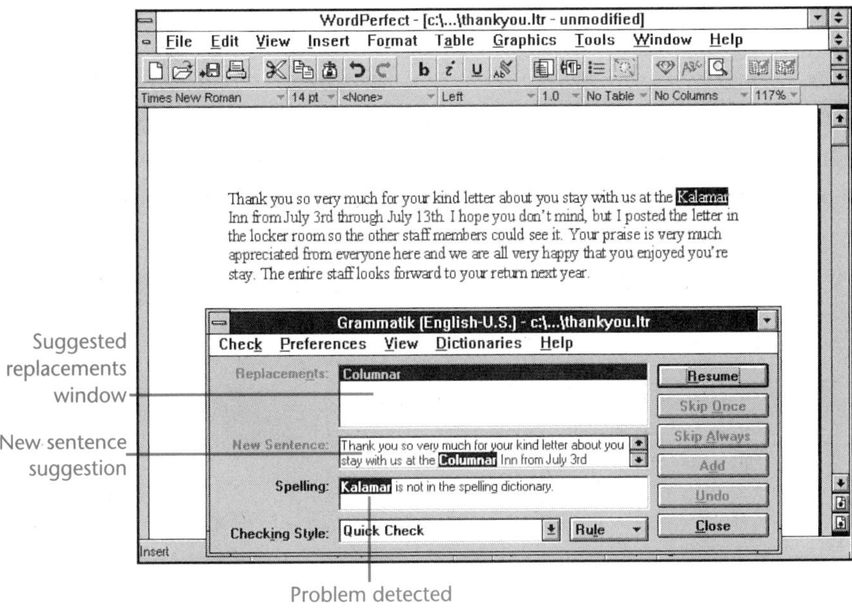

Fig. 6.13
When Grammatik locates a problem in the document, it tells you what type of problem exists and may offer suggestions for correcting the error.

When Grammatik encounters a grammatical error in your document, the program stops and highlights the text in question (see fig. 6.13). In the Grammatik dialog box, the program identifies the Rule Class and offers suggestions for correcting the problem. In some cases, Grammatik suggests replacement words or punctuation marks. You can choose one of the suggested replacements, edit the text to correct a mistake, or skip the problem and continue checking.

Moving Past a Problem

Grammatik follows a strict set of grammatical rules when checking your document for problems. Many good writers, however, often bend grammatical rules to make a point. In addition, Grammatik has its own dictionary, separate from WordPerfect's dictionary. To Grammatik, any word not in the program's dictionary is a misspelled word. In the sample text shown in figure 6.13, Grammatik stops on the word *Kalamar*—the correct spelling of the inn's name—and identifies it as a misspelled word. Since this word is correctly spelled, you don't want to change it. If Grammatik identifies a problem that you don't want to change, you have three options:

- Choose Skip **O**nce to skip the word and go to the next error. Grammatik skips this single occurrence; if Grammatik encounters the word again, it will stop on it.

- Choose Skip **A**lways if you don't want Grammatik to stop on the word again during this session.
- Choose A**d**d to add the word to the Grammatik dictionary.

Editing a Problem

In many cases, to correct a grammatical problem you must edit the document to reword a phrase or to delete extraneous words. For example, Grammatik may advise against using passive voice, in which case, you can revise the phrase to use active voice.

The next problem Grammatik finds in the document is in the date format used in July 3rd and 13th. Take the advice offered by Grammatik and edit the two dates to read `July 3` and `July 13`.

Follow these steps to edit the sample text:

1. Click the highlighted text to move the pointer into the document window.
2. Make your correction. In this case, delete the `rd` and `th` after the dates.
3. Choose **R**esume in the Grammatik dialog box to resume checking the document.

In the sample text, Grammatik stops and highlights the phrase `kind letter` (see fig. 6.14). Grammatik identifies a rule class of Missing Modifier and displays a suggested replacement sentence.

The real problem, however, is a simple typo: `you stay` should have been `your stay`. Because the suggested replacement sentence doesn't work here, you must edit the document to correct the problem. Click the document window and change `you` to `your`, and then click **R**esume to continue the grammar check.

Replacing a Word

Grammatik offers suggested replacements for words and punctuation marks whenever possible. In the sample text shown in figure 6.15, Grammatik stops on the word `you're`, which is used incorrectly in the third sentence. Grammatik identifies the problem as a homonym, describes why the program believes the word is incorrect, and suggests a replacement word. To replace a word (or punctuation mark), select the correct replacement and choose **R**eplace. Since the suggested replacement word is correct in this case, all you have to do is choose **R**eplace.

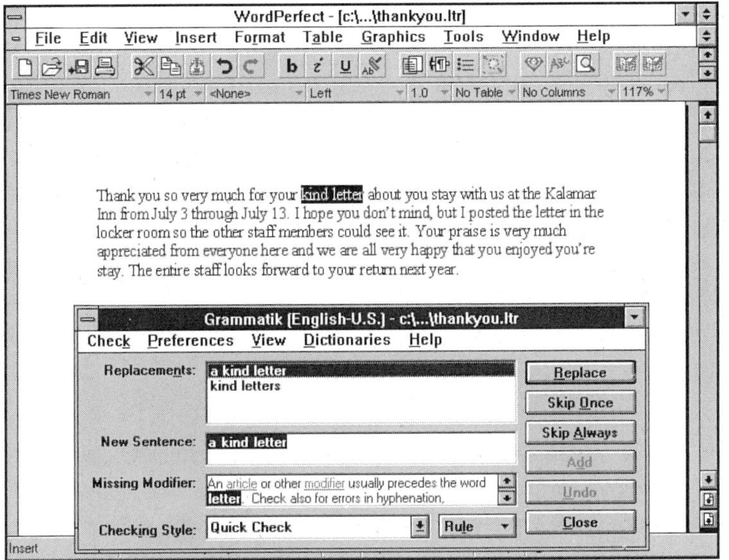

Fig. 6.14
You can choose a suggested replacement and have Grammatik insert the replacement in the document.

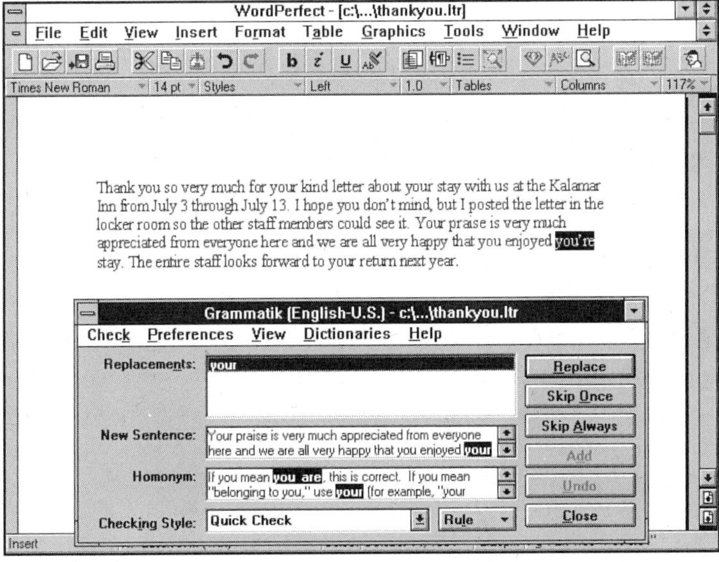

Fig. 6.15
Instead of choosing a replacement word to correct the missing modifier problem, you need to edit the document and change the you to a your.

Using the Undo Option

If you make a correction to a problem and later change your mind, you can use the **U**ndo option to reverse the last action taken by Grammatik. To undo an action on your document, choose **U**ndo. Remember, you can only reverse the very last action taken.

Disabling a Rule Class

If you want to disable checking for a particular rule class, select the Ru**l**e drop-down list and choose **T**urn Off. This change is temporary; it will only affect the current Grammatik session. You can repeat this action to disable as many rule classes as necessary.

Getting Help

Grammatical rules are quite complex, and most of us need explanations and examples to understand them. The Grammatik program has a comprehensive Help system to help you understand the program and to assist you in your writing.

The Grammatik Help system provides explanations and examples for all of the rule classes. If you want more information about the rule class of a problem upon which Grammatik has stopped, move the mouse pointer over the Rule Class name. The mouse pointer changes to a pointer with a large question mark attached. When you see this mouse pointer, click the mouse button to display a help screen on that rule class. Alternatively, you can choose **H**elp from the Ru**l**e drop-down list.

The Help system includes information on the types of problems that Grammatik identifies, explanations and examples of rule classes, advice on improving your writing, a glossary of grammatical terms, and instructions on using Grammatik commands. The Help system also includes an option that displays the parts of speech being used in a document; this information can help you understand the problems that Grammatik identifies.

Customizing Grammatik for the Current Document

Grammatik enables you to change many of its settings to better meet your specific needs. The Chec**k** menu has options that enable you to check only a portion of a document. You can choose to check a sentence, a paragraph, selected text, or all text from the insertion point to the end of the document. These settings only affect the current Grammatik session.

The **P**references menu contains setup options that will affect the current and future Grammatik sessions. The **P**references menu options are as follows:

- ***C**hecking Styles*. Select and edit the ten predefined styles.
- ***E**nvironment.* Select to have Grammatik provide spelling suggestions, show help prompts, prompt before an automatic replace, and start checking immediately.

Working with Writing Styles

Different types of documents must conform to different grammatical rules and require different levels of formality. To accommodate these differences, Grammatik recognizes ten predefined writing styles: Quick Check (the default writing style), Spelling Plus, Very Strict, Formal Memo or Letter, Informal Memo or Letter, Technical or Scientific, Documentation or Speech, Student Composition, Advertising, and Fiction. Each writing style has a preset formality level, which you can change when you edit the writing style.

To edit a writing style, choose **P**references from the Grammatik dialog box. Choose **C**hecking Styles to display the Checking Styles dialog box, as shown in figure 6.16.

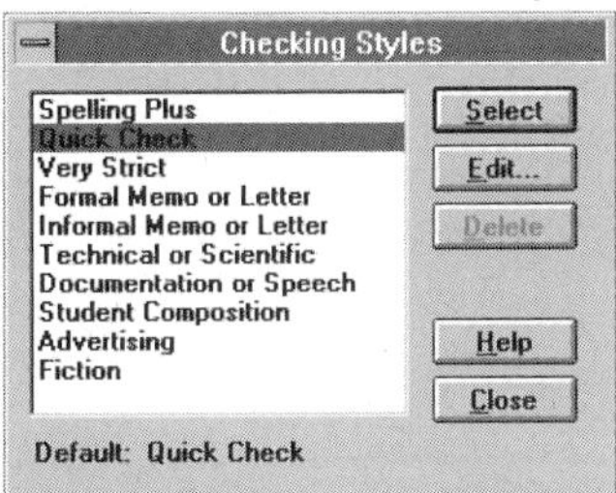

Fig. 6.16
You can select another writing style in the Checking Styles dialog box.

To edit a writing style, select the writing style, and then choose **E**dit to display the Edit Rules dialog box (see fig. 6.17). This dialog box has a list of Rule **C**lasses, a series of threshold settings, three formality levels, and a section where an example of each rule class is displayed. You use Rule **C**lasses check boxes to turn the rule classes on and off (scroll through the list if necessary). The right side of the dialog box is reserved for Maximum Allowed settings. These settings specify what conditions have to be met for Grammatik to identify a particular problem. For example, sentences containing over 99 words are identified as long sentences. You can select and change each of these five settings to accommodate your specific requirements.

If you want to change the formality level for a writing style, choose a formality level of **I**nformal, S**t**andard, or **F**ormal. The S**t**andard Formality Level is adequate for most business correspondence, and a level of Informal might be used for personal letters. The bottom left side of the dialog box is reserved for an example of the selected rule class.

The changes that are made to the writing style can be saved to the selected **C**hecking Style or to a custom checking style. If you opt to save changes to an existing checking style, those changes are permanent. The checking style is shown with an asterisk next to it in the checking style list so you can identify a style that has been modified. Fortunately, you can use the **R**estore option in the Edit Rules dialog box to restore the default settings for a modified style.

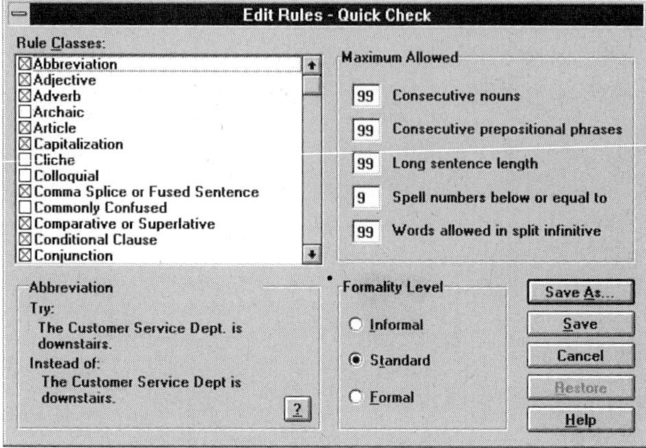

Fig. 6.17
Use the Edit Rules Quickcheck dialog box to modify writing styles.

Getting Statistical Information

Grammatik can compile a list of statistics about your document by running a statistics check. To run a statistics check, choose **V**iew, **S**tatistics. When Grammatik finishes the check, it produces a Basic Counts dialog box with counts and averages (see fig. 6.18). Select **R**eadability to generate a readability score. This information can help you determine the length and complexity of the document. For example, a document with an average sentence length of 25 words is harder to read than one with an average sentence length of 15 words because the sentences are longer and more difficult to follow. Choose **F**lagged to view a list of the potential errors that are found in the document.

Troubleshooting

I made some changes to one of the writing styles, but I can't seem to save the change.

Any of the ten writing styles can be modified, but you must be sure you choose **S**ave or Save **A**s before you exit the dialog box. If you choose **S**ave, the changes will be saved to the selected writing style. If you choose Save **A**s, you can specify another name for the writing style. A modified writing style will be shown with an asterisk (*) next to it in the Checking Styles dialog box.

Grammatik always stops on my company name and flags it as a spelling error. How can I tell Grammatik that the name is spelled correctly so it won't stop on it again?

Just as you can in Spell Check, you can add correctly spelled words to the Grammatik dictionary so Grammatik will no longer flag the word as a spelling error (unless, of course, the word is misspelled). Choose A**d**d the next time Grammatik stops on your company name to add it to the dictionary.

Grammatik is constantly flagging long sentences in my documents. Is there any way I can change this?

Each Checking Style has its own threshold settings in the Maximum Allowed section of the Edit Rules dialog box. You can increase the number of words in the Long Sentence Length (maximum of 99) text box to change the threshold setting for long sentences.

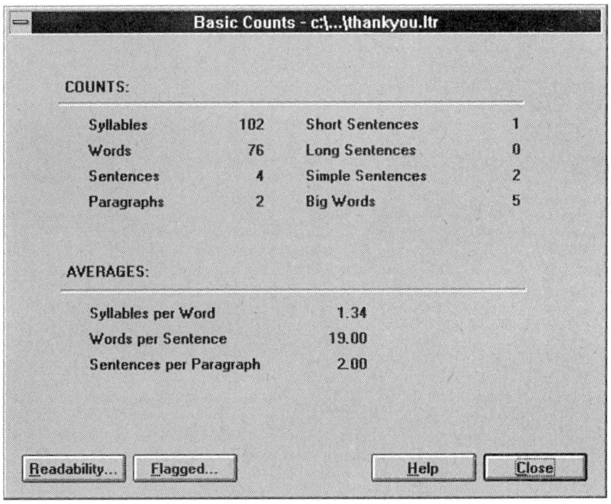

Basic Counts - c:\...\thankyou.ltr

COUNTS:

Syllables	102	Short Sentences	1
Words	76	Long Sentences	0
Sentences	4	Simple Sentences	2
Paragraphs	2	Big Words	5

AVERAGES:

Syllables per Word	1.34
Words per Sentence	19.00
Sentences per Paragraph	2.00

Readability... Flagged... Help Close

Fig. 6.18
Grammatik can calculate statistics on the different elements of your document's text.

Using the Thesaurus

A thesaurus helps you find the right words to express your thoughts. Some thoughts and ideas are more complex than others, and most ideas can be expressed in a number of ways. Using the right words enables you to convey exactly the message you want to get across to the reader.

The WordPerfect Thesaurus searches for and displays *synonyms* (words with the same or similar meanings) and *antonyms* (words with opposite meanings) for a word found in your document. You also can type in a new word for the

Thesaurus to look up. The Thesaurus displays a list of words from which you can choose a replacement for the word in the text.

Because the Thesaurus is a separate Windows application, you can start the Thesaurus without running WordPerfect first. You cannot use the WordPerfect Thesaurus in another Windows application, but you can copy a word to the Windows Clipboard and then paste it into the Thesaurus.

If you plan on using the Thesaurus again in the current writing session, you can minimize the application by clicking the Minimize button in the upper right-hand corner. This action reduces the Thesaurus window to an icon but doesn't close the application. When you maximize the Thesaurus, you see the window almost immediately.

Looking Up a Word in the Thesaurus

You can start the Thesaurus from a blank screen, or with the insertion point on the word you want to look up. In the sample text, position the insertion point on the word `kind`.

To start the Thesaurus, choose **T**ools, **T**hesaurus. The Thesaurus window appears on-screen with a list in the first column of synonyms and antonyms for the word `kind` (see fig. 6.19).

Fig. 6.19
The Thesaurus window displays lists of synonyms and antonyms for a word.

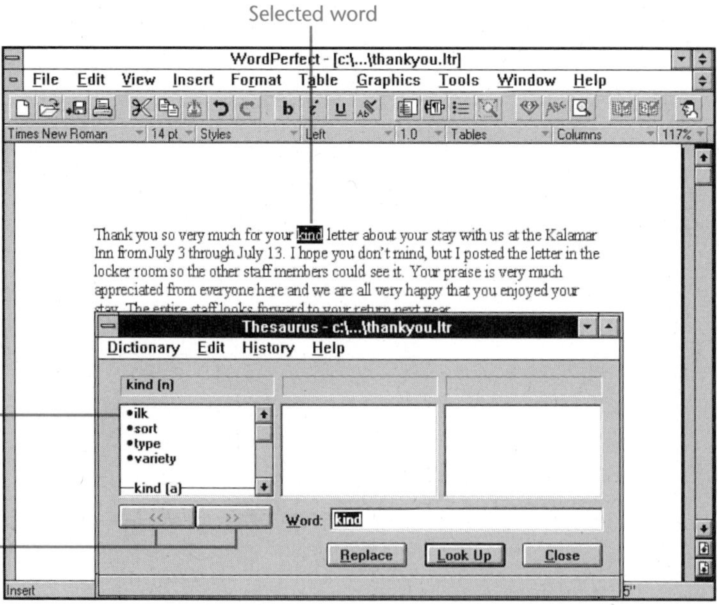

Understanding the Thesaurus Window

When you look up a word, the Thesaurus defines that word as the *headword*. A headword has its own list of synonyms and antonyms that you can display. The Thesaurus lists the headword at the top of the column and displays a list of references below it. If all the references cannot fit in the list box, use the scroll bar to scroll through the list.

Note

If you look up a word that is not in the Thesaurus, the program cannot provide a list of references. When this situation occurs, the Thesaurus displays a message at the bottom of the screen indicating the word could not be found. The insertion point remains in the **W**ord text box so you can immediately enter another word for the Thesaurus to look up. You can try looking up the root of the word the Thesaurus could not locate (for example, *success* instead of *successfully*), or you can move on to the next word you want to look up.

Several of the references shown in figure 6.20 are marked with a bullet. The bullet indicates that these references are also headwords that you can select to display additional references. These additional references can help you in your search for the right word. The Thesaurus can display as many as three headwords and their references at one time. You can use the left and right arrow buttons (<< and >>) under the first column to move between columns.

Thesaurus identifies the listed references as nouns `(n)`, verbs `(v)`, adjectives `(a)`, or antonyms `(ant)`. If the headword can be more than one of these word types, the headword appears again in the reference list with the appropriate identification. If a headword has more than one meaning, Thesaurus divides the references into subgroups by meanings.

You use the **W**ord text box to look up a headword from the references list or to look up a word that you type in. When you select a headword from the list, the word appears in the **W**ord text box. You can also select **W**ord and type in a word that does not appear in the list. If necessary, you can edit the word in the text box before inserting it into your document.

Replacing a Word

You can easily replace a word in your document with a word from a Thesaurus reference list. If the Thesaurus reference word is an exact replacement, select the word to insert it into the **W**ord text box, and then choose **R**eplace.

In some situations, however, you need to make minor changes to the replacement word. Suppose that you look up the word *assigning*. The Thesaurus produces the reference lists shown in figure 6.20. The program shows the headword as `assign` (a verb) and lists the reference word `distribute`. You want to use this reference word, but not in its current form; you want to use `distributing`. Select the word `distribute` to move it to the Word text box, delete the `e`, and insert `ing`. Choose **R**eplace to replace `assigning` with `distributing`.

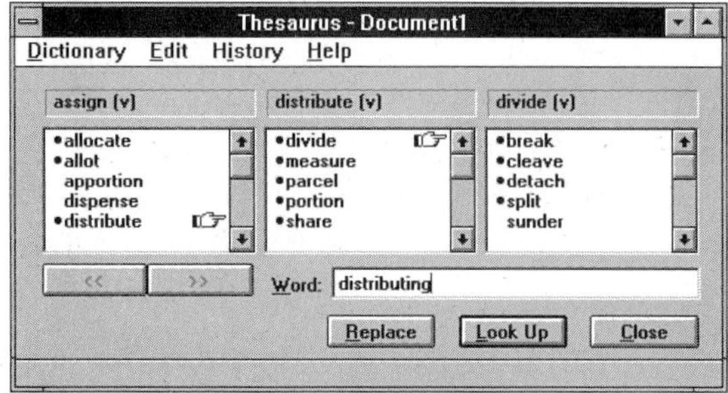

Fig. 6.20
The Word text box is used to edit the word before inserting it in the document.

Looking Up Reference Words

If the list of reference words does not contain the word you want to use, you can select any of the headwords in the reference list to look up additional references. You can use either of the following methods to look up a headword:

- Select the headword (marked with a bullet) to move it into the **W**ord text box. Press Enter to look up the word.
- Double-click the headword to look up the word.

When you look up another headword, Thesaurus places a hand symbol next to the word (refer to fig. 6.20), and that word becomes the headword in the next column. This system enables you to see the synonyms and antonyms for several headwords as you look for the right word. Thesaurus can display only three columns at one time. Use the << and >> buttons below the first column to scroll the columns to the left and right.

When you have looked up several words in Thesaurus, you may want to review the headwords you have looked up, or you may want to go back to a previous headword and look up references for it again. Choose H**i**story to see a list of headwords that you have looked up since starting the current Thesaurus session. If you want to look up one of the words again, select the word. The Thesaurus displays the headword and lists its reference words in the first column.

Note

If all three columns are full and you look up a word in the last column, the columns will scroll to the left so that the left column is pushed off-screen and a right column appears. Otherwise, the far right column is used to display the list for the selected word. Use the left and right scroll arrows or H**i**story to move between columns.

Customizing the Appearance of the Writing Tools on the Tools Menu

WordPerfect enables you to configure how the writing tools appear on the **T**ools menu. Using the Writing Tools area of the Pr**e**ferences menu, you can change the order in which the writing tools appear on the **T**ools menu. You can even remove the writing tools from the menu.

To change the appearance of the writing tools on the **T**ools menu, follow these steps:

1. Choose **E**dit, Pr**e**ferences. The Preferences dialog box appears.

2. Choose **W**riting Tools and press Enter; or double-click the **W**riting Tools icon. The Writing Tools dialog box appears, as shown in figure 6.21.

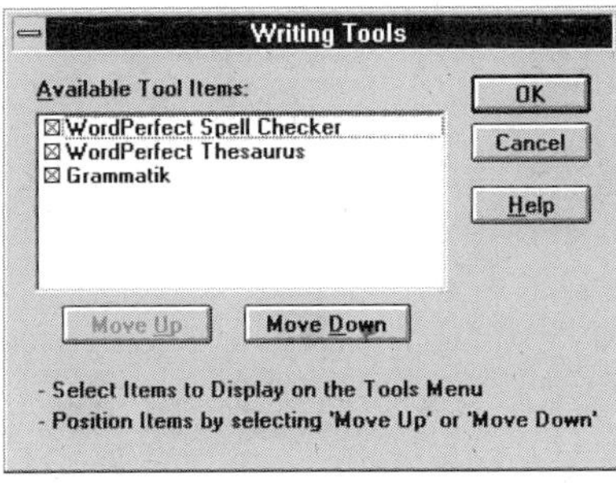

Fig. 6.21
The Writing Tools dialog box enables you to customize the appearance of the writing tools on the Tools pull-down menu.

3. Select the writing tools you want to appear on the menu from the **A**vailable Tool Items list. Selecting the box next to each item causes it to appear on the **T**ools menu; deselecting the box removes the tool from the menu.

4. To change the order in which the tools appear on the **T**ools menu, select the tool you want to move from the **A**vailable Tool Items list, and then choose Move **U**p or Move **D**own to change the tool's position.

   The order in which the tools appear in the **A**vailable Tool Items list is the order they appear on the **T**ools menu.

5. When you finish making your changes, choose OK and then choose **C**lose to return to your document.

   If you decide not to make your changes, choose Cancel from the Writing Tools dialog box.

Working with Other Languages

Writing in different languages involves more than being able to enter, display, and print non-English characters. You also need to be able to correct the spelling, look up terms in the Thesaurus, and check the grammar, in addition to using the proper date conventions and currency symbols. WordPerfect supports multiple languages in several ways:

- You can buy WordPerfect for a particular language. The menus, prompts, and other messages are in that language, as are the dictionaries that come with WordPerfect.

- You can mark a section of the document as being in one of the more than 30 languages supported by WordPerfect. Language modules containing additional files can be used in conjunction with the Spell Check, Thesaurus, Grammatik, Document Information, and Hyphenation features.

- A Language Resource file, included with the program, inserts dates in the customary style of the selected language and performs sorts based on that alphabet. If you use the footnote continued messages, they are printed in the new language. You can edit the Language Resource file to change what is printed for the continued message used when footnotes are carried over to the next page, for the currency symbols, and for the spelling of the days of the week and months of the year used in the Date feature.

Note

If you select text before selecting a language, WordPerfect inserts a code at the beginning of the text to change to the new language and inserts another code at the end of the text to change back to the original language. Otherwise, a single language code is inserted at the insertion point position in the document.

Using the Language Feature

You use the Language feature to specify the new language, which in turn tells WordPerfect which language module should be used with the writing tools. You can change languages as often as necessary in a document, or you can specify one language for the entire document.

Most language modules contain a separate dictionary for the Spell Check, Thesaurus, and Hyphenation features. Some modules also include files that can be used with Grammatik and Document Information. When you run Spell Check, Thesaurus, or Grammatik, the program checks for the appropriate language module. If the module is not available, WordPerfect displays an error message. In response to the message, you can attempt to locate the necessary files or opt to skip the language section during checking.

To change the language in the document, follow these steps:

1. Position the insertion point where you want to change the language or select the text you want affected.
2. Choose **L**anguage from the **T**ools menu to open the Language dialog box, as shown in figure 6.22.
3. Scroll through the list and select the appropriate language.

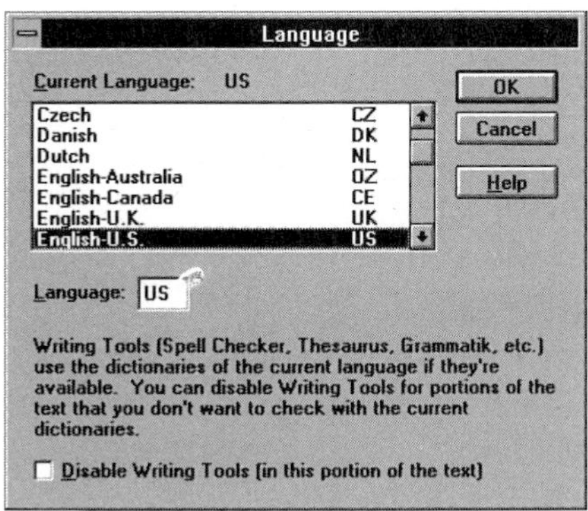

Fig. 6.22
Language codes placed in the document affect the Date format and the currency symbols used in tables. If the Language code is placed in the Initial Codes Style area, it also affects the footnote continued messages, Grammatik, and Sort.

Language codes can also be used to skip sections of a document when using the writing tools. This may be necessary if the appropriate language module is not available or if the sections contain technical references or unusual grammatical styles that will not be recognized in the current language.

Using the Language Resource File

The Language feature can also be used to change the conventions used for the Date, Sort, Footnote, and Tables features to those of another language. A Language Resource File (WP.LRS) is included with the program for this purpose, so an additional language module is not necessary. This file is a WordPerfect data merge file and can be edited like any other data file to suit your specific requirements.

► See "Understanding Data Files from Other Sources," p. 658

The Language Resource File contains the correct spelling for the days of the week and months in the year, in addition to the proper date format for many languages. (For example, in U.S. English, the correct format for a date is February 5, 1994; in French, the date should appear as 5 février 1994.) There is also information to modify sort conventions and adjust currency symbols for the chosen language. Finally, the continued messages used with footnotes are included for each language.

Using QuickCorrect

The QuickCorrect feature is an exciting new addition to WordPerfect for Windows. This feature automatically corrects common mistakes while you type. QuickCorrect cleans up extra spaces between words, fixes capitalization errors, corrects common spelling mistakes, and substitutes WordPerfect characters for special symbols. QuickCorrect also replaces regular quotation marks with typeset-quality quote marks (see the next section, "Using SmartQuotes," for more information).

Choose **T**ools, **Q**uickCorrect to display the QuickCorrect dialog box, which displays an extensive list of substitutions that are already defined for you (see fig. 6.23). Scroll through the list to get an idea of the type of substitutions that will be made. When you type a word that matches a word in the **R**eplace list, WordPerfect substitutes the word in the **W**ith list as soon as you press the spacebar. If you don't want QuickCorrect to make these substitutions while you type, deselect the R**e**place Words as You Type check box.

You can add additional combinations with the **A**dd Entry option. Simply type words that you misspell or mistype, or an abbreviation that you want to expand, as you type in the **R**eplace text box. Type the replacement in the

With text box, and then choose **A**dd Entry. See the "Using Abbreviations" section later in this chapter for more information on the Abbreviations feature, which can also be used to expand abbreviations in your documents.

As you'll recall, you can add misspelled words and their correct spelling to the QuickCorrect dictionary with the QuickCorrect option in the Spell Checker dialog box. If necessary, you can delete an entry from the list with the **D**elete Entry option.

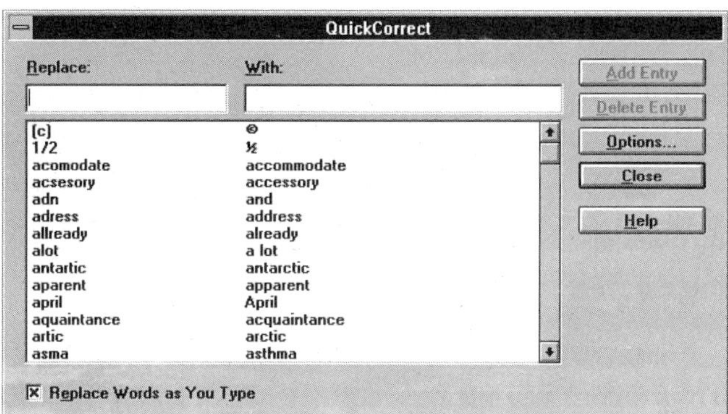

Fig. 6.23 QuickCorrect comes with a long list of substitutions that can be made as you type.

Choose **O**ptions to display the QuickCorrect Options dialog box, which allows you to specify the type of corrections you want made (see fig. 6.24). The Sentence Corrections options are all turned on by default. To disable a particular correction, select the option to remove the X in the check box. The default, End of Sentence Corrections, is set to **N**one. You can choose to have a single space changed to a double space or a double space changed into a single space. The changes made in this menu are permanent, so they will stay in effect until you change them again.

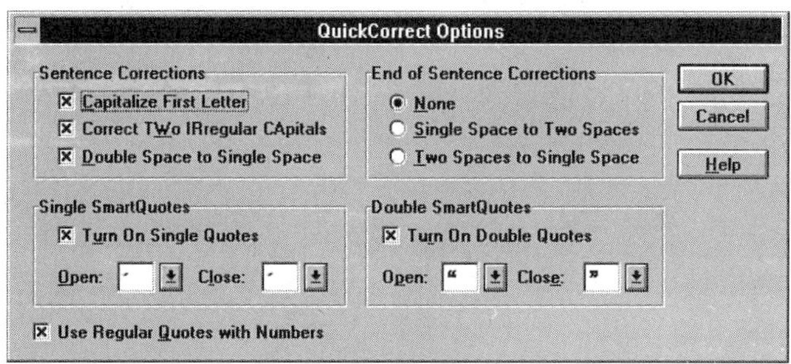

Fig. 6.24 The QuickCorrect Options dialog box displays all the corrections you can have QuickCorrect make for you.

Note

You can use the Replace Words as You Type option to turn off QuickCorrect if you prefer not to use it on a particular document.

Using SmartQuotes

The SmartQuotes feature automatically replaces the straight single and double quote marks you type in using the keys on the keyboard with typeset-quality quote marks. Options for the SmartQuotes feature are found in the QuickCorrect Options dialog box. To display the QuickCorrect Options dialog box, choose **T**ools, **Q**uickCorrect, **O**ptions.

In the Single SmartQuotes section, make sure the T**u**rn on Single Quotes option is selected (refer to fig. 6.24), and then select the quote mark you want to use in the **O**pen and C**l**ose drop-down lists. In the Double SmartQuotes section, make sure the Tu**r**n On Double Quotes option is selected, and then select the quote mark you want to use in the O**p**en and Clos**e** drop-down lists.

You also have the option of deleting the character shown in either of the Open and Close drop-down lists and using a WordPerfect character instead. Just press Ctrl+W, select a character, and then choose Insert **a**nd Close for each quote you want to change. The Use Regular **Q**uotes with Numbers option can be turned off if you don't want the straight quote mark used after numbers.

Checking Document Information

Submission requirements often limit grant proposals, research papers, and other projects to a specific number of words or pages. WordPerfect can check your document and compile an impressive list of statistics, including a word count.

To gather information on your document, choose Document **I**nfo from the **F**ile menu. The Document Information dialog box appears, as shown in figure 6.25.

Document Information displays a list of figure counts for characters (excluding spaces, returns, and codes), words, lines (including blank lines), sentences, paragraphs, and pages in the body of your document. Document

Information also calculates the average word length, average words per sentence, and the maximum words per sentence (the longest sentence in the document). This information can give you a general idea of the complexity of your writing.

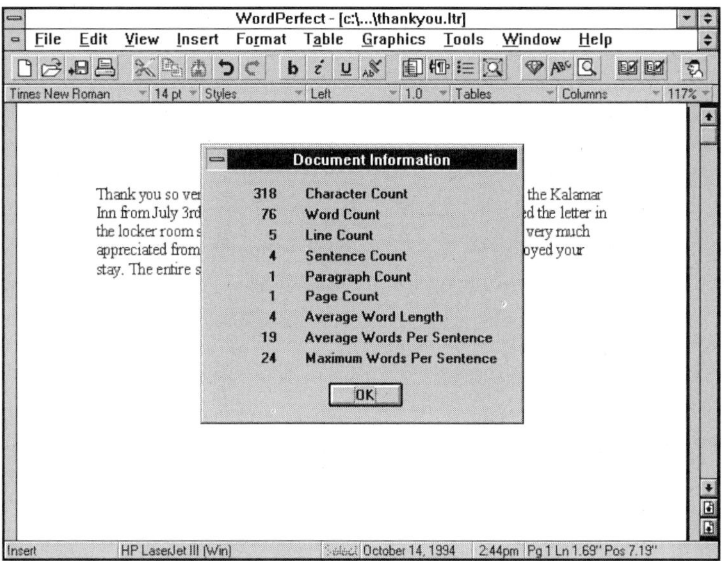

Fig. 6.25
The Document Information dialog box provides important information on the length and readability of a document.

When you are finished looking at the information, choose OK to close the Document Information dialog box. You can compile a new set of statistics at any time during the creation and modification of a document.

Note

Document Information counts only words in the body of the document, not words in document comments, text boxes, page headers and footers, footnotes, and endnotes.

Caution

Counts may not be accurate if your document contains section titles (just a few words without punctuation preceding a paragraph), which will be counted as paragraphs, or footnotes and endnotes, whose note numbers are counted as words.

Using Other Writing Tools

This section covers other types of tools that can be used while you are writing. You can use Document Comments to insert comments, suggestions, or directions in a document. The Hidden Text feature enables you to insert hidden text into a document, and then choose to display and print the text as necessary. You can use Abbreviations to reduce repetitive typing of long or complex phrases. Finally, an Insert Filename feature enables you to insert the file name (with or without the path name) anywhere in a document for reference purposes.

Using Document Comments

Most people are familiar with the sticky little note papers that office workers use to attach comments to documents. The electronic equivalent of these sticky notes is the Comment feature in WordPerfect.

As a writing tool, comments can be quite useful. If you use the sticky notes, you can imagine how you can use document comments. Consider the following uses:

- Store an idea as a comment, then return to the comment later to develop the idea.
- Create a comment to remind yourself (or someone else) to come back and check a statement's accuracy.
- Place instructions inside comments throughout on-screen forms to eliminate the need for printed instructions on how to use the form.

Creating a Comment

To create a comment, follow these steps:

1. Position the insertion point where you want the comment to appear.
2. Choose **I**nsert, Co**m**ment, **C**reate. The Document Comment window appears and displays the Document Comment feature bar (see fig. 6.26).
3. Type the text of the comment. You can use different fonts and font enhancements just as you would in the document.

   Use the feature bar in the Document Comment window to insert your N**a**me and **I**nitials (provided they are specified in the Environment Preferences menu), current **D**ate, and **T**ime. You also can move to the **N**ext or **P**revious comments in the document.

4. Choose **C**lose to insert the comment in the document.

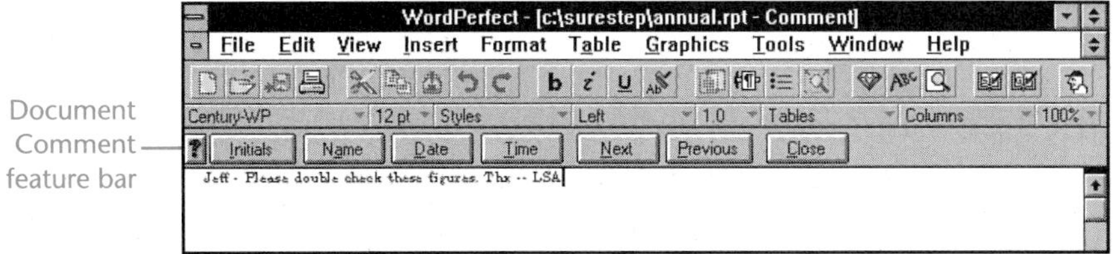

Fig. 6.26
The Document Comment feature bar enables you to create and edit comments.

WordPerfect inserts a comment icon, which represents the comment, in the left margin of the document (see fig. 6.27). Note that the comment icon can only be seen in the Page or Two Page View mode. If you use the Draft View mode, comment text shows up on-screen with a shaded background.

If you have supplied your initials in the User Info for Comments and Summary area of the Environment Preferences dialog box, they are displayed in the comment icon. In addition, if you specified a User Co**l**or in the User Info for Comments and Summary section, the comment icon and the comment itself are displayed in that color. To view a comment, click the comment icon. To hide the comment, click the comment or the comment icon.

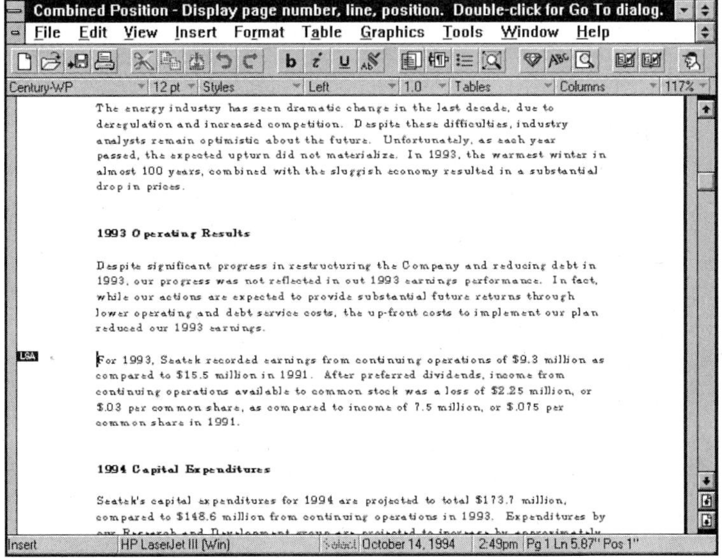

Fig. 6.27
The comment icon in the left margin marks the position of the comment in the document.

> **Note**
>
> It may be necessary to use the Horizontal scroll bar to scroll the screen over to the right until you can see the comment icon in the left margin.

Editing and Deleting Comments

The comment text is contained in a code (see fig. 6.28) that you can move or delete as necessary. If changes are necessary, you edit comments in the Document Comments window. You can use either of the following methods to edit a comment:

- Position the insertion point on the line with the comment icon. Choose **I**nsert, Co**m**ment, **E**dit.
- Double-click the comment icon.

Make the necessary changes; choose **C**lose from the Comment feature bar to close the Document Comment window and insert the revised comment in the document.

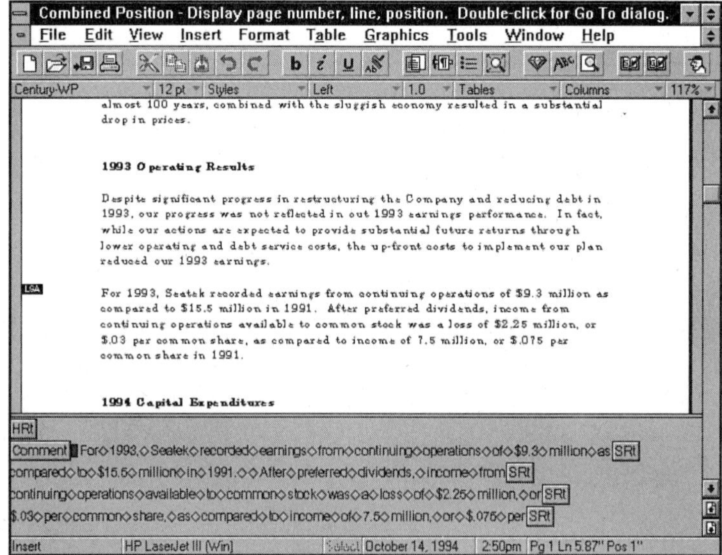

Fig. 6.28
Document comment text is contained in a comment code.

To delete a comment, position the insertion point at the beginning of the line with the comment icon. Turn on the Reveal Codes screen (choose **V**iew, Reveal **C**odes), locate the Comment code, and delete the code. For more information on deleting codes, see Chapter 3, "Retrieving and Editing Documents."

You can move a comment to another place in the document by deleting it and restoring it. To accomplish this task, locate the Comment code in the Reveal Codes screen, delete the code, reposition the insertion point, and restore the code (**E**dit, U**n**delete, **R**estore).

If you want to remove all the comments from a document, use the Find and Replace feature. First, position the cursor at the top of the document. Choose **E**dit, **F**ind and Replace to open the Find and Replace Text dialog box. Choose **M**atch, C**o**des to display a list of codes for which you can search. Scroll down the list until you find Comment. Select Comment; then choose **I**nsert to insert the Comment code in the F**i**nd text box. Leave the Replace **W**ith text box blank, so the code will be replaced with nothing. Choose Replace **A**ll to replace all comment codes with nothing. This action deletes the comment from the document.

Converting Comments to Text and Text to Comments

One of the major advantages of using document comments is that they do not print with the rest of the document. In some situations, however, you may want to print the comment text with the rest of the document. To answer this need, you can convert comments to regular document text. If you later want to convert the text back to comments, you easily can do so in WordPerfect.

To convert a comment to text, position the insertion point at the beginning of the line where the comment icon appears; choose **I**nsert, Co**m**ment, Convert to **T**ext.

To convert text to a comment, select the text you want to place in the comment; choose **I**nsert, Co**m**ment, **C**reate.

Using Hidden Text

Another feature in WordPerfect 6.1 for Windows is Hidden Text.

You can use hidden text to enter notes to yourself or to include text that you want to appear in some, but not all, copies of the document. If you are creating a test, for example, you can use hidden text to print the answers on the teacher's copy but not on the students' copies.

Unlike comments, which do not print unless you convert them to text, you display hidden text to make it printable. You can turn on and off the display of hidden text by choosing **V**iew, Hidden Te**x**t.

Follow these steps to insert hidden text:

1. Before you create hidden text, turn on the display of hidden text by choosing **V**iew, Hidden Te**x**t (a check mark indicates the option is on).
2. Choose Fo**r**mat, **F**ont; or press F9. Choose the Hidd**e**n Text attribute.
3. Type the text you want to hide.
4. Choose Fo**r**mat, **F**ont. Choose Hidd**e**n Text again to turn off the attribute.

You can easily change existing text to hidden text by following these steps:

1. Select the text you want to hide.
2. Choose Fo**r**mat, **F**ont; or press F9.
3. Choose Hidd**e**n Text.

Follow these steps to delete hidden text:

1. Turn off the display of hidden text.
2. Turn on Reveal Codes and locate the hidden code.
3. Delete the code.

Because the hidden text was not displayed, the text is deleted with the code.

Follow these steps to convert hidden text to regular document text:

1. Turn on the display of hidden text.
2. Turn on Reveal Codes and delete the hidden code.

Because the hidden text is currently displayed, the hidden text is converted to normal document text.

Note

You must display hidden text if you want to include it in page counts, QuickFinder searches, or if you want to check it with any of the writing tools (Spell Check, Grammatik, Thesaurus, or Document Information).

Using Abbreviations

Abbreviations simplify the insertion of frequently used words and phrases. You assign a short abbreviation to a phrase, use the abbreviation when typing the document, and then expand the abbreviation later. If you must frequently type your company name in a document, for example, you can assign it a short abbreviation. When you type the document, you can type the abbreviation in place of your company name. You can then press Ctrl+A to expand the abbreviation into the full company name.

Follow these steps to create an abbreviation:

1. Select the text for which you want to create an abbreviation.
2. Choose **I**nsert, **A**bbreviations. The Abbreviations dialog box appears, as shown in figure 6.29.

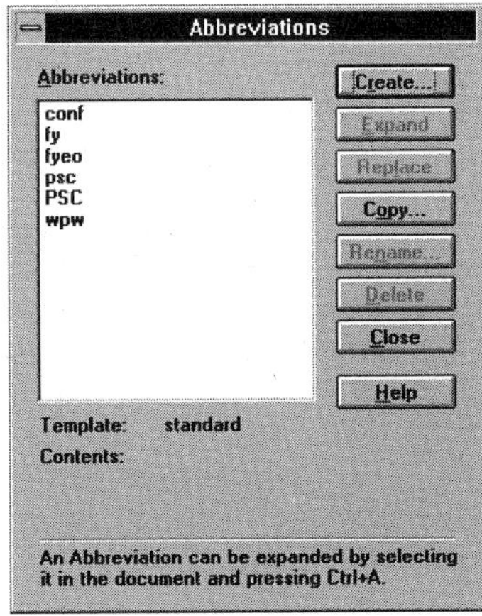

Fig. 6.29
The Abbreviations dialog box enables you to create abbreviations that save time and help reduce typing errors within your documents.

3. Choose C**r**eate to display the Create Abbreviations dialog box.
4. Type a name for the selected information in the **A**bbreviation Name text box.

5. Choose OK, and then **C**lose to return to the document.

Note

Abbreviations are case-sensitive. This attribute enables you to use within the same document, for example, the abbreviation "psc" for "post-sales contact" and "PSC" for "Peter Stewart contract."

You can expand a typed abbreviation at any time. To expand an abbreviation, position the insertion point anywhere in the abbreviation. Choose **I**nsert, **A**bbreviations, **E**xpand; or press Ctrl+A. WordPerfect includes a macro that will expand all of the abbreviations in the document at one time. To run the macro, choose **T**ools, **M**acro, **P**lay. Select the **expndall.wcm** macro file and choose **P**lay.

You can easily change the information associated with a particular abbreviation. To replace an abbreviation, select the text you now want associated with the abbreviation. Choose **I**nsert, **A**bbreviations, Rep**l**ace. For example, if your company name has changed, you will want to update the abbreviation with the new name.

WordPerfect saves abbreviations to the particular template in which you are working. You can set up different abbreviations for different templates. For example, you may have a set of abbreviations for an expense report template and another set for a sales proposal template. See Chapter 11, "Using Templates," for more information on the Template feature.

If you want to copy an abbreviation to another template, follow these steps:

1. Choose **I**nsert, **A**bbreviations to display the Abbreviations dialog box.
2. Highlight the abbreviation in the Abbreviations dialog box and choose C**o**py. The Copy Abbreviation dialog box appears.
3. Choose **S**elect Abbreviation To Copy and highlight the abbreviation.
4. Choose Template To Copy **T**o and select a template from the drop-down list; then choose **C**opy.

Inserting the File Name

Inserting the DOS file name in a printed document can help you and others who use your printed document find the document's file in the computer system. Many users include the file name in a document header or footer, or on the line just above the author/typist initials. You can insert the file name alone, or you can insert both the path and the file name. The *path* is the location of the file on the system; for example, in the path and file name

C:\NEWACCTS\TAYLOR\WELCOME.LTR

C:\NEWACCTS\TAYLOR is the path, and WELCOME.LTR is the file name.

To insert the DOS file name anywhere in your document, position the insertion point where you want the file name to appear. Choose **I**nsert, **O**ther; then choose **F**ilename if you want to insert just the file name; or choose **P**ath and Filename if you want to insert the path with the file name.

At the insertion point, WordPerfect inserts a code that represents the current DOS path and file name. If you rename the file or save it to a different location, WordPerfect automatically updates the file and path names to show the new path or file name.

Troubleshooting

I want to create Hidden Text, but when I choose Format Font, Hidden Text is dimmed. Why can't I use it?

To create or view Hidden Text, make sure Hidden Te**x**t is selected on the **V**iew menu.

I inserted the file name in my document. Why doesn't it appear?

You inserted the file name before saving the document. As soon as the file is saved, the file name will appear.

◄ See "Saving a Document to Disk," p. 72

◄ See "Understanding WordPerfect's Hidden Codes," p. 95

► See "Customizing Environment Options," p. 324

You can insert the code for the file name or path and file name even if the document has not been saved (and named) yet. When you name the document, WordPerfect automatically inserts the name wherever you have placed file name codes in the document.

From Here...

In this chapter, you learned how to use WordPerfect's writing tools to improve your writing accuracy, speed, and efficiency. You learned how to use Spell Check to catch typos and spelling errors and how to manage multiple dictionaries. You learned how to use Grammatik to catch grammar and style mistakes; and the Thesaurus, to look up synonyms and antonyms for a word to add variety or more clearly state your message. You also learned how to use QuickCorrect and SmartQuotes to polish your written materials.

This chapter discussed how to gather statistics on the document by using the Document Information feature, and how to use document comments, hidden text, and abbreviations to assist in your writing efforts. Finally, you learned how to insert the name of the file in the document to help you locate the file later.

For related information, please refer to the following chapters:

- Chapter 4, "Formatting Text," discusses the default formatting settings and how to use the Toolbar, Power Bar, and Ruler to perform formatting tasks quickly. Setting margins and tabs, controlling justification, and using the hyphenation feature are also explained.

- Chapter 5, "Formatting Pages and Documents," shows you how to assign formatting commands to pages or to the entire document. Centering a page, adding headers and footers, inserting page numbers, using paper definitions, modifying initial document settings, and using document summaries are also explained.

- Chapter 8, "Basic Output: Printing, Faxing, and E-mail," explains how to print, fax, and e-mail your documents. The Zoom feature and View modes, which enable you to preview your document before you send it, are also discussed.

Chapter 7

Integrating Text and Graphics

by Sue Plumley and Gordon McComb

It starts with text. In previous chapters, you learned to create, edit, and format text in documents, such as letters and memos. The way you assemble the words on the page defines the message of your document.

It gets better with graphics. With just a sprinkling of graphics, such as lines, borders, and images, you can greatly enhance the message of your document, without adding more words. Graphics emphasize important items, separate sections of text, and make the text more interesting to look at.

You use graphics lines, borders, and images to enhance your text. A page consisting entirely of text can be monotonous and cause the reader to lose interest in the message. A page containing lines or images, on the other hand, attracts the reader and supports the text. Use graphics, for example, to attract attention to an important announcement in a letter or to dress up a memo.

WordPerfect enables you to add a variety of graphics lines, borders, and images to your documents. You can create horizontal and vertical lines, paragraph and page borders, and boxes that hold text or images. This chapter introduces you to adding basic lines, borders, and images to your document.

Chapter 21, "Using Advanced Graphics Techniques," delves deeper into using and customizing WordPerfect's graphics capabilities.

In this chapter, you learn how to:

- Use horizontal and vertical lines
- Use paragraph and page borders

- Understand the types of graphics boxes
- Create, size, and move a graphics box

Using Graphics Lines

Use graphics lines in your documents to add emphasis, separate text, or dress up the page. You can use lines in most documents, such as letters, memos, newsletters, brochures, and reports. WordPerfect for Windows enables you to create various styles, thicknesses, and lengths of lines and to easily change line position, spacing, and color.

Note

Make sure that all graphics complement the message and add to the overall comprehension of the message. Unorganized use and placement of graphics confuses the reader. For more information on using WordPerfect for Windows as a serious desktop publishing tool, see Chapter 23, "Desktop Publishing with WordPerfect."

WordPerfect enables you to add horizontal and vertical lines to the page by using the **G**raphics menu, a keyboard shortcut, or the Graphics Toolbar; WordPerfect inserts the line at the position of the insertion point. After you insert a line, you can easily move the line on the page and resize the line by using the mouse. This section shows you how to create horizontal and vertical lines and move and size lines using the mouse. For more information about customizing lines, see Chapter 21, "Using Advanced Graphics Techniques."

Note

To display the Graphics Toolbar, choose **V**iew, **T**oolbar if the Toolbar is not already shown on-screen. Use the right mouse button to click anywhere over the Toolbar. A list of available Toolbars appears in the QuickMenu. Find the one that says Graphics, and click on it with the left mouse button.

Using Horizontal Lines

You can use horizontal lines to guide the reader's eye from page to page, to border pages or paragraphs, or to emphasize important text. You can use horizontal lines, for example, in a memo above and below the heading to make it stand out or to separate the banner lines and the message of the memo. Figure 7.1 illustrates a memo that uses horizontal lines to separate text and add pizzazz.

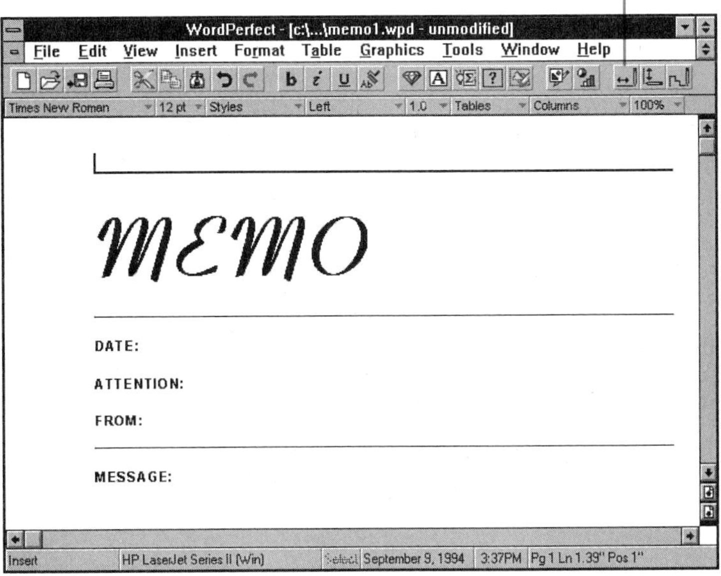

Fig. 7.1
Horizontal lines separate text and attract attention to the memo. A shortcut for creating a horizontal line is to use the Horizontal Line button on the Graphics Toolbar.

Try creating horizontal lines on a practice document; use a document created previously, or create a new document using the memo in figure 7.1 as a guide. After you create and format the text in the document, add horizontal lines by following these steps:

1. Position the insertion point.

2. Choose **G**raphics, **H**orizontal Line; or press Ctrl+F11.

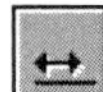

   The default settings of the line are horizontal extending the length between the left and right margins, single line style, black, and with no spacing above or below the line.

3. Reposition the insertion point and insert another horizontal line.

Note

To avoid crowding the text, create horizontal lines on a blank line—a line containing only a paragraph return (press the Enter key to make the paragraph return). Placing graphics lines on a blank line provides space between the text and the graphic. Alternatively, you can place the line on the same line as the text.

Using Vertical Lines

You can also create vertical lines in documents to separate text, emphasize text, or dress up the page. For example, use a vertical line to emphasize left text alignment in a business letter, or use short vertical lines to draw attention to important items in a report. Figure 7.2 illustrates a business letter with a vertical line near the left margin.

To create a vertical line in a document, use a letter you already created, or create a new one using figure 7.2 as a guide. After creating and formatting the text, follow these steps to add the vertical line:

1. Position the insertion point, preferably in front of all text.

2. Choose **G**raphics, **V**ertical Line; or press Ctrl+Shift+F11. The vertical line appears.

   The default line is a single-style vertical line, positioned at the left margin and extending from the top to the bottom margins. The vertical line also uses an offset—to separate it from the text—of 0.125-inch.

Vertical Line button

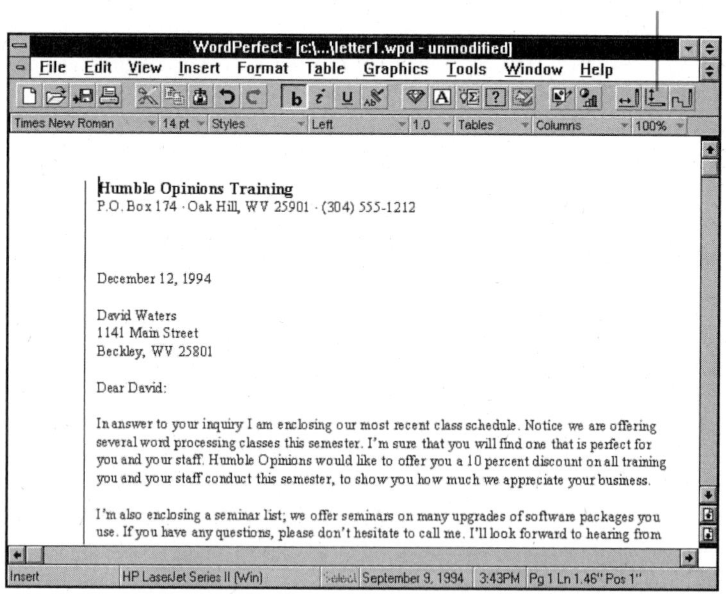

Fig. 7.2
Use a vertical line to dress up or emphasize the text. Use the Vertical Line button in the Graphics Toolbar as a quick and easy shortcut for creating vertical lines.

Customizing Lines Using the Mouse

WordPerfect enables you to alter the length, thickness, and position of a line by using the mouse or a dialog box. Using the mouse to customize lines is quick and easy, although not as precise as using the dialog box. This chapter covers using the mouse to customize graphics lines. For more information about using the dialog box to customize lines, see Chapter 21.

◀ See "Formatting Lines and Paragraphs," p. 134

▶ See "Customizing Lines," p. 706

Note

Add consistency to your document by using the same line style and thickness throughout the document. Occasionally, you may want to use two line styles—such as thick and thin, or thick-thin and thin-thick—but using more than two line styles may distract the reader and make the document look unprofessional.

To use the mouse to customize horizontal or vertical lines, open a document such as the memo you created previously, and follow these steps:

1. Use the mouse to select the line; the mouse cursor changes to a pointer when you move it over a line (see fig. 7.3). Click the line to select it.

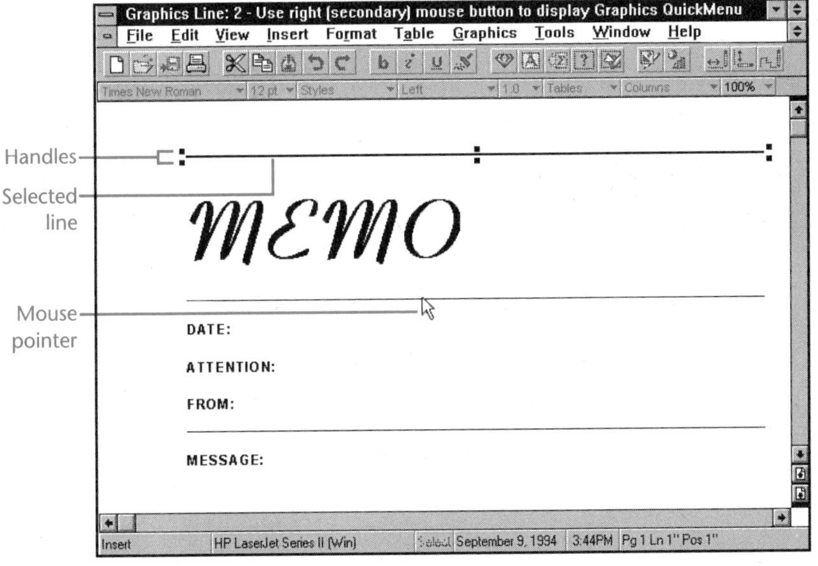

Fig. 7.3
When you select a line, small black boxes called handles appear at the ends and in the middle of the line. Use the handles to resize the line.

2. Position the mouse arrow on the bottom right handle; the mouse arrow changes to a double-headed arrow. Click and drag the handle towards the center of the line to shorten the line length.

3. Position the double-headed arrow on the bottom middle handle; click and drag the arrow down 1/4-inch to make the line thicker.

4. Position the mouse arrow on the line so that it changes shape to a four-headed arrow (see fig. 7.4). Use this arrow to move the line to any position on the page by clicking and dragging the line to its new position.

Tip
It takes a little time to get used to positioning the mouse pointer just right so that you get the double arrow; with practice, however, you'll have no problem.

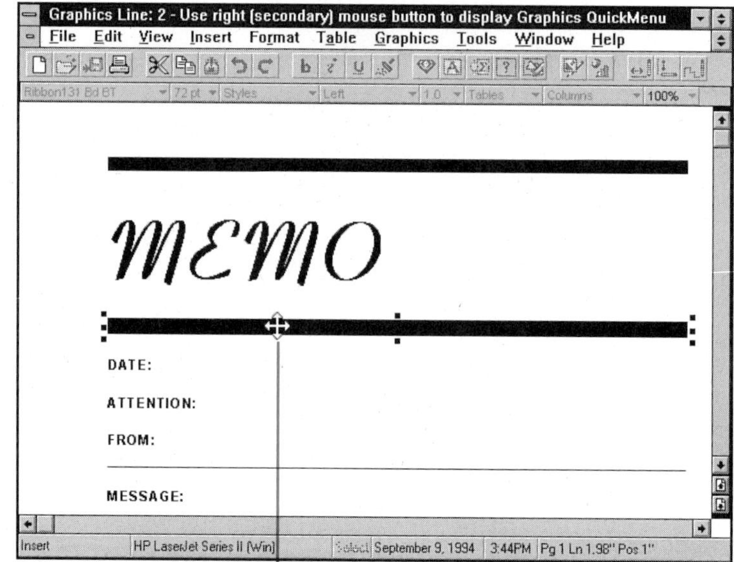

Fig. 7.4
Use the mouse to change the length and width of the line by first selecting the line and then manipulating the handles; you can also use the mouse to move the line.

Deleting Lines

You can easily delete lines in WordPerfect by deleting the code that represents the line, selecting the line with the mouse and pressing the Delete key, or by using a special menu.

Tip
If you accidentally delete the wrong line, press the Undo shortcut Ctrl+Z to reverse the action or choose **E**dit **U**ndo from the menu.

To delete a line using the right mouse button menu, follow these steps:

1. Point the mouse at the line to be deleted.
2. Click the right mouse button; the QuickMenu appears (see fig. 7.5).
3. Choose **D**elete.

Using Graphics Borders

A graphics border is a box that surrounds text to emphasize your message, separate text, or add pizzazz to the page. In addition, you can use borders, actually graphics boxes, to contain images. For more information about graphics boxes, see the "Using Graphics Boxes" section later in this chapter.

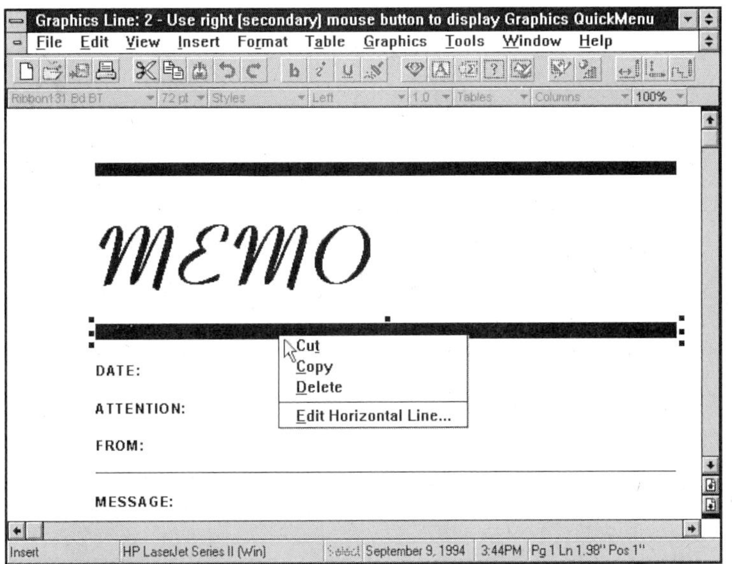

Fig. 7.5
Delete a line quickly by clicking the right mouse button while pointing to a graphic. You can also cut or copy the line, or edit the line using the Edit Graphic Line dialog box.

Tip
You can use a variety of line styles and thicknesses with page and paragraph borders. For more information about customizing border lines, see Chapter 21.

You can use a paragraph border to attract attention to one particular paragraph of text in a letter, for example, or you can add a page border to each page of a report to guide the reader and create consistency within the report. Figure 7.6 illustrates an advertising letter that uses both a page border and a paragraph border.

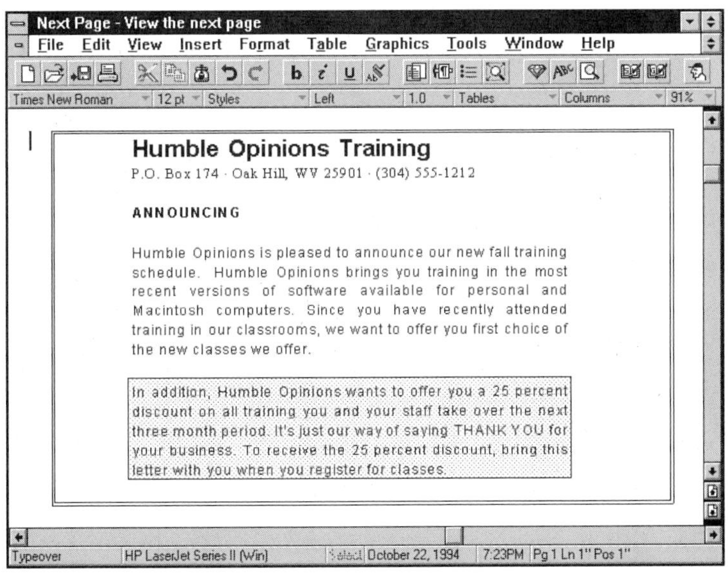

Humble Opinions Training
P.O. Box 174 · Oak Hill, WV 25901 · (304) 555-1212

ANNOUNCING

Humble Opinions is pleased to announce our new fall training schedule. Humble Opinions brings you training in the most recent versions of software available for personal and Macintosh computers. Since you have recently attended training in our classrooms, we want to offer you first choice of the new classes we offer.

In addition, Humble Opinions wants to offer you a 25 percent discount on all training you and your staff take over the next three month period. It's just our way of saying THANK YOU for your business. To receive the 25 percent discount, bring this letter with you when you register for classes.

Fig. 7.6
The page border dresses up the page and makes it more interesting to look at. The paragraph border emphasizes the text announcing a discount to the customer.

Using Paragraph Borders

► See "Customizing a Toolbar," p. 455

◄ See "Understanding WordPerfect's Hidden Codes," p. 95

A paragraph border is a frame, or box, that surrounds only the selected text. WordPerfect defines a paragraph as any amount of text followed by a hard return. Therefore, you can select one character or word followed by a hard return and surround it with a border; or you can select two, three, four, or more paragraphs to surround with a border.

Note

A paragraph border extends from the right margin to the left margin.

You can create paragraph borders in two different ways with WordPerfect. First, you can position the insertion point and create the border. Each subsequent paragraph is then surrounded by a border. Alternatively, you can select specific text and create the border; only the selected text contains a border, as shown earlier in figure 7.6.

Tip
Generally, use single or thin lines for paragraph borders; you don't want to overwhelm the text with a thick or double-lined border.

To add a paragraph border to a document, open a document previously created, or begin a new document using the one in figure 7.6 as a guide. After you format the text, follow these steps to create the paragraph border:

1. Select the paragraph of text to which you want to apply a border.
2. Choose Fo**r**mat, P**a**ragraph. A cascading menu appears.
3. Choose **B**order/Fill. The Paragraph Border dialog box appears (see fig. 7.7).

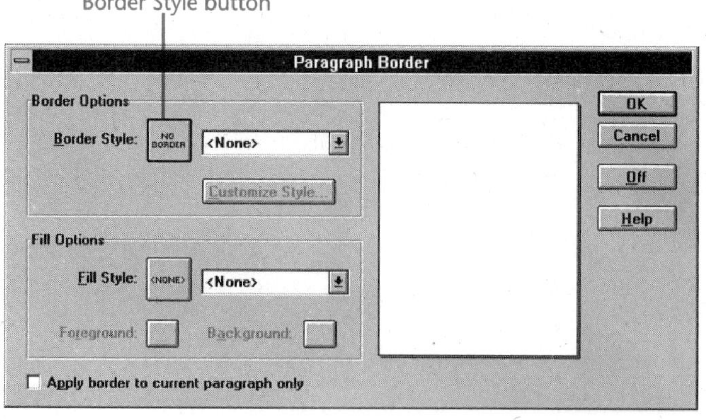

Fig. 7.7
Choose the **B**order Style button to view available styles; click on the style you want.

4. In the Border Options area, choose the button beside **B**order Style or choose the drop-down list to select the border by name. Choose the border style you want by clicking on the style.

5. Choose OK to accept the change and close the dialog box. WordPerfect returns to the document with the appropriate border style surrounding the text.

Adding Paragraph Fill

Often, you will want to include a fill or shade to the paragraph border to emphasize the text even more. WordPerfect makes it easy to add fill to a border. WordPerfect offers two methods of adding fill to a document.

The first method is to position the insertion point at the location you want the fill to start. When you choose the fill in the Paragraph Border dialog box, the fill begins at the insertion point and continues through the rest of the document. The second method is to select the text and apply the fill.

If you add fill with the cursor in the middle of a paragraph border area, a new paragraph border is created. If you have a border around three paragraphs and place the cursor in the third paragraph, for example, that paragraph is separated from the other two. In addition, the fill doesn't necessarily begin at the insertion point location. If the insertion point is in the middle of a paragraph, the fill begins at the beginning of that paragraph.

To apply fill to a paragraph of text, follow these steps:

1. Select the text.

2. Choose Fo**r**mat, P**a**ragraph. From the cascading menu, choose **B**order/Fill. The Paragraph Border dialog box appears.

3. In the Fill Options area, choose the **F**ill Style button or choose a fill percentage from the drop-down list of names. In the Fill Style palette (see fig. 7.8), click on the appropriate fill for the border and choose OK. WordPerfect returns to the document.

Tip

Never add more than a 30 percent shade to black text; fill that is too dark makes the text difficult to read.

Fig. 7.8
Even though WordPerfect provides various fill styles for a border, be careful to choose a fill that enables you to read the text easily.

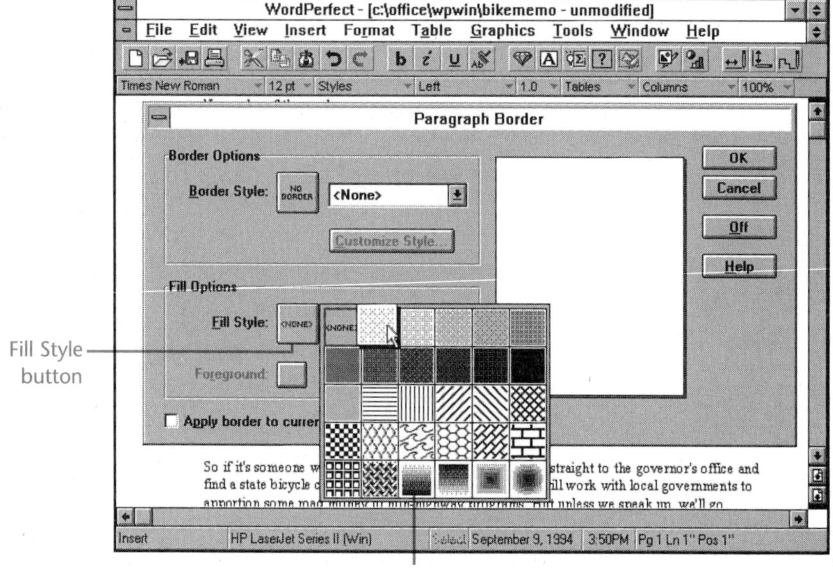

Fill Style palette

Adding a Page Border

Use a page border to add pizzazz to any document—such as letters, newsletters, menus, reports, and flyers. Normally, you repeat the page border—same line style, thickness, and so on—on all pages of a document. You may not want a page border on some pages, however—a page of a report containing several tables, images, or spreadsheets, for example. In that case, you can turn off the border for a particular page; see "Turning Off a Border" later in this chapter. Usually, try to be consistent with borders throughout a document.

> **Note**
>
> When using a page border, you can use a heavier border than the single line you use for paragraph borders, as long as you allow plenty of white space. *White space* is the breathing room in the margins, between paragraphs, below headlines, and so on that helps to balance heavy lines.

A page border extends from the top to the bottom margin and from the right to the left margin. When you create a page border in WordPerfect, the program automatically allows space between the text and the border so that the text is not crowded or difficult to read.

For this exercise, use any letter or memo document you have created, or create a new document using figure 7.6 as a guide. After the text is formatted, add the page border by following these steps:

1. Choose Format, **Page**. A cascading menu appears.
2. Choose **Border**/Fill. The Page Border dialog box appears (see fig. 7.9).
3. Choose the **Border** Style button or use the drop-down list of border styles; select the border style for the document.
4. Choose OK to return to the document.

Tip
To set page margins, choose Format, **Margins**; or press Ctrl+F8.

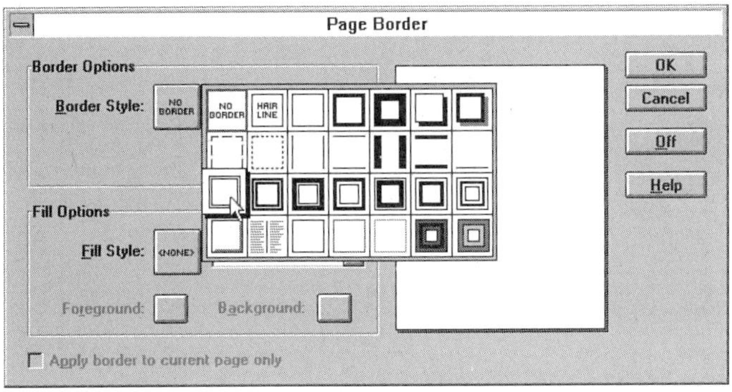

Fig. 7.9
Choose the **Border** Style button to select the border style for the document; alternatively, you can view the list of styles beside the Border Style button.

Adding Page Fill

You can use a fill or shade with a page border just as you can with a paragraph border. A fill attracts attention to the entire page. A page fill does not extend past the margins of the page. In addition, you can create a fill without using a line around the border.

To add a page fill to a document, follow these steps:

1. Position the insertion point at the top of the page.
2. Choose Format, **Page**, and then choose **Border**/Fill. The Page Border dialog box appears.
3. In the Fill Options area, choose the **Fill** Style button or use the list box and select the appropriate fill.
4. Choose OK to return to the document.

Tip
Be careful when using the fill. Too much fill—as in every page of a newsletter or report—can make the message difficult to read.

Turning Off a Border

Sometimes you may not want a border on a particular page—for example, on a page that contains a complicated graph or a large image. You can turn the page border off on any page in your document by using the Page Border dialog box. You can also turn off a paragraph border if you decide not to use it.

◀ See "Selecting Paper Size and Type," p. 186

Before turning off a paragraph border, position the cursor anywhere in the paragraph for which you want to turn off the border. If you're turning off a page border, position the insertion point on the page containing the border you want to turn off. To turn off a border, follow these steps:

▶ See "Customizing Borders," p. 714

1. Choose Fo**r**mat and then either **P**age or P**a**ragraph. From the cascading menu, choose **B**order/Fill.
2. In the Page or Paragraph Border dialog box, choose the command button labeled **O**ff.

Deleting a Border

You can delete a page or paragraph border in WordPerfect by deleting the code that represents the border. To practice deleting a border code, use a document you created previously and follow these steps:

Tip
When you delete a border containing the fill, both the border and the fill are deleted.

1. Choose **V**iew, Reveal **C**odes; or press Alt+F3.
2. Position the cursor in front of the Page or Paragraph border code (see fig. 7.10).
3. Press Delete.

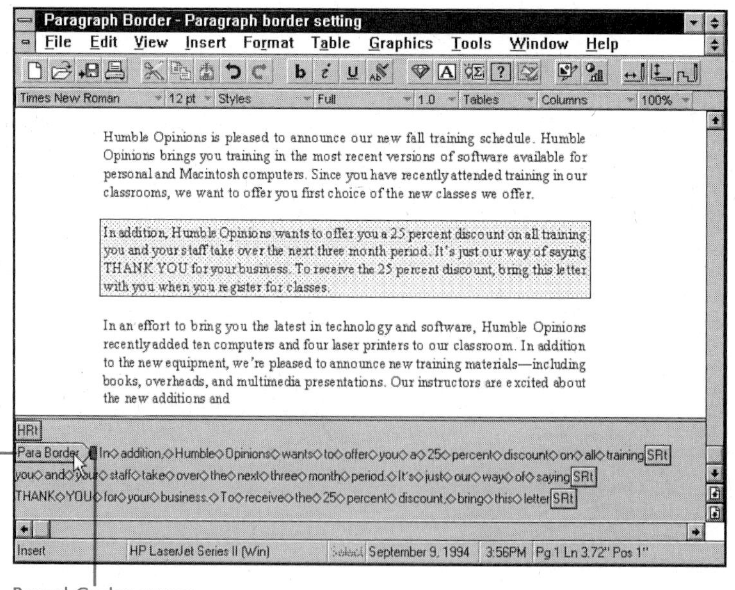

Fig. 7.10
Deleting the code of the border deletes the border; press Alt+F3 to reveal codes.

Troubleshooting

I can't delete a graphics line by pressing Backspace or Delete.

This is the way WordPerfect works. Normally, when you press the Backspace (or Delete) key, WordPerfect skips over the codes for graphics lines. This applies to both vertical and horizontal graphics lines. If you want to delete the graphics line, first turn on Reveal Codes by choosing **V**iew, Reveal **C**odes. Now you can use the Backspace and Delete keys to delete the codes for graphics lines. These codes appear as [Graph Line] in Reveal Codes.

When I turn off paragraph border, WordPerfect removes the paragraph border completely.

WordPerfect turns off the paragraph border in the current paragraph. The current paragraph is defined as the one that contains the flashing insertion point (or cursor). If you are done writing the text you want in a paragraph border, make sure that you press the Enter key first. This inserts an extra blank paragraph. You can now turn the paragraph border off by choosing Fo**r**mat, P**a**ragraph, **B**order/Fill, and then **O**ff.

When I print my document, I can't see the text inside a paragraph that has a filled border.

Exercise care when using a background fill inside a paragraph border. The more solid the fill pattern, the harder it is to see the text when you view or print the document. Depending on your printer, text within a filled pattern may be easier or harder to see than on the screen. You must experiment with your printer to find the optimal background fill pattern. A good fill pattern to start with is 5 percent, which means the fill pattern is five percent gray.

Using Graphics Boxes

A graphics box is a box that holds images or text—such as clip art, drawings, callouts, text files, equations, tables, and spreadsheets. Graphics boxes are different from borders. A graphics box holds text or images that you can change and move with the box; you add a graphics box and its contents to a document, and then adjust the contents of the document to make room for the box. A border, on the other hand, is an added ornamental frame that surrounds text already in your document.

Tip
To format the text in a graphics box, select the text and choose the F**o**rmat menu. Then choose **F**ont, **L**ine, or P**a**ragraph to format the text.

Adding graphics boxes to your documents illustrates the text, draws attention to the message, and adds interest to the document. Images, for example, help the reader understand the text; text callouts attract the reader's attention to the text. WordPerfect enables you to add several types of graphics boxes to your documents, each with a style and purpose of its own.

Understanding Graphics Box Styles

WordPerfect supplies eight graphics box styles you can use in your documents. Each graphics box style is designed to work best with one particular type of image or text—for example, the figure box style looks good with an image in a document. Any box, however, can hold any type of image, text, table, equation, and so on. The box style is simply a suggestion for the box's use.

Each box style has specific defaults; however, you can change the characteristics of any box. The primary box style defaults are defined by the box's line style and position. Line style refers to the width and type of line used as a border for the box—thick, single, none, and so on.

Positioning refers to how the box is anchored—to what element on the page the box is attached. A box can be attached, or anchored, to a page, paragraph, or character. A box anchored to the page means that its location is relative to the top and left edges of that page. A box anchored to a paragraph moves with the text in the paragraph to which it is attached. Finally, a box attached to a character acts just like any other character in the paragraph—it moves within the line left to right, and within the paragraph up and down, whenever text is edited around the box.

Note

You can customize any box; see Chapter 21 for more information.

The following list describes each graphics box style and the default line styles:

- *Figure Box*. Single line, anchored to the paragraph; generally holds clip art, drawings, or WPG files (see fig. 7.11).

Fig. 7.11
The figure box contains one of WordPerfect's many clip art files; you can also use image files from other programs.

- *Text Box*. Thick line on top and bottom, anchored to a paragraph; normally holds text such as a callout, announcement, or imported text files (see fig. 7.12).

Text added in a graphic box attracts attention to your message!

1 Use a caption with a text box when you want to identify the origin of the text, for example

Fig. 7.12
You can add a caption to a text box to identify the author or origin of the text.

- *Equation Box*. No border or fill, anchored to a paragraph; holds mathematical or scientific equations or text (see fig. 7.13).

$2a + 2b = 16$ (1)The default equation box with default caption.

Fig. 7.13
You can resize and move an equation box so that it best suits your document.

- *Table Box*. Thick line on top and bottom, anchored to a paragraph; normally holds a table (see fig. 7.14).

Table 1. Create a caption to describe the table or spreadsheet.

Sales Progress for 1st Quarter

Rep.	January	February	March	April
Clyde	$10,000	$12,065	$11,654	$14,500
Dave	$ 9,800	$ 9,006	$ 7,099	$ 8,500
Jim	$ 7,900	$ 7,800	$ 8,454	$ 7,898
Scott	$ 2,000	$ 1,284	$ 1,098	$ 989

Fig. 7.14
You can format text in any graphics box just as you would text in your document.

- *User Box*. No border or fill, anchored to a paragraph; perfect for contour text wrap-around images (see fig. 7.15).

Fig. 7.15
You'll probably use the user box most often; it's easier to start with the User's defaults and customize the box to suit your purposes.

- *Button Box.* Single line border with Button Fill, anchored to a character; can contain images or text (see fig. 7.16).

Fig. 7.16
Use a button box within a paragraph to illustrate a keystroke, icon, or other symbol; you can add text or an image to a button box.

- *Watermark Box.* No border or fill, anchored to the page; contains images or text screened so that it creates a background for the document (see fig. 7.17).

Fig. 7.17
A watermark box screens the logo, clip art, or other image in the background of the page; you can enter text over the image or use a contour text wrap.

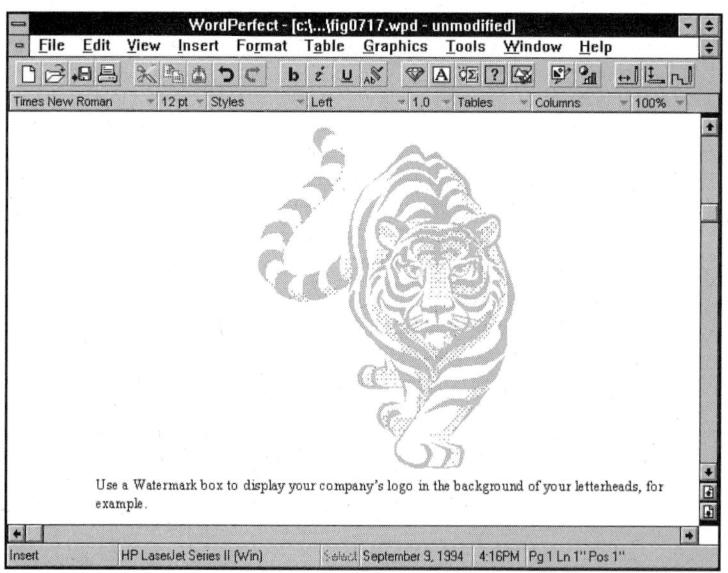

- *Inline Equation.* No border or fill, anchored to a character; contains an equation for placement within a paragraph of text—treated like a character (see fig. 7.18).

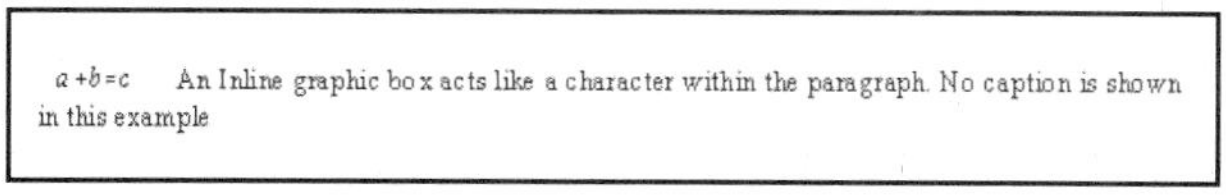

a+b=c An Inline graphic box acts like a character within the paragraph. No caption is shown in this example

Fig. 7.18
You can create a caption for an inline graphics box, but because the inline box is a character within the paragraph, the caption is difficult to read.

WordPerfect makes it easy to create any box style and add any contents you want to the box. After you create the box, you can change the box style, border, fill, content, position, size, and text wrap options. This section shows you how to create a graphics box, and how to move, resize, and delete a box using the mouse. For more information about other customization options, see Chapter 21.

Creating a Graphics Box

You can create a graphics box by using the Graphics Toolbar or the **G**raphics menu. After you create the box, you can move, resize, and delete the box by using the mouse. To create a simple figure box, for example, follow these steps:

1. Choose **G**raphics, I**m**age. The Insert Image dialog box appears (see fig. 7.19).

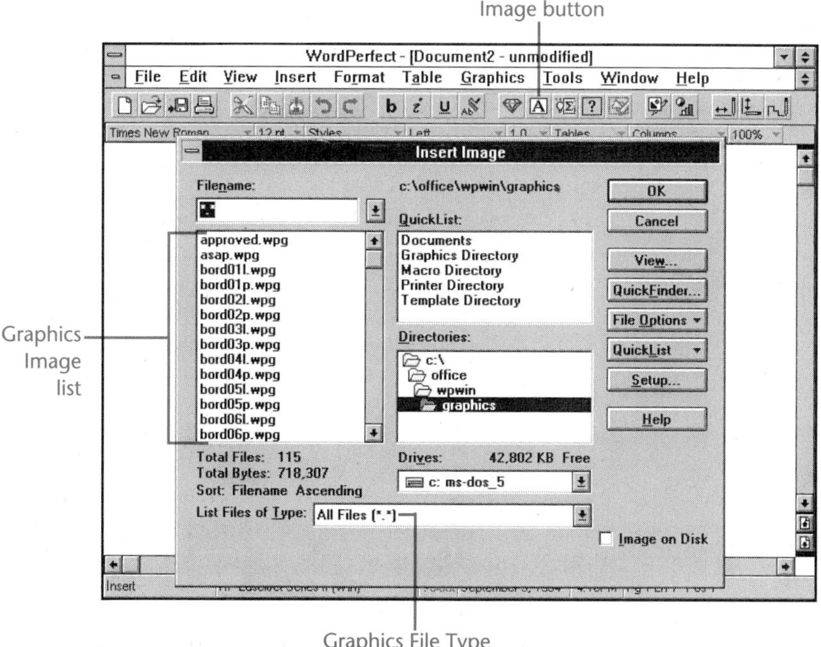

Fig. 7.19
Choose one of WordPerfect's clip art images, or choose a different file type—such as EPS, PCX, DRW, PIC, BMP, or TIF—from your own store of graphics images.

Tip
You can double-click on the image file name as a shortcut to choose the image and close the dialog box.

2. Select one of the listed images.

Tip
While in the Insert Image dialog box, choose a graphics file, then choose View to preview the graphic before you insert it in your document.

3. Choose OK or press Enter to close the dialog box and return to the document.

See Chapters 21 and 22 for information about creating other types of graphics boxes.

To perform any alterations to the graphics box—move, resize, or delete, for example—you must first select the graphics box. To select the box, click the mouse cursor on the box. Eight small black handles—or boxes—appear on the corners and in the center of each border line (see fig. 7.20). To deselect a box, click the mouse anywhere on the page other than in the graphics box.

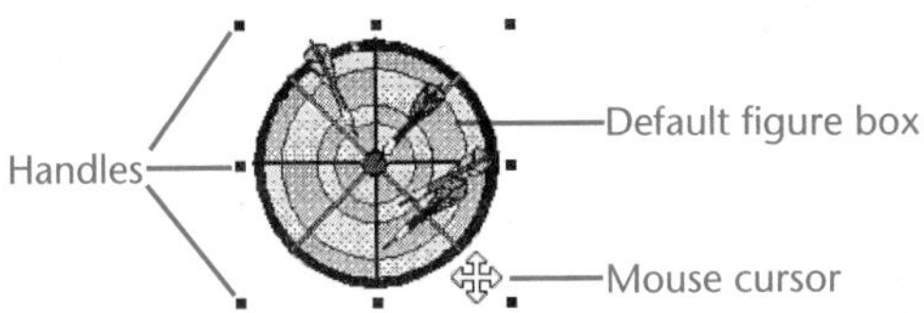

Fig. 7.20
When you position the mouse cursor over the graphics box, a four-headed arrow appears; drag the arrow to reposition the graphic.

Moving a Graphics Box

You can easily move the graphics box by dragging it to a new position with the mouse. When you position the mouse cursor over the graphics box—anywhere but on a small black handle—you can move the box around your document. To move the graphics box, follow these steps:

Tip
When you drag the graphics box, the box appears with a dashed line for the border so that you easily can move it to a new location.

1. Select the graphics box if the handles are not showing.
2. Position the mouse cursor over the box until you see a four-headed arrow.
3. Drag the mouse and the box to its new location.
4. Release the mouse button.

Resizing a Graphics Box

▶ See "Customizing Graphics Boxes," p. 719

▶ See "Retrieving and Positioning Clip Art," p. 750

You can resize a graphics box by using the mouse or a dialog box. For more information about using a dialog box to edit a graphics box, see Chapter 21.

Use the handles to resize the graphics box with the mouse. If you use one of the four corner handles to resize the box, the box and the image resize proportionally—both in height and width. If you use only one handle located in the middle of each border line, the box enlarges but the figure does not enlarge proportionally. To correct this problem, enlarge the other side of the box proportionally.

To use the mouse to resize the graphics box, follow these steps:

1. Click the mouse on the graphics box if the handles are not showing.

2. Move the mouse cursor over one of the handles until a double-headed arrow appears. Drag the handle to resize the graphics box (see fig. 7.21).

   You see the dashed border of the figure box when you drag the mouse, indicating the new size of the graphics box.

Tip
If you want the image to resize proportionally, use the corner handles.

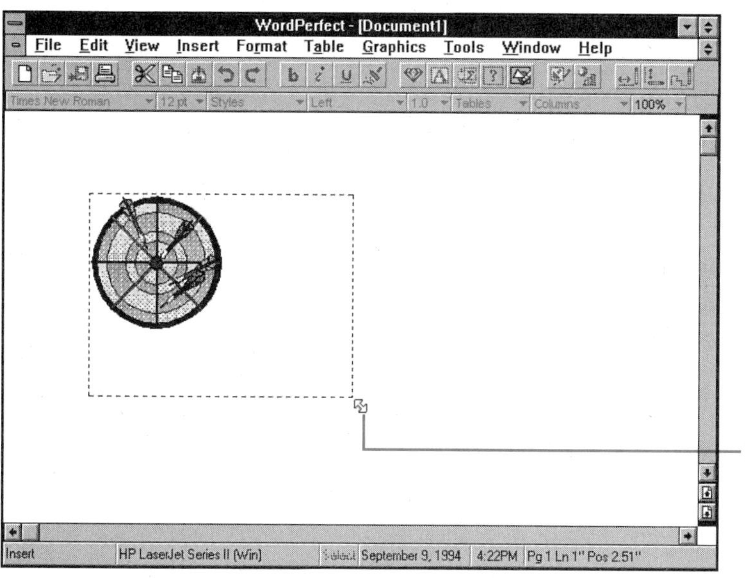

Fig. 7.21
This graphics box was resized using the right side handle; therefore, the image is not proportionally sized to the box. To correct the problem, drag the bottom middle handle down about two inches.

Deleting a Graphics Box

It's easy to delete a graphics box and image by using the mouse. Alternatively, you can use Reveal Codes and delete the graphics box code; but this method is much easier. To delete a graphics box, follow these steps:

1. Select the graphics box to be deleted.

2. Press the Delete key.

Tip
If you have trouble getting the double-headed arrow, move the mouse cursor slowly back and forth over the handle until the arrow appears.

Using a Graphics Box in a Letter

Thus far you have seen how to create, resize, move, and delete graphics boxes, but not how to apply a box to a document. It's easy to add graphics to your documents in WordPerfect. Figure 7.22 illustrates an advertising letter with two graphics boxes: a text box and a figure box.

The following instructions review creating a figure box. The text box in the figure has been customized—the border has been changed and fill has been added.

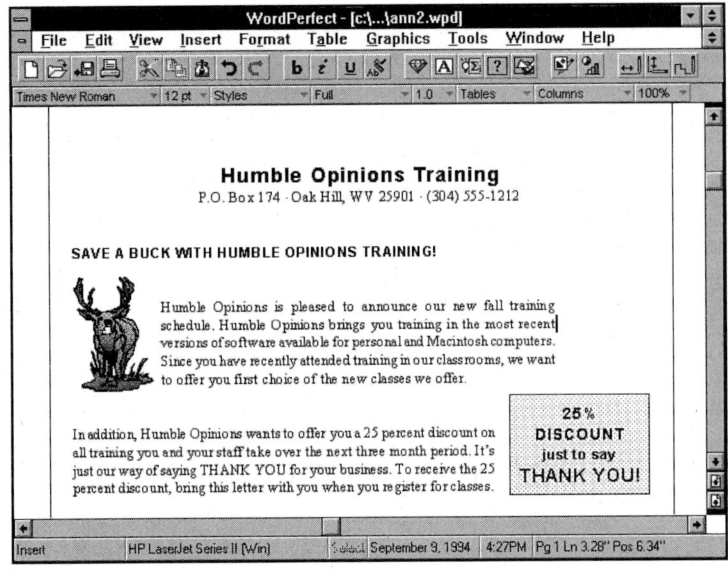

Fig. 7.22
Both the graphics boxes and the page border use a single line style to create consistency; the ten percent fill added to the text box attracts the reader's attention.

Tip
If you accidentally delete a graphics box, immediately choose **E**dit, **U**ndo to restore the box; or press Ctrl+Z.

For this exercise, use a document you already created or create a new document using figure 7.22 as a guide. After you enter and format the text, follow these steps to insert the figure box:

1. Position the insertion point at the point you want the first graphic to appear—at the beginning of the paragraph.

2. Choose **G**raphics, **Im**age. The Insert Image dialog box appears.

3. Select the graphics image and choose OK or double-click the mouse on the image name to close the dialog box and return to the document.

4. Using the mouse, resize and move the graphic.

Using Watermarks

A watermark is a custom graphic box that contains either text or graphics but prints in the background. The contents of the watermark box screens lightly so that text you enter in the foreground is readable.

There are many ways you can use watermarks. You can dress up a letter to a customer with your company logo or a screened border; add clip art in the background of fliers, newsletters, or brochures; add screened text to the background of notices, memos, reports, letters, and so on. You can use any of WordPerfect's 30 watermark files, create your own images or text to use as watermarks, or use images and text from other applications.

Tip

The graphics box attaches to the paragraph in which the insertion point is located. You can easily attach—or anchor—the graphics box to another paragraph by moving the box to a new position.

Using a Text Watermark

Most of WordPerfect's watermark files (WATER01.WPG, WATER02.WPG, and so on) consist of text; a few have screened lines, arrows, rectangles, and such. Following is a list of some of the text watermarks included in WordPerfect:

A.S.A.P.	Draft	Proof
Classified	Duplicate	Proposal
Confidential	Estimate	Reply Requested
Confirmation	File Copy	Thank You
Copying Prohibited	Past Due	

You can use WordPerfect's Watermark text or create your own. For more information about creating text in a graphics box, see Chapter 21. Figure 7.23 illustrates one of WordPerfect's Watermarks (WATER18.WPG) in a notice to employees.

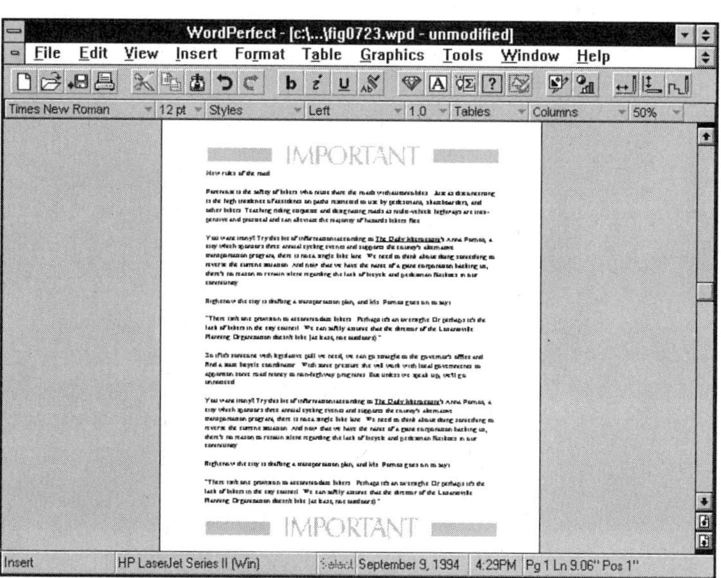

Fig. 7.23
Although the text in this figure does not overlap the watermark, it very well could. The watermark is screened lightly in the background.

Using Images as Watermarks

Try using other WordPerfect images as watermarks. Many of the borders are excellent as watermarks; use borders with a *p* in the file name for portrait (BORD03P.WPG, for example), *l* for landscape. You also can use any of the WPG images in WordPerfect's GRAPHICS directory. Figure 7.24 illustrates one of WordPerfect's image files—CRANE_J.WPG—used as a watermark in a bank report.

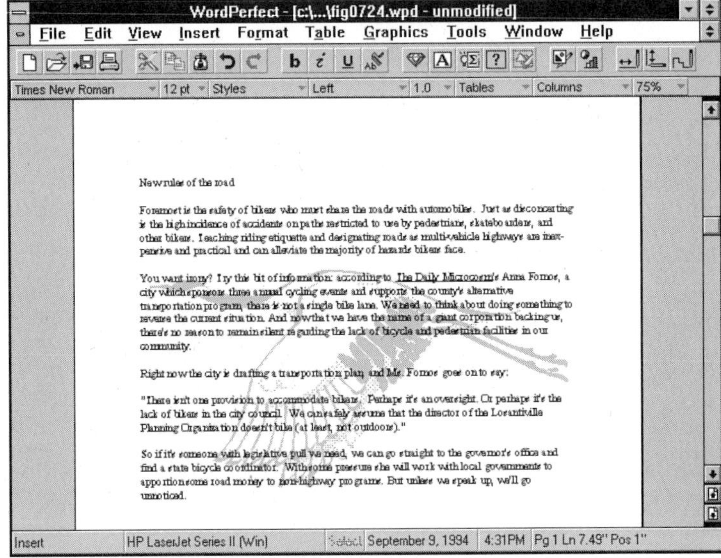

Fig. 7.24
In addition to using WordPerfect images, you can use clip art, scanned art, drawings from other programs including WP Draw and TextArt, and text in a watermark graphics box.

Figure 7.25 illustrates a small watermark added to a letterhead. You can size and position the image within the graphics box. For more information, see Chapter 22.

> **Note**
>
> When using watermarks, all editing options are available to you in the Graphics Editing screen. You can add a caption, reposition the contents of the screen, change the size and position of the graphics box, add a border, use the toolbox, and wrap text. For more information on the Graphics Editing screen, see Chapter 21.

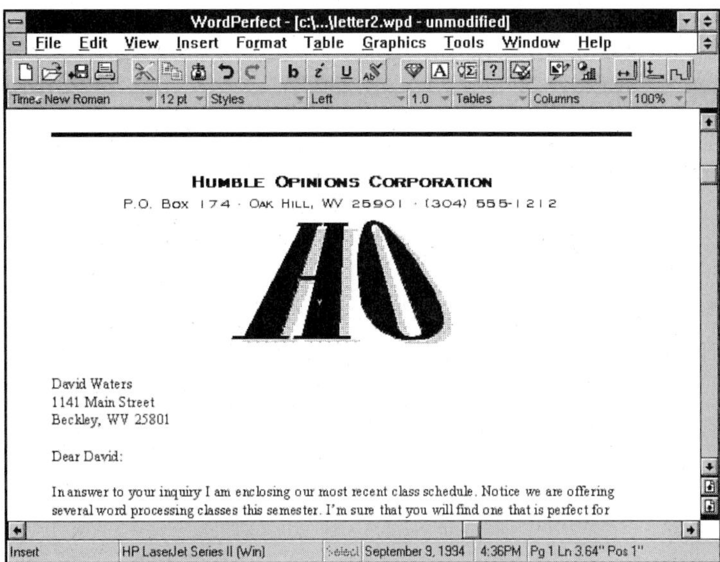

Fig. 7.25
This company logo was created with WordPerfect's TextArt, saved as a BMP file, and imported to the watermark graphics box.

Troubleshooting

I created the wrong type of graphics box and want to change the box type.

WordPerfect enables you to easily change the type of an existing graphics box, with little regard to what's inside the box. For example, you can change a figure box (that contains a graphics image) to a text box. Changing the box type can come in handy when you want to use the default style of another box, or if you accidentally create the wrong type of box in the first place. To change the box type, click the right mouse button over the graphics box. Choose S**t**yle from the QuickMenu. The Box Style dialog box appears. Choose New Box Style and then click OK.

I can't select a graphic by clicking on it with the mouse.

The easiest way to work with graphics boxes is by using the mouse. Select the box you want to edit by clicking on it. Sometimes you may click and the box is not selected. The usual reason is that the box was defined with the No Wrap option in the Text Wrap dialog box. To select the graphics box, you must choose **G**raphics, **E**dit Box; or press Shift+F11. Locate the box you want to edit by entering the number.

Creating a Watermark

Before creating a watermark, enter all text and format it. When the watermark appears on-screen, text editing slows considerably. To add a watermark to a document, follow these steps:

1. Choose **G**raphics, **C**ustom Box. The Custom Box dialog box appears.

2. In the Style **N**ame list box, choose Watermark and choose OK. The dialog box closes and the Graphics Editing screen appears with a new feature bar.

3. Choose C**o**ntent from the Graphics feature bar. The Box Content dialog box appears (see fig. 7.26).

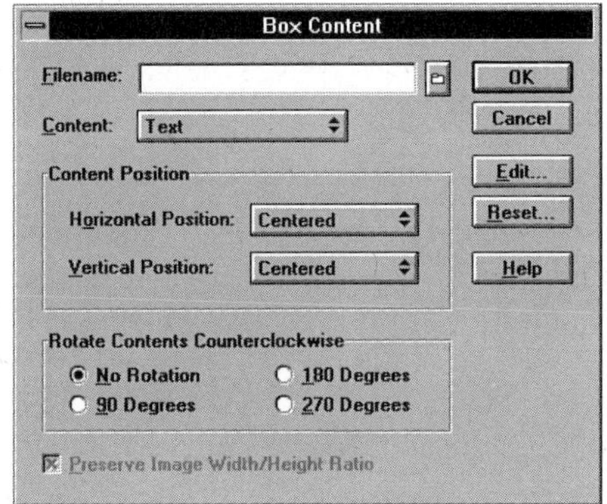

Fig. 7.26
The Box Content dialog box enables you to choose various images and to position those images within the watermark box.

4. Choose the file icon next to the **F**ilename text box. The Insert Image dialog box appears (see fig. 7.27).

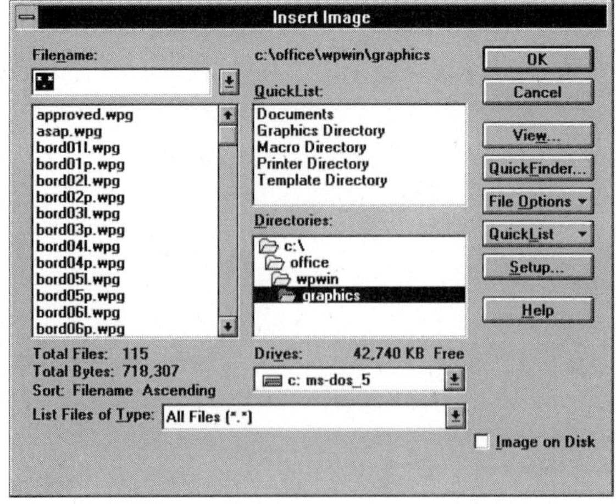

Fig. 7.27
In the Insert Image dialog box, you can view each watermark before you open it, thus saving time and energy. To view each WPG file, select the file and choose View. Continue to select files in the file list until you find one you like.

5. Choose any of the images to use for a watermark.

6. Choose OK to close the dialog box and return to the Box Content dialog box. Choose OK to return to the document.

7. To edit, format, or view your document, exit from the Graphics Editing screen by choosing the red question mark (?) in the Graphics feature bar. Choose **C**lose from the menu.

From Here...

In this chapter, you learned to use graphics to enhance your documents. You learned how you can add horizontal and vertical lines to separate text or dress up a page, and how to alter and move those lines by using the mouse. You also learned how to apply a border to a paragraph of text or to an entire page. You know you can easily change the border line styles and even add fill to any border you add to your document. In addition, this chapter showed you how to delete a border and how to turn off borders on specific pages.

Finally, you learned the different graphics box styles you can create in WordPerfect and how to add figure boxes to add pizzazz to your documents and emphasize text. After creating a graphics box, you learned how to resize, move, and delete the graphics box by using the mouse.

For more information on using the graphics features of WordPerfect, you may want to review the following chapters of this book:

- Chapter 14, "Working with Text Columns," shows you how to format text in columns, a common requirement when producing desktop-published documents combining both text and graphics.

- Chapter 17, "Creating and Modifying Charts with WP Draw," explains how you can produce and edit business charts (such as pie charts and line charts) to use in any WordPerfect document.

- Chapter 21, "Using Advanced Graphics Techniques," discusses the advanced graphics features of WordPerfect, including editing graphics.

- Chapter 22, "Using WP Draw and TextArt," provides information on using the drawing tools included with WordPerfect, Draw, and TextArt.

- Chapter 23, "Desktop Publishing with WordPerfect," shows you how to use WordPerfect's text and graphics feature to produce desktop-published documents.

Chapter 8

Basic Output: Printing, Faxing, and E-Mail

by Rick Hellewell and Read Gilgen

The paperless office isn't with us quite yet. In fact, printed output is the end objective of nearly every WordPerfect document you create. In this chapter you learn how to print great-looking documents, whether you use a dot-matrix printer, or the latest in color laser printer technology. You also learn how to select and set up your printer definitions, and to output your documents via fax or e-mail.

In this chapter, you learn about the following:

- Setting up WordPerfect 6.1 for Windows for your printer
- Using basic printing skills
- Using Zoom
- Printing specific pages
- Using WordPerfect's special print options
- Controlling print jobs
- Printing on a network
- Faxing from within WordPerfect
- Sending documents via electronic mail

Using Basic Printing Skills

Certain basic printing procedures apply to nearly all of the documents you print. In this section you learn to select the right printer, preview your document before printing, print one or more copies of your document, and cancel printing when something goes wrong.

Selecting a Printer

WordPerfect is a WYSIWYG (*What You See Is What You Get*) program. However, in order to truly see on-screen what your document will look like, WordPerfect has to know what printer you are planning to use so it can display the proper fonts and print attributes.

To select a printer, follow these steps:

1. Choose **F**ile, **P**rint to display the Print dialog box (see fig. 8.1).

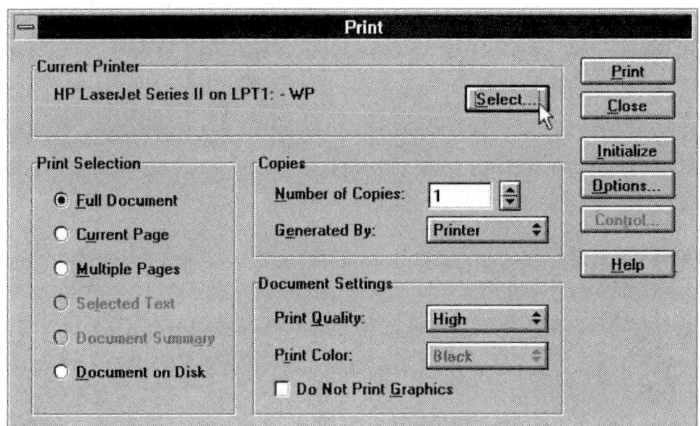

Fig. 8.1
Use the Print dialog box to select a printer definition and to specify the part of the document you want to print, along with the number of copies and the print quality of the text.

2. In the upper left corner of the dialog box, WordPerfect displays the current printer. If the printer name displayed is the printer you will be using, press Esc and continue to the next section.

3. If the printer is not correct, choose **S**elect. WordPerfect then displays the Select Printer dialog box (see fig. 8.2), which shows the current default Windows printer and a drop-down list of other installed printers. These are printers that you (or someone else) set up when you installed Windows (those printers with the Windows logo to the left) or when you installed WordPerfect (those printers with the "WP" logo to the left).

4. Click the printer to which you want to print.

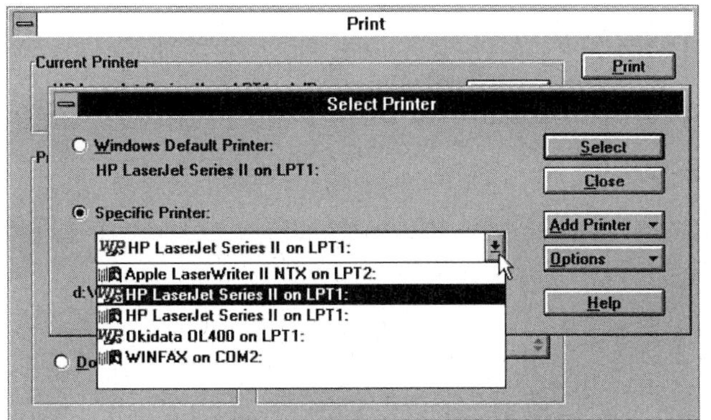

Fig. 8.2
Use the drop-down menu in the Select Printer dialog box to select the printer to which you intend to print your document.

Note

For the moment, don't worry about the "WP" or "Windows" designations. Generally, the Windows printers give you more flexibility and print the same in WordPerfect and other Windows applications.

5. Choose **S**elect to close the Select Printer dialog box, and choose **C**lose to close the Print dialog box.

Now you can create or format your document, knowing that the fonts and other formatting you see on-screen will match what your printer can print. See "Selecting and Configuring Your Printer" later in this chapter for more information on selecting a printer definition.

Using Zoom and View To See the Printed Output

In previous versions of WordPerfect, you had to use a separate Print Preview to see what your document would look like when printed. Because WordPerfect 6.1 for Windows is a WYSIWYG program, the text on-screen accurately represents what you get when you print the document. You see the fonts, sizes of characters, and character attributes (such as italic) on-screen as those parameters are selected. You also see graphics elements on-screen, such as pictures and lines. Seeing your document correctly before you print reduces printing errors, thus saving you time and also helping to save trees.

To see how everything in your document will print, you first should choose **V**iew, **P**age; or press Alt+F5. This enables you to see not only the text, but also any headers, footers, page numbers, or footnotes you might have. If you choose **D**raft, you see everything except what would appear in the margins. T**w**o Page enables you to see two facing pages side by side.

Now you also can use WordPerfect's Zoom feature to reduce or enlarge the size of the document on your screen to see more of the document, or to see more detail.

You can view the document in varying sizes by changing the zoom percentage with the **V**iew, **Z**oom command. This displays the Zoom dialog box (see fig. 8.3). You specify the *zoom percentage,* or a percentage of the actual size of the printed document. For example, if you select a zoom percentage of **1**00%, your document appears full-size on-screen. If you choose 90%, you see more of the document because the type and page are smaller.

The Zoom dialog box has several preset percentages: **5**0%, **7**5%, **1**00%, 15**0**%, and **2**00%. Other settings are:

- *M**a**rgin Width.* The full width of the text is displayed on-screen, with the left margin at the left edge of the screen, and the right margin at the right edge of the screen.

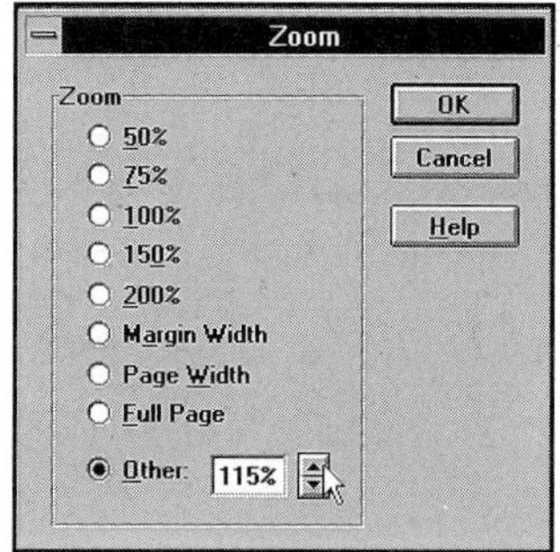

Fig. 8.3
The Zoom dialog box lets you select how the document is sized on-screen. The percentage values indicate the size of the document on-screen relative to the actual printed output.

- *Page **W**idth.* Shows the width of the page on-screen, including the left and right margin areas.
- ***F**ull Page.* The full page is displayed on-screen, including the top, bottom, left, and right margins.
- ***O**ther.* With this option, you can enter any percentage value, or use the up or down arrows to increment or decrement the value 5 percent at a time. The available range is 25 to 400 percent.

You use the Zoom settings to display the area of the document at the size you need. If you want to see the whole page, choose the **F**ull Page zoom. Some of the text in Full Page zoom may not be readable, depending on the resolution of your screen and the size of the text. While you are entering or changing text, you may want to choose the Page **W**idth or M**a**rgin Width zoom.

Tip
Switch between a full page view of your document and the zoom percentage you're using for editing by clicking the Page/Zoom Full button on the Toolbar.

Printing: The Basics

You have selected the proper printer, and viewed your document to determine that it's ready to be printed. In most cases, you now can print the current document in its entirety. You can start the Print process in one of several ways:

- Choose **F**ile, **P**rint.
- Press F5.
- Press Ctrl+P.
- Choose the Print button on the Toolbar.

Each of these choices displays the Print dialog box (refer to fig. 8.1).

You can change each of the settings in the Print dialog box according to your needs. In most cases, however, the default settings shown in figure 8.1 are suitable. To send the entire document to the printer, using the default settings, simply click the **P**rint command button. This prints one copy of the entire document, with high-quality text, and any graphics in the document. The document prints to the current printer.

Printing Multiple Copies

Use the Copies section of the Print dialog box to specify the number of copies to print and how those copies are generated. Specify the number of copies in the **N**umber of Copies box. You can enter the value or use the increment or decrement arrows to set the number of copies.

The G**e**nerated By option in the Print dialog box specifies how the copies are generated: By WordPerfect or by the printer. The G**e**nerated By options are explained as follows, using a value *x* you have specified in the **N**umber of Copies box:

- *Generated by* ***W****ordPerfect.* The entire document prints once, and then reprints until *x* copies are printed. This results in *x* collated sets of printed copies.

Tip
If you have a laser printer, let the printer generate multiple copies, especially if printing tables or graphics. WordPerfect generates each copy, while the printer duplicates the first copy.

- *Generated by **P**rinter*. Each page of the document prints *x* times, resulting in *x* copies of page 1, then *x* copies of page 2, and so on. This setting has no effect when printing with a dot-matrix printer.

Canceling a Print Job

Each time you tell WordPerfect to print something, you create a *print job*. Nearly everyone, at some time or another, begins a print job and then immediately realizes they don't want to print just yet, or have mistakenly printed the wrong thing. Fortunately, WordPerfect lets you cancel your print job.

If you are printing a single page on a fast printer (for example, a laser printer), you might just as well let it print because you may not be quick enough to cancel the print job. If you want to cancel printing several pages, you can try the following:

1. Choose **F**ile, **P**rint; or press F5.
2. In the Print dialog box, choose Con**t**rol. WordPerfect displays the WordPerfect Print Job dialog box (see fig. 8.4).
3. Choose **C**ancel Print Job.

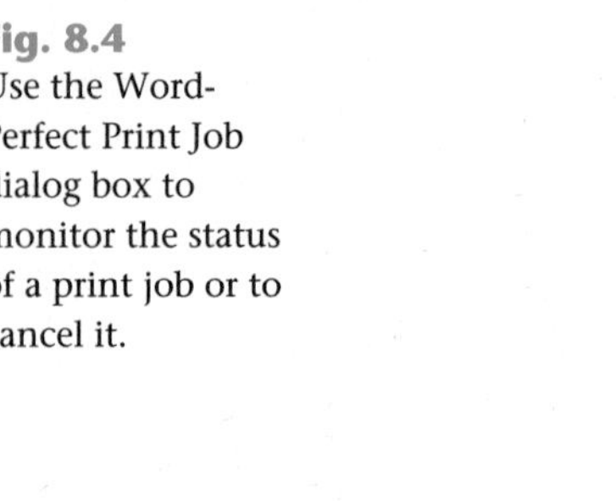

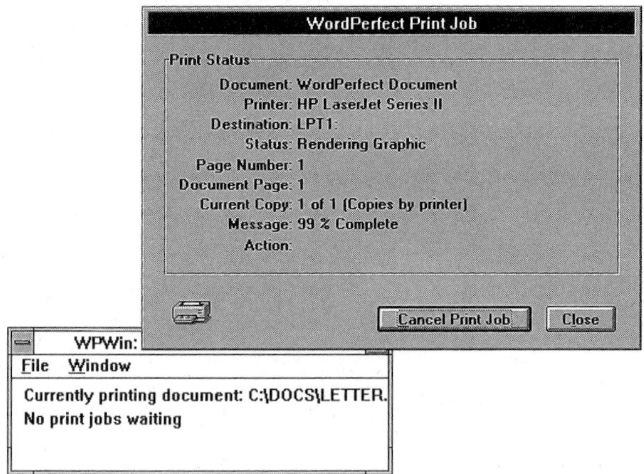

Fig. 8.4
Use the WordPerfect Print Job dialog box to monitor the status of a print job or to cancel it.

For more information on controlling your print jobs, see "Controlling the Printer and Print Jobs" later in this chapter.

Troubleshooting

I chose Print from the Print menu, but nothing happened.

First make sure you have selected the proper printer. Also, make sure your printer is on-line. Usually, if a printer is not available or is off-line you get an error message telling you so. However, if you are connected to a network, selecting the wrong printer may send your print job to someone else's printer.

When I try to print a document, everything comes out garbled, with wrong letters and fonts.

Correct printing depends on a complex interaction between the printer and WordPerfect. Sometimes either can get confused, resulting in improper printing. When this happens, you should try exiting WordPerfect (and even Windows if necessary), and turning off the printer to clear up the confusion. Turn on the printer and restart WordPerfect (and Windows), and try printing again. In most cases this corrects the problem.

Printing Specific Document Pages

Most of the printing you do follows the pattern described in the preceding section. However, WordPerfect also enables you to print only specific pages of your document. For example, you may need to print just a portion of a document because you made a change that affected only one page, or to check graphics or text placement, or to proofread.

Printing the Current Page

The easiest way to print a single page of a large document is to use the Print dialog to print just the current page. To do this:

1. Position your cursor anywhere on the page you want to print. The location of the cursor indicates the current page.
2. Access the Print dialog box (choose **F**ile, **P**rint; or press F5).

3. Choose C**u**rrent Page.
4. Choose **P**rint.

Printing Multiple Pages

WordPerfect 6.1 for Windows lets you print a portion of the document by specifying a range of pages to print. From the Print dialog box, choose **M**ultiple Pages. This displays the Multiple Pages dialog box shown in figure 8.5. After filling in the values, choose **P**rint to print the pages you specified.

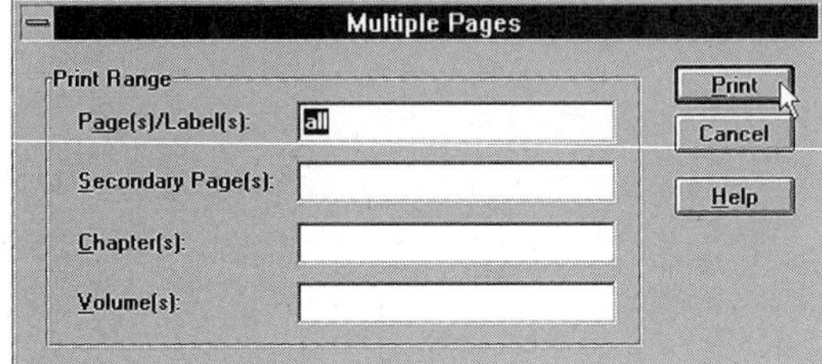

Fig. 8.5
The Multiple Pages dialog box is used to print specific pages from the document or file by specifying the page range.

Printing multiple pages by specifying a range in the Multiple Pages dialog box is much faster than moving to the desired page, choosing **F**ile, **P**rint, C**u**rrent Page, **P**rint, and then repeating those steps to print the next page.

You can specify in several different ways which pages you want to print:

- Print individual pages by separating the page numbers with commas or spaces, as in **3,15,23** or **3 15 23** to print pages 3, 15, and 23.
- Print a group of pages by separating the pages with a hyphen, as in **4-8** to print pages 4 through 8.
- Print all pages starting with a specific page number by typing a hyphen after the number, such as **3-** to print all pages starting with page 3.
- Print all pages up to a specific page number by typing a hyphen before the page number, such as **-15** to print the pages up to and including page 15.

You can combine page ranges by separating them with spaces or commas: **2-5 10-12** or **2-5,10-12** prints pages 2 through 5, and pages 10 through 12.

WordPerfect 6.1 for Windows allows you to format page numbers with Roman numerals, using the Page Numbering command. You can specify a range for such pages in the Multiple Pages dialog box. For example, to print the fourth through ninth pages of a document preface that you numbered with Roman numerals, specify **iv-ix** as the page range.

When using the Multiple Pages dialog box, make sure that you specify the pages in numerical order. If you specify a page range of **12-15 4**, only pages 12 through 15 print because page 4 comes before page 12 in the document. However, if an inserted code sets the page number to 4 somewhere after page 15, that page 4 which comes later does print.

If you print a document that is divided into chapters or volumes, be sure to specify the chapter or volume number. For example, if you have four chapters of twenty pages each, and specify 13-17 as the page range, only pages 13 through 17 of Chapter 1 print. To print specific pages of a chapter or volume, put a colon between the chapter or volume number and the page number, as in **4:10-14** to print pages 10 through 14 of Chapter 4.

The Multiple Pages dialog box lets you specify ranges for secondary pages, chapters, or volumes. Use the **S**econdary Pages, **C**hapters, or **V**olumes choices if you have divided your document into these page types. When you specify volume and chapter settings, remember that volumes have priority, followed by chapters, secondary pages, and pages. If you specify a volume of 4, and pages of 3 through 12, only pages 3 through 12 in Volume 4 print. Chapter 5, "Formatting Pages and Documents," covers the use of these page types.

Printing Odd or Even Numbered Pages

Normally, all the pages that you specify in the page range print. You can print just the odd or even numbered pages by selecting **O**ptions from the Print dialog box. This displays the Print Output Options dialog box shown in figure 8.6. This is useful for printing double-sided documents on a printer that can only print on one side of the page.

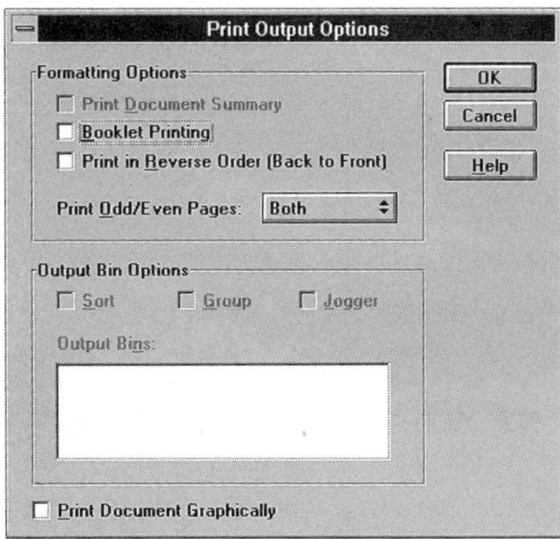

Fig. 8.6
You use the Print Output Options dialog box to print odd or even pages, along with other formatting and output options.

Note

You can print a double-sided document on a printer only capable of single-side printing. Or you can print a document so that you can bind and fold the pages as a booklet.

To print double-sided documents on a printer with only single-side printing capability, first print all the odd pages by setting Print **O**dd/Even Pages to **O**dd. Choose OK to close the Print Output Options dialog box, and then choose **P**rint from the Print dialog box. After all pages have printed, reload the printed pages into the printer and repeat the preceding steps, choosing **E**ven from the Print Output Options dialog box to print the even pages.

You have to determine how to reload the printed pages in your printer so that the pages print properly. To figure this out, create a four-page document with the page numbers on each page. Print the odd pages, reload the paper, and print the even pages. If the pages are not in the proper order (page 2 on the reverse of page 1), you need to print the even pages in reverse order by choosing the Print in **R**everse Order (Back to Front) check box in the Print Output Options dialog box. In each test, make sure that you reload the paper the same way.

Using Printing Options

WordPerfect's printing options enable you to print as much or little of your document as you want. You also can print your most complex documents, just the way you want them.

Printing Selected Text

If you have selected a block of text, choosing **F**ile, **P**rint (or one of the other ways discussed earlier in this chapter) displays the Print dialog box with the Se**l**ected Text radio button enabled. Choose **P**rint to print the selected block of text. Printing blocks of text is useful when you need to see text that spans a page boundary, or need to print only a part of the text on a page.

The selected text prints on a page in the same position that it occupies in the document. So if you block a paragraph at the bottom of a page, the text prints at the bottom of a page. If you select text across a page boundary, the text is printed on different pages in the same locations as it appears in the document. Printing selected text allows you to check the placement of the text, without having to print the entire page or document.

Printing Booklets

The **B**ooklet Printing check box in the Print Output Options dialog box allows you to print your document as a booklet. You should set up the subdivided pages and other formatting commands as described in Chapter 5, "Formatting Pages and Documents." When the document has printed, you can staple the pages together into a booklet without having to rearrange the pages. Dialog boxes tell you which pages to insert into the printer so that the text in the completed booklet is in the correct order.

Printing Documents with Graphics or Color

You use the Document Settings section of the Print dialog box to specify the print quality of the text and graphics, how color text or graphics print, and whether graphics print with the document.

The Print **Q**uality setting choices are **H**igh (the default), **M**edium, or **D**raft. The actual print quality depends on the capabilities of your printer; some printers may have only draft and high-quality print modes.

The P**r**int Color setting determines whether colored text or graphics print in full-color or in black. This option is available only if your printer has color printing capability.

The Do Not Print **G**raphics check box is available, in case you don't want to print any graphics in your document. This is useful for proofreading documents without being distracted by graphics, and may also result in faster printing, especially on a dot-matrix printer.

WordPerfect 6.1 for Windows has full support for color printing if you have a color printer. You can place colored text or graphics in your document even without having a color printer. The Print dialog box includes a P**r**int Color setting that is normally set to the color capability of your printer. If your printer does not support color, the P**r**int Color setting is set to black. This prints colored text or graphics as shades of gray.

You can set the P**r**int Color to black even when you do have a color printer. This is useful for draft copies of your document, because it usually takes longer to print a document with colors than one without colors. To print without colors if a color printer is selected, just change the P**r**int Color setting to black in the Print dialog box.

Printing the Document Summary

The Document Summary is a special page of your document that you create with the **F**ile, Document Summar**y** command. If you have created a document summary, it alone prints when you choose Document Summ**a**ry from the Print dialog box. If you want to print the Document Summary along with some or all of the rest of the document, choose **O**ptions from the Print dialog box and select the Print **D**ocument Summary check box on the Print Output Options dialog box. The Document Summary prints first, followed by the rest of the document or pages that you specified. The document summary does not print if you have not created it, or if only the author name has been entered in the Document Summary dialog box. The Document Summary is explained in Chapter 5, "Formatting Pages and Documents."

Specifying the Output Bin Options

Output Bin Options on the Print Output Options dialog box enable you to control how the pages are sorted on printers that have an output bin for collating printed pages. If your printer definition doesn't support this option, the choices are unavailable.

- ***S**ort*. Collates the output pages in each output bin.
- ***G**roup*. Groups multiple copies of one page in each output bin.
- ***J**ogger*. Puts each page into a separate bin.

Adding Printer Commands to Your Document

You may want to add certain printer commands to your document to take advantage of some of the special features of your printer. You can insert these printer commands in the document, and they won't affect the formatting of your document. For instance, you might have a special font cartridge with your signature or company logo on it. You can send out the command to the printer to access them.

You can place the printer commands in the document by first placing the cursor at the point in the document where you want the printer command to be sent. Then choose Fo**r**mat, **T**ypesetting, **P**rinter Command to display the Printer Command dialog box. You can then place your printer commands in the **C**ommand box. Or you can store the printer commands in an ASCII text file, and place the file name in the **P**rinter Command Filename text box.

You also can check the P**a**use Printer check box if you want the printer to pause at that point in the document. This allows you, for example, to load paper of a different color, or to change the printer ribbon.

Printer commands are listed in your printer manual and are different for each type of printer. They are usually listed as decimal or hexadecimal characters, or text. Put decimal printer commands in a pair of angle brackets, such as **<23>** to insert the decimal printer command of "23." Enter text commands as the text shown for the command.

For example, the HP LaserJet printer uses an Esc+E command to reset the printer. Because the Esc command is decimal 27, you enter the following printer command:

<27>E

WordPerfect does not check the syntax or correctness of the printer commands. If, when you print, part of the printer command syntax you entered appears as text in the middle of your printed document, you need to fix the invalid printer command.

You may want to place often-used printer commands in a printer command file. This is an ASCII file that contains the properly formatted printer commands. You can use WordPerfect 6.1 for Windows to create the file. Then choose **F**ile, Save **A**s; or press F3. In the Save As dialog box, change the format of the file to ASCII Text (DOS).

Caution

If you are connected to a shared printer, be aware that the printer commands you use may affect other users. For instance, a "Reset Printer" command may clear any downloaded soft fonts in the printer that other users may need to use.

Setting Up Printing Parameters

You can change the default settings used in the Print dialog box by choosing **E**dit, Pr**e**ferences, P**r**int, and then changing the settings in the Print Preferences dialog box (see fig. 8.7).

The Print Preferences dialog box includes Copies and Document Settings sections. You set values here the same way as in the Print dialog box, discussed previously.

The Print Preferences dialog box is where you also set the size attribute ratios. These settings are percentage multipliers used to scale the current font whenever relative size attributes are applied. For example, if the current font has a size of 10 points, and the **L**arge size attribute ratio in the Print Preferences dialog box is set to 120%, then anywhere the **L**arge attribute is applied in the document, the character size changes to 12 points, which is 120 percent of 10 points (10 * 120% = 12).

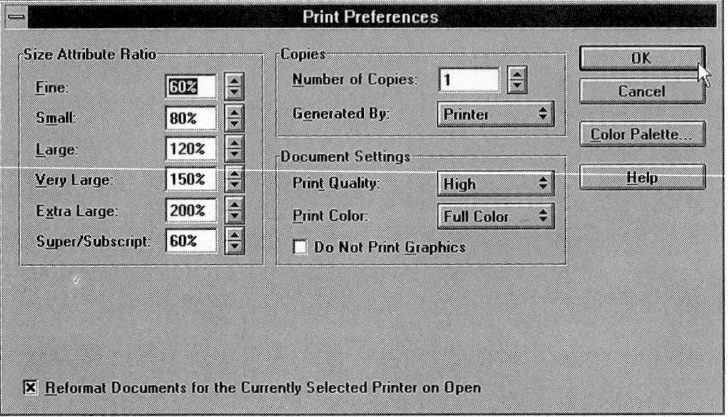

Fig. 8.7
The Print Preferences dialog box lets you specify the default Print dialog box settings. Whenever the Print dialog box next appears, the new defaults are used.

> **Caution**
>
> You can change these values, but they become permanent for the current and future WordPerfect 6.1 for Windows editing sessions. These settings are not saved with any document, so a user on another computer working with your document has his or her own size attribute ratios applied when printing.

When you open a document, by default WordPerfect reformats the document to match the currently selected printer. If you want the document to keep the printer settings that were used to create it, deselect the **R**eformat Documents for the Currently Selected Printer on Open check box. This is particularly useful if you are only editing the document and then returning to the original author for printing.

The **C**olor Palette options are used to specify the range of colors that you want to print in your document. You can select different color palettes, or create and edit color palettes. The colors that you place in your document are printed only if you have a printer with color capabilities. See Chapter 23, "Desktop Publishing with WordPerfect," for more information on using color in your documents.

Troubleshooting

When I print a document with graphics, the graphics don't look good even though I'm using a high quality laser printer.

There may be two problems. First, make sure you have Print **Q**uality set to **H**igh in the Print dialog box. Second, you may want to switch to the WordPerfect printer definition for your printer rather than using the Windows printer definition.

I'm trying to print envelopes, but my printer won't print them and I get an error message on my printer's display.

If you have a separate envelope bin on your laser printer, you won't have this problem (unless, of course, the bin is empty). On a single bin laser printer, WordPerfect assumes you will feed an envelope through the manual feed (top of the tray). If you insert the envelope in the manual feed before you print the envelope, you will avoid the error message. If you insert the envelope after you get the message, usually you can press the printer's On Line button (or an equivalent button) to continue printing the envelope.

Controlling the Printer and Print Jobs

WordPerfect 6.1 for Windows enables you to look at information about the current print job and to control multiple print jobs. WordPerfect 6.1 for Windows supports both the WordPerfect Print Manager and the Windows Print Manager. However, the procedures for controlling the printer with each of these managers are different.

Using the WordPerfect Print Manager

When you print a document or file, the WordPerfect Print Process is in charge of sending the information to the printer. You can look at the progress of the print job by choosing Con**t**rol from the Print dialog box. The Print Job dialog box shows you information about the current print job, including the following:

- The name of the document being printed, if it has been previously saved
- The name of the currently selected printer

- The destination of the print job (for example, your local printer which probably is connected to your computer at the LPT1 printer port location)
- The current status of the print job, such as `Printing`
- The number of the page currently being printed
- The number of the copy currently being printed
- The completion percentage of the current print job

If you want to cancel the current print job, choose **C**ancel Print Job.

Using the Windows Print Manager

If you have enabled the Windows Print Manager through the Windows Control Panel Printer program, WordPerfect 6.1 for Windows sends the print job through the WordPerfect Print Process to the Windows Print Manager. You can switch to the Print Manager after the print job has been sent, so you can look at the status of the print job and perform other actions on the print job. If your Windows installation has disabled the Print Manager through the Windows Control Panel Printer program, the WordPerfect Print Process sends documents directly to the printer. Your Windows manual has detailed information about using the Windows Print Manager.

Note

The WordPerfect Print Process returns control of WordPerfect to you more quickly than does the Windows Print Manager. Leaving the Windows Print Manager activated may give you more time to cancel your print jobs, but it also requires more time to print a document. Unless you use the Windows Print Manager for other Windows programs, you really don't need to use it.

Selecting and Setting Up Your Printer

Whether what you print turns out right or not depends largely on whether you selected the right printer, and whether it has been set up correctly.

Understanding Printer Drivers

When you installed WordPerfect 6.1 for Windows, WordPerfect printer drivers were set up with some default values. When you installed Windows and selected your printer, that also set up your Windows printer drivers.

Your printer is controlled by a *printer driver* (a file) that contains special commands used to perform various functions. As an example, when you make a word boldface, the printer driver is responsible for sending out the special commands to tell the printer that the next word needs to be printed in bold, rather than normal characters. These printer commands can be very complex. The printer driver is responsible for translating the text that you type on-screen into commands that the printer uses to print your masterpiece.

WordPerfect 6.1 for Windows lets you select WordPerfect or Windows printer drivers. You can have both types of printer drivers installed, but only one can be selected to be active. Because the printer driver contains font information, the capabilities of the drivers may differ depending on the fonts you have installed with the drivers. Switching between the drivers may result in changes in the look of your document, due to differences between available fonts.

The WordPerfect printer drivers support a larger variety of printers than the standard Windows printer drivers. You may find your printer on the WordPerfect printer driver list if it is not on the Windows printer list. If you work primarily in Windows and don't share your documents, you may want to use the Windows printer drivers. If you share your documents with other users who don't use Windows, use WordPerfect printer drivers. This allows WordPerfect 6.0 for DOS users to share your document without the problems caused by using different printer drivers. If you plan on faxing your document, you can use the Windows fax driver that was installed with your Windows-based fax software.

Selecting and Configuring Your Printer

When you have multiple printers installed, you can select the current printer by accessing the Print dialog box and choosing **S**elect. This displays the Select Printer dialog box (see fig. 8.8).

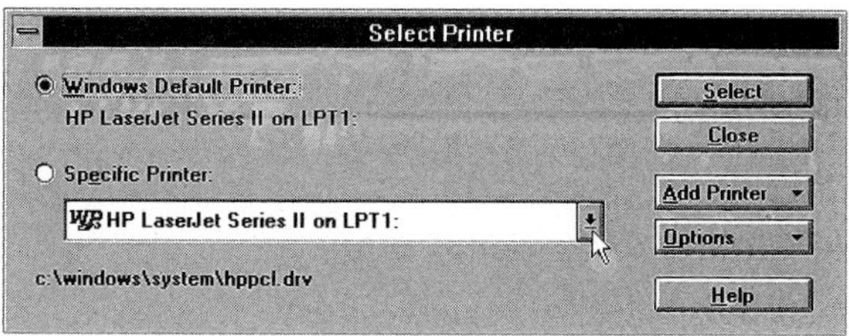

Fig. 8.8
The Select Printer dialog box enables you to choose the current printer.

The Select Printer dialog box displays two radio buttons: one for the current **W**indows Default Printer (as set up in the Windows Control Panel), and the other for a specific printer of your choice, either a Windows printer or a WordPerfect printer. In the lower left corner of the dialog box you see the actual printer driver file (for example HPPCL.DRV, a Windows driver, or HP2.PRS, a WordPerfect driver).

To select a specific printer, click the drop-down menu button on the Sp**e**cific Printer box. Windows drivers are marked with a Windows logo, while WordPerfect drivers are marked with a "WP" logo. Click the printer driver you want and WordPerfect automatically marks the Sp**e**cific Printer radio button. The buttons on the right side of the Select Printer dialog box enable you to **S**elect the chosen printer, **C**lose the dialog box, or **A**dd either a WordPerfect or a Windows printer definition to the list of available printers.

The **O**ptions button pop-up menu includes the following, most of which are covered in detail in this section:

- ***I****nitial Font.* Select the base font that is used for all documents created with the printer definition selected. Selecting this option displays the Printer Initial Font dialog box, in which you can choose the font face, style, and size values to be used as defaults for the current printer. Chapter 20, "Using Fonts and Special Characters," contains detailed information on using fonts in your documents.

- ***S****etup.* Change the printer name, specify cartridges and fonts for the printer, choose a sheet feeder, turn on color for color printers, and select the printer port.

- ***I****nfo.* Show information about WordPerfect printers, such as hints for using the printer and the printer's capabilities. Information on the printer's sheet feeder also is available.

- ***C****opy.* Make a copy of the currently selected printer so you can make changes to the copied printer without affecting the original printer's configuration.

- ***D****elete.* Delete the currently selected printer. For WordPerfect drivers, you can optionally delete the PRS file. For Windows drivers, select the printer, and then choose Remove from the Windows Printer dialog box.

Caution

Deleting a Windows printer driver makes that printer unavailable to all other Windows programs, regardless of whether they still need access to that printer.

- ***Network.*** Configure the printer for use on your network. The dialog box enables you to select a printer connection that works with your network from the list of printer queues available in WordPerfect.
- ***Update.*** Rebuild the Printer Resource file and update font information from the printer's ALL file. Applies only to WordPerfect printer drivers.
- ***Preferences.*** Another method of accessing the Print Preferences dialog box. See "Setting Up Printing Parameters," earlier in this chapter.

Changing the Printer Settings

To change the settings of a printer, first highlight the printer in the Select Printer dialog box, and then choose **O**ptions, **S**etup. If you select a WordPerfect printer driver, the WordPerfect Printer Setup dialog box is displayed (see fig. 8.9). Selecting a Windows printer driver results in the Setup dialog box being displayed for that driver.

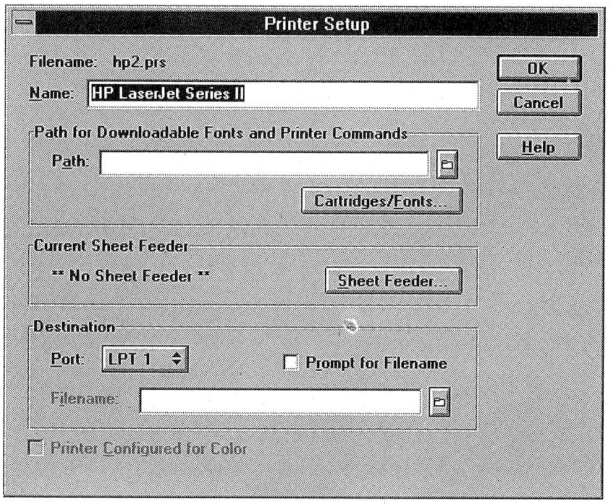

Fig. 8.9
The Printer Setup dialog box is used to configure the printer's fonts and sheet feeder, enable color printing, and specify the output port for the printer. You can also change the printer's descriptive name.

This dialog box shows the name of the PRS file that contains the commands used to control the printer. In the **N**ame text box, the descriptive name of the printer is shown. You must change this name if you are installing multiple copies of the same printer driver—for instance, if there are two HP 4si's on your network. You might call one, HP 4si in Accounting, and the other, HP 4si in Shipping. All printer names must be unique.

The Destination box shows the currently selected port for the printer. From the **P**ort pop-up list, you can choose any of the LPT1 through LPT3 or COM1 through COM4 ports, or File, to print to a file. When you choose a serial port

(COM1 through COM4), there are no changes to COM port settings such as baud rate. These COM port parameters must be set up through the Windows Control Panel Ports program.

To change the settings for a Windows printer driver, select the printer, and then choose **O**ptions, **S**etup. WordPerfect displays the Windows Control Panel dialog box which enables you to make changes to the printer driver. See your Windows manual for information on setting up Windows printer drivers.

Adding a New Printer to Your List of Available Printers

When you installed WordPerfect 6.1 for Windows, you selected a printer from the list of available printers. The install program then installed the WordPerfect printer driver files for the printer you selected. The printer family file ALL file was also installed. The ALL file contains information about similar printers. So if you selected an HP LaserJet 4 printer, for example, the ALL file contains information about a wide variety of laser printers.

After you start WordPerfect 6.1 for Windows, you can add additional printers to your list of available printers. You do this by first choosing **S**elect. Then from the Select Printer dialog box, choose **A**dd Printer. From the pop-up list, choose whether to add Word**P**erfect or **W**indows printers.

Adding WordPerfect Printers

When you choose to add Word**P**erfect printers from the **A**dd Printer pop-up list on the Select Printer dialog box, the Add Printer dialog box is displayed, as shown in figure 8.10.

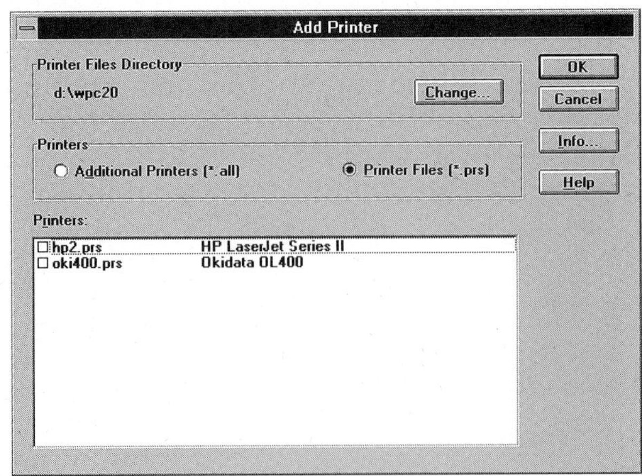

Fig. 8.10
The Add Printer dialog box displays a list of installed printer drivers' files (.PRS files). If you choose the Additional Printer (*.all) button and select a printer, WordPerfect creates the .PRS file for that printer.

The Add Printer dialog box shows the location of the Printer Files directory that WordPerfect created during the installation process. If you want to look at printer files that are stored in another directory, choose **C**hange and enter the directory name.

The Printers area of the dialog box enables you to display the ALL files (containing the printer information for printer families) when you choose A**d**ditional Printers (*.all), or the PRS files (the Printer Resource file containing printer information about one printer) when you choose **P**rinter Files (*.prs).

When you choose **P**rinter Files, the P**r**inters list box shows the list of printers that have already been installed. Each installed printer in the P**r**inters list box has a check box, the name of the PRS file, and the corresponding printer description. You can add several printers at once; selected check boxes indicate the printer(s) you have chosen. If you choose OK, WordPerfect adds the selected printer(s) to your available printers list. The output port assignment(s) for the new printer(s) are different from those already in use.

Choosing **I**nfo displays information about the highlighted printer. This information can include instructions on using colors to create text with patterns, using sheet feeders, or other topics.

When you choose A**d**ditional Printers, the P**r**inters list box of the Add Printer dialog box changes to show the list of printers available that are contained in the ALL files (see fig. 8.11). Notice that in this list, the description accompanies the check box, and the file names are in the rightmost column.

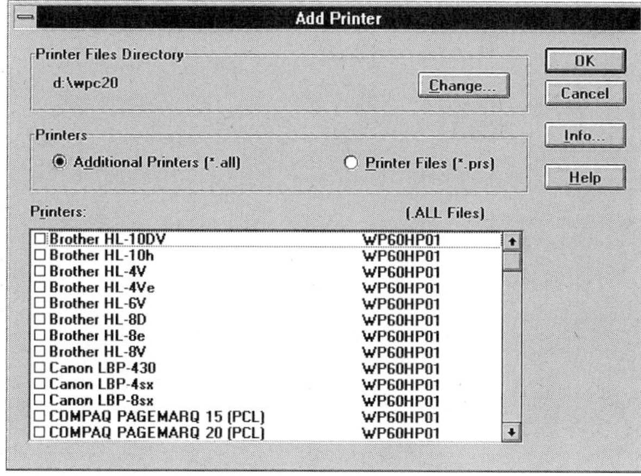

Fig. 8.11
When you choose A**d**ditional Printers, the Add Printer dialog box displays a list of printers available. These are the printers available in the ALL files that were copied to the printer files directory during installation.

To add a printer, scroll through the list until the desired printer is displayed. Click the printer name and choose OK. The Select Printer dialog box is displayed, with the new printer added to the list.

New printers are initially configured for the LPT1: port. If you add the same printer as one already installed, the new printer is then configured to LPT2:. To change the port assignment, highlight the printer in the Select Printer dialog box, and then choose S**e**tup, **P**ort to configure the printer port, as discussed in the next section.

If you have additional printer files stored in a directory other than the one displayed in the Printer Files Directory box, you can choose **C**hange and enter a new directory name to view the list of printer files in that directory. If you don't see your printer on the list, you can use the WordPerfect 6.1 for Windows installation program to install the needed file.

Adding Windows Printer Drivers

WordPerfect 6.1 for Windows lets you add additional Windows printer drivers by choosing Windows from the **A**dd Printer pop-up list on the Select Printer dialog box. This starts the Windows Control Panel Printer program. From the Windows Printer program, you can add or change the settings of Windows printers as described in your Windows manual. You may need the Windows installation disks to add additional Windows printers.

Adding Fonts for Your Printer

Each printer that you add comes with the default fonts installed for that printer. If you purchase additional font cartridges or soft fonts, you should add those fonts to your WordPerfect printer definition. From the Select Printer dialog box, choose **O**ptions, **S**etup to access the Printer Setup dialog box. Use the Path for Downloadable Fonts and Printer Commands to specify the directory where the soft fonts files are stored.

The Cartridges/**F**onts button in the Printer Setup dialog box lets you specify the fonts and font cartridges that you purchased for your printer. This displays the Select Fonts dialog box that allows you to select the Built In Fonts, Font Cartridges installed, and any Soft Fonts that are available.

To add fonts or cartridges to your Windows printer drivers, access the Font program from the Windows Control Panel. Chapter 20, "Using Fonts and Special Characters," contains detailed information about installing and selecting fonts.

Using Other Forms of Output

While most people print documents to their own dot-matrix or laser printer, some print to network printers or simply send their documents via fax or electronic mail.

Printing on a Network

If you or your network administrator have previously installed a network printer, you can select it from the Select Printer dialog box. The WordPerfect Print Process will send the print job to the network printer. You can choose **F**ile, **P**rint, Con**t**rol to see the progress of the print job in the network queue. You can also use your network's printer queue program to look at print jobs that are waiting in the network printer queue.

You can select a different network printer by choosing **N**etwork from the Select Printer dialog box. The **P**rinter Connections list box shows the port and printer queue for your current connection and any other printer connections available on your network. You can make any of these the current connection. If the desired network printer connection is not available, choose Attach to specify another available file server that has the desired connection.

You may want to set up several different available printers, each to a different printer queue. You can then select the appropriate network printer from the Select Printer dialog box.

Printing to a File

There are times you want to print to a file because that printer is not connected to your system. By printing to a file, all the printer commands are stored in the file along with the text. You can then take the file to a system that is connected to that type of printer, and "print" it to the printer (as covered later in this section), even if that system doesn't have WordPerfect 6.1 for Windows.

For instance, if you need to work on a Postscript-formatted document, you don't need to have a Postscript printer connected to your computer. Just install a Postscript printer driver, and print the document to a file. Then take the file to a computer that is connected to a Postscript printer. Installing a Postscript printer driver and using it with your Postscript document is much easier than trying to format the document with different printer drivers.

To set up printing to a file, choose **A**dd Printer from the Select Printer dialog box and add the printer to your list of available printers. Then select the printer and choose **O**ptions, **S**etup to display the Printer Setup dialog box. Choose **P**ort, **F**ile. If you want to print to the same file name each time, enter the file name in the F**i**lename text box. To specify a file name each time you "print" the document, choose the P**r**ompt for Filename check box. Choose **N**ame and change the printer's descriptive name to something like **HP Post-script definition, print to File**, so that you can identify it from others.

When you print to a file, be sure that you have selected the "file" printer from the Select Printer dialog box. If you have selected P**r**ompt for Filename, the file name is requested at print time.

After the document has printed, use the Open File dialog box to copy the file to a floppy disk. Then take the disk to another computer, and use the DOS COPY command to print the file. For example, if you call the print file PRNFILE.DOC on the A drive, and the computer's printer is connected to the LPT1 port, you type this command at the DOS prompt:

COPY A:PRNFILE.DOC /B LPT1:

The document then prints on the printer, just as if you used WordPerfect 6.1 for Windows and were connected to that printer. The /B parameter ensures that the entire file prints.

Faxing from WordPerfect 6.1 for Windows

WordPerfect 6.1 for Windows has the capability to fax documents when the following conditions are met:

- A fax board is installed in your computer or connected to your network
- A Windows-based fax program is installed on your computer (so that the fax "printer" is available from the Select Printer dialog box)

To fax a document, follow these steps:

1. With the document that you want to fax in the active window, choose **F**ile, **P**rint; or press F5. If you want to fax a block of text, first select the text and then choose **F**ile, **P**rint; or press F5.
2. Make sure that the fax printer is shown as the current printer in the Print dialog box. Choose **S**elect to select your fax printer driver, if it is not the current printer.
3. Specify the portion of the current document to fax by choosing C**u**rrent Page or **M**ultiple Pages, or leave **F**ull Document selected to fax the entire document.

4. Choose **Print** to fax the document. The document is *rasterized*—converted to a faxable format—and then handed off to your fax driver for faxing.

5. Your Windows fax program may display a dialog box for the fax destination information. If not, switch to your Windows fax program with Alt+Tab.

6. Fill in the destination information in the fax program's dialog box, and then send the fax. Figure 8.12 shows the dialog box for the WinFax fax program.

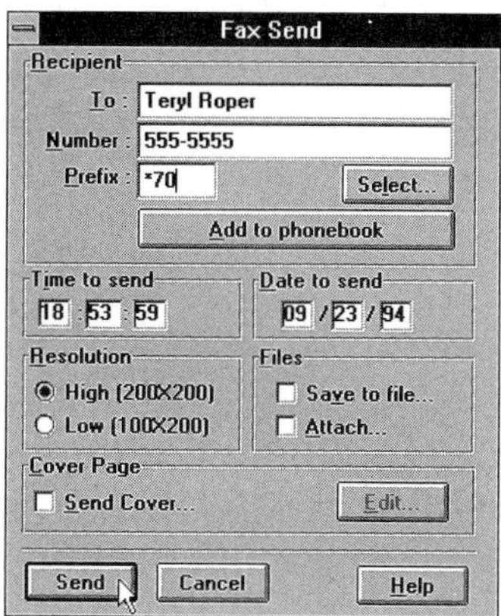

Fig. 8.12
The WinFax program "prints" to a fax/modem. Your fax dialog box may be different, but should include most of the same information.

After the document is sent to the fax driver, you can use the fax program's commands to learn the status of the fax, to look at the send or receive log, or to cancel the fax before it is sent.

Using Novell GroupWise 4.1 and WordPerfect Office E-Mail

If you are connected to a network, WordPerfect 6.1 for Windows can send mail to others on your network through WordPerfect Office 3.0, 3.1, or 4.0, or its more recent successor, Novell GroupWise 4.1. The program also supports any mail system that uses the VIM or MAPI mail standards.

When you want to mail the current document, choose **F**ile, S**e**nd. If the S**e**nd command is not available, you will need to use the WordPerfect 6.1 for Windows Installation program to install mail support after you have installed your mail program. Refer to your WordPerfect documentation for more information.

If you have WordPerfect Office 4.0 or Novell GroupWise 4.1 for Windows, the Mail To dialog box is used to prepare and send a copy of the current document as an attached file to your mail message (see fig. 8.13). Fill in the Address, Subject, and Message boxes. The current document is saved as a temporary file and attached to the message. You can attach other files and sound objects to your mail message. When you have completed the items in the Mail To: dialog box, use the Send button to send the message.

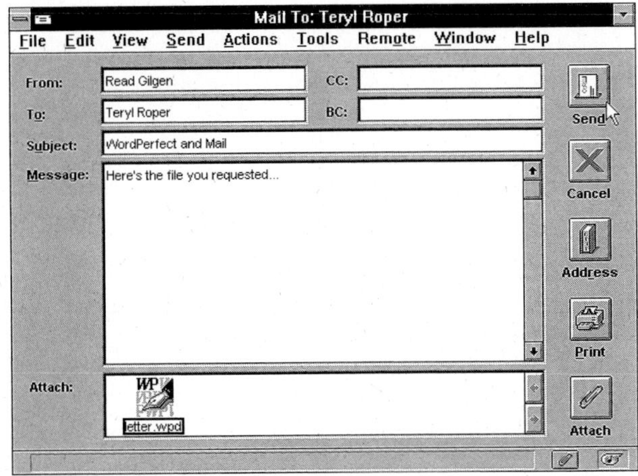

Fig. 8.13
If you use WordPerfect Office 4.0 or Novell GroupWise 4.1, you can choose **F**ile, S**e**nd to mail documents directly from WordPerfect as attachments to mail messages.

For more information about using WordPerfect Office 4.0 or Novell GroupWise 4.1 for Windows, see the program manual or contact your network support staff.

From Here...

Printing is the culmination of your document preparation. For additional information on processes mentioned in this chapter that help you prepare for printing, you may want to refer to the following chapters:

- Chapter 5, "Formatting Pages and Documents," teaches you how to select paper size and type, including subdivided pages, using page numbers, and document summaries.
- Chapter 20, "Using Fonts and Special Characters," shows you how fonts affect your document, and how to add them to your printer drivers.
- Chapter 23, "Desktop Publishing with WordPerfect," covers advanced printing techniques, including working with graphics and color, and improving print quality.

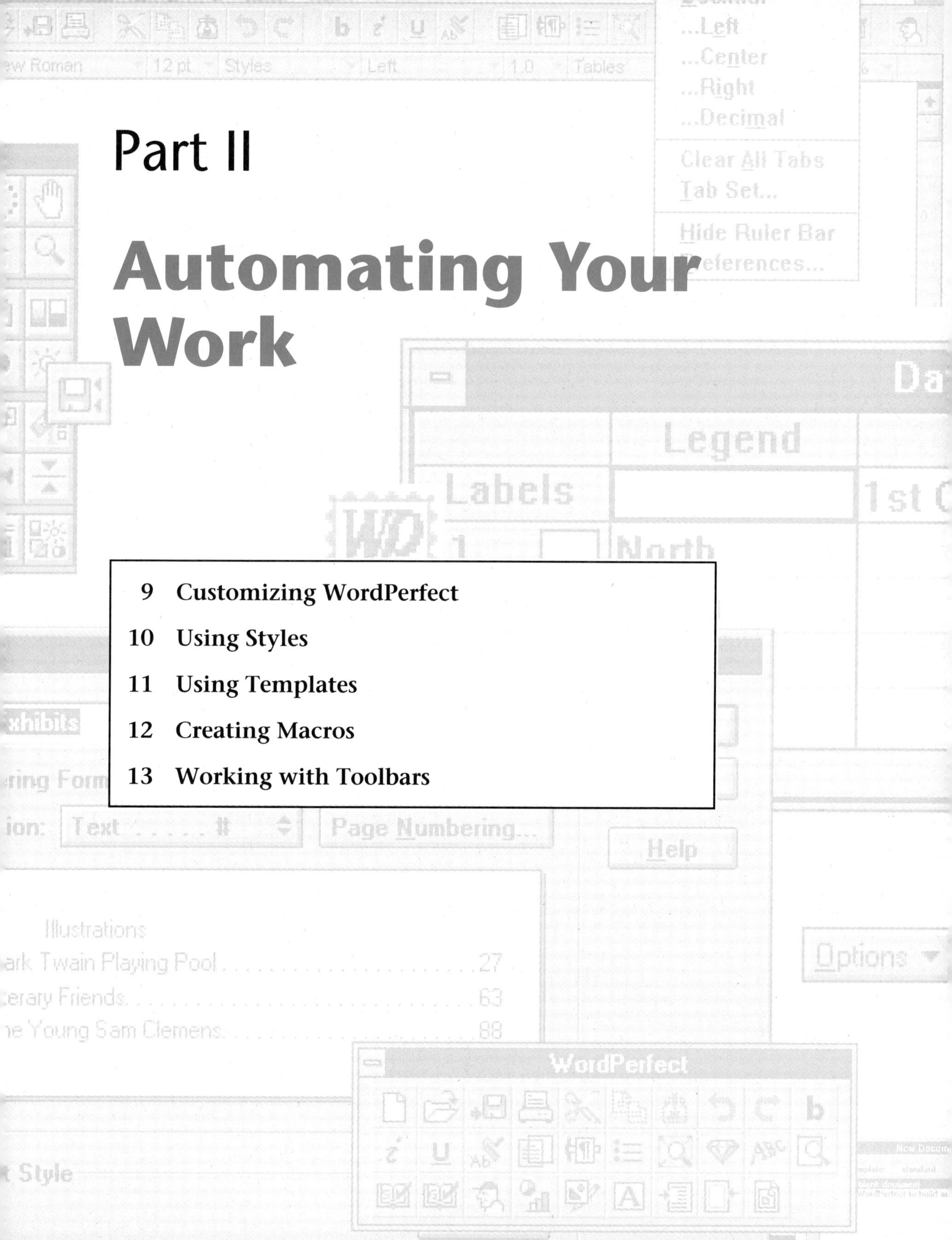

Part II

Automating Your Work

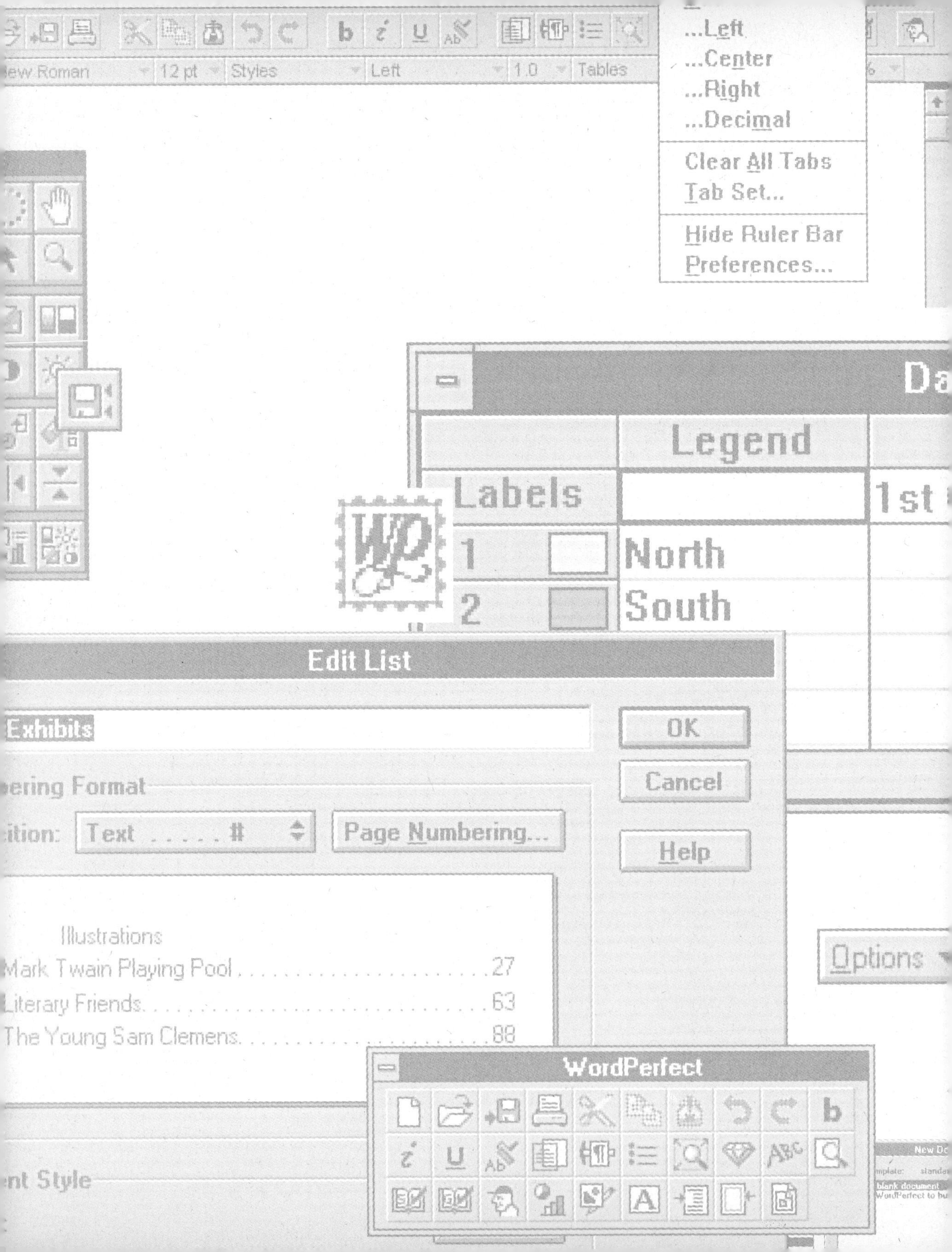

...Left
...Center
...Right
...Decimal
Clear All Tabs
Tab Set...
Hide Ruler Bar
Preferences...
12 pt
Styles
Left
1.0
Tables
Legend
Labels
1st
1 North
2 South
Edit List
Exhibits
OK
Cancel
Help
Text . . . . . ##
Page Numbering...
Illustrations
Mark Twain Playing Pool 27
Literary Friends. 63
The Young Sam Clemens. 88
Options
WordPerfect

Chapter 9

Customizing WordPerfect

by Judy Petersen

The customizing options in WordPerfect enable you to set up WordPerfect's features to match your most frequent needs. In a specific document, you make these changes using the regular WordPerfect menu options. Or you can use the Preferences options to customize how the feature works for all new documents.

You can customize these options and more using the Preferences feature. The changes you make in Preferences remain in effect until you change them again.

In this chapter, you learn to customize the following:

- What is displayed on-screen
- Environment options
- The location of files, default file extensions, and backing up your work
- Document summaries
- Default print settings
- Windows features

Customizing the Display

Using Display Preferences, you can customize the way various features, such as hidden text and graphics, are displayed in the document window, and set options for Zoom and the default view, the Reveal Codes window, the Ruler Bar, and the Merge code display. When you choose **E**dit, Pr**e**ferences, the features you can customize are displayed as icons in a dialog box that works like a Windows program group (see fig. 9.1), including the addition of a menu bar with the **P**references command. Choose the icon for the option you want or make your choice from the **P**references pull-down menu.

When you choose **D**isplay from the Preferences dialog box or pull-down menu, the Display Preferences dialog box shown in figure 9.2 opens with **D**ocument as the default choice.

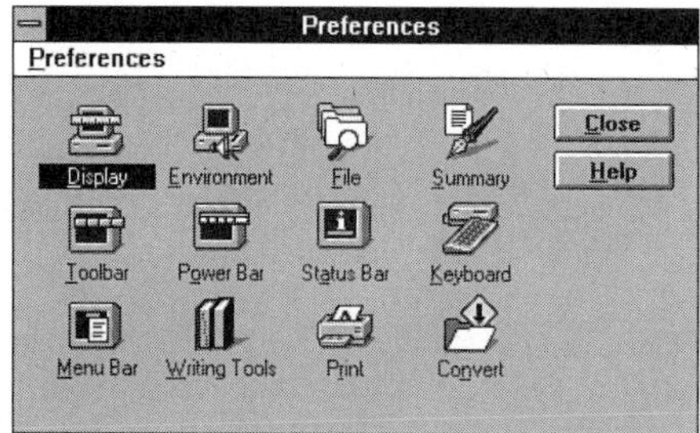

Fig. 9.1
To configure a feature, choose the icon for the feature or display the Preferences pull-down menu in the Preferences dialog box.

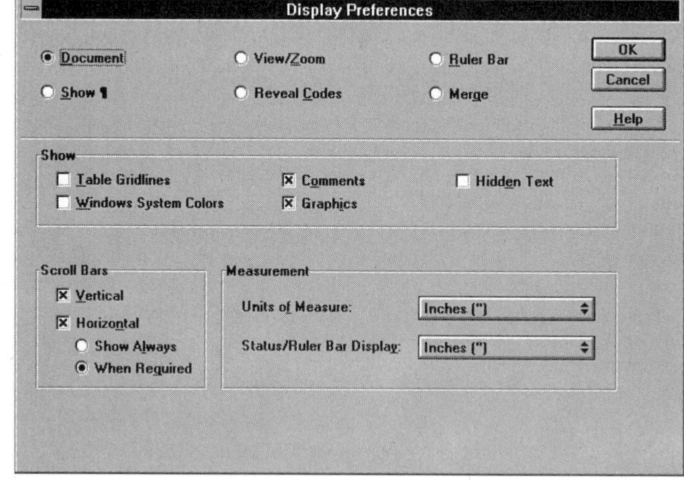

Fig. 9.2
To use the Display Preferences dialog box, choose an option and WordPerfect changes the Display Preferences dialog box to show the specific options you can customize for that option.

Note

Each time you choose an option from the top of the Display Preferences dialog box, the choices for that option are displayed in the remainder of the box. Each of these displays is illustrated later in this chapter in sections describing the options. When you have made your choices in one configuration of the Display Preferences dialog box, choosing OK brings back up the Preferences dialog box. If you want to make further display configuration choices, do not choose OK. Rather, choose another option from the top of the dialog box. Continue choosing from the top of the box until you have indicated your preferences for all six options. Then choose OK to exit the dialog box.

Document Display

With the Document radio button selected, you can customize the document window to change the text color; show or suppress the display of comments, graphics, and hidden text; add or remove scroll bars; change the way measurements are stated; and change the appearance of dialog boxes.

Show

The options in the Show group of the dialog box control the color of document text, and whether document features such as cell guides, graphic images, comments, and hidden text are visible in the document window. Choose as many of the options as you want to use by clicking on the option or pressing Alt plus its mnemonic key. When a check appears in the option's check box, the feature is selected. Choose the option again to toggle it off.

The following five options are available in the Show area:

- ***T****able Gridlines.* When you use the Tables feature to create a project such as an organizational chart where some of the cell lines are removed by choosing None for line style, it can be difficult to determine where the cursor is located in the table. Choose this option to display cell guides. Any removed cell lines display as dotted lines.
- ***W****indows System Colors.* The default color for text used by WordPerfect in document windows is black. The text color can be changed by customizing Window Text using the Color option available in Control Panel in the Windows Program Manager Main program group. To cause WordPerfect to use the text color you specify in Control Panel, choose **W**indows System Colors to place a check in its check box.

Note

In addition to text color, you can customize the colors for the active and inactive window title bar, the button faces and shadows, and other elements that make up a window, or select one of the many color schemes provided with Windows 3.1. The color scheme you create or choose in the Color dialog box controls the appearance of WordPerfect for Windows.

- *Comments.* You can add nonprinting comments to documents to remind you or others of printing instructions or other document features. These comments are, by default, displayed in the document window as an icon at the left edge of the screen at the comment location. If you use comments to add information to a document that you do not want viewed, choose Comments to suppress the display. The comment code is visible in the Reveal Codes window, but there is no other indication of its existence. Refer to Chapter 6, "Using Writing Tools," for more information about the Comments feature.

- *Graphics.* A major reason for the popularity of the Graphical User Interface is the display along with text of all document graphics such as lines and figures. When you are working with older systems, in large documents, or editing a document, the display of graphics can slow the screen refresh rate. Graphics images are displayed by default. To speed your work, suppress the display of graphics by choosing Graphics to remove the check from the adjacent check box.

- *Hidden Text.* Hidden text is not available in WordPerfect for Windows by default. Choose this option to enable you to use hidden text. Choosing Hidden Text adds the Hidden Text option to the Font menu. Refer to Chapter 6, "Using Writing Tools," for more information about using and displaying hidden text.

Note

To quickly turn the display of graphics back on to preview a document, choose **V**iew, **G**raphics. If hidden text display is turned off, you can view the hidden text in the Reveal Codes window or choose **V**iew, Hidden Te**x**t to see the hidden text displayed in the document.

Scroll Bars

A vertical scroll bar is displayed by default in the document window. A horizontal scroll bar is displayed when the document layout causes a portion of the document to not be visible on-screen. This can happen when you use a landscape orientation or a wide paper size. You can choose from the following options in the Scroll Bars group to customize the display of scroll bars:

- ***V**ertical.* You can turn off or on the display of the vertical scroll bar.
- *Horizo**n**tal.* You can turn off or on the display of the horizontal scroll bar. When you choose Horizo**n**tal, the display of the scroll bar can be configured. Choose Show A**l**ways to display the horizontal scroll bars all the time. Or choose When Re**q**uired to display horizontal scroll bars only if document features extend past the right edge of the document window.

Measurement

When you install WordPerfect, the program is set to display all measurements in decimal inches. This is reflected in the Ln and Posinformation in the status bar, the format of the Ruler Bar, and wherever you enter measurements, such as margins and line height. You can change the way measurements are displayed in dialog boxes and have the status bar display measurements in another format. This is a handy way to use points to enter measurements when creating a newsletter, yet have the status bar and Ruler Bar use the more familiar inches format.

To change the way measurements are displayed, choose either Units **o**f Measure or Status/Ruler Bar Displa**y** in the Measurement group of the Display Preferences dialog box (refer to fig. 9.2) to open the pop-up menu. From the menu, choose one of the following units of measurement:

WordPerfect Unit	Description
Inches (")	(8.50")
I**n**ches (i)	(8.50i)
Centimeters (c)	(1/100th of a meter)
Millimeters (m)	(1/1000th of a meter)
Points (p)	(In WordPerfect, there are 72 points per inch rather than 72.27)
1200ths of an inch (w)	(300w is 1/4")

Tip

Working with 1200ths of an inch allows you to specify very small increments, and the amounts can be very easy to calculate (600 = 1/2", 1200 is 1/10").

WordPerfect calculates measurements to six decimal places, although only three decimal places are displayed in any numeric text box. You can enter measurements in any format and WordPerfect converts the measurement for you. If you enter an amount in centimeters followed by a c and are working in inches, WordPerfect converts the centimeters to inches. Better still, if you use a standard ruler to measure a margin or binding offset, you can enter the measurement as a fraction of an inch, and WordPerfect converts the entry to the decimal equivalent.

Show Formatting Symbols

◀ See "View Modes," p. 30

◀ See "Customizing Formatting Options," p. 149

Tip

A quick way to turn the display of symbols off or on is to choose **S**how ¶ from the **V**iew pull-down menu or press Ctrl+Shift+F3.

The **S**how ¶ option in the Display Preferences dialog box causes WordPerfect to display symbols in place of spaces, hard returns, tabs, indents, or codes for center, flush right, soft hyphen, advance, or center page, every time you start WordPerfect. This feature is turned off by default. Enabling the display of symbols can help you locate incorrect codes and understand how portions of the document were formatted to create a specific appearance.

Choose the desired feature (spaces, hard returns, and so on) to toggle each on or off; then choose Sho**w** Symbols on New and Current Document to enable the display of symbols.

The steps for customizing the display of symbols used for each formatting code and ideas on using this feature in your work are discussed in Chapter 4.

View/Zoom Display

By default, the document window display is in Page mode. Using Page mode, the document margins are visible, and you can see and edit headers, footers, page numbers, and other features on the page. Two-Page mode is available, which also operates as a print preview mode. WYSIWYG (What You See Is What You Get) is also used in Draft mode, but margins, headers, footers, and other features are not displayed. To use View/Zoom to change the default view and to specify the default Zoom percentage for all documents from the Display Preferences dialog box, complete the following steps:

◀ See "Show Spaces, Tabs, and Hard Returns," p. 43

1. Choose View/**Z**oom to display the Default View and Zoom options in the Display Preferences dialog box (see fig. 9.3).

2. To change the document window view mode for all documents, choose Dr**a**ft, **P**age, or **T**wo Page. A dot appears in the option button next to your selection.

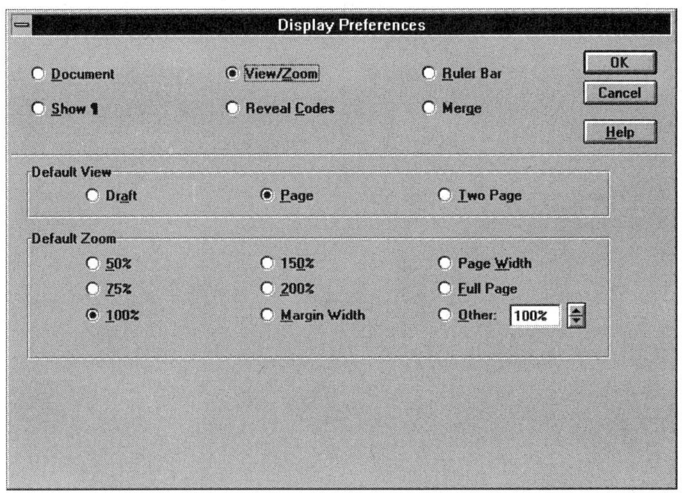

Fig. 9.3
View/**Z**oom options include Dr**a**ft, **P**age, or **T**wo Page view in the document window, a list of Zoom percentages, and a text box where you can enter a custom percentage.

3. Choose one of the predefined Zoom percentages or enter your preference in the **O**ther text box (from 25% to 400%). Using the mouse, you can click on the adjacent increment or decrement arrows to change the amount in increments of five.

   Alternatively, choose a page display format:

   - ***M**argin Width.* Displays the text aligned on the left edge of the screen. The number of lines displayed depends on the font being used, but is about 20 lines for a 12-point font.

   - *Page **W**idth.* The text is centered on-screen with the page margin width visible on the left and right edges. About 26 lines of text are visible when using a 12-point font.

   - ***F**ull Page.* The entire page is visible. This is equivalent to a print preview of a single page.

For information on using the different screen display modes and the effect of the Zoom options on each mode, refer to Chapter 1, "Getting Started."

Reveal Codes Display

Using the Reveal **C**odes option in the Display Preferences dialog box, you can customize the text font, background and text color, window size, and other options for the Reveal Codes window. For detailed information, refer to Chapter 3, "Retrieving and Editing Documents."

Ruler Bar Display

◀ See "Customizing Reveal Codes To Meet Your Needs," p. 100

WordPerfect includes a Ruler Bar you can choose to display at the top of the document window. The Ruler Bar shows the placement and type of tab stops, the current margins and, if the cursor is in a table or columns, the margins of the columns or table columns. By choosing **R**uler Bar in the Display Preferences dialog box, you see several options for customizing the way the Ruler Bar functions. Refer to Chapter 4, "Formatting Text," to learn how to customize the ruler display. Chapter 4 also discusses the tab features and using the Ruler to set tabs.

Merge Codes Display

◀ See "Customizing Formatting Options," p. 149

◀ See "Using Other Writing Tools," p. 254

▶ See "Understanding Merge Codes," p. 643

When working with merge documents, WordPerfect displays abbreviated merge codes in the document window. You may prefer to display merge codes as markers, or you can hide them completely. Choose Mer**g**e in the Display Preferences dialog box to display the available Merge Code options and choose one of the following:

- D**i**splay Merge Codes (the default setting)
- Disp**l**ay Merge Codes As Markers (red diamond bullets)
- Hid**e** Merge Codes

Customizing Environment Options

In the Environment Preferences dialog box, you can change your personal user information, decide when WordPerfect should beep, change the way menus are displayed, indicate when WordPerfect should prompt for confirmation of actions, set save options, turn on Hypertext capability, and choose Code Page options. Choose **E**nvironment from the Preferences dialog box, or the pull-down menu to display the Environment Preferences dialog box, shown in figure 9.4.

Note

If you are a regular WordPerfect user and want to immediately set up document backup protection, the backup options can now be found by choosing **F**ile in the Preferences dialog box to display the **D**ocuments/Backup options in the File Preferences dialog box.

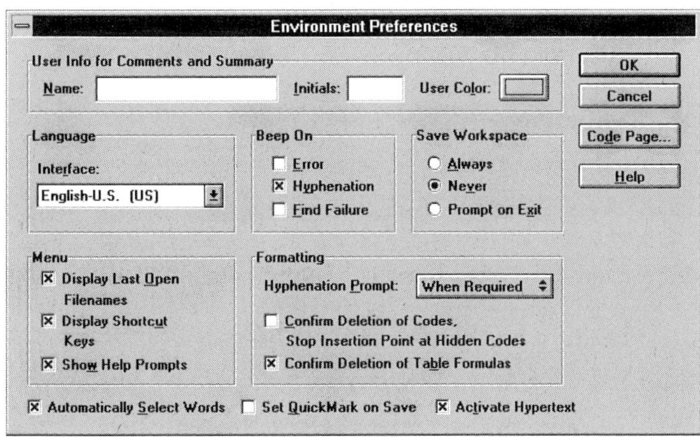

Fig. 9.4
Provide your name and initials, set beep, formatting, menu and save options, and open the Code Page dialog box from the Environment Preferences dialog box.

User Information

The User Info for Comments and Summary section of the dialog box enables you to attach your initials and a personal color to any document comments you insert, and provide your name to be included in the Typist and Author fields in document summaries you create. To configure or edit user information options, follow these steps:

1. Choose **N**ame, and enter your name in the text box.

2. Choose **I**nitials, and enter your initials in the text box.

3. Choose User Co**l**or, and choose a color from the color palette using either of these methods:

   - With the mouse, click on User Co**l**or to open the color palette. Click on the color you want to use.

   - With the keyboard, press Alt+l to choose User Co**l**or. Press the space bar to open the color palette. Using the arrow keys, move the box-shaped cursor to the color you want. Press Enter to return to the dialog box.

Refer to Chapter 6, "Using Writing Tools," for information on how to add your initials to a comment, and to Chapter 5, "Formatting Pages and Documents," for instructions on creating document summaries.

Language

WordPerfect is used in offices and homes throughout the world, as evidenced by the astonishing number of languages in which it is written. If you purchase another language version of WordPerfect, choose Inte**r**face and select the language you want from the pop-up list.

Beep Options

◀ See "Using Document Summaries," p. 210

◀ See "Using Document Comments," p. 254

You can change the sound of your computer's beep, or you can eliminate all sound effects. The default configuration is to beep only when prompted for a hyphenation decision. To change the beep, choose one or more of the following options to place or remove the check from the adjacent check boxes:

- ***E**rror.* Beeps when WordPerfect displays an error message.
- *H**y**phenation.* Beeps when WordPerfect prompts for a hyphenation decision.
- ***F**ind Failure.* Beeps when a search fails to find a match.

Formatting Options

In the Formatting section of the Environment Preferences dialog box, you can customize the action taken when a hyphenation question arises and whether you must confirm the deletion of formatting codes or of formulas in tables.

Hyphenation Prompts

◀ See "Customizing the Hyphenation Prompt," p. 157

You can customize the circumstances under which WordPerfect asks you for hyphenation decisions. WordPerfect uses a dictionary with hyphenation rules to decide how to hyphenate a word. Refer to Chapter 4, "Formatting Text," for more information about the options for customizing hyphenation prompts.

Confirmation Deletion Options

Using the WordPerfect default settings, you can navigate through your document and delete, move, and otherwise rearrange codes with little difficulty. If you prefer to protect the codes you have inserted and the formulas you have entered in tables, two options are available in the Environment Preferences dialog box:

- ***C**onfirm Deletion of Codes, Stop Insertion Point at Hidden Codes.* To turn on this option, WordPerfect stops at every code you try to delete and displays a confirmation dialog box that names the type of code and provides **Y**es and **N**o buttons. If you are editing with the Reveal Codes window open, the codes are not deleted but no confirmation prompt is displayed.

- *Confirm Deletion of Ta**b**le Formulas.* Choose this option to guard against accidentally typing text over the formulas you have created in tables or floating cells. Again, a confirmation dialog box is displayed asking whether you want to overwrite the formula already in the cell.

See Chapter 16, "Working with Tables," for information about entering and deleting table formulas, and Chapter 4, for instructions on inserting and deleting format codes.

Menu Display Options

What is displayed with the pull-down menus can be configured by you. By default, WordPerfect shows keyboard shortcut keys for commands on the pull-down menus, includes a list of most recently opened files at the bottom of the File menu, and shows a help prompt in the title bar for all menu and Power Bar commands. These menu options are available in the Environment Preferences dialog box (refer to fig. 9.4) for you to customize, as follows:

- *Display Last **O**pen Filenames.* When you choose this option, the names of the last four open files are listed at the end of the File pull-down menu. The file names remain on the menu when you close WordPerfect. To quickly retrieve a file on the list, press the number by the file name to retrieve the file.

- *Display Shortc**u**t Keys.* The default for pull-down menus is to display any keyboard shortcut keys next to the menu command. Choose this option to turn off this feature.

- *Sho**w** Help Prompts.* As you move the mouse pointer over the Power Bar buttons or move the highlight bar to available menu selections, a brief explanation of the command or button feature appears at the left end of the title bar. To turn off this feature, choose Sho**w** Help Prompts.

Save Workspace

With the advent of software that enables the user to have more than one document open at the same time, it is a common occurrence to have several related documents open simultaneously. Using the Save Workspace options, you can save all the currently open documents as a workspace. The next time you start WordPerfect, you can open all the related documents at once. Following are the options for Save Workspace:

- ***A**lways.* WordPerfect automatically saves the workspace every time you exit.

- *Never.* WordPerfect does not save the workspace when you exit.
- *Prompt on Exit.* A dialog box prompt appears when you exit, in which you can choose to save the workspace.

Choose one of these options from the Environment Preferences dialog box. Ne**v**er is the default setting.

Automatically Select Words

The I-beam mouse pointer is particularly helpful when you are trying to click the insertion point into place between small, thin, proportionally-spaced characters. Unfortunately, we still sometimes miss the first or last letter of a word when selecting several words.

Beginning with WordPerfect 6.1 for Windows, when you select more than one word of text, WordPerfect automatically extends the selection to include entire words. To see how this works, try using the mouse to select several words. You can see the reverse video highlight jump to the end of the current word as you move from word to word. Similarly, try selecting several words, beginning in the middle of the first word.

This feature does not apply to selecting text when you use the keyboard. Although Automatically Select Words can be of benefit when you are first learning to work with the mouse, not everyone will find it helpful. To turn off the feature, choose Automatically **S**elect Words to remove the check mark from the adjacent box.

Set QuickMark on Save

When you save a document you need to work with further, you can configure WordPerfect to place a QuickMark at the cursor location every time the document is saved. When you later retrieve the document, choose **I**nsert, **B**ookmark, **F**ind QuickMark to move the cursor to its previous location. To turn on this feature, choose Set **Q**uickMark on Save in the Environment Preferences dialog box to place a check in the adjacent check box.

Activate Hypertext

▶ See "Understanding Hypertext," p. 1068

You can highlight text or insert buttons, called *hypertext links*, in your document that are linked to other locations in the same or another document or to a macro. To use hypertext, the feature must be active, which is the WordPerfect default setting. To turn off hypertext, choose Ac**t**ivate Hypertext from the bottom of the Environment Preferences dialog box to remove the check from the adjacent check box.

If hypertext is not active and you are working with a document containing hypertext links, when you choose **H**ypertext from the **T**ools menu, WordPerfect displays a Hypertext bar that includes an **A**ctivate button. Using this method to reactivate hypertext does not restore the Activate Hypertext option in the Environment Preferences dialog box.

Code Page

When you install DOS on your computer, the operating system includes character sets for almost 20 different international languages. The character sets are designated by a three- or four-digit code page number. WordPerfect and DOS use the ASCII (or U.S. IBM) Character Set for the basic text characters, some symbols, Greek letters, and simple line drawings used in your documents. WordPerfect also provides its own graphical characters that can be inserted using the WordPerfect Character Set. Windows uses its own code pages that differ from those used by DOS.

Using the code page defaults for the DOS and Windows code pages, you can copy data freely from spreadsheets to WordPerfect for Windows. This is true even though the character numbers are different for the DOS and Windows U.S. character sets. The paragraph symbol (¶), for example, is character 20 in the ASCII character set but is character 187 if you want to display it in an Excel spreadsheet using the =CHAR( ) function.

The Co**d**e Page option enables you to choose a different character set, or code page, when creating, importing, or outputting documents created using a different language. To change the code page, choose Co**d**e Page to display the Codes Page Preferences dialog box. The current settings are for the U.S. language. To change the **D**OS Code Page or the **W**indows Code Page, choose the language you want from the pop-up menu that is displayed when you make your choice.

Change the **I**nput File Code Page if a source file uses a language other than those specified for the DOS or Windows Page Code. Change the **O**utput File Code Page to export a file to another language format. Otherwise, input and output files use the DOS and Windows Page Codes as the default.

Customizing File Preferences

As you continue to add programs on your computer, hard-disk management becomes more important. WordPerfect offers disk management support by enabling you to have separate directories for documents, backup files, printer files, and others. You can also specify supplemental directories for use with network installations.

The directories used by WordPerfect are created at installation. Refer to Appendix A, "Installing and Setting Up WordPerfect 6.1 for Windows," for information on how you can specify the directories using the custom installation feature. You can change the default directories at any time in the File Preferences dialog box for the specific file type. When you choose **F**ile from the Preferences dialog box, the File Preferences dialog box appears, with a menu of file types at the top of the dialog box. When you choose a file type to customize, such as **S**preadsheets, the lower portion of the box changes to display the options for that file type (see fig. 9.5).

You can specify a different directory for each of the nine file types in the File Preferences dialog box. If you use WordPerfect on a network, you can access files on your personal hard disk as well as files that are shared by everyone using the network. Use the S**u**pplemental Directory option to enter the path used to access network files for all file types except the hyphenation files.

The default for all file types is to update the QuickList feature with new directory locations or file extensions you provide. For instructions on creating and using the QuickList, see Chapter 28, "Advanced File Management." If you choose not to use the QuickList, you can select this option to turn it off.

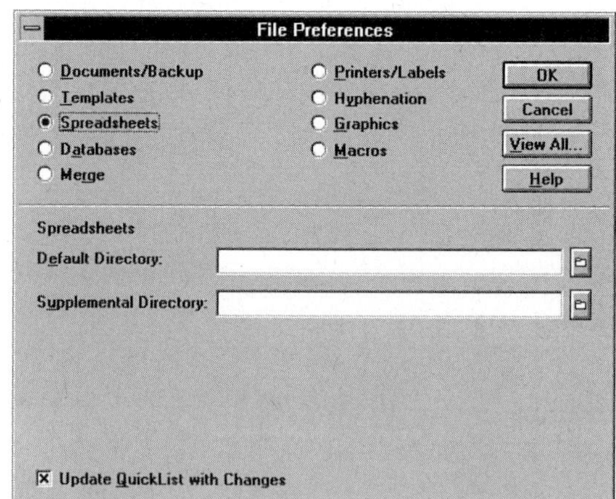

Fig. 9.5
The File Preferences dialog box displaying the options for spreadsheet files. Enter a default and supplementary directory in the appropriate text boxes.

To change a directory for a specific file type, follow these steps:

1. Choose **F**ile from the Preferences dialog box. The File Preferences dialog box appears.

2. Choose the file type from the list of file types marked with radio buttons in the top of the dialog box. Figure 9.5 shows the File Preferences dialog box for the **S**preadsheets option.
3. Choose D**e**fault Directory, and enter the path for the directory where WordPerfect will find the spreadsheet files, or choose the Files button at the right of the text box to choose the directory from the Select Directory dialog box (shown later in fig. 9.7).
4. Choose S**u**pplemental Directory, and enter the path for the directory location for spreadsheet files to be shared on a network, or choose the Files button at the right of the text box to choose the directory from the Select Directory dialog box.
5. *Optional:* Choose Update **Q**uickList with Changes to remove the check from its check box if you do not want the QuickList updated automatically.
6. Repeat Steps 2 through 5 to customize the file preferences for other file types.
7. When you have finished changing directories, choose **V**iew All to view the results in the View File Location Preferences dialog box (see fig. 9.6). Choose **C**lose or press Enter to exit the dialog box.
8. Choose OK or press Enter to return to the Preferences dialog box.

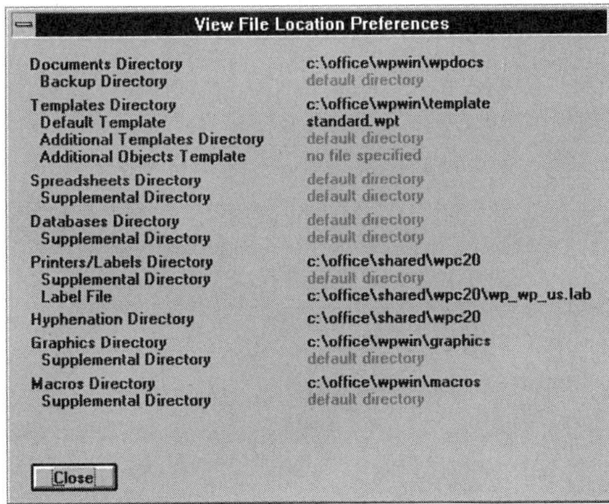

Fig. 9.6
The View File Location Preferences dialog box lists the information you have provided for the various file preferences, including default file names.

When you browse for the directory you want to use, click on the Files button at the end of one of the File Preferences text boxes, or press Alt+down arrow to open the Select Directory dialog box (see fig. 9.7).

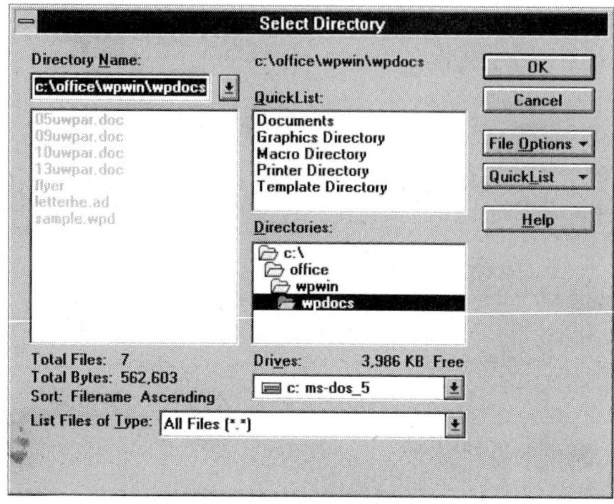

Fig. 9.7
In the Select Directory dialog box, scroll through the list of directories or the QuickList to find the directory you want.

Try using the following suggestions for working in the Select Directory dialog box:

- Choose **D**irectories and scroll through the list of directories available on the current drive. Click on another directory name to display the subdirectories included in that directory.
- To choose a network drive or use a floppy disk for backup or macro files, choose Dri**v**es and choose a different drive letter from the drop-down list.
- If the directory you want has a QuickList name, choose Quick**L**ist and choose the name of the directory.
- Although you cannot change `All Files (*.*)` in the List Files of **T**ype text box, check in the list box under the Directory **N**ame text box for a grayed list of file names to see whether the files you want to access are indeed saved in the highlighted directory.

Information for customizing File Preferences options for D**a**tabases, Me**r**ge, H**y**phenation, **G**raphics, **M**acros, and QuickFinder Index files is available in the chapters where these features are discussed. However, in addition to file location information, the File Preferences dialog boxes for **D**ocuments/Backup, **T**emplates, and **P**rinters/Labels file types also include options for creating document backups, default file names, and default file extensions. The following sections describe these three dialog boxes in more detail.

Documents/Backup Files

When you choose **F**ile from the Preferences dialog box, the File Preferences dialog box initially displays the Document/Backup File Preferences options shown in figure 9.8, in which you can specify a default document directory and file extension, authorize the creation of timed backups as well as original document backups, and specify a default directory for backup files.

◄ See "Customizing the Hyphenation Prompt," p. 157

► See "Specifying the Macros Directory in Location of Files," p. 444

► See "Using the QuickFinder File Indexer," p. 980

Document Directory and Extension

At installation, WordPerfect creates a WPDOCS directory in the main WordPerfect directory and uses it as the default directory for saving documents, although you use the Custom installation option to specify a different directory. To change the default document directory later, at the bottom of the File Preferences dialog box, choose D**e**fault Directory and enter the path for the directory in the text box.

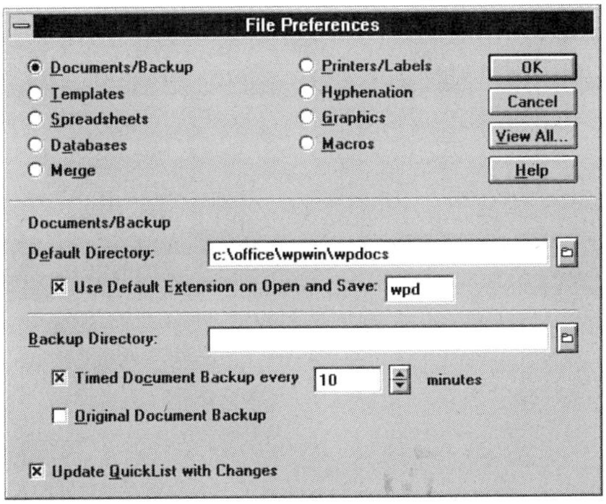

Fig. 9.8
The File Preferences dialog box opens to display the Document/Backup file options.

WordPerfect 6.1 for Windows uses WPD as the default file extension. Choose Use Default E**x**tension on Open and Save to turn off this feature. To save documents using a different default extension, enter the extension you prefer in the adjacent text box. If you change extensions, bear in mind that WordPerfect and Windows are set up to use the WPD extension with the Object Linking and Embedding (OLE) and Dynamic Data Exchange (DDE) features of Windows. OLE and DDE are used when you create links between a WordPerfect document and an object, such as a spreadsheet or a graphic image, in a document created using a different application. Consider the material in Chapter 18, "Importing Data and Working with Other Programs," before deciding to change the WPD extension.

The QuickList is automatically updated to incorporate any changes you make in the default file directory and extension. Choose Update **Q**uickList with Changes to remove the check from the check box if you do not want the QuickList updated.

Backup Options

WordPerfect offers two types of backup features to help you protect your files: Timed Do**c**ument Backup and **O**riginal Document Backup. Use Timed Do**c**ument Backup to guard against losing work because of power or equipment failure. WordPerfect is set up at installation to make a backup copy of the current document every 10 minutes, but you can specify another time interval or turn off Timed Do**c**ument Backup. To change the interval, enter the number of minutes in the adjacent text box from the keyboard or click on the up or down arrow buttons to change the default interval of 10.

Tip

Backup features are not a substitute for regularly saving your work and making backup copies of document files on separate disks.

Use **O**riginal Document Backup to guard against accidentally replacing work. For example, if you save a document, then edit it and save it again, the edited version (on-screen) normally replaces the original version (on disk). **O**riginal Document Backup saves the edited version of the document with the original file name and the original version with a BK! extension.

Templates

When you choose the **N**ew command on the **F**ile pull-down menu to open a new file, you can create new document templates, or form files, for newsletters, monthly reports, financial statements, or other standard document formats. The templates you create and use are saved in the directory you specify for templates in the File Preferences dialog box shown in figure 9.9. At installation, WordPerfect created a default directory for template files, a default template file named `standard.wpt`, and a default template extension of `wpt`.

The directories specified for templates are also used as the default directories for Styles. See Chapter 10, "Using Styles," for more information on creating, sharing, and applying styles.

To change the information in the templates Files Preferences dialog box, follow these steps:

1. Choose D**e**fault Directory, and enter the path for the directory where templates are to be stored, or choose the Files button at the right of the D**e**fault Directory text box to use the Select Directory dialog box (refer to fig. 9.7) to find the directory you want.

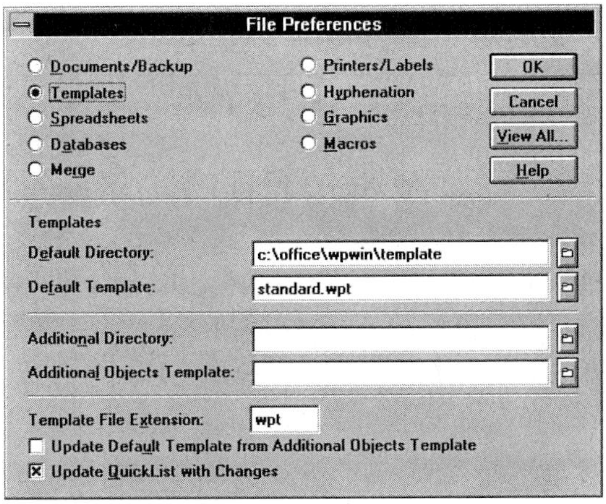

Fig. 9.9
When you choose Templates in the File Preferences dialog box, you can provide a default and supplemental (network) directory and file name, as well as change the default template file extension.

2. Choose De**f**ault Template, and enter the file name for the default template file, or choose the Files button at the right of the De**f**ault Template text box to use the Select Files dialog box to locate the file you want. The Select Files dialog box is identical to the Open Files dialog box. Refer to Chapter 3, "Retrieving and Editing Documents," for instructions on using the Open Files dialog box.

   If you enter a template name that does not exist, WordPerfect will create a template based on the template STANDARD.WPT, or on the template specified as the Additional Object Template, if you have provided one.

3. To specify an additional directory for storing templates, choose Additio**n**al Directory and enter the path for the directory, or choose the directory list button at the right of the text box to use the Select Directory dialog box (refer to fig. 9.7) to find the directory you want.

4. Choose Additiona**l** Objects Template, and enter the file name for an additional template file which contains additional objects such as keyboards, menus, template macros, toolbars, and styles; or choose the file list button to use the Select Files dialog box to find the file you want to use in addition to or in place of those in your default template.

5. Choose Template File E**x**tension and enter the extension you want WordPerfect to add automatically to all template files you create.

6. To cause the standard template to be continually overwritten by the additional objects template, select Update Defa**u**lt Template from Additional Objects Template.

7. Choose Update **Q**uickList with Changes if you do not want to update the QuickList.

Printers/Labels

The File Preferences options for printer and labels files offer some additional customizing preferences. At installation, WordPerfect places printer and labels files in the \WPC20 directory along with other files that are shared with other applications, such as the Speller and Thesaurus. The directory can be changed by choosing **P**rinters/Labels to open the File Preferences dialog box shown in figure 9.10.

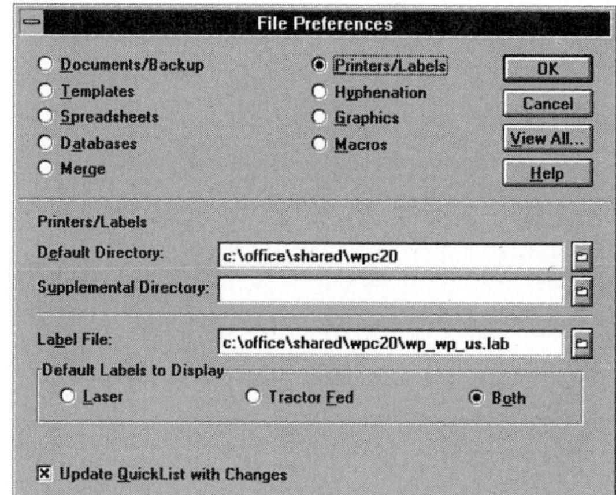

Fig. 9.10
Choose Printers/Labels in the File Preferences dialog box to specify directories for printer files, a default label file, and to choose the type of labels you want displayed in the Labels dialog box.

When you choose La**b**els from the Fo**r**mat pull-down menu, the Labels dialog box displays a list of approximately 130 custom label definitions for both laser and dot-matrix printers. Although you can limit the label list to only one printer type from within the Labels dialog box, you can change the default for the list if you have only one type printer.

To customize the preferences for printer and labels files, follow these steps:

1. Choose D**e**fault Directory, and enter the directory name where you want WordPerfect to look for printer and label files, or choose the Files button at the end of the text box to choose the directory from the Select Directory dialog box.

2. Choose S**u**pplemental Directory, and enter the directory name where you want WordPerfect to look for network printer and label files. You can also choose the Files button to choose the directory from the Select Directory dialog box.

3. If you create a label file of custom labels, change the default label file name by choosing La**b**el File, and enter the file name in the La**b**el File text box. To browse your drive for the file, choose the file list button at the end of the La**b**el File text box.

4. To limit the list of labels displayed in the Labels dialog box, choose **L**aser, Tractor **F**ed, or leave B**o**th selected.

5. If you do not want the QuickList updated with your changes, choose Update **Q**uickList with Changes to remove the check from the adjacent check box.

► See "Using the QuickList Feature," p. 978

Customizing Document Summaries

Document summaries are used to create a database of information about your documents without the necessity of retrieving each document. Instructions for creating document summaries are in Chapter 5, "Formatting Pages and Documents," including more detailed information about the Document Summary features that you can customize here. A review of that discussion will help you make appropriate configuration decisions.

◄ See "Using Document Summaries," p. 210

To configure the document summary preferences, choose **S**ummary from the Preferences dialog box to open the Document Summary Preferences dialog box shown in figure 9.11.

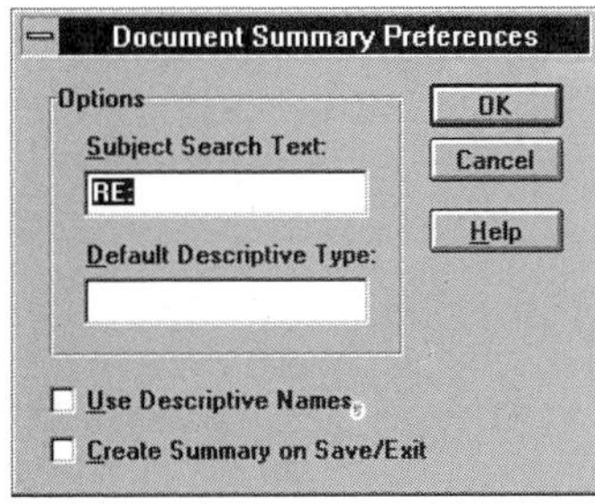

Fig. 9.11
The Document Summary Preferences dialog box enables you to specify how you identify the subject of a document, provide a descriptive type, and also use descriptive names.

Subject Search Text

One category of information is the subject of the document. The Document Summary feature automatically retrieves, or extracts, into the Subject field the text (until a hard return is encountered) that follows RE: in the document. If you want to use "Subject:," "Reference:," or other text in your document, enter the text you prefer to use in the **S**ubject Search Text text box.

Default Descriptive Type

WordPerfect can provide you with a default descriptive type such as "letter" or "proposal." If one type of document is predominant in your work, specify your most frequent descriptive type as the default. To do this, enter the document type in the **D**efault Descriptive Type text box.

You can override this default entry by typing a different descriptive type in the Descriptive Type text box in the Document Summary dialog box.

Use Descriptive Names

When you find the familiar eight-character filename format to be insufficient for your work, you can choose to use descriptive, or longer, names for files. You enter the descriptive name in the Descriptive Name field available in the document summary.

The Descriptive Name feature can be turned on by choosing **U**se Descriptive Names in the Document Summary Preferences dialog box. When active, the Descriptive Name feature causes the document summaries to be saved in a Speedup file. The document summary information can be searched more quickly, and is also used to display long file names in the Open File file list window. You can find more information about Descriptive Names in Chapter 28, "Advanced File Management."

Create Summary or Save/Exit

You can choose to have WordPerfect open the Document Summary dialog box when you save or exit your document. The dialog box continues to be displayed each time you save or exit until you fill it in. Choose **C**reate Summary on Save/Exit to turn on the option. Choose it again to turn off the option.

Customizing Window Features

A major attraction of the graphical user interface is that so many features are available at the click of a mouse or a shortcut keystroke. The Power Bar and Toolbars are designed to place as many features as possible only a click away. However, as WordPerfect continues to grow in power and size, you may find that your most frequently used features are being buried at the end of submenus or at the bottom of several layers of dialog boxes. To help you with this dilemma, WordPerfect enables you to add and remove buttons from the Power Bar and Toolbars, and to create your own Toolbars for special projects.

If your preference is to move that feature up to one of the main pull-down menus, you can do that too. You can add features, scripts, and macros to the main pull-down menus and submenus, and even launch other programs directly from the WordPerfect menus. For users who are more comfortable with the keyboard, features, scripts, macros, and other programs can also be assigned to keystroke combinations.

Whether you are customizing a Toolbar, the Power Bar, the keyboard, or menus, the features you can add open dialog boxes that are otherwise accessed from the pull-down menus and submenus, play a text script, launch another program, or play a macro.

Finally, to help you keep track of the status of various operations, you can customize the status bar to show the date, show that Insert, Select, or Outline mode is active, and show other useful information.

Note

You can open the Preferences dialog box for each of these features by clicking directly on the desired screen feature with the right mouse button.

Toolbars

WordPerfect 6.1 for Windows comes with 15 specialized Toolbars. You can copy and edit any of them, or make your own creations from scratch. You can choose to display text only, pictures only, or both, and change the location of the Toolbar or convert it to a palette you can move around the screen as necessary. Choose **T**oolbar from the Preferences dialog box to open the Toolbar Preferences dialog box shown in figure 9.12.

◄ See "The Toolbar," p. 24

► See "Customizing a Toolbar," p. 455

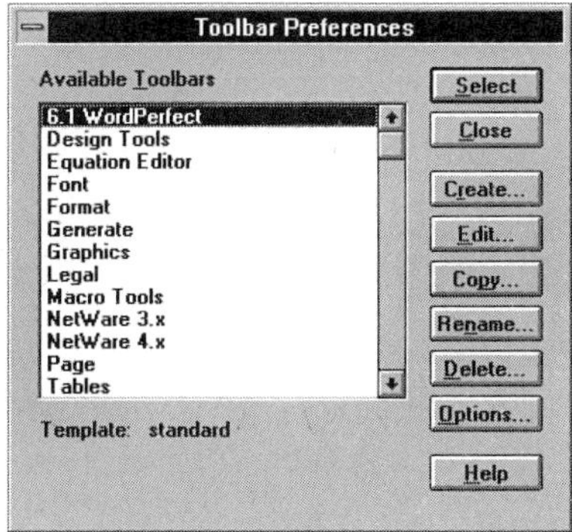

Fig. 9.12
In the Toolbar Preferences dialog box, you can choose from the 15 Toolbars available with WordPerfect, or create your own.

Using the Toolbar Editor to edit existing Toolbars and create your own designs is the subject of Chapter 13, "Working with Toolbars." There you can find instructions for using the Toolbar Editor to better suit your needs.

The Power Bar

◀ See "The Power Bar," p. 25

▶ See "Customizing the Power Bar," p. 462

By choosing P**o**wer Bar from the Preferences dialog box, you can choose from about 100 features to add to the Power Bar. You can choose features to add buttons, move buttons by dragging them to new locations on the Power Bar, and delete buttons by dragging them off the Bar.

See Chapter 13 for instructions on customizing the Power Bar for the way you work.

The Status Bar

◀ See "The Status Bar," p. 26

At the bottom of the WordPerfect screen is a sculptured status bar. By default, the status bar displays the current font on the far left, Insert mode indication at left center, the position of the cursor in the document on the right, and the Select mode indicator in gray at right center. When you use the mouse to select text or choose Se**l**ect from the **E**dit menu, `Select` is displayed in black letters to show that WordPerfect is in Select mode. The default status bar also displays information about the status of features such as columns, macros, merges, paragraph style, and tables when appropriate. Refer to Chapter 1 for more information on the status bar.

You can easily customize the status bar to notify you about other WordPerfect operating modes. Choose St**a**tus Bar from the Preferences dialog box, or click with the right mouse button on the status bar and choose **P**references to open the Status Bar Preferences dialog box (see fig. 9.13).

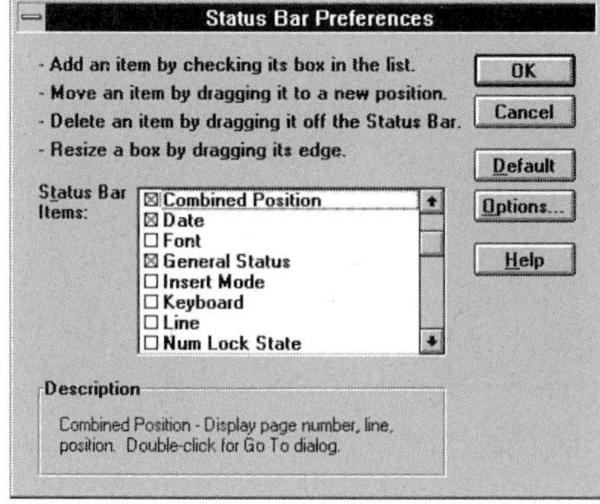

Fig. 9.13 The Status Bar Preferences dialog box lists the features you can include on the status bar.

To change the features or the appearance of the status bar, follow these steps:

> **Tip**
> Scroll the highlight bar through the features in the Status Bar Items list to see a description of each feature at the bottom of the dialog box.

1. To add items to the status bar, you must first make room for them. When the Status Bar Preferences dialog box is open, use the mouse to do the following:

   - Drag the left or right side of each box on the status bar to change the size of existing items.
   - Drag an item off the status bar.
   - Drag an item to a new position to change its order.

2. In the **St**atus Bar Items list box is a checklist of features that can be included in the status bar. Choose as many of the features as you want to add or remove from the status bar by selecting each to add or remove the check in the adjacent check box.

3. Choose **O**ptions to display the Status Bar Options dialog box (see fig. 9.14).

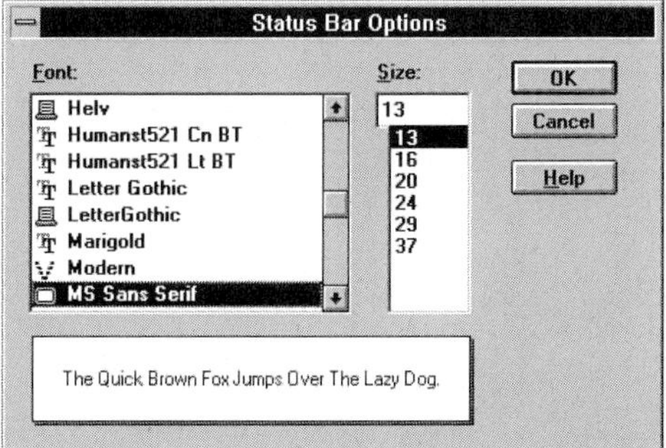

Fig. 9.14
Use the Status Bar Options dialog box to change fonts for the status bar text and to customize the appearance of the status bar.

4. Choose **F**ont, scroll through the list of fonts, and choose the font for the status bar text.

5. To change the font size, choose **S**ize and enter a size in the text box or choose a size by scrolling through the list of available sizes.

6. Choose OK twice to return to the Preferences dialog box.

When making your choices of what to display, you may find that you are dissatisfied and want to start over. Rather than trying to remember what features to remove, choose **D**efault to return to the original items.

The Pull-Down Menus

Using the Menu Editor, you can add commands to the menu bar or to any level of the pull-down menus. Choose **M**enu Bar from the Preferences dialog box to open the Menu Bar Preferences dialog box shown in figure 9.15.

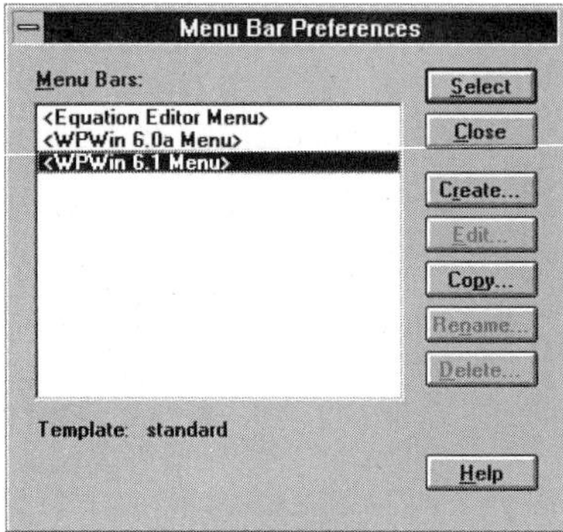

Fig. 9.15
Use the Menu Bar Preferences dialog box to select a different menu, copy or edit an existing menu, or create new menus for specific applications.

Menus are stored as part of a template. WordPerfect includes three menus in the Standard Template: the default WPWin 6.1 Menu, the WPWin 6.0a Menu, and the Equation Editor Menu, which is displayed automatically when you open the Equation Editor.

You can open the Menu Editor, which is used to create and edit menus, from the Menu Bar Preferences dialog box or by using the Create Object command in the Template Editor. Instructions for creating and editing menus are found in Chapter 11, "Using Templates."

Customizing Keyboards

WordPerfect comes with three keyboard layouts:

◄ See "The Pull-Down Menus," p. 23

► See "Using Objects in Templates," p. 404

► See "Associating Features and Events," p. 407

- The *WPWin 6.1 Keyboard* (the default) contains the commands described in this book.
- The *Equation Editor Keyboard* features a selection of Greek characters, symbols, and commonly used equation commands such as SQRT. You can use the Equation keyboard during document creation and while working in the Equation Editor.
- The *WPDOS Compatible* uses the WordPerfect for DOS function keys and cursor movements such as F4 to Indent, and Home, Home, Up arrow and Home, Home, Down arrow to move to the top and bottom, respectively, of a document.

The Keyboard Preferences dialog box also includes command buttons to open the Keyboard Editor you can use to redefine the function of every key on the keyboard. You can copy existing keyboards or create a keyboard that begins with the WPWin 6.1 default keyboard layout, and then customize the new keyboards to suit your needs.

Selecting Another Keyboard

During installation, WordPerfect selects the default WPWin 6.1 keyboard for your use. You can change keyboards at any time by following these steps:

1. From the Preferences dialog box, choose **K**eyboard. The Keyboard Preferences dialog box appears (see fig. 9.16).

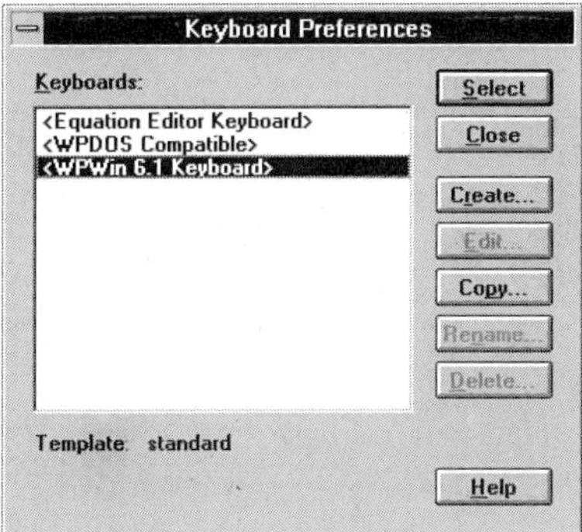

Fig. 9.16
When you open the Keyboard Preferences dialog box, the highlight bar indicates the name of the active keyboard.

2. Choose the name of the keyboard layout you want to use. To quickly move the highlight bar to a keyboard name, or if you created so many keyboards that not all are visible in the list box, type the first letters of the name of the keyboard in the text box that opens at the top of the list.

3. Choose **S**elect or press Enter to begin using the keyboard.

The newly chosen keyboard remains active every time you start WordPerfect until you choose another keyboard layout.

Creating, Copying, and Editing Keyboards

As you become comfortable with adding buttons to Toolbars and the Power Bar and using other keyboards, you might decide you are ready to add a few shortcuts of your own to the keyboard. Creating and editing a keyboard is easy because the Keyboard Editor does much of the work for you.

You cannot edit the keyboards that are installed by WordPerfect. To begin working with keyboards, you must create a new keyboard based on one of the WordPerfect keyboard definitions. To create a new keyboard definition that you can customize, follow these steps:

1. In the Keyboard Preferences dialog box, move the highlight bar to the keyboard definition you want to use as the basis for a new keyboard, and choose C**r**eate. The Create Keyboard dialog box appears.

2. In the **N**ew Keyboard Name text box, enter a name for your proposed keyboard. (In this example, the name is "Newsletter.")

3. By default, the keyboard you create is stored with the current template. If you prefer to store the keyboard with the default template, choose **T**emplate, **D**efault Template. Choose OK or press Enter to return to the Create Keyboard dialog box.

4. Choose OK or press Enter. The Keyboard Editor appears, in which you can customize the new keyboard (see fig. 9.17).

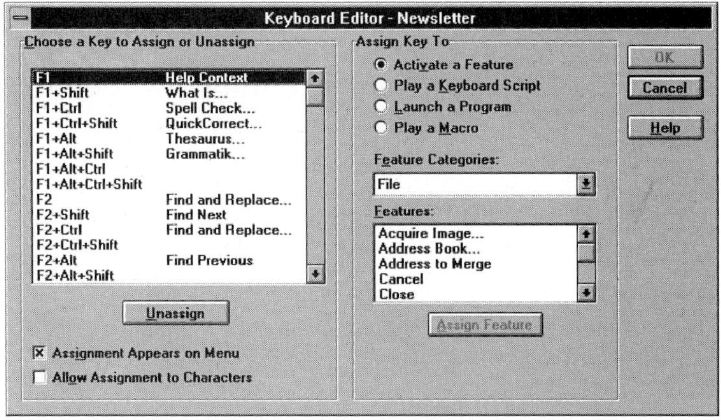

Fig. 9.17
The Keyboard Editor displaying the key assignments in the upper-left corner for the WPWin 6.1 keyboard definition used to create the Newsletter keyboard.

You can edit any of your personal keyboard creations. In the Keyboard Preferences dialog box, highlight the keyboard you want to edit and choose **E**dit to open the Keyboard Editor.

Making Keyboard Assignments

In the Keyboard Editor, you can create new key assignments, edit key assignments that already exist, and delete an assignment. The keys available to use as shortcut combinations include the Alt or Ctrl key pressed with letters, numbers, keypad keys, punctuation marks, or other keys, such as End, PgUp, and arrows.

Using the Keyboard Editor, you can assign any of the following functions to a keyboard:

- *Activate a Feature.* WordPerfect provides a comprehensive list of the commands on the pull-down menus and submenus so you can assign keyboard shortcut keystrokes to open dialog boxes or insert codes. For example, when you use chapter numbers, seven steps are needed to increment the chapter number and return to the document. Assigning the Chapter Number Increase feature to the keyboard causes WordPerfect to insert the `[Chap Num Inc]` code at the cursor location when you press the key assignment.

Note

While you are editing and testing a keyboard, assign the Keyboard Preferences feature to the keyboard, perhaps to Alt+K, to enable you to move from your document back to the dialog box quickly.

- *Play a Keyboard Script.* WordPerfect provides a text box in which you enter text to assign to a keystroke. You can remap Alt+C, for example, so that it types your company name. Then when you need to type your company name, press Alt+C instead. Or try assigning a standard closing paragraph to the keyboard. You can assign a sizeable paragraph of text to a key, and the text can include hard returns such as for a signature block, but otherwise must be unformatted.

- *Launch a Program.* You can start another program from within WordPerfect for Windows. For example, if you use an address book program to store the addresses for correspondents, you might assign the program to Alt+A. You can, of course, use the Windows Shortcut Key feature found in File Preferences and the Program Information Files, but the shortcut combinations allowed by Windows require three keys, whereas WordPerfect allows two-key shortcuts.

- *Play a Macro.* You can assign macros to any key on the keyboard, which enables you to use more than just the Alt+letter combinations for two-key macros. You can also make keys "smart," allowing a macro

Tip

If you use only a few letters from the Greek alphabet, assign these characters to keys on your standard keyboard rather than switching to the Equation keyboard when you need a character or two.

to figure out what the key should type. You can remap the asterisk, for example, so that WordPerfect types a bullet when you press the * key at the left margin.

To make a keystroke assignment, follow these steps:

1. In the Keyboard Preferences dialog box, use the C**r**eate, Co**p**y, or **E**dit command described earlier to display the Keyboard Editor shown in figure 9.17.
2. Click on the combination of keys to which you want to make an assignment, scroll through the keys in the **C**hoose a Key To Assign Or Unassign list box, or type the first letters of the keys to open a text box at the top of the list and move the highlight bar to the first key beginning with those letters.
3. Choose one of the following options for the type of assignment you want to make:
   - Acti**v**ate a Feature
   - Play a **K**eyboard Script
   - **L**aunch a Program
   - Play a **M**acro
4. If the item you assigned appears on a pull-down menu or you have added it to a custom menu, choose Ass**i**gnment Appears on Menu at the bottom of the Keyboard Editor to display the keystrokes to the right of the menu command.
5. If a key assignment is not correct, highlight the key and choose **U**nassign.
6. Repeat steps 2 through 5 until you have made all the key assignments you want.
7. Choose OK or press Enter to return to the Keyboard Preferences dialog box.
8. Choose **S**elect to use the keyboard immediately, or choose **C**lose to return to the Preferences dialog box.

The procedure used to make a key assignment varies markedly based on the type of assignment. The following sections examine each type individually.

Assigning Features

When you want a key assignment to perform a feature, follow these steps from the Keyboard Editor:

1. In the Assign Key To group box, choose Acti**v**ate a Feature.
2. In the F**e**ature Categories drop-down list, choose the name of the main menu in which the feature you want can be found.
3. Choose **F**eatures; then move the highlight bar to the feature you want to assign.
4. Select **C**hoose a Key To Assign Or Unassign, and move the highlight to the key to assign.
5. When the correct key and correct feature are both highlighted, choose **A**ssign Feature.

In addition to commands available on the various pull-down menus, you can also make any of these assignments:

- If you want to assign a feature that is on a submenu to a key, choose SubMenus from the end of the F**e**ature Categories drop-down list and choose the submenu you want displayed.
- To have a key assigned to select a specific amount of text, choose Selection from the list of F**e**ature Categories; from the list displayed next, choose the desired select action, such as Select Paragraph Next.

Assigning Keyboard Scripts

A keyboard script is a small amount of text that is typed into the current document when you press the keys to which the script is assigned. From the Assign Key To group box, choose Play a **K**eyboard Script to open a typing text box; then choose **T**ype the Script This Key Plays. Enter the text you want assigned to the keyboard.

When you type the script, the text wraps unless you press the Enter key to insert a hard return. Wrapped text conforms to the margins of your document when you play the script. Choose the **A**ssign Script command button when you have entered all the text.

You can assign special characters to a keystroke combination or include special characters in text, such as accented letters in a French or Spanish company name or city. Use either of these methods to include special characters in a script:

- To include characters from the WordPerfect Character Set, place the cursor where you want the character and press Ctrl+W.
- To insert characters from the IBM Character Set, hold down the Alt key while you type the character number, using the numeric keypad. If you use the section symbol (Alt+21) frequently, for example, assign it to a key.

See Chapter 20, "Using Fonts and Special Characters," for instructions on working in the WordPerfect Characters dialog box.

Assigning Programs

First, choose the key to which you want to assign a program. Choose **L**aunch a Program; then choose the **S**elect File button to open the Select File dialog box. Use the **D**irectories list box to scroll through directories to find the application file. Choose the application EXE or COM file; the file name appears in the File**n**ame text box. Choose OK to assign the program to the key.

Be sure that the programs you assign to the keyboard are all Windows applications.

Assigning Macros

When you assign macros to the keyboard, you first create the macro. The macro can be stored in a template or saved on a disk. Follow these steps to assign a macro:

Tip
If you use a named macro frequently, consider assigning it to a keyboard where you can provide a shortcut combination—using the Ctrl or Alt key, for example.

1. First, choose the key to which you want to assign a macro.
2. Choose Play a **M**acro; then choose the **A**ssign Macro button to open the Select Macro dialog box.

   To see instead a list of macros that have been stored in the current template, choose Assign **T**emplate Macro. If the macro you want is not displayed, choose **L**ocation, then choose one of these locations for the macro you want:

▶ See "Creating a Macro," p. 419

   - **C**urrent Template (*template.wpt*)
   - **D**efault Template (*template.wpt*)

To use your choice as the default location for macros, choose **U**se as Default. Choose OK.

4. Enter the name of the macro you want to assign in the **N**ame text box or choose it from the M**a**cros in Template (template.wpt) list box.

5. Choose **S**elect to assign the macro to the keystroke combination.

► See "Understanding Where Macros Are Recorded," p. 424

► See "Understanding Macro Storage," p. 992

Caution

Be careful when you delete macros or change the default directories if the directory contains macros. If the affected macros are assigned to a keyboard, the keyboard no longer functions properly when you try to execute those macros.

Deleting and Renaming Keyboards

To delete a keyboard definition you no longer use, highlight the keyboard name in the Keyboard Preferences dialog box and choose **D**elete. WordPerfect asks whether you want to `Delete keyboard from list?` Choose **Y**es.

Customizing the Writing Tools

Using the options available by choosing **W**riting Tools from the Preferences dialog box, you can select the writing tools and arrange their order of appearance on the **T**ools menu.

◄ See "Customizing the Appearance of the Writing Tools on the Tools Menu," p. 247

Customizing Print Preferences

If you regularly print two copies of every document or want to use high-quality graphics printing for all documents, you can customize print job features in the Print Preferences dialog box, and the changes become the default settings for individual print jobs in the Print dialog box. You can still customize an individual print job in the Print dialog box to override those set in Preferences.

In most instances, customizing using Preferences changes all the new documents. Customizing in the Print Preferences dialog box changes all future print jobs, even for documents created before the changes were made. To customize print settings, choose P**r**int from the Preferences dialog box; the Print Preferences dialog box appears (see fig. 9.18).

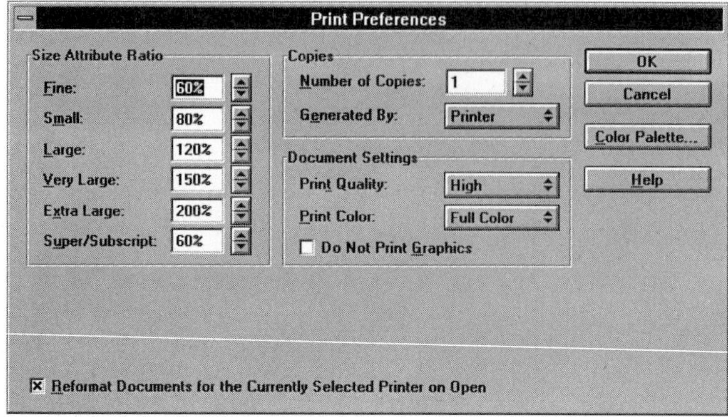

Fig. 9.18
In the Print Preferences dialog box, you can change the font size ratios, enter a number of copies to print, set print quality and color, and customize the color printing palette.

Size Attribute Ratio

▶ See "Font Mapping," p. 690

Using the **P**osition or the Relative Si**z**e option in the Font dialog box, available on the Fo**r**mat pull-down menu, you can place text as a subscript or superscript, or change to a smaller or larger font size. WordPerfect determines what font size to use for larger and smaller font sizes based on preset ratios.

The preset ratios may not be satisfactory for your most frequent jobs. If you often combine headings and text in your documents, you may prefer to have the heading appear only slightly larger than the body text. The heading font size will be 120 percent larger if you choose **L**arge. You may prefer a ratio of 110 percent. You can customize these ratios in Print Preferences.

To change the Size Attribute Ratio for all future Font Relative Size choices, choose from among **F**ine, S**m**all, **L**arge, **V**ery Large, E**x**tra Large, or S**u**per/Subscript size, and enter a new amount in the adjacent text box. You can click on the arrow buttons with the mouse to change the number in the text box. If you omit the percent symbol, WordPerfect inserts it for you.

Copies

If you print a standard number of copies of almost every document, here is the place to automate that process. Some printers will generate multiple copies for you and if you want to use this feature, change the G**e**nerated By option also. If WordPerfect generates multiple copies, each collated copy is printed separately. If the printer generates multiple copies, the chosen number of each page is printed before the next page, rather than being collated.

1. In the Print Preferences dialog box, choose **N**umber of Copies, and enter the number of copies you most frequently require. You can click on the arrow buttons with the mouse to change the number in the text box.

2. If you want your printer to generate the multiple copies, choose G**e**nerated By, **P**rinter.

◄ See "Controlling the Printer and Print Jobs," p. 303

◄ See "Changing the Printer Settings," p. 307

Document Settings

If most of your print jobs are printed at draft quality using a dot matrix printer, or if you can change the print quality to other than High on your laser printer, you can change these default settings for future print jobs. To do so, choose Prin**t** Quality. Then from the pop-up menu, choose from among **H**igh, **M**edium, or **D**raft quality printing.

Although you have a color printer, you may prefer to use colors only for special print jobs. Black-and-white graphics are usually quite exceptional and are sensible if you intend to use the original to make multiple photocopies using a black-and-white copier. To change the color printing option, choose **P**rint Color. Then from the pop-up menu, choose **F**ull Color or **B**lack.

When you print graphics, your laser printer takes longer to assemble your document or your dot-matrix printer takes longer to print the job. Graphics can tax—or even surpass—your printer memory. The number of graphics and the size of each one makes escalating printer memory demands. If you want draft printing without graphics or plan to have graphics printed professionally, you can turn off graphics printing by choosing Do Not Print **G**raphics so that a check appears in the adjacent text box.

Define Color Printing Palette

◄ See "Printing Documents with Graphics or Color," p. 299

The **C**olor Palette option in the Print Preferences dialog box displays the Define Color Printing Palette dialog box containing options that you can use to customize the colors for printing colored text with a color printer. (Not all color printers enable you to adjust the print colors, however. Refer to your printer manual for information about your printer's capabilities.) Using the **C**olor Palette option, you can adjust the color printing capabilities to meet your needs, perhaps to match a color used in the company letterhead.

Reformat Documents for Default Printer on Open

You can have any number of printer drivers installed in WordPerfect, even though some of those printers may never be attached to your computer. This feature enables you to create files designed to be printed on a printer at a different location, at another computer or office, using printer-specific formatting, such as the font selection.

If you installed fonts or set up cartridge fonts in each printer driver, you can use these driver files to create documents at home that are ready to print when you return to the office if you have the printer drivers on your home computer. You can apply the fonts when you create the document by choosing the appropriate printer driver, even though you don't have the fonts on your computer. When you finally print the job, the fonts and the printer must be available. Refer to Chapter 8, "Basic Output: Printing, Faxing, and E-mail," for information on setting up printers and installing fonts.

When you create documents using a variety of printer drivers, you usually want to retrieve your documents formatted for the printer you used when you created the document. In documents created with proportional-spaced fonts, text in columns created using tabs may word-wrap unexpectedly, and soft page breaks may occur at undesirable locations. This happens when the same font in one manufacturer's printer or cartridge differs slightly from the font the printer used when creating the document.

◀ See "Understanding Printer Drivers," p. 304

By default, when you retrieve a document, WordPerfect reformats the document for the currently selected (default) printer. To turn off this feature so that WordPerfect retrieves the printer driver that was current when the document was saved, choose **R**eformat Documents for the Currently Selected Printer on Open to remove the check in the check box.

Customizing Convert Options

▶ See "Setting File Preferences for Imported Files," p. 592

You can merge a WordPerfect merge form file with data files created in other programs and saved as DOS text. To do so, you must tell WordPerfect about the codes and characters used to divide fields (individual pieces of information, such as phone numbers) and records (a group of fields containing information about one subject) in the DOS text file. All records contain the same group of fields arranged in the same order.

Database and spreadsheet programs usually provide options for saving data as DOS text files, enabling you to specify characters or codes to insert at the end of fields (or columns) and records (or rows). Use the Delimited Text Options command to customize WordPerfect to look for the characters and codes you use most frequently. Choose Co**n**vert from the Preferences dialog box to display the Convert Preferences dialog box.

From Here...

In this chapter, you learned how to control the elements displayed on the screen, in the status bar, in a document, and in the Reveal Codes window; how the Ruler Bar displays; and whether merge codes are visible. You learned how to personalize features with your name, initials, or personal color; how to personalize the information included on pull-down menus; and whether to save all open documents when you exit. In addition, you learned how to create and customize your own keyboards to set up the location of directories for personal and shared network files. Finally, you learned of other features in WordPerfect that can be customized for the way you work and where in this book to find instructions for doing so.

For information relating to the features in this chapter, consider reviewing these chapters:

- Chapter 3, "Retrieving and Editing Documents," shows you WordPerfect's hidden codes and how to customize the Reveal Codes display.
- Chapter 6, "Using Writing Tools," shows you how to use and customize the Spell Check, Thesaurus, and Grammatik writing tools.
- Chapter 8, "Basic Output: Printing, Faxing, and E-mail," provides more information about printing options and how to best customize them.
- Chapter 12, "Creating Macros," describes how to create and save macros that you can then assign to keyboards.
- Chapter 13, "Working with Toolbars," shows you how to create additional toolbars, customize additional toolbars, and customize the Power Bar.
- Chapter 19, "Assembling Documents with Merge and Sort," teaches you the fundamentals of merge files and merge operations.

Chapter 10

Using Styles

by Rick Winter and Judy Petersen

Styles are the best-kept secret of WordPerfect for Windows. Simple to apply, yet challenging to master, styles are extraordinarily powerful and woefully underused. If you hope to master WordPerfect for Windows, you have to master styles; it's that simple. Because styles can incorporate nearly any WordPerfect formatting feature—as well as text, graphics, and even other styles—you need a good foundation in WordPerfect to define your own styles.

If you are new to WordPerfect for Windows, or if you have never bothered with styles, you can save a great deal of time and trouble by learning to use styles now, before you create many documents with manual formatting.

After providing an overview of styles and style classifications, this chapter teaches you how to create, edit, and use styles. Read this chapter with the templates feature of WordPerfect for Windows in mind. A template can include styles, as well as macros, text, menu items, feature bars, and abbreviations. The next chapter introduces templates.

In this chapter, you learn how to:

- Use document, paragraph, and character styles
- Create styles
- Work with documents and templates
- Edit styles with the Styles Editor
- Use styles from other files

Understanding Styles

Styles are primarily formatting tools. Think of a style as a named collection of formatting codes, graphics, text, and other elements. By defining styles for the formatting combinations that you use most often, you save time by reducing the number of steps necessary to format your documents. Because most of us produce the same types of documents repeatedly, a small investment of time in creating a library of custom styles pays off handsomely.

A style consists of various defined formatting elements that you apply collectively to all or part of a document. These elements might include type size, text enhancements (such as boldface or italics), text alignment, line spacing, and graphics.

Figure 10.1 shows a newsletter with five styles. The Letterhead style includes page margins, the Jeep graphic, and the address text with large caps in individual text boxes. The Dateline style includes the horizontal lines and enables you to type the volume, issue, and date information between the lines. The Head/Text style includes centering the text and 14-point bold. The Subheading style includes centering and bold. Finally, the column format is the Flyercolumns style.

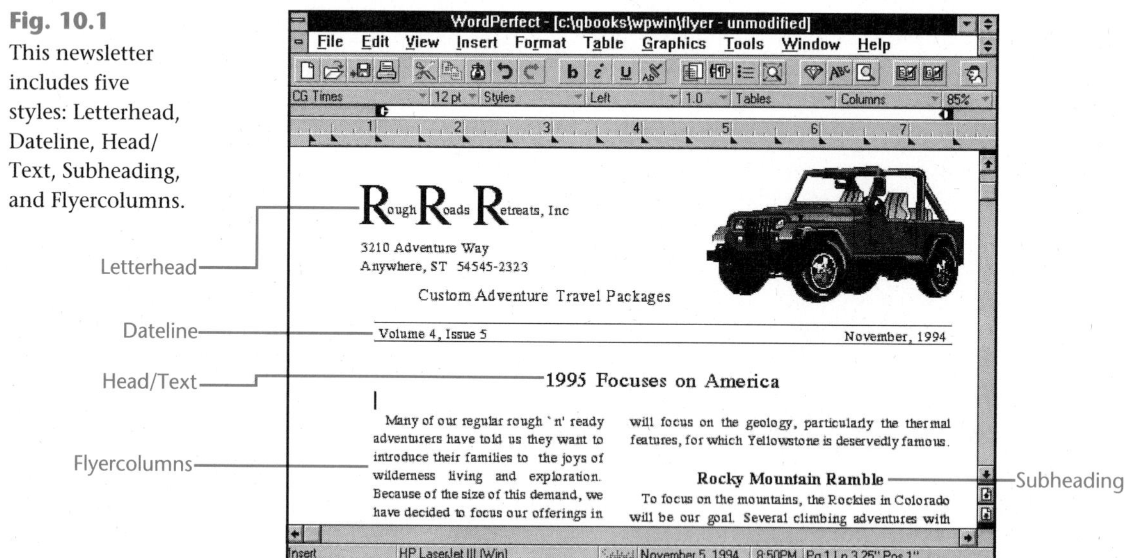

Fig. 10.1
This newsletter includes five styles: Letterhead, Dateline, Head/Text, Subheading, and Flyercolumns.

Benefits of Using Styles

One of the most important features of styles is that when you want to change formatting, you change the style instead of the individual formatting around the text. If you want to change bylines from italic to bold, for example, you edit the Byline style, and all text formatted with that style throughout the document changes from italic to bold.

If you work repeatedly with the same type of document, or if you work with long documents, styles offer many benefits, including the following:

- Saving time and keystrokes
- Creating a consistent look within a single document
- Creating a consistent look within groups of documents of the same type, allowing your organization to present a more professional image
- Allowing groups of writers who work together to standardize their formatting easily
- Providing a familiar road map to regular readers, thus helping them find important information quickly
- Making document revisions easier and less time-consuming
- Allowing you to see how a revision affects an entire document, not just a portion
- Allowing you to save a number of format codes, text, and graphics with memorable names

Styles versus Macros

You might be asking yourself, "What's the difference between styles and macros?" You also may ask, "If I already have macros for formatting my documents, why should I use styles instead?"

Although macros can automate some formatting tasks, save keystrokes, and help achieve consistency, macros are less useful than styles for formatting. Macros insert regular formatting codes, just as you chose the formatting options one by one from the menus. After you run a macro, the document formatted by the macro is indistinguishable from a document formatted by hand, and you cannot easily reformat the document if you change your mind. When you use styles, on the other hand, you retain control over the formatting because you can redefine the styles as often as you please. Styles thus provide more flexibility and control than macros.

► See "Comparing Templates to Macros, Merges, and Styles," p. 390

► See "Using Macros for Common Formatting Tasks," p. 437

► See "Creating a Macro," p. 419

Considering Types of Styles

WordPerfect for Windows styles can be classified in several ways. One way to classify styles is by the sections of documents that the styles affect. Paragraph styles, for example, apply only to complete paragraphs.

Another way to classify styles is by their location. Styles can be built into the current document, including initial styles at the beginning of a document. Styles are also part of the entire program (system styles), and part of templates.

Yet another way to classify styles depends on where you create and edit them. For example, you create document, paragraph, and character styles through the Style List dialog box. You create outline styles through the Outline Bar. You create graphics box and line styles through the graphics dialog boxes and feature bars.

Document, Paragraph, and Character Styles

WordPerfect for Windows offers three main types of styles: *document, paragraph,* and *character*. The style type determines how you apply the style and how it affects your document's formatting.

Document Styles

Document styles are most often used at the beginning of a document or a document section to control features such as paper size, margins, tabs, justification, line spacing, and page numbering. Document styles primarily contain formatting codes that stay in effect indefinitely, along with text, graphics, and other style codes. In previous versions of WordPerfect, document styles were defined as "open" styles.

You cannot turn off document styles, but you can override their effect by using another style or by manually inserting formatting codes into the document after the document style code. If, for example, you use a document style to change to landscape paper size, the landscape paper size remains in effect until you use another document style that changes the paper size or manually insert a different Paper Size code into the document.

Note

WordPerfect's formatting codes fall into two categories: *paired* and *document*. Paired codes consist of an On code and an Off code, and apply only to a portion of a document. Font attributes—including boldface, italics, and underlining—are paired codes. You cannot insert or remove one of the codes without inserting or removing the other. When you apply bold to a section of text, for example, WordPerfect inserts a bold code at the beginning of the section and another at the end of the section.

Document codes are single formatting codes that affect all following text until another code later in the document changes that formatting. Margins, Page Numbering, and Tab Set codes are examples of document codes.

Paragraph and Character Styles

The paired styles of WordPerfect 5.x are divided into two categories beginning with WordPerfect 6.0: *paragraph* and *character*. Paragraph styles, as you would expect, affect entire paragraphs. You typically use paragraph styles for titles, subtitles, items in numbered or bulleted lists, and bibliographic entries. Character styles can affect any amount of text. You use character styles to enhance a single character, a phrase, or an extended text passage.

When a paragraph or character style is turned off, the formatting options revert to the settings that were in place before the style was turned on. If you turn on the bold attribute as part of a paragraph or character style, for example, the bold attribute is turned off when the style is turned off. This also applies to open codes—such as margin changes, tab settings, and line spacing—when they are used in paragraph or character styles.

Paragraph and character styles differ in two other ways: how you turn them on and off. Because paragraph styles always apply to entire paragraphs, you do not need to select the current paragraph in order to apply a style to it; you can position the cursor anywhere in the paragraph to apply the style. Selecting text in one or more paragraphs before applying a paragraph style also works. If you already assigned a paragraph style to that paragraph, the new style replaces the old one. If you select text to turn on a paragraph style, the style automatically turns off at the end of the paragraph. However, if you turn on a paragraph style at the end of the document or beginning of a new document, you need to turn off the paragraph style by selecting the paragraph style `<None>`.

You can apply a character style to text as you type by turning on the style, typing the text, and then turning off the style. To apply a character style to existing text, however, you must select the entire text and not just position the insertion point in a paragraph. For more detailed instructions, see "Using Styles" later in this chapter.

A new type of style, the paragraph (paired-open) style, is introduced in WordPerfect 6.1 for Windows. If you change the format of a paragraph that uses a paragraph (paired-open) style, the style itself is immediately modified to incorporate the change(s) you made to the paragraph in the document. As with all other types of styles, once the style is edited, the change is reflected wherever the style is used in the document.

Initial Style

At the beginning of each document is the `[InitialStyle]` code. This code allows you to group the starting codes for the document in one place. You can edit the `InitialStyle` code the same way as other codes through the Style List dialog box (see "Editing Styles" later in this chapter) or by selecting the menu choices Fo**r**mat, **D**ocument, Initial Codes **S**tyle. To make this `[InitialStyle]` apply to all new documents, select the Use as Default check box on the Styles Editor dialog box. For more information on initial styles, see Chapter 5, "Formatting Pages and Documents."

System Styles

WordPerfect 6.1 for Windows controls the default settings for most document elements through types of styles called *system styles*. System styles represent the built-in settings for features such as headers, footers, endnotes, footnotes, and outline styles, as well as the settings for graphic boxes, text boxes, graphic captions, watermarks, equations, lines, borders, and graphic fills. System styles also control the format of generated features, including indexes, tables of contents, lists, and tables of authorities.

You can change the settings for these elements by editing the system style, or you can modify the settings by copying a system style to a document or to a template and then editing the copy.

A common complaint about earlier releases of WordPerfect was that although the program provided exceptionally precise control over certain kinds of formatting, such as kerning and letter spacing, you could not change many of the program's default settings. A graphic box, for example, always was positioned on the right and was half as wide as the space between the left and right margins. You could not automatically include a Tab or Indent code in a footnote or endnote. There was no foolproof way to ensure the use of a particular font for document substructures such as headers, footers, footnotes, endnotes, and box captions. In WordPerfect for Windows, however, you can change these and other default settings by modifying the system styles (more accurately, by modifying a *copy* of the system styles).

Template Styles

All documents created using WordPerfect for Windows are based on a template. *Templates* are a collection of styles, macros, abbreviations, Toolbars, keyboards, and menu choices. Instead of saving only styles in a style library, as in previous versions of WordPerfect, you now can save styles, as well as all the other features, in a template. You create, edit, and apply styles in a template just as you would in a document (see "Creating Styles," "Editing Styles," and "Using Styles" later in this chapter). You can use styles within templates as you would with any document. (For more information, see Chapter 11, "Using Templates.")

Outline Styles

Outline styles are a special category of text styles. WordPerfect for Windows has improved the original design of outline styles by integrating them with collapsible outlining and the Outline Bar. The result is that outline styles in this version are far more powerful, yet easier to apply. Because the topic of outlining and outline styles is covered indepth in Chapter 15, "Organizing Documents with Outlining," this chapter discusses outline styles only in relation to other types of styles.

Outline styles are potentially confusing because you define and apply them differently from non-outline styles. You can edit and apply outline styles through the Style List dialog box (choose Fo**r**mat, **S**tyles, and make sure that **O**ptions, **S**etup, Sy**s**tem Styles is selected) or through the Outline Style List dialog box (choose **T**ools, **O**utline, **O**ptions, **D**efine Outline, **E**dit, **E**dit Style). But you can define new outline styles and assign a hierarchical level to outline styles only through the Outline Define List dialog box.

◄ See "Setting the Initial Font," p. 207

◄ See "Creating the Initial Codes Style," p. 207

◄ See "Understanding Graphics Box Styles," p. 276

► See "Understanding Templates," p. 388

Graphics Styles

Although the casual user need not be aware of the fact, styles also control paragraph, column, and page borders, as well as tables, lines, boxes, and fills. (For detailed instructions on creating and editing graphics styles, see Chapter 21, "Using Advanced Graphics Techniques.") These styles control line attributes such as thickness, color, line spacing, spacing between lines and text or graphics, shading, and pattern (such as solid, dashed, or dotted).

Creating Styles

► See "Editing a Template," p. 399

WordPerfect provides several methods for creating new style definitions. You can base a style on a paragraph; enter formatting codes directly into a style; embed one style in another style; copy a style to a new name and modify the copy; or copy formatting codes, text, and graphics from your document into a style definitions.

Working with a Document or a Template

You create styles for a document or a template in the same way: through the Style List dialog box. The first step is to open the appropriate document or template.

Opening a Document

If you want to create or edit styles in an existing document, choose **F**ile, **O**pen; or press Ctrl+O. Then choose the name of the file that you want to retrieve.

If you want to create or edit styles in a new document, choose **F**ile, **N**ew; or press Ctrl+N.

Accessing a Template

To create or edit styles in a template, follow these steps:

1. Choose **F**ile, **N**ew; or press Ctrl+N. The New Document dialog box appears (see fig. 10.2).

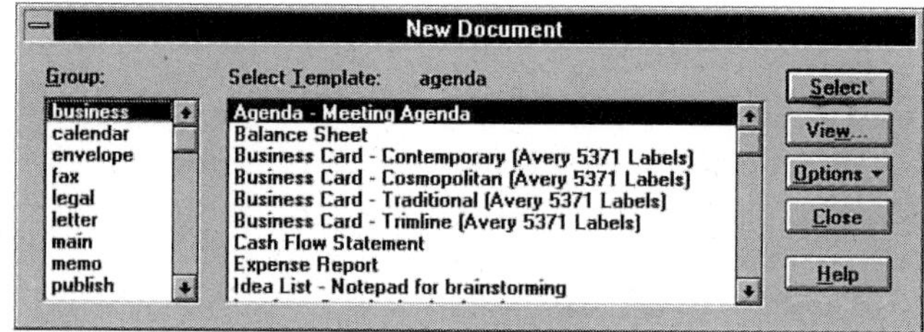

Fig. 10.2 The New Document dialog box lists 60 templates that ship with WordPerfect 6.1 for Windows, as well as any templates that you add.

2. Highlight the appropriate template in the Select **T**emplate list box, selecting a more specific category of templates from the **G**roup list box to show only templates of that type.

3. Choose **O**ptions, **E**dit Template (refer to fig. 10.2). The Template Feature Bar and any text and graphics within the template appear (see fig. 10.3).

Template Feature Bar

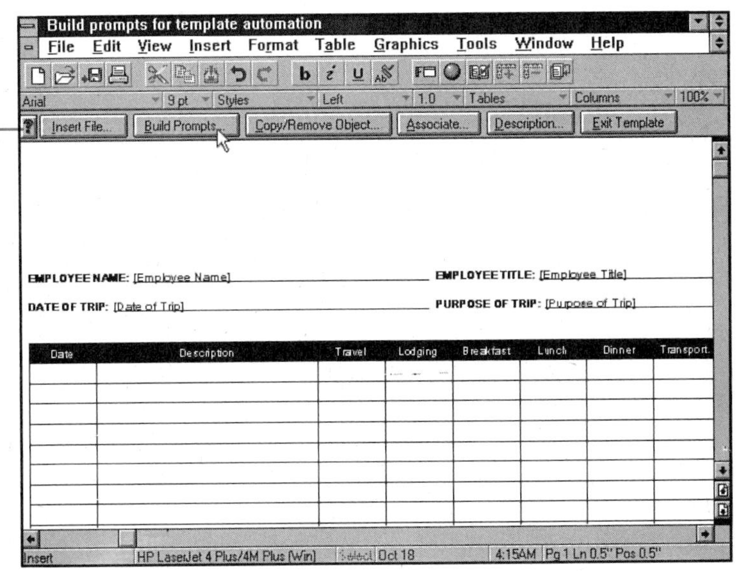

Fig. 10.3
The Template Feature Bar appears below the Power Bar. This figure shows text and table features associated with the EXPENSE.WPT template file. Notice that some of the buttons on the Toolbar have changed.

Bringing Up the Style List Dialog Box

After you open a new document, an existing document, or a template, the next step is to bring up the Style List dialog box.

To access the Style List dialog box, choose Format, Styles; or press Alt+F8 (see fig. 10.4). Many procedures in this chapter start from the Style List dialog box.

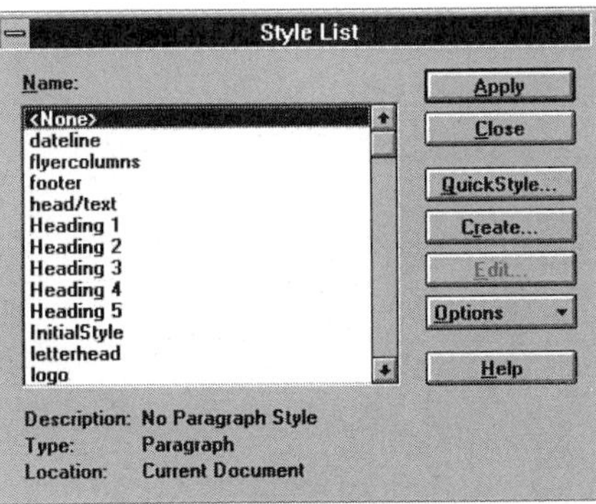

Fig. 10.4
The Style List dialog box showing the system style `<None>`, InitialStyle, and heading styles that come with the Expense Report template.

For instructions on listing existing styles, see "Displaying Style Names" later in this chapter.

Using QuickStyles with Existing Text and Codes

One of the easiest ways to create a style is to first format some text as you want the style to look and then use the QuickStyles feature.

To use QuickStyles, follow these steps:

1. Format a text selection or a paragraph with the features that you want to include in the style, as shown in figure 10.5.

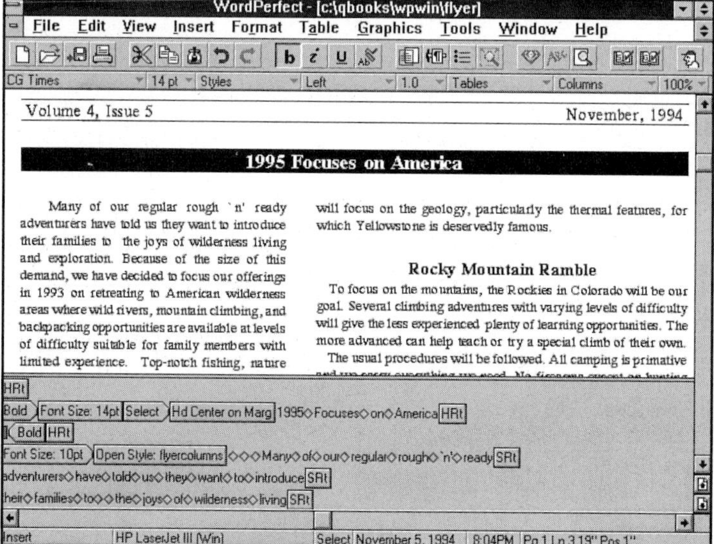

Fig. 10.5 In this example, the line is centered, and the text is made bold.

2. Position the cursor anywhere in the formatted text.

   You do not have to select the text, whether you are creating a character or paragraph style.

3. Bring up the Style List dialog box as described in the preceding section.

4. Choose the **Q**uickStyle command button on the Style List dialog box. The QuickStyles dialog box appears.

5. In the Style **N**ame text box, type the name of the style, using 12 or fewer characters.

6. If you want to include a description of what the style does, type it in the **D**escription text box.

7. Choose the appropriate radio button to indicate whether you want a **P**aragraph or **C**haracter style.

Figure 10.6 shows how the QuickStyles dialog box might look at this point.

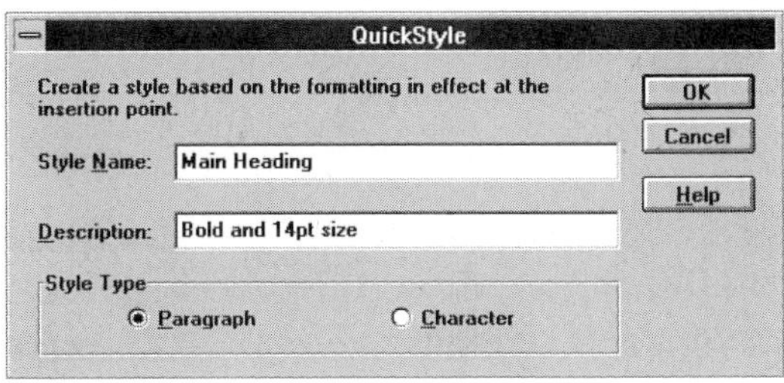

Fig. 10.6
A completed QuickStyles dialog box shows that this style will be a paragraph style good for headings.

8. Choose OK to return to the Style List dialog box.

The newly created style appears in the **N**ame list box. From here, you can **C**lose the dialog box, C**r**eate another style, or **E**dit another style.

To see information about the style you just created, highlight its name in the **N**ame list box. The information appears below the list box, as shown in figure 10.7.

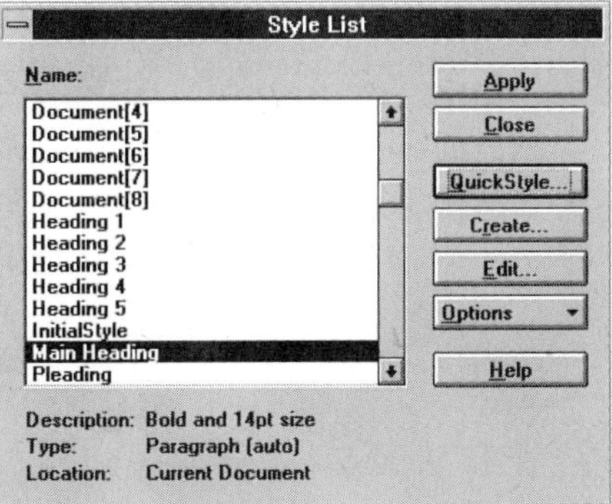

Fig. 10.7
The description supplied in step 6 appears, and the Type appears as Paragraph.

Creating a Style Through the Style List Dialog Box

In addition to using QuickStyles to generate a style, you can enter your own codes directly with a new style.

From the Style List dialog box, follow these steps:

1. Choose C**r**eate. The Styles Editor dialog box appears, as shown in figure 10.8.

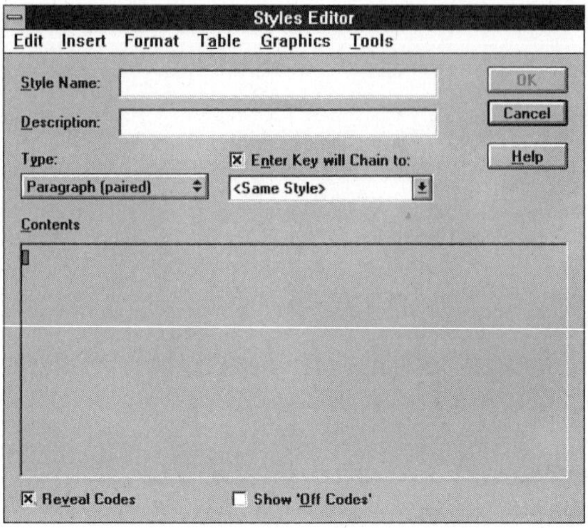

Fig. 10.8
The Styles Editor dialog box includes a menu bar, a Contents box in which to insert codes, and check boxes to see the codes and to control the Enter key action.

2. In the **S**tyle Name text box, type the name of the style, using 12 or fewer characters.

3. If you want to include a description of what the style does, type it in the **D**escription text box.

4. Choose the type of style that you want to create from the T**y**pe pop-up list. WordPerfect's default style type is **P**aragraph, but you can choose **D**ocument or **C**haracter instead.

5. Move to the **C**ontents box, and type text or choose items from the pull-down menus (see fig. 10.9).

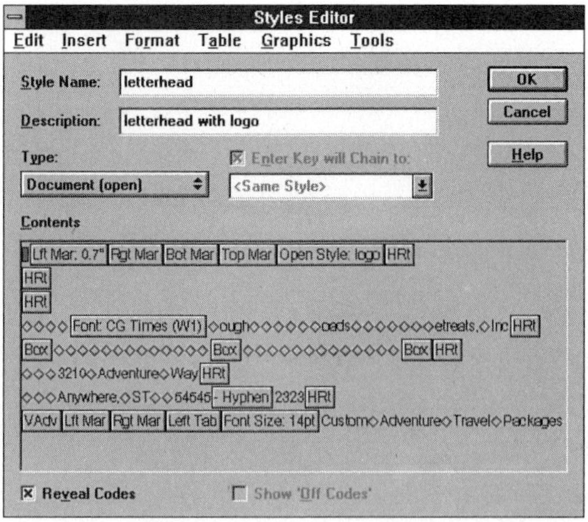

Fig. 10.9
In this example, the Contents box shows that graphics, formatting, and text are entered for the style *`MLetterhead`*.

If you make a mistake, you can edit any choice in the Styles Editor dialog box. (This procedure is described in the following section.)

6. When you finish creating a style, choose OK to return to the Style List dialog box.

7. In the Style List dialog box, you can create another style, edit an exiting style, or apply a style. When you finish with the Style List dialog box, choose **C**lose to return to the document window.

◄ See "Keeping Text Together," p. 167

◄ See "Using Headers and Footers," p. 172

◄ See "Numbering Pages," p. 177

Editing Styles

In addition to creating styles, you can use the Style List and Styles Editor dialog boxes to edit a style. You can delete the entire style, or delete and insert codes within the style. In the Styles Editor dialog box, you can change the name, description, or style type. In the Style List dialog box, you can copy information into the style from the document, copy the entire style and make changes, use the style as a code within another style, or link the style to another style. Remember that you can reach the Style List dialog box by choosing Fo**r**mat, **S**tyles; or by pressing Alt+F8.

Displaying Style Names

When you edit styles, you need to keep in mind the three types of styles: current document, template, and system. When you edit a style for the current document, the style changes for only that document unless you copy the style to another document or template. Do not confuse current document as a location for styles with document as a type of style (as opposed to paragraph and character styles).

If you edit a template style, all text formatted with the style in any document changes. You can change a system style to affect all documents by editing the style in the default template.

You cannot permanently change a system style that would affect all documents. When you edit a system style, WordPerfect creates a copy of the style and changes the style for the current document or template.

To display different kinds of styles, follow these steps:

1. In the Style List dialog box, choose **O**ptions.

2. Choose **S**etup from the pop-up list.

The Style Setup dialog box appears, allowing you to choose which styles are displayed (and, therefore, accessible).

3. To display styles of different types, choose one or more of the following check boxes in the Display Styles From area, as shown in figure 10.10:

   - *Current Document.* Displays styles associated with the current document.
   - *Default Template.* Displays styles associated with the template that you are editing or with the template that defines the current document.
   - *Additional Objects Template.* Displays the styles associated with an additional template for the current document, if you have specified one using Preferences.
   - *System Styles.* Displays styles for the program such as graphic captions, headers and footers, outline styles, and much more.

Note

To define the default and additional objects templates, choose **E**dit, Pr**e**ferences, **F**ile, **T**emplates, and then indicate the file names in the appropriate text boxes. For more information, see Chapter 9, "Customizing WordPerfect."

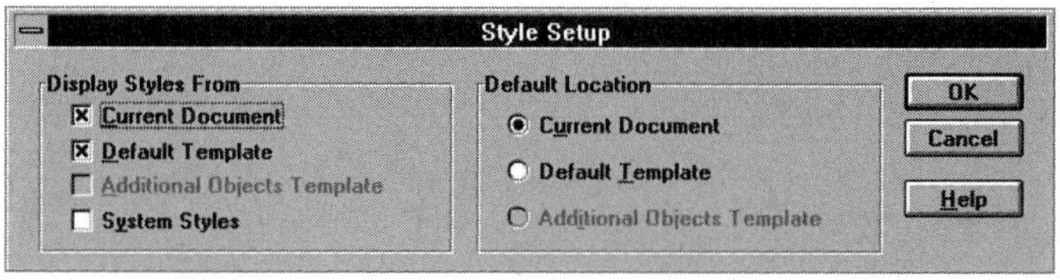

Fig. 10.10
To show styles for only the on-screen document and to save styles only to this document, choose Current Document in both locations in the Style Setup dialog box.

4. To save new styles to a specific file, choose one of the following options in the Default Location area:

   - *Current Document.* Saves the style only to the current document.
   - *Default Template.* Saves the style to the template that defines the current document.
   - *Additional Objects Template.* Saves the style to a supplemental template file if you have specified one.

5. When you finish with the Style Setup dialog box, choose OK.

> **Note**
>
> An Additional Objects Template must be designated in **E**dit, Pr**e**ferences, **F**ile, **T**emplates, to activate Additional Objects Template in the various Options features in the Style List dialog box.

Deleting a Style

When you no longer need a style, or if you make an irreparable mistake, delete the style from your style list as follows:

1. In the **N**ame list box of the Style List dialog box, highlight the style to be deleted.

   Pay attention to the information at the bottom of the dialog box. Make sure that you delete the style for the current document. If you want to delete the style for all documents based on the same template, make sure that the Location area indicates template.

2. Choose **O**ptions, **D**elete. WordPerfect displays the Delete Styles dialog box, which contains two options (see fig. 10.11).

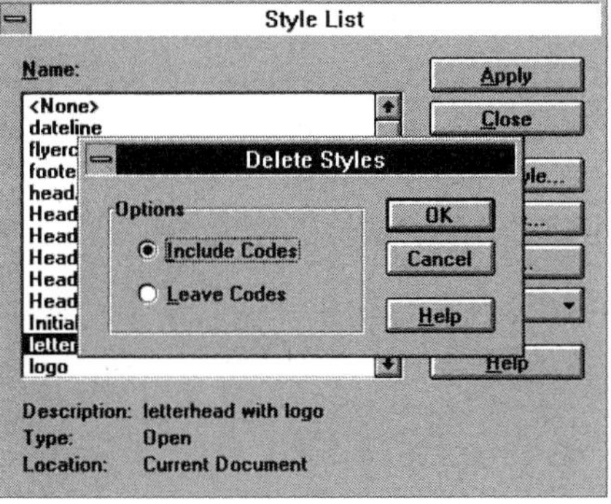

Fig. 10.11
If you choose Include Codes in the Delete Styles dialog box, your style is gone and cannot be brought back with Edit, Undo.

3. Choose one of the following options:

   - *Include Codes.* Deletes the style definition as well as all the style codes used in the document.

   - *Leave Codes.* Deletes the style definition but converts the style codes in the document to regular formatting codes.

4. Choose OK.

WordPerfect returns to the Style List dialog box. The deleted style is removed from the **N**ame list box.

Copying and Modifying a Style Definition

Suppose that you want to create a style similar to another style already created for the existing document, or that you want to copy a style to your template or supplemental template file.

To copy a style, follow these steps:

1. In the **N**ame list box of the Style List dialog box, highlight the name of the style. Choose **O**ptions, **C**opy. The Styles Copy dialog box appears, containing three options (see fig. 10.12).

Fig. 10.12
To avoid overwriting existing styles in your templates, choose Current Document in the Styles Copy dialog box.

2. Choose one of the following Copy To options:

   - *Current Document.* Copies the style to a new name. You will be prompted for the name (see step 4 below).
   - ***T**emplate.* Copies the style name and contents to your template.
   - ***A**dditional Objects Template.* Copies the style name and contents to your additional object template if you have specified one.

3. If you chose **T**emplate or **A**dditional Objects Template in step 2 and the name already exists, a confirmation box appears, asking whether you want to overwrite the current styles. Choose **Y**es to change the template style or **N**o to return to the Style List dialog box.

4. If you choose **C**urrent Document in step 2, the Styles Duplicate dialog box appears, as shown in figure 10.13. Type the name of the style in the **S**tyle Name text box, and then choose OK. Both styles—the old name and the duplicate name—appear in the Style List dialog box. If you want to, you can edit the copied style.

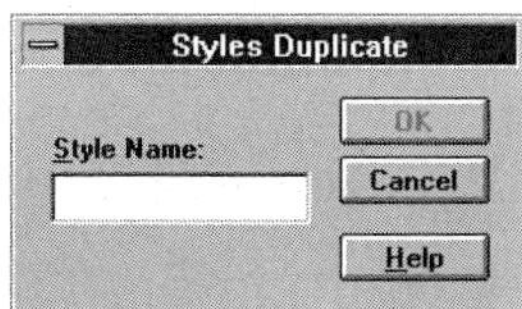

Fig. 10.13
In the Styles Duplicate dialog box, the style name can include up to 12 characters, just as when you create a style.

Copying Text, Graphics, and Formatting into the Clipboard

If you want to copy text, graphics, or formatting codes from the document to a style, first copy these elements to the Windows Clipboard by following these steps:

1. If you want to turn on Reveal Codes to assist your selection, choose **V**iew, Reveal **C**odes; or press Alt+F3.

2. Position the insertion point before the codes or text, and then use the keyboard or mouse to select the text and codes that you want to use.

3. Choose **E**dit, **C**opy; or press Ctrl+C to place a copy of the selected text and codes in the Clipboard.

◀ See "Working with Reveal Codes," p. 96

◀ See "Understanding WordPerfect's Hidden Codes," p. 95

Bringing Up the Styles Editor

Whether you copy from the Clipboard or make direct changes to the style definition, you need to bring up the Styles Editor dialog box for any style you want to change.

1. Choose Fo**r**mat, **S**tyles; or press Alt+F8 to bring up the Styles List dialog box.

2. In the **N**ame list box, highlight the style that you want to change.

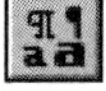

> **Note**
>
> You need to have the appropriate style type (Current Document, Template, or System) selected from the Style Setup to display your style. See "Displaying Style Names" earlier in this chapter.

3. Choose **E**dit.

   The Styles Editor dialog box appears, as shown in figure 10.14.

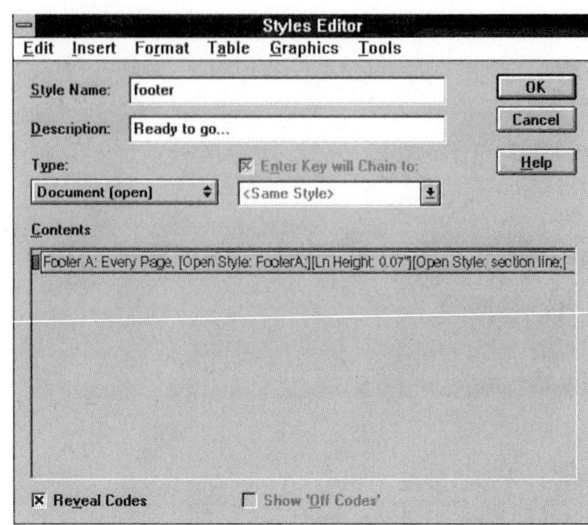

Fig. 10.14
To replace the description, press Tab until you reach the Description text box, or use the mouse to highlight the description. Typing the first letter of the new description removes the old description.

Editing a Style Definition

Tip
To edit a system style so that the edited style will be available in future documents, be sure to choose Default Template in the Default Location section of the Style Setup dialog box.

You can edit a style in several ways, including inserting or deleting text and codes, or changing the style name, style description, or style type. If you edit the contents of the style, make sure that the **R**eveal Codes check box is selected on the Styles Editor dialog box.

To edit the style, perform one or more of the following steps:

- Choose **S**tyle Name, and then type a new style name.
- Choose **D**escription, and then type a new style description.
- Choose T**y**pe, and then use the pop-up list to change the style type to **D**ocument, **P**aragraph, or **C**haracter.
- Edit the **C**ontents box by following the procedure in the following section.
- Place another style into the current style definition by following the procedure in "Nesting Styles" later in this chapter.
- Have another style turn on automatically when you turn off this style by following the procedure in "Chaining Styles" later in this chapter.

When you finish editing the style, choose OK in the Styles Editor dialog box, and then choose **C**lose in the Style List dialog box.

Editing Styles Editor Contents

To edit the codes and text of the style, follow the same procedure that you would use to edit text and codes with the Reveal Codes feature. For more information, see Chapter 3, "Retrieving and Editing Documents."

Place the insertion point in the **C**ontents box. The insertion point becomes a blinking rectangle. Perform one or more of the following steps:

- Move the insertion point with the mouse or arrow keys.
- Press Backspace to delete the text or codes before the insertion point.
- Press Delete to delete the text or codes after the insertion point.
- Choose **E**dit, **P**aste to bring information from the Clipboard into the Contents box.
- Choose other items from the Styles Editor menu bar to add codes and graphics.
- To place special text or formatting codes after a paired style (paragraph or character) is turned off, mark the Show '**O**ff Codes' check box and position the insertion point after the `[HPg]` code in the Contents box. This is useful to add spacing, formatting, or a graphic line below the text that is formatted with the paired style.

Note

Choose **I**nsert and choose **P**age Break, **H**ard Return, or **T**ab to add these codes to the Contents box.

Nesting Styles

When you are in the **C**ontents box of the Styles Editor dialog box, choose Fo**r**mat, **S**tyles (or press Alt+F8) to bring up the Style List dialog box. Highlight the style you want, and then choose **A**pply. A copy of the highlighted style appears at the location of the insertion point in the Contents box of the Styles Editor dialog box.

Tip

A paragraph style cannot be nested in another paragraph style.

Embedding one style in another is a very efficient way to control groups of related styles. For example, you might have a dozen styles based on a single style that contains your logo. If you ever change the logo style, all styles containing the logo style instantly reflect the change.

Chaining Styles

In some cases, you want not to embed one style in another, but to have one style turn on immediately after another turns off. For example, you might use a linked style for a newsletter in which each article title in one style is always followed by a byline in a different style.

> **Note**
>
> You can link only from a paragraph or character style. When you edit a document style, the E**n**ter Key Will Chain To option is dimmed.

To link two styles, follow these steps:

1. In the Style List dialog box, highlight the first style.
2. Choose **E**dit to bring up the Styles Editor dialog box.
3. Make sure that the E**n**ter Key Will Chain To check box is selected.
4. Use the drop-down list below this check box to choose the style to link to (see fig. 10.15). Only styles that you have created specifically for this document show in this list; template and system styles do not appear.

Tip
A system style cannot be chained to another style.

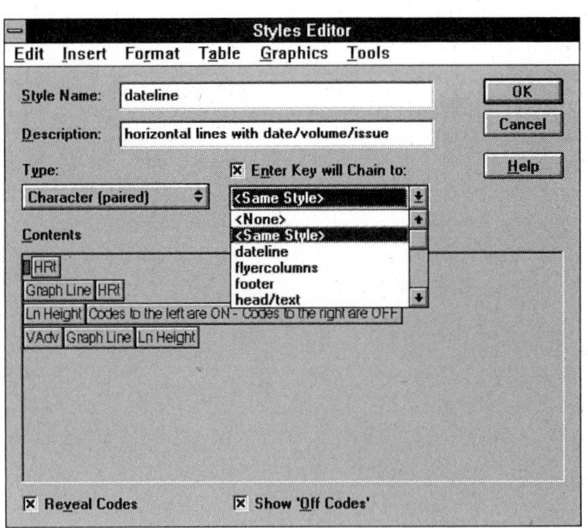

Fig. 10.15
In this example, you might choose to have the Head/Text appear when you press Enter after typing the text in the Dateline style.

5. If you have no further editing to do in the Styles Editor dialog box, choose OK to return to the Style List dialog box. Then choose **C**lose to return to the document window.

> **Note**
>
> The default selection for the Enter Key Will Chain To pop-up list is `<Same Style>`. This is useful for body text where you can press Enter, and the style will continue for all paragraphs. To turn off this style, apply the `<None>` paragraph style.

◄ See "Formatting Lines and Paragraphs," p. 134

◄ See "Formatting Characters," p. 130

◄ See "Customizing File Preferences," p. 329

> **Troubleshooting**
>
> *I have created a section heading style for the financial report I write every month. I am creating a new report and cannot find the new heading style.*
>
> When creating a style you want to be available in the future, be sure to choose Default **T**emplate in the Style Setup dialog box. To make this choice in the Style List box, choose **O**ptions, **S**etup. Alternatively, you can create a template for the monthly report. Create the style while creating the template and the style will be available when you use the report template but not in any other documents.
>
> *I've edited a system style and now I am unhappy with how it works.*
>
> You can quickly restore the original system style by selecting the style in the Style List dialog box, then choosing **R**eset from the **O**ptions drop-down list.

II

Automating Your Work

Using Styles

As you create and edit styles, you most likely will apply the styles to your document to see the results and then make further editing changes in the styles. You generally can apply a style in either of two ways: turn on the style code at a position in the document, or highlight text and then insert style codes. To use chained styles and styles that chain back to the same style, turn on the style and type your text. To apply text enhancements (bold, change in fonts), it may be easier to type the text first and then highlight the text to apply the style.

Inserting Styles

To turn on any type of style, follow these steps:

1. Choose Fo**r**mat, **S**tyles; or press Alt+F8. The Style List dialog box appears.

2. Highlight the style name in the **N**ame list box (see fig. 10.16).

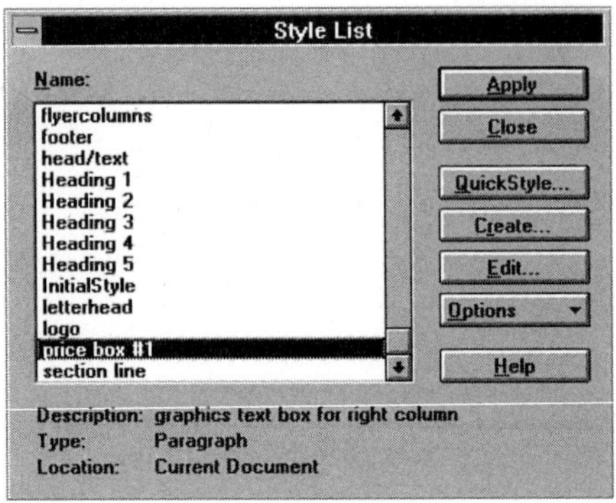

Fig. 10.16
When you highlight the style, notice the information area at the bottom of the Style List dialog box.

3. Choose **A**pply.

The steps for turning on a style are simple. However, the following factors affect you when you turn off the style:

- Whether the style is a document, paragraph, or character style
- Whether the style is inserted amid text
- Whether the style is chained to another style

The following sections explain how these factors influence the way each type of style is turned off.

Using Power Bar Buttons

The Power Bar includes buttons to help you work with styles. To use the Styles button, click on the pull-down arrow or the button face and scroll through the list of styles. After you choose your style, the button face displays the name of the current style.

◀ See "The Power Bar," p. 340

▶ See "Customizing the Power Bar," p. 462

The list of styles displayed using the Styles button includes only the current document styles, several WordPerfect heading styles, and any system styles you have used so far.

Applying Document Styles

Because document styles do not have an Off code, there is no sense in highlighting text. The document style code appears in the document, and all text following the code takes that code's formatting.

Applying Paragraph Styles

Unlike document styles, paragraph styles do have On and Off codes. The procedure for turning off the paragraph style depends on whether you first apply the style and then type text, or just select existing text. The procedure also depends on whether the paragraph style is linked to another style.

> **Note**
>
> A paragraph in WordPerfect for Windows is defined as any text followed by a hard return, so even a short line of text without any punctuation can be a paragraph.
>
> In a standard letter, for example, the date, each line of the address, and the closing, as well as full paragraphs within the letter, are all considered to be paragraphs for style-type purposes.

If you want to apply a paragraph style to an existing paragraph, position the insertion point anywhere in the paragraph, and then follow the procedure in the preceding section. If you want to apply the paragraph style to more than one paragraph, highlight the paragraphs first and then insert the style. As long as you highlight any portion of a paragraph, the style is applied to the entire paragraph. If you apply a paragraph style within existing text, the E**n**ter Key Will Chain To check box (style linking) has no effect.

If you apply a paragraph style before you type the text, what occurs when you press Enter depends on the status of the E**n**ter Key Will Chain To check box:

- If the check box is empty or indicates that the style will chain to itself with `<Same Style>`, the style remains turned on.
- For paragraph styles that chain to the `<Same Style>`, if you have added text or codes after the style off code in the Contents part of the Styles Editor, these style off codes will take effect after you press Enter, and the style on codes turn on at the beginning of the next paragraph.
- If the check box is marked and indicates a different style, pressing Enter links to the chosen style by turning off the first style and turning on the next.

In either case, if you want to turn off the paragraph style or not use the chained style, insert the `<None>` style after you press Enter. The `<None>` style is a special style that turns off any paragraph style and prevents chaining.

Caution

Be careful when you edit a paragraph formatted using a paragraph (paired-open) style. If you make a change that affects the entire paragraph, such as changing the font size or indenting the paragraph, the paragraph (paired-open) style is immediately edited to include the change.

Applying Character Styles

Character styles should apply only to a portion of text, not to specific paragraphs. Although it makes sense to chain paragraph styles, it is less appropriate to chain character styles (but the program allows you to do this). A better procedure is to choose E**n**ter Key Will Chain To <None> for character styles. This option allows you to turn on the character style, type text, and then press Enter to turn off the style. If you want to insert a hard return, you have to press Enter a second time.

To apply a character style to existing text, first select the text, and then follow the procedure in the preceding section.

◀ See "Finding and Replacing Formatting Codes," p. 124

◀ See "Formatting Characters," p. 130

◀ See "Formatting Lines and Paragraphs," p. 134

Working with Styles from Other Files

As mentioned earlier in the chapter, styles come from one of four places: the document, the template, the supplementary template, or the system. Templates allow you to create and save styles, macros, or menus, and to add generic text and graphics for each type of document you work with, such as letters, memos, and reports. (For more information on templates, see Chapter 11, "Using Templates.")

System styles are associated with WordPerfect features such as captions, line styles, and outline styles throughout the program. You can change a copy of the system styles for each template.

You can change a copy of the template and system styles only for the current document. You can make any changes you want to the styles for the current document, but the changes occur only in that document.

Using System Styles

If you change a system style in a document, you change the style only for the current document. If you change a system style for a template, however, only new files you create will be affected. Files you created before the style change will not be affected.

Using Templates

As mentioned in the preceding section, changing a template or a system style in a template affects all files that are based on the template. To edit a template (not a document based on the template), choose **F**ile, **N**ew; or press Ctrl+T. Then choose **O**ptions, **E**dit Template.

When you now follow the directions in this chapter for editing styles, the styles displayed are those in the current template.

Saving Styles to Another File

If you want to use your styles for other documents, you can save the styles into a document, a style library, or a template.

To save a style to a document, follow these steps:

1. In the Style List dialog box, choose **O**ptions, Save **A**s. The Save Styles To dialog box appears.
2. Type the name of the file in the **F**ilename text box, or click the File button (see fig. 10.17) and choose a file in the list of files.

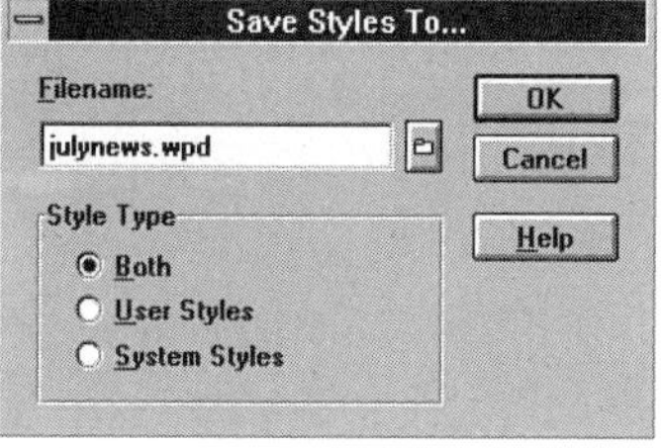

Fig. 10.17
The File tool accesses a list of existing files. After you select the tool, the Select File dialog box allows you to scroll through a list of files, change directories, and view the files.

3. The Style Type area of the Save Styles To dialog box allows you to save some or all of your styles. Choose one of the following options:
   - ***B**oth.* Saves all styles to the specified document.
   - ***U**ser Styles.* Saves current document styles and template styles to the specified document.
   - ***S**ystem Styles.* Saves only system styles to the specified document.
4. After you finish making choices in the Save Styles To dialog box, choose OK to save the styles and return to the Style List dialog box.

Note

You also can save the styles in a blank document by typing a new file name; previous versions of WordPerfect refer to such a file as a *style library*. One function of templates in Version 6.1 is to offer more flexibility than style libraries do, but if you want to save only styles (and no other features associated with the template), simply type an unused file name in the **F**ilename text box. Because the new file contains only styles, choose an extension such as STY. The new file is saved to the same directory as your template.

To copy the styles to the default or supplemental template, choose **O**ptions, **C**opy in the Style List dialog box. The Styles Copy dialog box contains options for copying to the **T**emplate or **A**dditional Objects Template (refer to fig. 10.12).

Retrieving Styles from Another Document or Template

You can combine the styles in your current document with styles from another document or template.

To retrieve styles into the current document, follow these steps:

1. In the Style List dialog box, choose **O**ptions, R**e**trieve. The Retrieve Styles From dialog box appears.

2. Type the name of the file in the **F**ilename text box, or click the file tool on the dialog box and choose a file in the list of files.

   You can choose a WordPerfect document (with a .WPD extension) or a WordPerfect template file (with a .WPT extension).

3. The Style Type area of the Retrieve Styles From dialog box allows you to retrieve some or all of the styles. Choose one of the following options:

   - ***B****oth*. Retrieves all styles from the specified document.
   - ***U****ser Styles*. Retrieves document styles and template styles from the specified document.
   - ***S****ystem Styles*. Retrieves only system styles from the specified document.

▶ See "Applying Templates to Documents," p. 392

▶ See "Finding Files," p. 965

4. After you finish making choices in the Retrieve Styles From dialog box, choose OK to retrieve the styles and return to the Style List dialog box.

Troubleshooting

I have created a master document that contains several subdocuments. Several of the styles in the subdocuments are not working and now when I try to edit one of these styles in a subdocument, the style has been changed.

You have probably repeated style names in the master document and the subdocuments. The master document style takes precedence over styles of the same name in the subdocuments. When the subdocument is condensed and saved, the master document style replaces the style in the subdocument. Be sure you use different names or use the same styles in master documents and subdocuments.

I want to edit the format of a bulleted paragraph but cannot find these styles in the Styles List box.

Bulleted and numbered paragraphs are edited from within the Bullets & Numbers dialog box accessed through the **I**nsert pull-down menu.

Examining Some Styles in Use

The four examples that follow illustrate how you can use some of WordPerfect's formatting capabilities in document, character, and paragraph styles.

Letterhead Document Style

A letterhead is an excellent application for styles, especially if you take advantage of the formatting capabilities of WordPerfect for Windows. Creating a letterhead in WordPerfect is helpful if your printer does not have a paper bin or if you want to fax files without printing them.

The example Letterhead style is an open style that uses a Delay code to change the top margin beginning on page 2 and includes text and a graphics image (see fig. 10.18). The Letterhead style uses an advance code to force the letter to begin exactly 2 1/2 inches below the top of the page.

Tip

Because Letterhead style is used so frequently, avoid wasting disk space by using WordPerfect's Image on Disk option instead of including the actual image in each file.

See Chapter 21, "Using Advanced Graphics Techniques," to learn about the Image on Disk option.

Note

If you use text in a style definition, WordPerfect does not see that text during a search, spell check, or grammar check.

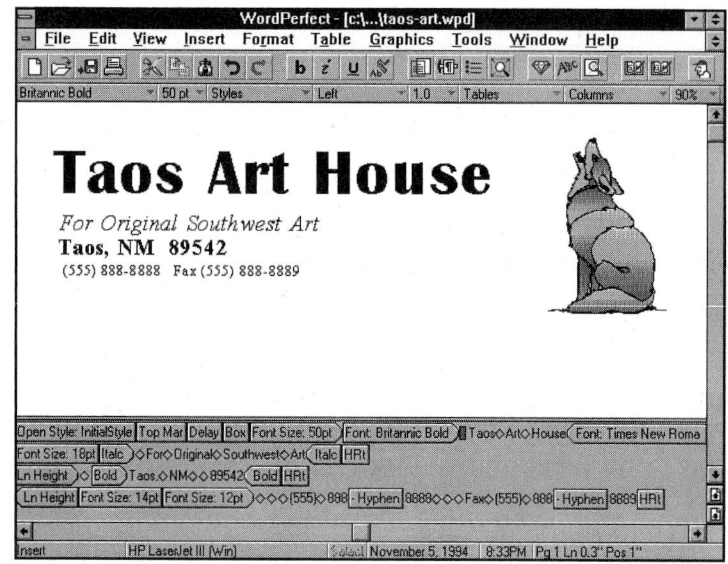

Fig. 10.18 The figure shows the letterhead produced by the codes and text shown in the Reveal Codes area. First create the letterhead as a document and then fine-tune it before replicating the codes in the Style Editor.

Quotation Character Style

The Quotation style shown in figure 10.19 controls the formatting for quoted text in a scholarly article. The Quotation style was created as a character style, but it could have been created as a paragraph style as well.

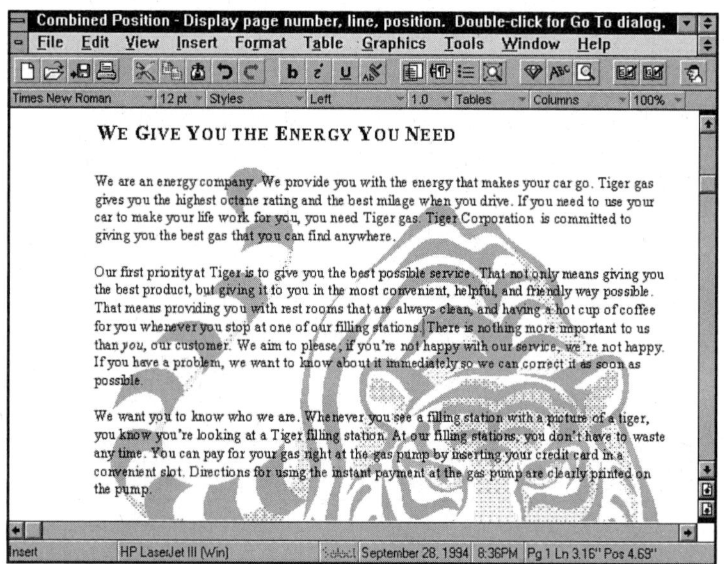

Fig. 10.19 The Quotation style makes it easy to format embedded quotations. If you want to change the style for all quotations, you can edit the style.

The Quotation style shown in figure 10.19 turns on italics, chooses the small-font attribute, and inserts a code that tells WordPerfect to skip text governed by this style during a spell or grammar check. The Quotation style also takes advantage of WordPerfect's new paragraph format feature to change the paragraph left and right offsets to 1/2 inch, the interparagraph spacing to 1 1/2 inches, and the first-line indent to 1/2 inch. To override the first-line indent, press Shift+Tab.

Border Text Paragraph Style

The Border Text style (see fig. 10.20) is a paragraph style that uses a dashed paragraph border and Block Protect to keep the paragraph together on a page. Because this style is designed for use with single paragraphs, E**n**ter Key Will Chain To is set to `<None>` to turn off the style. Justification is set to `Full` because a border looks better with full justification than with left justification.

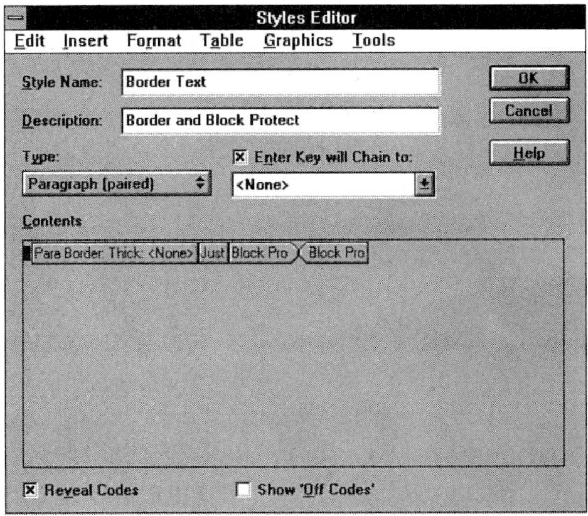

Fig. 10.20
The Border Text style adds a thick border and Block Protect to a paragraph. The Block Protect code prevents the paragraph from splitting when a page break occurs.

Q&A Linked Paragraph Styles

The Q&A style is a linkage of two paragraph styles—Q and A—that are designed to help you to format a series of questions and answers (see fig. 10.21). This illustrates style linking, a powerful capability of WordPerfect for Windows.

The Q style consists of an Italic code, the text `Q.`, and an Indent code. The A style consists of the text `A.` and an Indent code. The A style also contains a Hard Return code with the Style Off codes, to add space between the answer and the next question.

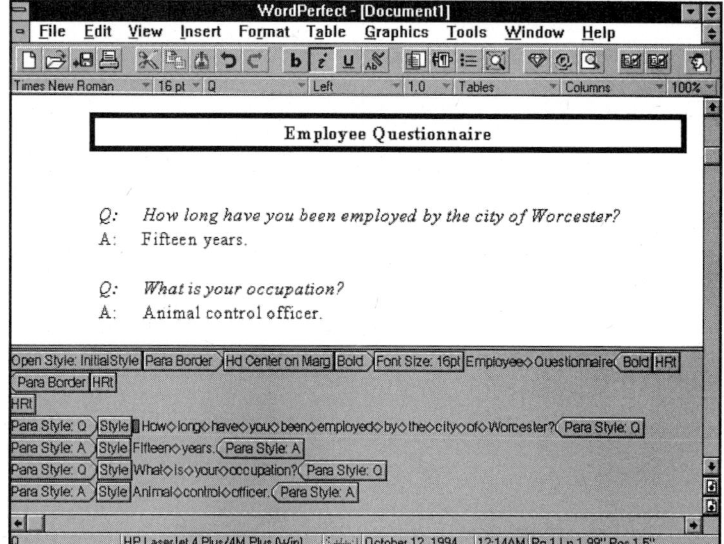

Fig. 10.21
The Reveal Codes area shows the style codes for the Q and A styles that create the format displayed in the document window. Notice that the Border Text style from figure 10.20 also appears in this example.

The Q style is linked to the A style, which in turn is linked to the Q style (see fig. 10.22). To use these styles, turn on the Q style and type your question. When you press Enter, WordPerfect turns off the Q style and turns on the A style. Type the answer to the question, and then press Enter. WordPerfect turns off the A style and turns on the Q style again. When you finish typing the questions and answers, open the Style List dialog box and choose `<None>`.

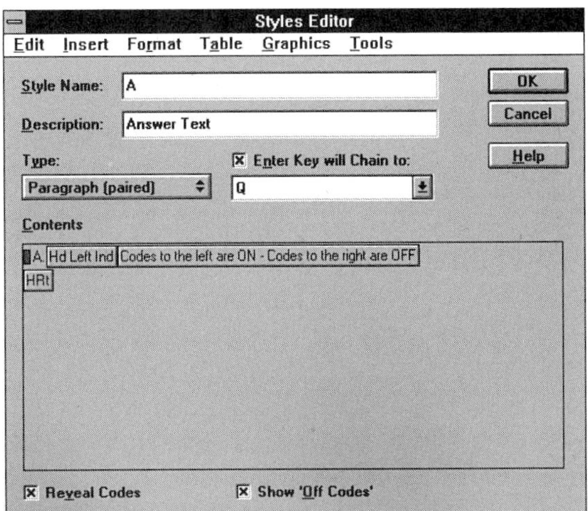

Fig. 10.22
The Enter Key Will Chain To text box in the Styles Editor dialog box shows that these styles are linked. By using a link of this sort, you can alternate between two styles by pressing Enter.

From Here...

WordPerfect 6.1 styles are far more flexible, comprehensive, and powerful than ever before. Although some aspects of styles are difficult to master, they are worth the effort. Styles reduce keystrokes and formatting time for all but the simplest documents. Styles enable you to modify the formatting in one document or many documents quickly and easily. Many projects, such as long reports, technical documentation, group writing projects, and desktop publishing applications, are more difficult in WordPerfect when you don't use styles.

For information relating to the features in this chapter, consider reviewing these chapters:

- Chapter 5, "Formatting Pages and Documents," introduces you to the many features you can use in WordPerfect to format your document.
- Chapter 11, "Using Templates," shows you how to edit the templates in WordPerfect and create custom templates to standardize your work.
- Chapter 15, "Organizing Documents with Outlining," teaches you how to use WordPerfect's outline feature and to create and edit outline styles.

Chapter 11

Using Templates

by Gordon McComb

WordPerfect lets you create documents based on previously designed templates—a sort of "write by the numbers," where the document gives you the basic framework. Fill in the missing text, and your document is done.

You can create a memo template, for example, that contains the basic formatting and text for your company's inter-office memos. To write a new memo, just create a document that is based on the memo template. Fill in the blanks—who the memo is to, the subject of the memo, and so on—and the document is ready to be saved or printed.

WordPerfect comes with many templates that you can use immediately, and you also can edit these templates to better suit your taste. You can, for example, provide your own name and phone number in several of the templates (such as the memo and fax cover sheet) so you don't need to retype this information each time you use the template. You also can create custom templates if you don't find what you want in the template assortment that accompanies WordPerfect.

This chapter explores templates, covering the following topics:

- Understanding the rationale behind the use of templates
- Applying templates to documents
- Editing templates to your specifications
- Creating new templates
- Adding Toolbars, keyboards, and other tools to templates
- Adding a "trigger" to a template so that it plays a macro when you perform an action in WordPerfect
- Using WordPerfect's Letter Expert feature

Understanding Templates

A *template* is a preformatted page or document layout, used as a model for other documents. Templates contain text that does not vary between documents of a certain type. Templates also can contain a number of WordPerfect for Windows tools, including styles, abbreviations, macros, keyboards, Toolbars, or menus. These tools are customized specifically for use with that particular type of document. By using a template, you can keep all the tools you need for a particular type of document close at hand, while ensuring that the correct document formatting is consistently used.

The result of using templates is that all copies of a particular type of document look much the same. All memos, for example, have a similar form. Company standards are automatically followed, the possibility of style mistakes is almost eliminated, and standard text is entered without typographical errors (assuming, of course, that you designed the template properly).

Regarding the memo example from the introduction of this chapter, for instance, you can have a memo template that contains the company letterhead, as well as address and date information. When you use this template, a "memo" Toolbar and style library are activated to help you to format the body of the memo. These tools are specifically designed to assist your work with memos.

The template feature is complex, especially if you probe its more elaborate variations. Learning to make the feature work for you is easy, however, and well worth the time, considering the time you can save and the consistency you can achieve with documents in future typing sessions. You don't need to master the advanced uses of templates just to be able to build a memo from a memo template.

The simplest definition of templates is *prefab forms*. WordPerfect 6.1 includes five dozen templates for commonly used documents and forms. You can change these templates to your specifications. You also can create new templates for other types of documents that you use often. When the time comes to create a document, you retrieve the proper template and edit it to meet your needs.

A template can contain text only, formatting only, or both. A letter template, for example, might contain only your return address or company letterhead. A report template may contain a single embedded code to force double-spacing.

A template for bulletin board announcements might consist of the word *Announcement*, a graphic, and a text box that contains codes for a certain font.

A purchase order template might include a table complete with formulas to compute the extended cost, amount due, and other critical information. In fact, this template is one of the many that comes with WordPerfect for Windows (see fig. 11.1).

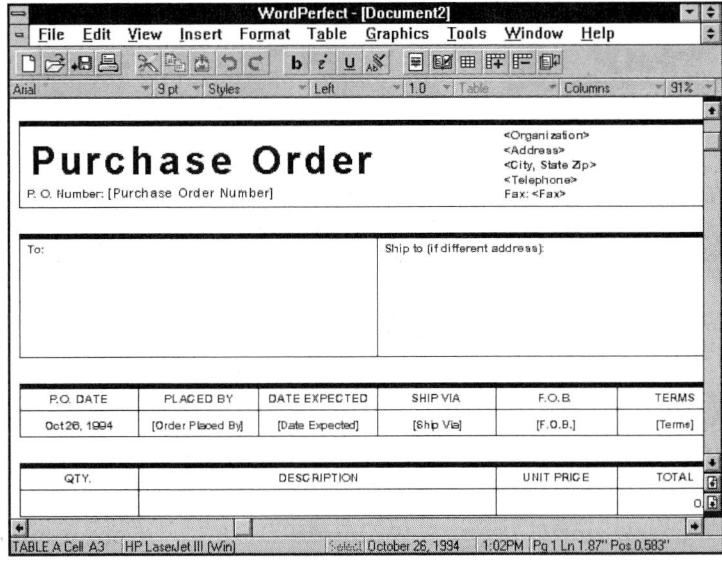

Fig. 11.1
The purchase order template, before use.

Templates are just WordPerfect files. By convention, template files are given a WPT file extension, and are stored in the TEMPLATE directory under the main WPWIN directory (these directory names assume that you chose the **S**tandard option when installing WordPerfect for Windows). Individual templates may also be stored in additional directories under the TEMPLATE directory. These additional directories, such as MEMO and CALENDAR, serve to group like templates together.

Because templates are WordPerfect files, you can open, edit, and print the files just like any other WordPerfect file.

Whether or not you have explicitly used the template feature of WordPerfect, you have used templates to create new documents. Every new document you start with WordPerfect is based on the default template, which is usually STANDARD.WPT. That is, choose **F**ile and then choose **N**ew. WordPerfect displays the New Document dialog box, shown in fig. 11.2. Choose Create a blank document, then choose **S**elect.

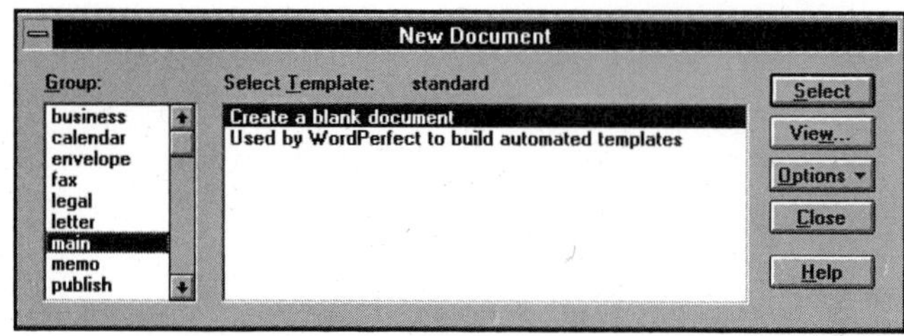

Fig. 11.2
The New Document dialog box. As you scroll through the list of templates you see that each one is summarized in the Select **Template** box.

WordPerfect creates a new, blank document. The document is based on all formatting and text that may be in the STANDARD.WPT file. If STANDARD.WPT contains the text, "This is WordPerfect for Windows," all the new documents you create in WordPerfect automatically contain this text.

Note

If you want to quickly start a new, blank document without the trouble of going through the New Document dialog box, press Ctrl+N (for New document), or click the New Blank Document icon in the Toolbar. Either of these methods bypasses the New Document dialog box, and immediately starts a new, blank document.

You can edit the STANDARD.WPT default template to suit your individual taste, adding as many features as you like. You can change margins, tabs, or the base font, or add text to the template.

Comparing Templates to Macros, Merges, and Styles

▶ See "Creating a Macro," p. 419

▶ See "Using Merge," p. 624

▶ See "Understanding the Merge Process," p. 646

Templates are yet another link in WordPerfect's long list of document automation features, which includes macros, merges, and styles. It may be convenient to lump templates with macros, merges, and styles, but it is also important to note that each automation feature has its own special set of uses and limitations.

Although templates can be used to solve a lot of problems and provide a great deal of flexibility, other automation features may be better suited for the task. It's also important to note that both macros and styles can be "embedded" in a template, so you can use all three together.

In fact, an ideal use of templates is to "package" all these elements into one file, to make it easier to distribute document building tools. For example, you can distribute a memo template to all employees, ensuring that they all use the same form, styles, and macros for memos.

Templates are best suited for creating documents that contain specific text or formatting, or both. The fax cover sheet is an excellent example of a perfect template; the template includes the words FAX COVER SHEET at the top and has places to type the name of the person to receive the fax, the subject of the fax, and so on. When you use the template, WordPerfect inserts this text—along with all accompanying formatting, such as centered text, font changes, or font attributes—into a new document. You need only fill in the blank parts (who the fax is for and so on), and then print the document.

Templates are not as well suited when you need the user to enter information in a specific order, or when you must be sure that the user provides the correct information. Macros and merges are better suited for this task because you can include intelligence that ensures proper entry.

Conversely, a benefit of templates is that the template contains the overall text and formatting of an entire document. If the template is a form that the user fills in, the formatting—as an integral part of the document—is automatically applied. This process is unlike styles, which must be applied manually.

Note

There's no rule that says you must use styles, macros, or templates. In fact, many document-building chores require that you combine all of WordPerfect's features for maximum benefit.

When deciding on whether to use templates, macros, merges, or styles, keep the following points in mind:

- Templates define the text and formatting for a whole document. If you need to insert only a line or two of text, use a macro.
- The same applies to styles. If you want to apply the formatting for only a portion of a document, use one or more styles rather than a complete template.
- By themselves, templates have no intelligence. A template cannot insert one graphic if a certain set of criteria is met and another graphic if another set of criteria is met. Macros and merges can be endowed with intelligence. If needed, you can embed a macro in a template if you want to combine the features of a template with the smarts of a macro.

- Templates cannot connect to a data file and therefore cannot be used as part of a merge. If you need to prepare a form letter to send to clients, use the merge feature instead. The form document becomes the "template," and the data document provides the information you want to insert into the template when the two documents are merges.

Applying Templates to Documents

When the time comes to create a particular type of document—a memo, for example—choose **F**ile, **N**ew; or press Ctrl+T. The New Document dialog box appears, containing a list of available templates and template groups (refer to fig. 11.2).

Highlight the template you want; then choose **S**elect. A new document, based on the template you selected, opens for you.

If you want to choose a template that is contained in a different group, such as a template in the *memo* group, select the template group you want in the **G**roup list. Templates within that group are shown in the Select **T**emplate list.

Tip
If the text in the Select **T**emplate list doesn't tell you enough about a template, highlight a template, and then choose Vie**w**. The View window appears, showing you the text and basic formatting of the template.

You can immediately use templates that contain only formatting and regular text. After WordPerfect opens the document, just write text as usual. However, templates that must be filled in require that you respond to one or more prompts to provide the information needed for the template.

As you highlight the templates in the Select **T**emplate list, the template file name (minus the WPT extension) appears above the Select Template list. This information can help you identify the actual template file, should you wish to copy it, move it to another directory, and so on.

Almost all of the templates that come with WordPerfect for Windows are designed as forms for filling in. For example, when you use the Fax Cover Sheet-Traditional template (filename FAX1.WPT), you are asked whom the fax is for, the fax number, the subject, and the total number of pages in the fax.

Note

The first time you use a template that requires your filling in information, WordPerfect asks you to provide personalizing information, such as your name, company name, address, and phone number. You enter this information once; thereafter, each time you use a template, WordPerfect inserts this information for you in the proper spots in the template.

Suppose that you want to write a memo, using one of the memo templates. To do so, choose **F**ile, **N**ew; or choose Ctrl+T. Choose memo in the **G**roup list, then one of the memos listed in the Select **T**emplate List, such as Memo-Trimline. Choose **S**elect.

WordPerfect for Windows creates a new document based on the Memo-Trimline template. It also automatically runs a macro (contained within the template) that displays the Template Information dialog box, which prompts you to fill in the document (see fig. 11.3)—who the memo is to, the name(s) of those who should receive a copy of the memo, and the subject of the memo. You need to write only the actual text of the memo and then save or print the document when you are done.

Note

You can refill the template at any time. Simply click the Template Fill button in the Toolbar. The Template Information dialog box appears, where you can re-enter the data you want included in the document. WordPerfect replaces the old data you previously provided with the new data.

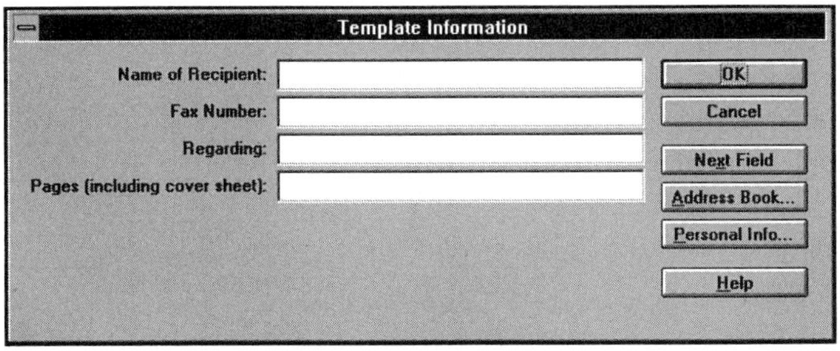

Fig. 11.3
Choose **P**ersonal Info to change your personalized information, such as name or company. Choose **A**ddress Book to add, delete, or select a name from an "address book" of often-used names.

Using the Template Feature Bar

When editing or creating a template, WordPerfect displays the Template Feature Bar, which consists of seven option buttons (see fig. 11.4). The Feature Bar helps you access the special features of templates. Table 11.1 describes the Template Feature Bar options.

Fig. 11.4
Use the Template Feature Bar to access advanced template editing features.

Table 11.1 The Template Feature Bar Options

Button	Function
?	Displays a menu list of Template Feature Bar functions.
Insert File	Allows you to insert text and graphics from another file at the current insertion point.
Build Prompts	Allows you to create your own Template Information dialog boxes for filling data into a template.
Copy/Remove Object	Copies object (such as style or macro) from another template, or deletes selected object.
Associate	Associates a macro with any of more than a dozen "events," such as saving a file, closing a file, or leaving WordPerfect.
Description	Describes the template; this descriptive text appears in the Description box in the Templates dialog box.
Exit Template	Saves any changes to the template and closes the template.

When using the Template Feature Bar, keep the following in mind:

- If you use a mouse, you can access any option in the Template Feature Bar by clicking the appropriate button.
- If you use the keyboard, you can access an option button by pressing Alt+Shift, then the letter associated with the button (such as C for **C**opy/Remove Object or A for **A**ssociate).

Using the Templates Provided with WordPerfect for Windows

As you read previously, WordPerfect for Windows comes with five dozen ready-made templates. Table 11.2 lists these templates and what they do.

Table 11.2 WordPerfect for Windows Predefined Templates

Template	Group	Description
AUTOTMP	main	Used by WordPerfect to build automated templates
AGENDA	business	Agenda—Meeting agenda
BALANCE	balance	Balance Sheet
BROCHUR1	publish	Brochure—Traditional
BROCHUR2	publish	Brochure—Elegant
BUSCARD1	business	Business Card—Traditional
BUSCARD2	business	Business Card—Contemporary
BUSCARD3	business	Business Card—Cosmopolitan
BUSCARD4	business	Business Card—Trimline
CALENDAR	calendar	Calendar Expert—Creates monthly calendars
CAL_SIDE	calendar	Monthly Calendar—Landscape orientation
CAL_UP	calendar	Monthly Calendar—Portrait orientation
CASHFLOW	business	Cash Flow Statement
CERTIF1	publish	Certificate of Achievement—Landscape Orientation
ENV1	envelope	Envelope—Traditional
ENV2	envelope	Envelope—Contemporary
ENV3	envelope	Envelope—Cosmopolitan
ENV4	envelope	Envelope—Trimline
EXPENSE	business	Expense Report
FAX1	fax	Fax Cover Sheet—Traditional
FAX2	fax	Fax Cover Sheet—Contemporary
FAX3	fax	Fax Cover Sheet—Cosmopolitan
FAX4	fax	Fax Cover Sheet—Trimline
FAX_EX	fax	Fax Expert—Creates fax cover sheets

(continues)

Table 11.2 Continued

Template	Group	Description
GREETING	publish	Greeting Card
IDEALIST	business	Idea List—Notepad for brainstorming
INVOICE	business	Invoice—Standard sales invoice
LETTER0	letter	Letter—Blank Letterhead
LETTER1	letter	Letter—Traditional Letterhead
LETTER2	letter	Letter—Contemporary Letterhead
LETTER3	letter	Letter—Cosmopolitan Letterhead
LETTER4	letter	Letter—Trimline Letterhead
LTR_EX	letter	Letter Expert—Creates letters
MEMO1	memo	Memo—Traditional
MEMO2	memo	Memo—Contemporary
MEMO3	memo	Memo—Cosmopolitan
MEMO4	memo	Memo—Trimline
MEMO_EX	memo	Memo Expert—Creates memos
NEWSLTR1	publish	Newsletter—Traditional
NEWSLTR2	publish	Newsletter—Traditional (White on Black Heading)
NEWSLTR3	publish	Newsletter—Cosmopolitan
NEWSLTR4	publish	Newsletter—Trimline
NWLTR_EX	publish	Newsletter Expert—Creates newsletters
PLEADING	legal	Pleading Paper
PRESS1	business	Press Release—Standard press release
PRESS2	business	Press Release—Press release with bold heading
PURCHASE	business	Purchase Order—Standard purchase order
REPORT1	report	Report—Traditional
REPORT2	report	Report—Contemporary

Template	Group	Description
RESUME1	resume	Resume—Traditional
RESUME2	resume	Resume—Contemporary
RESUME3	resume	Resume—Cosmopolitan
SIGN1	publish	Sign—General announcement, landscape orientation
SIGN2	publish	Sign—Southwestern style
SIGN3	publish	Sign—Seminar announcement
STANDARD	main	Creates a blank document
TERM1	report	Term Paper—Modern Language Assoc.
TERM2	report	Term Paper—Chicago Manual of Style
TERM3	report	Term Paper—American Psychological Assoc.
THANKYOU	publish	Thank You Card

Most of the templates supplied with WordPerfect for Windows are stored in separate directories to create template "groups." All of these directories are contained under a "master" template directory, usually TEMPLATE. This directory is identified in the File Preferences dialog box. If you don't see a list of template names when you choose **F**ile, **N**ew (or press Ctrl+T), one of two things might have happened:

- You performed a custom installation of WordPerfect and did not choose to include template files in the WordPerfect directory. To include these files, start the install program, choose **C**ustom install, Files, and then select the Template Files box. Click any other boxes that contain Xs to deselect them so that when you start the installation, only templates transfer.

- WordPerfect was not looking in the proper directory for the template files. Choose **E**dit, Pr**e**ferences, **F**ile, **T**emplates. The lower part of the File Preferences dialog box changes to show which directory Word-Perfect is using for templates. Enter the proper directory (for example, C:\OFFICE\WPWIN\TEMPLATE) in the default directory text box.

Note

Saving the new memo document has no effect on the template. The original memo template is unchanged and available for you to write more memos without erasing the text that you typed in the new memo.

Troubleshooting

When I choose File, New, no templates appear.

The template documents must be placed in specific directories. These directories are set up when you first install WordPerfect. The main template directory (usually \OFFICE\WPWIN\TEMPLATE) is identified in the File Preferences dialog box. Make sure this directory is specified in the File Preferences dialog box, or else WordPerfect won't be able to locate your template files.

When I choose File, New, all the templates appear at once, rather than in groups.

WordPerfect uses subdirectories under the main TEMPLATE directory to create "groups" for template files. As it comes "out-of-the-box," WordPerfect comes with over half a dozen group subdirectories, including BUSINESS, LETTER, MEMO, and REPORT. The individual templates are supposed to be placed within these subdirectories. However, if for some reason the files are moved to the main TEMPLATE directory, they will appear all together in the Select Template dialog box. If you'd like your templates in groups, you must create the group subdirectories as specified in this chapter, and move the files to their associated groups.

When I create a new document with a template, WordPerfect fills it with personal information for someone else, but not me.

WordPerfect stores one set of personal information. If someone else has used your copy of WordPerfect, that personal information may not be up to date for you. You can change the personal information by choosing the **P**ersonal Info button any time a Template Information dialog box appears. Make any necessary changes, and choose OK.

I can't find one or more of the templates that are supposed to come with WordPerfect.

Templates are files; and therefore they can be deleted. If a template you want to use is missing from the list of templates, you will need to reinstall the template files from the original WordPerfect disks or CD-ROM.

Working with Templates

You are not limited to working with WordPerfect for Windows default templates. You can edit the predefined templates to suit your needs or create your own templates. The new template can be one that you create from scratch or one that you base on a predefined WordPerfect template. When you no longer need one or more templates, you also can delete them.

Editing a Template

Most of the templates that come with WordPerfect for Windows can be used straight "out of the box," without modification, as long as you have previously provided personalized information (see the Note in the earlier "Applying Templates to Documents" section). For example, the Memo-Traditional template (filename MEMO1.WPT) is formatted so that when you use it, WordPerfect automatically inserts your name in the From: field.

Although WordPerfect's templates don't require modification before you can use them, you may still want to add or modify text or formatting to suit your tastes. For instance, you may want to use a different font, or change the word MEMO to INTEROFFICE MEMO, or perhaps even ELECTRONIC MEMO if you send memos via the company's electronic mail system.

To edit a template, choose **F**ile, **N**ew; or press Ctrl+T. Choose the template you want to edit (select a new group if the template you want is in another group) and choose **O**ptions, **E**dit Template. The selected template document opens showing you the contents of the template, as well as the Template Feature Bar (see fig. 11.5).

After the template document is open, you can edit it as you would any WordPerfect document. You may add or remove text, change the formatting, and so on.

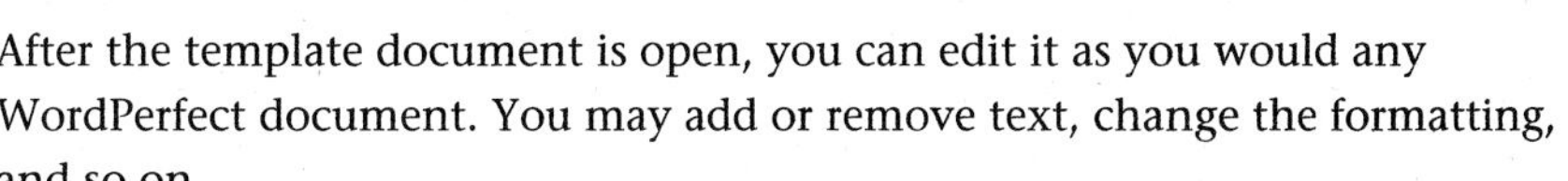

Note

The changes that you make in a template by following the steps in this section make permanent changes in the template, but not in any document you've previously created using the template. Be careful not to delete template elements that are hard to replace or add features that are not useful.

When you finish editing the template, save it so that it is available for future use. Choose **E**xit Template in the Template Feature Bar. WordPerfect asks whether you want to save the changes; choose Yes. The program saves and then closes the edited template.

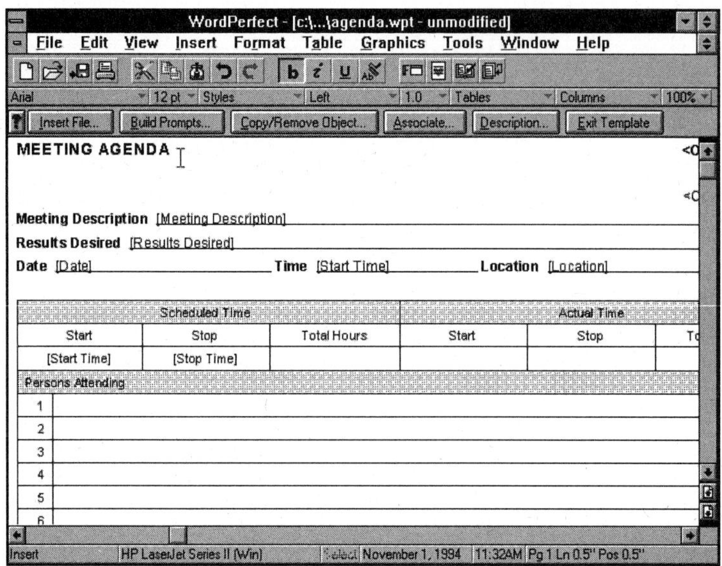

Fig. 11.5
An opened template, ready for editing. Templates are like regular WordPerfect documents, so you can use any formatting features to make the template look the way you want. Feel free to experiment with template designs.

Creating a New Template

Just because WordPerfect for Windows comes with previously made templates doesn't mean you can't create your own. You'll want to create your own templates if the ones that come with WordPerfect are not suitable for your needs, or if you regularly produce specialized documents.

For example, you can create a template for quickly producing "standard operating procedure" documents for your company. You might use another custom template for making it easier to write the notes for the weekly meeting. In short, there is no limit to the number and type of templates you can create for use in WordPerfect.

Creating a Template from Scratch

To create a new template, in the New Document dialog box, choose **O**ptions and then **N**ew Template. Once again, WordPerfect starts a new document for you, and displays the Template Feature Bar.

Select the formatting and text of the document as desired. After you finish with your changes, choose **E**xit Template. Answer **Y**es to save the changes. The Save Template dialog box appears (see fig. 11.6)

In the Save Template dialog box, provide a name for the template (don't use an extension; WordPerfect will do that for you). Provide a brief description of the template and indicate which existing template group to store your new template under. Choose OK when done. The template is saved, then closed.

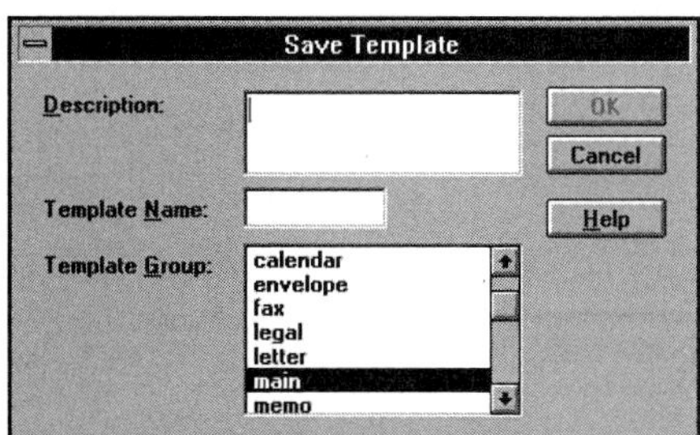

Fig. 11.6
The Save Template dialog box. Provide a name and description for your new template, and specify the group you want to store the template under.

> **Note**
>
> You can create a new template from any standard WordPerfect document. Just follow the previous steps, and then insert the document you want to use into the template document, using the **I**nsert File button on the Template Feature Bar.

Basing a New Template on an Existing Template

When you create a new template, WordPerfect doesn't base it on another template—unless you specifically ask it to. This means that the new template doesn't carry forward any formatting or text of another template. In most cases, this method is how you want to create most new templates.

However, WordPerfect also enables you to create a new template based on an already existing template. The new template *inherits* all the traits of the *parent*, or original, template. You can keep the new template as is (as a clone of the parent), or you can change formatting, text, and other features to customize the new template.

To base a new template on an existing one, follow these steps:

1. Choose **F**ile, **N**ew to display the New Document dialog box.

2. Locate the template you want to use as the basic template.
3. Choose **O**ptions, **E**dit Template. The template is opened for you.
4. Immediately choose **F**ile, Save **A**s. The Save Template dialog box appears, where you provide a new name for the template. You may also provide a new description and new location.
5. Choose OK to save the template.

You may now alter the template as you want. Remember that the new template has all the features of the original template. You can delete these features, or add to them, and so on. After you finish, choose the **E**xit Template option button in the Template Feature Bar. Answer **Y**es to save the changes you've made to the template. You now may use the new template as usual.

Basing a Template on _AUTOTMP

By now you may have discovered that WordPerfect for Windows offers an alternative choice in the *main* template group. The description of the template is "Used by WordPerfect to build automated templates." The file name associated with this template is _AUTOTMP.WPT.

The _AUTOTMP template has a unique purpose. It is designed to make it easier for you to create other templates that offer automated fill-in. Most of the templates that come with WordPerfect for Windows were originally based on _AUTOTMP. If you want your template to fill in personalized data, or display a dialog box asking for you to provide information, you should also base your new template on _AUTOTMP.

_AUTOTMP is an ordinary template, except that it contains a single embedded macro: <dofiller> (this macro cannot be edited or viewed). The job of <dofiller> is a simple one—it makes a few checks about WordPerfect's current state; it then displays the Template Information dialog box so that the template can be filled in.

Basing your new template on _AUTOTMP is only half the story. You also want to design your template so that it uses the same automated field-entry syntax found in the templates that come with WordPerfect.

Fortunately, you don't need to understand the field-entry syntax, because WordPerfect comes with a feature to assist you in providing the field-entry prompts in templates you create or edit. To use the automatic field-entry feature, choose the **B**uild Prompts button in the Template field bar. In a moment, the Prompt Builder dialog box appears (see fig. 11.7). After using the Prompt Builder dialog box, choose OK to close the box. WordPerfect updates the prompt information in the template.

When using the Prompt Builder, keep the following in mind:

- Ask for user information in the Template Information dialog box (this is the dialog box that first appears after choosing a template from the New Document dialog box), choose **B**uild Prompts from the Template

Feature Bar. In the Prompt Builder dialog box, choose **A**dd. The Add Template Prompt dialog box appears. Type the text of the prompt, and choose OK.

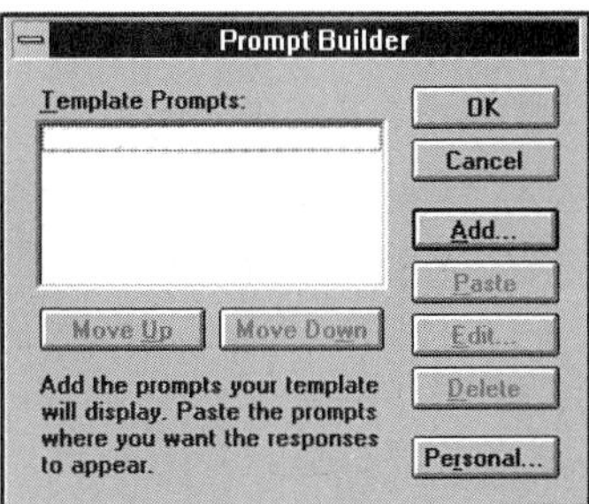

Fig. 11.7
Use the Prompt Builder dialog box to insert your own prompts and entry fields for automatic template fill-in.

- Reorder the prompts in the Template Information dialog box, select the prompt you want to reposition in the Template Prompts list, and then choose Move **U**p or Move Do**w**n.
- Specify where you want the user's data for a particular prompt inserted, place the insertion point at the desired spot in the document. Choose Build Prompts from the Template Feature Bar. In the Prompt Builder dialog box, select the prompt you want to insert in the Template Prompts list, and then choose **P**aste.
- Edit the text of a prompt, choose Build Prompts from the Template Feature Bar. In the Prompt Builder dialog box, choose the prompt to delete in the Template Prompts list, then choose **E**dit. Edit the prompt text, and then choose OK.
- Delete a prompt (it will no longer appear in the Template Information dialog box), choose Build Prompts from the Template Feature Bar. In the Prompt Builder dialog box, choose the prompt to delete in the Template Prompts list, and then choose **D**elete.
- Specify where the user's personal data will appear (such as the user's name, phone number, and so forth), and then place the insertion point at the desired spot in the document. Choose Build Prompts from the Template Feature Bar. In the Prompt Builder dialog box, choose Pe**r**sonal. The Personal Fields dialog box appears. Choose the field to use, and choose OK.

Note

The Add Template Prompt dialog box gives you the option of typing a prompt into the user's personal address book. If you want, you can associate a prompt with an address book entry, so that the template information is automatically provided if the user elects to use an address book entry when filling out the template. To tie an address book field to a template prompt, choose one of the field names in the **L**ink to Address Book Field button.

When writing the prompt text be sure to keep it short—no more than 20 or 30 characters. In addition, keep the number of prompts to a minimum—no more than four or five is ideal (12 is the maximum).

Deleting Templates You No Longer Need

You can delete templates you no longer need so they don't clutter the Templates dialog box. In the New Document dialog box, highlight the template you want to delete. Choose **O**ptions and then **D**elete Template. Confirm that you want to delete the template by answering **Y**es.

Creating New Template Groups

WordPerfect allows you to create new groups for storing templates. You might create a new group for templates you regularly use in your office, such as templates for filling out regular reports, or producing documentation for a client.

To create a new template group, in the New Document dialog box choose **O**ptions, then New **G**roup. Specify the name of the group (eight characters or less), and choose OK.

Choose **O**ptions, **R**ename Group to rename an existing group. You cannot rename the *main* group. Choose **O**ptions, De**l**ete Group to delete an existing group. You cannot delete the *main* group.

Using Objects in Templates

One of the greatest features of WordPerfect for Windows templates is that you can *embed* styles, macros, abbreviations, Toolbars, keyboards, and menus in the template. Whenever you use the template, these styles, macros, and other *objects* are available. If you have the Toolbar displayed, for example, and the template contains its own embedded Toolbar, WordPerfect removes the default bar and displays the bar from the template in its place.

Conversely, if you aren't using the template, the objects are not available, so they don't get in the way. Objects embedded in templates let you create styles, macros, abbreviations, Toolbars, keyboards, and menus that are context-sensitive. These specific objects are available to you only in the context of the template.

Of course, you do not need to use objects to use templates. But it's nice to know this powerful feature is available should you want to use it.

Note

If you do not specify an embedded object for a template, WordPerfect uses the object (if any) in the default template (usually, STANDARD.WPT). For example, if you do not specify a new keyboard layout for your template, WordPerfect merely uses the standard keyboard layout in the default template.

Adding an Object to a Template

Objects are added when creating or editing a template. You can add any type of object; the object does not have to already exist to be able to add it to the template.

To add an object to a template, follow these steps:

1. Create or edit the template in the usual manner (see the previous sections, "Editing a Template" and "Creating a New Template," in this chapter for more information).

2. Create the object you want by defining it using WordPerfect's normal feature editing tools. For example, to create a new menu, choose **E**dit, Pr**e**ferences, and then choose **M**enu.

3. Define the object in the same way that you change WordPerfect's preferences, such as with Toolbars and macros.

◄ See "Templates," p. 334

► See "Creating a Macro," p. 419

► See "Working with the Toolbar," p. 452

Objects are defined in the same way you use the corresponding feature outside of templates. If you are creating a macro object, choose **T**ools, Tem**p**late Macro, **R**ecord. Record the macro in the usual fashion. If you are creating a style, display the Style List dialog box, where you create the style as you do for a regular WordPerfect for Windows document.

The following table shows how to create the individual objects using WordPerfect's commands:

Object	Displays	Choose
Style	Style List	Fo**r**mat, **S**tyles
Template Macro	Record Template Macro	**T**ools, Tem**p**late Macro, **R**ecord
Abbreviation	Abbreviations	**I**nsert, **A**bbreviations
Toolbar	Toolbar Preferences	**E**dit, Pr**e**ferences, **T**oolbar
Keyboard	Keyboard Preferences	**E**dit, Pr**e**ferences, **K**eyboard
Menu	Menu Preferences	**E**dit, Pr**e**ferences, **M**enu Bar

Copying Existing Objects from Other Templates

WordPerfect for Windows lets you borrow objects contained in other templates. This feature saves you the time of re-creating objects that you may want to use over again.

To copy an object from another template, follow these steps:

1. Create or edit the template in the usual manner (see the previous sections, "Editing a Template" and "Creating a New Template" for more information).

2. Choose **C**opy/Remove Object in the Template Feature Bar, or press Alt+Shift+C. The Copy/Remove Template Objects dialog box appears (see fig. 11.8).

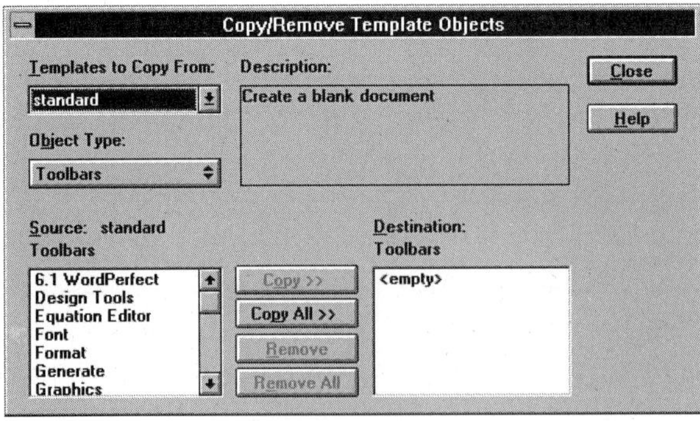

Fig. 11.8 Use the Copy/Remove Template Objects dialog box to copy objects from existing templates and to remove objects you no longer need from the template you are currently editing.

3. In the **T**emplates to Copy From list, choose the template that contains the object you want to copy.

4. Choose O**b**ject Type and specify the type of object you want to copy: Menu Bars, Macros, Toolbars, Abbreviations, Styles, Keyboards, or Macros on Disk.

5. Locate the object you want to copy in the **S**ource box and highlight it. Choose C**o**py to move the objects to the **D**estination box. Or, if you want to copy all of the objects in the Source box, choose Co**p**y All.

6. After you make your choices, choose **C**lose.

Removing Objects from the Current Template

The Copy/Remove Template Objects dialog box, described in the preceding section, also is used to delete objects no longer needed in the template. The following series of steps assumes that you are already editing the template.

To delete an object, follow these steps:

1. In the Template Feature Bar, choose **C**opy/Remove Object. The Copy/Remove Template Objects dialog box appears.

2. Choose O**b**ject type, and specify the type of object you want to delete.

3. In the **D**estination box, select the object you want to delete and choose **R**emove, or—if you want to delete all the objects listed in the **D**estination box—choose R**e**move All.

4. After you finish, choose **C**lose.

Associating Features and Events

In the previous section you learned how to embed objects into templates. Embedded objects—such as styles, macros, Toolbars, and keyboard layouts—are context-sensitive to the template you are using. Only when using a given template are the embedded objects available to you. This restriction helps to avoid clutter and streamlines your use of WordPerfect.

Besides embedding objects in templates, you can associate macros, Toolbars, menus, and keyboards to specific WordPerfect for Windows editing modes (called *features*). You can associate a particular Toolbar, for example, so that it appears whenever you use the Equation Editor or the Tables Editor. As you change modes, the Toolbar also changes.

To give templates even more of a power boost, you can associate a macro with any of 15 different *events*, or triggers. When one of these triggers occurs, the specified macro is played.

Associating to a Feature

As far as templates are concerned, WordPerfect has numerous main editing modes. These modes are shown in the following list:

Main editing window (normal document editing)
Comment box
Equation Editor
Footnotes
Endnotes
Graphics
Headers
Footers
Outline
Tables
Watermark

Using templates, you can associate a different Toolbar, menu, and/or keyboard to each of these editing modes. As you change modes, the Toolbar, menu, or keyboard layout changes dynamically and automatically.

To set an editing mode association, follow these steps:

1. Create or edit the template in the usual manner (see the "Editing a Template" and "Creating a New Template" sections earlier in the chapter for more information).

2. Choose **A**ssociate in the Template Feature Bar or press Alt+Shift+A. The Associate dialog box appears (see fig. 11.9).

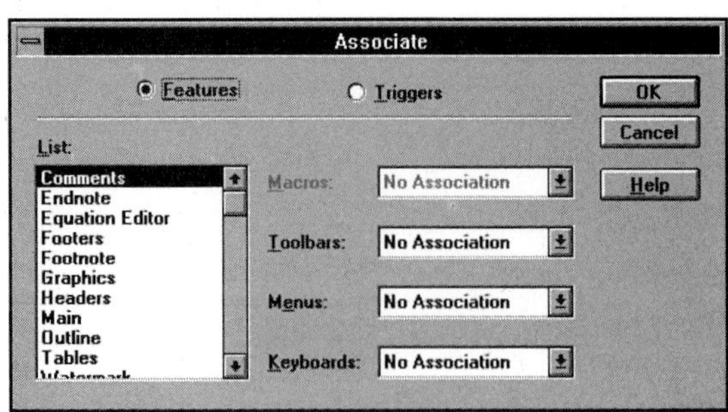

Fig. 11.9
The Associate dialog box permits you to associate certain WordPerfect for Windows features (editing modes) to Toolbars, menus, and keyboard layouts.

3. If not already selected, choose the **F**eatures option.
4. Choose the editing mode you want to associate, such as Comments, Equation, or Watermark.
5. In the respective lists, choose the **T**oolbars, M**e**nus, or **K**eyboards to specify the object you want to associate to. If no association is desired, choose No Association.

> **Note**
>
> The Toolbar, menu, or layout object already must be embedded in the template before an editing mode can be associated to the template. If you don't see the object you want to use, close the Association dialog box (choose Cancel), and create or copy the object to the template you are editing. See the previous section, "Using Objects in Templates," for more information.

6. Repeat steps 4 and 5 for each additional association.
7. Choose OK when you finish.

Associating Macros to Triggers

Macros are not associated in the same manner as Toolbars, menus, and keyboard layouts. Rather than associate a macro to a given editing mode, macros are associated to triggers. WordPerfect for Windows recognizes the following events as triggers to which you can associate a macro.

Trigger	Macro runs...
Post Close	After document is closed (choose **F**ile, **C**lose)
Pre Close	Before document is closed
Post New	After opening a new document (choose **F**ile, **N**ew)
Pre New	Before opening a new document
Post Open	After opening a document
Pre Open	Before opening a document
Post Print	After printing begins (choose **F**ile, **P**rint)
Pre Print	Before printing begins
Post Startup	After WordPerfect starts (note there is no Pre Startup, for obvious reasons)

(continues)

Trigger	Macro runs...
Post Switch Doc	After switching to a different document (choose Doc in Window)
Pre Switch Doc	Before switching to a different document
Post Tables	After switching to table edit (choose T**a**ble)
Pre Tables	Before switching to table edit

To associate a macro to one of these triggers, follow these steps:

1. Create or edit the template in the usual manner (see the sections "Edit a Template Using the Edit Template Option" and "Create a New Template Using the Create Template Option," earlier in this chapter, for more information).

2. Choose **A**ssociate in the Template Feature Bar, or press Alt+Shift+A. The Associate dialog box appears.

3. Choose the **T**riggers option.

4. In the Triggers list, choose the trigger you want to use, such as Pre Open or Post Startup.

5. In the **M**acros list, choose the macro you want to associate with the selected trigger. If no association is desired, choose No Association.

Note

The macro object already must be embedded in the template before it can accept a trigger association. If you don't see the macro you want to use, close the Association dialog box (choose Cancel), and create or copy the macro to the template you are editing. See the previous section, "Using Objects in Templates," for more information.

6. Repeat steps 4 and 5 for each additional macro trigger association.

7. Choose OK when you finish.

Planning for Embedded Macros

While there are no serious side-effects of using objects in templates, you should keep the following in mind:

- Avoid embedding more than a few macros (especially large ones) in a single template. Embedded macros can cause the template file to become larger (an increase of between 5K and 10K for even a relatively simple macro is not uncommon). The larger the template, the slower WordPerfect is in using it.

- If you must associate or embed more than a few macros in a template, consider using a "starter macro" in the template, and placing the full macro as a separate disk file. For the starter macro, use the macro CHAIN command and follow it with the name of the macro you want to use. Enclose the name in quotes, as in: CHAIN ("mymacro.wcm"). This causes WordPerfect to immediately play a macro called "mymacro.wcm" (the macro is assumed to be in the default macros directory).

- To edit an embedded macro, edit the template as described in "Editing a Template." Choose **T**ools, Tem**p**late Macro, **E**dit. Highlight the macro you want to edit, and then choose **E**dit. The macro is opened for you. You may now edit the macro. Save the changes when you are done, and close the document window.

Using the Letter Expert

The Letter Expert is something of a "hidden" feature of WordPerfect, and is new in version 6.1. With the Letter Expert, you can write and format entire business letters in a matter of minutes. WordPerfect comes with over a dozen pre-written business letters; you just insert the letter you want and fill in the blanks.

To use the Letter Expert, follow these steps:

1. Choose **F**ile, **N**ew; or press Ctrl+T. The New Document dialog box appears.

2. Choose the Letter group in the **G**roup list.

3. Select the Blank Letterhead (LETTER0.WPT) template.

4. In a few moments, WordPerfect displays the Letter dialog box (see fig. 11.10). In this dialog box, type the name and address of the person to whom you're sending the letter.

5. Specify the format of the letter: Full Block, Modified Block, Semi-Block, or Simplified.

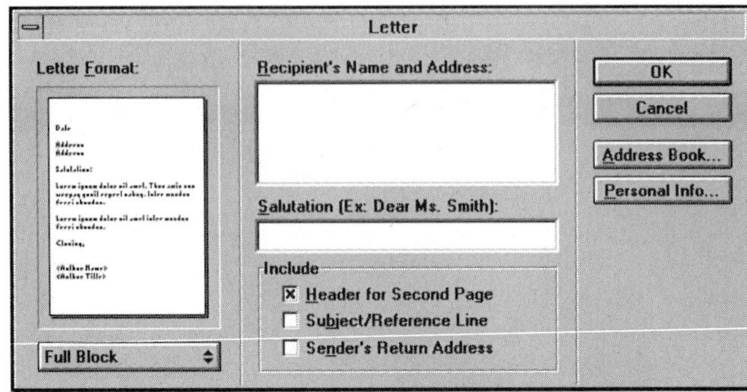

Fig. 11.10 Start the letter by filling in the Letter dialog box, including the name and address of the recipient of the letter.

6. Specify any options you want: to include a reference line with the sender's name and address, or a header for the second page. Then choose OK to close the dialog box.

7. Choose OK to start the letter.

   WordPerfect starts the letter for you and inserts the opening of the letter.

8. To enter the body of the letter, do one of the following:

   - Type the letter manually.
   - Choose **I**nsert, F**i**le, and specify the file name of a pre-written letter you want to insert as the body of the letter.

   - Choose the Pre-Written Letter icon in the Toolbar. A list of letters appears (see fig. 11.11). Highlight the letter you want to use, and choose **I**nsert.

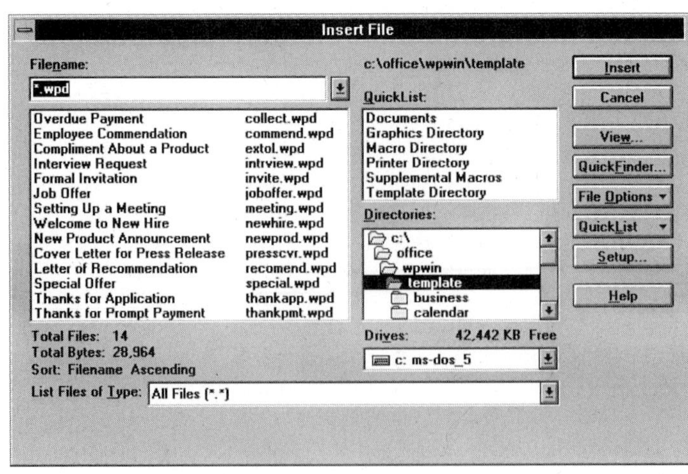

Fig. 11.11 WordPerfect comes with many pre-written business letters you can use. Specify the letter you want from the list in the Insert File dialog box.

9. At the prompt, choose **Y**es to confirm that you want to insert the selected file into the document.

10. If WordPerfect prompts you to provide information, type the response and choose OK. Your answer is inserted in the letter.

11. When done, be sure the insertion point is at the end of the letter. Choose the Letter Closing icon in the Toolbar. The Letter Closing dialog box appears (see fig. 11.12).

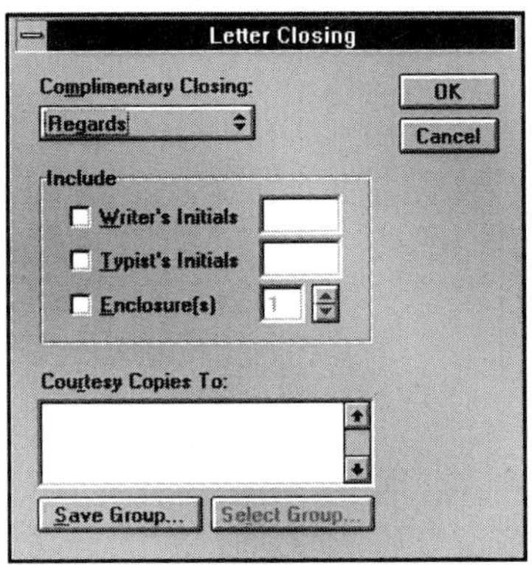

Fig. 11.12
Use the options in the Letter Closing dialog box to "close" your letter, including the complimentary close of the letter, and whether you want to send copies of the letter to other people.

12. Specify the complimentary closing to use, as well as any other letter closing options you want. Choose OK when you are done.

You can now spell check the letter, save it, and print it, as desired.

Note

WordPerfect stores the Letter Expert letters in the template directory (usually \OFFICE\WPWIN\TEMPLATE), as specified in the File Preferences dialog box. You can add your own letters by placing them in this directory, and giving them the standard WordPerfect document extension—WPD. Use the Document Summary of WordPerfect (choose **F**ile, Document Summar**y**) feature to provide a description of your letter. The text in the Document Name entry in the Document Summary dialog is what you see in the list of letters.

Note

If you want to create an envelope for your letter, choose the Envelope icon in the Toolbar. Fill out the envelope information as required, and choose **A**ppend to Doc.

Using WordPerfect's Other Template Experts

In addition to the Letter Expert described in the preceding section, WordPerfect comes with several other template experts that can make your work faster and easier. The following experts work in about the same way and prompt you for the information needed to complete each step:

- Memo Expert (choose <Memo Expert> in memo template group). Use the Memo Expert to quickly prepare memos.
- Newsletter Expert (choose <Newsletter Expert> in newsletter template group). Use the Newsletter Expert to create any of several styles of newsletters.
- Fax Expert (choose <Fax Expert> in the fax template group). Use the Fax Expert to prepare a fax cover sheet.

Troubleshooting

I can't associate two macros to the same trigger.

This is working as designed. WordPerfect only lets you trigger an event (like opening a new template) to one macro at a time. If you want to use more than one macro, you need to use the CHAIN command to play the macros one after another. If you want to run a macro and use the built-in <dofiller> macro, edit your macro so that the last command is TemplateFill(). Use this macro as the trigger association, rather than <dofiller>. WordPerfect will play your macro, then run the <dofiller> macro so the template can be filled in.

When I try to insert a Letter Expert letter, no letter appears.

The Letter Expert documents must be placed in the TEMPLATES directory (usually \OFFICE\WPWIN\TEMPLATE). Make sure this directory is specified in the File Preferences dialog box, or else WordPerfect won't be able to locate your Letter Expert files.

I can't find one or more of the Letter Expert files that are supposed to come with WordPerfect.

Letter Expert files are files, and therefore they can be deleted. If a letter you want to use is missing from the list of letters, you will need to reinstall the template files from the original WordPerfect disks or CD-ROM.

From Here...

Templates offer a great deal of power and flexibility to WordPerfect for Windows, allowing you to create documents in seconds rather than minutes. Whether you use just the basic features or the advanced features, you will find that judicious use of templates saves you many hours of work and improves the appearance of documents.

For information on creating and editing objects in templates (such as styles, menus, and keyboards), review the following chapters of this book:

- Chapter 9, "Customizing WordPerfect," details how to create and edit your own menus, keyboard layouts, and Toolbars.
- Chapter 10, "Using Styles," discusses how to create a new style, and how to edit existing styles.
- Chapter 12, "Creating Macros," teaches you the basics of recording and playing macros, including disk macros and template macros.
- Chapter 13, "Working with Toolbars," gives you details on using WordPerfect's Toolbars, including creating your own.
- Chapter 29, "Advanced Macro Techniques," takes advantage of WordPerfect's more in-depth macro features.

Chapter 12

Creating Macros

by Gordon McComb

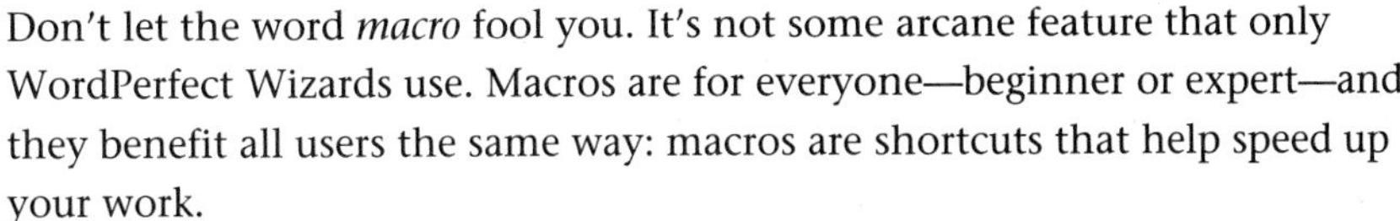

Don't let the word *macro* fool you. It's not some arcane feature that only WordPerfect Wizards use. Macros are for everyone—beginner or expert—and they benefit all users the same way: macros are shortcuts that help speed up your work.

The simplest *macro*—the kind you will use the most—is a recording of the keys you press and the commands you choose. When you *play back* your macro, your keystrokes and commands are repeated, and much faster than when you originally recorded them. With a macro, you can automate the time-consuming and dreary tasks you do every day with WordPerfect for Windows. You can, for example, set up letters, prepare fax cover sheets, or write memos.

The main purpose of macros is to make WordPerfect 6.1 for Windows do the work for you. The more menial tasks you can get WordPerfect to perform, the more time you can spend improving the content and look of your documents. If sheer output is your goal, macros enable you to speed up the preparation of documents so that you can turn out more work in the same period of time.

In this chapter, you learn how to do the following:

- Record and play back macros
- Re-record macros that don't work correctly
- Use macros for common writing, editing, and formatting tasks
- Access macros

Where did the word *macro* come from? Knowing the origin of the word helps you understand what macros are and why you shouldn't fear them. The term *macro* is a computer programmer's word for a collection of commands used to make a big programming job easier. You know that many of the documents you write with WordPerfect for Windows are little more than repetitions of the tasks you did yesterday, and the day before, and the day before that, and so on.

Computer programs are the same, using common sets of commands over and over again. To make their job easier, programmers create building blocks out of often-used commands, and they call these building blocks *macros*. When the programmers added a similar feature to WordPerfect several years ago, they named the feature *macros*. Many other names are more descriptive of the important role macros play.

You already know that macros help save you time. Now take a brief look at the other benefits macros provide:

- *Increase your productivity.* Instead of spending several minutes writing and formatting a cover sheet for every fax you send, a macro can help you write and print the cover sheet in seconds.

- *Improve your accuracy.* Although WordPerfect's built-in spelling checker helps you find spelling and typographical errors, it will not locate wrong phone numbers, shipping addresses, or social security numbers. If you type this kind of information often, you can use a macro to ensure that it is accurate every time.

- *Enhance consistency.* Did you use a 14-point font or an 18-point font for the title of last month's meeting notes? With a macro, you never have to worry about forgetting the formats you used the last time you wrote the meeting notes. Your documents will be more consistent and, therefore, more professional. While the style and template features of WordPerfect can also be used to make sure your documents look the same, a macro is often easier to set up and use.

- *Reduce complex tasks.* WordPerfect for Windows isn't known for making all tasks especially easy. Take, for example, the steps required to retrieve a graphic file, position it on the page, and set a particular border and background color. A job like this requires several dozen steps and can take minutes to perform. A macro, however, enables you to accomplish the same job in seconds and with little more effort than pressing two keys.

If you used the macro feature of WordPerfect for Windows Version 5.1 or 5.2, you will find only a few changes in the way you record and play back macros in WordPerfect 6.1. Version 6.1 also uses a similar approach to its macro language—the way your actions are recorded and stored. If you plan on writing your own macros, as opposed to just recording them, you'll find you don't have to relearn everything from scratch.

Creating a Macro

WordPerfect for Windows requires very little preparation before you can record a macro. Usually, you don't have to do anything more than start the macro recorder. As a precaution, save any documents you're currently working on. Unless you specifically want to do so, don't record your macros using a document that already contains text you don't want to change. The macro you record may change the contents of your document in ways that you may not anticipate.

Important Considerations

Although recording macros is simple and straightforward, don't use the macro record feature of WordPerfect for Windows in a haphazard fashion; if you do, you may accidentally change the document you are currently working on. Keep the following points in mind before recording your macros:

- *Save any documents you have open.* Although serious glitches during macro recording are rare, don't take chances. This step is particularly important if you are recording a macro that will modify existing text. If you save the document first and something goes wrong while you record the macro, you can retrieve the saved version and try again.

- *Unless your macros modify existing text, open a new document before starting macro recording.* This precaution helps ensure that the macro does not disturb another document you are working on.

- *If your macro modifies existing text, note the conditions that are present when you record the macro.* Be sure to reproduce those conditions before you play the macro. If you record a macro that changes wording in a form letter you send out to customers, for example, be sure to retrieve the form letter the next time you play the macro.

- *Be aware of where you are in WordPerfect for Windows before you start macro recording.* Consider WordPerfect's operating state so that you can remember to always play back your macro in the same way. If, for example, you record a macro in the header window, remember to only play the macro in a header, not at the main document screen.

- *Before recording a macro, make a dry run of the steps you want to record.* WordPerfect cannot tell if you make a mistake or choose the wrong command. Although minor mistakes usually pose no harm and can remain in your macro, you want to record your macros with the fewest number of mistakes possible. If you are making a macro of some complex task, write down the steps as a script you can follow during recording.

- *WordPerfect for Windows records the keys you press and the commands you choose.* The program does not record the amount of time you take to perform the steps. Go slow and take your time.

Note

Recording macros using standard conditions is highly recommended. If your macro is supposed to add text to a header, for example, start recording at the main document screen, and then open the header window. Type the text you want, and close the header window. By following this procedure, your macro includes all the commands needed to reproduce the conditions required for successful playback.

Steps To Record a Macro

You can use the keyboard or the mouse to record your macro. Either way, recording a macro requires the following five steps:

1. Choose **T**ools, **M**acro, **R**ecord; or press Ctrl+F10. The Record Macro dialog box appears (see fig. 12.1).

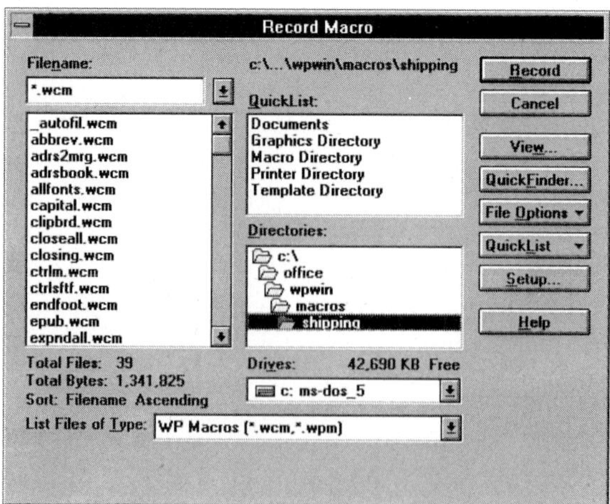

Fig. 12.1
The name you type in the File**n**ame text box becomes the macro's file name.

2. In the File**n**ame text box, type a name for your macro. This name is the macro's file name, which can include from one to eight characters and any valid character for DOS file names. Macros are automatically given a WCM extension.

3. Choose **R**ecord or press Enter. After a few moments, WordPerfect for Windows activates the macro recorder. Look for the `Macro Record` indicator in the status bar to let you know that your actions are being recorded. (This prompt does not appear if your status bar is not set to show the General Status group.)

4. Perform whatever action you want your macro to record. You can use the keyboard to enter text or choose commands from menus. Or you can use the mouse to choose commands from menus. However, when a macro is recording, *WordPerfect for Windows does not allow you to use the mouse to move the insertion point or block text.*

5. After you have entered the keystrokes, stop the macro recorder by choosing **T**ools, **M**acro, **R**ecord; or press Ctrl+F10. The `Macro Record` prompt disappears and your macro is complete.

Note

Immediately after you end a macro recording session, WordPerfect saves your macro and compiles the commands contained in the macro file. During this compiling phase, WordPerfect displays a `Compiling Macro` message, which usually appears for less than a second. On a very fast computer and a short macro, the message may just flash briefly on-screen.

A Practical Application Using Macros

A simple and common writing job is typing the complementary close and your name on a letter, as shown in the following:

Very truly yours,

Milton Farnsworth III, Esq.

Typing this example takes about 10 seconds, not including typographical errors. Although 10 seconds doesn't seem like a long time, consider the number of times that you may need to type this block of text each day, or week, or month. The 10 seconds can add up to many extra hours by the end of the year.

Because typing a closing is a common task in WordPerfect for Windows, recording a macro to type the close for you makes sense. Follow these steps to create a macro for this task, but feel free to use your own name (or your employer's name) instead of the name shown in the example:

1. As a safeguard, save any document you are currently working on.
2. Choose **F**ile, **N**ew to open a new document.
3. Start macro recording by choosing **T**ools, **M**acro, **R**ecord; or press Ctrl+F10. The Record Macro dialog box appears (refer to fig. 12.1).
4. For the name of the macro, type **vty**, for Very truly yours. You do not need to type a file extension.
5. Choose **R**ecord or press Enter. Wait a few moments for the `Macro Record` prompt to appear in the status bar.
6. Type **Very truly yours**. If you make a mistake, press Backspace to clear the error, and retype the text.
7. To add space between the close and your name, press the Enter key three or four times.
8. Type **Milton Farnsworth III, Esq.** (or any other name).

9. Stop macro recording by choosing **T**ools, **M**acro, **R**ecord; or press Ctrl+F10. The `Macro Record` prompt disappears.

Note

During macro recording, what you type is entered into the current document. Because you don't need this text, you can close the document window without saving the document.

Tip
If the document you're currently working on might be disrupted by the macro, be sure to save and close the document before you play the macro.

Now that you have recorded this macro, you can add a closing to any letter just by positioning the insertion point and executing the macro. The next section explains in detail how to play back a macro.

Playing a Macro

Macros are even easier to play than they are to record. You just tell WordPerfect you want to play back a macro, specify the name of the macro you want, and press Enter.

To play back a macro, follow these steps:

1. Choose **T**ools, **M**acro, **P**lay; or press Alt+F10. The Play Macro dialog box appears (see fig. 12.2).

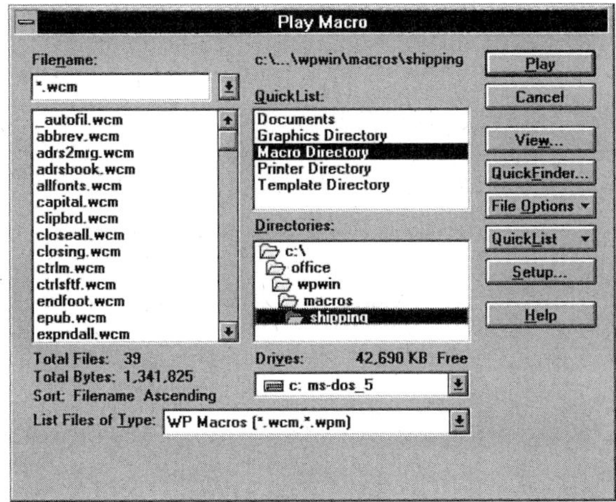

Fig. 12.2
In the Play Macro dialog box, you type the name of the macro you want to play.

2. In the File**n**ame text box, type the name of the macro you want to use. If, for example, you want to play the macro you recorded earlier, you simply type **vty**.

   Because WordPerfect for Windows always adds the WCM extension to macros that you record, you do not need to type this extension when you specify the name of the macro you want to play.

3. Choose **P**lay or press Enter. WordPerfect plays the macro.

As you use the macro feature of WordPerfect for Windows, you will eventually forget the names you gave your macros. Fortunately, WordPerfect helps you locate the macro you want by letting you scan through the available macro files. To scan the list of available macros, follow these steps:

1. Choose **T**ools, **M**acro, **P**lay; or press Alt+F10. The Play Macro dialog box appears (refer to fig. 12.2). This is the standard "open file" dialog box you see when you open a file, so you use it in the same way. Locate the file you want, or choose a different directory or disk drive to see the macro files there.

   In the Play Macro dialog box, you can use the scroll bar to scroll through the list of macros.

2. In the listing of files, highlight the macro you want to play, and choose OK or press Enter.

Re-Recording a Macro

Suppose that you are recording a macro and you make a mistake—you cut and paste instead of copy and paste, for instance. Don't worry. You can just stop macro recording and try again. When you make a mistake while you record a macro, you can simply re-record over the mistake.

You may also want to re-record a macro that isn't current. If you get promoted from vice president to president, for example, you will want to re-record any macro that identifies you as a V.P.

Consider these points before you re-record a macro:

- If you're re-recording a macro because you made a mistake the last time, the mistake may not be bad enough to warrant a new macro. Suppose, for example, that you entered one too many hard returns and had to remove it. The extra hard return and the deletion are recorded, but they have no ill effect when the macro is played back.
- Some mistakes aren't recorded. Suppose that you open the wrong dialog box. You immediately realize your mistake and choose the Cancel button. Under most circumstances, WordPerfect does *not* record this action. As a general rule, actions are recorded only when you make a change in a dialog box or type text in the document.
- WordPerfect for Windows does *not* record your fishing through various menus with the mouse or keyboard.

To re-record a macro, follow the steps in the earlier section "Steps to Record a Macro." When WordPerfect tells you that you already have a macro with the same name, answer Yes, that you want to replace it.

Understanding Where Macros Are Recorded

WordPerfect for Windows can record macros in any of several places. So far, you've read how a macro is recorded and stored as its own separate file, with a WCM file extension. The file is stored in the directory specified for macros in Preferences. (If no directory is specified, the macro is stored in the current document directory.)

This is just one way to record a macro for future use. Macros can also be recorded in a template document. To record a macro in a template:

1. Choose **T**ools, Tem**p**late Macro, **R**ecord. The Record Macro dialog box appears.
2. Choose **L**ocation. The Macro Location dialog box appears (see fig. 12.3).

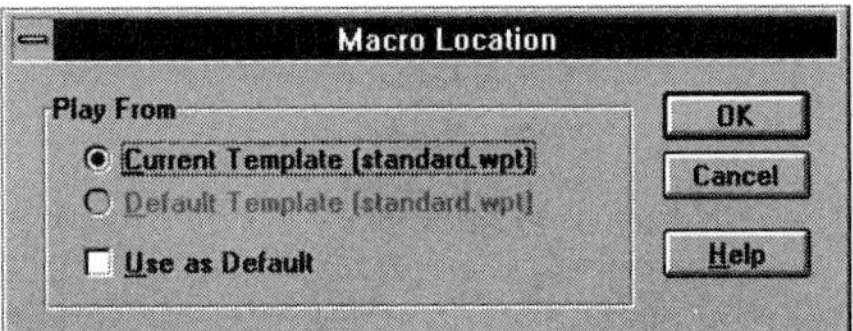

Fig. 12.3
In the Macro Location dialog box, specify where you want to store the macro when you record it.

3. Select either **C**urrent Template or **D**efault Template (usually STANDARD.WPT). If you're new to the subject of templates, see Chapter 11, "Using Templates."
4. If you want to choose a new default location, be sure to check the **U**se As Default option.
5. Choose OK or press Enter.
6. Type the name of the macro you want to record in the **N**ame box. The macro name can be up to 31 characters, and may contain spaces.
7. Choose **R**ecord or press Enter to start recording.

The Current Template Location Option

Use the **C**urrent Template location option to record the macro in whatever template file is being used for the currently open document. For example, if the currently open document is based on the resumé template (you chose **F**ile, **N**ew, choose the *resumé* group, then one of the several resumé template selections), the macro is recorded in the selected resumé template file. The macro is only available when you use the resumé template.

Even if you didn't use a template for the currently open document, by default all new documents are based on the STANDARD template (the STANDARD.WPT template file). If you didn't select a different template, the STANDARD template is the current template; therefore, recording a macro to the current template stores it in the STANDARD.WPT file.

Use the **C**urrent Template option when you want to store a macro that you plan to use only with that template. For example, if you use a resume template, you may want to record a macro that inserts your education history. Such a macro has little use outside a resume template, so storing it with the template consolidates files.

The Default Template Location Option

Use the **D**efault Template location option to record the macro in the template file used to create all new documents (normally STANDARD.WPT). This option is dimmed (unavailable) if the current template and the default template are the same.

◄ See "Understanding Templates," p. 388

Use the **D**efault Template option when you want to store a macro that you can access when using any template. Storing macros in the default template helps you consolidate files, while at the same time ensuring that the macros are always available to you.

Understanding Macro File Names

When using the File On Disk location option, you must give a name to every macro you record. WordPerfect for Windows uses that name as the file name for the macro. Each macro you record is stored on your computer's hard disk drive as a separate file. Storing the macros separately makes copying, renaming, or deleting your macros easier, because they are treated like any other file on your computer.

Note

When using the **C**urrent Template and **D**efault Template macro location options, you still must name the macro, but you are not limited to valid DOS file names. You can include spaces, punctuation, and other characters not allowed in file names (up to 31 characters).

The remainder of this section assumes that you are using file macros recorded and played with the **T**ools, **M**acro commands (as opposed to the **T**ools, Tem**p**late Macro commands).

The following sections introduce points you should keep in mind when naming your macros.

Unless Noted Otherwise, Macros Use the WCM Extension

WordPerfect for Windows uses a standard naming scheme for macros. All macros end with a WCM extension, which stands for *W*ordPerfect *C*orp *M*acro.

The WCM extension is not *mandatory*; however, it is highly recommended. When you use the WCM extension, you do not need to provide a unique extension when specifying the macro you want to play. If you use a different extension, you must also explicitly type the extension.

For example, if your macro is named TEST.WCM, you need only type **TEST** in the Play Macro dialog box, and WordPerfect plays the TEST.WCM macro. However, if the macro is named TEST.MAC, you must type **TEST.MAC** in order to tell WordPerfect the exact file name you want to use.

Ordinarily, you never have to give much thought to the WCM file extension requirement, unless you write your macros from scratch or rename a macro file. In these cases, ensure that the file names you specify include the required WCM extension.

All Macros Use Only Valid DOS File Names

Because WordPerfect for Windows macros are individual files (except those macros that are stored in templates; see the previous section for more information), you must follow standard DOS file-naming practices and give your macros names that DOS can accept. Keep in mind the following as you name your macros:

- The macro name can contain from one to eight characters.
- The macro name can contain any printable character except the following:

  A space

  A period (WordPerfect for Windows uses the period between the file name and extension)

  The characters **^ + = \ / [ ] " ; : ? * < > |**, which are either used in DOS or reserved for future use and, therefore, cannot be used in names of files

Creating Instant Play Macros

If you have a macro that you use fairly often, you may find the routine of playing macros (choosing **T**ools, **M**acro, **P**lay; typing the macro name; and pressing Enter) tedious. WordPerfect 6.1 for Windows provides a shortcut to playing commonly used macros—the Ctrl+key method.

Recording a Ctrl Macro

If you are recording a macro you know you will use often, you can give the macro a special name so that WordPerfect plays it back when you use the Ctrl+key method. At the Record Macro dialog box, press and hold the Ctrl key, press a letter key (A to Z), and then release the Ctrl key. WordPerfect automatically inserts the name Ctrl*X*, where *X* is a letter from A to Z. Press Ctrl+Y for instance, and WordPerfect inserts *ctrlywcm* in the Record Macro dialog box. You can also type the text **ctrly.wcm** in the Record Macro dialog box.

Note

The Ctrl+key method also works with number keys, giving you up to 36 possible macros you can store and access. For an additional 36 quick-access macros, you can press the Ctrl and Shift keys at the same time; this creates macros named ctrlsft*x*.wcm, where *x* is a letter from A to Z or a number from 0 to 9. Remember that WPWin already uses many Ctrl+key combinations for its menu commands, so you must exercise care in picking a combination that is not already used.

To play a Ctrl+key macro, just press Ctrl+the appropriate letter. To play the macro CtrlY, for example, just press Ctrl+Y. The Play Macro dialog box does not appear.

Renaming a Previously Recorded Macro for Ctrl+Key Playback

You might not discover how often you'll use a certain macro until you have used it for a while. Although you gave the macro a regular name when you first recorded it, you can still play the macro by using the Ctrl+key method. All you need to do is rename the macro file.

To rename a previously recorded macro so that you can play it using the Ctrl key, follow these steps:

1. Choose **F**ile, **O**pen; or press Ctrl+O. The Open File dialog box appears.

2. Find and select the macro you want to rename. If the file is not listed, change directories and disk, as needed.

3. Choose File **O**ptions. A pop-up menu appears.

4. Choose **R**ename. The Rename File dialog box appears, showing the current name for the file.

5. In the **T**o text box, type **ctrl*x*.wcm**. For the *x*, substitute the letter you want to use with the Ctrl key to play that macro (see fig. 12.4). If you want to play the macro by pressing Ctrl+Y, for example, rename the file **CTRLY.WCM**. *Be sure to include the WCM file extension!*

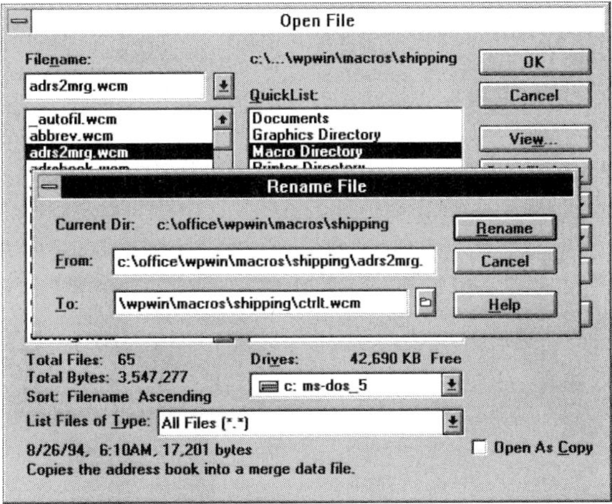

Fig. 12.4
Use the Rename File dialog box to rename macro files. Be sure to include the WCM file extension when using Ctrl and CtrlSft macros.

6. Choose **R**ename or press Enter.

Note

Be careful not to use a Ctrl+letter combination already in use by WordPerfect 6.1 for Windows for accessing a feature. Ctrl+key macros are ignored if WordPerfect already has a shortcut feature assigned to the same keys. For example, if you name a macro *ctrlo.wcm*, pressing Ctrl+O displays the Open File dialog box, rather than runs the **ctrlo.wcm** macro.

Ctrl+Key and Shift+Ctrl+Key Combinations Already in Use

Table 12.1 lists the Ctrl+key and Shift+Ctrl+key combinations that WordPerfect already uses for shortcuts to features (when using the standard WordPerfect 6.1 keyboard layout, as defined in **E**dit, Pr**e**ferences, **K**eyboard).

Do not use these combinations for Ctrl+key and Shift+Ctrl+key macros; otherwise WordPerfect will ignore the macro and execute the shortcut instead, as described in the preceding note.

Table 12.1 Ctrl+key and Shift+Ctrl+key Combinations Already in Use

Key	Pressing Ctrl+Key	Pressing Ctrl+Shift+Key
A	Expand abbreviation	*<None>*
B	Bold	Insert bullet
C	Copy text	*<None>*
D	Date text	Date code
E	Center justification	*<None>*
F	Font	*<None>*
G	Go to	*<None>*
H	Outline body text	*<None>*
I	Italic	*<None>*
J	Full justification	*<None>*
K	Case toggle	*<None>*
L	Left justification	*<None>*
M	*<None>*	*<None>*
N	New document	*<None>*
O	Open document	Outline define
P	Print	Page number
Q	Find QuickMark	Set QuickMark
R	Right justification	*<None>*
S	Save document	Save all
T	Template	*<None>*
U	Underline	*<None>*
V	Paste	Paste simple

Key	Pressing Ctrl+Key	Pressing Ctrl+Shift+Key
W	WP Characters	*<None>*
X	Cut	*<None>*
Y	*<None>*	*<None>*
Z	Undo	Undelete

Playing Macros in Other Ways

WordPerfect for Windows provides four other methods with which you can play macros without using the Play Macro dialog box. They are as follows:

- *Assign a macro to a keyboard layout. Keyboard layouts* are special WordPerfect 6.1 for Windows files that enable you to change the meaning of the keys on your keyboard. You can assign a macro—that is tell WordPerfect to play a macro whenever you press a certain key or key combination—to any of several hundred key combinations.

- *Add a macro button to a Toolbar.* When you click on the button for the macro, the macro plays. The Toolbar, however, can only be used with the mouse. If you don't have or use a mouse, you cannot take advantage of this option.

- *Choose any of up to the last four recently played macros by picking it from the Macro submenu.* Choose **T**ools, **M**acro. The menu that appears is the Macro submenu. At the bottom of this submenu WordPerfect automatically places up to the last four macros you replayed, with the most recently played macro shown first.

For more information on the first two methods, see the section "Playing Macros Using Other Methods," later in this chapter.

Stopping a Macro

Stopping a macro is sometimes necessary if something goes wrong during recording or playback. You may discover, for example, that the macro is adding text to the wrong part of your document, so you want to stop it from doing any more damage. You may just need to pause the macro if, for instance, you need to leave your desk or perform some other task while recording your macro.

Stopping a Macro During Recording

If you need to stop recording, choose **T**ools, **M**acro, **R**ecord; or press Ctrl+F10. (If you are in a dialog box, you must exit the dialog box before you can stop macro recording.)

Tip
If pressing Esc has no effect, press Ctrl+Break. Not all keyboards have a Break key. If yours does, it may be labeled Pause on the top and Break on the side.

You can stop a macro at any time, even before WordPerfect 6.1 for Windows has a chance to record any of your actions. Although the macro may be *empty* (it has no commands to tell WordPerfect what to do), the macro file is created anyway. You may delete this file or record over it.

Stopping a Macro During Playback

To stop a macro during playback, press the Esc (Cancel) key. If you press the Esc key soon enough, you may be able to limit the damage. Keep in mind, however, that most macros play very quickly, and you probably will not have time to press the Esc key before the macro ends.

Using the Macros that Come with WordPerfect

Tip
For details on how to use the macros that come with WordPerfect for Windows, choose **H**elp, **M**acros, and then select List of Shipping Macros.

WordPerfect for Windows comes with a small selection of macros. Many of these macros are handy additions to what WordPerfect can already do for you. Included, for example, are macros that help you prepare a memo or convert spaces to tabs. The macros that come with WordPerfect also include more complex macros that you can use as examples of how to write more sophisticated macros. (If you are interested in learning more about sophisticated macros, see Chapter 29, "Advanced Macro Techniques.") Table 12.2 lists some of the more useful macros that come with WordPerfect 6.1 for Windows and their functions.

Table 12.2 Selected List of Macros Included with WordPerfect

Macro	Function
ALLFONTS.WCM	Creates a document listing the name and some sample text from every font available to the current printer.
CAPITAL.WCM	Capitalizes the first letter of the current word.
CLOSEALL.WCM	Closes all documents currently open and prompts to save any that have been modified.
CLOSING.WCM	Closes a letter.

Macro	Function
ENDFOOT.WCM	Converts endnotes to footnotes in a document or Macro Function.
FILESTMP.WCM	Places the file name and path of the current document in a header or footer.
FONTDN.WCM	Decreases the font size of the selected text by two points.
FONTUP.WCM	Increases the font size of the selected text by two points.
INSERT.WCM	Inserts a letter (or other document) in the current document.
LETTER.WCM	Addresses and formats a standard business letter.
PAGEXOFY.WCM	Places "Page x of y pages" (or other formats) in specified position on paper.
PARABRK.WCM	Inserts graphical paragraph breaks between paragraphs.
PGBORDER.WCM	Creates decorative page borders with WordPerfect graphics.
PLEADING.WCM	Formats a standard legal "pleading paper."
REVERSE.WCM	Creates white text on black background (or other color options as set by the user) in document text or tables.
SAVEALL.WCM	Saves all documents currently open and prompts to save any that have been modified.
TRANSPOS.WCM	Transposes two visible characters. (This macro is much more elaborate than the TRANSP.WCM macro described in this chapter.)
WATERMRK.WCM	Aids in creating a watermark using a WordPerfect .WPG file.

Troubleshooting

I can't find a macro that I just recorded.

WordPerfect stores macros either on the computer's hard disk drive, or in the current template. If you record a macro in a template, you will not be able to find it if you later try to play a macro on disk, and vice versa. Be mindful where you are recording

(continues)

(continued)

the macro, either on disk or in a template. Be sure to choose the appropriate macro play command, in the Tools menu, to play back your macro. For example, to play a disk file macro, choose **T**ools, **M**acro, **P**lay. To play a template macro, choose **T**ools, Tem**p**late Macro, **P**lay.

I can't find the macros that come with WordPerfect.

When WordPerfect is installed, the macro files are placed in a directory of their own, usually called MACROS. If you selected the Standard install option, this directory is located in the OFFICE\WPWIN subdirectory. The files may be missing if they were not installed in the first place (meaning that the person who installed WordPerfect elected not to include them). You will need to install the macros from the original WordPerfect disks if you want to use them. Or, the files may not be found if WordPerfect is looking in the wrong place for the macro files. Check the directory specified for macros in the Files Preferences dialog box (**E**dit, Pr**e**ferences, **F**iles).

Using Macros for Writing and Editing Tasks

The most common macros are those that help you write and edit your documents. If you find yourself performing the same task repeatedly—you type the same list of names, or addresses, or other information one or more times a day, for example—consider the job a good candidate for a macro. You can play the macro rather than retype the same information.

Listed in this section are several macros you can use to start your writing and editing macro collection. These macros perform common tasks, and you will probably use them quite often. For this reason, consider giving them Ctrl*X* names, as described in "Creating Instant Play Macros" earlier in this chapter.

Caution

The macro examples detailed in this chapter are given full names rather than Ctrl*X* names in the event that you already have a Ctrl*X* macro of the same name. If you do use Ctrl*X* names, be sure to use a name that's not currently in use; otherwise, you may accidentally erase a macro you want to keep.

A Macro To Transpose Two Characters

The fingers of even the world's best touch typists sometimes get ahead of one another, and the result is tranpsosed—oops, transposed—characters. Perhaps the most commonly transposed word is *the* (as *teh*).

For all its other features, WordPerfect 6.1 for Windows lacks a built-in system to switch transposed characters. Most typists make the extra effort to delete and then type over the transposed characters. But you can record a simple macro that switches the positions of the characters and saves several keystrokes.

To record the transpose macro, first type two characters, such as *ab*. Make sure the cursor is to the immediate right of the *b*. After you record the macro, the characters will be reversed to *ba*. To create the transpose macro, follow these steps:

1. Choose **T**ools, **M**acro, **R**ecord; or press Ctrl+F10. The Record Macro dialog box appears.
2. In the File**n**ame text box, type **transp**, and choose OK or press Enter to start recording.
3. Press Backspace + ←.
4. Press the left-arrow key (←).
5. Choose **E**dit, U**n**delete. The Undelete dialog box appears.
6. Choose **R**estore to undelete the previously deleted character.
7. Press the right-arrow key (→).
8. Choose **T**ools, **M**acro, **R**ecord; or press Ctrl+F10.

The letter transpose macro is complete.

To use the transpose macro, position the insertion point after the transposed characters. Then play the macro.

Note

Rename the transpose macro so that you can run it by using the Ctrl+key shortcut, as explained in the earlier section "Creating Instant Play Macros." One possible name is CtrlSftT.WPM; you play the transpose macro by pressing Ctrl+Shift+T.

A Macro To Write a Memo

Writing memos is such a common job that most people don't think twice about the mechanics involved in preparing a memo. But each memo you write contains a great deal of the same *boilerplate* text, or text that doesn't change, from memo to memo. A macro makes the perfect memo-writing assistant, typing the boilerplate text for you. All you have to do is fill in the blanks.

In addition to the message, most memos contain four fields of information that you fill in:

- The date of the memo (Date:)
- Who the memo is from (From:)
- Who the memo is to (To:)
- The subject of the memo (Subject: or Re:)

To be most useful, you can make the memo-writing macro stop so that you can fill in each of the four fields of information. After you fill in the blanks, you can press the Enter key, and the macro continues.

You can tell WordPerfect for Windows to pause a macro during playback so that you can type the needed text. Whenever WordPerfect encounters a pause instruction, the macro stops temporarily and lets you type. When you press Enter, the macro starts again. For the memo-writing macro, you tell WordPerfect to pause two times so that you can enter the memo information. You will make the macro enter the fourth field of information—the date—by itself.

To record the memo macro, follow these steps:

1. Choose **T**ools, **M**acro, **R**ecord; or press Ctrl+F10. The Record Macro dialog box appears.
2. In the File**n**ame text box, type **mymemo**, and choose **R**ecord or press Enter to start recording.
3. Type **Date:** and a space.
4. Choose **I**nsert, **D**ate, Date **T**ext; or press Ctrl+D. This inserts the current date.
5. Press Enter twice to add a blank line between the Date field and the field that follows.

6. Type **From:** and your name. Press the Enter key twice.
7. Type **To:** and a space.
8. Choose **T**ools, **M**acro, Pa**u**se. Choose **T**ools, **M**acro, Pa**u**se again. This inserts a pausing command.
9. Press the Enter key.
10. Type **Subject:** and a space.
11. Repeat steps 8 and 9 to insert another pause instruction.
12. Choose **T**ools, **M**acro, **R**ecord; or press Ctrl+F10.

The memo macro is finished. Clear the document by choosing **F**ile, **C**lose, **N**o.

To play the memo macro, choose **T**ools, **M**acro, **P**lay; or press Alt+F10. Type **mymemo**, and press Enter. The macro inserts the date and the `From:` line (with your name). It then inserts the `To:` line, and pauses and waits for you to enter text.

Type the text, and press Enter. The Enter key unpauses the macro, which continues to the next memo field, where you type the name of the memo's recipient.

Repeat this process until you have filled in all the memo fields. When the macro finishes, you can complete the rest of the memo.

Using Macros for Common Formatting Tasks

As with writing and editing, you can simplify common formatting tasks—changing the margins, for example—by recording them as macros. To change the margins of a document from the regular one-inch margins to two-inch margins on all sides, you must perform at least ten steps—more if you use the mouse. If you must change the margins of your documents often, you can save a great deal of work by recording the margin change as a macro and then playing the macro whenever you want the new margins.

◄ See "Understanding Styles," p. 356

◄ See "Creating Styles," p. 362

Note

Another time-saver is the styles feature of WordPerfect 6.1 for Windows, discussed in detail in Chapter 10, "Using Styles." You can use styles to change the formatting of your documents. A style can contain one or many formatting changes. In fact, if you need to make many formatting changes (set new margins, new tab stops, set a header and footer, and so on), use styles instead of macros.

Follow these steps to record a macro that changes the left and right margins to 1 1/2 inches.

1. Choose **T**ools, **M**acro, **R**ecord; or press Ctrl+F10. The Record Macro dialog box appears.
2. In the File**n**ame text box, type **marg15**, and choose **P**lay or press Enter to start recording.

3. Choose Fo**r**mat, **M**argins; or press Ctrl+F8. The Margin Format dialog box appears.
4. Change the **L**eft margin to 1.50".
5. Change the **R**ight margin to 1.50".
6. Press Enter until the program returns to the main WordPerfect for Windows editing screen.
7. Choose **T**ools, **M**acro, **R**ecord; or press Ctrl+F10 to complete the recording of the margin setting macro.

To use the macro, place the insertion point where you want to change margins, and play the macro.

Playing Macros Using Other Methods

In this chapter, you have learned how to play macros by using the Play Macro dialog box, and by pressing the Ctrl key and a letter key. Two more ways exist to play macros: using a keyboard layout and using the Toolbar. Both methods enable you to play your favorite macros without using the Play Macro dialog box.

Assigning a Macro to a Keyboard Layout

WordPerfect for Windows is a "do it your way" kind of program; you can personalize it so that it behaves in the way *you* want, not the way some programmer thought it ought to be. One of the ways to personalize WordPerfect for Windows is to create a *keyboard layout.* With a keyboard layout you can change the meaning of almost any key on the keyboard. You can assign unused key combinations to favorite macros. Your keyboard layout is saved in a special file, to which WordPerfect refers each time it starts. You can change keyboard layouts whenever you want and turn this feature off when you no longer want to use it.

Chapter 9, "Customizing WordPerfect," details keyboard layouts—how they work and how to create them. In this chapter, you concentrate on creating a new keyboard layout and assigning a macro to a normally unused key combination. You use the TRANSP character-transposing macro detailed earlier in this chapter as the macro to assign to the keyboard layout; however, you can substitute any other macro.

Note

Only the keys that you specifically change in a keyboard layout differ from the original layout that WordPerfect for Windows uses. The functions of all the other keys remain the same.

(***Note:*** The following instructions assume that you are assigning a macro on disk, rather than a template macro, to a keyboard layout.)

To create a keyboard layout and assign a macro to it, follow these steps:

1. Choose **E**dit, Pr**e**ferences. The Preferences dialog box appears.
2. Choose the **K**eyboard icon. The Keyboard Preferences dialog box appears (see fig. 12.5). At least one keyboard layout is listed: <WPWin 6.1 Keyboard>. This keyboard layout is the one built into WordPerfect 6.1 for Windows and cannot be deleted or edited.
3. Choose C**r**eate. The Create Keyboard dialog box appears.
4. Provide a name for your new keyboard layout. The name can be up to 32 characters, and can contain spaces.
5. Choose OK or press Enter. The Keyboard Editor appears (see fig. 12.6).

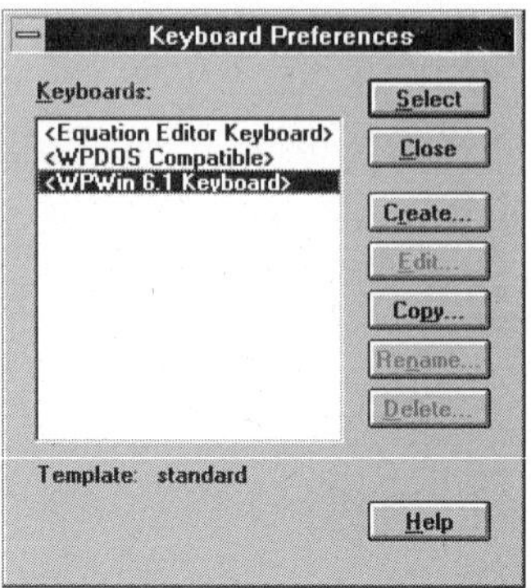

Fig. 12.5
The Keyboard Preferences dialog box lets you select and create new keyboard layouts.

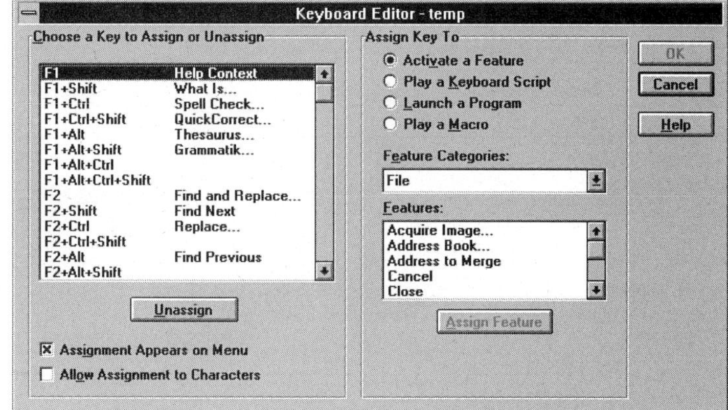

Fig. 12.6
The Keyboard Editor allows you to change the functions of just about any key and key combination on the keyboard.

6. In the **C**hoose a Key to Assign or Unassign list (on the left side of the Keyboard Editor), find and select the key or key combination you want to use.

7. In the Apply Key To group, choose Play a **M**acro. The Assign Macro button appears.

8. Choose **A**ssign Macro. The Select Macro dialog box appears.

9. Type the name of the macro you want to play (in this case **TRANSP.WCM**), and choose Select.

10. When WordPerfect asks if you want to save the macro name with the full path, answer **Y**es or **N**o. Answering **Y**es records the macro with its path; answering **N**o records just the name of the macro. As a general rule of thumb, choose **Y**es unless you are going to share your keyboard layouts and macros with other people.

11. Choose OK to close the Keyboard Editor.

12. Highlight the new keyboard, and choose Select.

The selected macro is now accessible by pressing the key or key combination you chose.

To play the TRANSP macro, type some text (so that you have something to transpose), and press the keys you assigned in step 6. If you used Ctrl+F12, for example, press these keys to transpose two characters.

You can assign additional macros to your custom keyboard layout by repeating steps 6 through 10.

Tip
To turn off your custom keyboard layout, choose **E**dit, Pr**e**ferences; then choose Keyboard. Highlight <WPWin 6.1 Keyboard>, and choose **S**elect.

Troubleshooting

I want to record a macro that exits WordPerfect, but when I try, the Exit command in the File menu is dimmed out (unavailable).

WordPerfect will not allow you to leave the program while a macro is recording. A macro that exits WordPerfect is not possible.

I tried recording a macro where I switch to another Windows program. When the macro is played back nothing happens.

WordPerfect only records actions inside the WordPerfect program, and other selected Novell applications (such as Quattro Pro and Presentations). As long as you stay within WordPerfect or one of these other applications, your actions are recorded in the macro. Once you leave these programs, macro recording is suspended until you come back. If you need a macro that controls other Windows programs, use the Macro Recorder facility that comes with Windows.

A macro that has worked before is now ending in an error message.

Macros must be played back under the same circumstances they were recorded under. The most common reason for a macro ending in an error message is that the macro searches for text that it can't find in the current document. Other reasons a macro can end in an error message include:

- A macro that opens a document when nine documents are already open
- A macro that creates a header when played in the Header window
- A macro that selects a font that is not supported by your printer
- A macro that opens a document that no longer exists on your computer's hard disk drive

Adding a Macro to a Toolbar

◀ See "Customizing Keyboards," p.342

▶ See "Customizing a Toolbar," p. 455

If you use a mouse with WordPerfect 6.1 for Windows, you have another option to playing macros: you can click a button on a Toolbar. Unlike the keyboard, which requires that you remember the key combinations you used, the Toolbar has the advantage of showing you the available macros. The disadvantage to the Toolbar is that you are limited to the number of buttons you can display at one time. Although you can scroll the Toolbar to see more buttons, it's better to use the Toolbar when all your regular buttons are always in view.

Associating a macro with a Toolbar is a little easier than assigning a macro to a keyboard layout. Chapter 13, "Working with Toolbars," discusses Toolbars in depth, but a few basic steps exist. The following exercise adds a button to the current default Toolbar. Unless you have switched to a different Toolbar, the default is WordPerfect, which comes with WordPerfect 6.1 for Windows. You can use a different Toolbar, however, or create a Toolbar of your own. Chapter 13 provides more details on how to do this.

(***Note:*** The following instructions assume you are assigning a macro on disk, rather than a template macro, to the Toolbar.)

To add a macro button to the current Toolbar, follow these steps:

1. Choose **E**dit, Pr**e**ferences; then choose **T**oolbar. The Toolbar Preferences dialog box appears (see fig. 12.7).

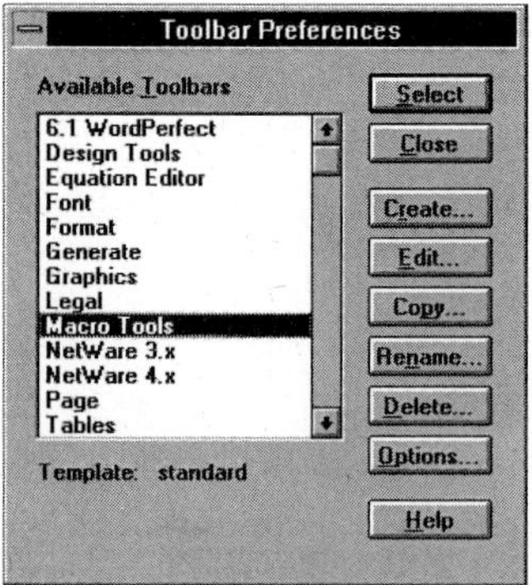

Fig. 12.7
Use the Toolbar Preferences dialog box to create and edit Toolbars.

2. Choose **E**dit. The Toolbar Editor appears.

3. Choose Play a **M**acro. The Add Macro button appears.

4. Choose **A**dd Macro. Type the name of the macro you want to play (such as TRANSP.WCM), and choose Select.

5. When WordPerfect asks if you want to save the macro name with the full path, answer **Y**es or **N**o. Answering **Y**es records the macro with its path; answering **N**o records just the name of the macro. As a general rule of thumb, choose **Y**es unless you are going to share your Toolbars and macros with other people.

6. Choose OK to close the Toolbar Editor.

7. Choose Close until you are back at the document window.

To use the new button on the Toolbar, display the Toolbar if necessary by choosing **V**iew, **T**oolbar. Locate and then click on the new button on the Toolbar. Your macro plays.

Tip

To select the macro you want from the Macro menu, choose **T**ools, **M**acro, and the name of the macro; or press Alt+T, M, and the number of the macro.

Note

WordPerfect for Windows also includes a handy Feature Bar you can use when writing and editing macros. When you edit a macro file (choose **T**ools, **M**acro, **E**dit), the Macro Feature Bar automatically appears. Or you can manually display the Feature Bar by choosing **T**ools, **M**acro, **M**acro Bar. For information about the Macro Feature Bar, see Chapter 29, "Advanced Macro Techniques."

Managing Macro Files

After you begin to use the macros feature of WordPerfect 6.1 for Windows, you will want to give some thought to how you can best manage your macro files; otherwise, you may forget what macros you have and lose track of where they are on your computer's hard disk drive.

When you record a macro, WordPerfect places it in one of two places:

- *The main WordPerfect for Windows directory.* This directory contains the bulk of WordPerfect's files, including WPWIN.EXE (the WordPerfect program itself).

- *A special directory just for macros.* This directory is specified in the Location of Files dialog box. To see this dialog box, choose **E**dit, Pr**e**ferences; then choose **F**ile. The File Preferences dialog box appears. Choose **M**acros to see the directory (or directories) used for macros.

The more macros you record, the more reason you have to create a directory just for them. A good place for your macro directory is under the \OFFICE\WPWIN directory (this directory contains the main WordPerfect for Windows files; the exact name of the directory may be different on your computer, depending on how WordPerfect 6.1 for Windows was installed). A MACROS directory under \OFFICE\WPWIN directory is automatically created for you if you use the "Standard" option when installing WordPerfect.

Creating a Directory for Macros

You can use the Windows File Manager to create a new directory for your macros. Follow the instructions provided in the Windows User Guide. Alternatively, you can use WordPerfect's Open File dialog box to create new directories by choosing **F**ile, **O**pen, File **O**ptions, then Crea**t**e Directory. See Chapter 28, "Advanced File Management," for more information.

Check to see whether a directory for macros already exists. The directories are always listed first in the File Manager list of files. A likely name for the macros directory is MACROS, and is probably located under the WPWIN61 directory.

Moving Files into the MACROS Directory

A MACROS directory is useless unless macro files are placed there. You must scan through the list of files using the Windows File Manager (or WPWin's Open File dialog box) to pick out the macro files.

Note

WordPerfect also places files for the coach feature in the MACROS directory. These files—which are really macros—have a .WCH extension. Be sure to move these files to the new macro directory so that you can access the coaches.

Specifying the Macros Directory in Location of Files

You need to tell WordPerfect where to find the macro files by following these steps:

1. Choose **E**dit, Pr**e**ferences; then choose **F**ile. The File Preferences dialog box appears.

2. Choose **M**acros (see fig. 12.8).

3. Choose D**e**fault Directory.

4. Type the full path of the directory that contains the macro files, such as C:\OFFICE\WPWIN\MACROS.

5. Press Enter or choose OK.

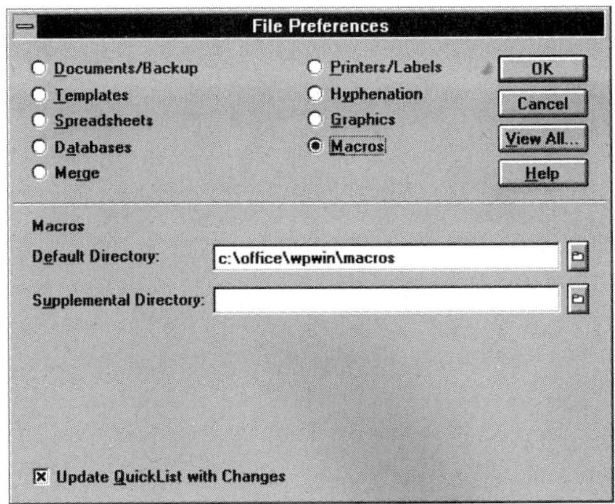

Fig. 12.8
Use the File Preferences dialog box to tell WordPerfect for Windows where to look for macro files.

> **Note**
>
> If you are on a network, you can also specify an alternate directory for *shared* macros, which are macros stored on a network server that your entire office might use. To specify a path for shared macros, choose S**u**pplemental Directory. Type the full path of the directory that contains the shared macros, and press Enter.

6. Choose OK or Close until you return to the main WordPerfect for Windows editing screen.

Giving Macros Descriptive File Names

Placing your macros in a central repository directory is the first step in managing your growing macro library. If you create many macros, however, after a period of time, you may forget what certain macros do, and you may even forget that you recorded a macro to handle a particular task.

You can guard against macros falling into obscurity by always giving your macros descriptive file names, which is not quite as easy as it sounds because you are limited to a maximum of eight characters for each name. Whenever possible, give your macros abbreviated names that reflect the tasks they perform, such as DBLSPACE for a macro that sets line spacing to two, or SPELLWRD for a macro that performs a spell check on the current word.

Avoid generic terms like MYMACRO or TEST, and be specific in describing the macros function. A macro named FONTCHNG probably changes fonts, but to what font?

Deleting Macros You No Longer Need

Recording a macro doesn't mean that you have to keep the macro around forever. Unnecessary macro files clutter up your computer's hard disk drive, and they take up valuable space that can be better used by the files you do want to keep. Delete macro files you no longer use.

To delete a macro you no longer want to keep, follow these steps:

1. Choose **F**ile, **O**pen, or press Ctrl+O. The Open File dialog box appears.
2. Find and highlight the file you want to delete (change the directory and drive, if necessary).
3. Choose File **O**ptions, **D**elete.
4. WordPerfect for Windows asks whether you want to delete the file; answer **Y**es.
5. Repeat steps 2 through 4 for each additional macro file you want to delete.
6. Choose Cancel.

Tip
You may select multiple files to delete at the same time by pressing the Ctrl key while you select the files.

Note

Macros that were recorded into either the default or current template are not deleted by removing a file on your computer's hard disk drive.

Rather, to delete a macro in a template, choose **T**ools, Tem**p**late Macro, **P**lay. A list of the macros contained in that template is displayed. Choose the macro you want to delete; then choose **D**elete.

From Here...

You have learned that WordPerfect for Windows macros can be used to save a great deal of time and extra keystrokes. In this chapter, you learned how to record and play macros, how to manage macro files, and how to create and use "instant play" macros.

For additional information on macros and other automation features of WordPerfect, refer to the following chapters in this book:

- Chapter 9, "Customizing WordPerfect." In this chapter you learn how to assign macros and "key scripts" to menus, Toolbars, and keyboards.

- Chapter 10, "Using Styles." Refer to this chapter for information on using WordPerfect's style feature, which allows you to provide consistent formatting to text.
- Chapter 11, "Using Templates." This chapter shows you how to use templates to quickly create documents, including fax cover sheets, memos, and letters. It also discusses WordPerfect's Letter Expert feature, which enables you to write complete business letters in a matter of minutes.
- Chapter 13, "Working with Toolbars." Refer to this chapter for specifics on using WordPerfect Toolbars to speed up your work, including attaching macros to Toolbar buttons.
- Chapter 19, "Assembling Documents with Merge and Sort." In this chapter, you learn how to use the merge feature to create personalized form letters.
- Chapter 29, "Advanced Macro Techniques." In this chapter you learn more about macros, including the vast WordPerfect for Windows macro language. A sample macro, using the macro language, is provided.

Chapter 13

Working with Toolbars

by George Beinhorn and Judy Petersen

Toolbars are an innovative way to carry out commands. Instead of searching through menus or issuing multiple keyboard commands, you simply click a button with the mouse to carry out the desired function. WordPerfect comes with 18 preconfigured Toolbars for specialized tasks, such as editing equations, working with fonts, or using outlines. You can configure your own customized Toolbars, and you can place any WordPerfect feature on the Toolbar. You can even assign macros to a button, and you can quickly switch between Toolbars.

In this chapter, you learn how to:

- Use Toolbar and Power Bar buttons
- Switch between Toolbars
- Add, delete, and move Toolbar and Power Bar buttons
- Move the position of the Toolbar on-screen
- Create new, specialized Toolbars
- Assign macros to Toolbars

Why Use the Toolbar and Power Bar?

WordPerfect 6.1 for Windows makes locating program commands easy. Using the mouse with pull-down menus soon becomes natural, and after you become familiar with the menu structure, you can quickly access commands with keystrokes.

Tip
To display other supplied Toolbars, right-click the Toolbar and choose a Toolbar from the pop-up QuickMenu.

So why use buttons? Toolbars are unique in that you can make them perform multiple commands, and you can customize them with your own most-used program functions and macros. You can create several Toolbars for specific tasks, and you can toggle the Toolbar display on and off with a single mouse click on the Power Bar. Figure 13.1 shows the default WordPerfect 6.1 for Windows Toolbar.

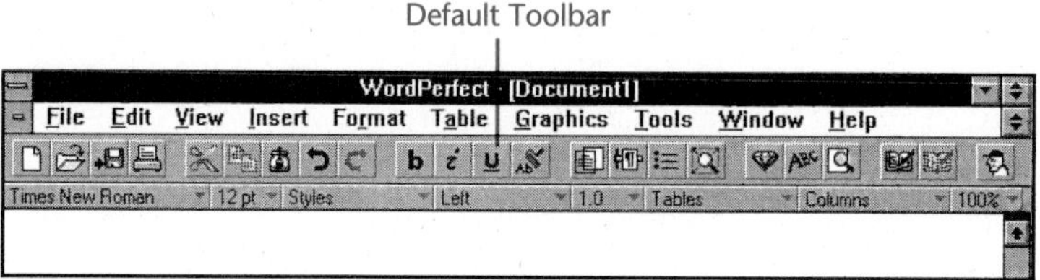

Fig. 13.1
The default Toolbar includes buttons for common WordPerfect commands.

The Power Bar is equally convenient but serves the slightly different purpose of performing common, everyday chores that mostly have to do with creating and formatting text and turning on special features such as tables and columns.

In practice, you will probably find that you prefer to perform some tasks with the keyboard and others with the Toolbars and the Power Bar. A unique advantage of the Toolbars and Power Bar is that you never forget a program command. In fact, moving the mouse cursor onto a button displays a description of its function in the title bar.

Above and beyond the Toolbars' everyday utility, clicking buttons to execute complicated program commands and macros is fun!

Hiding and Viewing the Toolbar

You can turn the Toolbar on and off in four ways:

- Choose **V**iew, **T**oolbar.
- Click the right mouse button anywhere on the Toolbar to display the QuickMenu, and choose **H**ide Toolbar.
- Add the Toolbar button to the default Toolbar, then click the Toolbar button.
- Choose **V**iew, **H**ide Bars; or press Alt+Shift+F5.

Tip
To quickly toggle the Toolbar on and off, add a Toolbar button to the Toolbar.

When you choose **V**iew, **H**ide Bars or press Alt+Shift+F5, WordPerfect displays the Hide Bars Information dialog box. If you choose OK on this dialog box, the following items are removed from the screen: menu bar, Power Bar, Scroll Bars, Toolbar, Ruler Bar, and status bar. To restore the bars to the screen, press Esc; or press Alt+V and choose **H**ide Bars.

Hiding all bars is useful when you need to view a larger area of a document.

Tip

To temporarily turn off all bars for a "clean screen," choose **V**iew, **H**ide Bars; or press Alt+Shift+F5. Choose OK. To turn bars on again, press Alt+Shift+F5; you don't have to choose OK.

Switching between Toolbars

WordPerfect provides 15 predefined Toolbars. You can use two ways to switch to a different Toolbar:

- You can choose **E**dit, Pr**e**ferences, **T**oolbar; then highlight a Toolbar in the list and choose **S**elect.
- You can click the right mouse button on the Toolbar to display the QuickMenu and switch to another Toolbar by clicking its name. Figure 13.2 shows the Toolbar QuickMenu.

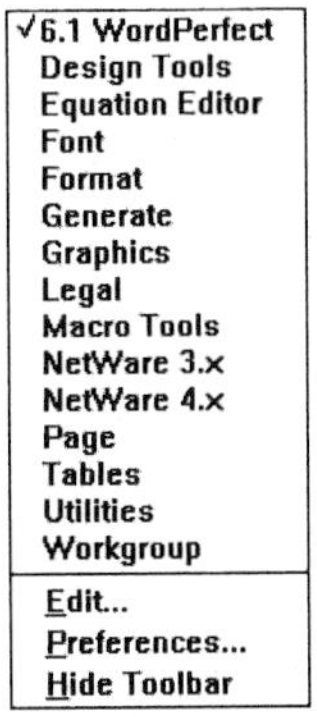

Fig. 13.2
To quickly switch to another Toolbar, click the Toolbar with the right mouse button to access the Toolbar QuickMenu. The default is the WordPerfect 6.1 Toolbar.

You can customize the Power Bar, but you cannot switch to another Power Bar, and you can display only one row of Power Bar buttons. To access a greater number of program operations with the mouse, customize the Toolbar.

Examining the Toolbar and Power Bar Icons

If you look closely at Toolbar icons, you notice that their design identifies the type of task they perform. For example, the first two buttons on the Toolbar are New Document and Open. Both have to do with files; therefore, their icons contain file folders, as does the icon for Save. Similarly, the Print button contains a printer.

Just as WordPerfect grays out unavailable menu options, Toolbar buttons currently unavailable are grayed.

Some buttons serve as visual indicators, for example the font attribute buttons, such as Bold, Italic, and Underline. Whenever your insertion point is between a pair of attribute codes, the button for that attribute appears pressed in.

The default appearance for the buttons on the Power Bar is text only. The text describes the current status of each button, such as the name of the font face in use, the font size, the number of columns, if any, and the zoom percent.

Working with the Toolbar

Tip
You can select common formatting functions by clicking the Ruler Bar, Power Bar, or Toolbar, or by using a QuickMenu.

You may want to customize one of WordPerfect's supplied Toolbars, removing buttons that you seldom use and installing buttons that perform frequently used tasks. You can also rearrange the buttons to suit your personal preference.

Positioning the Toolbar On-Screen

By default, the Toolbar is displayed horizontally at the top of the screen, under the main menu. You can move the Toolbar to the bottom edge of the screen, under the horizontal scroll bar, or vertically at the left or right edge of the document window. Additionally, you can display the Toolbar in a rectangular "palette" anywhere on-screen.

You can also reposition the Toolbar with the mouse. Move the mouse pointer to a space between buttons on the Toolbar until it becomes a hand, and drag the Toolbar to a new location. You can position the Toolbar at the top, left, bottom, or right edge of the screen.

If you drag the Toolbar into the document window, the bar outline becomes a rectangle. When you release the mouse button, the Toolbar becomes a palette. To move the palette, point to its title bar and drag it to a new location. To resize the palette, move the mouse pointer onto an edge until it becomes a double-headed arrow, and drag the edge of the palette to the desired size. Figure 13.3 shows the Toolbar displayed in a palette.

Tip
If the palette obscures options on the dialog box, use its title bar to drag it to a new location.

Fig. 13.3
Whether the Toolbar is displayed as a bar or a palette, you can drag it to a new location. As you drag, the Toolbar's shape is indicated by a gray-lined box.

To move the Toolbar using the keyboard, complete these steps:

1. Choose **E**dit, Pr**e**ferences to display the Preferences dialog box.
2. Choose **T**oolbar, then choose **O**ptions.
3. In the Options dialog box (shown in fig. 13.4), choose **L**eft, T**o**p, **R**ight, **B**ottom, or P**a**lette; then choose OK.
4. Choose **C**lose; then choose **C**lose again to return to the editing screen.

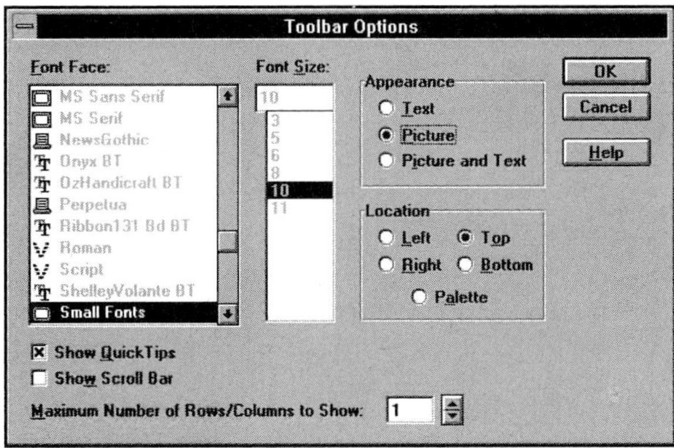

Fig. 13.4
You can place the Toolbar at the top, left, right, or bottom edge of the screen. Placing the Toolbar in a palette enables you to drag it out of the way of on-screen text.

To restore the palette to a horizontal or vertical Toolbar, drag it to an edge of the screen until the outline becomes an elongated horizontal or vertical bar, and release the mouse button.

Working with Large Toolbars

Half the Toolbars supplied with WordPerfect, including the default Toolbar, contain more buttons than can fit in a single row or column on-screen. If a Toolbar extends off the edge of the screen, WordPerfect displays scroll arrows at the right end of the Toolbar (for a horizontal Toolbar) or at the bottom of the Toolbar (for a vertical Toolbar). To scroll the Toolbar, you click the arrows.

If you prefer to avoid scrolling the Toolbar, you can display up to three rows of buttons on-screen by following these steps:

1. Choose **E**dit, Pr**e**ferences, **T**oolbar, **O**ptions.

   Or click the right mouse button on the Toolbar to display the QuickMenu, and choose **P**references, **O**ptions.

2. Choose **M**aximum Number of Rows/Columns to Show, and enter **1**, **2**, or **3**.

3. Choose OK, **C**lose, **C**lose.

WordPerfect reformats the Toolbar with the indicated number of rows.

Toolbars with more than one row displayed take up much room on-screen. To conserve editing space, you can change the style of Toolbar buttons, as described in the following section.

Note

Try this alternative to coping with rows of Toolbar buttons. Add the Toolbar button on the Power Bar so that you can quickly hide (and later unhide) the Toolbar when you need to see more of your document. You will need to remove a button from the Toolbar to make room for the Toolbar button.

Tip

Buttons formatted with the Picture option take up the least space on horizontal Toolbars; the Text option takes the least space on vertical Toolbars.

Changing the Button Style

WordPerfect can display Toolbar buttons with text and pictures (the default), or with pictures or text only. Switching to text-only or pictures-only saves screen space and displays more buttons on-screen without the need for scrolling.

To change the button style, perform the following steps:

1. Choose **E**dit, Pr**e**ferences, **T**oolbar, **O**ptions.

Or click the right mouse button on the Toolbar to display the QuickMenu, and choose Pr**e**ferences, **O**ptions.

2. In the Toolbar Options dialog box (refer to fig. 13.4), choose **T**ext, **P**icture, or P**i**cture and Text.

   Your changes are reflected on-screen behind the dialog box.

3. Choose OK, **C**lose, **C**lose to return to the editing screen.

Figure 13.5 shows the same Toolbar formatted as pictures only, text only, and pictures and text.

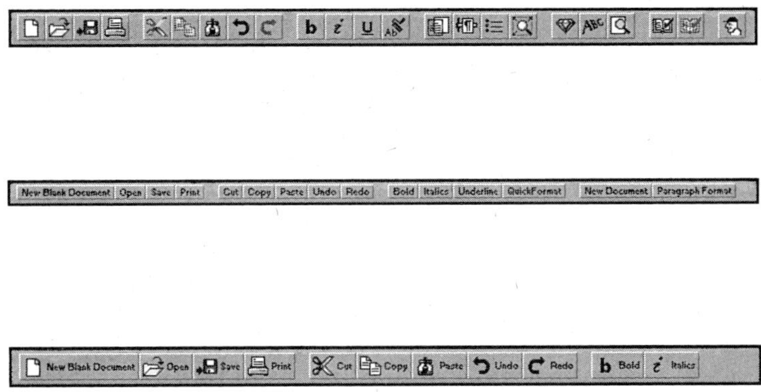

Fig. 13.5
Toolbars formatted with pictures only, text only, and pictures and text. Choose text only and move the Toolbar to the left or right edge of the screen to display the greatest number of buttons. You also can display more than one row of buttons.

Customizing a Toolbar

You can reposition buttons on a Toolbar, and you can assign program functions, keystrokes, or macros to buttons. Before you customize the Toolbar, however, remember that you can perform many common WordPerfect operations with the Power Bar and Ruler Bar.

WordPerfect allows you to restore the default Power Bar, and the WordPerfect Toolbar cannot be edited permanently, but you cannot restore another Toolbar to its default configuration. It's therefore a good idea to make a backup copy of a Toolbar before you edit it by following these steps:

1. Choose **E**dit, Pr**e**ferences, **T**oolbar.

2. In the Toolbar Preferences dialog box, choose Co**p**y.

3. In the Copy Toolbars dialog box, select a Toolbar from the **S**elect Toolbars To Copy text box, and choose **C**opy.

4. In the Overwrite/New Name dialog box, type a new name for the copied Toolbar in the **O**bject text box.

5. Choose OK.

WordPerfect lists the copy of the Toolbar in the Available Toolbars list box, where you can now select it (or the copied Toolbar) and choose **E**dit to customize.

Moving Toolbar Buttons

You can move the buttons on the Toolbar. You might want to place the buttons you use most frequently at the left end of the bar, for example. You can group buttons by adding spacers between the groups.

To reposition buttons on the Toolbar, follow these steps:

1. Choose **E**dit, Pr**e**ferences, **T**oolbar, **E**dit.

   Or click the Toolbar with the right mouse button to display the QuickMenu, and choose **E**dit.

   WordPerfect displays the Toolbar Editor dialog box (see fig. 13.6).

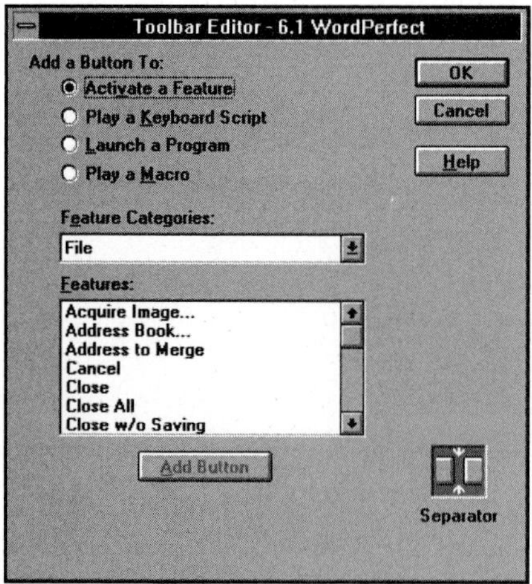

Fig. 13.6
You can use the Toolbar Editor dialog box to move buttons. You can also delete a button by simply dragging it off the Toolbar.

2. With the Toolbar Editor displayed, drag a button to a new location.

3. To insert a spacer between buttons, drag the spacer symbol at the bottom of the dialog box between two buttons on the Toolbar and release the mouse button.

4. To delete a button, drag it off the Toolbar; or click with the right mouse button and choose Delete.

5. Choose OK, **C**lose, **C**lose to return to the editing screen. Or choose Cancel to return the Toolbar to the way it was before editing.

Assigning Program Features to Buttons

You can assign any WordPerfect program feature to a Toolbar button. For example, you might decide to add a Save All button to the Layout Toolbar if you frequently perform page layout operations with several files open at once. To assign a program feature to a Toolbar button, follow these steps:

1. Choose **E**dit, Pr**e**ferences, **T**oolbar, **E**dit.

   Or click a button on the Toolbar with the right mouse button and choose **E**dit.

2. In the Toolbar Editor dialog box (refer to fig. 13.6), choose Acti**v**ate a Feature.

3. Choose F**e**ature Categories and choose a category from the list.

   The categories correspond to the WordPerfect menus. When you choose a category, WordPerfect displays the commands from the corresponding menu in the **F**eatures list.

4. Choose **F**eatures and select a feature from the list.

   WordPerfect highlights the **A**dd Button and displays the button's graphic and title. The title explains the button's function and appears in the document window's title bar when you move the mouse cursor onto the button.

5. Choose **A**dd Button to add the button to the bar.

6. Move the buttons and add optional spacers as described in the preceding section, "Moving Toolbar Buttons."

7. Choose OK, **C**lose, and **C**lose again to return to the document window.

Tip

If you make a mistake while editing a Toolbar, press Esc to remove all newly added buttons from the Toolbar.

You can also add a new button by choosing a feature from a WordPerfect menu while the Toolbar Editor dialog box is displayed. To move the Toolbar Editor out of the way of the program menus, click on the dialog box title bar and drag it. You also can click an empty area or spacer in the Toolbar and drag it to a new location.

Assigning a Text Script to a Button

You can create buttons that play back text by following these steps:

1. Choose **E**dit, Pr**e**ferences, **T**oolbar, **E**dit.

   Or click a button on the Toolbar with the right mouse button and choose **E**dit.

2. Choose Play a **K**eyboard Script.

3. Choose **T**ype the Script this Button Plays, and type the script in the text box.

   WordPerfect word-wraps the text in the box. You cannot apply formatting. Text entered with a Script button takes on the formatting currently in effect at the cursor location in a document.

4. Choose **A**dd Script.

   WordPerfect creates a new button for the script.

5. Choose OK, **C**lose, **C**lose to return to the document window.

Move the mouse pointer to the new script button, and you see a box with the first word of the script. Refer to the later section on customizing the button pictures for instructions on how to edit this button.

Assigning Macros to Buttons

◄ See "Adding a Macro to a Toolbar," p. 442

You can create Toolbar buttons that insert text and carry out complex strings of program commands. For example, you could create a button that retrieves a memo template and moves the insertion point to the first text-entry area. Another button could open a new document and retrieve an invoice form. To learn more about macros, see Chapter 12, "Creating Macros," and Chapter 29, "Advanced Macro Techniques."

To create a Toolbar button that runs a macro, follow these steps:

1. Choose **E**dit, Pr**e**ferences, **T**oolbar, **E**dit.

Or click a button on the Toolbar with the right mouse button and choose **E**dit.

WordPerfect displays the Toolbar Editor dialog box.

2. Choose Play a **M**acro and then choose **A**dd Macro.

   WordPerfect displays the Select Macro dialog box (see fig. 13.7).

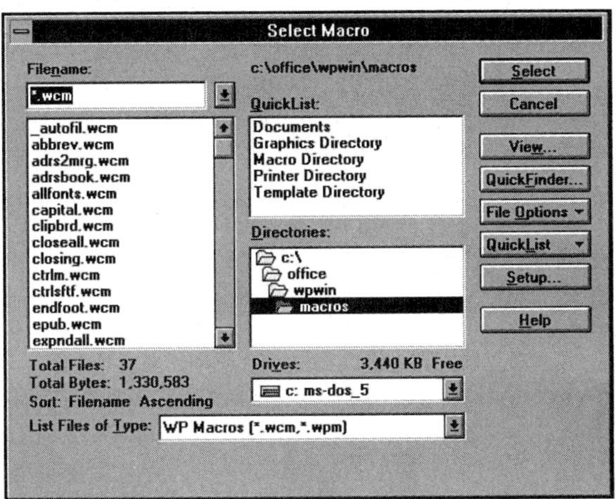

Fig. 13.7
The Select Macro dialog box. With Toolbar macros, you can perform complex series of commands by clicking once with the mouse.

3. To add a macro, type its name or select it from the File**n**ame list box and choose **S**elect.

You can also add a macro that is part of a template. Template macros are useful for performing document-specific tasks such as moving from a Date: field to a Name: field on an employee health insurance records form. Follow these steps:

1. Choose Add **T**emplate Macro in the Toolbar Editor dialog box.

2. Enter the name of the macro in the **N**ame text box or choose the macro from the M**a**cros In Template list box, which includes all the macros in the template.

   If the macro you want is in the default template rather than the current template, choose **L**ocation and select **D**efault Template. You also can choose to use the current template as the default by choosing **U**se as Default.

   Choose OK. The macros from the template you selected are now listed.

3. After selecting a macro, choose **S**elect to return to the Toolbar Editor dialog box.

WordPerfect creates a new button and places it on the Toolbar. Because all the macro buttons look alike, try customizing the picture if you add more than one button.

Customizing a Button's Text and Picture

Not only can you create a new Toolbar button as described in the preceding section, you can also customize its appearance with your own text graphic symbol.

To customize a button's appearance, follow these steps:

1. Choose **E**dit, Pr**e**ferences, **T**oolbar, **E**dit.

   Or click a button on the Toolbar with the right mouse button and choose **E**dit.

   WordPerfect displays the Toolbar Editor dialog box.

2. Double-click the button you want to customize; or right-click the button and choose Customize from the QuickMenu.

   WordPerfect displays the Customize Button dialog box (see fig. 13.8).

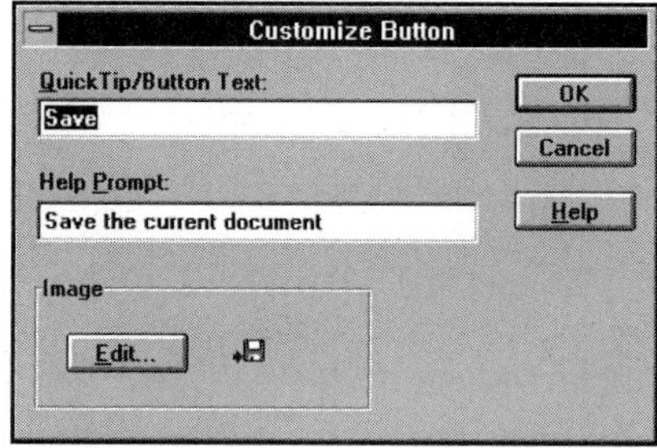

Fig. 13.8
You can customize the text or graphic image of a button. To maintain a look consistent with other WordPerfect task-specific buttons, you may want to copy and customize existing buttons.

3. To change the button's text, choose **Q**uickTip/Button Text and type the new text.

   You can type up to 25 characters, but WordPerfect uses only the amount of text that can fit on a button in one line on the current button display mode: text and picture, picture only, or text only.

4. To change the long description that WordPerfect displays when you move the mouse cursor onto the button, choose Help **P**rompt, and type the new description. You can type up to 130 characters.

5. Choose OK, **C**lose, **C**lose to return to the document window.

Tip
To create a button graphic from scratch, choose C**l**ear to clear the Zoomed Image display.

You can edit a button's graphic icon, or create a button with a graphic image of your own design by following these steps:

1. From the Customize Button dialog box (refer to fig. 13.8), choose **E**dit. WordPerfect displays the Image Editor dialog box (see fig. 13.9).

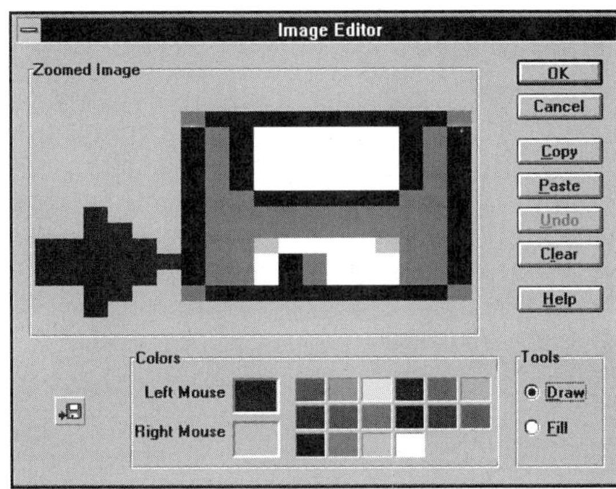

Fig. 13.9
The Image Editor dialog box. In its default configuration, clicking in the Zoomed Image area draws, and clicking the right mouse button deletes.

2. To draw, first click the left mouse button on a color in the Colors area. The Left Mouse sample display changes to the color you selected.

3. Move the cursor into the Zoomed Image image area and click the left mouse button to insert a square of color.

4. To erase, make sure that the Right Mouse sample display shows the same background color as the Zoomed Image display, and click with the right mouse button on the area of color that you want to remove.

5. To use fill colors, choose **F**ill, point the mouse cursor to an enclosed area in the Zoomed Image display, and click.

   WordPerfect fills the enclosed area with the color that's currently assigned to the left mouse button.

Tip
You can drag to "paint" with the mouse, but clicking on one area at a time is safer—you're less likely to run over and change an adjoining area's color unintentionally.

Your changes are shown in the small sample button in the lower left corner of the dialog box. You can paint in the sample button, but you cannot add colors outside the area covered in the Zoomed Image display. For example, you cannot fill a button with a color.

6. To undo your most recent changes, choose **U**ndo.

7. After you finish drawing, choose OK until you return to the editing screen.

Customizing the Power Bar

The Power Bar is intended as a tool for invoking a handful of frequently used functions, such as choosing fonts, applying styles and justifying text. The Power Bar handles these common chores so that you can place more advanced commands on the Toolbar.

You can customize the Power Bar just as you can the Toolbar; however, you cannot move the Power Bar to a new location on-screen.

Hiding and Viewing the Power Bar

You can toggle the Power Bar on and off in three ways:

- Choose **V**iew, P**o**wer Bar.
- Click the right mouse button anywhere on the Power Bar, and choose **H**ide Power Bar.
- Choose **V**iew, **H**ide Bars; or press Alt+Shift+F5.

Choose this third option if you need to view a larger area of a document. Refer to the earlier section, "Hiding and Viewing the Toolbar," for more information about this technique.

Customizing Power Bar Button Faces

As with the Toolbar, you can change the font face and size of the text on the Power Bar buttons to display text, pictures, or both. To customize these buttons, follow these steps:

1. Choose **E**dit, Pr**e**ferences, P**o**wer Bar.

   Or click the Power Bar anywhere with the right mouse button and choose **O**ptions.

   WordPerfect displays the Power Bar Options dialog box shown in figure 13.10.

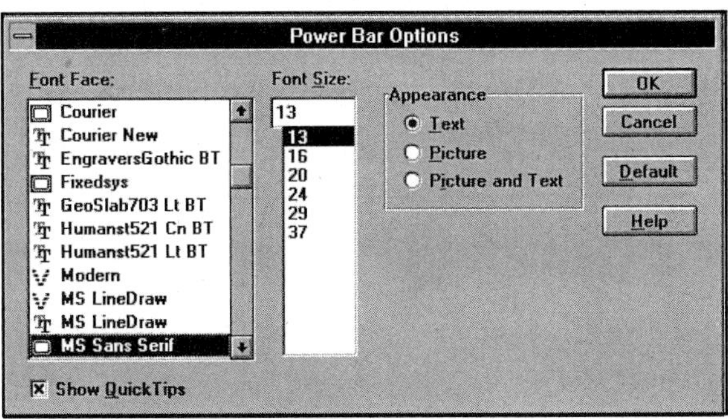

Fig. 13.10
Use the Power Bar Options to select a font face and size and change the appearance of the button face.

2. Select a font to use for the button text from the **F**ont Face list box.
3. From the Font **S**ize list box, select a new size for the button text.
4. Select whether to display **T**ext, **P**icture, or P**i**cture and Text on the face of the button.
5. Choose OK to close the dialog box.

Using only pictures enables you to add many more buttons to the Power Bar. In fact, with all the shortcut keys now available in WordPerfect, you can easily include all your frequently used features that require multiple keystrokes to access. Then dispense with the Toolbar altogether.

You also can edit the pictures on the button faces if you want. The instructions are the same as for customizing the Toolbar text and pictures.

Adding, Moving, and Deleting Power Bar Buttons

To add, move, or delete a Power Bar button, follow these steps:

1. Choose **E**dit, Pr**e**ferences, P**o**wer Bar, **E**dit.

   Or click the Power Bar anywhere with the right mouse button and choose **E**dit.

   WordPerfect displays the Toolbar Editor-Power Bar dialog box shown in figure 13.11.

2. To add a button to the Power Bar, choose whether you want to Acti**v**ate a Feature, Play a **K**eyboard Script, **L**aunch a Program or Play a **M**acro. Follow the instructions earlier in this chapter for adding buttons to the Toolbar.

3. To move a button, drag the button to the new location while the Toolbar Editor-Power Bar dialog box is displayed.

Tip
To quickly edit the Power Bar, click it with the right mouse button and choose **E**dit from the QuickMenu.

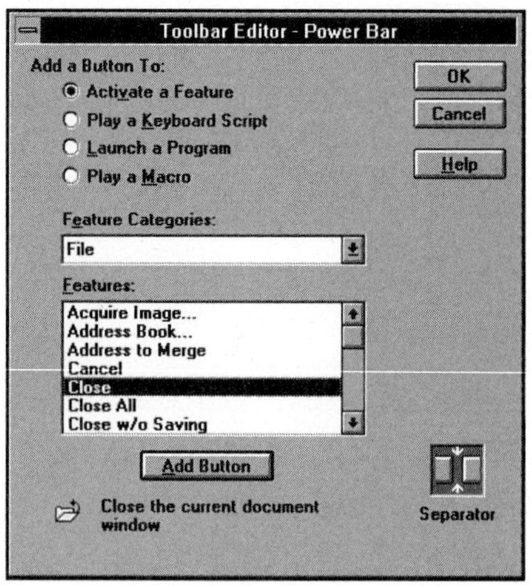

Fig. 13.11
Using the Toolbar Editor-Power Bar dialog box, you can add special Power Buttons, a variety of commands from the menus, macros, and scripts to the existing Power Bar.

◀ See "Using Power Bar Buttons," p. 376

4. To delete a button, drag the button off the Power Bar while the Toolbar Editor-Power Bar dialog box is displayed.

5. To add a spacer between buttons, drag the Separator symbol to the desired location on the Power Bar.

6. Choose OK to return to the document window.

To restore the default Power Bar buttons, choose **D**efault from the Power Bar Options dialog box. Before you close the Editor dialog box, move the box out of the way of the Power Bar and check the results of your editing. If you are unhappy, choose Cancel and all the changes you made are removed.

Troubleshooting

When I add buttons to the Power Bar, they aren't on the Power Bar when I return to the document window.

Be sure you click **A**dd Button each time you choose a feature to add. It's easy to just choose OK after choosing a feature when you want to add only one.

*I tried again, making sure to click **A**dd Button, and the button is still not on the Power Bar.*

If the Power Bar is full, additional buttons you add won't be visible. You'll need to return to the Editor and remove one or more buttons to make room for your additions. Study your word processing needs carefully. You may find that you rarely use standard newspaper columns, change justification, or zoom. To remove a button, just grab it with the mouse and drag it off the Power Bar.

I don't want to remove any buttons. Is there another solution?

If you still can't make room for the button you want, move a feature such as Zoom, or add the button you want to the Toolbar you use most often. The Toolbar contains scroll arrows that allow you to display more of the Toolbar, or you can display the buttons in several rows.

From Here...

Using the Toolbar and Power Bar, you can select many program options with the mouse—a way of working that can be quicker than using menus and the keyboard. A Toolbar button can operate any menu option, no matter how many menu levels deep, so that you can activate the option with a simple mouse click.

In this chapter, you learned to add, delete, and move buttons on the Toolbar and Power Bar and to switch between Toolbars by using a QuickMenu. You learned to position the Toolbar on-screen and to change the appearance of buttons. In addition, you learned how to create specialized Toolbars and how to assign macros to Toolbar buttons.

You also learned how to customize the Power Bar and how to view and hide the Toolbar, Power Bar, or all bars temporarily.

As with any WordPerfect feature, the more you use the Toolbar and Power Bar, the more useful you find it. Don't be afraid to experiment with creating and positioning your own buttons. See the following chapters for more information:

- Chapter 9, "Customizing WordPerfect," shows you how to use all the customizing features available in WordPerfect.
- Chapter 10, "Using Styles," teaches you about styles, the styles available with WordPerfect, and how to use them to standardize your work.
- Chapter 20, "Using Fonts and Special Characters," discusses font faces, proportional and monospaced fonts, type sizes, and when to use these features to enhance the appearance of your documents.

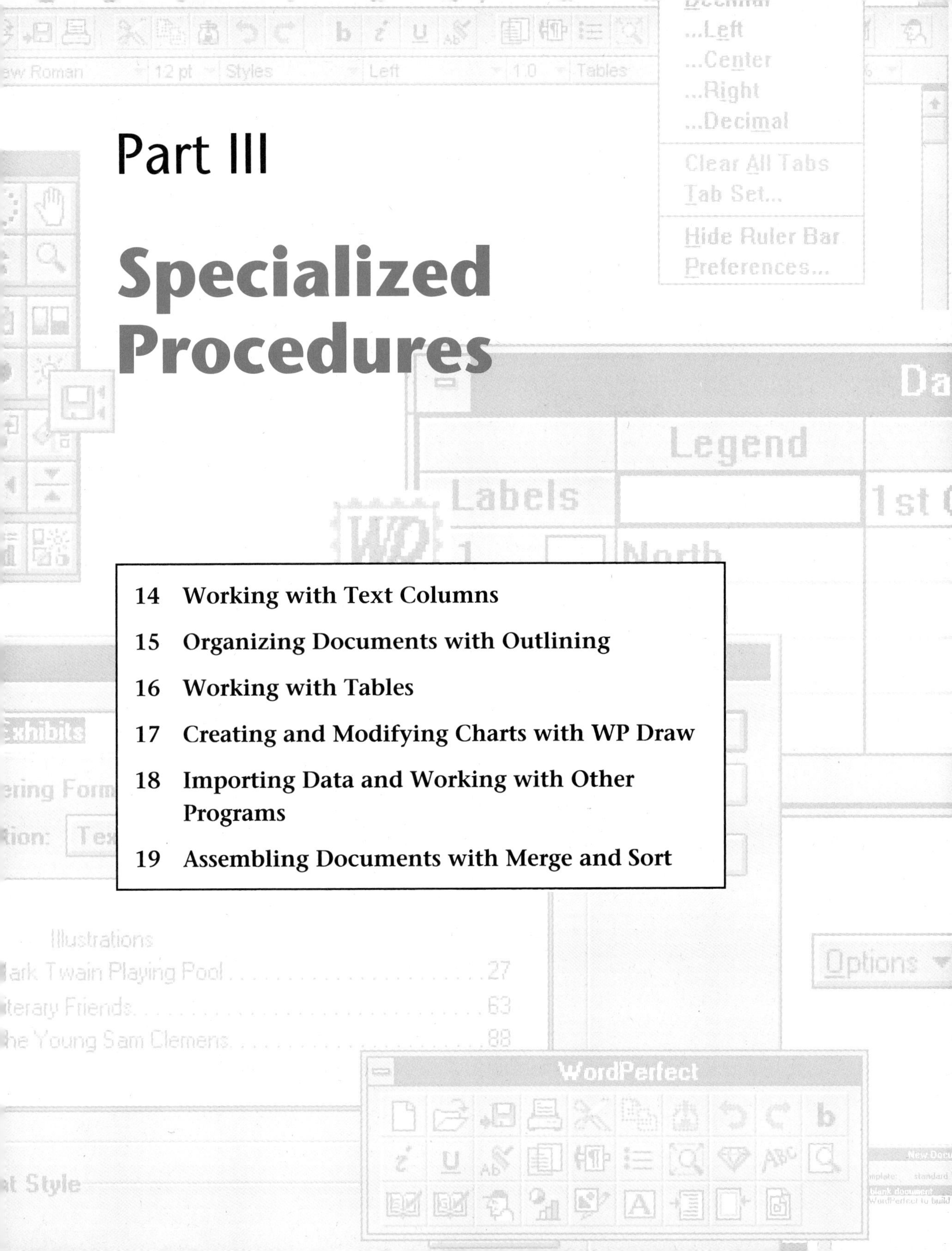

Part III

Specialized Procedures

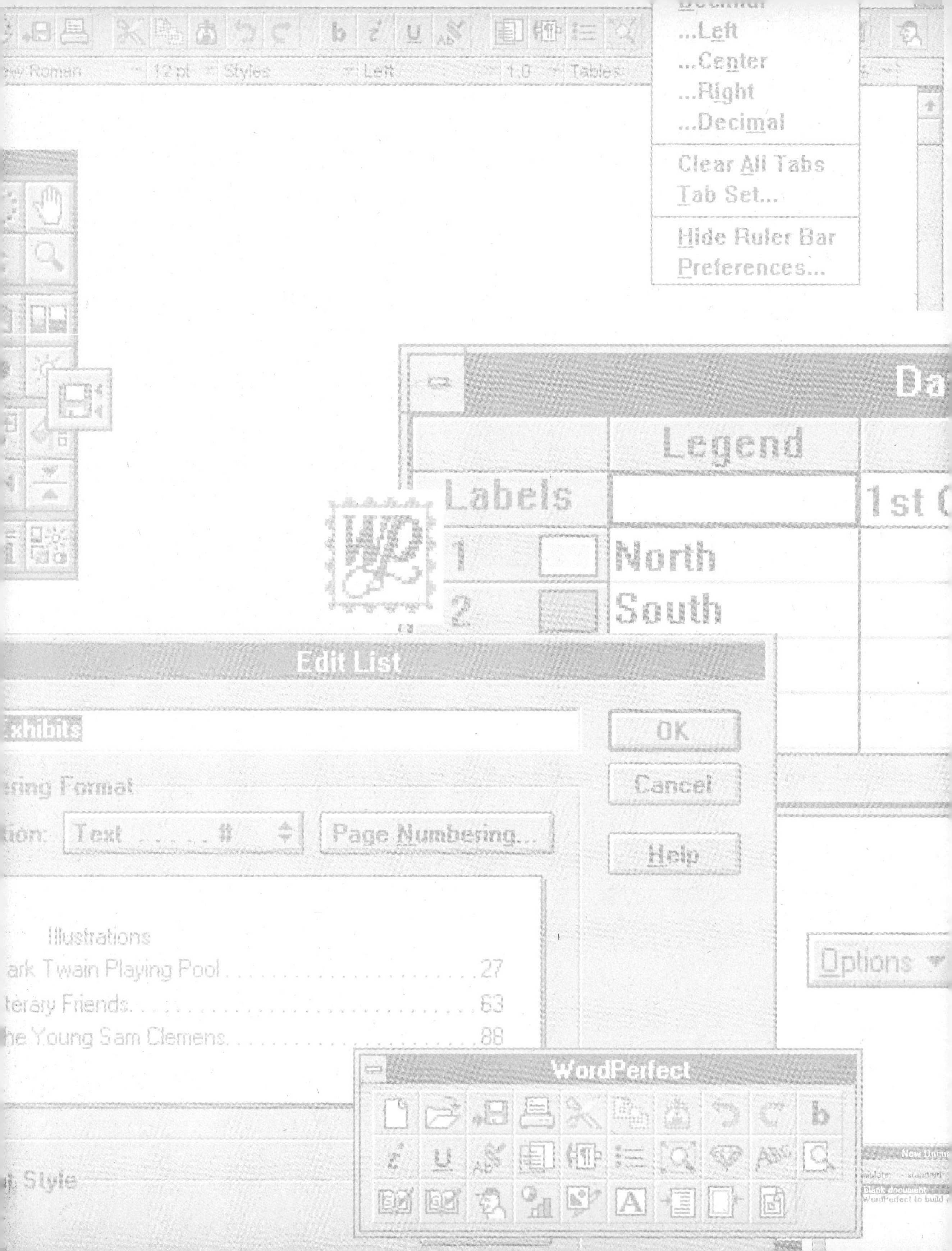

...Left
...Center
...Right
...Decimal
Clear All Tabs
Tab Set...
Hide Ruler Bar
Preferences...
12 pt
Styles
Left
1.0
Tables
Legend
Labels
1st
1
North
2
South
Edit List
OK
Cancel
Help
Text
Page Numbering...
Illustrations
27
63
88
Options
WordPerfect

Chapter 14

Working with Text Columns

by Gordon Nelder-Adams
and Gordon McComb

Suppose you're creating a newsletter, schedule, or script. Your document isn't like a memo or letter where all the paragraphs of text stack on top of one another. Yours requires columns of text neatly assembled on the page.

At first glance, it may seem that putting text into columns is a rather difficult chore. Fortunately, WordPerfect 6.1 for Windows is equally as comfortable formatting text in multiple columns as it is in single columns.

Columns can add visual impact to documents and make text easier to read. With WordPerfect's powerful Columns feature, you can format all or part of a document into columns. You can choose the number and width of columns, the manner in which text flows from column to column, and the width of the gutters (the empty spaces between columns). You can also print lines between your columns, put borders around them, and use background shading or patterns.

In this chapter, you learn about four types of columns in WordPerfect: newspaper columns, balanced newspaper columns, parallel columns, and parallel columns with block protect.

Figure 14.1 shows examples of WordPerfect's column types. *Newspaper columns* typically contain continuous text that flows down the complete length of each column on a page and then wraps to the top of the next column or to the top of the first column on the next page. *Balanced newspaper columns* are similar, but if the columnar text doesn't fill a page, WordPerfect adjusts the amount of text in each column to make them as close to the same length as possible. *Parallel columns* contain short blocks of text side-by-side in rows, like a table. *Parallel columns with block protect* are similar, except that if a column in one row extends past a page break, WordPerfect moves the whole row to the next page.

In the sections that follow, you learn more about using WordPerfect's column feature and controlling column formatting by using the Power Bar, the Columns dialog box, and the Ruler Bar.

Fig. 14.1
A newsletter using three types of columns.

Newspaper columns

The
Depth Gauge

Vol. 5, No. 8

Dive Trip to Cozumel!

That's right, folks, this year No Sierra Divers is taking its Fall dive trip to the island of Cozumel. If you've never been there, Cozumel is an island off the coast of Mexico's Yucatan Peninsula, about 30 miles south of Cancún. It has one small city, a dozen or so hotels, twice as many dive shops, and miles and miles of coral reefs.

While the locals at other popular diving locations may disagree, the inhabitants of Cozumel will cheerfully tell you that it's the number 2 dive spot in the world, second only to Australia's Great Barrier Reef. Without getting into the argument too heavily, we've never had a better time anywhere in this hemisphere.

The water is 80° down to 100 feet, so you won't need a wetsuit! That means less weight, too. You may want to wear a t-shirt to keep your straps from chafing, but otherwise all you'll need are mask, fins, snorkel, regulator, and BC (and a swim suit, of course). You can rent tanks anywhere.

By law you *can't* wear gloves or a dive knife into the water. The entire island is a National Park, and *everything* underwater is protected: fish, plants, and especially coral. Believe me, it's a *lot* harder to grab a piece of coral for a souvenir without gloves. So, while they can't watch every diver under water every minute, they *can* stop you from going under equipped to do damage.

There's a good reason for it, too. Did you know that coral only grows a fraction of an inch per year? At Palancar Gardens, you will see blocks of coral the size of apartment buildings. The reefs are thousands of years old. Yet it only takes one careless move to break off a piece of fan coral that took hundreds of years to grow. (We're assuming that no one's going souvenir hunting on purpose, right?)

The itinerary on the back page details all the stops and all the dives—including Carlos & Charlie's, one of the world's great scuzzy bars. We hope you like tequila slammers. We'll start with a checkout dive at Chancanab Lagoon, before working our way up to boat trips to Palancar and other spectacular reefs. Since we'll be staying at La Ceiba, another easy dive is the sunken airplane, just 100 yards offshore. It was put there for a Mexican disaster movie, but now it's in the process of becoming a reef.

Then, get ready for the boat dives. Nearly everything is a drift dive; they drop you at one end of a reef, and let the current move you (you don't have a lot of choice). The boat follows your bubbles, and when you surface there's a guy

No Sierra Divers, 66 Minor Street, Grass Valley, CA 95945

In this chapter, you also learn how to:

- Define newspaper columns
- Define parallel columns
- Type and edit in columns
- Edit column definitions
- Use column border and fill styles
- Preview your document in final form

whose sole purpose in life is to help you out of the water and hand you a Coke. You'll drift for miles over coral teeming with fish: parrotfish, rock beauties, grunts, sergeant majors, surgeons, and an occasional barracuda (don't worry, they're shy).

Some of the reefs we'll visit include Paraiso, Tormentos, Yocab, Maracaibo, and the Santa Rosa Wall. Watch your depth gauge on that one; it goes down a *long* way! And if you're used to California conditions, where 25-foot visibility is a good day, you won't believe how far you can see— several hundred feet is common, and there's really no such thing as *bad* visibility.

For those of you who can bear to spend a day out of water, there is an optional day trip to Tulum, a Mayan archaeological site on the mainland. The day won't be a complete waste, however, since the trip includes a stop at Xelha ("shell-ha"), a protected lagoon that has to be seen to be believed. Bring your mask, snorkel and flippers, and leave them on the bus at Tulum. Salt and fresh water mix naturally in the lagoon, which creates an inversion layer. You'll think you need prescription lenses for your mask, but in fact the water is just naturally blurry. Still, there's lots to see, including rays and giant parrot fish.

Balanced newspaper columns

Cozumel Dive Trip Itinerary

Date	Time	Place	Comments
9/29	8:00 AM	Meet at SFO; check in for flight	Don't forget your ticket and passport!
9/29	9:44 AM	Departure, Mexicana Flight 823	It's an 8 hour flight; bring a book or a game to pass the time.
9/29	2:16 PM	Arrive Cozumel; go through Customs; take bus to hotel; check in	
9/29	9:00 PM	Carlos & Charlie's downtown	Don't come on an empty stomach
9/30	10:00 AM	Meet at Chancanab State Park for check-out dive	Dive shops are available to rent tanks and other gear. Wetsuit not necessary!
9/30	8:00 PM	Costa Brava	The best seafood on the island! (and cheap)
10/1	8:30 AM	Meet at Tropical Divers for boat trip to Palancar Reef	Back at 5:00
10/1	7:30 PM	Meet back at Tropical Divers for night dive	They will provide underwater flashlights

Parallel columns

Newspaper Columns

With WordPerfect's newspaper columns feature, you can lay out an entire document—or sections within a document—in columns. Columnar format adds visual appeal and is often easier to read than text that spans the full width of the page, especially at smaller point sizes. When you read text printed on a normal page, your eye often has trouble scanning from the end of one line to the beginning of the next. For this reason, newspapers and most large-format magazines are printed in several columns.

Defining Newspaper Columns by Using the Power Bar

WordPerfect lets you control every aspect of column formatting, including the number and width of columns, the width of the gutter (the space between columns), and border and fill styles. If you find WordPerfect's default values acceptable, with a single mouse action you can select two, three, four, or five evenly spaced, parallel columns by using the Columns button on the Power Bar (see fig. 14.2).

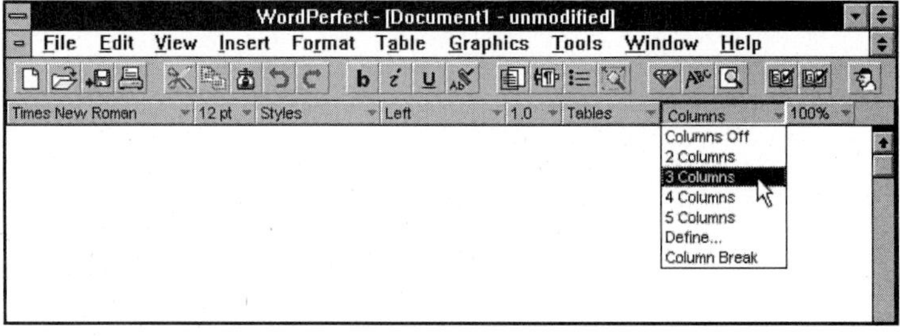

Fig. 14.2 You can choose the most commonly used column settings by using the Power Bar.

To select parallel columns by using the Power Bar, follow these steps:

Tip
If you select a block of text before you define columns, WordPerfect puts the column definition code at the beginning of the block and automatically turns columns off at the end of the block.

1. If the Power Bar is not displayed, choose **V**iew, P**o**wer Bar.
2. Start with a new document, or place the insertion point in an existing document where you want columns to begin.
3. Using the mouse, click and hold the Columns button. A drop-down list appears.
4. Drag down to select the number of columns you want.

WordPerfect inserts a column definition code into your document, at the beginning of the current paragraph. The column definition code specifies the type and number of columns. If you are editing an existing document,

WordPerfect reformats all text below the code in columns with a half-inch gutter space between each pair of columns. If you are creating a new document, all subsequent text you type is formatted into columns.

To turn columns off, choose Columns Off on the Power Bar's Columns button, or use WordPerfect's main menu to choose Fo**r**mat, **C**olumns, **O**ff. If the insertion point isn't in the last column, WordPerfect inserts one or more `[THCol]` codes (temporary hard column) to preserve the column structure. The program then inserts the column off code.

In effect, turning off columns is the same as defining a single newspaper column.

◄ See "Creating the Initial Codes Style," p. 207

Defining Newspaper Columns by Using the Columns Dialog Box

You can use the pull-down menu on the Power Bar to choose 2, 3, 4, or 5 evenly spaced parallel columns. In each case, however, the gutter width remains fixed at 0.5 inch. If any of these default settings are not acceptable, you can specify the settings you prefer by using the Columns dialog box (see fig. 14.3).

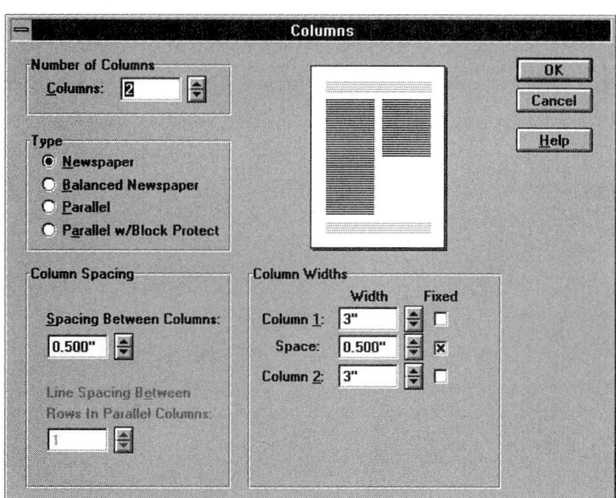

Fig. 14.3
You can specify all column settings in the Columns dialog box.

Tip
If you want your entire document to be in columns, place the Column Def code in your document's Initial Codes style. This makes it harder to delete the code accidentally and is less distracting in Reveal Codes.

Before calling up the Columns dialog box, you should decide how many columns you need, how much space you want between columns, and whether you want all columns to be the same width. You can change these column layout settings at any time, but a little thought before defining columns can save you a lot of work later on.

To select more than five newspaper columns or change the distance between columns, follow these steps:

1. Position the insertion point where you want the columns to begin.
2. Choose Fo**r**mat, **C**olumns, **D**efine. WordPerfect displays the Columns dialog box. If the insertion point is in columnar text, the box displays the current settings. Otherwise, the settings displayed are WordPerfect's defaults.
3. The Number of Columns text box is highlighted when the Columns dialog box appears. The default is 2 columns. If you want 3 or more columns, type the desired number in the text box, or use the increment/decrement arrows to change the number. You can define up to 24 columns.
4. Newspaper is the default column type. If another type is selected, choose **N**ewspaper.
5. The default 0.5-inch gutter between your columns is usually too wide. To change this value, choose **S**pacing Between Columns and type a new value, such as 0.2 or 0.25. You can insert a decimal value or a fraction, such as 1/3 or 1/5. You can also click on the increment arrows to change the value by 0.1 inch at a time. Because some gutter space is necessary, avoid settings that approach 0. WordPerfect doesn't accept a value that, multiplied by the number of gutters, is greater than the document's width.
6. Choose OK or press Enter when you are satisfied with your settings.

Tip
You can also call up the Columns dialog box by choosing Define from the Columns button in the Power Bar, or by double-clicking on the Columns button.

WordPerfect inserts the column definition code. If you are not satisfied with your column margins when you see the formatted text, you can return to the Columns dialog box and change the settings. With the insertion point anywhere within the defined columns, repeat the preceding steps, and make the desired changes.

To turn columns off, choose Fo**r**mat, **C**olumns, **O**ff; or choose Columns Off from the Columns button on the Power Bar. WordPerfect inserts a column off code into your document.

Defining Newspaper Columns with Custom Widths

When you define columns, WordPerfect automatically calculates the width and position of each column based on the number of columns, the distance between columns, and the current settings for left and right margins.

For example, if you select 2 columns, leaving the distance between columns at 0.5 inch and margins at 1 inch on each side, each column will be 3 inches wide. If you change the side margins to 0.5 inch, WordPerfect adjusts the column widths to 3.5 inches. If you adjust the width of one column, WordPerfect automatically adjusts the width of the other columns to keep them between the margins.

The gutters—the spaces between columns—are not available for text, and you always have one less gutter than the number of columns. With two columns, you have one gutter; with six columns, you have five gutters. The total amount of gutter space lost from a page is the **S**pacing Between Columns value multiplied by the number of gutters. In general, therefore, the more columns you have, the smaller the space you want between them. If you have six columns on a page with standard 1-inch margins, for example, and the **S**pacing Between Columns is set to 0.5 inch, you lose 2.5 inches of usable space. With the spacing set to 0.2 inch, only 1 inch is lost.

Therefore, you can control the width of columns to some extent by changing the settings for margins and **S**pacing Between Columns. If either setting is changed, WordPerfect automatically recalculates the column widths and reformats the document accordingly. If you want more precise control, you can specify exact widths for each column and each gutter in the Column Widths section of the Columns dialog box.

WordPerfect displays a thumbnail sample of the columns' appearance above the Column Widths settings in the dialog box. When you change the width of one or more columns or gutter spaces, WordPerfect changes the sample's appearance to reflect the current settings (see fig. 14.4).

You can also change the width of each column or gutter space and select whether that width should remain fixed. Before you set any custom widths, the dialog box shows the WordPerfect-calculated widths of the columns, with the widths of the spaces between columns set to the current **S**pacing Between Columns value; the width of each gutter space is fixed. Whenever WordPerfect adjusts column widths, it does not adjust the width of any column or gutter marked as Fixed.

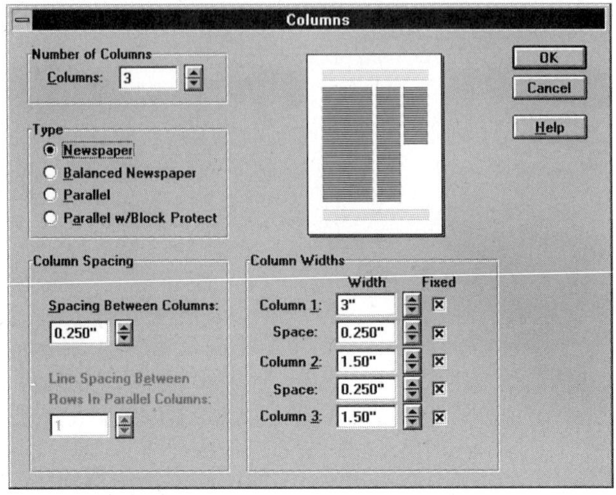

Fig. 14.4
When you change the column widths, WordPerfect changes the thumbnail sample in the Columns dialog box to show the effect of your changes.

To set custom column widths, follow these steps:

1. Place the insertion point where you want the columns to begin, and choose Fo**r**mat, **C**olumns, **D**efine. Leave Column Type set to **N**ewspaper.

2. Choose **C**olumns, and enter a value, such as **3**.

3. Choose **S**pacing Between Columns, and enter a value, such as **0.25**.

4. To change the width of the first column, choose Column **1**, or click in the text box to the right. Then type a value, such as **3**, or click on the increment/decrement buttons to change the current value by 0.1-inch increments. If you want to fix the column width, click on the check box to the right of the column value.

5. If you want to change the width of the space between Column 1 and Column 2, press Tab until WordPerfect highlights the current value, or click in the text box below the value for Column 1. Type a value, or click on the increment buttons to change the current value by 0.1-inch increments.

6. To change the width of other columns or gutter spaces, repeat steps 4 or 5. When you define more than 3 columns, a scroll bar appears that enables you to scroll to display additional column width values. You can also press Tab or Shift+Tab to move forward or backward through the column width values.

7. Choose OK, or press Enter. WordPerfect inserts a column definition code and returns to the document screen.

If you later change your margins, WordPerfect adjusts your custom column widths but maintains them in their relative proportions. If you fix the width of one column and then change your margins, WordPerfect adjusts the widths of the remaining columns and maintains them in their relative proportions. If you prefer to fix your column widths, but let the gutter space between them vary with margin changes, mark all columns Fixed and remove the marks from the gutter spaces. If you don't want WordPerfect to adjust any column or gutter widths, mark all columns and gutter spaces as Fixed. In this case, WordPerfect begins the first column at your left margin setting, and ignores the right margin setting.

You can also adjust column and gutter widths by dragging their guides in the Ruler Bar with your mouse. See "Changing Column Widths Using the Ruler" later in this chapter.

Adding Borders or Shading to Columns

You can "dress up" the appearance of a document by adding borders between or around columns. Background shading or a pattern can be added as well. You can choose any of WordPerfect's default line or fill styles, or customize them according to your own desires.

Column borders are similar to paragraph and page borders. Like paragraph borders, column borders do not surround headers, footers, or page numbers, but column borders let you put lines between columns, which the other border types do not. You may want to experiment to find which border types are appropriate for a particular document.

◀ See "Using Graphics Borders," p. 268

▶ See "Customizing Borders," p. 714

▶ See "Customizing Graphics Boxes," p. 719

You can select a border style, a fill style, or both, from the Column Border dialog box. You can select either style by name from a drop-down list box or from a display of thumbnail images of the most common styles. Not all border styles, however, are available from the thumbnail image display. As with the Columns dialog box, when you choose an option, WordPerfect displays an image of the current settings in the dialog box.

To add column borders or a fill, follow these steps:

1. Choose Fo**r**mat, **C**olumns, **B**order/Fill. WordPerfect displays the Column Border dialog box.

2. To add a border, place the mouse on the **B**order Style button, and drag to select one of the displayed border style images (see fig. 14.5). If you prefer to use the keyboard, choose **B**order Style, and then press the space bar to display the thumbnail images. Scroll to highlight a desired border style, and press Enter to select it.

Alternatively, click on the drop-down list box arrow, or tab to highlight the list box and press Alt+down arrow, to display the list of border style names. Then select a style name from the list. If you create your own border styles, you must choose them by name, because WordPerfect does not add them to the thumbnail image display.

3. To add a fill, click the **F**ill Style button with your mouse, and then drag to select one of the displayed fill style images (see fig. 14.6). If you prefer to use the keyboard, choose **F**ill Style, and then press the space bar to display the thumbnail images. Scroll to highlight a desired fill style, and press Enter to select it.

Alternatively, choose the drop-down list box, or tab to highlight the list box and press Alt+down arrow, to display the list of fill style names. Then select a style name from the list. If you create your own fill styles, you must select them by name, because WordPerfect does not add them to the thumbnail image display.

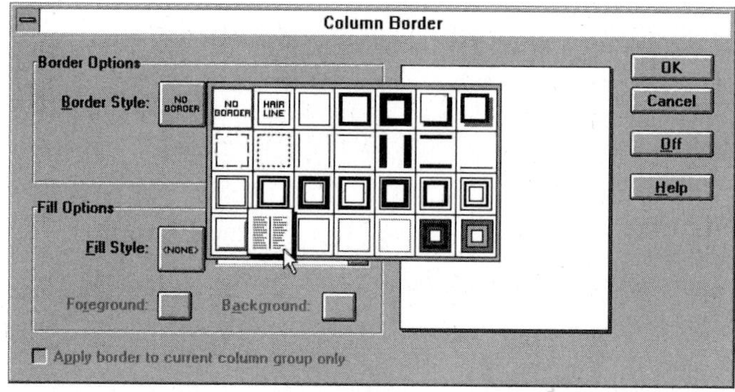

Fig. 14.5
Use borders to add interest to your columns.

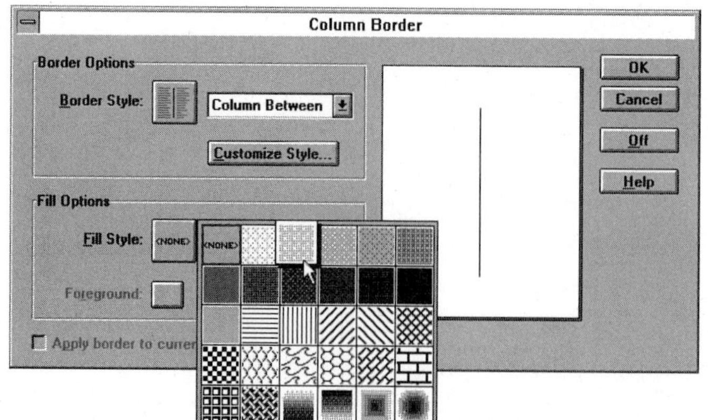

Fig. 14.6
Fill styles provide a variety of options to choose from.

4. Click OK, or press Enter.

Most column border styles are nearly identical to the paragraph and page border styles, but two particular styles are designed specifically for columns. The Column Between style places a vertical line between each pair of columns; these lines do not extend beyond any columnar text. The Column All style places a rectangle around the columns and vertical lines between columns; the lines between columns extend to meet the outside border. You can select the Column Between style from either the drop-down list or thumbnail images, but you can select the Column All style from only the drop-down list.

WordPerfect's default fill styles are shaded fills varying from 10% to 100%, as well as a variety of fill patterns and gradients. If your output device is a 300 dpi laser printer, the 10% Shaded Fill style provides a light gray background, which is quite noticeable without making your text harder to read. A 20% shaded fill is significantly darker, and a 30% shaded fill begins to make your text hard to read. In general, 30% and darker fills are useful only on higher-resolution printers and typesetters. If your printer is capable, however, you can choose the 100% shaded fill and set your text color to white to achieve white text on a black background. If you have a color printer, you can choose any two colors for the foreground and background, respectively, which is particularly effective with the gradient fill styles.

If none of the existing border styles seems appropriate for a particular document, you can choose **C**ustomize Style from the Column Border dialog box. From here, you can change the line style individually for top, bottom, left, right, or interior lines; select a color for any of your lines; add lines; change line thickness; modify the spacing between text and lines; add a drop shadow; or select round or square corners for lines and shading. For more details on creating, editing, and using border and fill styles, see Chapter 7, "Integrating Text and Graphics," and Chapter 21, "Using Advanced Graphics Techniques."

Working with Columnar Text

Entering text in columns is the same as entering text in a normal document. Text automatically wraps at the end of each line within the column and from the bottom of one column to the top of the next.

Because columnar text generally has a much narrower line width, you may need to adjust other formatting elements, such as the type size or type face. If your type size is too large for the column width, left-justified text may have a ragged right margin, and with justification set to Full, some lines may look abnormally spread out or compressed. Text set in a point size too small for the column width is difficult to read. In general, the more columns you define, the smaller your point size should be. As a good rule of thumb, you should average 10 or 12 words per line. Proportionally spaced fonts also adjust better than fixed-width fonts, and some fonts at the same point size are narrower than others.

Note

Previous versions of WordPerfect did not allow certain features to be used within columns. Footnotes and tables were not allowed, although endnotes were permitted. WordPerfect 6.1 has removed these restrictions.

You may want to hyphenate some words manually; however, avoid placing hyphens on several successive lines. If WordPerfect is hyphenating for you, you may need to adjust the Hyphenation Zone settings in extreme cases for tighter hyphenation. (Hyphenation is covered in Chapter 4, "Formatting Text.") Again, this problem is far less troublesome with proportionally spaced fonts than with fixed-width fonts.

If necessary, consider decreasing the number of columns to make each remaining column wider. Although you should make such overall layout decisions in advance to avoid such problems, appearance is the final guide.

Moving the Insertion Point

Insertion point movement within a column is the same as in a normal document, but moving between columns is not. The easiest way to move from one column to another is to select a new insertion point with your mouse. If you do not have a mouse, or if you prefer to use the keyboard, WordPerfect offers several commands for moving the insertion point between columns. If you create a macro to move between columns, you must use these commands, because macros don't record mouse movement.

Alt+right arrow moves the insertion point one column to the right, and Alt+left arrow moves the insertion point one column to the left. More powerful but more complex is the Go To command (Ctrl+G). Typically, you use the Go To dialog box to go to a specified page number or to the top or the bottom of the current page. When the insertion point is located within a column, however, the following additional options become available:

Top of Column

Bottom of Column

Previous Column

Next Column

First Column

Last Column

To choose one of these Go To options from the keyboard, follow these steps:

1. Choose **E**dit, **G**o To; or press Ctrl+G. The Go To dialog box appears.
2. Choose **P**osition; or press Shift+Tab.
3. Highlight the desired option.
4. Choose OK, or press Enter. WordPerfect moves the insertion point to the desired location.

WordPerfect displays columns side-by-side on-screen, exactly as they will print. When you scroll down through text in a column and reach the bottom, WordPerfect automatically moves the insertion point to the top of the next column. If that column is only partially visible on-screen, however, WordPerfect does not move the text on-screen to make the entire column visible. This problem is particularly noticeable if you zoom the display to a setting higher than 100%. If you need to see the full-column width, press the End key to move the insertion point to the right edge of the column. WordPerfect adjusts the screen so that the insertion point is visible.

Editing in Newspaper Columns

Editing text within columns is not much different from editing standard text. WordPerfect has no special keys for selecting text within columns. You must be aware, however, of the codes that create the columns themselves. Deleting a `[Col Def]` code reformats the document as normal text to the end of the document or to the next `[Col Def]` code, if any, and can drastically alter the pagination of the document due to the additional space that is no longer taken up by the gutters. If Reveal Codes is not active, however, deleting `[Col Def]` codes by accident is unlikely. (See Chapter 9, "Customizing WordPerfect," for more information on insertion point movement options.)

In Reveal Codes, formatting codes can be deleted by accident or on purpose. If several parts of your document have different column structures, and you want to change the format of one part to match that of the preceding section, delete the intervening `[Col Def]` code or codes.

If you delete a `[Col Def]` code accidentally, immediately select Undo (Ctrl+Z) or Undelete (Shift+Ctrl+Z). Undo reverses your last action, while Undelete enables you to restore any of your last three deletions. If you don't Undo or Undelete immediately, you must re-create your column definition.

If the insertion point is in columnar text, WordPerfect treats page break commands as column breaks. If you want to force a column break at some point, choose Column Break from the Power Bar's Columns button or the Fo**r**mat, **C**olumns menu; or press Ctrl+Enter. This code forces the following text to the top of the next column and leaves the remainder of the column below the break empty.

You can turn columns off by choosing Fo**r**mat, **C**olumns, **O**ff; or by choosing Columns Off from the Power Bar's Column button. If you want to turn columns back on at some later point in the document, choose Fo**r**mat, **C**olumns, **D**efine; or choose Define from the Power Bar's Columns Button. WordPerfect retains the previous column settings; you can accept or change them as you choose. If you choose a specific number of columns from the Power Bar, you lose any custom column widths.

◀ See "Using Hyphenation," p. 152

◀ See "Centering and Flush Right," p. 147

◀ See "Using Justification," p. 151

Justification and alignment codes also work in columns the same as in normal text. To center a heading, for example, you can use Center Align (Shift+F7) for a single-line heading or Center Justify (Fo**r**mat, **J**ustification, C**e**nter) for a multi-line heading. In either case, WordPerfect centers the text between the current margins, whether they are full-page or column margins. The other alignment and justification commands act in a similar manner. (See Chapter 4, "Formatting Text," for more information on aligning and justifying text.)

Troubleshooting

When I change the widths spacing between columns in the Columns dialog box, the column widths change as well.

WordPerfect tries to automatically adjust the columns widths to ensure that the columns will span the width of the page. As you change column widths and spacing, other column widths and spacing may be adjusted so that everything fits properly on the page. If you set a column width or spacing and don't want it to be changed, click the Fixed box next to the column width or spacing.

Setting the Border Style to lines between columns places a line between all of the columns. I just want lines between some of the columns.

To insert a vertical line between any column in a document, place the insertion point in the column to the left of where you want the column line to appear. For example, if your document has three columns, and you want the line to appear between the center and right columns, place the insertion point in the center column. Choose Graphics, Custom **L**ine. The Create Graphics Line dialog box appears. Choose **V**ertical under Line Type, then choose Column **A**ligned in the Ho**r**izontal pop-up button. Choose OK to return to the document. A line appears between the columns.

Balanced Newspaper Columns

As the name suggests, balanced newspaper columns are a special type of newspaper column. When you enter text in standard newspaper columns, the text fills the first column, then the second column, and so on. When you enter text in balanced newspaper columns, however, WordPerfect continually adjusts the length of each column to keep the lengths of all columns as even as possible.

For example, with standard newspaper columns, if the document has two columns and you turn columns off in the middle of the second column, WordPerfect leaves the first column as it is and forces any text that follows onto the next page, leaving the remainder of the second column empty (see fig. 14.7). With balanced newspaper columns, WordPerfect adjusts the length of all columns so that they end at approximately the same line (see fig. 14.8). In addition, any text that follows a column off code appears on the same page. When you use balanced newspaper columns, you see immediately how this column type affects text formatting.

You create balanced newspaper columns by using the Columns dialog box in the same way that you create normal newspaper columns, except that you choose the **B**alanced Newspaper type instead of **N**ewspaper. (You cannot create balanced newspaper columns using the Power Bar.) Typing balanced newspaper columns is very different, however.

As soon as you type past the first line, the cursor wraps to the second column instead of wrapping to the next line. If you choose three columns, when you fill the first line in the last column, WordPerfect adjusts the text in the second column backward, making it the second line in the first column and moving the text you just typed in the third column back to the second column. As you continue typing, the insertion point now remains in the third column, and each time you fill a line, WordPerfect adjusts the previous text backward, adding a line to each column in turn.

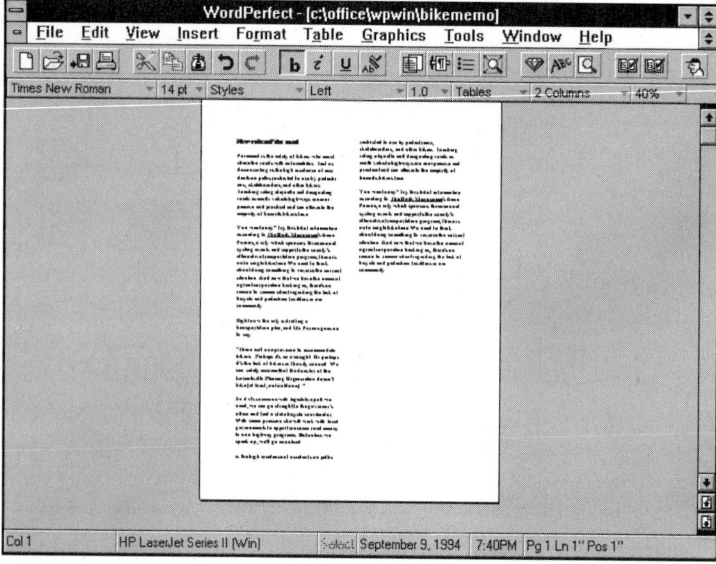

Fig. 14.7
In newspaper columns, WordPerfect fills each column before beginning the next one.

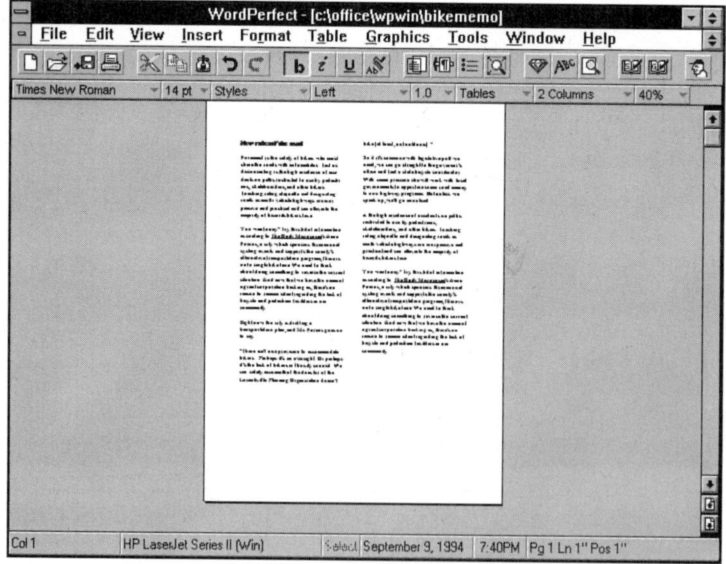

Fig. 14.8
In balanced newspaper columns, WordPerfect adjusts the length of each column as you type so that all columns are approximately the same length.

To turn off balanced newspaper columns, choose Format, Columns, Off, or choose Columns Off from the Power Bar's Columns button. WordPerfect moves the cursor to the left margin, a double space below the end of the first column. When you turn off normal newspaper columns, the cursor moves to the top of the next page. When you turn off balanced newspaper columns, you can add additional text below the columnar text.

Tip
Typing balanced newspaper columns can be painfully slow, because WordPerfect continually adjusts your column lengths. You may find it easier to type your text first and then add the column definition.

Note

Even though you select balanced newspaper columns, all your columns may not be exactly the same length. For example, fitting four lines of text evenly into three columns is impossible. Additionally, widows and orphans, paragraph spacing, and larger type sizes for headings can all cause your columns to have slightly uneven lengths. However, no column should be more than one line shorter or longer than the average number of lines in all columns.

Parallel Columns

Parallel columns, though closely related to newspaper columns, also have much in common with WordPerfect's Tables feature. Whereas newspaper columns typically feature large amounts of text flowing continuously from column to column, parallel columns contain shorter blocks of text that are read across the page from left to right (see fig. 14.9). These blocks of text can be any length, from individual words and short phrases to long paragraphs. You can use parallel columns for a wide variety of documents, from itineraries to screenplays.

► See "Incorporating Columns," p. 779

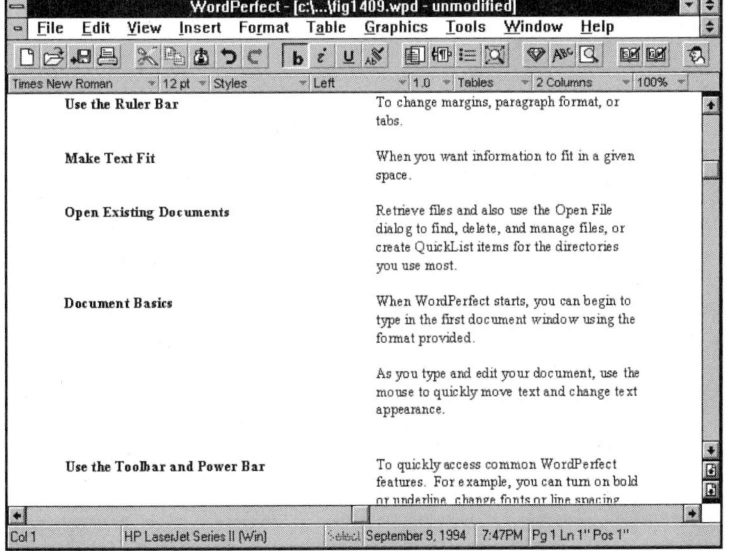

Fig. 14.9
An example of parallel columns.

Defining Parallel Columns

The steps for defining parallel columns are similar to those for creating newspaper columns. You can define parallel columns, however, only through the Columns dialog box. You cannot use the Columns button on the Power Bar as a shortcut, as you can for simple newspaper columns. Also, whereas newspaper columns usually are spaced evenly and need little, if any, adjustment after definition, parallel columns are usually of greatly differing widths. The best column width settings for parallel columns depend on the actual contents of each column. For the best appearance, you usually need to edit your parallel columns definition after you enter some text. Although you should plan in advance the number of columns you need and their approximate widths, don't spend a lot of time making complex calculations that you probably will change anyway.

WordPerfect inserts a `[Col Def:Parallel]` or `[Col Def:Parallel w/Blk Pro]` code, depending on which type of parallel columns you selected. The Ruler Bar, if visible, now displays your column margins between your page margins. You can change the widths of your columns by dragging the column guides in the Ruler Bar, but before doing so, you should type several rows of text.

Typing Text in Parallel Columns

When you type text in newspaper columns, as your text fills a column, WordPerfect automatically wraps the following text to the next column, but you also can force a column break at any point by pressing Ctrl+Enter. Although in normal text this keystroke inserts a `[HPg]` code, in columnar text Ctrl+Enter inserts a `[HCol]` code instead. You can also insert a `[HCol]` code by choosing Column Break from the Power Bar's Columns button.

When you type text in parallel columns, you must insert a column break at the end of each block of text. This tells WordPerfect where to break text between columns. If you do not insert a column break, WordPerfect treats all text that follows as part of the same column. Therefore, after you finish typing the block of text in the first column, insert a column break, and WordPerfect moves the insertion point to the second column. Do the same for each subsequent column. After you finish the text block in the last column, again insert a column break. WordPerfect moves the insertion point to the beginning of the first column and below any text you have entered.

When you choose the **P**arallel column type in the Columns dialog box, WordPerfect allows blocks of text to extend over a page break. This situation is acceptable in screenplays and other documents in which a single text block may be several paragraphs or even several pages long. In many other cases, however—particularly when your text blocks are relatively short—you may want to prevent blocks of text from being split by a page break. To do so, choose the P**a**rallel with Block Protect column type when you define columns.

Parallel columns with Block Protect look and act almost exactly the same as standard parallel. In Reveal Codes, the column definition code appears as `[Col Def:Parallel w/Blk Pro]`, but WordPerfect provides no other indication that block protection is active. Each text block still ends in a `[HCol]` code. If a text block extends past the page break at the bottom of a page, however, WordPerfect moves the entire row of text blocks to the next page.

To create the itinerary shown in figure 14.9, follow these steps:

1. Define parallel columns as described in the preceding section. Choose 4 columns with 0.25-inch space between them. You need not adjust column widths.
2. Turn on Bold, and then type **Date**.
3. Press Ctrl+Enter to go to the next column. In Reveal Codes, you can see a `[HCol]` code.
4. Type **Time**, and press Ctrl+Enter to go the third column.
5. Choose Fo**r**mat, **L**ine, **C**enter; or press Shift+F7. Type **Place**, and press Ctrl+Enter to go to the final column.
6. Again choose Fo**r**mat, **L**ine, **C**enter; or press Shift+F7. Type **Comments**, and turn off Bold.
7. Press Ctrl+Enter to return to the first column.
8. Continue to enter text in column format, pressing Ctrl+Enter at the end of each column. You can use any text attributes, choose justification or alignment options, change line spacing, and so on.
9. If you finish typing in columns and want to resume typing normal text, turn columns off by choosing Fo**r**mat, **C**olumns, **O**ff.

Tip
You can use the Columns button on the Power Bar to turn off columns or to insert a column break.

If you forget to turn off columns, and press Ctrl+Enter instead, delete the final `[HCol]` code, then turn off columns as in step 9 or by using the Columns button on the Power Bar.

Adding Space between Rows in Parallel Columns

When you create parallel columns, WordPerfect essentially turns columns off at the end of each row and turns them back on immediately at the beginning of the next row. (WordPerfect 5.1 literally did just that, but WordPerfect 6.1 only displays its standard `[HCol]` column code between rows.) If you choose borders or a fill for parallel columns, however, these features affect only the rows of text and not the lines between rows.

By default, WordPerfect 6.1 leaves one blank line between rows of parallel columns. You can increase or decrease that value in the Columns dialog box. When either parallel column type is selected, you can choose Line Spacing Between Rows in Parallel Columns and type in any decimal value; or click on the increment buttons to increase or decrease the value by 0.1-inch increments. You can type any standard line spacing value, such as 1.5 or 2.0, or you can decrease the space by typing values such as 0.5 for a half space or 0, which removes the space between rows completely.

The actual amount of space WordPerfect leaves between rows is a multiple of the value you enter and the current type size. If you later select larger or smaller type, the distance between rows changes accordingly.

Editing Parallel Columns

Editing in newspaper columns is essentially the same as editing in normal text. When you edit parallel columns, however, you must remain aware of the codes that give the columns their structure and work within that structure. You can then cut and paste text between columns, insert new groups of columns between existing ones, and move groups of columns to different locations.

You can cut and paste text from one location to another with few restrictions. You must pay attention, however, to your location within the columns. Because each column ends with a `[HCol]` code, if you block and copy text from more than one column at a time, your block includes a `[HCol]`. When you paste that block into another column, WordPerfect pastes the `[HCol]` code as well. The code ends the column, moves any following text to the next column, and moves each subsequent text block in the column structure one column to the right. As a result, text that was in the last column is now in the first column. Fortunately, to restore your column structure you can merely delete the extra `[HCol]` code, and the following text reverts to its previous position. In the same manner, if you delete a `[HCol]` code by accident, you can press Ctrl+Enter to insert a new code.

If you need to add a new event to the middle of the itinerary, simply place the cursor at the beginning of the following event, and begin typing. After you finish the first column, press Ctrl+Enter to move to the second column. WordPerfect pushes the following blocks of text ahead of you. Continue on in this manner, pressing Ctrl+Enter at the end of each column. At the last column, insert a column break, which moves the following text block to the beginning of the next row.

Moving Parallel Columns

Moving rows of parallel columns is not difficult, although you need to be sure that you preserve the column structure. When you move one or more rows of parallel columns, make sure that you include the `[HCol]` code at the end of the last column in any row. You can see exactly which codes are selected by using Reveal Codes.

To move a row of parallel columns, follow these steps:

1. Place the insertion point before the first character in the group of columns you want to move. Then press Shift+down arrow; or press Select (F8) and the down-arrow key.

2. Choose **E**dit, Cu**t**; or press Ctrl+X.

3. Press the up-arrow or down-arrow key to move the insertion point to the beginning of a different row. Then choose **E**dit, **P**aste; or press Ctrl+V. WordPerfect pastes the block at the new location.

Tip
You cannot move a row of columns above a column definition without losing the column format.

Alternatively, point just to the left of the first character in a row with the mouse pointer, and drag downward to select the row. Then point at the selected text and drag to the beginning of a different row. WordPerfect moves the block to the new location.

Changing Column Widths Using the Ruler

After you enter some text into columns, you can see which columns are too wide and which are too narrow. Figure 14.10 shows text formatted with default column widths.

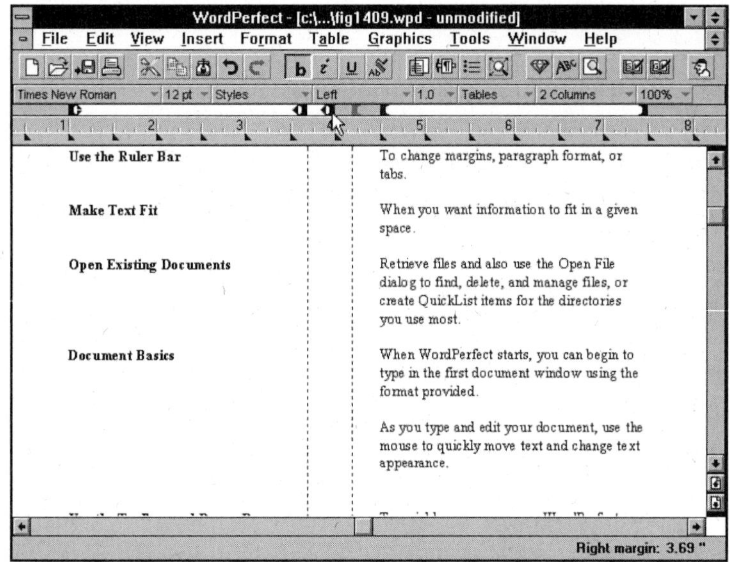

Fig. 14.10
You can drag column guides in the Ruler Bar to change the width of columns and gutters.

The Ruler Bar displays margin and column information along its top edge. You can drag the column markers or the gutter spaces with your mouse to adjust the widths of your columns and gutters. You can also drag a gutter space completely off the Ruler Bar to combine two columns into one. Whenever you drag a margin or column guide in the Ruler Bar, a vertical line appears down the screen to aid in placing the setting with respect to the existing text. When you drag a gutter space, a double-line appears (refer to fig. 14.10).

When you drag a column guide to narrow a column, WordPerfect makes the adjacent gutter wider by the same amount. When you drag a gutter, WordPerfect makes the column on one side of the gutter wider and makes the column on the other side narrower by the same amount.

To adjust the columns, follow these steps:

1. Place the insertion point in the first row of text blocks. If your insertion point is not in the first row, changing column widths inserts a new column definition in the current row, instead of editing the first column definition.

2. If the Ruler is not displayed, choose **V**iew, **R**uler Bar; or press Alt+Shift+F3.

3. Using the mouse, drag the gutter space between the first two columns. Two vertical lines appear; drag to the left until the left-vertical line approaches the text in the first column.

4. Release the gutter space, being careful not to drag it down off the Ruler Bar (which would delete it). The text in column 2 moves to the left; columns 3 and 4 remain unchanged.

5. Drag the gutter between columns 2 and 3 to the left the same way that you dragged the first gutter.

6. Finally, drag the gutter between columns 3 and 4 so that the two columns are about the same width.

Columns 1 and 2 are now much narrower, although the text in those columns is unaffected. Columns 3 and 4 are now much wider, and blocks of text that were 4 and 5 lines long are now mostly 1 or 2 lines long, and none is longer than 3 lines. The entire document takes up far less space, and the text is reasonably well balanced between columns. You can make further adjustments at any time to fine-tune column widths, remembering first to select an insertion point in the first block of text.

From Here...

In this chapter, you learned how to define and use newspaper columns and parallel columns. You learned to use the Power Bar to turn columns on and off from the document editing screen and to use the Columns dialog box to create and edit custom column widths. You also learned how to display borders around your columns and shading within them. You learned how to work most effectively in newspaper and parallel columns. Finally, you learned how to adjust column widths by dragging items in the Ruler Bar.

When you need a columnar format for text, WordPerfect's Columns feature is powerful and flexible. This chapter covers only the basic mechanics of creating and working in columns. In combination with such features as multiple fonts, headers and footers, graphics lines and boxes, tables, figures, and tables of contents, columns turn WordPerfect into a powerful desktop publishing engine rivaling more specialized programs.

For information relating to formatting text in WordPerfect, see the following chapters in this book:

- Chapter 4, "Formatting Text," details the basics of formatting text in WordPerfect, including formatting lines and paragraphs.

- Chapter 5, "Formatting Pages and Documents," shows you how to apply formatting to entire pages and documents. Included are discussions on creating headers and footers and using subdivide page, which is another way to create column text.
- Chapter 7, "Integrating Text and Graphics," shows you how to combine text and graphics in a document. When used with multiple-column formatting, this makes WordPerfect a particularly handy desktop publishing tool.
- Chapter 23, "Desktop Publishing with WordPerfect," provides tips and techniques for using WordPerfect 6.1 for Windows as a desktop publishing aid, including using multiple-column formats.

Chapter 15

Organizing Documents with Outlining

by Eric Baatz and Gordon McComb

An outline is an effective tool with which to present the main points and organization of a document. Additionally, the act of creating an outline enables you to determine what information you want your document to contain and in what order the topics should be presented.

WordPerfect enhances both aspects of outlines by making your final outline look good and by providing active, intelligent assistance that speeds up the mechanics of outline creation beyond anything you can do with a pen and paper.

In this chapter, you learn how to:

- Make simple lists using WordPerfect's Bullets & Numbers capability
- Create a variety of simple and multilevel outlines using WordPerfect's built-in capabilities
- Manipulate outlines
- Create customized outlines

Understanding What Outlines Can Do

A WordPerfect outline consists of more than Roman numerals. Figure 15.1 is an example of how WordPerfect outlines can look.

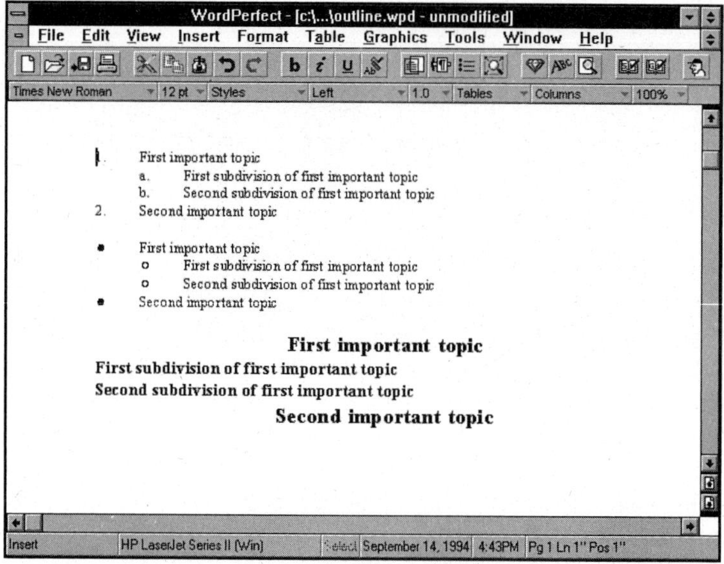

Fig. 15.1
Three different WordPerfect outlines. The only difference is that each uses a different outline style.

In addition to making the final appearance of an outline look sharp, WordPerfect makes outlines dynamic. The simplest consequence is that you can concentrate on writing particular points by hiding other parts of the outline and showing the whole outline only when you are done. The most general consequence is that you can construct documents from outlines by adding text and ideas as you go. Of course, when you insert or delete material, WordPerfect automatically maintains whatever, if any, numbering you are using.

Using Bullets & Numbers

Outlines may seem too complex if you only want a simple list, such as one of the lists shown in figure 15.2. Those lists, and similar ones, can be produced by choosing **I**nsert, Bullets & **N**umbers, selecting a bullet or number to insert, and choosing OK.

Tip
Click the Insert Bullet button on the default Toolbar to insert a small circle bullet at the location of the cursor.

However, it is not that much harder to use outlines to produce the same type of lists. See the "Creating Numbered and Bulleted Lists" section later in this chapter.

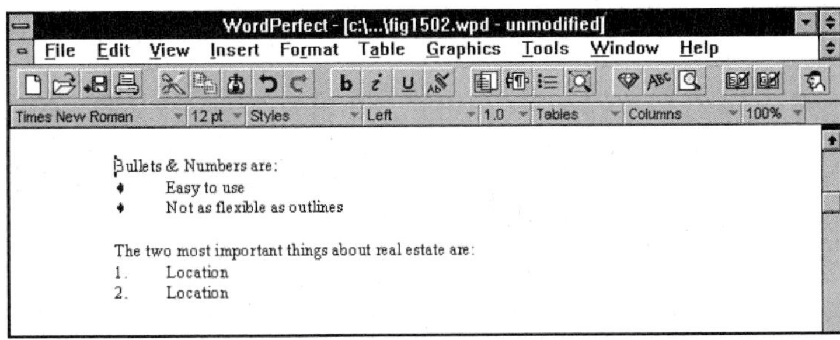

Fig. 15.2
Two simple lists that are easy and quick to make with Bullets & Numbers.

Creating a Simple List with Bullets & Numbers

A *simple list* is one or more paragraphs that have bullets or numbers at the left margin and no indented paragraphs under them. If numbers are used, they increase from paragraph to paragraph.

WordPerfect predefines five types of bullets (Small Circle, Large Circle, Diamond, Square, and Triangle) and five types of numbering styles (Numbers, Uppercase Roman, Uppercase Letters, Lowercase Roman, and Lowercase Letters), as shown in figure 15.3.

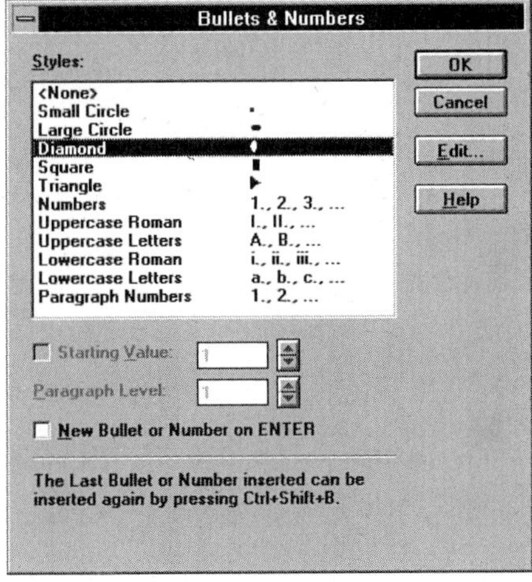

Fig. 15.3
The Bullets & Numbers dialog box. One or two clicks produces a number.

The general steps for creating a simple list are as follows:

1. Move the insertion point to the left margin of the line in which you want to create the simple list.

2. Choose **I**nsert, Bullets & **N**umbers. The Bullets & Numbers dialog box appears (refer to fig. 15.3).

3. Select the style you want. If it is a numbering style, look at the value in the Starting **V**alue field. If it is not 1, check the Starting **V**alue check box and enter **1** in the Starting Value field. Choose OK. WordPerfect returns to your document with the insertion point ready for you to enter text.

4. Type your text and press Enter.

5. If you want a blank line, press Enter again.

6. If you want another bullet of the same type or the next number, press Ctrl+Shift+B and then enter more text.

You also can create a simple list by first entering the text and then applying a Bullets & Numbers style. The general steps are as follows:

1. Move the insertion point to the left margin of the line in which you want to create the simple list.

2. Enter the text for each item, then press Enter. (Press Enter twice if you want a blank line between items.)

3. Select all the items.

4. Choose **I**nsert, Bullets & **N**umbers. The Bullets & Numbers dialog box appears (refer to fig. 15.3).

5. Select the style you want. If it is a numbering style, look at the value in the Starting Value field. If it is not 1, check the Starting **V**alue check box and enter **1** in the Starting Value field. Choose OK.

Note

To change the level of the paragraph numbers you insert—for example, to change *1.* to *a)*—choose the Paragraph Numbers style in the Bullets & Numbers dialog box. You can define a starting paragraph level by changing the value in the **P**aragraph Level box.

Making Fewer Keystrokes with Bullets & Numbers

You can create a series of bullets or numbers with fewer keystrokes than in the previous steps by checking **N**ew Bullet Or Number On ENTER in the Bullets & Numbers dialog box. Then, whenever you press Enter after typing your text, you immediately get a new bullet or number without having to press Ctrl+Shift+B.

The tradeoff is that you no longer have the option of inserting blank lines between bulleted or numbered paragraphs by pressing Enter. You solve that problem by temporarily setting the spacing between paragraphs to 2 by choosing Fo**r**mat, P**a**ragraph, **F**ormat and changing **S**pacing Between Paragraphs to 2.

See the next section for another way to automatically add blank lines between bulleted or numbered paragraphs.

To terminate the automatic numbering of paragraphs if you have checked **N**ew Bullet or Number on ENTER, choose **I**nsert, Bullets & **N**umbers. The Bullets & Numbers dialog box appears. Select `<None>` in the **S**tyles list box. Choose OK. The previously generated bullet or number disappears.

Modifying Bullets & Numbers

The simplicity of Bullets & Numbers is that it has only a few options. However, you can make a variety of modifications to the results of using Bullets & Numbers by using the two following general techniques:

- Because bulleted or numbered paragraphs are paragraphs, you can use any applicable WordPerfect layout technique to modify their look. For example, the previous section used paragraph formatting to change the spacing between bulleted or numbered paragraphs. You also can choose Fo**r**mat, P**a**ragraph, **F**ormat and modify the **L**eft Margin Adjustment to indent lists.

- You can edit the styles that Bullets & Numbers invoke. See the section "Editing and Creating Outline Styles" later in this chapter for the general techniques.

Caution

When you edit a Bullets & Numbers style, you are editing the style in your document's template, not in the document itself. Thus you are affecting future documents, not just the current one.

As an example of editing a Bullets & Numbers style, you can add a blank line after a numbered paragraph by following these steps:

1. Move your insertion point to the left margin of the line in which you want to create the numbered list.

2. Choose **I**nsert, Bullets & **N**umbers. The Bullets & Numbers dialog box appears.
3. Highlight Numbers and choose **E**dit. The Styles Editor dialog box appears.
4. Check the Show '**O**ff Codes' box. Move the insertion point after the codes in the **C**ontents field. Press Shift+Enter to insert a Hard Return code. Choose OK.

> **Note**
>
> Shift+Enter is necessary to insert a Hard Return code because just pressing Enter chooses OK.

5. Look at the value in the Starting Value field. If it is not 1, check the Starting **V**alue check box and enter **1** in the field. Choose OK. WordPerfect returns to your open document with the insertion point ready for you to enter text.
6. Type your text and press Enter.

Troubleshooting

I chose a bullet or number in the Bullets & Numbers dialog box; now every time I press the Enter key, WordPerfect inserts another bullet or number.

The **N**ew Bullet or Number on ENTER option in the Bullets & Numbers dialog box has been selected. To insert just one bullet or number (pressing Enter starts a new line, without a number), choose **I**nsert, Bullets & **N**umbers, then remove the check mark beside the **N**ew Bullet or Number on ENTER option.

I selected a number style in the Bullets & Numbers dialog box, but WordPerfect won't let me specify a paragraph number level.

Only one of the number styles in the Bullets & Numbers dialog box supports paragraph number levels. In the Bullets & Numbers dialog box, choose the Paragraph Numbers style. You can set an initial paragraph level in the **P**aragraph Level box. Once the number has been inserted in the document, you can alter the paragraph level by pressing Tab to decrease the level, and Shift+Tab to increase the level.

Introducing the Vocabulary of Outlines

There are two ideas at the heart of outlining:

- Information is presented hierarchically, meaning that a general idea is presented first, and then a related, more specific idea is indented under the first idea. Ideas on the same level, therefore, have the same amount of indentation from the left margin.

- Information at a given level of the outline looks similar to information at the same level elsewhere in the outline.

In WordPerfect, an *outline* is a series of paragraphs, called outline items, in which each paragraph has an optional *number*, an indentation level that is the same as the text's logical level in the hierarchy, and text. You can think of the number as a counter; you can format it to look like an Arabic numeral, a Roman numeral, an uppercase or lowercase letter, a bullet, and more.

Tip
Where a tab or indent positions text depends on how you set up your tab settings (see Chapter 4, "Formatting Text").

For many styles of outline, the indentation level corresponds directly to the number of tabs or indents that separate the beginning of the indented text from the left margin. In the Paragraph outline style, for example, the Level 1 number is at the left margin, and the text is preceded by one indent. The Level 2 number is preceded by one indent and the text by two indents (see fig. 15.4).

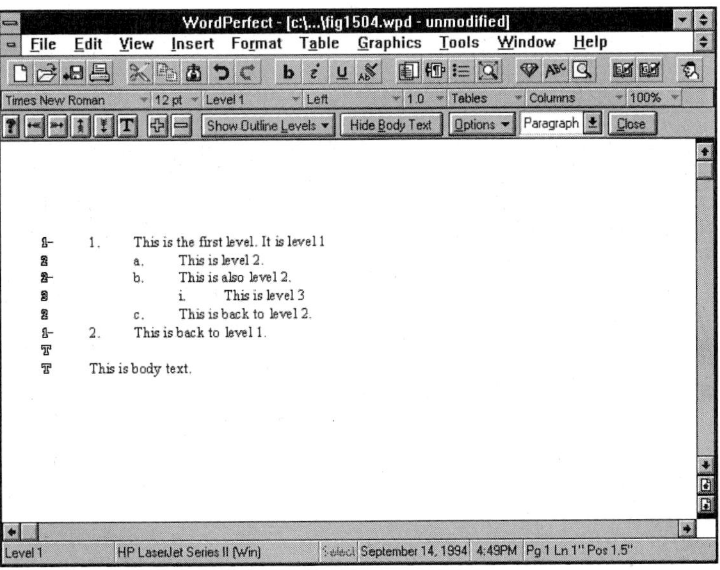

Fig. 15.4
A Paragraph style outline. The text for each item describes that item.

◀ See "Setting and Using Tabs," p. 141

Note

Although Tab and Indent both move the insertion point to the next tab stop, they are different. Indent causes second and subsequent lines to be aligned directly under the beginning of the first line, Tab does not. You must use the correct one immediately before entering text.

The following terms are related to WordPerfect's outlining feature:

- *Outline item.* A paragraph of an outline.
- *Body text.* A paragraph within an outline that does not have a number and may not have the same level of indentation as pieces of the outline that surround it. With WordPerfect, you can easily change normal text into a part of an outline and back again.
- *Family.* A group of related material consisting of all the numbered paragraphs and body text that are indented directly underneath the first item of that group. With WordPerfect, you can easily renumber, show, move, and delete families.
- *Outline mode.* A state in which you have access to the Outline Feature Bar, visual indications of the level of each outline item and whether some outline items are hidden, and support for selecting and moving outline families. Outline mode is entered by selecting **T**ools, **O**utline. Figure 15.4 shows Outline mode.
- *Outline Feature Bar.* A WordPerfect-defined set of buttons that makes it easy to define an outline and to manipulate its structure. The Outline Feature Bar automatically appears near the top of your screen when you enter Outline mode. Unlike a Toolbar, you cannot modify it. Figure 15.4 shows the Outline Feature Bar just above the text.
- *Outline style.* A group of styles, each of which uniquely defines the appearance of the number and text for each level of the outline. WordPerfect provides several predefined outline styles that you can use, modify, or refer to as examples of how to use many of outlining's features; for example, Paragraph, Headings, and Outline.

Introducing the Outline Feature Bar and Outline Toolbar

The *Outline Feature Bar* provides keyboard and one-button access to many of outline's capabilities and is the gateway to all of outline's functionality. Choose **T**ools, **O**utline, click on the Outline button, or double-click on the Status Bar Outline On/Off item to display the Outline Feature Bar (see fig. 15.5). It is used constantly when you create and manipulate outlines.

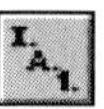

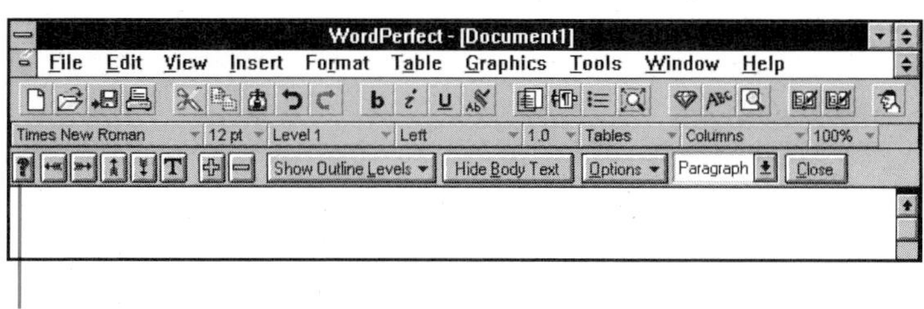

Fig. 15.5
The Outline Feature Bar provides keyboard and one-button access to many of outline's capabilities.

Table 15.1 describes the individual buttons on the Outline Feature Bar.

Table 15.1 Summary of the Outline Feature Bar

Icon	Keystroke	Function
	Alt+Shift+F10	Allows access to other feature bars, provides menu access to Outline Feature Bar functionality, lists the Outline Feature Bar keystrokes, and provides access to Help.
	Alt+Shift+P	Decreases the outline item's level by one. This is the equivalent of pressing Shift+Tab. (Decreasing an item's level may cause its formatting to change; for example, the form of its number and indentation from the left margin.)
	Alt+Shift+N	Increases the outline item's level by one. This is the equivalent of pressing Tab. (Increasing an item's level may cause its formatting to change; for example, the form of its number and indentation from the left margin.)

(continues)

Table 15.1 Continued

Icon	Keystroke	Function
	Alt+Shift+M	Moves the outline item or selection up one item without changing its level.
	Alt+Shift+W	Moves the outline item or selection down one item without changing its level.
T	Alt+Shift+T	Changes an outline item to body text that starts at the left margin or changes body text to an outline item.
	Alt+Shift+S	Shows/redisplays the collapsed family under the current outline item.
	Alt+Shift+I	Hides/collapses the family under the current outline item.
Show Outline Levels	Alt+Shift+L	Hides or shows levels 1 through 8.
Hide Body Text	Alt+Shift+B	Hides or shows body text.
Options	Alt+Shift+0	Displays the Outline Options menu, which allows you to change or define the current outline type, end the outline, and change the outline level and current paragraph number.
Paragraph	Alt+Shift+D	Defines the outline styles for each level of the outline.
Close	Alt+Shift+C	Removes the Outline Feature Bar from the window.

Tip

To add an Outline button to a toolbar, choose **E**dit from the Toolbar QuickMenu. Choose Tools in the F**e**ature Categories field, and select an Outline item in the **F**eatures field.

Rather than trying to define, in a rather abstract fashion, what each Outline Feature Bar button and pull-down menu does, the following sections simply use them in concrete examples.

Creating an Outline

The general steps for creating an outline using one of the built-in WordPerfect outline styles are as follows:

1. Move your insertion point to the left margin of the line in which you want to create the outline.

2. If the Outline Feature Bar is not already visible, choose **T**ools, **O**utline. The Outline Feature Bar appears, a level 1 outline item is created in your document, and the insertion point is placed so you can enter your text.

   If the style of the inserted outline item is not the one you wanted, choose **O**ptions, **D**efine Outline; or press Shift+Ctrl+O. The Outline Define dialog box appears. Highlight the outline style you want and choose OK or press Enter.

   or

   If the Outline Feature Bar is already visible, choose **O**ptions, **D**efine Outline; or press Alt+Shift+O. The Outline Define dialog box appears. Highlight the outline style you want, check S**t**art New Outline, and choose OK or press Enter. An outline item is created and the insertion point is placed so you can enter your text.

3. Type the text; then press Enter. The insertion point is automatically positioned at the same level to enter the text for the next item.

4. To enter text for a lower level, before you enter any text, press Tab; or choose **O**ptions, **C**hange Level. Enter the desired level into the Outline **L**evel field of the Change Outline Level dialog box. Each Tab increments the current level by one (and probably indents your text to the next tab stop, although whether that happens depends on the style of outline you are using). If you increment the level too many times, you can decrease the level by pressing Shift+Tab; or by choosing **O**ptions, **C**hange Level and entering the desired level into the Outline Level field.

5. If you want body text in an outline, click on the Outline Feature Bar's body text button, or press Ctrl+H any time before pressing Enter to end your text.

   If you want the body text to look like an unnumbered paragraph of an outline item, you should Indent (F7) or Tab at the left margin of the body text to align it with the outline item. Use Indent if the outline item's text is indented with an Indent and use Tab if the text is indented with a Tab.

6. After entering the last item's text, choose **O**ptions, **E**nd Outline.

Tip

If you want to insert a blank line between outline items, press Enter a second time immediately after entering an item's text.

Table 15.2 summarizes the keystrokes that have special meaning within an outline.

Table 15.2 Special Keystrokes for Creating and Editing Outlines

Keystroke	Function
Enter	When pressed following text, Enter ends the outline item. When pressed twice, Enter inserts a blank line between outline items.
Tab	When Tab is the first character of an outline item, it increases the item's level (which frequently increases the item's indentation and changes the format of its number).
Shift+Tab	When Shift+Tab is the first character of an outline item, it decreases the item's level (which frequently decreases the item's indentation and changes the format of its number).
Ctrl+H	Changes an outline item to body text that starts at the left margin or changes body text to an outline item. If the Outline Feature Bar is visible, you can also use Alt+Shift+T to toggle between outline text and body text.

Creating Numbered and Bulleted Lists

A list is really an outline with one level. You can easily create lists by using WordPerfect's built-in outline styles.

To create an unindented, numbered list, such as the one shown in figure 15.6, complete the following steps:

1. Move the insertion point to the left margin of the line in which you want to create the outline.

2. If the Outline Feature Bar is not already visible, choose **T**ools, **O**utline. The Outline Feature Bar appears, and an outline item for the default outline style is inserted into your document.

   Choose **O**ptions, **D**efine Outline. The Outline Define dialog box appears. Highlight Paragraph, and then choose OK or press Enter.

   or

   If the Outline Feature Bar is already visible, choose **O**ptions, **D**efine Outline. The Outline Define dialog box appears. Select Paragraph, select the S**t**art New Outline check box, and then choose OK or press Enter.

3. After entering each item's text, press Enter. The next number is automatically generated.

4. After entering the last item's text, choose **O**ptions, **E**nd Outline rather than pressing Enter.

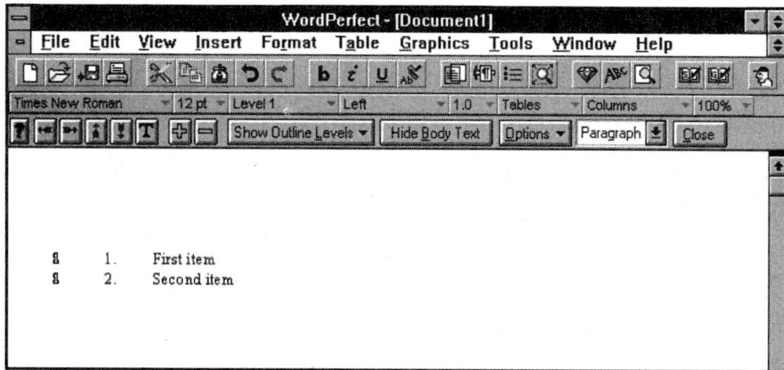

Fig. 15.6 A simple unindented, numbered list created using the WordPerfect-supplied Paragraph outline style.

To create an unindented bulleted list, as shown in figure 15.7, follow the same procedure to create an unindented numbered list, except highlight Bullets instead of Paragraph in step 2.

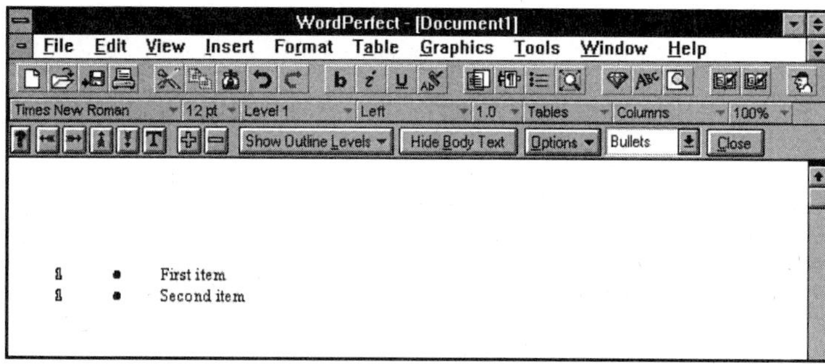

Fig. 15.7 A simple unindented, bulleted list created using the WordPerfect-supplied Bullets outline style.

If you want to use a different bullet than the WordPerfect default, see the section "Creating Your Own Bulleted List" later in this chapter.

Creating Incrementing Numbers in Normal Text

To create incrementing numbers within a paragraph, complete the following steps:

1. Enter the text that comes before the first incremented number.

2. If the Outline Feature Bar is not already visible, choose **T**ools, **O**utline. The Outline Feature Bar appears.

3. Choose **O**ptions, **D**efine Outline. The Outline Define dialog box appears.

4. Highlight Numbers; then choose OK or press Enter.

5. Choose **O**ptions, **C**hange Level. Accept the Outline **L**evel field default of 1 by choosing OK or pressing Enter; or enter your own value into the Outline **L**evel field, and then choose OK or press Enter.

6. Enter the text that comes after the incremented number.

7. Repeat step 5 when you need an incremented number.

You can change the style of the numbers—for example, from 1 to "(1)"—by editing the format of the numbers used by the Numbers outline style or by creating your own outline style (see the section "Editing and Creating Outline Styles" later in this chapter).

Displaying and Editing an Outline

Long and complicated outlines can be annoying to work with because their length or depth makes it difficult to see only the part in which you are currently interested. Several options available on the Outline Feature Bar control what portion of an outline is displayed. Using the Outline Feature Bar, you can:

- Hide/collapse individual families under their first outline item
- Hide all outline items of a specified level and their families
- Hide the entire outline excluding body text
- Hide only body text

You can mix these options. For example, you can hide all Level 3 outline items, and then collapse one or more individual Level 1 items. Figure 15.8 is an example of the hiding and showing techniques that follow.

Hiding and Showing Families and Levels

Sometimes it is advantageous to hide parts of an outline while working on other parts. WordPerfect lets you hide entire outline families, body text, or the entire outline.

Hiding an Outline Family

To hide an outline family—that is, to collapse the family so only its first level item is visible—place the insertion point in the first level of the family and choose the Outline Feature Bar's Hide Family button, or press Alt+Shift+I.

You also can move the cursor to the left of the first level of the family, until the cursor changes to a vertical, double-headed arrow; then double-click the primary mouse button.

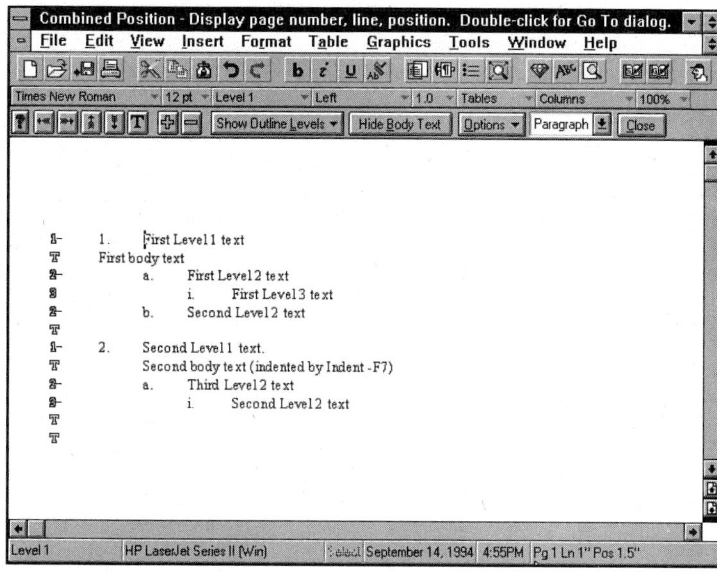

Fig. 15.8
The complete outline used in the hiding and showing examples.

Figure 15.9 shows the result of collapsing the first Level 1 family and the vertical, double-headed arrow cursor.

Showing a Hidden Outline Family

To show/redisplay a collapsed outline family, place the insertion point in the visible outline item and choose the Outline Feature Bar's Show Family button, or press Alt+Shift+S. You also can move the cursor to the left of the visible outline item until the cursor changes to a vertical, double-headed arrow; then double-click the primary mouse button.

Hiding All Outline Families under a Specified Level

To hide all the outline families under a specified level for the entire outline, place the insertion point in the outline and choose the Show Outline Levels button. Choose the lowest number that you still want shown. All levels underneath your specified level (that is, all the families of your specified level) are hidden. Figure 15.10 shows the result of showing only Level 1 for the outline in figure 15.8.

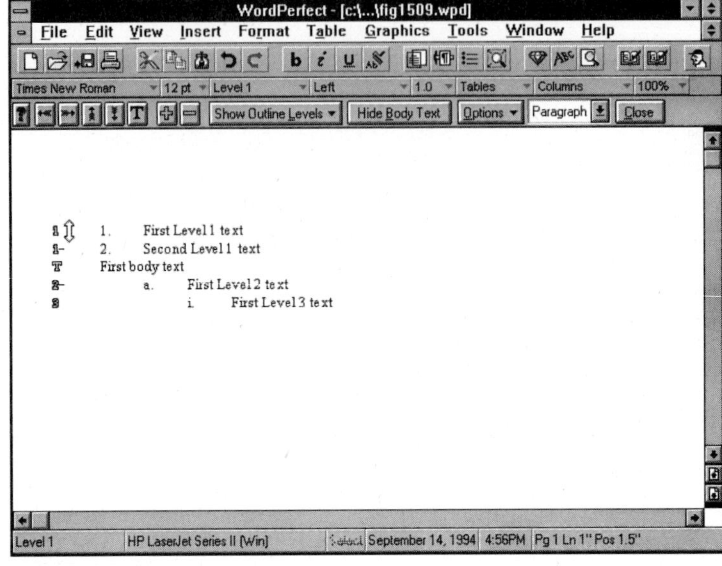

Fig. 15.9 Hiding the first Level 1 family shown in figure 15.8. The minus sign to the left of the first level 1 indicates hidden members of that outline family.

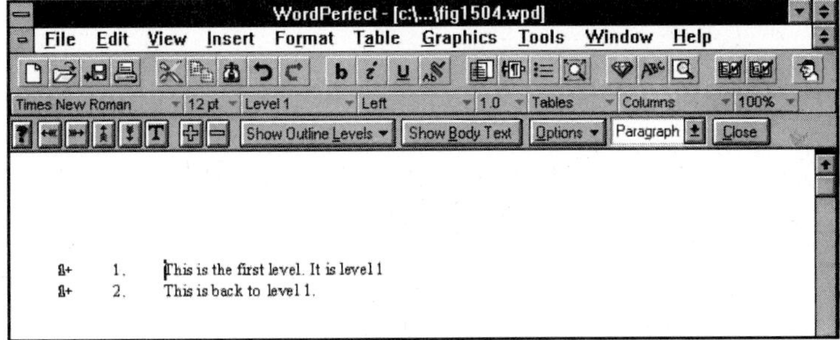

Fig. 15.10 The result of showing only Level 1 of the outline shown in figure 15.8.

Showing All Hidden Outline Families

To show/redisplay all the hidden levels of an outline, place the insertion point in a visible outline item and choose the Feature Bar's Show Outline **L**evels button; then choose 8 (all levels).

Hiding Body Text

To hide an outline's body text, as in figure 15.11, place the insertion point in the outline and choose the Outline Feature Bar's Show Outline **L**evels 8 button, or press Alt+Shift+B, then 8.

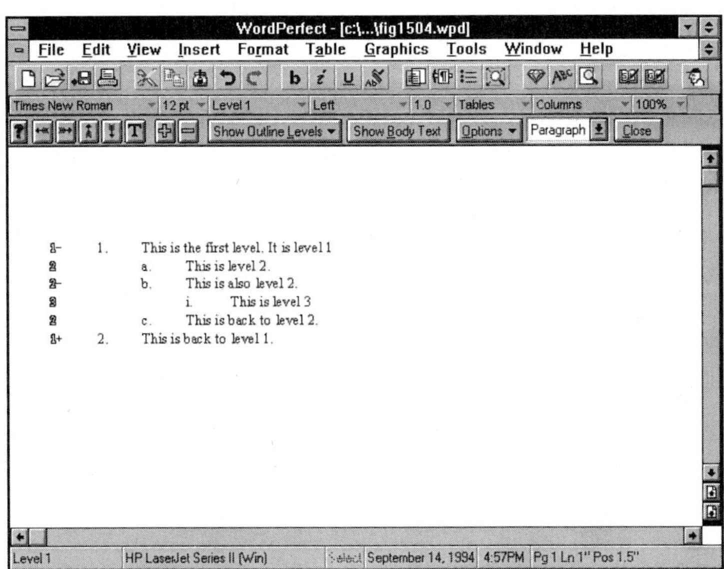

Fig. 15.11 The result of hiding body text of the outline shown in figure 15.8.

Showing Hidden Body Text

Because body text is an integral part of an outline level, the only way to show/redisplay hidden body text is to show the level that contains it. For example, to show all of the body text in an outline, put the insertion point in the outline and choose the Outline Feature Bar's Show All button, or press Alt+Shift+S.

Editing Outline Text

Because outline items are just normal text with an outline style applied to them, you edit text in outline items just as you do any other text.

Modifying an Outline's Structure

Modifying an outline's structure refers to renumbering and rearranging an outline's individual items and its families, rather than changing the text in an item. Although you can manipulate an outline by cutting and pasting the outline's text and hidden codes, doing so is very difficult because selection of normal text does not pick up the hidden codes that describe an outline's structure. Working around that by using the Reveal Codes display or by using the left margin's QuickMenu to select paragraphs is tedious, at best. However, when the Outline Feature Bar is visible, it is easy to select families for copying, deleting, and cutting, and it is especially easy to move a family without worrying about hidden codes. Of course, WordPerfect automatically adjusts the numbering of the outline to reflect each change made.

Adjusting Levels

To increase the level of an outline item by one, position the insertion point anywhere in the item and click on the Outline Feature Bar's Next Level button, or press Alt+Shift+N. If the insertion point is positioned just in front of an outline item's text, you also can press Tab.

To decrease the level by one, position the insertion point anywhere in the item and click on the Outline Feature Bar's Previous Level button, or press Alt+Shift+P. If the insertion point is positioned just in front of an outline item's text, you also can press Shift+Tab (Back Tab).

To increase or decrease several levels at once, position the insertion point anywhere in the outline item and choose **O**ptions, **C**hange Level.

Changing to and from Body Text

Tip
You can use Ctrl+H to change to or from body text if the Outline Feature Bar is not active.

To change an outline item to body text, place the insertion point anywhere in the outline item you want to change and click the Outline Feature Bar's Change to Body Text button, or press Alt+Shift+T. The text is placed at the left margin. You may want to adjust its indentation using Tab or Indent (F7).

To change body text to an outline item, place the cursor anywhere in the body text you want to change and click the Outline Feature Bar's Change to Body Text button, or press Alt+Shift+T. The text is given the next number at the same level as the outline item that immediately precedes the text. You may want to adjust the level.

Moving, Copying, Cutting, Deleting, and Pasting Families

To cut, copy, or delete an outline family, select the family and then use normal WordPerfect techniques to perform the cut, copy, or delete. Selecting a family is easiest if the Outline Feature Bar is visible. Then you can move the cursor to the left of the top item of an outline family, until the cursor becomes a double-headed arrow; then click to select the entire family. Two ways to access cut, copy, and delete are to hold down the secondary mouse button to get a QuickMenu that contains **C**ut, C**o**py, and **D**elete (see fig. 15.12), or press Ctrl+X, Ctrl+C, or Delete.

Tip
If you delete something accidentally, immediately choose **E**dit, **U**ndo, or press Ctrl+Z, to restore it.

To move a family within an outline, complete the following steps:

1. If the Outline Feature Bar is not visible, choose **T**ools, **O**utline.

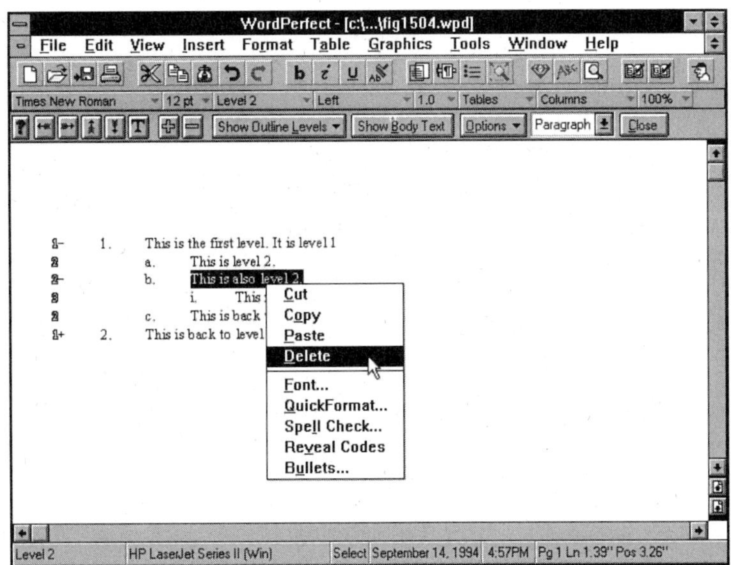

Fig. 15.12
Ready to delete the highlighted outline family using a QuickMenu.

2. Move the cursor near the outline level number in the left margin, across from the top item of the family that you want to move. It will change to a double-headed arrow. Hold down the primary mouse button to select the family.

3. While continuing to hold down the primary mouse button, move the cursor in the direction in which you want to move the family. A thin horizontal line will appear. Continue to hold down the primary mouse button and move the cursor until the thin horizontal line is where you want the family to be positioned (see fig. 15.13). Release the primary mouse button.

To move only the first item of a family requires selecting just the paragraph that is the outline item, and doing a normal cut and paste. Getting the selection just right may require turning on Reveal Codes by choosing **V**iew, Reveal **C**odes.

To move a family or an individual item between outlines, you must cut and paste.

Move, Copy, and Cut place the family into the paste buffer. To insert the paste buffer into your document, place the insertion point where you want the paste buffer to be inserted, and choose **E**dit, **P**aste; or choose **P**aste from the QuickMenu. Alternatively, press Ctrl+V.

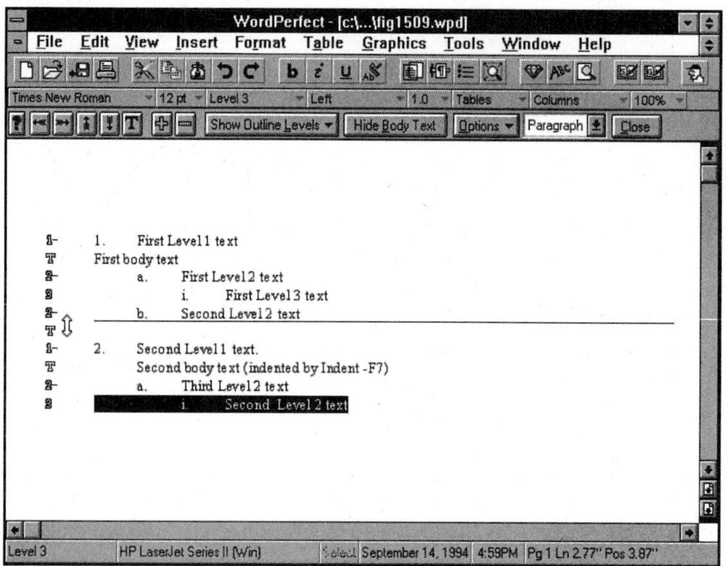

Fig. 15.13
Ready to move the highlighted outline family to the position of the thin horizontal line.

> **Note**
>
> The paste buffer is not cleared when you insert from it, so you can place multiple copies of an outline family into your document by copying the family to the paste buffer and inserting multiple times.

Renumbering an Outline

The values of outline numbers are normally automatically maintained by WordPerfect. You can, however, force an outline item to have a particular number and force succeeding outline numbers to start from particular numbers by doing the following:

1. Place the insertion point anywhere in the outline item whose number you want to change.

2. If the Outline Feature Bar is not visible, choose **T**ools, **O**utline.

3. Choose **O**ptions, **S**et Number. Enter the number you want in the Set Paragraph Number dialog box, and choose OK or press Enter.

The number you enter has a special format because it specifies values for all the levels, not just the one you want to change. Setting the paragraph number gives you complete control over the automatically generated outline numbers that follow your set paragraph number. The format of the number is Arabic numerals or a question mark separated by commas, spaces, or periods. The value of the first number specifies the value for the current Level 1; the value of the second number specifies the value for the current Level 2; and so on. A question mark means that the current value should not be changed. Figure 15.14 shows an outline and how it changes after setting several paragraph numbers.

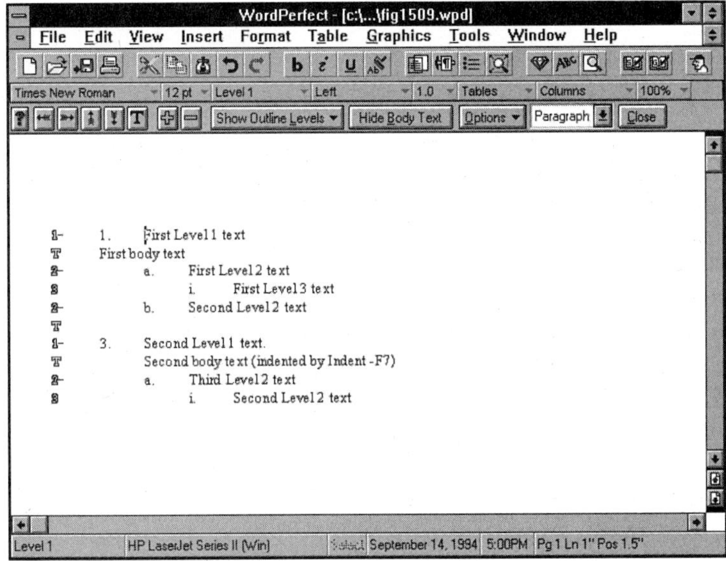

Fig. 15.14
You can control the value of an outline item's number by changing paragraph numbers for one or more levels.

Changing an Outline's Style

To change an outline's style, follow these steps:

1. Place the insertion point anywhere in the outline.

2. If the Outline Feature Bar is not visible, choose **T**ools, **O**utline.

3. Pull down the outline styles menu and select the new outline style. Alternatively, you can press Shift+Ctrl+O, and then make your choice from the Outline Define dialog box.

Troubleshooting

I don't see the outline numbers and symbols that are supposed to appear on the left side of the document window.

The outline numbers and symbols only appear when WordPerfect is in outline mode. To change to outline mode, choose **T**ools, **O**utline. The outline numbers and symbols will appear along the left edge of the document window, and the Outline Feature Bar will appear along the top of the document window.

I don't see all the levels in my outline.

One or more levels have been hidden. Levels can be hidden when WordPerfect is in regular editing mode or in outline mode. If the Outline Feature Bar is not already visible, choose **T**ools, **O**utline to switch to outline mode. Choose Show Outline **L**evels (or press Alt+Shift+L). Choose **8** to see all levels.

I want to insert a bulleted item in my numbered outline, but when I change to the bullet style, my entire outline changes from numbered to bullet format.

WordPerfect is working as designed. The easiest way to insert a bulleted item in a numbered outline is to insert a new line where you want the bullet to appear. Change the format to body text. Then choose **I**nsert, Bullets & **N**umbers. Find the bullet style you want to use, and choose OK.

Introducing Outline Styles

The preceding sections have shown what can be done with WordPerfect's predefined outline styles. Understanding outline styles reveals how predefined outlines accomplish what they do and allows you to create outlines to fit your needs. Ultimately, styles enable outlines to escape the rigid box of numbers and indentation levels to become simply a systematic way of controlling the look of your document.

The following sections assume that you already understand what styles are and how to use them in general (see Chapter 10, "Using Styles"). They concentrate on how you access outline styles, how styles relate to the basic pieces of an outline, and how to create several popular types of outlines.

A fundamental idea of WordPerfect is that every paragraph has a style associated with it that determines the paragraph's formatting. When you begin an outline, you are simply saying that each succeeding paragraph is formatted according to an outline style. Depending on how the outline style is defined, it may or may not display a number, and it may or may not indent the paragraph.

Although most outlines have numbers and step-like indentation, you will not have discovered the full power of outlines until you realize that WordPerfect outlines do not have to have numbers and indentation. The WordPerfect Headers outline style is a good example. Take a detailed look at it by bringing up the Outline Define dialog box, choosing **E**dit, and then backing out by pressing Esc.

The following examples generally assume that you have chosen **O**ptions, **S**etup from the Outline Define dialog box and checked the S**y**stem Definitions box so that you can see the predefined WordPerfect outline styles.

Using the Define Outline Dialog Box

The Outline Define dialog box (see fig. 15.15) is the place from which to start manipulating outline styles.

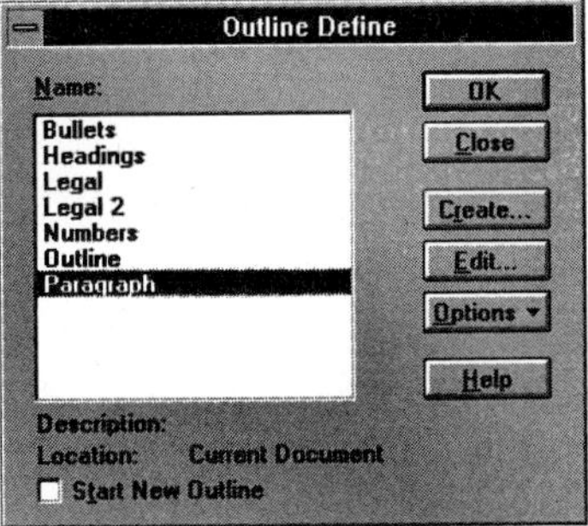

Fig. 15.15 The Outline Define dialog box showing the system definitions. Use this to start an outline or to create, modify, or copy an existing outline style.

To access this dialog box, do one of the following:

- Press Alt+Shift+O.
- If the Outline Feature Bar is not visible, Choose **T**ools, **O**utline. Then choose **O**ptions, **D**efine Outline.
- Click on the OutlineDef button on a toolbar—for example, the WordPerfect-supplied Outline Toolbar.

- Using the secondary mouse button, choose **O**utline from the left margin's QuickMenu.

Table 15.3 summarizes the controls in the Outline Define dialog box, many of which are discussed more fully in other sections.

Table 15.3 Controls in the Outline Define Dialog Box

Control	Function
OK	The highlighted style becomes the default. This is the equivalent of double-clicking on a listed style. To generate a number in your document you should check Start New Outline before choosing OK, or do a Change Level afterward.
Create	Begins the process of creating your own outline style. You specify its name. WordPerfect specifies its initial attributes. You edit the attributes to your specifications.
Edit	Begins the process of modifying the highlighted style.
Options	Presents a pop-up list of Setup, Copy, Delete, Reset, Retrieve, and Save As. *Setup.* Allows you to specify the sources for outline styles (the current document, the default template, or the supplemental template) and the type of outlines you want displayed. *Copy.* Allows you to copy and rename the highlighted outline style to the current document, the template, or the supplemental template. You can then edit it to your specifications. *Delete.* Deletes the highlighted outline style. You cannot delete one of the WordPerfect-supplied system definitions. *Reset.* Restores an edited WordPerfect-supplied system definition to its unmodified state. You cannot reset an outline style you create. *Retrieve.* Retrieves user and/or system outline styles from a file. *Save As.* Copies all the user or system outline styles, or both, to a file.
Start New Outline	If this is checked when OK is chosen, the highlighted style becomes the default and an outline level is inserted into your document to start the outline. If this is not checked when OK is chosen, the highlighted style simply becomes the default. Because of Autocode, this can affect outline items in front of the insertion point.

Editing and Creating Outline Styles

◀ See "Outline Styles," p. 361

Creating an outline style gives you complete flexibility in specifying every aspect of a style. Editing an outline style lets you modify every aspect of an existing style. Copying an existing style that does almost what you want, and then editing the copy, allows you to create a new outline style without having to specify every aspect of the style.

◀ See "Editing Styles," p. 367

To edit an outline style, complete the following steps:

1. From the Outline Define dialog box, highlight the style you want to edit.

2. Choose **E**dit. The Edit Outline Definition dialog box appears (see fig. 15.16).

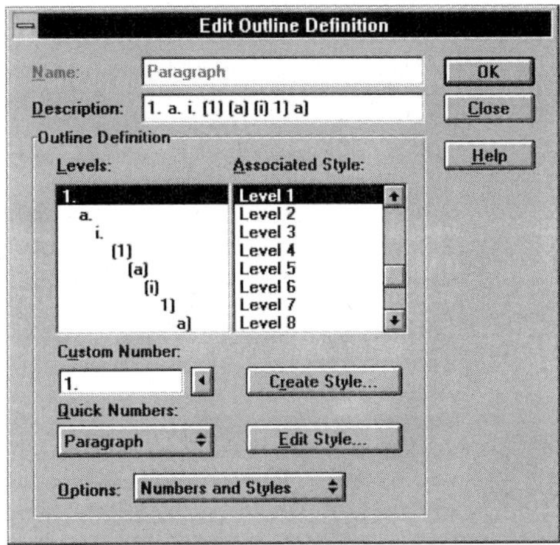

Fig. 15.16
The Edit Outline Definition dialog box showing the system Paragraph style. From here, you can modify every aspect of an outline style.

3. Work your way through the Edit Outline Definition dialog box, making appropriate choices. (See table 15.4 for the editing operations of this dialog box.) Then choose OK.

   Modifications to an outline style in the current document do not affect other documents. Modifications made to an outline style in the template or supplemental template file affect future documents. However, you can always reset system styles to their unmodified state.

Tip
You can back out of any part of a dialog box without making a change by pressing Esc.

4. If desired, copy the modified style to a template or a supplemental template.

Table 15.4 Items in the Edit Outline Definition Dialog Box

Item	Function
Name	Identifies the outline style. Editing this field renames the style. If the selected style is predefined by WordPerfect, this option is grayed so you cannot edit it. (However, you can rename an outline style when you copy it.)
Description	Allows you to enter the text you want displayed in the Description field for the style in the Outline Define dialog box.
Levels	Shows the number for each level. Clicking on a number highlights the associated style in the Associated Style field.
C**u**stom Number	Allows you to enter the format of the number you want for the highlighted level in Levels. In general, what you enter will appear literally in your document. However, the pop-up list allows you to insert six special characters and four bullet characters. The special characters have the following meanings: *1*—Numbers (for example, 1, 2, and 10) *A*—Uppercase ASCII letters (for example, A, B, and Z) *a*—Lowercase ASCII letters (for example, a, b, and z) *I*—Uppercase Roman numerals (for example, I, II, and X) *i*—Lowercase Roman numerals (for example, i, ii, and x) *0*—Numbers with leading zeroes (for example, 01, 02, and so on) The bullets are *Bullet* (WordPerfect character set 4, character 0), *Hollow Bullet* (4,1), *Square Bullet* (4,2), and *Small Bullet* (4,3). By pressing Ctrl+W, you can pop up the WordPerfect Characters dialog box, so you can insert any WordPerfect character into Custom Number. Whether a number is displayed depends on whether the corresponding level style includes `[Para Num]` and `[Para Num Disp]` hidden codes.
Quick Numbers	Allows you to choose **P**aragraph, **O**utline, **L**egal, or **B**ullets to set all eight entries of the Levels item to predefined values. Choosing **U**ser defined allows you to modify the first Levels entry by editing the Custom Number field.
Associated Style	When a Level *N* outline item is created, the style specified by the *Nth* entry of Associated Style is applied to the paragraph. To associate an Associated Style with a level, highlight the level in the Levels field, highlight the desired style in Associated Levels, and then choose OK.
C**r**eate Style	Brings up a Styles Editor dialog box in which you can begin defining a new style from scratch. The Styles Editor dialog box is explained in Chapter 10.

Item	Function
Edit Style	Brings up a Styles Editor dialog box in which you can begin modifying the style that is highlighted in Associated Style. The Styles Editor dialog box is explained in Chapter 10. When you modify a style, you are affecting all the documents that use that style.
Options	Controls which of the preceding fields are active. Choosing **N**umbers Only deactivates **A**ssociated Style, C**r**eate Style, and **E**dit Style. Choose this when you do not want the creation of an outline item to change the formatting of the paragraph. This allows you to embed a series of numbers that WordPerfect manages into a paragraph. (For example: I want (a) some candy and (b) a toothbrush.) Choosing **S**tyles Only deactivates Custom Number and Quick Numbers and clears Levels. Choosing Numbers **a**nd Styles activates all the fields.

Tip

The styles are also visible in the Style List dialog box when you choose Fo**r**mat, **S**tyles; or press Alt+F8 when you are back in your document.

Note

Your printer may not be able to print all the characters you want to use as bullets, or you may not like how it prints them. Before using bullets, therefore, print a test document that uses all the bullet characters at all the point sizes you will use.

To create your own outline style, perform either of the following series of steps:

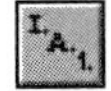

1. From the Outline Define dialog box, highlight the style that is closest to what you want. Choose **O**ptions, **C**opy. The Outline Definition Copy dialog box appears.

2. Choose the destination of the copy (**C**urrent Document, **T**emplate, or **A**dditional Objects Template) and choose OK or press Enter. The Outline Definition Duplicate dialog box appears.

3. Enter a name for your copy and choose OK, or press Enter.

4. Highlight the newly named style in the Outline Define dialog box. Choose **E**dit, and edit the style following table 15.4. Choose OK.

5. If desired, copy the style to a template.

Alternatively, perform the following steps:

1. From the Outline Define dialog box, choose C**r**eate. The Edit Outline Definition dialog box appears.

2. Type the name of the new style and fill in the other fields by following table 15.4. Choose OK.

3. If desired, copy the style to a template.

Creating Your Own Bulleted List

You can either modify the predefined WordPerfect Bullets style or create a new one. This section illustrates how to modify the WordPerfect style. The next section illustrates how to create a new style.

1. From the Outline Definition dialog box, highlight the Bullets style, and choose **E**dit.

2. In the Edit Outline Definition dialog box, choose **L**evels and then highlight the bullet that you want to change.

3. Choose C**u**stom Number. Enter the new character by typing it or by using the WordPerfect Characters dialog box.

Creating an Outline that Uses Tabs and Not Indents

The predefined WordPerfect outline styles use indents to produce outline text that aligns to the right of an outline number. For example, the first item in a Paragraph style looks like the following:

■ This line of text is long

 enough to wrap to two lines.

You may prefer a style that produces text like:

■ This line of text is long

enough to wrap to two lines.

The following steps create a new style that is a modification of the predefined WordPerfect Paragraph outline style. The basic idea is to replace the style's indents with tabs.

1. From the Outline Edit dialog box, highlight the Paragraph style; then choose **O**ptions, **C**opy.

2. In the Outline Definition Copy dialog box, choose **C**urrent **D**ocument, and then choose OK or press Enter.

3. In the Outline Definition Duplicate dialog box, name the copy ParaTab, and then choose OK or press Enter.

4. In the Outline Define dialog box, highlight ParaTab; then choose **E**dit. 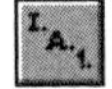

5. In the Edit Outline Definition dialog box's **A**ssociated Style field, choose Level 1; then choose **E**dit Style.

6. In the Styles Editor dialog box's **C**ontents field, place the insertion point to the right of the rightmost `[Hd Left Ind]`. Press Backspace. Choose Fo**r**mat, **L**ine, **O**ther Codes to access the Other Codes dialog box. Choose **L**eft and then **I**nsert to insert a `[Hd Left Tab]`. Choose OK or press Enter to return to the Edit Outline Definition dialog box.

7. Repeat steps 5 and 6 for Levels 2 through 8. In the Edit Outline Definition dialog box, choose OK or press Enter; then in the Outline Define dialog box, choose **C**lose.

Exploring Outline Styles

This section briefly presents two concepts for creating outline styles.

In standard outline styles, the numbering for levels within a family resets whenever a new family begins. However, you might want an outline where the numbering is consecutive, like the following sections:

I. First Chapter

  1. A Section

  2. Another Section

II. Second Chapter

  3. Yet Another Section

You can accomplish this by explicitly setting each level's first number, but that loses the flexibility of having WordPerfect renumber the outline if you modify it. It is better to edit an outline style by using a counter that is incremented independently of the outline numbers, and then to display the counter as part of a level style.

Bullets do not have to be characters. You can use a wide variety of graphics as bullets by putting them into custom graphic boxes with which you replace the bullet characters in level styles.

Saving Your Styles

If you create an outline style that you find useful, you may want to save it so you can reuse it in another document. WordPerfect provides two methods for doing this. From the Outline Define dialog box, you can choose **O**ptions, **C**opy to copy an individual outline style to the document, the template file, or the supplemental template file (if you have one assigned). You also can choose **O**ptions, Save **A**s to copy all the outline styles to a file, from which you can later retrieve them as a unit by choosing **O**ptions, R**e**trieve.

From Here...

For more information on modifying and organizing your documents, see the following chapters in this book:

- Chapter 3, "Retrieving and Editing Documents," provides the basics on using the editing tools to change the text in a document, including cutting and pasting.
- Chapter 10, "Using Styles," shows you how styles work, and how they are used to control the appearance of bulleted and numbered lists and outlines.
- Chapter 26, "Assembling Document References," shows you how to prepare references within a document to create a table of contents, index, list, cross-reference, or table of authorities.

Chapter 16

Working with Tables

by Read Gilgen

16

Of all WordPerfect's special features, the Tables feature offers more practical uses and enables you to enhance the effectiveness and attractiveness of your documents more than any other feature. That statement is a bold one, but as you learn in this chapter, it is easily substantiated.

In this chapter, you learn how to do the following:

- Create tables consisting of any number of rows and columns
- Enter text and move around in a table
- Add and delete cells, rows, and columns
- Modify the table structure by joining and splitting cells and changing column widths

Understanding Tables

Just what is a table? Although people use the term in many different contexts, in WordPerfect a table consists of rows and columns of data arranged and formatted to make the data easy to read or understand. For example, consider the following list:

Item	**Part#**	**Bin#**
Widget	34-222	24-A
Gadget	33-245	26-B
Doodad	33-249	13-F

In the past, most word processing programs could format this list only by separating the columns with tabs and by using underlining and different fonts to make the information easier to follow. Not only are such lists boring, but as you read them, you can easily lose your place, especially if the lists are wide and contain many details.

On the other hand, consider the same list as a printed WordPerfect 6 table (see fig. 16.1). Already you can see a difference—the program separates the items clearly, and the entire table is neat and attractive.

Fig. 16.1
An example of a WordPerfect table.

Item	Part#	Bin#
Widget	34-222	24-A
Gadget	33-245	26-B
Doodad	33-249	13-F

The structure of a table is very much like the structure of a spreadsheet, and in fact, you can even use WordPerfect tables for spreadsheet functions (see Chapter 30, "Advanced Tables"). In a table, WordPerfect labels the rows with numbers (1, 2, 3...) and the columns with letters (A, B, C...). The intersection of a column and a row is a *cell*. You identify each cell according to the row and column in which it resides (A1, B3, C14, and so on). In figure 16.1, for example, the word *Widget* is in the first column (A) and the second row (2); therefore, *Widget* is in cell A2.

All other table features are options. For example, you can change the lines that WordPerfect uses to separate table cells, or you can omit them altogether. You can change text justification, and you can add text attributes such as boldface or italic. You can adjust the width and height of any column or row. You can even create formulas to calculate numeric information.

Using WordPerfect's table formatting options, you can create any kind of table—from simple lists to complex invoices, from schedules to calendars, from programs to scripts, and more.

In this chapter, you first learn how to create and modify a table using a sample invoice as a model (see fig. 16.2). You learn how to enter text into tables, change the table structure, format table text, and convert existing data into a table format. Designing, creating, and modifying a table is a visual and artistic venture. Although this chapter describes how to obtain certain results when creating a table, you have your own needs and opinions of what looks good. Don't be afraid to experiment.

Badger Tours, Inc.
1234 Rose Bowl Avenue
Madison, WI 53700
(608) 555-4321

December 1, 1994

Quantity	Description	Unit Cost	Amount
2 ea	Deluxe Tour Packages	834.00	$1,668.00
2 ea	Tickets in End Zone	63.50	$127.00
1 ea	Rose Bowl Football (autographed)	75.00	$75.00
			$0.00
Comments: Deposit must be received 14 days prior to departure. Thank you for your business.		Subtotal	$1,870.00
		Tax (5.5%)	$102.85
		TOTAL	**$1,972.85**

Fig. 16.2
An invoice created with WordPerfect's Table feature.

Before you actually create a table, you can save a great deal of time by doing some preliminary planning. First, ask yourself what you want to accomplish with your table. Do you merely want to present straightforward information more clearly, or do you want to design a more complex, heavily formatted form?

Next, determine the approximate number of rows and columns you want. You can have up to 64 columns and 32,767 rows (or 2,097,088 cells), although it's unlikely you'll ever use that many. You do not need to know the exact number of rows or columns because you can add or insert them while you work with your table. Knowing this information in advance, however—especially the number of columns—can make creating, modifying, and using your table much easier.

You also can benefit from determining and selecting the font style and size you want to use before you begin. Again, this is not critical because you can change fonts as you work with your table.

Finally, consider the number and placement of your tables. You may need to place two tables of dissimilar structure one after the other, rather than trying to create just one table. Also, you may need to place two tables beside each other, in which case you may want to use columns or graphics boxes (see Chapter 14, "Working with Text Columns" or Chapter 21, "Using Advanced Graphics Techniques," for information on table boxes).

Creating and Using Tables: The Basics

▶ See "Using Basic Math and Formulas in Tables," p. 1039

Even in their simplest form, tables are easy to create and can be quite effective. Mastering the basic procedures described in this section is important. The more complex procedures, explained later in this chapter and in Chapter 30, "Advanced Tables," build on what you learn here.

◀ See "Parallel Columns," p. 485

▶ See "Customizing Graphics Boxes," p. 719

Creating a Table

At least two different methods of creating a table are available. You can use WordPerfect's menu system to specify the number of rows and columns you want in the table. Or you can use the mouse to choose the table size you want from the Power Bar.

To use the menus to create a table, follow these steps:

1. Position the insertion point in your document where you want to insert the table.

2. Select T**a**ble, **C**reate; or press F12. WordPerfect displays the Create Table dialog box which prompts you to specify the number of columns and rows you want in your table (see fig. 16.3).

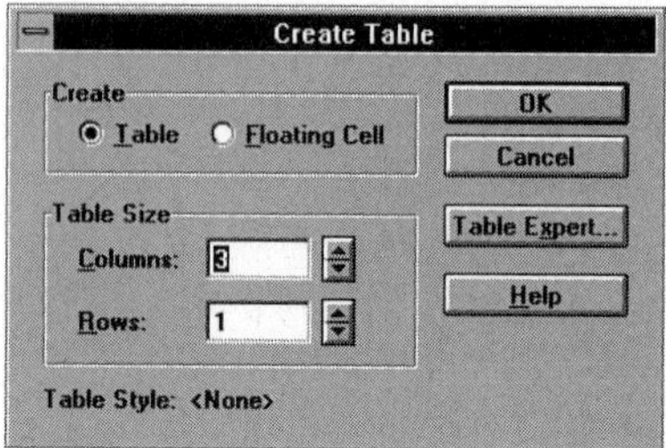

Fig. 16.3
The Create Table dialog box lets you specify the number of columns and rows you want in your table.

3. In the **C**olumns text box, type the number of columns you want (for example, **4**).

4. In the **R**ows text box, type the number of rows you want (for example, **5**). Choose OK or press Enter to display the table you have defined.

If you specify four columns and five rows, WordPerfect displays the table shown in figure 16.4.

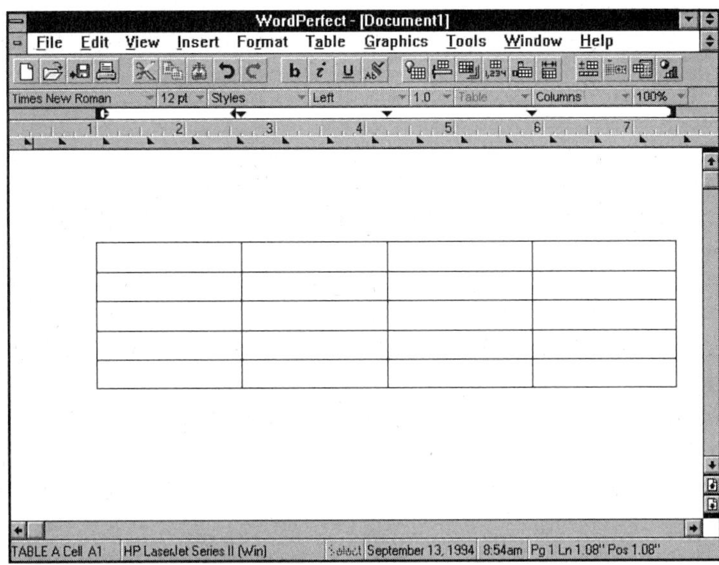

Fig. 16.4
A simple table with four columns and five rows. Notice that the columns are evenly spaced and extend from margin to margin, and the Toolbar now shows table-specific functions.

By default, all the cells in a WordPerfect table are surrounded by single lines, and the table has no border.

To use the Power Bar to create a table, follow these steps:

1. If the Power Bar isn't already displayed, select **V**iew, P**o**wer Bar.

   WordPerfect displays several buttons on the Power Bar. One of the default buttons is the Tables button, located between the Spacing (1.0) and Columns buttons (see fig. 16.5).

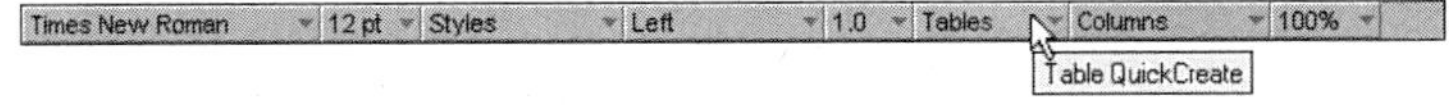

Fig. 16.5
The Power Bar includes the Tables button.

2. Position the insertion point in your document where you want to insert your table.

3. Click the Tables button, and hold down the mouse button to display a large grid.

4. Drag the mouse down and to the right until the pop-up grid highlights the number of columns and rows you want (see fig. 16.6). If you need more columns or rows than is displayed on the grid, keep dragging the mouse; WordPerfect expands the grid up to 32 columns by 45 rows. At the top of the grid, WordPerfect specifies the number of columns and rows, in that order, that you have selected (`4 x 5`, in this example).

Fig. 16.6
The Table button pop-up grid. Click the button and drag the mouse to select the number of rows and columns you want in your table.

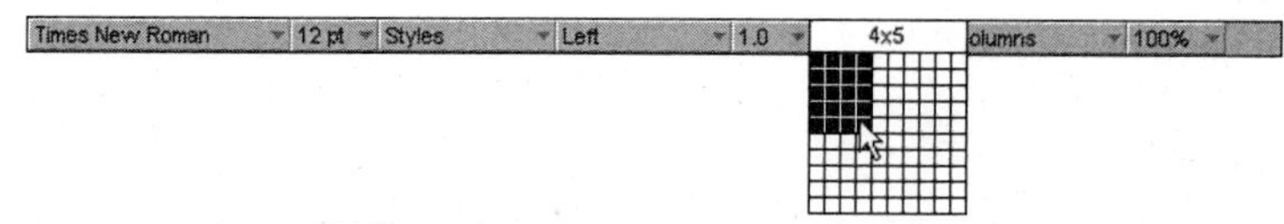

5. After you have displayed the number of columns and rows you want, release the mouse button. WordPerfect creates the table according to the size you indicated.

Tip
If you decide not to create a table, simply drag the mouse pointer to the top of the grid and when `No Table` appears, release the mouse button.

Converting Tabular Columns to Tables

You may have existing text you want to place in a table, and you don't want to retype the text. Fortunately, WordPerfect provides a simple method for creating a table from text that is formatted in tabular columns. In fact, this capability may be the easiest, yet most practical use for tables you will have.

Suppose that you have a list of company employees that includes their names, offices, and telephone numbers. The columns of data are separated by single tabs (see fig. 16.7).

Fig. 16.7
A list formatted in tabular columns.

Jones, Mary	VH246	3-2435
Tishler, Bob	VH295	3-2555
Hytry, Terry	VH390	3-5454

To convert data in tabular columns to a table, follow these steps:

1. Position the cursor at the beginning of the first line of data. Using the employee list as an example, place the cursor just before the letter J in `Jones`.

2. With the mouse or keyboard, select all the text to the end of the last line of data—for example, just after the 4 in `3-5454`. Don't include the final hard return, or you end up with an extra row in your table.

3. Choose T**a**ble, **C**reate; or press F12. WordPerfect displays the Convert Table dialog box (see fig. 16.8).

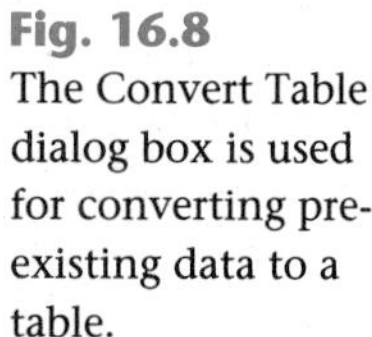

Fig. 16.8
The Convert Table dialog box is used for converting pre-existing data to a table.

4. Choose **T**abular Column (the default), and choose OK. WordPerfect converts your tabular columns of data into a table (see fig. 16.9).

Jones, Mary	VH246	3-2435
Tishler, Bob	VH295	3-2555
Hytry, Terry	VH390	3-5454

Fig. 16.9
A table converted from tabular columns.

This procedure seems quite easy because it *is* easy; however, the key to successfully converting tabular columns to a table lies in the format of the original text. Make sure that each column is correctly aligned by a tab setting. Also, make sure that only one tab separates each column of data. If, for example, you use WordPerfect's default half-inch tab settings and use two tabs to separate the office numbers from the short employee names and only one tab to separate the office numbers from the long names, WordPerfect adds extra cells in the table for the blank tabs. Consequently, the result can be quite messy.

After you convert your data to a table, you can use the procedures learned earlier to change column widths, modify column and cell attributes, and use line and fill options to format your table.

Moving within a Table

When you first create a table, WordPerfect positions the cursor at the upper-left corner of the table, in cell A1. Notice that the status bar, at the bottom of the screen, displays the name of the current Table (`Table A` in this case) and the cell location of the cursor, `Cell A1`. When you move the cursor to a new cell, WordPerfect indicates on the status bar the location of the new cell.

To move the cursor one cell to the right, press the Tab key. The status bar now indicates that the cursor is in cell B1. To move the cursor one cell to the left, press Shift+Tab. If the cursor is in the rightmost column, pressing Tab moves the cursor back to column A and down to the next row. Pressing Shift+Tab while the cursor is in the first column moves the cursor to the rightmost column and up one row.

Sometimes using the mouse to position the cursor in the cell is a quicker and easier way to move from one cell to another. If you are typing, however, using the Tab key usually is easier. You also can use the arrow keys to move from one cell to another. If the cells are filled with text or numbers, however, using the Tab key or mouse generally is easier. Using the Tab key, the mouse, or the arrow keys to move within a table provides the same results. Choose the method which is easiest and most efficient for you.

Entering Text

When you enter text into your table, think of each cell as a miniature document with its own margins and formatting. As you enter text, WordPerfect wraps the words within the cell, vertically expanding the row to accommodate what you type (see fig. 16.10). You can enter and edit text in a cell just as you do in any document.

Fig. 16.10
A table with more than one line of text in a cell. Notice that the row automatically expands to accommodate the text you enter.

Quantity of items Ordered (Units)			

Suppose that you want to create a four-column invoice table in which you list the quantity, description, unit price, and extended cost of various products. You simply move the cursor from cell to cell and type the information you want in each cell.

Note

As you follow the development of the sample invoice table, you may not see explicit instructions to enter text. Nevertheless, when you see new text in the sample figures, enter that text into your own invoice table. Refer to figure 16.2 to see the completed invoice.

Adding Rows to a Table

If you planned your table carefully, you probably have the right number of columns, but even the best planning often cannot predict the number of rows you will need. Fortunately, WordPerfect makes adding extra rows in a table easy.

Suppose that you have filled your entire table and need an additional row at the end. With your cursor in the last cell of the last row (in cell D5, for example), simply press Tab. WordPerfect adds a row and advances the cursor to the first cell of the next row. You now can enter information in the empty cells of your new row. (See the section "Editing the Table Structure" for more information on inserting and deleting rows and columns.)

Selecting Text and Cells

Within a single cell, you select text the same way you do in a document. You can use the mouse to select text, you can hold down the Shift key and use the cursor keys, or you can press Select (F8) and use the cursor keys.

To select text from more than one cell, you must use the Select key (F8). This key allows you to precisely select the text you want. If you use the other methods of selecting, after you cross a cell boundary, WordPerfect begins selecting entire cells. For example, if you click the mouse in the middle of the text in cell A1 and begin dragging the mouse toward cell B1, WordPerfect highlights just the text until the mouse pointer crosses over into cell B1. At that point, the entire cells (A1 and B1) are highlighted and the mouse pointer changes to an arrow (see fig. 16.11). As you continue to drag the mouse to other cells, these cells also become part of a block.

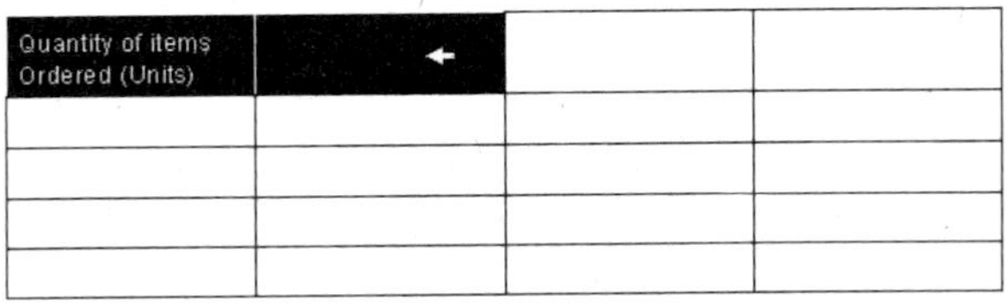

Quantity of items Ordered (Units)	←		

Fig. 16.11 You can select entire cells by dragging the mouse pointer across the edge of the cell until the pointer turns into an arrow. Continue dragging the pointer across cells to select multiple cells at once.

You also can select single cells, rows of cells, columns of cells, and entire tables of cells using this method. To select a single cell, position the mouse pointer within the cell you want to select and move the pointer slowly toward the left line of the cell until the pointer changes to a single arrow. This arrow indicates that you are about to select cells rather than just contents.

Click once to select the cell. Click twice to select the entire row of cells. Click three times to select the entire table.

To select a column, move the pointer toward the top line of any cell in the column until the pointer turns into a single upward-pointing arrow. Click once to select the cell, twice to select the column, and three times to select the entire table.

Deleting Text from Cells

To delete text from a cell, you can position the cursor anywhere in the cell and use Backspace or Del. You also can use Undelete (choose **E**dit, U**n**delete, **R**estore; or press Ctrl+Shift+Z) or Undo (choose **E**dit, **U**ndo; or press Ctrl+Z) to restore deletions made in this manner.

A quicker and easier method for deleting the contents of entire cells is to select the entire cell using the method described in the preceding section. For example, if you want to remove all the text from cell A1 of the invoice table, move the mouse pointer to the left side of the cell. When the pointer turns into a single arrow, click once and then press Backspace or Del; WordPerfect removes the entire contents of the cell.

Note

If you delete the entire contents of a cell, you cannot use Undelete to restore the deleted text. However, you can Undo the action if you do so immediately.

You can use the same method for deleting the contents of an entire row, column, or table. However, because deleting the contents of rows or the entire table can be a bit more destructive, WordPerfect displays a dialog box asking exactly what you want to delete. For example, if you select all of row 1 and press Del or Backspace, the Delete dialog box appears with the **R**ows radio button selected (see fig. 16.12). If you choose OK, you actually remove the entire row from the table. If you first choose the C**e**ll Contents radio button, then choosing OK removes only the contents of that row; the row itself remains.

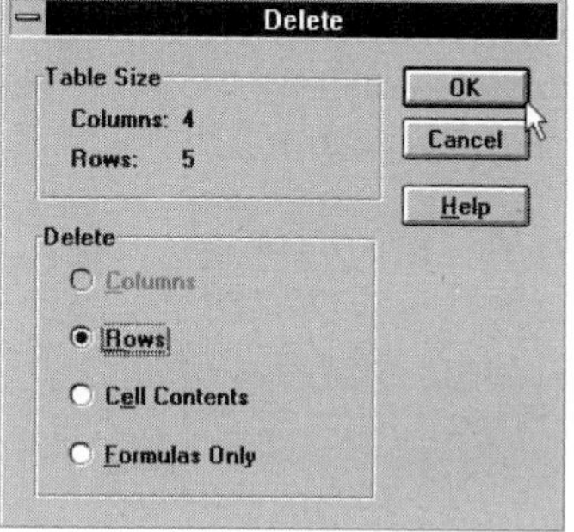

Fig. 16.12
The Delete dialog box enables you to delete the contents of cells or entire rows or columns.

If you select all the cells in the table, WordPerfect displays the Delete Table dialog box (see fig. 16.13), which offers several options:

- **E**ntire Table
- Table **C**ontents
- **F**ormulas Only
- **T**able Structure (leave text)

- C**o**nvert to Merge Data File
- Co**n**vert to Merge Data File (first row becomes field names)

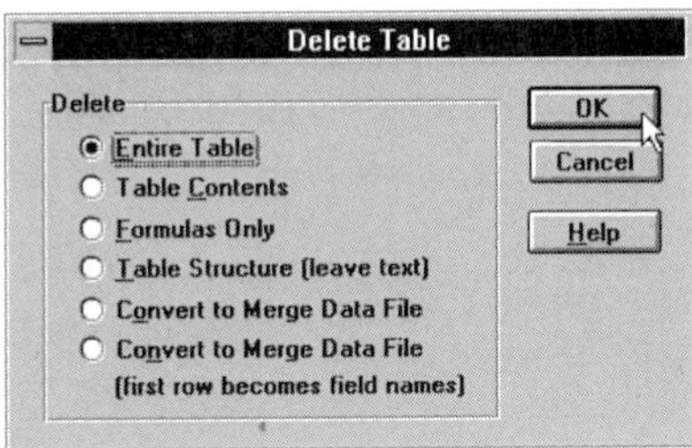

Fig. 16.13
The Delete Table dialog box enables you to delete the entire table, all the data in the table, or convert the table to a merge data file.

Cutting, Copying, and Pasting Text

You can cut, copy, and paste text to and from table cells the same way you do in text documents. Within a single cell, select the text you want to cut or copy, and use any of the various methods for cutting or copying. Then position the cursor in the destination cell and paste the text. You can move text from a cell to the document, from one cell to another, or from the document to a single cell.

By selecting entire cells, you can quickly and easily cut or copy all the text along with its formatting to a new location. For example, suppose that you want to copy all of row 1 to row 2. Select the entire row by dragging the mouse pointer across all the cells or by moving the mouse pointer toward the left edge of the cell. When the single arrow appears, click twice. Then when you choose Cut or Copy, the Table Cut/Copy dialog appears (see fig. 16.14).

Tip
Use Undo (choose **E**dit, **U**ndo; or press Ctrl+Z) if you mistakenly cut or copy the wrong text.

In this dialog box, you can choose to move the current selection (single cell or block of selected cells), the entire row, or the entire column. To cut the entire row, choose the **R**ow radio button, and then choose OK. Position the cursor where you want to paste the row, and choose Paste to paste the contents of the cells you just cut or copied.

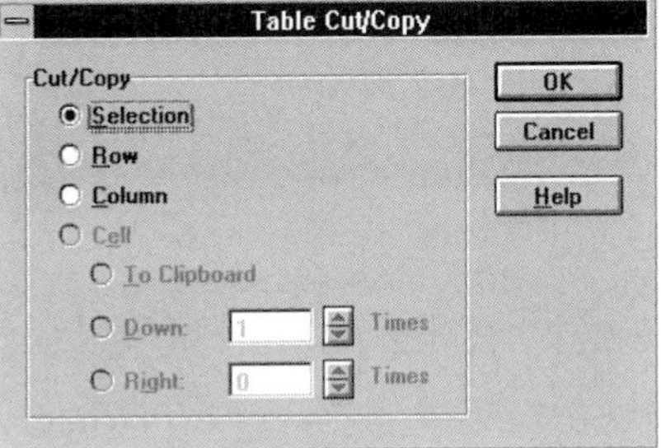

Fig. 16.14
You can use the Table Cut/Copy dialog box to cut and paste entire rows, columns, or groups of cells.

Using the Tables QuickMenu

When the insertion point is positioned inside a table, you can access a QuickMenu that is specific to table operations. All you have to do is click the secondary (right) mouse button. For example, to quickly perform a copy operation, you can select the cells you want to copy, access the QuickMenu by clicking the secondary (right) mouse button (see fig. 16.15), and choose the Cop**y** option from the QuickMenu.

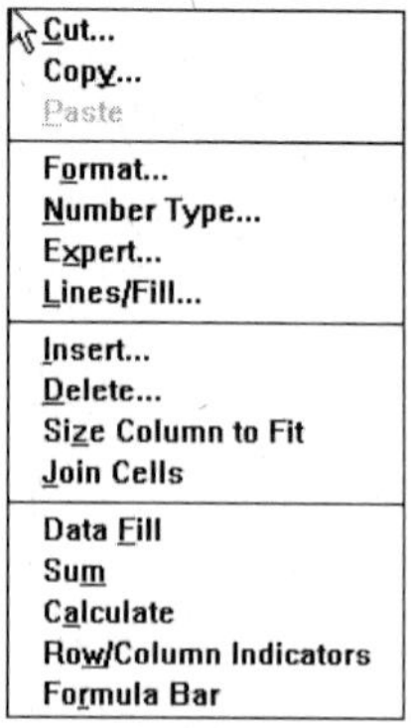

Fig. 16.15
The QuickMenu for working with tables. With the cursor in a table, click the secondary (right) mouse button to access this time-saving menu.

Cut...
Copy...
Paste
Format...
Number Type...
Expert...
Lines/Fill...
Insert...
Delete...
Size Column to Fit
Join Cells
Data Fill
Sum
Calculate
Row/Column Indicators
Formula Bar

Deleting, Cutting, or Copying a Table

To delete, cut, or copy an entire table, including its structure, position the cursor before the table, press Select (F8), and move the cursor to extend the selection beyond the end of the table; then delete, cut, or copy the table.

To restore a deleted table, you can use Undo (Ctrl+Z). If you cut or copied the table, you can paste it in the new location. You also can Undelete the table if you deleted it.

Note

If you select all the cells in a table and press Backspace or Del, WordPerfect offers you the options of deleting the data, the entire table, or converting the data to another format.

Saving and Printing a Table

A table always is part of a document, even when the table is the only element in the document. The procedure for saving tables, therefore, is exactly the same as the method for saving documents (see Chapter 2, "Creating and Saving a Document," for more information).

If you want to save just a part of your table, first select the cells you want to save, and then choose **F**ile, Save **A**s (or press F3). WordPerfect asks if you want to save the **E**ntire File or just the **S**elected Text. If you choose **S**elected Text and provide a file name, WordPerfect saves just the selected cells along with their format and contents. Although you print tables the same way you print other kinds of text, keep in mind the following points:

- WordPerfect never splits table rows with page breaks. The entire last row on a page always prints with a line at the bottom of the row of cells, and the next entire row prints at the top of the next page with a line at the top of the row of cells.
- Table lines print properly, regardless of the font you use or the format of the text and graphics in the cells.
- Because WordPerfect prints table lines graphically, you can print tables on any dot-matrix or laser printer.
- Graphic printing takes longer than regular text printing without graphics. Depending on the printer you use, printing tables can dramatically increase the printing time of your document. On laser printers, tables do not slow printing significantly.
- You can decrease printing time on a slow printer by turning off table lines (see the next section, "Editing the Table Structure"). However, choosing dotted or dashed lines actually increases printing time over solid single or double lines.

Troubleshooting

I'm not too steady with the mouse. When I try to use the Table grid to create a table, I sometimes get the wrong number of rows or columns.

As you practice, you'll get better at choosing just the right size. If you make a mistake, just click the Undo button on the Toolbar (or choose **E**dit, **U**ndo). The table goes away and you can try again.

Sometimes when I try to select cells in a table, the content of those cells ends up in some other part of the table.

You're probably inadvertently using WordPerfect's "drag and drop" feature. After selecting part of the cells you want, you're letting the mouse button go, and then clicking the already selected cells again and dragging to what should have been the last cell in your selection. When you let the mouse button go, the first selection of cells is moved ("dropped") into the new location. If this happens, just click the Undo button on the Toolbar (or choose **E**dit, **U**ndo) and try again.

Editing the Table Structure

Up to this point, you have learned about the default WordPerfect table settings, which include the following:

- Evenly spaced columns and rows that fit neatly between the margins of your document
- No special formatting of the contents of the cells
- Single lines that separate the cells of the table
- No special border around the table
- Left-justified tables (the tables themselves are justified at the left side of the document)

The real beauty of the Table feature, however, is that you can easily make all kinds of adjustments to these default settings. When you make changes to the shape and size of table cells, columns, and rows, you are editing the layout of the table, or the table structure.

Tools for Editing a Table

WordPerfect offers several methods for changing the layout of your table: the menu system, QuickMenu, mouse, Table Toolbar, and Ruler Bar. Indeed, the only difficulty in editing your tables may be choosing which method to use.

Before you can access any of these tools, you must position the cursor somewhere inside the table. You then can access the tools in these different ways:

- Display the Table menu by choosing T**a**ble from the main menu (see fig. 16.16).
- Select the QuickMenu by clicking the secondary (right) mouse button (refer to fig. 16.15 for an example of what the QuickMenu looks like).
- Move the mouse pointer toward the edge of a cell until the pointer turns into a single or double arrow, enabling you to select cells and to move column lines.
- When you create a new table using the default WordPerfect document template, WordPerfect automatically displays the special Table Toolbar which contains several buttons for editing table format and structure. If you use some other template or see another toolbar, you can select the Table Toolbar by choosing **V**iew, **T**oolbar. You then can position the

cursor anywhere on the Toolbar and click the secondary (right) mouse button for a QuickMenu of Toolbars. From here you can choose the Table Toolbar.

- Select the Ruler Bar by choosing **V**iew, **R**uler Bar.

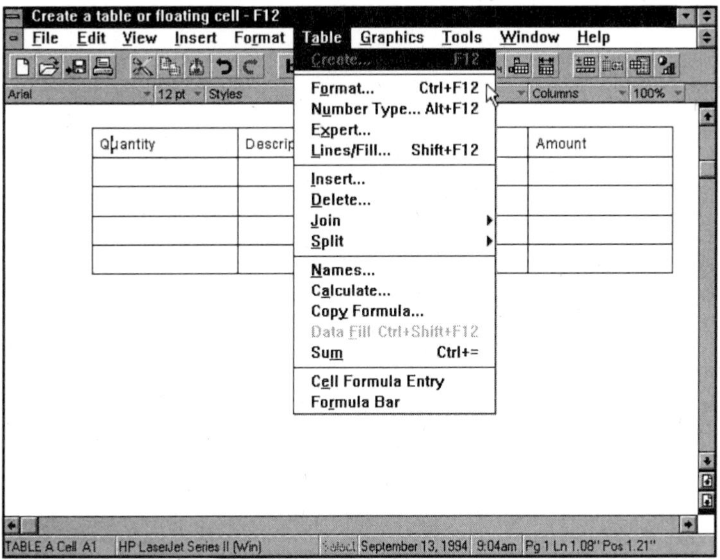

Fig. 16.16
The main WordPerfect Table menu, selected from the Menu Bar.

Although the Table menu is fairly accessible, learning to use these other tools can save you lots of time as you edit and format your tables.

Changing Column Widths

Often, instead of evenly spaced columns, you need a table with columns of unequal width. To change the width of a column quickly, position the mouse pointer directly on the line separating two columns until the pointer changes into a double arrow (see fig. 16.17). When you click and hold down the mouse button, WordPerfect displays a dotted guide that helps you position the new column margin. Notice that the status bar also displays the exact position of the column separator line: `Position: x.xx"`. Simply drag the column divider right or left until you have the desired width.

You can perform this same task by dragging the inverted triangles on the Ruler Bar (see fig. 16.18).

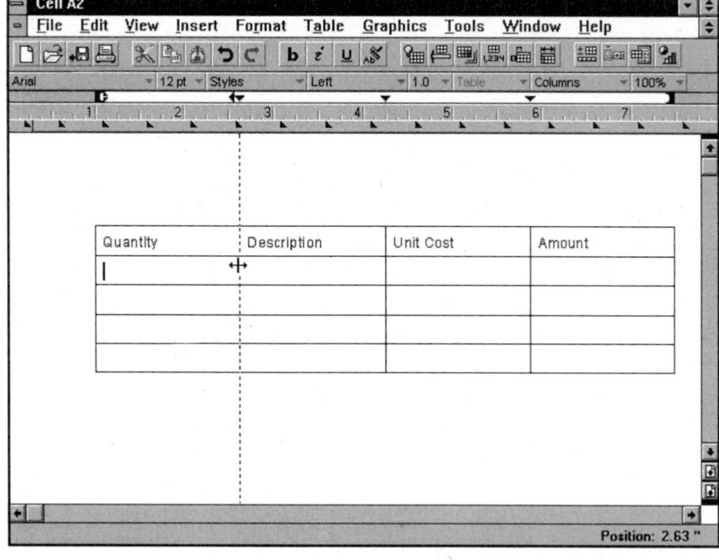

Fig. 16.17 You can change column widths by dragging the column divider with the mouse.

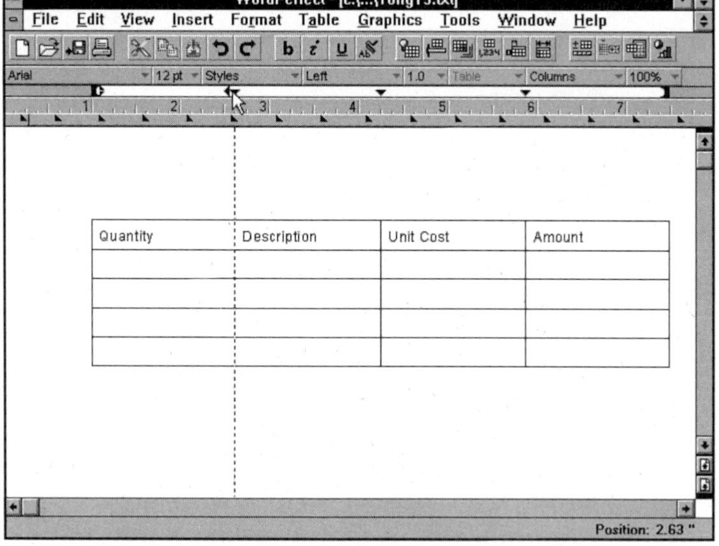

Fig. 16.18 Use the mouse to drag the inverted triangles on the Ruler Bar to size your table columns.

To change column widths proportionally, hold down the Shift key while moving the column separators. In the invoice form, for example, hold down Shift and drag the line between columns B and C to the right until the last two columns are about 1 inch wide. Notice that column A also expanded. Now, without holding down Shift, move the line between columns A and B to the left until column A is about 1 inch wide.

> **Note**
>
> If you prefer to use the keyboard to size your column widths, you can position the cursor in the column you want to change and press Ctrl+, (Ctrl and the comma key) to reduce the width of the column, or press Ctrl+. (Ctrl and the period key) to expand the width of the column.

Tip

You can choose the Format dialog box from the QuickMenu or from the Format Table button on the Toolbar.

Adjusting column width in this manner is not very precise. If you already have text in the columns and can see that the columns are wide enough, or if the measurements don't really matter, this method is adequate.

Sometimes you simply want to be sure that the columns are wide enough to display each cell's information on one line (for example, a list). To adjust a column's width to fit the text in its cells, position the cursor in the column you wish to adjust, click the secondary (right) mouse button, and from the QuickMenu choose Si**z**e Column to Fit. Columns adjusted in this manner expand to the right, thus reducing the width of columns to the right.

If, on the other hand, you want exact column measurements, position the cursor in any cell of the column you want to adjust and select T**a**bles, F**o**rmat. WordPerfect displays the Format dialog box. This is called a *dynamic dialog box*, which means that the bottom portion of the dialog box changes depending on which radio button is selected at the top. Choose the Co**l**umn radio button, and WordPerfect displays the dialog box shown in figure 16.19.

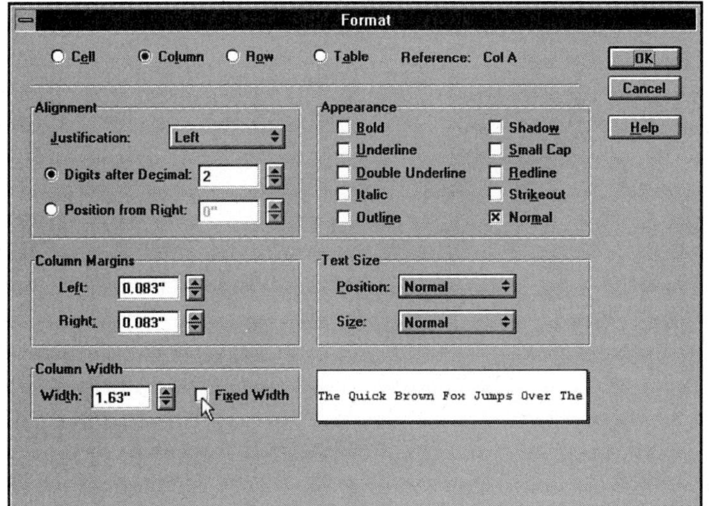

Fig. 16.19
The Format dialog box is used in this case for formatting table columns.

In the lower left corner of the dialog box, choose Wid**t**h and type **1"**. Also, choose the Fi**x**ed Width check box to prevent proportional sizing of columns from affecting this particular column.

For the sample invoice form, type **3.5"** in column B. You then can select both columns C and D, and set both columns to 1" at the same time.

> **Note**
>
> You can specify the column width measurement in decimals (the default unit of measurement) or in fractions of an inch, such as 1 5/16. Other units of measurement include centimeters (2.55cm = one inch), points (72p = one inch), or WordPerfect units (1200w = one inch). WordPerfect automatically converts these measurements into the measurement type you are using as a default.

Changing the Table Size

After you create a table, you often discover that it has too many or too few columns or rows. You learned earlier how to add rows at the end of a table by pressing Tab while in the last cell of the table. You also can insert or delete many rows or columns at one time. For example, suppose that you created an invoice table with five rows, and you now discover that this table must have at least eight rows.

To add three rows to the end of the table, position the cursor in any cell of the last row and choose T**a**ble, **I**nsert. WordPerfect displays the Insert Columns/Rows dialog box (see fig. 16.20).

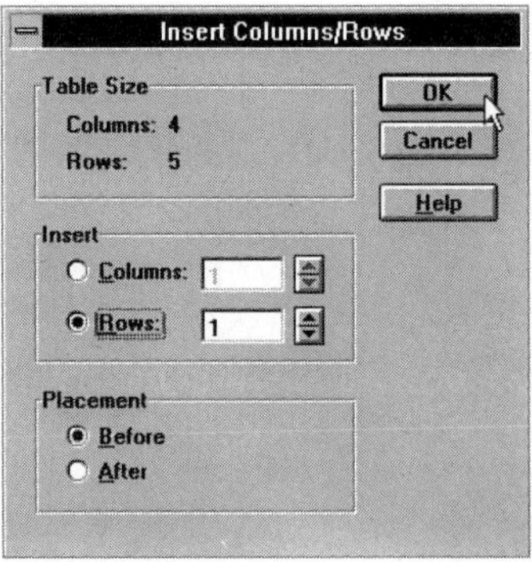

Fig. 16.20
The Insert Columns/Rows dialog box enables you to add rows or columns to your table.

By default, WordPerfect assumes you want to insert a single row preceding the current cursor position. In this case, you want to add three rows after the current cursor position; type **3** in the **R**ows text box, choose the **A**fter radio button, and choose OK.

Choosing **B**efore inserts the specified number of rows or columns at the location of the cursor, pushing the rows down or columns to the right to make room for the new rows or columns. Suppose, for example, that you already typed the column heading information, but now wish to add an extra row for your company name at the beginning of the table. Position the cursor anywhere in the first row and choose **I**nsert from the QuickMenu (or from the T**a**ble menu). From the Insert Columns/Rows dialog box—which by default inserts one row before the cursor—choose OK. WordPerfect inserts a row at the top of the table, and the row that contains Quantity, Description, and so on, becomes the second row.

Tip

You can move an entire row or column by selecting it, choosing **E**dit, Cu**t**, or **E**dit, **C**opy, and then pasting the row or column in the new location.

Note

Be aware that columns or rows you add or insert assume the special formatting attributes—such as lines and text formats—of the column or row that is selected when you choose **I**nsert.

To decrease the size of the table, you can delete rows or columns. Position the cursor in the row or column you wish to delete, and from the T**a**ble or QuickMenu choose **D**elete. Specify the number of columns or rows you wish to delete and choose OK. The Delete dialog box also enables you to delete only the contents of specified rows or columns.

Caution

You cannot use Undelete to restore deleted rows or columns. Instead, if you accidentally remove a row or column, immediately choose **E**dit, **U**ndo (or press Ctrl+Z) to restore that column or row.

Joining Cells

Suppose that you want the row at the top of your invoice to consist of one cell that extends all the way across the top of the table. You want one cell, rather than the four currently displayed, because you need more room to display your company name and logo. WordPerfect enables you to join two or more cells into one. To join the top four cells of the table, follow these steps:

1. Position the cursor in cell A1.
2. Select all the cells in the first row from cell A1 to cell D1.
3. Access the T**a**ble menu or the QuickMenu, and choose **J**oin Cells.

WordPerfect joins the cells, and the first row now consists of one large cell, A1. Cells B1, C1, and D1 no longer exist (see fig. 16.21).

Quantity	Description	Unit Cost	Amount

Fig. 16.21
The invoice table contains several joined cells which become one cell.

You can use this method to join any number of cells in rows, columns, or blocks. Joined cells become one cell, occupying the space formerly occupied by the individual cells. Suppose, for example, that in the lower left corner of your invoice you want a box for comments. Select cells A7, A8, A9, B7, B8, and B9; then use **J**oin Cells to create one large cell for your comments (refer to fig. 16.21). Any text you enter in this cell must fill it entirely before the cell expands.

Splitting Cells

WordPerfect also enables you to split a cell into two or more cells. Suppose that you now want to split the top cell into two cells: a small cell on the left for a graphic of your company's logo, and a longer cell on the right for your company's name and address. Position the cursor in cell A1, and from the T**a**ble menu choose **S**plit, **C**ell, or from the QuickMenu choose **S**plit Cell. WordPerfect displays the Split Cell dialog box (see fig. 16.22).

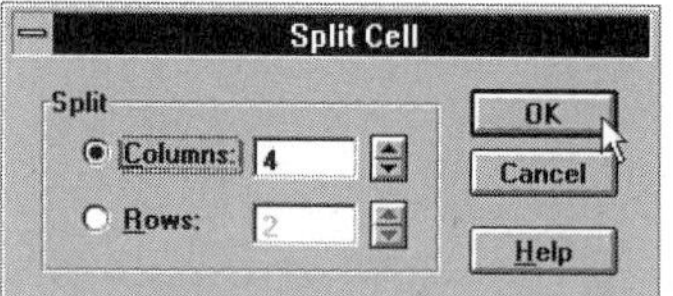

Fig. 16.22
The Split Cell dialog box enables you to split a cell into two or more rows or columns.

Because you want two columns, type **2** in the **C**olumns text box and choose OK. WordPerfect evenly divides the cell into two cells, but the left cell is as wide as columns A and B, and the right cell extends across columns C and D. To get the results you really want—a small cell on the left corresponding to column A and a wide cell on the right extending across columns B, C, and D—follow these steps:

1. Split cell A1 into two cells. WordPerfect now displays three cells in the top row.

2. Join cells B1 and C1. You now have the cells you want in row 1 (see fig. 16.23).

You also can split a cell into two or more rows. Simply position the cursor in the cell, choose **S**plit Cell from the QuickMenu, and in the Split Cell dialog box choose **R**ow and specify the number of rows you want.

Quantity	Description	Unit Cost	Amount

Fig. 16.23
Row 1 is split into a small and a large cell. You may have to split a cell into smaller units and then join cells to create the combination of small and large cells on the same row.

Joining and splitting cells may take some getting used to, but the procedure is easy and the effect can be quite attractive.

Changing Row Height

WordPerfect automatically determines the amount of vertical space in a row, based on the amount of text in its cells. The cell requiring the most vertical space sets the height for the entire row.

Sometimes you need to set a specific row height, either to limit the amount of text you can enter into the row's cells or to make sure that a row contains a minimum amount of space, regardless of whether the cells contain data. A good example of the latter situation is a calendar in which you may want a fixed row height, regardless of the number of events on any given day. (See the sample calendar in the section "Exploring Other Uses for Tables" later in this chapter.)

For the invoice example, you want the top row of your invoice to occupy 2 inches of vertical space, even though the logo and address really need only 1 1/2 inches. To set a specific row height in row 1, follow these steps:

1. Position the cursor in row 1.

2. Choose T**a**ble, F**o**rmat (or choose F**o**rmat from the QuickMenu).

3. From the Format dialog box, choose the R**o**w radio button. WordPerfect displays the options for formatting a row (see fig. 16.24).

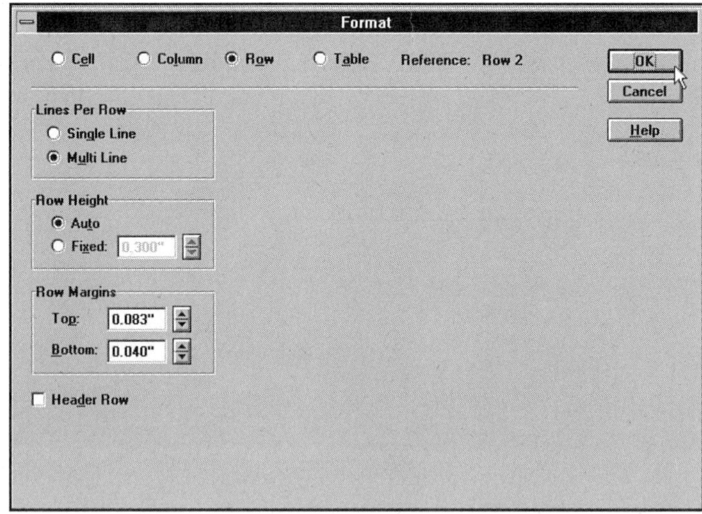

Fig. 16.24
The Format dialog box with the Row radio button selected.

In this dialog box you can select the following combinations of options:

- *Auto Row Height and Multi Line Lines Per Row.* This combination, the default, automatically adjusts the row height to accommodate as many lines as necessary.
- *Fixed Height and Multi Line Lines Per Row.* This combination uses a fixed height and enables you to enter multiple lines, but only up to the specified height. You use this combination, for example, when you create a calendar.

> **Caution**
>
> Make sure that any fixed height you select is high enough to accommodate at least one line of text. Otherwise, text which may appear on-screen will not print.

- *Auto Height and Single Line Lines Per Row.* Choosing this combination automatically adjusts the row height to accommodate a single line of text, regardless of the text's height (font size). If you choose these options and press Enter while entering text in your table, the cursor automatically advances to the next cell.
- *Fixed Height and Single Line Lines Per Row.* This combination maintains a fixed height but enables you to enter only one line of text. The font size for that line of text must be small enough to fit into the specified row height.

4. Because you want a fixed height of 2 inches, select Fi**x**ed and type **2** in the text box. Leave the M**u**lti Line box checked so that you can have as many lines as can fit within 2 inches.

5. Choose OK to set the row height for your first row.

Creating Header Rows

Because tables can consist of up to 32,767 rows, a table may span several pages. If you create a long table, you may want certain information (such as column headings) to repeat at the top of each page. If the table extends to multiple pages, suppose that you don't want the company logo to repeat, but you do want the column heading information to appear at the top of each page. To accomplish this, you specify this row as a *header row*. To create a header row, follow these steps:

1. Position the cursor in the row you want to designate as a header row (for example, row 2).

2. Choose T**a**ble, F**o**rmat, or choose F**o**rmat from the QuickMenu.

3. Choose the R**o**w radio button.

4. Choose the Hea**d**er Row check box so that an X appears.

5. Choose OK.

WordPerfect displays an asterisk next to the cell reference on the status bar (for example, `Cell A2*`) to indicate that the row is a header row.

Note

You don't have to begin with the first row, but if you want more than one header row, the rows you specify must follow one another.

Formatting Table Text

The preceding section focuses primarily on features that help you create the layout, or structure, of a table. You also want to make sure that the text itself contributes to the effectiveness of your presentation. Therefore, you need to understand how text attributes and text alignment apply to table cells.

Understanding Formatting Precedence

Each time you choose a text formatting option, you have to consider whether that attribute should apply to the entire table, to a column, or to a cell or group of cells. Whether an attribute you assign to a table affects a given cell depends on the priority of what you assign. Changes you make to a specific cell or group of cells have precedence, or priority, over changes you make to columns. Changes made to cells or to columns have precedence over changes made to the entire table.

Suppose, for example, that you specify that the data in a single cell should be centered (the heading of a column, for example) and then specify that the data for the entire column should be decimal-aligned. The change made to the column has no effect on the center alignment change you made to the individual cell.

Keep this in mind, especially as you format columns. Any changes to a cell you may have made (and forgotten about) are not changed when you specify something different with Columns or Tables formatting.

Accessing the Format Dialog Box

To format a cell, column, row, or entire table, you can access the Format dialog box in one of three ways: by choosing T**a**ble F**o**rmat from the menu, F**o**rmat from the QuickMenu, or the Table Format button from the Toolbar. WordPerfect displays the Format dialog box (see fig. 16.25).

The dialog box controls at the bottom of this dialog box depend on which radio button is selected at the top. Most of the procedures in the following sections take place in the Format dialog box. From there, simply choose the appropriate radio button for the procedure being discussed (for example, Co**l**umn).

Formatting Columns

To modify the text formatting of all the cells in a column, position the cursor in the column you want to format, access the Format dialog box, and choose Co**l**umn. WordPerfect displays dialog controls for formatting columns (see fig. 16.26).

To format several adjoining columns simultaneously, position the cursor in any cell in the leftmost column of the columns you want to format. Next, select that cell and the cells on the same row in columns to the right that you want to include. Then access the Format dialog box and choose Co**l**umn.

The options in the Appearance section of the Format dialog box enable you to assign the listed attributes to text entered into any of the cells in the column. These options include **B**old, **U**nderline, **I**talic, and so on. You can select any combination of attributes and see what they will look like in the Preview Box in the lower right corner of the dialog box; however, whether these attributes print and how they print depends on your printer and printer drivers.

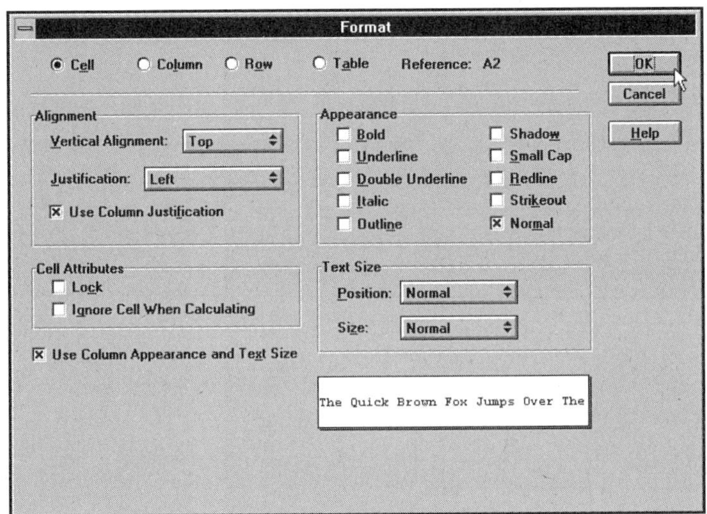

Fig. 16.25
The Format dialog box is a "dynamic" dialog box that changes depending on the radio button you have selected.

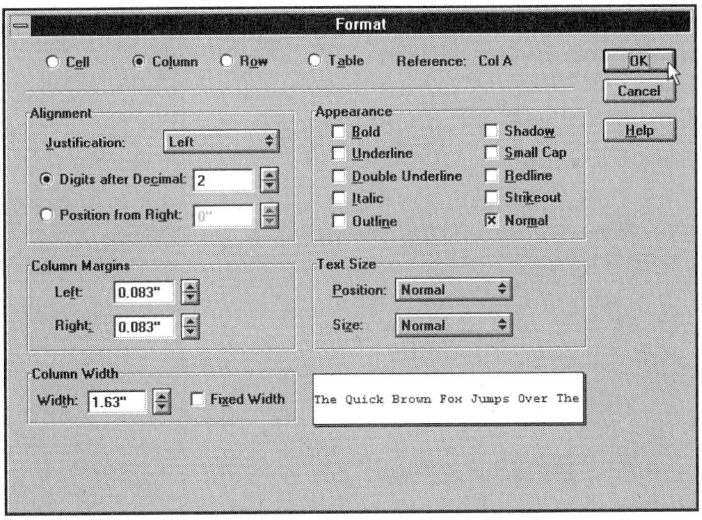

Fig. 16.26
To format columns, use the Column radio button in the Format dialog box.

The options in the Text Size section enable you to specify a variation of the current document font. If your document (table) is formatted in 12-point

Helvetica, for example, selecting Large from the Size pop-up menu may change the type size to 14 points for any text entered into cells in that column. The **P**osition pop-up menu includes Normal, Subscript, and Superscript. For a greater variety of effects, combine Text Size attributes with Appearance attributes.

Perhaps one of the most commonly needed column formats is **J**ustification, found in the Alignment section. Choose from the following options:

- ***L**eft.* Used for most kinds of text.
- ***R**ight.* Used for certain kinds of whole numbers and text headings for columns of right-aligned numbers.
- ***C**enter.* Useful for columns containing data that you will probably scan vertically—columns listing Yes, No, and N/A, for example.
- ***F**ull.* Used sparingly in tables, because text that extends to both margins in relatively narrow columns often has large gaps of white space between words.
- ***A**ll.* Enables you to evenly space letters of a title or heading between both margins. Use this setting as sparingly as you use **F**ull.
- ***D**ecimal Align.* Enables you to align numbers at the decimal point, normally two digits from the right edge of the column. You can specify the actual distance in terms of digits (the default is two) or by a specific measurement.
- ***M**ixed.* If you have selected two or more columns and the justification differs in either column, **M**ixed displays as the default.

Using your invoice as an example, align your columns so that the Quantity column is right-justified and the two Cost columns align at the decimal point. To right-justify the Quantity column, for example, follow these steps:

1. Position the cursor in any cell in column A.
2. Access the Format dialog box and choose Co**l**umn.
3. In the Alignment section of the dialog box choose **J**ustification, **R**ight.
4. Choose OK to right-justify the column.

To align both the cost columns at the decimal point, position the cursor in any cell in column C, and select that cell and the cell to the right in column D. From the Format dialog box, choose Co**l**umn, **J**ustification, **D**ecimal Align to align the two columns at the decimal point.

The column headings now assume the new column alignments, as does the text or numbers you type into any cell in these columns. As you enter text, the program right-justifies the text on the left side of the decimal. As soon as you type a period, WordPerfect left-justifies the text on the right side of the decimal point.

By default, WordPerfect displays decimal-aligned text two digits from the right edge of the cell. To change this setting, in the Format dialog box, select Co**l**umn, Digits after De**c**imal to specify the distance from the right edge of the cell in terms of digits. Notice that this setting does not specify how many digits are displayed after the decimal, but instead how far from the right edge of the cell the decimal will line up. You can specify instead the actual distance from the right edge of the cell by choosing Position from Ri**g**ht and typing the measurement.

In addition to column width, explained earlier in the chapter in the section "Changing Column Widths," you also can specify the left and right text margins for your columns. The default is 0.083" (1/12 inches).

Formatting Cells

After you format a column of cells, you may find that you need to change the justification or attributes of a single cell or group of cells within that column. For example, although the two price columns in your invoice now align text at the decimal point, the headings in those columns would look better if they were right-justified. To right-justify these headings, you need to change the formatting of the two cells containing these headings.

To change the format of a single cell, position the cursor in the cell you want to change, access the Format dialog box, and choose the C**e**ll radio button. WordPerfect displays the controls for formatting cells (refer to fig. 16.25).

To change the format of a group of cells, select the cells you want to change before you choose C**e**ll from the Format dialog box. The changes you choose apply to all the cells you selected.

Note

Although it might seem logical to choose R**o**w to format all the cells in a row, you must select all the cells first and then choose C**e**ll from the Format dialog box to format the row of cells.

To right-justify the column headings in columns C and D of your invoice, first select the two cells, and then from the Format dialog choose C**e**ll, **J**ustification, **R**ight. Then choose OK to apply the change to the two cells.

Many of the options for formatting cells are identical to those used for formatting columns, especially the Appearance, Text Size, and Justification options. Other options used only for formatting cells include:

- *Vertical alignment.* By default, WordPerfect vertically aligns all text in a cell at the **T**op of the cell. Choose **B**ottom or **C**enter to change the vertical alignment of the text in a cell.
- *Use Column Justification* and *Use Column Appearance and Text Size.* By default, each cell assumes the attributes that are in effect for the column in which it resides. Thus, when you first choose the Format (Cell) dialog box, both Use Column options are selected. If you select an attribute, justification, or number type that differs from the column type, WordPerfect deselects the appropriate box. To reassign the column defaults, choose the Use Column Justi**f**ication or Use Column Appearance and Te**x**t Size check boxes. WordPerfect automatically turns off any cell attributes that conflict with the default column formats.
- *Lock.* The lock option protects a cell from being altered.
- *Ignore Cell When Calculating.* If the cell contains numbers that you don't want calculated during a math operation, you can specify that WordPerfect ignore the numbers. (For details on Lock or Ignore When Calculating, see Chapter 30, "Advanced Tables.")

Formatting the Entire Table

► See "Locking Table Cells," p. 1049

Most of the changes you make to tables are to columns and cells. Sometimes, however, you may want to use a certain format as a default for your entire table. When you choose T**a**ble from the Format dialog box, WordPerfect presents the same controls used for columns and cells (see fig. 16.27).

The options you select apply to the entire table, except, of course, in columns or cells you already modified.

Three options that apply only to tables are:

- *Disable Cell Locks.* This option lets you quickly disable any cell locks you may have set. After you finish modifying the locked cells, select this box again to reset the locks.

- *Table Position.* By default, tables are left-justified in your document. This option lets you change the justification of the table itself, not the text in the cells of the table.

- *Auto Row Insert.* Deselect this check box to prevent WordPerfect from adding a new row to the table when you press Tab in the last cell of the table.

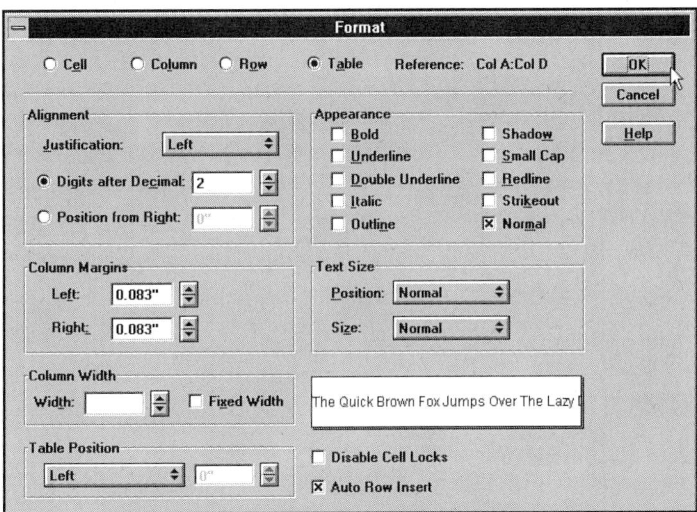

Fig. 16.27
The Format dialog box has the Table radio button selected.

Troubleshooting

I changed the format of my table column to decimal-aligned, but the text still appears left-aligned.

This is an easy mistake to make. When you used the Format dialog box, you probably forgot to choose the Co**l**umn radio button, so all you formatted is a single cell.

To correct the problem, position the cursor in that column again, and then choose F**o**rmat from the QuickMenu. This time, click the Co**l**umn radio button and make the desired changes.

After making format changes to a column, one of the cells doesn't seem to accept the new changes.

This is usually because you formatted a single cell at some point. To make the cell match the rest of the column, position the cursor in that cell, choose F**o**rmat from the QuickMenu, and with the C**e**ll radio button selected, make sure the Use Column Appearance and Te**x**t Size check box is selected.

Changing Table Lines, Borders, and Fills

One part of a table's effectiveness is the lines that help the reader better understand the information. For tables in which a user needs to fill in information, lines also help the user know where to enter appropriate data. By default, WordPerfect surrounds each cell with a single line, giving the appearance that the table also is surrounded by a single line. In fact, there is no border at all around a WordPerfect table. In addition to lines, you also can fill the entire table or individual cells with varying patterns and colors of shading. WordPerfect's lines, borders, and fill options provide nearly limitless control over the appearance of your tables.

Changing Lines

Tip

You can select multiple cells with the mouse by dragging the mouse pointer from one cell to another.

Changing the default single line between cells is simple. You can change to another line style or decide to use no line at all. Suppose, for example, that you want to use a thick line to separate the first row that contains your company address from the body of the invoice. To change the line style, follow these steps:

1. Position your cursor in the cell (or select the group of cells) you want to change. In your invoice table, for example, move to cell A1 and select the entire first row of cells.

2. Choose T**a**ble, **L**ines/Fill. Alternatively, you can press Shift+F12, or you can click the secondary (right) mouse button and choose **L**ines/Fill from the QuickMenu. WordPerfect displays the Table Lines/Fill dialog box (see fig. 16.28).

3. You can choose the line segment you want to change (for example, **B**ottom) from a palette of line styles by choosing that line's line style button. You also can choose from a drop-down list for each line.

4. After choosing each line style you want (for example, Thick), choose OK or press Enter. WordPerfect makes the change to your table.

Note

Depending on the resolution of your computer's monitor or the scale of your document display, single lines may not appear at all, or double lines may appear as a thicker single line. To be sure you have the correct line, you can increase the zoom percentage of your document.

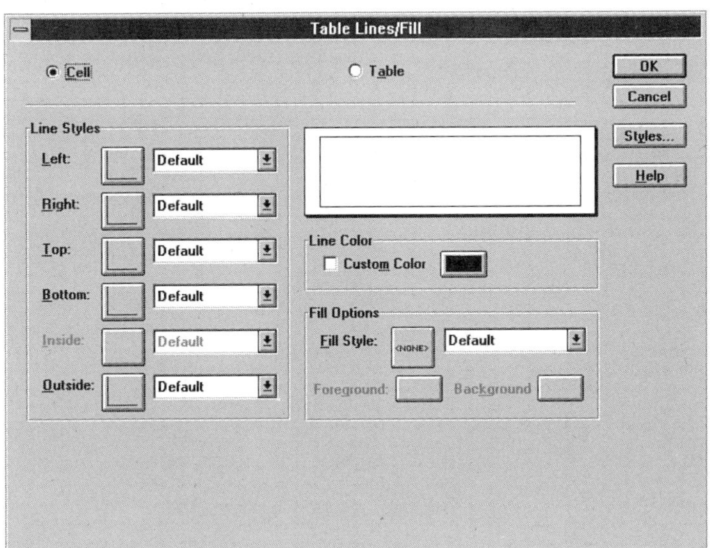

Fig. 16.28
The Table Lines/Fill dialog box is used to change line styles for cells, groups of cells, the entire table, or the table border.

Turning Off Cell Lines

You may find that you want to format text by using cell margins, but you don't want to print the lines. In your invoice, for example, you want to place your company's logo in cell A1, and use the left side of cell B1 as the left margin for your company's name and address. To turn off the line between the two cells, position the cursor in cell B1, choose **L**ines/Fill from the QuickMenu, and change the **L**eft line segment to <None>.

To turn off all the cells in a table, select all the cells, select **L**ines/Fill from the QuickMenu, and change all the **I**nside and **O**utside lines to <None>. Using this method, none of your table lines print.

Tip
If you use parallel columns to format your text, consider using tables without lines instead. The effect is the same, but working with tables is much easier than working with parallel columns.

You also can change the default line style to None by choosing **L**ines/Fill from the QuickMenu, then choosing T**a**ble, Line **S**tyle, and choosing None. Note, however, that any changes you made to individual line segments still print.

Using Table Cell Guides

If you still want to know where the cell lines are located, even though you don't want to print them, you can choose to display table cell guides. Choose **E**dit, Pr**e**ferences, **D**isplay. From the Display Preferences dialog box, choose **D**ocument and select the **T**able Gridlines check box in the Show area. Choose OK, and then Close to return to your table. In the invoice table, for example, you now see a dashed line between cells A1 and B1. However, this line does not print.

Understanding Default Line Styles

The default style for table lines is a single line. Although it may seem that a single line appears on all four sides of a cell, only two sides typically make up a cell: the left and the top. If you were to "explode" a typical table of three rows and three columns, the cells would resemble the cells shown in figure 16.29. (Notice that lines appear on the right and bottom sides of cells on the right and bottom of the table.)

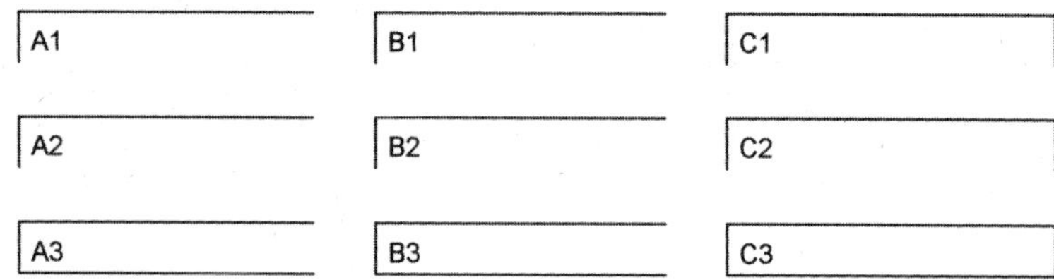

Fig. 16.29 An "exploded" WordPerfect table, showing default line segments.

When you specify a line style other than the default, you force WordPerfect to display that style at the location you specify. But you must be careful: if you specify a single line for the right side of a cell, even though its adjoining single cell line does not print, the line does not align with the other single lines in that column. In figure 16.30, for example, notice that the single line between cells A3 and B3 does not align with the other lines between columns A and B. To avoid this situation, make changes only to the top and left sides of cells whenever possible.

If you change both adjoining cell sides, you can create interesting effects because both lines print. Suppose, for example, that in your invoice table you select the Double Line style for the bottom of row 2 and select the Single Line style (not Default) for the top of row 3. You force WordPerfect to print both styles of lines, a single line beneath a double line.

This cell's default right line (none) has been replaced by a single right line.		

Fig. 16.30 If you change lines other than the default left and top lines, your table lines may not align properly.

Changing Borders

The border around a WordPerfect table is separate from the lines that surround each of the cells in the table. By default, a WordPerfect table border has no border style. Suppose that you want a double line around the outside edges of your table. To change a border style, follow these steps:

1. From the Table menu or from the QuickMenu, choose **L**ines/Fill.
2. From the resulting Table Lines/Fill dialog box, choose the T**a**ble radio button to display table-related lines and fill options.
3. In the Border Lines area, choose the Double line style from the Border list.
4. Choose OK or press Enter to return to your table.

Default border lines interact with default cell lines differently than described in the preceding section. For example, if you leave the outside cell lines at their default Single Line style and choose <None> for the default Border style, the single lines still print. If you choose specific styles for both the Border and the outside table cell lines, both styles print.

WordPerfect's Tables Border feature is both powerful and flexible. In addition to the standard list of styles, you can customize your border to include special combinations of lines, shading, and even drop shadow border effects. (See Chapter 30 for details.)

Changing Fills

WordPerfect enables you to fill individual cells, groups of cells, or the entire table with black, colors, or shades of black or color. Unless you have a color printer, however, the most practical use for this feature is to shade cells you want to set apart from the rest of the table. Suppose, for example, that you want to set off the column headings (Quantity, Description, and so on). To shade a cell or group of cells, follow these steps:

1. Position your cursor in the cell (or select the group of cells) you want to change. In your invoice table, move to cell A2 and select the entire second row of cells.

Tip

If you plan to print text in the cell you are filling, choose 20% fill or less. Higher percentages of shading usually make reading text contained in that cell difficult.

2. From the Table menu or the QuickMenu, choose **L**ines/Fill. WordPerfect displays the Table Lines/Fill dialog box (refer to fig. 16.28).

3. From the Fill Options area, choose the **F**ill Style button and from the palette of shading styles, choose 20% Fill (the fourth button from the left of the palette). Choose OK to return to your table.

You can select different shading or fill styles for any number of cells in your table. You can even create your own custom fills, including gradient shading and special patterns. WordPerfect provides expert help so you can choose special formats for entire tables from a list of predefined or customized table format styles (see Chapter 30 for details).

Adding Other Enhancements to a Table

You can add graphics and text with different attributes to a table. The only remaining task before you can use your invoice table is to add the graphic image for your company logo and enter the company name and address.

Adding Graphics to a Table

▶ See "Customizing Table Lines and Borders," p. 1033

▶ See "Customizing Cell and Table Shading," p. 1037

Each cell of a table is a self-contained miniature document, and you can place both graphics and text within a cell, just as you do in a document. To add pizzazz to the invoice table by adding a graphic to the upper left corner of the invoice (see fig. 16.31), follow these steps:

1. Position the cursor in cell A1, the cell in which you want to place the image. Although you easily can move the graphics to another cell, beginning in the cell where you want to place the graphic is best.

2. Choose **G**raphics, I**m**age. WordPerfect displays the Insert Image dialog box.

3. Choose the graphic file you want (ROSE.WPG, for example, is a graphic figure that comes with WordPerfect for Windows). Choose OK.

4. Position the mouse pointer on the graphic, and click the secondary mouse button. From the QuickMenu choose **B**order/Fill and change the Border Style to <None>. Alternatively, you can choose the **B**order/Fill

button on the feature bar that WordPerfect displays when you add a graphic to your document. You can make other changes to the graphic as you desire, using other tools you see on the Graphics menu or on the feature bar. (See Chapter 7, "Integrating Text and Graphics," for more information on adding graphics to your document.)

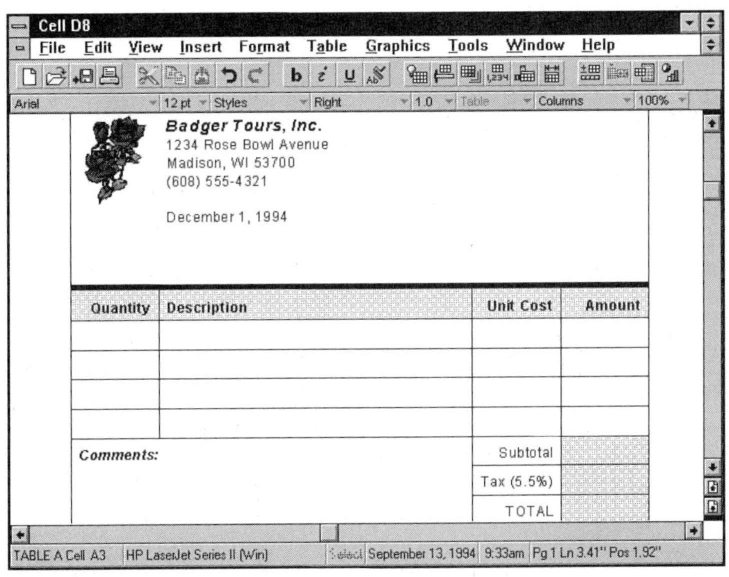

Fig. 16.31
The invoice table contains graphics and special text effects.

To get the exact results you want, you may have to experiment further, adjusting the size of the graphic and its position.

◄ See "Using Graphics Borders," p. 268

Adding Text with Different Attributes

Normally when you add text to a cell it takes on the attributes assigned to that cell. Sometimes, however, you must enter text with different attributes. For example, you may want to use a large boldface italic font for the company name, but normal text for the rest of the text in the cell (refer to fig. 16.31).

In this case, you enter the text into the cell just as you would enter text in any document. Then select the company name and choose Fo**r**mat, **F**ont; or press F9. In the Font dialog box, click the Relative Si**z**e pop-up menu and choose **L**arge. Select the **B**old and **I**talic check boxes. You also could choose a different **F**ont Face. Choose OK, leaving the remainder of the address in the normal font and size.

Troubleshooting

I turned off all my table lines, but now I can't tell where the different cells are.

Just choose **V**iew, Table Grid**l**ines to display the cell grid. These lines won't print, but they'll let you see what you're doing.

I can't seem to position my graphic image properly in a table cell.

Graphic images require enough room to display properly. You may have to reduce the size of the graphic image or increase the width or height of the table cell. There is no exact rule for accomplishing this task, so keep trying (and using Undo) until you get it the way you want it.

Exploring Other Uses for Tables

In the preceding sections, you learned the basics of creating and modifying tables by using a sample invoice. So many potential uses for tables exist that an entire book could be written describing samples and exploring tables options. This section gives you a taste of some specific and common practical applications for tables. In Chapter 30, you learn how to build on these basics.

Creating Calendar Forms

A good use for a table is as a personal calendar. Determine first whether you want your calendar in portrait or landscape orientation. Set your margins, and then divide by seven the available space to determine how much room you have for each day of the week. If you need more room, reduce your margins or the size of your font.

Create the table with seven columns and six rows (one row is for the day-of-the-week column headings). Select rows 2 through 6; from the Tables QuickMenu, select F**o**rmat, R**o**w, Fi**x**ed, and specify the vertical height you want (for example, 1 1/2 inches). To change the width of any column, position the cursor in the column you want to change, and from the Tables QuickMenu choose F**o**rmat, Co**l**umn, Wid**t**h, and then specify the width you want.

After you add your text attributes and line and fill changes, and enter text in the column headings, save the table as a blank form so that you can use it again. Next, add the month, dates, and events. You might even use a watermark graphic to visually represent the current month. Save your modified calendar under a different name and print it. Figure 16.32 shows an example of a simple printed calendar. See Chapter 30 for information on how you can automatically fill in the days and dates.

JUNE 1995

Sunday	Monday	Tuesday	Wednesday	Thursday	Friday	Saturday
				1	2	3
4	5	6	7	8	9	10
11	12 Summer Session Begins	13	14	15	16	17
18	19	20	21	22	23	24
25	26	27	28	29	30	

Fig. 16.32
A sample calendar can be created using the Tables feature.

Creating Phone Message Forms

The Tables feature is an excellent tool for creating preprinted forms. If, for example, standard phone message forms don't meet your needs, you can create your own (see fig. 16.33).

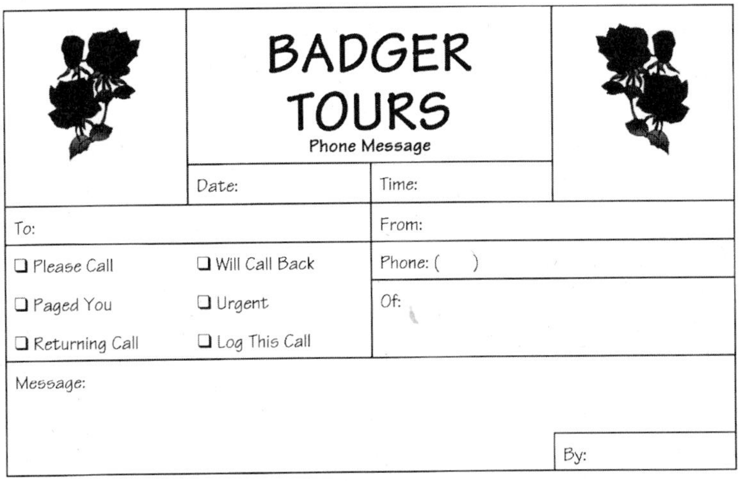

BADGER TOURS
Phone Message

Date: Time:

To: From:

❑ Please Call ❑ Will Call Back Phone: ( )

❑ Paged You ❑ Urgent Of:

❑ Returning Call ❑ Log This Call

Message:

By:

Fig. 16.33
A sample preprinted phone message form can be created with the Tables feature.

See "Using Data Fill To Simplify Data Entry," p. 1064

You want your forms (and tables) to be both functional and attractive. The advantage to creating your own forms with WordPerfect is that, before you print a large quantity of the forms, you can test several versions of the form on the people who actually will use it.

Creating Forms for Electronic Fill-In

The invoice form you created in this chapter can be printed and filled in manually, but you also can fill in such forms on the computer and print the result.

WordPerfect offers special math and spreadsheet functions that you can add to a form to provide greater functionality. Figure 16.34 is an example of the invoice form that contains formulas. You only have to enter the quantity and the unit price; then the form calculates the extended price, sums the charges, adds the sales tax, and gives the total for the invoice. (See Chapter 30 for more information on WordPerfect's math capabilities.)

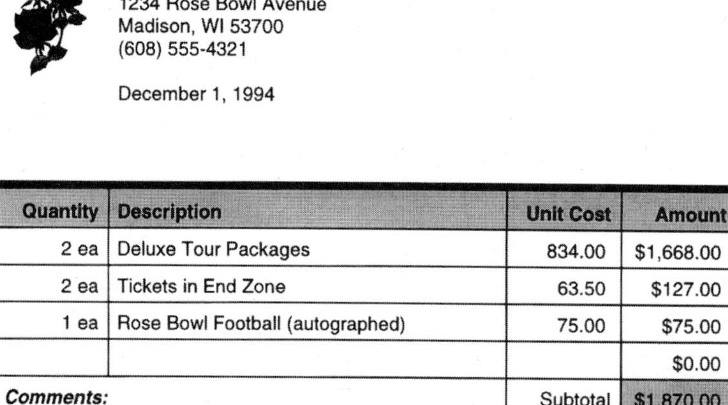

Badger Tours, Inc.
1234 Rose Bowl Avenue
Madison, WI 53700
(608) 555-4321

December 1, 1994

Quantity	Description	Unit Cost	Amount
2 ea	Deluxe Tour Packages	834.00	$1,668.00
2 ea	Tickets in End Zone	63.50	$127.00
1 ea	Rose Bowl Football (autographed)	75.00	$75.00
			$0.00
Comments: Deposit must be received 14 days prior to departure. Thank you for your business.		Subtotal	$1,870.00
		Tax (5.5%)	$102.85
		TOTAL	$1,972.85

Fig. 16.34
The complete invoice table uses math functions to calculate the total amount of the invoice.

From Here...

In this chapter, you learned about the Tables feature, one of WordPerfect's most powerful and useful features. You learned how to create tables consisting of any number of rows and columns; enter text and move around in a table; and add and delete cells, rows, and columns. You also learned how to modify the table structure by joining and splitting cells and changing column widths. You now can format text in cells with font attributes and alignment, and can dress up your tables with lines, borders, and shading.

For information relating to additional uses for tables, you may want to review these chapters:

- Chapter 18, "Importing Data and Working with Other Programs," shows how to import spreadsheets into tables.
- Chapter 19, "Assembling Documents with Merge and Sort," shows how to use tables to create data files, and also how to sort tables.
- Chapter 23, "Desktop Publishing with WordPerfect," tells you how to enhance tables to be used as forms.
- Chapter 30, "Advanced Tables," takes you to the next level of table formatting and also shows you how to create spreadsheet-like tables.

Chapter 17

Creating and Modifying Charts with WP Draw

by Pat Freeland and Alan Westenbroek

Profits are up sharply! The Denver office is leading the company in sales! Jones is the best salesperson by far!

These statements may be wonderful news, but you need to add more information to help your reader understand their meanings. One way is to add several paragraphs of text to make your points.

You can illustrate your points more quickly, however, with charts. A chart can replace mountains of words and make the point more clearly. WP Draw, which enables you to create charts and drawings, has been included with WordPerfect 6.1. Now it is possible to create a chart in WordPerfect based on data you supply from a table, a spreadsheet, or right in WP Draw.

In this chapter, you learn how to:

- Identify the parts of the chart
- Identify the types of charts available and their uses
- Create the chart
- Change the underlying data in the chart
- Add text to the chart
- Change the appearance of the chart
- Place the chart in a document

Understanding Chart Basics

A *chart*, sometimes called a *graph*, is a picture of numeric data. In WordPerfect 6.1 for Windows, the data must be in a table or spreadsheet.

You can create a table in WordPerfect. (See Chapter 16, "Working with Tables," to learn how to create a table.) You can also import into WordPerfect a spreadsheet you created in programs such as Microsoft Excel or a database created in a database program such as Paradox.

It is up to you whether the table appears in the document itself; in some cases it isn't necessary to display both the chart and the data. You may be interested in illustrating the growth of profits, for example. A chart with a line gracefully sweeping upward may do the job perfectly without a table of figures close by.

Note

A table or spreadsheet is a series of rows and columns. The rows are designated with numbers, the columns with letters. The intersection of a row and column is a cell. Labels, values, and formulas are entered into these cells.

Figure 17.1 is a simple bar chart with the important parts labeled. Each bar in the chart refers to a single number in a table. The top of a bar is called a *data point*. Naturally, each type of chart represents data points differently. A line chart, for example, shows data points as marks on a line, sometimes at a place where the direction of the line changes.

Along the left side of the chart is the vertical Y-axis. Numbers appear next to this axis, generally starting with zero and ending slightly higher than the largest number in the table. Each data point is compared in height to the numbers on the Y-axis.

The bottom of the chart is the X-axis. In most charts, the names of the items being compared appear along this axis. In figure 17.1, the performance of several offices is being compared for the four quarters of the year. The names of the quarters are along the X-axis.

The little box on the left side of the chart is the *legend*, which matches the pattern or color of each data point with one of the series in the table. In figure 17.1, the legend tells which color or pattern is associated with which office.

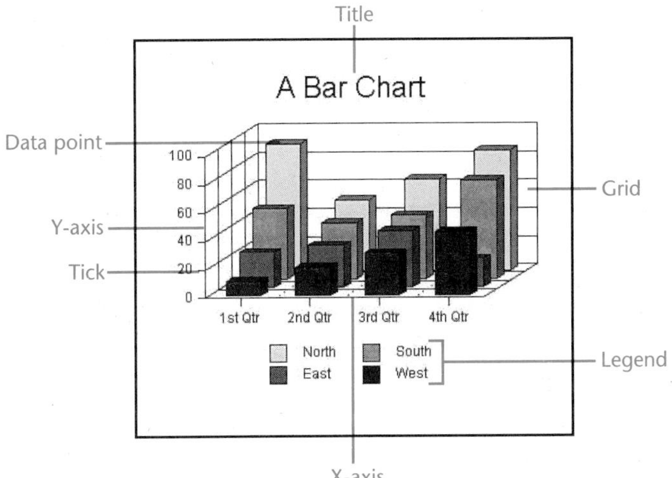

Fig. 17.1
A simple three-dimensional bar chart.

The horizontal lines running across the chart are the *grid,* which is used to help compare data points with the Y-axis and each other.

◄ See "Creating and Using Tables: The Basics," p. 526

► See "Importing and Working with Spreadsheet/Database Data," p. 606

Understanding How Data Affects a Chart

The way you arrange data in a table determines how WordPerfect displays the data in the chart. Table 17.1 shows the data used for the chart in figure 17.1. The names of the items being compared—the quarters—are in the top row of the table. They are the labels that appear on the X-axis.

Table 17.1 Data Used to Create the Graph in Figure 17.1

	1st Qtr	2nd Qtr	3rd Qtr	4th Qtr
North	90	50	65	85
South	50	40	45	70
East	25	30	40	20
West	10	20	30	45

The series are the numbers entered in the rows. One number is in each series for each quarter. The name of the series is in the left column. In table 17.1, there are four series: North, South, East, and West. When you create the chart, each number in the series is converted into a data point. One data point from each series is grouped with data points from the other series. In figure 17.1, the data points for each series of each quarter are displayed in a group of four bars.

Table 17.2 contains the same data as table 17.1, but it has been rearranged so that the series are now the offices, not the quarters. The chart in figure 17.2 is based on the data in table 17.2 and allows the reader to see the data represented differently. Office names are on the X-axis, not quarters.

Table 17.2 Data with Quarters, instead of Offices, Represented in Rows

	North	South	East	West
1st Qtr	90	50	25	10
2nd Qtr	50	40	30	20
3rd Qtr	65	45	40	30
4th Qtr	85	70	20	45

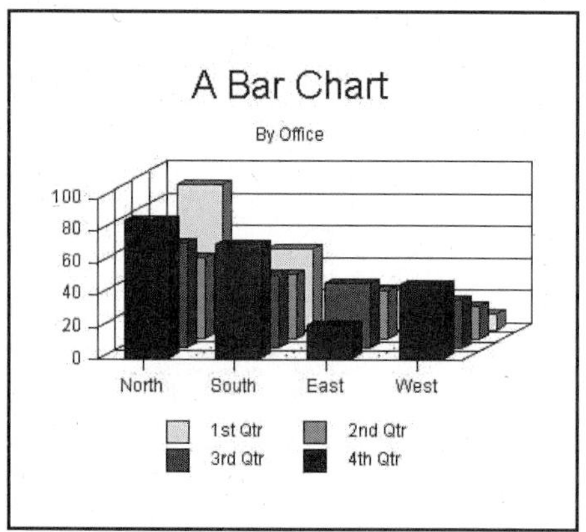

Fig. 17.2
A new bar chart based on rearranged data makes a different point. The bars are grouped by quarter in figure 17.1 and by regional office in figure 17.2.

Understanding the Chart Types

You can add features and make changes to a chart. WordPerfect 6.1 enables you to choose seven basic chart types: bar charts, line charts, high/low charts, area charts, scatter charts, pie charts, and radar charts. The following list describes the seven types of charts and explains why you might choose each.

- *Bar chart.* Each data point is represented by a bar that starts at the X-axis and rises parallel to the Y-axis to a height corresponding to the value it represents (refer to fig. 17.2).

  Bar charts are used for a quick comparison of related information or for showing trends in groups of related information. Generally, this type of chart should be used only when small amounts of data are involved; otherwise, a bewildering collection of tiny bars appears, looking like a cluster of match sticks.

  Stacked bar charts are a variation of bar charts. Stacked bar charts stack all bars in one bar to enable the user to see the contribution of each to the whole.

- *Line chart.* Figure 17.3 shows a line chart based on the data in table 17.1. Each data point is a marker on a line; one line for each series connects the data points for that series. Line charts are commonly used to display trends.

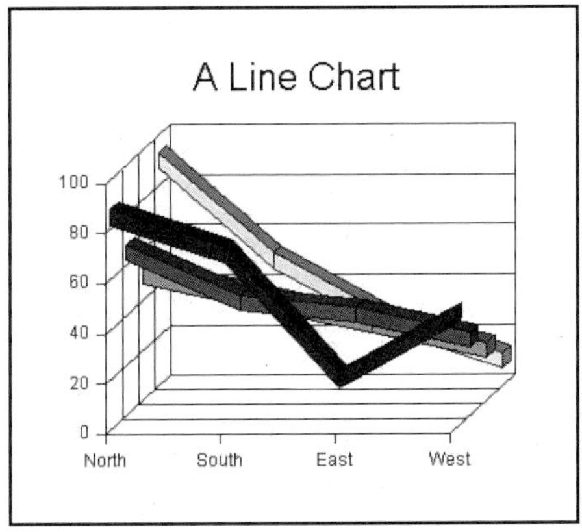

Fig. 17.3
A line chart. Each data point is a marker on a line; one line for each series connects the data points for that series.

- *Radar chart.* Each data point is represented by a mark that can be placed anywhere within the X-axis and Y-axis. Radar charts are used to show data over a period of time. They can be used to show variations and are ideal for plotting trends.

- *High/Low chart.* Figure 17.4 shows a high/low chart. Each figure displays four separate numbers in a series. The vertical bar represents the spread between the highest and lowest value of an item, the left "wing" of the bar represents the value of the item at the beginning of a specified time period, and the right "wing" represents its value at the close of the time period.

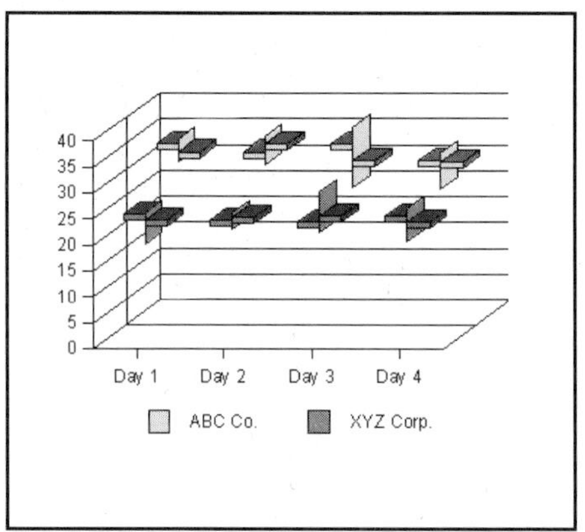

Fig. 17.4
A high/low chart, which is commonly used to show the performance of individual stocks for a given period of time.

- *Area chart.* Figure 17.5 shows an area chart. It is really a line chart with the space between the line and the X-axis filled with a color or pattern. Area charts are used to display broad trends. The contrast between the areas below and above the line call attention to the trend illustrated by the slope of the line.

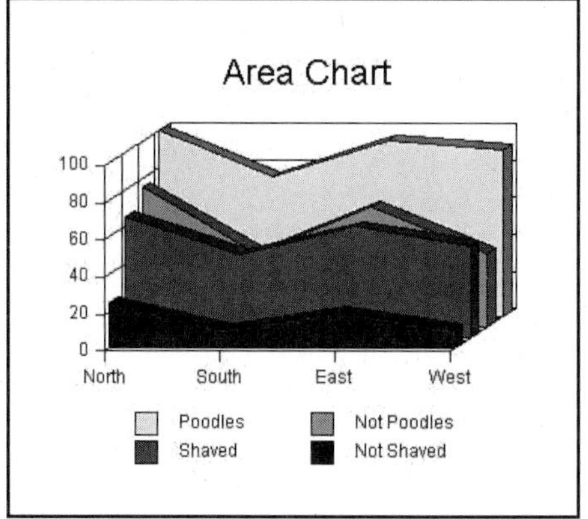

Fig. 17.5
An area chart, which really is a line chart with the space between the line and the X-axis filled with a color or pattern.

- *Scatter chart.* This type of chart is unique in that the top row of the table on which the chart is based contains values, not labels. The data points in the chart represent the relationship between the data in the series and the data in the top row of the table that appears on the X-axis.

  For example, you might want to show the relationship between temperature (entered in the top row) and sales of gloves, hats, mittens, and suntan cream (each item entered in the left column).

- *Pie chart.* Figure 17.6 is a pie chart. Pie charts are used to show the contribution of each part to the whole. Only one set of values can be displayed in a pie chart. Pieces of the pie correspond to values entered in a column below the label at the top of the column. Negative numbers cannot be displayed by a pie chart because you cannot have a negative piece of pie.

  Generally, it is best to use no more than six numbers for a pie chart—too many pieces can cause confusion. If more than six numbers are involved, it is better to create several separate pie charts or use one label for several of the smaller pieces.

Tip

Negative numbers may be used in bar, line, area, and scatter charts, but they won't be displayed correctly in high/low and pie charts.

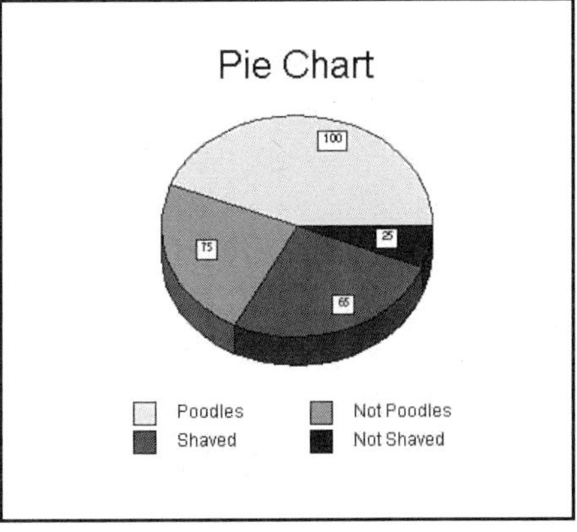

Fig. 17.6
Pie charts are used to show the contribution of each part to the whole. Only one set of values can be displayed in a pie chart.

Note

Sometimes one series may deserve special attention. The sales of one product, for example, may need to be displayed in a different way to set it apart. To differentiate one piece of data in a pie chart, the piece can be "exploded," or separated from the rest of the pie.

Another way to set one series apart from the other series is to represent its data with a chart type different from the type used for the others. In a bar chart, the sales figures for the company's flagship product could be displayed as a line rather than as a bar. (See the section "Making Changes to a Series" later in this chapter for details on how to change the chart type for one series.)

Creating the Chart

Before you create a chart, you need to create a table of data for the chart to represent. This table can be a spreadsheet created in a dedicated spreadsheet program such as Microsoft Excel; it can be entered in a table created in WordPerfect; or it can be data you enter directly into the Datasheet when you're using the Chart Editor. See Chapter 16, "Working with Tables," for information on how to create a table and enter data. Be sure you also read and understand the section "Understanding How Data Affects a Chart" earlier in this chapter.

Choose **G**raphics, Cha**r**t from the main menu. WordPerfect 6.1 changes the menus and toolbars to show that you're editing a chart object and a chart with the default type appears in the document with a heavy border around it.

If you created a spreadsheet in another program, click in the Datasheet window and then choose **D**ata, I**m**port. In the dialog box that appears, you must select the correct drive, directory, and file type. From the list of file names that appears, choose the name of the spreadsheet file. The data from that file appears in the Datasheet and replaces the data currently visible.

Tip
To get data from a program saved in a format not supported by the importer, copy it to the Clipboard and paste it into the Datasheet with **E**dit **P**aste.

The Import dialog box also displays any named ranges contained in the selected spreadsheet. This enables you to bring only a portion of an entire spreadsheet file into the Datasheet without the need to delete any unwanted data.

It is also possible to start entering data in the table section of the editing window. Place the cursor in a cell and type the data you want to place in that cell. You move from cell to cell by pressing the appropriate arrow key or by clicking on the desired cell. For long-distance moves, choose **E**dit, **G**o To Cell, or press Ctrl+G, from the chart edit menu bar. Type the cell address of the cell you want to change and press Enter.

The table feature in WordPerfect 6.1 enables you to create a table with more features, such as formulas, than is possible in the table section of the chart edit window. Therefore, you may prefer to create a table in the document, generate a chart, and then later delete the table from the document if you don't want it to be visible.

Note

After the chart has been created, it does not look at the data in the document to place its data points. Therefore, the chart isn't affected by data deletions.

After you place the table in the document, put the cursor anywhere in the table and choose **G**raphics, Cha**r**t. WordPerfect changes its menus and toolbars to reflect the fact that you're editing an embedded chart object. The Datasheet appears with the data from your table already loaded along with a chart (see fig. 17.7). By default, WordPerfect generates a bar chart.

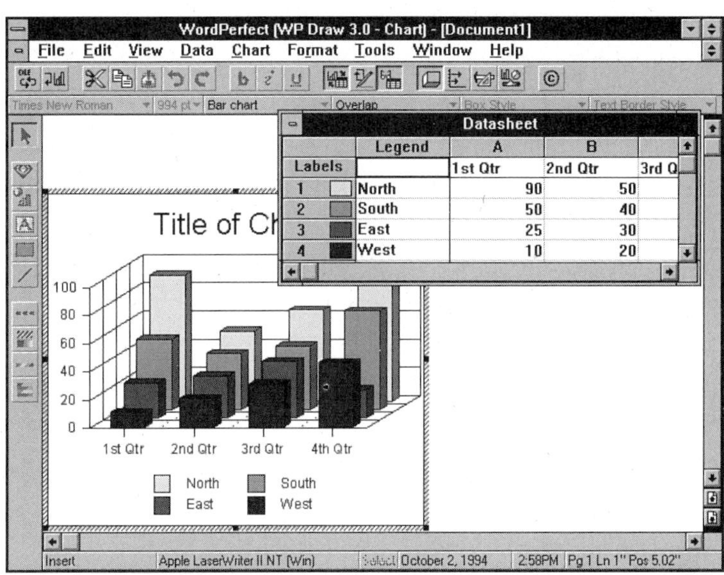

Fig. 17.7
WordPerfect in WP Draw Chart Mode. Notice the Datasheet is a separate window that you can close or move around.

Touring the WP Draw Interface

The major features of the WP Draw interface are explained in the following list:

- *Menu.* Across the top of the window is the pull-down menu bar, which WordPerfect alters to provide the commands you need while editing a WP Draw object. Items in this menu enable you to make changes to the chart, the data, and the display of the editing window. You access and utilize this menu the same way you use any other of WordPerfect's pull-down menus.

- *Main Toolbar.* WP Draw replaces WordPerfect's default Toolbar with its own. This Toolbar is similar to the one used in WordPerfect, but it uses functions relating to WP Draw. Many of these buttons provide quicker ways to accomplish the tasks included in the menu. If the Toolbar is hidden, you make it visible by choosing **V**iew, **T**oolbar.

- *Drawing Toolbar.* At the left side of the chart editing window is a palette of tools. These buttons enable you to make changes to the style, format, and appearance of objects in your drawing.

Note

You can move the tool palette, which is to the left of the window by default. Notice the mouse cursor changes to a hand as you move it across a blank area of the Toolbar. You can place the mouse pointer in that area and click and drag the entire palette to another area of the screen. If the WP Draw window is not maximized, you can place the palette outside of the WP Draw window.

Note

You can customize WP Draw's Toolbar just like any other. Choose **E**dit, Pr**e**ferences, **T**oolbar to access the Toolbar Preferences dialog box. You can add, delete, or move buttons and change the bar's position. Also, you can hide or display the Toolbar by choosing **V**iew, **T**oolbar.

Troubleshooting

I can't find the toolbar.

WordPerfect provides the flexibility to show or hide different elements of the screen, including toolbars. If you are missing one, choose **V**iew, **T**oolbar.

WP Draw either takes forever to start or it won't start at all.

The good part about OLE 2.0 is how easy and seamless it makes integrating data from different places. The bad part involves the amount of memory and system resources it requires. The performance of machines with less than 8MB of memory usually suffers when using OLE 2.0. If WP Draw starts slowly or fails to start, you may need more memory in your computer. Sometimes you can get around this by closing other applications you don't need at the moment. Exiting Windows and restarting can also free up system resources and get you going.

My chart looks great on-screen, but I can't read it once it's printed.

Many black-and-white printers don't do a very good job of translating colors to differing shades of gray. To do it yourself, select the chart object in your document, right-click, and choose **I**mage Tools. Select the black & white tool and adjust the threshold settings until you see a clear difference in the different elements of your chart.

Moving between the Chart and the Rest of the Document

When you want to return to the document, click Close from the Toolbar. You can also click anywhere outside the chart's borders and WordPerfect will return to editing the document.

To leave the document and reenter chart edit mode, select the chart you want to edit. With the chart selected, choose **E**dit, Chart **O**bject, **E**dit from the WordPerfect menu bar. Double-clicking the selected chart also switches to Chart edit mode.

Tip
Click anywhere in the chart and selection handles appear around the chart's frame. Any commands used affect the selected chart.

Changing the Underlying Data

After you create a table and generate a chart, you may need to change some of the data. It is possible that you either made a mistake in data entry or some of the numbers changed since you created the chart.

For any data change to be reflected in the chart, you must make the change in the Datasheet. Any change made to data in the document's table is not reflected in the chart, even if you change data in the table and then switch back to Chart edit mode.

Caution

Changes made in the Datasheet do not automatically appear in the table in the document. You must edit the table separately so that the chart accurately displays the data in the table that the readers see.

Note

If you make numerous changes to the table in the document, it makes more sense to create a new chart based on the new data and delete the old chart rather than editing the table in Datasheet. Use the Chart button or choose **G**raphics, Cha**r**t to create a new chart and enter Chart edit mode. After you return to the document, select the old chart by clicking on it and then press Del to remove it.

To change data in the Datasheet, move the cursor to the cell in which you want to enter new data and type the correction. You can also use the Edit

Cell button or double-click the cell. The advantage to using the Edit Cell button is that the contents of the current cell appear separated from the rest of the table, making it easier to concentrate on the contents of one cell at a time. A small cell edit window appears on-screen with the contents of the current cell in an edit box in the middle. When you complete the correction, click OK or press Enter.

To navigate around the Datasheet, use the arrow keys, the Go To Cell feature (Ctrl+G), or the scroll bars. Be careful when using the scroll bars; they move the focus of the screen but do not move the cell highlighter, so be sure to click a cell in the visible window before pressing an arrow key or entering data. If you don't click a cell, use an arrow key to return to the area of the screen previously visible. Otherwise, the data you type is entered in a cell off-screen.

Tip
To select an entire column or row, click the row number or column letter.

The **E**dit menu enables you to choose Cu**t**, **C**opy, and **P**aste to move and copy data from cell to cell. You can also access these features from the Toolbar. By clicking and dragging across several cells and then using the **E**dit menu, you can copy and move the contents of several cells at once. To move the data in column A to column E, for example, click and drag across all the cells in column A that have data. Selected cells appear black with white text. Choose **E**dit, Cu**t** (Ctrl+X). Move the cell highlighter to the top cell in column E and choose **E**dit, **P**aste (Ctrl+V).

Caution

Choosing **E**dit, Cle**a**r removes the contents or formatting, or both the contents and formatting, from selected cells but does not place them in the Clipboard. They are erased permanently and cannot be pasted elsewhere. The Clear button can be even more disastrous because it completely removes all data from the entire Datasheet. Notice that a prompt appears when you click the Clear button, asking if you really want to clear all data. Make sure you really want to empty the table before answering the prompt.

Formatting Data

When numbers are entered in cells, they may appear without any formatting (dollar signs, commas, or extra decimal places) or with the wrong formatting. You apply formatting to the current cell—or to a selected group of cells—by choosing **D**ata, F**o**rmat or pressing Ctrl+F12. Standard formats available include comma separators, currency symbols, and percent signs. Choosing one of the main formats enables you to determine the number of decimal places the data has in the cells and how negative numbers are displayed.

To change the number of decimal places, choose Precision and then type the number of decimal places you want for the highlighted numbers. Choose Fl**o**ating to allow WordPerfect to determine the number of decimal places in a number.

Format settings can also be accessed by right-clicking on the cell, row, or column and choosing F**o**rmat.

You display negative numbers with a minus sign or parentheses by clicking the appropriate box in the Negative #'s section of the Format dialog box.

Applied formats become visible in the chart after you click OK. To see what effect your settings have, choose Pre**v**iew. You can click OK or Cancel after you've seen the results.

Tip
Typing a format symbol like a dollar sign automatically applies the currency format to a cell. The format remains the same, even if the number is changed.

Widening Columns

Some columns may have data that is too long for the cell's width. If you need to see the whole cell entry, widen the columns. This has no effect on the table in the document or on the chart; it affects only the Datasheet. The easiest way to widen or narrow a column is to click and drag the right side of the box in which the column letter appears. Drag it to the right to widen the column. Widening one column widens all columns.

Another method for changing column width involves choosing **D**ata, **C**olumn Width and typing the width in number of characters. Clicking and holding on the increment/decrement arrows next to the **W**idth text box increases or decreases the number in the box. This new width is applied after you press Enter or click OK.

Tip
To widen columns, drag a column divider (the vertical line between the column letters) to the right. For narrower columns, drag a column divider to the left.

Removing or Adding Columns and Rows

After entering data and creating a chart, you may discover you forgot to enter a set of numbers. If this set goes in the middle of the table, you need to insert a row or column.

To insert a row or a column, select a cell in the row or column in which the insertion will be made. If you want to insert a blank column before column C, for example, select a cell anywhere within column C and choose **E**dit, **I**nsert, **C**olumn. An empty column appears and existing data is moved to the right. To insert multiple columns or rows, type into the number box the number of rows or columns you want to insert.

Selecting a cell and choosing **E**dit, **D**elete, **R**ow or **C**olumn removes the row or column and its data from the table. Data that is either in rows below the deleted information or in columns to the right of the deleted information

Tip
The quickest way to insert or delete a column or row is to right-click its label and choose **I**nsert or **D**elete.

moves up or to the left to fill the vacancy created by the deletion. Use the **D**elete command carefully—you can easily remove data that you did not intend to delete.

Note

It is not necessary to add a column or row if you plan to add data at the edge of the Datasheet. If, for example, you have data in the first three rows and want to add data to row four, simply go to the correct cell and enter the data. Insert rows and columns only when data must be added between existing rows or columns.

Changing the Appearance of the Chart

After the chart is created, it is time to stand back, look at the chart with a critical eye, and determine what needs to be done to make its message clear and its appearance pleasing.

In the sections that follow, you learn how to make changes to the entire chart and how to change one series to make it stand out. Because of the number of available changes, it's tempting to pile modification after modification on the chart. Be careful—your point could be lost in a bewildering flurry of enhancements.

Adding Titles

Adding some descriptive titles to your chart is a good idea. You will at least want to change the title of the chart, which reads "Title of Chart." Keep the titles simple and be sure they emphasize no more than one point, such as "Sales Are Up" or "Regional Sales Performance."

Add titles to the chart by choosing **C**hart, **T**itles or right-clicking on the default title and choosing **E**dit Titles. In the dialog box that appears, type the text for the main title, a subtitle, the X-axis, and either or both Y-axes. (See the section "Making Changes to a Series" later in this chapter for more information about adding a second Y-axis.)

To change the font, choose **O**ptions in the Titles dialog box. In the Titles Options dialog box, choose the **F**ont button. A new dialog box appears that includes a list of fonts and font sizes, a choice of alignments, and the option to add bold, underline, or italic to the font. Be sure you select the specific title you want to change before selecting the changes. Font settings are also available directly from the Title's QuickMenu. Right-click on the title and choose **F**ont.

As you make your choice of fonts and attributes, click Pre**v**iew to give you an idea how the title appears. There is no difference between choosing a font style named Bold or changing the appearance of the font by choosing Bold.

When you select the title or subtitle, you can place it at the left, right, or center at the top of the chart. You can make the axis titles vertical or horizontal. Choosing horizontal for a long Y-axis title or vertical for a long X-axis title squeezes the chart to make way for the title.

Tip

The chart looks better if you use one font for all text. If you use several fonts in a small area, the chart looks confusing and cluttered.

You'll find an item labeled Attributes in the box section of the Titles Options dialog box. Attributes, which appears in many other dialog boxes, enables you to put the title in a box and add color to the box.

Alignment and Attributes settings are available directly from the Title's QuickMenu.

Including a Legend

By now you've got an attractive chart with lots of colors and a meaningful title, but the effectiveness of the chart is lost if you don't know what the data points represent.

The legend removes any doubt about which data point goes with which element in the series. Each series has its own color or pattern. The legend shows which color or pattern goes with which series. If, for example, all the bars in a chart corresponding to North are red, the legend shows the word `North` next to a red box.

Choose **C**hart, L**e**gend or right-click the legend and choose **E**dit Legend. The dialog box that appears enables you to make changes to the legend. Choose Displa**y** Legend to activate the other items in the dialog box if it is not already selected. (If they are grayed, they are not active.)

Placement enables you to place the legend inside or outside the actual chart. Choosing **O**utside Chart makes sense if the chart is already cluttered or if the legend hides some data points. Choosing **O**utside Chart is not a good idea if the legend forces the chart to squeeze too much to the right.

Orientation places each color or pattern in a vertical or horizontal arrangement. If, for example, you choose Hori**z**ontal, the legends are displayed beside each other rather than above or below each other, giving you a rather wide legend box.

The name of the legend box is Legend. Choose Display **N**ame and type in some other text if you prefer to give the box a different title. **F**ont, as described earlier, enables you to change the type style, size, and attributes of the legend box title.

Using Labels

Labels are numbers placed near parts of the chart that tell the exact number associated with that part. Labels can be displayed or suppressed for the X-axis and Y-axis and for data points. When placed near data points, they are called *data labels*. Figure 17.8 shows a bar chart with data labels at the top of each bar. Notice that the display of the labels normally displayed with the Y-axis is suppressed, partially to show that such suppression is possible, but also to show that having numbers at data points and at the Y-axis is superfluous. Notice also that the display of the X-axis labels is staggered.

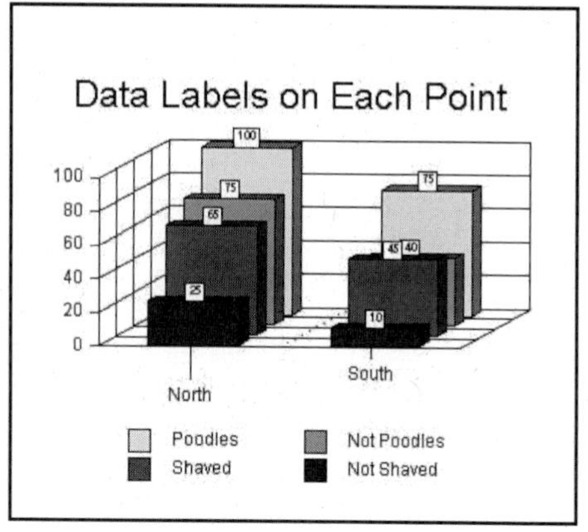

Fig. 17.8
A graph with data labels added to data points and removed from the Y-axis. Labels on the X-axis are staggered.

To make choices about each type of label, select the type in the dialog box that appears after you right-click the label or choose **C**hart, La**b**els. An X in the Disp**l**ay box means that the label will be visible.

If you choose to display data labels, you can also determine where the label will appear relative to the data points.

Displaying data points on the X-axis allows several choices. Staggering is useful when each label is long enough to interfere with the display of adjacent labels. If staggered, labels are placed at varying distances from the chart so that they have more space to be displayed.

Ti**c**ks on Intervals determine whether every label in the top row of the table is displayed. When the labels are very long, or when the display of every label becomes monotonous, you can choose to display only some of those labels. Choosing **2** from the **I**nterval box means that you display every other one; **3** displays every third label, and so on.

Changing Chart Types

WP Draw enables you to quickly change your chart type by choosing **Ty**pe from the **C**hart menu. You can also take advantage of several predefined chart types and styles in the Chart Gallery. For example, figure 17.9 shows a horizontal bar chart.

To change a chart from one type to another, Choose **C**hart, T**y**pe, and the chart type you want. Keep in mind that not all chart types are appropriate for all data. If, for example, your Datasheet contains two or more series, you wouldn't want to use a pie chart.

The Chart Gallery has a range of chart types already defined for you. To access it, choose **C**hart, **G**allery. You can select from different types on the left of the dialog box and apply specific style and formatting options by choosing the button with the sample chart you want. Check the 3-D box to make a **3**-D chart or clear it for a two-dimensional chart.

Note

You can fine-tune the options preset in the Chart Gallery by choosing **C**hart, **L**ayout.

Caution

One reason for choosing a two-dimensional display is that some smaller values may be hidden behind larger ones. A forest of high bars in the front can completely conceal a short bar in the back.

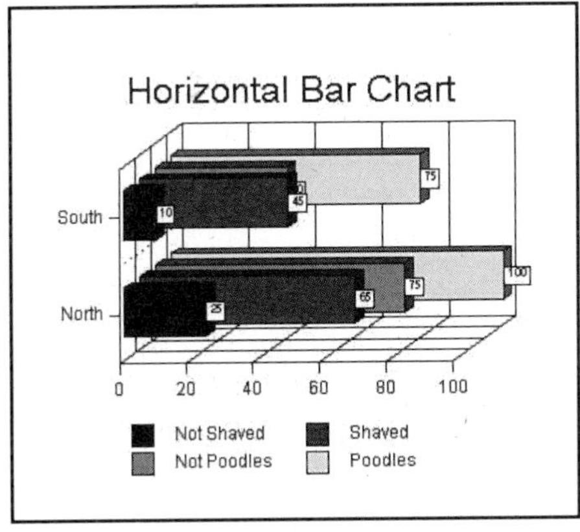

Fig. 17.9
The bar chart from figure 17.8 is displayed horizontally with the same clarity as when displayed vertically. Other charts, such as line charts, may appear confusing when rotated to the horizontal position.

The four styles available in the Layout dialog box include the following:

- *Cluster*. This style spreads the bars out so that they don't overlap and no bars are hidden by the others.
- *Overlap*. This style is opposite of cluster. The bars are permitted to overlap and some may be hidden.
- *Stacked*. This style takes all the bars for one range and stacks them so that the reader can see how each bar contributes to the whole. Each stacked bar is a true representation of the total value for the stack.
- *Stacked 100%*. This style stacks the bars and makes all composite bars the same height. The contribution of each component to the whole is shown as a percentage rather than as an actual amount.

Making Other Changes

The WP Draw **C**hart menu contains four other items that change the entire chart. They are **A**xis, G**r**id/Tick, **F**rame, and **P**erspective.

Modifying the Axes

Choose **C**hart, **A**xis and select the axis you want to change. You can make the following types of changes:

Tip

Create a Y-axis title to remind readers that the numbers on the Y-axis are in the millions, if you use the label scale factor to divide each by one million.

- *Scaling method*. You can choose **L**inear, which is the default, or Loga**r**ithmic. Logarithmic displays each tick on the axis as a power of the one below. For example, the numbers might be 10, 100, 1000, 10000, and so on. All numbers will be the same distance apart.
- *Auto Maximum Value*. An X in the box means the program automatically sets the highest axis value a bit higher than the highest value in the data. You can type in a number higher (but not lower) than the highest value in the data. The higher the number you type, the smaller the data points.
- *Auto Minimum Value*. This is generally set at zero, but you can set it to a negative value or to a value just below the lowest value in the data so that the differences between data points are more noticeable.
- *Major Grid Value*. A grid line crosses the chart for each major value. If the maximum value in a chart is 100 and you set the major grid value at **2**, a line appears every two numbers.

- *Minor Grid Lines.* This determines how many grid lines appear between the major grid lines.
- *Label Scale Factor.* This is a number divided into each number on the axis to make it appear smaller. If the numbers along the Y-axis ranged from 1 million to 10 million, dividing each by 1 million displays them as 1 through 10, which is easier to read.

Click on the Preview button to see the results of the changes. Clicking on the Grid/Tick button switches to the Grid/Tick dialog box.

Changing the Grid and Tick

You use the Chart, Grid/Tick menu to add or remove the grid and tick. The grid is the set of lines that appears across the chart. The tick is the little extension of the grid along the axis that points away from the axis. You can change the grid color and line style and change the tick so that it points inward, outward, or does not appear at all.

Modifying the Frame

The frame is the box in which the chart appears. When the chart is two-dimensional, there is only one frame. Change the chart to three-dimensional and a left side of the frame appears. Choose Chart, Frame to add or remove a frame at the right side, the front, the top, the bottom, the left side, or the back. The base height command raises the floor of the chart.

Adjusting the Perspective

After choosing Chart, Perspective, you can rotate the display of the chart. Choosing the Right Angles Axes box toggles between displaying the chart so that the X-axis and Y-axis are displayed as though they are at right angles. To rotate the display of the chart horizontally or vertically, change the number of degrees in the Horizontal or Vertical box. A quicker way to rotate the chart is to use the sliders next to the chart in the center of the dialog box.

Making Changes to a Series

A table often contains not only the data for each series and item, but also the totals. At times you may want to include the totals in your chart, but the data points for the totals will be much higher than the data points for the other series.

To keep totals from looking like just another series—and to keep the data points from looking disproportionately large—consider changing the graphic display of the total.

Figure 17.10 shows WP Draw Chart edit mode with a table that includes totals. The chart in the edit window contains a bar for the totals row, which is considerably higher than the bars for the other series.

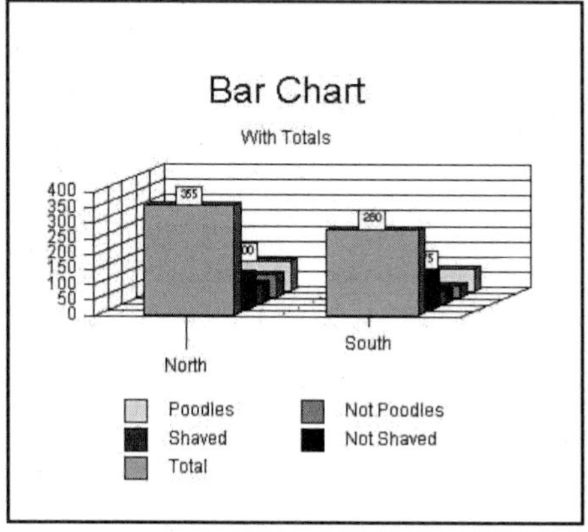

Fig. 17.10 A bar chart showing data and totals. The totals line is a series with its own set of bars, but they are disproportionately large.

In this chart, the large bar for totals does not look correct next to the bars for the other series. To keep totals from looking like just another series—and to keep the data points from looking disproportionately large—consider changing the graphic display of the total.

Note

Changing the display of one series is a good idea if that series deserves special attention. For example, you may want to alert readers to the performance of one product, the data concerning one corporate location, or the contribution of foreign sales.

Depending upon the point you are trying to make and the nature of the data displayed in the chart, there are several ways to change the appearance of the data points for one series.

To change the display of one series, choose **C**hart, **S**eries or use the QuickMenu of the series you want to change.

To use the QuickMenu, point the mouse at the series you want to change, click the right mouse button, then choose Edit Series.

The C**u**rrent Series text box in this dialog box contains the name of one of the series. Any changes you make affect the series whose name appears, so be sure that the name of the series you want to change appears there. Simply type the name of the series in the box or click Previous or Next until the proper name appears. The Series Options dialog box has the following functions:

- *Elements.* (The corners of the bars, for example) or any other lines visible in the chart. What you change is determined by which item the menu you are using refers to. If you are changing one series in a bar chart, for instance, **L**ine refers to the lines at the corners of the bars. The **L**ine menu allows you to select the color, style, and thickness of the line, and whether the line has arrowheads.

- *Fill.* This function enables you to choose two colors for whatever pattern you selected—a foreground color and a background color. You can also display the colors as a pattern or as a gradient. Choose **P**attern and the two colors are displayed consistently across the whole chart element.

  Choose Gradient in the Fill Attributes dialog box to separate the colors and they will blend together. One color becomes the center color and the other becomes the outer color. Using one of the F**i**ll Type options, you can choose to blend the two colors in linear fashion (from one side to the other of the chart element), in circular fashion (the two colors form a circular pattern blending from the center outward), or in rectangular fashion (similar to circular, except that the two colors form a rectangle).

Note

Choosing **X** and **Y** Offset in the Fill Attributes dialog box (visible when Gradient is selected) moves the center color left or right as you change the percentage. Setting offset higher than 50% moves the center color right; setting offset lower than 50% moves the color left. Changing the **Y** offset moves the center color up if you set it higher than 50% and moves it down if you set it lower than 50%.

Further fine-tuning is possible with the An**g**le and Blending commands. An**g**le, an active choice with Linear and Rectangular patterns, enables you to rotate the two colors around each other. Blending is usually **A**uto-Step, in which the two colors gradually blend together. When you choose Fix**e**d, you set a number into the window that determines how many stripes will appear in the chart element. Rather than gradually blending the colors, each stripe is a distinct step in the blending of the two colors.

- ***Pattern.*** This function offers a choice of 32 designs, each of which displays the color you choose in the pattern you select.
- *Color.* This function is the main color used to fill the chart element. You can choose from 256 colors—some solid, some with a muted pattern.
- *Shap**e*** (only available when a bar chart is selected). This function enables you to change the shape of the bar in a bar chart.

To see the results of the changes, click the Pre**v**iew button.

Caution

The appearance of a chart on a color monitor is much different from its appearance when it is printed in black and white. Be sure that your changes do not make the printed copy more difficult to interpret.

The C**u**rrent Series box is also where you select the type of chart for the one series. Figure 17.11 shows the results of choosing Li**n**e as the type of chart for the Totals series.

In figure 17.11, the line is floating above the bars because all numbers for all data points correspond to the numbers on the Y-axis to the left. You may want to display the line for totals in front of the bars, which makes the bars appear higher. To display the line in front of the bars, select Y2 as the axis for the Totals series. A second Y-axis appears at the right side of the chart and is used only for the Totals series.

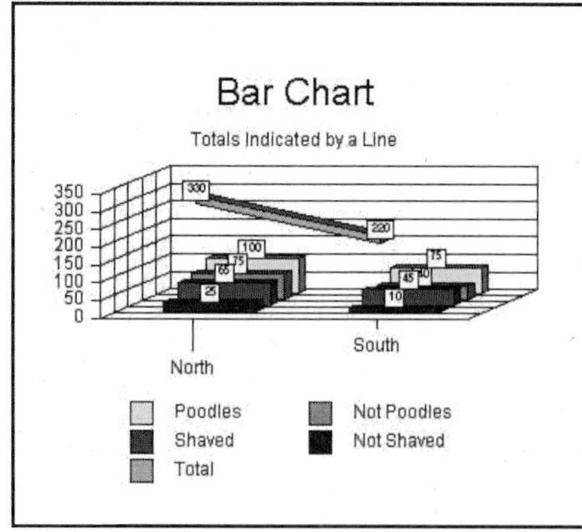

Fig. 17.11
The totals series has been changed so that it is now represented by a line chart. A second Y-axis represents the values for the total series so that it does not float too high above the bars.

Note

When you use two y-axes, be sure to give each a title so that the reader knows what data series goes with which axis. Select **C**hart, **T**itles or right-click the chart and choose **T**itles. Choose Y1 and type its title, then choose Y2 and type its title.

Making Changes to Individual Chart Types

The changes listed in the preceding section are possible with all the chart types, but each type has unique qualities that can be changed by choosing **C**hart, **L**ayout or **C**hart, **S**eries. Some changes are possible with several types of charts. Degree of overlap, for example, is part of the **C**hart, **L**ayout menu for line, area, and bar charts.

Pie Chart Changes

Choose **C**hart**,** **L**ayout to make the pie chart three-dimensional, to tilt the pie, or to explode pieces.

Tip
Clicking 3D toggles the pie between three- and two-dimensional.

To explode a pie piece, type the number of the piece (trial and error will determine which piece is which number) and type the distance between the piece and the pie.

Under Appearance in the Pie Layout dialog box, the following choices are available:

- *De**p**th*. This is the thickness of the pie. Maximum is 100.
- *Size*. This is the overall diameter of the pie. Maximum is 100.
- *Angle*. This is when the pie is rotated about its center. The number is in degrees, therefore the maximum is 360.
- *Ti**l**t*. This determines the degree to which the back of the pie appears higher than the front. Values range from 10 to 90 degrees.

Scatter Chart Changes

The only unique change possible in a scatter chart involves using **C**hart, **S**eries, picking one series, and changing the appearance of the individual data points. Eleven styles of points are available, including an X, a box, a triangle, and several types of stars. Use the Si**z**e box to change the size of the data points on a scale from 1 to 10.

High/Low Changes

The normal display of the high/low data points is a vertical bar with two wings. Change this default by choosing **B**ar/Error Bar, **E**rror Bar, or **A**rea options from the **C**hart, **L**ayout menu. Change the size of the resulting data points with the size options.

Placing the Chart in the Document

When the chart looks like you want it to, you must decide how it should be placed in the document. Chapter 7, "Integrating Text and Graphics," and Chapter 23, "Desktop Publishing with WordPerfect," deal with the options and considerations important to the placement of any graphic within a document.

After you place the chart in the document, you can still make changes. Double-click the chart and you switch back to WP Draw's Chart edit mode. Click the chart with the right mouse button to open the QuickMenu, which allows changes to the chart.

Items in the lower part of the QuickMenu are used to affect the appearance of the chart in the document. For example, you can add a caption outside of the chart box.

Although size is one of the choices in the menu, you may prefer to click and drag one of the selection handles to resize the chart box.

◄ See "Using Graphics Boxes," p. 275

► See "Printing Graphics," p. 802

You can also choose Feature Bar from the QuickMenu to show a row of buttons that performs the same function as some items in the QuickMenu.

Choose **I**mage Tools from the QuickMenu. A small Toolbar appears that enables you to make several changes to the chart. To see the function of a button, place the mouse arrow in the button and look in the upper-left corner of the WordPerfect window. A short description of the button function appears.

From Here...

In this chapter, you learned how to use data in a table to create a chart. The creation and modification of charts in WordPerfect 6.1 for Windows is a powerful tool for allowing the reader to interpret data.

For more information, refer to the following chapters:

- Chapter 7, "Integrating Text and Graphics," shows how to combine text and graphics in a document.
- Chapter 21, "Using Advanced Graphics Techniques," discusses using the advanced graphics features and includes editing graphics.
- Chapter 23, "Desktop Publishing with WordPerfect," covers advanced printing techniques, including working with graphics and color, and improving print quality.

Chapter 18

Importing Data and Working with Other Programs

by Judy Felfe and Alan Westenbroek

In many offices, several types of programs are used—word processing, spreadsheets, graphics programs, and databases, for example. Exchanging data between programs, therefore, becomes more and more important.

Most programs create data files in unique formats. Each program understands its own format but usually requires an interpreter to exchange its information with other programs, especially if the data contains complex formatting instructions. The process of interpreting a data file into the style used by other programs is called *document conversion*. Most word processing programs, including WordPerfect, include built-in document conversion from—and to—many other word processing formats.

One reason for the success of Windows is that it establishes standards for the sharing of data. For example, Windows requires programs to use certain data formats in the Clipboard—a utility that stores data and oversees data exchange between programs. Because of these standards, the Clipboard can perform document conversions of simple text, complex formatting, detailed graphics, or spreadsheets that other methods cannot.

In this chapter, you learn to perform the following tasks:

- Set file preferences for importing files
- Import files created by other programs

- Export documents to other programs
- Import documents via the Clipboard
- Import and link documents with DDE
- Embed, link, and edit objects with OLE
- Import and link data from spreadsheet and database programs

Windows also offers Dynamic Data Exchange (DDE), another method of sharing data. DDE creates a link between the Windows program that created a data file and another Windows program, such as WordPerfect. When data is changed in the originating program, you can update the linked data. (If both programs are memory-resident, the data could be updated automatically.)

Object Linking and Embedding (OLE) is still another way for programs running under Windows to share data. An OLE link creates an embedded object that is linked to data in another location. When you create an OLE link in WordPerfect to data from another program, you can open the source application and change the linked data while you're editing the WordPerfect document. Because data is updated at the source, it stays current in both places.

WordPerfect 6.1 supports the newest specification for Object Linking and Embedding, OLE 2.0. Version 2 offers several enhancements to OLE, including improved speed, an improved interface, and *in-place editing*. In-place editing allows you to create or edit an OLE document from within another document without the need to switch programs. For more information on OLE, see the section "Creating an OLE Link to Data in Another Program" later in this chapter.

In addition to supporting the Windows Clipboard and both DDE and OLE, WordPerfect for Windows has its own tools for importing data and working with other programs. WordPerfect converts documents written in more than 50 other text (word processing and ASCII) file formats into its own format, and it converts its own documents into those same formats. WordPerfect also directly imports data from spreadsheet programs and database programs. New formats are added to WordPerfect's list of supported formats on an ongoing basis.

Even with the powerful data-exchange methods provided by WordPerfect and Windows, the results of a conversion are not always perfect; complex formatting can complicate the conversion process. Formatting elements such as special tab settings, font changes, columns, mixed text justification, headers, footers, page numbering, styles, bullets, hypertext (links to other places in a document or other documents or to macros), sound clips, graphics elements, graphics text boxes, tables, and equations all contribute to the complexity of conversion.

Converting a word processing document offers one set of challenges; importing data from a spreadsheet or database document offers a different set of challenges. Importing a wide spreadsheet or a database with many fields, for example, poses the challenge of making the width of the imported columns (fields) fit across a WordPerfect page.

Understanding the Conversion Process

WordPerfect makes document conversion as seamless as possible. You can open or insert a file into a WordPerfect editing window, and if the file is not in WordPerfect 6.1 format, the conversion process begins automatically.

Note

If you select a file after choosing **F**ile, **O**pen, the selected file opens in an empty document window. If you select a file after choosing **I**nsert, F**i**le (instead of **O**pen), the file is inserted into the current document at the cursor position.

To convert a file from—or to—another format, WordPerfect must store information about that format. WordPerfect stores information about many different text, spreadsheet, database, and graphic file formats. The WordPerfect program is updated by Novell on an ongoing basis to include support for additional formats.

Note

To update your copy of WordPerfect so that it includes any newly supported formats, you can contact Novell to obtain new disks with the updated information.

Using the information that is stored for the selected file format, WordPerfect automatically brings the document into the main editing window with most, if not all, of the original text and formatting intact. You may have to answer prompts regarding the conversion while it takes place. The time required to perform the conversion can range from a few seconds to several minutes, depending on the size of the file and the hardware configuration of the system on which you are operating WordPerfect (see fig. 18.1).

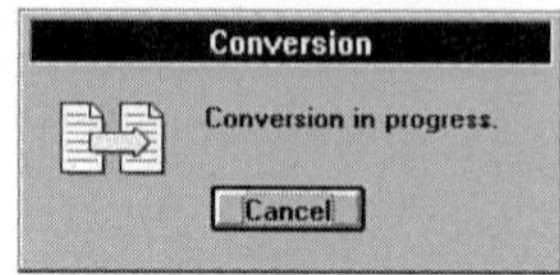

Fig. 18.1
The Conversion dialog box displays this message.

The amount of original formatting retained in the converted document depends on the complexity of the formatting in the original document.

Another way to convert a document from one format to another is to copy and paste data from the first document to the second by using the Windows Clipboard. To use this method, both the program using the original format and the program using the new format must be installed on the system on which the conversion takes place. The Clipboard conversion process is totally seamless. After data is selected and copied from the originating document—for example, from Ami Pro—it is stored on the Clipboard both in its native format and in standardized Windows format. If the data is pasted into another program—for example, WordPerfect—it is automatically converted to the format used by that program.

In addition to recognizing many document formats, WordPerfect recognizes many graphics formats and automatically converts files in those formats into WordPerfect format when the contents of a graphics file are placed in a WordPerfect graphics box. For general information on opening and retrieving documents, see Chapter 3, "Retrieving and Editing Documents." For information on integrating text and graphics, see Chapter 7, "Integrating Text and Graphics."

Setting File Preferences for Imported Files

This section discusses setting defaults for imported files. The types of files that are affected by these defaults are ASCII delimited text files, Windows Metafiles, and any file that is imported with an ASCII code page (character set) that is different from the expected character set.

Import preferences are customized in the Convert Preferences dialog box (see fig. 18.2). To display the Import Preferences dialog box, choose **E**dit, Pr**e**ferences; then choose Co**n**vert. (One option, **C**ode Pages, can be customized either by choosing the **O**ptions button in the Convert Preferences dialog box, or by choosing **E**dit, Pr**e**ferences, **E**nvironment, Co**d**e Page.)

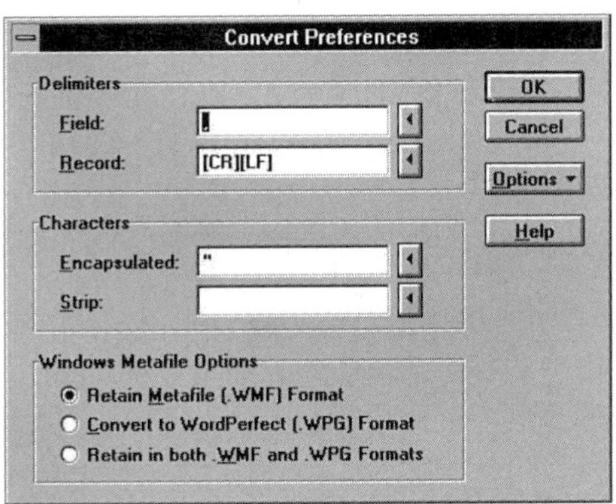

Fig. 18.2
In the Convert Preferences dialog box, you can customize import preferences.

When you import an ASCII delimited text file, you must accept or adjust the values of options that define the format of the file. When you import graphics data through the Clipboard, you accept options regarding the retention of Metafile data. When you import any data file, you accept the option setting for code pages. You can customize the defaults for these types of options in the Convert Preferences dialog box by choosing the pop-up list control and selecting a code from the list of common codes (refer to fig. 18.2) or by typing the information.

Setting Preferences for ASCII Delimited Text Files

The delimiters in an ASCII delimited text file separate the data into fields and records. The data also may contain extra characters (typically quotation marks) that encapsulate field values. Not all ASCII delimited text files have the same field and record separators or the same, if any, encapsulation. When you import an ASCII delimited text file, WordPerfect prompts you to accept or change the format settings. You can avoid customizing these settings every time you import an ASCII delimited text file if you adjust the default settings to match the settings for your incoming data.

If the database or spreadsheet file that you want to import is not formatted in one of WordPerfect's supported file formats, you still can import it by converting the database or spreadsheet from its native format to an ASCII delimited text file format.

Tip
Many database and spreadsheet programs have a built-in export option that creates an ASCII delimited text file from a database or spreadsheet file.

Setting Preferences for Metafiles

When graphic data is copied (or cut) to the Clipboard, that data is automatically formatted in Metafile format, a standardized Windows format. When you paste the graphic data into a WordPerfect document, the data is retained according to your Metafile option settings. You can adjust the default

Metafile options by choosing **E**dit, Pr**e**ferences, Co**n**vert. You can ask WordPerfect to retain Windows Metafiles in both Metafile format (WMF) and WordPerfect Format (WPG) (the default) or in just one of these two formats.

The default setting for the Windows Metafile option, Retain **M**etafile.WMF Format, keeps the original format. This setting uses the most disk space, but it is the most flexible. An image retained in WPG format can be displayed in WordPerfect on other platforms, and when it is edited with WordPerfect's Image Editor, more editing options are available than when the image is retained in WMF format. The appearance of an image usually is close to identical in either format. Some images look slightly better in one format; others look better in the other format.

Setting Preferences for Code Pages and Other Options

You can set four different types of convert options by choosing the **O**ptions button in the Import Preferences dialog box. These option types include **C**ode Pages, **D**ocument, **W**P 4.2 Fonts, and DCA/Display Write **F**onts. To see or change the settings for any of these options, choose **O**ptions in the Convert Preferences dialog box, and then choose an option type.

Code pages are DOS-defined lists that define the character sets used in different languages. Every file contains a code-page definition in its prefix. If a document was saved with a code page for a language other than the one built into your hardware, the data may contain characters that WordPerfect does not recognize. Regardless of the file's format, when WordPerfect opens a document containing an unrecognized character, it usually replaces the character with a space.

As a partial solution to this problem, you can set WordPerfect's Convert feature to recognize different code-page definitions. You can set the Input Code Page to Hebrew, for example, before you import a file with a Hebrew code page. A file with a code-page format that is not in the list of input-supported code pages is automatically imported with the DOS code page—unless the file is in ANSI format, in which case it is imported in the Windows code-page format. You can customize the input and output files' code pages.

▶ See "Using Merge," p. 624

▶ See "Understanding Data Files," p. 633

▶ See "Understanding the Merge Process," p. 646

Other types of options in the **O**ptions list are applied when a conversion is performed to or from a specific file format. Changing any of these options to match imported or exported files results in a more accurate conversion.

After you change any of the options on the **O**ptions list, choose OK to save changes and return to the Convert Preferences dialog box.

After you finish setting preferences in the Convert Preferences dialog box, choose OK; then, in the Preferences dialog box, choose **C**lose.

For information on importing spreadsheet/database files, see the section "Importing and Working with Spreadsheet/Database Data," later in this chapter.

Importing and Working with Word Processing Data

In this section, you learn to import and work with word processing data. The section covers the following topics:

- Importing documents with WordPerfect's Convert
- Saving converted documents
- Converting documents to an intermediate format
- Importing documents with the Clipboard
- Importing documents with Dynamic Data Exchange (DDE)
- Embedding document objects with OLE

Importing Documents with WordPerfect's Convert Feature

This section discusses the use of WordPerfect's Convert feature to import document files that are saved on disk. WordPerfect 6.1 for Windows converts files from and to more than 50 other word processing formats. The following formats are supported by the WordPerfect 6.1 Convert feature:

Ami Pro 1.2-3.0

ANSI, delimited/generic

ASCII, delimited/generic

Excel Spreadsheet, 3.0, 4.0

Lotus 123 Spreadsheet, 1.0-4.0 for Windows

Microsoft Word 1.0-2.0C

Quattro Pro 1.0, 5.0, 6.0

RTF

RTF Help File

Windows Write

WordPerfect 5.0, 5.1/5.2, 6.0/6.1

Note

If you need to convert a large number of documents to or from the WordPerfect 6.1 format, consider using ConvertPerfect 2.0 or a third-party conversion program that supports the WordPerfect 6.1 format and converts documents in a batch process. ConvertPerfect is a stand-alone utility program available from Novell.

Note

Whenever a new file format appears on the market, it takes time for other programs to provide support for that format. While this lack of support exists for the WordPerfect 6.1 format, the only way to translate a document from another word processing program to WordPerfect 6.1 format, or to translate from WordPerfect 6.1 to another word processing program, is to perform the conversion with WordPerfect (or with ConvertPerfect 2.0, a WordPerfect utility). As other programs provide file support for the new WordPerfect format, these programs will be able to perform conversions to and from WordPerfect 6.1.

Starting the Conversion Process

The conversion process begins as soon as you choose a document for editing and WordPerfect determines that the file is not in WordPerfect format. To convert a document file from another format to WordPerfect format, follow these steps:

1. Choose **F**ile, **O**pen; or press Ctrl+O.

   Alternatively, choose the name of the document you want to open from the bottom of the **F**ile menu; or choose **I**nsert, F**i**le to display the Insert File dialog box.

2. In the Open File dialog box, change the default directory, if necessary, to the directory that contains the document to be converted. For example, in the **F**ilename text box, type **c:\amipro\docs** and press Enter. Alternatively, you can browse directories or choose a directory using the **Q**uickList.

3. Scroll through the list of files until the file that you want to convert is highlighted (for example, AMINEWS.SAM).

4. Double-click the file name or press Enter. Depending on the actual format, one of the following actions occurs as soon as you choose a file:

   - If the file uses a WordPerfect 6.1 format, the program automatically brings it into an editing screen, using the WordPerfect 6.1 format.

   - If the file uses a WordPerfect 5.x format, a `Conversion in progress` message appears in a Conversion message box while the file is being converted to WordPerfect 6.1 format. The message disappears when the converted document is brought into an editing screen.

   - When the file uses any other text file format that WordPerfect recognizes—including a WordPerfect 4.2 format—the program displays the Convert File Format dialog box (see fig. 18.3), which displays a suggested format. In almost every case, the suggested format is correct; all you do is double-click its name or choose OK.

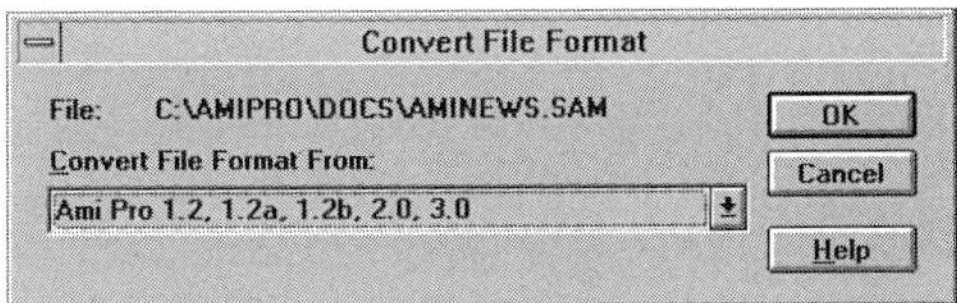

Fig. 18.3
If WordPerfect needs to convert a file's format from what appears to be a word processing program's file format, it suggests a format that seems to match the format of the incoming file.

   - If the file uses a supported spreadsheet or database format, WordPerfect automatically displays the Import Data dialog box. For more information on importing spreadsheet and database files, see "Importing and Working with Spreadsheet/Database Data," later in this chapter.

   - If the file seems to use an unsupported format, an `Unknown Format` message appears in the Convert File Format message box. In this case, you need to determine the original file format and whether you can bring its information into WordPerfect. For detailed information, see "Converting Documents to an Intermediate Format" and "Importing Documents with the Clipboard" later in this chapter.

Tip
If the document is password-protected, you'll get the Password dialog box. Type the password and press Enter to continue with the conversion process.

5. As soon as you see that Convert has correctly identified the format of the document, choose OK. The conversion begins.

Note

In the rare case that WordPerfect incorrectly detects the file's format, the conversion is unsatisfactory. To use a conversion format other than the one suggested by WordPerfect, scroll the list of formats and select another one. If you don't know for sure what the actual format is, and if the document is in the data directory of another word processing program, try converting from the format for that program.

During the conversion, you may need to answer questions about the conversion process. The Position Hyphen dialog box, for example, may prompt you to make a decision about hyphenating a particular word. You can temporarily disable the hyphenation feature by choosing the Suspend Hyphenation option. If, after the conversion is complete, the result is unsatisfactory, you may want to try the conversion again, this time supplying different answers to these conversion questions.

After the conversion process is complete, the document appears on-screen.

Editing a Converted Document

Before you edit a converted document, examine the new document carefully to determine whether the conversion result is acceptable. If important formatting or other details have been lost or incorrectly converted, consider trying another conversion approach.

Document conversion works best on documents with simple formatting and a minimum of graphics. The success of the conversion depends on the formatting complexity of the original document.

The document shown in figure 18.4 contains many elements found in complex documents. The newsletter-style page has a masthead, two graphics images, and a columnar layout. The types of problems that occur when you convert a document with formatting as complex as this are the same whether the document originates in Ami Pro, Word for Windows, or another word processing program for which WordPerfect has a conversion format.

Chappy Trails

Issue 1 **Chappaquidick Publishing, Ltd** **January, 1994**

Typical Winter Weather

After a particularly balmy fall, the weather here on Chappaquidick has settled into our usual pattern of dark, gray days followed by long, cold nights. We've seen very little sunshine since

Mostly Cloudy, Little Snow

Thanksgiving, but very little snow, either.

The few residents hardy enough to withstand the solitude have settled in for the winter, happy to enjoy the peace and quiet.

Fishing is Better than Average

Fishermen report that seas have been relatively calm for this time of year, and the nets have been full. This is good news, since past years have seen a depleted stock of good fish in these waters.

Shellfishermen have been seeding new areas in Edgartown harbor. They hope to replenish a once fruitful natural resource. Up Island, similar seeding programs have been successful in Mnemsha Harbor.

Looking forward to the summer tourist season, most charter boats have been taken out of the water for cleaning and repairs.

Building Permits Approved

Town hall announced that five requests for building permits for new construction were filed and approved; eight requests for permits for renovation are still pending.

Applications must be received by February fifteenth if you want to have approval before the Spring building season starts.

Community Center Activities

The Community Center is planning its summer schedule. Any one interested in offering classes or sponsoring any kind of an event is asked to stop in or give a call. Programs for children are especially welcome.

Also, the Center is looking for a secretary. If you are interested, or know someone, please call.

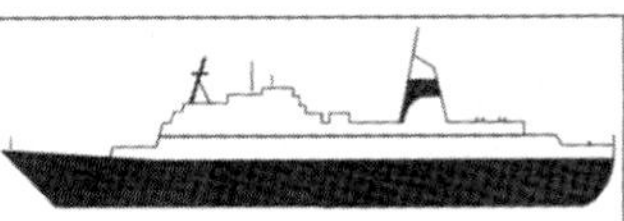

The Steamship Authority Announced its Schedule For 1994 is now Available.

Ferry Reservations: February 1!

Fig. 18.4
An Ami Pro document that has complex formatting.

After this newsletter (an Ami Pro 3 document) is converted by WordPerfect's Convert function, the resulting document appears as shown in figure 18.5. All the body text in the editing screen is retained, although minor font adjustment is needed. The graphic image in the masthead, however, is missing. (The masthead itself is not displayed on the document screen, but it does print out at the end of the document.) The text that appeared in Ami Pro frames is not converted. You can use the Clipboard to import the text in frames. (Hint: In the Ami Pro document, select the text in the frame; don't select the frame itself.) Copy the selected text to the Clipboard and paste it into the converted document in WordPerfect. You also can import the graphic image via the Clipboard.

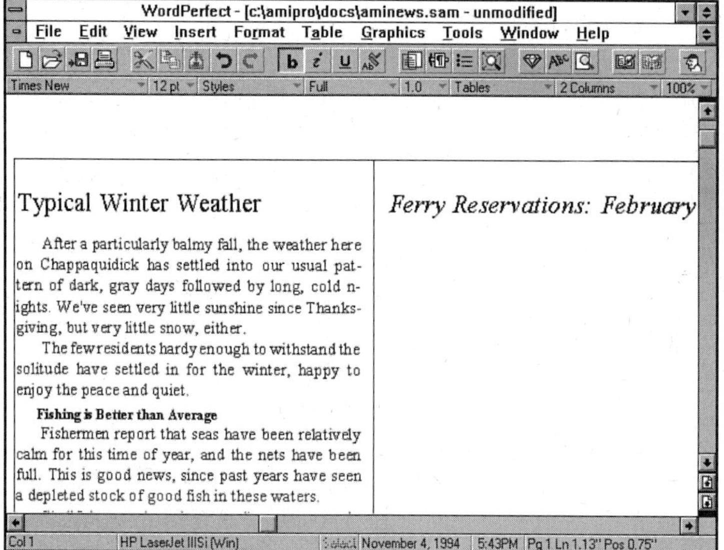

Fig. 18.5
The Ami Pro document shown in figure 18.4 after it is converted by WordPerfect for Windows. Body text is imported successfully; the graphic image and text in frames must be copied and pasted into the converted document.

With documents as complex as this newsletter, however, the best method may be to simply copy and paste text and graphics separately via the Clipboard. Converting the document text by copying and pasting sometimes results in a better conversion than the one performed by WordPerfect's Convert function.

For detailed information on combining text with graphics, refer to Chapter 7, "Integrating Text and Graphics."

Saving a Converted Document

When you use the Save feature (**F**ile, **S**ave; or press Ctrl+S) to save a file that is converted from another format, WordPerfect displays a message box stating the original format of the file and asking whether you want to overwrite it in WordPerfect 6.1 format. If you choose OK to the overwrite question, WordPerfect replaces the original file with the converted file. If you want to save the file back in its original file format, choose that format and then choose OK.

Exporting Documents with WordPerfect's Convert Feature

You convert a WordPerfect document to another supported format by bringing the document to an editing window and using the Save As feature to save it in another format. To convert the document in the current WordPerfect editing window, follow these steps:

1. Choose **F**ile, Save **A**s; or press F3. The Save As dialog box appears.

2. In the Save As dialog box, change the directory, if desired.

3. If necessary, select the File**n**ame option and then type a new file name.

4. The Save File as **T**ype entry suggests a WordPerfect 6.0/6.1 format (unless the document on-screen is an imported ASCII text file, in which case the original format is the suggested format). Use the Format list to choose the appropriate export format.

5. Choose OK or press Enter. A `Conversion in progress` message is displayed while the convert and save operations take place.

The only situation in which WordPerfect wants to save a document in a format other than its own format is when you resave a file that was opened as an ASCII-formatted file. The rationale for this exception is that the system and software programs store information in ASCII-formatted files (for example, the CONFIG.SYS and AUTOEXEC.BAT files) and cannot read these files if they are stored in any other format. When the system or programs fail to find a readable file containing essential information, the result can be a serious malfunction or total system failure. To guard against this potential problem, WordPerfect defaults to using the ASCII format for saving opened ASCII files.

> **Caution**
>
> The ASCII fail-safe protection doesn't work when an ASCII document is inserted into an editing window containing text or formatting that is not in ASCII format. In this situation, WordPerfect defaults to using its native Version 6.1 style when the document is saved, even if it replaces a document in ASCII format.

When you save a document in the WordPerfect 6.1 format, all its formatting feature and function codes remain intact. The next time the document is opened or inserted into a WordPerfect 6.1 editing window, its appearance onscreen is the same as when it was saved, unless one of the following problems occurs:

- The program cannot locate the printer definition that was active when the document was saved.
- The program is set for automatic document formatting and for using an active printer driver other than the driver that was active when the document was saved.

In either of these situations, WordPerfect attempts to format the document in a manner that duplicates its original appearance.

When a document is edited in WordPerfect and saved in any other format, however, the save operation automatically and permanently removes all WordPerfect formatting or feature and function codes not recognized by the file format in which it is saved. If the document contains a table and is saved in WordPerfect 4.2 format, for example, the program automatically replaces the table structure with protected parallel columns that simulate the structure, if not the appearance, of the original table. Even if you immediately retrieve the document and resave it in WordPerfect 6.1 format, the original table structure is lost unless you manually re-create it.

Converting Documents to an Intermediate Format

If WordPerfect cannot convert its documents to another word processing program's format, and if the other word processing program cannot convert its own documents to WordPerfect format, a possible solution lies in using an intermediate format that is supported by both programs. The extent of formatting that is preserved depends on several factors, including how well the first program handles the conversion to the intermediate format.

Using RTF as an Intermediate Format

Tip
If WordPerfect can't read a document created in another program and no intermediate shared format exists, use the Clipboard to convert the document.

Rich Text Format (RTF) is a standard document format used by Windows programs. RTF is designed to let programs use the same codes to represent document formatting details such as margins, indents, columns, justification, typeface, font size, boldface, italics, and underlining. In theory, word processing programs that use this common format can exchange documents with virtually all formatting elements transferring intact. RTF is not perfect, but it does a good job of translating documents between word processing programs.

You can convert documents to RTF format either with WordPerfect's **O**pen/**I**nsert F**i**le features or with the Clipboard.

The major limitation of the RTF format is that it does not support conversion of graphics images, graphic text boxes, or table structures. When RTF proves to be the best conversion alternative for the text in a document, use RTF for text conversion and import the graphics separately, using a format supported by WordPerfect.

Using ASCII Text or ANSI Text as an Intermediate Format

When all else fails, save the document to be converted in ASCII text or in ANSI text format. These categories produce lowest-common-denominator results. Very little, if any, of the original formatting is preserved, but the ASCII/ANSI formats retain most (if not all) of the original document's text. It can be easier to convert a very long document to ASCII text or ANSI text and then convert it again to the second word processing program than it is to retype the document. Use ANSI text format as an intermediate format between two Windows programs; otherwise, use ASCII text as an intermediate format.

Importing Documents with the Clipboard

The Windows Clipboard provides a quick and easy way to transfer data from one program to another. You can transfer both formatted text and graphics from one word processing program to another via the Clipboard. Because Windows programs are required to use certain standardized data formats when transferring information to the Clipboard, the Clipboard also can be an important conversion tool.

In many cases, the Clipboard preserves formatting features such as margins, indents, columns, typeface, and font size, as well as boldface, italics, underlining, and other complex elements. The Clipboard also can transfer tables and graphics from one document to another. Text on the Clipboard is retained in RTF (Rich Text Format) as well as in the originating program's format.

When you copy a document to the Clipboard and then paste the document into another word processing program, you can preserve all the text and graphics simultaneously. When the document is too complex to be translated successfully all at once, you can try breaking down the translation into more than one operation—that is, you could translate the text first and then the graphics.

The Clipboard has different capabilities, depending on whether you are transferring data between two Windows programs or from a DOS program to another program. When you are copying a document from a DOS program, the Clipboard can transfer only unformatted text.

The following sections explain how to copy with the Clipboard. Notice that you must follow different procedures for copying data to the Clipboard from Windows programs, DOS programs when Windows is running in 386 Enhanced mode, and DOS programs when Windows is running in Standard mode. You must use the correct procedures, or the Clipboard does not work correctly.

Placing Text on the Clipboard

To copy data to the Clipboard from a Windows program or a DOS program with Windows running in 386 Enhanced mode, follow these steps:

1. Start the program from which you want to copy data, and open the file containing the data that you want to copy.

2. If you are running a Windows program, maximize it to full screen.

   If you are running a DOS program in 386 Enhanced mode, the program should be running in a window; if the program has started full screen, press Alt+Enter to reduce the program to a window.

3. Select the data that you want to copy.

4. Copy the selected data to the Clipboard.

   If you are copying data from a Windows program, choose **E**dit, **C**opy; or press Ctrl+C. The data is copied to the Clipboard.

When Windows is running in Standard mode, DOS programs can run only full screen or minimized to an icon, so the preceding procedure does not work. You can, however, press the Print Screen key to copy an entire screen to the Clipboard.

Pasting Data from the Clipboard

After data is copied to the Clipboard, the next step is to paste the data into the destination program. Notice that you must follow different procedures for pasting data from the Clipboard into Windows programs, into DOS programs when Windows is running in 386 Enhanced mode, and into DOS programs when Windows is running in Standard mode. You must use the correct procedures, or the Clipboard does not work correctly.

To paste data into a Windows program or a DOS program when Windows is running in 386 Enhanced mode, follow these steps:

1. Start the program into which you want to paste data from the Clipboard. If you are copying into a DOS program, make sure that the DOS program is running in a window.
2. Open the document into which you want to paste the data.
3. Place the insertion point in the document where you want to insert the data.
4. Paste the data into the program.

   If you are pasting into a Windows program, choose **E**dit, **P**aste; or press Ctrl+V.

   If you are pasting into a DOS program, use the Control menu and choose **E**dit, **P**aste. Data from the Clipboard is pasted into the destination document.

To paste data from the Clipboard into a DOS program when Windows is running in Standard mode, follow these steps:

1. Start the program and open the document into which you want to paste the data, and position the insertion point at the point where you want to paste the data.
2. Press Alt+Esc to switch back to Windows. The target program is reduced to an icon at the bottom of the Windows Desktop.
3. Click the target program's icon once to open its Control menu.

   Alternatively, press Alt+Esc until the description line below the program's icon is highlighted, and then press Alt+space bar to open the Control menu.
4. Choose **E**dit, **P**aste. Data from the Clipboard is pasted into the destination document.

To copy data from one DOS program to the Clipboard and paste it into another DOS program from the Clipboard, follow the preceding directions for copying data from a DOS program, and then follow the preceding directions for pasting data into a DOS program.

Importing Documents with DDE

Windows Dynamic Data Exchange (DDE) is useful for importing document information into WordPerfect when the important consideration is current information rather than appearance. After you import data with a DDE link, the imported data can be updated (that is, replaced) from the source data. You can make any changes you want to the linked data in WordPerfect without affecting the source data (for example, you could reformat it). Keep in mind, though, that any changes made to linked data are lost whenever the linked data is updated from the source data.

WordPerfect is DDE-capable as a client; it can be linked to any Windows program that is DDE-capable as a server. Many Windows applications, including Ami Pro and Word for Windows, can be linked to WordPerfect with a DDE link.

For detailed instructions on creating a DDE link, see "Creating a DDE Link to Data in Another Program" later in this chapter.

For more information on opening and retrieving documents, see to Chapter 3, "Retrieving and Editing Documents." For more information on integrating text and graphics, see Chapter 7, "Integrating Text and Graphics." For more information on saving documents, refer to Chapter 2, "Creating and Saving a Document."

Importing and Working with Spreadsheet/Database Data

WordPerfect's built-in Spreadsheet/Database Import feature provides an easy-to-use, powerful tool for importing spreadsheet and database data. The imported data can be copied, or it can be both copied and linked at the same time. The Clipboard is another tool for importing spreadsheet and database data. In addition, because WordPerfect is DDE- and OLE-capable as a client, both DDE and OLE are available as tools for importing spreadsheet data from programs that are DDE- or OLE-capable as servers.

Figure 18.6 shows a WordPerfect document containing data that has been copied and pasted (via the Clipboard) from an Excel spreadsheet.

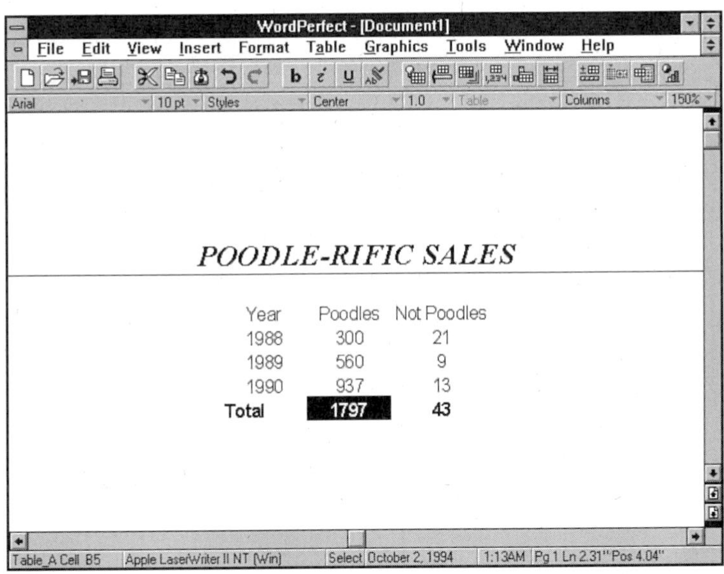

Fig. 18.6
A WordPerfect document containing data pasted from the Clipboard after being copied from an Excel spreadsheet. Calculations are retained as answers rather than as calculations; notice the cell contents on the WordPerfect status bar.

Copying Spreadsheet/Database Data

You can use WordPerfect's Spreadsheet/Database Import to copy data from a spreadsheet or a database, or you can use the Clipboard. When you copy data, the data in WordPerfect is independent of the data in the source file. You can change the data in WordPerfect without affecting the source data, or you can change the data in the spreadsheet/database file without affecting the document in WordPerfect.

Copying Spreadsheet/Database Data with the Import Feature

The Spreadsheet/Database Import feature has several advantages over the Clipboard in copying spreadsheet/database data. One advantage is that calculations in the source data are retained in the copied data. You also have the choice of copying the data into a table format, a merge data file format, or a text format; when you paste from the Clipboard, the data is formatted as a table. Another advantage of a WordPerfect Import is that you can copy from a file on disk; the source file does not have to be open when you perform the copy operation.

Note

Before defining the WordPerfect Import, start the program that was used to create the source data, and load the file containing the source data. If the file is a spreadsheet file, find the range of cells you want in the link, and record the range's address so that the information is available for reference during the link-definition process. If the file is a database file, decide which fields and records you want to import.

To copy spreadsheet/database data with WordPerfect's Import feature, follow these steps:

1. Place the insertion point where you want to place the imported data.
2. Choose **I**nsert, Sp**r**eadsheet/Database, **I**mport. The Import Data dialog box appears.
3. If the suggested Data **T**ype doesn't match the format of the file that you want to import, use the Data **T**ype option to select another type. Figure 18.7 shows the list of available data types.

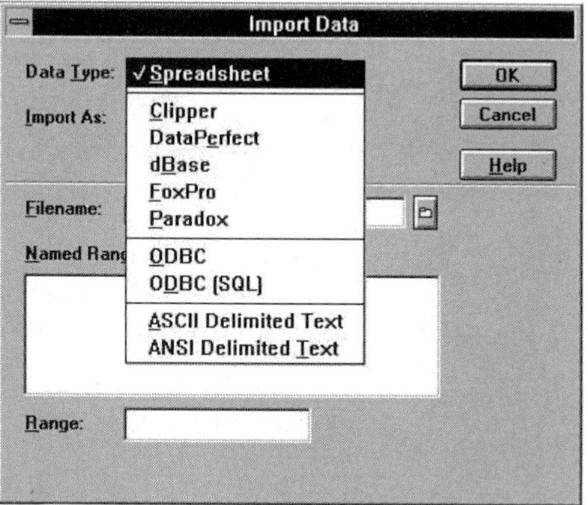

Fig. 18.7
The list of data types in the WordPerfect Import Data dialog box. The same Data Type options (and Import As options) are available when you choose **I**mport or when you choose **C**reate Link.

4. **T**able is the default setting for **I**mport As. Accept this setting if you want to preserve calculations in the imported data. If you would rather import the spreadsheet as a **M**erge Data File or as T**e**xt, make that choice from the **I**mport As list.
5. Choose the **F**ilename option, if necessary, and type the path and name of the file that you want to import, or choose the button to the right of the **F**ilename text box to open the Select File dialog box.

6. Select a file name and choose OK. WordPerfect examines the selected file.

7. If the detected file format belongs to a spreadsheet, the **N**amed Ranges list box displays the entire `<Spreadsheet>` range and any named ranges.

   In the **R**ange text box, type the range of cells that you are importing from the spreadsheet file, or choose a range from the **N**amed Ranges list. The default range is the entire spreadsheet. (If the range is very wide, follow the instructions in the section "Working with Wide Spreadsheets and Database Records," later in this chapter.)

   The completed information for copying spreadsheet data appears in figure 18.8.

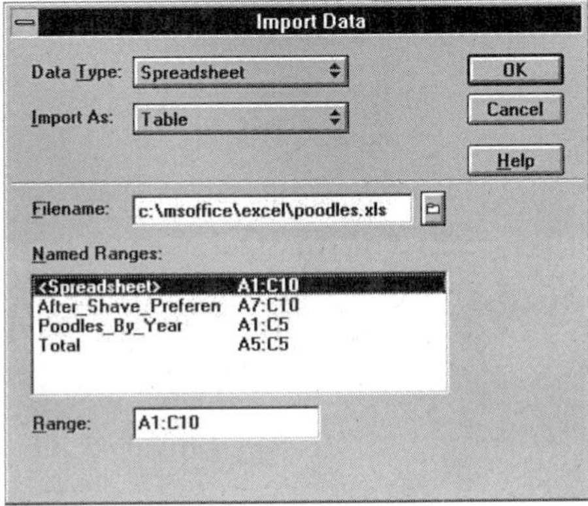

Fig. 18.8
The Import Data dialog box with completed information for importing the cell range A1:C10 from Microsoft Excel.

8. If the detected file format belongs to a database, a Fi**e**lds list box is displayed in the lower portion of the dialog box. All fields are listed and selected for import. (You can deselect fields you don't want to import.) Below the Fi**e**lds list box is an option for using field names as headings. When this option is selected, field names are used as headings in a table or as field names in a merge data file.

   Figure 18.9 shows the Import Data dialog box with completed options.

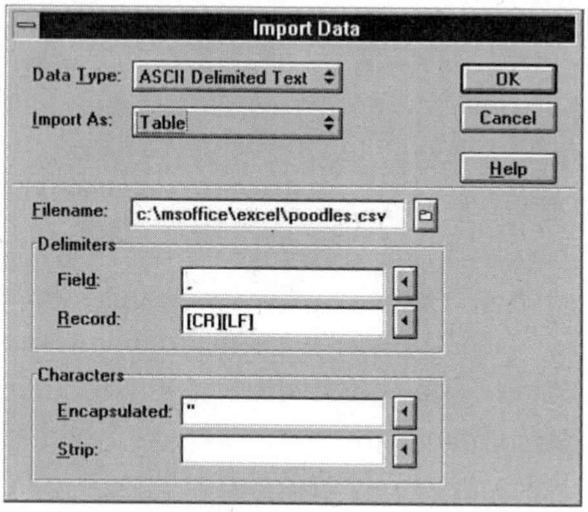

Fig. 18.9
The Import Data dialog box with completed information for importing data from an Excel file.

9. Choose OK to complete the import operation.

▶ See "Examining Advanced Merge Topics," p. 654

The specified data is copied from the source file on disk. A conversion message appears on-screen while the data is being converted to WordPerfect format. When the conversion is complete, the imported data is inserted into the WordPerfect document.

Note

Depending on your particular import task, one or more of the following points may be helpful:

- To convert mathematical functions as calculations rather than answers, import data as a WordPerfect Table. Always check mathematical operations for accuracy. Place the insertion point in a cell containing a calculation to see the calculation (on WordPerfect's status bar).

- You can customize option settings for imported ASCII delimited text files. See the section "Setting File Preferences for Imported Files," earlier in this chapter.

- If SHARE.EXE (a DOS utility program) is not loaded when you attempt an import from some programs, including Paradox, WordPerfect stops the import and identifies the problem. (This doesn't apply to Windows for Workgroups 3.11, which has SHARE built-in.) You can try the import again after exiting from Windows and loading SHARE. Do not attempt to run SHARE from a DOS command line window while Windows is running.

- When you import data from DataPerfect, in addition to choosing the file name, you must choose a Panel. A Panel list box is displayed beneath the **F**ilename text box.

- To access any of the SQL databases, you must log on to the database. After you select the SQL database from the list of data types, choose Logon, and type the Server Name or File Path and Directory Path for Netware SQL. Then type the User ID and Password, and choose Logon.

Copying Spreadsheet/Database Data with the Clipboard

Copying and pasting spreadsheet data with the Clipboard is quick and easy, especially when both programs are Windows products. You simply select and copy the source data, and then paste it into your WordPerfect document.

Note

When you copy and paste data that includes embedded graphics, the results are not perfect. If the results are not satisfactory, try copying the data without the graphics. An embedded graph can also be copied separately with the Clipboard, but the pasted graph is likely to be distorted no matter how it is copied.

Keep in mind that when you copy and paste with the Clipboard, formulas are not copied as formulas, as they are if you use WordPerfect's Import/Link feature and import the data as a table.

Most database programs make selecting an entire data record difficult, if not impossible. This places a severe limitation on the practicality of using the Clipboard for importing database data. Microsoft Access is a notable exception to this selection problem. Access enables you to choose record selectors to select a single record, contiguous records, or an entire table. (A database in Access consists of tables.) You can even hide columns (fields) that you don't want to import. After you complete the selection procedure, you can copy the selected data to the Clipboard and then paste it into a WordPerfect document.

For more information on using the Clipboard to copy data, refer to the section "Importing Documents with the Clipboard," earlier in this chapter.

Copying and Linking Spreadsheet/Database Data

If maintaining current spreadsheet/database information in a WordPerfect document is important, use WordPerfect's built-in Spreadsheet Import/Link feature to link data at the same time that it is copied. You can update the data in your document at any time to make sure that the data is current. Additionally, you can set the default link options so that WordPerfect automatically updates the linked data each time it opens or inserts the document. Keep in mind when you create a link that whenever you update the link, all data between the pair of link codes is replaced, including any formatting changes that you made for cosmetic reasons.

Creating a WordPerfect Spreadsheet/Database Link

To create a WordPerfect link, follow these steps:

1. Place the insertion point in your WordPerfect document where you want to copy and link the imported data.

2. Choose **I**nsert, Sp**r**eadsheet/Database, **C**reate Link. The Create Data Link dialog box appears. Except for its name, this dialog box looks exactly like the Import Data dialog box.

3. In the Create Data Link dialog box, take the same steps that you would take in the Import Data dialog box. (Refer to "Copying Spreadsheet/ Database Data with the Import Feature," earlier in this chapter.)

   The specified data is copied from the file on disk. A conversion message appears on-screen while the data is being converted to WordPerfect format. When the conversion is complete, the data is inserted between a pair of codes in the WordPerfect document. If Link Options are set to display link icons, the link icons are visible in the editing screen, just above and below the data. (See the section "Setting Options for WordPerfect Links," later in this chapter.)

Editing a WordPerfect Link

You can edit an existing WordPerfect link to change any of the link information that you specified in the Create Data Link dialog box. To edit an existing WordPerfect link, follow these steps:

1. Move the WordPerfect insertion point inside the link that you want to edit.

2. Choose **I**nsert, Sp**r**eadsheet/Database, **E**dit Link. The Edit Data Link dialog box appears.

3. Change any of the specifications that you defined in the Create Data Link dialog box. For example, you could reduce the linked spreadsheet range to remove blank rows.

Caution

Deleting either of the pair of codes removes both codes and destroys the link. The spreadsheet data continues functioning as an imported spreadsheet. The only way to restore the link is to delete the spreadsheet data and define a new link, as described in the preceding section, "Creating a WordPerfect Spreadsheet/Database Link."

Updating Data That Is Linked with a WordPerfect Link

To ensure that data is current in all WordPerfect spreadsheet/database links, ask WordPerfect to update all links. Follow these steps to update WordPerfect links:

1. Choose **I**nsert, Sp**r**eadsheet/Database, **U**pdate. You are prompted with `Update All Data Links?.`
2. To update links, choose **Y**es.

Setting Options for WordPerfect Links

You can adjust the default settings for WordPerfect spreadsheet/database link options in the Link Options dialog box. To adjust the settings of link options, follow these steps:

1. Choose **I**nsert, Sp**r**eadsheet/Database, **O**ptions. The Link Options dialog box appears.
2. The Link Options dialog box contains two options: **U**pdate on Retrieve (the default) and **S**how Link Icons. You can change either option or both options.
3. Choose OK to exit the dialog box and save your settings.

Handling Special Spreadsheet/Database Conditions

This section discusses special situations that can occur when you import spreadsheet/database data.

Working with Password-Protected Files

Password protection is part of a document's formatting that WordPerfect checks before allowing you to import a file. You must remove the password from a file created by a spreadsheet/database program before you can import or link to it, unless the file was created in PlanPerfect. If the file you are importing was created in PlanPerfect and it is password-protected, you are prompted for the password. Type the password and press Enter to continue the import operation.

Tip

Use the horizontal scroll bar and adjust the Zoom factor when you're working with a wide table in WordPerfect.

Working with Wide Spreadsheets and Database Records

WordPerfect tries to make imported spreadsheet/database data fit between the left and right margins of the document. When WordPerfect imports data that is wider than the document margins, formatting problems arise. One or more columns are compressed (table format) or data is wrapped to the next line (text format). If the data is too wide to fit between the margins, you can accommodate the data in any of the following ways:

- Reduce the column (field) widths in the source file.
- Reduce the font size or font type that is active at the location where WordPerfect inserts the imported data.
- Reduce the width of the left and right margins at the location where WordPerfect inserts the imported data.
- Choose a landscape-sheet definition for the page where WordPerfect inserts the imported data if the printer supports this mode, or choose a larger paper size, if possible.
- Use the methods described in Chapter 16, "Working with Tables," and Chapter 30, "Advanced Tables," to resize the table so that it doesn't exceed the space between the margins.
- Use more than one import operation, and import the data in sections. Import one cell range or one set of columns at one place in the WordPerfect document, and import another set at another place.

◀ See "Changing the Table Size," p. 540

◀ See "Editing the Table Structure," p. 536

Working with Unsupported Formats

To use a spreadsheet other than one created by Lotus 1-2-3, Excel 4.0 or before, Quattro/Quattro Pro, Quattro Pro for Windows, or PlanPerfect, you must convert the spreadsheet to one of the formats recognized by WordPerfect.

Most spreadsheet programs enable you to convert a spreadsheet to Lotus 1-2-3 format. For more information on converting a spreadsheet, see the documentation for the spreadsheet program.

If WordPerfect cannot convert data from the spreadsheet and the spreadsheet program cannot convert the file to a format supported by WordPerfect, converting the spreadsheet to an ASCII format first is a possible solution. Use the spreadsheet program to make an ASCII copy of the spreadsheet file. If the spreadsheet program can create an ASCII delimited text file, you can import the ASCII file into WordPerfect as a table or merge data file. If the ASCII file does not have delimiters, your only option is to open (or insert) the ASCII file as a text file.

When your database is not in one of WordPerfect's supported file formats, you can convert the file to an ASCII delimited text file and then import the ASCII file into WordPerfect. Many database programs have a built-in export option for converting their own database files to ASCII delimited text format. After the database file is in ASCII delimited format, you can import it as a table or merge data file, or you can merge the ASCII file without converting it first. See Chapter 19, "Assembling Documents with Merge and Sort," for information on merging.

Note

For information on setting defaults for imported ASCII delimited text files in WordPerfect, see "Setting File Preferences for Imported Files," earlier in this chapter.

Importing Spreadsheet Data with DDE

A Windows DDE link is an alternative to the WordPerfect spreadsheet link. (See "Copying and Linking Spreadsheet/Database Data," earlier in this chapter, for information on creating a WordPerfect spreadsheet link.) A DDE link gives you automatic updates when both programs are in memory at the same time and when the source (server) file is opened before the WordPerfect document is opened. This is the only advantage that a DDE link has over a WordPerfect spreadsheet link; with either type of link, you can update linked data simply by asking for an update. When the ability to have automatic updates under these circumstances is an overriding consideration, use a DDE link.

To create a DDE link in WordPerfect to data in any Windows spreadsheet program that is DDE-capable as a server (including Excel, Quattro Pro for Windows, and Lotus for Windows), follow the steps for creating a DDE link to data in another program, later in this chapter. While you are creating the link, the Paste Special dialog box is displayed. In the Paste Special dialog box, select the spreadsheet data and choose Paste Link. The data is imported and linked.

Importing Spreadsheet Data with OLE

When you want the convenience of being able to update linked spreadsheet data while you are editing the WordPerfect document that contains the link, you can have that convenience by creating an OLE link to the data. An OLE link creates an embedded object in your document; you can move and size the object with the mouse. Because the object is a graphics image of data rather than of text, its appearance may not be perfect. With a small and simple spreadsheet, the result may be acceptable. For more information on creating an OLE link to a spreadsheet, see "Creating an OLE Link to Data in Another Program," later in this chapter.

◄ See "Understanding Tables," p. 523

Windows DDE and OLE are not available as options for importing database data into WordPerfect.

◄ See "Creating and Using Tables: The Basics," p. 526

► See "Understanding the Merge Process," p. 646

Exporting Spreadsheet/Database Data

With WordPerfect 6.1's powerful built-in tables feature, the need to export data to a spreadsheet or database may never occur. One method for exporting data to a spreadsheet is to format the data in WordPerfect tabular columns (this works best if you use a monospace font), save the document in ASCII text format, and import the file into the spreadsheet. You then can parse the data into cells. See the documentation for your spreadsheet program for information on converting, translating, and importing data and on parsing data.

If a WordPerfect merge data file becomes too large and cumbersome to maintain in WordPerfect, you may want to export the merge data file to a database program. You can export data from WordPerfect to dBASE, for example, by converting the merge data file to ASCII delimited format with WordPerfect's internal convert process and then appending that file to a file with an appropriate structure. See your database program's reference manual for instructions on importing data from other programs.

Importing and Working with Graphics Data and Other Types of Data

Tip
To see which applications on your hardware installation support DDE/OLE, choose **I**nsert, Ob**j**ect and look at the Object **T**ype list in the dialog box.

The list of data types that can be imported into WordPerfect includes graphics images, text, charts, spreadsheets, database data, sound clips, and video clips. Guidelines for importing data from other word processing programs and from spreadsheet/database programs are presented earlier in this chapter. This section discusses the importation of data types—for example, graphics, sound, and video.

WordPerfect supports graphics formats from more than 75 of the most popular Windows and non-Windows graphics programs. Among the programs from which you can import graphics data are Freelance Graphics, Harvard Graphics, WordPerfect Presentations, CorelDRAW!, and Arts & Letters. You can import into a WordPerfect document a file saved in any compatible graphics format simply by placing that file in a graphics box. For a complete list of graphics formats supported by WordPerfect, and for more information about working with different graphics formats, see "Graphics: Formats and Programs" in the WordPerfect reference manual. For more information about working with graphics images, see Chapter 7, "Integrating Text and Graphics," in this book.

Tip
You can export data from WordPerfect 6.1 to another program by copying and pasting or by using DDE or OLE.

The quickest and easiest method of importing data into WordPerfect is to select the data in the source program, copy it to the Clipboard, and paste it into a WordPerfect document. If the data is clip art—that is, a graphics file on disk—you can create a graphics box and insert the image into the WordPerfect graphics box.

If you want to keep imported data current, and if the source program has DDE capability as a server, you can choose to import the data with a DDE link. If you want the convenience of editing the imported data while you are editing your WordPerfect document, and if the source program has OLE capability as a server, you can choose to import the data with an OLE link. Either of these techniques is appropriate, for example, for keeping data from an imported chart current in WordPerfect.

Note

The instructions in this section for creating Windows DDE and OLE links can be applied to the importation of data from any source that is DDE- or OLE-capable as a server. (If a program is DDE-capable as a server, it isn't necessarily OLE-capable as a server.)

Creating a DDE Link to Data in Another Program

To create a DDE link in a WordPerfect document to data in another program, follow the instructions in this section. The other program must be DDE-capable as a server, and the file containing the data to be linked must have a name (that is, it must have been saved). Creating the link is easiest if you have already started the server application and the data file containing the data to be linked is already open. After these conditions are met, follow these steps to create a DDE link:

1. Select the data that you want to link.
2. Copy the selected data to the Clipboard by choosing **E**dit, **C**opy or by pressing Ctrl+C.
3. Start WordPerfect. (Don't close the other program; you can minimize it or switch to the Program Manager.)
4. Open the document into which you want to import the data, and place the insertion point where you want to create the link.
5. Choose **E**dit, Paste **S**pecial. The Paste Special dialog box appears.
6. Choose Paste **L**ink to place a copy of the source data in the WordPerfect document. The beginning of the linked data is identified in Reveal Codes with a code, and the end of the linked data is identified with a code. The code contains an identifying link number.

A DDE link is updated automatically when the server file and the client file are open at the same time and the source file has been opened first. You can update the client file at any time, however, after saving any changes in the source data. Choose **E**dit, Lin**k**s to display the Links dialog box, highlight the name of the link that you want to update, and choose **U**pdate Now. Then choose OK to exit the Links dialog box.

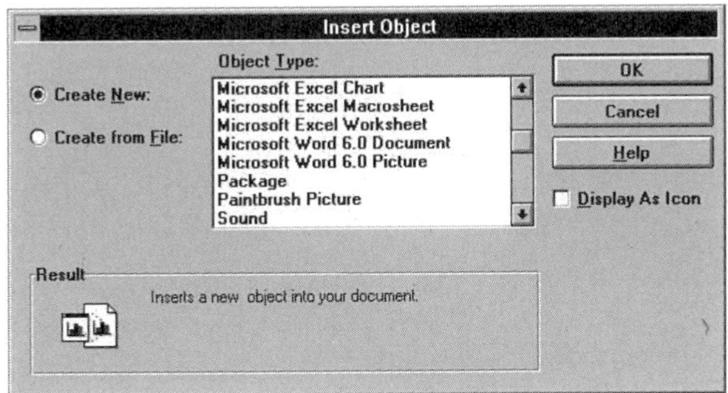

Fig. 18.10
The Insert Object dialog box displays a list of objects that can be inserted from the current hardware installation.

Creating an OLE Link to Data in Another Program

To create an OLE link in a WordPerfect document to data in another program that is OLE-capable as a server—that is, to embed an object in a WordPerfect document—follow these steps:

1. Choose **I**nsert, Ob**j**ect. The Insert Object dialog box appears (see fig. 18.10).

2. Select the Object **T**ype from the list of available object types on your hardware installation. The name of the type includes the name of its server application.

3. The server application starts, taking control of WordPerfect's menus and toolbar. Create the item (document, image, or sound clip, for example) that you want to embed in WordPerfect.

Tip
Another way to embed an object is to choose **E**dit, Paste **S**pecial (in WordPerfect) and select Object after placing the object in the Clipboard.

If the item you want to use has already been created and saved in a document, you can create an embedded object by choosing Create from **F**ile in the Insert Object dialog box.

4. Exit the server application by clicking in the document to deselect the object. WordPerfect's menus and toolbar return.

You can select the embedded object with the mouse and then move or resize the object.

To edit the embedded object at its source, double-click the embedded object. The source application starts, taking control of WordPerfect's menus and toolbar and displaying the embedded object in the WordPerfect document window. After you make your editing changes, exit the source application by clicking in the document to deselect the object. If the embedded object is a sound or movie clip, a double-click plays the clip.

For more information on combining text and graphics, see Chapter 7, "Integrating Text and Graphics."

Using Object Exchange To Publish and Subscribe Documents

Object Exchange (OBEX) is an advanced way of sharing data with other programs and users. OBEX lets you "publish" data in your document (much like creating an object) to members of a workgroup on a Novell NetWare network. Any time the data in your document is changed or updated, each member of your workgroup that has subscribed to that data is notified. Likewise, you may subscribe to data that has been published by any other member of your workgroup. Any time that data changes, you'll be informed.

Currently, OBEX only works with other applications in the Novell PerfectOffice suite (WordPerfect, Quattro Pro for Windows, and so on).

To publish data in your document, follow these steps:

1. Save the document.
2. Choose **F**ile, P**u**blish.
3. Choose the people you want to publish to from the **A**ddress list.
4. Type a meaningful description in the **D**escription box and click **P**ublish.

Be sure to type a good description because that's the way published documents are listed to other members of the workgroup.

To subscribe to data that has already been published, follow these steps:

1. Choose **F**ile, Su**b**scribe.

2. Select a document from the list of descriptions and click **I**nsert.

This will insert the published document into your document at the insertion point. Any time the original document changes, your document will be updated as well.

From Here...

As a user of WordPerfect 6.1 for Windows, you have many ways of sharing data with other programs. You can copy data, copy and link data, and embed an object that represents linked data. You have various tools to use with these methods, depending on the data to be shared. You can use WordPerfect's built-in internal conversion feature to convert a file from one format to another format; you also can use WordPerfect's Spreadsheet/Database Import/Link feature to copy or link and copy spreadsheet and database data. The Windows environment provides the Clipboard, Dynamic Data Exchange (DDE), and Object Linking and Embedding (OLE) as tools for sharing data with other programs.

In this chapter, you learned how to share data with other programs, how to plan for accurate conversion results, and how to work with problems involving the importation of data. These skills will help you share information created in WordPerfect, in other word processing programs, in spreadsheet programs, in database programs, and in graphics programs. See the following chapter for more information:

- Chapter 19 "Assembling Documents with Merge and Sort," shows how to use tables to create data files, and also how to sort tables.

Chapter 19

Assembling Documents with Merge and Sort

by C. Brian Scott and Judy Petersen

Consider the following situations:

You have just been appointed to chair a committee of your child's soccer club and your first task is to send a letter announcing the first meeting to the other committee members. How do you produce the letter and prepare it for mailing to everyone who should receive it?

You must design a new form for use in your office. How do you design the form to make sure that users get the right information in the right place, formatted the right way?

The WordPerfect 6.1 Merge feature provides an answer in both situations. Merge enables you to combine fixed information (the form, its text, and merge codes) with variable information. The variable information can come from a data file or it can be entered by the user.

This chapter explains the merge feature, tells you how to construct simple merges, and introduces advanced features that can be used in complex merges.

This chapter also explains the Sort feature. You can use Sort to order the information in files, whether or not the file is to be used as a data file for a merge operation.

In this chapter, you learn how to:

- Create data files and form files for merging
- Use merge to prepare a form letter mailing and to create envelopes and labels from a mailing list

- Use keyboard input in a merge
- Use only selected records from a data file in a merge
- Merge data into a table
- Use data from other programs

Using Merge

Merge is the process of combining variable information with a file containing fixed information to produce one or more new files. The file with the fixed information is referred to as a *form file*. The variable information can come from user input at the keyboard or from another file referred to as a *data file*.

Many people use a *mail merge* to create customized form letters together with envelopes or labels. In this type of merge, the form file is the letter and the data file is the mailing list. You also can use merge to create "fill in the blank" forms. You can design the forms to be filled in by users at the keyboard or with variable information from a data file.

Performing a Simple Merge

This section demonstrates a typical simple merge. The basic features shown here apply to any merge operation for a mass mailing. Later sections of this chapter provide detailed explanations of the various features used in the demonstration.

Refer to the committee letter example presented earlier in the chapter. To prepare the mailing, you need to create a letter (the form file), a mailing list (the data file), and envelopes for the letters.

Creating the Data File

Although you can create the data and form files in any order, creating the data file first is the easiest approach; you can name the fields in the file and use the field names in your form. For this example, you need the following information for each person who is to receive the letter: first name, last name, address, city, state, and ZIP code.

Note

A *field* is a single item of information (for example, a first name) that you use in your form. (See the "Understanding Data Files" section for more details.) You can combine the first and last names in a single field, but if you do, you can't use just the first name in the salutation of the letter.

To create the data file with the listed fields, follow these steps:

1. Choose **T**ools, M**e**rge; or press Shift+F9. The Merge dialog box appears (see fig. 19.1).

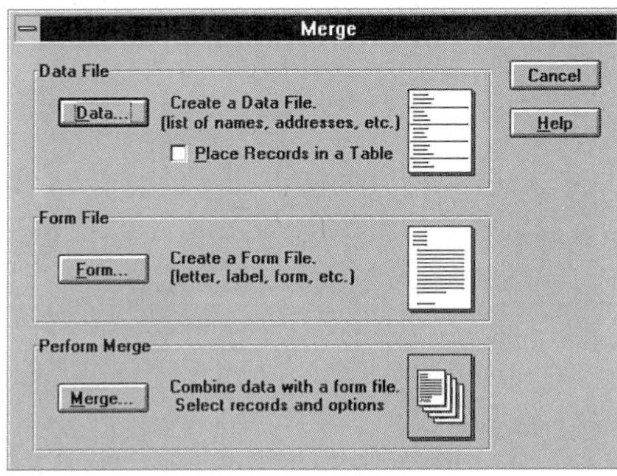

Fig. 19.1
In the Merge dialog box, select the type of merge file to be created and begin the merge.

2. Choose **D**ata. The Create Data File dialog box appears (see fig. 19.2).

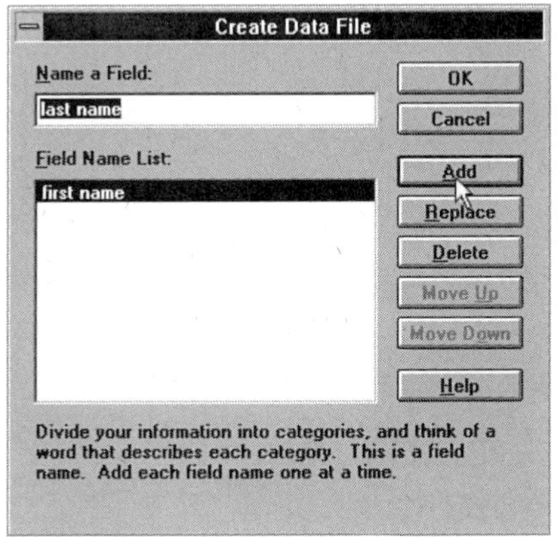

Fig. 19.2
Enter the names of the fields in **F**ield Name List. If this list contains too many names to display at one time, scroll through the field names. You can add, delete, edit, and rearrange the order of the fields by using the controls in this box.

3. Type **first name** in the **N**ame a Field text box, and then press Enter.

4. Continue to enter the remaining field names: **last name**, **address**, **city, state**, and **zip code**.

5. Choose OK. The Quick Data Entry dialog box appears (see fig. 19.3).

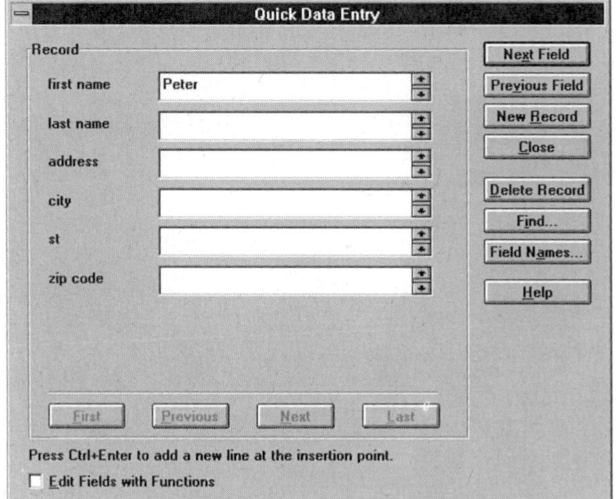

Fig. 19.3
Use the Quick Data Entry dialog box to enter information in your data file. You can enter, edit, and delete records or choose Field N**a**mes to open the Edit Field Names dialog box.

You are ready to type in the mailing list information. For this example, you need to mail the letter to three people: Peter Wilson, 3740 NE Alameda, Portland, OR 97212; John Reed, 3416 SE 117th Avenue, Portland, OR 97266; and Terry Macnamara, 2216 SE 57th Street, Portland, OR 97215. Proceed as follows:

6. Be sure the insertion point is in the text box next to the first name prompt. Click in the text box, use the Ne**x**t Field and Pre**v**ious Field controls, or press Tab or Shift+Tab to position the insertion point.

7. Type **Peter**, then press Enter. Because Ne**x**t Field is the default control when you begin data entry, pressing Enter moves the insertion point to the next field.

8. Continue entering the field information for Peter Wilson as shown previously. When you finish typing the ZIP code, press Enter to insert the completed record in the file. The insertion point returns to the first field prompt, and you can enter another record.

9. After you enter the data for all three records, choose **C**lose. A dialog box appears, asking if you want to save changes to disk.

10. Choose **Y**es. The Save As dialog box appears.

11. Type a suitable file name, such as **soccer.dat**, and then choose OK or press Enter to save the file.

Tip
If you want to keep your merge data files in a directory other than the current default directory, be sure to include the path to the directory.

Note

Use a DAT file extension for your merge data files; then you can see a listing of just the data files by choosing the WP Merge Data (*.dat) file type when you use any of WordPerfect's features for selecting a file. WordPerfect recognizes files with a DAT extension as merge data files, and files with an FRM extension as form files.

The completed data file resembles figure 19.4.

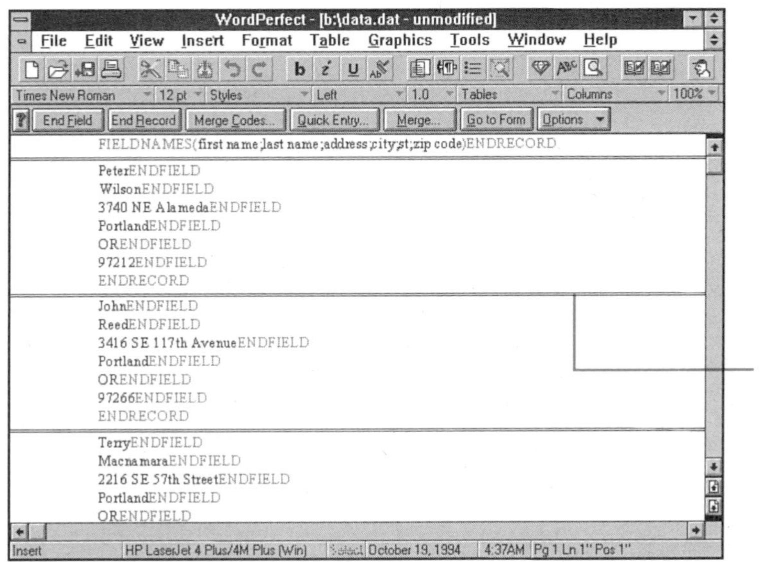

Fig. 19.4
A hard page break separates the records in the data file. Notice the field names in the first record at the beginning of the file.

Note

A WordPerfect 6.1 merge file is always displayed with a Merge Feature Bar. The Merge Feature Bar gives you quick access to the merge features you use most often with that file. See the section "Understanding the Merge Feature Bar" later in this chapter for more details. Use Alt+Shift+*L* (where *L* is the mnemonic letter of the Feature Bar control) to choose items on the Merge Feature Bar by using the keyboard.

Creating the Form File

You have completed the mailing list. Now, you need to prepare the letter about the date and time of the next meeting to send to the people on the list. You can draft a generic notice and use mailing labels to send it out, but personalized letters generally receive a more favorable response. To prepare a personalized letter that contains the meeting information, follow these steps:

1. Choose **G**o to Form from the Merge Feature Bar.

2. The Associate dialog box appears with a `No Associated File` message. Choose **C**reate.

3. Type the inside address as follows:

   Metro West Soccer Club

   Coach Development Committee

   P.O. Box 80317

   Portland, OR 97280

4. Press Enter four times to make three blank lines before the date.

5. To date the letter to the time of the mail merge (regardless of the date you type the form), use the DATE merge code. To insert the DATE code, choose Merge **C**odes from the Merge bar. The Insert Merge Codes dialog box appears. (This dialog box is covered in more detail in the section "Inserting Merge Codes" later in this chapter.)

6. Press D. WordPerfect highlights the DATE code (see fig. 19.5). Choose **I**nsert or press Enter to insert the code in your document at the insertion point.

> **Note**
>
> The Insert Merge Codes dialog box stays on-screen, but inactive, so that you can insert additional merge codes into your document as needed. You can move or close the dialog box if it gets in your way.

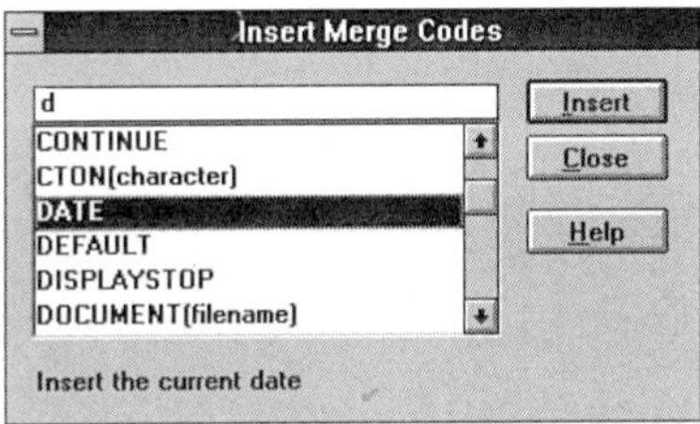

Fig. 19.5
Pressing the first letter of a code takes you to the first code that begins with that letter. Continue entering letters or use the arrow keys or scroll bar to move to the code you want.

7. Choose **C**lose in the Insert Merge Codes dialog box to close the box.

8. Press Enter four times to make three blank lines before the inside address.

9. Choose **I**nsert Field from the Merge bar. The Insert Field Name Or Number dialog box appears (see fig. 19.6).

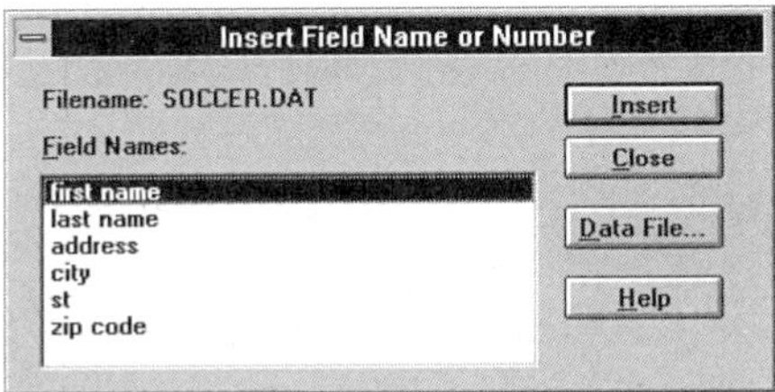

Fig. 19.6
The Insert Field Name Or Number dialog box lists the fields in the order in which they appear in the associated data file.

10. Move the highlight bar to `first name`, and choose **I**nsert or press Enter. The line `FIELD(first name)` appears in your document at the insertion point.

11. Press the space bar once to place a space between the first and last name, and then choose and insert `last name` from the Insert Field Name or Number dialog box.

12. Follow the same procedure to insert the field codes for the rest of the address. Press Enter to move down a line, then insert the address code. Press Enter to move down another line, then insert the field codes for the city, state, and ZIP code. (Do not separate the state and ZIP codes with a comma, or a comma will appear between them in the document.)

13. Press Enter three times to create two blank lines before the salutation. Type **Dear** and then insert the first name field code and type a colon. Close the Insert Field Name or Number dialog box.

14. Press Enter two times to position the insertion point for typing the body of the letter. The remainder of the letter is plain text, without merge codes. Type the following text, using your own name as the author:

    This will confirm our recent phone conference about the first meeting. We will hold an organizational meeting of the committee at 7:00 p.m. on Monday, January 16, 1995, at the Horsebrass Pub, 4832 SE Belmont. Whoever gets there first should try to secure a quiet corner where we can spread out some papers and discuss the issues before the committee.

    Bring your ideas for the coming season. I look forward to seeing you there!

    Sincerely,

    your name

    Chairman

Figure 19.7 shows the finished document.

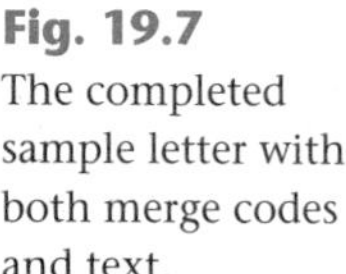

Fig. 19.7
The completed sample letter with both merge codes and text.

You have completed the form file.

15. Choose **F**ile, Save **A**s; or press F3 to save the file. Use an appropriate name, such as **orgmeet.frm**.

Creating Envelopes

Although you can create envelopes and letters separately, a form letter mailing is easiest to prepare when you create the envelopes as you perform the merge. To create envelopes for the sample merge, proceed as follows:

1. Choose **M**erge from the Merge Feature Bar. The Merge dialog box appears (refer to fig. 19.1).

2. Choose **M**erge. The Perform Merge dialog box appears (see fig. 19.8). WordPerfect 6.1 displays the name of the data file associated with the form file you just created.

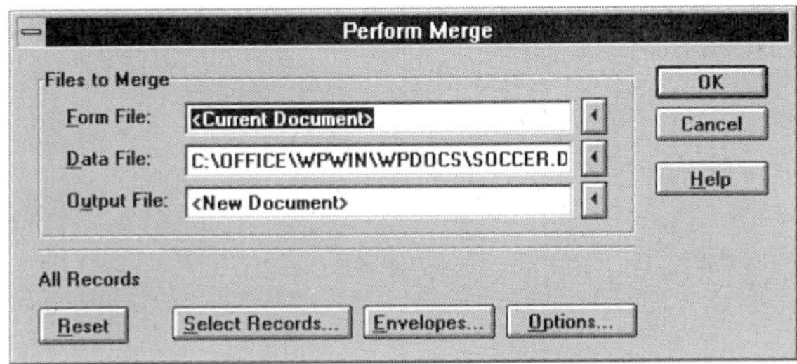

Fig. 19.8 The Perform Merge dialog box shows the data file associated with the current form file. Use this box to choose the files to be merged, direct the merge output, and create envelopes.

3. Choose **E**nvelopes. The Envelope dialog box appears (see fig. 19.9).

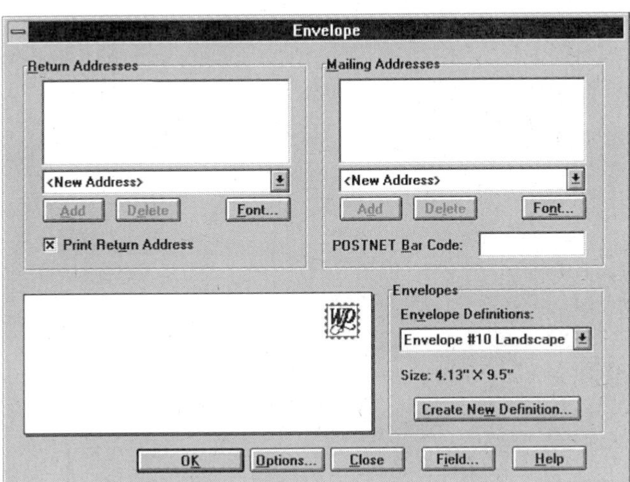

Fig. 19.9 The Envelope dialog box, which now includes a Field button, enables you to insert the return address and the mailing address into the form, save mailing addresses, choose saved addresses, and define envelopes.

4. Choose **R**eturn Addresses, and then type the return address as shown in the sample letter.

5. Choose **M**ailing Addresses, and then choose F**i**eld. The Insert Field Name or Number dialog box appears.

6. Choose `first name` from the Insert Field Name or Number dialog box, and then choose **I**nsert. The field `first name` is inserted into the Mailing Addresses text box (see fig. 19.10).

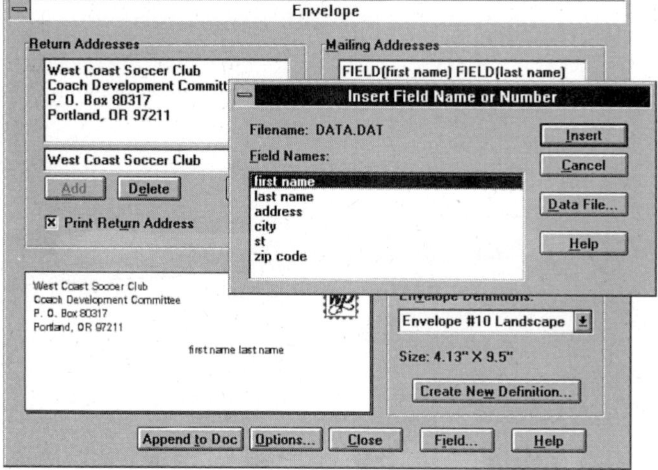

Fig. 19.10
By using the Insert Field Name or Number dialog box, you can quickly and accurately insert merge codes for the mailing address.

7. Continue to insert the fields for the remainder of the mailing address. Choose **C**lose after you finish to return to the Envelope dialog box.

8. To use postnet bar codes on the envelopes, choose POSTNET **B**ar Code; then choose F**i**eld. Choose and insert the ZIP code field in the **F**ield Names list of the Insert Field Name or Number dialog box.

Note

If you do not see the POSTNET Bar Code text box, choose Options; then choose whether to include U.S. POSTNET Bar Code above or below the address. Choose OK to return to the Envelope dialog box before performing step 8.

The envelopes are now defined for the merge, and your screen resembles figure 19.11.

9. Choose OK or press Enter. The program returns to the Perform Merge dialog box.

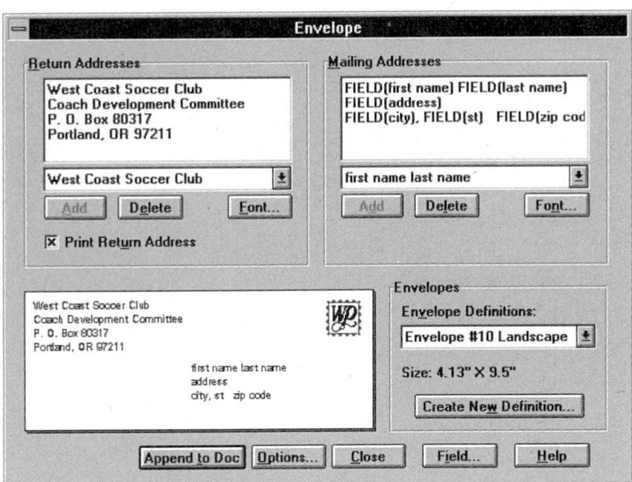

Fig. 19.11
The Envelope dialog box with the return address and mailing address completed for use with the sample merge.

Performing the Merge

You are ready to perform the merge. To merge the files you have just created, follow these steps:

1. Make sure that `<New Document>` appears in the O**u**tput File text box.

2. Choose OK or press Enter to complete the merge operation. The merge creates a file that contains a letter, immediately followed by an envelope, for each record. Each letter and envelope is separated from the others by hard page breaks.

Tip
If your printer doesn't have an envelope feeder, you may find it more efficient to create envelopes separately from the letters for larger printing jobs.

After the merge is completed, you can print the resulting file to generate the letters for mailing. You also can save the file, although in most situations saving only the form files and the data files is more efficient than saving the merged file.

Understanding Data Files

Data files hold the variable information used in a merge. That variable information can be of any type. The data may be personal information such as names, addresses, and phone numbers, or more varied data such as contract clauses, airline schedules, or recipes. For WordPerfect to use the information, you must organize the data into fields and records.

Understanding Records and Fields

Each *record* in a data file contains information that is related in some way. Each record in a mailing list, for example, contains information about one person or company. Records are subdivided into *fields*. A field contains the smallest item of information that you intend to deal with in a form file using that data file. Each field of a record in a mailing list contains a single item of information, such as a name, address, or phone number.

You decide the organizational structure for your data when you create the data file. As a result, when you create the data file, you must give careful consideration to what level of detail your fields must provide. You may choose to divide personal information, for example, into just three fields: name, address (including the city, state, and ZIP code), and phone number. You have much greater flexibility in using the data, however, if you divide the same information into more fields, for example: first name, last name, street address, city, state, ZIP code, and phone number. As a rule, the more fields you use, the more flexibility you have in using the data.

WordPerfect identifies fields by name and number (or relative position in the record). Use the same number of fields and the same field order in every record in your data files, even if some records have blank fields. WordPerfect identifies numbered fields only by their relative position in the record. If you have records with different numbers of fields in different orders, you may get unintended results when you perform a merge that calls for fields by number.

Understanding the Types of Data Files

◄ See "Creating and Using Tables: The Basics," p. 526

WordPerfect uses two types of data files: *data text* files and *data table* files. In a data text file, fields are separated from each other by an ENDFIELD code and records are terminated by an ENDRECORD code. In a data table file, each row of the table is a record and each cell is a field. You saw an example of a data text file in figure 19.4. Figure 19.12 shows the same data in a data table file format.

You use the same process to create a data table file that you use to create a data text file. If you want to use a data table file, choose **P**lace Records in a Table in the Merge dialog box before choosing **D**ata. WordPerfect then creates the table for you as you enter the field names.

first name	last name	address	city	st	zip code
Peter	Wilson	3740 NE Alameda	Portland	OR	97212
John	Reed	3416 SE 117th Ave.	Portland	OR	97266
Terry	Macnamara	2216 SE 57th Street	Portland	OR	97215

Fig. 19.12
This data table file holds the same data as the file shown in figure 19.4. The field names are the column headings in the first row of the table.

The two data file types have these relative features:

Feature	Data Text	Data Table
Field Delimiter	ENDFIELD code	table cell
Record Delimiter	ENDRECORD code	table row
Maximum Number of Fields	Unlimited	64
Maximum Number of Named Fields	255	64
Maximum Number of Records	65,535	65,535
Maximum Size of Fields	Unlimited	Must fit in cell (less than one page)

Your choice of data file type depends on the data you plan to use in the file. Data table files work best with a relatively small number of short fields. Although data table files can hold up to 64 fields, the font and paper you select (for the document window in which you create the table) limit the practical size of a table. If you create 64 cells in a data table row, you may not be able to read any of the data. The data table shown in figure 19.12 is close to the practical size limit for standard letter-size paper in portrait orientation with one-inch margins and a 12-point font.

Understanding Field Names

WordPerfect can recognize fields by number or by name. When you first create a data file, WordPerfect gives you the opportunity to enter field names before you move to the main document window. Entering field names is illustrated in the earlier section, "Creating the Data File." If you do not use field names, WordPerfect automatically numbers the fields. The program numbers the fields in a data text file sequentially, from the beginning of the record to the end; fields in a data table file are numbered sequentially by cell, from left to right.

Working with a form file is easier when you have created the file with named fields whose names correspond to the information in the fields. When you want to locate information or enter data into a specific field, the field name helps you find the right field quickly. When the main document window for a data file is active, the WordPerfect status bar identifies the field in which the insertion point is located. Further, the Quick Data Entry dialog box displays the fields' identification next to the data entry text boxes. If you haven't used field names, only field numbers appear in these displays.

Prior versions of WordPerfect limited you to 99 named fields in a data file. The program's new 255 named-field limit enables you to use named fields in virtually any project that uses merge.

Using the Quick Data Entry Dialog Box

WordPerfect 6 for Windows introduced an innovative way to make data entry simple and nearly foolproof. After you have entered field names in a new data file, WordPerfect displays the Quick Data Entry dialog box (see fig. 19.13). You also can access the Quick Data Entry dialog box by choosing **Q**uick Entry from the Merge Feature Bar that is present when you edit a merge data file.

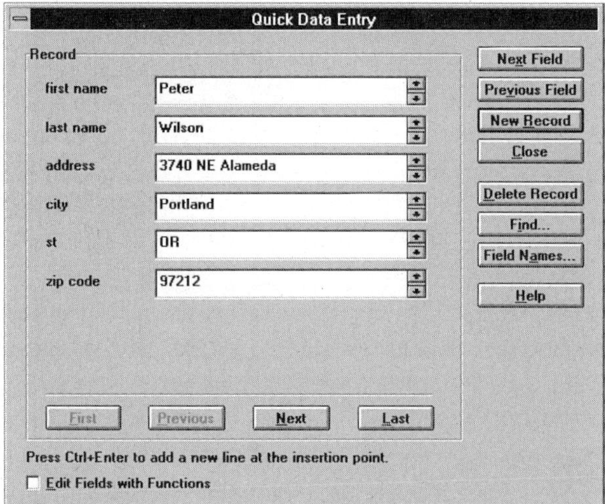

Fig. 19.13
The Quick Data Entry dialog box enables you to enter, delete, and edit records quickly in merge data files.

To enter data through the Quick Data Entry dialog box, position the insertion point in the text box for the first field, type the information for the field, and then press Enter. The insertion point advances to the text box for the next field. Repeat this process to enter data for each field. If you have no data for a field, press Enter to leave the field blank. When you complete the last field, press Enter to save the record in the data file. The insertion point moves to the text box for the first field to enable you to enter another record. This process is identical for both data text files and data table files.

The Quick Data Entry dialog box displays the record in which the insertion point is located when you choose **Q**uick Entry from an existing merge data file. You can position the insertion point in the displayed record by clicking in the text box for the field you want to edit, or by choosing the Ne**x**t Field or Pre**v**ious Field controls. The controls along the bottom of the dialog box enable you to quickly select the record you want to edit.

The following table lists and describes the Quick Data Entry dialog box options:

Control	Action
Ne**x**t Field	Moves the insertion point to the next field in the displayed record.
Pre**v**ious Field	Moves the insertion point to the previous field in the displayed record.
New **R**ecord	Clears the text boxes for entry of new record data (the new data is placed in the data file where the insertion point was located when you chose Quick Entry).
Close	Closes the Quick Data Entry dialog box, writes the data entries to the data file, and makes the data file the active window.
Delete Record	Deletes the displayed record from the data file.
F**i**nd	Opens the Find Text dialog box to enable you to search for text in the data file; displays the record in which the matching text is located.
Field N**a**mes	Opens the Edit Field Names dialog box in which you can add, delete, or edit field names; any changes you make in this dialog box apply to all records in the data file.
First	Displays the first record in the data file.
Previous	Displays the record that immediately precedes the currently displayed record.
Next	Displays the record that immediately follows the currently displayed record.
Last	Displays the last record in the data file.
Edit Fields with Functions	By default, fields containing merge functions are protected from change when the data file is edited. Choosing this option enables you to edit any field with a function.

Entering Data Directly in an Existing Data File

Adding or editing records in an existing data table file is similar to editing any table. Adding a row adds a new record; entering data in a cell edits the field defined by the column heading. Choose Row from the Merge Feature Bar, then choose Insert, to quickly insert a new row at the insertion point. For more details on editing tables, see Chapter 16, "Working with Tables."

Note

Use Alt+Shift+*underlined letter* to use the keyboard to choose Feature Bar buttons.

To enter a new record directly in an existing data text file, follow these steps:

1. Position the insertion point where you want to begin the record (begin either at the end of the data file or immediately after the record you want your new record to follow).

   Note

   Changing your View mode to Draft before editing a data text file enables you to see more than one record at a time. Records are separated by both an ENDRECORD code and a [HPg] (hard page break) code. In Page mode, the [HPg] codes cause only one page (therefore, one record) to appear on-screen at any one time. In Draft mode, the [HPg] breaks appear on-screen as double horizontal lines.

2. Type the data for the field. Notice that the status bar shows the name of the field in which the insertion point is located.

3. After you finish typing the data for the field, choose End **F**ield from the Merge Feature Bar. WordPerfect inserts an ENDFIELD code followed by a [HRt] code. The insertion point moves to the next line for the beginning of the next field.

4. Repeat steps 2 and 3 to enter data in each field.

5. After all the fields are complete, choose End **R**ecord from the Merge Feature Bar. WordPerfect inserts an ENDRECORD code followed by a [HPg] code, and moves the insertion point to the beginning of the next record.

Understanding the Merge Feature Bar

When you use the merge feature to create a file, WordPerfect identifies the file as a merge file and always displays it with the appropriate Merge Feature Bar. Figure 19.14 shows the Merge Feature Bars for data text files and data table files.

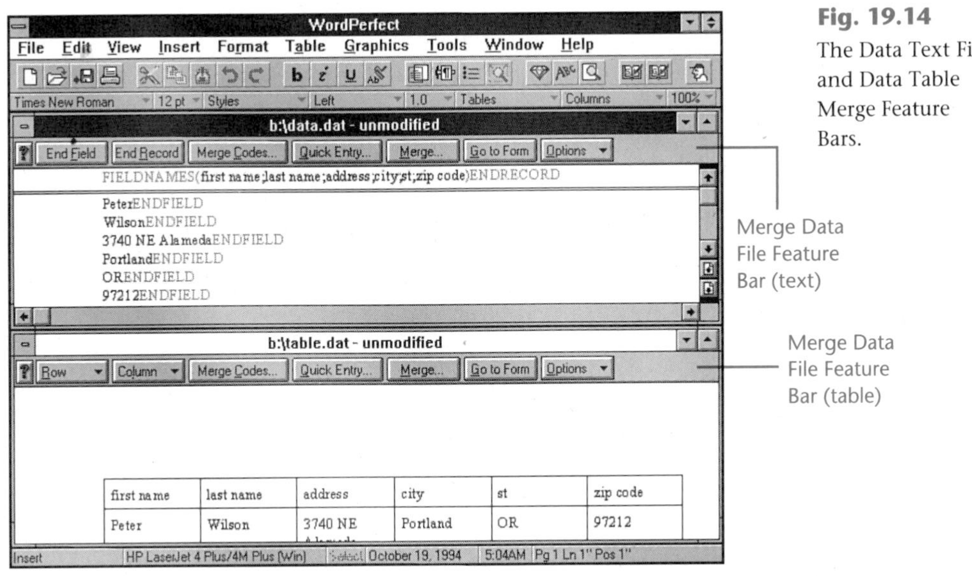

Fig. 19.14
The Data Text File and Data Table Merge Feature Bars.

The Merge Data File Feature Bar provides instant access to the most common merge actions. The following table lists and describes the controls on the Merge Feature Bar for data files:

Control	Action
?	Displays menu of choices for other Feature Bars.
Row	Enables you to insert or delete a table row (data table files only).
Column	Enables you to insert or delete a table column (data table files only).
Merge Codes...	Displays the Insert Merge Codes dialog box to provide access to all merge codes.
Quick Entry...	Displays the Quick Data Entry dialog box to enable you to enter and edit records.

(continues)

Control	Action
Merge...	Displays the Merge dialog box to enable you to create new merge files or begin a merge.
Go to Form	Displays the associated form file; if no form is associated, enables you to select or create an associated form file.
Options ▾	Displays a menu of these additional file manipulation options: Sort—Displays the Sort dialog box that enables you to sort the records in the data file (see the "Using Sort" section for more details). Display Codes—Displays full merge codes in the file. Display as Markers—Displays merge codes as a diamond icon. Hide Codes—Suppresses all display of merge codes (codes are visible only in Reveal Codes). Remove Merge Bar—Removes Merge bar to prevent WordPerfect from treating file as a merge file.

Note

Adding a row adds a record, and adding a column adds a field. You can insert a new row above or below the current row or at the end of the file. You can place a new column to the left or right of the current column, or at the end of the data file.

Understanding Form Files

Form files are WordPerfect 6.1 files that contain text, merge codes, or both. A form file serves two functions in a merge operation: it supplies the instructions for the merge process, and it holds the constant information that is combined with the data file to produce the final document. Most form files contain both text and codes, but you can use a form file that contains only merge and formatting codes.

Every merge requires a form file. The merge instructions come from merge codes placed in the form file. Merge instructions can be simple or complex; they can range from causing a pause for user input to controlling a complex application. WordPerfect's merge codes comprise a programming language with which you can create sophisticated applications. At the same time, the default merge setups make basic mail merges easy.

Using the Merge Feature Bar for Form Files

The Merge Form File Feature Bar, shown in figure 19.15, provides quick access to merge codes and other program functions you use to create form files.

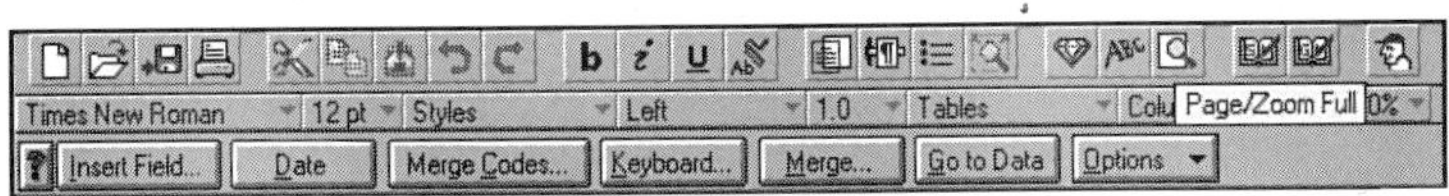

Fig. 19.15
The Merge Form Files Feature Bar gives you instant access to the merge codes and program functions you use most often in creating and editing form files.

You can choose the **I**nsert Field, **K**eyboard, and **D**ate codes directly from the Merge Feature Bar, and all other merge codes are readily accessible. The following table shows each of the choices available on the Merge Feature Bar for form files:

Choice	Action
?	Displays menu of choices for other Feature Bars.
Insert Field...	Places a FIELD(field name) code at the insertion point.
Date	Places a DATE code at the insertion point.
Merge Codes...	Displays the Insert Merge Codes dialog box from which you can choose any of WordPerfect's 81 merge codes.
Keyboard...	Inserts a KEYBOARD([prompt]) code at the insertion point (see "Understanding the Keyboard Code" for more details).
Merge...	Displays the Merge dialog box that enables you to create a data file or another form file, or begin a merge.
Go to Data	Makes the associated data file the active window; opens the associated data file if it has not been opened; if no associated data file exists, prompts you to select or create one.
Options	Displays a list of options, as follows: Display Codes—Displays full merge codes in the file. Display as Markers—Displays merge codes as a diamond icon. Hide Codes—Suppresses all display of merge codes, codes are visible only in Reveal Codes. Remove Merge Bar—Removes merge bar to prevent WordPerfect from treating file as a merge file.

Associating Form and Data Files

WordPerfect enables you to easily enter correct FIELD( ) codes in a form file by selecting fields from the Insert Field Name or Number dialog box when you designate a particular data file as the source of the field information. The data file you designate is *associated* with the form file. In the form file, WordPerfect stores an internal reference that points to the associated data file. When a data file is associated with a form file, the following features become available:

- Choosing **G**o to Data takes you to the associated data file. If you have not yet opened that data file in your current session, the file opens in an unused document window.

> **Note**
>
> The **G**o to Data feature works only if you saved the form file after you made the data file association.

- After a data file is associated with the form, choosing **G**o to Form from the Merge Feature Bar in the data file takes you to the associated form file. The link from the data file to the form file is not durable; the association lasts only until the data file is closed.

- Choosing **I**nsert Field causes the Insert Field Names dialog box to display the list of named fields from the associated data file.

When you first choose to create a form file, WordPerfect prompts you to designate an associated data file (see fig. 19.16). The program also prompts you to associate a data file when you choose **G**o to Data from the merge bar in a form file that does not already have an associated data file (see fig. 19.17). If you choose **I**nsert Field from the Merge Feature Bar, and you have no associated data file, you see the prompt shown in figure 19.18.

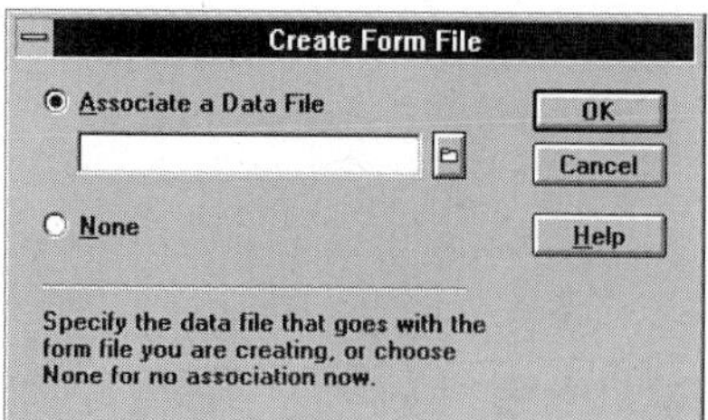

Fig. 19.16
When you first create a form file, WordPerfect prompts you to designate an associated data file.

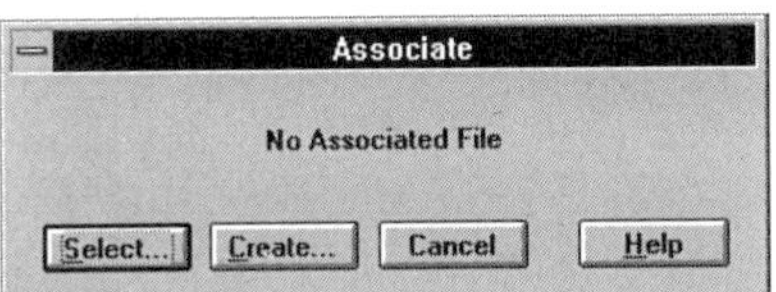

Fig. 19.17
WordPerfect prompts you to select or create an associated data file.

You need not associate a data file with every form file. The association is useful only when the form file uses FIELD( ) codes. Form files that use direct keyboard entry only do not need an associated data file.

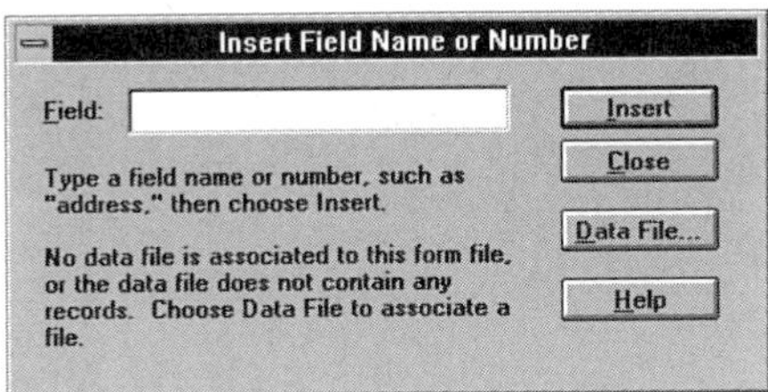

Fig. 19.18
This message appears if you choose **I**nsert Field when no data file is associated with your form file. Choose **D**ata File to select a data file.

Understanding Merge Codes

Merge codes are codes that direct the operation of WordPerfect's merge function. You cannot type merge codes directly into a WordPerfect 6.1 document; only the program can insert these codes.

Most merge codes require additional parameters, called *arguments*, to operate correctly. Arguments are enclosed in parentheses at the end of code names. The FIELD(*field*) code, for example, includes the argument (*field*). In this example, the code requires an argument, either a name or number, that identifies the particular field in the data file from which information is to be extracted during the merge. Some merge codes accommodate optional arguments, but do not require them. Optional arguments are displayed in square brackets in the Insert Merge Codes dialog box. The KEYBOARD([*prompt*]) code, for example, enables you to include a prompt, but does not require it. Other merge codes, such as ENDFIELD, do not accept any arguments.

Merge codes that take arguments appear in Reveal Codes as paired codes, similar to WordPerfect's paired formatting codes. For example, the code to insert the contents of the last name field in your document appears as `FIELD(last name)` on the editing screen. When viewed in Reveal Codes, however, you see a paired code surrounding the name of the field, as shown in figure 19.19.

Fig. 19.19
The FIELD(last name) merge code in the text. WordPerfect uses the redline attribute to distinguish merge codes from regular text.

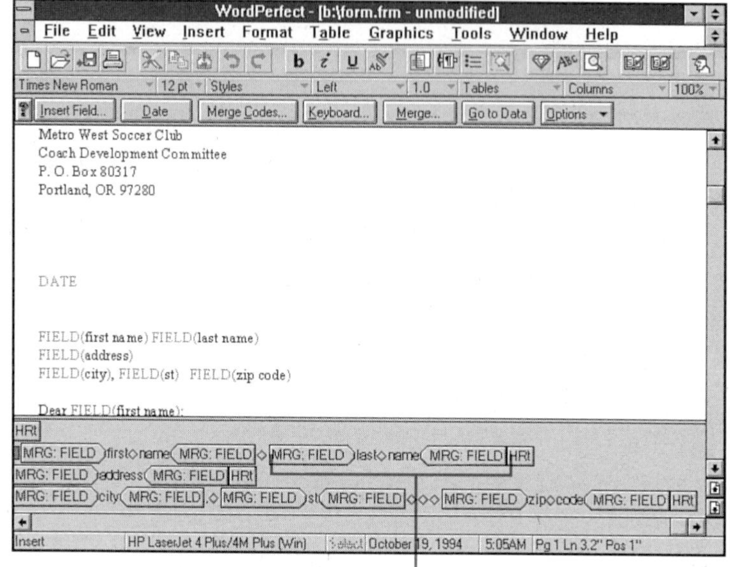

The FIELD(last name) merge codes in Reveal Codes

You need not insert the parentheses for merge codes. The parentheses are not actually characters, but are part of the codes. If no parentheses appear next to a merge code, that code does not require arguments.

You can insert the ENDFIELD, ENDRECORD, DATE, FIELD( ), and KEYBOARD( ) codes by choosing them from the Merge Feature Bar. You insert all other merge codes by choosing the desired code from the Insert Merge Codes dialog box. To access this dialog box, choose Merge **C**odes from the Merge Feature Bar. Type the first few characters of the code's name to jump to the code you want to use. Highlight the code, and then choose OK or press Enter to insert the code in your document. If the code accepts or requires parameters, a message prompts you to enter those. After you enter the parameter, WordPerfect inserts the code in your document.

Controlling Merge Codes Display

WordPerfect 6.1 enables you to control the display of merge codes in a file. The default setting is to show full merge codes. After you have fine-tuned the form file so that merges consistently work the way you expect, the full display of the merge codes may be distracting. If you prefer to use a file that does not display the merge codes, you can change the way the codes are displayed.

To change the way merge codes are displayed in your files, choose **O**ptions from the Merge Feature Bar. Among the options listed in the drop-down list are three that control the merge codes display. The default setting is **D**isplay Codes. Choosing Display as **M**arkers places a diamond-shaped marker in your file where each merge code is located. The marker hides the code, including any parameters or nested merge expressions. **H**ide Codes completely eliminates any display of the codes on the regular editing screen. To see codes you have hidden or displayed as markers, use Reveal Codes.

Note

If merge codes are displayed in full, you can edit parameters for the codes on the main editing screen. You cannot edit hidden codes or codes displayed as markers.

Understanding the Keyboard Code

The purpose of the KEYBOARD([*prompt*]) code is to pause the merge to allow input from the keyboard. You can use the optional prompt parameter to tell the operator what to type at the location of the pause. Prompt text appears in a Merge Message dialog box that remains visible until the operator closes it or continues the merge. By default, the window is located at the bottom center of the screen. You can drag the message dialog box to another location, resize it, or close it if it gets in your way.

When the merge pauses for keyboard entry, WordPerfect displays choices on the Merge Feature Bar that enable you to **C**ontinue from the pause, **S**top the merge, or **Q**uit. If your merge combines keyboard data entry with a data file merge, the Merge Feature Bar also includes a choice, Skip Current, to skip over the current record. Even if you close the Merge Message dialog box, the Merge Feature Bar remains displayed as a visible indication that you are in the middle of a merge operation. While the merge is paused, you can use nearly all of the program's functions, including opening and editing other files. When you have completed your actions during the pause, choose **C**ontinue to proceed with the merge.

If you choose **Q**uit while the merge is paused, the remainder of the form file is placed in your document, but the program processes no more merge codes. Any remaining merge codes are now in your new document, so you can complete the merge later using the new file as the form. If you choose **S**top while the merge is paused, the merge immediately terminates at the location of the insertion point, and the program inserts no further text or codes from the form file.

If you often write the same letter to more than one person, you can set up a form letter that prompts for the name, address, and salutation. WordPerfect inserts the prompt messages inside the parentheses of the KEYBOARD( ) code. You can modify the letter written in the section "Creating the Form File" earlier in this chapter for interactive use by changing the inside address and salutation prompts as follows:

> **KEYBOARD(*Type the Addressee's name, address, city, state, and ZIP code.*)**
>
> Dear **KEYBOARD(*Type the salutation.*)**

To enter the KEYBOARD( ) code, choose **K**eyboard from the Merge Form File Feature Bar and type the text for the prompt message. When you finish typing, choose OK or press Enter. When you merge this form file, the prompt text appears in the Merge Message dialog box and whatever you type in response is inserted in the document at the location of the KEYBOARD( ) code (see fig. 19.20). After you complete the response to the prompt, choose **C**ontinue to proceed with the merge.

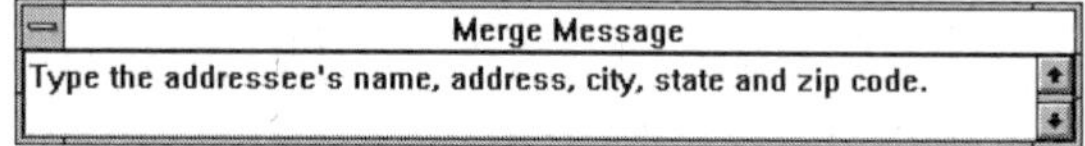

Fig. 19.20 The sample letter is paused for keyboard entry of the inside address.

Understanding the Merge Process

After you have prepared your form file and data file, you can perform a merge. To begin a merge from a screen that does not contain a merge file, choose **T**ools, M**e**rge, **M**erge; or press Shift+F9 and choose **M**erge. If you have a merge file in the active window, choose **M**erge from the Merge Feature Bar, and then choose **M**erge. The Perform Merge dialog box appears (refer to fig. 19.8). Use this dialog box to select the form file and data file and begin the merge process.

Understanding the Perform Merge Dialog Box

When you perform a merge from a window that does not contain a merge file, the Perform Merge dialog box appears, but the data file controls are grayed (see fig. 19.21). The insertion point is in the **F**orm File parameter entry box waiting for your entry. You can select general merge options, but before you can perform the merge, you must select a form file.

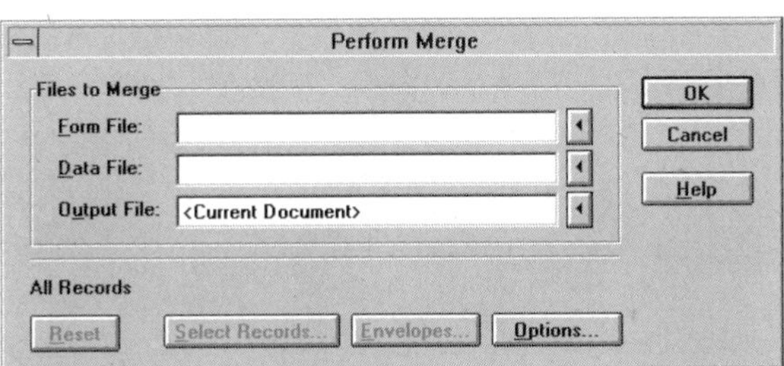

Fig. 19.21
The Perform Merge dialog box, before a form file is selected. You must select a form file before you can perform a merge.

Selecting the Merge Files

Type in the name (and path, if needed) of the form file you want to use. If you are uncertain of the name or location of the form file, or if you want to use the current document as the form file, click the arrow at the right end of the **F**orm File text box. A drop-down list appears, offering the following alternatives:

Tip
Press Alt+Down Arrow to use the keyboard to open the drop-down list.

- ***S****elect File*. Choosing this option produces the Select File dialog box. This dialog box enables you to search anywhere on your system to locate the form file you want to use. If you have used WordPerfect's suggested file extension of FRM for your form files, you can display only the form files in a directory by choosing WP Merge Forms (*.frm) from the List Files of **T**ype drop-down list.
- *<Current Document>*. Choose this option to use the document in the active window as the form file.
- *<Clipboard>*. This option enables you to use a form that has been previously copied to the Windows Clipboard. If you select a form that has an associated data file, the filename for the associated data file appears in the **D**ata File text box when you move the insertion point to that box.

If you have previously performed a merge during your current session, the name of the form file you most recently used is displayed in the **F**orm File text box, and the name of the data file you used with that form is displayed in the **D**ata File text box.

If you reached the Perform Merge dialog box by choosing **M**erge from the Merge Feature Bar of a merge form file, <Current Document> is the default in the Form File text box and the name of the form file's associated data file is in the Data File text box.

After you choose a form file, you can choose a data file (if you need a data file and have not yet chosen one). Choose the data file by using the same methods you use to choose a form file.

In most situations, you need not change the setting for the O**u**tput File text box. The default location is `<New Document>` if the active window is being used when Merge is chosen. If the active window is unused, the default location for merge output is `<Current Document>`. If you have many records to merge with the form file, you may want to change the destination to the printer. With this destination, each completed record goes immediately to the printer as a separate print job. You also can direct output to a disk file—a good arrangement if your computer has limited amounts of memory.

To change the default location, click the arrow at the right of the O**u**tput File text box and choose the desired destination from the drop-down list. If you choose to send the output to a disk file, you can enter the name of the file or use the Select File dialog box to choose an existing file.

Setting Merge Options

Choose **O**ptions to set options for the merge. The Perform Merge Options dialog box appears (see fig. 19.22). The options you set in this dialog box remain in effect during your current session (unless you change them).

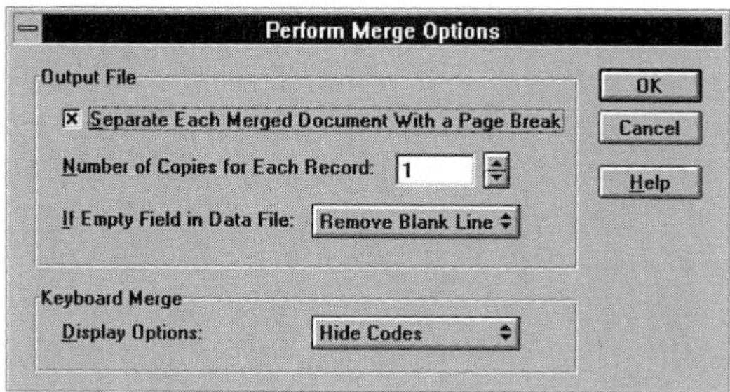

Fig. 19.22 The Perform Merge Options dialog box provides options with which you can determine how the merge operates.

Choose **D**isplay Options and then choose an option from the drop-down list to control how merge codes are displayed when a merge is paused for data entry from the keyboard. This choice affects the code display only during the merge process; it does not affect the display of codes in the form file or data file after the merge is completed. The default setting is **H**ide Codes. **S**how Codes enables you to see unprocessed merge codes in full while the merge is paused. Show as **M**arkers displays a diamond-shaped marker for each unprocessed code.

The **N**umber of Copies for Each Record option enables you to set the number of times each record in a data file is merged with the form.

By default, WordPerfect places a hard page break between each merged record. If you want the merged records to run together without a page break, choose **S**eparate Each Merged Document With A Page Break to deselect this option. A PAGEOFF code also suppresses the page break between merged records, but a PAGEOFF code permanently affects the form file in which you place it. A PAGEOFF code is not affected by the setting of this option.

You can choose how WordPerfect handles a blank field by choosing the **I**f Empty Field In Data File option. The default is to leave a blank line in the merged record. You can choose to have the blank line suppressed, however, by choosing **R**emove Blank Line from the drop-down list. This option is particularly useful when you are merging letters with an address list that may contain some blank fields, such as a list in which only some business owners use a separate business name in their address.

If you have changed the options, when you choose OK to return to the Perform Merge dialog box, you see the words `Options Modified` to the right of the phrase All Records; the **R**eset control is activated. Choosing **R**eset returns all options to their default settings.

Selecting Records

If you only want to use some of the records from the data file in the merge, choose **S**elect Records. The Select Records dialog box appears with the Selection Method option **S**pecify Conditions selected (see fig. 19.23). You can specify a range of records, select records by setting conditions, or select records by specifying both a range and setting conditions.

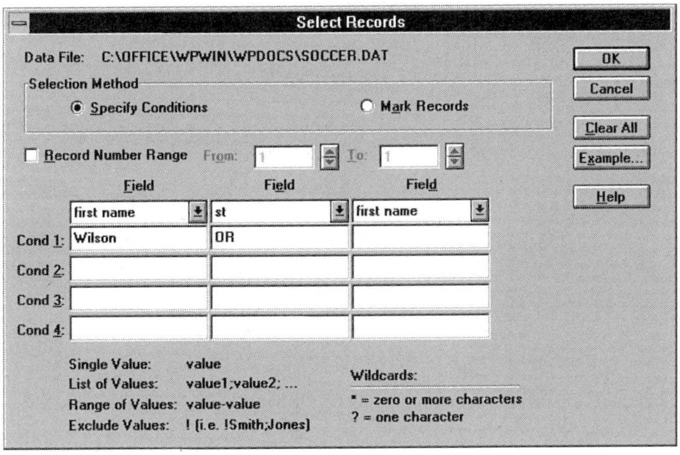

Fig. 19.23
Select **S**pecify Conditions in the Select Records dialog box to choose a record set that matches conditions you define. These conditions specify records for all persons with the last name "Wilson" and an Oregon address.

Specifying a Range

To specify a range of records, choose **R**ecord Number Range, then enter the record number in the Fr**o**m and **T**o boxes. WordPerfect sequentially numbers records in a data file from beginning to end. If you have an exceptionally large data file, you can specify a range to limit the number of records used during the selection and merge process.

Defining Conditions

Conditions are based on fields present in the data file. To set a condition, do the following:

1. Choose **F**ield.
2. Use the drop-down list on the **F**ield text box to choose the field you want to use as a condition (for example, last name).
3. Position the insertion point in the Cond **1** text box below the **F**ield column, and type the condition in the box.
4. Use the same procedure to set any other conditions you want to use.

Each condition line defines a set of records that is to be selected from the data file. You can define more than one condition for a single row; only records that meet all conditions in the row are selected. Specifying more than one row of conditions selects records that meet any row of conditions.

WordPerfect provides excellent help for defining conditions. The Help dialog box shown in figure 19.24, for example, provides examples of the records selected for various example conditions. You can access this Help dialog box by choosing E**x**ample in the Select Records dialog box. For additional guidance on selection statement syntax, you can choose **M**ore from the Example Select Records dialog box to produce the screen shown in figure 19.25.

Example Select Records

In this example, records that meet any of the following conditions will be merged:

1- Everyone up to and including the Lings who live in Iowa.
2- All of the Allens to the Cohens who live in Arizona and New York.
3- All people whose last name starts with "n", "o", or "p".
4- Everyone named Gonzales who does not live in California or Texas.

	Field	Field	Field
	Last Name	State	First Name
Cond 1:	-Ling	Iowa	
Cond 2:	Allens-Cohen	Arizona;New York	
Cond 3:	n*-p*		
Cond 4:	Gonzales	!California;Texas	

Close
More...
Help

Fig. 19.24 Examples of conditions for selecting records, provided by WordPerfect 6.1 after you choose Example from the Select Records dialog box while the Specify Conditions option is selected.

Example Select Records

The following are examples of valid entries:

1- A* - D*	All values that start with "A" "B" "C" or "D"
2- A*; B*; C*; D*;	Same as example 1
3- 840?7	84007,84017,84027....(not 8407 or 84000)
4- 84057-	All values greater than or equal to 84057
5- 84057-*	Same as example 4
6- >=84057	Same as example 4
7- *-84057	Values less than or equal to 84057
8- <84057	Values less than 84057
9- !Fred	All values that are not equal to Fred
10- !Julie;Fred	Values not equal to Fred and not equal to Julie
11- 84057-84068;84601	Values between 84057 and 84068 as well as 84601
12- "224-5643";"Test?"	The value 224-5643 as well as the value Test?

Close

Fig. 19.25 Examples of valid entries to use in defining the conditions for selecting records. This screen is provided by WordPerfect after you choose More from the Example Select Records dialog box.

Marking Records

You also can select records from the data file by marking them manually. This procedure is useful for selecting a relatively small number of records that share no consistent pattern for selection.

To mark records, follow these steps:

1. Choose M**a**rk Records at the Select Records dialog box; the dialog box changes to offer manual marking options (see fig. 19.26).

2. Set the range of records to be displayed.

   You can work with a range of records by setting the starting and ending numbers in the Fr**o**m and **T**o boxes for **D**isplay Records. The default is to display all records.

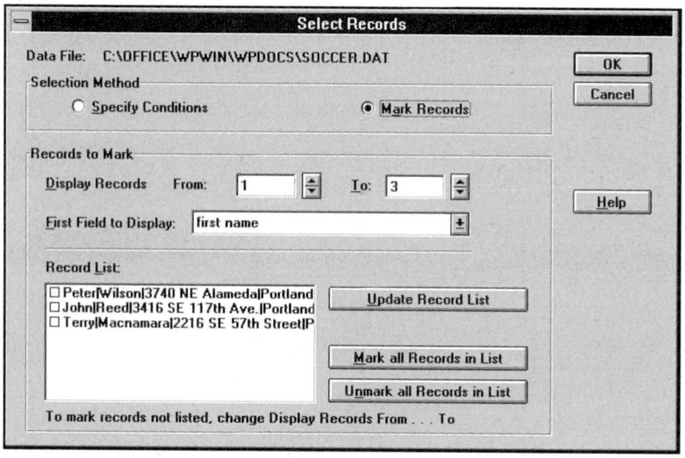

Fig. 19.26
If you choose the Mark Records option, the Select Records dialog box enables you to manually mark the records in the data file.

3. Choose **F**irst Field to Display.

   WordPerfect displays 39 characters of the selected range of records in the Record **L**ist text box. By default, the display begins with the first field defined in the data file. You can change the display to begin with any field in the data file.

> **Note**
>
> The display begins with the designated field and shows up to the next 80 characters in the record. If you choose the last field in the record as the first field to display, you see only the last field of the record.

4. Use the drop-down list of the **F**irst Field to Display text box to choose the field you want to display first—for example, the `last name` field.

5. Choose **U**pdate Record List. The selected range of records appears in the Record **L**ist list box, beginning with the field you selected.

6. Select the records you want to use. Choose **M**ark All Records in List to include all records in the Record List in the merge. To change an individual mark, click the record. Choose U**n**mark All Records in List to remove all record markings.

7. After you finish marking records, choose OK to return to the Perform Merge dialog box.

Creating Envelopes and Labels

Creating envelopes as part of a form letter merge is covered in detail in the section "Creating Envelopes" earlier in this chapter. The following sections describe how to create envelopes or mailing labels from a mailing list.

Merging Envelopes Only

To create an envelope form to merge with a mailing list, follow these steps:

1. Starting in an unused document window, choose **T**ools, M**e**rge; or press Shift+F9. The Merge dialog box appears.

2. Choose **F**orm, and then specify the data file containing the mailing list to associate with the form.

3. Choose OK. You now have a form file containing no text.

4. Choose Fo**r**mat, En**v**elope. The Envelope dialog box appears.

5. Complete the **R**eturn Addresses and **M**ailing Addresses areas of the Envelope dialog box, as described in the section "Creating Envelopes" earlier in this chapter.

6. Choose Append **t**o Doc. The Envelope dialog box closes and you see the envelope in the active document window. The form is ready to be merged with your mailing list.

Tip
If you saved a mailing address that contains field codes for the address you want to use, you can choose this mailing address from the drop-down list of addresses.

If you choose to include the POSTNET bar code, WordPerfect places the bar code above the mailing address.

Creating Mailing Labels

Creating mailing labels is essentially the same as creating any form file. When you create mailing labels, however, you work with a label-sized page. To create labels, choose Fo**r**mat, La**b**els, and then choose a label definition.

After you select the label form, you simply create a regular form file on a small page. Choose **T**ools, M**e**rge; or press Shift+F9. Choose **F**orm, and designate the associated data file. After you designate the current file as your form file, proceed as described in the section "Creating the Form File" earlier in this chapter, to insert field codes to define the address. For more details on choosing and editing labels, see Chapter 5, "Formatting Pages and Documents."

◄ See "Working with Labels," p. 194

Troubleshooting

I want to use a mailing label format to print a roster of members in alphabetical order. Neither the spacing nor the order of the addresses is correct.

Because there are several changes that must be made to a form that prints mailing labels to get what you want, try creating a new file. Select just the field codes and text and paste them into a new file. Begin the roster form file by setting up parallel columns. Then add an extra hard return at the end of the form so a blank line will be inserted between addresses, and end the form with a PAGEOFF code. Save the new form file. Now all you'll have to do is remember to sort the data file by last name when you perform the merge.

When certain fields in my data file are blank, I want the merge to insert specific information rather than just remove or leave a blank line.

You can set up options based on the presence or absence of data in a field. Use IFBLANK or IFNOTBLANK, as appropriate, to test for the presence or absence of data. At the end of the text or other instructions for the option, insert an ENDIF code.

Examining Advanced Merge Topics

WordPerfect's merge codes comprise a true programming language that enables you to create sophisticated applications. Exploring the extent of that language is beyond the scope of this chapter. The information in the following sections provides a sampling of some advanced merge topics.

Working with User Input

Merge is an excellent tool for creating forms that are to be filled in individually. Rather than taking variable information from a data file, you supply the variable information for these forms from the keyboard. Typing information from the keyboard in response to prompts can be inefficient, however, if the form repeatedly asks for the same information. You can easily make keyboard merges more efficient by capturing variable information the first time it is typed, and then reusing that information wherever necessary without additional user input.

Understanding Variables

WordPerfect uses *variables* to hold data that can be manipulated by merge programming codes or macros. Just as an algebraic variable can have many values, so too can a merge variable have different values. For example, the variable name can be assigned the value John Doe, or Richard Roe, or some other name.

You assign a value to a variable by using the ASSIGN(*var;expr*) code, the ASSIGNLOCAL(*var;expr*) code, any of the merge codes that work with user input, or a macro. For example, the merge code ASSIGN(name;John Doe) places the value of the expression "John Doe" in the variable "name." After a variable has a value, you use a merge code, such as VARIABLE(*var*), to insert the *value* of the variable identified by the *var* parameter in your text at any place you would otherwise type that information.

Capturing User Input

Suppose that you have an office form that uses KEYBOARD( ) codes to prompt the user through interactive completion of the form. The form uses the author's name several times in the document. You could use the KEYBOARD code to prompt for the author's name each time, but with minor effort you can capture the author's name to a variable when the name is first typed. The program then inserts the name wherever the variable appears in the document.

To capture the author's name the first time it is typed, position the insertion point where the author's name is first used, and then follow these steps:

1. Access the Insert Merge Codes dialog box and select the GETSTRING(*var[;title][;prompt]*) code. The Insert Merge Code dialog box appears, as shown in figure 19.27.

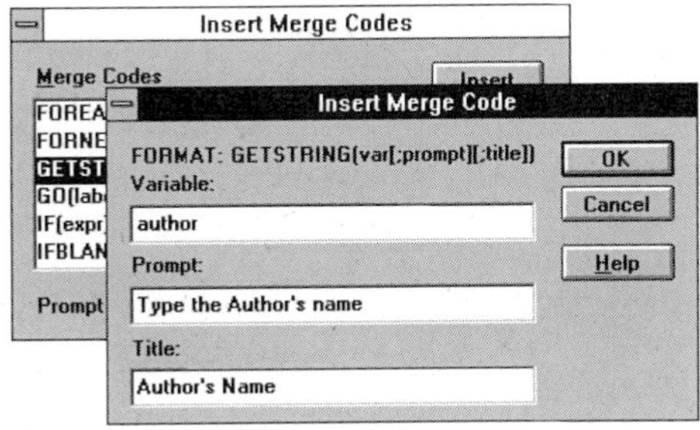

Fig. 19.27 The Insert Merge Code dialog box for the GETSTRING code assists you in entering parameters for the code.

2. In the Insert Merge Code dialog box, choose Variable, type **author** for the variable name, and then press Enter.

3. Choose Prompt, type **Type the Author's Name**, and then press Enter.

4. Choose Title, type **Author's Name**, and then press Enter.

5. Choose OK or press Enter to insert the code in your form. After the file is merged, whatever the user types in response to the prompt is assigned to the variable named *author*.

6. Insert a VARIABLE(*author*) code. This code is required to place the value assigned to the variable into the document. After the file is merged, the contents of the variable *author* are placed at the location of the VARIABLE(*author*) code.

7. Position the insertion point to the next place in the file where you need the author's name, and insert a VARIABLE(*author*) code.

8. When you perform a merge with the form file containing the GETSTRING code, WordPerfect prompts you for the author's name (see fig. 19.28). After the merge is complete, the text you typed in response to the Author's Name prompt is inserted at the location of the VARIABLE(*author*) code.

Fig. 19.28
When you are prompted for keyboard input, the dialog box title and prompt message are the entries you included in the GETSTRING code.

Please Wait...
Author's Name
Type the Author's name
OK
Cancel

Figure 19.29 shows an example of a memorandum form that uses the GETSTRING code to capture and use the author's name in both the heading and signature line.

Fig. 19.29
A sample memorandum shows how the GETSTRING code can be used to capture keyboard input to a variable.

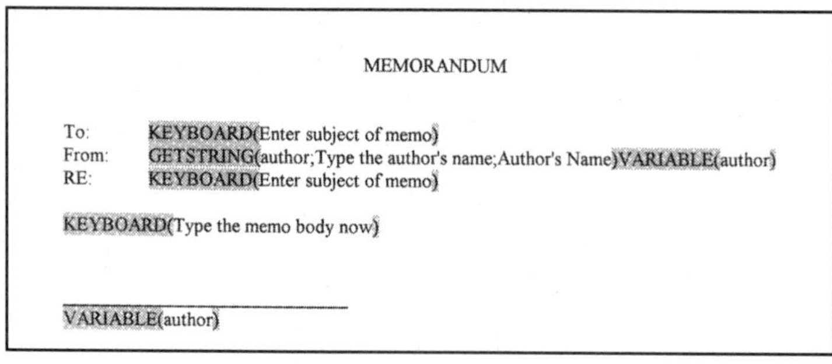

MEMORANDUM

To: KEYBOARD(Enter subject of memo)
From: GETSTRING(author;Type the author's name;Author's Name)VARIABLE(author)
RE: KEYBOARD(Enter subject of memo)

KEYBOARD(Type the memo body now)

VARIABLE(author)

Controlling User Input

The previous section shows how you can capture user input to a variable and then use that variable information in your document. The codes, however, do not control the appearance of text the user puts in the document. Whatever the user types in response to the prompt is assigned to the variable and is used throughout the document. You don't have to rely on the user, however, to enter text correctly. WordPerfect 6.1 has additional merge codes that enable you to control the appearance of text entered by a user.

The codes CAPS(*expr*), FIRSTCAP(*expr*), TOLOWER(*expr*), and TOUPPER(*expr*) enable you to force text input from a user to be inserted into the merged document in the way you want the text to appear. The word *expr* in these codes refers to data (an expression) that is to be acted upon by the code. Usually these codes operate on text contained in a variable. CAPS capitalizes the first letter of each word in the expression. FIRSTCAP capitalizes the first letter of the first word in the expression. TOLOWER and TOUPPER change all characters in the expression to lowercase and uppercase, respectively. CAPS and FIRSTCAP work only on text that is all lowercase; they cannot change the case of text in positions other than the first characters of words.

Suppose the corporate standard for the memorandum shown in the preceding section required that the names of the author and recipient be in small caps. You can put formatting codes in the form to apply the small caps attribute to text entered by the user. The small caps attribute, however, correctly formats text only if it has initial caps. WordPerfect makes it possible for you to get the result you want, regardless of how the user types the text. Figure 19.30 shows the merge codes in the memorandum that accomplish the desired result.

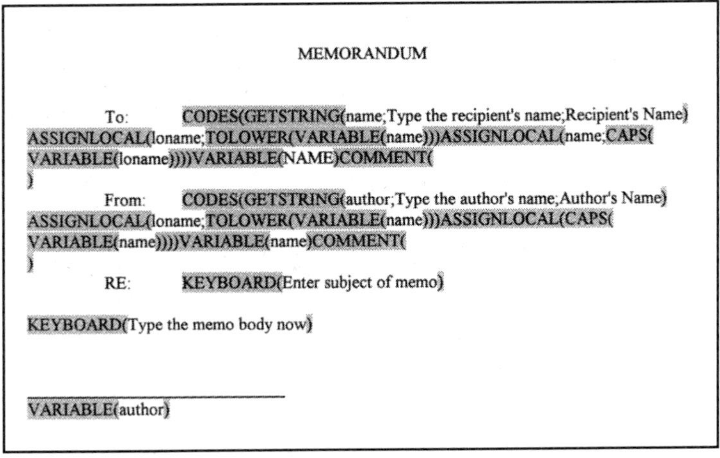

MEMORANDUM

To: CODES(GETSTRING(name;Type the recipient's name;Recipient's Name)
ASSIGNLOCAL(loname;TOLOWER(VARIABLE(name)))ASSIGNLOCAL(name;CAPS(
VARIABLE(loname))))VARIABLE(NAME)COMMENT(
)
From: CODES(GETSTRING(author;Type the author's name;Author's Name)
ASSIGNLOCAL(loname;TOLOWER(VARIABLE(name)))ASSIGNLOCAL(CAPS(
VARIABLE(name))))VARIABLE(name)COMMENT(
)
RE: KEYBOARD(Enter subject of memo)

KEYBOARD(Type the memo body now)

VARIABLE(author)

Fig. 19.30 A memorandum form with merge codes that force user input to appear in the document as small caps.

Using Data Files from Other Sources

With WordPerfect 6.1 for Windows, you can use data files produced by supported programs in merge operations, and you need not convert them prior to the merge. WordPerfect 6.1 converts supported files on the fly. You can use WordPerfect secondary merge format files (now known as data text files) from prior versions of WordPerfect and from WordPerfect Office Notebook as data text files. Data files created by most major word processing programs also can be used.

In addition to files from word processing programs, WordPerfect supports the import and use of data files created by spreadsheets and database programs. Field names used in the source application are recognized and used by WordPerfect as field names. To use a data file from another application, simply select the file as the data file either while performing a merge or associating a data file. WordPerfect performs any conversions necessary to make the file usable.

WordPerfect has an important feature that enables data files to be linked to your document. After you establish a link to a data file, the linked data in your WordPerfect file is updated whenever the source data file changes. To import or link to a spreadsheet or database file, choose **I**nsert, Sp**r**eadsheet/Database, and then choose either **I**mport or **C**reate Link. Figure 19.31 shows a list of the database formats that WordPerfect supports for import and linking.

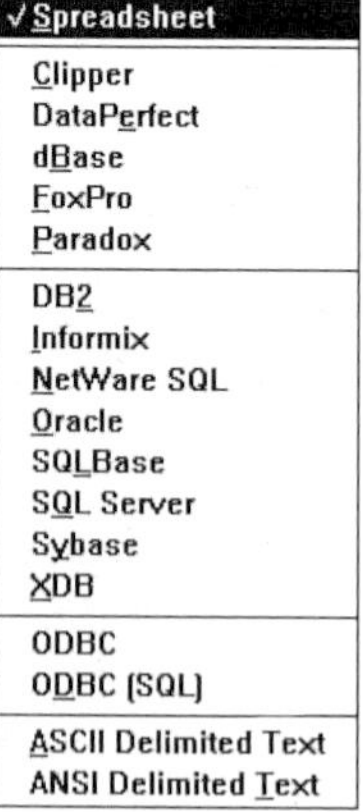

Fig. 19.31
WordPerfect enables you to create links to data files created by any of the supported programs listed.

In addition to direct use of files from other applications, WordPerfect can use ASCII delimited text as a data text file without prior manipulation. ASCII delimited text typically surrounds each field with quotation marks (" ") and separates fields with commas. Records are a single line of text terminated by a carriage return and a line feed. WordPerfect automatically recognizes DOS text and prompts you for the characters to be stripped during the merge.

Merging into Tables

Although you can maintain a data file in table format, at times you may need to merge data from a data text file into a table. When you merge text file data into a table in WordPerfect, a new row is automatically added to the table for each record.

Suppose you have a data text file with named fields in the following order: First Name, Middle, Salutation, Last Name, Spouse, Office, Address, City, State, ZIP Code, Work Phone, Home Phone, Fax Number, and Notes. You want to prepare a table from the data file that contains only the full name, address, and home phone. Follow these steps to prepare the table:

1. Starting in an unused document window, choose **T**ools, M**e**rge; or press Shift+F9.
2. Choose **F**orm, select the data file to associate with the form, and then choose OK.
3. Create a table of three columns and two rows. Make the first row a header row and enter column headings of **Name**, **Address**, and **Home Phone** in the first row. (See Chapter 16, "Working with Tables," if you are unsure how to create the table.)
4. Position the insertion point in the last cell of the first row. Choose Merge **C**odes from the merge bar and choose the LABEL(*label*) code.
5. Type a name for the label, such as **loop**, then choose OK or press Enter.
6. Position the insertion point in the first cell of the second row.
7. Choose **I**nsert Field from the Merge Feature Bar, then choose and insert the First Name field.
8. Press the space bar, then repeat step 7 to choose and insert the Last Name field.
9. Continue in the same way to insert the Address, City, State, and ZIP Code fields in the second cell, and the Home Phone field in the third cell.
10. With the insertion point positioned in the third cell following the Home Phone field code, insert the NEXTRECORD code.
11. Insert the GO(*label*) code. At the prompt, type the same label name that you used in step 5; the screen now resembles figure 19.32.

Name	Address	Home PhoneLABEL(loop)
FIELD(first name) FIELD(last name)	FIELD(address) FIELD(city), FIELD(st) FIELD(zip code)	FIELD(home phone) NEXTRECORD GO(loop)

Fig. 19.32 A table form file with merge codes in place to merge data into the table. The table automatically expands to accommodate the records from the data file.

12. Save the form with an appropriate name, such as **table.frm**.

13. Perform the merge in any of the ways described in the section "Performing the Merge" earlier in this chapter.

Using Sort

In addition to the WordPerfect 6 merge functions which can be used for sorting data files and selecting individual records when merging, you can sort the data file itself as well as other kinds of files. The Sort feature enables you to manipulate any file that is formatted in a way that WordPerfect can recognize. You can use Sort to arrange records, lines, columns, or other text alphabetically or numerically, based on the value of sort keys, and you can use Sort to extract text that meets conditions you define.

Understanding Sort Record Types

Sort recognizes five types of data files, described as follows:

Record type	Record termination	Record subdivisions
Line	Each line is a record, terminated by an HRt	Fields Words
Paragraph	Records are terminated by two hard returns	Lines Fields Words
Merge text data file	Records end with an ENDRECORD code	Fields Lines Words
Parallel columns	Records are a parallel row of columns	Columns Lines Words
Table	Each row is a record	Cells Lines Words

The terms used in the right column of the preceding table are descriptive terms for the recognized subdivisions of a record of the type shown in the left column. The list of recognized subdivisions for a particular record type is set out in order from largest to smallest. In a table, for example, a record (a single row) is divided into cells, which are subdivided into lines, which are themselves subdivided into words. Notice the difference between paragraph records and merge data records.

Fields and lines in ordinary text are usually the same. Tabs or indents on a line, however, separate the line into fields. ENDFIELD codes separate fields in merge data files. Words are separated by spaces, forward slashes (/), and hyphen characters; for example, the date 7/19/95 is actually three words.

Note

The regular hyphen is not treated as a word separator. To separate sort "words" with a hyphen, use the hyphen character (Fo**r**mat, **L**ine, **O**ther Codes, Hyphen Ch**a**racter, **I**nsert) instead. When you want to lock words together, such as "John Smith III" or "Van Nuys," replace the regular space between the words with a hard space (Fo**r**mat, **L**ine, **O**ther Codes, Hard S**p**ace, **I**nsert). Words joined by a hard space are treated as a single word during a sort.

Understanding Sort Keys

Sort keys are the definitions for the record subdivisions that you use to arrange a data file. Figure 19.33 shows a list of officers for a soccer club presently listed alphabetically by office held.

Awards Coordinator	Bernice Ardman	5772 SW Iowa St.	Portland, OR	97221	245-3026
Equipment Manager	Gary Williams	7220 SW 63rd Ave.	Portland, OR	97219	245-7923
Field Coordinator	Mike Van Luwen	2620 SW Nevada Ct.	Portland, OR	97219	245-9011
Head Coach	Dave Tonkon	5440 SW 53rd	Portland, OR	97221	244-4687
Librarian	Margie Albertson	4347 SW Flower St.	Portland, OR	97221	246-8954
Mailing	Kristi Stavropoulis	8137 SW 40th	Portland, OR	97219	244-9244
Newsletter	Mike Sanders	4925 SW 18th Dr.	Portland, OR	97201	246-3030
Picture Day Coord.	Noreen Bolger	6721 SW 36th Ave.	Portland, OR	97219	244-8842
President	Carol Rutan	6910 SW 11th Dr.	Portland, OR	97219	244-9824
PYSA Representative	Brian Brown	7410 SW 54th Ave.	Portland, OR	97219	246-9922
Registrar	Neal Radak	6446 SW Loop Dr.	Portland, OR	97221	245-3349
Secretary	David Scott	7810 SW 49th Ave.	Portland, OR	97219	245-3557
Small-Sided Fields	Perry Richardson	2912 SW Carolina	Portland, OR	97201	244-8034
Treasurer	Beth Cross	5720 SW California	Portland, OR	97219	246-5043
Uniform Coordinator	Chuck Carson	6023 SW Pendleton Ct	Portland, OR	97221	245-3753
Uniform Exchange	Sally Arditi	5325 SW Boundary St.	Portland, OR	97221	245-5394
Vice President	Andy Roberts	5313 SW Illinois	Portland, OR	97221	244-2241

Fig. 19.33
A list of club officers. Tabs separate the columns and hyphen characters separate the phone numbers.

You can sort this list to reorder it alphabetically by the officers' last names. To accomplish this task, begin with the file open on-screen, and follow these steps:

1. Choose **T**ools, So**r**t; or press Alt+F9. The Sort dialog box appears, as shown in figure 19.34.

   The default is set to order the records by the first word in the first cell in a table. In this case, the last names of the officers are not the first word of the first field. To use the last name as a key, you must create a new key statement.

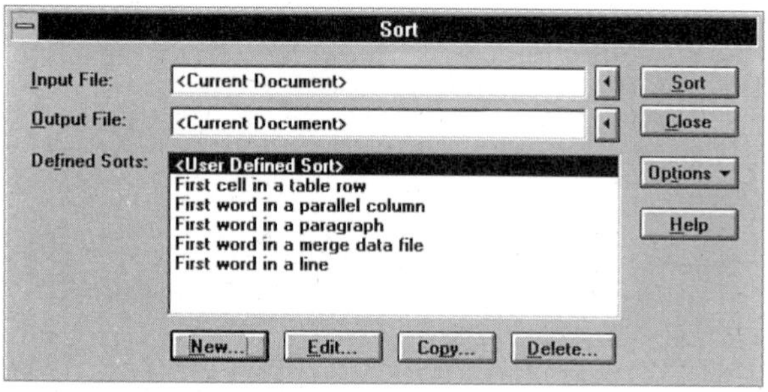

Fig. 19.34
The Sort dialog box enables you to select a predefined table, line, merge file, paragraph, column sort or one of your previous sorts. You can also create new sorts or edit an existing sort.

2. Choose **N**ew to open the New Sort dialog box shown in figure 19.35.
3. Enter **Last Name Sort** in the **S**ort Name text box. This descriptive name will be added to the list in the Sort box and will be easy to recognize in the future.
4. Type **2** in the Field text box.
5. Type **–1** in the Word text box. Use –1 rather than 2 for the Word box because not all the names have the same length. The –1 parameter directs Sort to count words from the right rather than the left.
6. Choose OK or press Enter to perform the sort. Figure 19.36 shows the sorted list.

Sorting merge data files is exactly the same process as the previously illustrated sort. In fact, you can use the same menu choices to begin either sort. You can also begin a sort of a merge data file by choosing **O**ptions, **S**ort from the Merge Feature Bar of the data file.

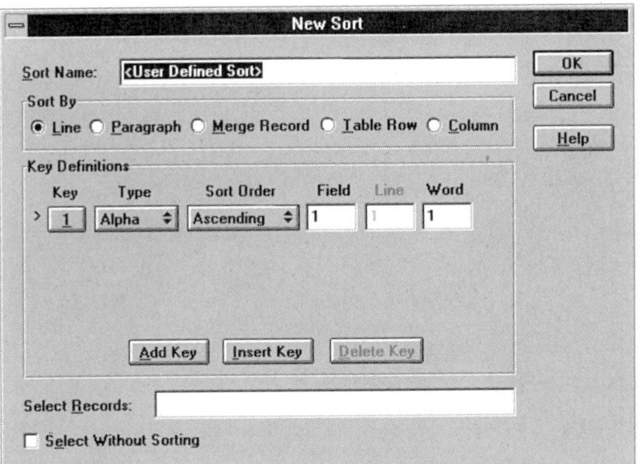

Fig. 19.35
The New Sort dialog box enables you to establish keys to sort and select records from data files.

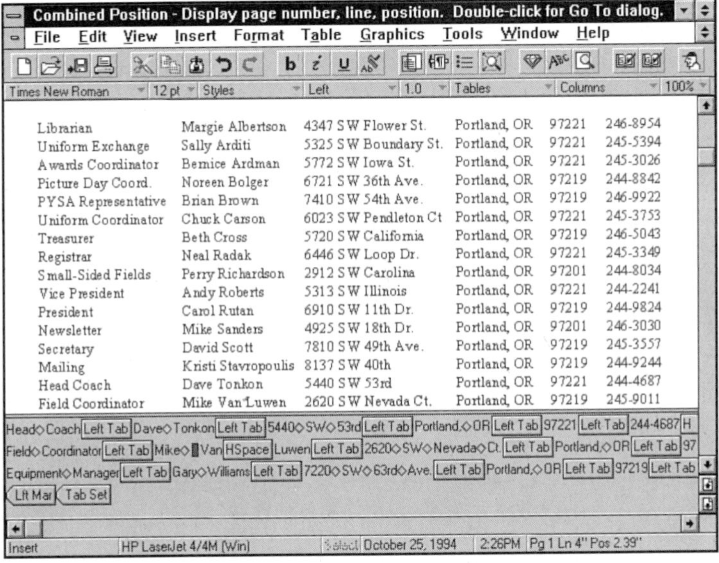

Fig. 19.36
The list of officers from figure 19.33 sorted by the last name of the officer. In this Reveal Codes view, notice the [HSpace] code between Van and Luwen that keeps this name together during the sort.

Using Multiple Keys to Sort and Select Records

Suppose that you have a mailing list containing more than 1,000 business names and addresses spread across five ZIP codes. The data is organized in the same way as the data file in the previous example, but the name of the business is in the column used for the office in the soccer club example. You want to send a marketing letter to those business owners in a single ZIP code whose business phone numbers match a particular prefix. You also want the list in alphabetical order by the owner's last name. Using the soccer club data file as an example, you can define the sort keys as follows:

1. Choose **T**ools, So**r**t; or press Alt+F9.
2. Select Last Name sort and choose **E**dit. Make sure that Sort By is set to **L**ine and that the first sort key is still set for Field 2 and Word –1.
3. Choose **I**nsert Key.
4. Type **5** in the Field text box (the Word text box contains 1). This sets the primary key to the ZIP Code field.
5. Choose Key **2**, and then choose **I**nsert Key.
6. Type **6** in the Field text box. This entry sets the second key to the phone number prefix.

Caution

Although the phone number and ZIP code fields in this example contain numeric data, the key type has been left as alphanumeric. These keys sort properly because the numbers are all the same length. When unequal length numbers are sorted as alphanumeric data, the numbers are ordered by the value of the leftmost digit, then the second digit, and so on. For example, the numbers 9, 124, 28, and 3029 would be sorted alphabetically as 124, 29, 3028, 9.

Now that the keys are set, you can enter select statements to extract the records you want from the data file. A select statement assigns a value to a sort key you defined and chooses from the file being sorted only those records in which the key data values match the select value.

Using the previous data file as an example, select all records with a 97221 ZIP code and phone numbers with a 245 prefix. To assign select values to extract the records that meet these conditions, follow these steps:

1. Position the insertion point in the Select **R**ecords text box.
2. Type **Key1=97221 & Key2=245** (see fig. 19.37).

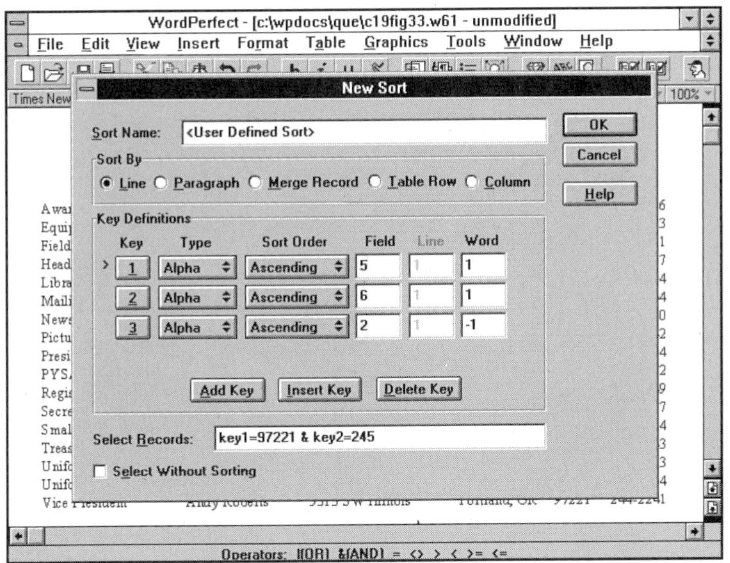

Fig. 19.37 The logical selection operators (¦(OR) &(AND) = <> > < >= <=) are displayed in the status bar while you create or edit selection statements in the New Sort dialog box.

3. Choose OK or press Enter. The results of the sort and select operation are shown in figure 19.38.

Uniform Exchange	Sally Arditi	5325 SW Boundary St.	Portland, OR	97221	245-5394
Awards Coordinator	Bernice Ardman	5772 SW Iowa St.	Portland, OR	97221	245-3026
Uniform Coordinator	Chuck Carson	6023 SW Pendleton Ct	Portland, OR	97221	245-3753
Registrar	Neal Radak	6446 SW Loop Dr.	Portland, OR	97221	245-3349

Fig. 19.38 The results of performing the selection. Notice that the selected records have been sorted in alphabetical order by the person's last name.

Troubleshooting

I have a file of employee names with the job title and social security number in tabular columns on the same line. I can't successfully sort the file by job title or social security number, only by first or last name.

Check in Reveal Codes to see if there is more than one tab code between columns. If you have not set tabs for the document, you often must press Tab more than once to line up the data. However, tabs are recognized as separating each line into fields. Set tab stops for the three columns of data and remove any extra tab codes to assure that only three fields of data are on each line.

I have multi-word names, including some that are followed with M.D. or Ph.D. How can I sort the list of names by last name?

It's simple. Use a hard space between each word in the last name and between the last name and the initials. Insert hard spaces from the **O**ther Codes dialog box found on the Fo**r**mat, **L**ines menu.

From Here...

This chapter provided a detailed description of basic merge functions and a brief introduction to some advanced merge programming codes. The WordPerfect 6.1 merge tools are even more powerful than this chapter has demonstrated (a full examination of the merge programming language can fill a lengthy book).

In addition to merges, this chapter examined sorting and selecting records from data files. You can use these features to make data and form file creation and management easier and more productive.

For information related to the features in this chapter, consider reviewing these chapters:

- Chapter 5, "Formatting Pages and Documents," discusses the many features you can use in WordPerfect to format your document.
- Chapter 8, "Basic Output: Printing, Faxing and E-Mail," shows how to choose and configure printers for specific jobs, set printer fonts and print selected pages and document summaries.
- Chapter 10, "Using Styles," shows you how to create styles you can use to quickly format documents and help standardize the appearance of your work.
- Chapter 13, "Working with Toolbars," discusses how to create additional toolbars, to customize additional toolbars and to customize the Power Bar.
- Chapter 16, "Working with Tables," shows you how to create and use tables, including formatting the appearance of cells, creating header rows, and other table features.

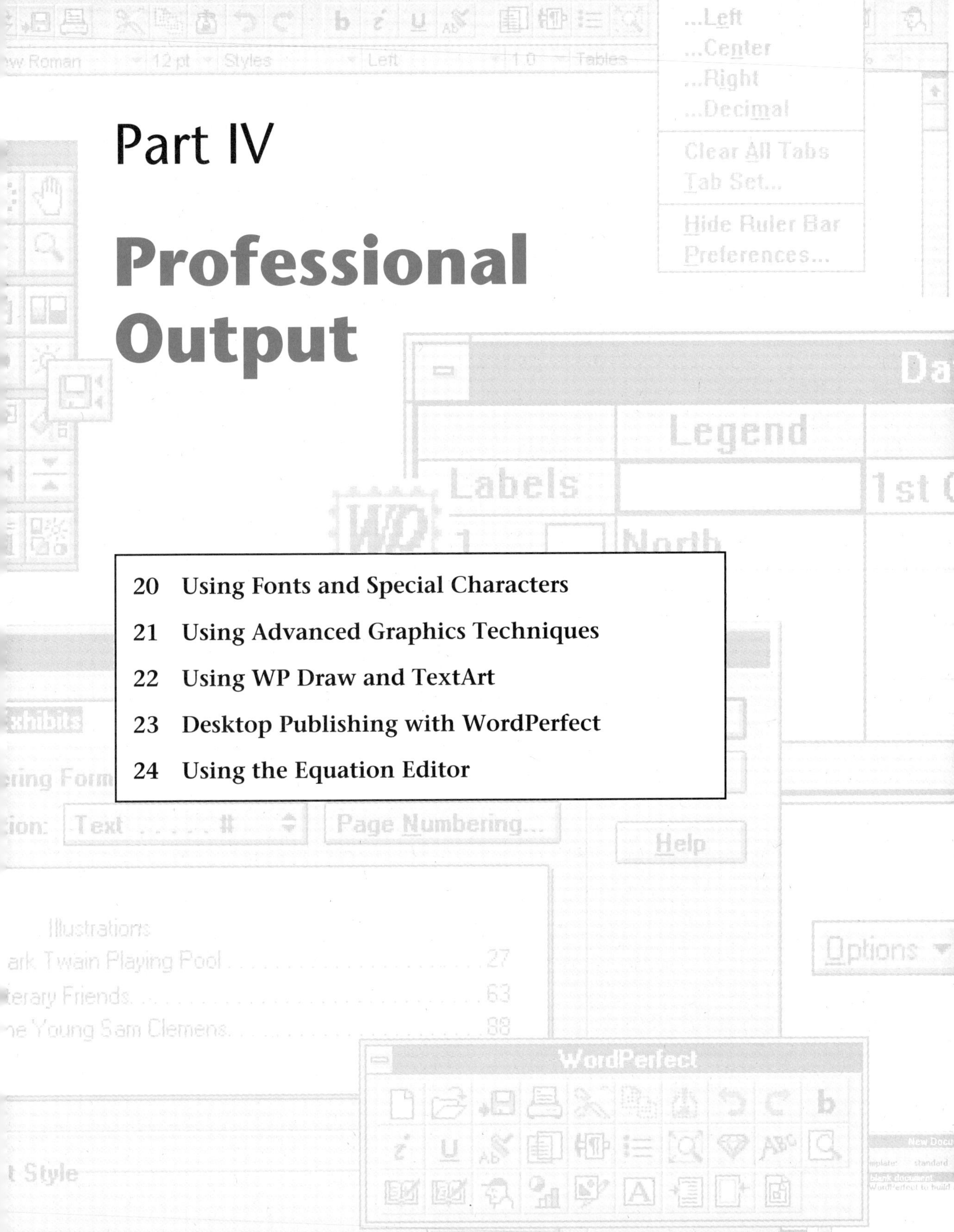

Part IV

Professional Output

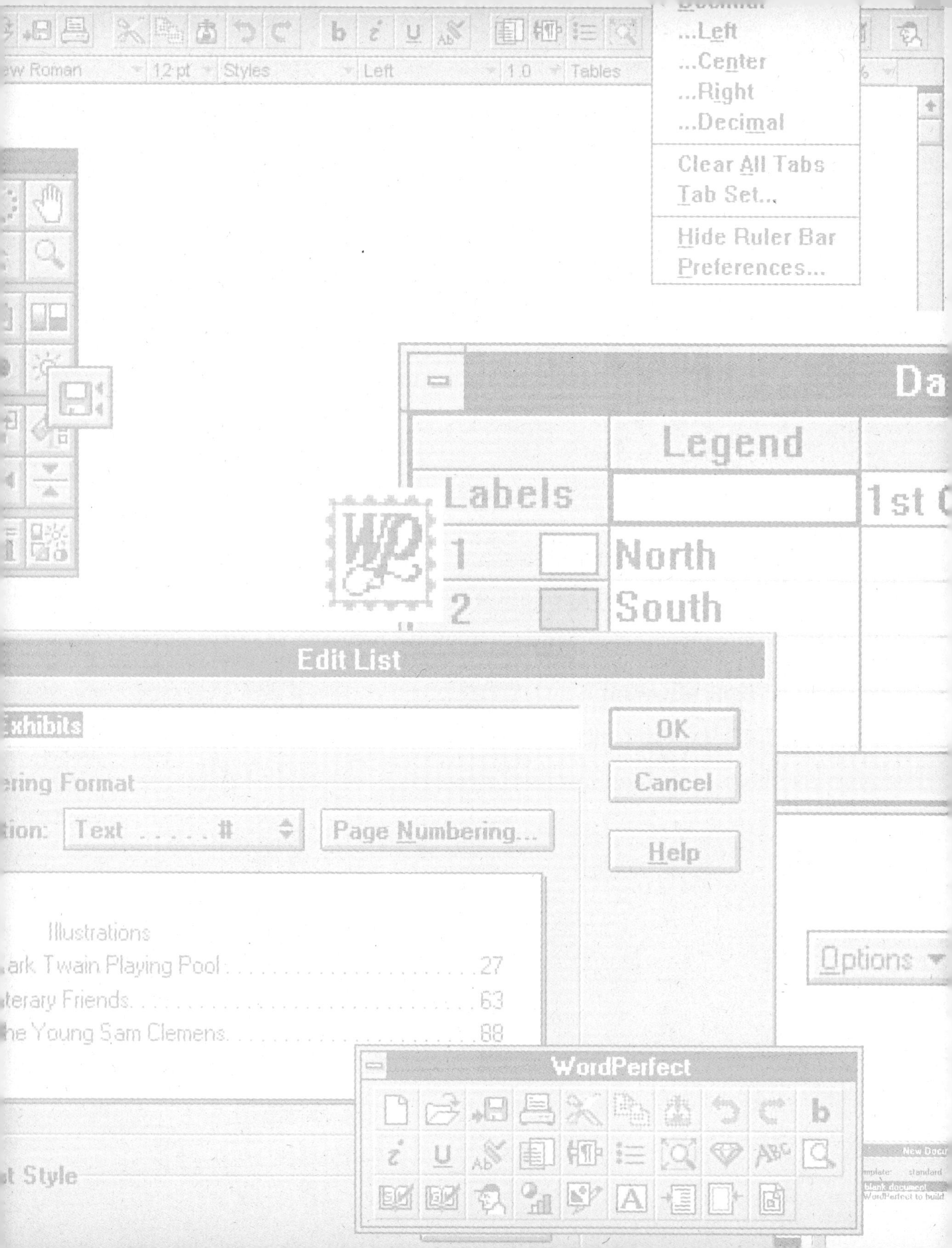
...Left
...Center
...Right
...Decimal
Clear All Tabs
Tab Set...
Hide Ruler Bar
Preferences...
Legend
Labels
North
South
Edit List
OK
Cancel
Help
Page Numbering...
Illustrations
Options
WordPerfect

Chapter 20

Using Fonts and Special Characters

by Gordon Nelder-Adams

Would you like a quick and easy way to spice up your documents? It's easy when you use fonts. You can change the appearance of a document dramatically by choosing a different font for its body text, headings, or other elements such as headers, footers, and captions.

WordPerfect 6.1 for Windows provides a great deal of flexibility and control over the fonts you can use, and their appearance on-screen and in printed text. You can use fonts that are built into your printer, installed into Windows, or provided by WordPerfect itself. You can also use additional fonts that you purchase in a fonts package, as well as fonts that come with a printer. WordPerfect also lets you insert thousands of characters and symbols into documents.

In this chapter, you learn how to:

- Choose which types of fonts are best for your needs
- Install printer fonts and graphics fonts
- Include special characters in your documents
- Create and edit overstrike characters
- Modify Automatic Font Changes (AFCs) to fine-tune the appearance of your documents
- Modify the links between printer fonts and graphics fonts

Understanding WordPerfect and Windows Font Management

Computer programs use fonts in two ways: to create printed output and to display text on-screen. All programs that run under Microsoft Windows, including WordPerfect 6.1 for Windows, use Windows itself to display fonts on-screen. Several add-on Windows font managers are also available, including Adobe Type Manager (ATM), FaceLift for Windows, and Intellifont for Windows. These font managers give Windows the capability to use fonts in several different formats. Figure 20.1 includes some of the fonts that are installed when you first set up WordPerfect on your computer.

WordPerfect 6.1 for Windows can create printed output using either a Windows printer driver or a WordPerfect printer driver. Windows printer drivers are installed as part of the Windows environment, and can be used by all Windows programs. WordPerfect printer drivers can only be used by WordPerfect Corporation programs. See Chapter 8, "Basic Output: Printing, Faxing, and E-mail," for more information on selecting printer drivers.

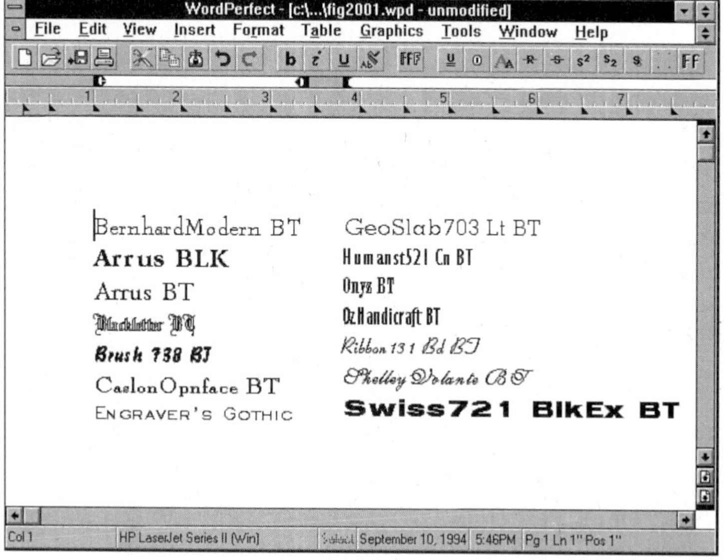

Fig. 20.1
WordPerfect installs some of these and other TrueType fonts when you first set up WordPerfect on your computer.

The Windows printer drivers provide font compatibility with other Windows programs. The WordPerfect printer drivers provide font compatibility with WordPerfect 6 for DOS. Therefore, if you share documents with users of the DOS version of WordPerfect, you may want to use the WordPerfect printer drivers. Otherwise, there is little reason to use the WordPerfect drivers. If you create a document with a Windows printer driver selected and give a copy of the document to a WordPerfect 6 for DOS user, the document content will be correct; but he or she may need to reselect the fonts.

Note

In previous versions of WordPerfect for Windows, there were significant differences between the Windows and WordPerfect printer drivers. The WordPerfect drivers offered much greater flexibility in paper handling, but did not work directly with Windows font management. In WordPerfect 6.0 and 6.1 for Windows, these differences no longer exist.

Microsoft Windows 3.1 directly supports the TrueType font format. When you use the Windows Control Panel to add TrueType fonts, Windows can immediately display those fonts on-screen, and your Windows printer driver can likewise use those fonts to print (unless your printer itself can't print graphics). If you use a font manager such as Adobe Type Manager, you install new fonts into ATM, which then works with Windows to display the fonts on-screen and with Windows printer drivers to send the fonts to your printer.

WordPerfect 6.1 for Windows can use any Windows printer driver, and thus can use any font you have installed into Windows. If you prefer to use the WordPerfect printer drivers, these drivers can also use any fonts installed into Windows. As a result, no matter which printer drivers you use, when you add a font using Windows or a Windows font manager, you can immediately print using that font.

Printer Fonts and Graphics Fonts

For font management purposes, you can divide fonts into two broad categories: printer fonts and graphics fonts.

Printer fonts are fonts in your printer's native font format. Printer fonts can be *internal fonts*, *cartridge fonts*, or *soft fonts*. *Graphics fonts* are fonts created "on the fly" (as needed) by Windows or WordPerfect. These fonts are called graphics fonts because they are often printed as graphics, and Windows uses them to display on-screen.

Internal fonts are built into your printer. All printers have one or more internal fonts, which almost always include a Courier font. Some printers have many internal fonts, and some have only one or two.

Cartridge fonts are similar to internal fonts, but are built into cartridges that can be inserted into a printer. Not all printers accept font cartridges. The most common cartridges are designed for use in Hewlett-Packard LaserJet (and compatible) printers.

You must purchase your printer and font cartridges separately. Although you can purchase many font cartridges, your printer probably has no more than one or two font cartridge slots, which limits the number of cartridge fonts you can use at one time. After you insert a font cartridge into the printer, the fonts are in effect "built in," and you can use them in exactly the same way you use internal fonts.

Soft fonts are fonts stored in files on your hard drive. Before your printer can use these fonts, they must be downloaded (copied) to your printer from your hard drive. WordPerfect does this for you automatically.

There are advantages and disadvantages to each type of font. Because internal fonts are built in, printing with internal fonts is extremely fast. Cartridge fonts are equally fast. Unfortunately, most printers can hold relatively few internal and cartridge fonts at one time. If you want to use other fonts, you often have to turn off your printer, remove a cartridge, and install a new cartridge.

Because soft fonts must be downloaded to your printer before they can be used, printing with soft fonts takes longer than printing with internal or cartridge fonts. You can save some time by downloading fonts to your printer's memory, making the fonts resident before printing. However, most printers can hold only a limited number of resident fonts in memory. Soft fonts also take up room on your hard drive.

Although printing with soft fonts is usually slower than printing with internal or cartridge fonts, soft fonts are usually far more flexible, because you can use any soft font stored on your hard disk at any time. If you have room on your hard drive, you can easily acquire and store hundreds of soft fonts.

Printing with graphics fonts is always slower than printing with internal or cartridge printer fonts. Depending on your printer, printing with graphics fonts may be slightly faster or slower than printing with soft fonts in your printer's native font format.

When adding fonts to WordPerfect, it's important to understand three important differences between printer fonts and graphics fonts:

- *One user's printer font can be another printer's graphics font.* A printer font is simply a font in your printer's native font format. If you own a PostScript printer, for example, it has some Type 1 fonts built in, and WordPerfect can download other Type 1 fonts directly to it. If you own a Hewlett-Packard LaserJet III printer, your printer doesn't recognize Type 1 fonts; however, with Adobe Type Manager, WordPerfect can use Type 1 fonts to generate temporary graphics fonts in your Hewlett-Packard's native format.

- *Printer fonts are printer and printer-driver specific.* If you add a printer font, WordPerfect adds it only to the currently selected printer driver. (See Chapter 8, "Basic Output: Printing, Faxing, and E-mail," for instructions on selecting printer drivers.) If you have two or more printer drivers capable of supporting the same printer fonts, you need to repeat the process of adding the printer fonts to each printer driver. You can use graphics fonts with any printer.

- *WordPerfect always uses graphics fonts for screen fonts, and can also use graphics fonts for printing.* When you select a graphics font to print with, WordPerfect also uses the font on-screen. In contrast, printer fonts are used only for printing. When you choose a printer font to print with, WordPerfect chooses a similar screen font to use on-screen. (See "Editing Display Font Mapping" later in this chapter for instructions on how to override WordPerfect's choice.)

Font Formats

Depending on the Windows font scaling program that you use, WordPerfect can use fonts in many supported formats—TrueType, Type 1, Speedo, Intellifont, and PCL (HP LaserJet). Of these, all but the latter are scalable fonts, meaning that either WordPerfect or your printer can print text in a wide variety of sizes from a single font file.

TrueType fonts are directly supported by Windows 3.1. They also can be used as printer fonts with the HP LaserJet 4 family of printers, and with the Microsoft Windows Printing System (an add-in cartridge for LaserJet Series II printers). Fonts in this format are available from many sources, including Bitstream, CompuGraphic, Monotype, and Microsoft. When you install WordPerfect, you automatically install several dozen additional TrueType fonts as well.

Type 1 is the PostScript font format invented by Adobe, and is the native font format of any printer that is PostScript-compatible. If you use Adobe Type Manager (ATM) with Windows, you already have some Type 1 fonts. If you prefer Type 1 fonts to TrueType fonts, you can obtain Type 1 versions of the WordPerfect fonts directly from Novell, makers of WordPerfect.

Bitstream Speedo is the font format used by FaceLift for Windows. Only Bitstream supplies fonts in this format. Each font contains over 500 characters; therefore, foreign language and mathematical characters are available to you in the same typeface. Speedo fonts are not native to any printer, so WordPerfect always treats them as graphics fonts.

The *CG Intellifont* font format was invented by CompuGraphic, and is the native font format of the Hewlett-Packard LaserJet III and 4 families of printers. In fact, Intellifont fonts purchased from Hewlett-Packard are really CompuGraphic fonts. A few other sources are available. Like Bitstream Speedo fonts, each font contains many characters. These fonts are directly supported by the Windows and WordPerfect printer drivers for the appropriate LaserJet printers, so you don't need an additional font scaling program to use them; however, you must use HP's Intellifont for Windows to display them accurately on-screen. Otherwise, Windows uses the closest available TrueType font to represent the equivalent Intellifont font.

PCL or HP LaserJet fonts are the native font format of Hewlett-Packard LaserJet, LaserJet Plus, and LaserJet Series II printers. These fonts are bitmapped, not scalable, which means that you need a different font file for each size, weight, and orientation of font. As a result, LaserJet bitmapped fonts take up far more room on disk than fonts in the other formats, and are far less flexible. Windows cannot use this font format to create screen fonts, either, and uses its own built-in screen fonts or TrueType fonts to display the closest equivalent font on-screen.

Installing Fonts

◄ See "Adding Fonts for Your Printer," p. 310

When you install WordPerfect, the Install program automatically installs a number of TrueType fonts into Windows, which makes the fonts available not only to WordPerfect, but also to all your other Windows programs. (See Appendix A, "Installing and Setting Up WordPerfect 6.1 for Windows.") These fonts include specialized fonts that contain the WordPerfect Character Sets, as well as a selection of body text and display fonts (refer to fig. 20.1).

The method for installing additional fonts depends on the format of the fonts you want to install. You install TrueType fonts into the Windows Control Panel, PostScript Type 1 fonts into Adobe Type Manager, and Bitstream Speedo fonts into FaceLift for Windows. You install both Intellifont and the older HP LaserJet bitmapped fonts directly into the Windows driver for an HP LaserJet printer.

TrueType

The TrueType font format was jointly developed by Microsoft and Apple, and TrueType font support is built directly into Microsoft Windows 3.1 and Apple System 7. TrueType fonts contain all the information necessary to use the font within the font file itself, so whenever you purchase additional TrueType fonts you can install them directly into Windows.

TrueType font files have a TTF filename extension. To install TrueType fonts, you simply tell Windows where the files are, and then mark which fonts you want to install. Windows then copies the fonts to the \WINDOWS\SYSTEM subdirectory, and builds a small FOT file for each font. Some font packages compress the fonts on the distribution disks, and typically have an Install program that decompresses the fonts and installs them directly to your \WINDOWS\SYSTEM directory. If the fonts are not compressed, you can install them directly from the floppy disks.

If you decide that you don't like a particular font, or that your list of available fonts is getting too long, you can remove one or more fonts. You can simply remove the font name from the list of available fonts, or have Windows remove the font file itself from your hard disk, thus freeing up disk space.

To install TrueType fonts in Windows 3.1, follow these steps:

1. Double-click on the Control Panel icon in the Program Manager (usually in the Main program group). Windows displays the Control Panel.

2. Double-click on the Fonts icon in the Control Panel. The Fonts dialog box appears (see fig. 20.2).

3. Choose **A**dd. The Add Fonts dialog box appears.

4. From the Dri**v**es drop-down list, select the drive that contains the fonts you want to install. If necessary, select the directory that contains the font files.

   Windows builds a list of the available fonts. If the drive or directory contains many TrueType files, Windows may take a few seconds to build the list.

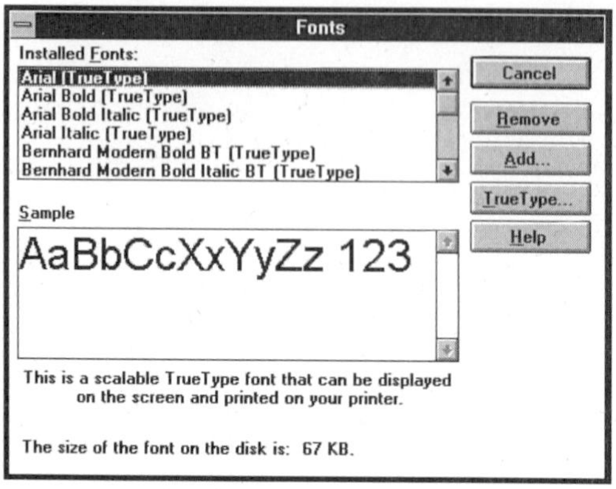

Fig. 20.2
The Fonts dialog box in the Control Panel displays a list of installed TrueType fonts. From here you can add or remove TrueType fonts.

5. Select the fonts you want to add. You can click on a single font to highlight it, then Ctrl+Click to highlight a second font; or Shift+Click to highlight a range of fonts (see fig. 20.3). Or choose **S**elect All to highlight the entire list.

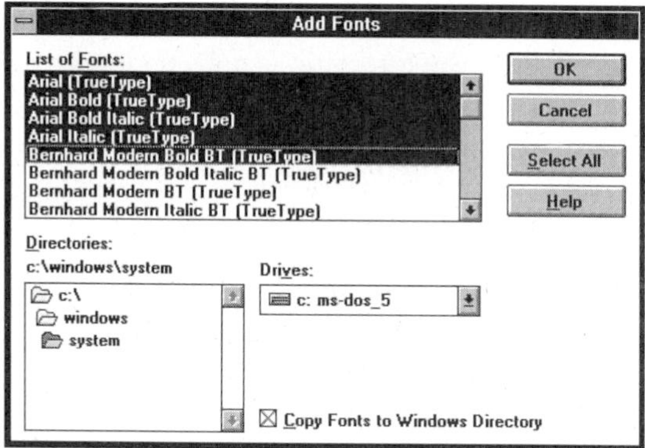

Fig. 20.3
You can highlight a range of fonts to install, or choose Select All to install all the fonts on the drive or directory.

6. Make sure that the **C**opy Fonts to Windows Directory check box is selected. Then choose OK.

   Windows copies the font files to the \WINDOWS\SYSTEM subdirectory, and adds the font names to the list of available fonts.

7. Choose Close to close the Fonts dialog box; then close the Control Panel.

You can use the newly installed fonts immediately; you do not need to restart Windows before the fonts are available.

To remove TrueType fonts from Windows 3.1, use the following steps:

1. Double-click on the Control Panel icon in the Program Manager (usually in the Main program group). Windows displays the Control Panel.
2. Double-click on the Fonts icon in the Control Panel. The Fonts dialog box appears (refer to fig. 20.2).
3. Select the fonts you want to remove. You can click on a single font to highlight it, then Ctrl+Click to highlight a second font; or Shift+Click to highlight a range of fonts.
4. Choose **R**emove. Windows displays a dialog box prompting you to confirm removal of the font(s).
5. If you want to delete the font files themselves, mark the **D**elete Font File From Disk check box. Otherwise, Windows removes the font names from the list of available fonts, but does not delete the font files from your hard disk.
6. Choose Yes to **A**ll to remove all selected fonts. Or choose **Y**es to remove the first selected font; Windows then prompts you to remove the next selected font.
7. When all selected fonts have been removed, choose Close to close the Fonts dialog box, and then close the Control Panel.

If you remove TrueType fonts from the list of available fonts but don't delete the font files themselves, you can later reinstall the fonts using the previous installation process.

Type 1

Whether or not you use a PostScript printer, you must use Adobe Type Manager (ATM) to display and print the PostScript Type 1 fonts in Microsoft Windows. If you do use a PostScript printer, ATM downloads the font files directly to your printer. If you don't use a PostScript printer, ATM automatically creates temporary fonts in your printer's native font format if possible, or otherwise prints the fonts as graphics.

When you purchase Type 1 fonts, the distribution disks typically contain several types of files. Files with a PFB filename extension are the Type 1 fonts themselves; and files with an AFM extension are font metrics files that describe which characters each font contains, the characters' relative sizes, and other information. When you install Type 1 fonts, ATM by default copies the

PFB files to the C:\PSFONTS directory, and the AFM files to the C:\PSFONTS\AFM directory. At the same time, ATM creates a Windows font metrics file for each font, with a PFM extension, and stores these files in the C:\PSFONTS\PFM directory.

To install Type 1 fonts using Windows 3.1, follow these steps:

1. Double-click on the ATM Control Panel icon in the Program Manager (usually in the Main program group). The ATM Control Panel appears (see fig. 20.4).

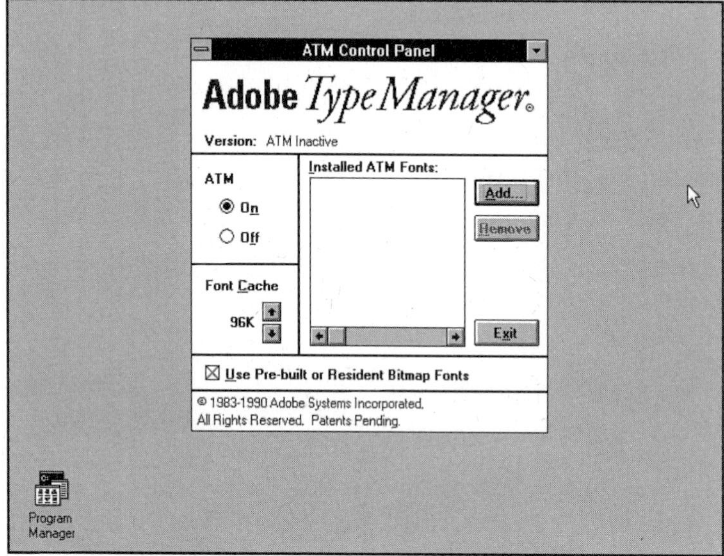

Fig. 20.4 The ATM Control Panel displays a list of installed ATM (PostScript Type 1) fonts. From here you can add or remove Type 1 fonts.

2. Choose **A**dd. ATM displays the Add ATM Fonts dialog box.

3. In the **D**irectories list box, double-click on the drive or directory that contains the fonts you want to install. ATM builds a list of the available fonts and displays them in the Available **F**onts window.

4. Select the fonts you want to add. You can click on a single font to highlight it, then Ctrl+Click to highlight a second font; or Shift+Click to highlight a range of fonts (see fig. 20.5).

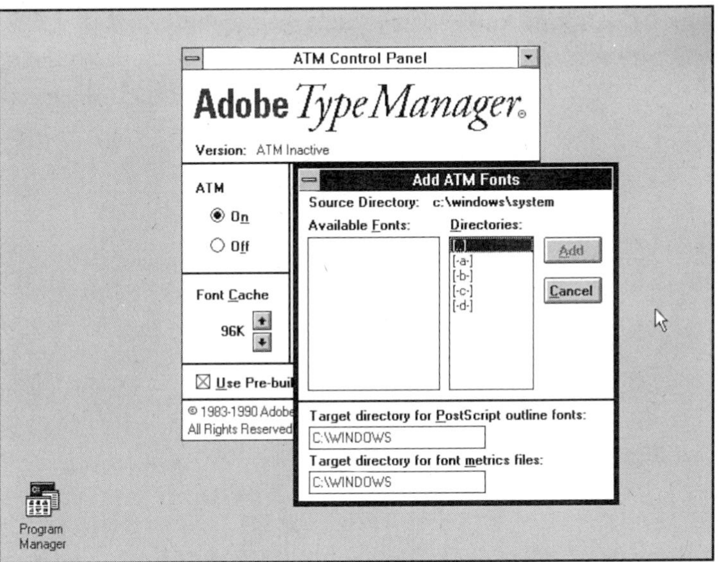

Fig. 20.5
You can highlight a range of fonts to install into ATM.

5. Choose **A**dd. ATM copies the font and font metrics files to the appropriate directories, and then returns to the main ATM Control Panel dialog box, where the new fonts now appear in the **I**nstalled ATM Fonts list.

6. When you have finished adding fonts, choose E**x**it. If you are using the current version of ATM, you return to the Program Manager and can use your new fonts immediately. If you are using an older version of ATM, you may see a message informing you that you must restart Windows for your changes to take effect. If you want to use the new fonts immediately, choose **R**estart Windows; otherwise, choose **R**eturn to Current Windows Session, and the new fonts will be available the next time you start Windows.

To remove Type 1 fonts using Windows 3.1, follow these steps:

1. Double-click on the ATM Control Panel icon in the Program Manager (usually in the Main program group). The ATM Control Panel appears.

2. Select the fonts you want to remove from the **I**nstalled ATM Fonts list. You can click on a single font to highlight it, then Ctrl+Click to highlight a second font; or Shift+Click to highlight a range of fonts.

3. Choose **R**emove. ATM displays a dialog box prompting you to confirm removal of the first selected font. Choose **Y**es to remove the font, and

have ATM prompt you to confirm removal of the next font; or select No **C**onfirmation to remove all font check boxes, and then choose **Y**es to have ATM remove all marked fonts without further confirmation.

4. When all selected fonts are removed, ATM returns you to the main ATM Control Panel. Choose E**x**it.

When you remove fonts in this manner, ATM does not delete the PFB and PFM files from your hard disk; if you want to free up hard disk space, you must remove the fonts using the Windows File Manager or a similar program. Unless you delete the font files from your hard disk yourself, however, you can later reinstall the removed fonts by using the procedure to install fonts.

Bitstream Speedo

Speedo is Bitstream's proprietary font format, which is used by Bitstream FaceLift. There are two versions of Bitstream FaceLift—FaceLift for WordPerfect, which works only with WordPerfect 5.1 for DOS, and FaceLift for Windows. If you have used FaceLift for WordPerfect and want to use the same fonts with WordPerfect 6 for Windows, you must install FaceLift for Windows.

Intellifont and PCL Fonts

PCL fonts are the native font format of older HP LaserJet (and compatible) printers, and Intellifont fonts are the native font format of newer HP printers, including the LaserJet III and 4 families. Because both types of fonts are printer fonts, you install them directly into the Windows driver for a specific printer, rather than into Windows as a whole.

If you want to display Intellifont fonts accurately on-screen, obtain a copy of Intellifont for Windows (IFW). If you own an HP printer that supports Intellifont fonts, HP will send you a free copy of IFW. IFW only displays Intellifont fonts in Windows; it does not control the printing of those fonts in any way, and you can use Intellifont fonts without using IFW. Without IFW, however, Windows will use the closest screen font or TrueType font to display Intellifont fonts on-screen.

To install Intellifont or PCL fonts, use the following steps:

1. In WordPerfect for Windows, choose **F**ile, **P**rint, **S**elect. The Select Printer dialog box appears.

2. Highlight the name of an installed Windows printer driver for a Hewlett-Packard LaserJet or compatible printer. If you highlight a WordPerfect driver, the following steps will not work.

3. Choose **O**ptions, **S**etup. The Windows Setup dialog box appears for the selected printer driver.

4. Choose **F**onts. The HP Font Installer dialog box appears (see fig. 20.6). The list box on the left displays installed fonts, and the list box on the right displays available fonts that you can add.

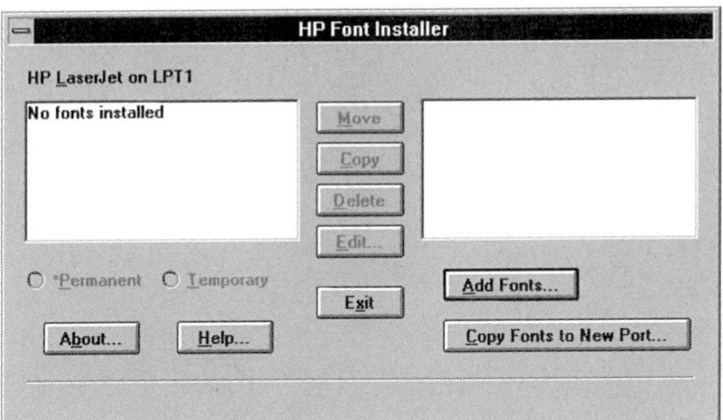

Fig. 20.6
The HP Font Installer dialog box displays lists of installed fonts on the left, and fonts available for installation on the right.

5. Choose **A**dd Fonts. The Font Installer displays a small dialog box asking for the location of the font files, and suggesting A:\ as the default location. If your fonts are in a different location, such as drive B, your hard drive, or a network drive, type the path to the correct location. Choose OK. The Font Installer scans the specified location and creates a list of available fonts in the Source list box.

6. Click on each font that you want to install. You do not need to Shift+Click or Ctrl+Click to select multiple fonts.

7. Choose **A**dd. If you selected Intellifont fonts to add, the Font Installer displays a Symbol Set Selection dialog box. For most fonts, the default WN: Windows selection is correct. If you are installing ITC Zapf Dingbats or some other font with a different symbol set, however, select the symbol set from the list box. Choose OK.

8. The Font Installer displays a dialog box asking where to copy the files. For both Intellifont and bitmapped PCL fonts, the default location is C:\PCLFONTS. If you are installing Intellifont fonts, the dialog box also asks for a location for screen fonts; the default location is C:\TD\TYPE. You can enter another location for one or both entries, or leave the default(s) unchanged. Choose OK. The Font Installer copies the selected fonts to the location(s) specified and adds the font names to Windows' list of installed fonts.

9. Choose E**x**it to leave the Font Installer. Then choose OK to close the Windows Setup dialog box, and choose Close to close the Select Printer dialog box.

   The fonts will not appear in WordPerfect's list of available fonts until you exit WordPerfect and reenter the program.

To remove PCL fonts, follow these steps:

1. In WordPerfect for Windows, choose **F**ile, **P**rint, **S**elect. The Select Printer dialog box appears.
2. Highlight the name of an installed Windows printer driver for a Hewlett-Packard LaserJet or compatible printer.
3. Choose **O**ptions, **S**etup. The Windows Setup dialog box for the selected printer driver appears.
4. Choose **F**onts. The HP Font Installer dialog box appears.
5. Click on each font that you want to remove. You do not need to Shift+Click or Ctrl+Click to select multiple fonts.
6. Choose **D**elete. The Font Installer displays a dialog box asking `Remove corresponding font file(s) from disk?` Choose **Y**es to delete the font files, or choose **N**o to remove the font names from the list of available fonts but leave the font files on disk. The Font Installer carries out the selected action.
7. Choose E**x**it to leave the Font Installer. Then choose OK to close the Windows Setup dialog box, and choose Close to close the Select Printer dialog box.

Accessing Special Characters

Although a computer keyboard has only several dozen keys, WordPerfect can access several thousand special characters, such as typographic or scientific symbols and letters in foreign alphabets. The program makes accessing non-keyboard characters simple. Most applications require that you know where and in which font each *glyph* (character, symbol, or anything else contained in a font) is located. WordPerfect simplifies this problem. Unlike almost any other program, WordPerfect does not make you remember which character is located where in which font. If you need to insert a plus or minus sign

(+ or –) in your document, the keystrokes needed are the same regardless of the printer and font you are using.

You can access all these characters through the WordPerfect Characters feature. WordPerfect groups the characters into 15 Character Sets. Each Character Set contains dozens or hundreds of related letters or symbols. Table 20.1 lists the Character Sets available in WordPerfect 6.1 for Windows.

Table 20.1 WordPerfect Character Sets

Character Set Number	Name of Character Set	Examples	Number of Glyphs
0	ASCII	Characters available from the keyboard	95
1	Multinational	Accented characters	242
2	Phonetic	International Phonetic Alphabet	145
3	Box Drawing	Single and double lines	88
4	Typographic Symbols	Quotation marks, em dash	102
5	Iconic Symbols	Dingbats, happy face	255
6	Math/Scientific	Less than, empty set	238
7	Math/Scientific Extensions	Large math symbols	229
8	Greek	Alpha, omega; includes breathing marks	219
9	Hebrew	Aleph, gimel; includes vowel points	119
10	Cyrillic	Characters for printing various Slavic languages	250

(continues)

Table 20.1 Continued

Character Set Number	Name of Character Set	Examples	Number of Glyphs
11	Japanese	Phonetic Japanese	63
12	User Defined	Usually empty	255
13	Arabic	Block printing version of Arabic	196
14	Arabic Script	Script version of Arabic	220

In total, WordPerfect's Character Sets contain 2,716 characters. Except for Character Set 12 (User Defined), all the characters are available to any user of WordPerfect who has access to a printer capable of printing graphics. The following list describes each Character Set:

- *ASCII (Set 0).* These characters are the normal typewriter characters available directly from the keyboard.

- *Multinational (Set 1).* Modified from previous versions of WordPerfect, two Multinational Character Sets have been combined into one larger set. In this Character Set, you find all the characters you need for writing in Western European languages and Central European languages that use the Roman alphabet. In addition to complete characters, the various accents and marks (diacriticals) are provided independently. See this chapter's later "Overstrike" section for an explanation of how to create additional characters you may need.

- *Phonetic (Set 2).* New with WordPerfect 6.x for Windows, this set consists of the characters in the International Phonetic Alphabet (IPA). Most users have no need for any of these characters, but if you do need to use the IPA, the characters are available to you. As with the Multinational set, the various diacriticals are provided both as independent characters and combined with the basic letter form.

- *Box Drawing (Set 3).* You seldom need to directly choose any of these characters. They were used for the Line Draw feature in earlier versions of WordPerfect and remain for compatibility with older documents.

- *Typographic Symbols (Set 4).* This Character Set contains common symbols such as bullets, daggers, currency symbols, and ligatures. Some of these characters are very useful. Perhaps the most often used are the true open and close quotation marks ("curly quotes"). Compare the use of straight quotation marks:

He said, "See Dick run."

with typographic quotation marks:

He said, “See Dick run.”

Other commonly used typographic symbols are the em dash (—) used to set off an aside or change of subject, and the en dash (–) used for dates such as 12–03–94. Several fractions and other useful symbols are also found in this Character Set.

Note

WordPerfect 6.1 for Windows includes a special "Smart Quotes" utility. This utility automatically substitutes typographical quotation marks for the straight keyboard quotation marks as you type. If you use typographical quotes often, you might consider activating the Smart Quotes utility. To do so, choose **T**ools, **Q**uickCorrect, **O**ptions. Then place check marks in the T**u**rn on Single Quotes and Tu**r**n on Double Quotes options. Choose OK then **C**lose to return to the document.

- *Iconic Symbols (Set 5)*. These characters include less commonly used symbols defined in your PC's ROM, such as the male (Z) and female (ζ) signs and the happy face (o), as well as the ITC Zapf Dingbats Character Set. Dingbats are a major addition from previous versions of WordPerfect, which did not include these symbols.

Tip

You can use Reveal Codes to see what the WordPerfect character number and set are for any special character. To enter a character by specifying its set and number, choose **I**nsert, **C**haracter; or press Ctrl+W.

Note

In WordPerfect 5.0 and 5.1, Dingbats were mapped to the User Defined Character Set (Set 12). If you edit a document created in WordPerfect 5.0 or 5.1 that contains Dingbats, you may need to edit the file to correct these characters. The character number is likely to be the same, but the Character Set is now 5 instead of 12. For example, if the character was 12,200, it is likely to be the character now found at position 5,200 in WordPerfect 6.1 for Windows. If there are several such characters in the document, you can use the Replace function to quickly correct the situation.

- *Math/Scientific (Set 6)*. Most often used to create equations. (See Chapter 24, "Using the Equation Editor.") However, you can use these characters at any place in a document. This Character Set includes a wide variety of symbols, including the plus or minus sign, degree symbol, and various symbols used in Set Theory.

- *Math/Scientific Extensions (Set 7).* Contains symbols almost never used outside of an equation. These characters are pieces of large mathematical symbols (such as the top, middle, and bottom of a summation sign), and are used by WordPerfect's Equation Editor. Certain large complete symbols are also defined in this Character Set.

- *Greek (Set 8).* Consists of normal capital and minuscule Greek letters used in mathematical expressions and also the accented letters (including breathing marks) used for writing Greek (classic and modern).

- *Hebrew (Set 9).* Consists of Hebrew. The vowel points are included.

- *Cyrillic (Set 10).* Consists of the characters necessary for Russian, Serbian, and other languages written in the Cyrillic alphabet.

- *Japanese (Set 11).* Includes the Hiragana and Katakana characters necessary for writing phonetic Japanese. This set does not include Kanji characters.

- *User Defined (Set 12).* This set is provided so that you can use fonts containing characters not included in WordPerfect's other Character Sets. If you install an "expert" font or a font containing typographical ornaments, the characters appear in Set 12. Foreign language fonts containing characters not defined elsewhere (such as Thai) could also use this Character Set. Unless you install such a font, the characters in this set print as blanks.

- *Arabic (Set 13) and Arabic Script (Set 14).* New with WordPerfect 6.1 for Windows, these characters are for writing in Arabic.

WordPerfect makes using special characters in your documents easy. You can select characters from a menu, enter a specific Character Set and character number, or use mnemonic shortcuts for common characters. Each method is discussed in subsequent sections.

WordPerfect Characters

If you are unsure of exactly where the character you need is located, you can use the WordPerfect Character feature. To access WordPerfect Characters, open **I**nsert, and choose **C**haracter; or press Ctrl+W. The WordPerfect Characters dialog box appears (see fig. 20.7).

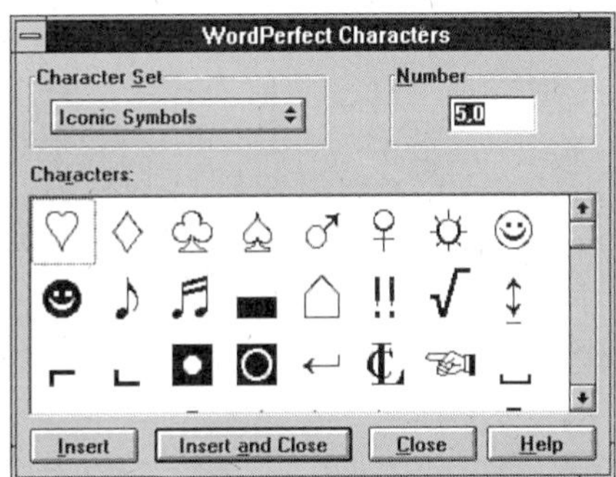

Fig. 20.7
Select any available character from the WordPerfect Characters dialog box.

In this dialog box, choose Character **S**et and select the desired Character Set from the pop-up list that appears. You then can double-click the appropriate character in the Cha**r**acters list box to have WordPerfect insert the character into your document.

Tip
If you know the set and number of the character you want, you can type the set and number in the **N**umber text box and press Enter. To insert a playing card club symbol, for example, type **5,2** and press Enter.

The WordPerfect Characters dialog box is *modeless*, which means that you can work in your document while the dialog box remains on-screen. If you simply double-click on a character, WordPerfect inserts the character and does not close the dialog box. If you don't intend to insert another character immediately, you can choose **C**lose to close the dialog box. You can also click once on a character to select it, and then choose Insert **a**nd Close to insert the character into your document and close the dialog box. If you select a character, the character's set and number appear in the **N**umber text box.

Compose

With over 2,500 characters available, remembering the Character Set and number of even frequently used characters can be difficult. Although you can always select a character directly from the Cha**r**acters list box, WordPerfect also provides some keyboard shortcuts for some of the most common characters. The Compose feature lets you use *mnemonics* to "assemble" characters from pairs of more common characters.

A mnemonic is a memory device. For example, the name Roy G. Biv is a common mnemonic to remind you of the colors of the rainbow: Red, Orange, Yellow, Green, Blue, Indigo, Violet. Many of the Multinational Characters and Typographic Symbols can be accessed with mnemonics. For example, to insert a u umlaut (ü), open the WordPerfect Characters dialog box by pressing Ctrl+W, type **u"**, and press Enter. The following table provides additional examples of mnemonics.

Keystrokes	Character	Keystrokes	Character
a"	ä	a'	á
a'	à	a^	â
n~	ñ	f-	ƒ
c,	ç	ss	ß
ao	°a	a=	ª
co	©	ro	®
rx	R_x	tm	™
m-	—	n-	–
!!	¡	??	¿
/2	1/2	/4	1/4
>>	»	<<	«
>=		<=	<
+-	±	~~	≈
**	●	.	■
*O	❍	*o	o
Y=	¥	L-	£
c/	¢	Pl	91
AE	Æ	ae	æ

Tip

If you frequently need to use certain special characters, add the characters in the preceding table to a keyboard layout. (See Chapter 9, "Customizing WordPerfect.")

Notice that many of these mnemonics are case-sensitive. Also, in most, but not all cases, the order in which you type the characters is not important.

Overstrike

WordPerfect offers a way to create characters that aren't otherwise available: combining two existing characters. When you create an overstrike, WordPerfect literally prints one character on top of another. This feature is seldom necessary because of the huge range of characters and symbols provided in the various Character Sets, but it can be useful in certain situations.

Creating Overstrikes

To create an overstrike character, follow these steps:

1. From the Format menu, choose **T**ypesetting, and then select **O**verstrike. The Overstrike dialog box appears (see fig. 20.8).

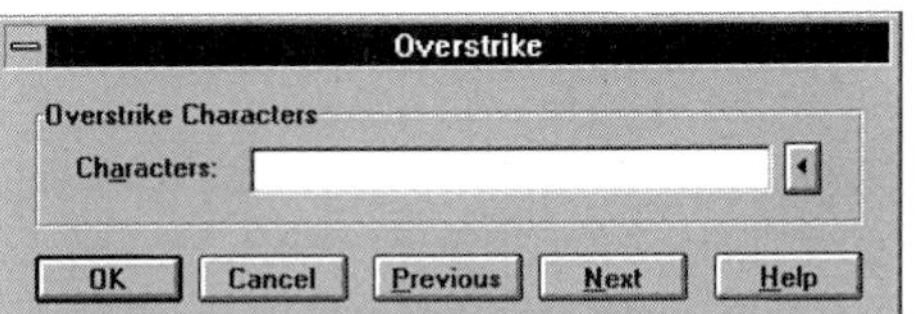

Fig. 20.8
You can combine two characters using the Overstrike dialog box.

2. Enter the characters you want to combine. You can enter the characters in any way you want. You can use WordPerfect Characters (Ctrl+W), use the Alt+number pad method, or type standard keyboard characters. You can enter as many characters as you like, although more than two or three characters printing on top of each other becomes illegible.

> **Note**
>
> When using the Alt+number pad method, press and hold the Alt key while entering the number in the numeric keypad. Release the Alt key when you are done entering the number. Press 0xxx (such as **0128**) to insert a character using the ANSI character set, and xxx (such as **128**) to insert a character using the ASCII character set. Note that WordPerfect does not support the IBM character set, such as the IBM box drawing characters.

3. After entering the desired characters, you can apply font attributes to the overstrike characters. Block one or more characters using either the keyboard or mouse. Then, from the Ch**a**racters pop-up menu, select an attribute. You can put different attributes around the individual characters that make up the overstrike character. By combining glyphs of different sizes, appearance, and positions (superscript and subscript), you can create exactly what you need.

4. Choose OK to insert the overstrike character into your document.

Tip
If you use an overstrike character frequently, create a macro that inserts the character into your document. (See Chapter 12, "Creating Macros.")

Editing Overstrikes

After an overstrike character is created, you may need to edit it. To do so, follow these steps:

1. From the For**m**at menu, choose **T**ypesetting, and then select **O**verstrike. The Overstrike dialog box appears.

2. Choose **P**revious or **N**ext until the desired overstrike character appears in the Ch**a**racters text box.

3. Add, delete, or change any of the characters or attribute codes in the overstrike sequence.

4. After you finish, choose OK. Alternatively, choose Cancel to abandon your changes.

◀ See "Using Find and Replace," p. 116

▶ See "Using the Equation Editor," p. 809

◀ See "Customizing Keyboards," p. 342

◀ See "Creating Macros," p. 417

Troubleshooting

I have collected a number of fonts, but I don't remember what they all look like.

WordPerfect comes with a macro that lets you create a "catalog" of available fonts. The macro is named ALLFONTS.WCM, and is contained in the macros directory (e.g., \OFFICE\WPWIN\MACROS). To use the macro, open a new, blank document. Play the macro by pressing Alt+F10, typing ALLFONTS, and pressing Enter. The macro takes a moment to make the catalog of fonts. Once the macro is done with the font catalog, you can print it out for future reference. You should, however, avoid using the ALLFONTS.WCM macro if you have more than 255 fonts installed in your system.

I don't get typographical (curly) smart quotes when I press the " key.

There are three reasons typographical open and close smart quotes may not appear when you press the " (quote) key. One obvious reason is that the smart quote feature has been turned off. To turn it on, choose **Q**uickCorrect from the **T**ools menu. In the QuickCorrect dialog box, choose **O**ptions. Place an X beside the T**u**rn on Single Quotes and Tu**r**n on Double Quotes options to turn smart quotes on. Another reason is that when you are editing a macro (the Macros Feature Bar appears), WordPerfect automatically turns smart quotes off. And finally, the smart quotes may seem not to appear if the font you are using—such as Courier—lacks curly quotes.

Font Mapping

When you use a font attribute such as bold or italic, WordPerfect actually selects a different font to print those characters. The program maintains a table of *Automatic Font Changes (AFCs)* for each font, which tells WordPerfect which font to choose for changes in Appearance, Relative Size, Orientation, and WordPerfect Character Sets. (See Chapter 4, "Formatting Text," for information on Appearance and Relative Size font attributes.)

When you first install a printer driver, and whenever you install additional fonts, WordPerfect selects default values for Automatic Font Changes. However, if you don't like the AFCs WordPerfect has selected, you can change them.

When you use fonts that are built into your printer, WordPerfect also has to choose which graphics font to display on-screen to represent the printer font. Finally, when a document calls for a font that isn't installed on your system, WordPerfect has to choose which installed font to use to represent the document font. Just as you can change WordPerfect's AFC selections, you can change its sections for display and document fonts.

Understanding AFC Attributes

Although you use completely different commands in WordPerfect to select font attributes, insert special characters, or print landscape fonts, the program uses Automatic Font Changes in each case. When you edit Automatic Font Changes, WordPerfect lists every type of AFC under one heading, but they can be grouped into four general categories—Appearance, Relative Size, Character Sets, and Orientation.

Appearance

Appearance includes such attributes as bold, italic, and small capitals. Combinations of appearance attributes are handled in a series. For example, if you apply the bold attribute and then the italic attribute, WordPerfect first finds the bold AFC font and then finds the italic AFC font for the bold font. For font families that don't contain a complete set of Regular, Bold, Italic, and Bold Italic font styles, this process can cause some unexpected results, because WordPerfect will choose a font outside of the immediate font family. As a result, you may obtain different results if you switch the order in which you apply the attributes.

Tip

If you need to use combinations of attributes that WordPerfect isn't selecting the way you want, you can create a character style that specifically selects the desired font.

WordPerfect tries to find an appropriate font when you choose an appearance attribute. For example, if your base font is Times Roman (Type 1) and you apply the bold appearance attribute to some text, WordPerfect chooses Times Bold (Type 1) when printing (and displaying) that text. If an appropriate font does not exist, WordPerfect attempts to approximate it. If you choose the bold attribute, for example, and no appropriate font exists, WordPerfect prints the text twice, using the base font, to make the printed text darker.

Relative Size

When you use the relative size or position font attributes, WordPerfect uses AFCs to select a font that is a specific percentage of the size of your base font.

Each relative size and position AFC is based on a different size ratio for each attribute. The Large font attribute is 120% of normal, for example. You can change the size ratios to affect these AFCs for all fonts, or edit AFCs for individual fonts.

If you are using a scalable font (such as Speedo, TrueType, Intellifont, or Type 1), you won't need to change relative size or position AFCs, because WordPerfect can generate fonts of almost any size from the same Base Font without using an AFC. You can change the size ratios for all fonts, however.

If you are using nonscalable fonts (such as HP PCL soft fonts), you may need to change size ratios as well as edit individual AFCs to suit your needs.

WordPerfect Character Sets

If a special character isn't available in the current font, WordPerfect uses an AFC to select a font that contains most or all of the Character Set in which that character can be found. If WordPerfect finds the desired character in any of the available fonts—not just the selected font—it prints the character. Nearly every WordPerfect character is available in the TrueType fonts that WordPerfect installs automatically, but other installed fonts may contain different versions of the same character; one of these versions may provide a closer match to the current body text font. As a result, you may want to change the AFC to select a more pleasing font to print special characters.

If the character isn't available, WordPerfect creates and prints a graphical representation of the character. The only exceptions to this process are characters in the User Defined Character Set. WordPerfect doesn't create graphical representations of these characters because it has no way of knowing what characters are defined in that set. WordPerfect also doesn't graphically create characters from Character Set 0 (ASCII).

Orientation

WordPerfect offers four orientations—Portrait, Landscape, Reverse Portrait, and Reverse Landscape. WordPerfect can use its graphics fonts in any orientation; however, dot-matrix printer fonts usually can only be used in Portrait mode. The only time you may need to adjust the Orientation Automatic Font Changes is for laser and inkjet printer fonts. Some lasers (such as PostScript and the Hewlett-Packard III and 4 series) can rotate fonts, while others (such as the LaserJet II and earlier Hewlett-Packards) cannot. Inkjet printers (such as the Hewlett-Packard DeskJet series) usually cannot rotate fonts.

Editing Size Ratios

WordPerfect selects Automatic Font Changes for the Size attributes based on the size ratios specified in Print Preferences. For example, the default for the **L**arge Size Attribute is 120%, which means that if the Base Font is 10 points, WordPerfect prints text marked as **L**arge at 12 points. If you change the default to 150%, WordPerfect prints text marked as **L**arge at 15 points.

If you don't like the sizes chosen by WordPerfect for all fonts, you can change the size ratios, and then have the program select new AFCs. If you use scalable fonts, WordPerfect will immediately begin using the new size ratios you select. If you use bitmapped fonts, you must tell WordPerfect to generate new AFCs after changing size ratios.

To change size ratios, follow these steps:

1. From the **E**dit menu, choose Pr**e**ferences. The Preferences dialog box appears.

2. Choose P**r**int. The Print Preferences dialog box appears (see fig. 20.9).

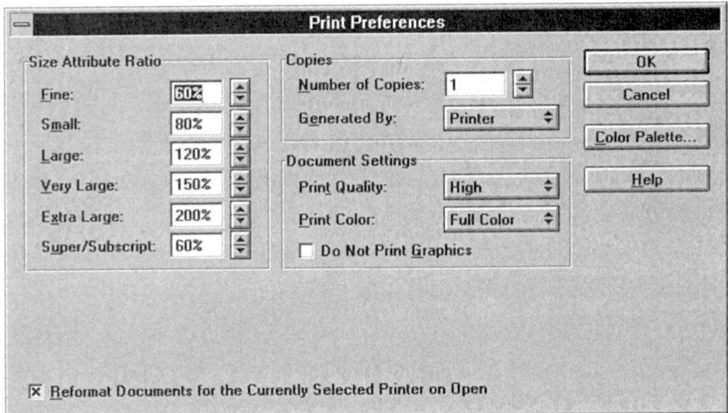

Fig. 20.9
You can change the size attribute ratios for font attributes in the Print Preferences dialog box.

3. Choose any Size Attribute Ratio option. Then type a different percentage or click on the increment or decrement buttons to change the value.

4. When you finish changing the ratios, choose OK to close the Print Preferences dialog box, and then choose Close to close the Preferences dialog box.

If you use bitmapped fonts with a WordPerfect printer driver, you now need to update that driver (PRS file). To do so, follow these steps:

1. From the **F**ile menu, choose **P**rint and then **S**elect. The Print dialog box appears.
2. Highlight the printer driver you want to update.
3. Choose **O**ptions, **U**pdate.
4. Close all open dialog boxes to return to the document window.

Updating Automatic Font Changes

WordPerfect automatically creates Automatic Font Changes when you create a printer driver. However, if you add graphics fonts, you may need to update AFCs for WordPerfect printer drivers, because you may want to use some of your new fonts as AFCs for existing fonts.

To perform this action, follow these steps:

1. From the **F**ile menu, choose **P**rint and then **S**elect. The Select Printer dialog box appears.
2. Highlight a WordPerfect printer driver.
3. Choose **O**ptions, **U**pdate. WordPerfect generates new AFCs for all graphics fonts for the selected printer.

Editing Automatic Font Changes

If you aren't happy with WordPerfect's choice of Automatic Font Change for a particular font, you can edit WordPerfect's AFC table. With previous versions of WordPerfect, editing Automatic Font Changes required using a separate program named PTR.EXE to change the Automatic Font Changes that WordPerfect chooses. Version 6.x provides you with this capability within WordPerfect itself.

To edit AFCs, follow these steps:

1. Open the Fo**r**mat menu and choose **F**ont; or press F9. The Font dialog box appears.
2. Choose Font **M**ap. The Edit Printer/Document Font Mapping dialog box appears (see fig. 20.10).

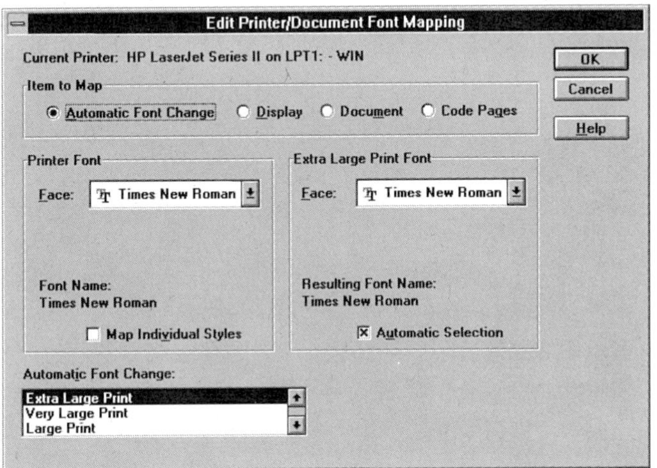

Fig. 20.10
The Edit Printer/Document Font Mapping dialog box lets you select different AFCs for any font.

3. Choose the **A**utomatic Font Change radio button in the Item to Map group. The **F**ace list box displays the currently selected font. The Automat**i**c Font Change list box at the bottom of the dialog box lists the available attributes and other Automatic Font Change categories. The **F**ace list box displays the currently selected Automat**i**c Font Change for the selected printer font and highlighted AFC option.

4. From the **F**ace drop-down list, under the Printer Font heading, select the font whose Automat**i**c Font Change you want to review or change.

Note

Most fonts are part of a font family made up of several font styles—usually Regular, Bold, Italic, and Bold Italic. By default, WordPerfect creates AFCs for font families as a group. If you want to review or change AFCs for the individual styles within a given family, mark the Map Indi**v**idual Styles check box. WordPerfect then adds Style and Size drop-down list boxes to the Printer Font group and the adjacent group.

5. Select the Automat**i**c Font Change category you want to review or change from the list at the bottom of the dialog box. WordPerfect displays the currently mapped font to the right of the printer font. If no font is listed, there is no font change for that particular AFC.

6. If you want to change the displayed AFC, select from the **F**ace drop-down list, under Extra Large Print Font, a different font from the list of available fonts. WordPerfect removes the check from the A**u**tomatic Selection check box immediately below this menu.

7. Repeat steps 4 and 5 to review or change the AFC for another AFC category for the same font; repeat steps 3 through 5 to review or change the AFCs for another font.

8. Choose OK to return to the Font dialog box and have WordPerfect save the changes in the printer driver and supporting files; or choose Cancel to abandon your changes.

If you aren't happy with a new AFC that you've chosen, you can repeat the preceding steps to map a different font for that particular AFC, or you can mark the A**u**tomatic Selection check box to return to WordPerfect's default AFC for that font.

Editing Document Font Mapping

Document font mapping is a feature that lets you use different fonts for printing than those actually selected in the document. If you edit a document formatted for a different printer driver and the fonts selected in the document aren't available for your printer, WordPerfect selects what it thinks is a close match for the fonts to substitute. You can change the document font mapping to quickly correct any erroneous guesses.

Notice that changing document font mapping only changes the font used to print a document. To change the font used on-screen, you can change the screen font mapping.

Caution

Document font mapping changes affect all documents. If you only want to change font mapping for a single document, make sure that you change the mapping back to its original state when you are done. Instead of changing document font mapping for a single document, you may want to use the Replace feature to select different fonts within the document.

To change document font mapping, follow these steps:

1. From the Fo**r**mat menu, choose **F**ont; or press F9. The Font dialog box appears.

2. Choose Font **M**ap. The Edit Printer/Document Font Mapping dialog box appears.

3. Choose Docu**m**ent. WordPerfect displays a modified version of the dialog box (see fig. 20.11).

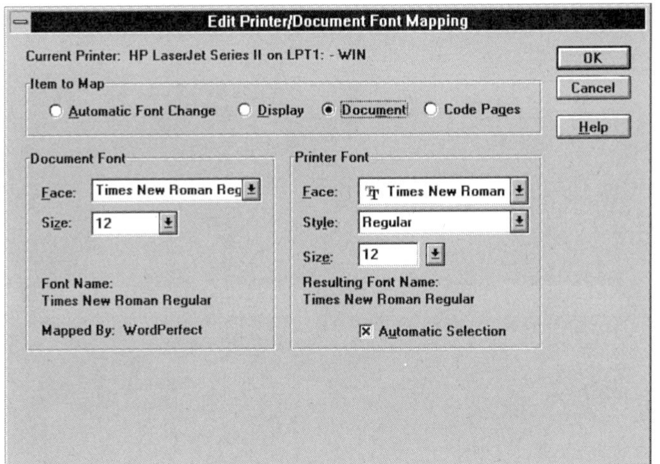

Fig. 20.11
If you don't have a font called for in a document you're editing, you can choose which font WordPerfect substitutes for the missing document font.

4. From the **F**ace drop-down list under the Document Font heading, select the font whose printer font you want to review or change. WordPerfect displays the currently mapped font in the **F**ace list box.

5. To change the printer font mapping for the document font, select a different font from the Printer Font **F**ace drop-down list of available fonts. WordPerfect removes the check from the A**u**tomatic Selection check box immediately below the menu.

6. Repeat steps 4 and 5 to review or change the printer font mapping for another document font.

7. Choose OK to return to the Font dialog box and have WordPerfect save the changes in the printer driver and supporting files; or choose Cancel to abandon your changes.

To undo the changes, repeat steps 1 through 4; then mark the A**u**tomatic Selection check box for the selected font, which returns the document font mapping for the selected font to WordPerfect's original choice.

Editing Display Font Mapping

When you use a font built into your printer, WordPerfect selects a similar graphics font to represent the printer font on-screen. If you disagree with a choice WordPerfect has made, you can change the display font mapping to choose any graphics font for the on-screen representation of any printer font.

To change the display font mapping, follow these steps:

1. From the Fo**r**mat menu, choose **F**ont; or press F9. The Font dialog box appears.

2. Choose Font **M**ap. The Edit Printer/Document Font Mapping dialog box appears.

3. Choose **D**isplay. WordPerfect displays a modified version of the dialog box (see fig. 20.12).

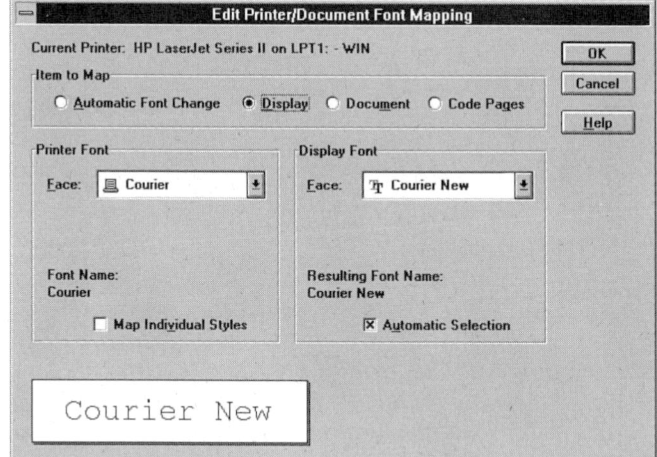

Fig. 20.12
You can choose which display font WordPerfect uses on-screen to represent fonts built into your printer.

4. Select from the **F**ace drop-down list under the Printer Font heading the printer font whose display font you want to review or change. WordPerfect displays the currently mapped font in the **F**ace list box.

5. To change the display font mapping for the printer font, select from the Display Font **F**ace drop-down list a different font from the list of available fonts. WordPerfect removes the check from the A**u**tomatic Selection check box.

6. Repeat steps 4 and 5 to review or change the display font mapping for another document font.

7. Choose OK to return to the Font dialog box and have WordPerfect save the changes in the printer driver and supporting files; or choose Cancel to abandon your changes.

To undo the changes, repeat steps 1 through 4; then mark the A**u**tomatic Selection check box for the selected font, which returns the display font mapping for the selected printer font to WordPerfect's original choice.

Troubleshooting

When I print my document the text looks all jagged, and printing is very slow.

Under normal circumstances, WordPerfect uses the fonts built into the printer or available through Windows (such as TrueType and ATM) to print the document. However, both WordPerfect and Windows can print text graphically—that is, by sending the dots that make up each character to the printer, rather than the characters themselves. Usually this is not advisable, because the text can look jagged, and it can take much longer to print a document. If you are using a Windows and TrueType fonts printer, turn graphical text printing off by opening the Printers icon in the Control Panel. Then choose **S**etup, **O**ptions, and remove the X that appears in the Print TrueType As **G**raphics. There is another setting you may need to change. In WordPerfect, open the **F**ile menu and choose **P**rint to display the Print dialog box. Choose **O**ptions; then remove the X that appears beside the **P**rint Document Graphically option.

WordPerfect uses the wrong fonts when I open a document created by someone else on another computer.

Not every computer has the same collection of fonts. If someone creates a document with a given font, but you don't, WordPerfect will attempt to match the missing font as best as it can with one you do have. Sometimes, this matching is not accurate. If you consistently get the wrong font, use the font mapping procedures outlined earlier in this chapter to force WordPerfect into substituting a different font, or install the missing font so it's on your computer as well.

◄ See "Formatting Characters," p. 130

Working with Multiple Languages

WordPerfect Corporation has released more than 30 foreign language versions of WordPerfect, including not only Western European languages such as French, Spanish, and German, but also versions such as Russian, Greek, and Japanese. No matter which version of WordPerfect you own, if you need to create or edit documents in more than one language, WordPerfect provides several kinds of support.

- You can enter, display, and print any of more than 2,500 foreign language characters and other symbols using the WordPerfect Characters dialog box. You can also use the Compose feature to insert common accented characters such as é (see the earlier sections "WordPerfect Characters" and "Compose").

- If you carry on correspondence in a foreign language, you need to be able to use dates, times, and currency in the correct formats. You can insert a language code into a document, and WordPerfect will use the appropriate conventions for that language.
- If you use a foreign language frequently, you will also want to check the spelling of the non-English portions of your documents. You can purchase a WordPerfect foreign language module that contains dictionary files for use with the Speller, Grammatik, and Thesaurus. Language modules also contain alternate keyboard layouts that let you type the characters used in that language far more quickly than using WordPerfect Characters or Compose.
- You can purchase a foreign language version of WordPerfect itself, in which all the menus, prompts, and dialog boxes appear in the foreign language as well.

Entering a WordPerfect Language Code

When you buy WordPerfect, you receive a version for a specific language and country. You can buy an English version of WordPerfect for the United States, for example, or an English version for Australia, or one for the United Kingdom. Likewise, you can purchase a French version or a French Canadian version. WordPerfect refers to the combination of language and country as the package language and abbreviates the language with a two-letter language code. The package language for the United States, for example, is English-U.S., and the corresponding language code is US. The Australian package language is English-Australian, and its language code is OZ; the British versions are English-U.K. and UK.

WordPerfect uses the language code in several ways. With any version of the program, you can insert a language code to tell WordPerfect to use foreign dates and times. For example, in U.S. English the standard date text is "September 19, 1994"; but in UK English the proper format is "19 September 1994." In French it's "19 septembre 1994," and in Spanish it's "19 de septiembre de 1994." In tables, WordPerfect uses the language code to insert the appropriate number formats and currency symbols, such as pounds (£) or yen (¥). This information is contained within the Language Resource File, WP.LRS.

If you have purchased a foreign language module, inserting a foreign language code also tells WordPerfect to use the appropriate dictionary for the Speller, Thesaurus, and other language features. If you have passages of a foreign language within an English-language document, you can insert multiple language codes to tell WordPerfect to switch back and forth between languages when spell-checking. See Chapter 6, "Using Writing Tools," for more information on using writing tools in a foreign language.

To insert a language code in a document, follow these steps:

1. Move the insertion point to where you want the change to take effect, or select a block of text.

2. From the **T**ools menu, choose **L**anguage. WordPerfect displays the Language dialog box (see fig. 20.13). The current language code is highlighted.

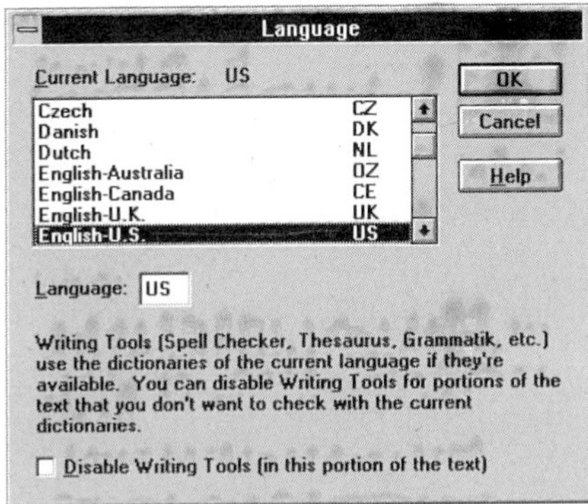

Fig. 20.13
Choose a different language code for WordPerfect to be able to insert dates, times, and currency correctly for that language.

3. Select a language.

4. Choose OK or press Enter.

WordPerfect inserts a `[Lang:XX]` code in your document, where XX is the two-letter language code. If you select French-National, for instance, the code is `[Lang:FR]`. The new language stays in effect until WordPerfect encounters a different language code. If you select a block of text, WordPerfect places the language code for the new language before the text and, at the end of the block, reverts the language to the original language.

If you then insert a date or time in the document, WordPerfect uses the format of the new language.

If you use footnotes that span more than one page and want WordPerfect to include "(continued...)" messages in a different language, you must insert a language code into the Initial Codes Style.

Understanding the Language Resource File

The Language Resource File, WP.LRS, is a WordPerfect merge data file. Each record contains many pieces of information for one language, including the names and abbreviations of the months and days of the week, the standard format for dates and times, currency symbols, and footnote continued messages.

Because WP.LRS is a merge data file, you can edit it as a normal WordPerfect file. If you make changes, however, you must not change the format in any way, including adding or deleting lines, end-of-field codes, and end-of-record codes. You can, however, edit any visible text.

Using Foreign Language Keyboards

When you type in a foreign language, you frequently use characters and symbols that aren't used in American English. You can certainly insert these characters using WordPerfect Characters or Compose. If you have to insert more than a few characters, however, this procedure quickly becomes tedious. If you are typing in a foreign alphabet such as Cyrillic or Greek, you would have to leave the WordPerfect Characters dialog box open to the correct alphabet and then double-click to insert each character, clearly not a practical solution.

Instead, you can use an alternate keyboard file. If you only need to insert an occasional foreign character, you may want to create your own keyboard file, adding the character(s) you need to use. If you do extensive work in a foreign language, however, you should purchase the appropriate language module from WordPerfect Corporation. The language modules include not only files to be used with the writing tools such as Speller, Thesaurus, and Grammatik, but also keyboard files customized for the language.

When you purchase a language module, you can use its keyboard file in several ways. If you will be creating entire documents in the foreign language, you can create a template designed for working in that language, and assign the foreign keyboard file to that template. You can then select that template whenever you want to create a foreign language document, and WordPerfect automatically selects the foreign keyboard. See Chapter 11, "Using Templates," for more information.

If you need to switch back and forth between languages and keyboards within a document, you must choose **E**dit, Pr**e**ferences, **K**eyboard, and then select the desired keyboard to change to a different file. To make this procedure easy to use, you should record a macro that selects the foreign keyboard and assign it to your normal keyboard file; then record a macro that selects the normal keyboard and assign it to your foreign keyboard file.

Working with Character Maps

Languages such as English, French, Spanish, and German all use the Roman alphabet. Although you can insert characters from other alphabets, such as Greek, WordPerfect assumes that most of the letters in your documents will use the standard Roman alphabet. If you use a foreign language module such as Greek, Hebrew, or Russian (which uses the Cyrillic alphabet), most of the characters in your foreign language documents will not be in the Roman alphabet.

◀ See "Customizing Keyboards," p. 342

◀ See "Using Templates," p. 387

◀ See "Creating Macros," p. 417

WordPerfect language modules for such languages contain a different character map for the foreign alphabet. Each character map contains a subset of the more than 2,600 WordPerfect characters most likely to be used in languages that use that alphabet.

When you use the standard character map for English, each Greek letter that you insert into a document takes up more room on disk than a character in the English alphabet. If you only insert an occasional Greek character, this extra room is a small fraction of the document's total size, but if you create an entire document in Greek, the document takes up much more room on disk than an equivalent document in English.

If you purchase the Greek language module, however, you can select the Greek character map, which tells WordPerfect to assume that most of the characters in the document will be Greek. In this case, the Greek letters take up less room on disk, and inserting an English character takes more. If you purchase a Russian or Hebrew language module, the same principle applies for the Cyrillic and Hebrew character maps.

You can only choose a different character map if you have purchased a language module for a language in a different alphabet. If you do have a different character map available, however, you should choose that character map whenever a document has more characters in that language than in English. To choose a different character map, open the Fo**r**mat menu and choose **D**ocument. Then choose Character **M**apping and select a character map from the list. (Without a foreign language module, this list will be empty.)

From Here...

◄ See "Working with Other Languages," p. 248

In this chapter you learned about the different font formats WordPerfect supports, and when you can use them as printer fonts or graphics fonts. You also learned how to install additional fonts. You learned about the WordPerfect Character Sets, and several methods to insert characters not found on the keyboard.

You also learned how to use Overstrike to combine two or more characters into one. You learned how to edit the Automatic Font Changes that WordPerfect uses to select fonts for changes in appearance, relative size, character set, or orientation. You also learned how to change the fonts WordPerfect uses to print or display the fonts selected in a document by changing the document and screen font mappings. You learned to customize the Power Bar's list of fonts and font sizes to display only the items you use frequently.

Finally, you learned how to insert a language code into a document for inserting correctly formatted foreign dates, times, and currency symbols, and to use a keyboard file or character map for a foreign language.

For additional information on using fonts and special text formatting with WordPerfect, refer to the following chapters in this book:

- Chapter 4, "Formatting Text," discusses the basics of text formatting, including changing character attributes such as bold and italics.
- Chapter 10, "Using Styles," shows you how to create and apply styles, which can be used to select a combination of text and paragraph formatting. Styles can also be used to quickly select commonly used fonts and character attributes.
- Chapter 22, "Using WP Draw and TextArt," explains how to use the TextArt drawing tool included with WordPerfect. The TextArt tool can be used to enhance the textual appearance of your documents.
- Chapter 23, "Desktop Publishing with WordPerfect," gives you tips and techniques for using WordPerfect 6.1 for Windows as a desktop publishing aid, including the proper use of font attributes.
- Chapter 24, "Using the Equation Editor," shows you how to use WordPerfect's powerful Equation Editor to create special effects for text.

Chapter 21

Using Advanced Graphics Techniques

by Susan Plumley and Alan Westenbroek

Using WordPerfect, you can add a variety of graphics to your documents: horizontal and vertical lines, paragraph and page borders, and graphics boxes that hold text, images, tables, equations, and spreadsheets. In Chapter 7, "Integrating Text and Graphics," you learned to add basic graphics to a document to create interest, separate text, and emphasize your message. This chapter shows you how to customize the graphics elements to get the most out of WordPerfect's capabilities.

Customizing graphics elements includes changing the thickness and color of lines and borders, adding shadows and fill to graphics boxes, setting margin spacing within a border, adding captions to graphics boxes, and much more. WordPerfect enables you to modify the graphics elements in your documents in many ways.

Even though you can create many varied lines, borders, and boxes in WordPerfect, keep some basic guidelines in mind when using graphics elements. First and foremost, you want to provide a consistent design with the graphics so the graphics won't overwhelm the message. Graphics lines, borders, and boxes should support the text, not confuse the reader or overwhelm the message. Be consistent with your use of graphics; that is, if you use single line styles and 10 percent fill on the first page, use that same formula throughout the document with little or no variation. Second, be careful not to crowd text and graphics on the page; a crowded page is difficult to read. Use plenty of *white space*—areas without text or graphics that provide a rest for the reader's eyes.

This chapter shows you how to customize the graphics elements—lines, borders, and graphics boxes—in your documents. In addition, this chapter gives you helpful tips on how to provide the most comfortable reading environment while adding interest and emphasis with graphics.

In this chapter, you learn to do the following:

- Insert a drop cap
- Customize graphics lines
- Customize borders
- Customize graphics boxes
- Retrieve and edit images
- Create Graphics with Drag to Create

Inserting a Drop Cap

One of the effects added in version 6.1 of WordPerfect is the ability to create drop caps. A *drop cap* is the large initial letter that sometimes begins a page or chapter. This is an easy way to add that extra "finished" look to a formal or fancy document.

To add a drop cap in WordPerfect, place your insertion point anywhere in the paragraph you want to begin with a drop cap and choose Fo**r**mat, D**r**op Cap. WordPerfect selects the first letter of the paragraph, makes it larger, and wraps the other text around it. WordPerfect also displays an additional Toolbar with options for changing the font, size, and border style of the drop cap. The default style is perfect for many occasions, but you can experiment with the options to get the look that's just right for your specific application.

Customizing Lines

WordPerfect enables you to customize the horizontal and vertical lines you add to your documents. In Chapter 7, "Integrating Text and Graphics," you learned to create lines and alter them by using the mouse. You also can alter, or edit, lines by using the Edit Graphic Line dialog box, which gives you more control over the changes you make.

Suppose you want to add several lines to separate related stories in a newsletter. You want to screen the lines and make them shorter than the column length; in addition, you want all three lines to be exactly alike. Use the Edit Graphic Line dialog box to make the changes to the lines, and all the lines will be the same. Figure 21.1 illustrates just such a situation; the figure contains a newsletter that uses screened lines to separate related stories. Notice, too, the use of thick lines to emphasize the nameplate.

In WordPerfect, you can change the style, position, color, and spacing of any horizontal or vertical line. The *style* of the line refers to whether the line is single, double, thick, extra thick, and so on. *Position* describes the placement of the line on the page—for example, whether the line starts on the left, right, or center of the page or column. If you have a color monitor, or better yet a color printer, you also can assign a color to the lines in your documents. Finally, *spacing* refers to any margin area you set above or below the line to separate it from text. This section shows you how to customize these options for horizontal and vertical lines.

Changing Line Style

Line style refers to the type of line you choose: single, thick, thick double, triple, thick triple, and so on. In Chapter 7, "Integrating Text and Graphics," you created the default horizontal and vertical lines—single lines. You can create a default line and then change the line style, or you can choose a line style as you create a line.

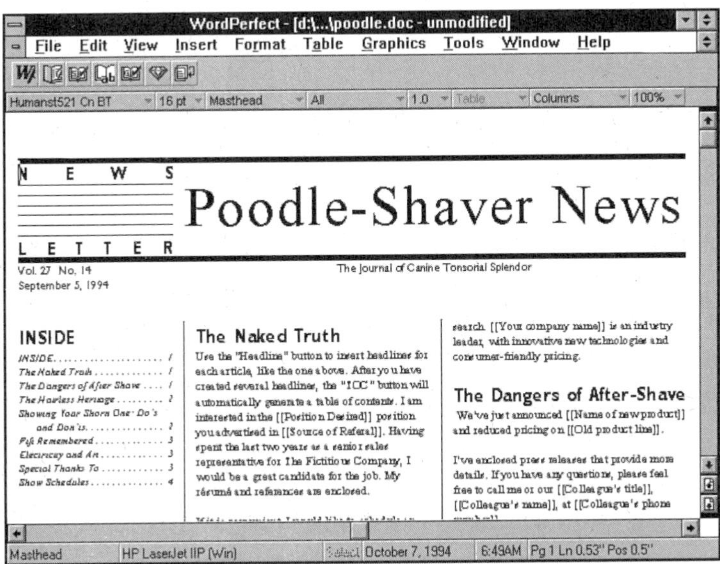

Fig. 21.1
All lines in the newsletter are thick, thus creating consistency.

Tip

To create a line, choose **G**raphics, **H**orizontal Line, **V**ertical Line, or Custom **L**ine.

> **Note**
>
> The following instructions can be used for either horizontal or vertical lines.

To create a line using a style other than the default Single, follow these steps:

1. Choose **G**raphics, Custom **L**ine. The Create Graphics Line dialog box appears (see fig. 21.2).

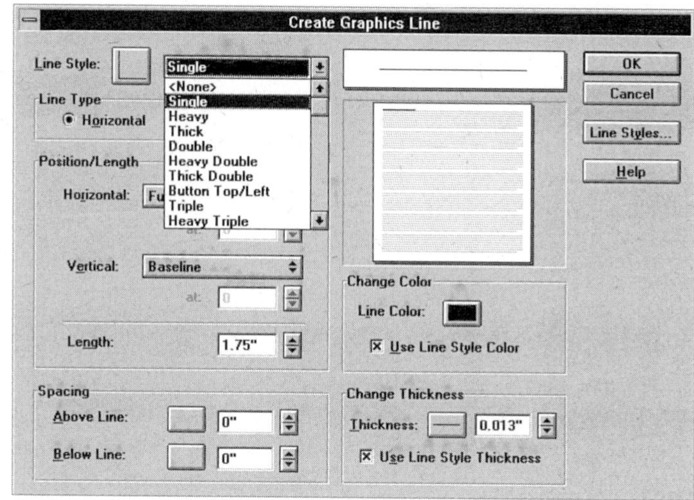

Fig. 21.2
WordPerfect offers two methods for choosing line style. The drop-down list gives the verbal description of the line style. By choosing the Line Style button, you can view and choose from line style examples.

2. In the **L**ine Style area, choose the style you want.
3. In Line Type, choose H**o**rizontal or **V**ertical.
4. Choose OK to close the dialog box and return to the document.

Tip

In the Create/Line Graphics dialog box, you can also set other options for the line, all of which are described in the following sections.

To change the line style of a line after the line is created, follow these steps:

1. Position the insertion point on the line to be edited.
2. Choose **G**raphics, Edit Li**n**e. The Edit Graphics Lines dialog box appears.
3. In the **L**ine Style area, choose the style of line you want.
4. Choose OK to close the dialog box and return to the document.

Changing Line Thickness

You can further customize a line by changing its thickness. When you select a line style, your choices for line thickness include Hairline, Single, Thick, and Extra Thick. You can control the thickness of any line by using the Create or Edit Graphics Line dialog box.

Tip
The Edit Graphics Line dialog box and the Create Graphics Line dialog box are identical.

To change line thickness, follow these steps:

1. In the Create or Edit Graphics Line dialog box, locate the Change Thickness area (see fig. 21.3).

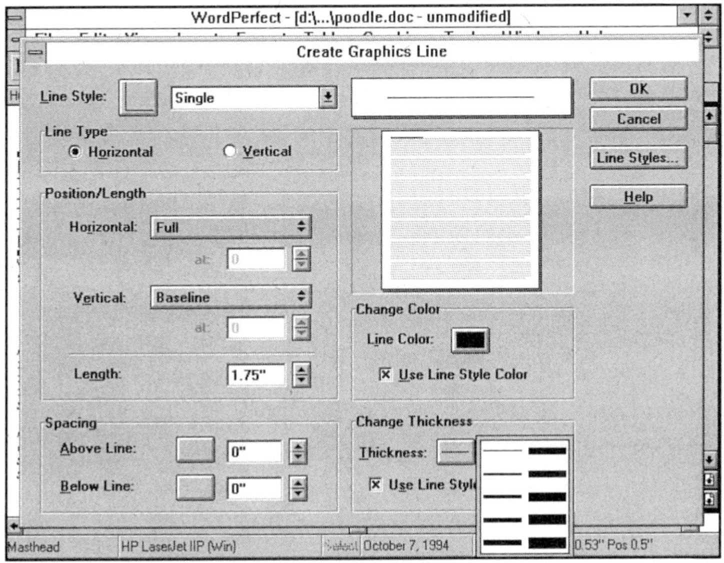

Fig. 21.3
Choose from sample thicknesses by using the Thickness button. Or use exact measurements by entering a value. As you change the thickness value, the sample in the thickness button changes so that you can view the change.

Note

All instructions from this point apply both to the Edit Graphics Line dialog box and the Create Graphics Line dialog box.

Tip
Alternatively, point at the graphics line and click the right mouse button to reveal a menu. Choose **E**dit Horizontal Line, and the Edit Graphics Line dialog box appears.

2. Choose OK to close the dialog box and return to the document.

Setting Line Color

You can change the color of any lines you add to your document to a shade of black or to an actual color such as red, blue, or yellow, plus many variations of each color. If you have a color monitor, you can see the colors on-screen. However, without a color printer, the colored lines print a shade of black or gray.

Tip
To change back to the default line style thickness, choose U**s**e Line Style Thickness.

Line color is especially useful if you want to use a line that's a shade of black—a screened line like the lines in the newsletter at the beginning of this chapter. To change a line's color, follow these steps:

1. In the Create or Edit Graphics Line dialog box, choose the L**i**ne Color button. The Line Color palette appears (see fig. 21.4).

Fig. 21.4
Use the Line Color palette to change the color of lines in your document. If you change your mind, choose the **U**se Line Style Color check box to revert back to the default color—black.

Tip
Don't use more than two different shades of black or two different colors for lines within a document. Remember to be consistent with your design so that the reader can concentrate on your message.

2. Choose the color you want by clicking the mouse on the color in the box.

3. Choose OK to close the dialog box and return to the document.

Customizing Horizontal Lines

WordPerfect includes some specific options you can customize for horizontal lines, including position, spacing, and line length. Using these options, you can place a horizontal line exactly where you want it, create short or long lines, and change the space above or below the line.

The default horizontal line you create extends from the left to the right margin and is located on the baseline. The line length is dependent on the area between the margins. In addition, the default line uses no spacing above or below the line. The following sections describe how to change the horizontal line defaults.

Horizontal Position

The horizontal position sets where the left end of the line begins. To customize the horizontal position of a line, follow these steps:

1. Choose **G**raphics, Custom **L**ine. The Create Graphics Line dialog box appears.

2. In the Position/Length area, choose Ho**r**izontal. A pop-up list of choices appears (see fig. 21.5).

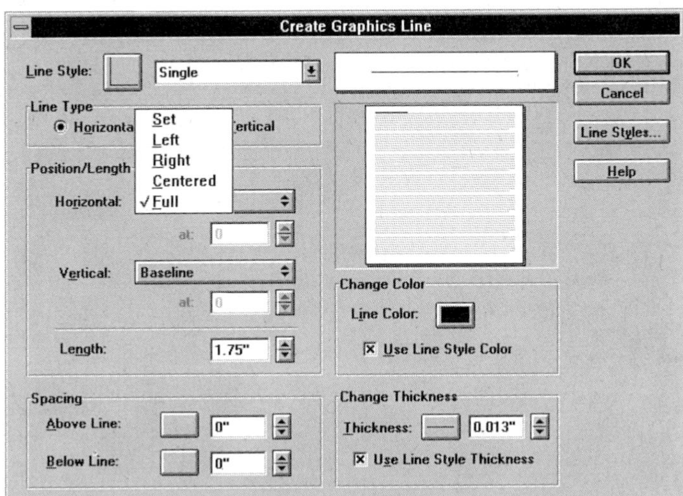

Fig. 21.5
When altering the horizontal position of a line, you may also need to change the line length to better fit the page.

The following table describes each of your Horizontal position choices:

Option	Results
Set	Sets a value in the At box to indicate where the left side of the horizontal line begins. When you choose **S**et, the At box becomes available.
Left	Sets the line to begin at the left margin.
Right	Sets the line to begin at the right margin.
Centered	Centers the line in the column or on the page.
Full	Sets the line to extend from the left to the right margin (default).

3. Choose the Ho**r**izontal position option you want and choose OK to close the dialog box and return to the document.

Note

The preceding steps apply both to the Create Graphics Line and the Edit Graphics Line dialog boxes.

Vertical Position

The vertical position sets the line position between the top and bottom margins. Adding or deleting text before a graphics line set to a vertical position of Baseline alters the position of the line. However, editing the text in front of a line set to a specific value does not alter the line's position. Figure 21.6 shows two lines, each set to a different vertical position.

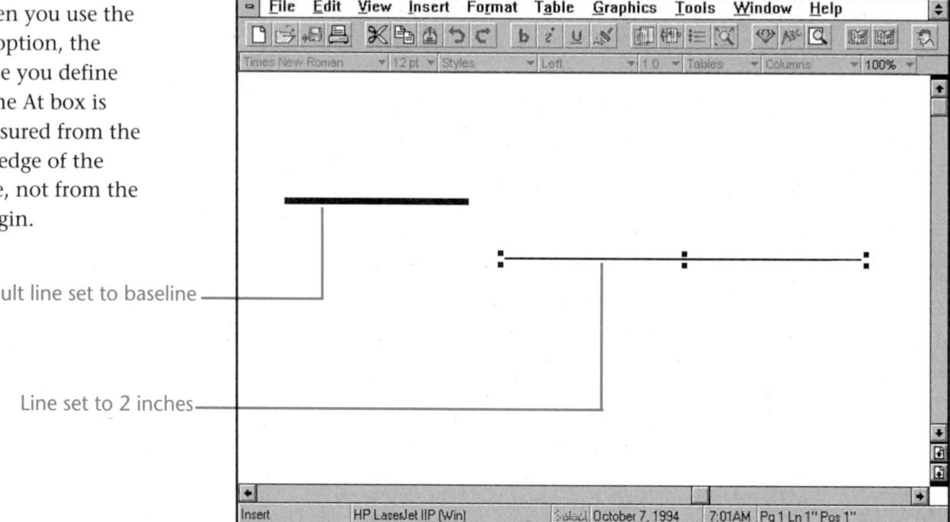

Fig. 21.6
When you use the Set option, the value you define in the At box is measured from the top edge of the page, not from the margin.

To alter the vertical position of a horizontal line, follow these steps:

1. In the Create Graphics Line dialog box, choose Vertical in Position/Length. The following table describes your choices:

Option	Result
Set	Appoints a specific value in the At box to define the vertical position of the line from the top edge of the page.
Baseline	Places the line on the baseline on which the insertion point is positioned (default).

2. Choose an option and choose OK to close the dialog box.

Line Length

You can adjust the length of a horizontal line to any length between the left and right margins. To change the line length, follow these steps:

1. In the Create Graphics Line dialog box, choose Le**n**gth in Position/Length.
2. Enter a new value, in inches, in the text box.
3. Choose OK to close the dialog box.

Customizing Vertical Lines

Just as you can change the position and length of a horizontal line, you can change the position and length of a vertical line. The vertical line options, however, are slightly different. This section explains how to change the horizontal and vertical position of a vertical line and how to change the line length.

Horizontal Position

You can change the horizontal position of a vertical line, but you must be careful how the line affects your text. A vertical line between columns works to separate text; a vertical line running through your text does not work at all. Experiment with changing the position of a vertical line to get the hang of it.

To change the horizontal position of a vertical line, follow these steps:

1. In the Create Graphics Line dialog box, choose Ho**r**izontal in Position/Length. The following table describes the options.

Option	Result
Set	Sets a specific value, in the At box, from the left edge of the paper.
Left	Sets the line along the left margin of the page (default).
Right	Sets the line on right margin of the page.
Centered	Centers the line on the page. If you have text in one column—stretching from the left margin to the right—the Centered line runs directly through your text.
Column **A**ligned	Sets the line to position after any column; sets the column in the After column text box. This is a handy option for placing lines between columns in a newsletter, report, and so on.

Tip

To insert a vertical line between columns, choose Fo**r**mat, **C**olumns, **B**order/Fill.

2. Choose an option and choose OK or press Enter to close the dialog box.

Vertical Position

The vertical position of a line describes where the top of the line begins. To change the vertical position, follow these steps:

1. In the Create Graphics Line dialog box, choose Vertical in Position/Length. The following table describes available options.

Option	Result
Set	Sets a specific value, in the At text box, from the top edge of the paper to describe where the vertical line begins.
Top	Sets the line to begin at the top margin, not top edge of paper.
Bottom	Sets the line to begin at the bottom margin of the page.
Centered	Centers the line between the top and bottom margins.
Full	Sets the line to extend between the top and bottom margins (default).

◄ See "Using Graphics Lines," p. 264

2. Choose an option and choose OK to close the dialog box.

Line Length

Setting the line length of a vertical line gives you more control over its vertical position. For example, set a line's vertical position to begin at the bottom. If the line length extends from the top to the bottom margins, you can't tell any difference. However, if you set the line length to three inches, the vertical positioning is more noticeable. To set the line length of a vertical line, follow these steps:

1. In the Create Graphics Line dialog box, choose Length in Position/Length.

2. Enter a value in the text box and choose OK to close the dialog box.

Customizing Borders

In Chapter 7, "Integrating Text and Graphics," you learned to create a paragraph and a page border, and even to customize the border somewhat. This section takes you a step further.

WordPerfect enables you to customize more than just the line style of a border; you can change each line of a border, add spacing to the inside and outside of a border, change the color of the lines, and add a drop shadow. In addition, you can customize the type of fill and the color of the fill in a border.

As explained in Chapter 7, to create a paragraph border, choose Fo**r**mat, P**a**ragraph, **B**order/Fill. To create a page border, choose Fo**r**mat, **P**age, **B**order/Fill.

Tip
The Page Border and Paragraph Border dialog boxes are the same when customizing borders. Therefore, even though the text refers to the Page Border dialog box, you can apply the steps to the Paragraph Border dialog box, as well.

Modifying Lines

As you know from Chapter 7, you have over 25 choices for line styles, including Single, Thick, Thick Shadow, Dashed, Dotted, Thick Right/Left, Thin Bottom, and Double. You also have the option of customizing the line style by using the Page Border dialog box.

To customize a border, follow these steps:

Tip
Although you can change the lines in a border, keep your design consistent by altering the lines in pairs—left and right, or top and bottom.

1. Choose Fo**r**mat, **P**age. A cascading menu appears.
2. Choose **B**order/Fill. The Page Border dialog box appears (see fig. 21.7).
3. In the Page Border dialog box, choose a border.
4. In Border Options, choose **C**ustomize Style. The Customize Border dialog box appears (see fig. 21.8).

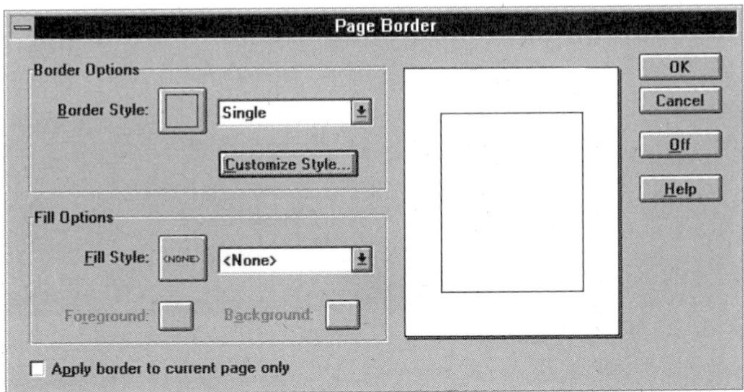

Fig. 21.7
The Page Border dialog box includes choices of preformatted borders. In addition, you can customize even more options by using the **C**ustomize Style option.

5. In Select Sides To Modify, choose the lines you want to alter by selecting Le**f**t, **R**ight, **T**op, Botto**m**, or **A**ll.
6. In Lin**e** Style, choose the style of line.
7. Choose OK to close the dialog box and return to the Page Border dialog box. Choose OK again to return to the document screen.

Tip
You can choose Lin**e** Style by selecting the button or the drop-down list.

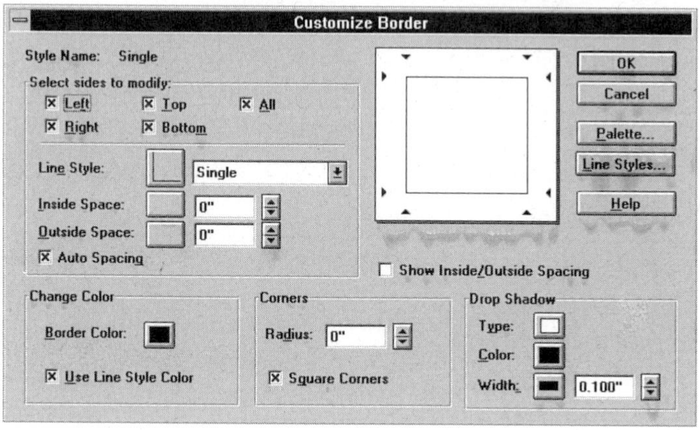

Fig. 21.8
Use the Customize Border dialog box to alter specific border lines, spacing, border color, corner styles, drop shadows, and more.

Setting Spacing

Tip
Be careful to leave space around a paragraph or page border to keep from crowding text and making it hard to read.

WordPerfect enables you to set the space between a border and outside text and the border and inside text. In addition, you can view the spacing in the example box as you change it. You can set the spacing as a numerical value or by sight, by using the Customize Border dialog box.

To change the spacing assigned to a border, follow these steps:

1. In the Page Border dialog box, choose **C**ustomize Style. The Customize Border dialog box appears (see fig. 21.9).

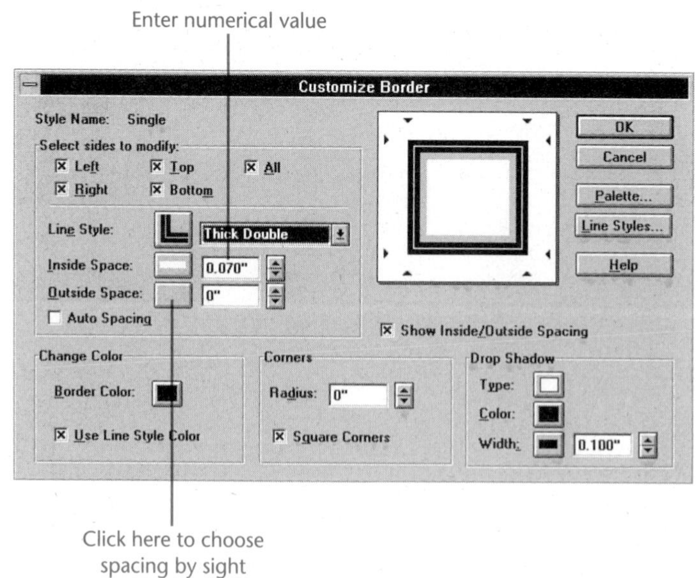

Fig. 21.9
Whether you set the spacing by sight or by numerical value, choose Show Inside/Outside Spacing to view the spacing in the example box. The example here shows 0.070-inch inside spacing in gray.

2. Choose the button or enter a value in the text box to set **I**nside Space and **O**utside Space.

3. Choose OK to accept the changes and close the dialog box. Choose OK again to return to the document.

Tip
If you change your mind about the spacing you set, choose Auto Spacin**g** to set the spacing back to the default.

Changing Color

You can apply one of a variety of colors to a paragraph or page border; you can even apply a shade of black to the border. Color is easy to add by using the Customize Border dialog box. To change the color of a border, follow these steps:

1. In the Customize Border dialog box, choose the **B**order Color button. An array of available colors appears (see fig. 21.10).

2. Drag the mouse pointer to the desired color.

3. Choose OK to close the dialog box and choose OK again to return to the document.

Tip
Limit colors of borders to two within each document to create consistency and unity.

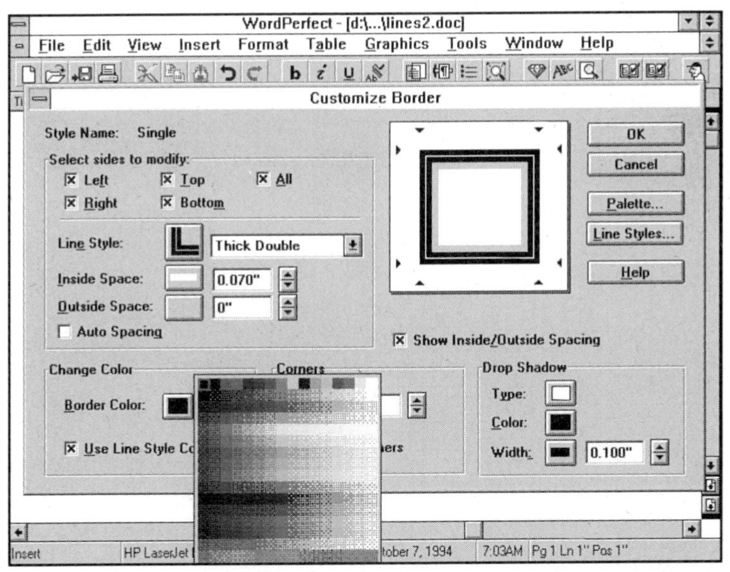

Fig. 21.10
If you don't use a color printer, try applying a shade of black—10%, 20%, 30%, and so on—to a border to add interest and diversity to the page. Use thicker and heavier borders with a 50% shade instead of solid black; to make it less overwhelming.

> **Note**
>
> You can't select sides to modify in different colors; all lines change to the color you choose.

4. Choose OK to close the dialog box and return to the document.

Tip
If you change your mind about the color you've selected, you can choose **U**se Line Style Color to change back to the default.

Changing Corners

Tip

As you change the curvature of the corners, watch the example box to get an idea of how much curve you want.

Round-cornered borders create an interesting effect in a document. You can change the border corners to anything from slightly rounded to almost circular. To change the corners of a border, follow these steps:

1. In the Customize Border dialog box, choose S**q**uare Corners to turn off the option.

2. In Ra**d**ius, enter a value for the curvature of the corners.

Adding a Drop Shadow

A drop shadow gives your document a professional look by adding depth to the page. For example, you can add a drop shadow to a paragraph border for special announcements, advertisements, or special areas of a form. A drop shadow also looks good when applied to a page border for a letterhead, title page, or flyer. To create a drop shadow, follow these steps:

1. In the Customize Border dialog box, choose T**y**pe in the Drop Shadow area (see fig. 21.11).

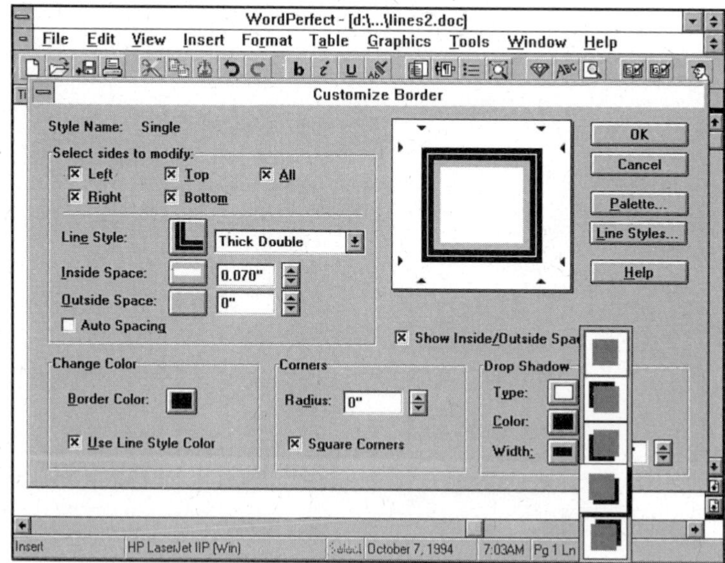

Fig. 21.11
Choose the top left, bottom left, bottom right, and top right shadow offsets according to their placement on the page. Choose a bottom right shadow for a paragraph border placed in the bottom right corner of the page.

Tip

Use a 30% or 40% shade of gray to add more perspective to a small border; the larger the border, the darker the gray drop shadow can be.

2. Choose the **C**olor of the border.

3. Accept the default width of the drop shadow, or choose Width and enter a value.

4. Choose OK to close the dialog box; choose OK to return to the document.

Adding Fill

As described in Chapter 7, "Integrating Text and Graphics," you can also add fill to a paragraph or page border. In addition to a variety of fills—including 10% through 100% shaded fill, lines, checkerboard, fish scale, waves, mesh, and more—you can add a variety of colors to your fill. To add fill to a border, follow these steps:

1. Choose Fo**r**mat, **P**age or P**a**ragraph, then **B**order/Fill. The Page or Paragraph Border dialog box appears.
2. In Fill Options, choose **F**ill Style; select any fill you want.
3. Choose Fo**r**eground; a color palette similar to that in the Border Line Color palette appears.
4. Choose the appropriate color and choose OK to close the dialog box.

Customizing Graphics Boxes

WordPerfect enables you to add graphics images—such as clip art, WP Draw images, scanned images, and so on—to your documents to add interest and diversity. You can add text boxes for callouts, quotes, announcements, and so on. You can also add graphics boxes to hold equations, tables, inline figures, even screened images to cover the entire page. WordPerfect offers many ways to spice up your documents. Chapter 7, "Integrating Text and Graphics," shows you how to create a variety of graphics boxes.

◄ See "Using Graphics Borders," p. 268

WordPerfect offers eight graphics box styles you can use. Using just one of these styles may not always work for your document. You may need to change line style, color, spacing, add captions, and so on. WordPerfect enables you to do all of this and more. You can adjust the text flow around the graphics box, for example, or rotate the contents within a box. This section shows you how to customize graphics boxes to suit your documents and purposes. Figure 21.12 illustrates three customized graphics boxes and their contents.

Tip

Point the mouse at the graphics box and press the right mouse button. A graphics menu appears from which you can choose any of the editing options.

When you create a graphics box, or when you choose to edit a graphics box, WordPerfect displays the box and the graphics editing screen as shown in figure 21.13. To edit a graphics box, select the box, and then choose **G**raphics, **E**dit Box (press Shift+F11).

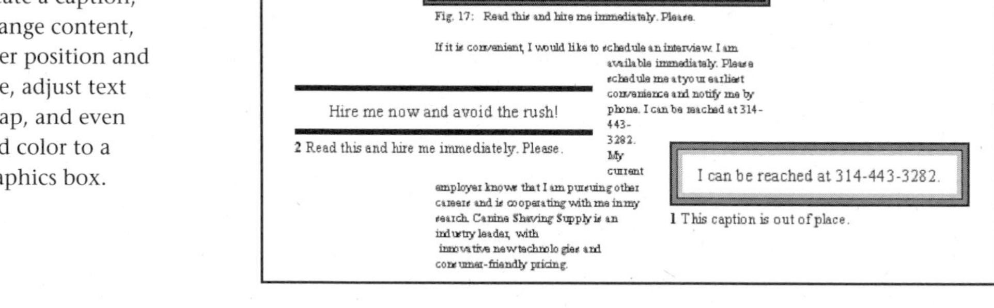

Fig. 21.12
You can customize borders and fill, create a caption, change content, alter position and size, adjust text wrap, and even add color to a graphics box.

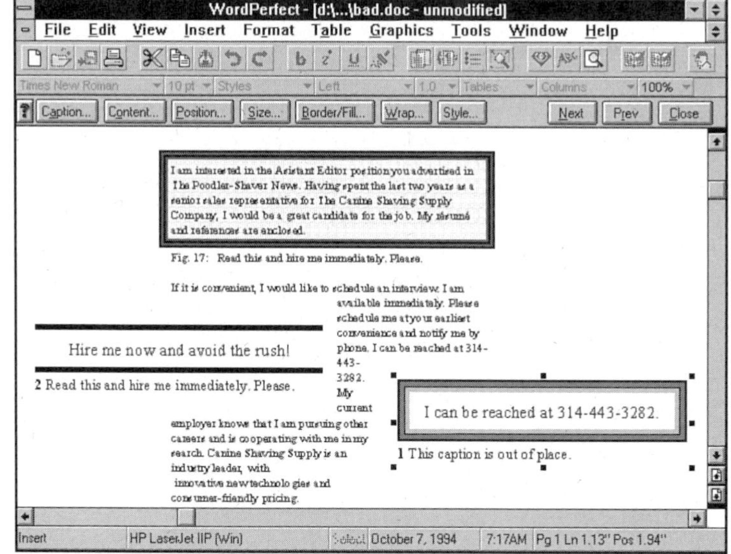

Fig. 21.13
The additional Feature Bar enables you to change the border, fill, style, size, position, text wrap, and content of the graphics box. You can add a caption or choose other graphics boxes to edit while in this editing mode.

Tip
You can add a box style you use often to the **G**raphics menu by choosing **G**raphics, **G**raphics Styles, **M**enu. Select the box style in the **I**tems list and choose OK.

Choosing a Box Style

You can choose the style of box you want by using the **G**raphics menu or the Toolbar. Both the **G**raphics menu and the Toolbar contain three box options: I**m**age, **T**ext, and **C**ustom Box—the **G**raphics menu also includes the E**q**uation box. If you do not want to use an I**m**age, **T**ext box, or E**q**uation box, choose **C**ustom Box and select the style of box you want to create.

You can choose a new graphics box style at any time by using the editing box screen. To change a box style, follow these steps:

1. When you create the graphics box, the graphics box editing screen appears (refer to fig. 21.13).
2. Choose the S**t**yle button on the Feature Bar. The Box Style dialog box appears (see fig. 21.14).

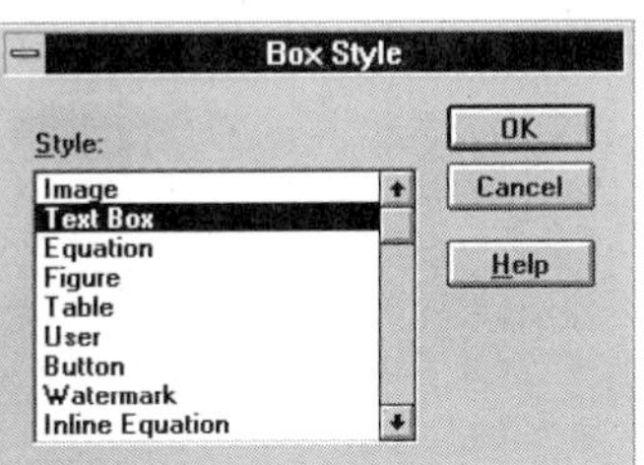

Fig. 21.14
Changing the box style means assigning different defaults to the graphics box. Any changes you make to border, spacing, fill, and so on are erased when you change the box style.

3. Choose a new style and choose OK to return to the editing screen.
4. To exit the graphics box editing screen, choose the Menu button (?) shown in figure 21.15, and choose **C**lose.

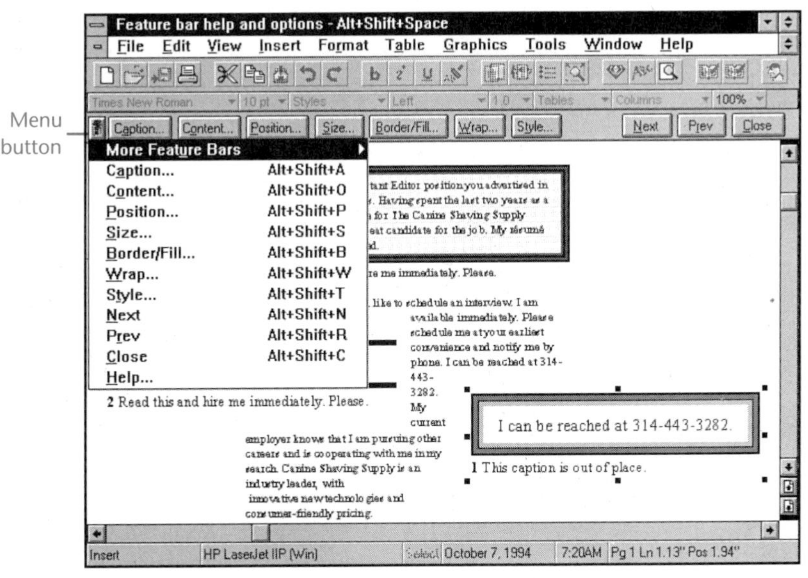

Fig. 21.15
The ? menu enables you to perform any option for editing or customizing a graphics box—such as adding a caption, changing content, size, position, border, and so on.

Choosing Contents

You can choose the contents of a graphics box—image, text, equation, or the box can remain empty. In addition, you can position the contents within the box horizontally and vertically. You can choose to center the contents horizontally, for example, or position the contents to the left or right of the graphics box. You can also center the contents vertically, or position the contents to the top or bottom of the box.

Tip
As long as you're in the graphics box editing screen, you can further customize the graphics box by changing C**a**ption, C**o**ntent, **P**osition, **S**ize, **B**order/Fill, **W**rap, and St**y**le using the Feature Bar.

Note

If the contents of the box consist of text, you can additionally rotate the contents 90, 180, or 270 degrees, if you want, as well as adjust the position of the text within the box.

To choose the contents of the graphics box, follow these steps:

1. In the graphics box editing screen, choose the C**o**ntent button. The Box Content dialog box appears (see fig. 21.16).

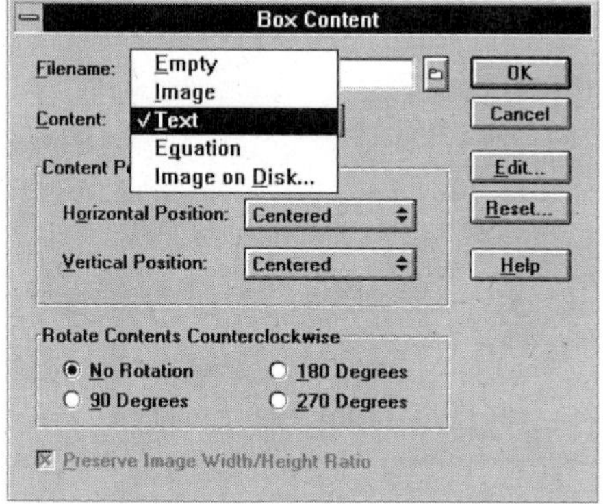

Fig. 21.16
You choose the Content category first—image, text, equation—and then you can either choose a file to import to the graphics box, or create your own text, image, or equation.

2. Choose **C**ontent and a pop-up list appears. Your choices are listed in the following table:

Tip
When using a Watermark box—used to screen a logo or image in the background of the page—you can position the image to the bottom right, for example.

Option	**Result**
Empty	The box remains empty.
Image	Choose an image file from the hard disk drive; the image can be clip art, WP Draw, scanned art, or any variety of other graphics.
Text	Choose a file name or create the text in the box.

Option	Result
E**q**uation	Create an equation for the box.
Image on **D**isk	Choose an image file from a floppy disk. The image will be linked to the document, meaning that you must insert the disk containing the image each time you open the document.

3. Choose any other options such as positioning or rotation.
4. Choose **F**ilename if you want to import a file and select a file. If you choose to create your own text, choose **E**dit.

Tip
For most graphic images, choose **P**reserve Image Width/Height Ratio to maintain the image's proportion when changing the proportion of the graphics box.

If the content you select is text, WordPerfect returns to the editing window with the insertion point in the graphics box. Enter and format the text.

If you choose to edit the equation contents of a box, the Equation Editor appears on-screen.

If you choose to edit the image contents of a graphics box, WP Draw appears on-screen.

Creating a Caption

WordPerfect enables you to add captions to the graphics boxes you create. You can position the caption on the left, right, top, or bottom of the graphics box. You can also place the caption inside, outside, or on the border of the box. In addition, you can left-, right-, or center-align the text in the caption, offset the text, rotate the text, and number the captions. To add a caption to the graphics box, follow these steps:

1. In the graphics box editing screen, choose C**a**ption. The Box Caption dialog box appears (see fig. 21.17).

Note

If you have a great deal of text to enter in a graphics box, consider entering the text in a WordPerfect document, formatting, and then saving it. Then use the **F**ilename option in the Box Contents dialog box to import the text.

2. Choose options for the placement, position, rotation, and so on of the caption.

IV

Professional Output

3. Choose **E**dit. The dialog box closes and returns you to the graphics box editing screen. The insertion point is in position for the caption; enter the text.

4. If you are finished editing, choose the "?" menu and choose **C**lose. If, however, you want to further edit the graphics box, remain in the Graphics Editing screen.

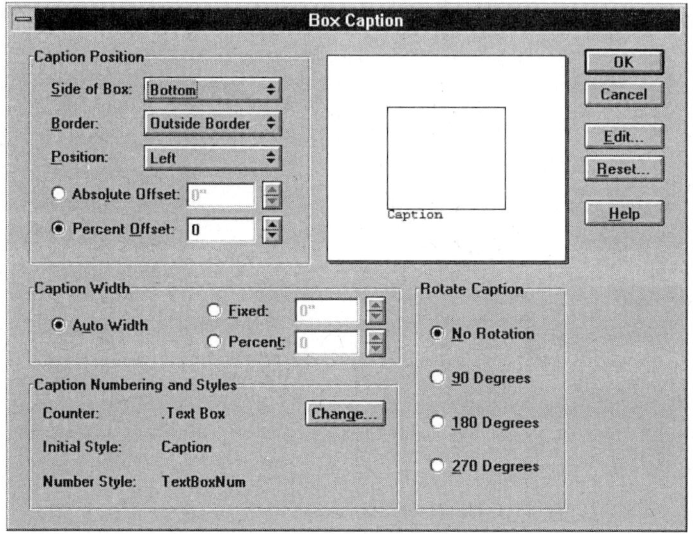

Fig. 21.17
When you create a caption, WordPerfect automatically numbers the caption according to the number of like box styles you have created. For example, if this is the third Figure box, the caption number is 3.

Choosing Position Options

Tip
To reposition a graphic with the mouse, click and hold the mouse button within the graphics box and drag it to a new position.

As you learned in Chapter 7, "Integrating Text and Graphics," you can easily position a graphics box by selecting it with the mouse and moving it to a new position. You can also reposition a graphics box by using the Box Position dialog box. To position a graphics box, follow these steps:

1. In the graphics box editing screen, choose **P**osition. The Box Position dialog box appears (see fig. 21.18).

2. Choose the type of Box Placement from the following options:

Option	Result
Put Box on Current Page	The box is anchored to the page no matter what text editing is performed.
P**u**t Box in Current Paragraph	The box remains with the paragraph that the insertion point is in when you create the box—a paragraph anchor.
Treat Box as Character	The box moves with surrounding text as if it were one of the characters on the line.

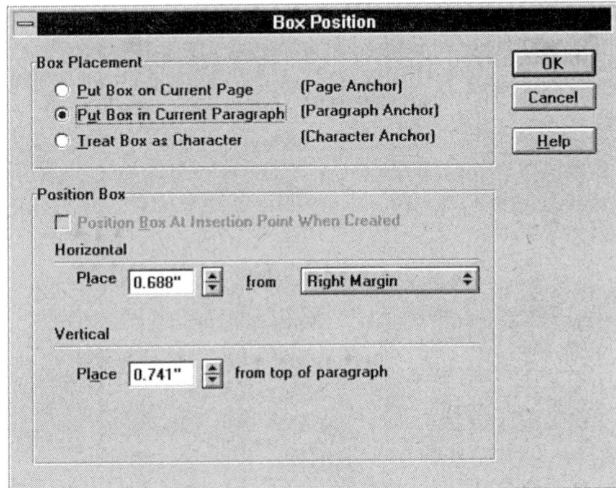

Fig. 21.18
You can position the graphics box horizontally and vertically by entering a value in inches. Horizontal placement can be measured from the right or left margin, center of paragraph, or left of the page. Vertical placement is measured from the top of the paragraph.

◄ See "Using Graphics Boxes," p. 275

3. In Position Box, enter a value for Horizontal placement and choose where the measurement should start. Enter a value for Vertical placement.

4. Choose OK to close the dialog box and return to the editing screen.

Choosing Size Options

Perhaps the easiest way to size a graphics box is with the mouse. However, you may want an exact size for fitting within a column, matching the exact width-height ratio, and so on. To set an exact size for the graphics box, follow these steps:

1. In the graphics box editing screen, choose **S**ize. The Box Size dialog box appears (see fig. 21.19).

Tip
To size a graphics box with the mouse, select the box. Click and drag one of the box's handles to resize.

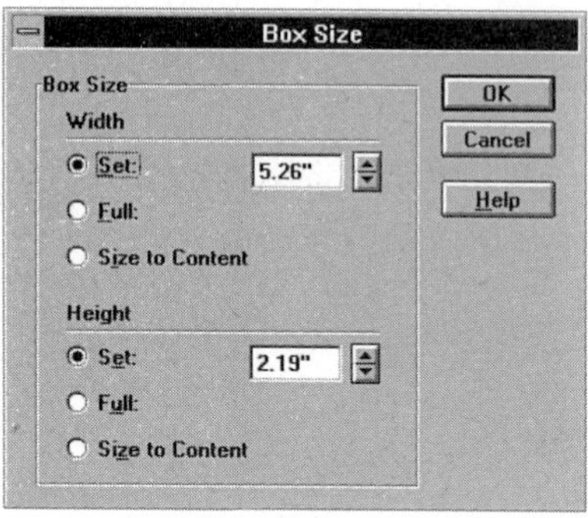

Fig. 21.19
Set the width and height of the graphics box by entering values in the text boxes. Choose **F**ull to fill the page with the image, or choose S**i**ze to Content to create a proportioned image.

2. Choose the Width and the Height of the graphics box.

3. Choose OK to return to the screen.

> **Note**
>
> You can mix and match sizing options. For example, choose Width to be **F**ull and Height to be S**i**ze to Content, which makes the image the full width between the margins and proportionally adjusts the height of the image.

Editing Border and Fill

Editing the border and fill of a graphics box is the same as editing the border and fill of a graphics border. For more information, see the earlier section, "Customizing Borders." To edit the border and fill of a graphics box, choose **B**order/Fill from the graphics box editing screen.

Adjusting Text Wrap

Graphics boxes you use in your documents are normally accompanied by text. When placing a graphics box in a page or column of text, you must decide how that text flows—or wraps around—the graphics box. WordPerfect gives you several choices for text wrap. To adjust text wrap for a graphics box, follow these steps:

1. In the graphics box editing screen, choose **W**rap. The Wrap Text dialog box appears (see fig. 21.20).

2. Choose the Wrapping Type, and then choose a Wrap Text Around option.

3. Choose OK to close the box and return to the screen.

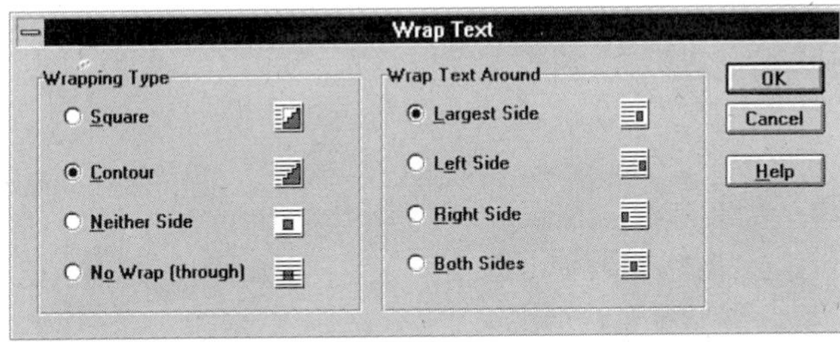

Fig. 21.20
Choose how the text wraps around the graphics box by choosing an option in Wrapping Type. Then, choose on which side of the graphics box the text will wrap by selecting an option in Wrap Text Around.

Figure 21.21 illustrates **C**ontour text wrap with the wrap occurring on the largest side of the graphics box.

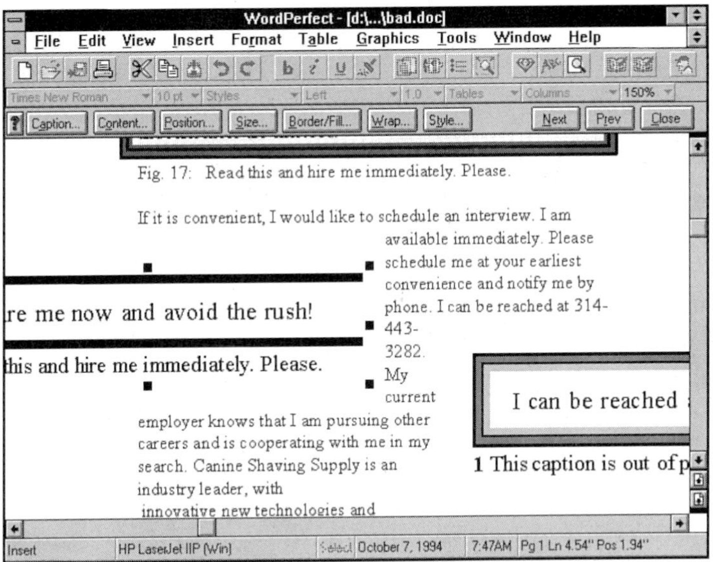

Fig. 21.21
Be careful when you use the text wrap option; the text may wrap in such a way as to make reading impossible.

Retrieving a Graphics Image

WordPerfect enables you to import many types of graphics files; you can import vector graphics (line art) and bit-mapped graphics (raster). *Vector graphics* are images created using an outline; thus, the edges of the image are smooth and sharp. *Bit-mapped graphics* are images created using a series of dots; the edges are usually rough and grainy. Figure 21.22 illustrates examples of vector and bit-mapped graphics.

Fig. 21.22
The image on the right (the beautiful, rare marsh crane) is a vector graphic; notice that the outlines are smooth. The image on the left (the dinosaur) is a bit-mapped image.

Tip
You can use images created in WordPerfect's applet WP Draw as an image file. See Chapter 22 for more information.

WordPerfect enables you to use a variety of files, including WP Graphics (WPG), Encapsulated Postscript (EPS), PC Paintbrush (PCX), Tagged Image Format (TIF), and more. Images from most drawing, painting, and scanning programs can be imported to WordPerfect for Windows.

If you want to quickly import a graphics image, you can create a default Figure box and retrieve an image without editing the graphics box as described previously. The box appears in the document, and you can resize and reposition it by using the mouse. Of course, you also can edit the graphics box by using the graphics box editing screen, if you find it necessary.

To retrieve an image into a Figure box, follow these steps:

1. Choose **G**raphics, I**m**age. The Insert Image dialog box appears (see fig. 21.23).

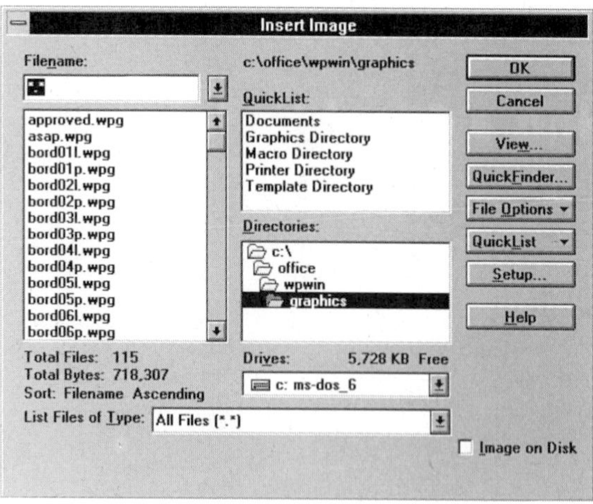

Fig. 21.23
If you don't have image files of your own, choose from the clip art provided with WordPerfect; the path to the WordPerfect clip art files is C:\OFFICE\WPWIN\GRAPHICS. All WordPerfect graphics use a WPG extension.

2. In List Files Of **T**ype, choose the file format.

3. In File**n**ame, enter the name of the file to be retrieved, or choose the file name from the list.

4. Choose OK to close the dialog box and return to the document.

Tip

To close the Image Tools tool box, double-click the control menu in the upper left corner of the box.

Editing a Graphics Image

When you retrieve a graphics image, you may find you need to adjust the image to make it more suitable to your document. Editing an image includes adjusting brightness or contrast, changing color or fill, even rotating, moving, and scaling the image.

Note

Editing also includes adding lines and shapes to the image with WP Draw, which you can learn more about in Chapter 22, "Using WP Draw and TextArt."

You can edit graphics images so that they complement and emphasize the text in your document. For instance, if you have an image of a ship that's facing the wrong way for its placement in your document, you can alter the position of the image by mirroring it. Suppose that your image is in color and you have a black printer; you can change the image to black-and-white for better resolution. This section shows you how to edit graphics images.

WordPerfect's graphics box editing screen includes a tool box—Image Tools—that enables you to customize and edit images. To display the Image Tools palette, choose Too**l**s in the Graphics Editing screen. Figure 21.24 illustrates the Image Tools.

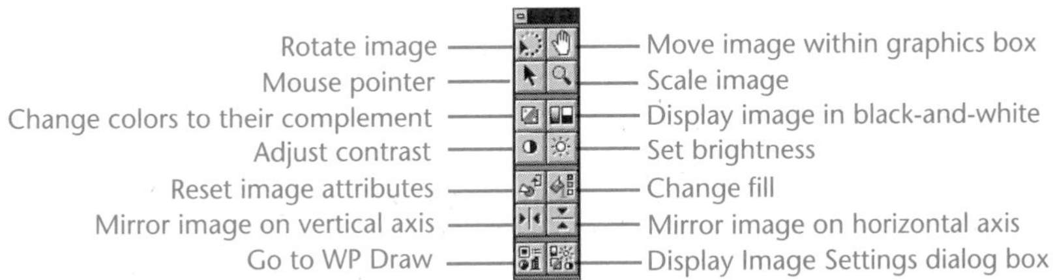

Fig. 21.24
Icons represent each tool in the Image Tools tool box. To discover the use of any tool, position the mouse pointer over a tool and view the title bar at the top of the screen.

You can reverse all editing effects at any time by choosing the button representing Reset from the Image Tools tool box.

Rotating Images

You can rotate an image within the graphics box by using the Rotation tool. Figure 21.25 illustrates an image being rotated.

Fig. 21.25 Drag any of the rotation handles to rotate the image. All handles enable the image to rotate on a center vertical axis.

To rotate an image, follow these steps:

1. In the graphics box editing screen, choose Too**l**s to display the Image Tools tool box.

2. Click the mouse pointer on the Rotation tool. Small double handles appear in the corners of the image.
3. Move the mouse over one of the new handles appearing inside the graphics box until the double-headed arrow appears. Click and drag the handle until the image is rotated the way you want.

Tip
You can point the mouse at the graphics box and press the right mouse button to display a QuickMenu. Choose **I**mage Tools.

Moving an Image

You can crop—or move the image within the graphics box—by using the grabber hand in the tool box. This tool is handy for repositioning the image to move unwanted areas out of view. To crop an image, follow these steps:

1. In the Image Tools Toolbox, choose the Moving tool.
2. Click and drag the image to a new position within the graphics box.

Scaling an Image

The Scaling tool is exceptionally handy for enlarging an area of an image to cover the entire graphics box. Suppose that an image contains one small section you want to enlarge; you want that small section to be all that shows. Use the Scaling tool by following these directions:

1. In the Image Tools tool box, choose the Scaling tool. A cascading tool box appears.

2. Choose the method of scaling. You have three choices of scaling the image:

   The magnifying glass enables you to draw a box around the area you want to enlarge (see fig. 21.26).

   The up/down arrows add a scroll bar to the figure box. Click the up arrow and the image becomes smaller; click the down arrow and the image becomes larger. Figure 21.27 illustrates the scroll bars.

   The 1:1 ratio button changes the image back to its original size.

Tip
To better see the image, especially when using the scroll bars to scale, move the Image Tools toolbox by clicking the window's title bar and dragging it to another location.

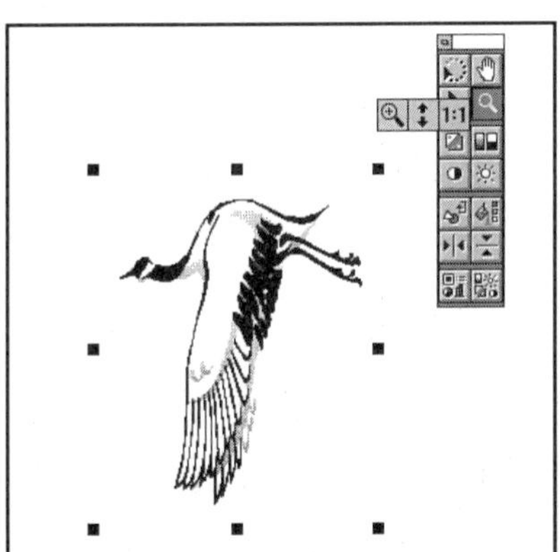

Fig. 21.26
Use the Magnifying Glass scale control tool for quick and easy image editing.

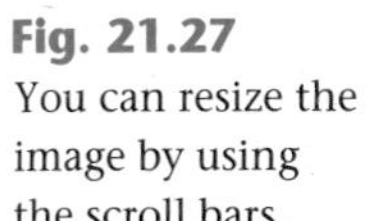

Fig. 21.27
You can resize the image by using the scroll bars.

Changing Colors

Using the Image Tools, you can change the colors of an image to its complementary colors or you can change an image to black-and-white. Complementary colors are those that are opposites on the color wheel: red and green, yellow and purple, and blue and orange, for example. Thus an image that is red and blue changes to green and orange if you change to complementary colors. For more control over the color of an image, use WP Draw.

To change colors of the image to its complementary colors, follow these steps:

1. Choose the tool that changes colors to complementary colors.
2. To change the colors back, choose the tool again.

To change a color image to black-and-white, follow these steps:

1. Choose the tool that displays the image in black-and-white.
2. To change the image back, choose the tool again.

Tip
If the image is in black-and-white, choosing to change to complementary colors switches black to white and white to black in the image.

Changing Contrast

Changing the contrast of an image changes the difference between the colors. For example, if you're using a black-and-white image, you can adjust the contrast so that everything is black-or-white. You can also adjust the contrast so that grays appear and the contrast is not so strong. Figure 21.28 illustrates the contrast tool and a black-and-white figure using a lesser degree of contrast.

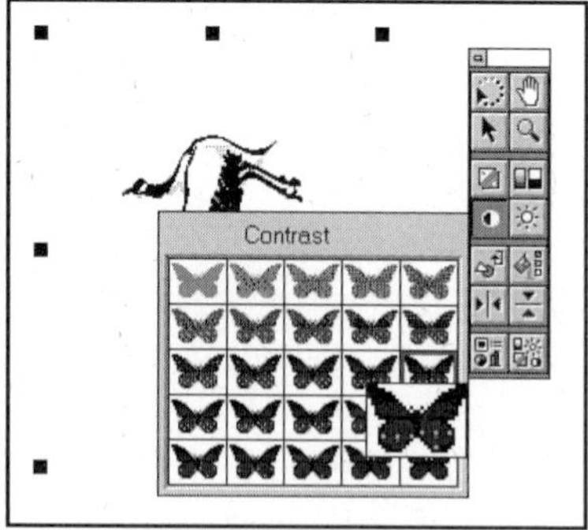

Fig. 21.28
When changing contrast, make changes in small increments—one step at a time—to see how the changes affect the image. Experimentation is the best guide because each image is different.

To change the contrast of an image, follow these steps:

1. Choose the contrast Image tool. A secondary tool box appears.
2. Choose any block and view the difference in the image.

Changing Brightness

Changing the brightness is similar to changing contrast, except that brightness refers to the intensity of the colors. Experiment with the brightness of the image as you would with the contrast before deciding which setting is best. To change the brightness of the image, choose the brightness button in the Image Tools toolbox. A secondary toolbox appears; choose the preferred brightness.

Setting Fill

The fill attributes button controls the lines and fill of the image. You can display the image with fill, as lines, or as a transparent object. To set the fill for an image, follow these steps:

1. Choose the Fill Image tool. A secondary toolbox appears.
2. Choose the fill you want. The first box represents color or black fill; the second box represents a transparent fill with only lines; the third box represents opaque white fill with lines.

Mirroring Images

You can choose to mirror an image on its vertical (up-and-down) or horizontal (left to right) axis. Use this mirror tool when you need to flip an image to better suit your document.

To flip an image, choose either the horizontal or vertical mirror tool in the Image Tools toolbox.

Using the Image Settings Dialog Box

You can accomplish all of the image editing techniques covered in this section through the use of the Image Settings dialog box. Choose the Image Settings button in the Image Tools toolbox to display the dialog box shown in figure 21.29. The main difference between editing the image with the tools and editing with the Image Settings dialog box is the difference between using the mouse and entering a value for the options. For example, to rotate an image with the Image Settings dialog box, you enter a value between 0 and 360 degrees.

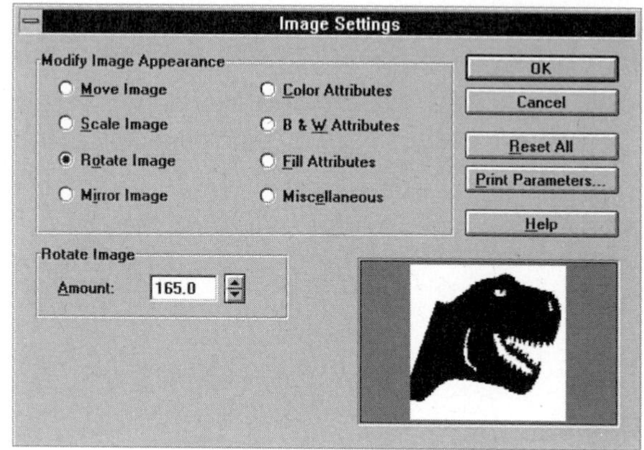

Fig. 21.29
As you choose an option in Modify Image Appearance, the options in the lower left half of the dialog box change. In addition, the image changes in the example box so that you can see the results of the editing.

Creating Graphics with Drag to Create

The Drag to Create feature allows you to quickly and easily size and position any type of box. Using Drag to Create, you simply click and drag anywhere in your document to create a graphics, text, or custom box.

To use Drag to Create, select **G**raphics, Drag t**o** Create. A check mark will appear next to the menu item when it is activated. Now choose the type of box you want from the **G**raphics menu as you normally would. Click the mouse in the document and drag to create an outline of the box you are creating. When you release the mouse button, the box appears.

From Here...

As you've seen, you can add a variety of graphics to your documents: horizontal and vertical lines, paragraph and page borders, and graphics boxes that hold text, images, tables, equations, and spreadsheets.

For more information on creating and manipulating graphics, see the following chapters:

- Chapter 17, "Creating and Modifying Charts with WP Draw," discusses how to create your own charts in WP Draw and how to edit them.

- Chapter 22, "Using WP Draw and TextArt," teaches you to create and edit shapes, retrieve clip art, and use a scanner.

Chapter 22

Using WP Draw and TextArt

by Rick Winter, Sue Plumley, and Alan Westenbroek

You have seen that working with graphics is fun and helps stimulate ideas, and that graphics add interest to your documents. In addition to the advanced graphics capabilities mentioned in the previous chapter, WordPerfect 6.1 for Windows now comes with WP Draw and TextArt. These modules cost nothing extra and add most of the capabilities that come with separate standalone programs such as WordPerfect Presentations and Harvard Graphics.

The key to using WP Draw and TextArt within WordPerfect is OLE (*Object Linking and Embedding*). OLE enables you to access one program from within another program. If you have inserted a WordPerfect graphic or text created with TextArt into a document, for example, you can double-click the graphic or text and enter WP Draw or TextArt, respectively. When you exit WP Draw or TextArt, the graphic or text remains linked to the document.

With version 6.1, WordPerfect adds support for OLE 2.0, which significantly improves on the interface and usability of OLE. OLE 2.0 features *in-place editing*, which allows one application to "take over" another, modifying its menus and toolbars. Now when you double-click to activate an embedded object, you remain in your document *in WordPerfect* with all the menu commands and toolbar buttons provided by the OLE application used to create the object.

A number of Windows programs now support object linking and embedding. In addition to WordPerfect for Windows, some other programs that support OLE 2.0 include Microsoft Word and Excel, CorelDRAW!, and Microsoft Video for Windows.

In this chapter, you learn how to:

- Start WP Draw
- Create and edit shapes such as lines, rectangles, and circles
- Retrieve clip art and make changes in the graphic
- Add text to your graphic
- Use a scanner to import images into WP Draw
- Use TextArt to create text with a variety of shapes and special effects

Starting WP Draw

As an OLE-based accessory program, WP Draw works only from an application that supports OLE 2.0 technology, such as WordPerfect 6.1 for Windows or Microsoft Excel. You can start WP Draw through WordPerfect for Windows or through another product. The technique you use to start WP Draw depends on whether you are editing an existing graphic or creating a new graphic.

Entering WP Draw from WordPerfect

Because the WP Draw module is an accessory of WordPerfect, you can enter WP Draw from the WordPerfect menu or by clicking the Draw button on the Toolbar. You also can enter WP Draw by double-clicking an existing graphic (as described later in this section).

To start WP Draw from WordPerfect, follow these steps:

1. Position the insertion point in your WordPerfect document where you want to insert your graphic.

2. Choose **G**raphics, **D**raw. WP Draw switches the WordPerfect menu and toolbar to its own and places a thick border around the drawing area.

Entering WP Draw from Other Programs

If you want to create a graphic for another program, you can enter WP Draw from the **E**dit or **I**nsert menus (if these menus are available). Look for a menu item named Insert Object.

Some examples of how to start WP Draw from various OLE-supported programs follow:

1. Look for an Insert Object menu choice and select it, as in the following examples:

   - For Lotus 1-2-3 for Windows and Microsoft Excel, choose **E**dit, Insert **O**bject.
   - For Microsoft PowerPoint, choose **E**dit, **I**nsert, **O**bject.
   - For Microsoft Word, choose **I**nsert, **O**bject.
   - For WordPerfect, choose **I**nsert, Ob**j**ect.

   In all cases, after you find and select Insert Object, you see an Insert Object dialog box (see fig. 22.1).

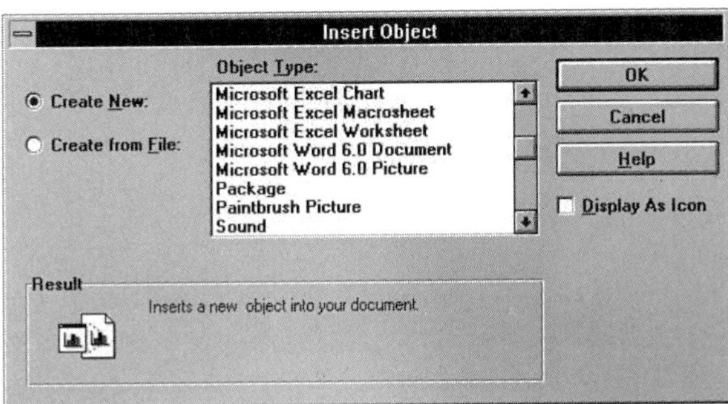

Fig. 22.1 The types of objects available within the Insert Object dialog box depend on what other OLE-compliant applications you have installed on your system.

2. In the Object **T**ype list box, scroll to and highlight WP Draw 3.0 Drawing.

3. Click OK or press Enter.

Note

You can use the procedure explained in the preceding numbered steps to insert any embedded object. To insert a Microsoft Draw object, for example, select `Microsoft Drawing` in step 2.

Editing an Existing Graphic

To start WP Draw in order to edit an existing graphic, you can double-click an embedded WordPerfect graphic (see fig. 22.2).

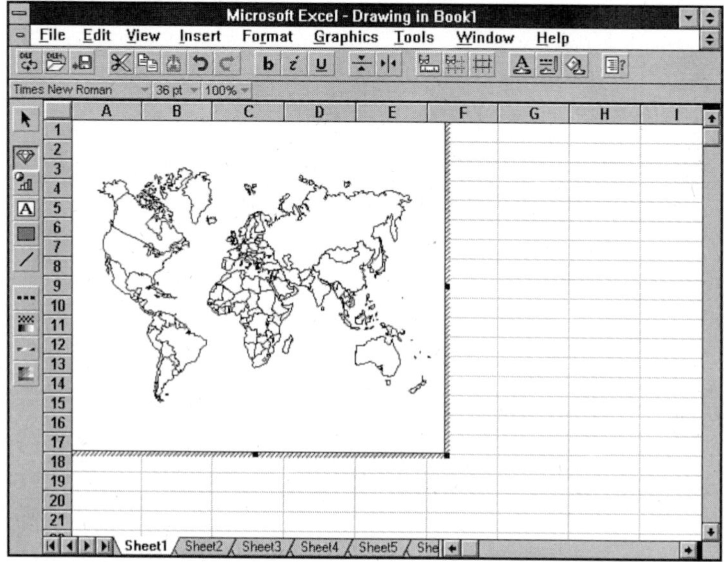

Fig. 22.2
If a figure is embedded in another program such as Microsoft Excel, when you double-click the figure, WP Draw launches and enables you to make changes in the figure.

Updating Your Document

After you start WP Draw and create or retrieve and edit a graphic, you can add the drawing to your document, spreadsheet, or presentation. To add the drawing, do one of the following:

- From the WP Draw toolbar, click **U**pdate to add the new or edited graphic to the document and continue working in WP Draw.

- Click OLE Close to add the new or edited graphic to the document and exit WP Draw.
- Click anywhere else in the document to de-select the graphic. WordPerfect will regain control of its toolbar and menus and update the drawing.

Remember, you have embedded the graphic in your document. If you do not save the document in WordPerfect (or the other program), the graphic and any other changes since the last save are lost.

Note

If you do not see your graphic in the document, you may be in draft view or have graphics turned off. In WordPerfect, for example, you must choose **V**iew, **G**raphics to see your graphics.

◀ See "Using Help," p. 47

Exploring WP Draw

Whether you enter WP Draw from WordPerfect for Windows or another program, you see the same WP Draw controls (see fig. 22.3). WP Draw works in much the same way as do other graphics products. The WP Draw controls are intuitive, and you quickly can become familiar with them, even if you are accustomed to using other graphics products.

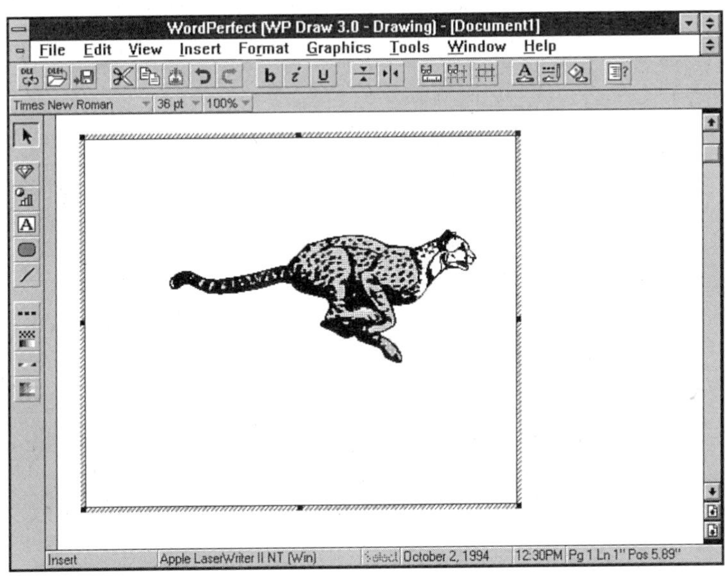

Fig. 22.3
WP Draw includes a Toolbar and Tool palette. To turn the Toolbar on, select **V**iew, Tool**b**ar.

◀ See "Understanding the Editing Screen," p. 18

◀ See "Working with Multiple Documents," p. 45

◀ See "Customizing a Toolbar," p. 455

Glancing at the Pull-Down Menus

WP Draw's menu bar is similar to WordPerfect's. Both menus begin on the left with **F**ile, **E**dit, and **V**iew options and end with **W**indow and **H**elp options on the right. The following list provides a general description for each of the items on the WP Draw Menu bar.

Item	Function
File	This menu remains unchanged from WordPerfect's default File menu.
Edit	Undo last command, cut, copy, paste, select, control links, and rotate selected items.
View	Show or not show tools such as Toolbar, ruler, grid, and reveal codes, and change view size of picture.
Insert	Inserts drawing elements, other objects, date, and time.
Fo**r**mat	Text and graphic styles and formatting.
Graphics	Changes the order and orientation of graphic elements and controls Contour Text.
Tools	Spell checker, thesaurus, and Macro tools.
Window	View more than one document window or move to a different document window.
Help	Find more information about WP Draw.

Using WP Drawing Tools

The WP Draw screen also includes its own Toolbar. The buttons provide you with shortcuts to the most frequently used procedures within WP Draw. Although the default for the program is having the Toolbar on, if the Toolbar does not show, choose **V**iew, Tool**b**ar.

The following table lists and describes the functions of the buttons on the Toolbar:

Button	Function
	Updates the OLE object in the document.
	Closes WP Draw.
	Saves the current drawing.
	Cuts the selected item(s) to the clipboard.

Button	Function
	Copies the selected item(s) to the clipboard.
	Pastes the contents of the clipboard.
	Undoes the last action.
	Redoes the last action.
b	Makes the selected text bold.
i	Makes the selected text italic.
U	Makes the selected text underlined.
	Flips the selected item horizontally.
	Flips the selected item vertically.
	Views or hides the ruler.
	Views or hides the grid.
	Snaps drawing objects and tools to the grid points.
A	Edits the text colors, pattern, and outline width.

Viewing the Tool Palette

The Tool palette on the left side of the screen enables you to select, view, create, and modify graphic items (see fig. 22.4). The tools are divided into three sections. The Selection section, the Drawing tools section, and the Attribute tools section.

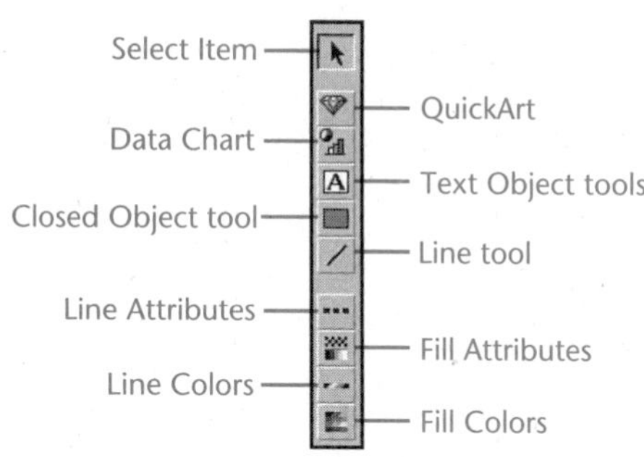

Fig. 22.4
The Tool palette enables you to create and edit graphics quickly.

Viewing the Ruler and Grid

The **V**iew menu offers two features that can help make your work more precise. These features are the WP Draw *ruler* and *grid* (see fig. 22.5). The ruler displays at the top and left side of the screen and is segmented into inches (or other units, as explained in the following tip). The grid marks off your screen's background display with evenly spaced vertical and horizontal lines. The grid helps you position graphics more accurately on the page.

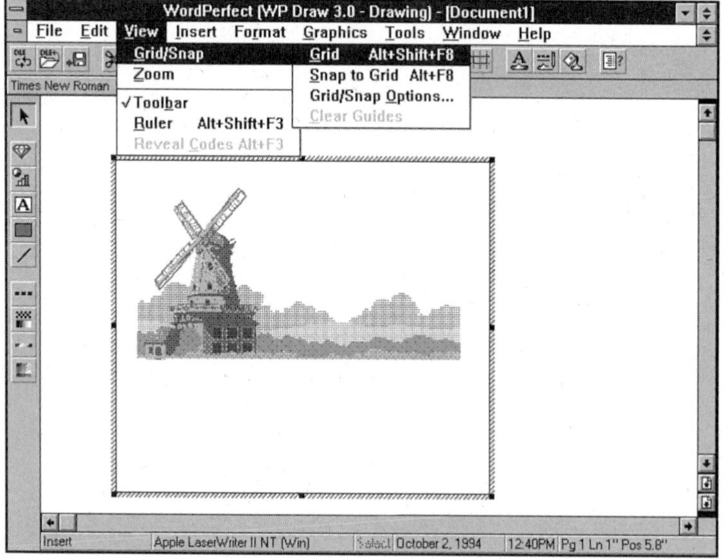

Fig. 22.5
The **V**iew menu enables you to display the ruler and grid. Use **V**iew, **G**rid/Snap, Grid/Snap **O**ptions to change the spacing for the grid.

 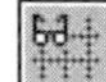 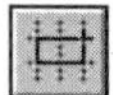

To turn the ruler on (or off if it is already on), choose **V**iew, **R**uler. To turn the grid on or off, choose **V**iew, **G**rid. If you want the lines and boxes you are creating to align with the grid, choose **V**iew, **S**nap to Grid.

Note

You can set WP Draw to turn on the ruler or grid automatically when you start up WP Draw. Choose **E**dit, Prefere**n**ces, **D**isplay. In the Display Preferences dialog box, choose Display **R**uler On Startup or Display **G**rid On Startup. The Display Preferences dialog box also enables you to change the ruler's measurement units to inches, centimeters, millimeters, points, or 1200ths of an inch by selecting the Display and **E**ntry Of Numbers pop-up list.

Creating Shapes

To draw a shape, you need to select the shape tool from the Drawing Tools palette or from the Draw menu. When you move the mouse pointer into the drawing area, the cursor changes to a crosshair. Depending on the shape you choose to draw, you click to start the object, click to add points, and double-click to end the object; or you click and drag the mouse to draw the object. The different kinds of shapes you can create are shown in figure 22.6.

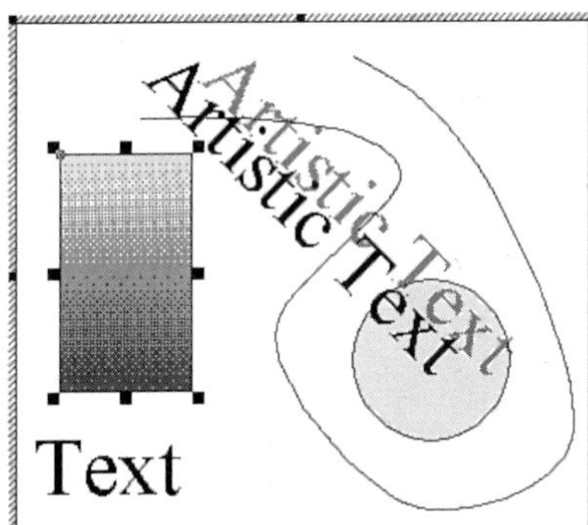

Fig. 22.6
An example of the shapes you can create by using a variety of WP Draw Drawing tools.

In WP Draw, you can choose attributes (such as line width, fill pattern, or font) before you begin drawing shapes or entering text, or you can apply the attributes after you finish creating the shape or text. If you choose attributes before you begin drawing, those attributes apply to all shapes you create (until you change the attributes). If you apply attributes after drawing, you select the shapes or text to which you want to assign the attributes.

You can select attributes by using the Attribute tools or the Attribute options in the Format menu in the WP Draw Menu bar. The Attribute tools provide basic choices; the Attributes menu options provide more specific choices.

For more information on changing attributes, see "Changing the Shape Attributes" later in this chapter.

Using the Drawing Tools

The Drawing tools are located in the Tool palette on the left side of the WP Draw screen. Each Drawing tool has a specific use, but some tools have more than one function. You can draw a rectangle or a perfect square with the Rectangle tool, for example, and you can draw an oval or a perfect circle with the Ellipse tool. To use a tool, you must first click it with the mouse.

The drawing tools are grouped into five categories: QuickArt, Charts, Text, Closed Shapes, and Lines. To select a specific tool from each group, click and hold down the mouse over the group tool you want. A fly-out menu will appear with the different choices for each group.

Here are the different tools in each group:

Tool name	Function
QuickArt	Inserts a WordPerfect QuickArt graphic.
Charts	Inserts a data chart in the default style.
Text	Choose either line (artistic) text, or a text box.
Closed shapes	Rectangle, rounded rectangle, circle, ellipse, polygon, and closed curve.
Line	Line, curve, and freehand tools.

As you select a tool, the mouse pointer appears as an arrow. When you move to the drawing area, the mouse pointer changes to a crosshair or a hand with a box.

Using the Mouse and Keyboard To Draw

The following information describes the general procedures for drawing with the mouse and the keyboard. The descriptions of these procedures assume that you use the default left mouse button. You need a mouse to draw an object, but you can control drawing by using the mouse and the keyboard together.

Drawing with the Left Mouse Button

Depending on which shape on the Drawing Tools palette you have selected to draw, you can use one of three general procedures to create the shape with the mouse:

- To create rectangles, rounded rectangles, ellipses, and elliptical arcs, and to define the area for a chart, figure, and text, press and hold the left mouse button and drag the mouse pointer from one corner to the opposite corner of the drawing.
- To create lines, polygons, closed curves, and curves, click the left mouse button for each corner or change in direction and double-click the mouse to end. If you want to completely start over before you double-click, press Esc. To remove a corner or change in direction, press Backspace.
- For freehand drawing, press and hold the left mouse button and drag the mouse pointer across the drawing area. When you release the mouse button, the drawing is completed.

Moving the Shape with the Right Mouse Button

If you are in the middle of drawing a shape and want to reposition the location of the shape, press and hold the right mouse button and drag the shape to the new location.

Deleting with Esc and Backspace

When you draw lines, polygons, closed curves, and curves, if you want to completely start over before you finish the shape, press Esc. To remove the last click action of the mouse that created a corner or change in direction, press Backspace.

To remove a shape immediately after you create it, choose **E**dit, **U**ndo; or press Ctrl+Z. This technique works only if you have not pressed any other keys or performed any other function since you created the shape.

Constraining the Shape with Shift

To draw a straight vertical, horizontal, or 45-degree line or polygon edge, hold down Shift before you click or drag the mouse. To create a square, rounded square, circle, or radius of a circle, hold down Shift when using the Rectangle, Rounded Rectangle, Ellipse, or Elliptical Arc tools or options.

◄ See "Using the Mouse," p. 17

Troubleshooting

WP Draw takes forever to start, or won't start at all.

WordPerfect uses OLE 2.0 to accomplish switching transparently between its different modules. OLE is a powerful tool, but has steep RAM requirements. Machines with less than 8MB of memory usually exhibit poor performance when using OLE 2.0. If WP Draw is slow starting, or fails to start, you may need more memory in your computer. Sometimes you can get around this by closing other applications you don't need at the moment. Exiting Windows and restarting also can free up system resources and get you going.

I get an "out of memory" or "application" error when I try to run WP Draw. Why?

These kinds of errors can be caused by running low on system resources. If you've been using Windows for a while, or you have a large number of documents or applications open, you may simply have exhausted Windows supply of memory. To find out, switch to the Program Manager and choose **H**elp, **A**bout from the menu. If your system resources are less than about 30 percent, save your work and then exit and restart Windows. This will refresh the available resources.

Drawing a Shape

After you start WP Draw, you can draw lines, rectangles, ellipses, curves, and add figures. You can even use the mouse as a crayon and draw freehand. If you don't have the time to create your own drawings, you can choose from over 100 figures from WordPerfect or from thousands of clip art figures available on the market.

A figure is a drawing you have created and saved from a graphic program or a figure that was created by someone else (also called clip art). You can save a graphic in WP Draw as a figure by itself; click the Save button in the Toolbar.

Drawing a Line

The Line tool allows you to draw a straight line. If you want to change the line into an arrow, choose **F**ormat, Li**n**e Attributes and choose **B**eginning, **E**nding, or B**o**th Ends under **A**rrowhead in the Line Options area to draw the arrowhead at the first point, the last point, or both ends, respectively.

To draw a line or polygon, follow these steps:

1. Select the Line tool from the Drawing tools.

2. Move the crosshair mouse pointer to the beginning of the line.
3. Click the left mouse button to begin the line or border.
4. Move the crosshair mouse pointer to the end of the line and double-click.

To create straight vertical or horizontal lines or to create a line with a 45-degree angle, hold down Shift before you double-click in step 4.

Drawing Lines, Polygons, Curves, and Closed Curves

In addition to drawing straight lines, you can draw a line with multiple changes in direction. You can draw other shapes that have multiple sides as well. These shapes include polygons, closed curves, and curves.

◄ See "Using Graphics Lines," p. 264

◄ See "Using Graphics Borders," p. 268

A *polygon* is a multiple-sided enclosed shape such as a triangle, pentagon, or hexagon. You can fill the polygon or leave it empty with only the border showing. Squares and rectangles are polygons, but WP Draw provides the Rectangle and Rounded Rectangle tools to help you draw those shapes.

The current line color and line pattern applies to curves as well as lines and become the border of polygons, closed curves, and other shapes. You can change the fill pattern, fill color, and turn the fill attribute on or off. For more information on this technique, see the "Filling Solids" section later in this chapter.

To draw a multiple-sided line, curve, polygon, or closed curve, follow these steps:

1. Select one of the following tools:

   Line

   Curve

   Polygon

   Closed Curve

2. Position the crosshair pointer where you want to begin drawing the line or shape and click the left mouse button.

3. Move the crosshair pointer to the position where you want to place the second point of the shape.

4. Click the left mouse button to begin the next side of the shape or a change in direction for the line (see fig. 22.7).

5. Repeat steps 3 and 4 for each change in direction of the line or side of the polygon.

6. Double-click the mouse for the last point of the line or polygon.

When you are drawing lines and polygons, to create straight vertical or horizontal lines or to create a line with a 45-degree angle, hold down Shift before you draw the line in step 3.

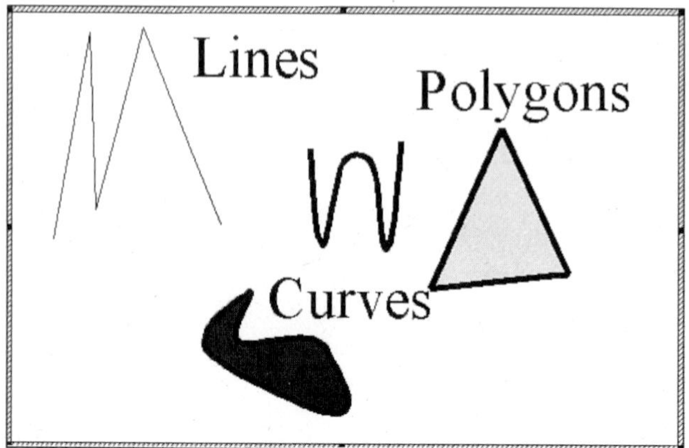

Fig. 22.7 Click the left mouse button to indicate a change in direction when you draw lines, curves, closed curves, and polygons. If you click in the wrong place, press Backspace. Press Esc to erase the shape.

Drawing Rectangles, Arcs, and Ellipses

◀ See "Changing Table Lines, Borders, and Fills," p. 552

◀ See "Creating the Chart," p. 570

A *rectangle* is a four-sided polygon. An *ellipse* is a shape with no corners. Ovals and circles are examples of ellipses. An *arc* is a portion of an ellipse's border. In WP Draw, you use the same technique to draw rectangles, ellipses, and arcs.

Note

You can use the Polygon tool to create a rectangle, but you have only your "eye" to vertically and horizontally align such a rectangle. When you print the rectangle, it may not be perfectly parallel to the sides of the paper. To help you draw rectangles that are parallel to the sides of the paper, use the WP Draw Rectangle tool and the Rounded rectangle tool.

To draw a rectangle, arc, or ellipse (as shown in fig. 22.8), follow these steps:

1. Select one of the following tools:

    Rectangle

    Rounded Rectangle

    Ellipse

    Elliptical Arc

2. Position the crosshair pointer where you want to begin the shape.
3. Press and hold the left mouse button, and drag the crosshair pointer toward the position where you want to create the opposite corner of the shape. An outline of the shape appears as you drag the mouse.
4. When the crosshair pointer reaches the position where you want the opposite corner of the shape, release the mouse button. The screen displays the completed shape.

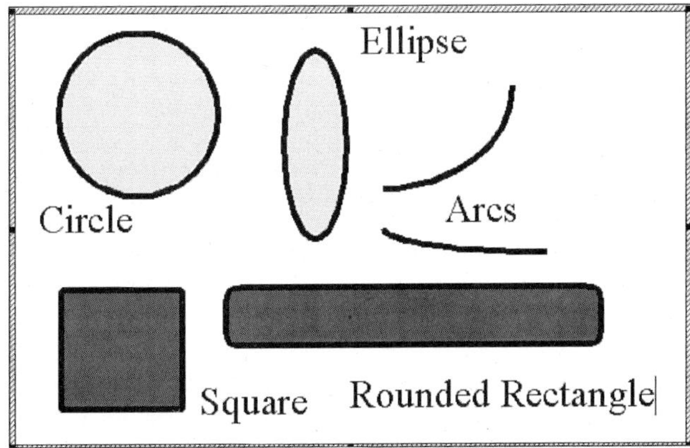

Fig. 22.8
Hold down Shift when you draw an ellipse to turn it into a circle. Use the circle tool to draw a circle from the center out. With a square, hold down Shift while you draw the rectangle.

Drawing Squares and Circles

A *square* is a rectangle that is of equal length on all sides. In WP draw, a *circle* is an ellipse in which all points of the border are an equal distance from the center point.

You use the same tools and techniques to draw a square or circle that you use to draw a rectangle or ellipse, except you hold down the Shift key as you draw.

Tip
Although you can draw rectangles with the Polygon tool, use the Rectangle or Rounded Rectangle tool if you want the rectangle's sides to be exactly horizontal and vertical.

Drawing Freehand

Using the Freehand tool is similar to drawing with a colored pencil. If you are a good artist and skilled at using the mouse, you can draw fairly sophisticated shapes in WP Draw.

To draw a freehand shape, follow these steps:

1. Select the Freehand tool.
2. Hold the mouse button down as you drag the crosshair across the drawing area to draw the shape.
3. Release the mouse button when you finish drawing the shape.

Retrieving and Positioning Clip Art

Most of us are not artists and are too unskilled with the mouse to create anything except crude drawings with the Freehand tool. Luckily for us, great libraries of clip art (or pre-drawn art) are available, including a number of figures that come with WordPerfect.

If you installed WordPerfect to the default directories, clip art is located in the C:\OFFICE\WPWIN\GRAPHICS directory. This directory contains well over 100 figures that you can place in your document directly through the Graphics Figure features (see Chapter 7, "Integrating Text and Graphics," and Chapter 21, "Using Advanced Graphics Techniques"). If you want to modify the clip art, you can bring the figure into WP Draw and change it.

To add clip art to your drawing within WP Draw, as shown in figure 22.9, follow these steps:

1. Select the QuickArt tool.
2. Move the mouse pointer into the drawing area; the pointer becomes a hand with a rectangle.
3. Drag the pointer from one corner of the area where you want to place the graphic to the opposite corner.
4. Release the mouse button; the Insert Figure dialog box appears (see fig. 22.10).
5. If necessary, change the Drives and Directories boxes to show the graphics directory. If you installed WordPerfect 6.1 for Windows in the default location, the graphics are in the C:\OFFICE\WPWIN\GRAPHICS directory.

Fig. 22.9
This picture shows the flying figures available from the C:\OFFICE\WPWIN\GRAPHICS directory. As you drag the mouse pointer, a dotted line appears where the new figure will appear.

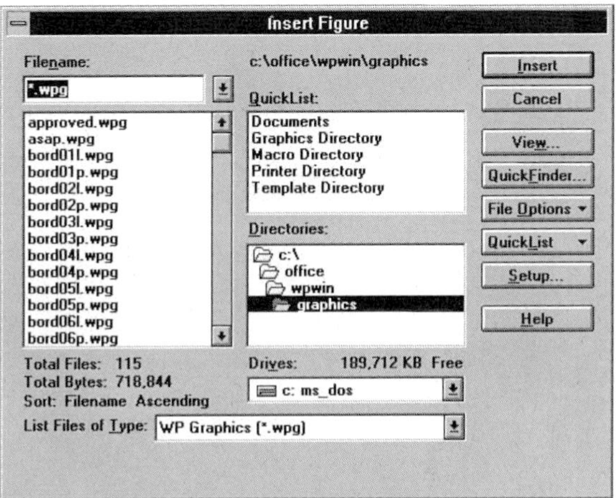

Fig. 22.10
Well over 100 clip art files come with WordPerfect. Scroll to the file you want in the File**n**ame list box.

6. If you have other clip art or different programs, you can change the file type in the List Files Of **T**ype pop-up list.

7. Select the name of the file by typing the file name in the File**n**ame text box or by choosing from the scroll list box. If you want to look at the graphic before you use it, choose the Vie**w** button.

8. When you have selected the file for the graphic that you want to use, choose **I**nsert.

◄ See "Retrieving a Graphics Image," p. 727

► See "Finding Files," p. 965

Note

An alternative way to bring a figure into the drawing area is to choose **I**nsert F**i**le, and then choose the figure's name from the Insert File dialog box. When you bring in a figure this way, you can edit individual pieces of the figure. For example, you can change colors on the butterfly's wings. When you use the Figure tool to retrieve a figure, the entire figure is grouped together, and you can only edit the entire figure, not portions of the figure. When you drag on the figure, the entire figure moves. To edit portions of such a figure, double-click the figure. A blue-hashed bounding box appears around the figure. During this mode you can edit portions of the figure.

The following is a list of available graphics file types. Next to each file graphics type is its extension:

WP Graphics (*.wpg)
AutoCAD (*.dxf)
Bitmaps (*.bmp)
Computer Graphics Metafiles (*.cgm)
Micrografx Draw/Designer (*.drw)
Adobe Illustrator/Encapsulated Postscript (*.eps)
HP Graphics Language (*.hpg)
Lotus PIC (*.pic)
Macintosh PICT (*.*)
PC Paintbrush (*.pcx)
Tagged Image Format (*.tif)
Truevision Targa (*.tga)
Windows Metafiles (*.wmf)
WordPerfect Masters (*.mst)
WordPerfect Presentations (*.shw)

Be certain that any clip art you purchase has one of the above file type formats available. Although you can retrieve and work with these file types in WP Draw, the best graphics type for editing is WordPerfect's own graphic file type, WPG.

Inserting a Chart into Your Drawing

As a rule, the easiest way to enter chart edit mode from WordPerfect is through the Chart button on the Toolbar or through the **G**raphics, Cha**r**t menu. You also can insert a chart into a WP Draw drawing, however, if you want to combine the chart with drawing shapes or figures.

To insert a chart into the drawing, follow these steps:

1. Double-click the drawing to display the drawing in WP Draw.
2. Choose the Chart tool.

3. Move the mouse pointer into the drawing area; the pointer becomes a hand with a rectangle.
4. Press and hold the left mouse button and drag the pointer from one corner of the graphic area to the opposite corner; release the mouse button. You are in the Create Chart dialog box.
5. Choose a chart type from the Chart Options section and choose OK; or choose the Gallery command button and then choose a chart type. The Datasheet will appear along with a chart in the default type.

◀ See "Creating the Chart," p. 570

◀ See "Changing the Appearance of the Chart," p. 576

◀ See "Changing the Underlying Data," p. 573

See Chapter 17, "Creating and Modifying Charts with WP Draw," for more instructions on making charts.

Editing a Figure

After you retrieve a figure or draw any of the shapes available with WP Draw, you may want to edit or delete all or parts of the drawing. If you want to change the attributes, see the section, "Changing the Shape Attributes" later in this chapter.

Selecting an Item

Before you can change an item such as a drawn shape or an imported figure, you first must select the shape or figure.

To select an item, follow these steps:

1. Choose the Select tool.

2. Click the item to select it (see figs. 22.11 and 22.12).

Fig. 22.11
When you select an item in the drawing window, small black selection markers surround the item.

3. If you want to select more than one item, hold down Ctrl and click another item.

Fig. 22.12
When you select more than one item, the black selection markers surround all objects and a small white rectangle appears next to each item selected.

You can select all items by choosing **E**dit, **S**elect, **A**ll or by clicking the right mouse button and choosing Select All.

Deleting an Item

After you have selected an item or items, you can delete them by pressing Delete. If you accidentally delete the wrong item, immediately choose **E**dit, **U**ndo; or press Ctrl+Z.

If you want to delete everything in the drawing area, choose **E**dit, C**l**ear; or press Ctrl+Shift+F4. At the Clear Drawing dialog box prompt, choose OK.

Moving an Item

If you have one or more items selected, you can move the selection.

To move items, follow these steps:

1. Select the item or items to move.
2. Press and hold the left mouse button and drag the mouse pointer from the center of one of the items.
3. As you drag, a gray outline of the shape moves with the mouse pointer.
4. Release the mouse when the item or items are in the proper position.

> **Note**
>
> If you are moving a single item, you can select and move the item in one step by dragging the item. If you try to move multiple items and they become unselected, you did not drag from the inside of one of the selected items.

Copying an Item

You can repeat an item on the same drawing, copy it to another drawing, copy it to a document within WordPerfect, or even copy the item to another program. The following sections explain the techniques for accomplishing these tasks in WP Draw.

Copying within the Drawing Area

To create a copy of an item within the same drawing, follow these steps:

1. Choose the Select tool.

2. Position the mouse pointer on the item you want to copy.
3. Hold down the Ctrl key and the left mouse button, and drag from the item to copy to the location for the copy's new position.

Copying to Another Document or Program

To copy an item directly to a document, follow these steps:

◄ See "Transferring Selected Text to Another Location," p. 109

1. Select an item on your drawing.
2. Choose **E**dit, **C**opy; or press Ctrl+C. Windows copies the item to the Clipboard.

3. Move to the document (within a program that accepts items from the Clipboard) by using Alt+Tab or Ctrl+Esc to go to the Task List.

4. Position the insertion point where you want to place the copy of the item.

5. Choose **E**dit, **P**aste from the menu bar in the new program.

> **Note**
>
> If the application you are pasting the WP Draw object into supports OLE, you can choose Paste **S**pecial from the **E**dit menu, then choose WP Draw 3.0 Drawing Object. This will paste the graphic as a WP Draw OLE object, which you can edit by double-clicking.

Changing the Size and Shape

You can make an object larger or smaller by dragging one of the black selection markers surrounding the object.

If you change only the width or height of a graphic image, you can significantly alter the proportions of the figure or shape (see fig. 22.13).

Fig. 22.13 You can create special effects by changing the width or height of an item. This example uses a widened figure (TIGER_J.WPG) and heightened text.

You also can alter the size, shape, and orientation of a selected figure by the following methods:

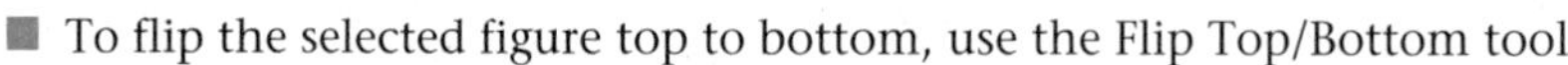

- To flip the selected figure top to bottom, use the Flip Top/Bottom tool.

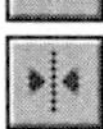

- To flip the selected figure to a mirror image, use the Flip Left/Right tool.

- To rotate the selected figure, choose **E**dit, R**o**tate and drag one of the selection markers.

◄ See "Editing a Graphics Image," p. 729

- If two items are stacked on top of each other, select one and choose **G**raphics, **O**rder, **F**ront to bring the select item in front of the other item, or choose **G**raphics, **O**rder, **B**ack to move the selected item behind the other item.

Changing the Shape Attributes

You can apply attributes such as colors and patterns to shapes before or after you create the shapes. If you select attributes before drawing the shapes, the attributes apply to all shapes you subsequently draw. To modify existing shapes, select the shape(s), and then change attributes. These changes affect only the shapes you selected; they do not affect non-selected shapes or shapes you draw later.

You can change an attribute with an attribute tool, or for more choices, you can change an attribute through the Fo**r**mat menu.

Applying Color

You can use a number of methods to apply color to a shape. WP Draw offers two color palettes as well as the **C**olor Attributes menu choice on the Fo**r**mat menu. You also can define colors from options on dialog boxes for line, fill, text, and shadow.

The easiest way to change colors is through the Line Color palette and the Fill Color palette. In WP Draw, *line color* refers to the color for lines, curves, elliptical arcs, and freehand drawing; the term also refers to the border surrounding closed curves, polygons, ellipses, and rounded rectangles. You can fill the area inside the border with a different color or colored pattern, referred to as *fill color*.

◄ See "Printing Documents with Graphics or Color," p. 299

► See "Using Color," p. 795

► See "Printing in Color," p. 803

Using the Color Palettes

To change the line color, follow these steps:

1. Click the Line Color tool; the current color palette appears.

2. Click the color you want to use for the line or border.

To change the fill color, follow these steps:

1. Click the Fill Color tool; the current color palette appears.

2. Click the color or colored pattern you want to use to fill your shapes.

Using More Options to Change Colors

If you select a pattern other than a solid for your shapes, the pattern can have two colors. One portion of the pattern (for example, the lines) is the foreground color and the other portion of the pattern (for example, the space between the lines) is the background color.

When you select the Fill Color palette, you can change the foreground color with the left mouse button and the background color with the right mouse button. To have more options for line and text colors, follow these steps:

1. Choose Fo**r**mat, **C**olor Attributes; the Color Attributes dialog box appears (see fig. 22.14).

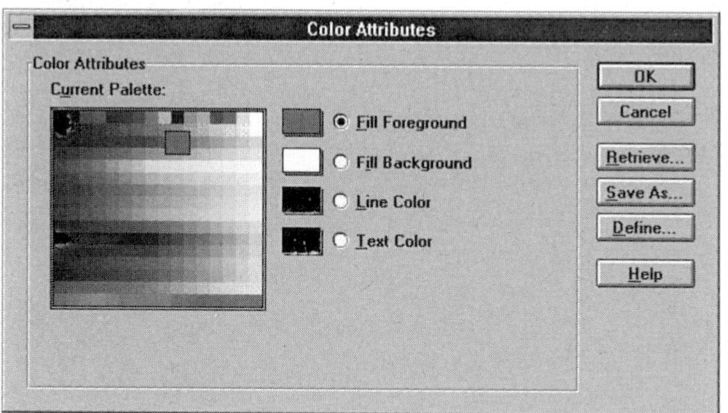

Fig. 22.14
The current choice for the selected option button (in this example, the Fill Foreground button) displays as an enlarged square.

2. If you saved a different color palette earlier (through the Save As command button), choose the **R**etrieve command button and select the appropriate color palette file name and choose OK to return to the Color Attributes dialog box.

3. Select one of the following option buttons:

   Fill Foreground for the patterned part of fill.

   F**i**ll Background for the other background part of fill.

   Line Color to change line or border colors.

   Text Color to change the color of text.

4. If you do not see the color you want on the current palette, choose the **D**efine command button to display the Define Color Palette dialog box (see fig. 22.15).

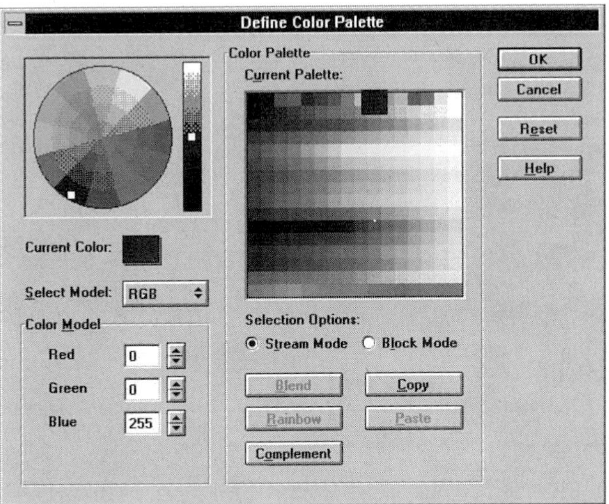

Fig. 22.15
In the Define Color Palette dialog box, a color wheel appears and the current color is displayed in a box under the color wheel.

5. Click the color in the Current Palette area that you want to change.

6. Change the current color by changing to one of the color model types (**R**GB - Red Green Blue; **H**LS - Hue Lightness Saturation; **C**MYK - Cyan Magenta Yellow Black) and by changing the values for each of the portions of the color models. You also can change the current palette by changing the Selection Options section below the palette. If you want more description on these options on the Define Color Palette dialog box, choose the **H**elp command button.

7. Repeat steps 5 and 6 for every color you want to change in the C**u**rrent Palette.

8. When you finish making your selections, choose one of the following:

   OK to save the changes.

   Cancel to ignore the changes.

   R**e**set to return the current palette to the default palette.

9. After you return to the Color Attributes dialog box, you can save your change to a palette name. Click the **S**ave As command button and

select a file name and directory for your palette. You need not add the extension; WP Draw automatically adds a PRC extension to your file name.

10. Choose OK to return to the drawing.

Filling Solids

As mentioned earlier, you can create a patterned fill for a solid, have an empty fill for the solid, or turn off the border for the solid.

To change the pattern for solids, follow these steps:

1. Click the Fill Attributes tool. The expanded Pattern palette appears.
2. Click one of the displayed patterns (see fig. 22.16). If you have a color monitor, the current pattern is surrounded by a red box.

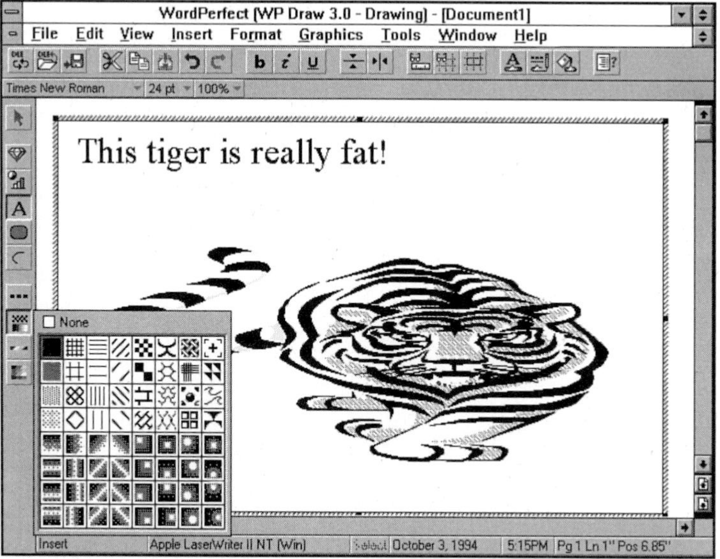

Fig. 22.16
In addition to the None choice, the pattern palette shows 64 different patterns.

> **Note**
>
> In addition to using the Pattern palette, you can change the pattern by choosing Format, Fill Attributes; a dialog box appears that enables you to change from pattern to gradient (a gradient ranges from a pattern to no pattern) and change the shape of the gradient. You also can change the background and foreground colors, as you did in the Attributes Color dialog box.

When your shape is a closed curve, polygon, ellipse, rectangle, or rounded rectangle, you have the choice of turning the border on or off around the shape, or you can turn the fill on or off. If the fill is off, your image shows only the border for the shape.

Click the Line Attributes tool and select *none* to turn the border on or off.

Click the Fill Attributes tool and select *none* to turn the fill on or off.

Changing the Line or Border Pattern

As mentioned above, when you change the line color, the change also affects the border surrounding solids. The same is true for the line pattern.

To change the line pattern, follow these steps:

1. Click the Line Attributes tool. The expanded Line Style palette appears.

2. Click one or more of the options on the Line Attributes palette (see fig. 22.17).

   ◄ See "Customizing Lines," p. 706

   Choose the **N**o Line check box to have no line show around solid shapes.

   Choose Line Options on the left side of the box to change the Line **W**idth.

   Choose one of the 16 **S**tyle options to change the line pattern.

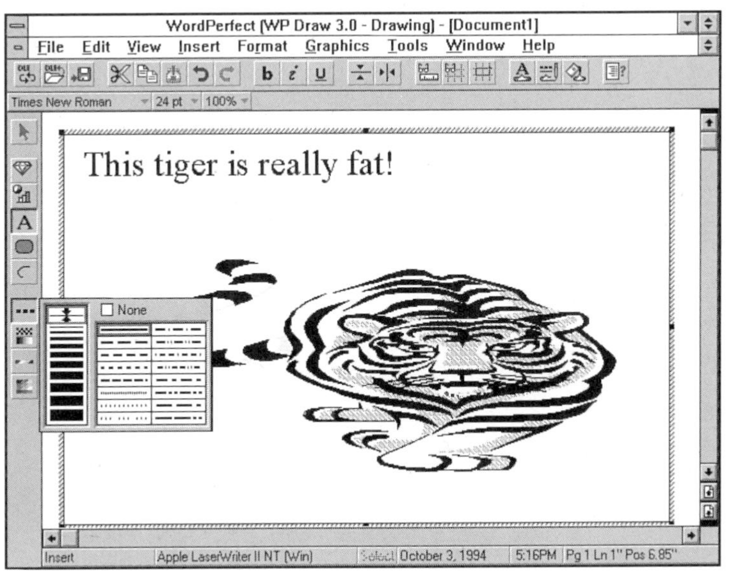

Fig. 22.17
The Line Attribute palette gives you three choices: none, 10 values of line thickness, and 16 values of line patterns.

◀ See "Changing the Appearance of the Chart," p. 576

◀ See "Customizing Borders," p. 714

You also can change the line color, thickness, and style from the F**o**rmat, Li**n**e Attributes menu selection. You can select an exact line thickness by typing a value in the Line **W**idth text box. In addition to the color, thickness, and style, you can select one or two arrowheads for your lines from the **A**rrowhead pop-up list.

Using Text in WP Draw

One of the frustrating aspects of working with graphics in prior releases of WordPerfect was the difficulty of placing text on a drawing. WordPerfect came with a number of diagrams to add text, but you had to work with advanced typesetting and graphics commands to line up the text with the graphic. Adding text to graphics is greatly simplified with WP Draw.

Adding Text to the Drawing

After you select the location for your text within a drawing, adding text to a graphic is just like adding text to a document.

To add text to your drawing, follow these steps:

1. Click the Text tool.
2. Position the mouse crosshair pointer in the upper-left corner of where you want the text to start.
3. Hold down the left mouse button and drag the mouse pointer from the upper-left corner of where you want text to appear to the lower-right corner. A text box appears on-screen.
4. Type text and place formatting characters within the text box.
5. When you finish typing the text, click outside the text box or click another drawing tool.

Using Common Text Features

Many of the text features available in WordPerfect for Windows also are available in WP Draw (see table 22.1). These features are covered throughout "Part I: Basic Tasks." For example, to delete or change the format of existing text, first select the text box, highlight the text with the mouse, and type the new text or add a format such as Ctrl+B for bold. The procedures are essentially the same for text within a WP Draw drawing. Any of the text formatting commands available from the Toolbar will affect your text in WP Draw.

Table 22.1 Text features available in WP Draw

Feature	Shortcut Keys	Description
Font	F9	Change font face, style, size, appearance, and attributes (color, pattern)
Normal	Ctrl+N	Change back to no changes in appearance
Bold	Ctrl+B	Bold selected text or type bold text
Italic	Ctrl+I	Italicize selected text or enter italicized text
Date	Ctrl+D or Ctrl+Shift+D	Place current date as text or a code
S**e**arch/Replace	F2	Find and/or replace existing text
Layout	**C**enter - Shift+F7 **F**lush Right - Alt+F7 **I**ndent - F7 Back Tab - Shift+Tab	Change line position of text
Advance		Move text a specified distance from insertion point
Justification		Change document justification to **L**eft, **R**ight, or **C**enter
S**p**eller	Ctrl+F1	Spell check the diagram
Thesaurus	Alt+F1	Look for a word
WP Characters	Ctrl+W	Add a special character such as a bullet, copyright symbol, or foreign letter

◀ See "Revising and Editing Text," p. 89

◀ See "Formatting Characters," p. 130

◀ See "Accessing Special Characters," p. 682

◀ See "Understanding WordPerfect and Windows Font Management," p. 670

▶ See "Choosing Fonts," p. 786

Wrapping Text Around an Object

If you want to mold your text into a non-linear shape, you can use WP Draw's new contour text capability. To change the shape of your text line, follow these steps:

1. Enter the text you want to contour.

2. Using one of the drawing tools, such as line or circle, draw the shape to which you want your text to conform.

3. Select your text.

4. Select the graphics object you drew. Figure 22.18 shows a line and text after both items have been selected.

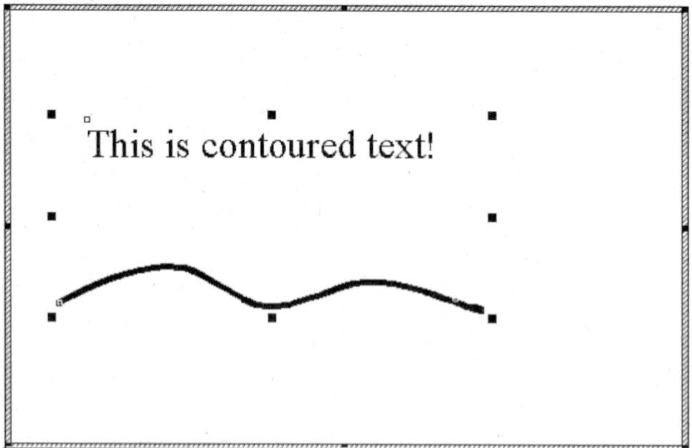

Fig. 22.18
Selected text and a graphics object that are about to be contoured.

5. From the menu bar, choose **G**raphics, Contour **T**ext. The Contour Text dialog box appears (see fig. 22.19).

   WP Draw allows you to specify where the text will be positioned in association with the selected graphics object. Choose **P**osition to select one of the following options: Top **L**eft, Top **C**enter, Top **R**ight, **B**ottom Left, B**o**ttom Center, and Bo**t**tom Right. These selections allow you to place your text on the top or bottom of the selected graphics object and also place your text left, right, or center justified on the graphics object. The default Position is Top Left.

   The option Displa**y** Text Only determines whether you will be able to see the graphics object used to contour the text. The default option is On, which means the graphics object will not be visible after you have performed the contour operation. If Displa**y** Text Only is not selected, you see both the contoured text and the graphics object.

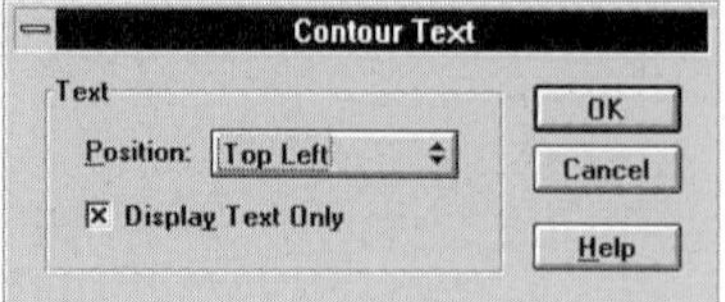

Fig. 22.19
The Contour Text dialog box allows you to specify how the text is contoured to the selected graphics object.

6. Accept the default options from the Contour Text dialog box. Your text appears as shown in figure 22.20.

To undo the contour, choose **G**raphics, **S**traighten Text.

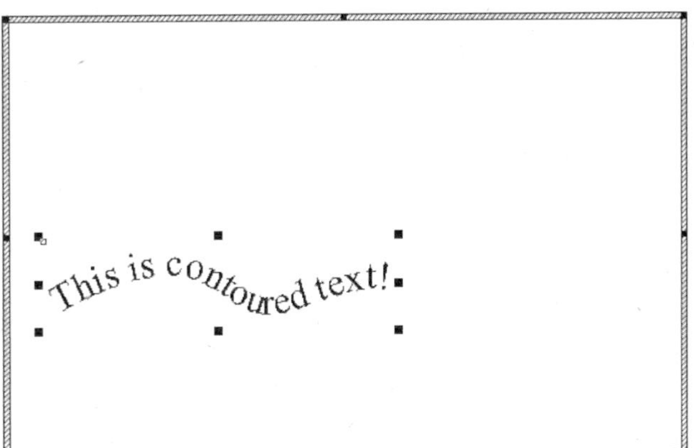

Fig. 22.20
Your text after using the default options of **P**osition Top Left and Displa**y** Text Only from the Contour Text dialog box.

Scanning or Capturing an Image into WP Draw

If you have a scanner and scanner program or video capture board, you can bring a copy of a photograph, typeset image, or still frame from video into your documents.

Selecting the Image Source

You must tell WP Draw what kind of scanner or video capture hardware you have. You need to select it only once; it will remain defined for all your WordPerfect sessions. To select the image source, choose **I**nsert, **S**elect Image Source. The Select Source dialog box appears, as shown in figure 22.21. Choose the device in the Source box, and click the Select command button.

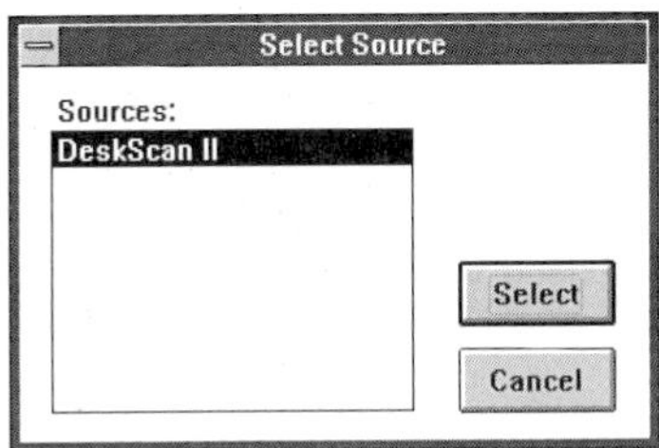

Fig. 22.21
The Select Source dialog box shows the name or names of your TWAIN software in the Sources section.

Acquiring the Image

After you select the source, you can capture an image by following these steps:

1. Place the photograph or object on the scanner, or cue up the videotape or laser disc if you are capturing from video.

2. Choose **I**nsert, Ac**q**uire Image. WP Draw brings up the TWAIN capture interface for the device you selected.

3. Complete the procedure for capturing the image according to the software instructions. The dialog box that appears depends on your software.

> **Note**
>
> WordPerfect uses the TWAIN interface for image capture. This means you see the same window and controls no matter which program you're using to acquire the image. If you can capture in CorelDRAW! or Photoshop, you can capture in WordPerfect.

Adding the Drawing to Your WordPerfect Document

◀ See "Customizing Graphics Boxes," p. 719

◀ See "Editing a Graphics Image," p. 729

▶ See "Printing Graphics," p. 802

After you finish creating and editing your drawing, you need to switch back from WP Draw and place the drawing in your WordPerfect document.

To place the drawing in your document, simply click anywhere else on the page to deselect the drawing.

When the drawing is in your document, you can use the procedures in Chapter 21, "Using Advanced Graphics Techniques" to resize, delete, and move the drawing around the document.

Using TextArt

TextArt is a module that WordPerfect has added to WordPerfect 6.1 for Windows. You can use TextArt to create company logos and display heads for your documents quickly and easily. TextArt enables you to change fonts, type styles, and alignment of the text on-screen; but more importantly, TextArt enables you to distort and modify the text so it conforms to various shapes. You also can add a shadow, use different outlines and fills, and resize the text in TextArt.

After creating the text, you can save the text in a file for use later, place it in a WordPerfect document in a movable frame, or insert it in a graphics box for a different effect such as a Watermark box.

Understanding the Tools

Figure 22.22 shows the TextArt interface. The TextArt menu and font formatting tools work similarly to those in WordPerfect. Choose the menu and then the command, or choose the drop-down Font or Style box and choose from the list. Additionally, you can click one of the text alignment buttons to apply that alignment to the text.

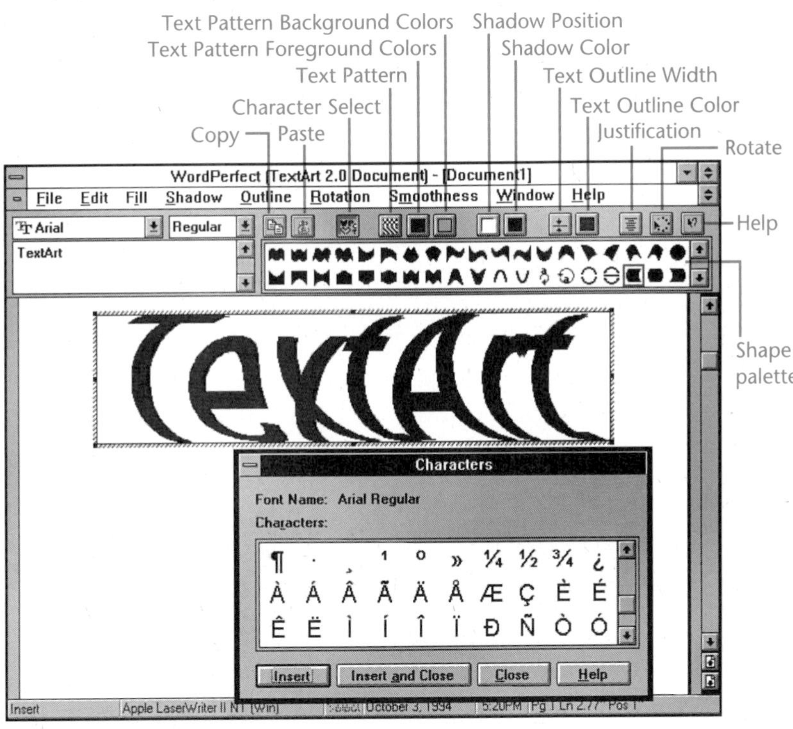

Fig. 22.22
You can add up to three lines of text—58 characters—to use in TextArt.

Tip
The more text you enter on one line, the more distorted the text becomes. Use short lines of text when possible.

To enter text for formatting, click the mouse in text box and type your text. The sample box illustrates the text you enter and the formatting. You don't have to select the text to apply formatting to it; TextArt applies any formatting you choose to all text in the text box.

Tip

Move the mouse pointer to any tool, and TextArt displays a brief description of the tool in the message bar.

After you enter the text, you can use the TextArt tools to change the shape, color, size, and so on. You also can change the font, style, and alignment at any time. TextArt will automatically redraw each time you make a change.

Following are brief descriptions of each of the tools in the TextArt module:

- *Copy.* Copies the text to the Clipboard.
- *Paste.* Pastes the text onto the screen.
- *Character Select.* Displays the character set in the character select dialog box. Use this to access characters not readily available from the keyboard like a copyright symbol.
- *Shape palette.* Choose a shape in which to mold the text; some fonts look better with certain shapes, so try several fonts when you find a shape you like. Figure 22.23 illustrates text molded in one of the shapes.

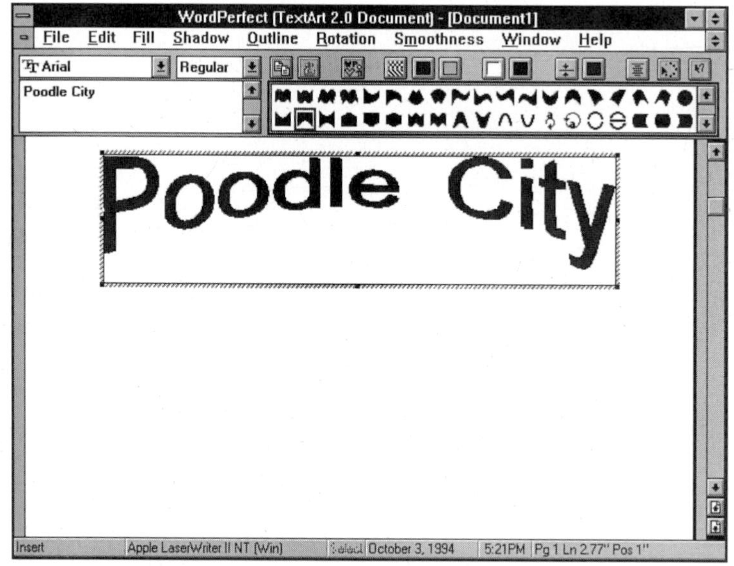

Fig. 22.23
The logo uses the Arial bold font in a TextArt shape; the Width is 5 inches, and height is 3 inches. The simple font keeps the text readable even in the flowing envelope.

- *Text Pattern.* Change the fill pattern used in the text.
- *Text Pattern Foreground and Background Colors.* Specify the colors used in the text fill pattern.
- *Shadow Position.* Control the location and offset of the shadow.
- *Shadow Color.* Specify the color used to create the text shadow (see fig. 22.24).

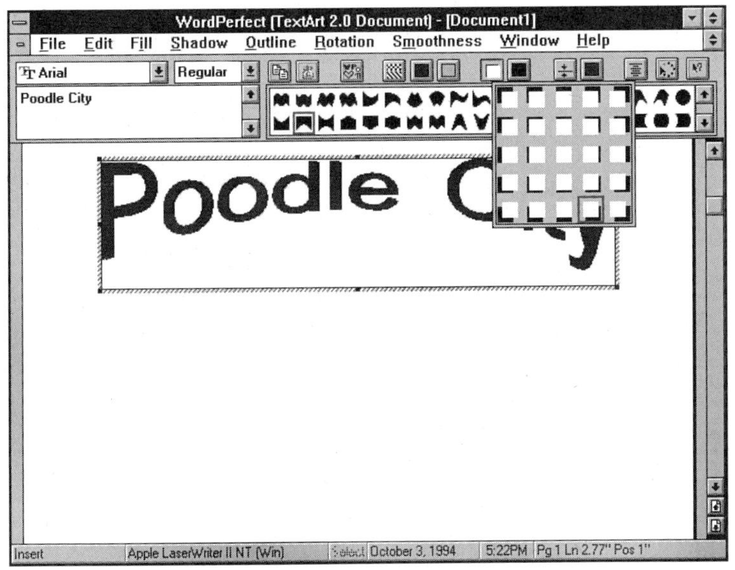

Fig. 22.24
Use the arrows in the Shadow Color button to adjust the shadow color.

- *Outline Width.* Choose whether you want an outline (left button) and if so, the thickness of the outline (right button).
- *Outline Color.* Specify the color of the text outline.
- *Justification.* Choose left, right, or centered.
- *Rotation.* Rotate the text from 0 to 360 degrees. Figure 22.25 illustrates text in an envelope rotated to 65 degrees.
- *Help.* Context-sensitive help. Click this button, then on the screen item you want help about.

Tip
Use a white outline if the letters seem too close or crowded.

Saving TextArt

After completing your design in TextArt, you can save your text as a file to use again in TextArt or as a graphic file to use in WordPerfect and other programs.

To save a copy of the text, choose **F**ile, Save **A**s. The Save As dialog box appears. This dialog box works like any other Save As dialog box.

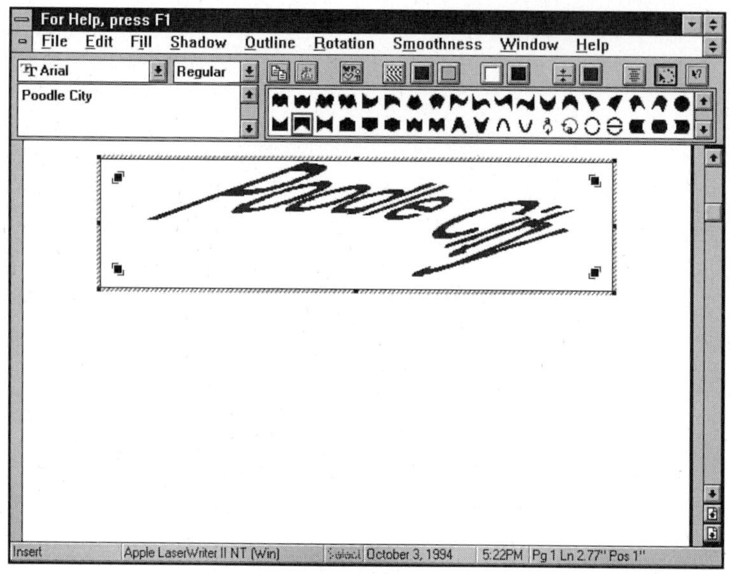

Fig. 22.25
When you rotate text in an envelope, experiment until you get the effect you want.

Using TextArt

Using TextArt is 90 percent experimentation. The more you explore and test the program, the better you will learn how to use it. No one can tell you exactly how to judge the height of text in any certain envelope. You have to explore the possibilities.

To use TextArt, follow these steps:

1. Choose **G**raphics, Te**x**tArt or click the TextArt tool. TextArt's menus and toolbar appear.
2. Type the text in the text box.

   If you need a special character, click Character Select and select the character to insert it in the text box. Choose **I**nsert, and then choose **C**lose.
3. Select a font, style, and alignment for the text.
4. Experiment with the shape envelopes, color, shadow, size, and so on.
5. To save the text, choose **F**ile, Save **A**s. The Save As dialog box appears. Choose the file type options and name the file; then choose OK to return to TextArt.

6. Click in your document to deselect the TextArt object if you want it to appear in the current WordPerfect document.

> **Troubleshooting**
>
> *TextArt creates my text OK, but won't display a shadow behind it.*
>
> Make sure you have a shadow selected with the Shadow Position tool, and make sure it has a color other than white.

From Here...

The addition of WP Draw and TextArt to WordPerfect 6.1 for Windows adds a whole new dimension to creating graphics and enhanced text for your documents. WordPerfect has solved many of the limitations of previous releases of WordPerfect. In your earlier releases if you wanted to edit or create graphics or include enhanced text in your WordPerfect documents, you had to be satisfied with the clip art that came with your program, or buy an additional graphics program. Now WordPerfect 6.1 for Windows will be sufficient for most graphics and special text needs.

- Chapter 4, "Formatting Text," describes the basics of formatting text, including lines and paragraphs.
- Chapter 7, "Integrating Text and Graphics," shows how to combine text and graphics in a document.
- Chapter 21, "Using Advanced Graphics Techniques," discusses using the advanced graphics features and includes editing graphics.

Chapter 23

Desktop Publishing with WordPerfect

by Susan Plumley

With desktop publishing, you can use a personal computer to create attractive, visually interesting, typeset-quality documents. Desktop publishing involves integrating text and graphics on the same page and printing to a high-resolution laser printer or image typesetter. Word processors enable you to enter and edit text; some word processors allow you to format the text and the page for a more professional look than a document created with a typewriter.

A word processor that enables you to accomplish true page layout—design a professional-looking document using various typefaces and type styles, columns, graphic lines, borders, images, and so on—is also a desktop publishing program.

WordPerfect 6.1 for Windows has many features you can use to perform desktop publishing. Among the most important of these features is WYSIWYG (*What-You-See-Is-What-You-Get*), which enables you to view on-screen exactly what will be printed. When you're laying out a page, you have a specific design to follow; you must be able to see the layout develop as you work. In addition, WordPerfect includes many other features that enable you to create a professional-looking document: styles, templates, columns and tables, fonts, various typographic controls, graphics, and advanced printing capabilities. Other chapters introduce many of these features.

This chapter offers guidelines for designing professional-looking documents and shows you how WordPerfect's features can help. You learn how to plan a successful document; lay out a page using design elements such as white space, emphasis, and balance; and refine the page by choosing typefaces, type size, and text alignment.

Color is another important element in desktop publishing. WordPerfect enables you to add color to your document on-screen and to print in color if you have a color printer. This chapter shows you how to use color effectively in your documents.

Finally, this chapter gives you information about printing your documents. Advanced printing techniques used for printing graphics and printing in color are very important for desktop-published documents. The purpose of desktop publishing is to create and print an attractive and interesting message to your audience.

This chapter discusses the following topics:

- Planning margins and columns in a document
- Aligning the text and using line spacing
- Choosing typefaces and type sizes
- Using kerning, letterspacing, and word spacing
- Adding color to your documents
- Printing graphics images
- Printing a document in color

Designing Successful Publications

A successful publication or presentation grabs the reader's attention and holds it. You can attract the reader's attention in a variety of ways: use very large text as an eye-catching headline, display a graphic image that entices the reader, or use color for emphasis.

After attracting the reader, the design of your document can also help sustain attention—although ultimately, it's your message that must maintain the reader's interest.

The first step in designing a professional-looking document is to plan the overall look of the document. How will the text appear—typefaces, type size, columns, text alignment? What graphics elements and images will appear—lines, borders, clip art, scanned art, art created in WP Draw? How do the graphics relate to the text—illustrate, separate, guide the eye, emphasize?

Will you use colors in your document—one, two, or more? If you are using color in your document, what division of color will you use—graphics borders one color, text another?

The next step is to plan each page of the document. Is there a logical sequence to the text and graphics? Does each page relate logically to the whole? Design each page of a document so that it can stand alone but also correspond with the whole. Guide the reader through the document page by page. Add graphics to enhance and reinforce the text. Balance text and graphics elements on the page to entice the reader.

Designing a professional-looking document takes time, experimentation, and the willingness to change what doesn't work. Consider the following points when planning your document:

- *Amount of copy.* Ascertain the amount of text and number of graphics to help you decide the type of document, number of pages, and so on.
- *Type of document.* Decide whether your message is best suited for a newsletter, brochure, flyer, on-screen presentation, or other type of document.
- *Page orientation.* Determine whether the type of document suggests a landscape or portrait orientation. Consider the copy as well as the graphics. If the graphics are taller than they are wide, use a portrait orientation; if the text consists of long paragraphs, it may be more readable using a multicolumn format in a landscape orientation.
- *Size of the document.* Determine document size based on the type of document (flyers are usually 8 1/2-by-11 inches, for example), method of reproduction (laser printer limits paper size), and method of distribution (mailings, for example, have size and weight limits).
- *Number and type of column.* Choose the number and type of columns that best fit the copy and type of document.
- *Type.* Determine typefaces, type size, and type attributes according to design guidelines.
- *Color.* If you can print in color and want to use color in your document, choose the number of colors for the final document and how the colors will be distributed within the document.

Tip
Look at other publications to get ideas for designs. Keep a folder of designs you like and don't like, and refer to them as you plan your documents.

In addition to the physical characteristics of the document, further aesthetic considerations—design guidelines—play a part in the page layout. These guidelines, which apply design principles to page layout, help you make your documents more effective. Consider the following topics when planning your documents in WordPerfect:

- *Consistency.* Whether your document consists of one page or many, you must establish a consistent format. Consistency creates unity in your documents and helps the reader maintain interest in your message. Design elements such as margins, columns, typeface, type size, spacing, and alignment must remain the same throughout your document to create consistency.

- *Emphasis.* You can emphasize certain elements of your document to create an area of interest. Emphasis keeps the document from being monotonous for the reader; too much emphasis can create chaos, however. Emphasize only *one* object—text or graphics—per page.

- *Balance.* Balance the text and graphics in the document to create an even, pleasing, and simple appearance. A balanced document leads the reader logically from topic to topic without distracting jumps in column number, text blocks, or graphic images.

- *Proportion.* Just as balance helps keep a page uniform, so too does proportion. A graphics image or a headline that is too large can overpower the other elements on the page. Keep all elements proportionally equal so that they work together instead of fighting each other for the reader's attention.

- *White Space.* White space—the area of the document that contains no text or graphics—is an important addition to any design. White space provides contrast, emphasis, and a rest for the reader's eyes. Text and graphics that are surrounded by white space have more impact. Margins and *gutters* (the space between columns, and the space between inside margins where pages come together) are the most effective ways of implementing white space; however, other methods include using left-aligned text, spacing between paragraphs, and adding space above and below a headline.

- *Color.* Adding color to a publication can enhance your message, improve readability, and attract attention—or it can create confusion in your document. Use no more than three or four colors per publication. Make sure the colors you use are not too bright or harsh—or too light or dark—to be read comfortably.

◀ See "Formatting Lines and Paragraphs," p. 134

◀ See "Selecting Paper Size and Type," p. 186

◀ See "Using Graphics Lines," p. 264

◀ See "Creating Styles," p. 362

◀ See "Editing Styles," p. 367

◀ See "Newspaper Columns," p. 472

◀ See "Retrieving a Graphics Image," p. 727

Figure 23.1 shows a desktop publication—a newsletter—that employs the design guidelines previously listed. Use the design guidelines listed in this section as you plan your publications and presentations. The remainder of this chapter explores desktop publishing with WordPerfect in more detail.

TRAIL NEWS

A Newsletter Especially for the Bicycle Enthusiast
Spring 1995

New rules of the road

Foremost is the safety of bikers who must share the roads with automobiles. Just as disconcerting is the high incidence of accidents on paths restricted to use by pedestrians, skateboarders, and other bikers. Teaching riding etiquette and designating roads as multi-vehicle highways are inexpensive and practical and can alleviate the majority of hazards bikers face.

Right now the city is drafting a transportation plan, and Ms. Fornos goes on to say:

A Quote

"There isn't one provision to accommodate bikers. Perhaps it's an oversight. Or perhaps it's the lack of bikers in the city council. We can safely assume that the director of the Losantiville Planning Organization doesn't bike (at least, not outdoors)."

We need to think about doing something to reverse the current situation ... now that we have the name of a giant corporation backing us...

You want irony? Try this bit of information: according to The Daily Microcosm's Anna Fornos, a city which sponsors three annual cycling events and supports the county's alternative transportation program, there is not a single bike lane. We need to think about doing something to reverse the current situation. And now that we have the name of a giant corporation backing us, there's no reason to remain silent regarding the lack of bicycle and pedestrian facilities in our community.

So if it's someone with legislative pull we need, we can go straight to the governor's office and find a state bicycle coordinator. With some pressure she will work with local governments to apportion some road money to non-highway programs. But unless we speak up, we'll go unnoticed.

Fig. 23.1
When designing a document, use guidelines such as consistency, emphasis, white space, and balance, as in this example.

Planning the Page

To create an effective publication or presentation, you must lay some groundwork. First, decide what you want to communicate. What is the purpose of your document? Do you want to sell, inform, announce, or explain? Who is your audience? Customers, potential customers, employees? Consider the type of document—is the final output a brochure for a few people, or a flyer mailed to thousands?

The next step is to write the text and select or create graphics—images, tables, spreadsheets, and so on—that support the text. When you are satisfied with the content of the document, you are ready to begin planning the page.

You must consider many factors when planning the page. Physical factors include the amount of copy, the size of the document, and the number of pages. In addition, keep in mind the design guidelines as you plan. This section gives you some guidelines and ideas for planning your page, as well as tips on how to use WordPerfect features to make your job easier.

Determining Page Margins

Margins—the areas surrounding text blocks and graphics—serve as a buffer zone, breathing room to contrast the text and graphics. Margins provide white space on the page to improve readability and emphasize the message. Plan the margins of the page as a first step to page layout.

Note

Use margins to help maintain consistency throughout your document. When you determine the margins, stay with that formula; don't change the margins for the sake of "design," and don't change the margins to squeeze in an extra bit of text.

The size of the margins depends on the amount of copy and the type of document. If you have a lot of copy and few pages to work with, for example, use smaller margins. If you're producing a brochure with two folds, the outer margins must reflect the margins between the panels. However, try to plan as much margin space as possible with all documents. Always leave at least a 3/8-inch margin on all sides of a page. More is better; margins of 1/2 inch or 1 inch are not only acceptable, they are preferable. The margin is the best way to add white space to your pages.

Tip

If you vary the margin on one page of a multi-page document, repeat the same margin on every page to ensure consistency.

You can vary the margins on the page for interesting white space. Suppose you design a one-page advertising piece. The minimal amount of copy gives you room to adjust the margins for a more interesting page layout. Figure 23.2 shows an advertising flyer that has wide left and bottom margins. The advertisement has an openness to it because of the wide margins, the added white space around the figure, and the right-aligned text.

> **Note**
>
> WordPerfect enables you to control the margins of your document from the Margin dialog box. (Choose Fo**r**mat, **M**argins.) For more information on setting margins, see Chapter 4, "Formatting Text."

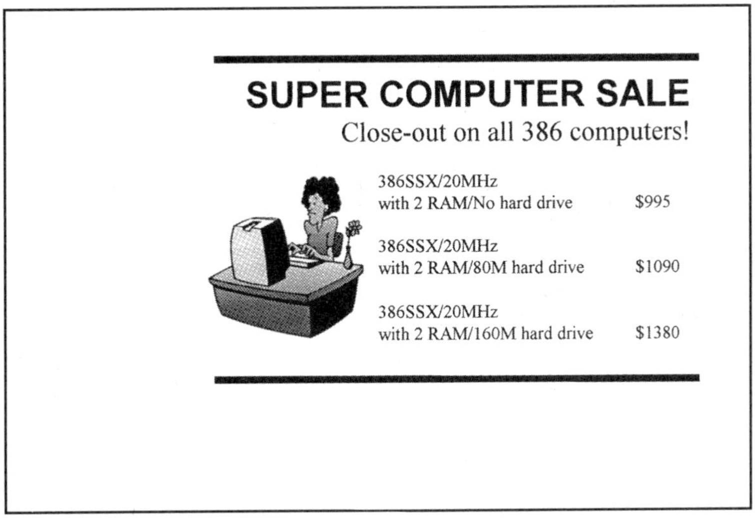

Fig. 23.2
Wide left and bottom margins create interest and attract attention in this advertisement; in addition, right-aligned text emphasizes the white space.

Incorporating Columns

As you learned in Chapter 14, "Working with Text Columns," WordPerfect enables you to use several types of columns in your documents. Columns add visual appeal, and columnar text can be easier to read than a full page of text. A full page of 10- or 12-point body text can be difficult to read because when you reach the end of the line, your eye must jump a long way to get to the beginning of the next line. Placing your text in columns alleviates this problem.

Choose the type of column that best suits your document's needs. Because the main purpose of any document is to present information to the reader in a format that is easy to understand and follow, text should flow in a logical order. Don't be so creative with your columns that you confuse the reader.

> **Tip**
>
> To format columns in WordPerfect, choose Fo**r**mat, **C**olumns, **D**efine.

Too many columns clutter the page. When using portrait orientation, generally use no more than three columns per page. In landscape orientation, which offers more flexibility, you can use four or five columns. This section gives examples of some types of columns you can use in your documents and when to use them.

Note

If the text is suited for more columns—such as lists consisting of short line lengths—you can fit four or five columns to a page using parallel columns.

Newspaper Columns

The text in a newspaper column flows the entire length of the first column and then wraps to the top of the next column. Use newspaper columns for a large amount of text, such as a newsletter, book, or report. Figure 23.3 shows a newsletter that incorporates newspaper columns.

Fig. 23.3
Newspaper columns in a newsletter promote the smooth flow of text and guide the reader's eye. Continuing a story from the third column to the next page may encourage the reader to open the newsletter.

TITLE

The Newsletter Subtitle
Vol. I No. I
February 1995

Main Heading

Foremost is the safety of bikers who must share the roads with automobiles. Just as dis-concerting is the high incidence of accidents on paths restricted to use by pedestrians, skateboarders, and other bikers. Teaching riding etiquette and designating roads as multi-vehicle highways are inexpensive and practical and can alleviate the majority of hazards bikers face.

You want irony? Try this bit of information: according to The Daily Microcosm's Anna Fornos, a city which sponsors three annual cycling events and supports the county's alternative transportation program, there is not a single bike lane. We need to think about doing something to reverse the current situation. And now that we have the name of a giant corporation backing us, there's no reason to remain silent regarding the lack of bicycle and pedestrian facilities in our community.

Right now the city is drafting a transportation plan, and Ms. Fornos goes on to say:

"There isn't one provision to accommodate bikers. Perhaps it's an oversight. Or perhaps it's the lack of bikers in the city council. We can safely assume that the director of the Losantiville Planning Organization doesn't bike (at least, not outdoors)."

So if it's someone with legislative pull we need, we can go straight to the governor's office and find a state bicycle coordinator. With some pressure she will work with local governments to apportion some road money to non-highway programs. But unless we speak up, we'll go unnoticed. Foremost is the safety of bikers who must share the roads with automobiles. Just as dis-concerting is the high incidence of accidents on paths restricted to use by pedestrians, skateboarders, and other bikers. Teaching riding etiquette and designating roads as multi-vehicle highways are inexpensive and practical and can alleviate the majority of hazards bikers face.

You want irony? Try this bit of information: according to The Daily Microcosm's Anna Fornos, a city which sponsors three annual cycling events and supports the county's alternative transportation program, there is not a single bike lane. We need to think about doing something to reverse the current situation. And now that we have the name of a giant corporation backing us, there's no reason to remain silent regarding the lack of bicycle and pedestrian facilities in our community.

Right now the city is drafting a transportation plan, and Ms. Fornos goes on to say:

"There isn't one provision to accommodate bikers. Perhaps it's an oversight. Or perhaps it's the lack of bikers in the city council. We can safely assume that the director of the Losantiville Planning Organization doesn't bike (at least, not outdoors)."

So if it's someone with legislative pull we need, we can go straight to the governor's office and find a state bicycle coordinator. With some pressure she will work with local governments to apportion some road money to non-highway programs. But unless we speak up, we'll go unnoticed. Foremost is the safety of bikers who must share the roads with automobiles. Just as dis-concerting is the high incidence of accidents on paths restricted to use by pedestrians,

CONTENTS

<< Contents Go here >>

Balanced Newspaper Columns

Balanced newspaper columns flow in the same way that newspaper columns flow, except the text lines up evenly across the top and bottom of the columns. You can use balanced columns on the last page of a newsletter or report to create an even appearance at the bottom of the page. You also can use this type of column if you need an even space to place a graphics box.

Tip
Any extra paragraph returns at the end of your text can throw off the balance. Remove extra blank lines before choosing the balanced newspaper option.

Custom Column Widths

With WordPerfect, you can create custom column widths. Using custom column widths breaks up the page so that it isn't monotonous to the reader. If you use custom column widths, however, plan them carefully so that you don't present a chaotic layout of text and graphics. Keep the layout simple. Just because WordPerfect lets you create up to 24 columns of varying widths doesn't mean the layout will look good.

Figure 23.4 illustrates a simple newsletter layout that incorporates custom-width columns. For more information on creating custom column widths, as well as adding borders or shading in columns, see Chapter 14, "Working with Text Columns."

Tip
Use the same custom widths throughout the document to avoid inconsistency. Use no more than two or three columns per page.

If the newsletter consists of more than one page, you can switch the position of the two columns on the second page—and the fourth page and the sixth page and so on. By doing this, the wide column appears on the left on odd pages and on the right on even pages. This *mirroring* adds interest to the layout while maintaining consistency.

Gutter Space and Columns

Consider the *gutter*, the space between columns, as additional margin space. Documents need gutters to separate the text, but gutter space also provides valuable white space that acts as a resting point for the reader's eye. Narrow gutters make text hard to read and may force the reader's eye to jump to the next column. On the other hand, very wide gutters may separate columns too much, thus separating related text.

Note

Don't substitute a graphics line for gutter space. If you use lines between columns, add extra gutter space to compensate. Also, be sure to use plenty of gutter space when you use justified text.

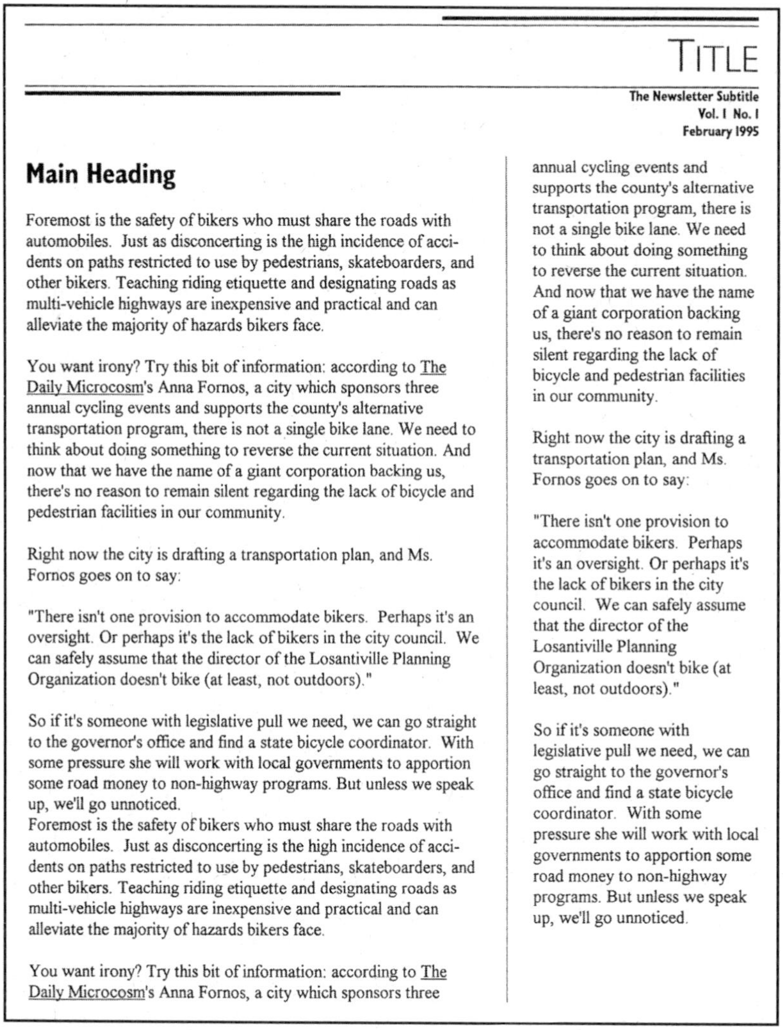

Fig. 23.4
Custom columns in a newsletter. The left column is twice the width of the right column—a simple formula that looks good.

TITLE

The Newsletter Subtitle
Vol. I No. I
February 1995

Main Heading

Foremost is the safety of bikers who must share the roads with automobiles. Just as disconcerting is the high incidence of accidents on paths restricted to use by pedestrians, skateboarders, and other bikers. Teaching riding etiquette and designating roads as multi-vehicle highways are inexpensive and practical and can alleviate the majority of hazards bikers face.

You want irony? Try this bit of information: according to The Daily Microcosm's Anna Fornos, a city which sponsors three annual cycling events and supports the county's alternative transportation program, there is not a single bike lane. We need to think about doing something to reverse the current situation. And now that we have the name of a giant corporation backing us, there's no reason to remain silent regarding the lack of bicycle and pedestrian facilities in our community.

Right now the city is drafting a transportation plan, and Ms. Fornos goes on to say:

"There isn't one provision to accommodate bikers. Perhaps it's an oversight. Or perhaps it's the lack of bikers in the city council. We can safely assume that the director of the Losantiville Planning Organization doesn't bike (at least, not outdoors)."

So if it's someone with legislative pull we need, we can go straight to the governor's office and find a state bicycle coordinator. With some pressure she will work with local governments to apportion some road money to non-highway programs. But unless we speak up, we'll go unnoticed.
Foremost is the safety of bikers who must share the roads with automobiles. Just as disconcerting is the high incidence of accidents on paths restricted to use by pedestrians, skateboarders, and other bikers. Teaching riding etiquette and designating roads as multi-vehicle highways are inexpensive and practical and can alleviate the majority of hazards bikers face.

You want irony? Try this bit of information: according to The Daily Microcosm's Anna Fornos, a city which sponsors three annual cycling events and supports the county's alternative transportation program, there is not a single bike lane. We need to think about doing something to reverse the current situation. And now that we have the name of a giant corporation backing us, there's no reason to remain silent regarding the lack of bicycle and pedestrian facilities in our community.

Right now the city is drafting a transportation plan, and Ms. Fornos goes on to say:

"There isn't one provision to accommodate bikers. Perhaps it's an oversight. Or perhaps it's the lack of bikers in the city council. We can safely assume that the director of the Losantiville Planning Organization doesn't bike (at least, not outdoors)."

So if it's someone with legislative pull we need, we can go straight to the governor's office and find a state bicycle coordinator. With some pressure she will work with local governments to apportion some road money to non-highway programs. But unless we speak up, we'll go unnoticed.

Troubleshooting

When I format text in two or more newspaper columns, the column(s) to the right are higher than the left column.

When WordPerfect formats newspaper columns, it begins the text for the first column at the insertion point, but wraps the text for the other columns at the top margin. If there are extra blank lines after the insertion point, the text won't be even across the tops of the columns. If you are not starting the columnar text at the top of the page, you should define the column, and add the extra blank lines (press Enter) before the Column Define code ([Col Def] in Reveal Codes; turn on Reveal Codes to see it). As you add blank lines to the page, the tops of all the columns are pushed down and remain even.

The text in my document looks scrawny when the document is formatted at more than two columns wide.

For most layouts, the maximum practical number of columns per page is four. With a two-column treatment, WordPerfect's default column spacing of half an inch is acceptable; but with three and four columns, the half-inch spacing makes the columns too narrow. When formatting the text to more than two columns, be sure to change the spacing between columns. Try a spacing of one quarter-inch between columns, and make adjustments until the text looks right. Use the ruler to see the effects of your spacing changes as you make them.

Refining the Page

Now that you have planned the page using margins and columns, refine the page layout by dealing with the text. This section describes working with text in blocks—as page elements rather than individual characters. Decide on the alignment and line spacing—the appearance of the paragraphs—before you decide on fonts. For information about choosing fonts, see the "Choosing Fonts" section later in this chapter.

The methods for organizing text elements depend on the amount of copy, the type of document, and the message you want to present. Justified text organized in columns, for example, lets you fit the most copy on a page. One-and-a-half or double-line spacing, for instance, makes the text more readable in an advertisement, but makes entire blocks of text in a newsletter harder to read. Short phrases in an advertisement may be better received if the text is center-aligned. Consider the design guidelines—white space, consistency, emphasis, and so on—when you organize text on the page.

This section contains tips on how to refine the page layout for a professional-looking document. WordPerfect features enable you to perform page-refinement tasks and experiment with options before deciding on the layout that best suits your document. This section discusses text alignment and line spacing.

Aligning Text

Text alignment is a method of organizing words in a document. You can also use text alignment to create consistency and emphasis in your documents.

All text—body text, headlines, tabs—requires an alignment (left- or right-aligned, centered, or fully justified). As always, make sure that the alignment remains consistent throughout the entire document; too many alignment changes can distract the reader. To change alignment, choose Fo**r**mat, **J**ustification.

Left Alignment

Left-aligned text—flush left and ragged right text—is perfect for body text and headlines. The ragged right edge adds valuable white space, and the flush left edge helps the reader find the next sentence. Left-aligned text, which provides a more open, informal feeling to your documents, is more readable. Use left-aligned text in newsletters, reports, advertisements, forms, or any other document.

Left-aligned text offers the following advantages:

- Word spacing is even, unlike word spacing with justified text, in which the spacing between words varies.
- With narrow columns, the reader's eye is directed quickly and easily to the beginning of the next sentence.
- Left-aligned heads and subheads enable the reader to find the next topic easily.

> **Note**
>
> Be sure that the ragged right text is not too ragged. Hyphenating left-aligned text helps keep the right margin somewhat uniform. Try not to hyphenate the ends of more than two lines in a row, however, because too many hyphens can make reading difficult.

Right Alignment

Right-aligned text—flush right and ragged left text—gives you eye-catching headlines when used with justified body text. You can use right-aligned text in documents with short phrases, such as an advertising piece (refer to fig. 23.2). Reserve right-aligned text for heads and subheads, single words, and occasionally short phrases; never use right alignment for body text because the reader must be able to find the beginning of each line easily—a task that is extremely difficult with right-aligned body text. When designing a document using right-aligned text, make sure the overall page design reflects the alignment. Notice in figure 23.2 that all elements—including the margins—reinforce the right alignment.

The advantage of using right-aligned text is that it's unique—because it's difficult to use successfully—and attracts attention.

Center Alignment

Centered text—ragged left and right text—is used primarily for headlines, subheads, and captions. Center alignment adds visual interest and an air of dignity to a document. You can use centered text for short lists, names and addresses, dates, and even invitations or announcements. Do not use center alignment for body text, however.

Centered text for a headline complements either justified or left-aligned body text (refer to fig. 23.4). When using centered headlines, make sure the text is large enough—24- or 36-point type with 10- or 12-point body text, for example—to differentiate it from the body text.

Centered text offers the advantages of even word spacing and visual interest. To turn on hyphenation, choose Fo**r**mat, **L**ine, Hyph**e**nation.

Full Justification

Full justification—flush left and flush right text—is perfect for long articles, reports, newsletters (refer to fig. 23.1), and books. A page of justified text appears organized and comfortable for the reader. Justified text is also more formal than left-aligned text and allows you to fit the most copy on a page. When you use full justification, *always* use hyphenation. Large gaps between the words in unhyphenated justified text can form "rivers" of white space that are distracting to a reader.

The advantages of using fully justified text are that you can fit more copy on a page and create an even, organized, formal page.

Using Line Spacing

Line spacing—also called *leading*—refers to the amount of space between lines of text. WordPerfect enables you to adjust the line spacing within a paragraph and between paragraphs. The default line and paragraph spacing in WordPerfect is 1. To change line spacing, choose Fo**r**mat, **L**ine, **S**pacing to access the Line Spacing dialog box.

The tallest character in a particular typeface and size is the guideline for measuring line spacing. Uppercase letters, *ascenders* (b, k, d, for example), and *descenders* (g, j, p, for example) must have enough space to prevent them from overlapping letters on lines below or above them. Typical line spacing is 20 to 30 percent of the size of the font, which allows a little extra space above and below a line. In WordPerfect, 1 (the default) is equal to the type size plus 30 percent.

The commonly used line spacing values are 1, 1 1/2, and 2; these are the values with which you're probably most familiar. WordPerfect, however, enables you to set line spacing to any measurement from .01 to 160. You seldom need to set line spacing at either extreme (.01 or 160); however, you may want to adjust line spacing at some point in your documents.

◄ See "Formatting Lines and Paragraphs," p. 134

◄ See "Using Hyphenation," p. 152

The majority of line spacing uses the default, 1. You can increase line spacing to make crowded text more readable. Decreasing line spacing may make the text unreadable. Figure 23.5 illustrates different line spacings.

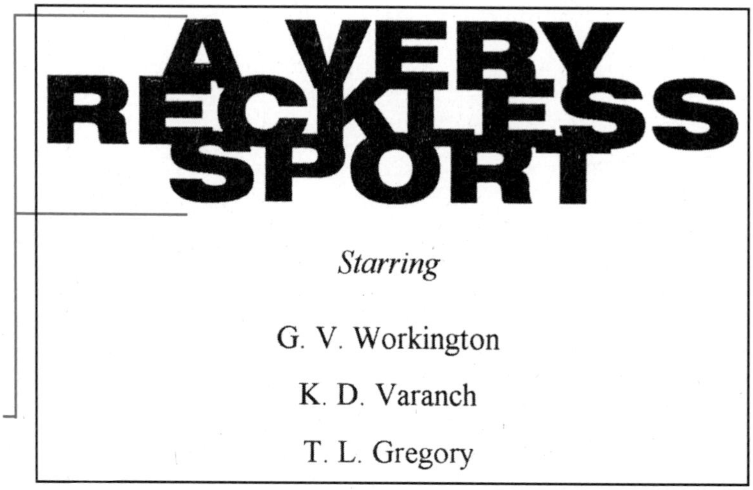

A VERY
RECKLESS
SPORT

Starring

G. V. Workington

K. D. Varanch

T. L. Gregory

Line spacing is 0.7

Fig. 23.5 Spacing at .7 overlaps the letters of each line, creating a unique artistic effect; however, don't use this line spacing unless you're striving for an effect such as this.

Choosing Fonts

A *font* (family) includes all sizes and styles of a particular typeface. A *typeface* is a specific style or design of letters; Helvetica and Times Roman are two different typefaces. Type styles, or attributes, include normal, italic, bold, or bold italic. A *type size* indicates the font's size, usually expressed in points (an inch contains 72 points). An example of a font is 8-point bold Times Roman; 48-point italic Times Roman is a member of the same font. Eight-point Helvetica and 12-point Courier are different fonts.

WordPerfect offers many different fonts for your documents. In addition to your printer fonts, WordPerfect includes several TrueType fonts. As with all elements of page design, following certain guidelines ensures that the chosen fonts complement, rather than confuse, your message. This section contains tips on how to use fonts to create a successful document.

Using Typefaces and Attributes

You're probably familiar with the typefaces available in WordPerfect. Depending on your Windows setup and printer, as few as five typefaces or as many as 500 may be available. No matter which typefaces you have, you need to follow basic guidelines when designing your documents.

In using typefaces and attributes, the first and most important rule is to never use more than three typefaces in one document. Too many typefaces not only distract the reader, but also interfere with the message. Remember that the consistency guideline applies to typefaces, as well.

Tip
Never use Courier, which has an unprofessional appearance, in a typeset document.

Generally, you use only two typefaces per document; a sans serif and a serif font work nicely together. A *serif*—a decorative component of some typefaces—is the fine stroke across the end of the main strokes of characters. Times Roman is a serif typeface. An example of a *sans serif* typeface—no serifs—is Helvetica.

Use a sans serif typeface for headlines, subheads, captions, callouts, and headers and footers. Use a serif typeface for body text. Serif type is easier to read because the serif adds a horizontal flow to the text, making the letters easily recognizable. You can use serif type for headlines, but avoid using sans serif for body text because it's difficult to read in small type sizes. Figure 23.6 illustrates Helvetica (sans serif) and Times Roman (serif) typefaces.

Helvetica

Times Roman

Fig. 23.6
Helvetica is good for headlines, subheads, and captions; Times Roman is perfect for headlines and body text.

As you choose typefaces for documents, you also choose type styles, or attributes. Common attributes include underline, bold, italic, and bold italic. Other attributes include condensed type, superscript, and subscript. Attributes emphasize a word or group of words; applying an attribute to a small amount of text is more emphatic than applying it to large blocks of text. Also, a large block of text that is bold or italic can be very difficult to read.

Avoid using many different attributes in a document. Also avoid overusing any attribute; using one too often diminishes its importance.

Note

Although underlining is a common attribute, limit its use in documents. Professional typesetters use underlining *only* at the bottom of a column of numbers. Use italic or bold instead of underlining for a more professional-looking document.

Using Type Sizes

Tip
One inch contains 72 points.

Type size is the size of a font measured in points from the top of the tallest ascender to the bottom of the lowest descender. Figure 23.7 shows some common type sizes and uses. All the type examples in the figure are regular type (no attributes). Generally, however, you use attributes such as bold or italic with subheads, headings, and display type (either large—60-point and larger—or especially decorative typefaces that are used to attract the reader to the document).

The following table describes common type sizes:

Tip
Create display type by entering the size in the Font Size text box (Font dialog box). Enter a number larger than 72 points only if your printer can support it.

Type Style	Size	Uses
Body text	9, 10, 11, 12	The majority of text in a document is body text.
Subheads	12, 14	Subheads categorize main topics or act as headlines. Use bold or italic type.
Headings	18, 36, 48	Represent main topics with headings. Headings can be bold, italic, or all uppercase.
Display heads	60, 72, 96, 126	Use display type—large and sometimes ornamental—sparingly in a document.

As with typefaces, limit the number of type sizes you use in any one document. Use no more than three type sizes if possible: one size each for body text, headings, and subheads, for example. Figure 23.8 illustrates a flyer that uses the appropriate number of typefaces, type sizes, and attributes.

Body Text

9-point
10-point
11point
12-point

Subheads

12-point
14-point

Headings

18-point
24-point
36-point
48-point

Display Type

60-point
72-point

Fig. 23.7
Use the sizes represented in the figure as a guideline for sizing text in your documents. You can also use bold and italic to emphasize text.

Fig. 23.8
A flyer using 18-point subheads, 24-point headings, and 72-point display type. Just two typefaces, two type styles, and three type sizes create an eye-catching, professional-looking advertisement.

Using Typographical Controls

Typography refers not only to typeface, type style, and type size, but to aesthetics and readability. When creating type for documents, your goal is to produce attractive and easy-to-read material that invites the reader and impels him or her to read further. To accomplish this task, you can use WordPerfect's typographical controls to adjust the type on the page.

WordPerfect's typographical controls include leading, kerning, letterspacing, and word spacing. Each of these options regulates the way the type appears in documents and the way the type prints. You won't use all three options at one time; and you won't use any of the options all the time. You will, however, need to control leading, kerning, letterspacing, and word spacing at some point in your desktop publishing projects. The following sections explain each of WordPerfect's typographical controls and when to use them.

Leading

Leading (pronounced LED-ing) is the same thing as line spacing, or the amount of space between two lines of text within the same paragraph. You're probably familiar with single-, one-and-a-half, and double-line spacing; these are common leading settings. WordPerfect, however, enables you to adjust the leading in smaller increments in the Word/Letterspacing dialog box.

To adjust the leading of your text, follow these steps:

1. Choose Fo**r**mat, **T**ypesetting.
2. From the cascading menu, choose **W**ord/Letter Spacing. The Word Spacing and Letterspacing dialog box appears.
3. In Line Height (Leading) Adjustment, choose Adjust **L**eading.
4. In Be**t**ween Lines, enter a value for the leading of your text, in inches.

Figure 23.9 shows three examples of leading set in the Word Spacing and Letterspacing dialog box. Leading is 0.020" in the first paragraph, 0.010" in the second paragraph, and 0.110" in the third paragraph.

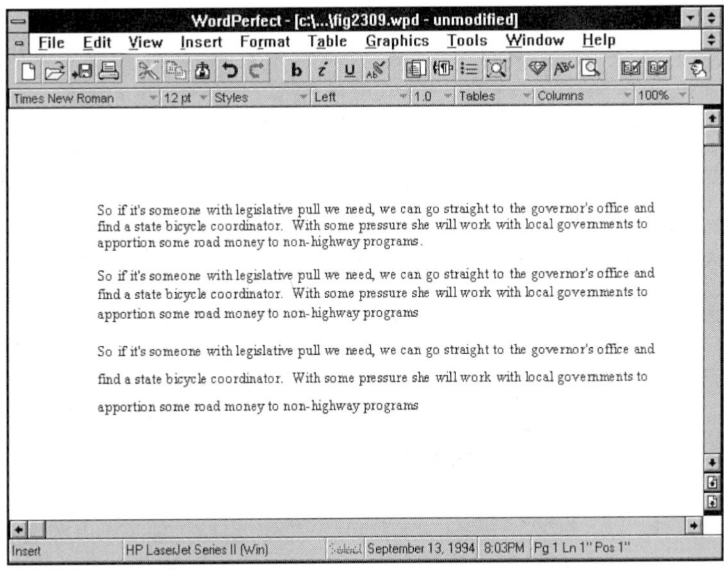

Fig. 23.9
Adjust leading to fit text on a page; decrease leading to fit more text, and increase leading to fit less text. Be careful not to sacrifice readability in the process.

Kerning

Kerning is the reduction of space between certain letter pairs so that the characters appear more pleasing to the eye. Some letters take up more space than others, which is not a problem when the text is small—for example, 14 points and smaller; however, kerning is sometimes necessary with larger text. Kerning is often useful with certain pairs of letters: for example, At, Av, AV, AW, LT, OA, Ta, Ya, and We. Figure 23.10 illustrates 24-point Times Roman letter pairs before and after kerning.

At Av AV AW LT OA Ta Ya We

At Av AV AW LT OA Ta Ya We

Fig. 23.10
Letter pairs before kerning (top) and after kerning (bottom). Kerning is most effective when used on large type—heads and display type.

Note

You can't kern monospaced fonts, such as Courier, because they allow the same amount of space for all letters.

To kern two letters in a heading or in display type, position the cursor between the two letters. Then follow these steps:

1. Choose Fo**r**mat, **T**ypesetting. From the cascading menu, choose **M**anual Kerning. The Manual Kerning dialog box appears.

2. In **U**nits of measure, choose the type of measurement you want to use: **I**nches, **C**entimeters, **M**illimeters, **P**oints, or **1**200ths.

3. In **A**mount, enter a value—either positive or negative—to adjust the spacing between the two letters.

   Note

   As you change the value in **A**mount, you can see the letters on-screen move closer together (negative value) or farther apart (positive value). The letter to the right of the cursor is the letter that moves.

4. When you are satisfied with the kerning, choose OK to close the dialog box.

Tip
You can turn on automatic kerning in the Word Spacing and Letterspacing dialog box. See the next section for more information about this dialog box.

Letterspacing

Using WordPerfect's letterspacing controls is a way of minimizing the large gaps of space that occur when you use full justification. *Justification*—aligning text both flush left and flush right—applies extra space between words to force the text to be flush with both margins. Figure 23.11 illustrates justified text before and after using letterspacing.

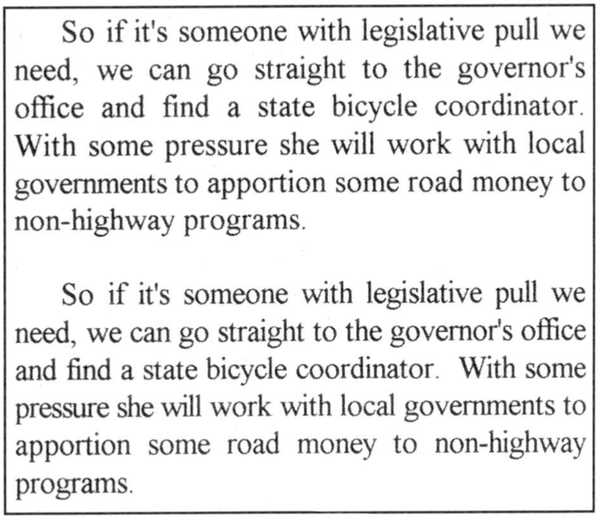

So if it's someone with legislative pull we need, we can go straight to the governor's office and find a state bicycle coordinator. With some pressure she will work with local governments to apportion some road money to non-highway programs.

So if it's someone with legislative pull we need, we can go straight to the governor's office and find a state bicycle coordinator. With some pressure she will work with local governments to apportion some road money to non-highway programs.

Fig. 23.11
Text before (top) and after (bottom) letterspacing is applied. To alleviate the rivers of white space, use letterspacing to add a fraction of space between characters and reduce the space between words.

To apply letterspacing to your text, follow these steps:

1. Either select the text to be adjusted, or position the cursor at the beginning of the text to be adjusted, in which case your action affects all text after the cursor.

2. Choose Fo**r**mat, **T**ypesetting. From the cascading menu, choose **W**ord/Letter Spacing. The Word Spacing and Letterspacing dialog box appears (see fig. 23.12).

3. In Letterspacing, choose Pe**r**cent of Optimal. Enter a value in the text box, or use the arrows to increase or decrease the value.

4. Choose OK to close the dialog box and view the results on the document screen.

WordPerfect **O**ptimal letterspacing is the default setting and is adequate in most instances. However, you can experiment with the settings. Start by changing the percentage in small increments—5 or 10 percent at a time. Then view the changes, and adjust the letterspacing if necessary.

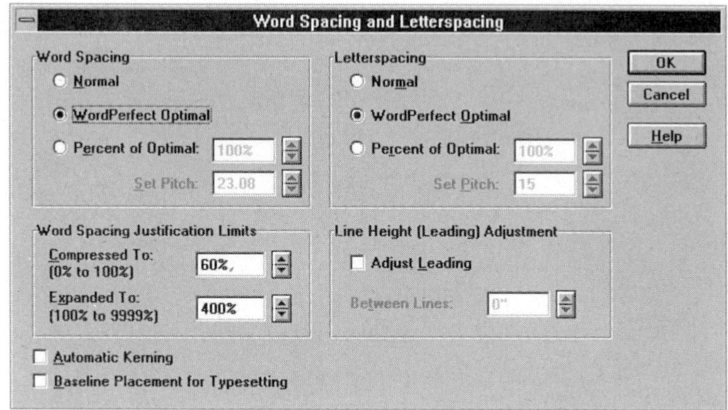

Fig. 23.12
You can adjust typographical controls for your text. When you change word spacing, letterspacing, or leading in a document, remember to be consistent, changing all text.

Word Spacing

Word spacing, like letterspacing, can be adjusted in justified text to create a more pleasing and readable block of text. Optimal word spacing is the width of the capital I. You can adjust the word spacing in the same way you adjust letterspacing. Figure 23.13 shows text before and after word spacing is applied.

To change the word spacing in WordPerfect, follow these steps:

1. Select the text or position the cursor in the text to be adjusted.
2. Choose Fo**r**mat, **T**ypesetting. From the cascading menu, choose **W**ord/ Letter Spacing. The Word Spacing and Letterspacing dialog box appears.
3. In Word Spacing, choose P**e**rcent of Optimal and enter a value.
4. Choose OK to close the dialog box and return to the document.

Optimal word spacing is the default setting in WordPerfect; however, you can experiment with the settings by choosing Percent of Optimal. Increase or decrease the percentage in small increments until you are happy with the word spacing.

The Word Spacing Justification Limits section of the dialog box enables you to set default word spacing limits for your document. The Compression limits refer to how much space can be reduced between words when the text is justified. You can set the limit from 0%, which is much too close to read easily, to 100%, which may be a bit too far apart. WordPerfect sets a default value of 60%, which provides comfortable reading.

◄ See "Formatting Characters," p. 130

Expansion limits refer to how much space can be added between words when the text is justified. The Expansion limits range from 100% or 9999%, with

WordPerfect's default set at 532%, or middle range. When set lower than 532%, the words begin to close up space; when set to higher than 532%, more space separates the words.

So if it's someone with legislative pull we need, we can go straight to the governor's office and find a state bicycle coordinator. With some pressure she will work with local governments to apportion some road money to non-highway programs.

So if it's someone with legislative pull we need, we can go straight to the governor's office and find a state bicycle coordinator. With some pressure she will work with local governments to apportion some road money to non-highway programs.

Fig. 23.13
Before (top) and after (bottom) word spacing is applied. Word spacing makes the text flow, enabling the reader to concentrate on the message.

In general, use the expansion and compression limits WordPerfect sets and use word and letterspacing to adjust the text. If you decide to try changing the compression and expansion limits, do so in small increments—such as 100% at a time—until you see the effects you want.

Using Color

WordPerfect enables you to use color in your documents, both on-screen and in printed materials. You can display text, lines, borders, fills, and graphic images in color on-screen. If you have a color printer, WordPerfect can print the same elements in color. Using color with documents is as easy as formatting text or adding graphics. You can use WordPerfect's palette of colors or create your own custom colors.

Naturally, as with other design elements—type, graphics, columns, and so on—be careful to present the color in your documents within the design guidelines and be sure not to overwhelm or distract the reader. Consider the following guidelines when using color in your documents:

- Limit the number of colors to two or three; consider the paper color as one of the colors if you use a paper color other than white.
- Be consistent with the use of color; if you choose dark blue for headings, use dark blue for all of the headings in the document.
- Use contrasting colors such as red and blue.
- Don't use light colors such as yellow or white for text because these colors make text difficult to read. Instead, use light colors for screens, lines, or graphic elements.
- Use a splash of color for emphasis; for example, use dark blue for text, and then use a splash of yellow for one element, such as a screen or thick graphic border.
- Don't forget white space in your designs. If you fill every area with color, the colors compete for the reader's attention; use white space to give the reader's eye a break.

This section shows how to apply color to type and graphics to create attractive, professional color documents. This section is a prerequisite to the "Printing in Color" section later in this chapter. Many of the techniques you learn here will be helpful when you are ready to print your document.

When applying color to a document, first apply the color on-screen. When you are satisfied with the way the text and graphics look on-screen, you can print your finished document. You can apply color to selected sections of text only, or you can apply color to all the text. You can use color with graphic elements—such as lines, borders, and fills (screens)—or you can use color with graphic images, such as clip art or art from WP Draw.

Using Color with Text

Tip
You can apply colors to styles for faster and easier formatting.

When using color with text, make sure the color enhances the text. The text must be easy to read. Use color sparingly: for example, red headings with black body text, green display type in an advertisement, or blue body text with red headings on white paper. If you must use three colors, use two colors consistently throughout the document and the third as an emphasis point.

The easiest way to apply color to text is after you have entered and formatted the text. When the document is complete, add color. To apply color to text, follow these steps:

Note

If you select the text before you change the color of the font, only the selected text is changed. If, however, you position the cursor within the text, all text following the cursor is changed until you change the font color again.

1. Choose Format, Font. The Font dialog box appears.
2. In Color Options, choose Color. The color printing palette appears (see fig. 23.14).

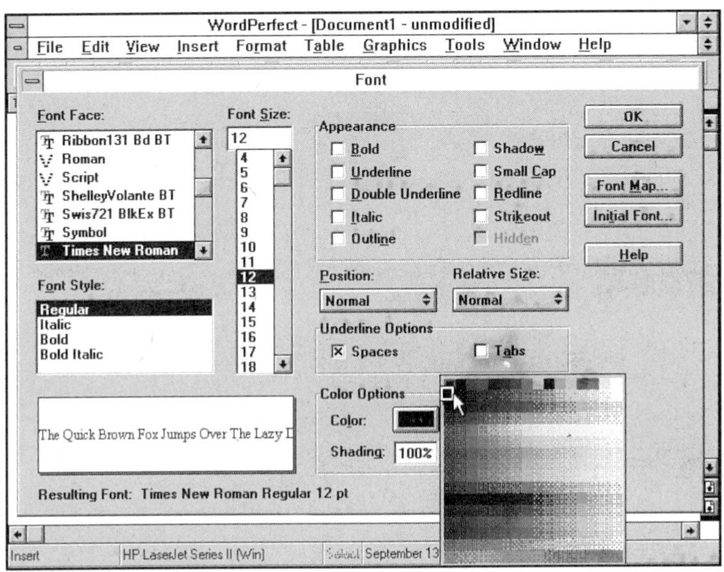

Fig. 23.14
The color printing palette offers various shades of colors you can apply to a font. You can choose a shade of black, creating a gray screened effect for interesting headings or display type.

3. Choose a color and choose OK to close the dialog box.

In addition to changing the color of a font, you can also change the shading of the selected font. In Color Options, change the value in the Shading text box; note the change in the Resulting Font box as you change the shading.

Furthermore, you can create your own custom colors and shades by choosing Palette in the Color Options area. Figure 23.15 illustrates the Define Color Printing Palette dialog box. You can choose various colors in the palette and change the composition, blend, copy, and invert colors. After you've created colors you plan to use often, save them as a Palette Name to use over and over in your documents.

Tip
You can also access the Define Color Printing Palette dialog box by choosing Edit, Preferences, Print. In the Print Preferences dialog box, choose Color Palette.

> **Note**
>
> When you create a palette in the Define Color Printing Palette dialog box, that palette replaces the original in the Color Options area of the Font dialog box, until you change it again.

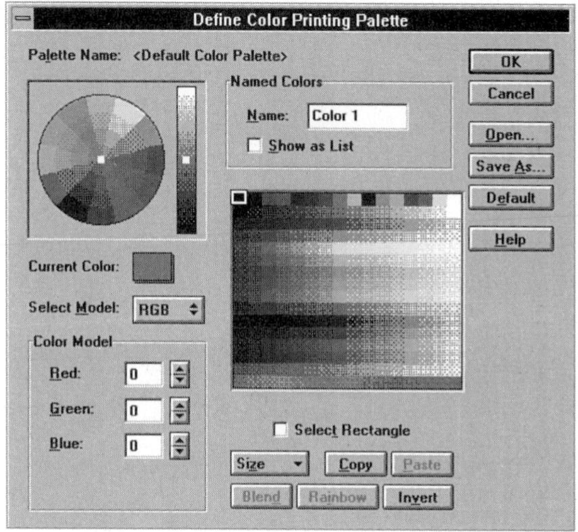

Fig. 23.15
The current palette is one created using four colors; choose colors from the color wheel or create the color by entering values in the Color Model.

> **Note**
>
> Size defines the number of colors in the palette. If you choose 16 or more colors, you can use the Blen**d** option to create shades of one color; you can use the Ra**i**nbow option to create complementary colors within the palette automatically.

Using Color with Graphics

You can also apply colors to graphic lines, borders, fills, and images using a color palette like the one used for fonts. The color palette you choose in **E**dit, Pr**e**ferences, **P**rint is the palette available for use with graphic lines, borders, and fills. In addition, you can change the color of images using WP Draw. For more information about WP Draw, see Chapter 22, "Using WP Draw and TextArt."

Lines

To change the color of a graphic line, create a line, or choose one to edit, follow these steps:

1. Access the Create/Edit Graphic Line dialog box by choosing **G**raphics, and then either Custom **L**ine to create a line or Edit Li**n**e to customize a line.

2. In Change Color, choose L**i**ne Color. The palette appears; choose the color for the line and choose OK to close the dialog box.

Tip
If you want to revert to the original line color, access the Edit Graphic Line dialog box. In Change color, choose **U**se Line Style Color.

Border

To change the color of a page or paragraph border, follow these steps:

1. Access the Paragraph/Page Border dialog box by choosing Fo**r**mat, P**a**ragraph or **P**age, **B**order/Fill.

2. In Border Options, choose **B**order Style and choose the line style of the border.

3. Choose **C**ustomize Style. The Customize Border dialog box appears.

4. In Change Color, choose **B**order Color. The palette appears.

5. Choose the color, and then choose OK to close the dialog box and return to the document.

Tip
Use the option **U**se Line Style Color to revert the border to its original color.

Fill

To change the fill within a paragraph or page border, follow these steps:

1. Access the Paragraph/Page Border dialog box by choosing Fo**r**mat, P**a**ragraph or **P**age, **B**order/Fill.

2. In Fill Options, choose **F**ill Style; then choose a fill.

3. Choose Fo**r**eground. The color palette appears (see fig. 23.16).

4. Choose the color for the fill and choose OK to close the dialog box.

Tip
Do not use a heavy fill—50 percent or more—when you use dark colors; you want the reader to be able to see the text through the fill.

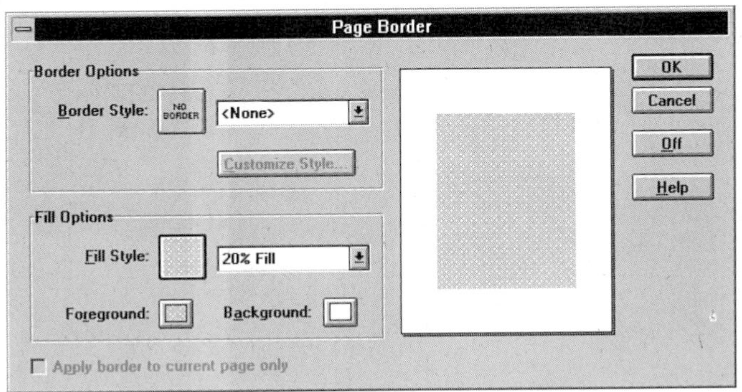

Fig. 23.16
Choose a fill style and color that complements the contents of the border. Don't choose a dark blue gradient or honeycomb fill for a border with text to be read.

Creating a Color Document

If you have a color printer, you can print your documents in a full range of colors. Although printing thousands of newsletters is not feasible using your own color printer, printing ten special reports to show the board members may be. You must consider the number of documents you'll print and the cost to print them before you decide to print in color.

Tip
Look at as many color publications—magazines, brochures, cards, newsletters, and so on—as you can. Use samples to give you ideas for your documents.

In addition, make sure you follow all design guidelines and suggestions to ensure that your document looks professional and attractive. Following is a list of considerations when applying color to a document:

- Bear in mind the number of printed copies and the number of pages per copy; judge the feasibility of color printing by calculating the cost per copy.
- Lay out the page and format all text before adding color. Use the design guidelines as you format the document.
- Choose only two or three colors for the entire document.
- Remember that the design guidelines—consistency, emphasis, balance, proportion, and white space—apply to color as well as to text and page formatting.

Using Advanced Printing Techniques

After creating your documents, you'll want to print them. In addition to the control Windows gives you in printing documents, WordPerfect offers some additional ways to control what you print. With WordPerfect, you can choose the print quality of the text and graphics, control whether graphics print, and control color printing.

Tip
If you print your document on a 600 dots-per-inch (dpi) laser printer or a high-resolution image typesetter, use the high-quality print resolution.

Naturally, the limits of control over printing your documents depend on the limits of your printer. If you use a 9-pin dot-matrix printer, for example, draft quality and high quality may look the same. On the other hand, if you use a color inkjet or a laser printer, you'll be able to take better advantage of the print quality. This section introduces you to WordPerfect's advanced printing techniques.

Choosing Print Quality

You can choose the print quality of text and graphics in your documents. If, for example, you print a proof—a first draft used to check wording, placement, and so on—you can direct WordPerfect to print in draft quality. A document printed in draft quality contains text and graphics that are not sharp—perhaps even ragged—but the document prints fast. If the document is completely finished, however, WordPerfect can print the text and graphics in high quality for a professional-looking final product.

You can choose the print quality you most often use in the Print Preferences dialog box; you also can change the print quality for each document by setting it in the Print dialog box. To choose the print quality in both the overall program setting and for each individual document, follow these steps:

1. Choose **E**dit, Pr**e**ferences. The Preferences dialog box appears.

2. Choose P**r**int and the Print Preferences dialog box appears (see fig. 23.17).

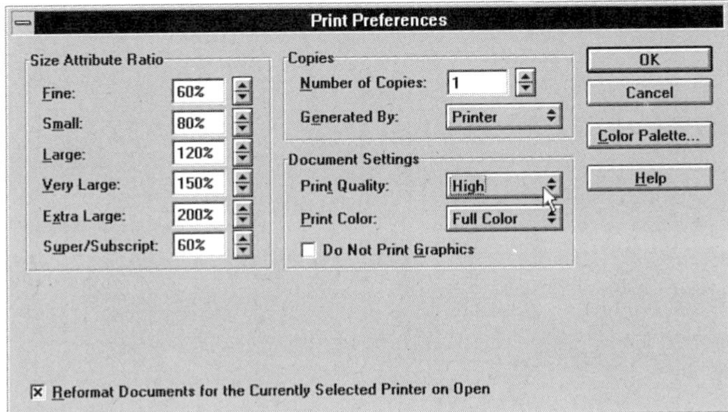

Fig. 23.17
Print your documents in high, medium, or draft quality. Choose high quality when you want the document to look its best and draft quality for proofreading the document.

3. In Document Settings, choose Prin**t** Quality. Choose either **H**igh, **M**edium, or **D**raft to specify the quality with which your document is printed.

4. Choose OK to close the dialog box and return to the Preferences dialog box. Choose **C**lose to return to the document.

5. Choose **F**ile, **P**rint. The Print dialog box appears.

6. In Document Settings, choose Print **Q**uality. Make a choice for the current document (see fig. 23.18); and choose OK to print the document.

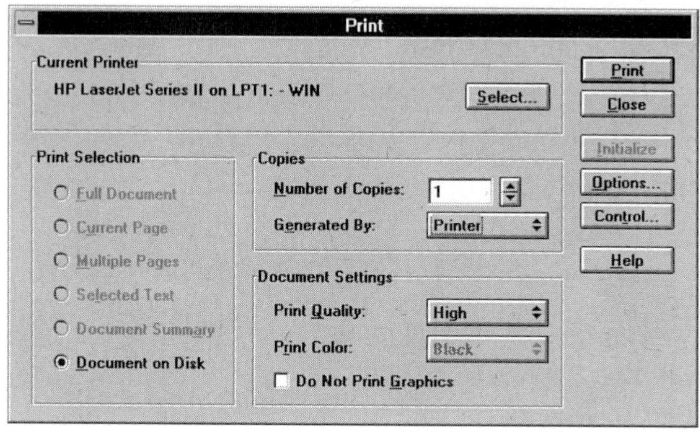

Fig. 23.18 Choose the quality in which you want to print the current document in the Print dialog box. This choice always overrules the choice in the Print Preferences dialog box.

Printing Graphics

As you have seen, you can print a document in high, medium, or draft quality. The print quality affects the text and the graphics. When you print text at different qualities on a laser (300 to 600 dpi), inkjet, or high-resolution printer (1200 to 2500 dpi), you probably notice very little difference. However, you can definitely tell a difference when graphics are printed at different print qualities.

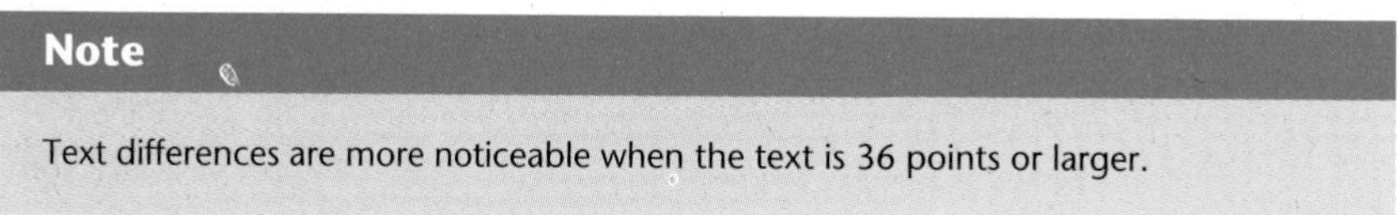

Note

Text differences are more noticeable when the text is 36 points or larger.

Print quality refers to the resolution of the image. Resolution is determined by the dot pattern used to form the image; the higher the resolution, the better the print quality. Therefore, high quality is high resolution; draft quality is low resolution. Although you most likely won't notice the differences between high and draft quality on a 300-dpi or lower printer, you'll notice the difference between high and draft quality on a 600-dpi or higher printer.

Tip
You can choose not to print graphics in a proof, thus showing only placement of the graphics and saving time in printing.

Another feature you can use when printing documents containing graphic images in WordPerfect is also in the Print dialog box. If you choose to print a draft-quality document for proofreading purposes, you can also choose not to print the graphics. Not printing graphics enables the program to print your document faster and more efficiently. To print a document without the graphics, follow these steps:

1. Choose **F**ile, **P**rint. The Print dialog box appears.

2. In Document Settings, choose Do Not Print **G**raphics.

3. Choose **P**rint to print the document.

The document prints showing all formatted text; however, WordPerfect prints empty boxes where the graphics would otherwise appear.

Printing in Color

If you have a color printer, WordPerfect can print text and graphics in color. WordPerfect supports any color printer that Windows supports, including Hewlett-Packard PaintJet series XL, IBM Color Printer, HP ColorPro Plotter, NEC Colormate, Seiko ColorPoint, and other printers using manufacturer-supplied printer drivers, including the Hewlett-Packard DeskJet 500C.

In WordPerfect, color is specified through the use of one of three color models—RGB (red, green, and blue), HLS (hue, lightness, and saturation), or CMYK (cyan, magenta, yellow, and black). Each model describes how the selected color is created.

CMYK

CMYK is normally used by commercial printers to mix inks, for example. When the first three colors—cyan, magenta, and yellow—are mixed in various combinations by overlaying dots of ink, they produce seven basic colors: black, red, green, blue, cyan, magenta, and yellow.

Suppose, for example, that you want red with the CMYK model. You must set Magenta to 255 and Yellow to 255; Black and Cyan are set to 0. Black is created by a setting of 255 for Black and 0 for the other three colors.

RGB

RGB refers to the amount of red, green, and blue ink mixed to form a color. For a bright red, for example, set Red at 255, Green to 0, and Blue to 0. The more blue you add, the more towards purple the color changes; the more green you add, the more towards orange—then yellow—the color changes.

When all three values are at 0, black is the current color. You can create any of the colors used in CMYK; the method of mixing is just different. Experiment with these mixtures to find the perfect color.

HLS

HLS is another method of mixing colors. Hue refers to red at 0, moving through orange, yellow, green, blue, and purple, and back to red at 360. In between the hue changes are colors like yellow-orange, yellow-green, blue-green, and so on.

Lightness refers to tint and shade; tint is the color plus white, whereas shade is the color plus black. Start with Lightness on 50 for bright vibrant colors. 0 Lightness is equal to black; 100 Lightness is equal to white.

Saturation refers to the brightness of the color. For example, to get a very bright red, you set saturation on 100; for a dull red, set saturation to 25. Setting saturation to 0 makes the color more gray.

Choosing Colors

The color model you use depends on how you want the colors to mix. If you're unsure of which model to use, experiment to find the one you like. As you change the values in each model, the color changes in the color wheel so you can view the change. You may find that the easiest way to choose the color is to click the mouse on the color in the selection box.

To choose color printing, follow these steps:

1. Choose **E**dit, Pr**e**ferences. The Preferences dialog box appears.
2. Choose P**r**int. The Print Preferences dialog box appears.
3. In Document Settings choose **P**rint Color, and then choose **F**ull Color.

To change the color models in the color palette, follow these steps:

1. In the Print Preferences dialog box, choose **C**olor Palette. The Define Color Printing Palette dialog box appears (see fig. 23.19).

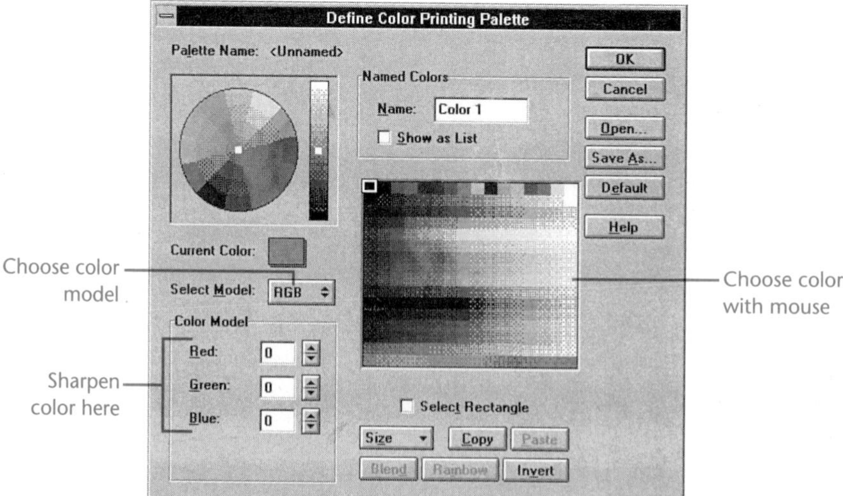

Fig. 23.19
Choose a model and enter values for each color, or choose the color by clicking the mouse on the color. You can refine the color using either method.

2. Choose the model in Select **M**odel and then enter a value for each color option; alternatively, you can use the mouse to choose the color.

3. Choose Save **A**s if you want to give your chosen colors a name and use them again later.

4. Choose OK to return to the Print Preferences dialog box; choose OK to return to the Preferences dialog box, and then choose **C**lose.

Improving Print Quality

If you print in color, you can improve the quality of your printed pieces by following a few simple guidelines.

- *Paper.* Use a cotton bond paper for best quality; copy paper has a hard surface that tends to allow *bleeding* (colors running together) of the inks.

- *Color Intensity.* Dark and intense colors print more ink to the page, sometimes causing the ink to spread or bleed. Use a cotton bond paper whenever you use intense colors.

- *High Quality Print Mode.* Printing in high-quality mode is slower but improves color quality immensely.

- *Color Palette.* Use a shade or tint—instead of fully intense colors—for a more professional look to your documents.

Troubleshooting

I looked for the fonts Helvetica and Times Roman, but WordPerfect doesn't offer these.

The names Helvetica and Times Roman are registered trademarks for popular typefaces. WordPerfect (and Windows in general) offers substitute typefaces (fonts) that are very nearly identical in appearance to the real Helvetica and Times Roman. Use New Times Roman as the equivalent of the Times Roman font; use Arial as the equivalent of the Helvetica font.

When I tried to change the kerning of a pair of letters, nothing happened.

WordPerfect offers a means to adjust the spacing between two letters. This is more often used in desktop publishing to adjust the kerning of the letter pair—for example, when kerned closer together the letters VA look more visually appealing, because the left side of the A tucks in neatly to the right side of the V. The kerning

(continues)

(continued)

adjustment—accessible by choosing Fo**r**mat, **T**ypesetting, **M**anual Kerning—works only with proportionally spaced fonts. These are fonts where characters take up only as much space on the line as they need to: i's take up less space than W's. Kerning will not work with monospaced fonts, such as Courier, because with these fonts all the characters take up the same amount of space on the line.

When I try to print a document with graphics, the text appears on the printed page, but not the graphics.

WordPerfect allows you to turn off graphic printing, and print just the text. Among other things, this feature lets you quickly create a "proof" of the text of a document, without spending the time to print the graphics that are in place. To enable graphic printing, choose **F**ile, **P**rint, and remove the check beside the Do Not Print **G**raphics option.

From Here...

In this chapter, you learned to design professional-looking documents, using WordPerfect as a desktop publishing program. You learned to plan the margins and columns of documents and the importance of choosing the right typefaces, type sizes, and alignment for text. In addition, you learned the importance of using kerning, letterspacing, and word spacing with some type sizes.

Using the design guidelines outlined in this chapter, you can create documents that are impressive and that attract the attention of the reader. This chapter also introduced you to using color in your printed documents. You can use WordPerfect's special color features and advanced printing techniques to produce a high-quality, professional document.

For more information on using WordPerfect as a desktop publishing tool, see the following chapters in this book:

- Chapter 4, "Formatting Text," details the basics of formatting text within WordPerfect, including formatting lines and paragraphs.
- Chapter 5, "Formatting Pages and Documents," provides specifics on applying formatting to entire pages and documents.

- Chapter 7, "Integrating Text and Graphics," shows you how to combine text and graphics in a document—the basis of using WordPerfect as a desktop publishing aid.
- Chapter 10, "Using Styles," shows you how styles work, and how they are used to control the appearance of text and graphics.
- Chapter 11, "Using Templates," discusses how WordPerfect uses templates as "boilerplate" files, which can be used as a starting point to creating desktop published documents.
- Chapter 14, "Working with Text Columns," shows you how to format text in columns, a common requirement when producing desktop-published documents combining both text and graphics.
- Chapter 21, "Using Advanced Graphics Techniques," discusses advanced graphics features of WordPerfect, including editing graphics.
- Chapter 22, "Using WP Draw and TextArt," provides information on using the drawing tools included with WordPerfect, Draw and TextArt.

Chapter 24

Using the Equation Editor

by Gordon Nelder-Adams

Everyone knows Einstein's famous equation, $E=MC^2$. Einstein had no trouble writing an equation like this on his chalkboard. But even a man of Einstein's genius may have had trouble figuring out to how show such equations in his favorite word processor (which undoubtedly would have been WordPerfect for Windows!).

Fortunately for the Einsteins of the world, WordPerfect 6.1 for Windows comes with an extremely powerful Equation Editor—a special tool designed just for creating equations of all shapes and sizes.

Mathematical equations have their own grammar and syntax, which is analogous to the grammar and syntax of written and spoken English. Just as you use a text editor to create and edit sentences, you can use WordPerfect's Equation Editor to create and edit equations. Although WordPerfect's text editing tools are ideal for creating words, sentences, and paragraphs, mathematical equations require more specialized tools to create multiple type sizes, special characters, varying line spacing, and complex alignment.

In this chapter, you learn to perform the following tasks with WordPerfect's Equation Editor:

- Type entries in the Editing Pane
- View equations in the Display Pane
- Insert commands, functions, and symbols from the equation palettes
- Create superscripts and subscripts, fractions, sums and integrals, roots, and matrices

- Number equations automatically
- Embed equations within text

Understanding the Equation Editor

You can use WordPerfect's Equation Editor to create complex, multilevel equations that would look perfectly at home in a calculus textbook, scientific paper, or engineering diagram. You can also use the Equation Editor to create simple fractions, square roots, and other common algebraic functions more likely to be helpful to the average user.

The Equation Editor uses a specialized syntax similar to the language you use to read equations out loud. For example, the syntax for creating a fraction is simply "a over b." After you enter a description of an equation, the Equation Editor performs all the formatting for you, automatically placing each element in the correct position, using the appropriate type sizes, and scaling mathematical symbols such as sums, integrals, roots, and parentheses to fit. The Equation Editor automatically positions, sizes, and aligns the elements in mathematical expressions such as complex ratios, built-up fractions, and multilevel subscripts and/or superscripts. The Equation Editor does not solve equations for you, nor does it check the mathematical validity of any equation you create.

When you create an equation, WordPerfect places it in a graphics box. You can then adjust the equation's size, shape, and position as you do any other graphics box. WordPerfect also provides all the symbol fonts necessary to display equations within your document exactly as they will print, so you can see an equation as you create or edit the surrounding text. The program can print equations on any printer, from a 9-pin impact printer to a PCL laser printer to a PostScript typesetter.

Starting the Equation Editor

The Equation Editor is a specialized graphics editor; therefore, the mechanics of creating, saving, and positioning equations are similar to those used for figures and other graphics boxes (see Chapter 7, "Integrating Text and Graphics," and Chapter 21, "Using Advanced Graphics Techniques").

Because you can choose which types of graphics boxes to include in the **G**raphics menu, before you can create an equation you must verify that E**q**uation is listed as an option. To do so, choose the **G**raphics menu. If E**q**uation is not listed, follow these steps to add the option:

1. With the **G**raphics menu still displayed, choose **G**raphics Styles.
2. Choose Bo**x** to display options for Graphics Box styles.
3. Choose **M**enu. The Edit Graphics Menu dialog box appears, which lists the available Graphics Box styles. Check boxes to the left of the styles indicate which styles appear in the menu (see fig. 24.1).

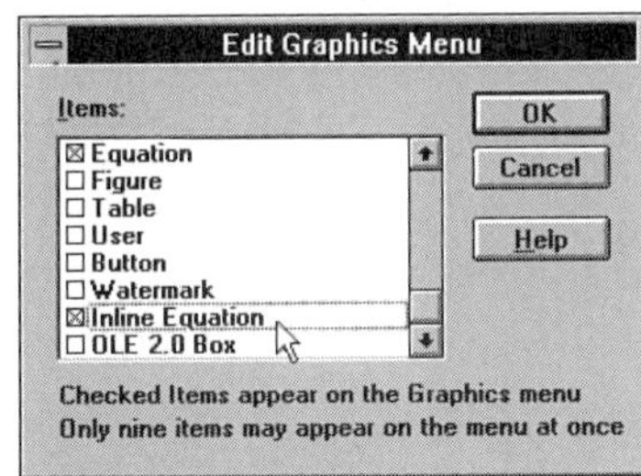

Fig. 24.1
The Edit Graphics Menu dialog box lets you choose which Graphics Box styles to display in the Graphics menu.

4. Select the Equation check box (if it is not already selected).
5. If you want to create inline equations, which can be embedded within a paragraph, select the Inline Equation check box.
6. Choose OK and then **C**lose to return to the document window.

To start the Equation Editor and create a new equation, choose **G**raphics, E**q**uation. The Equation Editor appears on-screen, temporarily replacing the normal document editing screen (see fig. 24.2).

Examining the Equation Editor

The Equation Editor consists of five main elements:

- The Editing Pane
- The Display Pane
- The Equation palette
- An abbreviated menu bar
- The Equation Editor Toolbar

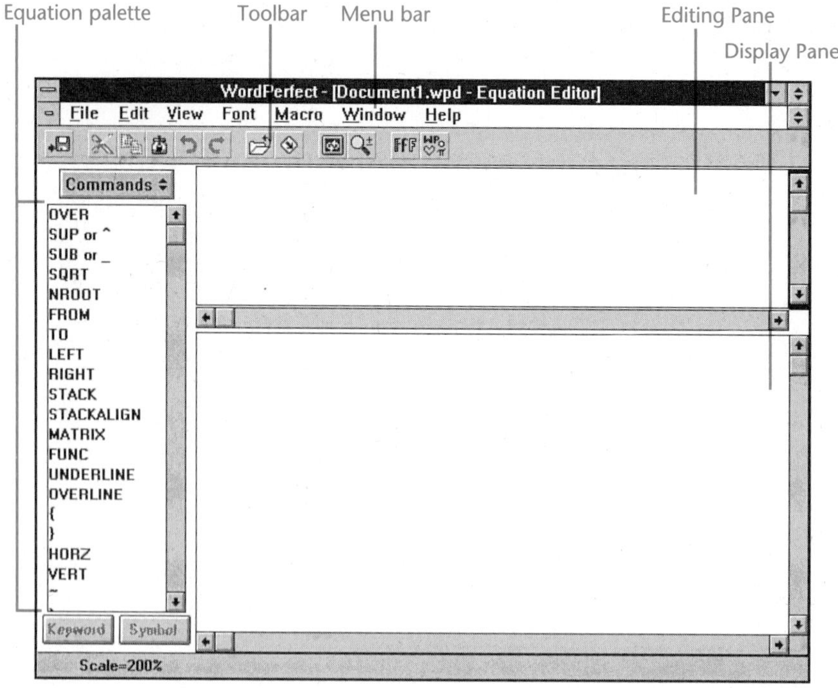

Fig. 24.2
The Equation Editor has its own menus and toolbars, equation palettes for inserting commands and special characters, an editing pane for typing equation texts, and a display pane for displaying equations as they will print.

◀ See "Using Graphics Boxes," p. 275

◀ See "Customizing Graphics Boxes," p. 719

Making full use of the Equation Editor requires using all five of its elements, as well as other available features, including the WordPerfect Characters dialog box and specialized equation keyboards.

When you call up the Equation Editor to create a new equation, the Editing Pane and Display Pane are empty (refer to fig. 24.2). You can switch between the Editing Pane, Display Pane, and equation palettes with the Next Pane and Previous Pane commands (F6, Shift+F6) or by using your mouse.

The Editing Pane, located at the top of the Equation Editor, is a simple text-editing window in which you type the text of an equation. The Editing Pane lets you use all the basic text-editing commands and techniques, but provides none of the normal formatting options. You can move by character, word, line, or to the top and bottom of an equation with the normal cursor-movement keys. You can select text by using Shift either with the cursor keys or with the mouse. You can delete selected text, or cut or copy it to the Clipboard, and paste it back once or many times. You can use Edit, Find (F2); or Edit, Replace (Ctrl+F2) to search for a word or number in a large equation or to replace it with an alternative throughout an equation. (You can also move information between the normal document screen and the Editing Pane by cutting or copying to the Clipboard.)

You cannot, however, use any of WordPerfect's normal formatting commands, such as font attributes or justification, in the Editing Pane. Instead, you type a text description of the equation you want to create, using special commands and symbols to format the equation. Each description can consist of text, variables, symbols, numbers, functions, and commands. You can insert these elements by typing directly from the keyboard, by selecting them from an Equation palette, or through the WordPerfect Characters dialog box.

You also can perform basic file operations in the Equation Editor. You can save the contents of the Editing Pane as a separate file, and retrieve other equation descriptions into the Editing Pane to modify or build upon.

When you want to see the current appearance of your equation, choose **V**iew, **R**edisplay; or press Ctrl+F3. WordPerfect displays the equation in the Display Pane (the lower half of the Equation Editor). If your equation is not syntactically correct, the program displays an error message instead of the equation.

As its name implies, the Display Pane displays an image of your equation as it will print. WordPerfect usually magnifies this image for ease of viewing, although you can zoom in or out to enlarge or reduce the view of a particular segment or the entire equation, and you can scroll within the window to display different parts of your equation. You cannot, however, make any changes in the Display Pane. If some part of your equation is incorrect, you must make changes in the Editing Pane.

Note

WordPerfect doesn't automatically display your equation in the Display Pane, nor does the program automatically update the display when you make changes in the Editing Pane. The Equation Editor cannot display an equation if its syntax is not correct, which is often the case while you are in the process of building an equation. After you create or change an equation, therefore, you should redisplay the equation to see the results.

When you need to insert a character, symbol, command, or function into an equation, you can type it from the keyboard or insert it from an Equation palette. The Equation Editor has eight palettes, similar in concept to the 15 character sets available in the WordPerfect Characters dialog box. Each palette provides quick access to a group of WordPerfect characters, formatting commands, or mathematical functions used frequently in the Equation Editor. You can browse through the palettes to find the symbol, command, or function you need, and then insert it into the Editing Pane.

The Equation Editor has a menu bar of its own, similar to WordPerfect's menu bar, but with fewer entries. The Equation Editor menu bar contains the following menus:

- ***File menu.*** Lets you save equations and return to the document, cancel changes, and save and retrieve equations as separate files.
- ***Edit menu.*** Lets you perform the standard editing undo, undelete, cut, copy, paste, find, and replace operations.
- ***View menu.*** Lets you redisplay equations in the View Pane, zoom the display of the View Pane, or turn the palettes and Toolbar off or on.
- ***Font menu.*** Lets you choose a font to be used in the Equation Editor, and call up the WordPerfect Characters dialog box.
- ***Macro menu.*** Lets you record or play macros to automate Equation Editor tasks.
- ***Window menu.*** Lets you switch between the Equation Editor and an open document, or tile or cascade all open windows.
- ***Help menu.*** Lets you call up the WordPerfect Help system.

Finally, the Equation Editor has its own Toolbar and keyboard, which are automatically activated whenever you call up the Equation Editor. Each contains features and functions useful in the Equation Editor.

Creating a Simple Equation

Before examining the Equation Editor's syntax and command structure in detail, create a few simple equations and observe how WordPerfect interprets them.

Creating Proper Spacing in an Equation

The Equation Editor doesn't interpret normal spaces between words in the same manner that WordPerfect does. Instead, you have to instruct the Equation Editor where to add spaces and how much space to add. To see how the Equation Editor uses spacing, follow these steps:

1. Choose **G**raphics, E**q**uation. The Equation Editor appears. The insertion point is in the Editing Pane, and the Equation palette is displayed.

2. Type the following equation, using the space bar to create the spaces before and after the plus (+) and equal (=) signs:

   2x + 3y = 24

3. Choose **V**iew, **R**edisplay; or press Ctrl+F3. Your equation appears in the Display Pane, but it doesn't look quite the way you typed it. Instead, it appears as follows:

   $2x{+}3y{=}24$

   The Equation Editor doesn't interpret spaces that you type in the Editing Pane as spaces in the printed equation. In many cases, equations require spacing far narrower than standard spacing, so the Equation Editor demands that you explicitly enter spacing instructions by using a tilde (~) to create a normal space and an opening single quotation mark (‘) to create a thin space, which is one-quarter the width of a normal space.

4. Edit your original equation so that it reads as follows in the Editing Pane:

   2x~+~3y~=~24

5. Choose **V**iew, **R**edisplay; or press Ctrl+F3. In the Display Pane your equation now appears like this:

   $2x + 3y = 24$

6. Choose **F**ile, **C**lose; or press Ctrl+F4.

   Your equation appears horizontally centered in your document.

The tilde (~) and left quote (‘) can be called formatting spaces, because they are the codes that control the spacing format of printed equations. If you do not use formatting spaces in your equations, WordPerfect runs the clauses in your equation together. As you work in the Editing Pane, however, the Equation Editor treats the formatting space codes as it does any other character for the purposes of cursor movement and text editing.

Normal spaces, created by pressing the space bar, don't affect the appearance of the printed equation, but make working in the Editing Pane much easier. Normal spaces separate items and improve readability of the text in the Editing Pane. They also break an equation up into "words," which you can move through quickly using the Ctrl+left arrow and Ctrl+right arrow keys, as in a normal document.

Just as pressing the space bar inserts a nonprinting space, pressing the Enter key in the Editing Pane inserts a nonprinting hard return. The hard return moves the cursor to the next line in the Editing Pane without affecting the appearance of the printed equation. Like normal spaces, hard returns improve the readability of equations in the Editing Pane by letting you put individual clauses on lines by themselves. If you want a printed equation to contain two or more lines, you must use the STACK or STACKALIGN commands. See the section "Creating Multiline Expressions with STACK and STACKALIGN" later in this chapter for more information.

In practice, you should use a combination of normal spaces and formatting spaces when you create and edit equations, to make the equation easier to work with in the Editing Pane, and to ensure the proper formatting of the printed equations.

Creating a Simple Fraction

You also use regular spaces in the Editing Pane to separate commands and variables. OVER, for example, is the Equation Editor command that creates a fraction. You type **a OVER b** to create the following equation:

$$\frac{a}{b}$$

Because the printed equation contains no spaces, you don't need to use tildes. You might assume, therefore, that you can omit regular spaces from the typed equation as well. Typing **aOVERb**, however, produces the following equation:

$$aoverb$$

Without the spaces around OVER, the Equation Editor cannot recognize it as a command, and instead treats the entire phrase as a single, six-letter variable.

Create the following sample equation using the OVER command:

$$\frac{2x}{3y} = 24$$

To create the equation, follow these steps:

1. Choose **G**raphics, E**q**uation.

2. In the Editing Pane, type the following equation:

 2x over 3y ~=~ 24

> **Note**
>
> You don't need to capitalize the OVER command; Equation Editor commands are not case-sensitive.

3. Choose **V**iew, **R**edisplay; or press Ctrl+F3. Your equation now looks like this:

$$2\frac{x}{3}y = 24$$

 Again, this is not quite what you want. The Equation Editor recognized the OVER command, but it did not recognize "2x" and "3y" as belonging together. The Equation Editor makes very few assumptions about which letters, characters, and symbols should be grouped together and which should not. Just as you must indicate formatting spaces by inserting tildes and left quotes, you must use braces ({ and }) around groups of characters on which you want the Equation Editor to perform some action.

4. In the Editing Pane, change the text again to read as follows:

 {2x} over {3y} ~=~ 24

5. Choose **V**iew, **R**edisplay; or press Ctrl+F3. Now the equation appears as desired.

Creating Superscripts and Subscripts

Superscripts and subscripts are as common as fractions in many equations. WordPerfect's normal text attributes do not work in the Equation Editor, so you must use commands to create superscripts and subscripts in equations. These commands are SUP and SUB, respectively. Because these two commands are used so frequently, WordPerfect provides abbreviated forms of the commands. In place of SUP you can use a caret (^) to create a superscript, and in place of SUB you can use an underline (_) to create a subscript.

Therefore, to produce the simple expression x^2, you can type **x SUP 2**, or simply **x^2**. To produce x_1, you can type **x SUB 1**, or simply **x_1**. As with OVER, you must use regular spaces around SUP and SUB. You do not need to use spaces around the caret and underline characters because their meanings are always clear, and the Equation Editor reserves their use for these commands.

You can nest multiple levels of super- and subscripts, using braces if necessary. Examine the following typed equations and their printed appearances:

(a)	**(b)**	**(c)**	**(d)**
x^e^n	x^e^n-1	x^e^{n-1}	x^e^n_1
$x^{e^{n}}$	$x^{e^{n}}-1$	$x^{e^{n-1}}$	$x^{e^{n_1}}$

As you can see, WordPerfect chooses a smaller point size for each successive level. Also, note the difference that adding braces makes between equations (b) and (c).

Finally, you can add both a superscript and a subscript to the same character. For example, to create the following expression:

$$x_1^2$$

you type the following:

x_1^2

To make the superscript appear immediately over the subscript, you must type the subscript first, then the superscript.

Editing Equations

If you discover a mistake in an equation after you have closed the Equation Editor and returned to your main document, or need to edit the equation for some other reason, you can return to the Equation Editor to make further changes in an equation.

To edit an existing equation, follow these steps:

1. Choose **G**raphics, **E**dit Box; or press Shift+F11. If you only have one graphics box in your document, WordPerfect immediately selects the box and displays the Graphics Box Feature Bar. (The feature bar is described in detail in the "Changing Equation Box Options" section later in this chapter.)

If you have more than one graphics box, WordPerfect displays the Edit Box dialog box. Choose Equation Box, and then enter the number of the equation you want to edit in the Counter Number box. WordPerfect selects the box and displays the Graphics Box Feature Bar.

2. Choose C**o**ntent; or press Alt+Shift+O. WordPerfect displays the Box Content dialog box.

3. Choose **E**dit. The Equation Editor appears, displaying the selected equation.

Tip

To edit an equation quickly, double-click the equation with your mouse. The Equation Editor opens and automatically retrieves the equation.

Reviewing Key Concepts

Now that you've created a few equations and have some feel for how the Equation Editor works, you are ready to examine some concepts and terminology in more depth. Although learning the syntax of individual commands is important, understanding the concepts on which those commands are based is equally important.

At first glance, many commands can appear to be confusing and arbitrary collections of symbols. With a little background knowledge, the command syntax becomes logical and necessary. In the following sections, you learn some definitions and general rules of syntax. Then you examine the parts of the Equation Editor in more detail, before returning to more specific examples of Equation Editor formatting commands.

Defining Terms

A *command* is a reserved word or character that tells the Equation Editor to perform a formatting action on the text that follows. OVER, SUP, and SUB (or ^ and _) are examples of commands. Table 24.1 contains a full list of Equation Editor commands and their meanings.

A *function* is a word recognized by the Equation Editor as a standard mathematical function, such as *log* or *sin*. A full list of functions can be found in table 24.3, located in the later section "Using Functions and Commands To Create Equations."

A *symbol* is any character that is not a standard letter or number. Symbols frequently used in the Equation Editor can be found in the Greek, Symbols, Arrows, Large, Sets, and Other equation palettes. The complete set of WordPerfect Characters is available by choosing Edit, Characters; or by pressing Ctrl+W.

A *keyword* is an alphabetic description of a command, function, or symbol. Commands and functions are keywords by definition. However, just as SUP and SUB can be represented by ^ and _, each symbol can be inserted as a keyword or an individual character. Thus, BETA is the keyword for the symbol Β. You can use either the keyword or the equivalent character in the equation text to make the symbol appear in the printed equation.

A *variable* is any sequence of letters and numbers that the Equation Editor doesn't recognize as a command, function, or other keyword. Variables can be one or more characters long and must start with a letter of the alphabet, but can contain numbers also. Any word not having a special meaning is treated as a variable. A variable must be followed by a nonalphabetic character, such as a symbol, a normal space, or a hard return. Examples of variables include *x*, *B1*, and *velocity*; by default, the Equation Editor prints variables in italic type.

A *number* is any non-negative integer (such as 0, 1, or 387) that is followed by a space, an alphabetic character, a symbol, or a period. Thus, although B2 is a variable, 2B is the number 2 followed by the variable B. The Equation Editor doesn't recognize real numbers (negative numbers and decimals, such as –2 or 3.1) as units, and treats minus signs and decimal points as separate characters. To make the Equation Editor treat real numbers as units, you must use braces around real numbers to group them, such as {–2} or {3.1}.

Table 24.1 Equation Editor Commands

Command Keyword	Description
OVER	Fraction
SUP or ^	Superscript
SUB or _	Subscript
SQRT	Square root
NROOT	Nth root
FROM	Limits
TO	Limits
LEFT	Left delimiter
RIGHT	Right delimiter
STACK	Vertical stack

Command Keyword	Description
STACKALIGN	Vertical stack with character alignment
MATRIX	Matrix
FUNC	User-defined function
UNDERLINE	Underline
OVERLINE	Overline
{	Start group
}	End group
HORZ	Horizontal move
VERT	Vertical move
~	Normal space
'	Thin space (1/4 of normal space)
BINOM	Binomial
&	Column separator
#	Row separator
MATFORM	Matrix column format
ALIGNL	Align left
ALIGNR	Align right
ALIGNC	Align center
PHANTOM	Place holder
.	No delimiter
\	Literal
BOLD	Bold attribute
ITAL	Italic attribute
OVERSM	Fraction small
BINOMSM	Binomial small
LINESPACE	Vertical (line) spacing

(continues)

Table 24.1 Continued

Command Keyword	Description
LONGDIV	Long division
LONGDIVS	Long division (square symbol)
SCALESYM	Scale symbol

Understanding Syntax

An equation text resembles a sentence. Commands act the part of verbs; numbers, variables, and other symbols take the place of nouns. Just as each language has its own rules of grammar and syntax, the Equation Editor has specific rules that govern how you combine the various elements of an equation. The Equation Editor doesn't check to see whether your equation makes sense, only that it is syntactically correct. In the Equation Editor, as in English, you can construct a sentence that is syntactically correct but means something other than what you intended, or one that is missing an essential part of speech and is meaningless. It is up to you to ensure that the equation makes sense.

Your equation text must provide the necessary commands for what actions are to be taken, and what groups of characters those commands should act upon. The Equation Editor then performs the mechanics of positioning the various elements of an equation, selecting the proper type sizes, and creating graphic symbols where necessary. As long as your equation's syntax is correct, the Equation Editor shows it in the Display Pane, although the displayed equation may not be exactly what you intended. If your syntax is faulty, however, when you choose **V**iew, **R**edisplay, the Editor displays an `ERROR: Incorrect Syntax` message in the status bar and moves the insertion point to a part of your equation text that it recognizes as faulty. If your equation has more than one error, you may have to edit and attempt to redisplay several times.

The following syntax rules apply to all equations. Some commands have additional syntax rules, as described in the "Using Functions and Commands To Create Equations" section later in this chapter.

- Commands are not case-sensitive. You can type a command in all uppercase, all lowercase, or in mixed case. **OVER**, **over**, and **Over** are all acceptable commands.

- All commands must be separated from variables that come immediately before and after them. You can use the space bar, press Enter, or insert a symbol to separate a command from a following variable or number.

  You can place a number immediately before a command, but if you place a number immediately after a command, the Equation Editor interprets the two elements as a single variable. For example, typing **3OVER 5** creates the fraction 3/5, but typing **3OVER5** creates the expression 3 OVER5. The best practice, therefore, is to use spaces around commands at all times. When you choose a command from the Equation palette, the Editor automatically puts a space before and after the command and displays the command in uppercase letters.

- Commands act only on individual elements of an equation, whether those elements are numbers, variables, or characters. If you want a command to act on several elements as a group, you must put braces ({}) around the elements you want to combine. The Equation Editor then formats everything between the pair of braces as a single group.

Tip
Putting spaces around commands is a good way to avoid syntax errors.

- You can create groups within groups by using additional pairs of braces.

- Braces must appear in pairs. Mismatched braces are the most common cause of syntax errors.

- When formatting equations, the Equation Editor groups elements in the following order of precedence:

  1. Groups formed by braces ({})
  2. Diacritical marks (such as overbars, vectors, and tildes)
  3. Primes, SUB, SUP, FROM, and TO
  4. Roots
  5. OVER, BINOM
  6. Other elements from left to right

  Groups formed by braces ({}) take precedence in all cases. When the Equation Editor doesn't format a clause as you desired, you can always override its defaults by establishing a group.

Working with the Equation Editor Features

As you saw in the examples earlier in this chapter, you can create and edit many equations in the Editing Pane using only the keyboard, without employing the other resources the Equation Editor provides. Making full use of the Equation Editor, however, requires making full use of its features: the keyboard, specialized equation keyboards, the equation palettes, the WordPerfect Characters dialog box, and the Equation Editor Toolbar.

Using the Editing Pane

The Editing Pane provides a full text-editing environment with most of the editing features available in a normal document. You can use the normal directional keys to move by character, word, line, or to the top or bottom of an equation, or you can select any insertion point with the mouse. You can select text by using Shift with the insertion point-movement keys or by using the mouse. You can delete selected text, or you can cut or copy it to the Clipboard and paste it back once or many times. You also can move information between the normal document screen and the Editing Pane by cutting or copying to the Clipboard.

You can enter letters, numbers, and other keyboard characters by typing directly in the Editing Pane. You can also insert many mathematical symbols and characters using the Equation palette, but if you need to include the following common characters in an equation you must enter them from the keyboard:

+ - * / = < > ! ? . | @ , ; :

Several other common characters must also be entered from the keyboard, but have special meaning to the Equation Editor. These are:

~ ‘ “ \ # & { } ( ) [ ]

You already have seen the tilde (~) and left quotation mark (‘) used. The meanings of the other characters are described in the later section “Using Functions and Commands To Create Equations.”

Using an Equation Keyboard

Just as WordPerfect supplies a Toolbar customized for use in the Equation Editor, the program also supplies an equation keyboard with keys mapped to Equation Editor functions. Although you cannot edit this keyboard, you can copy it and then edit the copy as you would any other keyboard, moving commands from one function key to another or assigning macros or special characters to Ctrl+key combinations.

While in the Equation Editor, you can select which keyboard it uses. To do so, follow these steps:

1. Choose **E**dit, Pr**e**ferences. The Preferences dialog box appears, with most options grayed.
2. Choose **K**eyboard. The Keyboard Preferences dialog box appears.
3. Highlight the Equation Editor Keyboard, and choose **S**elect.
4. Choose **C**lose to close the Preferences dialog box.

The new equation keyboard will now be selected whenever the Editing Pane is active. See the WordPerfect manual for a complete list of shortcut keys contained in the equation keyboard. You can add any command or other keyword you use frequently to this keyboard, and assign that text to a keystroke combination. See Chapter 9, "Customizing WordPerfect," for more information on editing keyboards.

Using the Equation Palettes

The equation keyboard lets you insert common characters and symbols with a single keystroke combination, but you are limited by the number of keys available on a keyboard. Unless you use the equation keyboard frequently, you may have trouble remembering which characters are assigned to which keys. Although not as quick to use, the Equation palettes provide access to many more symbols and mathematical functions, as well as to the main Equation Editor formatting commands.

The Equation Editor displays one palette at a time, at the left of the screen. At the top of the currently displayed palette is the Equation palette pop-up list, a large button that displays the name of the current palette. You can browse through the palette to find the symbol, command, or function you need; then you can insert the item you choose into the Editing Pane. Table 24.2 lists the names of the palettes and their contents.

Table 24.2 The Equation Palettes

Palette	Contents
Commands	The main Equation Editor formatting commands
Large	Large and small versions of common mathematical and scientific terms, including brackets, braces, sums, and integrals
Symbols	Common mathematical symbols
Greek	The entire Greek alphabet, in upper- and lowercase letters
Arrows	Single and double arrows pointing in various directions, as well as circles, squares, and triangles
S**e**ts	Mathematical set symbols
Other	Diacritical marks and ellipses
Function	Trigonometric and other mathematical functions

You can insert commands and functions only as keywords. You can insert items from the other groups as keywords or as the symbols their keywords represent. Symbols such as Greek letters and other characters always print as symbols, regardless of whether you enter them in the Editing Pane as keywords or symbols. Keywords are usually quicker to type than to select through an Equation palette, but they take up more room in the Editing Pane. If you use symbols, your equation text will more closely resemble the printed equation, but selecting symbols through the palettes takes longer than typing keywords (although you can insert some symbols quickly from the equation keyboard).

When you insert a command, function, or symbol into the Editing Pane from an Equation palette, the Equation Editor puts a space before and after the item, whether it is inserted as a keyword or as a symbol.

To use an Equation palette, move the insertion point in the Editing Pane to where you want to insert a command or symbol; then perform the following steps:

1. Choose the desired palette by pressing the Equation palette pop-up list button with your mouse. When the list of palettes appears, drag up or down and release to select the desired palette.

Alternatively, choose Next Pane (F6) to activate the Equation palette. Then press Alt+PgUp or Alt+PgDn to cycle through the palettes until you reach the desired palette.

2. Highlight a symbol or command in the selected palette using your mouse or the cursor keys. As each item is highlighted, its keyword appears at the bottom of the screen. If the entire menu will not fit in the space available on-screen, a vertical scroll bar appears that you can click with your mouse. You can also continue to scroll using the up- and down-arrow keys, or use PgDn and PgUp to move to the bottom or top of the palette.

3. At the bottom of the palette are two buttons labeled Keyword and Symbol. Click on either button with your mouse to insert the item in the form indicated. (Because commands and functions can only be entered as keywords, the Symbol button is grayed when either of those menus is displayed.)

   Alternatively, press Enter to insert the item as a keyword, or press Ctrl+Enter to insert the item as a symbol.

> **Note**
>
> You can double-click on an item to insert it as a keyword, or hold down the Ctrl key and double-click to insert the item as a symbol.

If you need more room on-screen, you can turn off the Equation palette by choosing **V**iew, **P**alette. Use the same actions to turn the palette back on.

Using WordPerfect Characters

Although the Equation palettes provide access to a wide variety of characters commonly used in equations, they do not contain every available WordPerfect character. If you need to enter some other character into an equation, you have access to the full set of nearly 2,000 characters that WordPerfect recognizes. To access these characters, choose F**o**nt, **C**haracter; or press Ctrl+W. The WordPerfect Characters dialog box appears in the lower right corner of the Equation Editor, partially obscuring the Display Pane.

You can choose from the 15 different character sets (0-14), select a character, and insert it into the Editing Pane in a manner nearly identical to using the Equation palettes. If you only need one special character, you can close the dialog box after you insert the character. To insert additional characters, you can leave the dialog box open and switch between it and the Editing Pane. You can redisplay equations while the WordPerfect Characters dialog box is open, but they will be partially hidden until you close the dialog box. See Chapter 20, "Using Fonts and Special Characters," for more information on WordPerfect Characters.

Altering the Equation Display

By default, the Equation Editor displays equations in the Display Pane at 200% magnification, or twice actual size. If you create large equations, however, your equations may not fit entirely within the Display Pane. You can change the degree that the Equation Editor magnifies equations, from a low of 10% (one tenth actual size) to a high of 1000% (ten times actual size). The status bar at the bottom of the screen displays the current degree of magnification.

To change the degree of magnification, choose **V**iew, **Z**oom Display. WordPerfect displays the Zoom Equation Display dialog box (see fig. 24.3). Choosing any percentage option from 50% to 200% changes the display to that magnification. You can choose one of several standard magnifications—**5**0%, **7**5%, **1**00%, 15**0**%, or **2**00%—or choose **O**ther, and enter any percentage from 10% to 1000%. You can type in a value, or click on the scroll buttons to change the percentage by 5% increments. The Equation **H**eight option increases or decreases the magnification so that the equation fills the entire height of the Display Pane. The Equation **W**idth option changes the magnification so that the equation fills the entire width of the Display Pane. The **F**ull Equation option changes the display height or width as necessary to display both the entire width and height of the equation within the Display Pane. At some magnifications, the entire equation may not fit within the Display Pane.

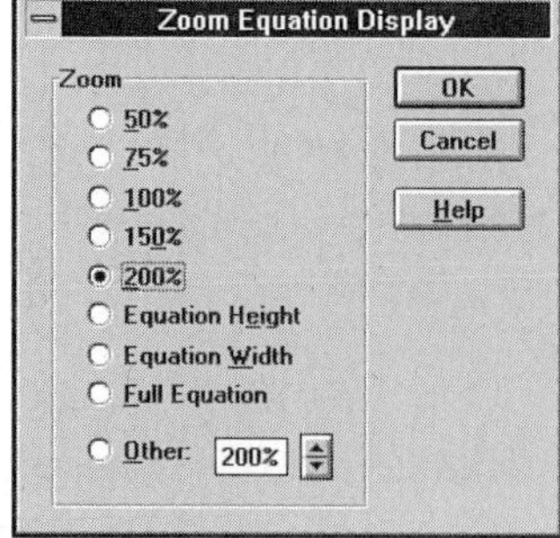

Fig. 24.3
You can change the view of the Display Pane to show an equation at several degrees of magnification, or the equation's full height or width.

The Equation Editor always displays scroll bars in the Editing Pane and View Pane. You can use these scroll bars to move the equation within the Display Pane without changing its magnification.

Moving or resizing an equation in the Display Pane does not affect the printed appearance of the equation. To change the printed size, see the "Changing Equation Box Options" section later in this chapter.

Using the Equation Toolbar

The Equation Editor has its own Toolbar, to which WordPerfect has already added buttons for the most useful Equation Editor options. Whenever you call up the Equation Editor, WordPerfect displays this Toolbar by default. You can switch to a different Toolbar once you are in the Equation Editor, although all buttons for features not available in the Equation Editor will be grayed.

◀ See "Customizing Keyboards," p. 342

◀ See "Working with the Toolbar," p. 452

◀ See "WordPerfect Characters," p. 686

As with any other Toolbar, you can edit the Equation Editor Toolbar to assign various menu commands, keyboard scripts, or macros to individual buttons. You can change its position on-screen, and choose to display button text, pictures, or both. If you need more room on-screen, you can turn off the Toolbar by choosing **V**iew, **T**oolbar.

Troubleshooting

When I insert a space in an equation, WordPerfect ignores it when it displays the equation in my document.

Spaces and other "white space"—like tabs and hard returns—are ignored in the Equation Editor. To insert a space in the equation, use the ~ (tilde) character for a full space, and the ` (grave accent) character for a half space.

When I use the ` key, it doesn't create a "half space" as it's supposed to.

The character for creating a half space in an equation is the ` character, or grave accent. It's not the apostrophe character. Using the apostrophe character instead of the grave accent character will lead to an error. On most computer keyboards, the grave accent character is in the upper left corner, on the same key as the ~ (tilde). You can also insert the grave accent by choosing it in the Commands list on the left side of the Equation Editor window.

I don't see an Inline Equations command in the Graphics menu.

As it comes "out of the box," WordPerfect doesn't display the Inline Equation command in the Graphics menu. If you want to create inline equations, you should add the command to the menu. See the section "Starting the Equation Editor" earlier in this chapter for details on adding the Inline Equation command to the Graphics menu.

Using Functions and Commands To Create Equations

Although the Equation Editor automatically performs certain formatting tasks, such as printing variables in italic and functions in standard type, you must provide most formatting instructions yourself. You have seen several commands used, including OVER, SUP, and SUB (^ and _). The following sections explore other useful commands, from basic to complex, that you can use to format equations to your exact needs.

Using Functions in the Equation Editor

The Equation Editor follows accepted mathematical rules in formatting equations. In particular, this requires setting recognized mathematical functions in regular type and setting variables in italic type. As a result, any word that the Editor doesn't recognize as a function, command, or other keyword is treated as a variable and is automatically set in italics. The words recognized by the Equation Editor as functions are standard terms for trigonometric, logarithmic, and other mathematical functions. Table 24.3 lists the functions and their descriptions.

Table 24.3 Equation Editor Functions

Keyword	Description
cos	Cosine
sin	Sine
tan	Tangent
arccos	Arc cosine
arcsin	Arc sine
arctan	Arc tangent
cosh	Hyberbolic cosine
sinh	Hyperbolic sine
tanh	Hyperbolic tangent
cot	Cotangent
coth	Hyperbolic cotangent
sec	Secant

Keyword	Description
cosec	Cosecant
exp	Exponent
log	Logarithm
ln	Natural logarithm
lim	Limit
liminf	Limit inferior
limsup	Limit superior
min	Minimum
max	Maximum
gcd	Greatest common denominator
arc	Arc function
det	Determinant
mod	Modulo

You can type functions directly or insert them from the Function Equation palette. The palette always uses lowercase letters when inserting functions into the Editing Pane, and automatically puts a space before and after each function. As with commands, functions require either a space, hard return, or symbol on either side to be recognized by the Equation Editor.

Although you can enter functions in either upper- or lowercase, the lowercase used by the Function Equation palette is the normal mathematical practice. In mathematical typesetting, functions are often separated from variables by a thin space ('), which is 1/4 the width of a normal space.

For example, you type

B'cos'theta ~+~ A

to produce the equation shown in figure 24.4.

The Equation Editor recognizes the letters *A* and *B* as variables and therefore italicizes them. It recognizes cos as a function and formats it in normal type. It recognizes theta as the keyword for a Greek letter. Thin spaces separate cos from the letter *B* and theta, but full spaces separate the plus sign from the whole first clause and from the letter *A* that follows.

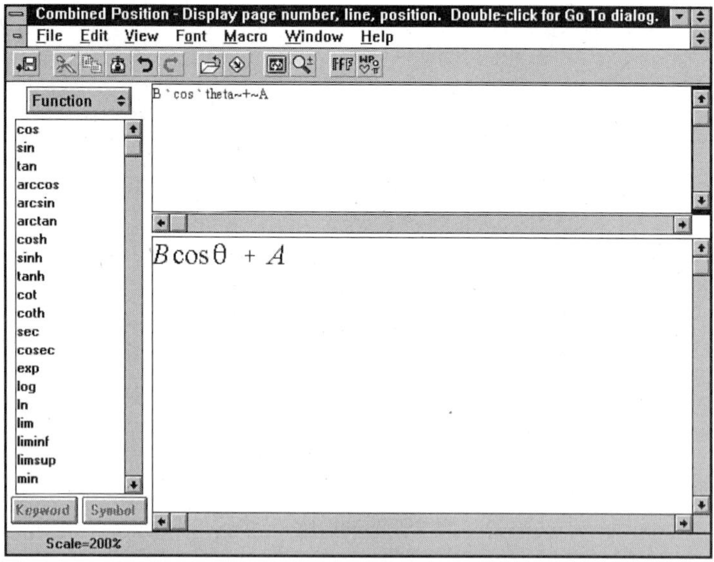

Fig. 24.4
The Equation Editor's Function Equation palette lets you insert trigonometric functions, which are commonly followed by a thin space.

Using FUNC, BOLD, and ITAL To Format Equations

The Equation Editor displays functions as typed, in normal (non-italic) font. Unfortunately, the Equation Editor treats everything it does *not* recognize as a function, command, symbol, or other keyword as a variable and italicizes it. Suppose that you want to create the following equation for Present Value:

You may be tempted to type the following:

$$\mathrm{Present\ Value} = \mathrm{Payment}\ (\frac{1 - (1 + \mathrm{interest\ rate})^{-\mathrm{number\ of\ payments}}}{\mathrm{interest\ rate}})$$

```
Present~ Value ~=~ Payment~ ({1 ~-~ (1 ~+~ interest~ rate)^...
{-number~ of~ payments}} over {interest~ rate})
```

The Equation Editor does not recognize any word except *over* as a keyword, and therefore treats the rest as variables, with the following result:

$$Present\ Value = Payment\ (\frac{1 - (1 + interest\ rate)^{-number\ of\ payments}}{interest\ rate})$$

To format this equation without italic type, you must use the command FUNC. FUNC instructs the Equation Editor to treat the item that follows it as a function. The item can be a single variable, a grouped word or phrase, or an entire equation. The Editor then formats the indicated text normally instead of italicizing it. To correct the preceding equation text, insert the command FUNC at the beginning and surround the rest of the equation with braces, as follows:

> **FUNC {Present~ Value ~=~ Payment[t]l ({1 ~-~ (1 ~+~ interest~ rate)^{-number~ of~ payments}} over {interest~ rate})}**

The equation now appears as desired. Whenever you use FUNC, make sure that you properly group the desired text with braces ({}).

Because the Equation Editor always formats functions in normal type by default, it also provides the command ITAL to italicize functions. You use ITAL in exactly the same manner as FUNC, and you can use both simultaneously. You can use FUNC on an entire equation, for example, and use ITAL to italicize a smaller group within the equation.

You can use a third command, BOLD, in a similar manner to set part (or all) of an equation in bold type. UNDERLINE and OVERLINE are similar to BOLD and ITAL in syntax and usage.

Note

WordPerfect's normal Bold (Ctrl+B), Italic (Ctrl+I), and Underline (Ctrl+U) commands have no effect in the Equation Editor.

Using \ To Format Literals

When you include a common word in your equation text that also happens to be a keyword for a mathematical symbol, such as *and*, *or*, *in*, or *not*, the Equation Editor formats the word as a symbol instead of as a word. You can correct this situation by placing a backslash (\) immediately before the misinterpreted word, in the following manner:

> **\and**

The backslash is a command that instructs the Equation Editor to treat the following symbol or command as a literal; that is, to render it exactly as typed. If you use braces ({}) in an equation, for instance, the Equation

Editor assumes that you are trying to group the text in between, and does not print the braces. To cause them to print, place a backslash before each brace, as in the following example:

\{ equation \}

You must also use a backslash if you want to print characters such as a tilde (~), ampersand (&), pound sign (#), the backslash itself (\), or other keywords such as BOLD or UNDERLINE.

Forming Fractions with the OVER, LEFT, and RIGHT Commands

You have already seen the OVER command used to create a fraction in the form

x over y

where x and y can be individual characters or groups. As with multiple levels of superscripts and subscripts, the Equation Editor can create fractions within fractions, as long as each successive level of fractions is properly grouped with braces so that it can be treated as a single item. For instance, the equation text

{{x^2 ~+~ 5} over y} over 2

creates the following result:

$$\frac{\frac{x^2 + 5}{y}}{2}$$

where $x^2 + 5$ is placed over y, and the entire fraction is then grouped and placed over 2.

You also can use a variant of the OVER command, OVERSM, to set the numerator and denominator in the next smaller size of type than the rest of an equation. In all other respects, OVERSM works in exactly the same manner as OVER.

More complex equations frequently use parentheses (( )), brackets ([ ]), and braces ({ }) as delimiters to enclose individual clauses. When surrounding a single line of text, these symbols can be used as they are (although each brace must be preceded by a backslash to print). Used by themselves, however, these characters are not tall enough to properly enclose multiple-line fractions.

You can use the commands LEFT and RIGHT with delimiters to create dynamic delimiters that automatically expand to the height of the equation they surround. Table 24.4 lists the available delimiters.

Table 24.4 Dynamic Delimiters

Delimiter	Description
(	Left parenthesis
)	Right parenthesis
[	Left bracket
]	Right bracket
< or LANGLE	Left angle bracket
> or RANGLE	Right angle bracket
\{ or LBRACE	Left brace
\} or RBRACE	Right brace
¦ or LINE	Single vertical line
DLINE	Double vertical line

You can rewrite the Present Value equation in an abbreviated form as follows:

```
PV ~=~ PMT~ LEFT [ {1 ~-~ (1~+~ i)^{-n}} OVER i RIGHT ]
```

with the following result:

$$PV = PMT\left[\frac{1 - (1 + i)^{-n}}{i}\right]$$

In this example, the parentheses ( ) are used normally, the brackets [ ] are used with LEFT and RIGHT to create dynamic delimiters, and the braces { } are used to group the numerator, and therefore do not print. The Equation Editor automatically expands the height of the brackets to match the enclosed text.

If you enclosed multiple levels of an equation with delimiters, the Equation Editor adjusts the height of each pair of delimiters to the appropriate height. For example, typing the following:

a ~+~ LEFT \{‘ b OVER {c ~+~ LEFT \{‘ d ~+~ e OVER {f ~+~
LEFT\{‘ g OVER {h ~+~ DOTSAXIS} ‘ RIGHT \} }
‘ RIGHT \} } ‘ RIGHT \}

creates the following equation:

$$a + \left\{ \frac{b}{c + \left\{ d + \frac{e}{f + \left\{ \frac{g}{h + \cdots} \right\}} \right\}} \right\}$$

The Equation Editor automatically positions and sizes the braces correctly. The DOTSAXIS keyword, located in the Other equation palette, creates the centered ellipsis (...).

You must always use the LEFT and RIGHT commands as a pair, although you do not need to use the same left and right delimiters. If you want to use a single delimiter, you can substitute a period (.) for the delimiter that you don't want to print. For example, typing the following:

LEFT . {7x} OVER {x~+~3} RIGHT LINE_0^5

creates the following equation:

$$\left. \frac{7x}{x + 3} \right|_0^5$$

Creating Sums and Integrals

Although you can create most of the equations you have seen thus far outside of the Equation Editor, specialized constructs such as sums and integrals are nearly impossible to create any other way. Using the Equation Editor, these constructs are no more difficult to produce than a simple fraction.

You use the SUM and INT operators with the FROM and TO commands to create a sum or an integral using the following syntax:

```
operator FROM x TO y
```

where operator is SUM or INT, and *x* and *y* are variables for the beginning and ending limits. For example, typing the following

INT FROM 0 TO inf ~ x^2 ~+~ 2

creates the following equation:

$$\int_{0}^{\infty} x^2 + 2$$

And typing the following

SUM FROM {i=1} TO N F_i ' DELTA t_i

creates the following equation:

$$\sum_{i=1}^{N} F_i \Delta t_i$$

The use of FROM and TO is optional. You can use none, one, or both, but you cannot use TO without FROM. You can trick the Editor, however, by using a space (~) after FROM.

FROM and TO always place the limits below and above the symbols, respectively. If you want the limits to appear to the side, use SUP and SUB instead. Notice that you must use braces around limits such as {i=1} for them to be treated as a single item.

Also, notice the use of keywords for symbols. INF is the keyword for infinity, and is not case-sensitive. The keywords for Greek letters, however, *are* case-sensitive, since the Greek alphabet contains both upper- and lowercase characters. Therefore, DELTA is typed in all capitals to create a capital Delta symbol.

If you want to enlarge a sum or integral symbol, you can use the command SCALESYM following the syntax:

```
SCALESYM (% of normal) operator
```

Therefore, the equation text

SCALESYM 200 INT

creates an integral sign twice the normal size. Although SCALESYM is most useful with SUM and INT, it can be used with any character.

You can use the FROM command to position items below other functions and symbols. For example, typing the following:

lim FROM {t-> inf} " x(t)

creates the equation:

$$\lim_{t \to \infty} x(t)$$

Notice that the combination of a minus sign and a greater than sign (–>) creates a right arrow in the equation. No keyword exists for this symbol, or for any other symbol in the Arrows Equation palette.

Creating Roots

Another mathematical construct difficult to create without the Equation Editor is the root. The command for creating a square root is SQRT, and the command for nth root is NROOT. The syntax for SQRT is shown in the following:

```
SQRT { expression }
```

Both SQRT and NROOT are dynamic operators and automatically expand in height and width to enclose any expression enclosed by braces ({}). You always need to use braces to group root expressions, unless you are creating the root of a single number. For example, the statement

SQRT {x^3+1}

creates the following equation:

$$\sqrt{x^3+1}$$

As with other constructs, the information within the braces can be simple or complex, and can include additional roots, fractions, or any other command or symbol the Equation Editor can use.

The syntax for NROOT is as follows:

```
NROOT n { expression }
```

where *n* denotes the root number. The root commands can also be nested. For example, typing the following:

NROOT 4 { a '+' SQRT { b '+' SQRT c }}

creates the following equation:

$$\sqrt[4]{a+\sqrt{b+\sqrt{c}}}$$

Using the Matrix Commands

Matrices and determinants contain elements that must be properly aligned in rows and columns. When you create a matrix, you must indicate the beginning of each new row with a pound sign (#), and within each row, you must separate each column with an ampersand (&). You can further specify the way in which each row is formatted by including the MATFORM command in conjunction with ALIGNC, ALIGNL, or ALIGNR. Table 24.5 describes the matrix commands and their functions.

Table 24.5 Matrix Commands

Command	Function
MATRIX	Creates a matrix structure in the Equation Editor by specifying the row and column location of every subgroup
MATFORM	Specifies the horizontal alignment format to be applied to each subgroup (left, right, or centered within the column) in combination with the commands ALIGNC, ALIGNL, and ALIGNR
ALIGNC	Aligns its accompanying variable in the center of the current subgroup or matrix column
ALIGNL	Aligns its accompanying variable on the left margin of the current subgroup or matrix column
ALIGNR	Aligns its accompanying variable on the right margin of the current subgroup or matrix column
&	Column separator
#	Row separator

To create a matrix with three columns and three rows, type the following:

MATRIX {a1 & b1 & c1 # a2 & b2 & c2 # a3 & b3 & c3}

which creates the following equation:

$$\begin{matrix} a1 & b1 & c1 \\ a2 & b2 & c2 \\ a3 & b3 & c3 \end{matrix}$$

You must surround the entire matrix with braces ({}), type an ampersand (&) between each column, and type a pound sign (#) between each row. Each row must have the same number of columns, and you can create a maximum of 48 columns.

Matrices are usually bounded by square brackets or vertical lines. In most cases, therefore, you will use the LEFT and RIGHT commands, in conjunction with the appropriate delimiters, to surround the matrix. Thus, the following text:

LEFT LINE ' MATRIX {aaa & bbb & ccc # 11 & 22 & 33 # x & y & z} ' RIGHT LINE

creates the following equation:

$$\left| \begin{matrix} aaa & bbb & ccc \\ 11 & 22 & 33 \\ x & y & z \end{matrix} \right|$$

If all the elements in a column are not the same width, the Equation Editor centers them around a common midpoint. If you prefer to have one or more columns aligned to the left or right, you can include a MATFORM command, which specifies the alignment of each column with the ALIGNL, ALIGNC, and ALIGNR commands. The syntax is as follows:

```
MATFORM { align1 & align2 & align3 ...}
```

where *align1* is either ALIGNL, ALIGNR, or ALIGNC to specify whether the column is aligned to the left, right, or center. The syntax of MATFORM used with MATRIX is as follows:

```
MATRIX { MATFORM { align1 & align2 & ... } a1 & a2 ... # b1 & b2
... # ... }
```

Place the command after the MATRIX keyword, immediately inside the left brace and before the contents of the matrix. If you use MATFORM to specify the alignment for one column in the matrix, you must specify the alignment for every other column in the matrix. To realign the first and last columns of the previous equation, you can change the equation text as follows:

LEFT LINE ' MATRIX {MATFORM {ALIGNL & ALIGNC & ALIGNR} aaa & bbb & ccc # 11 & 22 & 33 # x & y & z} ' RIGHT LINE

which creates the following equation:

$$\left| \begin{matrix} aaa & bbb & ccc \\ 11 & 22 & 33 \\ x & y & z \end{matrix} \right|$$

As with any other Equation Editor construct, each element in a matrix can be quite complex, as long as the entire expression that makes up the element is surrounded by braces to create a group.

Creating Multiline Expressions with STACK and STACKALIGN

The Equation Editor assumes that each equation text, no matter how complex, is a single equation centered on a common baseline. Spaces and hard returns in the Editing Pane can make your equation text easier to read but don't change the printed appearance of the final equation.

Often, however, you want to stack several shorter equations on top of one another within the boundaries of a single equation box. The Equation Editor provides two commands that perform this task in slightly different ways: STACK and STACKALIGN. STACK simply creates a vertical stack of expressions; STACKALIGN also creates a vertical stack of expressions, but requires that you identify on which character each expression should be aligned. The syntax for STACK is as follows:

```
STACK {line1 # line2 ...}
```

As with MATRIX, STACK uses the pound sign (#) as a row separator. To stack two equations, such as:

```
2x + 3y = 9

x - 2y = 8
```

you type the following:

STACK {2x ~+~ 3y ~=~ 9 # x ~-~ 2y ~=~ 8}

$$\begin{array}{c} 2x + 3y = 9 \\ x - 2y = 8 \end{array}$$

Notice that these two equations are centered around a common midpoint. This alignment is the default alignment, which you can change by using some of the same commands you use to align matrices: ALIGNL and ALIGNR. For example, to align the two equations along their left edges, you could edit the equation text as follows:

STACK {2x ~+~ 3y ~=~ 9 # ALIGNL x ~–~ 2y ~=~ 8}

to create the following result:

$$\begin{array}{l} 2x + 3y = 9 \\ x - 2y = 8 \end{array}$$

Usually, however, you want to align two or more equations along a specific point such as an equal sign, which you can accomplish by using the STACKALIGN command. The syntax for STACKALIGN is nearly identical to that for STACK, except that each line of the equation must also contain an ampersand (&) following the character upon which the equations should be aligned. The above equation text could again be edited as follows:

STACKALIGN {2x ~+~ 3y ~=&~ 9 # x ~–~ 2y ~=&~ 8}

to align the equations on their equal signs, as follows:

$$\begin{aligned} 2x + 3y &= 9 \\ x - 2y &= 8 \end{aligned}$$

The equations now line up in a pleasing manner. Another example:

STACKALIGN {DELTA f ~=&~ f(a ~+~ DELTA x) ~–~ f(a)

#=&~ SQRT {9 ~+~ 0.3} ~–~ SQRT 9

#=&~ SQRT {9.3} ~–~ SQRT 9 }

creates the following equation:

$$\begin{aligned} \Delta f &= f(a + \Delta x) - f(a) \\ &= \sqrt{9 + 0.3} - \sqrt{9} \\ &= \sqrt{9.3} - \sqrt{9} \end{aligned}$$

Notice that the equation text could have been written in a continuous string without affecting the printed output of the equation(s). Pressing Enter to place each part of the equation on a different line, however, makes the entire equation easier to read and work with. This technique is helpful when you work on large or complex equations.

You can also use the PHANTOM command to help align equations. PHANTOM tells WordPerfect to leave space in an equation for a character or group of characters, but not to actually print them. Thus

```
PHANTOM {x+1}
```

tells WordPerfect to leave a space in the equation the exact width of the clause x+1. This command is particularly useful in stacked equations for matching the same clause in the line above or below. PHANTOM can also be used to create placeholders in matrices.

Using Other Commands and Symbols

Although you will probably find the Commands, Functions, and Greek Equation palettes to be the most useful, do not overlook several other palettes.

The diacritical marks found in the Other palette can be considered either commands or symbols; each prints a characteristic mark, but prints that mark over another character. Common diacritical marks include vector (VEC), overbar (BAR), tilde (TILDE), hat (HAT), and left and right accent marks (ACUTE and GRAVE). The Other palette also contains keywords that create several kinds of ellipses, including horizontal, vertical, and diagonal. To add a diacritical mark to a character, press the space bar to add a space after the character; then type or insert the keyword for the mark. Typing the following:

x BAR DOTSLOW y VEC

creates the equation

$$\bar{x}..\vec{y}$$

Notice that a diacritical mark must be typed before a subscript or superscript. Typing a diacritical keyword after a subscript puts the diacritical mark on the sub- or superscript.

The Large palette contains symbols that are commonly used in a larger size (as well as smaller equivalents of each). Some examples are SUM and SMALLSUM for large and small sums, and INT and SMALLINT for large and small integrals.

The Arrows palette contains a wealth of single and double arrows pointing in all directions. For example, the left and right harpoons are useful in chemical equations, such as:

$$HCO_3^- \leftrightharpoons H^+ + CO_3^{2-}$$

The Symbols palette contains many other common symbols, from primes, mathematical operators such as the partial derivative, and multiplication and division symbols, to logical symbols such as therefore, and abstract symbols such as infinity.

The examples in this chapter provide only a small sample of the many characters and symbols available in the Equation palettes. Virtually any mathematical character or symbol is available, and you can access still more through the WordPerfect Characters dialog box.

Changing Equation Box Options

Although created by the Equation Editor, WordPerfect's equations are contained within graphics boxes that are functionally identical to a figure box or other graphics box. Each type of graphics box has its own graphics box style, which contains settings for default anchor type, position, size, border and fill styles, caption, and text wrap. The default equation box style anchors an equation to the current paragraph, and sets the box width to the full width of the page, even if the equation itself is only an inch or two wide. The height of the equation determines the height of the equation box. By default, the equation box has no border, fill, or caption.

As with any other graphics box, you can change an equation box's position, size, anchor type, border, or fill style individually, or even choose a different graphics box style. To change one of these options, click on the equation using the right mouse button. WordPerfect displays a QuickMenu from which you can choose the desired option. If you want to change several options, or change the options for more than one equation box, choose **F**eature Bar from the QuickMenu. WordPerfect displays the Graphics Box Feature Bar (see fig. 24.5).

The procedures for changing graphics box settings in general are described in detail in Chapter 21, "Using Advanced Graphics Techniques," and need not be repeated here. Several specific settings, however, are particularly useful for equations.

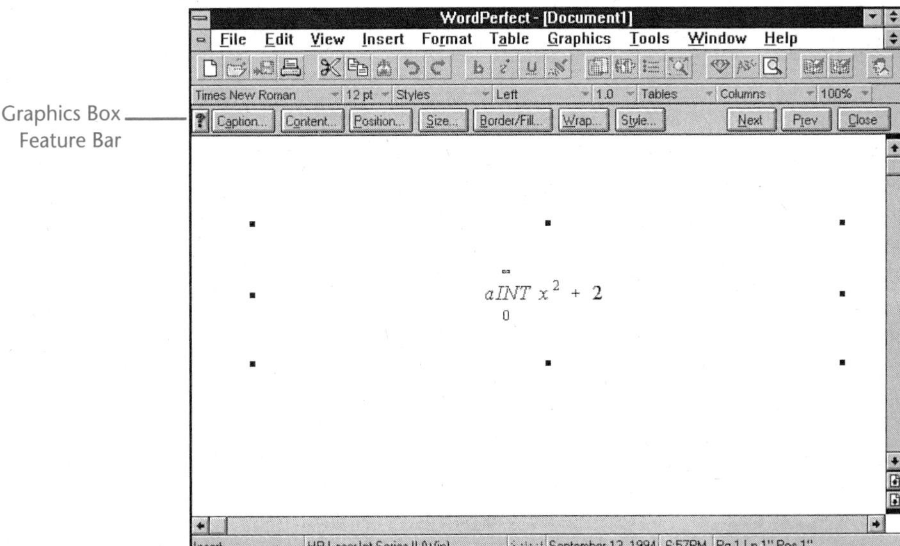

Fig. 24.5
The Graphics Box Feature Bar lets you change an equation's position, size, border, fill, and caption, among other options.

Numbering Equations

Although an equation doesn't have a caption when it's first created, you can add a caption after you return to the document screen. Why would you want to caption an equation? Because the default caption style for equation boxes is simply a number in parentheses, aligned flush right adjacent to the equation. This format is the standard format for numbering equations in journals and texts. Furthermore, equation boxes are automatically numbered in sequence just as are figure or table boxes.

You cannot create or edit an equation caption from within the Equation Editor; you must first close the Editor and return to the normal document window. To add an equation number caption, click on the equation using the right mouse button, and choose Create **C**aption from the QuickMenu. WordPerfect adds the caption in the form of an equation number.

WordPerfect automatically numbers equations in sequence. If you add or delete equations, the program automatically renumbers all equations. To change the equation numbering sequence, change the Equation Box counter. Choose **I**nsert, **O**ther, **C**ounter. Then highlight Equation Box, and choose **I**ncrease, **D**ecrease, or **V**alue. The first two options insert a code that increases or decreases the value of the following equation by 1, and automatically adjusts if you add or decrease equations. If you choose **V**alue, you must enter a specific number, and WordPerfect permanently sets the value of the following equation to that number.

Embedding Equations in Text

You may want a simple expression (such as the square root of a number) to appear within the text of your document, but even a simple equation created by the Equation Editor by default takes up the full width of the screen and is half an inch tall. By changing the graphics box settings, you can reduce the size of the equation box to the size of the equation itself, and include the equation in the text of your document. WordPerfect calls such an equation an *inline* equation, and includes a special box style for this type of equation.

You create an inline equation just as you would create a normal equation, except that you choose a different option from the Graphics menu. To create an inline equation, follow these steps:

1. From the editing screen, choose **G**raphics.
2. Choose **I**nline Equation. (If the Inline Equation option is not listed, follow the steps in "Starting the Equation Editor" to add Inline Equation to the Graphics menu.) WordPerfect displays the Equation Editor.
3. Create the inline equation as you would create a normal equation.
4. Choose **F**ile, **C**lose; or press Ctrl+F4. WordPerfect displays the inline equation embedded in your text at the cursor position.

If you have already created a normal equation, you can change it to an inline equation by changing its box style. To change a normal equation to an inline equation, follow these steps:

1. Choose S**t**yle from the Graphics Box Feature Bar.

   Alternatively, click on the equation using the right mouse button, and choose S**t**yle from the QuickMenu.
2. Choose Inline Equation.
3. Choose OK. WordPerfect shrinks the dimensions of the box to the size of the equation itself.

Changing the Equation Font

When you install WordPerfect, the program automatically installs TrueType fonts for all the WordPerfect Character Sets, which include the special characters and symbols necessary to print equations. As a result, unless the printer cannot accept either downloadable fonts or graphics, it can print WordPerfect equations.

By default, WordPerfect formats and prints equations in the same font and point size as a document's initial font. You can change the font or point size for an individual equation, or for all equations in a document.

To change the font for an equation, in the Equation Editor choose F**o**nt, Equation **F**ont. WordPerfect displays the Equation Font dialog box, a variant of the normal Font dialog box. You can choose a different font or size, or both.

To change the font for all equations in a document, you change the font settings in the Equation Box style. Follow these steps:

1. Choose **G**raphics, **G**raphics Styles. The Graphics Styles dialog box appears.
2. Highlight Equation; then choose **E**dit. WordPerfect displays the Edit Box Style dialog box.
3. Choose **S**ettings. The Equation Font Settings dialog box appears.
4. Choose a different **F**ont Face, Font **S**ize, or both.
5. Choose OK or **C**lose to close all open dialog boxes.

All equations in the document now print with the new font settings, unless you change the font for one or more individual equations.

◄ See "Customizing Graphics Boxes," p. 719

Saving and Retrieving Equation Files

If you create equations infrequently, or if the equations you create are significantly different from one another, you must create all your equations from scratch. If, however, you repeatedly use the same commands or frequently create equations that are slight variations of one another, you can make your task easier by reusing your work. From the Equation Editor, you can save part or all of an equation text to a file on disk. You also can retrieve previously saved equations—or even WordPerfect documents—into the Equation Editor.

To save an equation as a separate file, from within the Equation Editor choose **F**ile, Save **A**s. The standard Save As dialog box appears. WordPerfect automatically suggests *.EQN as the filename extension. You can use any file name or extension you want, although when you later insert a saved equation into the Equation Editor, the program likewise suggests files with an EQN extension to retrieve. You must type the EQN extension; WordPerfect does not add it for you automatically. You can save the equation in the current directory, or change the directory before saving. You also can save part of an equation by selecting a portion of the equation text before choosing Save As.

By default, the program saves equations as standard WordPerfect 6.0/6.1 documents. You can also save an equation as a WordPerfect 5.1/5.2 document, or in WordPerfect Graphics (WPG) 1.0 or 2.0—the graphics formats used by version 5.1/5.2 and 6.x, respectively. To save an equation in a different file format, in the Save As dialog box choose Save File As **T**ype; then choose a file type. If you save the file in one of the graphical formats, you can retrieve the file into a drawing program such as WordPerfect Presentations. You can then create technical illustrations containing equations.

Caution

If you save a WordPerfect equation in a graphical format, you cannot later retrieve the graphic into the Equation Editor. If you might need to edit an equation again, you should save it twice: once in the standard document format and once in the graphical format.

To insert a previously saved equation into the Equation Editor's Editing Pane, place the insertion point where you want the inserted equation text to appear; then choose **F**ile, Insert F**i**le. The Retrieve Equation Text dialog box—a variant of the standard Open File dialog box—appears, listing all files in the current directory with an EQN extension. If you don't see the equation you want, you can select a different directory or choose All Files to see all the files in the directory. When you find the correct file, double-click on the file name, or highlight the name and choose **R**etrieve. The contents of the file appear at the insertion point in the Editing Pane.

You can follow the preceding steps to insert a standard WordPerfect document into the Editing Pane also. The Equation Editor strips the inserted document of all codes and formatting, leaving only text, WordPerfect characters, and hard returns. Any soft returns are changed to hard returns, and the Equation Editor treats the result according to its usual rules.

If you save many equations as separate files, you may want to create one or more separate directories for those files and add the location(s) to your QuickList for easy access.

Troubleshooting

When I use an equation function, like "theta," WordPerfect displays the text of the function, rather than display the symbol for the function.

When using functions and commands, WordPerfect requires you to insert spaces so that it can understand the equation syntax you've provided. For example, typing **Btheta** displays the text "Btheta," rather than B and the theta symbol. To properly display the equation, insert either a space or a space character (~ or `) before and after all equation functions and commands, such as B theta or B~theta.

Nothing happens when I press Ctrl+B to make text bold in the Equation Editor.

Character formatting for bold and italics is ignored in the Equation Editor. Instead, use the BOLD and ITALIC command to format characters in an equation as bold or italics, respectively. Only the next character or symbol after a BOLD or ITALIC command is bolded or italicized. You need to repeat the BOLD and ITALIC commands to format additional characters and symbols in your equation as bold and italic.

The font that I use for equations doesn't match the font I use for the rest of the document.

The Equation Editor uses its own default font, and is separate from the font used in the body of the document. You can change the Equation Editor font to match the rest of the document by changing the style for Equation graphics boxes. See the section "Changing the Equation Font" in this chapter for details on selecting a different equation font.

From Here...

The Equation Editor is a specialized tool that makes the task of creating all equations, from the simplest to the most complex, quick and easy. In this chapter, you learned to type entries in the Editing Pane and view the equation in the Display Pane. You learned to insert commands, functions, and symbols from the Equation palettes, and enter characters from the normal keyboard, an equation keyboard, or the WordPerfect Characters dialog box.

You also learned the commands to create superscripts and subscripts, fractions, sums and integrals, roots, matrices, and multiline equations. You learned how to number equations automatically, how to embed inline equations within text, and how to change the equation font. Finally, you learned how to save, retrieve, and print equations.

For more information directly relating to the Equation Editor feature of WordPerfect, see the following chapters in this book:

- Chapter 7, "Integrating Text and Graphics," shows you how WordPerfect manages graphics boxes in a document.
- Chapter 10, "Using Styles," explains how styles work, and how they are used to control the appearance of graphics, including Equation Editor graphic boxes.
- Chapter 20, "Using Fonts and Special Characters," gives you information on changing the font for equations. The chapter also details using special characters, which can sometimes be used in lieu of an equation created in the Equation Editor.

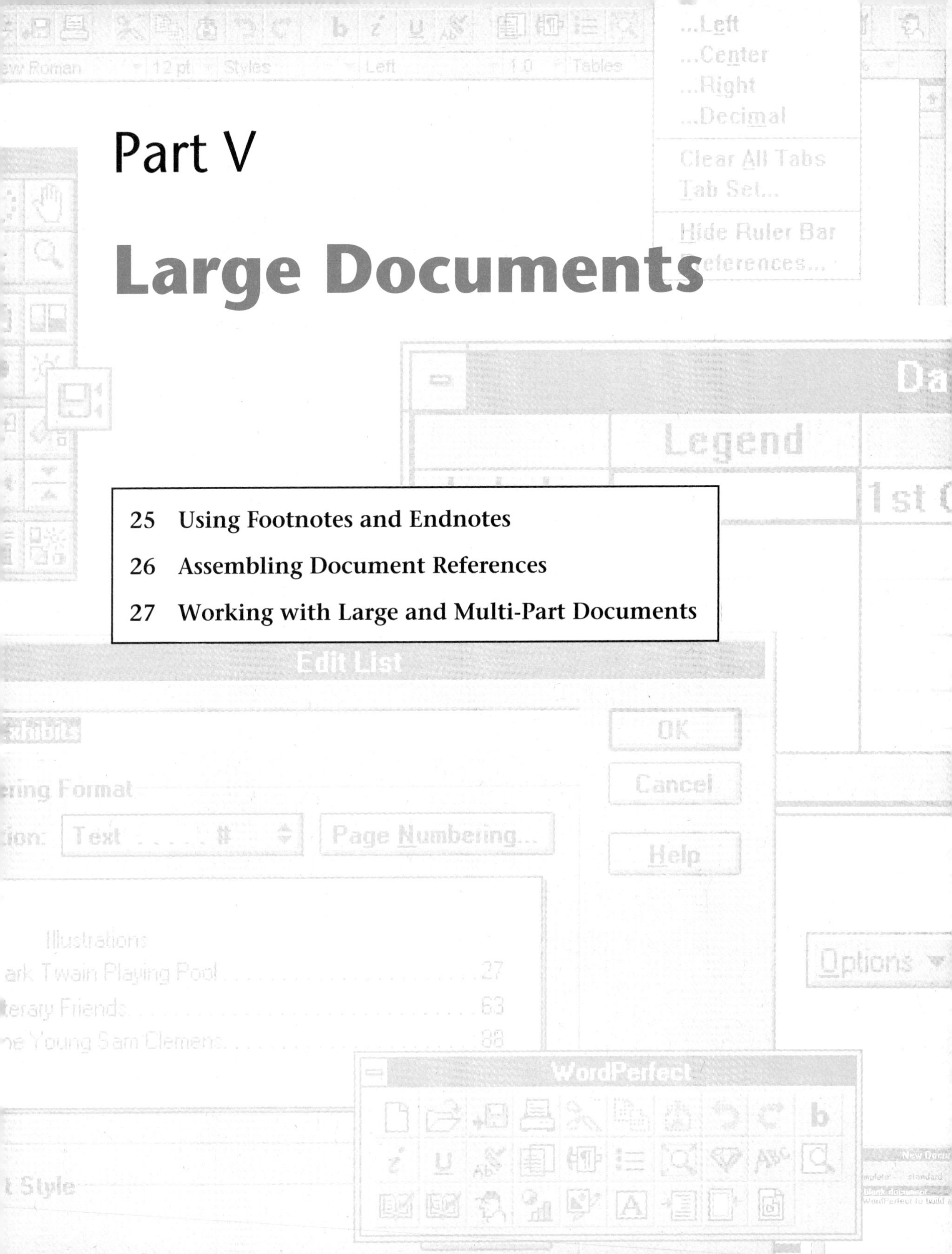

Part V

Large Documents

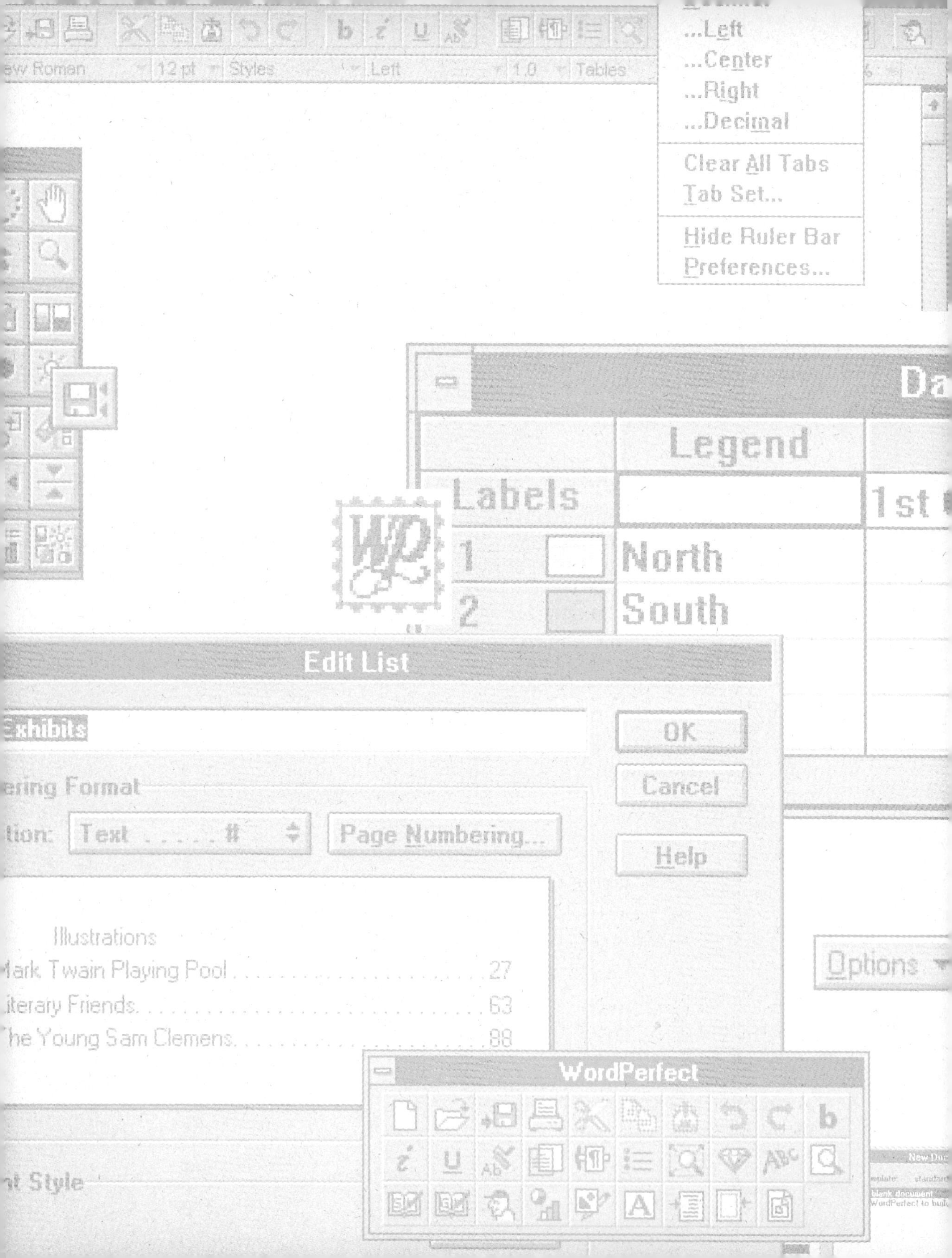

...Left
...Center
...Right
...Decimal
Clear All Tabs
Tab Set...
Hide Ruler Bar
Preferences...
Legend
Labels
1st
1
North
2
South
Edit List
Exhibits
OK
Cancel
Help
ering Format
tion:
Text . . . . . #
Page Numbering...
Illustrations
lark Twain Playing Pool 27
iterary Friends. 63
he Young Sam Clemens. 88
Options
WordPerfect
nt Style

Chapter 25

Using Footnotes and Endnotes

by Laura Acklen and Gordon McComb

Mention the word footnotes, and most people picture volumes of scholarly works laden with obscure references. Many people also remember—painfully, no doubt!—the difficult chore of typing footnotes for research papers. But with WordPerfect, footnotes (and endnotes) are easy to create, and they aren't just for academics anymore.

Footnotes and endnotes provide additional information about what is being said in the text's body without interrupting the flow of that text. They may contain reference details, such as the name of the author and the title of the work, the page number on which the reference is found, and so on. They may also provide parenthetical or interpretive explanations of technical material. Footnotes and endnotes should not contain essential information, however, because by their very location, the author is telling you that they are not required reading.

Typing footnotes and endnotes on a typewriter can be a tedious and frustrating process, especially if the references move around during editing. Fortunately, WordPerfect makes creating, editing, moving, and renumbering footnotes and endnotes easy.

Typically, footnotes are placed at the bottom of the page on which the footnote reference number appears. This arrangement makes it easier for the reader to find the additional information. Endnotes, on the other hand, are listed together on a page. They are usually at the end of the document, or, in the case of long documents, at the end of every section. This arrangement is easier for typists because they don't have to remember to allow room at the bottom of each page for the notes. In WordPerfect, the methods for working with footnotes and endnotes are virtually the same. Because footnotes are more widely used, this chapter focuses first on footnotes and then explains how endnotes differ.

In this chapter, you learn how to do the following:

- Create and edit footnotes and endnotes
- Move, copy, and delete notes from a document
- Restart note numbering
- Change the style of the footnote reference number and footnote text
- Continue notes across pages
- Place endnotes on a titled page

Using Footnotes

A footnote consists of two parts: the footnote reference number and the footnote text. The footnote reference number appears in the text. The footnote text, with a corresponding footnote number, is at the bottom of the page. If the footnote text is lengthy, WordPerfect splits the footnote and carries it over to the next page. Figure 25.1 shows a sample document with footnotes.

Note

You can use the Cross Reference feature to reference a footnote number anywhere in the text (see Chapter 26, "Assembling Document References"), for example, "See footnote number 13 on page 27." After you modify the document, you can update the page number and footnotes number references with the Generate option on the Tools menu.

Inserting Footnotes

You may choose to create footnotes as you type the text of the document, or you may create the notes later when you have the necessary information. A footnote should be inserted where you want the footnote reference number to appear in the text.

> **Caution**
>
> You can create footnotes in tables, but not in a header row. If you create a footnote in a table header row, WordPerfect converts it to an endnote. See Chapter 16, "Working with Tables," for more information.

If you want to experiment with footnotes but don't have text of your own to work with, type the text that appears in figure 25.1, without the footnote reference numbers or the footnote text at the bottom of the page. This chapter walks you through creating and modifying the footnotes in this sample section of text.

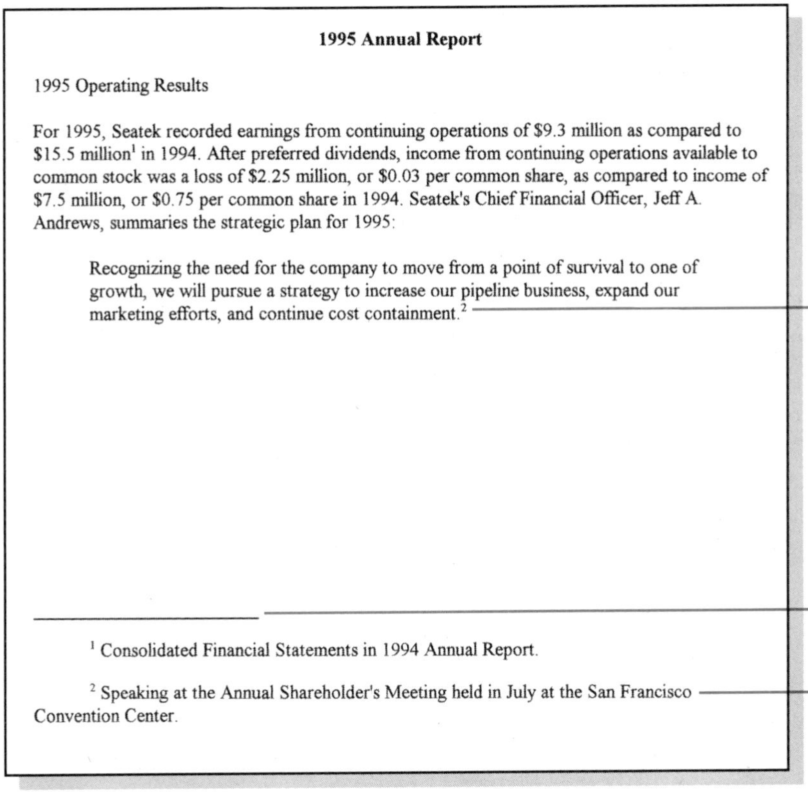

1995 Annual Report

1995 Operating Results

For 1995, Seatek recorded earnings from continuing operations of $9.3 million as compared to $15.5 million[1] in 1994. After preferred dividends, income from continuing operations available to common stock was a loss of $2.25 million, or $0.03 per common share, as compared to income of $7.5 million, or $0.75 per common share in 1994. Seatek's Chief Financial Officer, Jeff A. Andrews, summaries the strategic plan for 1995:

> Recognizing the need for the company to move from a point of survival to one of growth, we will pursue a strategy to increase our pipeline business, expand our marketing efforts, and continue cost containment.[2]

---

[1] Consolidated Financial Statements in 1994 Annual Report.

[2] Speaking at the Annual Shareholder's Meeting held in July at the San Francisco Convention Center.

The footnote reference number in the document text

The footnote separator line

The footnote text with the corresponding footnote number

Fig. 25.1
A sample document containing a footnote reference number and footnote text.

> **Note**
>
> Use Format, Paragraph, Double Indent, or press Ctrl+Shift+F7, to indent the quotation from both the left and right margins. If you use indented quotations often in your writing, create a Quotation style that indents, single spaces, and, if necessary, selects a smaller font. See Chapter 10, "Using Styles," for more information on creating and using styles.

To create a footnote, complete the following steps:

1. Position the insertion point where you want the footnote reference number to appear in the text. For the sample document, position the insertion point at the end of the indented quote.

2. Choose **I**nsert, **F**ootnote, **C**reate.

   WordPerfect moves the insertion point down to the footnote area of the document editing window. If you are using Draft View mode, the insertion point is moved into a separate Footnote window. The text `Footnote` appears in the title bar, and the Footnote/Endnote Feature Bar is added at the top of the window.

   > **Note**
   >
   > If you are using the Draft View mode, footnotes (or endnotes) don't appear in the document editing window. Therefore, creating and editing footnotes is accomplished through a separate Footnote window. You must change to the Page View mode or print the document to see the footnotes (and endnotes).

   Notice that WordPerfect has automatically inserted the correct footnote number underneath a separator line.

3. Type the text of your footnote. For the sample document, type the following footnote text, as shown in figure 25.2.

   Speaking at the Annual Shareholder's Meeting held in July at the San Francisco Convention Center.

4. After you finish typing the footnote text, choose **C**lose from the feature bar.

   WordPerfect moves the insertion point back to the document text area and inserts a superscript footnote reference number (see fig. 25.3).

Note

If you accidentally delete the footnote number in the footnote text, and it is too late to restore it by using the Undo or Undelete features, use the N**o**te Number button on the Footnote/Endnote Feature Bar to reinsert the footnote number. Don't retype the number yourself; you need to insert the correct code so that WordPerfect can update the note number automatically if you later change the order of the notes. Position the insertion point at the beginning of the footnote text, and choose N**o**te Number.

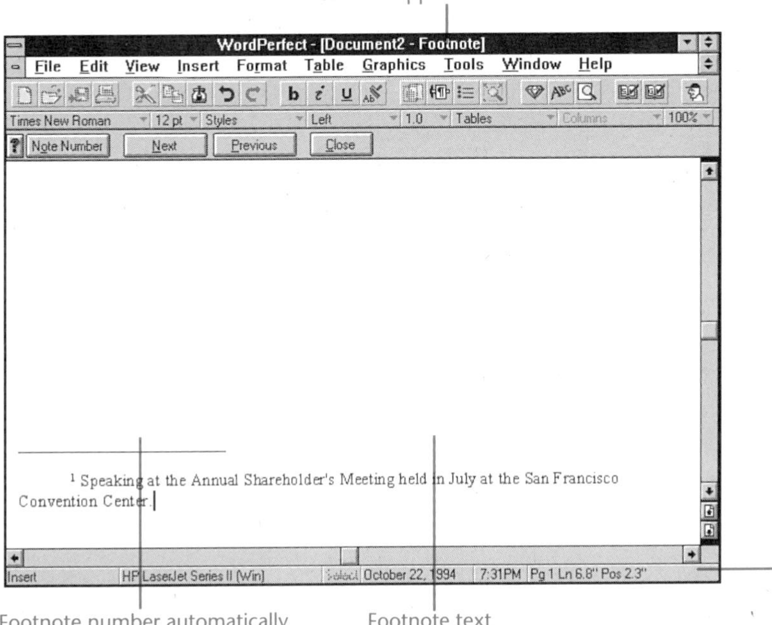

Fig. 25.2
If the Page View mode is selected, you can create and edit footnotes from the document editing window. The Footnote/Endnote Feature Bar is displayed when creating a footnote.

Note

If the text that you want to appear in a note already exists in a document (this one or any other), you can use several WordPerfect features to insert the text into a note without having to retype it. The Copy and Paste, or Delete and Undelete, features can duplicate text so that you can insert it into a note. You can even use the Insert File feature to insert an entire document in a note.

Tip
If you double-click a footnote (or endnote) code, the Edit Footnote (or Endnote) dialog box appears. Here you can type the number of the note you want to edit.

The footnote reference number in the text represents a footnote code that contains both the footnote reference number and the footnote text. Because a code is used instead of typing in a number, WordPerfect can update the footnote numbers as you insert or delete footnotes. To look at a footnote code, position the insertion point directly before or after the footnote number in the text and turn on Reveal Codes (see fig. 25.4).

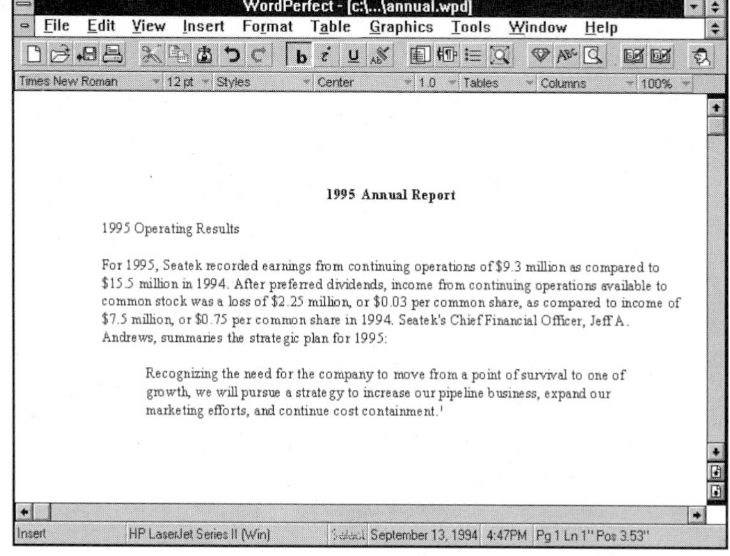

Fig. 25.3
The sample text with the first footnote reference number displayed at the end of the quotation.

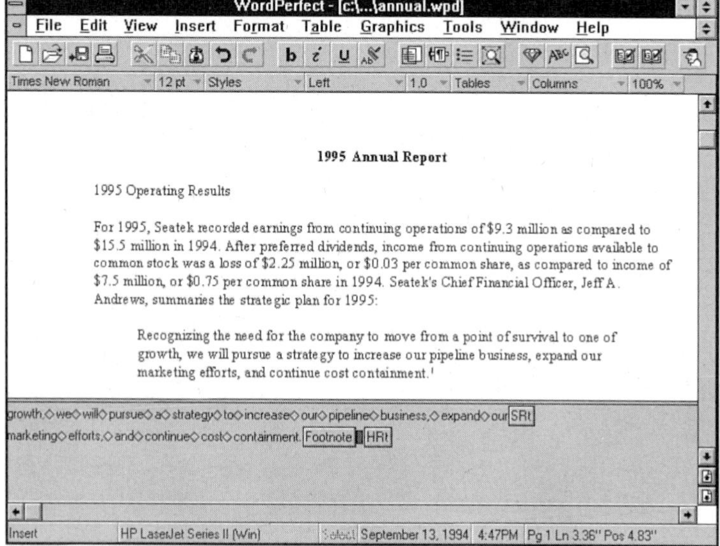

Fig. 25.4
The Reveal Codes screen with a footnote code displayed.

To insert a footnote before another existing footnote, you follow the same steps that you used to create a new footnote. In the sample document, insert a new note at the end of the phrase `$15.5 million` in the first sentence of the first paragraph. Type the following text for the note contents:

Consolidated Financial Statements in 1994 Annual Report.

Notice in figure 25.5 that WordPerfect has automatically numbered the new footnote as footnote number 1 and renumbered the existing footnote (underneath it) to footnote number 2.

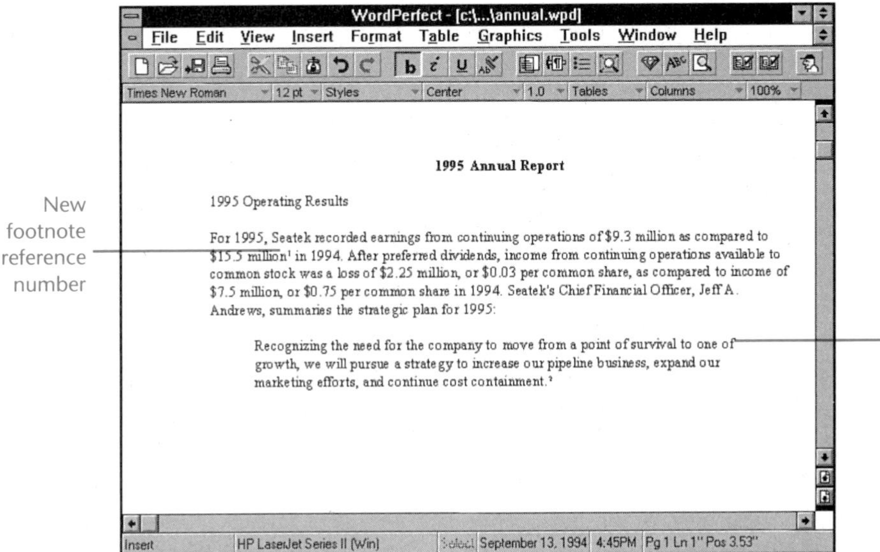

Fig. 25.5 WordPerfect automatically updates the footnote numbers as you insert and remove footnotes.

WordPerfect places the footnote text at the bottom of the page with a corresponding footnote number. The program automatically inserts a separator line and a blank line between each footnote. Use the scroll bar to move down to the bottom of the page to view your footnotes, as shown in figure 25.6.

Note

If there is too much space between the footnotes, edit the notes and look for an extra blank line after the footnote text. You probably pressed Enter after typing the footnote text. Look through the footnotes and delete the extra blank lines. Because WordPerfect automatically inserts one blank line between notes, extra lines are not usually necessary.

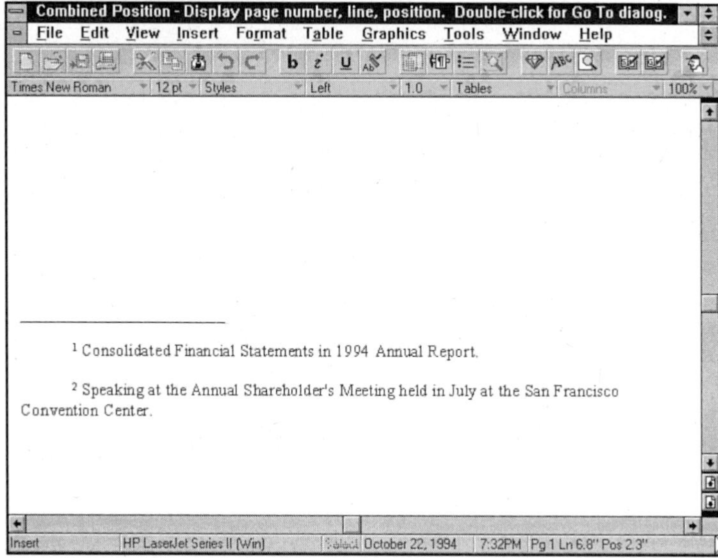

Fig. 25.6
Footnotes are separated from the rest of the text by a separator line. The alignment, length, and type of line can all be specified in the Line Separator dialog box.

WordPerfect prints footnotes (and endnotes) in the document initial font that may be different from the font you have chosen for the body text. The document initial font will be shown on the Power Bar when the insertion point is in the footnote (or endnote) area of the document editing window. If you want to change the font in the document and have the footnote (and endnote) text match it, you can change the font with Fo**r**mat, **D**ocument, Initial **F**ont, which affects both the document and the note text.

A second method is to insert a font code before the note text in the note area of the document editing window. Keep in mind that you have to do this for each note. Likewise, if you change the margins in the document and you want the note text to use those margins, you can either make the margin change with Fo**r**mat, **D**ocument, Initial Code **S**tyle, or set the margins in the note area of the document editing window for each note.

Editing Footnotes

If you use the Page View mode, footnotes are displayed at the bottom of the page, so you can edit footnotes from the document editing window. The Draft View mode does not display footnotes as part of the page, so you must use a separate Footnote window to edit them. The Footnote/Endnote Feature Bar automatically appears when editing footnotes in choosing **I**nsert, **F**ootnote, **E**dit.

To edit a footnote in the document editing window, scroll down to the bottom of the page and click in the footnote text. The insertion point moves into the footnote area of the document editing window. Insert or delete text as necessary to make the changes. Click in the text area of the document editing window to move back into the body of the document; or press Ctrl+F4.

If you are using the Draft View mode or if you are working in the Page View mode and want to add the Footnote/Endnote Feature Bar, use the following steps to edit footnotes. You can edit any footnote in the document, from any position in the document, by specifying the footnote number in the Edit Footnote dialog box. WordPerfect searches for that footnote and displays the footnote text for editing.

To edit a footnote, complete the following steps:

1. From anywhere in the document, choose **I**nsert, **F**ootnote, **E**dit. Figure 25.7 shows the Edit Footnote dialog box.

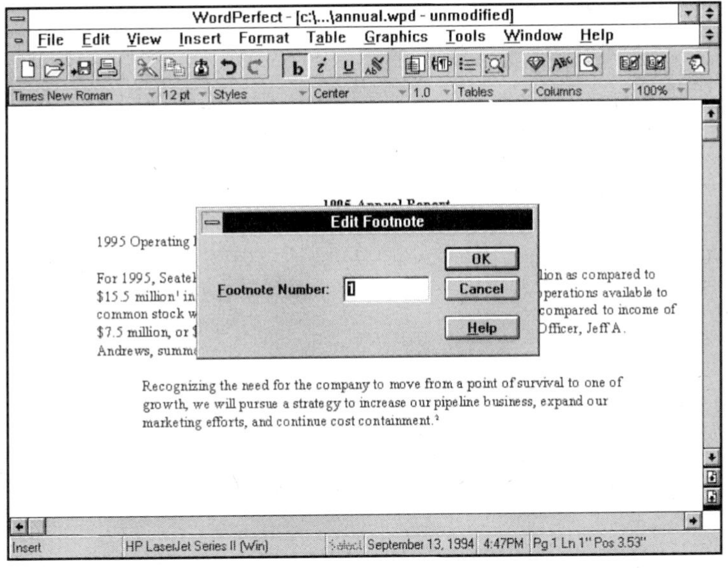

Fig. 25.7
Type the number of the footnote you want to edit in the Edit Footnote dialog box and let WordPerfect locate the footnote for you.

WordPerfect automatically displays the number of the next footnote found in the document. For example, if the insertion point is between footnotes 2 and 3, WordPerfect inserts the number 3 in the Edit Footnote dialog box.

Caution

If the cursor is positioned beyond all the footnotes, WordPerfect prompts you with the number of the next footnote you can create. If you choose OK or press Enter to accept that number, WordPerfect displays a Not Found dialog box. Choose OK or press Enter, and try again.

2. If the number of the footnote shown is the one you want to edit, choose OK or press Enter. Otherwise, type the appropriate number, and then choose OK or press Enter.

   WordPerfect moves the insertion point to the requested footnote text and displays the Footnote/Endnote Feature Bar across the top of the window.

3. Make the necessary changes.

   At this point, you have the option of returning to the document text or editing other footnotes.

4. If you want to edit or view other footnotes, choose **N**ext or **P**revious from the feature bar to browse through the notes.

5. Choose **C**lose from the feature bar when you are ready to return to the document text.

Tip
If you use footnotes often, use WordPerfect's Toolbar feature to create a toolbar with Create Footnote and Edit Footnote buttons already on it.

When you return to the document text area, the insertion point is positioned directly after the footnote reference number for the footnote text you just edited.

Copying Footnotes

◄ See "View Modes," p. 30

◄ See "Understanding WordPerfect's Hidden Codes," p. 95

◄ See "Selecting Text," p. 103

◄ See "Customizing a Toolbar," p. 455

If two or more footnotes have the same footnote text, you can create the first footnote and then copy that footnote to another location in the document. In the sample document, for example, you will use the text from the first footnote as the text for a new second footnote. Rather than typing that text a second time, copy the first footnote and insert it as the second footnote.

The Copy function is really a two-step process. First, select and copy the text. Then paste the text into a new location. Follow these steps to copy and paste the footnote:

1. Save the document (so that you can go back to your original if you make a mistake later).

2. Select the footnote reference number in the text. For this example, block the first footnote reference number in the sample document, making sure that only the 1 is highlighted.

3. To copy the footnote, choose **E**dit, **C**opy; or press Ctrl+C.

4. Move the insertion point to the location where you want to insert the copied footnote. In the sample document, position the insertion point after `7.5 million` in the second sentence of the first paragraph.

5. To paste the footnote, choose **E**dit, **P**aste; or press Ctrl+V.

Tip
You can also use the drag-and-drop method to copy footnotes.

You now have two footnotes with identical text. Notice that WordPerfect has automatically renumbered the footnote at the end of the quotation (formerly footnote number 2) to footnote number 3.

Tip
Once text is selected, you can also click the right mouse button and choose Cu**t**, C**o**py, and **P**aste from the QuickMenu.

Moving Footnotes

As you edit your document, you may have to move sections of text from one place to another. If the text contains footnotes, WordPerfect moves the footnotes along with the text and renumbers them according to their new locations.

> **Caution**
>
> If the footnote reference number is the last character in the selected text, be sure to extend the selection to include it, or the footnote will be left behind.

◄ See "Selecting Text," p. 103

Sometimes, however, you need to move only the footnote and not the text around it. For example, you might insert a footnote in the wrong place. Moving is a two-step process: cutting and pasting. First, select and cut the text (in this case, a footnote); then paste the text at the new location. The steps for moving a footnote follow:

1. Save the document (in case you later make a mistake).

2. Select the footnote reference number in the text. In the sample document, select the second footnote reference number in the second line of the first paragraph.

3. To cut the footnote, choose **E**dit, Cu**t**; or press Ctrl+X.

4. Move the insertion point to the new location for the footnote reference number. In the sample document, position the insertion point at the end of the second sentence of the first paragraph, after `1994`.

5. To paste the footnote, choose **E**dit, **P**aste; or press Ctrl+V.

Deleting Footnotes

If you decide that footnote information is unnecessary, or if you have created a footnote in error, you may need to remove a footnote. The footnote reference number and footnote text are both contained in a footnote code. If you delete the code, WordPerfect removes the footnote reference number, and the footnote text no longer appears at the bottom of the page.

To delete a footnote, position the insertion point to the right of the footnote reference number and press Backspace. Alternatively, position the insertion point to the left of the footnote reference number and press Del.

> **Caution**
>
> If you accidentally create a footnote without any footnote text, WordPerfect inserts a footnote reference number (for the blank footnote) at the insertion point position. Without moving the insertion point, press Backspace to remove the footnote reference number.

Setting a New Footnote Number

If you have a large number of footnotes in your document, you may decide to restart the numbering at the beginning of each section. Or you may opt to split a large document into several files (since WordPerfect runs faster with smaller files). If this is the case, you need to specify a new footnote number to use. When you specify a new number, WordPerfect numbers all subsequent footnotes beginning with that new number.

To specify a new number, choose **I**nsert, **F**ootnote, **N**ew Number. WordPerfect displays the Footnote Number dialog box, as shown in figure 25.8.

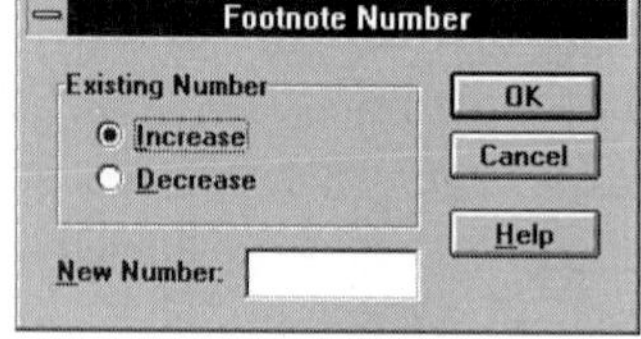

Fig. 25.8
Type a new footnote number to restart the numbering for all subsequent footnotes.

Using Footnote Options

You can change many aspects of your footnotes' appearance if WordPerfect's style doesn't suit your needs. For example, you may want to use a different numbering style or separator line.

To access the footnote options, choose **I**nsert, **F**ootnote, **O**ptions. WordPerfect displays the Footnote Options dialog box (see fig. 25.9).

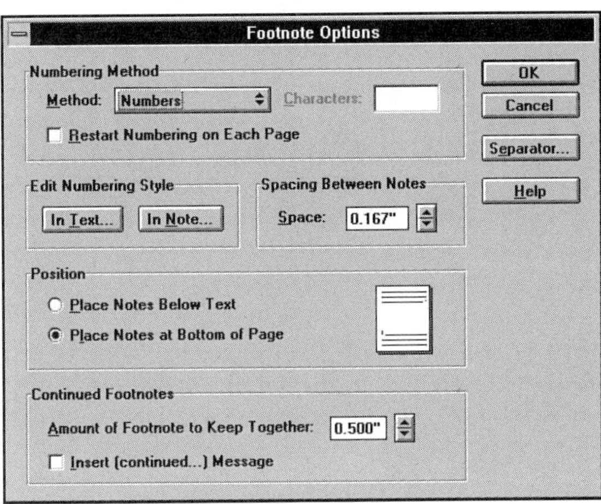

Fig. 25.9
The Footnote Options dialog box always displays the settings that are in effect for that particular area of the document.

Any changes that you make in the Footnote Options dialog box affect only the footnotes on that page through the end of the document. If you want the changes to affect all the footnotes, position the insertion point at the top of the document (or before any footnotes) before accessing the Footnote Options dialog box.

Changing the Numbering Style

WordPerfect offers several numbering styles for footnotes, the default being Arabic numerals (1, 2, 3). If you want to change to a different numbering style, choose **M**ethod in the Numbering Method section of the Footnote Options dialog box. A pop-up list of numbering styles appears. Choose the numbering or lettering scheme you want to use.

Note

If your document contains a mixture of footnotes and endnotes, you may want to use characters for footnotes and numbers for endnotes. Because characters can quickly become long and cumbersome, use a series containing a number of different characters or restart numbering on each page.

To use symbols other than numbers or letters, choose the **C**haracters option on the Numbering Method pop-up list. Next, in the Characters text box of the Footnote Options dialog box, type the characters you want to use. If you specify a series of characters like *#~, WordPerfect numbers footnotes *, #, ~, **, ##, ~~, ***, and so on.

Restarting Numbering on Each Page

If your document contains a large number of footnotes, you might want to restart the footnote numbering with 1, or with the first character in your character series, at the top of every page. Check the **R**estart Numbering on Each Page option in the Footnote Options dialog box (refer to fig. 25.9). This feature is especially useful if you are using asterisks or other characters (instead of numbers or letters) to number your footnotes.

Editing the Numbering Style in Text

The appearance of the footnote reference number in the text is controlled by a style that you can modify to suit your specific needs. By default, the footnote reference number appears in superscript in the text. If your printer doesn't support superscript, or you want to use another type of formatting, you can edit the style with the Style Editor. The Style Editor has its own pull-down menu for features that you can use in styles.

To edit the style for the footnote reference number in the text, choose In **T**ext under Edit Numbering Style in the Footnote Options dialog box. The Styles Editor appears with the contents of the style displayed, as shown in figure 25.10. If necessary, choose Reveal Codes to display the codes in the style. Insert or delete codes as necessary to make the desired changes. Choose OK when you are done.

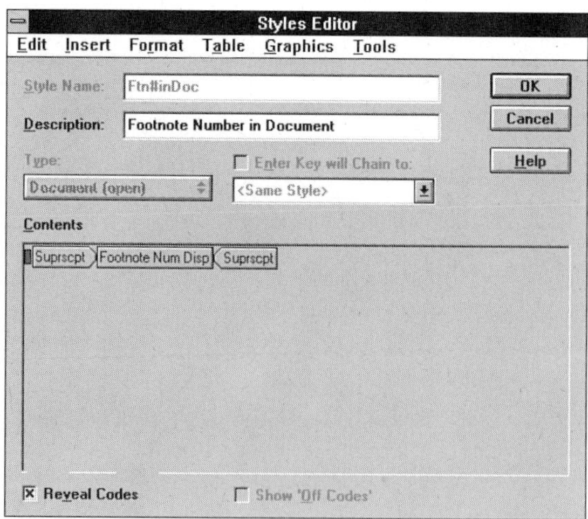

Fig. 25.10
As with other styles in WordPerfect, the Footnote Number in Text style can be edited with the Styles Editor.

WordPerfect does not insert a code in the document when you make changes to the footnote styles. Instead, the program makes changes to the document's Footnote System Style, which affects all footnotes in the document. See Chapter 10, "Using Styles," for more information on editing styles.

Editing the Numbering Style in Notes

The format of the footnote text (including the footnote number) is controlled by a style, which you can modify to suit your specific needs. You may want to change the style to match a change you made to the style for the footnote reference number in the document, or you may have to follow specific guidelines for formatting footnotes. The format assigned by default is a left tab followed by a superscripted footnote number, followed by the note text.

To edit the style for the footnote text, choose In **N**ote under Edit Numbering Style in the Footnote Options dialog box. The Styles Editor appears with the contents of the style displayed, as shown in figure 25.11. If necessary, choose Reveal Codes to display the codes in the style. Insert or delete codes as appropriate to make the format changes.

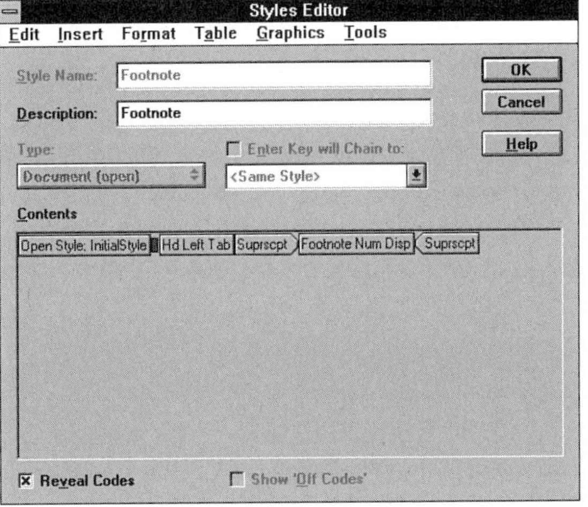

Fig. 25.11
The Footnote Number in Note style shows the codes displayed in the Styles Editor dialog box.

WordPerfect does not insert a code in the document when you make changes to the footnote styles. Instead, the program makes changes to the document's Footnote System Style, which affects all the footnotes in the document. See Chapter 10, "Using Styles," for more information on editing styles.

Changing the Spacing between Notes

WordPerfect automatically inserts a blank line between footnotes. If you want to increase or decrease the size of this space, choose **S**pace under Spacing Between Notes in the Footnote Options dialog box. Change the number by typing a specific measurement or by using the arrows to increase or decrease the size.

Specifying the Position for Footnotes

In most cases, footnotes should be at the bottom of the page; this is the default in WordPerfect. However, if you want your footnotes to print immediately below the last line of text, you can choose **P**lace Notes Below Text in the Footnote Options dialog box.

Splitting Long Footnotes

Normally, WordPerfect reserves enough space at the bottom of a document page for all the footnotes on that page. However, if a page has several footnotes that are particularly long, WordPerfect may split a footnote between the current page and the following page. You can specify how much of the footnote to keep together on the current page in the **A**mount of Footnote to Keep Together text box under the Continued Footnotes section. If there isn't enough room for at least three lines of text, WordPerfect moves the text and the footnote to the next page.

If a footnote is split between two pages, you can have WordPerfect automatically insert a `(Continued...)` message on the last line of footnote text on the current page and a `(...continued)` message on the first line of footnote text on the following page. To activate this option, check the **I**nsert (Continued...) Message option in the Footnote Options dialog box.

Note

WordPerfect can print the footnote continued messages in a different language if necessary. Specify the appropriate language in the Initial Codes Style menu by choosing **T**ools, **L**anguage; then select the language from the list.

Choosing a Separator Line

WordPerfect automatically places a line between the document text and the footnotes. This line helps the reader to distinguish between the two parts of the page. By default, the separator line is a single line, two inches long. There are a number of line styles and other options available for the separator line. Choose S**e**parator from the Footnote Options dialog box to open the Line Separator dialog box (see fig. 25.12).

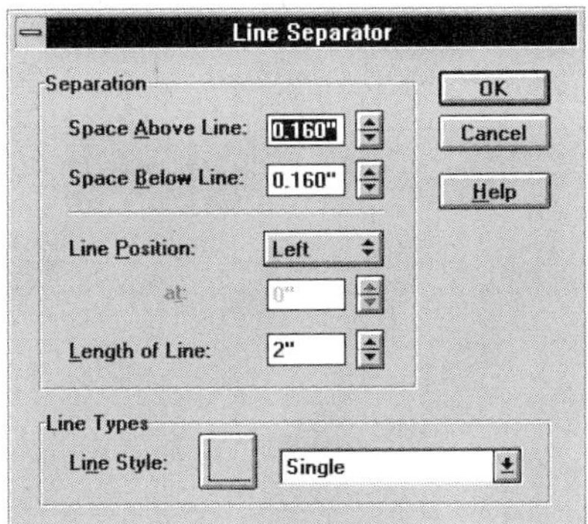

Fig. 25.12
The Line Separator dialog box is used to modify the separator line between the footnotes and the document text.

In the Line Separator dialog box, you can increase or decrease the amount of space above and below the separator from the standard one blank line. You can change the Line **P**osition from **L**eft (flush with the left margin) to **C**enter (center of the line), **R**ight (flush with the right margin), or **F**ull (extend from the left to the right margin). Or you can **S**et a specific position. You also can change the length of the line from the default of 2 inches. Finally, if you want to use something other than a single line, you can select from a long list of line styles.

If you make any changes in the Line Separator dialog box, WordPerfect inserts a code in the document at the top of the current page. Only the footnotes on the current page and subsequent pages will have the new separator line.

To change the separator line for the sample document, follow these steps:

1. From the Line Separator dialog box, choose Line **P**osition and set it to **C**enter.
2. Click the up arrow next to **L**ength of Line and set it to 3" (three inches).
3. Choose Li**n**e Style and then Thick/Thin 1.
4. Choose OK.

Figure 25.13 shows the modified separator line in the sample document.

Changing Footnote Options for the Entire Document

If you want to change the options for all the footnotes in a document, there are a couple of ways to do it. First, you can position the insertion point at the top of the document before making any changes in the Footnote Options dialog box. Second, you can place the Footnote Options codes in the Document Initial Codes style (Fo**r**mat, **D**ocument, Initial Codes **S**tyle). The advantage of placing the codes in the Document Initial Codes style is that the codes won't be accidentally deleted or moved during editing.

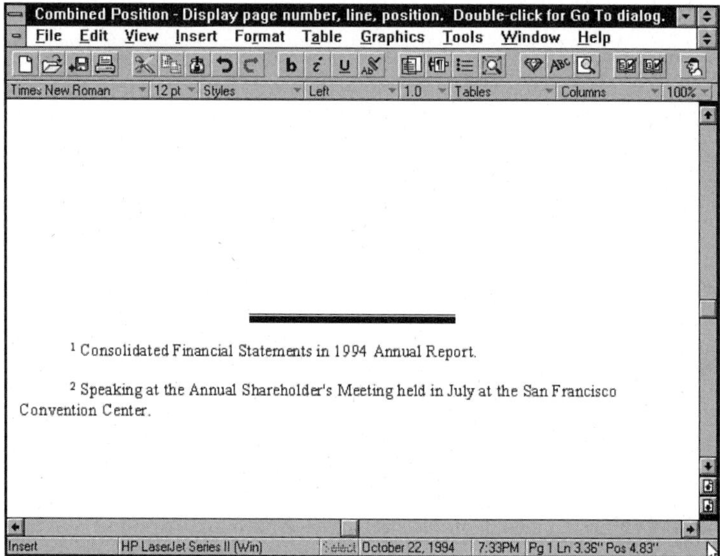

Fig. 25.13 The sample document with a new separator line.

Troubleshooting

When I insert a footnote number on a new page, the numbering starts again at 1.

The **R**estart Numbering on Each Page option is selected in the Footnote Options dialog box. To use continuously numbered footnotes for the entire document, choose **I**nsert, **F**ootnote, **O**ptions. In the Footnote Options dialog box, deselect the **R**estart Numbering on Each Page option.

I cannot edit the separator line between the text and footnote area by clicking the line.

The footnote separator line is not a standard WordPerfect graphic line. It is not edited by selecting it and then choosing a command from the Graphics menu. Rather, to change the separator line, choose **I**nsert, **F**ootnote, **O**ptions. In the Footnote Options dialog box, click S**e**parator to change the appearance of the separator line. If desired you can remove the line by choosing None in the Line Style palette.

I deleted a footnote but the footnote reference number remains in the text.

The footnote number in the footnote itself and the footnote number in the document are two separate entities. Deleting the text of the footnote and the number in the footnote area does not automatically remove the footnote reference number in the text of the document. You must remove the reference number manually. Or, if you want to remove a footnote entry entirely—both its reference number in the text and the footnote itself—simply delete the reference number. The text of the footnote is automatically deleted.

Using Endnotes

The methods for creating and editing endnotes are much the same as those for footnotes. The main difference between the two types of notes is that you can list endnotes together on a page by themselves. Usually found at the end of the document, endnotes can be listed anywhere in the document. For example, in long documents, it is common to print a page of endnotes at the end of each section.

Endnotes have several advantages over footnotes. If your footnotes are lengthy, they can be split between two pages, which makes them more difficult to read. In addition, multiple footnotes can reduce the amount of text available on a page. Since endnotes are grouped together on a page, lengthy notes are easier to read and they do not take up valuable space in the body of the document.

Inserting Endnotes

As with footnotes, you may choose to create endnotes as you type the text of the document, or you may create the notes later when you have the necessary information. You insert an endnote where you want the endnote reference number to appear in the text.

To create an endnote, do the following:

1. Position the insertion point where you want the endnote reference number to appear in the document text.

2. Choose **I**nsert, **E**ndnote, **C**reate.

WordPerfect moves the insertion point to the endnote area of the document editing window, which, by default, is one line below the last line of text on the current page. If you are using the Draft view mode, the insertion point is moved into a separate Endnote window. A Footnote/Endnote Feature Bar is available in the Endnote window.

WordPerfect inserts the correct endnote number in the endnote area. While the footnote number is a superscript number followed by a tab, the endnote number is normal size and followed by a period and a space to separate it from the text of the endnote.

Editing and Manipulating Endnotes

When editing, the only difference between footnotes and endnotes is that WordPerfect displays the Endnote window instead of the Footnote window. Deleting, moving, and copying endnotes works exactly the same way as for footnotes.

Using Endnote Options

The Endnote Options dialog box looks similar to the Footnote Options dialog box, with a couple of exceptions. Because endnotes are grouped together on a page, the Position options are not necessary. Also, there is not an option to print a continued message if a footnote is split between pages.

Note

Endnote text is frequently indented next to the endnote number. To indent the endnote text, insert an Indent (F7) after the period in the Note Number in Note style using the Styles Editor.

Placing Endnotes

In long documents, it is often preferable to compile a list of endnotes at the end of each section, rather than at the end of the document. You can specify where to insert the endnotes with the **P**lacement option on the **E**ndnote cascading menu. The Endnote Placement dialog box has two options: **I**nsert Endnotes at Insertion Point, and Insert Endnotes at Insertion Point and **R**estart Numbering.

To insert endnotes within the document, rather than at the end of the document, follow these steps:

1. Position the insertion point where you want the endnotes listed. If you want the endnotes on a new page, press Ctrl+Enter (Hard Page) to create a new page. If necessary, create a heading for the page (for example, "Notes," centered, underlined, and bold).

2. Choose **I**nsert, **E**ndnote, **P**lacement to display the Endnote Placement dialog box.

3. Choose either option: **I**nsert Endnotes at Insertion Point, or Insert Endnotes at Insertion Point and **R**estart Numbering.

4. Choose OK.

WordPerfect inserts an Endnote Placement code at the insertion point, followed by a Hard Page code. The Hard Page separates the endnote page from the rest of the text. If you want the following text on the same page, delete the `[HPg]` code. Figure 25.14 shows the sample document endnotes page.

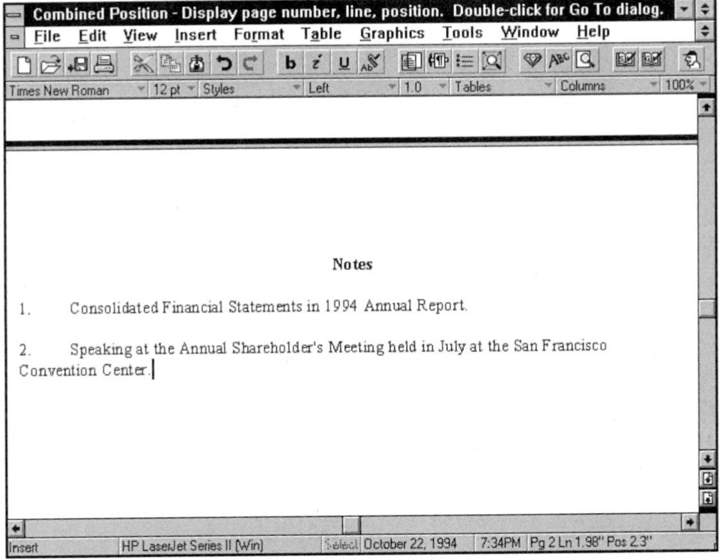

Fig. 25.14
The endnotes for the sample document are compiled on a titled page.

Troubleshooting

I deleted an endnote but the endnote reference number remains in the text.

The endnote number in the endnote itself and the endnote number in the document are two separate entities. Deleting the text of the endnote and the number in the endnote area does not automatically remove the endnote reference number in the text of the document. You must remove the reference number manually. Or, if you want to remove an endnote entry entirely—both its reference number in the text and the endnote itself—simply delete the reference number. The text of the endnote is automatically deleted.

When I insert an endnote, the endnote appears immediately below the insertion point.

Before inserting the first endnote of the document, place the insertion point where you want the endnotes to appear (usually at the very end of the document). Choose **I**nsert, **E**ndnote, **P**lacement, and choose one of the two placement options in the Endnote Placement dialog box. When done, move the insertion point back to where you want the endnote reference to appear, and then create the endnote.

Converting Footnotes and Endnotes

Tip
Also use the WordPerfect specially designed macros FOOTEND.WCM to convert footnotes to endnotes and ENDFOOT.WCM to convert endnotes to footnotes.

Sometimes requirements for a document can change, and you may find yourself needing endnotes instead of footnotes, or vice versa. If this is the case, you can cut and paste the text instead of typing it again.

To convert footnotes to endnotes, follow the steps listed below (the steps for converting endnotes to footnotes are exactly the same):

1. If you are working in the Page View mode, position the insertion point immediately after the footnote reference number.

   If you are working in the Draft View mode, choose **I**nsert, **F**ootnote, **E**dit. Type the number of the footnote you want to edit and choose OK. Position the insertion point immediately after the footnote number.

2. Select the footnote text.

3. Choose **E**dit, Cu**t**; or press Ctrl+X.

4. Choose **C**lose.

5. Press Backspace to delete the footnote reference number in the text.

6. Choose **I**nsert, **E**ndnote, **C**reate.
7. Insert a tab, indent, or a space (depending on the desired appearance).
8. Choose **E**dit, **P**aste; or press Ctrl+V.

9. Choose **C**lose.

From Here...

In this chapter, you learned how to create and edit footnotes and endnotes. You also learned how to move, copy, and delete notes from a document. You learned how to restart note numbering, change the style of the footnote reference number and footnote text, change the spacing between notes, continue notes across pages, and change the separator line between the document text and the footnote text. Finally, you learned how to place endnotes on a titled page.

For more information on special document formatting including advanced use of footnotes and endnotes, see the following chapters in this book:

- Chapter 5, "Formatting Pages and Documents." This chapter talks about document formatting that affects the entire page or document, including creating headers and footers.
- Chapter 10, "Using Styles." Refer to this chapter for information on using WordPerfect's style feature, which allows you to provide consistent formatting to text.
- Chapter 11, "Using Templates." This chapter discusses how WordPerfect uses templates as "boilerplate" files, which can be used as a starting point to creating documents with special formatting.
- Chapter 26, "Assembling Document References." Refer to this chapter to learn how to prepare references within a document, to create a table of contents, index, list, cross-reference, or table of authorities.
- Chapter 27, "Working with Large and Multi-Part Documents." In this chapter, you learn how to assemble a large document out of several smaller ones. When printed, WordPerfect combines footnotes and endnotes.

Chapter 26

Assembling Document References

by Gary Pickavet

WordPerfect 6.1 for Windows is a truly powerful word processor, yet its power doesn't stop with composing a document. WordPerfect also provides tools that enable you to perform complex document processing tasks, such as generating different kinds of references automatically, comparing versions of a document, and marking the changes.

WordPerfect provides a variety of document reference types: lists, tables of contents, tables of authorities, indexes, and cross-references. These references enable you to mark document text and have WordPerfect automatically create tables listing the items and their page numbers. WordPerfect can even mark graphics box captions automatically to be included in a list. When you revise a document, the power of the document reference feature is most apparent: you can add or delete information anywhere in the document without worrying about the page numbers assigned to the marked items. After you revise the document, you simply use the Generate feature when you want WordPerfect to update the tables.

Before computerized word processors, a significant amount of time was required at the end of a project for designing, creating, modifying, and proofreading tables of exhibits, tables of contents, indexes, and other reference materials. With automatic generation of references, WordPerfect makes creating references almost effortless and saves countless hours.

Lawyers preparing legal briefs once had to spend much time poring over a document, noting all the legal citations. After finding all the legal citations and noting their page numbers, the writer had to create a table of authorities listing each citation and the page numbers. WordPerfect's table of authorities feature was designed specifically to solve this problem and allow these tables to be created with minimum effort.

In this chapter, you learn how to do the following:

- Mark text for the various references
- Choose the numbering format of your tables
- Define the location for reference tables
- Change the reference tables' formatting styles
- Change the page number format in the reference tables
- Use Generate
- Use automatic cross-referencing
- Use redlining and strikeout

Showing the differences between old and new versions of a document by using strikeout and redlining is another time-consuming task often performed manually. WordPerfect includes a Compare Document feature that marks the new version of a document, indicating deleted material with the strikeout enhancement and new material with the redline enhancement.

Note

WordPerfect comes with several ready-made Toolbars. The Toolbars can be displayed on any side of your screen. One of these Toolbars, called Generate, enables you to quickly choose each of the WordPerfect document reference features. When you plan to be doing a great deal of document reference work, consider displaying the Generate Toolbar (see fig. 26.1). For more information about Toolbars, see Chapter 13, "Working with Toolbars."

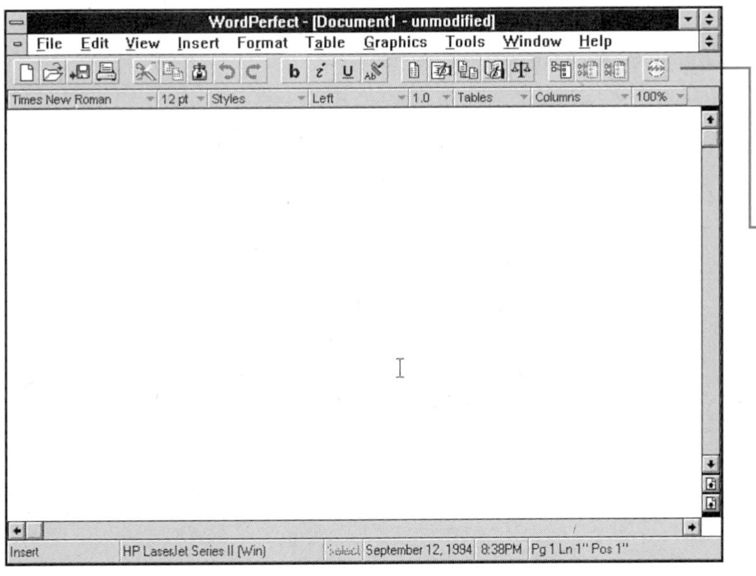

Fig. 26.1
Use the Generate Toolbar to choose document reference features.

Creating Lists

Lists are the most basic reference feature provided by WordPerfect. In a document, you use lists to create a table of exhibits, maps, or figures. You can create a list of any items you want to mark. WordPerfect generates a list of the marked items, with or without their page numbers.

When you create lists, follow these basic steps:

- *Mark.* Mark the text to be included in the list and specify the list on which it is to appear. (You can bypass this step if you only want lists generated from captions of the various graphics boxes provided by WordPerfect. WordPerfect finds the captions automatically.)

- *Define.* Indicate where you want WordPerfect to create the list and how you want the list to look.

- *Generate.* Run Generate to create and revise the list of marked items and, optionally, page numbers.

When WordPerfect generates a list, the items appear in the order in which they appear in the document. The list is created at the location you specify.

Marking Text for Lists

To create a list, you must mark the text you want included in the list. (This step can be bypassed if you only want lists generated from captions of the various graphics boxes provided by WordPerfect. WordPerfect finds the captions automatically.) WordPerfect includes the marked text as the item description in the list. If the marked text has any text enhancements (such as bold or italic), the enhancements also appear in the list. If, for example, you mark *Exhibit 1*, which is italicized, the text is italicized in the list.

> **Note**
>
> You don't need to mark graphics box captions. WordPerfect can include these elements automatically.

To mark text that you want to appear in a list, follow these steps:

1. Choose **T**ools, L**i**st. The List Feature Bar appears (see fig. 26.2).

Fig. 26.2
The List Feature Bar enables you to enter and select list names, mark list entries, define a list, or run Generate to create and update lists you've defined.

2. Select the text. Selected text appears highlighted on-screen.
3. Choose **L**ist to move the insertion point to the **L**ist text box. For a new list, type a descriptive name in the **L**ist text box.

   If this is the first list defined in your document, the **L**ist text entry box is empty. If you are marking subsequent occurrences of text for existing lists, the list name that you last used appears in the **L**ist text entry box. If the desired name of a previously entered list name is not displayed, click the pop-up list button to show the current list names. Select the desired list name.
4. Choose **M**ark on the List Feature Bar. The text is marked for inclusion in the selected list, and WordPerfect returns to your document.

Tip
To access the mnemonics in the Feature Bars, press Alt+Shift+*letter*.

When you mark text to be placed in a list, WordPerfect inserts the code `[Mrk Txt List]` at the beginning and end of the selected text. These codes do not print; however, you can see these codes by opening the Reveal Codes window (choose **V**iew, Reveal **C**odes; or press Alt+F3). To see which list the marked text belongs to, move the insertion point so that it immediately precedes the code before or after the marked text. The code expands and displays the name of the list to which the selected text belongs (see fig. 26.3).

Alternatively, click on the code in the Reveal Codes window to quickly place the insertion point before the code and expand it. You can change the Reveal Codes Display Preferences so that WordPerfect always shows codes in detail. Then the list name is always displayed in the code. Because this causes all codes to display expanded with their values, you may prefer to expand the codes when you need to know the list name rather than having WordPerfect display all codes as expanded.

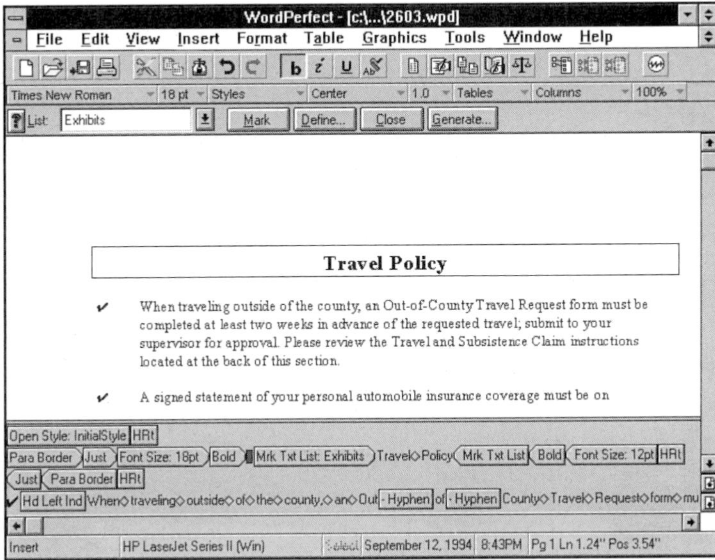

Fig. 26.3
A WordPerfect code showing marked text for a list called Exhibits.

If you use graphics boxes in your documents, you can define a list, and the captions can be included automatically in your list—you don't have to manually mark text. When you define the list, you indicate the type of graphics box you want automatically included in a list. You can mix captions that WordPerfect automatically selects with text that you select and mark with the same list name. Still, the better practice is to keep the lists for which you mark text separate from WordPerfect's automatically selected lists. See "Making a List of Graphics Box Captions" later in this chapter for more information.

If you change your mind about what you want the text in your list to say, edit the text between the mark text codes. If you decide you do not want an item included in the list, delete the code marking the list item. The next time you generate the list, WordPerfect modifies or removes the list text, as appropriate.

Defining a List

After you mark the text to be included in the list, or if you plan to use a list using only the captions from graphics boxes, you are ready to define where you want the list to appear in your document. You also can optionally edit the list definition to specify the numbering format you want to use for the list, the format of the page number, what type of graphics box captions you want included in the list, and the default settings for the style that determines how your list is formatted.

To define where you want the list placed and to use the formatting options, follow these steps:

1. Place the insertion point at the location in your document where you want the list to appear.

   To place the list on its own page, insert a hard page break (press Ctrl+Enter) and type a page heading that describes the list. (Although optional, typing a page heading is recommended.)

2. If the List Feature Bar is not displayed, choose **T**ools, L**i**st.

3. From the Feature Bar, choose **D**efine. The Define List dialog box appears. The lists you have already defined appear in the list box (see fig. 26.4).

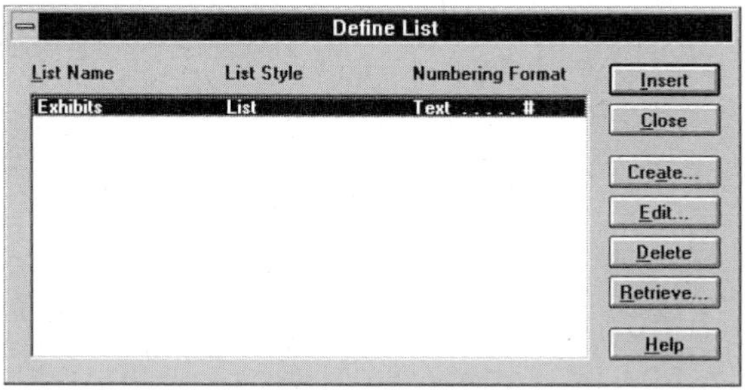

Fig. 26.4
The Define List dialog box shows the names of lists you have already defined, the style applied to the list, and the numbering format for the list.

4. Choose the list. Scroll the selection highlight bar to the desired list.

5. Choose **I**nsert. The Define List dialog box disappears, and WordPerfect returns to your document.

When you define a list, WordPerfect inserts a `[Def Mark]` code in your document. If you want to see which type of document reference is being defined and its name, click on the `[Def Mark]` code. The code expands, similar to the following:

```
[Def Mark: List, Exhibits: None]
```

The text << `List will generate here` >> is inserted into your document between two `[Gen Txt]` codes. This text is replaced by the list when you run Generate.

Tip
To see these codes, open the Reveal Codes window by choosing **V**iew, Reveal **C**odes; or by pressing Alt+F3.

Selecting and Editing How the List Looks

You can change the appearance of your lists by specifying the numbering format you want to use for the list, the format of the page number, and the default settings for the style that determines how your list is formatted.

To change the appearance of your list, follow these steps:

1. If the List Feature Bar is not displayed, choose **T**ools, L**i**st.

2. From the Feature Bar, choose **D**efine. The Define List dialog box appears.

3. Choose the list whose appearance you want to modify. Scroll the selection highlight bar to the desired list.

4. Choose **E**dit. The Edit List dialog box appears (see fig. 26.5).

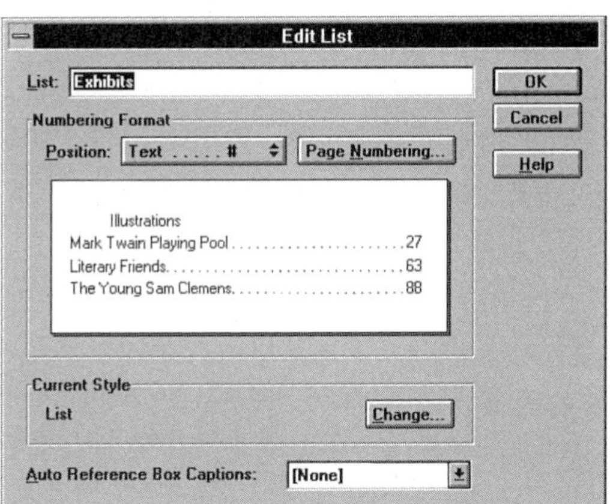

Fig. 26.5
The Edit List dialog box enables you to change the appearance of your list and select graphics box captions to be automatically selected for the list.

The following sections describe the various options for changing the appearance of your list. Follow the steps in the appropriate section.

Choosing the Numbering Position for a List

Five numbering positions for lists are available. The default numbering position is a right-justified page number with dot leaders.

To change the position of the page number, follow these steps:

1. From the Edit List dialog box, choose **P**osition.
2. Choose the desired page number option from the following table.

Numbering Format	Text Result
No Numbering	Map of the US
Text #	Map of the US 38
Text (#)	Map of the US (38)
T**e**xt #	Map of the US 38
Text . . . . . #	Map of the US.38

3. Choose OK and then Close to return to your document.

Changing the Page Number Format for a List

You can change the appearance of the page numbers for the items in a list. The page number format can be the same as the page number formatting in your document, or you may want the page number printed with your list items to use a different format. To change the page number format for a list, follow these steps:

1. From the Edit List dialog box, choose Page **N**umbering. The Page Number Format dialog box appears showing two choices: **D**ocument Page Number Format and **U**ser-Defined Page Number Format (see fig. 26.6).
2. Choose **D**ocument Page Number Format to format the page numbers in your list the same way page numbers are formatted in your document.

   Alternatively, choose **U**ser-Defined Page Number Format to set the page number format differently for this list.

   The code `[Pg #]` in the User-Defined Page Number Format text-entry box represents the page number. If you want text to appear before or after the page number, type the text. To have the page number appear as `- 1 -`, for example, type a dash and space before and after the page number code in the text entry box **(- `[Pg #]` -)**.

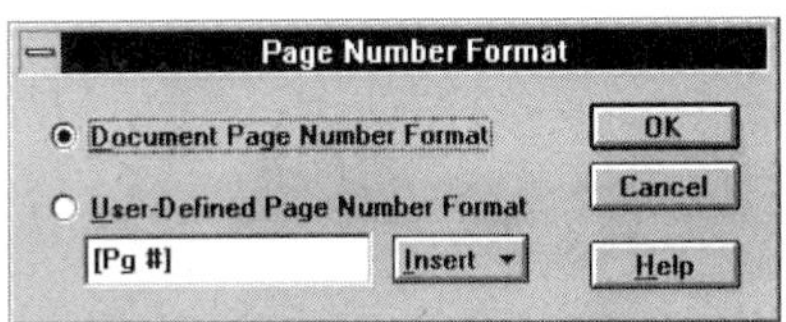

Fig. 26.6
The Page Number Format dialog box enables you to design custom page number formats for your lists.

By using the Insert pop-up list, you can also include a secondary page number, chapter numbers, and volume numbers (such as School Problems-Chapter 4 Page 12). For detailed information about working with page number formats, see Chapter 5, "Formatting Pages and Documents."

3. Choose OK to return to the Edit List dialog box.

4. Choose OK and then **C**lose to return to your document.

Changing a List's Default Style

WordPerfect provides a default style for each of its document references. The style name used for lists is appropriately called *List*. You can modify the List style, and WordPerfect applies your modifications to all lists that use this default style; or you can create a new style that you apply only to certain lists.

To modify the default style of a list, follow these steps:

1. From the Edit List dialog box, choose **C**hange. The List Style dialog box appears showing the various document reference styles as well as styles you have created. The style called List is highlighted.

2. Choose **E**dit. The Styles Editor dialog box appears.

   The default style for lists contains the codes to create a hanging indent (`[Hd Left Ind][Hd Back Tab]`). WordPerfect enables you to customize this List style as you would any style. For detailed information about styles, see Chapter 10, "Using Styles."

3. Make any desired changes and choose OK. WordPerfect returns to the List Style dialog box.

4. Choose **C**lose, OK, and **C**lose to return to your document.

In addition to editing the existing List style, from the List Style dialog box you can also highlight another style and choose **S**elect to change from the default style list to another existing style. Or you can choose C**r**eate to design a new style to be applied to a list. When you create a style, WordPerfect inserts the style in the Style Name box in the List Style dialog box.

Making a List of Graphics Box Captions

For most lists, you mark in your document text that you want to include in the list. Then when you generate the list, WordPerfect copies the marked text to the selected location and formats the list. If you use graphics boxes in your document, you can have WordPerfect automatically place the captions from each type of graphics box into a separate list.

> **Note**
>
> You can mix marked text in a list with graphics box captions. The better practice, however, is to keep separate the lists for which *you* mark text from WordPerfect's automatically selected lists.

To make a list of graphics box captions, follow these steps:

1. Place the insertion point at the location in your document where you want the list to appear.

2. If the List Feature Bar is not displayed, choose **T**ools, L**i**st.
3. From the Feature Bar, choose **D**efine. The Define List dialog box appears. The lists you have already defined appear in the list box.
4. Choose Cre**a**te. The Create List dialog box appears.
5. Type a list name in the **L**ist text box, and choose OK.
6. Choose **E**dit. The Edit List dialog box appears.
7. Choose **A**uto Reference Box Captions at the bottom of the Edit List dialog box.
8. Use the pop-up list button at the right of the Auto Reference Box Captions list box to display the list of WordPerfect graphics boxes.
9. Select the type of graphics box for which you want to have WordPerfect automatically select the box captions and place in the list.
10. Choose OK. The Define List dialog box reappears.
11. Choose **I**nsert. The Define List dialog box disappears, and WordPerfect returns to your document. WordPerfect inserts a `[Def Mark]` code in your document. The captions from the type of graphics box you selected are included in the selected list the next time you run Generate.

You are now ready to generate your list, as explained in the next section.

Using Generate To Create and Update Document References

After you mark text, determine which list to place the text on, and define the appearance and location of the lists, you are ready to create the lists.

◄ See "Working with Reveal Codes," p. 96

◄ See "Selecting Text," p. 103

◄ See "Numbering Pages," p. 177

◄ See "Using Graphics Boxes," p. 275

◄ See "Creating a Caption," p. 723

All references in a document—lists, tables of contents, tables of authorities, cross-references, indexes, and endnotes—are generated and updated each time you perform the Generate function. To ensure that all page numbers and cross-references are correct, you usually want to generate references immediately before you print. If you modified your document since the last time you generated references, WordPerfect reminds you that the references may need to be generated by displaying a dialog box with the message `Document may need to be regenerated. Print anyway?`. Choose Yes if you want to print the document with the references in their current state—as they were last generated. Otherwise, choose No and run Generate.

When you run Generate, WordPerfect creates new lists where you've indicated. WordPerfect deletes any lists previously generated and rebuilds new lists based on the text currently marked in your document. Tables of contents, tables of authorities, cross-references, and indexes are all deleted and rebuilt when you use Generate.

To create and update lists, follow these steps:

1. If the List Feature Bar is not displayed, choose **T**ools, L**i**st.

2. From the Feature Bar, choose **G**enerate. The Generate dialog box appears. The Generate dialog box enables you to have WordPerfect perform the job of locating, gathering, sorting, and listing all of a document's (and optionally its subdocuments') references. Doing this manually is very tedious and time-consuming.

   Alternatively, you can choose **T**ools, Ge**n**erate; or press Ctrl+F9.

3. Choose OK to create or update lists and any other references in the document.

   By default, Generate updates all document references in subdocuments. This task can be very time-consuming because WordPerfect must open each subdocument, generate any document references in the subdocument, and then save the subdocument. If you are using subdocuments and do not want WordPerfect to generate and save them, from the Generate dialog box choose **O**ptions. Then uncheck the **S**ave Subdocuments option. For more information about working with subdocuments, see Chapter 27, "Working with Large and Multi-Part Documents."

Creating a Table of Contents

WordPerfect enables you to form a comprehensive table of contents (ToC) for documents you create. Tables of contents can include as many as five levels of headings and subheadings. Each level is automatically indented to indicate the subordinate levels. As with a list, each marked item included in the table of contents can include the item's page number. When you perform the Generate function, WordPerfect creates, and subsequently updates, the table of contents entries and their page numbers.

Marking Text for a Table of Contents

Selecting items for a table of contents is as easy as highlighting text and any desired enhancement codes, and then selecting the desired ToC level.

WordPerfect provides five levels of headings and places a blank line before each level 1 ToC entry. Subordinate items with levels below 1 are not separated by blank lines (see fig. 26.7).

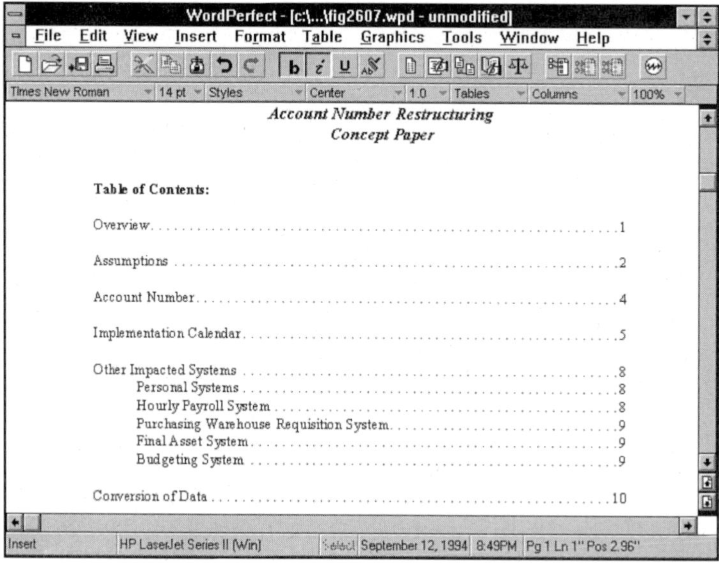

Fig. 26.7 A sample table of contents showing two levels and the default formatting, which places a blank line before each level 1 ToC entry.

To mark text for a ToC entry, follow these steps:

1. Choose **T**ools, Table of **C**ontents. The Table of Contents Feature Bar appears (see fig. 26.8).

Fig. 26.8
Use the Table of Contents Feature Bar to mark entries, define a table of contents, or run Generate to create and update the table of contents.

2. Select the text and include any enhancement codes to be applied to the text (for example bold or italic).

> **Note**
>
> Using Reveal Codes (choose **V**iew, Reveal **C**odes; or press Alt+F3), you can easily include or exclude text enhancement codes that occur at the beginning of selected text. When you mark a ToC entry with codes within the text, WordPerfect applies the code to the text in the ToC. If the code starts before the marked text, the enhancement will not be applied to the text that appears in the generated ToC. If you capture an item with a text enhancement code that you don't want to print in the ToC, you can edit the table of contents after it has been generated. However, any changes you make in the generated table of contents are replaced the next time you generate the document references because WordPerfect deletes the old ToC and creates a new one.

3. Choose the ToC level number (Mark **1** through Mark **5**) for this item; or press Alt+Shift+(1-5). The selected text is marked with the appropriate ToC code and level number.

To see the text and enhancement codes that are or will be included in the table, open the Reveal Codes window. The text and enhancement codes are surrounded by a `[Mrk Txt ToC]` code. To see the level number, click on the code in the Reveal Codes window. The insertion point moves to just before the code; the code expands; and the level number (1 through 5) appears at the end of the code. To change the ToC entry, edit the text between the codes. The next time you generate the document references, WordPerfect inserts the revised text in the table of contents.

If you decide that you no longer want the item included in the table of contents, delete either of the `[Mrk Txt ToC]` codes surrounding the text. WordPerfect deletes the other code and removes the item from the table of contents the next time you generate document references.

Defining a Table of Contents

After you mark the text to be included in the table of contents, you select the location of the table of contents and define its appearance.

To define where you want the table of contents to appear, follow these steps:

1. Place the insertion point at the location where you want to place the table of contents.

2. If the Table of Contents Feature Bar is not displayed, choose **T**ools, Table of **C**ontents.

   If you want the table of contents to begin on a new page with appropriate headings, as shown in figure 26.7, and any part of your document falls *before* your selected location for the table of contents, insert a hard page break (Ctrl+Enter).

3. Choose **D**efine. The Define Table of Contents dialog box appears (see fig. 26.9).

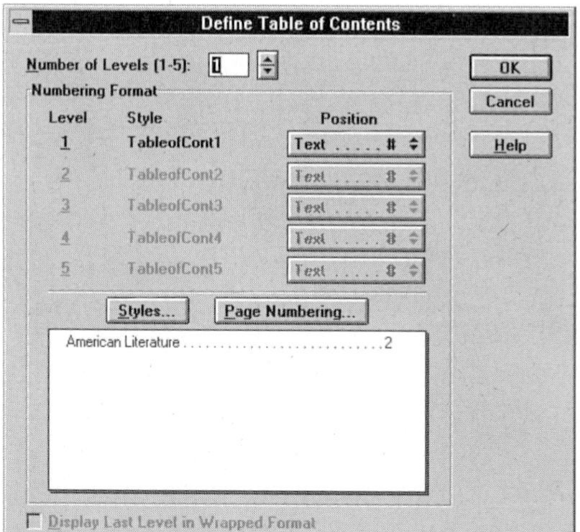

Fig. 26.9
The Define Table of Contents dialog box lets you choose how many levels to include in your table of contents and change the look of the ToC. A preview window shows you how the table of contents is formatted.

4. Choose **N**umber of Levels (1-5) and enter a number, 1 through 5, to indicate how many ToC levels you want included in your document's ToC. Alternatively, you can use the up and down arrows to change the value.

5. To change the default numbering position for any of the levels, select the level (1-5) you want to change and choose one of the five available numbering positions. (Level numbers are available only to the number of levels you indicate in step 4.) For a detailed description of the available formats, see the earlier section "Choosing the Numbering Position for a List." Repeat this step for each level that you want to change.

6. To change the default style for any of the levels, choose **S**tyles. Selecting, creating, and editing styles for each table of contents level is similar to editing styles for lists. For information on changing the default style or creating a custom style, see the earlier section "Changing a List's Default Style."

7. You can change the look of the page numbers for the items in a table of contents by following the same procedure used for changing page number format for lists. For information on changing the page number format, see the earlier section "Changing the Page Number Format for a List."

8. Choose **D**isplay Last Level in Wrapped Format if you want the ToC entries for the last level to wrap to the next line without indenting. If you choose this option, all last level headings and, optionally, their page numbers, follow one another as though they are one paragraph of information. If the entries are longer than one line, the text wraps.

> **Note**
>
> If you select the **D**isplay Last Level in Wrapped Format option, only the first three numbering formats in the Numbering Mode section are available for the last level.

9. Choose OK. The Define Table of Contents dialog box disappears, and WordPerfect returns to your document. The text `<< Table of Contents will generate here >>` appears between two `[Gen Txt]` codes. The text is replaced by the Table of Contents when you run Generate. WordPerfect also inserts a `[Def Mark]` code into your document.

> **Note**
>
> If you want to see which type of document reference is being defined and its name, click on the `[Def Mark]` code. The table of contents code expands, similar to the following:
>
> ```
> [Def Mark: TOC, 2: Dot Ldr #]
> ```

10. Press Ctrl+Enter to insert a hard page break at the end of the table of contents page.

11. If you place the table of contents before your document text, make sure that you set the page number to 1 at the top of the first page of document text to ensure that your document is properly numbered and has correct page numbers in the table of contents.

    Because the table of contents pages count as pages, if you don't reset the page number to 1, the document is misnumbered, and the numbers in the ToC will not be correct.

After you define the location and appearance of the table of contents, you are ready to generate it.

You can run Generate several ways. From the pull-down menus, choose **T**ools, Ge**n**erate; or press Ctrl+F9. Alternatively, from the feature bar, choose **G**enerate. WordPerfect generates all document references—including the table of contents. For complete instructions on generating document references, refer to the earlier section "Using Generate To Create and Update Document References."

Troubleshooting

When I generate a table of contents, only the first word in each heading in the table of contents appears.

When you defined the headings for the table of contents, you didn't select the entire heading first. If you merely put the insertion point at the beginning of the heading, WordPerfect will assume that's the extent of the text you want included in the table of contents. If you want the entire line, select it, and then choose the table of contents heading level you want (1 through 5).

All the headings in my table of contents are the same level, instead of level 1, level 2, and so forth.

You must be careful to specify the heading level you want for the table of contents. After selecting the text you want included in the table of contents, click the button in the Table of Contents feature bar for the level you want: Mark **1** for level 1, Mark **2** for level 2, and so forth. In addition, when defining the Table of Contents (choose **D**efine in the Table of Contents feature bar) make sure that you specify the number of headings you plan to use for the table of contents.

Creating a Table of Authorities

Few professions probably have to deal with more paperwork than the legal profession. Court cases require enormous amounts of correspondence, transcripts, and other written materials, such as legal briefs. A table of authorities is a table used to reference (or index) a legal brief.

The WordPerfect Table of Authorities (ToA) feature makes creating a table of authorities easier. The time savings to a legal office in automating this task is well worth the time required to learn how to use the feature.

Creating a ToA is not as difficult as it may seem at first. Although you must perform several steps, the steps are straightforward:

1. Decide what groupings or categories of legal citations you will have in the brief.
2. Mark the first occurrence of each legal citation. Define precisely what the citation reference should say and how it should be formatted when printed in the ToA. This task is called *marking the full form.*
3. Assign a unique keyword to be associated with that particular legal reference. This is the *short form.*
4. Mark all subsequent occurrences of a citation with the appropriate keyword to tie these occurrences to the full form. This task is called *marking the short form.*
5. Define where you want to place the ToA and what formatting options you want to apply.
6. Generate the document references (which creates the ToA).
7. Print the legal brief.

WordPerfect sorts the authorities within each section alphabetically. Figure 26.10 shows a sample table of authorities for a legal brief.

Marking Text for a Table of Authorities

Before you begin marking citations for the table of authorities (ToA), decide how many sections you plan to have. As you mark each citation the first time, you assign it to a section. Suppose, for example, that you decide to have three sections: one for Federal Cases, one for State Cases, and one for Other Authorities (see fig. 26.10).

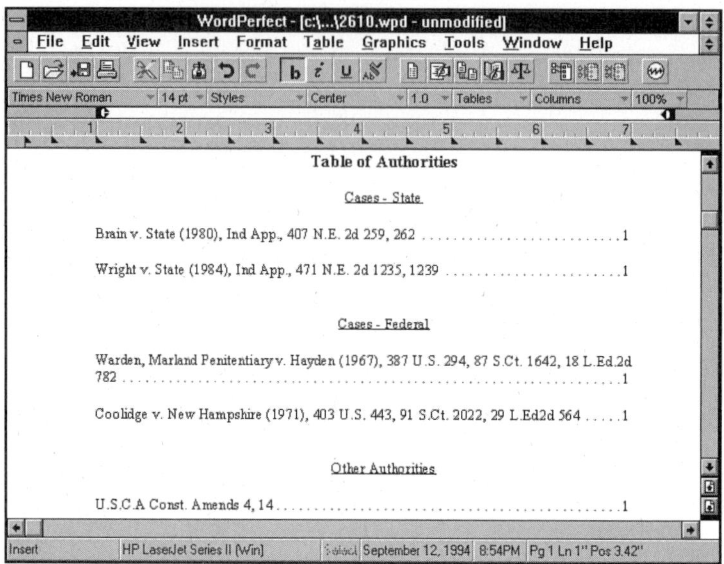
WordPerfect - [c:\...\2610.wpd - unmodified]

Table of Authorities

Cases - State

Brain v. State (1980), Ind App., 407 N.E. 2d 259, 262 1

Wright v. State (1984), Ind App., 471 N.E. 2d 1235, 1239 1

Cases - Federal

Warden, Marland Penitentiary v. Hayden (1967), 387 U.S. 294, 87 S.Ct. 1642, 18 L.Ed.2d 782 1

Coolidge v. New Hampshire (1971), 403 U.S. 443, 91 S.Ct. 2022, 29 L.Ed2d 564 1

Other Authorities

U.S.C.A Const. Amends 4, 14 1

Fig. 26.10
A sample table of authorities.

Before you begin marking text, you should understand how WordPerfect uses the ToA full form and ToA short form. The ToA full form, which you enter only once, contains the text of the complete citation as it appears in the generated table of authorities and the section in which the authority is to appear.

As part of the ToA full form code, you also assign a ToA short form. The ToA short form is a unique identifier you assign to tie citations together when the table of authorities is generated. Using the same ToA short form for more than one ToA full form causes the error message `A Full Form has already been defined with this Short Form.`

Note

If you allow WordPerfect to generate the ToA short form identifier for you as you mark the ToA full form, this error alerts you that you are attempting to mark the full form a second time.

After you create the ToA full form for a citation, you mark the location of subsequent occurrences of the same citation with the unique short form name assigned to the citation. By doing this, you enable WordPerfect to build the table of authorities with page numbers showing every place where the citation occurs.

Marking Full Form Entries

When you mark a citation for the first time, it's good practice to mark it as the ToA full form. This means that you define the actual text to be placed in the table of authorities. To mark a citation as a ToA full form, follow these steps:

1. Choose **T**ools, Table of **A**uthorities. The Table of Authorities Feature Bar appears (see fig. 26.11).

Fig. 26.11
Use the Table of Authorities Feature Bar to mark short form entries, create and edit full form entries, define a table of authorities, or run Generate to create and update the table of authorities.

2. Select all the text for the citation that you want included in the ToA.

3. Choose C**r**eate Full Form. The Create Full Form dialog box appears (see fig. 26.12).

   The first time you mark a full form, the Section **N**ame entry box is blank. You can use numbers to identify the sections where the full forms are to be included, or you can make them more descriptive—such as State, Federal, or Other.

Fig. 26.12
The ToA Create Full Form dialog box enables you to enter the section name and short form name for the ToA full form.

4. To enter the section name, choose Section **N**ame. For a new section, type the name.

   For an existing section name, you can select a section name from the list of existing section names. Choose the Section **N**ame pop-up list button, and a list of the currently defined section names appears. In this pop-up list, move the highlight bar to the desired section name (or number) in which you want to include this citation. Choose the desired section name. WordPerfect closes the list and places your choice in the Section **N**ame entry box.

5. An abbreviated portion of the citation text you highlighted appears in the Short **F**orm text box. If you want to use a different short form, you can edit the short form identifier. The short form name must be unique because it relates all occurrences of the same authority to this full form entry.

Tip
Open the Reveal Codes window to make sure that you mark the exact text you want to include as the full form.

6. Choose OK to view the full form. The ToA full form editing window appears. The text you selected in your document appears in the text editing area (see fig. 26.13).

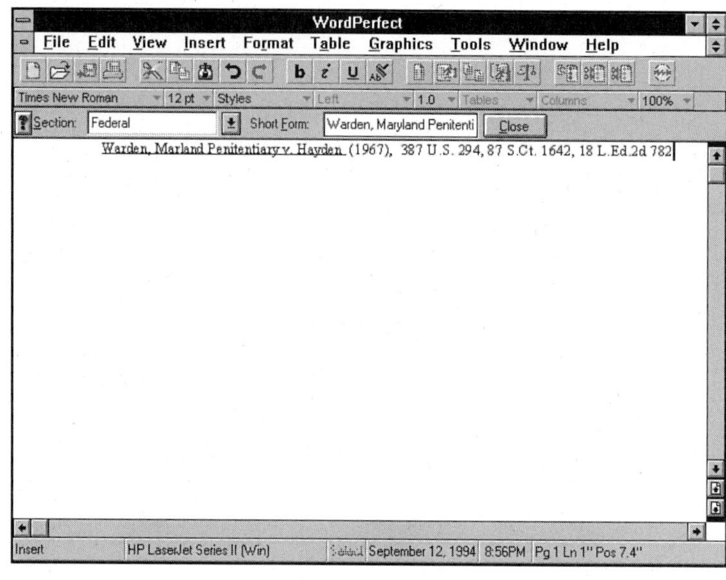

Fig. 26.13
The table of authorities full form editing window lets you view the full form text you've selected. In the full form editing window, edit the text until it looks exactly as you want it to appear in the generated table of authorities.

Tip
You can apply text enhancement codes (such as bold, italic, or small caps) or formatting codes (such as indent) to the full form citation.

7. Edit the citation so that it appears exactly as you want it to appear in the table of authorities. When you are finished, choose **C**lose. WordPerfect returns to your document.

When you mark text for a full form entry to be included in a table of authorities, WordPerfect inserts the code `[ToA]` at the beginning of the citation. If you want to see more information about the Table of Authorities code, click on the `[ToA]` code. The code expands, similar to the following:

```
[ToA:section name;short form text;Full Form]
```

Tip
These codes do not print. To see these codes, open the Reveal Codes window by choosing **V**iew, Reveal **C**odes; or by pressing Alt+F3.

Caution

If you edit the legal citation in your brief, the text in the full form is *not* modified. You must edit the full form to change the appearance of the citation in your table of authorities.

Editing Full Form Entries

After you mark a full form citation, you can edit its short form identifier, the section name it belongs to, or its full form text.

To edit a full form entry, follow these steps:

1. From the Table of Authorities Feature Bar, choose **E**dit Full Form. The Edit Full Form dialog box appears (see fig. 26.14).

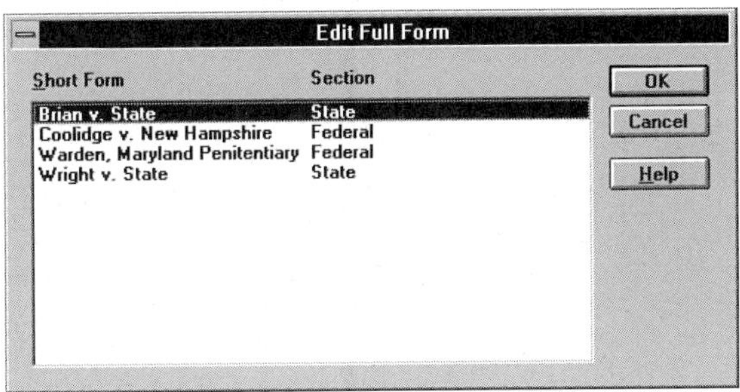

Fig. 26.14
The Edit Full Form dialog box lists the unique short form identifier and assigned section for each of the full forms you have marked.

2. Choose the citation you want to edit. Scroll the highlight bar to the desired citation.

3. Choose OK. The full form text editing window appears with the full form text. You can choose from the following options:

   - *Short **F**orm.* Changes the short form identifier. Edit the short form as desired.

   - ***S**ection.* Changes the section in which you want this full form entry to appear. Either type a section name or click the section pop-up list button to display and select from a list of available sections.

4. Choose **C**lose to save the changes.

The edited full form text and section changes do not appear in the table of authorities until you generate the document references.

Marking Short Form Entries

After you enter the ToA full form, you mark subsequent occurrences of the citation by using the ToA short form name that you associated with the ToA full form.

Note

Because WordPerfect displays the last short form used in the **S**hort Form text box on the Table of Authorities Feature Bar, you may find it more efficient to mark all related short forms for one citation before moving to the next. You can find each occurrence of the citation quickly by using Find (F2).

To mark a citation by using the ToA short form identifier, follow these steps:

1. Move the insertion point so that it immediately precedes the citation.
2. From the Table of Authorities Feature Bar, make sure that the short form displayed is the one you want to use. If not, type in or edit the short form as necessary.

   To select from a list of existing short form names, click the Short Form pop-up list button. Move the highlight bar to the desired short form name.
3. Choose **M**ark. WordPerfect inserts a hidden code into your document.
4. Repeat steps 1 through 3 until all citations are marked.

Note

The short form name must be unique for each full form, but it also should be descriptive so that you can easily associate the short form with the citation full form.

Tip

To see these codes, open the Reveal Codes window by choosing **V**iew, Reveal **C**odes; or by pressing Alt+F3.

When you mark a citation with a short form code, WordPerfect inserts the code `[ToA]`. If you want to see the short form name for the code, click on the code. The code expands and displays the name of the short form such as `[ToA:,short form text;]`. If you decide to delete the reference, simply delete the code. If you want a different short form name for a citation, delete the code and repeat the preceding steps.

Defining a Table of Authorities

Before WordPerfect can generate the table of authorities, you must define where you want the table placed. You may want to title the page and place headings before each section. The following steps show how to define the location and options for a table of authorities. The table of authorities shown in figure 26.15 is used as an example.

To define the location for a table of authorities, perform the following steps:

1. Move the insertion point to the end of the table of contents.

2. Press Ctrl+Enter to place a hard page break at the end of the table of contents and start the table of authorities on a new page. (The table of authorities should be a separately numbered part of the document.)

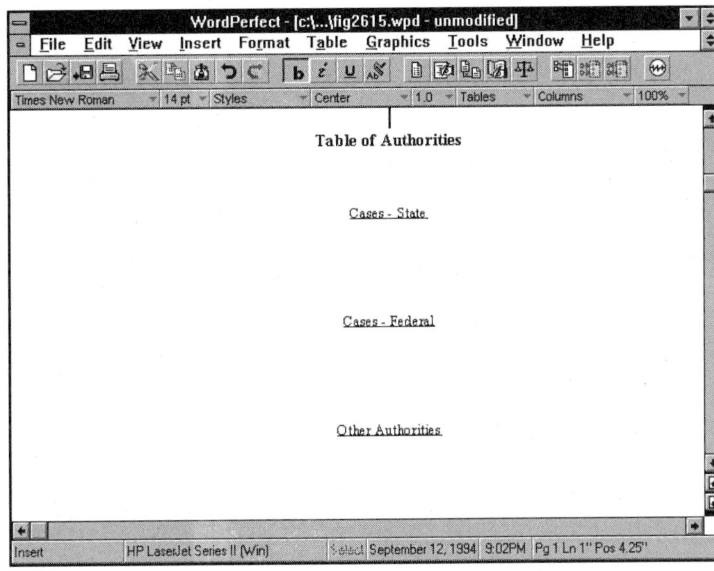

Fig. 26.15
The sections of a sample table of authorities. When you run Generate, WordPerfect builds the table of authorities and places the full form entries in the appropriate section.

To create a page heading for a table of authorities, follow these steps:

1. Choose Fo**r**mat, **L**ine, **C**enter; or press Shift+F7. Then choose Fo**r**mat, **F**ont, **B**old, OK; or press Ctrl+B.

2. Type **TABLE OF AUTHORITIES**.

   Mark the heading for inclusion in the table of contents if you want it included there.

3. To turn off bold, choose Fo**r**mat, **F**ont, **B**old, OK; or press Ctrl+B.

To create the first section for a table of authorities, follow these steps:

1. Press Enter three times.

2. Choose Fo**r**mat, **L**ine, **C**enter; or press Shift+F7. Then choose Fo**r**mat, **F**ont, **U**nderline, OK; or press Ctrl+U.

3. Type the heading for the first section (in this example, type **Cases - State**).

4. To turn off underlining, choose Fo**r**mat, **F**ont, **U**nderline, OK; or press Ctrl+U.

5. Press Enter three times to create blank space between your heading and the table of authorities for the section.

To define the location and options for a table of authorities section, do the following:

1. From the Table of Authorities Feature Bar, choose **D**efine. The Define Table of Authorities dialog box appears (see fig. 26.16).

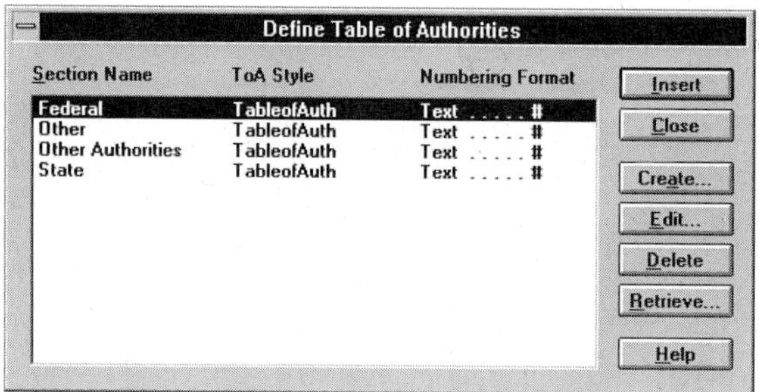

Fig. 26.16
The Define Table of Authorities dialog box lists the names of the sections you used when you marked the ToA full form entries.

2. Choose the section name you want to place at the current location. Scroll the selection highlight bar to the desired list.

3. Choose **I**nsert. The Define Table of Authorities dialog box disappears, and WordPerfect returns to your document. The text `<< Table of Authorities will generate here >>` and a `[Def Mark]` code are inserted into your document. The text is replaced by the Table of Authorities when you run Generate.

4. If you have more than one type of authority, repeat the steps for creating a section heading, and repeat steps 1 through 3 to define the location of a ToA for the other sections (in the example, section two is "Cases - Federal," and section three is "Other Authorities").

5. Press Ctrl+Enter to insert a hard page break at the end of the ToA page.

6. If the next page is your document text, restart the page number at 1 to ensure that your citations are referenced to the correct page numbers.

When you define a table of authorities, table of contents, list, or index, WordPerfect inserts a `[Def Mark]` code in your document. If you want to see which type of document reference is being defined by the code, click on the code. The code expands. For a table of authorities, the code resembles the following example:

```
[Def Mark: ToA, <section name>]
```

These codes do not print, but you can see these codes by opening the Reveal Codes window (Choose **V**iew, Reveal **C**odes; or press Alt+F3).

You can also change how a table of authorities is formatted. To change table of authorities options, follow these steps:

1. From the Table of Authorities Feature Bar, choose **D**efine. The Define Table of Authorities dialog box appears (refer to fig. 26.16).

2. Choose the section name for which you want to change options. Scroll to move the selection highlight bar to the desired list.

3. Choose **E**dit. The Edit Table of Authorities dialog box appears (see fig. 26.17).

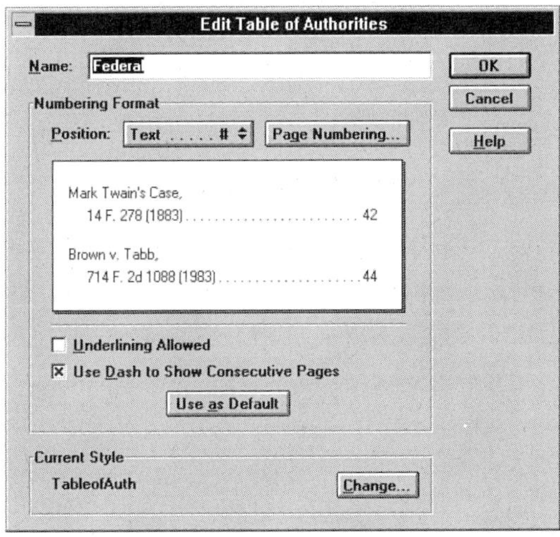

Fig. 26.17
The Edit Table of Authorities dialog box enables you to change the appearance of the table of authorities, including the numbering format and the style used to format the text.

4. The default numbering position is a flush-right page number with dot leaders. To change the numbering position, choose **P**osition from the Edit Table of Authorities dialog box. Choose from the five available numbering positions. For a detailed description of the available formats, see the earlier section "Choosing the Numbering Position for a List."

5. You can change how the page numbers look for the items in a ToA. Changing the page number format is the same for tables of authorities and lists. For information on changing the page number format, see the section "Changing the Page Number Format for a List," earlier in this chapter.

6. In the text of your brief, the court case references are normally underlined. You can display or omit the underlining in the ToA. By default, underlining does not appear in the ToA because **U**nderlining Allowed is disabled. If you want to use underlining in the ToA, choose this option.

7. If you want groups of sequential pages combined (for example, 7-10), instead of printed out separately (7, 8, 9, 10), choose Use **D**ash to Show Consecutive Pages.

8. If you want to use the current settings for underlining and dashes for sequential pages for all new table of authorities sections, choose Use **a**s Default.

9. To change the default style for a table of authorities, choose **C**hange. Selecting, creating, and editing styles for a table of authorities is similar to editing styles for lists. For detailed information on changing the default style, see the section "Changing a List's Default Style" earlier in this chapter.

10. Choose OK and Close until WordPerfect returns to your document.

Now that you have marked the citations and defined the table of authorities, you are ready to generate the table.

You can run Generate several ways. From the pull-down menus, choose **T**ools, Ge**n**erate; or press Ctrl+F9. Alternatively, from the Feature Bar, choose **G**enerate. WordPerfect generates all document references—including the table of authorities. For complete instructions on generating document references, refer to the earlier section "Using Generate To Create and Update Document References."

Note

If you incorrectly type a ToA short form or have no ToA full form corresponding to the short form, when you generate the table of authorities, WordPerfect displays the message `Generate TOA - Full form not found`. WordPerfect places the ToA short form name, preceded by an asterisk (*), at the beginning of the first section of the table of authorities when you generate it. If this situation occurs, simply locate the incorrect short form, delete the code, and enter the correct short form. If the full form is missing, find the first occurrence of the citation, delete the short form, and create a full form.

Creating an Index

Manually generating a good index is a time-consuming task. Sifting through a long document looking for each reference to a word or phrase can also be subject to error. WordPerfect makes this task much quicker and easier.

WordPerfect's Index feature creates an alphabetized list of index headings and subheadings for a document. You can manually mark the words to be included in the index, use a file with the words you want to use as index words for the document, or use a combination of both methods.

As an alternative to marking each occurrence of a word or phrase in a document for inclusion in the index, WordPerfect offers another way to build an index: the concordance file. A *concordance file* is a regular WordPerfect file into which you place words or phrases that you want to include in the index. WordPerfect reads the list of words in the concordance file, determines on what pages the words appear in your document, and places the entry in the index.

◄ See "Finding Words and Phrases," p. 117

You use the same procedure to create an index as you use to create a list or a table of contents. You mark the words to include—optionally, create a concordance file—define the location and formatting for the index, and then generate the index.

Marking Text for an Index

You can mark text for an index in two ways: you can manually mark each occurrence of the index word in the on-screen document, or you can list the words and phrases in a concordance file. Each method has advantages and disadvantages, and you can use the methods together if you want.

Marking each occurrence of a word manually draws your attention to misspelled words quickly. When WordPerfect generates the index, only exact matches appear together with the page numbers for each occurrence. Misspelled index entries do not match and will appear on separate lines.

Suppose that in your document you marked the text *Instructional Expenses Accounting* as an index entry, and elsewhere in your document you marked the text *Instructional Expense Accounting*. When you generate the index, the entries are listed separately because the text is not identical ("Expense" and "Expenses").

If you placed the text *Instructional Expense Accounting* into a concordance file, *Instructional Expenses Accounting* would not appear at all in the index because it is not an *exact* match.

Marking Text Manually

Marking each occurrence of an index word provides the greatest flexibility, but is the most time-consuming. This method requires you to find and mark every occurrence of the index word in the document. Items not marked are not included in the index.

To mark text manually as an index word, follow these steps:

1. Choose **T**ools, Inde**x**. The Index Feature Bar appears (see fig. 26.18).
2. Select the index text.

Fig. 26.18 Use the Index Feature Bar to mark index entries as headings and subheadings, define an index, or run **G**enerate to create and update the index.

> **Note**
>
> Any enhancements—bold or underline, for example—are not applied to the index text in the index.

3. Choose H**e**ading. The selected text is placed into the H**e**ading text box.
4. Choose **M**ark to insert an index code containing the selected text into your document.

   To place this reference as a subheading under another heading, type the text of the heading into the H**e**ading text box. Press Tab or choose **S**ubheading. The insertion point moves to the **S**ubheading text box, and the text you selected in your document appears as the subheading. Choose **M**ark to insert an index code containing the selected text into your document.

Note

The heading and subheading don't have to be the same as the marked text. You can highlight the text you want indexed, and then type the text you want to appear in the document index in the H**e**ading or **S**ubheading text boxes. When the index is generated, the text you typed appears in the index with the page number of the text you selected.

After you have created a heading or subheading, you can subsequently select the entries by choosing the H**e**ading or **S**ubheading pop-up list buttons to display and select the previously entered index items.

When you mark an entry as an Index heading, WordPerfect inserts the code `[Index]` at the location of the insertion point. If you want to see the text of the index, click on the code. The code expands and displays the heading such as `[Index: heading text]`. If you mark an entry as a subheading after typing a heading in the H**e**ading text box, the expanded WordPerfect code shows `[Index: heading text;subheading text]`. These codes do not print, but you can see these codes by opening the Reveal Codes window (choose **V**iew, Reveal **C**odes; or press Alt+F3).

Caution

When you mark text as an index entry, the heading and subheading text you type is inserted in the index code. If you subsequently modify the text that you selected for inclusion as an index item, the text in the index code does not automatically change. You must delete the index code to the left of the revised text in your document and re-mark the text for the index. If you no longer want the item included after you mark text for inclusion in the index, delete the `[Index]` code by dragging it out of the Reveal Codes window. WordPerfect removes the item from the index the next time you generate document references. Subheadings are listed alphabetically and normally indented under a heading. Suppose that you are indexing a document with a section describing computer training for Macintosh and IBM computers. You may want to mark *Training Opportunities* as the heading and *Macintosh* and *IBM* as subheadings for each separate occurrence. The resulting index is shown as follows:

Index:

Training Opportunities............................13

    IBM...................................13

    Macintosh...........................14

Note

If you want text to be displayed as a heading above subheading items but without a page number reference, use the text as a heading when you define subheadings but do not define the heading text in your document as an index. Use the text only in the H**e**ading text box when marking index items as subheadings.

Marking Text by Using a Concordance File

You can create an index without manually marking text by using the concordance feature. A concordance file contains the words and phrases that you want to use as index words in a document. When you define the index for your document, as explained in the section "Defining an Index" later in this chapter, WordPerfect enables you to specify a concordance file for use in generating the index. The words and phrases you place in the concordance file become your index items, and the referenced page numbers reflect all occurrences of the words in the document.

WordPerfect includes and shows the page numbers of only items that are an exact match with a concordance entry. An entry of *Print* in the concordance file, for example, does not match *Printing* in your document; consequently, WordPerfect doesn't create an index reference for *Printing*.

Tip
The fastest way to open a new blank document is to click the New Blank Document button in the Power Bar.

On the other hand, the match is not sensitive to upper- or lowercase letters. An entry in the document of *print* matches *Print* in the concordance file, causing that page number to be included in the index.

To create a concordance file, follow these steps:

1. Choose **F**ile, **N**ew; or press Ctrl+T. In the New Document dialog box, choose Create New Document, and then choose **S**elect. A blank file appears.

2. Type the entries that are your index items. Type one entry to a line, pressing Enter at the end of each line.

3. Choose **F**ile, **S**ave; or press Ctrl+S.

Note

Keep your concordance file and your primary document window open at the same time. Each time you use a word in your primary document that is appropriate as an index entry, click in the concordance file window, add the word to the list, click back in your primary document, and continue composing.

WordPerfect makes each entry in the concordance file a heading. Normally, you just enter the words in the concordance file; marking the words isn't necessary. However, if you want a concordance file entry to be listed in your document's index as a subheading, mark the concordance file entry as a subheading and type the heading under which the subheading is to be listed.

If you mark a concordance file entry as a subheading, it will not automatically create a heading in your document's index. If you want a word or phrase in the concordance file to be listed under a heading as described in the preceding paragraph and also want it listed as a heading, mark the concordance file entry again—this time as a heading. Two `[Index]` codes will precede the word in the concordance file.

Defining an Index

You define the index's placement and formatting. To define an index, follow these steps:

1. Place the insertion point at the location where you want to place the index (normally the end of your document).

   If you want to place the index on a page by itself, insert a hard page break (press Ctrl+Enter). You may want to type a page heading (such as **INDEX**).

2. From the Index Feature Bar, choose **D**efine (if the Index Feature Bar is not displayed, choose **T**ools, Inde**x**). The Define Index dialog box appears (see fig. 26.19).

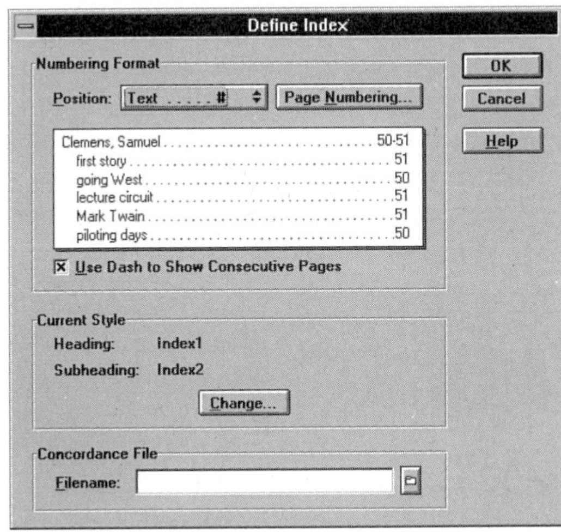

Fig. 26.19
The Define Index dialog box enables you to change the appearance of your index and specify a concordance file. A preview window shows you how the index is formatted.

V

Large Documents

3. If you want to use the default formatting options for your index and don't want to use a concordance file, choose OK.

   The Define Index dialog box closes, and you are returned to your document. The text `<< Index will generate here >>` is inserted into your document between two `[Gen Txt]` codes. This text is replaced by the index when you run Generate.

When you define an index, table of authorities, table of contents, or list, WordPerfect inserts a `[Def Mark]` code in your document at the location of the insertion point. If you want to see which type of document reference is being defined by the code, click on the code. The code expands. For an index, the code resembles the following example:

```
[Def Mark: Index, Dot Ldr #]
```

These codes do not print, but you can see these codes by opening the Reveal Codes window (choose **V**iew, Reveal **C**odes; or press Alt+F3).

You can also change how an index is formatted. To define an index with a different appearance, follow these steps:

1. From the Index Feature Bar, choose **D**efine. The Define Index dialog box appears (refer to fig. 26.19).

2. The default numbering position is a flush-right page number with dot leaders. To change the numbering position, from the Define Index dialog box, choose **P**osition. Choose from the five available numbering positions. For a detailed description of the available formats, see the earlier section "Choosing the Numbering Position for a List."

3. You can change how the page numbers for the items in an index will look. Changing the page number format is the same for indexes and lists. For information on changing the page number format, see the earlier section "Changing the Page Number Format for a List."

4. If you want groups of sequential pages printed out separately (for example 7, 8, 9, 10) instead of combined (for example, 7-10), uncheck the default **U**se Dash to Show Consecutive Pages option.

5. To change the default style for the index Heading or Subheading levels, choose **C**hange. Selecting, creating, and editing styles for an index is similar to editing styles for lists. For detailed information on changing the default style, see the earlier section "Changing a List's Default Style."

6. To generate the index by using a concordance file, choose **F**ilename and type the file name in the text box.

   Alternatively, choose the list button at the right of the **F**ilename text entry box. The Select File dialog box opens to help you find the desired file.

7. Choose OK until WordPerfect returns to your document.

If, after you define the index, you want to change its location or numbering format, you must delete the current `[Def Mark:Index]` code, and then define the index and desired format information at the new location. WordPerfect deletes the generated index information at the old location and places the newly generated index information at the new location the next time you generate.

Tip
You can quickly delete a code by dragging the code out of the Reveal Codes window.

Now that you have marked the index entries and optionally selected a concordance file of index entries, you are ready to generate the index.

You can run Generate several ways. From the pull-down menus, choose **T**ools, Ge**n**erate; or press Ctrl+F9. Alternatively, from the Feature Bar, choose **G**enerate. WordPerfect generates all document references—including the index. For complete instructions on generating document references, refer to the earlier section "Using Generate To Create and Update Document References."

Using Automatic Cross-Referencing

Using automatic cross-referencing makes a complex document much easier for a reader to understand. With automatic cross-referencing, you can let the reader know where a figure is located or provide a detailed explanation of a concept (for example, *See fig. 3 on page 22* or *See the detailed description of the widget that begins on page 114*). You can cross-reference any item. You control the definition of the referenced items (the targets) and the references to them.

In the past, writers often avoided using cross-references because the task was time-consuming and prone to errors. Each time the document was revised, the writers had to manually find, review, and correct the cross-references. Now, WordPerfect makes cross-referencing a snap. WordPerfect automatically and reliably updates references each time you run Generate.

When WordPerfect generates the document references, it matches *targets* (the location where you are telling the reader to look) and references using the *target name,* a unique identifier used to link the target with its reference. The target name must be an exact match. During document reference generation, a reference to the name *account* does not match and cross-reference if you entered the target name as *accounts.* The matching is not sensitive to upper- or lowercase letters, however. This means that a reference linked to the target name *Accounts* is matched with a target defined as *accounts.*

WordPerfect uses the target name to link references with their targets only when it generates document references. The target name is not printed with the document.

You can use cross-referencing in different ways. You can use simple cross-referencing in which there is one reference to one target (*See the detailed description of helium on page 234*). You can have a reference to multiple occurrences of a unique target name (*See the graphics check boxes on pages 2, 12, 20*). Or you can reference a single target in different ways (*See fig. 1 on page 4*).

To use cross-references, follow this basic procedure:

1. Define one or more references to each target.
2. Mark the referenced item(s) (the targets).
3. Generate the document references to update the page numbers for all references.

Depending on what works best for you, you can mark a target when you create it and mark the references to it later, or you can mark the references as you write them and mark the target later. Generally, if you are composing a new document and want to handle the references and targets as you write, mark the reference before the target. Then when you come to the place where you want the reader to look, mark the target.

Marking References and Targets

To mark a reference, follow these steps:

1. Type any desired introductory text such as **See description on page** at the desired location.
2. Place the insertion point where you want to insert the reference code.

3. Choose **T**ools, Cross-Re**f**erence. The Cross-Reference Feature Bar appears (see fig. 26.20).

Fig. 26.20
Use the Cross Reference Feature Bar to choose and work with types of references.

4. Choose a reference type from the **R**eference pop-up list (see fig. 26.21). For example, if you want the reference to show the page number of the target, choose **P**age. As you can see in figure 26.21, you can refer the reader to other than page numbers.

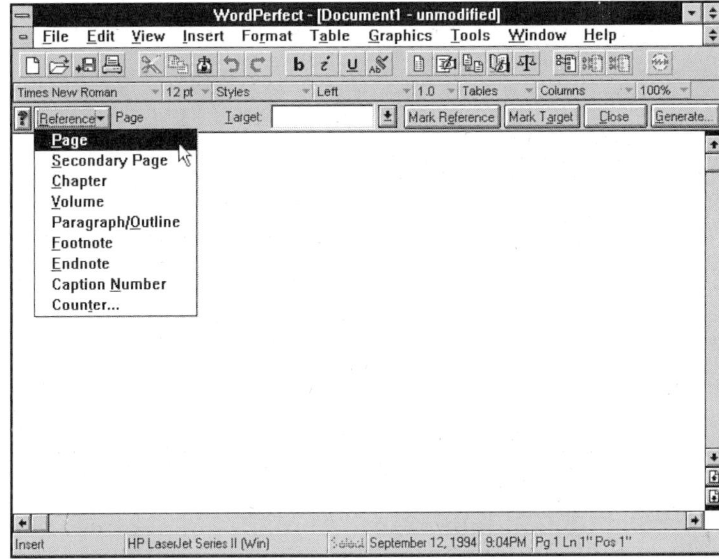

Fig. 26.21
WordPerfect provides several reference types to which you can refer readers.

5. Type the target name desired into the **T**arget text box.

   The last target name you used may already be in the **T**arget text box. If you previously entered a reference to the target you want to reference and it is not displayed, choose a target from the pop-up list.

6. Choose Mark Reference. WordPerfect inserts a hidden code into your document.

WordPerfect inserts a reference code such as `[Ref Pg: target name]` in your document. Initially, in the displayed text, a question mark appears. WordPerfect replaces the question mark with the page number of the target when you generate the document references. If more than one target exists with the entered target name, WordPerfect lists multiple page numbers separated by commas. If you make a mistake while you type the target name, delete the code and mark the reference again.

Tip
You can quickly delete a code by dragging the code out of the Reveal Codes window.

After you mark references to a target, you must mark the target before you generate the document references. If you don't, the question mark shown at the reference is not replaced with the document reference.

To mark a target, follow these steps:

1. Position the insertion point within the first word in the target text. If you are marking an item other than text (for example, a graphics box), position the insertion point to the immediate right of the graphics box code.

2. If the Cross-Reference Feature Bar is not displayed, choose **T**ools, Cross-Re**f**erence.

3. The last target name you typed appears in the **T**arget text box. If the name is correct, choose Mark T**a**rget.

   For a new target, type the name in the **T**arget text box. Or if you have already created the target, choose it from the pop-up list. Then choose Mark T**a**rget.

When you define a target, WordPerfect inserts a `[Target(target name)]` code in your document. If you made a mistake typing the target name, delete the code and mark the target again.

Marking References to Footnotes and Endnotes

Sometimes you want to reference a footnote in the main text of your document (*See discussion in footnote 4 on page 12*, for example). To mark a footnote as a target, you must be in the footnote editing window.

Tip
If you mark a target in the footnote editing window, the target moves to other pages with the footnote if you add or delete text in the document.

You mark endnotes the same way you mark footnotes. Be sure to place the target codes for endnote references in the endnotes themselves.

You can run Generate several ways. From the pull-down menus, choose **T**ools, Ge**n**erate; or press Ctrl+F9. Alternatively, from the feature bar, choose **G**enerate. WordPerfect generates all document references—including the cross-references. For complete instructions on generating document references, refer to the earlier section "Using Generate To Create and Update Document References."

To learn more about footnotes and endnotes, see Chapter 25, "Using Footnotes and Endnotes."

> **Troubleshooting**
>
> *When I generate an index (or any document reference) WordPerfect says "No def codes found."*
>
> In addition to marking entries for the index, you must make sure that you define the index somewhere in the document. The index is usually defined at the very end of the document, but it can be placed anywhere. To define the index, place the insertion point where you want the index to go. Choose **D**efine in the Index Feature Bar. If desired, choose the index options you want to use, and choose OK. After it is defined once, you do not need to define the index again unless you want to modify the index options.
>
> *When I generate a document with cross-referencing, WordPerfect displays a ? (question mark) where the reference is supposed to go.*
>
> The ? question mark denotes an unresolved cross-reference. The question mark is normal when you are defining the cross-references before the document has been generated. If a question mark remains after generating the document, it means that a reference was made to an undefined target. Check the target name of the unresolved cross-reference to make sure that it is spelled correctly. And make sure that the target exists someplace in the document. Click the arrow beside the **T**arget list to see a list of the targets in the document.

Using Compare Documents

When you revise a document, you may want someone to review the changes and provide feedback. Manually identifying every change, however, takes a great deal of time. Also, you must provide both the original document to show the removed text and the new document to show the new text. WordPerfect's Compare Document feature, however, compares an old version of a document on disk to the on-screen document. WordPerfect indicates which text has been added, deleted, changed, and moved in the on-screen document.

Deleted material is shown with the strikeout text enhancement. New text is marked with the redline text enhancement. If you have a color monitor, the new text appears in red on-screen.

> **Caution**
>
> Using this feature requires foresight. Many people perform revisions to a document by retrieving the current document, making the changes, and then replacing the old version of the document with the revised version. After you replace the old version of the document with the on-screen version, you cannot use the Compare Document feature because you have no old version to compare to the on-screen document.

If you plan to use the Compare Document feature after you revise an original document, save the revisions with a new name, rename the original document, or make a copy of the original document. By taking any one of these steps, you maintain the original version for use with the Compare Document feature.

Comparing a New Version to an Old Version

To compare the revised version of the document to the old version saved on disk, follow these steps:

1. Choose **F**ile, Compa**r**e Document, **A**dd Markings. The Add Markings dialog box appears with the current path and file name displayed (see fig. 26.22).

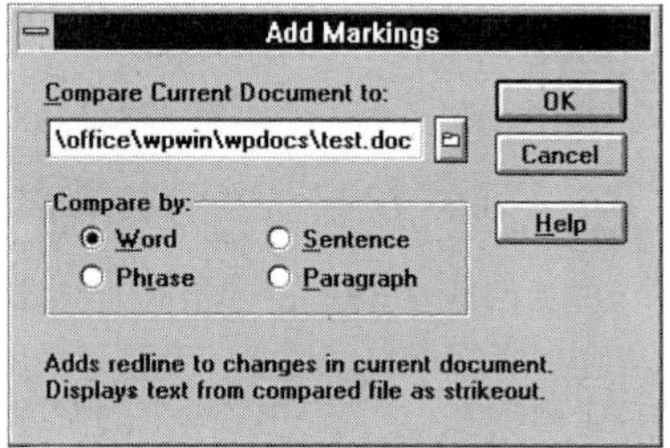

Fig. 26.22 Use the Add Markings dialog box to specify the file you want to compare the current document to and the method used by WordPerfect to compare the documents.

2. If necessary, change the file name to match the name of your original document.

   To search for another file, choose the list button at the right of the text box. The Select File dialog box appears to help you select another directory or file name. Select the desired file and choose OK.

3. In the Compare By section of the Add Markings dialog box, choose from the compare options to indicate how you want WordPerfect to compare the documents. The available Compare By options are **W**ord, **S**entence, Ph**r**ase, or **P**aragraph.

4. Choose OK. WordPerfect compares the documents, and the Document Compare Status dialog box appears showing you the progress of the comparison. When the comparison is finished, WordPerfect returns to your document.

   If instead of immediately returning to your document you want to review the statistics of the document comparison, from the Compare Status dialog box, choose Hold **D**isplay. When you are done, choose Hold **D**isplay again to return to your document.

Note

The Compare Document feature marks changes in footnotes, endnotes, and tables, but it doesn't mark changes in graphics boxes, watermarks, comments, headers, and footers.

WordPerfect modifies the on-screen version of the document and notes the differences. Removed text is marked with the strikeout enhancement. New text is displayed with the redline enhancement. Moved text is shown by two messages. The message at the beginning of the moved text says `THE FOLLOWING TEXT WAS MOVED`. The message at the end of the text says `THE PRECEDING TEXT WAS MOVED`. Figure 26.23 shows a document that has been marked using the Compare Document feature.

On laser printer, strikeout is shown as text with a line through it. Redlined text is shaded. The actual enhancements printed depend on your printer and the enhancements it supports. Consult your printer manual for more information.

WordPerfect also enables you to change the method of redlining to one other than the default WordPerfect printer driver method.

To change the way WordPerfect displays the redlining when your document is printed or displayed, follow these steps:

1. Choose Fo**r**mat, **D**ocument, **R**edline Method. The Redline dialog box appears (see fig. 26.24).

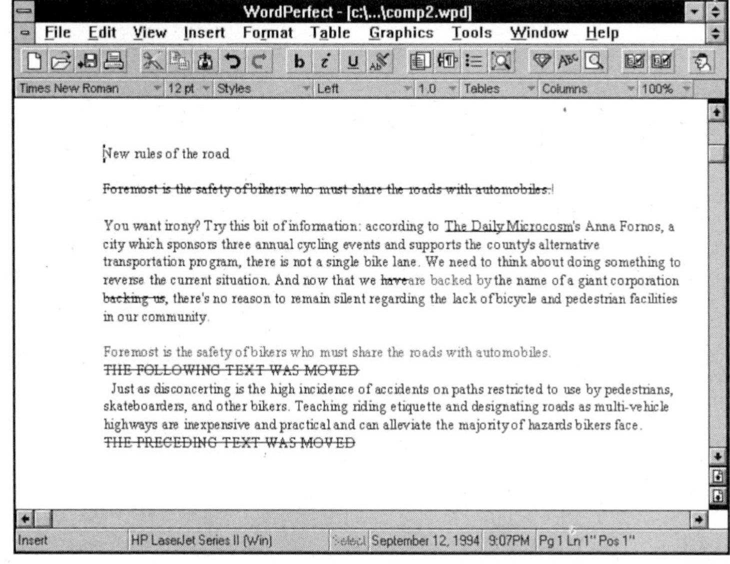

Fig. 26.23
A revised document with changed sentences marked in strikeout and redline and messages about moved text.

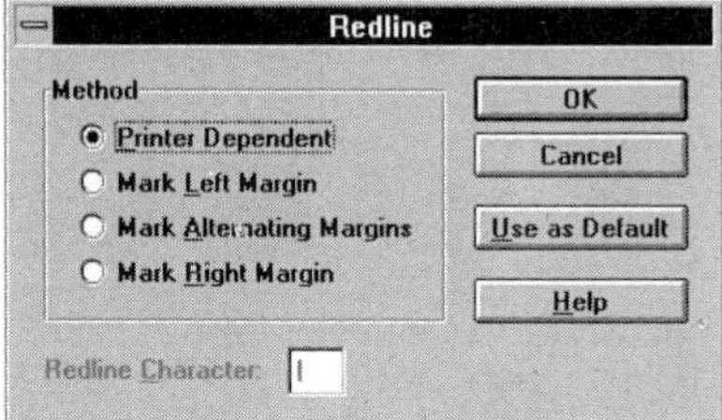

Fig. 26.24
The Redline dialog box showing a list of redlining display choices.

2. Optionally, choose one of the following:

   - ***P**rinter Dependent.* Uses the WordPerfect printer driver redlining method. Redlined text (which has been added) is printed on most laser printers as gray shaded text.

   - *Mark **L**eft Margin.* Places the selected redline character in the left margin of lines with added text.

   - *Mark **A**lternating Margins.* Places the selected redline character in the left margin of lines on even-numbered pages and right margin of lines on odd-numbered pages.

   - *Mark **R**ight Margin.* Places the selected redline character in the right margin of lines.

3. To change the redline character from the default vertical bar, choose Redline **C**haracter and type the desired character in the box. This option is available only if you choose to use a redline method other than Printer Dependent. You can press Ctrl+W to open the WordPerfect Characters dialog box and insert a special character.

4. Choose OK. WordPerfect applies the changes and returns to your document.

Tip
Choose **U**se As Default to have WordPerfect use the selected redline method for future editing sessions as well as the current one.

Purging Marked Changes from a Saved Document

If you saved your revised file immediately before using the Compare Document function, you have no reason to remove the redlining and strikeout from your document. After you print the document with the noted changes, simply close the document without saving it and open the latest version of the revised document. If you haven't saved the on-screen document or if you accidentally save the on-screen document after you have marked it and replaced the latest revision, you can remove the strikeout and the redline text enhancement from the document.

To remove Compare Document markings, follow these steps:

1. Choose **F**ile, Compa**r**e Document, **R**emove Markings. The Remove Markings dialog box appears.

2. To remove both the text marked with the redline and strikeout enhancements, choose Remove **R**edline Markings and Strikeout Text.

3. To remove only the text marked with the strikeout enhancements and leave the text marked with the redline enhancement, choose Remove **S**trikeout Text Only.

◄ See "WordPerfect Characters," p. 686

4. Choose OK to remove the Compare Document markings.

You can also remove the Compare Document text and redline enhancements by choosing **E**dit, **U**ndo; by pressing Ctrl+Z; or by choosing the Undo Power Bar button. If you choose this method, you must choose Undo immediately after you use the Compare Document function.

From Here...

In this chapter, you learned how to create lists, tables of contents, tables of authorities, and automatic cross-references. You also learned how to create indexes and control the entries included in them by marking text and using a concordance file. This chapter also showed you how to compare a current version of a document on-screen with an old version on disk.

For more information on creating documents with references to other text and graphics within the document, refer to the following major sections of this book:

- Chapter 7, "Integrating Text and Graphics." In this chapter, you learn how WordPerfect manages graphics boxes in a document.
- Chapter 10, "Using Styles." Refer to this chapter for information on using WordPerfect's style feature, which enables you to provide consistent formatting to text.
- Chapter 21, "Using Advanced Graphics Techniques." This chapter discusses advanced graphics features of WordPerfect, including editing graphics.
- Chapter 27, "Working with Large and Multi-Part Documents." In this chapter, you learn how to assemble a large document out of several smaller ones.
- Chapter 31, "Interactive Documents." This chapter details how to use WordPerfect's hypertext feature to create reference links to other parts of a document (or parts of other documents).

Chapter 27

Working with Large and Multi-Part Documents

by Gordon Nelder-Adams

You can create documents of any length—from a single address label to a manuscript hundreds of pages long—by using WordPerfect. WordPerfect imposes no specific limits on document size; the only real limit is the amount of available disk space.

Large documents can be awkward to work with because their size makes them cumbersome. Moving the cursor in a large document from one point to another can take several minutes, particularly on older computers or those that have less RAM. If you break a large document into smaller, more manageable files, editing becomes much easier. However, you must keep page numbers consistent from file to file, and you cannot easily generate a table of contents, list, or index of your entire document.

WordPerfect's Master Document feature provides the solution to this problem. This feature lets you work with smaller documents for ease of use and then, when you need to work with the document as a whole, combine the small documents into one large file.

In this chapter, you learn to do the following:

- Create a master document and subdocuments
- Save the master document
- Define and generate document references
- Use styles to ensure consistent formatting

- Insert page numbering codes
- Spell check and print the expanded document

You use two types of files with this feature: a master document and one or more subdocuments. A *subdocument* is a normal WordPerfect file that is one of the smaller pieces of your large document. The *master document* is essentially an outline of the final document and contains codes that identify each of the subdocuments. A master document also typically contains definitions for document reference features such as a table of contents, lists of tables or figures, or an index. You also can include text in a master document.

The Master Document feature is ideally suited for any large project—a college dissertation, a user manual, or a complex legal contract, for example. Writers often collaborate on a large project and then combine their work into one document. Without WordPerfect's Master Document feature, combining separate efforts is a time-consuming task that presents many challenges in numbering pages, creating a table of contents, and indexing the final document. These challenges take time away from the actual research and writing effort of the authors.

Document reference features such as tables of contents, tables of authorities, lists, indexes, and cross-references are particularly useful with long documents. (If you haven't already done so, read Chapter 26, "Assembling Document References," for a complete discussion of these features.) This chapter explains how to use document references with master documents and subdocuments.

Creating Master Documents and Subdocuments

The Master Document feature makes collaboration on projects more practical. Many people can work independently on their own subdocuments, and then one person can assemble the subdocuments into the whole document at the appropriate time. WordPerfect can then automatically handle tasks such as page numbering and indexing. Any document with parts logically maintained or managed in separate disk files is a good candidate for the Master Document feature.

Using the Master Document feature involves the following basic steps:

1. Create the individual subdocuments.

2. Create a master document with codes that identify the subdocuments and, if desired, definitions for document reference features.

3. Expand the master document. Expanding combines all the individual subdocuments into a single long document.

4. If necessary, edit the expanded document to create a consistent format throughout or add document references.

5. Print the master document.

6. Condense the master document. Condensing removes the subdocuments from the master document, optionally saving any changes you have made to subdocuments within the expanded master document.

You can use the Master Document feature with any document that can be divided into sections. Most books, for example, are divided into individual chapters. A class syllabus or training manual can be divided into individual lectures. For illustration purposes, this chapter creates an office procedures manual—a document used by most businesses.

An office manual may contain many types of information—from personnel policy to accounting, organization charts, floor plans, phone lists, and more. Several people or departments usually create or compile this information. Some parts of the manual, such as the personnel policy section, might be revised infrequently; whereas other parts, such as the phone list, might be updated monthly. These separate files are combined to produce a complete manual.

◄ See "Creating Lists," p. 879

Using the Master Document feature for this project is desirable for the following reasons:

- Sections can be created by a number of people in different departments, and then easily combined.
- The individual subdocuments can be created in any order, regardless of the order in which they will appear in the master document.
- The author or authors of each section can revise their documents at any time, and use them as separate files unrelated to the office manual.
- You can ensure consistent pagination throughout the manual and create a comprehensive table of contents and index that can be updated quickly each time a subdocument is revised.

Creating Subdocuments

A subdocument is a WordPerfect document of any length that contains any text or formatting codes. Unlike WordPerfect's Merge feature, which requires certain types of merge codes in data files, a subdocument requires no "Master Document feature" codes to make it act as a subdocument (although certain codes are required in master document files).

WordPerfect places no limits on the number of subdocuments you can combine into a master document. When you use a master document for a large project, divide the job into as many logical sections as you want and create a subdocument for each. In addition, a subdocument can contain links to other subdocuments, making a subdocument in one master document a master document in its own right. This concept is covered in the later section "Creating Subdocuments within Subdocuments."

When you expand a master document, WordPerfect retrieves a copy of the entire contents of each designated subdocument—each with its own set of format codes—into one large document. In any WordPerfect document, format codes—margins, tab sets, and fonts, for example—that you insert affect the format of all text that follows until another code of the same type appears. As a result, the format codes in each subdocument can affect the formatting of every following subdocument in the expanded master document.

When a subdocument takes its place in a master document, the subdocument's formatting may change substantially, depending on the format codes from preceding subdocuments. Likewise, any format codes you insert in one subdocument can affect subsequent subdocuments. Therefore, when you create a subdocument, use only formatting codes essential to your subdocument's appearance, and reset any formatting changes to the defaults whenever possible. For example, if you need to insert a nonstandard tab set for a particular group of paragraphs, remember to reset your tabs back to every half inch at the end of that group.

You can prevent many formatting errors by using styles. Paragraph styles can ensure consistency of headings and body text throughout a master document. You can create a "Begin Subdocument" style that sets defaults for all formatting that might change from subdocument to subdocument, and then use this style at the beginning of each subdocument. You can also create separate style libraries—with identical style names but different style contents—for master documents and subdocuments. When the subdocuments are expanded into the master document, the master document's styles take precedence over subdocument styles of the same name. These techniques are covered in the later section "Using Styles with Master Documents."

Caution

When it expands a master document, WordPerfect ignores each subdocument's Initial Codes style. Any codes placed in that subdocument's Initial Codes style will be missing in the master document. Therefore, place any codes essential for your subdocument's format in the body of the document, not in its Initial Codes style.

Building a Master Document

To build a master document, insert one or more subdocument codes into any normal document. The subdocument code identifies the file name of a subdocument and creates a link between the master document and subdocument. In practice, most master documents contain many subdocument links. Building a master document requires the following three basic steps:

1. Decide what files you want to use as subdocuments with the master document.
2. Create a new WordPerfect file or open an existing file to which you want to add subdocument codes.
3. Insert subdocument codes into the master document.

You can insert the subdocument codes in any order. When you expand the master document, individual subdocuments are retrieved in the order in which their codes appear in the master document. Table 27.1 lists the files to be included in the office procedures manual.

Tip
Establish naming conventions for your master document and subdocument filename extensions, such as MD for master documents, and SUB for subdocuments to indicate the type of file.

Table 27.1 Subdocuments Included in the Office Procedures Manual

File Name	Description
TITLE.PG	The title page
BACKGRND	The company's history and mission statement
OFFICE.PRO	The heart of the manual—a detailed description of office procedures
PERSONNL.POL	The company's personnel policies
EMERGNCY.PRO	Emergency procedures

(continues)

Table 27.1 Continued

File Name	Description
NETWORK.GDL	Guidelines for logging on to and using the company's local area network
ORG.CHT	The company's organization chart
PERSONNL.LST	A list of room numbers and phone numbers for all employees
MAP	A floor map of the building
CALENDAR	A list of office holidays and other scheduled events

To create a PROCEDUR.MD master document, begin with an empty document. If the active window is not empty, choose **F**ile, **N**ew, or press Ctrl+T. In the New Document dialog box, choose Create Blank Document, and choose **S**elect (as a shortcut, click the New Blank Document button on the Power Bar). WordPerfect displays a blank document. You can now begin to place the subdocument codes in the document. When you eventually expand the master document, WordPerfect retrieves the contents of each subdocument into the master document where you placed the appropriate code.

To insert a subdocument code, follow these steps:

1. Move the insertion point to where you want to place the subdocument. (If you are starting from a new document, skip this step and proceed to step 2.)

2. Choose **F**ile, Master **D**ocument, **S**ubdocument. WordPerfect displays the Include Subdocument dialog box, a variant of the Open dialog box (see fig. 27.1), which lists the files in the current directory.

3. Type a subdocument's file name; or highlight a name in the file list. Then choose **I**nclude, or press Enter. For the first subdocument in the office procedures manual, for example, you would include the file **title.pg**.

Note

A subdocument doesn't need to be present when you type its name in the Include Subdocument dialog box. When you expand the master document, however, the subdocument must be in the specified location.

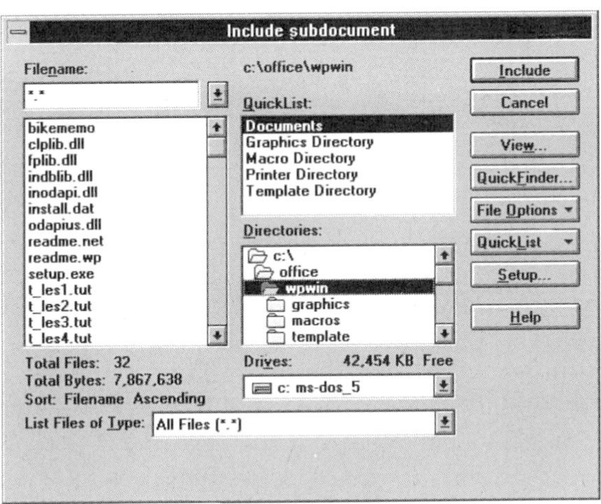

Fig. 27.1
Select a file name in the Include Subdocument dialog box to create a link between a master document and the selected file.

WordPerfect inserts a subdocument code into the master document. In Page mode or Two Page mode, the code appears as an icon in the left margin (see fig. 27.2). In Draft mode, the code can be seen in the document, resembling a document comment with the text `Subdoc:FILENAME`, where FILENAME is the complete path and file name of the subdocument file (see later fig. 27.3). In any mode, you can see a similar code in the Reveal Codes window.

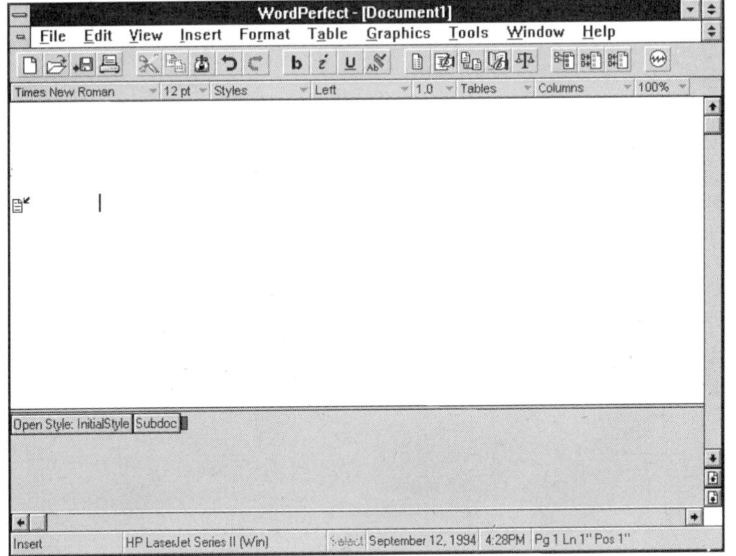

Fig. 27.2
In Page mode, a subdocument link appears as an icon in the margin, as well as a code visible in Reveal Codes.

Because the subdocument link includes the complete path to a subdocument, the subdocument need not be in the same subdirectory as the master document. In fact, none of your subdocuments need to be in the same subdirectory. However, if you move the subdocument from the directory designated in the code, WordPerfect cannot locate the subdocument when you expand the master document. You will need to move the file back to its original location, or delete and re-create the subdocument link.

Repeat the preceding procedure for each subdocument link you want to include in a master document.

You may want each subdocument to begin on a new page. In some books, for instance, each chapter begins at the top of a page. In other books, each chapter begins immediately after the preceding chapter, wherever on the page the division may fall. To force page breaks in your master document, simply press Ctrl+Enter to insert a Hard Page code before you insert each subdocument link.

You also can use WordPerfect's Force Page command, which lets you specify that a chapter start on a new page, an odd-numbered page (the right-hand page in a double-sided publication), or an even-numbered page (the left-hand page). To force page breaks in your master document, choose Fo**r**mat, **P**age, **F**orce Page, and then choose Current Page **O**dd, Current Page **E**ven, or New **P**age. If you specify Current Page **O**dd, and the page following the code falls on an even-numbered page, WordPerfect inserts a soft page break after the code to force the text to the following odd-numbered page.

After you have inserted all the subdocument links, save the master document. For this example, the file is saved with the name PROCEDUR.MD. For more information on saving master documents, see the section "Saving a Master Document" later in this chapter.

Figure 27.3 shows the first several subdocument codes in the PROCEDUR.MD master document, displayed in Draft mode on-screen. In this example, page breaks are used to separate the subdocuments, forcing each to begin on a new page.

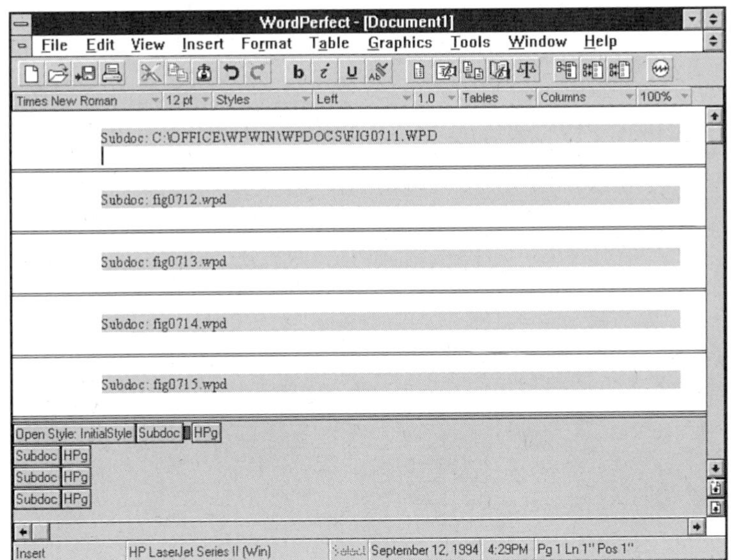

Fig. 27.3
A master document with subdocument links separated by page breaks.

Adding, Deleting, and Moving Subdocuments

You can change the structure of your master document at any time, regardless of whether your master document is expanded. You may need to add a new subdocument code, delete an existing code, or move a code to a different location in the master document.

To add a subdocument, move the insertion point to where you want to insert the code. Turning on Reveal Codes (choose **V**iew, Reveal **C**odes; or press Alt+F3) may help you position the insertion point precisely, particularly if your master document contains formatting codes for page numbering or headers and footers. Then follow the steps in the preceding section to insert the subdocument code. The next time you expand the master document, WordPerfect adds the new subdocument.

Deleting a subdocument is easier when the master document is condensed because you need to delete only one code. When the master document is expanded, each subdocument begins with a `[Subdoc Begin]` code and ends with a `[Subdoc End]` code, and deleting a subdocument requires deleting these two codes as well as all text and formatting between them.

To delete a subdocument from a condensed master document, turn on Reveal Codes (choose **V**iew, Reveal **C**odes; or press Alt+F3), and then move the insertion point immediately to the left of the `[Subdoc]` code. Press Del, and WordPerfect removes the code from your document. If you placed a `[HPg]` code (indicating a Hard Page break) after the subdocument code to separate it from the following subdocument, you also may want to delete this code to prevent a blank page from appearing in the middle of your document. Alternatively, you may want to insert a different subdocument code at the same position.

Deleting a subdocument from an expanded master document is more complicated. You can either block and delete everything from the `[Subdoc Begin]` code through the `[Subdoc End]` code, or you can follow the steps for condensing a single subdocument in the later section "Condensing a Master Document," and then delete the resulting `[Subdoc]` code.

You can move a subdocument from one location to another within your master document in several ways. First, you can delete any existing codes for the particular subdocument, and then insert a new code at the desired location. WordPerfect always retains the last three blocks of text or codes you delete, so you can undelete the old code or codes instead of inserting a new subdocument code. Second, you can block and move everything from the `[Subdoc Begin]` code through the `[Subdoc End]` code. See Chapter 3, "Retrieving and Editing Documents," for more information on blocking, moving, and deleting text and codes.

Caution

If you move a subdocument in an expanded master document, make sure that you move both the `[Subdoc Begin]` code and the `[Subdoc End]` code. If these codes are mismatched, WordPerfect cannot properly condense the master document.

After you delete a subdocument from a condensed master document, the next time you expand the master document, that subdocument will not be included. If you add, delete, or move a subdocument in an expanded master document, you need to regenerate any document references such as table of contents, lists, or index, to update the page numbers for the current subdocuments.

Expanding a Master Document

After you insert all the subdocument codes in the master document, creating links between the master document and each of the subdocuments, you can expand the master document. When you expand the master document, WordPerfect retrieves a copy of each subdocument into the master document, in effect combining the many smaller documents into one large document. You can then use several of WordPerfect's features and functions on the expanded document much more efficiently than on the individual subdocuments. You can use Find and Replace to change a particular phrase throughout the entire document in one operation, instead of repeating the operation for each subdocument. Likewise, spell checking an expanded master document is more efficient than individually checking each subdocument.

Most important, though, is that after you expand a master document, you can number pages, headers, and footers sequentially throughout the document. You can also easily generate document references across the entire master document. Both tasks are difficult, if not impossible, when working with subdocuments alone.

Note

As mentioned earlier, WordPerfect doesn't impose restrictions on the number of subdocuments you can include in a master document. However, the amount of free disk space on your computer does impose a practical limit on the combined size of the master document and all its subdocuments. As a rule of thumb, the free disk space should be at least three times the size of the combined size of your subdocuments. When you expand your master document, this document occupies as much disk space as the subdocuments, and WordPerfect requires an equal amount of space to hold temporary files while you work with the expanded document. If you run out of disk space while working in an expanded master document, you might be unable to save any changes you make.

WordPerfect provides the option of expanding all or only selected subdocuments in a master document. The procedure you follow to accomplish either task is much the same. To expand one or more of the subdocuments within a master document, follow these steps:

1. Open the master document.
2. Choose **F**ile, Master **D**ocument, **E**xpand Master.

   WordPerfect displays the Expand Master Document dialog box (see fig. 27.4). The **S**ubdocuments list box displays the names of all the subdocuments for which you have inserted a `[Subdoc]` code. The names appear in alphabetical order, not in the order the `[Subdoc]` codes are inserted in the master document. The check mark before each file name indicates that the file will be included when you expand the document. By default, all subdocuments are checked.

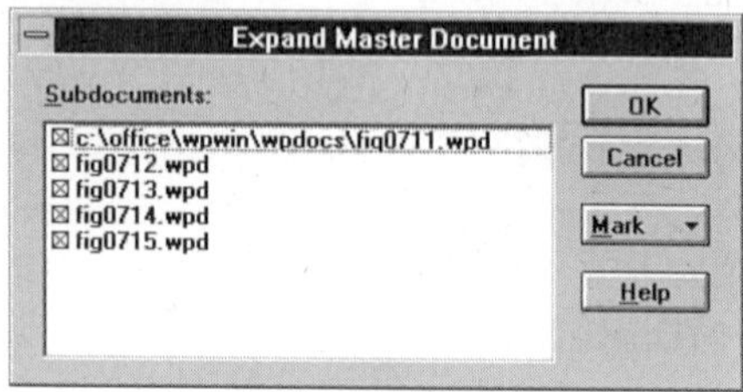

Fig. 27.4
The Expand Master Document dialog box lists all the subdocuments in alphabetical order.

3. If you do not want to expand all the subdocuments, you can choose which ones to expand. Do one of the following:

   - To unmark all selected subdocuments, choose **M**ark, **C**lear All. (To remark all subdocuments, choose **M**ark, **M**ark All.)

   - To mark an individual subdocument, unmark all subdocuments, and then click on the desired subdocument's name so that the box to its left is checked.

   - To unmark an individual subdocument, click on the desired subdocument's name so that the box to its left is unchecked.

   Figure 27.5 shows the Expand Master Document dialog box with three subdocuments marked.

4. Choose OK or press Enter.

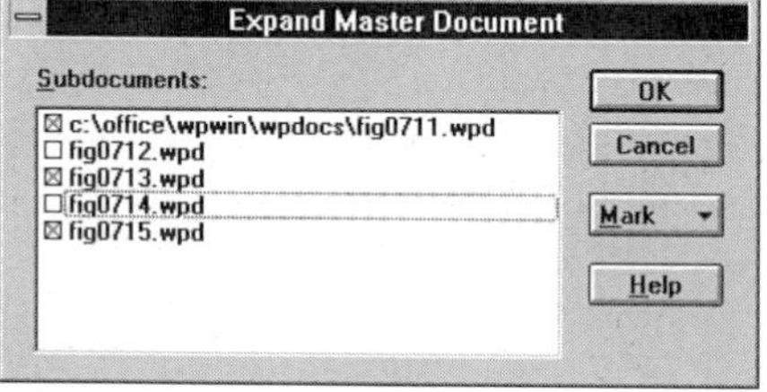

Fig. 27.5
You can expand selected subdocuments by marking them in the Expand Master Document dialog box.

WordPerfect retrieves a copy of each subdocument you marked. If the program cannot find a file, a Subdocument Error dialog box is displayed (see fig. 27.6). You can enter a new file name and/or location, or click on the file folder button to browse for the file. You can also choose Skip to tell WordPerfect to ignore the missing file and move on to the next subdocument, or Cancel to abandon the expansion process entirely.

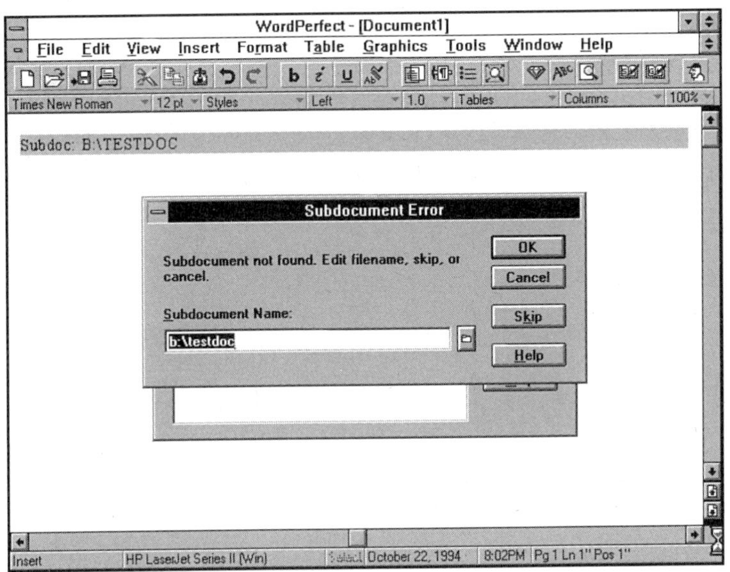

Fig. 27.6
If WordPerfect can't find a file while expanding a master document, this dialog box enables you to enter a new name and/or location.

When WordPerfect expands a master document, it retrieves each subdocument at the location of its `[Subdoc]` code. For each subdocument, the program removes the original `[Subdoc]` code and places a `[Subdoc Begin]` code at the beginning of the subdocument and a `[Subdoc End]` code at the end of the subdocument (see fig. 27.7).

Caution

Never delete an individual `[Subdoc Begin]` or `[Subdoc End]` code in an expanded master document. WordPerfect requires that these codes be in pairs to manage your subdocuments. When you condense a master document, the program removes subdocuments according to these paired codes, and if it can't find half of a pair, WordPerfect displays an error message and halts the procedure. If you delete a code by mistake, immediately choose Undelete (choose **E**dit, U**n**delete; or press Ctrl+Shift+Z) to restore the code. If you discover the deletion only while condensing, you must delete the remaining code before you continue condensing, and you must delete the contents of the subdocument or block and save them as a separate file. To delete a subdocument from your master document, see the earlier section "Adding, Deleting, and Moving Subdocuments."

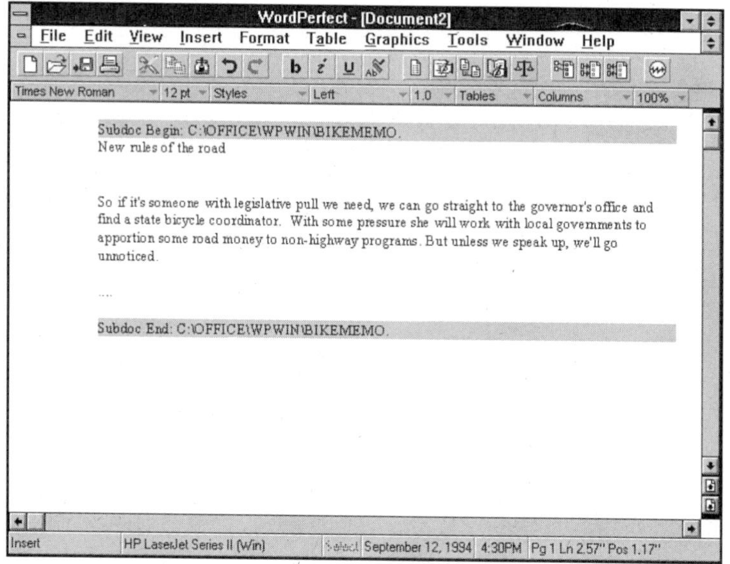

Fig. 27.7
When you expand a master document, WordPerfect places `[Subdoc Begin]` and `[Subdoc End]` codes at the beginning and end of each subdocument.

Troubleshooting

WordPerfect can't find a file when expanding a document, but the file is still on the computer's hard disk drive.

WordPerfect stores the complete path and name to a subdocument. If you move the file to a different directory, WordPerfect cannot find it when the master document is expanded. Two solutions to this problem are possible. First, you can move the file back into its original directory. Or second, remove the old Subdocument code in the master document file and insert a new Subdocument code using the file in its new directory.

In Draft display mode, some files are shown with a complete path in the gray Subdocument comment box, and some are not.

WordPerfect is working as designed. The files shown with a full path—such as C:\OFFICE\WPWIN\WPDOCS\MYFILE.TXT—already existed when you inserted them as subdocuments. Files not shown with a full path (name only) did not yet exist when you inserted them as subdocuments. Because nonexistent files are inserted with their names only, you must make sure that when you finally create the files, they are placed in the documents directory. That way, WordPerfect finds them when you expand the master document.

Saving a Master Document

After you expand a master document, you can save it in its expanded or condensed form. If you only need to update page numbering and document references and then print—and you don't need to edit the expanded document—then no good reason exists to save an expanded master document. Because the expanded document takes up so much room, you may not want to save the document in its expanded form, particularly if you are low on disk space.

Tip
An expanded master document takes up as much space on disk as all its subdocuments combined.

If you do need to edit the expanded master document, however, you may find that saving the full document in its expanded form is practical. Expanding and condensing a large master document can waste time if you're not finished with the expanded document. If you plan to use the expanded document again soon, save the document in expanded form.

You save a master document just as you would save any other document. (See Chapter 2, "Creating and Saving a Document," for more information on file saving options.) If your master document is expanded, WordPerfect saves it in its expanded form. If you don't want to save the expanded document, either close the document without saving, or condense the master document before saving. The following section covers this process in detail.

Condensing a Master Document

When you have finished working with an expanded master document, you can condense it. When you condense a master document, WordPerfect reverses the operations it performed when expanding. The program removes the subdocuments from the master document, and replaces each pair of `[Subdoc Begin]` and `[Subdoc End]` codes with a single `[Subdoc]` code.

If you edited the subdocuments while they were part of the expanded master document, you can save the versions of the subdocuments contained in the master document over the earlier versions of the subdocuments on disk. If you save subdocuments while condensing, WordPerfect overwrites any earlier versions of the subdocuments without prompting for confirmation.

> **Caution**
>
> If you save subdocuments while condensing but don't want to overwrite the original versions of the subdocuments, you must move the subdocuments before condensing, or WordPerfect replaces them with the newer versions of the subdocuments contained in the master document.

If you don't save subdocuments while condensing, WordPerfect discards the versions contained in the master document, including any changes you made.

> **Caution**
>
> By default, WordPerfect doesn't save subdocuments when you condense a master document. If you made changes to the master document that you want saved in the subdocuments, mark the subdocuments you want to save during the condense process; otherwise, your changes will be lost.

Whenever you make changes to an expanded master document, save subdocuments while condensing, unless the changes were only temporary. If you make extensive changes to a colleague's document, however, he or she may not appreciate your replacing the original version. In this case, make sure that you move or copy the original version before condensing.

Just as you can choose to expand only selected subdocuments, you can also choose to condense and/or save only selected subdocuments. To condense an expanded master document, follow these steps:

1. Choose **F**ile, Master **D**ocument, **C**ondense Master.

   WordPerfect displays the Condense/Save Subdocuments dialog box, which closely resembles the Expand Master Document dialog box. In the Condense/Save Subdocuments dialog box, however, each subdocument is listed twice: one entry to be marked for saving the subdocument, and one entry to be marked for condensing the subdocument (see fig. 27.8).

2. Mark which subdocuments you want to save and which subdocuments you want to condense. You can perform any of the following actions:

   - To deselect a marked subdocument, click the subdocument's name. WordPerfect unchecks its box.

- To select an unmarked subdocument, click the subdocument's name. WordPerfect checks its box.
- To mark all items to be condensed, choose **M**ark, **C**ondense All. WordPerfect checks all subdocuments with an accompanying "condense" entry.
- To mark all items to be saved, choose **M**ark, **S**ave All. WordPerfect checks all subdocuments with an accompanying "save" entry.
- To unmark all items to be condensed, choose **M**ark, C**l**ear Condense. WordPerfect unchecks all subdocuments with an accompanying "condense" entry.
- To unmark all items to be saved, choose **M**ark, Cl**e**ar Save. WordPerfect unchecks all subdocuments with an accompanying "save" entry.

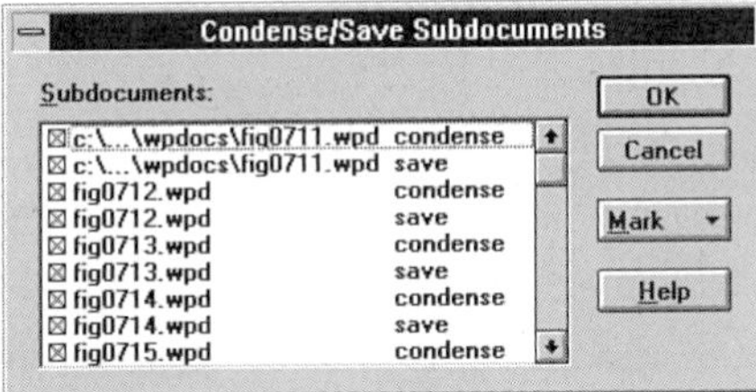

Fig. 27.8
By default, WordPerfect marks all subdocuments for condensing and saving.

3. Choose OK or press Enter.

   WordPerfect removes from the master document all subdocuments marked to be condensed, and saves all subdocuments marked to be saved. Any subdocument not marked to be saved is discarded.

Creating a Table of Contents, List, Index, or Table of Authorities

In Chapter 26, "Assembling Document References," you learn about features you can use to assemble document references. When you combine those features with the Master Document feature, you can create a table of contents that spans all the subdocuments in an expanded master document. You can also create a table of authorities, lists of tables, figures or other repeating items, an index, or cross-references that span the expanded master document.

This section describes the steps required to generate a table of contents for a master document. The steps to generate a table of authorities are nearly identical, and the steps to generate lists or an index are similar. For more detailed information about these features, refer to Chapter 26.

Creating a table of contents in a master document requires the following basic steps:

1. Mark the text to be included in the table of contents.
2. Select a location for the table of contents and insert a table definition code.
3. Generate the table (and any other document references).

> **Note**
>
> Create a Mark Text Toolbar to save time when you are marking many entries for table of contents or other document references. Add buttons for marking and defining the table of contents, lists, index, cross-references, and table of authorities (if needed), and a Generate button. For detailed instructions, see Chapter 13, "Working with Toolbars."

When you generate a document, WordPerfect scans the entire document for document reference marks, including table of contents marks. The program copies the text between each pair of codes and its table of contents level, assembles the marked text at the location of the table of contents definition mark, and formats the text according to the definition.

Tip
Instead of opening each subdocument and marking text for table of contents and other document references, expand the master document and mark the expanded document. Then compress and save the master document and modified subdocuments.

Marking Text for the Table of Contents

Marking the text to be included is the first step in creating a table of contents. You can mark any text in any document to be included in a table of contents. That text can be in an individual subdocument, a condensed master document, or an expanded master document.

Block the text and any format codes for each heading that you want to include in the table of contents. If you are marking a subdocument, save the subdocument and repeat for other subdocuments included in your master document. As you mark text for inclusion in the table of contents, note the highest level number you use so that you can define the table of contents properly.

Defining the Tables of Contents

After you mark the headings or other text for inclusion in the table of contents, you can define the table of contents and its options. The table of contents definition specifies the location of the table, the number of levels to include when the table is generated, and how WordPerfect should format each level.

To define the table of contents in a master document, follow these steps:

1. Open the master document, select a location for the table of contents, and move the insertion point to that location.

2. To place the table of contents on its own page, insert a `[HPg]` code (hard page) by pressing Ctrl+Enter. Type any desired heading, and press Enter several times.

3. Create the table of contents definition as described in Chapter 26, "Assembling Document References."

4. If necessary, press Ctrl+Enter to insert a hard page break at the end of the table of contents. If you want to add lists of tables, figures, or other items, define them on the following pages. When you generate the table and other document references, WordPerfect adds pages as needed to hold the entire table.

> **Note**
>
> Instead of marking each heading individually for inclusion in the table of contents, put the table of contents marks into styles, and use those styles to format your headings. See the later section "Using Styles with Master Documents" for more information.

5. Insert a new page number code where the body of your master document begins, so that your body text always starts with page 1. Generally, this position immediately precedes the subdocument code linking the first subdocument containing body text, and follows any definitions for table of contents or lists. (The title page may be a subdocu-ment, but comes before the table of contents, and is usually not considered body text.) For information on inserting a new page number code, see the later section "Inserting a New Page Number."

Caution

If you don't insert a page number code at the beginning of your body text, your table of contents and body text are part of the same numbering sequence. When you generate document references, any tables or lists that grow longer than one page change the body text page numbers, and the generated references are no longer correct.

6. Save the master document with the defined table of contents.

After you define the table of contents and any other formatting options, you are ready to generate the table.

Caution

If you create an index in a master document, you should place the index definition code at the end of the master document. Any text marked as index items must precede the index definition code; otherwise, WordPerfect doesn't include those items in the index. The program ignores any index marks located after an index definition. If you use a concordance file, all references in the document are included in the generated index regardless of where the text is referenced. See Chapter 26 for more information on index definition codes and concordance files.

Generating Tables, Lists, and Indexes

After you mark your master document and subdocuments for table of contents entries or other document references and define the location and formatting options for the table of contents and other lists and indexes, you can use the Generate command to create or update the actual table of contents, list, or index.

The first time you generate a table of contents, WordPerfect scans the entire document for table of contents marks. The program copies any text and codes between each pair of `[Mrk Txt ToC]` codes, noting the table of contents level for each mark. WordPerfect then assembles the marked text at the location of the table of contents definition mark and formats each item according to the style, numbering mode, and page number format you defined.

When you generate document references for a condensed master document, WordPerfect automatically expands the master document, generates the document references, and then condenses the master document again. If this procedure modifies any subdocuments, by default WordPerfect saves any modified subdocuments over the originals. If you don't want subdocuments modified by a Generate command to be saved over their original versions, you can tell WordPerfect not to save modified subdocuments when you generate.

Note

If you defined a list or index in addition to the table of contents, you cannot generate just the type of document reference. Whenever you use the Generate command, WordPerfect generates all references in a document. Each subsequent time you use the Generate command, WordPerfect deletes the entire contents of any previously generated tables, lists, or indexes and creates entirely new ones.

To generate or update the table of contents for your master document, follow these steps:

1. Choose **T**ools, Ge**n**erate; or press Ctrl+F9. WordPerfect displays the Generate dialog box.

2. If you don't want subdocuments modified by a Generate command to be saved over their original versions, choose **O**ptions. WordPerfect displays the Generate Options dialog box (see fig. 27.9).

   Uncheck the **S**ave Subdocuments option, and then choose OK.

3. Choose OK to create or update the table of contents and other references in the document.

◄ See "Creating an Index," p. 903

◄ See "Creating a Table of Contents," p. 888

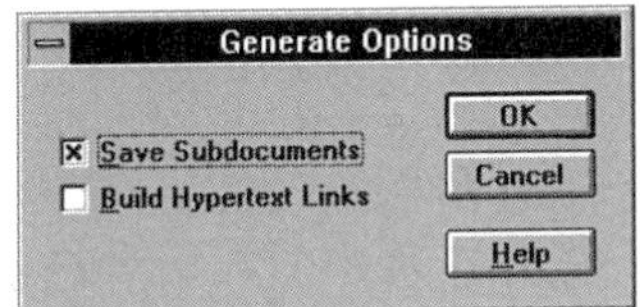

Fig. 27.9
Uncheck the **S**ave Subdocuments option in the Generate Options dialog box if you don't want modified subdocuments to replace the original subdocuments.

After you generate the table of contents, you may discover typographical or formatting errors in the generated table. Because each entry in the table of contents is copied from the body of the expanded master document, an error in the table of contents duplicates an error in the text. Instead of correcting the table of contents entry, fix the error in the body text and regenerate the table of contents.

Caution

If you edit any text in a generated table of contents, list, or index, the next time you generate the document your changes will be lost.

Using Styles with Master Documents

WordPerfect 6.1 for Windows makes extensive use of styles. A *style* is a named collection of format codes that you can apply to a group of text or graphics. WordPerfect formats all text marked with a particular style identically. If you edit the style definition, WordPerfect automatically reformats any text marked with that style.

Styles are useful for ensuring consistent formatting throughout a document or between several documents—an important capability when you work with master documents. This section covers several uses of styles particularly applicable to master documents. For more information about styles, refer to Chapter 10, "Using Styles."

You can use four types of styles with text: paragraph, paragraph-auto, character, and open. Paragraph styles format the contents of an entire paragraph. Character styles format any text that appears between paired `[Char Style]` codes, and essentially act like paired font attribute codes. Open styles, which are similar to character styles, contain all their formatting codes in a single `[Open Style]` code.

Note

In previous versions of WordPerfect, character styles were referred to as *paired* styles. In addition, WordPerfect 6.0 for Windows offered only the standard paragraph style, not paragraph-auto.

Whenever you combine many documents prepared by many people, you can expect the formatting of those documents to be different. If you have a collection of subdocuments in various formats, you can easily apply styles to those documents to reformat them according to the needs of your project. A more efficient method, however, is to create a template containing the styles for your project. You can then share that template with your colleagues so that they can use the styles when they create their subdocuments.

When a master document contains styles, those styles take precedence over any other styles of the same name in any of the subdocuments. Styles with unique names in subdocuments are added to the master document's styles, and if several subdocuments use a style name not used by the master document, WordPerfect uses the first style definition it encounters as it expands the subdocuments.

If all the subdocuments contain different style names, a master document's style list can become huge and unmanageable. When you edit the subdocuments, rename styles to ensure consistency or delete unnecessary styles. If the master document and all subdocuments use the same style names—even if the contents of those styles are different—WordPerfect reformats all the subdocuments according to the style definitions in the master document when a master document is created.

Although you can use styles in the master document, styles are more useful in the individual subdocuments—particularly the codes at the beginning of each subdocument and the headings within each subdocument.

Using Open Styles To Begin Subdocuments

When you expand a master document, each subdocument effectively becomes part of one large document, and WordPerfect ignores each subdocument's Initial Codes style and Initial Font. As a result, each subdocument assumes whatever formatting was in effect at the end of the previous subdocument, including font, justification, margins, line spacing, tab sets, and more. Likewise, any format changes made in the subdocument have a similar effect on all subdocuments that follow.

To ensure consistency of format throughout the master document, you should create a standard format for the entire document and insert all the codes that specify that format at the beginning of each subdocument. Each subdocument automatically begins with the preferred format options. Each author can then make necessary deviations from that format within his or her subdocument without affecting other subdocuments. By combining all these formatting codes into one open style, you can apply all the formatting codes in a single style. If necessary at a later date, you can edit the style and thereby reformat all the subdocuments in the master document.

You should create an open style for the beginning of each subdocument with a name, such as SubdocInit. In the style, include all the format codes that define your preferred master document's appearance and that may be changed within a subdocument. The following codes are a suggested minimum:

- Margins (top, bottom, left, and right)
- Tab set
- Line spacing
- Paragraph spacing
- Font
- Font size
- Paper size/type
- Page numbering

Other useful codes include the following:

- Force page
- Increment Chapter or Volume number
- Header or Footer discontinue
- Footnote numbering

You can place the style at the beginning of each subdocument or in a master document immediately before each subdocument code.

Using Paragraph and Character Styles To Format Headings

You can put nearly any WordPerfect formatting code into a paragraph or character style. These codes can determine font, font size, text alignment or indentation, chapter or outline number, and table of contents marks. For example, WordPerfect's default Heading 1 style, which is a paragraph style designed to be used on main titles, contains the following codes:

```
[Bold][Very Large][Hd Center on Mar][Mrk Txt ToC: 1]
```

The first three codes make the paragraph bold, very large (relative to the body text size), and centered. The `[Mrk Txt ToC]` code marks the paragraph as a first-level table of contents entry. As a result, whenever you apply the Heading 1 style to a paragraph, you automatically mark that paragraph for inclusion in the table of contents. Because the other formatting codes appear before the mark text codes, the table of contents entry includes only the following text, not the preceding codes.

Most main headings and high-level subheadings appear on a line by themselves and are followed by hard return codes ([HRt]), which, by definition, makes them paragraphs. Use paragraph styles to format such headings. For lower-level headings that are not paragraphs in their own right, use character styles. Character styles can contain the same types of codes as paragraph styles.

You can use WordPerfect's default styles, edit these styles to your liking, or create entirely new styles. In any case, by applying styles to your headings, you can quickly and consistently format the headings of any document. In addition, applying a style to a heading automatically marks the heading for inclusion in the table of contents if the style contains table of contents codes.

You can use styles most effectively with a master document project if you distribute a style library to everyone working on a subdocument. If this is not possible, you can still save time by using styles to format the subdocuments after you receive them.

◄ See "Considering Types of Styles," p. 358

Inserting Page Numbering Codes

Without the Master Document feature, sequentially numbering a master document is a monumental task: you need to count the number of pages in the first document, insert a page number code with the next sequential page number at the beginning of the second document, and repeat the process for each successive document. If you add pages to or delete pages from any document, you must renumber the pages in all subsequent files. With the Master Document feature, however, if you insert a new page number code into the master document, WordPerfect automatically renumbers all pages from that point forward.

Alternatively, if you frequently change the number of pages in a master document, you may not want to repeatedly print and duplicate the majority of the document simply to correct the page numbers. WordPerfect lets you insert codes that identify individual subdocuments as chapters or volumes and include the chapter or volume number with the printed page numbers, such as "II-1". You can then begin the numbering of each subdocument with page 1, and if you edit that document, you don't need to reprint the remainder of the master document.

Inserting a New Page Number

If you want your master document numbered sequentially, you must insert a new page number code in the document after any table of contents or list definitions and before the beginning of the body of the document. In the sample office procedures manual, for example, the first page after the table of contents is the company history and mission statement. If you place a new page number code with a value of 1 in the master document immediately before the BACKGRND subdocument code, the company history now begins on page 1. WordPerfect numbers all subsequent pages sequentially from that point. (See Chapter 5, "Formatting Pages and Documents," for detailed information on inserting page numbers.)

Note

WordPerfect prints page numbers where the top or bottom line of your document would otherwise print, shortening each page of your document by two lines. If you decrease the size of your top or bottom margin to approximately 2/3 inch (depending on the location of your page numbers), you can regain the lost space, and your page numbers will appear to print in the margin.

Inserting Chapter Codes

Just as you can have WordPerfect print the current page number, you can place a chapter code at the beginning of each subdocument and have WordPerfect insert the current chapter number into page numbers, headers and footers, or text. Chapter numbers are particularly useful if you don't need to sequentially number all pages in a master document. You can start numbering each chapter at page 1 and include the chapter number with the printed page number so that, for example, Chapter II, page 3 prints as II-3. (See Chapter 5 for detailed information on chapter numbering.)

Unlike page numbers, which WordPerfect automatically increments at each page break, chapter numbers do not change until you instruct the program. If you use chapter codes at the beginning of each subdocument, you must place a Chapter Number Increment code. If you want to start numbering each chapter at page 1, also insert a Page Number Set code. In the master document, at the beginning of the body text, insert a Page Number Position code as described earlier. Also insert a Chapter Number Method code to format chapter numbers using letters, numbers, or Roman numerals.

◀ See "Numbering Pages," p. 177

You also can have WordPerfect insert the current chapter number anywhere in body text, a header or footer, or a style by choosing Fo**r**mat, **P**age, **N**umbering, **O**ptions, and then checking the box for the I**n**sert Format and Accompanying Text at Insertion Point option. WordPerfect inserts a code that displays and prints as the current chapter number.

> **Note**
>
> Include a Chapter Number Increment code in your `SubdocInit` style so that each subdocument automatically starts a new chapter. If you include a chapter increment code for your subdocuments at the beginning of your master document, you must decrement the chapter number to 0. Choose Fo**r**mat, **P**age, **N**umbering, **V**alue; then set the **In**crease/Decrease Existing Chapter Number value to -1.

Using Headers and Footers with Master Documents

Headers and footers can make a large document easier to read. You can include almost any information in a header or footer, including chapter title or number, volume numbers, document headings, topics, author name, and page numbers. When you include this type of information in headers and footers, your readers can find relevant information more easily. Chapter 5 covers the process of creating and editing headers and footers in detail. This section discusses using headers and footers with master documents.

WordPerfect lets you use two headers and two footers simultaneously (Header A, Header B, Footer A, and Footer B) in addition to automatic page numbers. If you use two headers, you can print one header on odd-numbered pages and one header on even-numbered pages, or you can print both headers on all pages; footers function identically. Although you can only have one Header A and one Header B on a given page, you can have a different Header A or B for each chapter or section of your document. These options give you great flexibility.

In the office procedures manual, for example, Header A may read "Office Procedures Manual" and appear on even-numbered pages for the entire document. For the odd-numbered pages, you may want to create a different Header B for each subdocument containing a chapter number and title. The header for the first chapter might read "Part I—Company History and Mission Statement."

The document title would thus appear on all even-numbered (left-hand) pages, and the section number and title would appear on all odd-numbered (right-hand) pages. You can include page numbering codes within a header or footer, or you can use automatic page numbers, as described earlier in this chapter.

◄ See "Using Headers and Footers," p. 172

Printing a Master Document

Expanding your master document produces one large document containing all the text and codes of the condensed master document and each of the linked subdocuments. After you insert the appropriate page numbering codes and generate the document references, you have created a complete version of the document. Printing the expanded document produces a comprehensive final document.

Printing the Entire Document

You print an entire expanded master document just as you print any other document. First choose **F**ile, **P**rint; or press Ctrl+P. Then press Enter to select the default value of **F**ull Document and begin printing.

Printing Selected Pages or Chapters

As with any document, you can print selected pages of an expanded master document. If you have inserted a new page numbering code for your body text, however, you may have to specify the page range in a different fashion.

Every new page number code inserted in a document creates a new logical section for page numbering purposes. For example, if your title page, table of contents, and other prefatory material take up eight pages, and you insert a new page number code to start numbering the body text at page 1, your document now has two page 1s (one in the body and one in the front matter). If you simply tell WordPerfect to print pages 1-4, the program prints the title page and subsequent pages. If you specify pages 20 through 50, WordPerfect prints that page range from the body text, because the first section of the document doesn't contain pages numbered greater than 8. To print pages 1 through 8 of the body text, however, you must tell WordPerfect that you want pages 1 through 8 of the second section of the document. You specify that page range as 2:1-8 (meaning section 2, pages 1 through 8).

If you inserted chapter codes, you can print one or more chapters instead of printing a page range. You can also specify a page range within a specific chapter. To print selected pages or chapters, do the following:

1. Choose **F**ile, **P**rint. WordPerfect displays the Print dialog box.
2. Choose **M**ultiple Pages, **P**rint. WordPerfect displays the Multiple Pages dialog box.
3. To print a page range, choose P**a**ge(s)/Label(s) and enter the desired range, using dashes or commas.

4. To print one or more chapters, choose **C**hapter(s) and enter the desired chapter number or range of chapters.

5. Choose **P**rint.

Normally, you will not want to print a condensed master document. However, because a master document can contain text of its own as well as the generated table of contents, lists, and index, you may want to print the condensed master document to see those items. To print the condensed master document, print the document before expanding it. If the master document is already expanded, condense it and then print. Remember, the subdocument links are displayed as comments and do not print.

◄ See "Using Basic Printing Skills," p. 290

Using Search, Replace, and Speller in a Master Document

You can use many WordPerfect features with the Master Document feature. You can perform functions—a spelling check, search, and replace, for example—more efficiently on one expanded document than on many separate subdocuments.

The sample office procedures manual has many sections contained in separate subdocuments. Using search, replace, or spelling check functions without the Master Document feature requires that you open each subdocument, perform the desired operation, and save the revised file—a tedious and time-consuming task. Also, with so many separate files, you may forget to check some of the files. With the Master Document feature, however, you can expand the master document and perform operations knowing that all files will be checked.

To search, replace, or check spelling across all the subdocument files linked to your master document, you simply open and expand the master document, and then perform the necessary operation.

Adding Footnotes and Endnotes

Footnotes and endnotes also are useful with a master document. If you plan to use footnotes or endnotes, however, use caution with the codes you use to control their format. Footnote and endnote format are controlled in two ways. A default system style for each element controls such details as default font, margins, indentation, and appearance of the footnote or endnote number. You can have only one footnote or endnote system style per document. Footnote (or endnote) option codes control other options, such as spacing between footnotes, separator line, and whether numbers should restart on each page. You can have many option codes in a document.

Use footnote or endnote option codes only in the master document, not the subdocuments. Like many WordPerfect codes, an option code placed in the middle of a document changes the format of that feature for the remainder of the document. If you place a footnote or endnote option code in a subdocument, all notes before the code have one appearance, and all notes after the note have another.

For detailed information on creating and editing footnotes and endnotes, see Chapter 25, "Using Footnotes and Endnotes."

Numbering Footnotes

WordPerfect gives you the option of numbering footnotes sequentially throughout a master document or of numbering each chapter or section separately. Like page numbers, by default WordPerfect numbers footnotes sequentially throughout an entire document. If you print a subdocument by itself, its page numbering and footnote numbering both start at 1. If you print that same subdocument in its place in an expanded master document, its page and footnote numbers depend on how many of each appear in previous subdocuments.

Just as you can insert a new page number code, you can insert a new footnote number code to restart numbering at any given value. If you want all subdocuments to start numbering at 1, place this code in your SubdocInit style.

Placing Endnotes

◄ See "Using Footnotes," p. 854

◄ See "Using Endnotes," p. 871

By default, WordPerfect places endnotes at the end of a document. If you instead want endnotes to appear at a particular location within a document—such as the end of a subdocument—you can insert an endnote placement code. Any endnotes you create before the code are printed at the location of the code and any endnotes you create later in the document are printed at the end, or at a subsequent endnote placement code. You can insert an endnote placement code at the end of each subdocument, or you can insert a single code near the end of your master document—immediately before an index definition, for example.

The Endnote Placement dialog box contains two options: **I**nsert Endnotes at Insertion Point, and Insert Endnotes at Insertion Point and **R**estart Numbering. If you are placing endnotes at the end of each subdocument and want to restart numbering for each, choose the latter. If you are placing all endnotes near the end of your master document, choose the former.

Using Cross-References

When you combine individual documents by using a master document, you can cross-reference items in other subdocuments—a process that is impossible without the Master Document feature. You can reference chapter titles or section headings in other subdocuments, for example.

To cross-reference between subdocuments, insert a reference code with a particular target name into one subdocument, and then use that same target name for a target code in a different subdocument. If you are creating many cross-references, expand the master document so that reference and target are in the same large document. See Chapter 26, "Assembling Document References," for more information about cross-references.

Troubleshooting

I've expanded a master document and the formatting I used in the original subdocuments is lost.

If you use styles for formatting, WordPerfect gives precedence to the style definitions in the master document. If you have a StyleA defined in a subdocument, and a StyleA defined in the master document, WordPerfect ignores the definition for StyleA in the subdocument and goes with the definition in the master document. Because of this precedence, you should give styles unique names if you want their definitions to remain when they are expanded into a master document. Avoid using the InitialStyle style to define styles unique to the individual files.

WordPerfect takes an inordinate amount of time to generate a very large expanded master document.

The larger the expanded master document, the more time it takes to generate it. Long documents of several hundred pages are not uncommon, and these can take several minutes—depending on the speed of your computer—to generate. Because large documents can take so long to generate, it is advisable to do it just once, when you are putting the finishing touches on your document and preparing it for printing. If you must generate large documents often, consider ways to speed up the process by using a faster computer. A PC with no less than 16 megabytes of RAM also improves the speed of the generating process.

Creating Subdocuments within Subdocuments

Any subdocument can be a master document. If, for example, the personnel policy section of the office procedures manual, PERSONNL.POL, becomes very large, you can break it into individual sections covering sick leave, vacation, holidays, overtime, and so on. Then you can treat the personnel files both as a separate document and as part of the larger office manual.

When you expand PROCEDUR.MD (the office procedures manual master document), if WordPerfect finds subdocument links within the PERSONNL.POL file, the program expands those subdocuments into PERSONNL.POL. When you condense PROCEDUR.MD, WordPerfect also condenses the subdocument files in PERSONNL.POL.

From Here...

This chapter showed you how to use WordPerfect's Master Document feature to manage large and complex documents. You saw that breaking a large document into smaller, easy-to-handle pieces and then combining these pieces when necessary, can save time.

In addition, you learned how to create a table of contents in the master document, including the use of styles and page numbering codes.

For more information on working with WordPerfect files and multi-part documents, see the following chapters in this book:

- Chapter 1, "Getting Started," gives you information on working with WordPerfect documents, including viewing multiple document files at once.

- Chapter 2, "Creating and Saving a Document," shows you how to store a document on disk.

- Chapter 3, "Retrieving and Editing Documents," details opening and editing documents, including opening documents in new document screens and combining files with text already in the document.

- Chapter 19, "Assembling Documents with Merge and Sort," shows you how to create one or more personalized form letter documents using WordPerfect's merge feature.

- Chapter 26, "Assembling Document References," discusses how to prepare references within a document and to create a table of contents, index, list, cross-reference, or table of authorities.
- Chapter 28, "Advanced File Management," details working with files within WordPerfect, including using the QuickList and QuickFinder features.

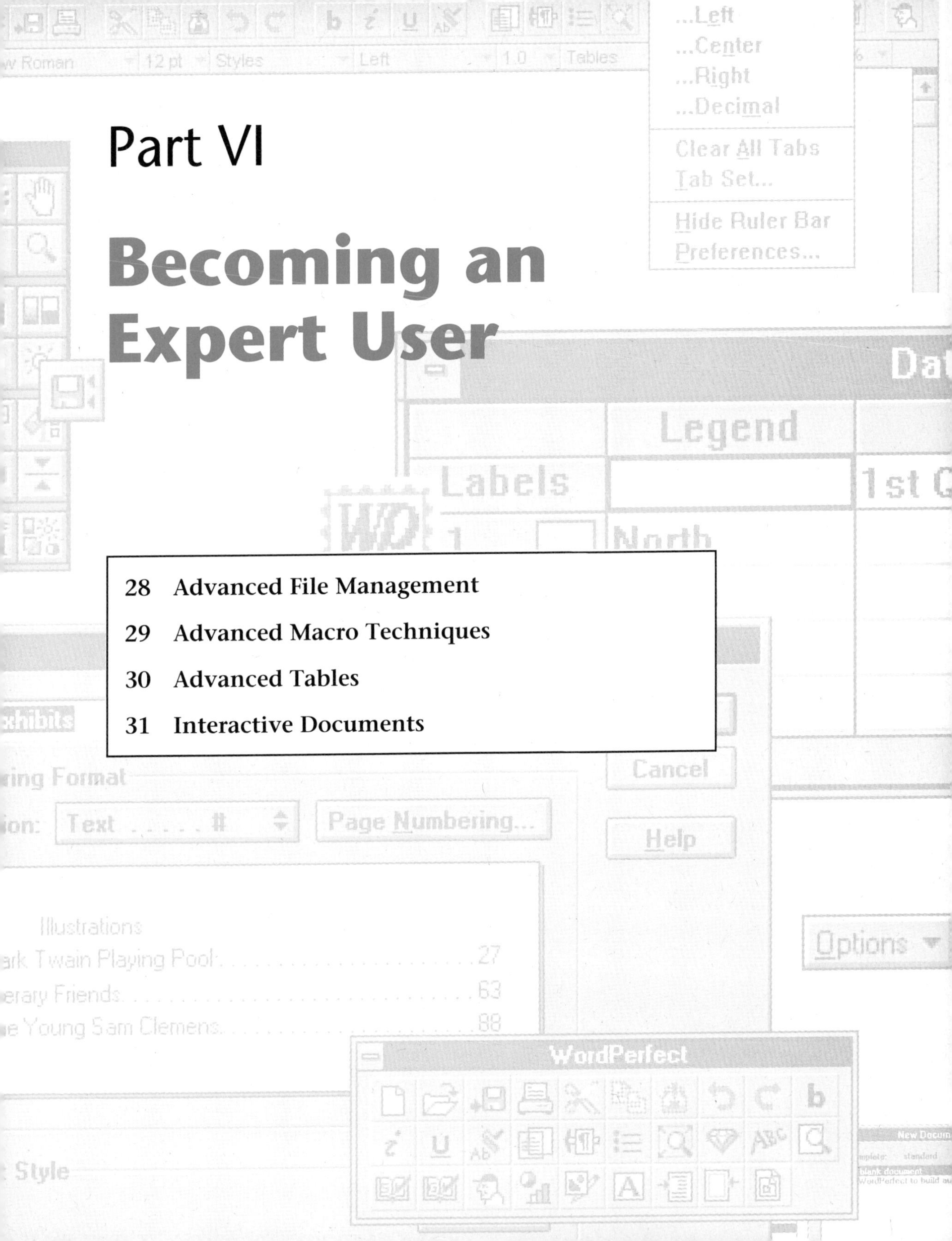

Part VI

Becoming an Expert User

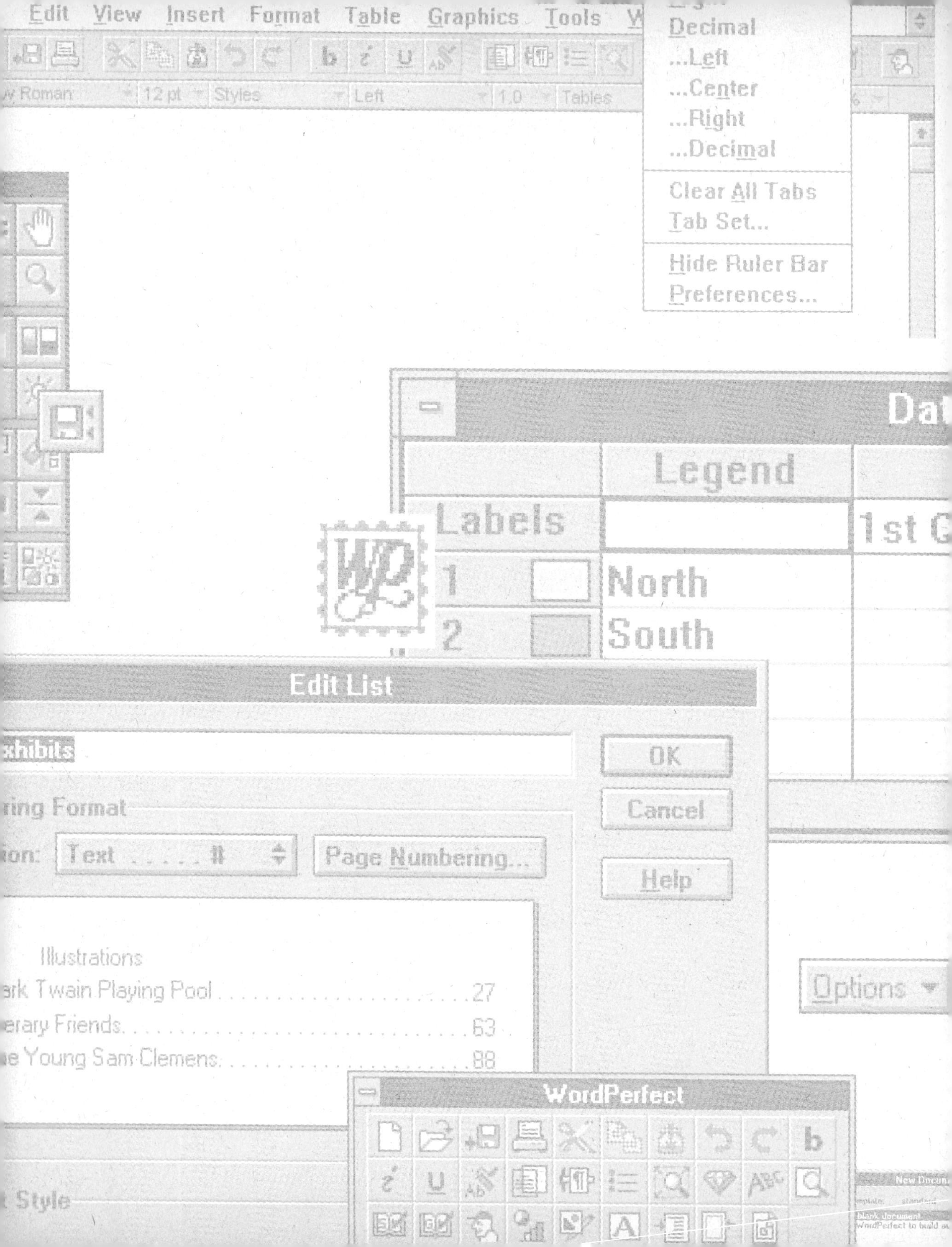

Edit View Insert Format Table Graphics Tools
Decimal
...Left
...Center
...Right
...Decimal
Clear All Tabs
Tab Set...
Hide Ruler Bar
Preferences...
Legend
Labels
1 North
2 South
Edit List
OK
Cancel
Help
Page Numbering...
Illustrations
WordPerfect
Options

Chapter 28

Advanced File Management

by Laura Acklen

In the early chapters of this book, you learned how to perform basic file-related tasks such as retrieving, saving, and closing documents. You soon will have quite a collection of files, however, and will discover that you need to organize your work. Learning how to manage files is one of the most important skills you can acquire.

WordPerfect's file management tools are powerful and easy to use. To understand how these tools can help you, suppose that you go to a library that has no card catalog and whose books are randomly placed on the shelves. Finding what you need requires a very special librarian who has read *and* remembers everything in the collection and who knows exactly where to find each book.

Fortunately, librarians have shelving systems, catalogs, and references to find and retrieve information efficiently. Likewise, effective use of your collection of documents depends on your ability to find and retrieve only the information you need. WordPerfect's file management tools actually surpass the skills of most librarians. To ignore these important skills is akin to searching for information in a library merely by browsing the shelves.

In this chapter, you learn how to use WordPerfect's file management tools and perform the following tasks:

- Move, rename, copy, and delete files
- Create, rename, and remove directories
- Customize the file and directory lists

- Locate files with the QuickFinder
- Set up and use QuickLists
- Use the QuickFinder File Indexer to create indexes to locate files quickly

Using the File Options Menu To Perform File Management Functions

Tip
You can also press Ctrl+O to open the Open File dialog box.

In WordPerfect 6.1, the file management functions are incorporated into each directory dialog box. Directory dialog boxes appear when you use Open, Save As, Insert File, Insert Image, Select File, Retrieve Equation Text, or any other feature that requires you to specify a file. The File Options menu is used to move, copy, rename, delete, print, and change the attributes for a file. It's important to note that you can work with virtually any file on your system, not just WordPerfect files. If you need to work with more than one file, you can mark a series of files and then work with them as a group. You also can create directories to organize related files into groups.

Although the File Options menu is available in several directory dialog boxes, this section uses the Open File dialog box as an example. To access the Open File dialog box, click the Open button on the Toolbar; or choose **F**ile, **O**pen. Choose File **O**ptions; a pull-down list of menu items appears (see fig. 28.1).

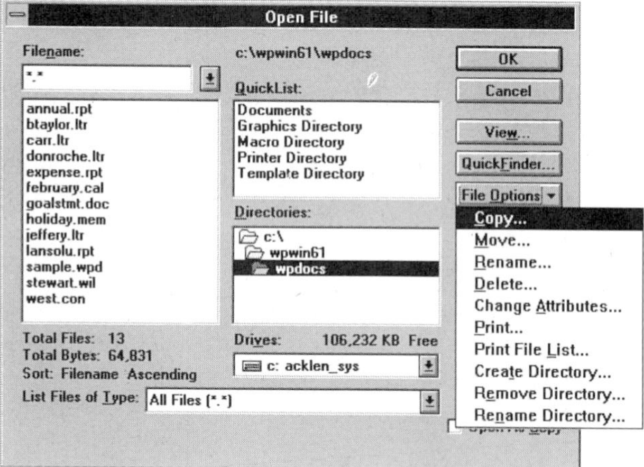

Fig. 28.1
The File **O**ptions menu lists the file management functions you can perform.

Tip
You can also point at the file list (in a directory dialog box) and click the right mouse button to display the File Options menu.

Copying Files

A file can be copied to a new location with the **C**opy option on the File **O**ptions pull-down menu. If you select a file in the list, WordPerfect places the name of the file in the **F**rom text box on the Copy File dialog box (see fig. 28.2). If the file does not appear on the list, you can type in the path and name of the file in the **F**rom text box.

Fig. 28.2
You use the Copy File dialog box to copy a file to another drive or directory.

You can copy a file to another directory or drive (back up a file to a floppy disk, for example). If you don't want to replace an identical file in the destination directory, check the **D**on't Replace Files with the Same Size, Date, and Time check box. If you can't remember the name of the destination directory, click the Files icon to the right of the **T**o text box to access the Select Directory dialog box, where you can look through the directories on your system.

Tip
Make a copy of a file before making heavy revisions. Then if anything happens to the document during revision, you can always return to the original copy.

Moving Files

If you accidentally save a file to the wrong directory or if you are reorganizing your files, you may need to move a file to another directory. Just select the file in the File**n**ame list and choose **M**ove from the File **O**ptions menu. Type the name of the destination directory in the **T**o text box or click the Files icon to access the Select Directory dialog box, where you then can select a directory.

Renaming Files

You can rename a file by selecting the file and choosing **R**ename from the File **O**ptions menu. To keep the file in the current directory, simply type a new file name in the **T**o text box. To rename the file to another directory (essentially to move it), type the name of the destination directory and the file name in the **T**o text box. The Files icon, which accesses the Select Directory dialog box, is also available here if you can't remember the name of the destination directory.

Note

Renaming a file to a different directory and moving a file accomplish the same result.

Deleting Files

Tip
Selecting a file and pressing the Delete key will also open the Delete File dialog box.

If you no longer need a file, you can delete it from the system by using the **D**elete option. You can delete almost any file; the only exceptions are some program files and files marked specifically so they cannot be deleted. Use this option with extreme caution. After you delete a file, only an Undelete utility can bring it back, if then. Instead, use the **M**ove command to move a file (or group of files) to a floppy disk, which you can then store in a safe location. This technique is known as *archiving*.

Changing File Attributes

Every file is assigned certain attributes that tell the Disk Operating System (DOS) how to deal with the file. In WordPerfect 6.1, you can set and clear four file attributes: archive, hidden, read-only, and system. Choose Change **A**ttributes from the File **O**ptions pull-down menu and check the corresponding check box in the Change File Attributes dialog box (see fig. 28.3).

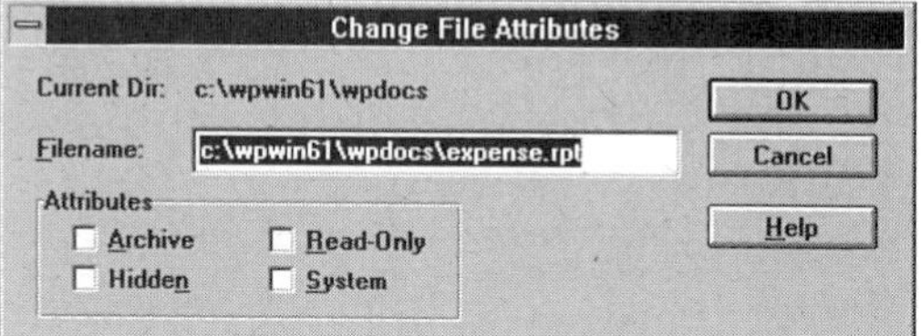

Fig. 28.3
You can use the Change File Attributes dialog box to set and clear four DOS attributes.

The **A**rchive attribute acts as a reminder—such as DOS BACKUP, Microsoft's Backup, or Fastback Plus—that this file needs to be backed up. If you deselect the **A**rchive option, the file is excluded from the backup—even if it was modified.

The Hidde**n** attribute designates a file as being hidden, so it will not be shown in directory listings. You must know the name of the file to work with it. This attribute is helpful if you are working on confidential files.

The **R**ead-Only attribute prevents a file from being modified or deleted. These files can be retrieved and edited in WordPerfect, but they must be saved under a new name. They can also be copied to a new file name. Either way, the original file remains unchanged.

The **S**ystem attribute designates a file as a system file. Files with this attribute are not shown in a directory listing.

Opening a File as a Copy

As an alternative to setting a **R**ead-Only attribute on a file, you can use the Open as **C**opy option to open a file as a copy, so that the original cannot be modified accidentally. This is a new feature added in the WordPerfect 6.1 release. When a file is opened as a copy, it cannot be saved to the original filename. This prevents accidental modification of important files, such as form files or contracts.

To open a file as a copy, choose the Open As **C**opy option in the Open File dialog box (see fig. 28.4) before selecting a file to open. The Open As **C**opy check box should now have an X in it so you know the option has been selected. If the X is not present, try choosing Open As **C**opy again.

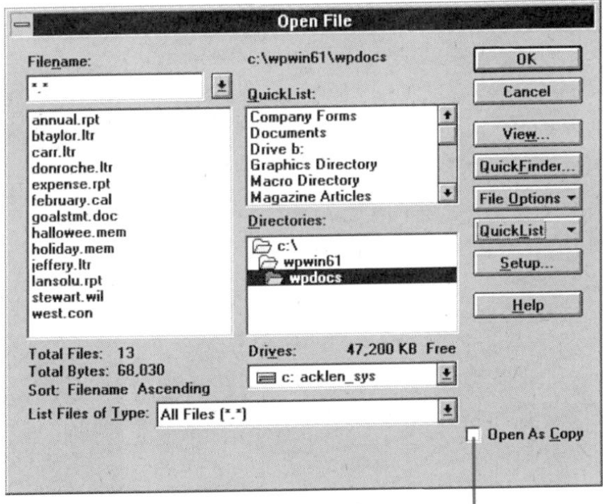

Fig. 28.4
Use the Open As **C**opy option to open a file as Read-Only so you don't accidentally modify the original.

The title bar for the document window contains the name of the file and the text (Read-Only) so you know the file has been opened as a Read-Only file. When you save the file, the Save As dialog box opens automatically, and you will have to type a new name for the file. If you accidentally type the original filename, WordPerfect will display a message box indicating that the file is Read-Only and cannot be saved to the original filename.

Printing a File

You can print a file without retrieving it into the document edit screen by highlighting the file and choosing **P**rint from the File **O**ptions pull-down menu. After the Print File dialog box appears, you confirm that you want to print the file, and WordPerfect sends the file to the printer.

> **Note**
>
> The Print File **L**ist option sends a copy of the file list to the printer. This option is ideal for documentation purposes. A good example is printing a list of all the files to be archived off the system.

Working with More Than One File

If you need to perform a file management function (copy, move, delete, print, or change attributes) on more than one file, you can select, and then work with, the files as a group. To select a file, click the file name; or use Tab to move to the File**n**ame box and then use the arrow keys to move the selection bar to the correct file. To select a series of contiguous files (files that are next to each other in the list), click the first file name and drag down to the last file name; or use the arrow keys to highlight the first file, and hold down the Shift key and use the arrow keys to highlight additional files. To select noncontiguous files, click the first file name; then hold down the Ctrl key and click the other file names. If you want to select all the files, click in the file list; then press Ctrl+/ (forward slash).

Creating, Renaming and Removing Directories

◄ See "Saving a Document to Disk," p. 72

Setting up a directory system is like setting up a filing system. Just as you take out and then label a manila file folder, you can create a directory and give it a name. Organizing files into directories by account, subject, or project helps you later locate the files you need quickly and easily.

◄ See "Saving a Document with a Different Name or File Format," p. 76

To create a directory, select Crea**t**e Directory from the File **O**ptions pull-down menu. To create the directory under the current directory (listed at the top of the Create Directory box), just type the name of the directory in the **N**ew Directory text box. If you want to create the directory elsewhere, type the full path name for the new directory (for example, **C:\NEWACCTS\TAYLOR**) in the text box.

While a directory name may seem appropriate when you create the directory, over time, the contents of that directory can change. It makes sense to update the name of the directory to match the contents.

To rename a directory, select the directory name in the **D**irectories list box, then choose Re**n**ame Directory from the File **O**ptions pull-down menu. Type the new directory name in the **T**o text box in the Rename Directory dialog box, then choose OK.

◀ See "Using Insert File To Combine Files," p. 88

If you decide that you no longer need a directory, you can remove it from the hard disk. When you archive files that are no longer current, for example, you may choose to remove the directory also.

To remove a directory, select the directory name in the **D**irectories list box, then choose R**e**move Directory from the File **O**ptions pull-down menu. If the directory contains files and/or subdirectories, you are asked to confirm the removal of the directory. If you do so, the files and/or subdirectories are deleted and the directory removed.

Troubleshooting

I moved (or copied) a file to another directory, but now I can't find it.

There is a chance that you accidentally renamed the file when you moved it, so you may be looking for the wrong file name. Or, you may be looking in the wrong directory. Either way, the fastest way to find the file is to use QuickFinder to search for it. You can either search for the filename, or if you are unsure about the filename, you can search for it based on the text in the file. See the "Finding Files" section later in the chapter for more information on QuickFinder.

I accidentally deleted an important file—can I get it back?

First of all, don't do anything else on your computer after you accidentally delete a file. Don't save a file, open another file, print a file—don't do anything until you have tried to undelete the file with an Undelete utility. If the utility isn't successful, you can restore the file from your latest backup. If you don't have a backup with that file on it, as a last resort, you can retype the document from a printed copy.

I changed the attributes for a file, and now I can't find it.

Files with the **H**idden or **S**ystem file attribute will not show up in your file lists. To show these files, select the Show Hidden/**Sy**stem Files option in the Open/Save As Setup dialog box, which is discussed in the next section.

I can't seem to select more than one file in my file list. When I try to select the second file, it deselects the first one.

Selecting multiple files can be tricky. You have to remember to hold down the Ctrl key when you select the second and subsequent files. If the files are all in a row, you can click and drag through them with the mouse, or select the first one, then hold down the Shift key when you select the last one.

Using the Setup Menu To Customize the File List Display

The **S**etup button opens the Open/Save As Setup dialog box, which is used to specify how you want files listed in the directory dialog boxes. The changes you make in the Open/Save As Setup dialog box affect all directory dialog boxes, not just the box in which you made the changes. Choose **S**etup from a directory dialog box to display the Open/Save As Setup dialog box (see fig. 28.5). If you choose **S**etup from the Save As dialog box, a slightly different Open/Save As Setup dialog box appears (see fig. 28.6). An additional option for a default save file format is available.

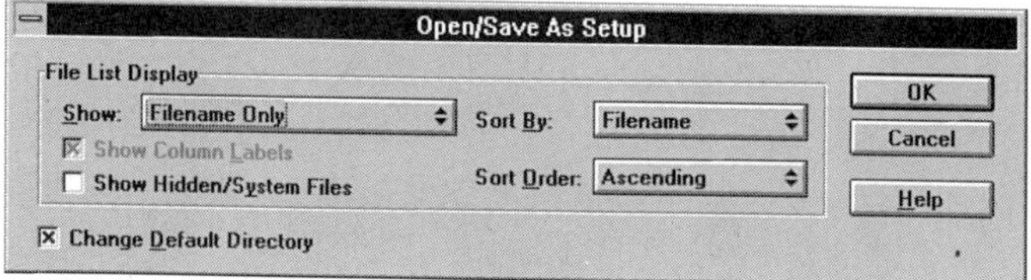

Fig. 28.5
You use the Open/Save As Setup dialog box to customize the file list for all directory dialog boxes.

Note

You can select the Change **D**efault Directory check box to change the default directory each time you change to a different directory in a directory dialog box. The default directory is the directory WordPerfect uses to save a file if only a file name is given (instead of the full path name) and also is the directory that is selected when you open a directory dialog box. If you don't want to change the default directory each time you change directories, deselect this option.

Open/Save As Setup
File List Display
Show: Filename Only
Show Column Labels
Show Hidden/System Files
Sort By: Filename
Sort Order: Ascending
OK
Cancel
Help
Change Default Directory
Default Save File Format
Format: WordPerfect 6.0/6.1 (*.wpd;*.wpt;*.doc;*.wp)

Fig. 28.6
An option to specify a default save file format is available on the Open/Save As Setup dialog box when called from the Save As dialog box.

Setting Up the File List Display

The File List Display section controls which type of file name is displayed and how the files are sorted in the File list. If you use descriptive file names and types, you can display this information. You also can create custom columns to display file information in a certain order.

Choosing Which Kind of File Name To Display

You can assign two kinds of file names in WordPerfect: a DOS file name and a descriptive name. The DOS file name, which is mandatory, has a maximum of eight characters, followed by a period and a three-letter extension. It can be difficult to describe the type of file with just eleven characters, so WordPerfect includes the Descriptive **N**ame and Descriptive **T**ype options in the Document Summary to create a longer, more descriptive file name and file type.

Choose **S**how under the File List Display section to display a drop-down list (see fig. 28.7). If you prefer working with DOS file names, you can have them displayed with or without the size, date, and time information. If you use descriptive names in the document summaries, you can have WordPerfect display the descriptive name next to the DOS file name.

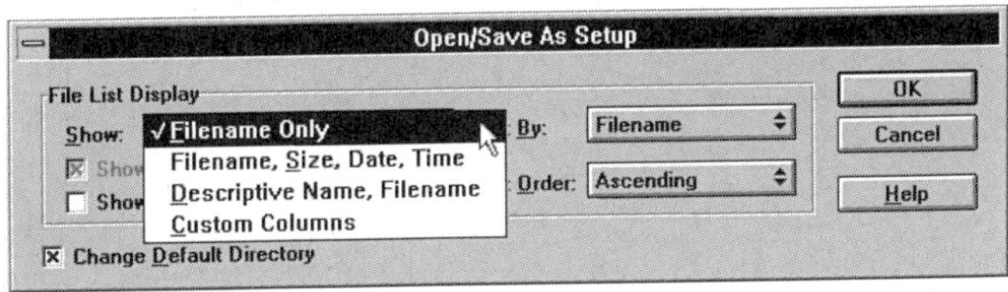

Fig. 28.7
You can choose the information to be displayed in the file list by choosing an option in the **S**how drop-down list.

The **C**ustom Columns feature displays the file list in the directory dialog box with separate columns for file name, size, date, and time. Unless you deselect the Show Column **L**abels check box in the Open/Save As Setup dialog box, each column heading label appears as a button that you can click and drag to resize and rearrange the columns. To add another column, click the gray area between buttons with the right mouse button and select from the drop-down list. Click and drag a button off the screen to delete a column.

If you decide to display either descriptive names or custom columns, the Open/Save As Setup dialog box expands to show an additional section for Speedup files. Speedup files are discussed later in this section.

Sorting the File List

In the Sort **B**y option, you can specify the method for sorting files in the list. You can sort files by file name, extension, size, date/time, descriptive name, and descriptive type in either ascending or descending order. If the Descriptive **N**ame and Descriptive **T**ype items are grayed on the menu (see fig. 28.8), they are not currently displayed in the file list.

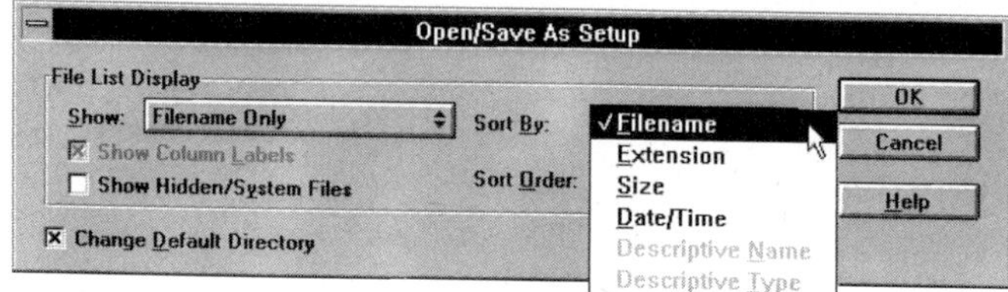

Fig. 28.8
You use the Sort **B**y options to sort the file list by different pieces of file information.

Using Speedup Files

If you elect to display Descriptive **N**ames or **C**ustom Columns, an additional section called Descriptive Name Speedup Files Location appears in the Open/Save As Setup dialog box (see fig. 28.9). A *Speedup file* is an index file that contains descriptive name information for each file in the list. Scanning the index to display descriptive names is much faster than scanning the document summaries each time you display a list of files.

The first time you choose to show Descriptive **N**ames in the file list, or add a column for descriptive names in **C**ustom Columns, WordPerfect prompts you to create a directory for Speedup files. The default directory is WPSPEED; you can specify another directory if necessary.

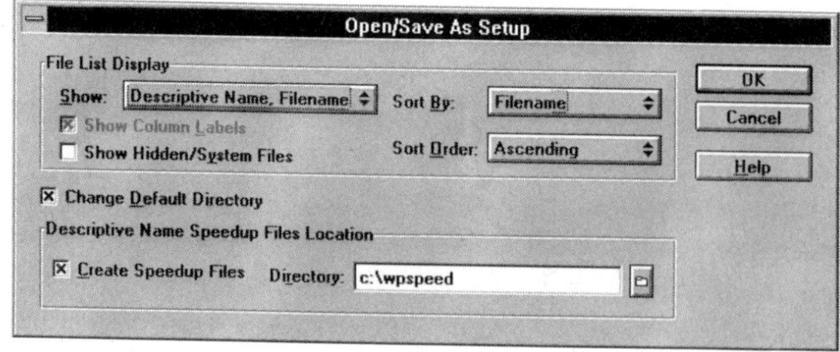

Fig. 28.9
You can turn off Speedup files or specify another directory to use in the Descriptive Name Speedup Files Location section.

Setting a Default Save File Format

If you frequently save files in a format other than WordPerfect 6.1, you can change the Default Save File Format to that format. This will eliminate the need to choose the correct format from the Save File as **T**ype drop-down list each time, speeding up the saving process. You will still have the ability to choose another file format in the Save As dialog box, if necessary.

To specify the default file format, choose **S**etup from the Save As dialog box; then select the proper format from the **F**ormat drop-down list. WordPerfect will change the default in the Save As dialog box for the current and all new documents.

Finding Files

With today's large hard disks, you can store literally thousands of files on one disk, which makes the task of locating files a daunting one. Learning the methods that you can use to search for files is one of the most important skills you can master. In previous chapters, you learned how to browse through file lists in the directory dialog boxes. You scrolled through the current list of files and changed directories to look at lists of files in other directories. This approach has several major disadvantages:

- Disk drives may contain so many directories that looking through each directory is tedious and time-consuming.
- Directories may contain so many files that scanning the file names to find the file you want is impractical.
- You may have assigned a file name that, at the time, seemed to adequately describe the file contents. Days later, however, the file name may not seem meaningful.
- You may not remember the name of the file.

Although organizing files into directories and subdirectories can help reduce the time you take to find a particular file, this method isn't always foolproof. WordPerfect provides a number of methods that you can use to locate files in a directory, subtree, or disk. From displaying a specific file list to using the search options in the QuickFinder dialog box, you are sure to find the file(s) you are looking for. In addition, WordPerfect also includes a QuickFinder File Indexer and QuickList feature, described in later sections in this chapter.

Listing Files by Type

The List Files of **T**ype option appears on most directory dialog boxes. A drop-down list of file types (such as text, macros, or documents) is available (see fig. 28.10). This list references certain file name extensions that are assigned to files, indicating the file type (for example, WPD for WordPerfect Documents). When you select an option, WordPerfect displays a new file list with only the files that have the selected extension.

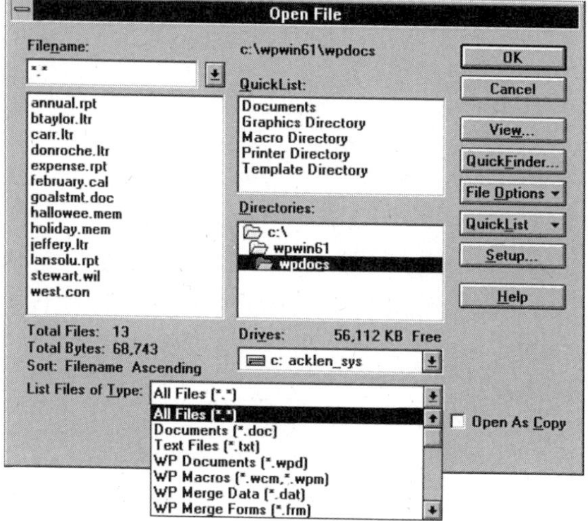

Fig. 28.10
The List Files of **T**ype option lists files with a particular extension.

Creating a Partial Directory Listing Using DOS Wild-Card Characters

Occasionally, you may need to be able to work from a specific list of files rather than from the list of every file in a directory. You can create a custom list of files by using DOS wild-card characters to represent a portion of the file name. By listing only files that match the pattern, you can narrow down the list to a manageable size.

Two DOS wild-card characters—* and *?*—are available. The asterisk (*) stands for *any number* of characters, and the question mark (?) stands for *any one character*. The following examples use these wild cards:

Wild Card	Locates
.	All file names
*.LTR	All files names with an LTR extension
REPORT*.*	All files names that begin with REPORT, such as REPORT95.LST, REPORT.TBL, and REPORTS.FIN

Wild Card	Locates
M*.FRM	All files that begin with an M and have an FRM extension, such as M.FRM, MEMO.FRM, MINUTES.FRM,MISSING.FRM, MBTA.FRM
L?ST.WPD	LIST.WPD, LAST.WPD, and LOST.WPD, but not LEAST.WPD

You can create a custom list of files from any directory dialog box. Type the file pattern you want to display in the File**n**ame text box, and then choose OK or press Enter.

Using QuickFinder To Search for Files

Although the previously mentioned features are helpful and easy to use, the QuickFinder feature provides the real muscle for locating files. QuickFinder goes beyond searching for patterns in file names to searching for patterns of words in documents. If you complete the document summary information, you can search any item in the summaries. You can expand the search for files from the current directory to a subtree of the drive or even the entire drive. You can use the QuickFinder File Indexer to create indexes of files that can be searched much more quickly. (The QuickFinder File Indexer is covered in the later section "Using the QuickFinder File Indexer.")

To access the QuickFinder dialog box, choose Quick**F**inder from a directory dialog box. The QuickFinder dialog box appears (see fig. 28.11).

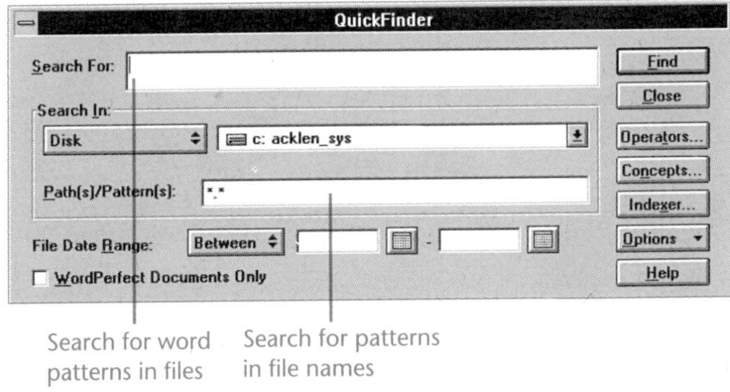

Fig. 28.11
Use the QuickFinder dialog box to specify the criteria for a file search.

> **Note**
>
> The Inde**x**er option on the QuickFinder dialog box takes you directly to the QuickFinder File Indexer utility where you can create and edit index files.

Searching for Word Patterns in Documents

To search for a particular word or word pattern, choose the **S**earch For option on the QuickFinder dialog box and type the word pattern in the text box. If you type **Taylor**, for example, WordPerfect searches for files that contain the word *Taylor* anywhere in the file.

Tip
If you prefer, you can type the operator symbols with the keys on the keyboard, rather than selecting them from the Search Operators dialog box.

You can build more complex searches by using options in the Search Operators dialog box, accessible by choosing Opera**t**ors. The Search Operators dialog box has six different options, each with a list of operators that you can insert to build a word search pattern. When you select an operator from the list, a symbol that represents the operator is inserted in the **S**earch For text box. Choose **I**nsert to insert an operator and leave the dialog box open; choose Insert **a**nd Close to insert the operator and close the dialog box; choose **C**lose to close the dialog box.

Using Operators

By default, the **O**perators option is selected, so the list of operators is shown (see fig. 28.12).

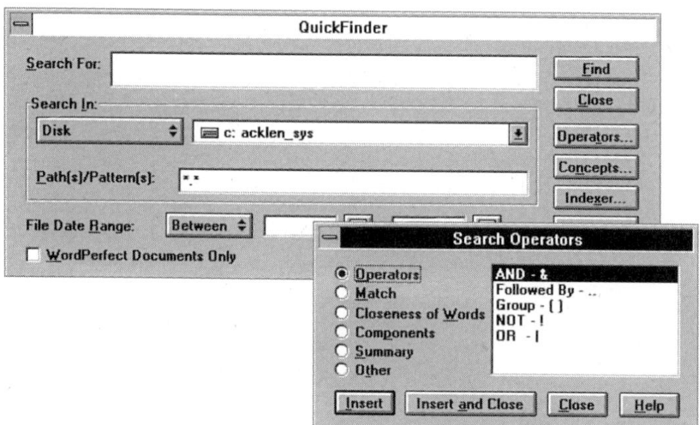

Fig. 28.12
You can use the operators listed to create a very specific word search.

The following table provides a list of the operator symbols and their descriptions:

Search Operator	Description
&	AND
|	OR
!	NOT
..	Followed by
( )	Group

The following examples show valid search patterns that use operators:

Pattern	Files Selected Contain
Benjamin&Taylor	*Benjamin* and *Taylor*
Benjamin|Taylor	*Benjamin* or *Taylor*
Benjamin&Taylor|Andrews	*Benjamin* and also *Taylor* or *Andrews*
Benjamin&"recycling efforts"	*Benjamin* and the exact phrase *recycling efforts*
!Taylor	Does not contain *Taylor*
Taylor!Andrews	*Taylor* but not *Andrews*
Benjamin..Taylor	*Benjamin* followed by *Taylor*
(recycling plastic paper)	All three words, in any order
"election"	Only the exact phrase: *election*

Specifying Case-Sensitive Searches

The **M**atch option allows you to specify whether or not you want a case-sensitive search. The default search is not case-sensitive. Position the insertion point before the word pattern for which you are searching and choose **M**atch to open the list of options (see fig. 28.13). If you choose Case Sensitive, /Case is inserted into the **S**earch For text box. If you choose Case Insensitive, /Nocase is inserted into the text box.

Tip

If you prefer, you can type **/Case** or **/Nocase** in the **S**earch For text box, rather than selecting them from the menu.

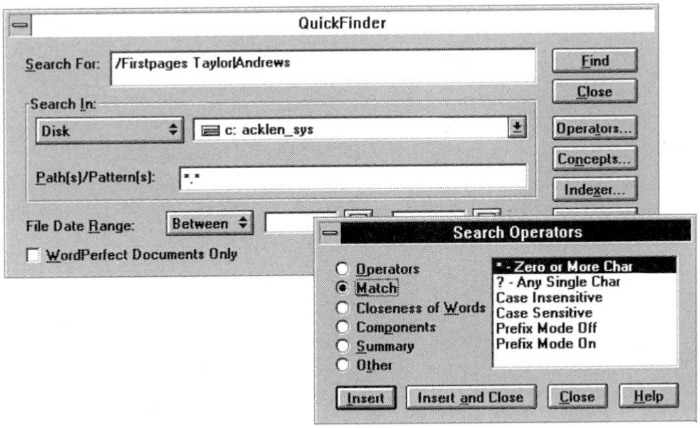

Fig. 28.13
Options on the **M**atch list will turn case-sensitivity on and off.

Tip
If you prefer, you can type a ? or * in the **S**earch For text box, rather than selecting them from the menu.

Using Wild-Card Characters

The ? and * are called *wild-card characters* and can also be used to limit a list of files (see the section "Creating a Partial Directory Listing Using DOS Wild-Card Characters" earlier in this chapter). The **M**atch menu has two options that use these characters: Any single char—? and Zero or more char—*. Use these wild-card characters to search for partial words, which will further limit your search.

The following examples show valid search patterns that use wild-card characters:

Pattern	Files Selected Contain
ta?	tan, tar, tab, tad and so on
expen*	expense, expenditure, expend
"elect*"	Finds the exact pattern as a portion of something longer: *elect, election, electoral, electing, electricity.*

Using the Prefix Mode

The **M**atch menu has the options to turn Prefix Mode on and off. The Prefix Mode setting eliminates the need to type an asterisk after a partial word in the **S**earch For text box. For example, if you are searching for "tree, water" and you turn Prefix Mode on, QuickFinder will locate all words with "tree" and "water" in the beginning of a word. The same thing can be accomplished by typing "tree*, water*". Prefix Mode simply eliminates the need to type an asterisk after every word. If you turn Prefix Mode off, QuickFinder will only locate the words "tree" and "water".

Specifying the Closeness of Words

You can limit the search to finding words and word patterns only if they are found within certain boundaries. Position the insertion point before the word pattern you want affected by the search limitation and choose Closeness of **W**ords to display a list of options (see fig. 28.14).

When chosen, each option inserts a backslash (\), followed by the selection's name. The exception is the Within # Words option, which inserts a backslash (\), followed by the number 5, which you can change to the desired number.

Specifying Which Part of the Document To Search

You can restrict the search to a certain part of a document, rather than searching the entire document, which can greatly reduce the time taken to perform the search. You might decide to limit the search, for example, to the first page only or to the document summary.

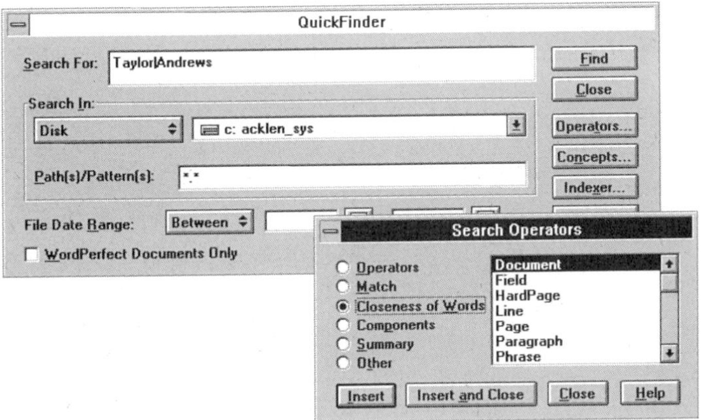

Fig. 28.14 The options on Closeness of **W**ords limit the search to certain boundaries within the document.

Note

You can select the **W**ordPerfect Documents Only option to limit the search to WordPerfect documents only.

Tip If you prefer, you can type the backslash and the document component name rather than choosing them from the menu.

To specify what part of the document to search, position the insertion point before the word pattern you want affected by the search limitation and choose Com**p**onents to display a list of options (see fig. 28.15). Select an option from the list and choose either **I**nsert or Insert **a**nd Close. When chosen, each option inserts a backslash (\), followed by the selection's name.

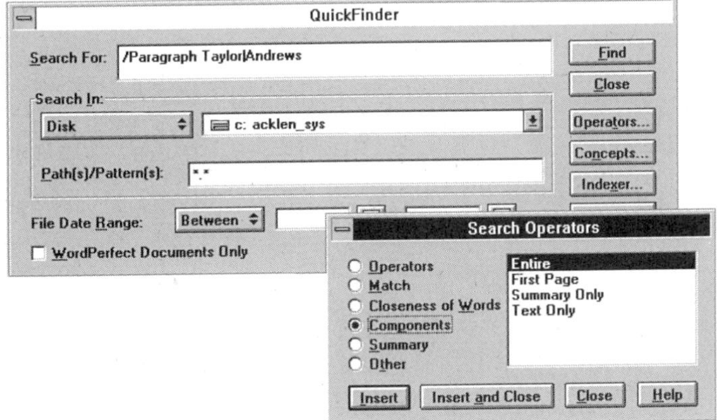

Fig. 28.15 You can use the Com**p**onents options to limit the search to a certain part of the document.

The Entire option searches the document text and all substructures (headers, footers, and so on). The First Page option searches only the first page, and the Summary Only option searches only the document summary information. The Text Only option limits the search to the document text (no substructures).

Searching Document Summary Fields

The **S**ummary option displays a complete list of document summary fields (see fig. 28.16). Searching through a particular document summary field is much faster than searching through the document text or the entire summary, so use this option as often as you can.

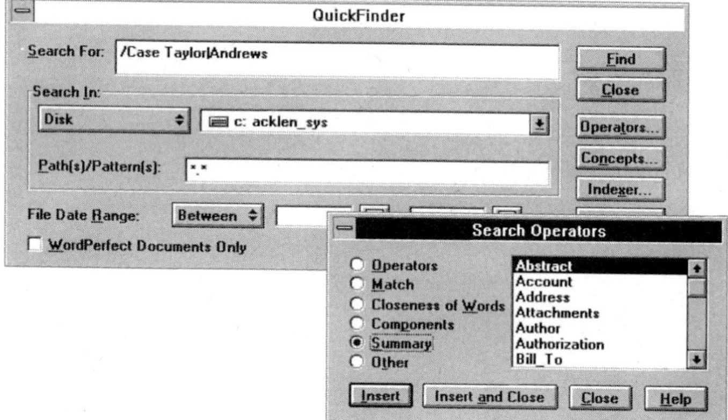

Fig. 28.16 Use the **S**ummary option to select one or more document summary field(s) you want to search from the list.

Type the text you want to search for, then insert the Document Summary field. When a document summary field is selected from the list, it appears in the **S**earch For text box with a backslash (\) in front of it.

Turning the Wild-Card Search On and Off

As previously mentioned, you can use the asterisk (*) and the question mark (?) to search for partial words. However, if you need to search for a word that actually contains an asterisk or a question mark, you'll need to turn off the wild-card search. Use the Wild card Off and Wild card On options on the O**t**her menu to turn the wild-card search capability on and off.

Using Scan Off

The Scan Off option on the O**t**her menu disables part of the internal scanning that takes place during index searches where the index level prompts a two-level scan. For example, if you search for "Jon Crain", QuickFinder performs a preliminary scan through the index for files that contain the words "Jon" and "Crain", but not together. Then, a second scan is done through these files for files that contain the words "Jon Crain" together. If you select Scan Off, the initial scan will be disabled.

Specifying Where To Search

The Search **I**n option is used to specify where you want to search for files. You can opt to search the current directory (the default), the subtree, the disk, an index file, or the Search Results list. You use the QuickFinder File Indexer to create an index file (see the section "Creating QuickFinder Indexes" later in this chapter).

Changing the Search In Selection

Select Search **I**n to display the pull-down list. The **D**irectory option searches the current directory. The **S**ubtree option searches the current directory and all related subdirectories. The D**i**sk option displays a new window with the current drive name displayed and a pull-down list of other available drives from which you can select. The **Q**uickFinder Index option expands the QuickFinder dialog box to include a drop-down list of available indexes. If you just completed a search, another option for S**e**arch Results List also appears on the menu so that you can perform a search on the previous search results and continue to narrow down the list.

> **Note**
>
> If you have not yet created a QuickFinder index file, the **Q**uickFinder Index option is dimmed on the menu.

Searching for File Name Patterns

The **P**ath(s)/Pattern(s) option is used in the same way as the File**n**ame option on the directory dialog boxes: to limit which files are searched. You can use the previously mentioned DOS wild-card characters to search for a particular pattern in a file name.

Setting a Date Range

You can limit the search for files with a creation date within a certain range. The default selection is to search for files created between two dates. You can click the drop-down list to select **A**fter, **B**efore, Be**t**ween, or **O**n so you can search for files created before, after, or on a specific date. Specify a date or dates by either typing the date in the two text boxes; or clicking the Calendar icons to select a date. If you prefer typing the date, use the month/day/year format.

The Calendar icons display the current month's calendar with the current date outlined (see fig. 28.17). To move forward a month, click the single right arrow next to the month; to move forward a year, click the double right arrow. To move back a month, click the single left arrow; to move back a year, click the double left arrow. Although the process is significantly slower, you can also use the arrow keys on the keyboard to move around in the calendar.

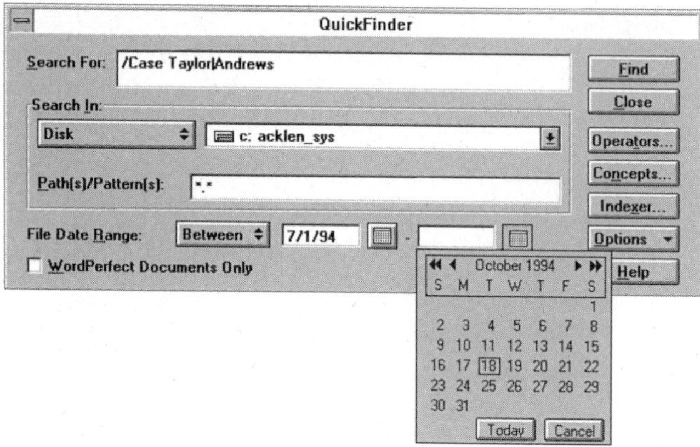

Fig. 28.17
Use the two Calendar icons to select the dates for the date range you use in your search.

Expanding Word Searches

The Co**n**cepts button opens the Concept Builder dialog box (see figure 28.18), which is used to expand QuickFinder searches by including alternative forms of words in the **S**earch For text box. This is helpful if you aren't exactly sure how the words are used in the document. This should reduce the number of searches you perform since you can include search words and selected alternatives in a single search.

Other spellings of the search words can be used, as well as synonyms and alternative word forms (or conjugations). For example, if one of the words in the Search **F**or text box is "distribute," alternative word forms would be "distributed," "distributes," "distributing," and "distribution."

The **T**hesaurus option will produce a list of synonyms for the original search word. The The**s**. -> Word Forms option will produce a list of alternative word forms for the synonyms. You can also use common misspellings and typos as alternative words. Finally, you can choose to include or exclude any of the listed alternative words in the search.

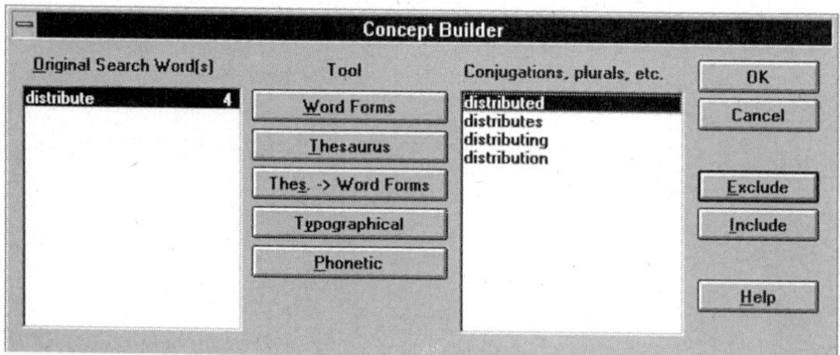

Fig. 28.18
The Concept Builder dialog box is used to expand word searches.

Using the QuickFinder Options Menu

The **O**ptions button opens a pull-down list of selections to expand the QuickFinder dialog box to select the relevance setting, include document summary fields, redisplay the last search results, and manage search queries. Choose **O**ptions from the QuickFinder dialog box to display the pull-down list of QuickFinder options (see fig. 28.19).

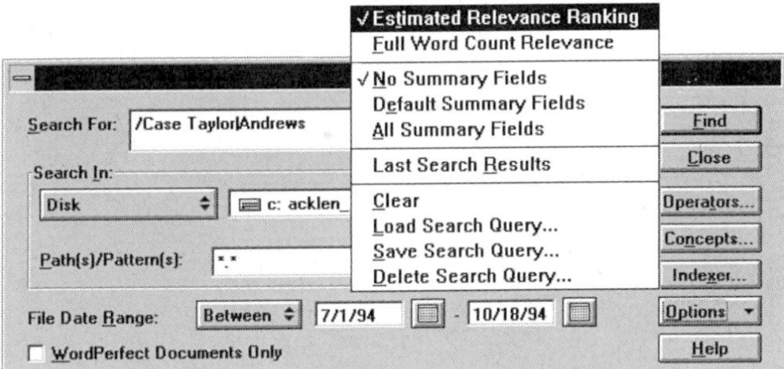

Fig. 28.19
You can manage search queries with the selections on the QuickFinder Options menu.

Use the Es**t**imated Relevance Ranking and **F**ull Word Count Relevance settings to let QuickFinder rank the documents matching the search query in order of relevancy, based on the number of words found. The default setting for relevance is Es**t**imated Relevance Ranking, as shown by the check mark next to the option. If this setting is selected during an index search, the S**e**arch Results List will display the number of search elements found, determined by the level of the index (line, paragraph, sentence, etc.). If this setting is selected during a scan search (one that does not search through QuickFinder indexes), the S**e**arch Results List will display the estimated number of search elements found (referred to as "hits"), per 1000 words. QuickFinder estimates how many hits a document contains in each 1000 words. If **F**ull Word Count Relevance is selected, QuickFinder will perform a scanning search automatically. The S**e**arch Results List will display the number of times the search text is found in the document. This search will take longer, but it is more precise.

The default summary selection is **N**o Summary Fields, as shown by the check mark next to the option. Choose D**e**fault Summary Fields to expand the QuickFinder dialog box to include a list of the default document summary fields. Choosing **A**ll Summary Fields from the **O**ptions menu adds a Document Summary Fields section to the QuickFinder dialog box that contains a complete list of document summary fields. You can search any field, or you can scroll to the appropriate field and type the information for which you want to search. You may fill in multiple fields to further narrow down the search.

◄ See "Using Document Summaries," p. 210

◄ See "Customizing the Document Summary Fields," p. 215

The Last Search **R**esults option displays the results of the last search query. This option works only if you checked the Save Search **R**esults check box in the previous S**e**arch Results List dialog box. This feature is helpful if you want to go back to the list of files from the previous search.

The **C**lear option clears the current search query so that you can start to build a new query.

After you build a search query, you can save it for later use, which is especially important when building complex search queries that require several steps to complete. After you create a search query, choose **S**ave Search Query, type a name for the search in the Search **N**ame text box, and choose **S**ave.

Existing search queries can be used later. Choose **L**oad Search Query from the **O**ptions menu to display the list of existing queries. Select a search query name in the S**e**arch Query List and choose **L**oad. You can delete existing search queries with the **D**elete Search Query option, when necessary.

Using the Search Results Dialog Box

The QuickFinder displays the results of a search query in a Search Results List dialog box (see fig. 28.20). The S**e**arch Results list has column heading buttons similar to the buttons in Custom Columns; you can move, resize, and add columns to the list to display the needed file information. Any changes made to the columns in the S**e**arch Results list are permanent.

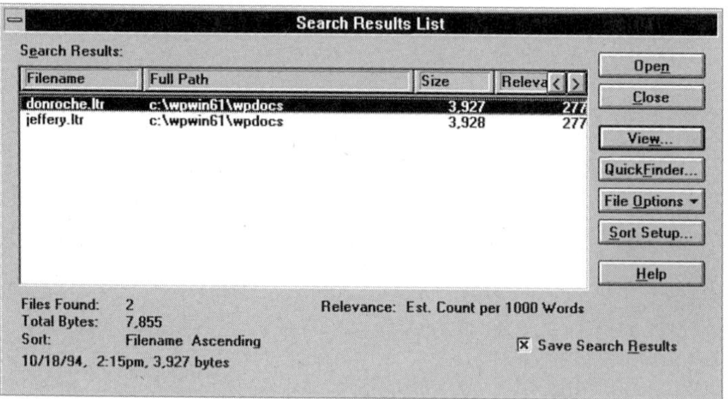

Fig. 28.20 The Search Results List dialog box displays a list of files from a search query.

The following options are available in the Search Results dialog box:

- The Vie**w** option loads the Viewer and displays the contents of a selected file.

- The QuickFinder option takes you back to the QuickFinder dialog box. The **A**dd Matching Files to Search Results List check box has been added so you can continue to build the list of files. Also, an option for the S**e**arch Results List has been included in the Search **I**n pull-down list so that you can continue searching only the files in the previous Search Results list and further narrow the search.
- You can use the File **O**ptions menu to manipulate the files in the Search Results list. You can copy, move, rename, delete, change attributes or print files, as well as print a list of the files in the Search Results list. (These options were discussed earlier in the section "Using the File Options Menu To Perform File Management Functions.")
- You can choose how you want the files sorted in the list with the **S**ort Setup option.
- Checking the Save Search **R**esults check box saves the results of the last search query so that you can return to it later. To redisplay the search results, choose Last Search **R**esults on the QuickFinder **O**ptions menu. The previous search results are saved even if you exit the program.

Note

If you choose the Quick**F**inder button in the Search Results List dialog box, an additional option, **A**dd Matching Files to Search Results, appears in the QuickFinder dialog box. If you check this box, the results of the next search query are added to the current S**e**arch Results list. Using this method, you can build a list of files from several search queries.

Troubleshooting

I'm trying to search for text on the first page of a file, and WordPerfect says it can't find the file. I know it's in the directory somewhere—what am I doing wrong?

Make sure the operators you are using are placed in front of the text you are searching for. Also, try using a partial word search using the * or ? so you have a greater chance of finding what you are looking for. Remember, the phrase you type must be found in the document, or WordPerfect will tell you the file is not found.

When I select the Last Search Results option in the QuickFinder Options menu, WordPerfect displays the results of the wrong search query.

Remember, this option works only if you checked the Save Search **R**esults check box in the previous Search Results List dialog box. You will have to re-create the search results, then make sure you check the Save Search **R**esults option this time.

Using the QuickList Feature

Although organizing files into directories and subdirectories is a good management practice, remembering the exact path and directory names can be difficult. The QuickList feature eliminates the need to remember these path names. You can use QuickList to assign a descriptive name to a directory. Rather than typing **C:\REPORTS**, for example, you can select the QuickList entry for "Reports."

You also can use the QuickList feature to display quickly a particular group of files. You might create a QuickList entry, for example, for all the letters to a certain client and another entry for all the notices (see the examples in the table).

QuickList is a powerful tool that you should take the time to learn. You can save time (and frustration) by using the QuickList entries to display files, rather than typing long-and often forgotten-path names. The following list shows some examples of QuickList entries:

Directory/File Name	QuickList Description
C:\FORMS	Company Forms
A:	Drive A:
C:\NEWACCTS\TAYLOR*.LTR	Letters to Taylor Engineering
C:\NEWACCTS\TAYLOR*.NOT	Notices to Taylor Engineering
C:\CALENDAR*95.TRN	Training Calendars for 1995

Displaying and Using the QuickList

Tip

You can open a QuickList pull-down menu of options by pointing at the QuickList and clicking the right mouse button.

Directory dialog boxes have a QuickList button that opens a pull-down list of options to display the directory list, the QuickList, or both lists. There are also options to add, edit, and delete QuickList entries. Choose Quick**L**ist from a directory dialog box, and then choose Show **Q**uickList to display the QuickList (see fig. 28.21).

Note

The QuickList replaces the Directory List in the dialog box unless you choose to display both, in which case both the lists are split in half to share the space.

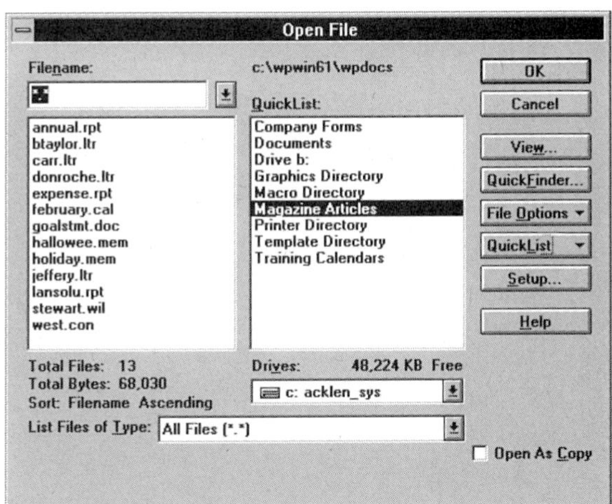

Fig. 28.21
A **Q**uickList entry is a descriptive name assigned to a directory or group of files.

The first time you display the QuickList, you may have entries for the WordPerfect program files. These entries were created when the program was installed. Some of these entries may be helpful to you, although others can be deleted (see the later section "Editing or Deleting QuickList Entries").

To display the list of files for a **Q**uickList entry, double-click the entry; or highlight the entry and choose OK. The new directory name is displayed at the top of the directory dialog box, and the new list of files appears in the File**n**ame window.

Note

If the QuickList entry is no longer valid (the directory was deleted or renamed), WordPerfect displays an error message, and the file list remains the same. Choose OK to continue.

Adding QuickList Entries

You can add as many **Q**uickList entries as you need. Any directory (or group of files) on any drive can be referenced by a **Q**uickList entry. You can even create a **Q**uickList entry for a directory that hasn't been created yet.

To add a QuickList entry, choose Quick**L**ist from a directory dialog box. First, choose Show **Q**uickList to display the QuickList in the dialog box. Second, choose Quick**L**ist again, and then **A**dd Item to display the Add QuickList Item dialog box (see fig. 28.22). Type in the name of the directory or group of files and a description for the QuickList entry, and then choose OK.

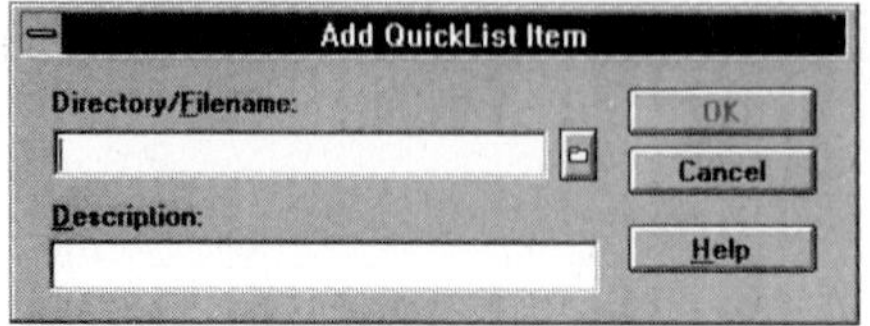

Fig. 28.22 You use the Add QuickList Item dialog box to specify a directory or file name and a corresponding description.

> **Note**
>
> If you use a directory name that does not exist when creating or editing a QuickList entry, WordPerfect stops and displays a message indicating that the directory does not exist. If you choose to use the directory name anyway, WordPerfect creates the QuickList item. If you choose not to use the name, WordPerfect returns to the Directory/**F**ilename text box so you can type another name.

Editing or Deleting QuickList Entries

As your files and directories change, so must the QuickList entries. QuickList entries can only be edited or deleted if the QuickList is displayed. Choose Quick**L**ist, and then **S**how QuickList. Select the entry in the QuickList, choose Quick**L**ist, and then choose **E**dit Item. Make the necessary changes in the Directory/**F**ilename or **D**escription text boxes, and then choose OK.

To delete a QuickList entry, select the entry in the QuickList, choose Quick**L**ist, and then choose De**l**ete Item.

Printing QuickList Entries

The ability to print your QuickList entries is a new feature in WordPerfect 6.1 for Windows. If you want someone in your office to set up QuickList entries similar to your own, you can print your QuickList and give them the hard copy to follow. To print your QuickList, choose Quick**L**ist, **P**rint QuickList.

Using the QuickFinder File Indexer

Earlier in the chapter, you learned how to use the QuickFinder feature to locate files with certain word patterns. As powerful as this feature is, the File Indexer takes the concept one step further by creating indexes of all the words in your files so WordPerfect has to reference the *index* only rather than search through each individual file. The result is a dramatic increase in the speed of the search.

Note

The QuickFinder File Indexer program is a separate utility that runs from the Windows Program Manager. Although you can access the QuickFinder File Indexer from within WordPerfect, you also can start it from Windows, without starting WordPerfect. To start the File Indexer from Windows, double-click the QuickFinder File Indexer icon in the WPWin program group.

Creating QuickFinder Indexes

You have to create an index before you can use it in a QuickFinder search. You can access the QuickFinder File Indexer dialog box (see fig. 28.23) from the QuickFinder dialog box by choosing Inde**x**er, or you can start it from the Windows Program Manager.

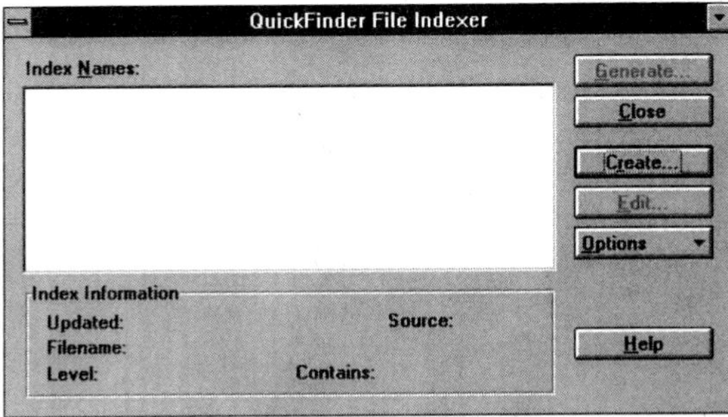

Fig. 28.23
The QuickFinder File Indexer dialog box. Any existing indexes are listed in the Index **N**ames window.

During the installation of WordPerfect 6.1, a directory is created specifically for the QuickFinder index files (C:\OFFICE\SHARED\WPC20\QFINDEX). If you want to use another directory, you can do so by specifying that directory in the QuickFinder Preferences menu.

Caution

Unless your computer has large amounts of memory and disk space, you probably should not try to index your entire hard disk. Instead, create indexes for the different classes and types of documents you have.

Setting Preferences in the QuickFinder File Indexer

When creating indexes, you can specify what the index will contain, which files to exclude, what level of indexing will be done, and how to handle extended characters. To change these options for all new indexes, choose

Preferences from the **O**ptions pull-down list in the QuickFinder File Indexer dialog box (see fig. 28.24). To change the preferences for a new index, choose **O**ptions in the Create Index dialog box (see fig. 28.25). The preferences for an existing index file can also be changed. Choose **O**ptions in the Edit Index dialog box; the changes will be reflected the next time the index is generated.

Fig. 28.24
Changes made in the Preferences menu affect all new indexes.

Preferences
Show Indexing Progress Every 10 Files
Location for Index Files:
c:\office\shared\wpc20\qfindex\
Location for Shared Indexes:
Expand Browse Dialog
Index Defaults
File Selection
Exclude Files: *.EXE, *.COM, *.DLL, *.BMP
WordPerfect Documents Only
Index Contents
Index Contains: Entire Document
Index Level: Document
Include Numbers in Index
Extended Characters in Unknown Formats: Exclude
OK
Cancel
Advanced <<
Help

Fig. 28.25
Changes made in the Options menu affect the current index only.

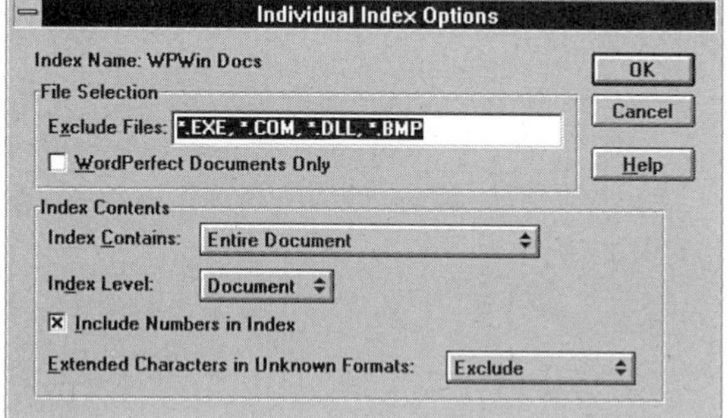

The Preferences dialog box, with the **A**dvanced options displayed, contains the following components:

- ***Show Indexing Progress Every n Files***. In this option, *n* can be increased to 5, 10, 25, or 50. A higher number may slightly decrease indexing time on slower computers, but it makes little difference on faster ones.

- *Location for Index Files.* This text box lists the directory **C:\OFFICE\SHARED\WPC20\QFINDEX** by default. If you want the index files created in another directory, type another directory name.
- *Location for **S**hared Indexes.* This text box does not list a directory by default. Since this directory contains shared files, it is probably located on a network drive. Ask your system administrator for the correct drive and directory to use here.
- *Expand **B**rowse Dialog.* When you create a QuickFinder Index, a Browse option is available on the Create Index dialog box. This option expands the Create Index dialog box to include a file list, directory list, and drive list. If you check this option, the Create Index dialog box is expanded, without your having to select Browse.
- *E**x**clude Files.* Certain files should be excluded from your indexes because they function as program files. By default, WordPerfect has excluded files with the EXE, COM, and DLL extensions. You can add to the list if necessary by typing in additional file extensions after these existing ones. Make sure you separate each entry with a comma and a space, and that you include the asterisk and the period before the extension. For example, you might add ***.BAT** to the list so you don't include DOS batch files in your indexes.
- ***W**ordPerfect Documents Only.* Check this box if you want to index WordPerfect 5.1/5.2/6.0/6.1 documents only.
- *Index **C**ontains.* This pop-up list controls what information about the file is indexed. You can choose **E**ntire document (all text and substructures) or Entire **D**ocument - Summary Fields (includes the document summary information). You can also choose to index **T**ext Only, **S**ummary Fields Only, or **F**ilename Only.
- *In**d**ex Level.* The level selected when the index is created defines the setting for the **C**loseness of Words option when a search for multiple words is performed. If, for example, you select an index level of Paragraph, WordPerfect flags only the files in which the words are found in the same paragraph.
- ***I**nclude Numbers in Index.* Check this box to include numbers in the index.
- ***E**xtended Characters in Unknown Formats.* This setting is Exclude by default. If necessary, you can change it to interpret the extended characters as ASCII (DOS standard) or ANSI (Windows standard).

Creating an Index

If you have been organizing your files into directories and subdirectories, your files are already grouped together by subject and are quite easy to index. You might, for example, want to index your archive files for the month of July before taking them off the system. Follow these steps to create an index for the archive files:

1. From the QuickFinder File Indexer dialog box, choose C**r**eate. The Create Index Name dialog box appears.

2. Type a descriptive name for the index file in the **N**ame text box. For this example, type **July Archive Files**. Choose OK or press Enter. The Create Index dialog box appears.

3. You need to tell WordPerfect which directories (and files) to include in the index. In the Add **D**irectory (and File Pattern) text box, type the full path name of the directory you want to include. For this example, type **C:\ARCHIVE**. Choose **A**dd; or press Enter to add the directory to the Directories **t**o Index window (see fig. 28.26).

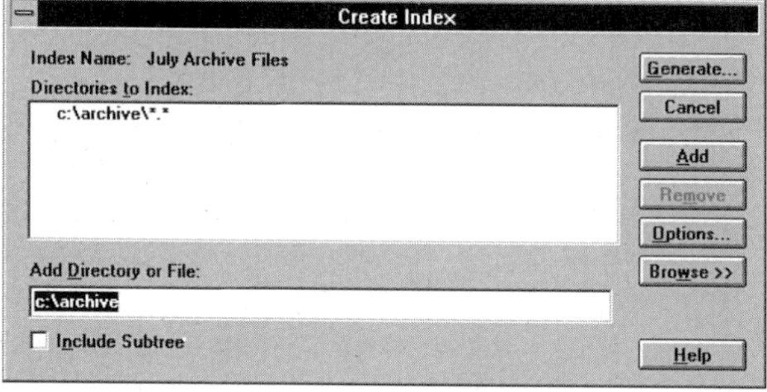

Fig. 28.26
The Create Index dialog box with the information to create the archive file index.

> **Note**
>
> If the directory you are indexing contains subdirectories, you can automatically include the files in the subtree by selecting the I**n**clude Subtree option in the Create Index dialog box.

4. If necessary, add additional directories to the Directories **t**o Index list.

5. If necessary, use Bro**w**se to display a file, directory, and drive list from which you can select additional directories.

6. If necessary, choose **O**ptions to change the settings for the archive index file.

7. Choose **G**enerate to create the index file.

WordPerfect displays the Building Index dialog box with information on the index progress, such as what percentage of the index is complete and approximately how long the process will take.

When indexing is complete, the Index Completed message box appears showing the number of files indexed and the time it took to complete the index process. Choose OK to clear the message and add the new index to the list of QuickFinder indexes.

If you want to add more indexes right now, repeat steps 1 through 7 in this section. If you want to use the new index file with QuickFinder right away, close the QuickFinder File Indexer dialog box, and then choose Inde**x**er from the QuickFinder dialog box. Otherwise, choose Close twice to return to the Open File dialog box (or Windows if you were running the QuickFinder File Indexer outside of WordPerfect).

Editing QuickFinder Indexes

As you add new files and directories to your system, you may want to edit your existing QuickFinder indexes to add these new directories or remove the directories that are no longer applicable.

Note

If you want to add a new QuickFinder index file for a new project, follow the steps in the earlier section "Creating QuickFinder Indexes."

To edit an existing QuickFinder index file, choose Inde**x**er from the QuickFinder dialog box or start QuickFinder File Indexer from the Windows Program Manager. Select the index file in the Index **N**ames window, and choose **E**dit. Add or remove directories in the Directories **t**o Index window. Choose **G**enerate when you finish making the changes. WordPerfect prompts you with an Index Method dialog box. Choose **U**pdate Index With New or Modified Files or **I**ndex All Files to add only those files that have changed since the last index.

Updating QuickFinder Index Files

Searching for files with QuickFinder indexes can be effective only if you maintain current indexes. Indexes can quickly become outdated as documents are added and deleted from the directories.

To update a QuickFinder index file, choose Inde**x**er from the QuickFinder dialog box or choose QuickFinder File Indexer from the Windows Program Manager. Highlight the index file in the Index Names window, and choose

Generate. WordPerfect prompts you with an Index Method dialog box. Choose **U**pdate Index with New or Modified Files or **I**ndex All Files. If you have deleted files or directories in the index, you should index all files.

Importing QuickFinder Index Files

You can use index files created by another WordPerfect 6.1 user by importing the index file. To import another user's index file, choose **O**ptions on the QuickFinder File Indexer dialog box, and then choose Imp**o**rt. Either type in the name of the index file or use the Drive, Directories, or QuickList lists to locate the file.

Note

You will be able to use an imported index file for searching purposes only; you cannot make any changes to this index file.

Working with QuickFinder Index Files

Existing index files can be renamed, moved, and deleted. Select the index file, and then choose **D**elete, **R**ename, or **M**ove from the **O**ptions pull-down list in the QuickFinder File Indexer dialog box.

Using Kickoff To Update QuickFinder Indexes

WordPerfect includes a program called Kickoff to automate the process of updating the index files. Although Kickoff can be used to start an event or to open a file at a specified time and repeat interval, this discussion is limited to using Kickoff to automatically update the QuickFinder Index Files.

Kickoff is a separate program that you start from the Windows Program Manager. Each task that you want accomplished is considered to be an *event* in Kickoff. You can add and remove events as necessary.

The Kickoff program must be running to launch your events. You will probably want to start Kickoff at the beginning of the day and keep it minimized and out of the way. Alternatively, you could add Kickoff to the Startup group in Windows so that it is always started with Windows. The Kickoff Options menu has a selection to start Kickoff minimized, so you don't have to minimize it each time.

Follow these steps to set up the Kickoff program to update the QuickFinder index files automatically at regular intervals:

1. Double-click the Kickoff icon in the WPWin 6.1 program group. The Kickoff dialog box appears.

2. Choose **A**dd. The Edit/Add dialog box appears (see fig. 28.27).

Fig. 28.27
You use the Edit/Add dialog box to create and edit Kickoff events.

The following table describes several startup options that can be used to run the QuickFinder File Indexer.

Startup Option	Purpose
/ra	Rebuilds all indexes listed in the QuickFinder Index Names list box.
/r-[*index name*]	Rebuilds only the specified index file. Index names must be separated by a comma and a space.
/ia	Updates all the indexes listed in the QuickFinder Index Names list box with new or modified files.
/i-[*index name*]	Rebuilds the specified index with new or modified files. Index names must be separated by a comma and a space.

3. Choose **C**ommand Line and type the following:
C:\OFFICE\SHARED\WPC20\QFWIN20.EXE /RA
This tells Kickoff to run the QuickFinder File Indexer program and rebuild all the indexes.

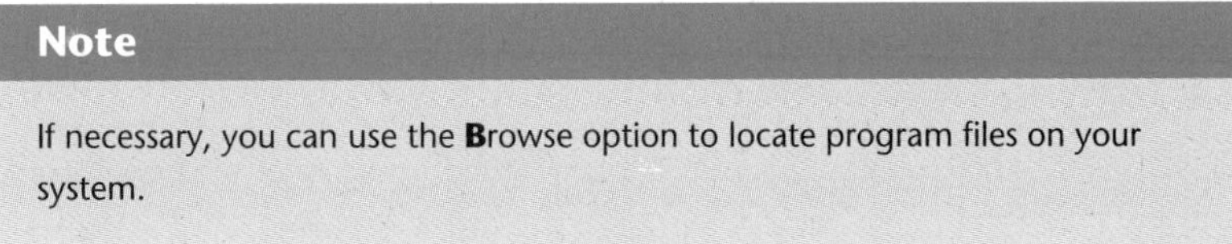

Note

If necessary, you can use the **B**rowse option to locate program files on your system.

4. The current date and time are already inserted in the Start Time section. If necessary, choose **D**ate and/or **T**ime and make adjustments. Be sure you verify the **A**M or **P**M setting.

5. Choose Da**y**s in the Repeat Interval section and type the number of days to wait before repeating the event. For this example, type **3** to set the interval to three days.

6. If necessary, choose Hrs:**M**ins and type the number of hours and minutes to wait before repeating the event.

> **Note**
>
> Make sure the D**i**sable check box is not checked before choosing OK in the Edit/Add dialog box. If D**i**sable is checked, the launching of the event is disabled.

7. If you check the **R**un Minimized check box, the specified program or event is reduced to an icon upon startup from Program Manager.

Kickoff adds the new event to the list in the Events window. In the Selected Event's information section, Kickoff displays the status of the event and the date/time the event will be launched (see fig. 28.28).

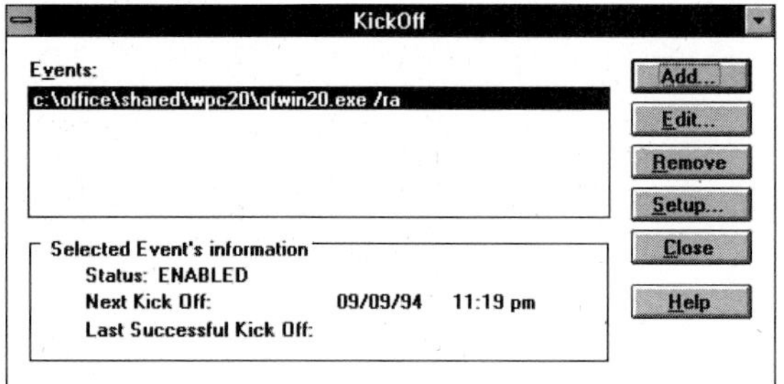

Fig. 28.28
The Kickoff dialog box with an event to automatically update the Quick-Finder Index files.

From Here...

In this chapter, you learned procedures for organizing and managing your files. You learned to use the Options menu to move, copy, rename, print, and delete files, as well as to create, rename, and remove directories. You also learned how to use the Setup menu to customize the file and directory lists.

You learned how to find files by searching for file names or words and phrases contained in those files with the QuickFinder feature. You also learned how to create and use QuickList entries to identify and change directories quickly. Finally, you learned how to create and maintain QuickFinder File Indexes to speed up file searches.

- Chapter 2, "Creating and Saving a Document." This chapter covers creating, printing and saving a new document to disk as well as moving around in the document.
- Chapter 3, "Retrieving and Editing Documents." You learn how to open existing files that have been saved to disk, insert and delete text and how to work with WordPerfect codes.
- Chapter 5, "Formatting Pages and Documents." This chapter covers the features for formatting pages and entire documents.
- Chapter 9, "Customizing WordPerfect." This chapter shows you how to customize the WordPerfect operating environment to suit your specific needs.

Chapter 29

Advanced Macro Techniques

by Gordon McComb

WordPerfect for Windows macro feature goes far beyond recording the keys you press and the commands you choose. You can write macros from scratch, using a sophisticated and powerful macro language. This language is similar to other computer programming languages such as BASIC or Pascal, except that the macro programs you write are designed to be used solely in WordPerfect.

These and other macros are detailed in this chapter. Along with these macros, you learn the basics of WordPerfect's powerful macro programming language. You learn about several dozen of the most important programming commands and how to use them to construct your own sophisticated macros. You also learn how to open and print macros for future reference.

In this chapter, you learn how to:

- Store macros for easier access
- Use macros in templates
- Print and edit macros
- Use the Macro Feature Bar
- Create advanced macros with the macro programming language
- Use macro variables
- Create a macro that automatically formats a fax cover sheet, prompting you for the information needed to fill out the sheet

Understanding Macro Storage

In Chapter 12, "Creating Macros," you learned that macros can be stored either inside a template or as a separate file. When stored inside a template, the macro becomes part of the template file. The commands that make up the macro are placed in a special area of the template so that you can access the macro while you are using the template.

Macros that are separate files are really WordPerfect documents. Because of this, you can readily open and edit your macro files.

Whether your macros are embedded in a template or recorded as a stand-alone file, you do not need a separate "macro editor" facility. This is different from the macro feature in earlier versions of WordPerfect for DOS, in which macros are contained in their own special file format. In these earlier versions, you had to use a special editing window to write and edit macros.

Opening a Macro Stored in a Template

To open a macro stored in a template document (to view, edit, or print it), follow these steps:

1. Choose **T**ools, Tem**p**late Macro, **E**dit.
2. Type the name of the macro you want to open.
3. Choose **L**ocation.
4. Choose the location of the template, either **C**urrent or **D**efault; then choose OK. (If the template that contains the macro is not listed, you need to create a new document based on the template before following these steps.)
5. WordPerfect displays the macros contained in the template. Select the template you want, and choose **E**dit. The macro is opened.

Opening a Macro File

To open a stand-alone macro file (to view, edit, or print it), follow these steps:

1. Choose **F**ile, **O**pen; or press Ctrl+O. The File Open dialog box appears.
2. Type the name and path of the macro file you want to open.
3. Choose OK or press Enter.

With either method, WordPerfect opens the macro file and displays it in the document window (see fig. 29.1). The strange words you see are part of WordPerfect's macro programming language.

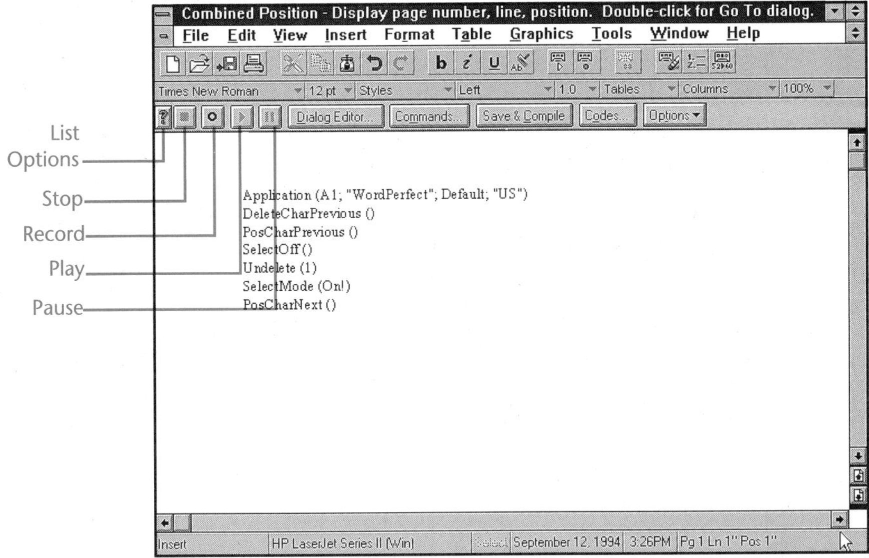

Fig. 29.1
Macros are stored in standard Word-Perfect for Windows documents or within templates.

Don't worry if the language looks complex or indecipherable. The language actually is straightforward and logical. After a time, you will learn it and will be able to speak it fluently. The remainder of this chapter is devoted to helping you understand the language.

Printing a Macro File

Macros can be printed as you would print any WordPerfect document. This lets you create a "hard copy" version for future reference. Printing also is handy when you are working with longer macros. Putting the macro on paper enables you to trace its operation more easily and track down any problems that may occur.

> **Note**
>
> You can print a file macro directly from the Print dialog box. After displaying the Print dialog box, choose **D**ocument on Disk, then choose **P**rint. WordPerfect prompts you for the name of the file. Type the full name and include the directory path. Choose **P**rint to begin printing.

Using the Macro Feature Bar

WordPerfect for Windows includes a handy Feature Bar you can use when writing and editing macros. When you edit a macro file (choose **T**ools, **M**acro, **E**dit), the Macro Feature Bar automatically appears (refer to fig. 29.1). You can also manually display the Feature Bar by choosing **T**ools, **M**acro, **M**acro Bar.

Note

If you are editing a template macro, choose **T**ools, Tem**p**late Macro, **T**emplate Macro Bar. The Macro Bars for file macros and template macros are actually the same.

The Macro Feature Bar offers the following ten option buttons (the labels on the first five buttons are icons; the labels on the remaining buttons are text):

- *?*. Lists the available options in the Macro Feature Bar.
- *Stop*. When playing a macro, click this button to stop the macro.
- *Record*. Click this button to start recording a macro. The macro is recorded in a new document window. (*Note:* you can stop the macro only by clicking the Stop button in the Macro Feature Bar. *Use this feature with care!*)
- *Play*. Click this button to play the macro currently shown on the screen. The macro must have already been saved and compiled first. (WordPerfect must first *compile* a macro before it can be played; this step is automatic and done entirely by WordPerfect.)
- *Pause*. When playing a macro, click this button to temporarily pause the macro. This is the same as choosing **T**ools, **M**acro (or Tem**p**late Macro), Pa**u**se.
- ***D**ialog Editor*. Click this button to create or edit a dialog box.
- *Co**m**mands*. Click this button to display the WordPerfect Macro Command Inserter dialog box, which makes it easier to insert macro commands.
- *Save & **C**ompile*. Click this button to save the current macro file and compile it.

- *Codes*. Click this button to display the Codes dialog box, which allows you to insert special macro codes.
- *Options*. Click this button to choose one of four options: save as file macro, save as template macro, close macro, remove Macro Bar.

Troubleshooting

I recorded a macro that opens a dialog box and makes some changes in the box. When I look at the macro, the command for opening the dialog box isn't there.

WordPerfect records complete actions, not the separate steps it takes to perform the action. So, if you record a macro that includes opening a dialog box, what WordPerfect records is what you actually do inside the dialog box. If you like, a WordPerfect macro can open a dialog box and pause there, waiting for you to manually choose options. If you'd like to record a macro that opens a dialog box and waits, follow this procedure. First, turn on macro recording and open the dialog box. Find the check box in the upper right corner of the dialog box (the check box appears only when recording a macro), and click in it. Close the dialog box by choosing Cancel. Stop macro recording. The resulting macro includes the command to open the dialog box. When you play the macro, it stops after opening the dialog box, letting you choose the options you want yourself.

I need to save a macro in progress, but because it's not done yet, WordPerfect finds lots of syntax errors in it and fails to save the file.

As long as WordPerfect recognizes the document as a macro (it does this if the Macro Feature Bar is visible), it will attempt to compile the macro each time you save it. If there are errors in the macro, you'll get syntax errors. If you need to save the macro even though it contains errors, choose Options in the Macro Feature Bar, and choose Remove Macro Bar. Now when you save the file, WordPerfect saves it as an ordinary document and does not try to compile it first.

Introducing the WordPerfect Macro Language

Macros are composed of commands that tell WordPerfect what to do. When you record a macro, WordPerfect inserts a command for every complete action you take, such as opening a file, entering text, or deleting a paragraph. Because each step is a complete and separate action, each action is recorded in the macro as a separate command.

Recording a Sample Macro

To record a macro, follow these steps:

1. Choose **T**ools, **M**acro, **R**ecord; or press Ctrl+F10. The Record Macro dialog box appears.
2. Type **TESTMAC** and press Enter. After a few moments, the `Macro Record` prompt appears in the lower left corner of the screen.
3. Type **This is a test** and press Enter.

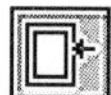

4. Choose Fo**r**mat, **M**argins; or press Ctrl+F8. The Margins dialog box appears.
5. Set the **L**eft and **R**ight margins to 0.5" and choose OK.

6. Choose Fo**r**mat, **F**ont, **B**old, and then choose OK or press Ctrl+B.
7. Type **This is bolded text** and press Enter.
8. Choose Fo**r**mat, **F**ont, **B**old, and then choose OK or press Ctrl+B.

9. Choose **T**ools, **M**acro, **R**ecord; or press Ctrl+F10. Macro recording stops.

Now look at the commands WordPerfect recorded in the macro file. Open the TESTMAC.WPM macro as detailed earlier in "Opening a Macro File." You should see the following text:

```
Application (A1; "WordPerfect"; Default; "US")
Type ("This is a test")
HardReturn ()
MarginLeft (0.5")
MarginRight (0.5")
AttributeAppearanceToggle (Bold!)
Type ("This is bolded text")
HardReturn ()
AttributeAppearanceToggle (Bold!)
```

These nine lines make up the entire TESTMAC macro.

Examining the TESTMAC Macro

The following list examines the commands WordPerfect recorded in the TESTMAC macro. Some commands are followed by a set of parentheses and text inside the parentheses. This is important, as you learn later in the chapter.

- `Application (A1;"WordPerfect"; Default;"US")`. The Application command is always inserted at the beginning of recorded macros. It provides specifics on how to translate the macro commands.

- `Type("This is a test")`. This command inserts the text `This is a test` at the current cursor position. You use the Type command whenever you want a macro to insert text.

- `HardReturn()`. This command enters a hard return at the current cursor position. You use the HardReturn( ) command (notice the open and close parentheses) whenever you want to start a new line.

- `MarginLeft(MarginWidth:0.5")` and `MarginRight(MarginWidth:0.5")`. These commands set the left and right margins to one-half inch. Notice that there are two margin commands: one for the left margin, and one for the right margin.

- `AttributeAppearanceToggle(Bold!)`. This command toggles bold on or off, depending on the previous state. As bold was off, the command turns bold on.

- `Type("This is bolded text")`. Another Type command; this one prints the text `This is bolded text`. A HardReturn( ) command follows.

- `AttributeAppearanceToggle(Bold!)`. As with the previous AttributeAppearanceToggle command, this command turns bold on and off (in this case off, because bold was previously on).

Note

Most commands are fairly self-explanatory, but they may appear more cryptic in some macros you record. As long as you remember what you did to record the action, you can readily decipher the meaning of most macro commands. Remember this when writing your own macros. If you are not sure what command to use, simply record the action you want your macro to take. When you are done, open the file and look at the macro command WordPerfect recorded for you.

Using Two Kinds of Commands

On a broad scale, WordPerfect for Windows uses two types of macro commands: product function and programming.

- *Product function* commands control specific features of WordPerfect—therefore, the name *product function*. When you type on the keyboard to enter text, WordPerfect inserts a Type command. When you change the margins of a document, WordPerfect inserts a Margin command.

By convention, product function commands generally appear in mixed case (upper- and lowercase). The majority of WordPerfect's macro commands are the product function type.

- *Programming* commands work independently of any feature found in WordPerfect and are designed to add intelligence and control to your macros. By convention, programming commands generally appear in all uppercase.

From an operational standpoint, you don't have to concern yourself much with the difference between product function commands and programming commands. In fact, the remainder of this chapter refers to both as *commands*.

All macro commands are described in the Macros on-line help. Choose **H**elp, **M**acros to view Macros help. Choose the Macro Commands Index keyword to see an alphabetized list of the macro commands.

Comparing Product Commands versus the WordPerfect 5.1 Macro Model

As mentioned in the earlier section "Understanding Macro Storage," macros in earlier versions of WordPerfect for DOS (such as Versions 5.0 and 5.1) are recorded differently than in WordPerfect 6.1 for Windows.

In WordPerfect 5.1 for DOS, for example, your actions were recorded as keystrokes. The combination of the keystrokes determines the overall action, whether entering text into the document, setting margins, and so on.

In WordPerfect 5.1 for DOS, the TESTMAC macro looks like the following:

```
{DISPLAY OFF}
This is a test{Enter}
{Format}170.5"{Enter}
0.5"{Enter}
{Enter}
{Enter}
{Bold}This is bolded text{Bold}
```

The problem with recording macros as a series of keystrokes is that they are tied to the keyboard. What if you are using a mouse or some other input device? Because you are not always clear what they do, keystroke macros are harder to maintain. You have to be very familiar with WordPerfect, for example, to know that `{Format}170.5"` means "change the left margin to half an inch." Compare the readability of the WordPerfect 6.1 for Windows macro with its clunky 5.1 counterpart.

Notice, too, that 5.1 commands are context-sensitive, making it harder to determine exactly what the macro is doing. For example, which `{Enter}` codes are used to navigate through menus, and which are used to insert hard returns in the document?

Finally, keystroke macros are highly dependent on WordPerfect's interface. During the lifetime of WordPerfect 5.1 for DOS, WordPerfect Corporation wanted to add a variety of features to the program. Doing so, however, would have "broken" a large number of macros—including many shipped with the product! This is no longer a problem in WordPerfect 6.1 for Windows.

If you are familiar with WordPerfect 5.1 for DOS macros, you will need a period of adjustment to become familiar with the way macros work in WordPerfect 6.1 for Windows. If you approach the change in macro languages with an open mind, you will find that the new way has great potential.

However, if you have some experience in the macro language of WordPerfect 6 for DOS, you will find striking similarities between it and the language used in WordPerfect for Windows. The languages are similar, but not identical. After you learn one language, you should have no trouble mastering the other.

Understanding the Syntax of Macro Commands

Macro commands follow a predictable format, called *syntax*. If you use the wrong syntax, WordPerfect refuses to play the macro because it doesn't understand what you are trying to do. This is similar to trying to speak in a foreign language and mixing up verbs, nouns, and other parts of speech.

The syntax of WordPerfect's macro commands is relatively simple and follows certain conventions:

- All commands are one word, with no spacing and no special characters. For example, AttributeAppearanceToggle is allowed, but Attribute Appearance Toggle is not.
- The capitalization of the command does not make a difference. The consistent capitalization is for your benefit. Type is the same as type, TYPE, TyPe, and all other variations.

- Proper spelling is an absolute must. WordPerfect for Windows doesn't know what you mean if you use the command HardRet rather than HardReturn. Spelling mistakes such as this cause WordPerfect to display a Syntax Error message when the macro is compiled (see fig. 29.2). This compiling stage is usually performed immediately before the macro is played the first time after it was written or edited.

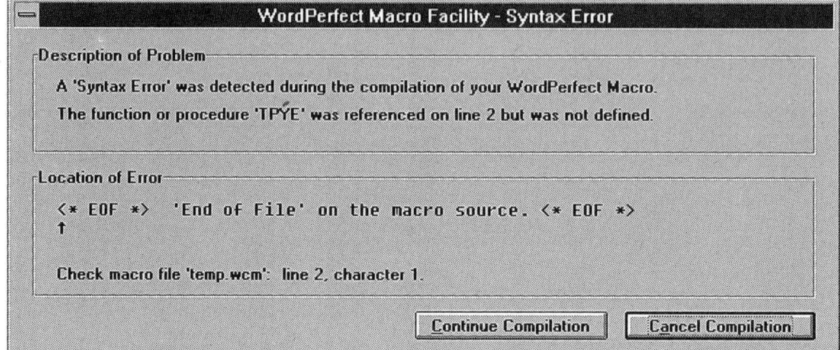

Fig. 29.2 WordPerfect for Windows warns you when you make a mistake in your macro. You must fix the mistake before the macro will play.

- Many commands consist of two parts: the command name and one or more *parameters*. The parameters, which tell WordPerfect exactly what you want to do with the command, are always enclosed in a pair of parentheses. The Type command, for example, uses one parameter—the text you want to type, such as `Type ("I am Text")`. This text is enclosed in double quotation marks.

- Some commands need two or more parameters. The parameters are separated from one another with a semicolon (;). The GETSTRING command, for example, uses four parameters, which look like this:

```
GETSTRING (Response;"This is the message";"Title";30)
```

- WordPerfect for Windows doesn't care about spaces between the command name, the parentheses, and the semicolon characters.

- Not all commands use parameters. With these, the parentheses are not absolutely required, but are highly recommended. HardReturn( ) and HardReturn do the same thing.

The *parameter name* is optional when writing your own macros.

Don't worry about remembering all these syntactical rules. The more you work with WordPerfect advanced macros, the more the special grammar of the macro commands becomes second nature to you.

Getting To Know the WordPerfect Macro Language

Although WordPerfect's macro language contains over 2,000 commands, most macros consist of the same small handful. This section details this core group of macro commands and how they are used.

Understanding Variables

Many macro commands use a *variable*. A variable is a special place that holds information in your computer's memory (see fig. 29.3). This information may change each time the macro is run. Some commands, such as GETSTRING and MENULIST, fill a variable so that its contents can be used elsewhere in the macro. Other commands, such as IF, CASE, Type, and several others mentioned in this chapter, peek inside the variable and use whatever information it contains.

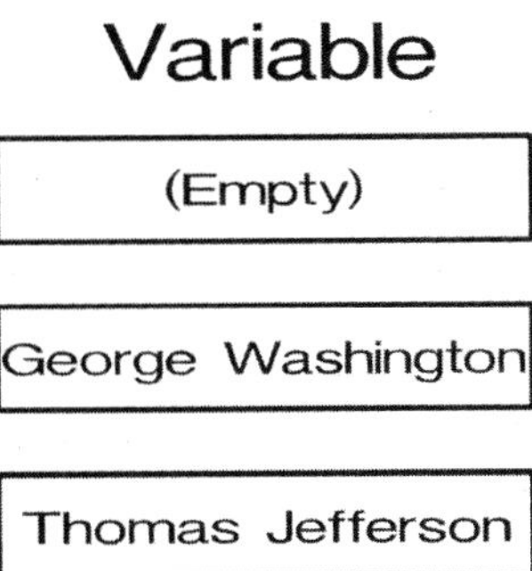

Fig. 29.3
Variables contain information that can vary each time the macro is played.

Variables are useful because they enable you to store information once and then use it many times in a macro. You can ask the user to enter his or her name, for example, and store the response in a variable whose contents can be reused many times during the macro.

Keep the following points in mind when using WordPerfect macro variables:

- Variables are identified by name, and you get to choose the name. You can have as many variables in a macro as you want—until WordPerfect runs out of memory and cannot store any more.

- You can use almost any word for a variable name, up to the maximum of 30 characters.

- Avoid variable names that conflict with existing macro commands. Don't use HardReturn as a variable name, for example, or WordPerfect could become confused.
- Variable names contain numbers and letters but cannot start with a number. Few special characters are allowed in variable names, except the underscore. You can use the underscore to break up a long variable name made up of several words—for example, This_Is_My_Variable. For ease of use, choose short, descriptive words for variable names.
- The contents of variables are erased when the macro ends.

System Variables

Asking for the user's name with a GETSTRING command is one way to give information to a macro. Another way is to use system variables. A *system variable* tells the macro something about WordPerfect, such as the number of the current page, the name of the current document, and the absolute location of the cursor on the page.

System variables are *read-only*; you can access the information contained within them, but you cannot store any information within them—that's WordPerfect's job.

WordPerfect 6.1 for Windows offers more than 200 system variables. These variables are listed in the Macros Commands dialog box, detailed in the section "The Macro Command Inserter" later in this chapter. All system variables start with a question mark (?), as in the following list:

- *?Page.* Provides the current page number.
- *?Name.* Provides the name, if any, of the current document.
- *?BlockActive.* Indicates whether block is turned on or off. The value obtained from ?BlockActive is True if block is on and False if block is off.
- *?DocBlank.* Indicates whether the current document is blank. As with ?BlockActive, the value obtained from ?DocBlank is False or True: False if the document is not blank; True if the document is blank.

As you can see in the preceding example, two general types of information are provided by system variables: actual values (?Page, ?Name) and the "logical" states True and False.

The large number of system variables makes it impossible to list all of them here. To learn more about WordPerfect's system variables and how they are used in macros, see the System Variables entry in the Macros on-line help. Choose **H**elp, **M**acros; then choose System Variable Index.

Commands That Ask for User Input

One common requirement of an advanced macro is that it interact with the user. This interaction is usually in the form of a dialog box or message prompt. WordPerfect provides several user input commands. The most common commands are GETSTRING and MENULIST.

Both commands display a message and save the user's response inside a variable. See the sections "Understanding Variables" and "System Variables" earlier in this chapter for more information on variables.

The GETSTRING Command

When the macro is run, the GETSTRING command displays a WPWin dialog box, which includes a prompt and an entry blank for text (see fig. 29.4). What the user types goes into the entry blank. The user's response is stored in a variable for later use. The following example displays a GETSTRING dialog box:

```
GETSTRING(Response;"Type your name";"WPWin";30)
```

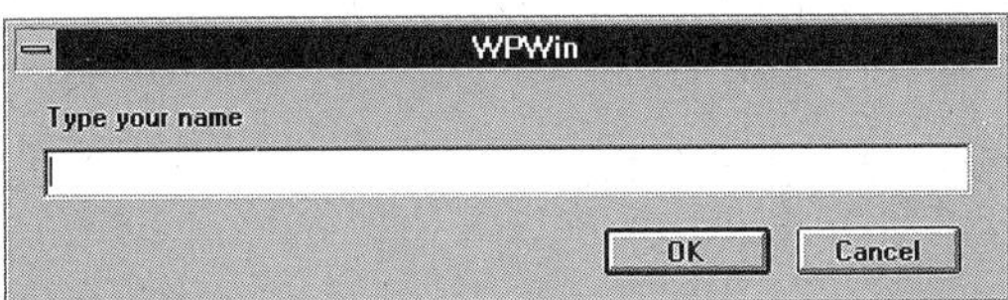

Fig. 29.4
The GETSTRING command displays a dialog box where you type text in response to a message that appears in the box.

This example prompts `Type your name`. The text `WPWin` is used for the title of the dialog box; the title appears at the top of the box. In response to this box, the user types his or her name and chooses OK. This text is stored in a variable named Response, which can then be used as the parameter in a Type command like:

```
Type (Response)
```

The last parameter in the GETSTRING command limits the length of the response to 30 characters. This parameter is optional. If you leave it out, WordPerfect limits the entry to 128 characters.

Response appears without quotation marks in the Type command. You are interested in the *contents* of the Response variable, so don't put the variable name Response in quotations.

The MENULIST Command

You use the MENULIST command to display a menu of choices. The menu appears in a pop-up dialog box and includes an OK button and a Cancel button. When you select an item from the menu, the number of that item is stored in a variable. Other commands in your macro—usually an IF command or a CASE command—determine the number in the variable and perform some specific action. See the next section, "Commands That Make Decisions," for more information on IF and CASE.

The syntax for MENULIST is somewhat complex because it has many parts. Some of its parameters are optional, meaning that you can leave them out if you don't want to use them. At a minimum, MENULIST needs you to fill in two items: the name of the variable that will hold the user's response and the text for one or more menu items, as in the following example:

```
MENULIST (Response; {"First Item";"Second Item";"Third Item"})
```

Response is the name of the variable that contains the number of the user's choice. The text for the three menu items is enclosed in quotation marks and is separated by semicolons. All three items are placed inside a pair of curly braces. Figure 29.5 shows how WordPerfect displays the MENULIST dialog box.

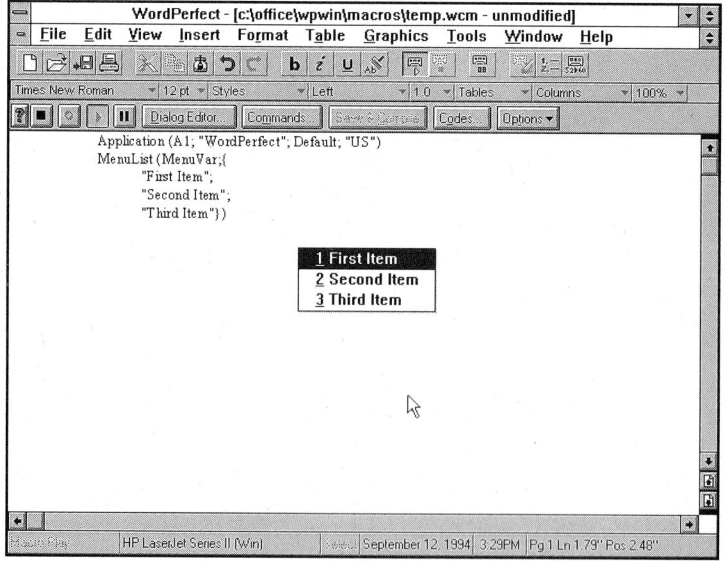

Fig. 29.5
The MENULIST command displays one or more options you can choose.

You can add more items inside the braces, up to a practical maximum of nine items. The items are automatically numbered 1 through 9. When the MENULIST dialog box is displayed, select any item, and the number of the item is stored in the Response variable. Pick the fourth item, for example, and the Response variable contains a number 4.

Tip
The MENULIST dialog box lets the user skip making a choice by choosing Cancel. In this case, Response contains the value –1.

You can use three additional parameters with the MENULIST command: the title of the MENULIST dialog box, the horizontal position of the box, and the vertical position of the box. See the MENULIST entry in the on-line help for more information on these additional parameters.

Commands That Make Decisions

You can make your macros "intelligent" by using commands that make decisions. Decision-making commands typically are used with user input commands, such as GETSTRING and MENULIST. Depending on the response from the user, the macro does either one thing or another. WordPerfect offers two powerful decision-making commands: IF and CASE.

The IF Command

The IF command is familiar if you have any experience with a programming language; it is found in all modern computer languages. The IF command determines whether a statement is true or false, which in turn enables your macros to make decisions. A typical IF statement tests whether one value is equal to another value, as in the following example:

```
IF (1=1)
```

The result of this statement is true: 1 equals 1. In a real-life macro, the IF statement contains one or more variables. Your macro may compare one variable against another, or it may compare a variable against a known value, as follows:

```
IF (Response=1)
```

Response is the name of a variable previously created and filled with the MENULIST command (see the earlier section "The MENULIST Command" for more information). This variable contains a number, and the IF statement tests whether that number is 1. If the number in Response is 1, then the IF statement is true. If the number in Response is something else, then the IF statement is false.

The IF command is never used by itself; it is always used with a matching ENDIF command. Commands between the IF and ENDIF commands are part of the IF structure—things for the macro to do if the IF statement is true.

See the following example:

```
IF (Response=1)
     Type ({"True"})
ENDIF
```

If Response is equal to 1, the macro types `True`; otherwise, the macro skips to the ENDIF command and performs any commands following it.

Note

Try to get into the habit of formatting the various parts of the IF structure. The indentation of the steps between the IF and ENDIF helps you visually see the relationships of all the commands and makes the macro easier to read.

The ELSE command also is used with IF and is optional. ELSE tells WordPerfect what you want the macro to do when the IF statement is false. Consider the following example:

```
IF (Response=1)
     Type ("True")
ELSE
     Type ("False")
ENDIF
```

Your macro types `True` or `False` depending on the outcome of the IF statement:

- If Response equals 1, the IF statement is true, and the macro types `True`.
- If Response does not equal 1, the IF statement is false, and the macro types `False`.

The equal sign (=) is an *operator*, which tells WordPerfect how you want the values in the IF statement evaluated. The = sign is the most common operator, but WordPerfect supports several other types. The most useful operators are shown in table 29.1.

Table 29.1 IF Statement Operators

Operator	Use	Example
=	Equals	Response=1
<>	Not equal to	Response<>1
<=	Less than or equal to	Response<=1
>=	Greater than or equal to	Response>=1

Note

You are not limited to just one command for the true and false parts of an IF structure; you can include as many commands as you need. The following macro, for example, beeps the computer's speaker and types a line of text if the IF expression is false. When the IF expression is true, the macro types several lines of text, with each line separated by a hard return.

```
IF (Response=1)
     Type ("This IF statement")
    HardReturn()
    Type ("Turned out to be true")
ELSE
     BEEP
    Type ("This IF statement turned out to be false")
ENDIF
```

The SWITCH Command

As you read in the preceding section, the IF command is used to determine whether a statement is true or false. If the statement is true, the macro does one thing; if the statement is false, the macro does another. The IF statement is limited to "either/or" tests. This is fine for most types of decision-making, but not all.

The SWITCH command does a job similar to the IF command, but it lets you compare a value against any number of possibilities. SWITCH also lets you define an action if the value doesn't match any of the possibilities. You are not limited to just two outcomes. With SWITCH, you can specify a different outcome for each possible value. Because of its flexibility in determining how the macro should respond depending on the test value, SWITCH is ideal for use with the MENULIST command, described in the earlier section "The MENULIST Command."

Like IF, the SWITCH command is never used by itself. SWITCH is always used with an ENDSWITCH command to mark the end of the SWITCH structure, and it's always used with at least one CASEOF command. You use a separate CASEOF command for every possible value you want to check for. The following example uses the SWITCH and CASEOF commands:

```
SWITCH (Response)
     CASEOF 1:   Type ("Response is 1")
     CASEOF 2:   Type ("Response is 2")
     CASEOF 3:   Type ("Response is 3")
ENDSWITCH
```

In this example, WordPerfect types `"Response is x"` (*x* is a number from 1 to 3), depending on the number in the Response variable.

To use SWITCH, follow these rules:

- Place the reference value (usually a variable) in parentheses after the SWITCH command. In the example, the reference value is a variable named Response.
- Place each test value after the CASEOF command, and follow it with a colon. The example has three test values: 1, 2, and 3.
- Following the CASEOF command, include the command(s) you want executed if the test value matches the reference value.
- You are not limited to just one command after each CASEOF, as shown in the preceding example. You can add any number of additional commands as needed. To make reading the macro easier, place each command on a line of its own.
- Place the ENDSWITCH command after the last CASEOF.

A handy but optional command you can use with SWITCH is the DEFAULT command. DEFAULT tells WordPerfect what command(s) you want executed if no test values match the reference value. Include the DEFAULT command after the last CASEOF and before the ENDCASE, as follows:

```
SWITCH (Response)
     CASEOF 1:   Type ("Response is 1")
     CASEOF 2:   Type ("Response is 2")
     CASEOF 3:   Type ("Response is 3")
     DEFAULT:    Type ("Response not 1, 2, or 3")
ENDSWITCH
```

The colon after the DEFAULT command is required.

Commands That Control the Flow of a Macro

The simplest macros start at the beginning and proceed to the end. All recorded macros work this way. In more advanced macros that you write yourself, particularly those that use the IF and CASE decision-making commands, you may want to redirect the flow of your macro so that WordPerfect executes different parts of it at different times.

WordPerfect provides several useful commands to control the flow of the macro. You can start at point A, then jump to a different part of the macro, depending on what you want the macro to do. The flow control commands can also be used to streamline the design of your macro. You can, for example, use the CALL command, detailed in a later section "The CALL Command," to repeat a set of commands two or more times.

Note

WordPerfect also supports the CASE command, which performs a similar job as SWITCH. The CASE command isn't as versatile and is mainly provided for compatibility with macros created with earlier versions of WordPerfect for Windows. See the Macros on-line help for more information on the CASE command.

Caution

When using the flow control commands, you must be careful that you don't create *spaghetti code*—macros that jump all over the place. Careless use of the flow control commands can make your macros harder to write and harder to fix if something goes wrong.

The LABEL Command

The LABEL command is used with the CALL and GO commands. The LABEL command specifies a certain spot in the macro—sort of like a street address—where you want the macro to divert control. The LABEL command uses one parameter, the label name, which optionally ends with an @ symbol. The name is your choice and can be up to 30 characters long (don't use spaces). The following example uses the LABEL command:

```
LABEL (MyLabel@)
```

The label name is MyLabel@. You now can use the CALL or GO commands to change the flow of the macro to this label.

Tip

Label names can be used only once in your macro. If you try to create two labels with the same name, WordPerfect displays an error message.

The CALL Command

The CALL command is used to branch temporarily to a different part of the macro, usually to perform some set of commands. Programmers refer to this as "branching to a subroutine." A *subroutine* is any self-contained group of commands. The start of the subroutine is identified with a LABEL command. The LABEL command tells WordPerfect exactly where in the macro you want to jump.

The CALL command uses one parameter, the name of the label you want to jump to, as follows:

Tip
The LABEL (MyLabel@) can be anywhere in the macro. It can be before or after the CALL command, but by convention, subroutines are usually placed toward the end of a macro.

```
CALL (MyLabel@)
```

Elsewhere in your macro, you write the following:

```
LABEL (MyLabel@)
```

The RETURN Command

WordPerfect needs to be told when a subroutine ends. For this you use the RETURN command. You place the RETURN command after the last command in the subroutine. When WordPerfect encounters the RETURN command, it returns execution to the spot immediately after the CALL command (see fig. 29.6).

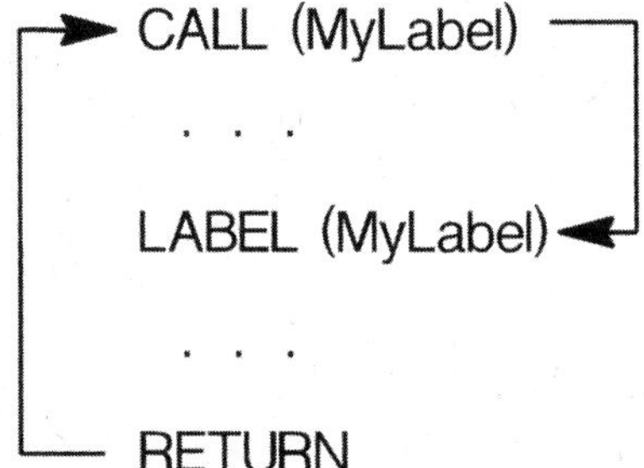

Fig. 29.6
The CALL, LABEL, and RETURN commands work together to precisely control the flow of macro execution.

Consider the following example:

```
CALL (MyLabel@)
Type ("I'm back from the subroutine")
HardReturn()
LABEL (MyLabel@)
Type ("This is the MyLabel subroutine")
HardReturn()
RETURN
```

In this example, WordPerfect calls the MyLabel@ subroutine. This subroutine types a line of text, `"This is the MyLabel subroutine"`. The RETURN command that follows tells WordPerfect to go back to the point immediately after the CALL command. The macro then types another line of text, `I'm back from the subroutine`.

The QUIT Command

If you try the preceding example, you find that WordPerfect types `This is the MyLabel subroutine` twice:

```
This is the MyLabel subroutine

I'm back from the subroutine

This is the MyLabel subroutine
```

After calling the MyLabel@ subroutine and printing the first two lines of text, WordPerfect continues the macro to the end. It encounters the LABEL(MyLabel@) command, which it ignores, and types `This is the MyLabel subroutine` again. When it reaches the RETURN command, WordPerfect stops the macro because there is no CALL to return to.

Although some macros are written so that a called subroutine is repeated before the macro ends, the usual requirement is that the macro stops before reaching any subroutines. Your macro may contain several subroutines, for example, but only one is executed whenever the macro runs. If you don't stop the macro before it reaches the subroutines, WordPerfect may erroneously execute the commands in the wrong subroutine.

Use the QUIT command whenever you want to stop the macro before it reaches the last command in the macro. The following applies the QUIT command, using the preceding example:

```
CALL (MyLabel@)
   Type ("I'm back from the subroutine")
   HardReturn()
   QUIT
   LABEL (MyLabel@)
   Type ("This is the MyLabel subroutine")
   HardReturn()
RETURN
```

This time, the macro types each line only once. The QUIT command ends the macro before it has a chance to continue through the LABEL command.

The GO Command

The GO command is similar to the CALL command in that you use it to redirect WordPerfect to a LABEL elsewhere in the macro. The difference between GO and CALL is that WordPerfect doesn't automatically return to the GO command after finishing the subroutine. With GO, you have to tell WordPerfect where you want to go next. The following example uses two GO commands and two LABEL commands:

```
GO (MyLabel@)
LABEL (ReturnToThisSpot)
Type ({"I'm back from the subroutine"})
HardReturn()
QUIT
LABEL (MyLabel@)
Type ({"This is the MyLabel subroutine"})
HardReturn()
GO (ReturnToThisSpot@)
```

The first GO command tells WordPerfect to branch to the MyLabel@ subroutine. At the end of the subroutine is yet another GO command, which redirects the macro back to a label called ReturnToThisSpot@.

Although the GO command has its use, you can see how it can lead to confusing and badly written macros, as control jumps from one spot to the other. Whenever possible, use the CALL command because it includes a mechanism for automatically returning control of the macro when the subroutine is over.

Commands That Run Other Macros

Most of the time you run macros by telling WordPerfect which macro to play. To select a macro, you first choose **T**ools, **M**acros, **P**lay; or press Alt+F10. Then you type the name of the macro and choose OK. In addition to this manual method of playing macros, one WordPerfect macro can also play another.

This is handy if you have two separate macros and each macro does a specific task. One macro may start a letter, and the other may type some standard paragraph of text. By linking the two macros you can have WordPerfect run them both, even though you play just one macro. WordPerfect 6.1 for Windows supports two commands that run other macros: CHAIN and RUN.

The CHAIN Command

The CHAIN command runs a second macro when the first macro is finished. The CHAIN command should be the last command in the first macro. Include the name of the macro as the parameter for the CHAIN command, as in the following example:

```
CHAIN ("mymacro.wcm")
```

This plays the macro MYMACRO.WCM, which WordPerfect assumes to be in the default macros directory, as specified in the File Preferences dialog box. (If you are not sure of the default macros directory, choose **E**dit, Pr**e**ferences, **F**ile, **M**acros.) Note the quotation marks that enclose the “mymacro.wcm” macro name.

Note

If you want to CHAIN to a macro in another directory, include the full path and the macro name, as in CHAIN (“c:\newmacs\mymacro”). This plays the MYMACRO.WCM macro, which is in the C:\NEWMACS directory.

The RUN Command

Like CHAIN, the RUN command plays a second macro, but the first macro doesn't have to finish first. When WordPerfect encounters the RUN command, it pauses the first macro and plays the second macro. When the second macro is finished, WordPerfect picks up where it left off with the first macro and continues executing it.

As with the CHAIN command, you indicate the macro you want to play as the parameter of the RUN command, as follows:

```
RUN ("mymacro.wcm")
```

Tip

WordPerfect 6.1 for Windows also supports the NEST command, which does the same job as RUN. The NEST command is provided for greater compatibility with WordPerfect 6 for DOS macros.

Caution

When nesting macros, be sure the second macro (the one you nest to) does not end with a QUIT command. If it does, WordPerfect will stop all macro execution and control will not return to the first macro. If you have a nested macro that includes a QUIT command, replace it with a RETURN command.

Other Useful Commands

Several other commands commonly used in macros defy easy categorization. These commands add "comments" to your macros, control the display, pause the macro at various points, display a short message at the bottom of the screen, and sound a beep on the computer's built-in speaker.

The // (Comment) Command

The macros you write today may look like hieroglyphics tomorrow. Two months from now, you may not remember what a particular command or subroutine does in your macro. Instead, add *comments* to your macros. The comments are annotations that you provide to help you remember how your macro works. Comments also are helpful for users who are not familiar with your macro.

To add a comment to a macro, type a double slash (//); then write the text for the comment. The comment ends when you press Enter.

You can write comments of any length, from one word to complete paragraphs. You can insert comments on a separate line in your macro or after a macro command. Several examples follow:

```
// The following is the "MyLabel@" routine
LABEL (MyLabel@)
Type ("This is the MyLabel@ subroutine")
HardReturn()
RETURN  // This returns to the command that CALLed MyLabel@
```

Note

While comments can span two or more lines (as long as you don't press Enter), limiting comments to a single line is a good idea. If you must write longer comments, add the double slash at the beginning of each line, as follows:

```
// This is the first line of the comment

// and this is the second line.
```

The DISPLAY Command

Use the Display command to control how and when WordPerfect updates the screen when a macro plays. With DISPLAY turned off, WordPerfect does *not* update the screen while the macro plays. Text, graphics, tables, and other elements inserted by the macro aren't shown until the macro ends.

With DISPLAY turned on, WordPerfect updates the screen while the macro plays. If the macro types some text, for example, each character is shown as it is inserted into the document.

Macros run faster when DISPLAY is turned off. But you may prefer to leave DISPLAY on so that you can see the progress of your macro.

Caution

Don't confuse the DISPLAY command with the CLS (CLear Screen) command found in some other programming languages, such as BASIC. Unlike the CLS command, WordPerfect's DISPLAY command does not blank the screen. DISPLAY merely turns off screen updating so that typing and editing changes aren't seen while the macro runs.

The DISPLAY command is used with one argument, either On! or Off!, as follows:

```
DISPLAY (On!)   // Turns display on

DISPLAY (Off!)  // Turns display off
```

Notice the exclamation point after the words On and Off. The exclamation point tells WordPerfect you are using a built-in parameter value rather than a variable. The parameter values On! and Off! have a significant meaning to WordPerfect and are equivalent to the numbers 1 and 0, respectively. If you prefer, you can use the numbers instead of the parameter values:

```
DISPLAY (1)  // Turns display on

DISPLAY (0)  // Turns display off
```

All macros recorded by WordPerfect start with a DISPLAY(Off!) command. If you want the screen to be updated as the macro runs, either remove this command or change it to DISPLAY(On!).

You can use the DISPLAY command any number of times in a macro to control precisely when you want the screen updated and when you don't. For example, you might start with DISPLAY turned Off! as the macro creates a table. Then, midway through the macro you can turn it On! to display several lines of text that the macro inserts into the table. You can turn DISPLAY Off! again for the remainder of the macro, as it completes other formatting tasks.

Keep the following points in mind when using the DISPLAY command:

- Use the DISPLAY (On!) command before that part of the macro that contains the commands you want to show. If you want to show text being entered in the document, for example, place the DISPLAY(On!) command before the Type command, as follows:

  ```
  DISPLAY (On!)

  Type ("This text shown as it is entered")
  ```

- Similarly, use the DISPLAY (Off!) command before that part of the macro containing the commands you do not want to show, as in the following example:

  ```
  DISPLAY (Off!)

  Type ("This text is NOT shown as it is entered")
  ```

- When you use the DISPLAY(On!) command, WordPerfect displays any typing and editing the macro may have done so far.

- Use DISPLAY(On!) DISPLAY (Off!)—both commands immediately following each other—if you want to update the screen with any typing and editing the macro has done so far and then turn DISPLAY back off.

The PauseKey Command

You were introduced to the PauseKey command in Chapter 12, "Creating Macros," where you learned how to insert a PauseKey command when recording a macro. You can use the PauseKey command in any macro you write. When WordPerfect encounters the PauseKey command, it temporarily stops the macro. Macro playback doesn't resume until you press Enter. Following is an example of the PauseKey command:

```
Type ("This is the first line of text")
HardReturn()
PauseKey(Enter!)
Type ("This is the second line of text")
```

See the FAXCOVER macro later in this chapter for a practical example of how to use the PauseKey command.

The MacroStatusPrompt Command

The PauseKey command commonly is used with another handy command: MacroStatusPrompt. The MacroStatusPrompt command displays a short, one-line message in the status bar, located at the bottom of the screen. (Of course, you can use one command without the other.)

Tip
For best results, limit the MacroStatusPrompt message to no more than 40 characters. Longer messages are harder to read.

To use the MacroStatusPrompt command, indicate the text you want to show. Make sure that the text is 80 characters or less. Enclose the message in double quotation marks, as follows:

```
MacroStatusPrompt (On!; "Type your name, then press Enter.")

PauseKey(Enter!)
```

WordPerfect for Windows automatically removes the message as the macro continues or when the macro ends.

The BEEP Command

Use the BEEP command to sound a tone on the computer's speaker. A common use of the BEEP command is to call attention to the message provided in a MacroStatusPrompt command. In the following example, WordPerfect sounds the beep, displays the prompt message, then pauses the macro:

```
BEEP

MacroStatusPrompt (On!; "Type your name, then press Enter.")

PauseKey (Enter!)
```

Dialog Box Commands

WordPerfect for Windows lets you create your own macro dialog boxes that look exactly like the program's own dialog boxes. There are two ways to create dialog boxes: using the dialog box commands, and using the Dialog Editor.

- To create a dialog box with commands, use the DialogCreate command, followed by one or more commands to insert "controls" into the dialog box. The dialog box displays with the DialogDisplay command.

- To create a dialog box with the Dialog Editor, you must create the basic macro first, then save and compile it. Using the Macro Feature Bar (choose **T**ools, **M**acro, **M**acro Bar), access the Dialog Editor by clicking the **D**ialog Editor button. You then create a new dialog box and add "controls" to it.

Because there are more than a dozen dialog box commands, requirements for their use—as well as using the Dialog Editor—are too lengthy to discuss here. For more information on creating dialog boxes for your macros, see the "User-Defined Dialog Boxes" entry in Macros on-line help that accompanies WordPerfect 6.1 for Windows.

The Macro Command Inserter

WordPerfect offers a convenient way to insert programming commands as you write your macros. Choose **T**ools, **M**acro, **M**acro Bar. The Macro Feature Bar appears. Choose Co**m**mands. The WordPerfect Macro Command Inserter dialog box appears (see fig. 29.7). Highlight a command, and its syntax is shown to the right of the Commands list.

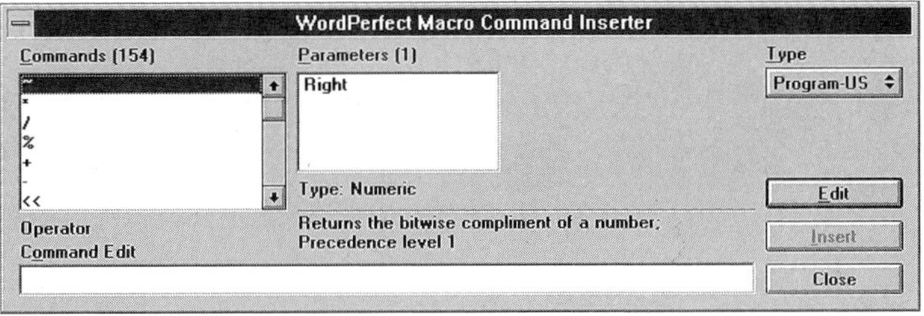

Fig. 29.7 Use the Macro Command Inserter dialog box to insert programming commands, system variables, and product function commands.

To insert a command, follow these steps:

1. Choose the command you want. You can use the keyboard or the mouse.

2. Press Enter.

3. If the command requires parameters, WordPerfect places the command name in the C**o**mmand Edit text box, where you can fill in the parameters (see fig. 29.8). Type the parameters and Choose **I**nsert. The command is inserted.

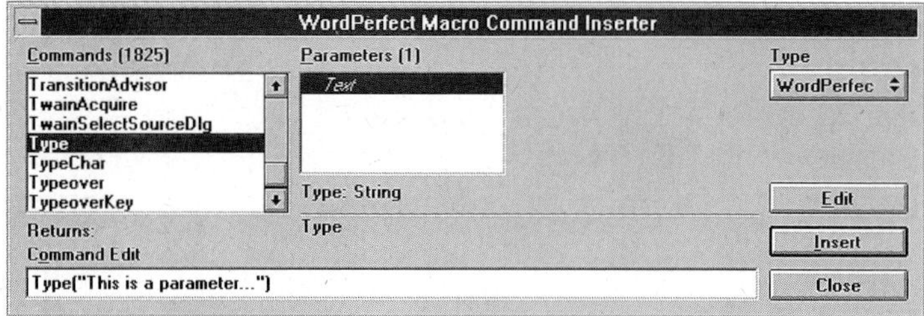

Fig. 29.8
The Macro Command Inserter dialog box helps you enter the correct parameters for each command that requires them.

Useful Product Function Commands

As you read earlier in this chapter, WordPerfect has two kinds of macro commands: programming commands and product function commands. So far, discussion has been limited to the most commonly used programming commands (exceptions include PauseKey and MacroStatusPrompt). Although more than 1,800 product function commands exist, only a handful are used regularly. A brief description of these commands follows:

Note

In addition to programming commands, the Command Inserter dialog box also lists system variables and product commands. To display the system variables and product commands, choose the **T**ype pop-up list and then choose WordPerfect. The commands in the Commands list change. System variables are listed first, followed by the product commands.

- *Close*. The Close command closes the current document window.
- *DeleteCharNext* and *DeleteCharPrevious*. These two commands delete the character (or code) to the right and left of the cursor, respectively.
- *FileNew*. The FileNew command opens a new document window.
- *FileOpenDlg*. The FileOpenDlg command displays the Open Document dialog box. When WordPerfect displays this dialog box during macro playback, it pauses the macro and waits for you to type the file name of a document to open.
- *FileSaveAsDlg*. The FileSaveAsDlg command displays the Save Document dialog box. When WordPerfect displays this dialog box during macro playback, it pauses the macro and waits for you to type the file name of the document to save.
- *HardReturn*. This command inserts a hard return in the document. It simulates pressing Enter.

- *PosCharNext* and *PosCharPrevious*. These two commands position the cursor to the right or left of the cursor, respectively. If SelectMode is on (using the SelectMode command detailed previously), these two commands are used to extend the block selection character by character.
- *SelectMode(On!)*. The SelectMode command turns block mode on and is the same as choosing **E**dit, Se**l**ect.
- *Tab*. This command inserts a tab in the document. It simulates pressing the Tab key.
- *Type(Text)*. The Type command inserts text into the document. The *Text* parameter indicates the text you want typed. The text can be the actual characters, or it can be the name of a variable, as in these examples:

```
Type ("This is a text") // Types the actual characters
This is a test

Type (Response) // Types the contents of the Response vari-
able.
```

Troubleshooting

WordPerfect displays an error when I try to play a macro I created with WordPerfect 6.0 for Windows.

While the macro language in WordPerfect 6.0 for Windows is almost identical to that in version 6.1, there are some changes and differences. Most macros created for version 6.0 of WordPerfect for Windows will run without hitch. If you encounter an error message, first try to recompile the macro. This can be done by opening the macro in WordPerfect 6.1 for Windows and resaving it. If that doesn't work, open the macro file and run the MCVTWIN.WCM macro conversion macro, which comes with WordPerfect 6.1 for Windows. It will go through the macro and correct for the changes between the two versions. For best results, when prompted by the MCVTWIN.WCM macro, save the converted macro under a new name. This keeps the original intact in case you need to edit the macro manually to make any necessary changes.

WordPerfect tells me a label was defined but not referenced.

When you use the LABEL command, WordPerfect expects you to reference it elsewhere in the macro. This is usually done with either a GO or a CALL command. Suppose, for example, you create a label called Start, with LABEL (Start). Elsewhere in the macro, WordPerfect will expect to see a CALL (Start) or GO (Start) command; a reference to the Start label. If you get the error message that a label was defined but not referenced, you can ignore it and the

(continues)

(continued)

macro will compile properly anyway. The message is a warning, not a "fatal" error. Just click Continue Compilation button to go on.

I can't see the text my macro types into the document.

WordPerfect normally does not display the text it types with the Type command until the macro is done. This helps speed up macro execution. If you wish to see the text before the macro has finished, insert a Display (On!) command prior to the Type command that you want to display.

Extending Your Macro Programming Skills

The best way to learn about WordPerfect macros is to practice writing them. Following is a sample that will help you understand how to create sophisticated WordPerfect macros. The macros are commented at key points so that you can better follow the techniques used.

Note

If you forget how to use a command listed in the Macro Commands dialog box, choose Macro Help, and WordPerfect displays the Macros on-line help. When you close the Help window, WordPerfect takes you back to the Macro Commands dialog box.

Tip

For more information on these and other macro commands, refer to the on-line Macros help that accompanies WordPerfect. To view this help, choose **H**elp, **M**acros.

Note

Some of the examples use commands not specifically discussed in this chapter. This is unavoidable because of the number of commands. If you encounter a command that is new to you, look it up in the Macros on-line help that accompanies WordPerfect. To access the Macros help, choose **H**elp, **M**acros. In the help screen that appears, choose Macro Command Index. The macro commands are listed alphabetically within this index.

Descriptive file names, such as DOTASK.WCM, are given for each macro. If you use a macro frequently, you should consider giving it a Ctrl*x*.wcm name, as detailed in Chapter 12, "Creating Macros." That way, you can play the macro by pressing the Alt key and a letter key.

The FAXCOVER.WCM macro automates most of the steps in creating a fax cover sheet. The macro automatically inserts the current time and date, and seeks the following pertinent information:

◀ See "Stopping a Macro during Recording," p. 432

- Who the fax is from
- Who the fax is to
- The fax number of the recipient
- The subject of the fax
- The total pages in the fax transmission

FAXCOVER.WCM uses the PauseKey command to temporarily stop the macro for each piece of information it needs. You know exactly what and when to type, thanks to the MacroStatusPrompt command, as in the following example:

```
Application (A1; "WordPerfect"; Default; "US")
     // Center and bold the text "FAX COVER SHEET"
Center ()
AttributeAppearanceToggle (Bold!)
Type ("FAX COVER SHEET")
AttributeAppearanceToggle (Bold!)
HardReturn ()
HardReturn ()
     // Insert date format (this part must be recorded)
DateText ()
HardReturn ()
HardReturn ()
     // Ask for and insert's the sender's name
Type ("Sender's Name: ")          // Type descriptive text
MacroStatusPrompt (On!;"Sender's Name")    // Display prompt
PauseKey(Enter!)     // Pause and wait for Enter key
HardReturn ()     // Insert two hard returns
HardReturn ()
     // Ask for and insert the receiver's name
Type ("Receiver's Name: ")
MacroStatusPrompt (On!;"Receiver's Name")
PauseKey(Enter!)
HardReturn ()
HardReturn ()
     // Ask for and insert the receiver's fax number
Type ("Receiver's Fax Number: ")
MacroStatusPrompt (On!;"Receiver's Fax Number")
PauseKey(Enter!)
HardReturn ()
HardReturn ()
     // Ask for and insert the subject
Type ("Subject: ")
MacroStatusPrompt (On!;"Subject")
PauseKey(Enter!)
```

```
HardReturn ()
HardReturn ()
     // Ask for and insert the total pages
Type ("Total Pages: ")
MacroStatusPrompt (On!;"Total Pages")
PauseKey(Enter!)
HardReturn ()
HardReturn ()
```

From Here...

Macros can greatly extend the features and functions of WordPerfect. Although writing your own macros is not for the faint-hearted, you will find many rewards in doing so if you plan to become a WordPerfect power user.

For more information on using macros and other automation-related tools in WordPerfect, refer to the following chapters in this book:

- Chapter 9, "Customizing WordPerfect," teaches you how to assign macros and "key scripts" to menus, toolbars, and keyboards.
- Chapter 10, "Using Styles," gives you information on using WordPerfect's style feature, which allows you to provide consistent formatting to text.
- Chapter 11, "Using Templates," shows you how to use templates to quickly create documents, including fax cover sheets, memos, and letters. It also discusses WordPerfect's Letter Expert feature, which enables you to write complete business letters in a matter of minutes.
- Chapter 12, "Creating Macros," provides an overview of the macro feature of WordPerfect.
- Chapter 13, "Working with Toolbars," shows you how to use WordPerfect Toolbars to speed up your work, including attaching macros to toolbar buttons.
- Chapter 19, "Assembling Documents with Merge and Sort," teaches you how to use the merge feature to create personalized form letters.

Chapter 30

Advanced Tables

by Read Gilgen

In Chapter 16, "Working with Tables," you learned something of the power and versatility of WordPerfect's Tables feature. You also learned the basics of designing, building, formatting, saving, and printing tables. In this chapter, you take the next step toward your mastery of WordPerfect Tables. You also learn how to create functional forms using WordPerfect's powerful spreadsheet and calculation capabilities.

In this chapter, you learn to do the following:

- Position, join, split, and sort tables
- Import spreadsheets to a table
- Add graphics and customize table lines
- Use basic math functions inside tables
- Design and use complex spreadsheets
- Work with floating cells

Creating and Using Tables: The Next Step

Working with tables is somewhat like an artistic experience. The procedures included in this section are the tools you need to turn your tables into works of art—documents that meet your needs both functionally and aesthetically.

Using the Tables Toolbar and QuickMenu

When working with tables, you can speed up your work considerably by using two special tools: the customized Tables Toolbar that comes with WordPerfect, and the Tables QuickMenu. By default, when you first create a table, WordPerfect displays the Tables Toolbar. If some other toolbar is displayed instead, select the Tables Toolbar by choosing **V**iew, **T**oolbar. Then position the mouse pointer anywhere on the Toolbar and click the right mouse button. From the QuickMenu list, select the Tables Toolbar. When you finish working with your table, you can quickly return to the WordPerfect—or any other Toolbar—by following the same steps.

To access the Tables QuickMenu, make sure your cursor is positioned anywhere inside the table and that the mouse pointer is positioned anywhere in the document editing screen. Then click the right mouse button, and WordPerfect displays the Tables QuickMenu (see fig. 30.1). Using the QuickMenu rather than first accessing the T**a**ble menu can save considerable time because you don't have to move the mouse to look for the menu.

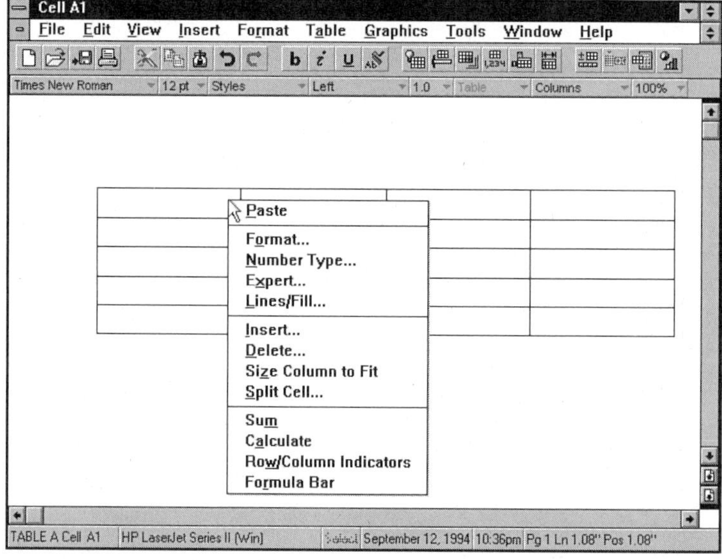

Fig. 30.1
The Tables QuickMenu. With the cursor in the table, click the secondary (right) mouse button to access this handy menu of table-related features.

Note

Unless specified otherwise, procedures described in the following sections assume you are using the QuickMenu. For example, "Choose F**o**rmat" means to first access the QuickMenu as described previously, and then to choose F**o**rmat from the QuickMenu. You also can use the keyboard to access the Table menu that contains the QuickMenu items.

Positioning Tables

By default, WordPerfect positions tables at the left margin. When you create a table, WordPerfect allocates all the available space between the margins you specify; if you change column widths, however, your table may not extend from margin to margin.

You can change the horizontal position of a table in your document by choosing F**o**rmat, and then selecting T**a**ble. Then from the Table Position pop-up menu, specify whether you want to align your table at the left margin, the right margin, or the center, or whether you want the table to extend from margin to margin (**F**ull). If you choose From Left **E**dge, you can specify the exact position of the table from the left edge of the paper. For example, 2" places the table two inches from the left edge of the paper, or one inch from the left margin.

If your table already extends from margin to margin, choosing **R**ight or **C**enter has no effect. If you choose **F**ull and then change your margins or move the table to a location that has different margins, WordPerfect adjusts the table so that it fits within the new margins.

Placing Tables Side by Side

In normal body text, you cannot place two tables side by side. You could place your tables in graphics boxes, but creating and positioning such boxes can be a bit complicated. Instead, you can simply turn on columns, create your tables, and then turn columns off.

To create side-by-side tables using newspaper-style columns, simply define your columns and turn them on. Then create the first of your tables, position the cursor just below the table you create, press Ctrl+Enter to advance to the next column, create the second of your tables, and turn off your columns. (See Chapter 14, "Working with Text Columns," for more information on creating and working with columns.)

Tip

You can define and turn on two columns easily by choosing 2 Columns from the Columns button on the Power Bar.

◀ See "Parallel Columns," p. 485

As you expand or edit your tables, the columns also expand so the two tables are always parallel. Be aware, however, that such tables cannot extend across page boundaries. To prevent page breaks from rearranging side-by-side tables, choose Fo**r**mat, **P**age, **K**eep Text Together from the main menu.

Splitting Tables

Sometimes you need to position part of a table by itself in a different location. You can copy the whole table to the new location and then delete the rows or columns you don't need. An easier method, however, is to split the table into two separate tables and then move the part you want to its new location.

To split a table, position the cursor in the row of the table that you want as the first row of the second table. From the pull-down menus, choose T**a**ble, **S**plit, **T**able. WordPerfect splits the table into two tables and adds the current border around each (see fig. 30.2). Notice, however, that because of the way table lines appear, the break between the tables may be barely noticeable.

Fig. 30.2
A WordPerfect table after being split.

Cell A1			
Cell A2			
This used to be cell A3, but now is A1 of the second table.			

Joining Tables

If you decide you don't want split tables, or if you create two separate tables and later decide to join them, follow these steps:

1. Position the two tables one immediately after the other. There can be no text (even blank lines) between the two tables.
2. Make sure the two tables have an equal number of columns. Tables with different numbers of columns cannot be joined.
3. Position the cursor in the last row of the first table.
4. Choose T**a**ble, **J**oin, **T**able from the main menu. WordPerfect joins the two tables.

If the tables cannot be joined, WordPerfect displays an error message to tell you why. For example, if you get the error message, `Table to be joined must immediately follow this table`, make sure your cursor is in the first table and that no text separates the tables.

Note

The joined tables take on the format characteristics of the first of the two tables.

Creating Forms with Irregular Columns

You sometimes want to use tables to create forms that have somewhat irregular columns. You can split and join cells to accomplish the task, but you must remember that WordPerfect splits and joins cells along existing column lines. An easier method for creating a form with irregular columns is to create two separate tables, one immediately following the other; the result looks like a single table.

For example, to create a form that begins with three columns and then changes to four, create the first table with three columns; then position the cursor immediately below that table and create a second table with four columns. Change the bottom line style in the first table to <None> to complete the illusion of only one table. When printed, the two tables look like a single table (see fig. 30.3).

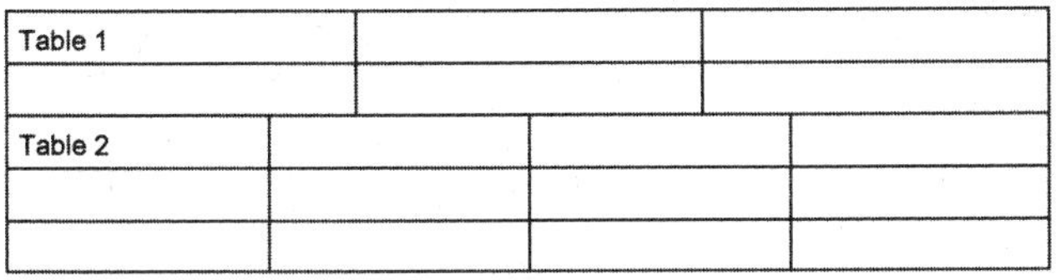

Table 1		

Table 2			

Fig. 30.3
Two tables of dissimilar column structure can be made to appear as one table by creating one table immediately following the other.

Merging and Sorting Data in Tables

WordPerfect tables are perfect for rosters or lists of inventory parts, addresses, and so on. You can create table forms to which you can merge the information from your data files to create such lists. You also can easily sort lists of data in tables. See Chapter 19, "Assembling Documents with Merge and Sort," for more information on merging data to a table.

You also can use other merge codes in a table, just as you do in any form file. Suppose that you want to automate the Invoice table form you created in Chapter 16. You can place a DATE code in the form, along with a KEYBOARD( ) command to prompt for the invoice number, or another to prompt for the person who is being billed. You also can create a macro to start the merge automatically, and even assign that macro to a button on your Toolbar so that one click of a button brings up your invoice. This is just one of the many creative ways you can use Tables to make your work easier and to produce quality documents.

Tip
To sort all rows except for certain rows at the top of the table, before starting Sort, select the rows you want to exclude. From the QuickMenu, choose F**o**rmat, R**o**w, and select the Hea**d**er Row check box.

Importing a Spreadsheet to a Table

Spreadsheets have the same kind of layout as tables. To convert a spreadsheet to a table, open or insert the spreadsheet just as you open or retrieve any other document.

You can open any spreadsheet that is in a format recognized by WordPerfect. As of this printing, allowable formats are PlanPerfect (Versions 3.0-5.1), Lotus 1-2-3 (Versions 1A-3.1) and Lotus 1-2-3 for Windows (Version 4.0), Microsoft Excel (Versions 2.1-4.0), Quattro Pro (Versions 3.0-4.0), Quattro Pro for Windows (Version 1.0-6.0), and Spreadsheet DIF. Most other spreadsheets are compatible with one of these formats, or can be saved in a compatible format.

When you attempt to open a file that WordPerfect recognizes as a spreadsheet, WordPerfect first displays the Import Data dialog box (see fig. 30.4). Here WordPerfect enables you to specify how much of the file you want to import, and even lists any named ranges found in the spreadsheet. By default, spreadsheets are imported in table format.

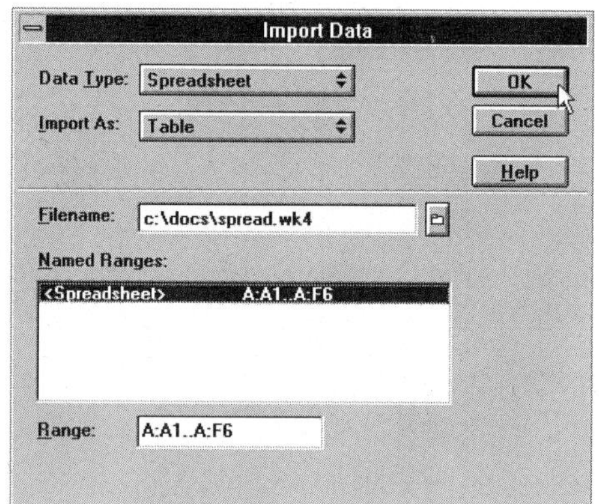

Fig. 30.4
The Import Data dialog box enables you to specify the file or named ranges you want to import into your document.

When you convert a spreadsheet to a table, the spreadsheet's blank rows convert to blank cells, as shown in figure 30.5.

WORDPERFECT COSTS					
	License	Manual	Workbook	Complete	%Discoun t
List Price	N/A	N/A	N/A	$495.00	0.0%
Mail Order	N/A	N/A	N/A	$235.00	52.5%
Site License	$50.00	$25.00	$25.00	$100.00	79.8%

Fig. 30.5
A table imported from a spreadsheet. Some editing of cell and column formats may be required before the data displays correctly.

In addition, if the spreadsheet is too wide to fit within the margins, WordPerfect imports the whole spreadsheet, but does not print whatever extends beyond the right margin. Some useful strategies for importing spreadsheet data into tables include the following:

- Consider changing the paper orientation. More data can fit horizontally on a landscape page (11 × 8 1/2 inches) than can fit on a portrait page.

- Reduce the margins to allow more room for data. Remember, however, that most laser printers have minimum margin requirements, usually about 0.3 inches.

- Change to a smaller sans serif font. Helvetica, for example, requires less horizontal room than Times Roman. An 8-point font usually is adequate for spreadsheet information.

- Have the person who creates the original spreadsheet assign names to blocks or ranges of cells. Then as you import the spreadsheet, you can simply choose from the list of named ranges and import just the range of cells you need.

◄ See "Merging into Tables," p. 659

◄ See "Importing and Working with Spreadsheet/Database Data," p. 606

For more information on importing spreadsheets, see Chapter 18, "Importing Data and Working with Other Programs."

Troubleshooting

Sometimes when I click the right mouse button to get a QuickMenu, the menu flashes onscreen, disappears, and then strange things happen.

When your mouse pointer is in the lower-right area of the screen, there isn't enough room to display the QuickMenu. When you click the right mouse button, the menu appears, and WordPerfect executes whatever menu item happens to be at the point

(continues)

(continued)

of your mouse pointer (for example, **D**elete). To avoid this, hold down the right mouse button when choosing the QuickMenu and slide the mouse pointer to the menu item you want before releasing the mouse button.

I tried to open a spreadsheet but got an error message saying the file is not a supported format.

Although WordPerfect supports many different spreadsheet formats, you must be sure that the necessary conversion files are installed when you install WordPerfect. Use the installation disks, choose a Custom install, choose File Options, and select the file conversion types you need.

Using Custom Table Styles

In Chapter 16, you learned to use basic line and fill styles to modify the appearance of your tables. WordPerfect also enables you to select a variety of predefined table designs.

Using Table Expert Styles

WordPerfect's "expert" styles are predefined table styles that make it easy to add lines, fills, and other formatting to existing tables. To access these expert designs, position the cursor in your table and from the QuickMenu choose E**x**pert. WordPerfect displays the Table Expert dialog box (see fig. 30.6).

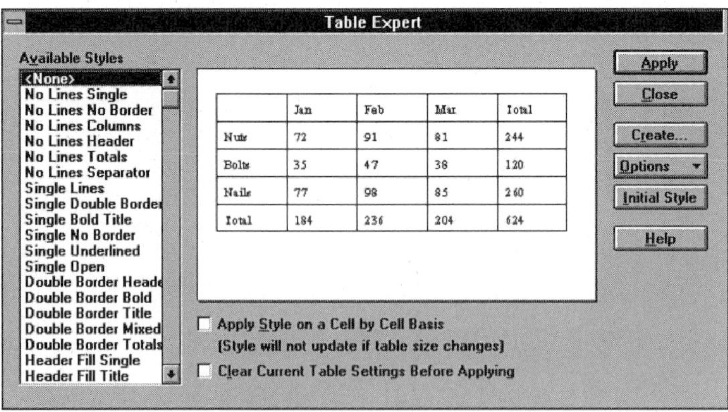

Fig. 30.6
Use the Table Expert feature to select predefined table format styles or to create your own expert styles.

Listed under A**v**ailable Styles are several predefined table formats. When you click a style, WordPerfect displays a sample table in the preview box. For example, if you select the "Fancy Totals" style, WordPerfect formats your table with a colored title bar and no lines except to set off the totals (see fig. 30.7).

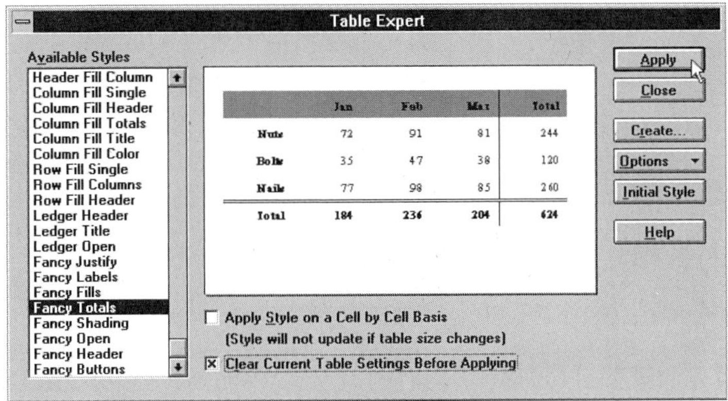

Fig. 30.7
When you select an Expert Table style, such as "Fancy Totals," you apply a predefined set of formats, lines, and fills to your table.

You can clear all formatting first and then apply the expert style you choose by checking the C**l**ear Current Table Settings Before Applying check box. You also can simply select the style and add it to any formatting changes you already have made to the table.

Finally, if you create a certain table format that you particularly like, you can save that style as an "expert" style and use it again as often as you like. To create your own expert style, follow these steps:

1. Make any format changes you wish, including justification, text size, lines, and fills.
2. With the cursor in your table, choose E**x**pert.
3. In the Table Expert dialog box, choose C**r**eate. WordPerfect displays the Create Table Style dialog box.
4. In the **N**ame text box, type a name for your table style.
5. Choose OK to save the new table style.

You can make this or any other table style the default by choosing **I**nitial Style and choosing **Y**es.

Using Alternating Fills for Rows or Columns

One of the more popular styles for tables is an alternating pattern of filled rows or columns. Computer programming printouts, for example, used to use a "green bar" pattern to help readers follow the data. WordPerfect enables you to establish an alternating pattern of your choice, and as you expand your table WordPerfect automatically continues alternating that pattern.

To create alternating rows of dark green and light green, for example, follow these steps:

1. With the cursor in your table, choose **L**ines/Fill from the QuickMenu.
2. In the Table Lines/Fill dialog box, choose T**a**ble.
3. In the Fill Options section, choose **R**ows from the Al**t**ernating Fill pop-up menu. WordPerfect then displays a modified Table Lines/Fill dialog box (see fig. 30.8).

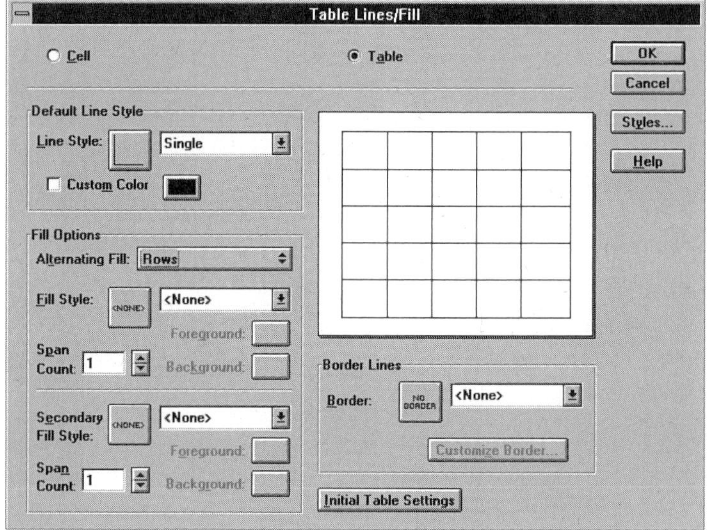

Fig. 30.8
Choose T**a**ble in the Table Lines/Fill dialog box to access the alternating fills feature. Your table then continues to alternate fills as it expands.

4. Now choose the pattern and colors you want. For the first **F**ill style, for example, choose 100% fill, and choose green as the foreground color. (The background color is not important unless you are using a patterned fill.)
5. For the Se**c**ondary Fill Style, choose 10% fill, and again choose green as the F**o**reground color.

6. If you want to make this your default table style (for this and all subsequent tables you create), choose **I**nitial Table Settings, and choose **Y**es.

7. Choose OK to apply the alternating style to your table.

Now, as you enter data in your table, and expand the rows in your table, every other row will be solid green and alternating rows will be light green.

Customizing Table Lines and Borders

You also can significantly enhance the appeal of tables by modifying the lines that separate their cells and by customizing their borders.

Customizing Lines

In addition to the predefined line styles described in Chapter 16, "Working with Tables," WordPerfect enables you to create your own custom line styles and effects. Furthermore, you can save your custom lines in style templates or in expert table styles and use them over and over again.

Suppose that you want to separate the top row of your invoice (the column header row) from the rest of the table with something fancier than a simple thick line. You can create a style that includes, for example, two thick black lines separated by a thicker gray line, with no white space in-between (see fig. 30.9).

Badger Tours, Inc. 1234 Rose Bowl Avenue Madison, WI 53700 (608) 555-4321 December 1, 1994			
Quantity	**Description**	**Unit Cost**	**Amount**
Comments:		Subtotal	
		Tax (5.5%)	
		TOTAL	

Fig. 30.9
A customized table line that consists of two thick black lines separated by a thicker gray line.

To create a custom line, follow these steps:

1. Position the cursor in the cell, or select the group of cells where you intend to use the new style. (This is not terribly important, however, because you can create the style first and then use it later.)

2. From the QuickMenu choose **L**ines/Fill, and from the Lines/Fill dialog box choose St**y**les. WordPerfect displays the Graphics Styles dialog box. Choose C**r**eate and WordPerfect presents the Create Line Style dialog box (see fig. 30.10).

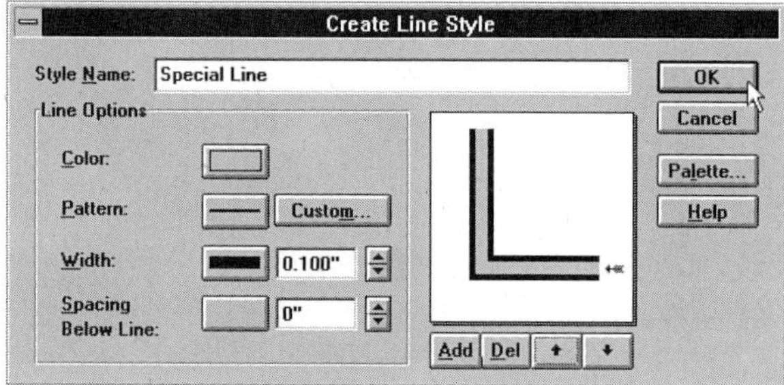

Fig. 30.10
The Create Line Style dialog box appears after following the steps to create a custom line.

3. In the Style **N**ame text box, type a unique name (for example, **Special Line**).

4. In the **W**idth text box, enter **.05**". Also, in the **S**pacing Below Line text box enter **0**".

5. Choose **A**dd twice. This adds two more lines to the style, each 0.05 inches wide, with no spacing between them. Notice that in the preview box, an arrow points to the inside line. Move this arrow using the mouse or the up- and down-arrow buttons until it points to the middle of the three lines.

6. Choose **C**olor and change the color to gray. Also, change the **W**idth of this line to **.1**"

If you want to keep your new line style with just the current document, simply save the document. However, if you think you want to use this line style over again, you can save it in your personal line styles library. (See Chapter 10, "Using Styles," for details on working with customized styles.)

Customizing Table Borders

Table borders are separate from the lines of the table, and you change them separately from table lines. By default, WordPerfect displays no border at all around tables. The border you see is actually the default outside single lines of the table cells themselves. The advantage of this approach is that if you add or delete rows or columns, or sort your table, any border you have selected remains a border and does not affect, nor is it affected by, table cell lines.

◀ See "Changing Table Lines, Borders, and Fills," p. 552

◀ See "Working with Styles from Other Files," p. 378

Unless you actually change the outside cell lines to something specific, their default single lines yield to any border style you select and do not display. For example, to change the appearance of the table to look like tables in WordPerfect 5.1 or 5.2, you change the border style to double lines.

Suppose you want to surround your table with a three-line border and create a shadow effect. Perform the following series of steps to create a customized table border.

1. From the QuickMenu, choose **L**ines/Fill.
2. Choose the T**a**ble radio button so the bottom part of the dynamic dialog displays the table-related options (see fig. 30.11).

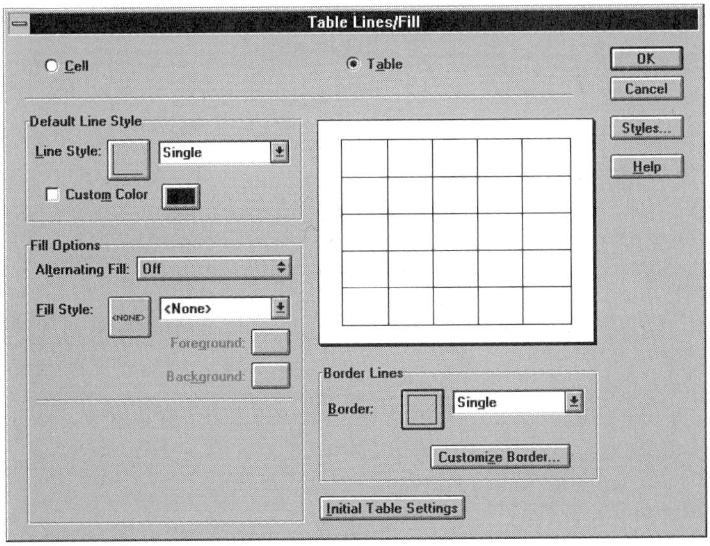

Fig. 30.11 Customizing a table border style from the Table Lines/Fill dialog box.

Normally you just select a Border Lines style either from the button or from the drop-down list. However, the style you want isn't there (for example, "Triple" is actually a thin-thick-thin triple with no shadow).

3. Choose the Styles button. WordPerfect displays the Graphics Styles dialog box.

> **Note**
>
> If you don't intend to save your custom border as a style, you can simply choose Customize Border and skip forward to steps 6-8.

4. Choose Create to display the Create Border Style dialog box.

5. In the Style Name text box, type the name of your special style—for example, **Triple-Shadow**.

6. Choose Line Style and using either the button or the drop-down list, choose Triple (three regular thin lines).

7. You also can specify the type of drop shadow you want. Choose Drop Shadow Type, and choose a drop shadow style—for example, with the shadow to the left and bottom.

8. Note how your newly defined border looks in the preview window (see fig. 30.12). If no further changes are needed, choose OK.

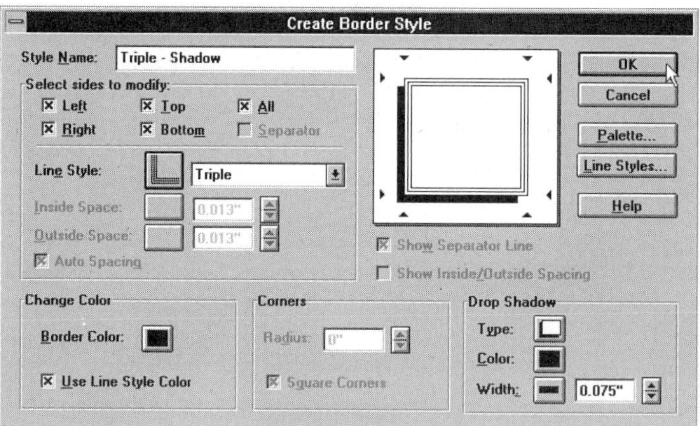

Fig. 30.12 Customizing a border style in the Create Border Style dialog box.

9. In the Graphics Styles dialog box, you can choose **O**ptions, Save **A**s, and follow the procedures described for custom lines for saving this border style for future use. If, however, you want this style just for this document, choose **C**lose.

10. Finally, in the Table Lines/Fill dialog box choose **B**order, and from the drop-down list choose the style you just created—for example, Triple-Shadow. Choose OK to return to your document.

Customizing Cell and Table Shading

WordPerfect uses the term *fill* to refer to shading cells, tables, and graphics boxes. By default, WordPerfect tables are not shaded, or filled. But WordPerfect offers a wide variety of shading options, including percentages of shading, colors, and even gradient shading.

Suppose that you want to change the shading on the column heading row of your Invoice table. Follow these steps for changing cell shading, which are similar for changing table and graphics box shading:

1. Select all the cells in the row you want to shade—for example the column headings row.
2. From the QuickMenu, choose **L**ines/Fill.
3. Choose the St**y**les button. WordPerfect displays the Graphics Styles dialog box.
4. Choose the **F**ill radio button.
5. Choose C**r**eate to display the Create Fill Style dialog box.
6. Choose the **G**radient radio button to display the gradient shading portion of the dynamic dialog box.
7. In the Style **N**ame text box, type the name of your special style—for example, **Special Shading**.
8. Under Pattern Options, from the **F**oreground Color palette choose gray, and leave the **B**ackground color at white.
9. Leave the Gra**d**ient at Linear, but change the **V**ertical Offset to 0%.
10. Notice what your style looks like in the preview box (see fig. 30.13), and when everything is the way you want it, choose OK.
11. In the Graphics Styles dialog box, you can choose **O**ptions, Save **A**s, and follow the procedures described for custom lines for saving this fill style for future use. If, however, you want this style just for this document, choose **C**lose.

12. Finally, in the Table Lines/Fill dialog box choose **F**ill Style, and from the drop-down list choose the style you just created, for example, Special Shading. Choose OK to return to your document.

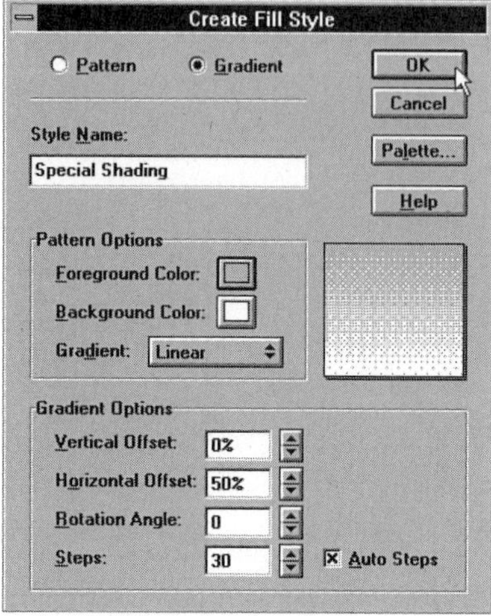

Fig. 30.13
Previewing custom cell and table shading from the Create Fill Style dialog box.

Remember that you are not limited to just one fill style (shading) in a table. For example, if you have a color printer, you could shade certain rows light green, others slightly darker green, and even others solid green. Appropriate uses of shading can have a dramatic impact on the readability of a table.

Note

Don't forget that you can save your custom table format as an expert style. See "Using Table Expert Styles," earlier in this chapter.

Troubleshooting

When I create a custom line, it overlaps the text of the cell.

Thick lines, in particular, will overlap text in a cell because the cell doesn't automatically expand to accommodate the new line. You'll need to increase the cell margins (from the Format dialog box, choose Co**l**umn and change the Le**f**t or Right column margins, or choose R**o**w and change the To**p** or **B**ottom margins). You may also need to increase the column width or the row height in order to have enough room for the line and the text.

After I change the fill for a row of cells, I can't read the text in those cells.

If you choose a shading that is too dark (30% or more, or a color such as blue), black text will be hard to read. Instead choose a lighter shade (10%, for example) or color (yellow is quite light). If you really want a dark background, select the cells you want to fill and then play the REVERSE macro. This macro enables you to choose, for example, a black background with white printing.

Using Basic Math and Formulas in Tables

WordPerfect does such a great job with formatting text that it's easy to forget the many features that can take advantage of your computer's native capability to work with numbers. In this section you learn not only how to add and subtract numbers in a table, but also to use the table as a simple spreadsheet. This section also prepares you for the next section, in which you explore more complex formulas.

Understanding Spreadsheets

If you use spreadsheet programs, you probably have noticed the similarity between WordPerfect's tables and a typical spreadsheet layout. Both arrange data in rows and columns, and the intersection of a row and a column is a cell.

Up to this point you have learned about tables which allow you to arrange and format information. To use a table as a spreadsheet requires you to rethink the function of the table. In other words, you must switch from thinking about a table as a text formatter to thinking of it as a number processor. For example, you must consider whether cells are text only, or whether they have numeric values.

In the case of numeric cells, you specify number type and then let WordPerfect add formatting such as dollar signs, commas, or percent signs. If you use formulas, you must decide what you are trying to calculate. You also must be ready to analyze your table to make sure the numbers you see make sense, and be prepared to modify formulas that aren't functioning properly or that don't produce correct results.

Designing a Spreadsheet

For simple tasks, jumping right in and building the layout and formulas in a table is okay. But often you find that the table's complexity increases as you begin to add functionality. In such cases, consider planning your table before you start to create it. A bit of planning during the early stages makes creating a functional table much easier.

On a separate sheet of paper, sketch the layout of your table. Pencil in the locations of calculations and the bits of information used to make those calculations. For example, when planning the formulas for your Invoice table, you might say to yourself, "I want to multiply the quantity times the unit cost to get the extended amount. I then want to add all the extended amounts, 5 1/2 percent sales tax, and shipping fees, and then produce a total amount due."

Don't be afraid to think in the broadest terms. WordPerfect's tables functions are very flexible and powerful. Whether you need to perform complex interest payment schedules or simply add prices, WordPerfect's tables functions are up to the task. Browse through the *WordPerfect Reference* appendix to see just what functions are available and what they can do.

Determine the number of columns you need and, if possible, the number of rows. Given the number of columns, try to determine how wide those columns must be and whether you need to change your paper size or orientation (for example, landscape) or reduce the size of your font (for example, 8-point Helvetica). Other format considerations, such as text attributes, lines, borders, and fills can be determined later. At this point focus on the functionality of the table.

Adding Spreadsheet Capabilities to a Table

By default, WordPerfect considers as text all information typed into a table cell, even numbers. When you begin to add formulas to tables, WordPerfect recognizes the values of any numbers you have entered and can use these numbers in formulas and calculations.

In WordPerfect, you really don't convert a table into a spreadsheet, as much as you begin to use the tools that add spreadsheet functionality to your table: Cell Formula Entry and the Formula Bar.

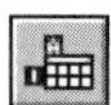

To explore how WordPerfect handles numbers in tables—with and without these tools—begin by creating a simple three-column by four-row table. Also, before you continue, access the Tables QuickMenu and choose Ro**w**/Column Indicators (see fig. 30.14). These indicators help you know what cell you are looking at. Now try the following steps:

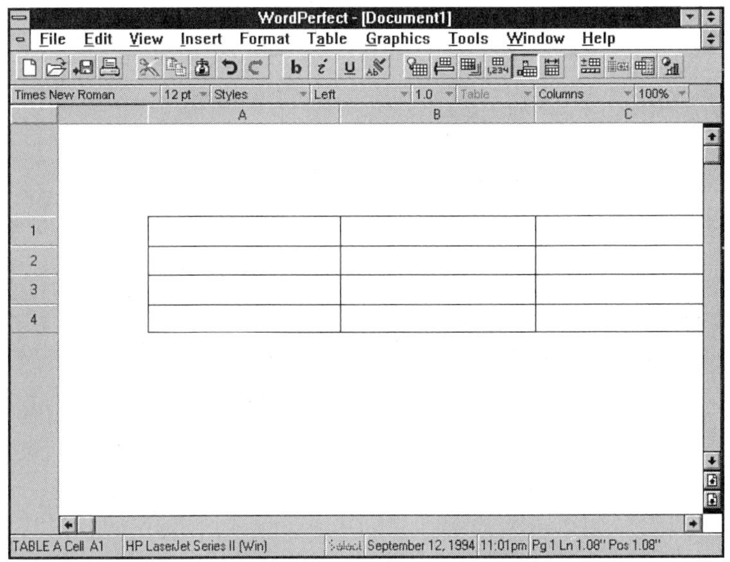

Fig. 30.14
Use Row/Column Indicators when working with tables to better see your exact column and row location.

1. Type **2** in cell A1, and **3** in cell B1. Notice that the numbers appear just as you would expect them to. Later they can be used as reference values for formulas.

2. Type **7/1/94** in cell A2, and **555-1234** in cell B2. Notice that although these could be interpreted as numbers (for example, 7 divided by 1 divided by 94), WordPerfect displays them as text.

3. Type **a1*b1** in cell C1. Again, WordPerfect sees the formula as text, displaying `a1*b1` in the cell.

4. Choose T**a**ble, C**e**ll Formula Entry. This changes the default cell entry mode so that numbers that look like formulas are treated as formulas.

5. Now type **7/1/94** in cell A3 and **555-1234** in cell B3. Because Cell Formula Entry is on, these numbers result in `0.07446808511` and `Å679`, respectively.

6. Delete the contents of cell C1 and type **a1*b1**. When you move to another cell, WordPerfect views what you typed as a formula and displays the result of multiplying those two cells (for example, `6`).

   C**e**ll Formula Entry remains selected even if you exit your document or WordPerfect. To turn this feature off and return to the default text entry mode, choose T**a**ble, C**e**ll Formula Entry.

VI

Becoming an Expert User

7. Access the Formula Bar by choosing Formula Bar from the QuickMenu or from the Table menu. WordPerfect's Formula Bar (see fig. 30.15) aids in entering formulas, and does not require that the Cell Formula Entry feature be active.

Fig. 30.15
Use WordPerfect's Formula Bar to enter and edit table cell formulas.

8. Delete the contents of cell C1. Click the mouse pointer in the formula edit box, located to the right of the green check mark on the Formula Bar. WordPerfect displays the message `Formula Edit Mode is On` on the Formula Bar.

9. Now type the formula **a1*b1** in the formula edit box. Click the green check mark or press Enter to place the formula in the table. To cancel the formula, click the red X or press Esc. The result of the formula, `6`, appears in cell C1.

10. Position the cursor in cell C2. Remember that the values in cells A2 and B2 were entered as text. Click the formula edit box, type **a2*b2** and press Enter. The result, 3885, comes from multiplying the first separate number in each of the two cells (7 times 555).

Fortunately, formulas do recognize numbers in cells that also contain text, so you can enter, for example, **2 ea**. in a Quantity column and a formula would recognize the 2 but ignore the text. However, you have to be careful because you may not expect such numbers to calculate. For example, if you add a list of numbers in a 2nd Quarter column, you may inadvertently add an extra 2 to your total.

In summary, there are two methods for entering formulas in a cell:

- Use the Formula Bar and enter formulas by way of the formula edit box.
- Activate the Cell Formula Entry feature and enter formulas directly in the table.

Which is best? Unless the primary use of your table is for spreadsheet-like formulas, you probably should leave the Cell Formula Entry feature turned off. The Formula Bar is easy to access, provides virtually the same functionality, but still enables you to enter dates and phone numbers without having WordPerfect interpret them as formulas.

Tip

For easiest formula entry, turn on and use the Formula Bar, but turn off the Cell Formula Entry feature.

Formatting Numeric Data

You can use standard table formatting such as attributes and alignment for all table cells, both text and numeric, by choosing F**o**rmat from the QuickMenu. You also can add additional formatting to numeric cells by choosing **N**umber Type from the QuickMenu.

Consider the Invoice table you created in Chapter 16, "Working with Tables" (see fig. 30.16). The information in the Quantity column contains both numbers and text and needs no special formatting beyond right alignment. The Description column is all text. The Unit Cost and Amount columns, however, are best formatted as currency, whether for numbers or for formulas. To format either of these columns, position the cursor in the column you want to change and choose **N**umber Type from the QuickMenu (or press Alt+F12). When WordPerfect displays the Number Type dialog box, choose the C**o**lumn radio button (see fig. 30.17).

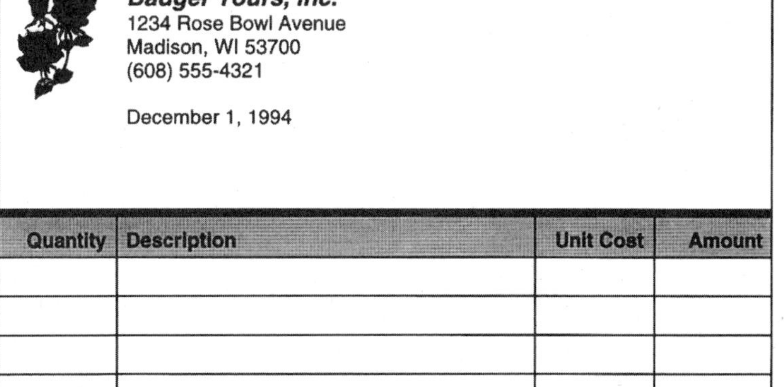

Badger Tours, Inc.
1234 Rose Bowl Avenue
Madison, WI 53700
(608) 555-4321

December 1, 1994

Quantity	Description	Unit Cost	Amount
Comments:		Subtotal	
		Tax (5.5%)	
		TOTAL	

Fig. 30.16
A table used as an invoice. Use Number Type from the Tables menu to format the cells for currency.

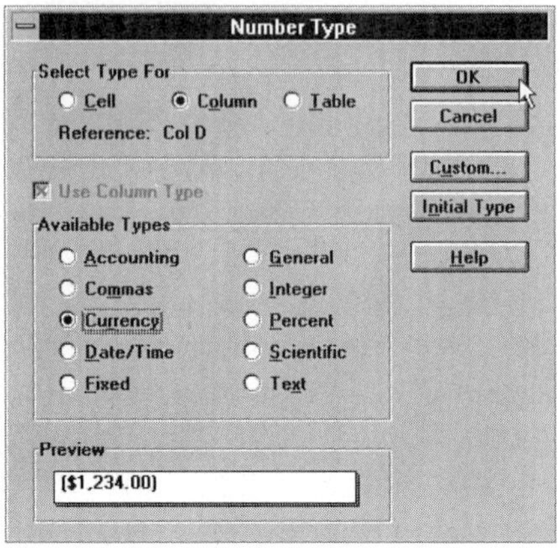

Fig. 30.17
The Number Type dialog box in which you choose the numeric format for tables cells.

Because you are displaying currency values, choose Cu**r**rency from the list of Available Types. In the Preview box you can see what the format is for the number type you choose (for example, $1,234.00).

You can choose additional numeric formatting options by choosing C**u**stom. WordPerfect displays the Customize Number Type dialog box (see fig. 30.18). Here you can specify how you want to display negative numbers (minus sign, parenthesis, or CR/DR symbols); whether to use the currency symbol and how it is to be aligned in the cell; how many digits to display and whether to round to this digit for calculation purposes (be careful, you can lose money if you do this!); and whether to use commas to separate thousands. You even can choose from a list of 40 international currency symbols.

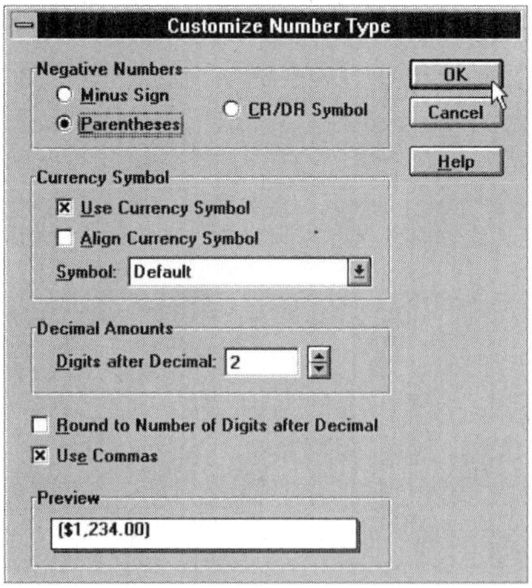

Fig. 30.18
The Customize Number Type dialog box can be used for additional numeric formatting of table cells.

When you have chosen the format and options, choose OK to return to your document.

Unfortunately, WordPerfect does not automatically align numbers according to the number type you select. Therefore, to complete the formatting of the Unit Cost and Amount columns, choose F**o**rmat from the QuickMenu, choose the Co**l**umn radio button, and then choose **J**ustification, **D**ecimal Align. Here you also can specify how far from the right margin of the cell you want to align your decimal point. By default, WordPerfect allows room for two digits. If you change this (for example, to 4) you aren't specifying how many digits to display, but instead how many digits from the right margin you want your decimal point.

Finally, the Unit Cost and Amount column headings may not look correct if you change the alignment of the columns. To correct this, select the two column heading cells, choose F**o**rmat from the QuickMenu, and choose **R**ight from the **J**ustification pop-up menu.

Forcing Text Mode for Cells That Contain Numbers

Normally, WordPerfect considers combinations of text and numbers to be text, but does recognize the first separate numbers in such cells and uses them in calculations if you reference that cell in a formula. For example, if your column heading is **Bin 1** and you add the column's values, the total equals one more than you expect because the value 1 in **Bin 1** is added to the total. You can avoid this problem in two ways:

1. Using the Formula Bar, enter the text in the formula text box, enclosed in quotes (for example, **"Bin 1"**). WordPerfect then inserts Bin 1 in the cell and treats it completely as text.

2. If you have many such cells, this process could be quite tedious. Instead, select all the cells you want to force into text mode, and from the QuickMenu choose **N**umber Type. From the Number Type dialog box, choose the Te**x**t type from the Available Types. The result of this is that any number entered in text-type cells is entered as text and ignored in all calculations.

If you want to enter numbers as values but ignore the value during calculations, you can enter the number as a regular value, then choose F**o**rmat from the QuickMenu, and choose I**g**nore Cell When Calculating. The advantage to this method is that when you deselect the I**g**nore check box, the value then can be calculated in a formula. Changing the **N**umber Type to Te**x**t, as described previously, does not permit this.

Creating Formulas

You now are ready to create formulas that range in complexity from simple adding or multiplying of cells, to the use of functions such as PMT( ), which is used to calculate loan payments. Begin with something basic. For example, use the Invoice table again and calculate the extended amount (Quantity times Unit Cost). Then add the Amounts column, and calculate and add the tax.

The first step in creating formulas (after creating the basic table, of course) is to choose the Cell Formula Entry method, or the Formula Bar method. Suppose that you choose to enter formulas directly into the cells. Choose T**a**ble, C**e**ll Formula Entry (if the feature already is checked, don't select it again).

In your Invoice table, position the cursor in cell D3. Here you want the results of multiplying cells A3 and C3, so enter **A3*C3**. WordPerfect displays the result of the formula in cell D3. On the General Status button of the status bar, WordPerfect displays the Table and Cell location along with the actual formula contained in the cell at that location.

Because you knew that you wanted to multiply cell A3 times cell C3, you entered the formula directly into cell D3. However, what do you do if you forget the cell locations (for example, a large table in which you can't see all the different cells that you want to include in the formula)? Fortunately, WordPerfect provides the Formula Bar that aids in "pointing" at the cells you want as you "compose" your formula. To turn on the Formula Bar, choose Fo**r**mula Bar from the QuickMenu (refer to fig. 30.15). You might also want to turn off the C**e**ll Formula Entry feature; you can do this from the T**a**ble menu.

To enter a formula using the Formula Bar, follow these steps:

1. Position the cursor in the cell where you want your formula—for example in cell D3.

   If you already entered a formula in the cell, WordPerfect displays the formula in the formula edit box (to the right of the green check mark on the Formula Bar). Otherwise, the edit box is empty.

2. Click the mouse pointer in the formula edit box area. Delete any formula you see there. Notice that on the Formula Bar, WordPerfect displays the message `Formula Edit Mode is On`.

3. Begin composing the formula by clicking the cells you want to include and typing any required math or function symbols in the formula edit box.

For example, click the mouse pointer in cell A3. WordPerfect displays A3 in the formula edit box. Click the formula edit box and press asterisk (*). Finally, click the mouse pointer in cell C3. WordPerfect now displays A3*C3 in the formula edit box.

4. When you have the formula you want, enter the formula in the target cell (for example, D3) by clicking the green check mark just to the left of the formula edit box, or by pressing Enter.

   If you decide to cancel the formula, click the red X on the formula bar, or press Esc.

> **Caution**
>
> When you first enter a formula, WordPerfect automatically calculates the formula and displays the result. Subsequent changes to cells referenced by this formula do not change the calculated result. Before you depend on the results you see, always choose C**a**lculate from the QuickMenu or the Calcula**t**e button from the Formula bar to update your table formulas.

Copying Formulas

You now want to repeat this formula in the three remaining Amount rows. Fortunately, WordPerfect does not require that you enter this formula three more times. Instead, you can copy the formula by following these steps:

1. Position the cursor in the cell that contains the formula you want to copy (for example, in cell D3).

2. Choose Co**p**y Formula from the Formula Bar or choose Cop**y** Formula from the T**a**ble menu. WordPerfect displays the Copy Formula dialog box (see fig. 30.19).

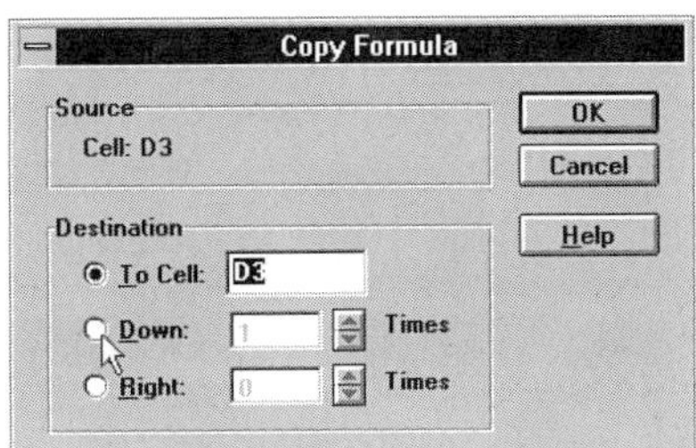

Fig. 30.19
The Copy Formula dialog box enables you to copy a formula from one cell to another. WordPerfect automatically adjusts the cell references in the formula to reflect its new location.

3. Note the location of the Source Cell (for example, D3) to make sure you are copying the correct formula.

   You can copy the formula to a cell, **D**own *n* times in the same column, or to the **R**ight *n* times in the same row.

   Choose **D**own and specify how many cells you want to copy the formula to (3, for example).

4. Choose OK. WordPerfect copies the formula to all three cells immediately below the current cell.

Tip
The displayed results of your copied formulas may not be correct because they have not yet been calculated. Choose the Calcula**t**e button from the Formula Bar or C**a**lculate from the QuickMenu to update the results.

WordPerfect automatically adjusts the cell references in formulas to reflect the new location of the formula. This is called *relative referencing*. For example, move the cursor to cell D4 and notice that the formula reads `A4*C4`. In cell D5 it reads `A5*C5`, and so on.

Using Functions in Formulas

Already you can see the power of formulas in WordPerfect tables. But WordPerfect goes even further by providing nearly 100 special functions that you can use in your formulas to manipulate and calculate your data in exactly the same way you do in a full-featured spreadsheet. In this section, you learn the basics of working with functions.

To total the Amounts column in your Invoice table, follow these steps:

1. Position the cursor in the cell in which you want the subtotal (for example, in cell D7). Always start a formula in the exact cell in which you want to display the result.

2. If the Formula Bar is not displayed, choose Fo**r**mula Bar from the QuickMenu or from the T**a**ble menu.

3. In the formula edit box on the Formula Bar, type **sum(** and then type the range of cells to include—for example **d3:d6**. Type the closing **)** and press Enter, or click the green check mark on the Formula Bar.

A different but perhaps easier method is to use the mouse to select the functions and the cell range to include. Rather than step 3, simply click the formula edit box, and then choose the **F**unctions button on the Formula Bar and from the list select SUM(List). WordPerfect places the function in the formula edit box, with `List` highlighted. Using the mouse, select the cells you want to include (for example, cells D3 through D6). WordPerfect automatically displays `D3:D6` in place of the word `List` in the formula edit box. Press Enter or click the green check mark to enter the formula SUM(D3:D6) in the table.

The results may be correct, but don't forget to choose **C**alculate to make sure.

The remaining formulas in the Invoice table are quite easy compared to using functions. In cell D8, you want to calculate the tax using the formula C7*.055 (5 1/2 percent tax). In cell D9, you want the total of the amounts plus the tax, so you use the formula C7+C8.

Tip
To add numbers directly above the formula cell, choose **S**um from the Formula feature bar, or simply enter + as the formula for the cell. WordPerfect adds any numbers in the same column above the + sign.

Modifying, Deleting, and Calculating Cells and Formulas

When you finish building your table and its formulas, recalculate one more time. Choose C**a**lculate from the T**a**ble menu or from the Formula Bar. Then examine the table to make sure the results make sense. Most mistakes in formulas produce obviously wrong results. The best time to find and correct any mistakes is while the table and what you are trying to do are fresh in your mind. To correct or change a formula, position the cursor in the cell that contains the formula. In the formula edit box on the Formula Bar, make any necessary corrections or even start over. When you are through, click the green check mark or press Enter to insert the updated formula in your table. Because you are replacing a formula, WordPerfect prompts you that you are about to replace a formula. Choose **Y**es.

To correct or change values in a referenced cell, move to that cell and make the changes. For example, if your unit costs just rose from $12.36 to $13.24, change the amount in the appropriate cell.

After making any changes to formulas or cell values, recalculate your table so that the information you see is the latest and most up-to-date version.

Locking Table Cells

After you finish setting the formulas and attributes for a cell, you can lock the cell to protect it from further changes. Suppose that in the invoice table you don't want the user to be able to change the formulas in the Amount column cells. To lock a cell, follow these steps:

1. Position the cursor in the cell you want to lock.

2. From the QuickMenu, choose F**o**rmat.

3. In the Format dialog box, choose C**e**ll if it isn't already selected and select the Lo**c**k check box.

4. Choose OK to return to your document. At this point, you cannot modify the contents of the cell without deselecting the Lock feature.

> **Note**
>
> You can use the Lock feature to speed data entry. After designing the entire form—for example, an Invoice form—lock the header cells and all the formula cells. When you fill in the form, pressing tab advances you past any locked cells to the next unlocked cell.

Designing More Complex Tables: The Grade-Tracking Table

The power and versatility of WordPerfect's formula functions could fill an entire book. Therefore, this limited space focuses more on some of the procedures used to build a more complex table, and also introduces some of the powerful functions available in WordPerfect tables.

Suppose that you have to keep grades for your Spanish class. You don't have a grade-tracking program, nor do you have a spreadsheet. WordPerfect comes to your rescue by helping you build a table that can keep track of grades, provide totals and averages, and even create and print a report card that includes the student's letter grade.

Consider the grade-tracking table in figure 30.20. The purpose of this section is to explore the formula and other spreadsheet functions of tables, rather than review table-creating and formatting procedures. If you aren't sure of something you see, refer to Chapter 16, "Working with Tables," or preceding sections in this chapter.

Fig. 30.20
A grade-tracking table uses special functions to calculate totals, averages, percentages, and even letter grades.

STUDENT NAME October 24, 1994	Quizzes			Quiz Points	Exam 1	Exam 2	Paper	Total Points	Average %	Letter Grade
Possible Points	85	70	100	100	150	150	200	600	100.0%	
Berndobler, Gary	83	65	92	94	136	130	175	535	89.2%	B
Bresser, Deborah	76	55	76	81	125	110	165	481	80.2%	C
Houghton, Sam	85	69	96	98	144	143	190	575	95.8%	A
Larson, Jerry	66	50	60	69	120	110	155	454	75.7%	D
Prochniak, Maria	83	68	90	95	140	138	190	563	93.8%	A
Rinzelli, Dennis	50		70	47	130	110	150	437	72.8%	D
AVERAGES	73.8	61.4	80.7	80.7	132.5	123.5	170.8	507.5	84.6%	C

The following summarizes the layout and format of the grade-tracking table:

- Accommodate in 11 columns the student names; each of the quizzes, tests, and papers; averages; and letter grades.
- Create enough rows to accommodate each member of the class, plus three rows for column headings, possible points, and averages.
- Measure and then specify a fixed width for each of the columns.
- Right-justify all the columns except the first (left-justified) and the last (centered).
- Join three cells for the quizzes heading, and center the joined cell.
- Add line and fill changes after the entire table is built.

Understanding Functions

Functions are both versatile and powerful, and can be divided into six basic groups or types: Arithmetic (AVE, SUM, QUOTIENT, and so on); Calendar (DATE and TIME, for example); Financial (NPV, PMT, and so forth); Logical (such as AND and FALSE); Special (BLOCK and LOOKUP, for example); and Text (CHAR, LENGTH, and so on).

Most functions also require one or more arguments to complete the function. Multiple arguments must be separated by commas. For example, the SUM() function requires one argument: the list or range of cells to total. The PMT() function, on the other hand, requires five arguments: rate, present value, periods, future value, and type. All functions require a pair of parentheses following the function name, even when no argument is required—for example DATE(). When you omit or mistype any part of the function, its arguments, or its punctuation, WordPerfect displays an error message suggesting how to correct it.

Thorough coverage of all WordPerfect table functions is beyond the scope of this book. See the *WordPerfect Reference* or the Help menu for information on functions. As you learn in the next section, a listing and mini-Help feature is available when you create formulas. Because the spreadsheet functions in WordPerfect are identical to those found in PlanPerfect, WordPerfect Corporation's spreadsheet program, you also can refer to the PlanPerfect Reference if you have it.

Using a Function

Perhaps not the first, but one of the easier formulas in your grade-tracking table is the one that gives a class average for each quiz, test, and paper.

To create a formula to report an average, follow these steps:

1. If you haven't done so already, choose Fo**r**mula Bar from the QuickMenu to display the Formula Bar. All of the following procedures assume use of the Formula Bar.

2. Position the cursor in the last row of the first column of grades—B9 for example.

3. Click the mouse in the formula edit box; or press Alt+Shift+E.

4. Click the **F**unctions button; or press Alt+Shift+F. In the Functions dialog box, WordPerfect displays a list of nearly 100 functions. As you scroll through the list, WordPerfect displays a brief description of each function's purpose or use. When you find the function you want—for example AVE(List) (for averaging a list of numbers)—choose **I**nsert.

5. Specify the list, or range of cells, that are included in the average. You can type the range (for example, **B3:B8**) but it is much easier to use the mouse to select the cells in that range, because WordPerfect then automatically inserts B3:B8 in place of the word `List` in the formula.

6. Click the green check mark or press Enter to insert the formula in the table. If you haven't entered any student grades, the formula calculates to 0.

Your next task is to copy the AVE( ) formula eight times to the right. (You use another formula in the Letter Grade column.) After you copy the formula, notice that it changes automatically to reflect its new location. For example, in C9, the formula reads `AVE(C3:C8)`. As explained earlier in this chapter, relative referencing enables you to copy formulas without having to edit them to match their new location.

Using Formulas with Absolute References

Before you proceed, you should understand something about the difference between relative and absolute references so that your formulas work the way you expect them to when you copy them to other cells.

Each time you copy a formula, WordPerfect uses relative referencing, thus automatically changing the formula to reflect the formula's new location. Sometimes, however, you don't want one or more references in a formula to change. If you place brackets ([ ]) around a cell reference, it remains constant even when copied to a new location. This is called *absolute referencing*. You also can specify only the row or the column as absolute. For example, [A]2 means that row 2 changes relative to the new row as you copy down; however, as you copy the formula to the right, column A remains absolute in the copied formulas.

In the grade-tracking table, each instructor assigns different values to different testing activities. Assume that you grade the three quizzes using varying point values, but plan to give only 100 points total for all the quizzes. The formula for each student in column E, therefore, must divide that student's total quiz points by the total possible quiz points (the sum of all the points in cells B2 through D2), and multiply by 100. Because each formula in the column references the same cells (B2:D2), you use absolute referencing.

To create a Quiz Points average formula using an absolute reference, follow these steps:

1. Position the cursor in cell E3 (the first student row) and then click the formula edit box.
2. Choose **F**unctions, find SUM(List), and choose **I**nsert. You also can simply type **sum(** (opening parenthesis) in the formula edit box.
3. Use the mouse to select the range of cells you want to include (for example, B3:D3). If you type the range, be sure to type a **)** (closed parenthesis) after D3—for example, **sum(B3:D3)**.
4. Type the division symbol (/).
5. Choose **F**unctions, SUM(List) from the list, and **I**nsert.
6. Use the mouse to select the range of cells by which you divide the student's scores, for example, sum(B2:D2).
7. Type ***100**. The formula now reads `sum(B3:D3)/sum(B2:D2)*100`.
8. Finally, to make the sum of the cells in the range B2:D2 an absolute reference, type brackets on each side. The formula now reads `sum(B3:D3)/sum([B2:D2])*100`. With the sum of possible scores now established as an absolute reference, you can choose OK and safely copy the formula down to the other cells in column E. You even can copy the formula from E3 to E2 (the column heading row) to show the total possible points (100).

Using the SUM( ) Function To Create a Total Points Formula

The formula for total points is relatively simple. You can use the SUM() function to add the range of cells from Quiz Points through the Paper (columns E through H). For example, the formula can read `SUM(E2:H2)`.

That formula, however, works best for a final summary grade. To create a formula that reflects only the points possible to this point in the term, you can use a formula that lists only the cells of completed items—for example, SUM(E2, F2, H2). With this formula, the percentage averages and letter grades reflect a student's current standing in a more meaningful way.

The formula used on the student rows of column I should follow the pattern SUM(E3:H3). Although they may not have all the assignments completed or grades recorded, this formula gives a sum of what they have completed compared with the total number of points possible so far (at the top of the column).

Creating the Percent Formula and a Percent Format

You calculate a student's final percentage average by dividing his or her total points by the total possible points in cell I2. Once again, you use absolute referencing to make sure each formula in the column divides by I2. For example, the formula in row three reads `I3/[I2]`. Copy the formula to the other student rows.

A perfect score results in 1, whereas most scores result in a decimal number less than 1. You can multiply the result by 100 to display a number that looks more like a percentage. But you also can format the entire column so that any number in the column appears as a percentage. To format a column for percentage, you change the number type as follows:

1. Position the cursor in the column you want to format, or column J here.

2. From the QuickMenu, choose **N**umber Type. Choose C**o**lumn, and from the list of number types choose **P**ercent.

   Remember that number types enable you to predetermine the format of numbers you enter in a column.

3. You also can specify the decimal precision you want to display. For this example, choose C**u**stom, and specify **1 D**igits After Decimal. None of the other options apply here, but note them for future reference.

4. Choose OK twice to return to your document.

The value, for example .892, now displays as a properly formatted percentage: 89.2%. Remember, however, that if you reference a percentage cell in another formula, you must refer to the decimal value, not the displayed percentage (for example, .892, not 89.2).

Using the IF( ) Function To Calculate the Letter Grade

One of the more powerful functions is the IF( ) statement, which you use to determine a result based on certain conditions. The syntax for this function is as follows:

```
IF(CaseAisTrue, ThenResultB, OtherwiseResultC)
```

In column K of the grade-tracking table, for example, you want to indicate that the person receives a letter grade of "A" if his or her average is 92 percent or higher. In cell K3, you enter **IF(J3>=.93,"A","F")**. In plain English, this formula reads, "If the value of J3 is greater than or equal to .93, print an A in this cell, otherwise print an F." The percentage is entered as the decimal value to match properly the actual values in column J. Also, text strings can be part of a formula, but they must be surrounded by quotation marks.

This formula is a good start, but obviously you have a wider range of grades than just A's and F's. You need to use another IF statement in place of the F. In English you say, "Otherwise, if J3 is greater than or equal to .85, print a B; otherwise, if J3 is greater than or equal to .76, print a C," and so on. The final formula looks like this:

```
IF(J3>=.93,"A",IF(J3>=.85,"B",IF(J3>=.76,"C",IF(J3>=.7,"D","F"))))
```

Notice that the formula ends with four parentheses. For each opening parenthesis, you must add a closing parenthesis. If you enter the formula incorrectly, WordPerfect prompts you to modify it so all its functions, arguments, and punctuation are correct.

Copy this formula to all the student rows, as well as to the AVERAGES row at the bottom. Functionally, the grade sheet is completed. Add lines and other cell formatting, lock formula cells, and save the grade sheet. You are ready to begin entering student names and grade scores.

Using Names To Create a Report Card Table

As useful as the grade-tracking table is for monitoring student progress and how well the class is doing on your exams and quizzes, you can extend its power even further by using it to generate simple report cards. One method for doing this is to use floating cells (see "Using Floating Cells To Create a Mortgage Loan Approval Letter" later in this chapter). But another effective way is to use the Names feature to help transfer data from the master grades table to a report card table on a separate page in the same document.

Creating the Form

Use the grade-tracking table as a model to create the report card table; make sure that the master grade-tracking table is completed and formatted just the way you want it. Then follow these steps:

1. Move to the bottom of your document and press Ctrl+Enter to create a new page.
2. Copy the entire grade-tracking table to this newly created page.
3. Position your cursor in row four of the copied table.
4. From the QuickMenu, choose **D**elete and specify the number of rows you want to delete. Remove all but the first three rows. (Alternatively, split the table and delete the second of the two resulting tables.)
5. Be sure to save your work. Figure 30.21 shows the completed table.

STUDENT NAME October 24, 1994	Quizzes			Quiz Points	Exam 1	Exam 2	Paper	Total Points	Average %	Letter Grade
Possible Points	85	70	100	100	150	150	200	600	100.0%	
Berndobler, Gary	83	65	92	94	136	130	175	535	89.2%	B

Fig. 30.21 The student report card table is created by copying the grade-tracking table and deleting unneeded rows.

Creating Names in Tables

Every table has a name, and you can reference or go to a table in your document by using the name of the table. Unless you specify otherwise, WordPerfect names your tables Table A, Table B, and so on. When you copied your table in the preceding section, however, you ended up with two tables named Table A. (WordPerfect also copied the table name.)

You can easily assign descriptive names to your tables that makes it easier to reference them in macros, formulas, and so on. To change the names of your tables, follow these steps:

1. Position the cursor in either table.

2. From the pull-down menus choose Table, Names. WordPerfect displays the Table Names in Current Document dialog box (see fig. 30.22).

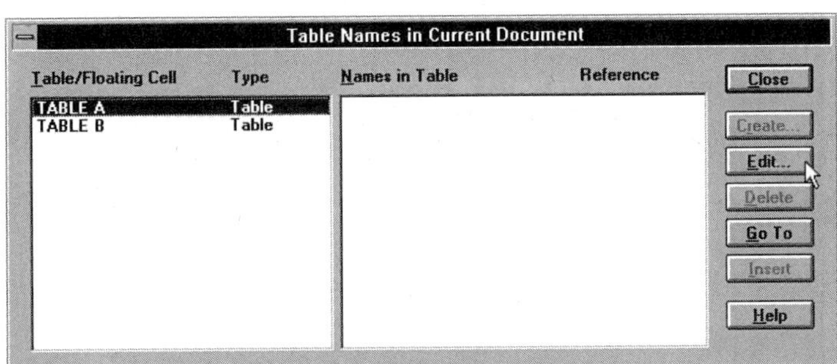

Fig. 30.22
The Table Names in Current Document dialog box lets you change the names of tables and cells, and then use those names as reference points for formulas, macros, and so on.

Note

You cannot create or edit table names from the QuickMenu.

3. Select the first Table A entry from the **T**able/Floating Cell list, and choose Edit.

4. From the Edit Name/Reference dialog box, enter **Grade Sheet** in the **N**ame text box and choose OK.

5. Select the second (remaining) Table A entry and choose **E**dit. Enter **Report Card** and choose OK.

6. Choose **C**lose to return to your document.

You also need to name the first cell in the third row of the Report Card table as a reference point to which you can copy student data. To name a cell, follow these steps:

1. Position the cursor in the cell you want to name—for example cell A3 of the Report Card table.

2. Choose T**a**ble, **N**ames. WordPerfect displays the Table Names in Current Document dialog box (refer to fig. 30.22).

3. Select the Report Card table from the **T**able/Floating Cell list and choose C**r**eate. WordPerfect displays the Create Name dialog box (see fig. 30.23). In this dialog box, you can name a cell, a range of cells, or an entire row or column. You also can use the text in the cell to be named, as the name for that cell.

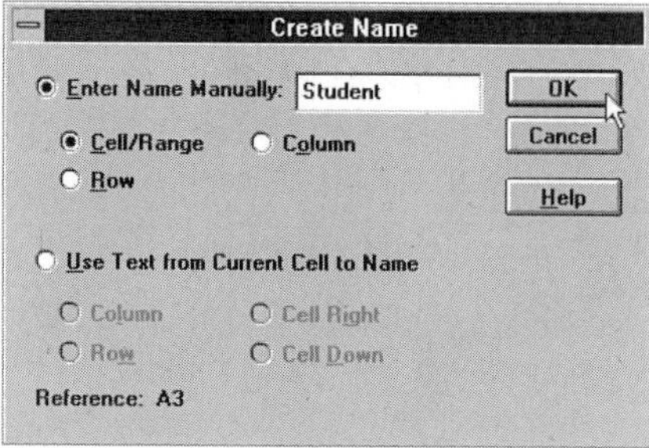

Fig. 30.23
The Create Name dialog box is used for naming cells, rows, and columns in a WordPerfect table.

4. In the **E**nter Name Manually text box, enter **Student** and choose OK.
5. Now when you select the Report Card table in the Table Names in Current Document dialog box, STUDENT followed by A3 should appear in the **N**ames in Table list.
6. Choose **C**lose to return to your document.

Using Names in Tables

Table and cell names make it much easier to move from one location to another. For example, you can use the Go To command (Ctrl+G) to move from one table to another.

If you are in the Report Card table, press Ctrl+G and from the list of tables, choose Grade Sheet, and then choose OK. If you want to go to a specific cell in another table, press Ctrl+G and choose both the table and the cell, and then choose OK (see fig. 30.24).

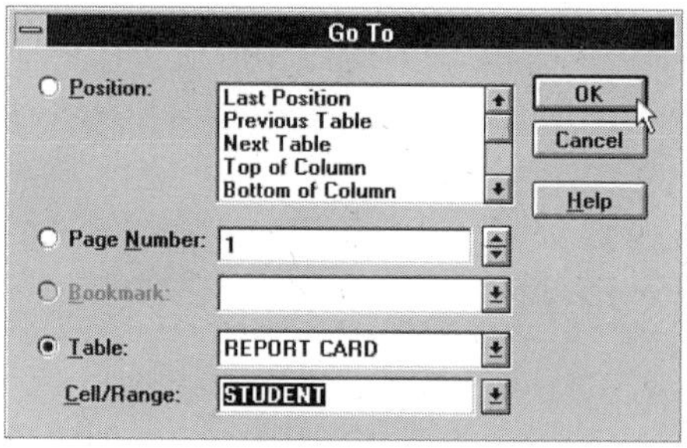

Go To
Position: Last Position / Previous Table / Next Table / Top of Column / Bottom of Column
OK
Cancel
Help
Page Number: 1
Bookmark:
Table: REPORT CARD
Cell/Range: STUDENT

Fig. 30.24
Use the Go To dialog box to select a destination table and cell location.

You also can use table/cell names as reference points in formulas. For example, if in your INVOICE table you have a value in a cell named TOTAL, and have another cell named TAX, you can calculate the sales tax in your table by ending the formula **INVOICE.TOTAL*TAX**. The table and cell are separated with a period.

Finally, you can use table and cell names as reference points in macros for copying data from one location to another. For example, you want to create a report card for each student by copying the data from his or her row on the master GRADE SHEET table to the STUDENT row on the REPORT CARD table. After you position the cursor at the beginning of any row of grade information in the GRADE SHEET table, include these basic steps in your macro (you also can perform these steps without using a macro):

1. Press Ctrl+Shift+Q to set a QuickMark bookmark.
2. Select the entire row of data by pressing Shift+F8 and then pressing Ctrl+right-arrow key. You also can hold down the Shift key and press End twice.
3. Choose Copy (Ctrl+Insert), and from the Table Cut/Copy dialog box, choose OK (to copy selection).
4. Press Ctrl+G, and choose the REPORT CARD table and the STUDENT cell. Choose OK.
5. In the STUDENT cell, choose Paste (Shift+Insert).
6. Press Ctrl+Q to return to the original QuickMark bookmark location.

As you can see, table names and named cells give you tremendous power and flexibility as you work with table math and functions.

Using Floating Cells To Create a Mortgage Loan Approval Letter

One of WordPerfect's unique new features, floating cells, allows you to use table functions and formulas in the body of your text. For example, you can use these cells to reference other floating cells or cells in any table such as in a mortgage loan letter that calculates payments based on current interest rates.

Understanding and Creating Floating Cells

A *floating cell* is nothing more than a pair of codes that surround the same kind of information that you put in any table cell. Floating cells also can be formatted for number type, the same as in table cells.

To create a floating cell, position the cursor in your document text where you want to create the cell. Then follow these basic steps:

1. Choose T**a**ble, **C**reate. From the Create Table dialog box, choose **F**loating Cell. Then choose OK.

2. If you know the format you want for the floating cell, choose T**a**ble, N**u**mber Type and choose the number format you want to use. Choose OK.

3. WordPerfect automatically names floating cells—for example FLOATING CELL A. If you plan to use the cell in a formula, you may want to use the Names feature to give it a more descriptive and shorter name—for example, AMOUNT.

4. You can now enter the actual data in the floating cell. However, if you have turned on the Formula Feature Bar, you can enter the information more easily in the formula edit box. If you plan to create several floating cells, using the Formula Feature Bar can make the task easier.

> **Note**
>
> If the check mark next to the formula edit box is not green, then your cursor is positioned outside the pair of floating cell codes. Turn on Reveal Codes, move the cursor between the pair of codes, and the check mark turns green.

5. After you create the floating cell, assign the number type, and enter the data you want into the cell, you must move your cursor to the right, outside of the pair of floating cell codes. Press End or click the mouse to the right of the floating cell and continue with the text of your document.

Using Calendar Math in a Floating Cell

Suppose you want to include in your letter a sentence stating that the loan offer is good for two weeks from today's date. You need to create two floating cells, one for today's date and one for the offer expiration date. The first cell contains the function MDY( ), using the Date/Time number type to display the current day. The second cell, also using the Date/Time number type, simply adds the contents of the first cell plus 14. To create the closing paragraph of the loan letter (see fig. 30.25), follow these steps.

1. Type the paragraph until you reach the location of today's date (`...beginning today, July 1, 1993,`).

2. Turn on the Formula Feature Bar by choosing T**a**ble, Fo**r**mula Bar.

3. Choose T**a**ble, **C**reate, **F**loating Cell, and choose OK.

4. Choose T**a**ble, N**u**mber Type, select **D**ate/Time and choose OK.

5. Choose T**a**ble, **N**ames and edit the name of the floating cell to **Today**. Choose **C**lose.

6. Click the formula edit box on the Formula Feature Bar and type **mdy()**. Press Enter or click the green check mark to enter the formula into your document. The document should display today's date (for example, `November 15, 1995`).

7. Continue typing the paragraph until you reach the location of the expiration date (`...of this loan by`).

8. Repeat steps 3-5 to create a floating cell, formatted for Date/Time, and named **Expires**.

9. Click the formula edit box on the Formula Feature Bar and enter **today+14**. Press Enter or click the green check mark to enter the formula into your document. The document should display today's date plus 14 days (for example, `November 29, 1995`).

10. Finish typing the paragraph and save the document.

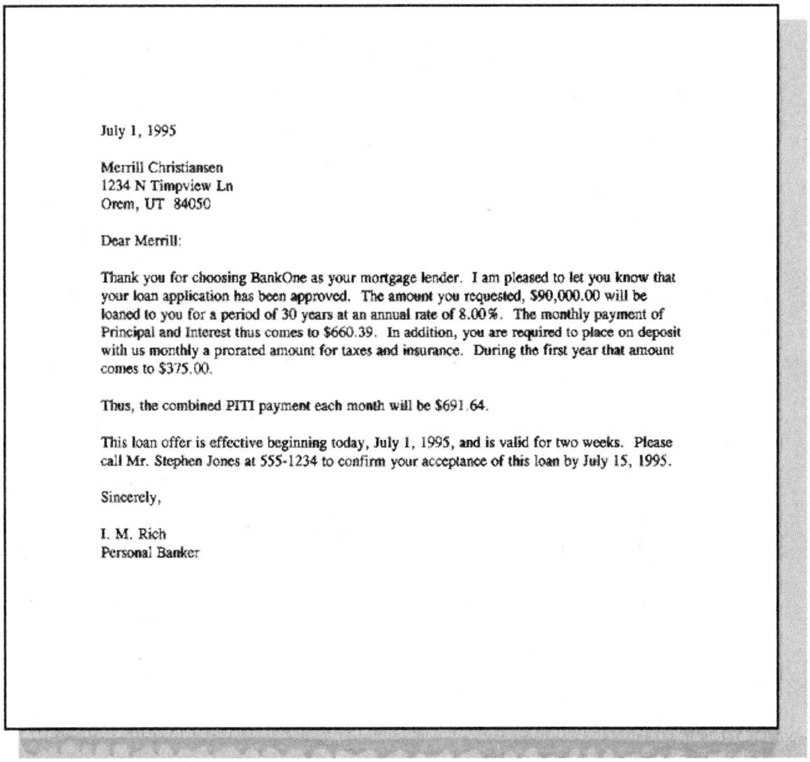

July 1, 1995

Merrill Christiansen
1234 N Timpview Ln
Orem, UT 84050

Dear Merrill:

Thank you for choosing BankOne as your mortgage lender. I am pleased to let you know that your loan application has been approved. The amount you requested, $90,000.00 will be loaned to you for a period of 30 years at an annual rate of 8.00%. The monthly payment of Principal and Interest thus comes to $660.39. In addition, you are required to place on deposit with us monthly a prorated amount for taxes and insurance. During the first year that amount comes to $375.00.

Thus, the combined PITI payment each month will be $691.64.

This loan offer is effective beginning today, July 1, 1995, and is valid for two weeks. Please call Mr. Stephen Jones at 555-1234 to confirm your acceptance of this loan by July 15, 1995.

Sincerely,

I. M. Rich
Personal Banker

Fig. 30.25
A loan letter that uses functions in named cells to calculate a mortgage payment and the offer expiration date.

Using the PMT( ) Function To Calculate a Loan Payment

The same principles you used to create the expiration date apply when using more complex formulas:

- Determine what arguments are required for the function
- Create the floating cells (or table cells) that supply the information needed for the arguments
- Name those cells so you can reference them easily
- Create the floating cell that contains the function, assign a number type, and use named cells to create the formula

The PMT() function is a good example of a powerful, yet relatively simple function. This function requires the following syntax and arguments:

```
PMT(Rate,Present Value, Periods, Future Value, Type)
```

- *Rate.* The annual interest rate. If you use periods other than years, the rate must be prorated. For example, 8 percent annual interest over 12 monthly periods must be expressed as 8%/12 (or .08/12)
- *Present Value.* The current or initial value of the loan (for example, $90,000).
- *Periods.* The number of periods to be used in the calculation. A loan paid monthly for 30 years is for 360 periods (or 30*12).
- *Future Value.* The amount of the loan when it is paid off—usually zero (0).
- *Type.* This indicates whether the payment is made at the end of a loan period (the default, 0), or at the beginning of the loan period (any non-zero value). This argument can be omitted altogether.

Thus for a loan of $90,000, at 8 percent interest over 30 years, you use the following formula:

pmt(.08/12, 90000, 360, 0, 0)

Using the loan letter as a sample, enter the text you see until you reach each of the locations that contains a part of the PMT() arguments. At that location, create a floating cell that contains the following:

- *Amount.* Name this **Amount**, choose Cu**r**rency as the number type, and enter **90000** as the formula.
- *Period.* Name this **Years**, enter **30** as the formula (leaving the number type **G**eneral).
- *Interest.* Name this **Interest**, choose **P**ercent as the number type, and enter **8%** as the formula. Because the cell is formatted for percent, WordPerfect displays `8.00%` and also establishes the value of the floating cell as `.08`.

When you arrive at the payment amount, create the Payment floating cell, formatted for **C**urrency, and enter the following formula: **pmt(interest/12, amount, years*12, 0, 0)**.

If you entered everything as indicated, the result should read `$660.39`.

Simplifying Data Entry in a Floating Cell Letter

The amount of work required to enter each of the preceding entries is almost more work than it is worth. For example, to change the loan amount to 90000, you must position the cursor between the `Flt Cell` codes. Then you delete the text that already is there and replace it with the new amount. You must do this in Reveal Codes to ensure that the new amount appears between the two floating cell codes.

A much easier method is to create a merge form using KEYBOARD( ) merge codes placed between the floating cell codes. Then when you merge the form, WordPerfect prompts you for the needed data and automatically inserts it in the proper floating cell location. (See Chapter 19, "Assembling Documents with Merge and Sort," for information on creating a form file, how to insert KEYBOARD( ) merge codes, and how to merge to a form from the keyboard.)

You also can create a custom template document that prompts you for the necessary data and then fills it in at the proper locations. (See Chapter 11, "Using Templates," for information on creating custom templates.)

> **Caution**
>
> Make sure your floating cell formulas and formats are the way you want them before you add the KEYBOARD( ) merge codes. If you change the formula, name or number type in a floating cell, WordPerfect deletes any other data such as the merge code that may be in the cell.

◀ See "Understanding Form Files," p. 640

Don't forget, after filling in the data, to update all the floating cells by choosing Table, Calculate, and choosing Calc Document.

Troubleshooting

After I create my table and formulas, the results don't appear to be correct.

There are no easy rules for making sure a table calculates correctly. However, try calculating the document first. Then examine each formula to make sure cell references and logic are correct. Finally, make sure you aren't inadvertently including a text cell that contains numbers in your formula (for example, adding a column that includes "2nd Quarter" so that the "2" is added to the total.) Proofreading formulas is as important as proofreading text, since incorrect formulas could cost you a lot of money.

When I enter a dollar amount in a column, the cents sometimes wrap to the next line even though the original 0.00 displays properly.

Make sure the column is wide enough for the new number. The easiest method is to choose Size Column to Fit from the QuickMenu. If the numbers are in the last column, you'll probably have to change the width of the column. You also may need to change the amount of space reserved for numbers following the decimal point by going to the Format, Column menu.

Using Data Fill To Simplify Data Entry

In Chapter 16, "Working with Tables" you created a calendar form using tables with fixed row height (see fig. 30.26). Although you could type in the days and dates by hand, WordPerfect's spreadsheet functions once again offer a simpler solution, as you learn in this section.

Understanding Data Fill

The idea behind the data fill procedure is that WordPerfect can examine the first few entries in a series and automatically determine the pattern that is being used. The program then fills in the remaining blank cells in the series based on that pattern.

For example, if you want to enter a series of numbers in 15 cells, and the first three of those cells are 1, 3, and 5, WordPerfect would fill the remaining cells with 7, 9, 11, and so on.

JUNE 1995

Sunday	Monday	Tuesday	Wednesday	Thursday	Friday	Saturday
				1	2	3
4	5	6	7	8	9	10
11	12 Summer Session Begins	13	14	15	16	17
18	19	20	21	22	23	24
25	26	27	28	29	30	

Fig. 30.26
A calendar table. Use WordPerfect's Data Fill feature to automatically fill in days of the week and the calendar dates.

Using Data Fill To Enter the Days of the Week

In your calendar, the first row of seven cells should contain the days of the week. To automatically fill in these days, follow these steps:

1. Position the cursor in cell A1.
2. Type **Sunday**.
3. Select all of the cells on the first row.
4. Choose T**a**ble, Data **F**ill; or press Ctrl+Shift+F12.

WordPerfect automatically fills in Monday, Tuesday, Wednesday, and so on.

Filling in the Dates of the Month

You can automatically fill in the dates of the month, although not quite so cleanly as you fill in the days of the week. To fill in the dates of the month, follow these steps:

1. Position the cursor in the cell that corresponds to the first day of the month and type **1**.
2. If this day falls on any day other than Sunday, you must then type at least two more days by hand, then select the first row and choose T**a**ble, Data **F**ill. If the first day falls on Sunday, skip this step.

3. Fill in the first three days of the first full week of the month (for example, 4, 5, and 6).

4. Select all the cells in the first full week through the end of the month and choose T**a**ble, Data **F**ill.

5. Delete the "extra" days at the end of the month.

Other Uses for Data Fill

Anywhere you need a series of values and want to avoid typing them by hand, you can use the Data Fill feature. In addition to number sequences, you also can enter Days and Months:

Monday, Tuesday, Wednesday, ... (or Mon, Tue, Wed, ...)

January, February, March, ... (or Jan, Feb, Mar, ...)

For example, you could create a mortgage payment schedule, a weight reduction schedule, a jogging progress schedule, and more. In short, let WordPerfect do the work for you.

From Here...

In this chapter, you have gone far beyond the basics of creating and formatting a table. You have learned much about the flexibility and power of tables. Specifically, you learned to properly position tables in a document; split and join tables; customize tables by modifying lines, borders, and fills; use formulas in tables; create spreadsheet-like tables and forms; and use the powerful floating cell feature.

For information relating to additional uses for tables, you may want to review these chapters:

- Chapter 16, "Working with Tables," reviews some of the basics of table layout and formatting.
- Chapter 18, "Importing Data and Working with Other Programs," shows how to import spreadsheets into tables.
- Chapter 19, "Assembling Documents with Merge and Sort," shows how to use tables to create data files, and also how to sort tables.
- Chapter 23, "Desktop Publishing with WordPerfect," teaches you more about how to enhance tables to be used as forms.

Chapter 31

Interactive Documents

by Mitch Milam

Paper is fast becoming passé.

Document technology—the art of presenting textual information—has evolved greatly in the past few years. No longer must users read volumes of paper documents to find something that interests them. They can now view the documents on their computer screens in a format that is a very close, if not exact, representation of the printed output.

Even more importantly, references to related topics can be embedded directly into the document allowing the reader to move around the document much the way they would flip through a book using the table of contents, index, and other references to find related topics. The term used for interactive documents is *Hypertext.*

Computer-based documentation not only saves our forests, but also provides companies and individuals a medium for presenting information that is easily distributed and updated.

Most modern computer applications show a trend toward large and complex on-line help systems and a reduction in the amount of printed material shipped with the product. After all, why print out the manual when it is already at the user's fingertips under the Help option?

This chapter shows you how to:

- Use WordPerfect's Hypertext feature to create links to different parts of the same document and to parts of other documents
- Run a WordPerfect macro from your document using a Hypertext link
- Explore the process of embedding sounds in documents to emphasize a topic

Understanding Hypertext

Hypertext is a generic computer term that means a document's capability to immediately and automatically display nonsequential text when requested. WordPerfect takes this generic term and applies it to the creation of WordPerfect documents. Using WordPerfect's Hypertext feature, you can link, or connect, one section of a document to other sections of the same document or to sections of a different document; you can also run a macro. Figure 31.1 is a flow chart showing Hypertext's text-switching and macro-running capabilities.

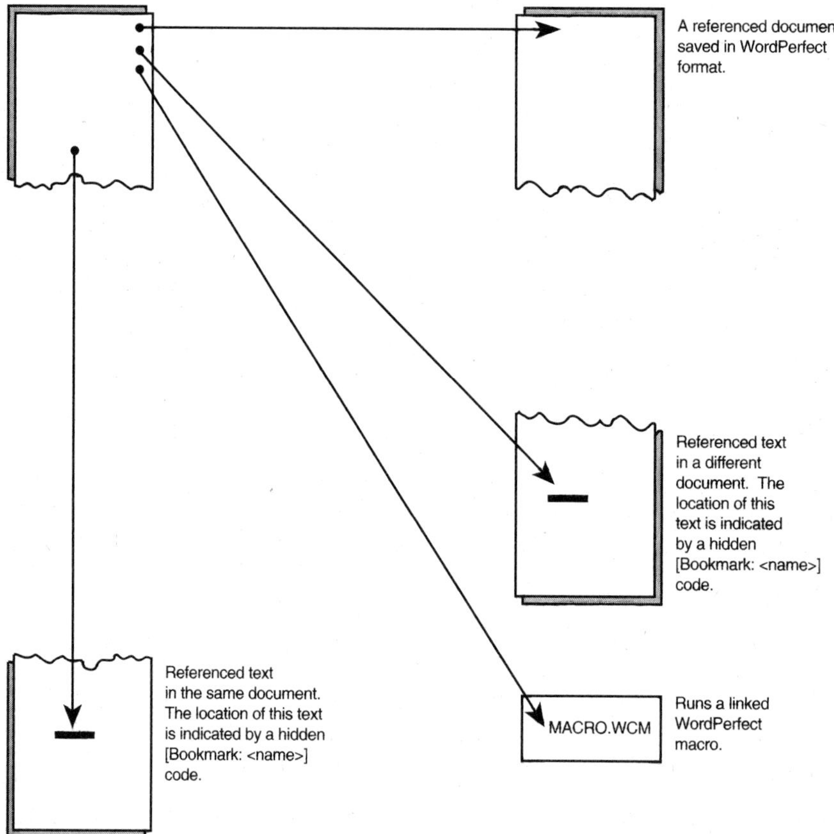

Fig. 31.1
A flow chart showing Hypertext's capabilities.

WordPerfect uses the Bookmark feature to mark the locations that are referenced by the Hypertext engine. A bookmark is a hidden code that marks a location in the document. In Reveal Codes, you see the `[Bookmark:<name>]`

code that marks the location of the bookmark. Bookmarks allow you to immediately jump from any position in the document to the bookmark. You can place bookmarks anywhere in a document.

WordPerfect uses a *button* to mark a Hypertext link. A button can appear as either emphasized text or as an actual graphical button, like those found in Windows dialog boxes.

As you read this discussion on the Hypertext feature, keep in mind the following terms:

- A *link* is the connection between a button, a word, or a group of words marked in the document with emphasized text, or the connection between a graphic image and its target.
- A *jump* is the switching operation that displays the target. You can invoke a jump by moving the cursor to the Hypertext button and pressing Enter, or by clicking the Hypertext button.
- A *return* is the switching operation that redisplays the original text passage.
- A *run* is a special type of jump that starts a WordPerfect macro.

Working with WordPerfect's Hypertext Feature

WordPerfect provides an additional tool called a Feature Bar that appears below the ruler. The purpose of the Feature Bar is to provide additional buttons for quick access to features specific to the tool you have chosen. The Feature Bar changes depending on the tool you have selected. Figure 31.2 shows a WordPerfect document containing Hypertext links with the Hypertext Feature Bar active.

The Hypertext Feature Bar buttons perform the following actions:

- *?* allows you to select the same functions contained in the Feature Bar's buttons and also to select other WordPerfect feature bars.
- *Perform* activates the Hypertext action of the current Hypertext button.
- *Back* returns to the point where the cursor was located before you performed a Hypertext jump.
- *Next* jumps to the next Hypertext button in your document.

- ***Previous*** jumps to the preceding Hypertext button in your document.
- *Crea**t**e* allows you to create a new Hypertext button.
- ***E**dit* allows you to modify an existing Hypertext button.
- ***D**elete* removes an existing Hypertext button.
- ***A**ctivate/De**a**ctivate* switches the current Hypertext mode of the document.
- ***S**tyle* allows you to change the appearance of the text version of a Hypertext button.
- ***C**lose* removes the Hypertext Feature Bar.

You can select these buttons by clicking them or by pressing the Alt+Shift+*letter* combination.

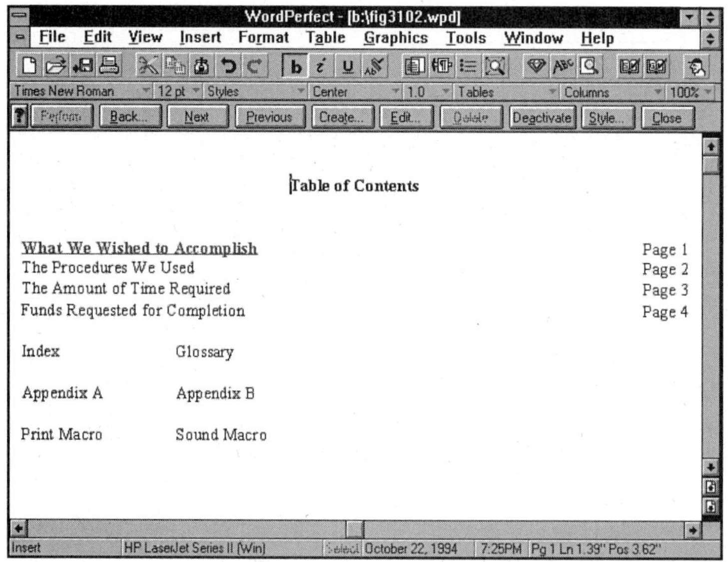

Fig. 31.2
The WordPerfect Hypertext Feature Bar supplies buttons for the different Hypertext functions. You can select the button with the mouse or by pressing an Alt+Shift+letter combination.

When you first load a Hypertext document, it is *deactivated*, meaning that you can edit the document, including the Hypertext buttons, as you would any other WordPerfect document. Choosing **A**ctivate in the Hypertext Feature Bar switches the document from Edit mode to Hypertext mode and changes the Activate button to Deactivate. When a Hypertext document has been activated, clicking a Hypertext button or pressing Enter with the cursor on the Hypertext button performs that link. Choosing De**a**ctivate switches the document back to Edit mode.

> **Note**
>
> Selecting the **C**lose button removes the Hypertext Feature Bar, but because there are no menu equivalents to the Feature Bar, you will lose most of the Hypertext functionality. If Hypertext was active when you closed the bar, it will remain active, but the only feature available to you is selecting a Hypertext button in your document.

Creating an Interactive Report

The best way to learn about Hypertext is by using it, so let's take an everyday report and make it interactive. Reports of any length have a table of contents at the beginning that allows the user to determine the contents of the report and on what page each topic starts. Figure 31.3 shows a report in WordPerfect before any Hypertext features have been added.

The table of contents is the main jumping-off point in your document.

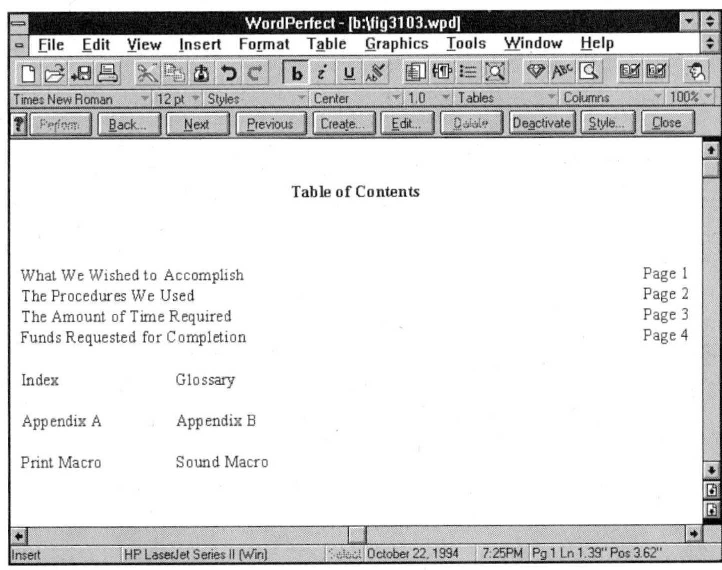

Fig. 31.3
A report in WordPerfect before adding Hypertext features.

Designing Your Hypertext Document

The first step in creating a Hypertext document is creating the document itself. Follow whatever formatting and layout conventions you would use when creating a normal WordPerfect document. After you complete this step, print the document so that you have a working hard copy. The example used in this chapter is a project report. The report has four sections: an index, a glossary, and two appendixes. Each has an entry in the table of contents. The table of contents is located at the top of the document and will be used by the reader as the starting point for the document. From the table of contents, the user may jump to any section of the document.

Tip
You can create a jump map at any time during the document's assembly. Waiting until the document is completed keeps you from wasting time modifying the jump map due to document editing changes.

The next step is creating a *jump map*. Like a road map that allows you to visually see the best way to navigate the roadways, a jump map allows you to define points of interest that are referenced with the Hypertext links. A jump map consists of a table of entries defining the following information:

- Topic name
- Page number
- Bookmark name
- Locations where the topic can be referenced

Note

If you are creating a multiple-document Hypertext system, add the name of the document to the list of jump map entries.

To create a jump map, perform the following steps:

1. Find a topic of interest. This topic could be the beginning of a chapter or section, a graphics image, or a relevant paragraph.
2. Create a named bookmark for the location. Remember that bookmark names must be unique. The actual bookmark is created in the next section of this chapter, "Marking a Hypertext Target with a Bookmark."
3. Review the document and create a list of locations that could benefit from a reference to the current topic.
4. Repeat steps 1–3 until all topics of interest have been covered.

Table 31.1 shows an example of a jump map.

Table 31.1 An Example of a Jump Map

Topic	Page	Bookmark	References
Wishes	1	Wishes	Table of Contents, page 1
Procedures	2	Procedures	Table of Contents, page 1
Time	3	Time	Table of Contents, page 1
Funds	4	Funds	Table of Contents, page 1
Index	99	Index	Table of Contents, page 1
Glossary	97	Glossary	Table of Contents, page 1
Appendix A	90	Appendix A	Table of Contents, page 1

Now that you have created a jump map, you are ready to create the bookmarks that will be used as targets for Hypertext links.

Note

Always work on a copy of the document or documents. This procedure allows you to be creative without the worry of damaging the original work. You'll also have a backup in case you make a major editing mistake.

Marking a Hypertext Target with a Bookmark

Using the jump map that you created in the preceding section, you can insert the bookmark targets that are referenced by your Hypertext buttons. For example, to insert a bookmark at the section "What We Wished to Accomplish," one of the specified jump map locations, you can perform the following steps:

1. The first topic in your jump map is located on page 1 of the report. Move the cursor to the top of page 1.

2. From the **I**nsert menu, choose **B**ookmark, and then select Cr**e**ate. Enter the name of the bookmark Wishes and choose OK. WordPerfect inserts the hidden bookmark code at the current cursor location. This bookmark will be used by the Hypertext feature as a jump target.

If you have text selected when you create the bookmark, WordPerfect will use the selected text as the bookmark name. If you don't have text selected, WordPerfect will select text for you and supply it as the name. You may edit the name once the Create Bookmark dialog box is displayed.

3. Repeat steps 1 and 2 for each of the bookmark names in the jump map.

> **Note**
>
> If you select text before accessing the Bookmark feature, only the text within the selection is offered as the default bookmark name. If you press Enter, WordPerfect marks the text in the document with beginning and ending bookmark codes instead of the default single code. The Hypertext feature works with both types of bookmark codes.

Linking Text within a Document

After you create all your reference bookmarks, you are ready to insert the Hypertext links that will provide the links to the bookmarks. To create a Hypertext button using the default settings, perform the following steps:

1. From the **T**ools menu, select **H**ypertext. The Hypertext Feature Bar appears.

2. Select the text "What We Wished to Accomplish," to be used as the Hypertext button. In some cases, you will probably want to type text specifically for a button; at other times, you will want to use existing text in the document. In this case, the existing text will be used for the button.

   If you are using the text style of the Hypertext button, you can simply select the text, and then create the Hypertext button. The only change to the original text of your document will be in its appearance (font, bold, and underline). The button form of the Hypertext button makes it stand out from the surrounding text but is also practically limited to a single word or two. You can create larger buttons, but in most cases a large button distracts from the presentation of the text.

3. Choose Crea**t**e from the Hypertext Feature Bar. WordPerfect displays the Create Hypertext Link dialog box (see fig. 31.4).

4. The dialog box contains three options that create different actions. For this example, choose Go To **B**ookmark.

5. Enter the name of a bookmark and press Enter, or choose OK. For a list of bookmarks, use the Go To **B**ookmark drop-down list.

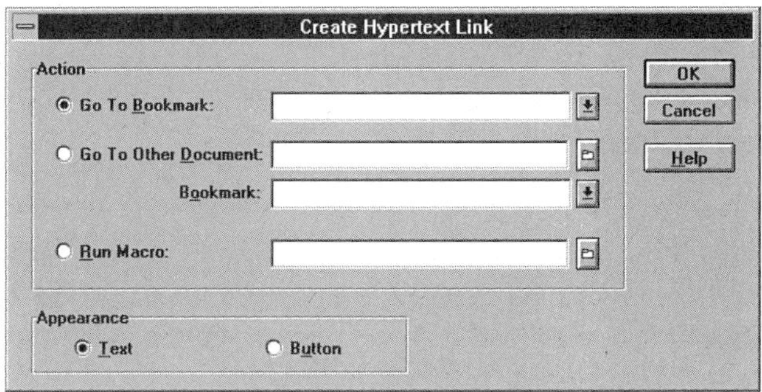

Fig. 31.4
Use the Create Hypertext Link dialog box to define or change the Hypertext links in your document.

Notice that the selected text has a changed appearance. On a color monitor, the text is green, boldfaced, and underlined. Figure 31.5 shows the effect of this operation. Notice the Hypertext On and Hypertext Off codes in the Reveal Codes window.

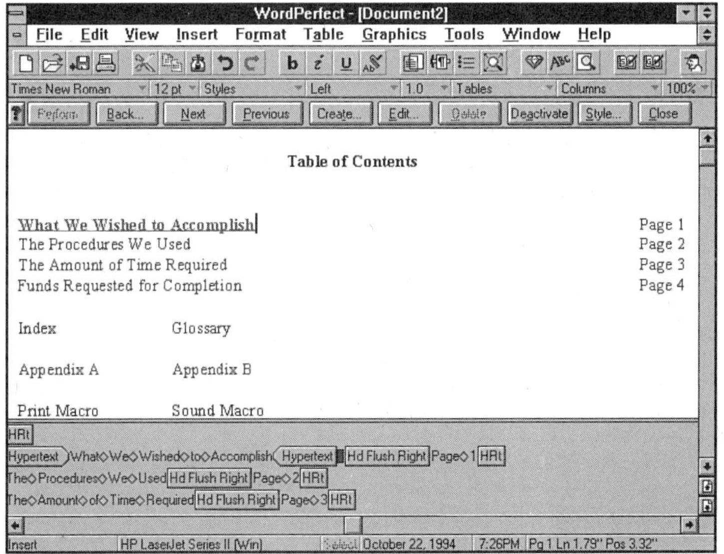

Fig. 31.5
The sample report shows a Hypertext button created using the default style and appearance (text).

Note

The appearance of the Hypertext button may be changed by modifying the Hypertext style. Refer to the section later in this chapter "Changing the Style of Hypertext Buttons," and Chapter 10, "Using Styles," for more information.

The default appearance WordPerfect has chosen for Hypertext buttons is as text. You also can create a Hypertext button that is displayed graphically. When you create the button, select B**u**tton as the Appearance instead of **T**ext.

Graphical Hypertext buttons can be blank or can contain text that you blocked before creating the button. Refer to figure 31.2 for examples of text and graphical Hypertext buttons.

Functionally, the graphical Hypertext buttons are different from text Hypertext buttons in two ways. First, a character text box is created for the appearance of the button. If you blocked text that will appear on the button, you will find that text inside the text box. Second, when Hypertext is active, clicking anywhere on the box activates the link.

The graphical Hypertext buttons are actually text boxes used by the Hypertext feature. You may edit these buttons the same way you would edit a normal text box.

Deleting the Hypertext button removes the text box and restores the text inside the document.

Editing Hypertext Links

To edit an existing Hypertext button, perform the following steps:

1. Look at the Hypertext Feature Bar to make sure that Hypertext is not active. If the Activate button appears in the bar, Hypertext is inactive, and you can continue with step 2. Otherwise, choose De**a**ctivate to return to Edit mode.

Tip
You can also double-click on the Hypertext codes in Reveal Codes to edit the link.

2. Place the cursor on the Hypertext button that you want to edit.

3. Choose **E**dit from the Hypertext Feature Bar. The Edit Hypertext Link dialog box appears (see fig. 31.6). In this dialog box, you can make any changes necessary.

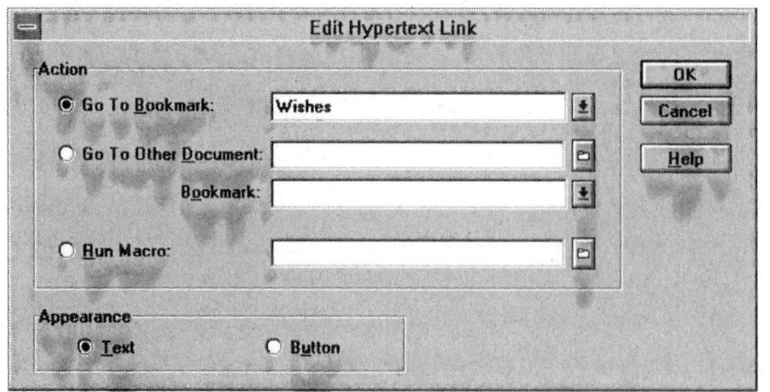

Fig. 31.6
The Edit Hypertext Link dialog box allows you to change the jump location and the appearance of the Hypertext button.

To remove the Hypertext button and restore the text of the button to normal, perform the following steps:

1. Place the cursor on the Hypertext button that you want to edit.
2. Choose **D**elete from the Hypertext Feature Bar. The Hypertext button is removed, restoring the text to its original form.

Linking Documents with Hypertext

The Hypertext feature can link the main document with one or more other documents. If the other document is a WordPerfect document, you can define a link to specific text, using bookmarks, within the second document. If you want to link to a non-WordPerfect document, the most you can do is display the entire document for the user to browse through.

You would create a multiple-document Hypertext system if you had a variety of information stored in separate files that you wanted the user to view; or if the system was extremely large and you had broken the documents into smaller pieces for easier management.

To create a Hypertext link to another document, perform the following steps:

1. Create bookmarks in the destination document. Refer to the earlier section in this chapter "Marking a Hypertext Target with a Bookmark."
2. With the Hypertext Feature Bar active, choose Crea**t**e.
3. Choose Go To Other **D**ocument.
4. Enter the name of the document. You can select the document name from a file list by selecting the folder icon located to the right of the edit box.
5. Choose B**o**okmark.
6. Enter the name of the bookmark to which you want to jump. If you entered the name of a WordPerfect 6.1 document, a list of available bookmarks appears in the list. If you entered a document that is not in WordPerfect 6.1 format, no bookmarks are listed. If you do not select a bookmark, when the Hypertext button is selected, the new document is loaded and your cursor placed at the top of the document.
7. Choose OK to return to the document.

> **Note**
>
> If you distribute the Hypertext document to other users through a network, try to put the linked secondary documents in a subdirectory common to all users. If a common subdirectory is not available to all users, do not add path names to the secondary document's file names, but be sure to distribute all the other documents with the Hypertext document.

Linking Hypertext to Macros

WordPerfect's Hypertext feature also can run a WordPerfect 6.1 macro. This capability can be useful to display information that is not part of the document or to perform certain commands you feel would enhance the function of the document. To create a Hypertext run link, perform the following steps:

1. Choose Crea**t**e from the Hypertext Feature Bar. The Create Hypertext Link dialog box appears.

2. Choose **R**un Macro.

3. Enter the name of the macro. Alternatively, select the macro from a file list by selecting the folder icon located to the right of the edit box.

4. Choose OK.

> **Note**
>
> In multiple-document Hypertext systems, you must be careful to distribute the macros along with the Hypertext documents. On a network, all users must have access to the macros as well as the documents. A solution to this problem is to save the macros as part of the document. This ensures that the macros will always accompany the document wherever it goes.

Changing the Style of Hypertext Buttons

WordPerfect associates a style with the Hypertext button. The default style is green, boldfaced, and underlined. In certain situations (if you are using a monochrome or LCD display, for example), you might find this style unacceptable. To change the Hypertext style, perform the following steps:

1. With the Hypertext Feature Bar active, choose the **S**tyle button. WordPerfect displays the Styles Editor dialog box (see fig. 31.7).

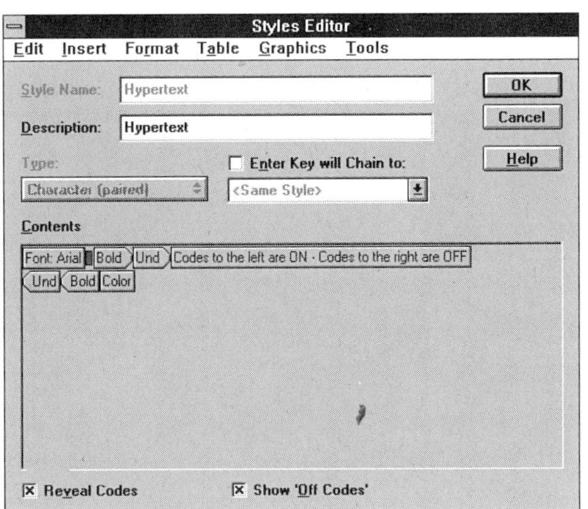

Fig. 31.7
The Styles Editor dialog box allows you to change the Hypertext Style.

2. Modify the Hypertext style in any way you want. Figure 31.7 shows the style after `[Color:Green]` was changed to an Arial font.

3. When you finish editing, choose OK to close the dialog box and return to the document screen.

> **Note**
>
> When you modify the Hypertext appearance style, it is modified for all Hypertext buttons. You cannot modify the style of a single Hypertext button. The Hypertext style is a WordPerfect system style and can be edited like any other style. Refer to Chapter 10, "Using Styles," for more information.

◀ See "Editing Styles," p. 367

Activating a Document with Hypertext

The final step in creating a document with the Hypertext feature is activating the document's automatic links. To activate the link, follow these steps:

1. Choose **T**ools, **H**ypertext. WordPerfect displays the Hypertext Feature Bar.

◀ See "Activate Hypertext," p. 328

2. Choose the **A**ctivate button. Hypertext is now active.

Navigating a Hypertext Document

A WordPerfect document containing Hypertext buttons offers two methods of navigating the Hypertext links: manual and automatic. The manual navigation method allows you to perform a Hypertext link when the Hypertext feature is inactive. When Hypertext is active, you can automatically navigate the document by using the mouse or the Tab key, as well as the Hypertext Feature Bar buttons.

Jumping and Returning in an Active Hypertext Document

When Hypertext is active (and when the Hypertext Feature Bar is displayed), you can switch between different locations of the document with a single keystroke or mouse click, as described in the following list:

- To use the mouse to jump to the link's target location, click the Hypertext button.
- To use the keyboard to jump to the target, move the cursor to the left edge of a graphic Hypertext button or within the text Hypertext button, and press Enter.
- To return to the position of the Hypertext button that you last selected, choose **B**ack from the Hypertext Feature Bar.
- To move to the next Hypertext button, choose **N**ext in the Hypertext Feature Bar, or press Tab. Then press Enter or use the mouse to activate the jump link for that button.
- To move to the preceding Hypertext button, choose **P**revious or press Shift+Tab. Press Enter or use the mouse to activate the jump link for that button.

Tip
The **N**ext and **P**revious feature buttons find the next available Hypertext button located either above or below the current cursor position, even if the cursor is not located at a link code.

Note

Tab and the Shift+Tab key combination perform their normal functions when the cursor is located at any position in the document other than the left edge of the graphic Hypertext button or within the text Hypertext button.

Jumping and Returning in an Inactive Hypertext Document

Even when Hypertext is inactive, the links still are functional. To jump to a target in an inactive Hypertext document, perform the following steps:

1. If the Hypertext Feature Bar is not active, display it by selecting **H**ypertext from the **T**ools menu.

2. Move the cursor to the left edge of a graphic Hypertext button or within the text Hypertext button.

3. Choose Pe**r**form from the Hypertext Feature Bar.

To move from the target back to the Hypertext button, choose **B**ack from the Hypertext Feature Bar.

The **N**ext and **P**revious feature buttons function in the same manner as when the Hypertext document is active.

Jumping and Returning between Documents

Jumping between documents is simply an extension of jumping around a single document. The major difference occurs when the document has been modified by any of the actions of either the Hypertext system or the user. If the current document has been modified and the user selects a jump to another document, a dialog box appears offering the following options:

- **Y**es saves the changes in the document and continues the jump.
- **N**o abandons the changes in the document and continues the jump.
- Cancel abandons the changes and cancels the jump.

Running Macros with Hypertext

Running a macro from a Hypertext document is exactly like using any of the other Hypertext link options. If the macro modifies the current cursor position, just select the feature button **B**ack to return to the preceding location.

Troubleshooting

Nothing happens when I click a Hypertext link.

WordPerfect lets you enable or disable the Hypertext feature. With the feature disabled, clicking a Hypertext link does nothing. To enable the Hypertext feature so that you can click a Hypertext link, choose **H**ypertext from the **T**ools menu. Choose **A**ctivate in the Hypertext Feature Bar. Choose **C**lose to close the Hypertext Feature Bar. Hypertext is now active.

(continues)

(continued)

WordPerfect displays a `Macro XXX Not Found` *error when I click a Hypertext link.*

The macro you specified for the Hypertext link cannot be found. Either the macro is missing completely, or it's not in your regular macros directory (usually \OFFICE\WPWIN\MACROS). If your macro is on your hard disk drive, locate it and copy it to the macros directory.

When I click on a Hypertext link, WordPerfect displays a `Bookmark Not Found` *error.*

The bookmark you specified for the Hypertext link could not be found. If you linked to a bookmark in the current document, be sure the bookmark is in the document. If it's not, place the insertion point at the proper spot in the document and create a bookmark there. If you linked to a bookmark in another document, open it and check that the bookmark is there.

Embedding Sound in a Document

Just as the Hypertext feature allows you to create interactive documents, WordPerfect's sound feature allows you to enhance a document by embedding sounds that the user can play. You can use sounds to emphasize a point or to provide additional information that is understandable only in an audio presentation.

You should remember several things about using sounds in your documents. First, sound clips occupy a large amount of space. How the sound clip was recorded and its length determine its file size. The higher the sound quality and the longer the clip runs, the larger the file size.

WordPerfect relies on the Windows Sound Recorder to record sounds. In most cases, however, the software shipped with the sound board provides superior recording and editing functions. This means that you must use another program to record and edit sound clips before you insert the clip into a document.

Using WordPerfect with a Sound Board

Microsoft Windows provides a link between the Windows environment and the various sound boards available today. Because Windows controls the hardware, any application that can speak to the Windows sound drivers can use sound; WordPerfect is such an application. The program provides the interface between the user and the software that drives the sound hardware so that you can embed, record, and play sound clips as part of a WordPerfect document.

The configuration and setup of a sound card in a PC depends on the type of card being used and on its feature set. Follow the installation instructions to configure the sound card for your PC and Windows. Due to the number of sound cards on the market, this chapter cannot use the installation procedure for a specific card as a blanket example.

Linking Sound Files to a Document

To insert a sound clip into your document, perform the following steps:

1. Select **S**ound from the **I**nsert menu. WordPerfect displays the Sound Clips dialog box (see fig. 31.8).

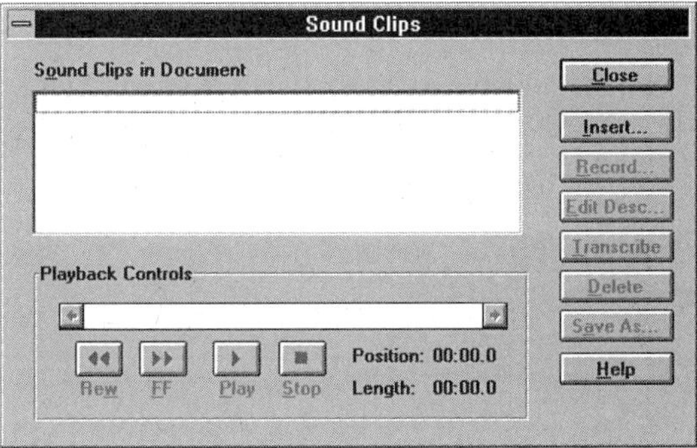

Fig. 31.8
The Sound Clips dialog box allows you to insert, record, and play back sound clips.

2. Choose **I**nsert. WordPerfect displays the Insert Sound Clip into Document dialog box (see fig. 31.9).

Fig. 31.9
Select a sound clip to be inserted into a WordPerfect document.

3. Type the name of the sound clip in the **F**ile text box, or select the folder icon to display the Select File dialog box.

4. The **N**ame text box is the name that WordPerfect will use when referring to the sound clip. The default naming scheme is Clip #X, with X being the next sequence number of the sound clips. You can change the name to allow you to identify the sound clip. In most cases, you can just enter the name of the sound clip file.

5. Choose either of the two clip-insertion options. The first option—**L**ink to File on Disk—merely establishes a connection to the disk file that contains the sound clip. The second option—**S**tore in Document—actually retrieves and stores the sound clip inside your WordPerfect document.

> **Note**
>
> Storing a sound clip in a document makes the document larger and could make managing the document cumbersome. Also, if the original sound clip is modified for any reason, you must reinsert the re-recorded sound clip to incorporate the latest changes. However, using **L**ink to File on Disk means that you must ensure that the clip doesn't change locations on disk and is distributed with the document.

6. Select a file in the file list box, and then choose OK. You return to the document screen.

When you insert a sound clip into a document, WordPerfect places a small speaker icon in the document to inform you that a sound clip resides there (in Page view). Also, Reveal Codes shows a Sound code at the location of the inserted sound clip.

Exploring the Sound Clips Feature

When you choose **S**ound from the **I**nsert menu, the Sound Clips dialog box appears (see fig. 31.10). Take a moment to review the features of this dialog box.

The S**o**und Clips in Document list contains the names of all sound clips in the current document and also the description and storage method for each sound clip.

The Playback Controls buttons—Rewind (Re**w**), Fast Forward (**F**F), **P**lay, and **S**top—perform the same functions as their counterparts on a tape recorder. The horizontal scroll bar represents the current location in the sound clip when you choose **P**lay. The Position indicator displays the current position, in minutes and seconds, as you play the sound clip. The Length indicator shows the duration of the sound clip.

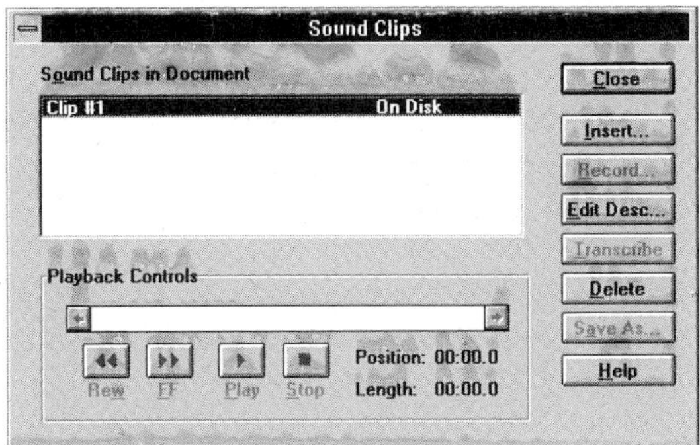

Fig. 31.10
The Sound Clips dialog box provides a central location from which you can insert, record, edit the description of, transcribe, delete, and play back sound clips within a Word-Perfect document.

The dialog box also contains the following buttons:

- ***C****lose*. Returns to the document screen.
- ***I****nsert*. Adds a new sound clip to the document.
- ***R****ecord*. Launches the Windows Sound Recorder, which allows you to play, record, and edit sound clips. (Your sound board might include its own software for recording sounds).
- ***E****dit Desc*. Allows you to edit the sound clip's description.
- ***T****ranscribe*. Removes the Sound Clips dialog box and activates the Sound Feature Bar, which allows you to access the Playback Controls from the document editing screen.
- ***D****elete*. Removes a sound clip from the document.
- *S****a****ve As*. Creates a file on disk containing a sound clip that is currently stored inside a document.
- ***H****elp*. Displays help information on the sound feature.

Playing a Sound Clip

To play a sound clip from the document edit screen, click the speaker icon that represents the clip. Figure 31.11 shows a WordPerfect document with an embedded sound clip.

To play a sound clip from the Sound Clips dialog box, highlight the sound clip in the S**o**und Clips in Document list, and then choose the **P**lay button.

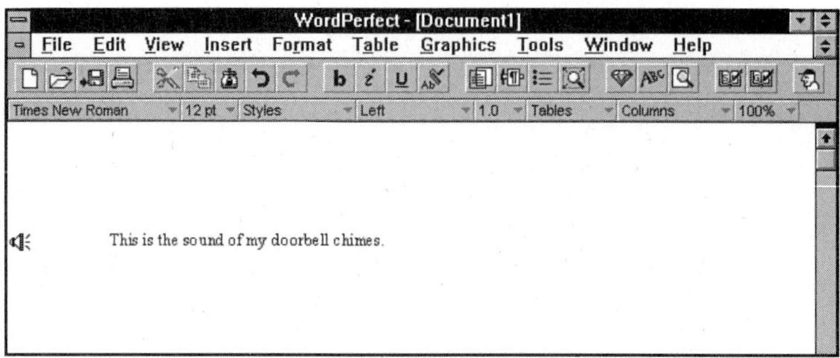

Fig. 31.11
When a sound clip is embedded in a WordPerfect document, and the display view is set to Page, a speaker icon appears in the left margin (in Draft mode, the sound clip is a gray comment box).

Troubleshooting

When I click on a sound to play it, WordPerfect displays a `WAVE sound output not available` *error message.*

WordPerfect uses the sound capabilities of Windows to play sounds. You must have a suitable sound card properly installed in your computer before you can play sounds.

After inserting sound clips, my files get very large and take up a lot of space on my hard disk drive.

You specified the **S**tore in Document option in the Insert Sound Clip into Document dialog box. This places the entire sound file in your document. Sound files can be quite large; the longer the sound, the larger the file. To prevent your documents from growing in size when you insert a sound file, be sure to choose the **L**ink to File on Disk option in the Insert Sound Clip into Document dialog box.

From Here...

For more information on using links and references in WordPerfect documents, see the following chapters in this book:

- Chapter 12, "Creating Macros," provides an overview of the macro feature of WordPerfect.
- Chapter 18, "Importing Data and Working with Other Programs," describes how to set up DDE and OLE links with other programs so you can share data between them.
- Chapter 26, "Assembling Document References," shows you how to prepare references within a document to create a table of contents, index, list, cross-reference, or table of authorities.

- Chapter 27, "Working with Large and Multi-Part Documents," describes how to assemble a large document out of several smaller ones.
- Chapter 29, "Advanced Macro Techniques," gives you more information about macros, including the vast WordPerfect for Windows macro language.

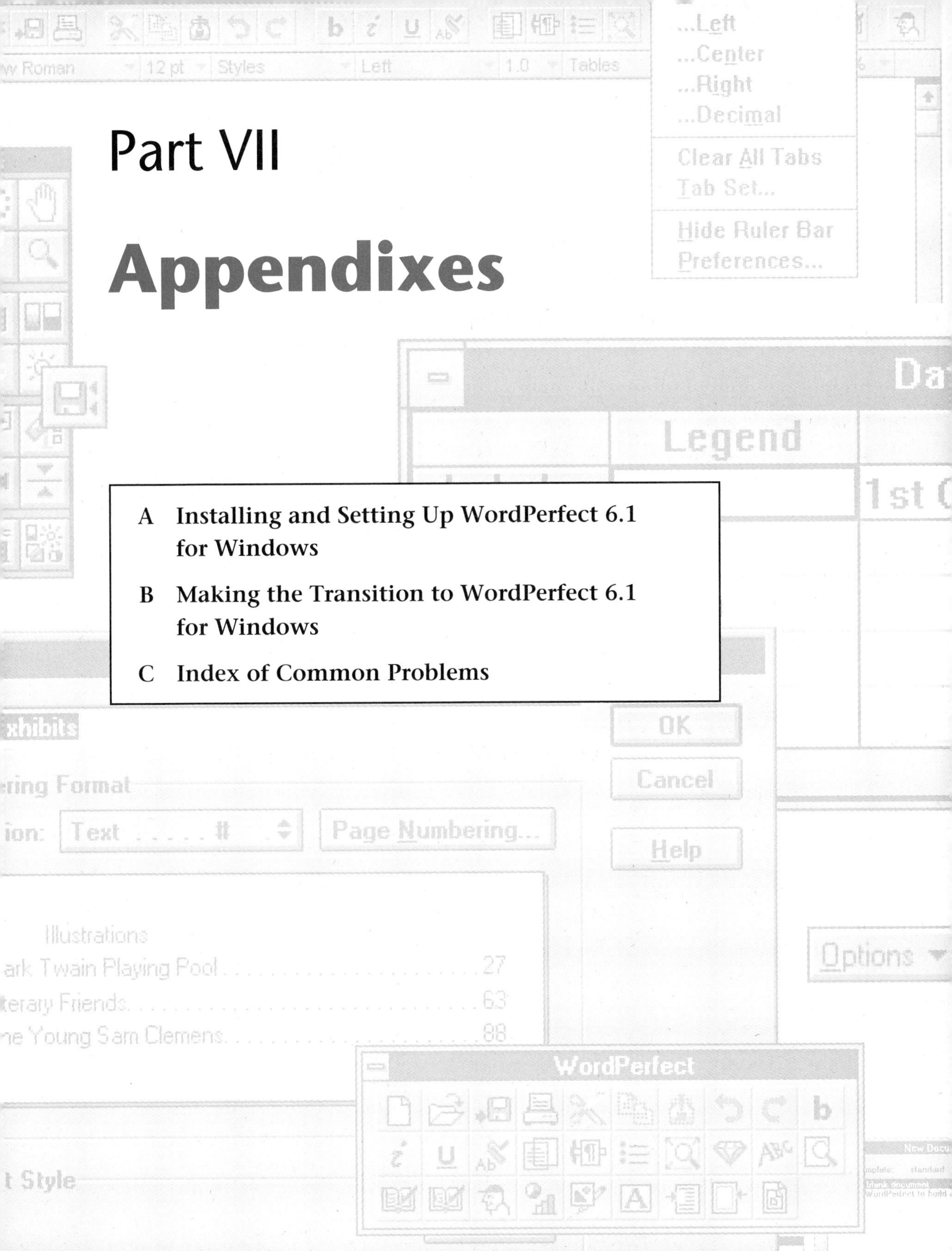

Part VII

Appendixes

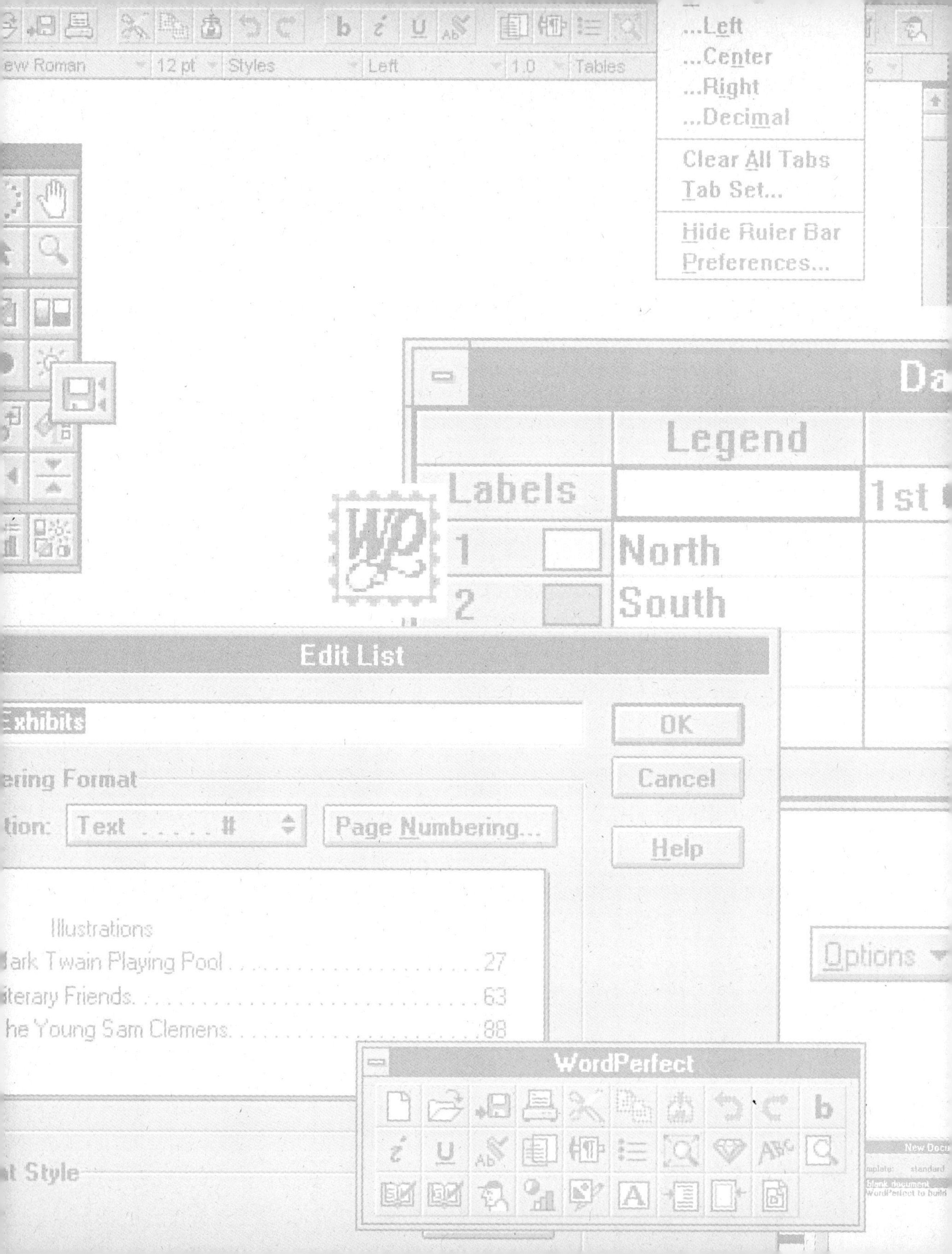

...Left
...Center
...Right
...Decimal
Clear All Tabs
Tab Set...
Hide Ruler Bar
Preferences...
Legend
Labels
1st
1 North
2 South
Edit List
Exhibits
OK
Cancel
Help
Text
Page Numbering...
Illustrations
Options
WordPerfect

Appendix A

Installing and Setting Up WordPerfect 6.1 for Windows

by Tony Rairden and Cathy Kenny

Whether you are a novice computer user, a power user with an intense dislike for "automatic" install programs, or someone in between, WordPerfect's Install options can accommodate your needs and preferences. This appendix helps you with the initial installation of WordPerfect and with setting up WordPerfect for Windows. This chapter also shows you how to use the new Uninstall program, which enables you to remove all or specific components of WordPerfect for Windows.

Installing WordPerfect for Windows

WordPerfect's files are shipped compressed on 3 1/2-inch high-density (1.44M) or 5 1/4-inch high-density (1.2M) disks. The disks are divided into two sets: Install and Program. The Install disk starts the installation procedure while the program disks contain the WordPerfect program files. These sets have no significance to you as an end user, but Install looks for specific components of WordPerfect on specific disks within a specific set. If you later add another WordPerfect printer driver or reinstall specific files, Install will call for specific disks from within the sets.

Caution

You must use WordPerfect's Install program to install WordPerfect on your system. You can't decompress and install the individual files without the program. To access WordPerfect easily, you also need the changes that Install makes to your Windows initialization file and the Program Manager group Install creates.

The WordPerfect Install program does the following:

- Decompresses and installs the program files into the appropriate subdirectories.
- Installs the WordPerfect 6.1 for Windows Group file (from which you can start WordPerfect) in the Windows subdirectory and modifies Windows to recognize the new group and to support WordPerfect.

Don't be concerned about overwriting your WordPerfect 6.0, 5.1 or 5.2 for Windows installation. WordPerfect 6.1 for Windows generates a totally separate installation, with its own discrete directory structures and a completely separate Windows group. You may continue to use the earlier version(s) without difficulty.

Initial Installation

For a full installation of WordPerfect, you need at least 34M available on the hard disk to which you're installing the program. A full installation of WordPerfect includes the supplied TrueType fonts, WPDraw, Templates and Macros, the tutorial files, and the Writing Tools—the spell checker, the thesaurus, and Grammatik. The full installation itself requires approximately 32M. You also need another 2M for temporary, backup, and data files.

In addition to the preceding space requirements, if you have less than 6M of total RAM, you should have at least 2M of free space on the drive on which the directory indicated by your `Temp=` variable (set in your AUTOEXEC.BAT) is found; if this is the same drive as that on which you are installing WordPerfect, you need a total of at least 36M free on that drive to run a full installation.

If you don't have the required space, you can use the Custom Installation option for a less-than-full installation, but you sacrifice some of the program's capabilities. You may save considerable space, for example, by leaving out WP Draw (2.6M), the Template Files (1.7M), the Coach/Tutorial Files (3.3M), the Graphics Files (.5M), or TextArt (.5M). Even with all five of those groups left out, however, you still need about 25M available hard disk space. Leaving out other file groups saves even more space—the Grammatik Files save 1.2M or the TrueType fonts 1M.

Caution

If you choose not to install the TrueType fonts, the Templates don't display or print correctly and WordPerfect doesn't have access to its full character set.

Use the **M**inimum Installation option if you have extremely limited space, such as a small hard drive on a notebook computer. The Minimum Installation requires approximately 11M for WordPerfect plus 2M workspace and the 2M "Temp" space. To get WordPerfect into that limited space, you sacrifice many of the program's more useful features and capabilities. The Minimum Installation includes only the essential program files, and the fonts. You basically can just input, edit, save, and print documents. You can, however, use the Custom Install feature to install additional components at a later date. This option is discussed later in the section, "Choosing Minimum Installation."

For the best performance from WordPerfect for Windows—and Windows in general—your CONFIG.SYS file should contain the directive FILES=60 (minimum), and you should have SmartDrive or an alternative disk cache active.

Note

You should defragment your hard drive before installing WordPerfect and then periodically (weekly works well for many people) with a utility such as MS-DOS 6's Defrag, Norton's SpeedDisk, or Central Point's Optimize.

WordPerfect 6.1 for Windows is a Windows application and requires that Microsoft Windows 3.1 or higher first be installed on your system and be running in 386 Enhanced mode. After you make sure that your system has the necessary hardware (see Chapter 1, "Getting Started," in this book, and "Installing WordPerfect" in the Introduction to the WordPerfect for Windows Reference Manual), software, and disk space for WordPerfect, follow these steps:

1. Access the Windows Program Manager.

2. Insert the WordPerfect Setup 1 disk into drive A or drive B.

3. Choose **F**ile, **R**un.

4. Type **a:setup** (or **b:setup**) and press Enter.

The Windows delay hourglass momentarily appears, followed by the WordPerfect 6.1 for Windows Setup screen with the WordPerfect 6.1 for Windows Setup dialog box in its center (see fig. A.1). Choose **I**nstall to start the setup procedure.

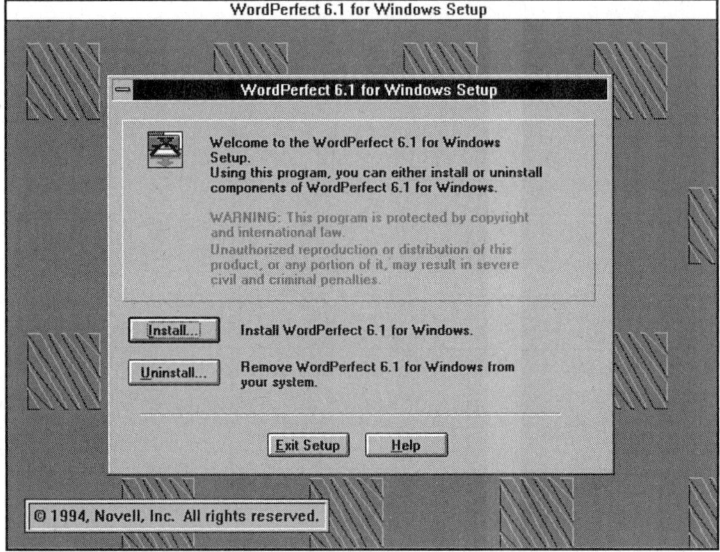

Fig. A.1
Choose **I**nstall in the WordPerfect 6.1 for Windows dialog box to install WordPerfect.

The Registration Information dialog appears (see fig. A.2). Type in your name, then press Tab or Enter, type in your company name, then press Tab or Enter, and then type in your license number. Press Enter or choose C**o**ntinue.

Note

Your license number can be found on the Certificate of License that came in the WordPerfect box if this is your initial WordPerfect purchase. If you're upgrading from an earlier version of WordPerfect, use the license number from that earlier version. If you can't find your license number, enter your name and bypass the license number box. The program runs without a license number.

The Installation Type dialog box appears (see fig. A.3). You perform your initial installation from this dialog box. You also use this box to install interim and maintenance updates on the entire program or on specific portions only. Use this dialog box for both stand-alone and network installations. (This appendix deals with stand-alone installations only. If you are installing to a network, refer to the WordPerfect for Windows Reference Manual for more information.)

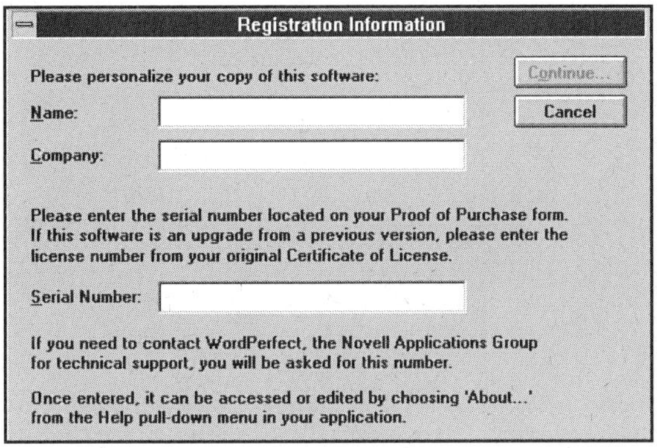

Fig. A.2
The Registration Information dialog box appears only on your first use of Install. The License Number you enter here is displayed in the Help, About WordPerfect dialog box.

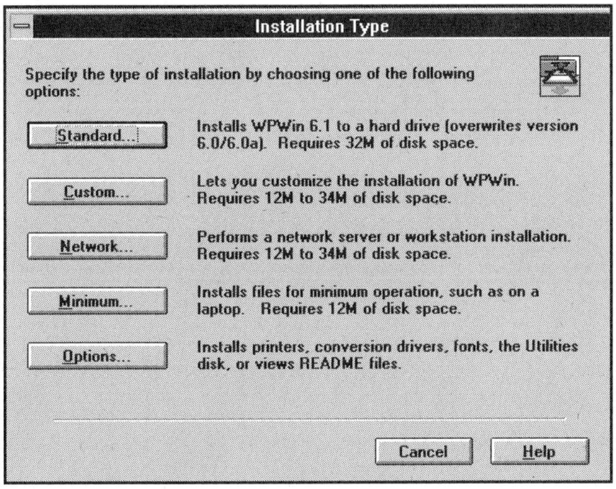

Fig. A.3
Both initial and update installations are performed from the Installation Type dialog box.

The following installation options are available:

- ***Standard.*** Standard installation installs the many program and ancillary files to the drive of your choice in a default, predefined directory structure.

- ***Custom.*** Custom installation gives you considerable control over which files are installed and where they are placed. This option also enables you to save space by not installing WordPerfect features you know you won't use.

- *Network.* This option enables network administrators to customize installation onto a network server. It also allows installation of files from a network server to a workstation.
- *Minimum.* A Minimum installation, as discussed earlier in this chapter, uses less than half the hard disk space of a full installation. Because many program functions are eliminated, use this option only when available disk space is extremely limited.
- *Options.* These additional installation options normally are used after the initial installation. Use them to install additional or updated WordPerfect printer drivers and language modules or to install WordPerfect's TrueType fonts to Windows and the WordPerfect printer drivers.

These options and those for most dialog boxes in Install also are described in the Install Help system, accessed from the dialog boxes by choosing **H**elp.

Note

Help must be accessed in WordPerfect's Install by choosing the **H**elp buttons offered in most dialog boxes. Install doesn't have a menu bar, and the F1 keystroke does nothing in Install. If the dialog box doesn't have a **H**elp button, Help is not available from that point in the installation.

For your initial installation of WordPerfect for Windows, use either the **S**tandard or the **C**ustom option if you have the necessary disk space. If you don't have enough disk space for a full installation, use **C**ustom and deselect file groups under the Files option, or use **M**inimum. (For information about the **C**ustom Files option, see the section "Choosing Custom Installation," later in this chapter.) The following sections cover these three installation options. The later sections on README files and recovering disk space also pertain to the initial installation process.

Choosing Standard Installation

If you choose **S**tandard Installation, Install presents the Select Drive dialog box (see fig. A.4). The Select Drive dialog box also displays the available space on each drive. Select or type in the drive on which you want to install; then press Enter or choose OK. If you don't have enough space for the installation type you prefer, an Error dialog box is displayed. You either have to remove enough files from your drive to make room or change your installation plans.

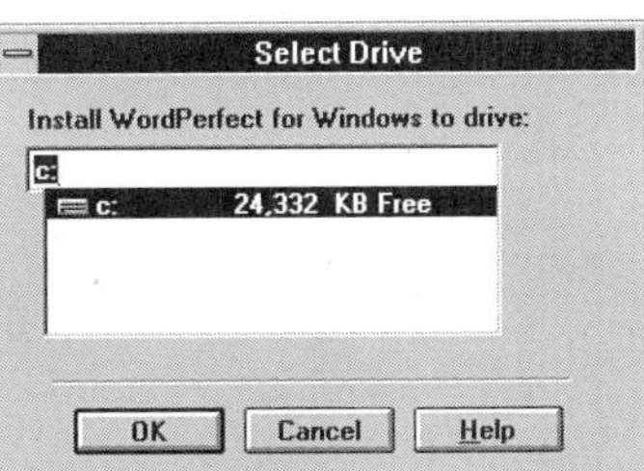

Fig. A.4
In the Select Drive dialog box, you may select any hard disk on your system for your WordPerfect installation.

Proceeding with the Actual Installation

After making your drive selection and choosing OK, the installation begins with the file decompression and transfer routines, prompting you only when you need to swap disks. As the installation proceeds, you see a series of screens containing helpful and informative messages about WordPerfect 6.1 for Windows. In each screen, an Install Files progress dialog box indicates what file is being installed to what directory. Moving bar graphs in the dialog box indicate how much of the individual disk installation and the total program installation have been accomplished (see fig. A.5).

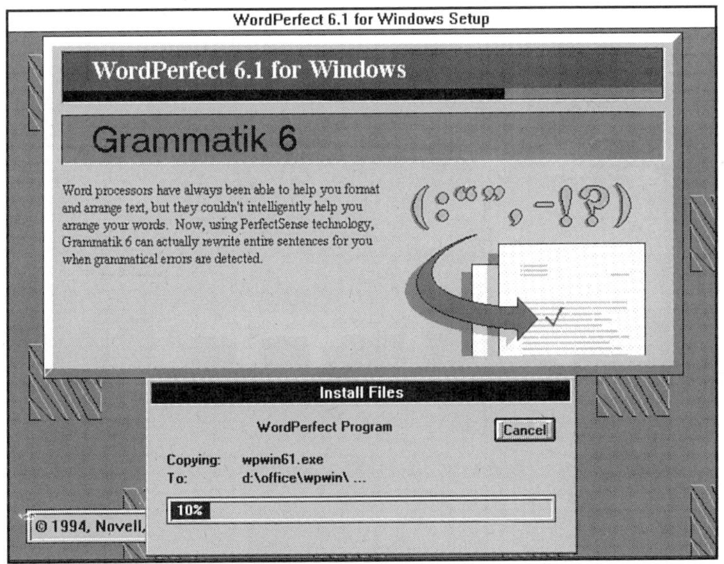

Fig. A.5
During the installation, a series of informative and useful messages appears in the Install Files progress dialog box.

The Install Files progress dialog box also contains a Cancel button, which enables you to abort the installation at any point. If you do abort, you end up with a partial installation of WordPerfect that is unlikely to run. Your best course of action following an aborted installation is to use a file management utility to delete all the WordPerfect files and their directories, then start over.

Install adds more than 540 files in close to 32M to your hard drive for a full installation. After all files have been expanded and transferred, you briefly see a System Initialization message box. Install modifies Windows' WIN.INI and REG.DAT files to accommodate WordPerfect.

The System Initialization message box is followed by an Installing WordPerfect Character Set Fonts message box and an Installing Bitstream TrueType Fonts message box, each of which displays the name of each of its respective TrueType fonts as it is installed into Windows.

Viewing the README Files

The new WPWin 6.1 group box briefly appears on-screen; then Setup displays a dialog box asking if you want to view the README files. Choose **Y**es, and then review each of the files at least briefly to familiarize yourself with their contents. After you Close the View README Files dialog box, the WordPerfect for Windows Installation Complete dialog box appears. Click OK.

The installation process then ends, leaving the WPWin 6.1 group box on-screen (see fig. A.6). This box displays the icons for WordPerfect 6.1 for Windows, the Spell Checker and Thesaurus utilities, the QuickFinder File Indexer, Kickoff, and the WordPerfect 6.1 for Windows Setup. (Kickoff is a WordPerfect Windows utility that can be used to launch any Windows application or file at a scheduled time and at regular intervals.)

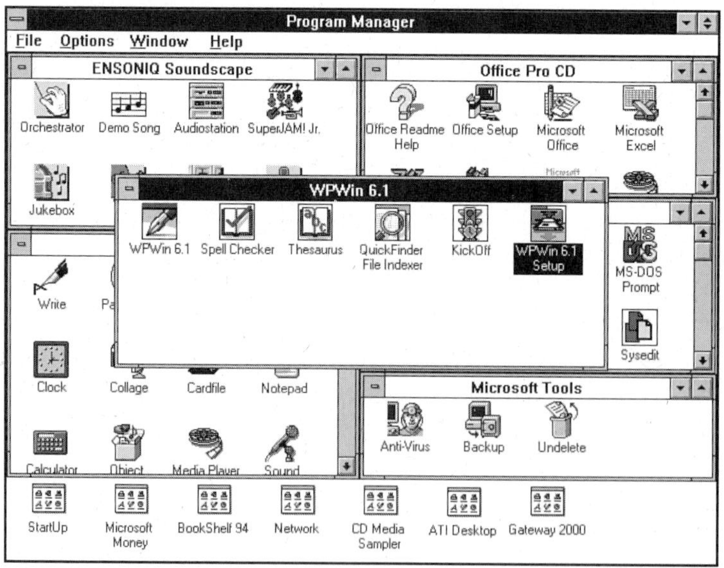

Fig. A.6
The WordPerfect 6.1 for Windows group in Windows' Program Manager includes the principal "shared applications," along with WordPerfect itself and the WordPerfect Setup program.

Opening WordPerfect

Open WordPerfect 6.1 for Windows by either double-clicking on its icon or selecting it in the group and pressing Enter. Choose **Y**es in the WordPerfect for Windows dialog box to view the QuickStart Coach.

The QuickStart Coach dialog box is displayed (see fig. A.7). You can select a coach or tutorial to familiarize yourself with WordPerfect. Select a coach or choose Skip This Coach then click OK. WordPerfect continues to its default editing screen. You are ready to begin work.

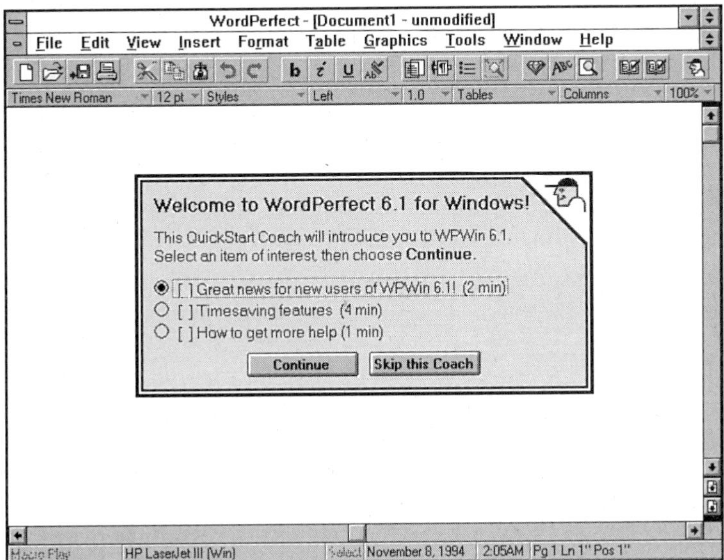

Fig. A.7
The first time you open WordPerfect after installing it, the QuickStart Coach dialog box is displayed. Select a coach to learn how to use WordPerfect.

Choosing Custom Installation

If you choose the **C**ustom installation from the Installation Type dialog box, the Custom Installation dialog box appears (see fig. A.8). Use Custom Installation when you want to control directly the extent and locations of the installation. Because Install does not include an Update or Interim option, you also use Install's **C**ustom option for updating any prior custom installation with an interim release of WordPerfect 6.1 for Windows.

The Custom Installation dialog box contains three entries: WordPerfect, Shared Components, and PerfectFit Components. The default drive and directory locations for these files also appears. WordPerfect program files are installed in C:\OFFICE\WPWIN, the shared components are installed in C:\OFFICE\SHARED, and the PerfectFit Components are installed in C:\OFFICE\SHARED\WPC20.

If you change the directory and/or the drive for the WordPerfect program files, all other default locations are changed to create the same structure in the new location. The same holds true for the Shared Components directory. The TrueType Font Files and Initialization Files directories are unaffected by changing the PerfectFit Components directory on a given drive. This is because they are assigned to the Windows directory structure (where Install expects any other TrueType font and INI files to be found) rather than to a WordPerfect directory structure.

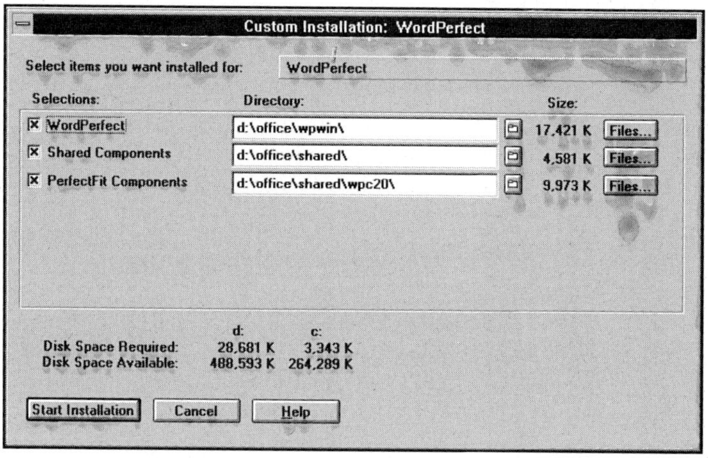

Fig. A.8
From the Custom Installation dialog box, you can control the selection and the locations for WordPerfect.

To change any of the file group locations, select the group by tabbing to it or double-clicking in its Directory text box. Make each change and then select the next group to change. If you specify directories that don't yet exist, you are prompted for the creation of each new directory when you start the Install; press Enter or choose Yes at each such prompt.

The Files option takes you to the next step of the Custom Installation: WordPerfect dialog box, shown in figure A.9. The dialog box shows the total WordPerfect file set broken down into separate groups, each pertaining to a specific function or set of functions in WordPerfect. You may select or deselect individual file groups for installation. The Disk Space Required tally at the bottom of the dialog box is continuously updated as you select and deselect file groups. You do so either by tabbing to them and pressing the space bar, or simply by clicking in the check boxes.

Note

To install a single file, go to the Custom Installation: WordPerfect dialog box, and select Files in Custom installation. Unmark all the groups, select the group containing the files you need and press Enter.

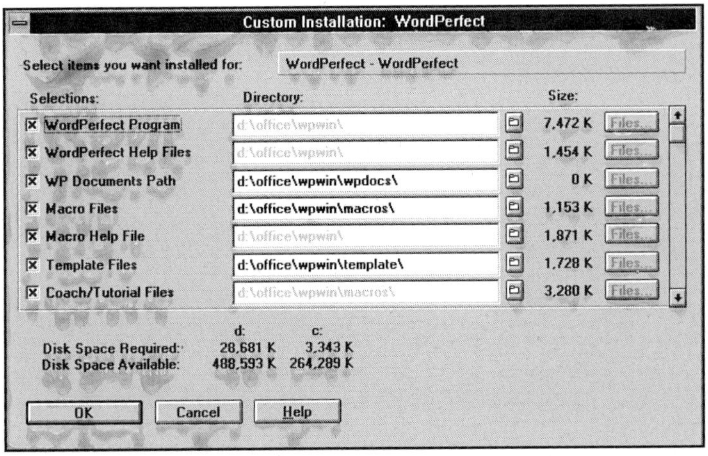

Fig. A.9
If you don't have the 36M of space required for a usable full installation, but still want as much functionality in WordPerfect as your space affords, select the components you want to install from this dialog box.

After you finish selecting or reviewing the file groups you want to install, click OK to return to the first screen in the Custom Installation: WordPerfect dialog box (refer to fig. A.8), and choose Start Installation. The file expansion and transfer is accomplished as described earlier, in the section, "Proceeding with the Actual Installation." This process is followed by the appearance of a dialog box in which you can designate the name of your WordPerfect 6.1 for Windows group file. The dialog box then provides you an opportunity to view the README files.

Choosing Network Installation

The Network Installation selection enables you to install WordPerfect to a network environment on either a server or a workstation. This appendix, however, deals only with stand-alone installations. See "Appendix K: Networking WordPerfect," in the WordPerfect Reference Manual, and the README.NET file if you are installing to a network or if you want to use some of WordPerfect's network-oriented features, such as multiple Preferences profiles.

Choosing Minimum Installation

If your hard disk space is extremely constrained, or you simply want a basic text entry and editing installation on your notebook computer, use Minimum Installation. In exchange for its 12M size, Minimum Installation leaves out spell checking, the thesaurus, macros, graphics files (clip art), most file format conversions, font installation, grammar checking, the tutorial and workbook files, Help files, QuickFinder, WPDraw, and TextArt.

Minimum Installation essentially enables you to input, revise, save, format, and print documents. You also can record and edit macros and toolbars, but no shipping macros are installed. (The Macros README file is also not available from the View README Files dialog box, since that file covers the shipping macros.)

You still need to allow about 2M additional space for temporary, backup, and data files, so even the Minimum Installation actually requires almost 14M of available space on your hard drive. (If you find yourself still short on drive space, see the section, "Recovering Disk Space after Installation," later in this chapter.)

Choosing **M**inimum from the Installation Type dialog box brings up a Minimum Installation dialog box warning you of the extreme limited functionality of a Minimum installation. Press Enter or choose **Y**es to proceed; you return to the Select Drive dialog box to specify the location for the installation. After choosing the disk partition on which to install WordPerfect, press Enter or choose OK.

File transfer and expansion begins immediately upon exiting the Select Drive dialog box. The Minimum installation then parallels the other installation options.

Note

After using the **M**inimum Installation option to install WordPerfect, you can use the **C**ustom Installation option at a later date to install additional components of WordPerfect if you have freed up the necessary disk space.

Choosing Options

Install's **O**ptions selection is used for updating or adding printers, fonts, and language modules after the initial installation. The selection is discussed later in this appendix under "Updating and Adding onto WordPerfect 6.1 for Windows."

Viewing the README Files

When you have the opportunity at the end of your installation sequence to view the README files, do so. Don't skip this step. These files usually contain useful and valuable information about features and capabilities that were included in the program too late to be covered in the printed documentation.

Install has put the README files onto your hard drive already. This menu option gives you the opportunity to view them during your installation so that you can become familiar with their contents.

You also can access the README files later, whenever you want to, simply by opening them from within WordPerfect. (The files are in ASCII Text (DOS) Format. You will see them being converted as WordPerfect loads them. You may need to reset your margins or font size if the lines are breaking inappropriately.) You also may want to print the README files to keep in the back of your WordPerfect Reference Manual.

Recovering Disk Space after Installation

If you are short of hard disk space, you can recover a fair amount after your installation. Use the file management capabilities of the File Open dialog box (see Chapter 28, "Advanced File Management,") or another file management utility to delete files you don't need.

The WordPerfect documentation identifies most of the more than 540 files that Install places on your hard disk. In carefully reviewing that listing, you may identify a number of files you don't need on your system.

If you'll never use WordPerfect's Grammatik grammar and style checker, for example, you can recover approximately 1.2M by deleting the files associated with it. You also, of course, have the option in Custom Install of deselecting Grammatik for installation.

You are unlikely to need all of the file format conversion filter DLLs (CV*.DLL files, in your \WPC20 or designated WPC Shared Components directory). Many other opportunities for eliminating unneeded files are suggested in the files list in the WordPerfect documentation.

Updating and Adding onto WordPerfect 6.1 for Windows

Novell Applications Group is constantly working on new versions of its products. Major additions to the capabilities of the program are indicated by new "major version" numbers, which precede the decimal point in the version number: 5.0, 6.0. Lesser, but still significant, enhancements are indicated by minor version numbers, which follow the decimal point. This version of WordPerfect is 6.1 for Windows; it surpasses the capabilities and features of WordPerfect 6.0 and 5.2 for Windows and 5.1 for DOS, and has a broader feature set than 6 for DOS.

In addition to major and minor version releases, Novell Applications Group regularly adds enhancements and fixes minor problems with all its software products. The company occasionally incorporates a series of those changes and fixes into what is called an interim, or maintenance, release. Interim releases are identified by a letter after the minor version digit.

Novell Applications Group also constantly adds new printer drivers to support new printers and revises previously released printer drivers to improve functionality or performance. The new and updated drivers are available from Novell Applications Group as soon as they are completed. Periodically, a new printer driver set is released, incorporating all the latest changes and additions into a new set of disks with all file dates revised to the date of the driver release.

Obtaining an Interim Release

If you have a specific problem with the program or a printer driver that an interim release resolves, Novell Applications Group provides the update to you free of charge. The Problems Resolution group, part of the Customer Support staff on the Technical Support phone lines, handles these updates. If you simply must have the "latest and greatest" version and don't have a specific problem that the update fixes, you may order the update for a nominal charge from Novell. (Refer to the Introduction of this book for a list of toll-free phone numbers.)

Installing an Interim Release

If you obtain an interim release from Novell Applications Group install it following the initial installation routines described earlier in this appendix. Install contains no selection specifically for updates and maintenance releases. Install does, however, prompt you before overwriting some program files you may have modified.

Printer Additions and Updates

To change WordPerfect printer drivers, add a printer driver, or update your printer driver from a new WordPerfect Printer disk, choose **O**ptions from the Installation Type dialog box. This takes you to the Additional Installation Options dialog box. Choose **P**rinters, select the Printer Driver you want to install and click OK. Install calls for whichever floppy disk(s) it requires.

If you are updating an existing printer driver, a printer driver overwrite warning dialog box appears. This box provides an opportunity to change your mind if you have put a lot of work into fine-tuning the driver.

For a more detailed discussion of adding, selecting, setting up, and deleting WordPerfect printers, see Chapter 8, "Basic Output: Printing, Faxing, and E-mail." If you want to change, add, or delete Windows printer drivers, refer to Chapter 8 and to the Windows User's Guide.

Installing Additional Language Modules

WordPerfect can support multiple languages, either for separate documents or in the same document. Install's Language option enables you to install dictionary (spell checking and hyphenation) and thesaurus files for languages in addition to that with which your copy of the program shipped. After these files are installed, use the Language Code function in your documents to tell the spell checking and thesaurus facilities which language support to use. With the Language option, you also can switch back and forth between languages within the same document. This capability is covered in detail in Chapter 20, "Using Fonts and Special Characters."

Installing Fonts

Type 1 fonts are based on the PostScript page description language. They are generally of very high quality, and literally thousands of them are available. Postscript-based printers can output Type 1 fonts directly, while other printers, such as most of the HP LaserJet family, cannot. Type 1 fonts also don't inherently display smooth images on-screens. Adobe Type Manager (ATM) solves both of these problems by using a process known as rasterizing, which converts the Type 1 font outlines to pixels suited for display screens and then outputs the necessary information (raster or downloaded fonts) for non-PostScript printers. Many Windows users have obtained ATM and have developed extensive libraries of Type 1 fonts.

TrueType, which was co-developed by Microsoft and ships with Windows 3.1, is a competing technology that many users have found meets their needs quite well. These users, therefore, are not concerned with Type 1 fonts or ATM.

Installing TrueType Fonts

WordPerfect utilizes TrueType scalable fonts extensively, both as the basis for the 1,700+ characters in its 15 character sets and in the design of its ExpressDocs templates. If you elected not to install these fonts during your initial installation, you can use the Fonts option, accessed from Install's Options dialog box, to install these character set fonts and the Bitstream fonts into both WordPerfect and Windows at a later time. The Fonts option also can be used if you have deleted or corrupted your installed fonts files or if you receive an updated fonts disk from Novell Applications Group.

Obtaining and Installing Type 1 Fonts

WordPerfect 6.1 supports Type 1 fonts and ATM as well as TrueType fonts, but at this point, TrueType appears to have the leading role in WordPerfect for Windows. (WordPerfect 6 for DOS also supports both Type 1 and TrueType fonts.) If you want to work in a PostScript-dominated environment, and thus use PostScript fonts rather than TrueType for the WP character sets and for ExpressDoc templates, Novell Applications Group can supply you with ATM and Type 1 replacements for the TrueType fonts.

For more information on using fonts, see Chapter 20, "Using Fonts and Special Characters," and Chapter 23, "Desktop Publishing with WordPerfect."

Setting Up and Starting WordPerfect

Now that you have installed WordPerfect for Windows, put the program to work. Open Windows, double-click on the WordPerfect group icon, and double-click the WordPerfect icon.

WordPerfect's Initial State

WordPerfect appears on-screen with all its defaults at the factory settings (see fig. A.10). WordPerfect reflects your preferences and needs at this time only in the location of its various files—and in that aspect only if you used the **C**ustom option of Install.

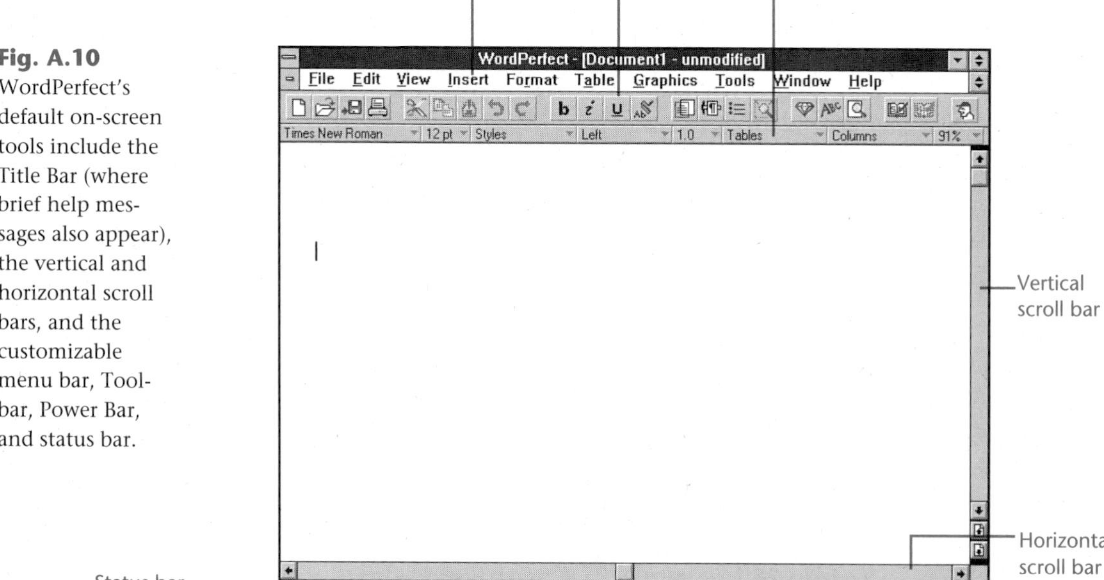

Fig. A.10 WordPerfect's default on-screen tools include the Title Bar (where brief help messages also appear), the vertical and horizontal scroll bars, and the customizable menu bar, Toolbar, Power Bar, and status bar.

WordPerfect can be extensively fine-tuned to suit your personal tastes and needs. Chapter 9, "Customizing WordPerfect," discusses customizing in depth. In this appendix, however, the emphasis is strictly on what you need to do to begin working effectively.

Having loaded Windows and WordPerfect, you may want to refer to Chapter 1, "Getting Started," before you proceed in this appendix.

Activating the Ruler Bar

The Ruler Bar is an on-screen tool that many users heavily rely upon, but it isn't in WordPerfect's default screen configuration. This tool is discussed and referred to in several chapters of this book, particularly Chapter 4, "Formatting Text." Figure A.11 shows the WordPerfect editing screen with the Ruler Bar activated.

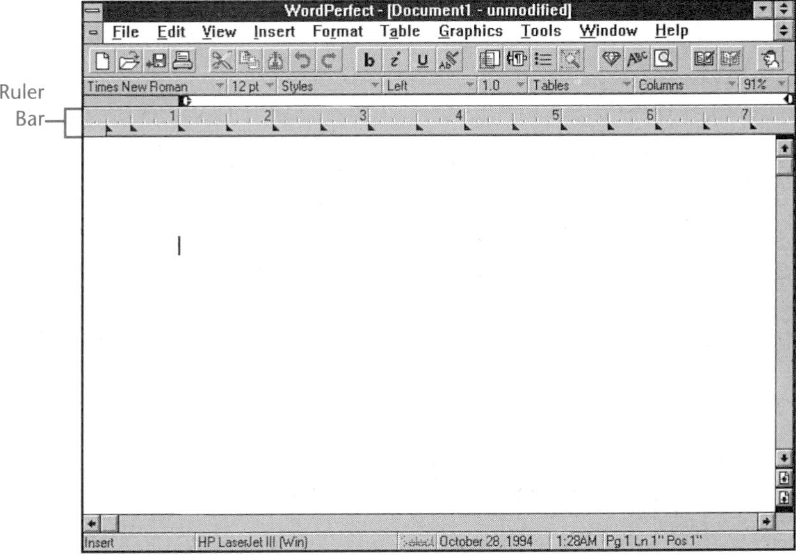

Fig. A.11
The Ruler Bar provides access to many of WordPerfect's formatting features.

The Ruler Bar provides a visual reference for the horizontal formatting (margins, tab stops, columns, and so on) in effect at the insertion point.

To activate the Ruler Bar for the current WordPerfect session only, choose **V**iew, **R**uler Bar. To activate it permanently, follow these steps:

1. Choose **E**dit, Pr**e**ferences, **D**isplay and press Enter.

2. From the Display Preferences dialog box, choose **R**uler Bar.

3. Choose Sho**w** Ruler Bar on New and Current Document, then press Enter or click OK.

Using WordPerfect Start-Up Switches

WordPerfect has several start-up options you can use by adding the appropriate switch to the command line you type to load the program (see table A.1). More than one switch may be used at a time—just make sure to put spaces between them. To use one or more of the switches when launching WordPerfect via its icon in a group in the Windows Program Manager, follow these steps:

1. Access the Windows Program Manager.
2. Click once to select the WordPerfect icon. (Clicking twice launches WordPerfect.)
3. Choose **F**ile, **P**roperties (or press Alt+Enter).
4. In the **C**ommand Line text box of the Program Item Properties dialog box, add the switch and its parameters (/m-START, for example) to the end of the command line, and then choose OK or press Enter. (The command line may extend beyond the initially visible space in the box.)

Add the start-up switch(es) to the end of your command line string if you use a single command to load Windows and run WordPerfect from the DOS command line or if you run WordPerfect from the Windows Program Manager's File Run dialog box. (This procedure is the best way to invoke the switches for one-time use.)

Table A.1 Start-Up Options for WordPerfect 6.1 for Windows

Option	Description
:	Starts WordPerfect, bypassing the "billboard" opening display screen.
filename	Starts WordPerfect with a specific file already open. Include the full path if the file isn't in your document default directory.
/m-*macroname*	Executes a specific macro when WordPerfect starts.
/d-*drive\directory*	Specifies the drive\directory where you want WordPerfect to store the temporary buffers, print queue, and overflow files it creates.
/x	Overrides Preferences settings with WordPerfect "out of the box" default settings (for the current session only).

Option	Description
/nb	Turns off Original Backup (to save disk space).
/sa	Turns on Stand-alone mode; disregards network environment and settings. This option may provide greater speed of operation when the network facilities are not required.
/nt	Tells WordPerfect to operate in network mode; also accesses network-oriented features for a stand-alone system.
/pi-*path*	Accesses a path to personal preferences files (WPCSET.BIF or XXXX####.BIF) so that an individual user can override the network-wide settings established in the master preferences file WPCNET.BIF. Use with the /u switch.
/u-*username*	Identifies specific network user and machine. Stand-alone users may create multiple configurations of WordPerfect by using a combination of /nt, /pi- , and a different four-character /u-*username* for each configuration.

Uninstalling WordPerfect for Windows

WordPerfect 6.1 for Windows also provides an Uninstall feature which enables you to remove all or selected components of WordPerfect. (WordPerfect 6.0A also provided this feature.) Unlike previous versions of WordPerfect, which installed files in selected subdirectories, WordPerfect 6.1 for Windows installs files in additional subdirectories, including \WINDOWS and \WINDOWS\SYSTEM. To remove previous versions of WordPerfect, you had to not only delete the program subdirectories and the files within, but also the various files that are installed in other directories of your hard disk. The Uninstall feature removes all traces of WordPerfect and its files from your hard disk.

Tip
Use the Uninstall feature to remove selected file groups from your hard disk. For example, if you need to recover disk space you can use Uninstall to remove WP Draw or other files from the installation.

Uninstall deletes all unmodified WordPerfect files—it won't remove any modified program files unless you specify that it do so. During the Uninstall procedure, WordPerfect compares the dates of each file to its original creation date. If the file was saved after the original date, then that file won't be removed. So for example, if you modify a document template, it won't be removed during installation.

Uninstall also removes the icons from the program group and the program group itself. It also removes WordPerfect file information from the WIN.INI and REG.DAT files.

To start the Uninstallation procedure, double-click the WordPerfect for Windows 6.1 Setup icon in the WordPerfect Program Group or select the icon and press Enter. In the WordPerfect 6.1 for Windows Setup dialog box choose **U**ninstall. The Uninstall dialog box is then displayed (see fig. A.12).

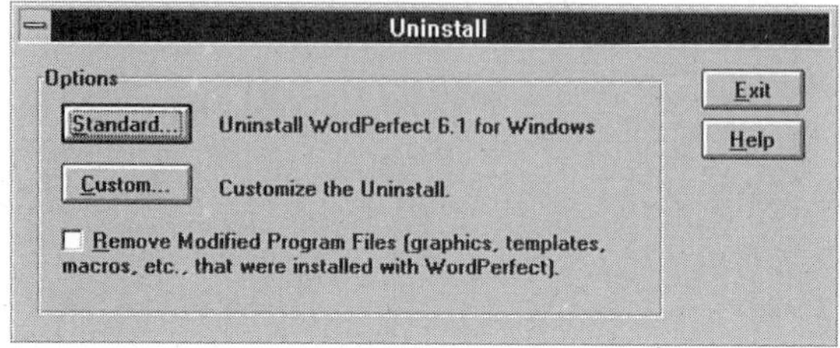

Fig. A.12
The Uninstall dialog box enables you to remove WordPerfect in its entirety or its components from your hard disk.

Uninstall provides two options: **S**tandard and **C**ustom. The **S**tandard option removes WordPerfect in its entirety; the **C**ustom option allows you to select the specific files you want to delete.

Choosing Standard Uninstall

To remove WordPerfect and all its program files choose **S**tandard from the Uninstall dialog box. If you want to remove any modified program files as well, choose **R**emove Modified Program Files before you choose **S**tandard. A message box is displayed, alerting you that WordPerfect will be removed from your system (see fig. A.13).

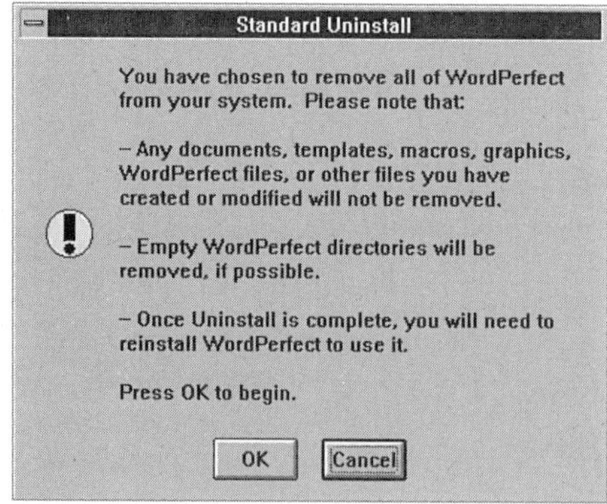

Fig. A.13
A Standard uninstall removes all WordPerfect files from your hard disk.

To remove WordPerfect from your hard disk, click OK. WordPerfect, all its accompanying program files, and program group are deleted from your system.

Choosing Custom Uninstall

If you want to remove selected WordPerfect files from your hard drive, choose the **C**ustom option in the Uninstall dialog box. If you want to remove any modified program files as well, choose **R**emove Modified Program Files before you choose **C**ustom. The Uninstall Files dialog box is displayed (see fig. A.14).

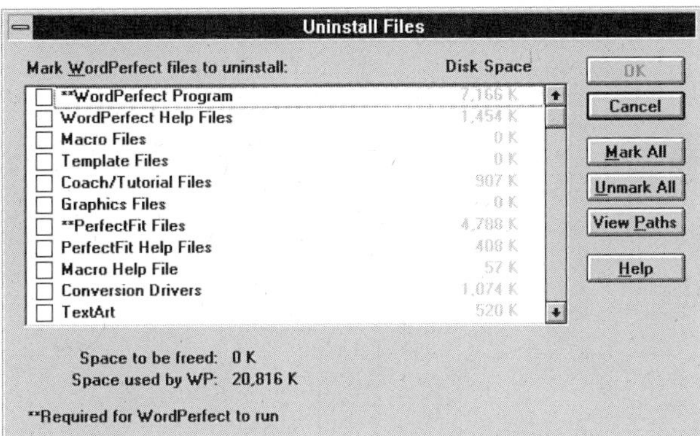

Fig. A.14
Select the files you want to remove from your hard disk with the Uninstall Files dialog box.

The Uninstall Files dialog box displays each of the WordPerfect components that are currently installed on your system. Click the View **P**aths button to expand the listing in the dialog box to display the directories in which each file is stored (see fig. A.15.)

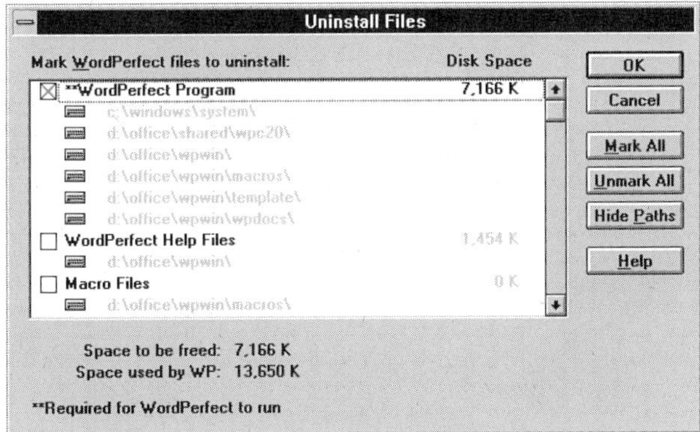

Fig. A.15
The View **P**aths option displays the WordPerfect files and the directories in which they are stored.

Selecting the Files to Remove

To remove a component from WordPerfect, click the check box to the left of the file group to select it. Choose the **M**ark All button to remove all files. As you select each file group, the space freed up by its removal is displayed in the lower half of the dialog box.

When you have selected the files you want to remove, choose OK. A message box is displayed alerting you that the Uninstall is ready to begin (see fig. A.16.) Choose OK to start the process; click Cancel to stop the Uninstall.

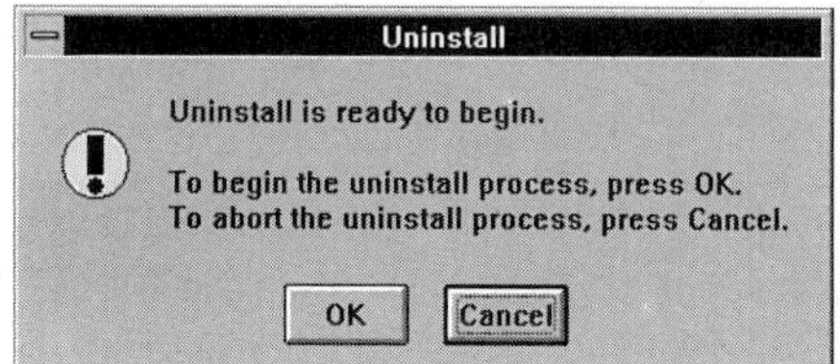

Fig. A.16
Click OK to start the Uninstall procedure and remove the files from your system.

The Custom Install Status dialog box appears and WordPerfect proceeds to remove the selected files from your hard disk. You can click Cancel at any time to stop the Uninstall, however, you may be left with an incomplete program that may not run properly.

When all of the selected files are removed, the Uninstall dialog box reappears alerting you that the Uninstall procedure is complete (see fig. A.17). Click OK.

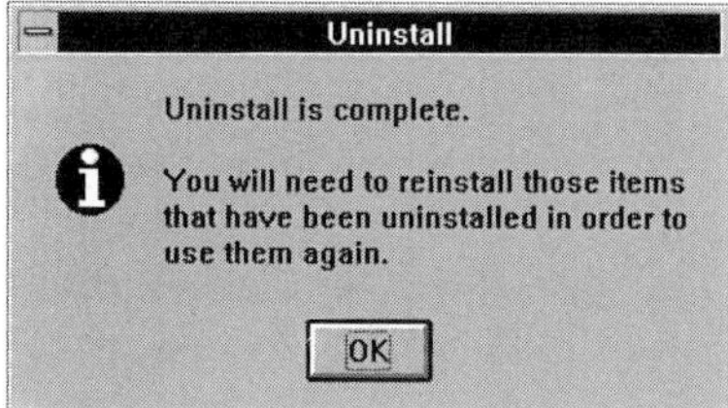

Fig. A.17
This dialog box appears when the Custom Uninstall has finished.

Appendix B

Making the Transition to WordPerfect 6.1 for Windows

by Read Gilgen

If you are currently a WordPerfect user, making the switch to WordPerfect 6.1 for Windows may take some getting used to. For those coming from the DOS version, just getting used to the Windows interface will be a challenge. But even for those upgrading from WordPerfect 5.2 or 6.0 for Windows, there are plenty of new and changed features to not only challenge you, but to enable you to take your word processing skills to new heights.

Why Make the Switch

You've spent a great deal of time learning and using your current version of WordPerfect. Is changing to WordPerfect 6.1 for Windows really worth the effort? Is it worth the cost? What will you lose in the process?

Advantages

Perhaps the biggest advantage in moving to WordPerfect for Windows is the huge number of new and improved features. This appendix lists some of the more interesting and significant ones.

"But," you protest, "I've switched to WordPerfect 6.0 for DOS. What else could there be?"

The answer is "Plenty!" Although WordPerfect 6.0 for DOS made giant strides forward, much of what it contains already was present in WordPerfect 5.2 for Windows. WordPerfect 6.1 for Windows has added many features and improved the interface in ways that WordPerfect 6.0 for DOS has not.

One reassuring point is that WordPerfect for Windows files and WordPerfect for DOS files are compatible, so you really don't have to make an immediate choice. Experiment with both programs and determine which one makes the most sense for you.

Costs

Hardware costs might be the biggest factor in deciding whether to upgrade. Consider the following:

- If you currently use a PC XT computer, there is no consideration of using Version 6.1 of WordPerfect for either Windows or DOS—neither program runs on a PC XT computer.

- If you use a 286 (AT) computer, don't consider using WordPerfect 6.1 for Windows. However, WordPerfect 6.0 for DOS works reasonably well in text mode on this machine. The same consideration applies to 386SX computers.

- If you own a fast 386 computer (or 486 or Pentium) with at least 4M RAM (8M RAM is a more realistic minimum), then you should consider WordPerfect 6.1 for Windows, because these are the recommended minimum requirements for WordPerfect 6.1 for both DOS and Windows. As you examine WordPerfect 6.1 for Windows' feature list, ask yourself if you really want to remain with a DOS-based word processor, as good as it may be. Now might be the time to switch.

Another cost to consider is training time. If you already use WordPerfect 5.2 for Windows, upgrading to WordPerfect 6.1 for Windows should be quite easy. For those coming from the DOS world, the learning curve is steeper. Experience shows, however, that if you already know any version of WordPerfect, making the switch to the latest Windows version is relatively painless.

New (and Improved) Features in WordPerfect for Windows

Whether you're switching from WordPerfect for DOS or upgrading from WordPerfect 5.2 or 6.0 for Windows, you want to know what's new in WordPerfect 6.1 for Windows. Although a complete listing of all new features is impossible in this section, you find here a brief description of some of the more important and intriguing new features. Features that are completely new to either versions 6.0a or 6.1 are listed here, along with previously available features that saw significant enhancements. Features you may have missed by not upgrading to WordPerfect for Windows 6.0 or 5.1/5.2 are listed in separate following sections.

Drop Cap

You now can quickly create a drop cap (a large letter that drops down one or more lines) for either the first letter of a word or for the entire first word. You can choose from 12 pre-defined drop cap styles, or you can customize your own. (For information on Drop Caps, see Chapter 21, "Using Advanced Graphics Techniques.")

Find/Replace

Find and Replace are now combined in the same dialog box. More significantly, however, WordPerfect integrates its PerfectSense technology to let you match word forms as well as exact word patterns. For example, you now can replace "fly" with "drive" and Replace will also replace "flew" with "drove." (See Chapter 3, "Retrieving and Editing Documents" for information on changes to Find and Replace.)

Grammatik

One of the leading grammar checking programs, Grammatik, is owned now by WordPerfect Corporation and became fully integrated into WordPerfect beginning with version 6.0. This feature complements the Speller and Thesaurus tools that have made WordPerfect so valuable to writers. No longer do you need to be embarrassed by dangling participles or mismatched subjects and verbs. The version that ships with WordPerfect 6.1 for Windows (Grammatik 6) has been significantly enhanced to provide more complete and accurate grammar checking, and to even suggest complete replacement sentences. Refer to Chapter 6, "Using Writing Tools," for more information about Grammatik.

Graphics

In addition to full visual manipulation of graphic images (see "Graphics" in the next section), you now can choose Drag to Create and then specify the exact location where you want your graphic image by dragging with the mouse. In this latest version of WordPerfect for Windows, graphic figures are now called *images*.

Integration with Other Programs

WordPerfect 6.1 for Windows now integrates more completely with other PerfectOffice 3.0 applications (such as GroupWise 4.1 and Presentations 3.0). It also provides support for network Universal Naming Conventions (UNC), mail (MAPI and VIM as well as WP/Novell products), OLE 2.0 objects, OBEX (for Quattro Pro and Paradox, for example), ODBC database technology, TWAIN (for scanning images directly into your document), and ODMA support for document management software. (For more information about integrating WordPerfect for Windows 6.1, see Chapter 18, "Importing Data and Working with Other Programs.")

Also, although WordPerfect does not come in an OS/2 version, an optional OS/2 Integration tools disk makes it possible to seamlessly integrate WordPerfect 6.1 for Windows with the OS/2 Workplace Shell.

Macro Dialog Editor

Along with its powerful macro commands, including those that enable you to create custom dialog boxes, WordPerfect now sports a handy Macro Dialog Editor that enables you to create custom dialog boxes by design and example, rather than by programming commands. (For information on the Macro Dialog Editor, see Chapter 29, "Advanced Macro Techniques.")

Make It Fit

This handy feature enables you to squeeze your document into a specified number of pages by reformatting automatically such things as font size, line spacing, and margins. For example, if you have two pages plus three lines on the third page, you can "Make It Fit" into two pages with just one command.

Outline

While the outline feature was enhanced significantly with version 6.0, now you also can collapse outlines and still leave text such as hard returns and titles.

Performance

In response to many concerns expressed by early users of WordPerfect 6.0 for Windows, WordPerfect Corporation focused on speed and reliability enhancements for version 6.0a. Similar improvements in performance appear in version 6.1. The program shows noticeable speed increases in basic formatting, scrolling, tables, graphics, outlines, printing, and opening large documents.

Reliability issues that were addressed include more accurate conversion of fonts in documents created by earlier versions of WordPerfect, and stability of the program when using certain video drivers.

QuickCorrect

This handy feature, which was added to version 6.0a, quickly corrects common mistakes as you type them. For example, "teh" becomes "the." It also corrects initial capitalization problems (for example, "TErry"). You can add words to the QuickCorrect list, and even use this feature as a shortcut for abbreviations. The QuickCorrect feature also includes SmartQuotes which gives you typographically correct quote marks as you type. (For information on QuickCorrect, see Chapter 6, "Using Writing Tools.")

QuickFormat

A significant addition to the QuickFormat feature (see "QuickFormat" in the next section) is that you can specify that formats are being applied to Headings. QuickFormat thus links all such formatted sections so a change to one heading also changes all other headings. (For information on QuickFormat, refer to Chapter 4, "Formatting Text.")

Speller

The Speller just continues to get better. Words from your supplementary dictionary now appear in the suggested replacements list. You also can link your QuickCorrect list (see "QuickCorrect" in this section). Not only is the Speller faster in this version, but when you check a document for the second time it checks only words that have changed.

Tables

Many significant enhancements have been made to the Tables feature, in addition to the spreadsheet functions discussed in the next section.

The most important is the addition of the Table Expert feature which lets you choose from predefined table layouts (formats, line, and fills) or create your own. (For more information on Table Experts, see Chapter 30, "Advanced Tables.") Another welcome feature is the command Size Column to Fit, where WordPerfect automatically adjusts column widths to match the longest line of text in that column.

Several other nifty additions include the ability to specify alternating fills in rows or columns. You also can display table row and column indicators just as in a spreadsheet program. You now can save selected cells to a file in table format. Calculate has been added to the QuickMenu, and you can turn off Auto Row Insert (where pressing Tab automatically adds a row at the end of your table).

TextArt

The TextArt program (see "TextArt" in the next section) has been significantly enhanced with many additional shapes and several new options, including "smoothing" to remove image "jaggies." TextArt also is an OLE 2.0 server. Images created with TextArt in WordPerfect 6.1 for Windows cannot be used with earlier TextArt versions. (See Chapter 22, "Using WP Draw and TextArt" for more information.)

Thesaurus

When you select a replacement word from the Thesaurus, it now replaces the existing word with a grammatically correct equivalent. For example, if you choose "thrill" to replace "exciting," you get "thrilling."

Templates

Templates were a significant addition to version 6.0 (see "Templates" in the next section). In version 6.1, you have many new templates as well as more ease-of-use features. For example, templates are now listed in groups rather than in one huge list.

Also, creating your own templates has been made easier with a Prompt Builder feature, along with the ability to record macros directly into a template. (For additional information on Template documents, see Chapter 11, "Using Templates.")

Toolbar

The Button Bar is now called the Toolbar. Its look has changed dramatically in that the buttons are smaller. Placing the mouse pointer over a button pops up a Quick Tip description of the button. Toolbars are now also shared among PerfectOffice 3.0 applications. (See Chapter 13, "Working with Toolbars," for more information.)

Undo

The Undo feature has been changed to allow, by default, ten levels of Undo. If that's not enough, you can change that to 300 levels. If you accidentally undo too many changes, you can use the new Redo feature to rebuild what you have undone. (For details on the Undo feature, see Chapter 3, "Retrieving and Editing Documents.")

Upgrade Expert

This handy Help feature enables you to learn how your previous word processor compares with WordPerfect for Windows. Pick a feature and the expert shows you how to do it, or even does it for you. Earlier versions of WordPerfect are supported, as well as Ami Pro and Word.

The Upgrade Expert supplements the QuickStart coach, Help Tutorial, and special transition template documents, all of which make learning WordPerfect for Windows much easier than you imagined.

Uninstall

Most people never need to remove WordPerfect for Windows from their computer; but if you do, Uninstall does so quickly and easily. (For more information, see Appendix A, "Installing and Setting Up WordPerfect 6.1 for Windows.")

Window Tile

You now can display tiled documents either horizontally (one above the other) or vertically (side by side). In addition, you now can "drag and drop" text to cut and paste text from one window to another.

WPDraw

You now can save images you create in WP Draw as separate .WPG files (in WPG 2.0 format). (See "WP Draw" in the next section.)

If I Didn't Upgrade to WordPerfect 6.0 for Windows, What Did I Miss?

Several new features appeared in WordPerfect for Windows, version 6.0, most of which surpassed the feature set of WordPerfect 6.0 for DOS. If you haven't used WordPerfect for Windows before, or if you didn't upgrade from version 5.1/5.2, these are some of the features you've been missing.

Abbreviations

You can define abbreviations for nearly any text, even text that includes attributes or other formatting. For example, you can tell WordPerfect that "asap" means "as soon as possible." When you later type "asap" and press Ctrl+A, WordPerfect expands the abbreviation.

Bookmarks

You now can insert bookmarks into your text, which you then can use as reference points. Either search for the bookmarks directly, or run macros that use these bookmarks as reference points. A variation on the named bookmark is the QuickMark bookmark, which is set easily by pressing Ctrl+Shift+Q, and found easily by pressing Ctrl+Q. A QuickMark bookmark also is inserted at the point of the cursor any time you save your document.

Borders

In addition to borders that surround graphics boxes, you can add borders to paragraphs, whole pages, columns, and tables. You can create custom borders with special styles that include drop shadows and rounded corners (see Chapter 21, "Using Advanced Graphics Techniques," for more information on graphic borders).

Coaches

WordPerfect's help system always has been good. But coaches give the term "help" a whole new meaning. Custom coaches not only provide information about a feature, but also "coach" you as you learn to use the feature. For example, a coach may tell you how to perform a certain procedure, and then ask you to try it; but, if you prefer, the coach actually shows you step-by-step how it's done. A separate utility available from WordPerfect Corporation enables you to create custom coaches. Consider, for example, how procedural coaches could help your company's new employees to learn how to format documents that match company standards.

Comments

The comments feature has a completely new look. First, in Preferences you can specify your full name, initials, and a color identification code. Then, when you create a comment, instead of displaying the comment, WordPerfect displays your initials with a small, color-coded tab in the margin. When you click on the comment tab, the full comment is displayed. When you create the comments, a feature bar assists you to insert your name, the date, or the time, along with your comments. (For information on comments, see Chapter 6, "Using Writing Tools.")

Delay Codes

WordPerfect now enables you to insert codes on the first page of your document, but to delay their implementation for *n* number of pages. For example, if you don't want page numbering to start until the fourth page of your document, you can specify that the page numbering code you enter on page one is delayed four pages. The advantage of this, of course, is that all such codes are located in one easily found location, making editing much easier.

Document Summary

The Document Summary feature enables you to customize the fields of information required in the summary. You can choose from 51 different fields—more than enough for even the most demanding corporate situations. (For information on document summaries, see Chapter 5, "Formatting Pages and Documents.")

Envelope

WordPerfect for Windows used to rely on a separate macro for addressing and printing envelopes. Now, this is a regular WordPerfect for Windows feature. Using the Envelope feature, you can capture an address from your document, add a return address, and print these on an envelope in the font of your choice, with or without a postal bar code. In addition, you can store up to 100 commonly used addresses, as well as up to 100 return addresses, so that you can create and print envelopes without first creating a document.

File Management

Although WordPerfect Corporation has decided not to develop further the separate File Manager program, it has included the majority of File Manager features in the Open dialog box. You now can Copy, Delete, Move, or even Open or Print multiple files. You also can display a directory tree (using visually attractive folder icons) along with your Quick List entries. You can sort files by size, date, or time, and can print a listing of your files. Finally, you can display just the file name, or choose which bits of file information (date, time, size, and so on) you want to display. (For more information on file management, refer to Chapter 28, "Advanced File Management.")

Floating Cells

You can create separate spreadsheet-capable cells right in the text of your document. For example, a mortgage loan approval letter could tell the customer that her loan for *x* amount is now approved at *y* percentage for *z* years. It could then use a fourth floating cell to calculate the mortgage payment with a spreadsheet function, using the values of *x*, *y*, and *z*. See Chapter 30, "Advanced Tables," for details on this exciting new feature.

Fonts

WordPerfect 5.2 shipped with several Adobe Type 1 fonts. WordPerfect 6.1 for Windows now ships instead with several Bitstream TrueType fonts, such as Bernhard Modern, Arrus, Brush, Caslon, Humanist, Swiss, and others. In addition, the program includes several WordPerfect fonts, including Arabic, Cyrillic, Greek, Hebrew, and other fonts that match the WordPerfect character sets. Of course, any other fonts you currently use with Windows will work well with WordPerfect 6.1 for Windows.

Graphics

In addition to being able to create and edit graphics and charts with a full-featured graphics editor (see "WP Draw" in this section), you also can wrap text on both sides of a graphic figure, and even contour text to the figure's shape. For information on graphics procedures, see Chapter 7, "Integrating Text and Graphics," and Chapter 21, "Using Advanced Graphics Techniques."

Hidden Text

You can hide text that you don't want to display or print by adding a Hidden attribute from the Font menu. Then from the View menu, choose to display or hide everything found between the Hidden codes. (For information on hidden codes, see Chapter 3, "Retrieving and Editing Documents.")

Hypertext

Hypertext refers to text that is "linked" to bookmarks in your document, to macros, or to other documents. When you click on a hypertext link, WordPerfect automatically jumps to a linked location within your document or in another document. This feature is particularly useful for training or reference materials. You can also use hypertext to create buttons in your text to run macros.

Interface Bars

Although WordPerfect introduced the Button Bar in WordPerfect 5.2 for Windows, the program now has several specialty bars that aid you in creating and editing your document:

- *Toolbar.* The Button Bar is now called the Toolbar. Each shipping Toolbar includes basic editing tools (File Open, Cut, Paste, Print, Undo, and so on). You can drag the Toolbar to the left, right, top, or bottom with the mouse. You also can drag the Toolbar to the center of the screen, where it becomes a floating palette of buttons. In addition to being able to add or remove buttons from any Toolbar, you can modify existing Toolbar buttons (both the names and the bit-mapped graphic icons).

- *Power Bar.* Many basic format functions (for example, Font, Justification, Tables, or Zoom)) now are found on the Power Bar. This means that you don't lose these basic functions when you change from the basic Toolbar to a specialty Toolbar.

- *Feature Bars.* Feature Bars appear on demand, or sometimes automatically when you select a certain feature. For example, if you choose Outline or Merge, Feature Bars related to these features appear. Or, when creating formulas in a table, you can display a Formula Bar to help you enter and edit the formulas.

- *Ruler Bar.* The feature buttons are gone from the Ruler Bar, making it less cluttered. Adding tabs to the Ruler Bar is easier, because to place a new tab you simply click on the desired location. The QuickMenu lets you change the tab type or access other Ruler Bar features.

- *Status Bar.* Long a hallmark of the WordPerfect interface, the status bar now can be customized to meet your needs. Double-clicking with the mouse on status bar indicators takes you directly to an appropriate dialog box (Fonts, Go To, and so on).

Keyboard

Changing key definitions in earlier versions of WordPerfect was nothing short of torture. Now, changing key assignments could hardly be easier. All you do, essentially, is to match features from a list with keys on a simulated keyboard. The only two keys you can't reassign are Tab and Enter. For information on customized keyboards, see Chapter 9, "Customizing WordPerfect."

Labels

This feature used to be a special macro that helped to create the Paper/Size definitions you needed. When you want to create labels now, simply choose a label definition from a WordPerfect list of commercially available label sizes and types. Furthermore, when you are in Page mode, you see the exact size and layout of the labels you create. (For information on labels, see Chapter 5, "Formatting Pages and Documents.")

Merge

The merge feature has a completely revamped interface. First, primary files now are called Forms, and secondary files are called Data Files. Each must be identified by its type. You associate Data Files with Form files, and save the associations, which makes merging a breeze—once you specify a form file, the data file name appears automatically. Data entry is simplified by using the Quick Fill dialog box, which acts like a database input screen, using field names to prompt for the correct information. You can create Data Files in table format also.

The merging process is also changed dramatically. Now you can selectively merge, without having to Sort/Select separately. You can merge to a letter and to the envelope for that letter in the same merge. See Chapter 19, "Assembling Documents with Merge and Sort," for details on these improvements.

Mouse

WordPerfect 6.1 for Windows takes even more complete advantage of the mouse than earlier versions did. For example, you can move column margins in tables by dragging the column separators directly. You can point and click on cells to add them to formulas. You can click on Comments, Sound Clips, or Hypertext buttons to activate these features. And last, but certainly not least, you can click the right (secondary) mouse button to access QuickMenus (see "QuickMenus" in this section).

Outlines

WordPerfect's outline feature has been made more powerful, yet easier to use. Using the Outline Feature Bar, you can change text to outline entries, and vice versa. You also can "collapse" your outlines. For example, if you want your students to have only the first and second levels of your outline of class notes, you can collapse the outline to two levels, print it for the students, and then print an expanded version for yourself. The default outline style is a numbered list (1., 2., 3., . . .). See Chapter 15, "Organizing Documents with Outlining," for more information on outlining.

Page Mode

True WYSIWYG editing is now possible when you use the Page mode in WordPerfect for Windows. In this mode, you can directly enter and edit headers, footers, footnotes, and page numbers. Because you can see these objects on-screen, simply click on any of them (for example, a footnote), and begin editing. When you finish, click on your text to continue editing your document. There is, of course, a Draft mode for doing things "the old way." (For information on Page mode, see Chapter 1, "Getting Started.")

Printing

Because you see everything in Page mode, WordPerfect no longer needs a Print Preview mode. In fact, Page mode *is* a preview mode.

WordPerfect now has a special Print Management program that returns control of the editing screen to you much faster than the Windows Print Manager does. In addition, WordPerfect now uses the Windows printer drivers by default, and the program comes with several special Windows-capable typefaces.

Finally, you can print documents in reverse order, as well as in booklet format (sequenced for back-to-back, camera-ready copy).

Refer to Chapter 8, "Basic Output: Printing, Faxing, and E-mail," for details on printing improvements.

QuickFinder/Kickoff

Although QuickFinder was added to WordPerfect 5.2, it now is an integral part of WordPerfect 6.1 for Windows, and can be accessed like any other feature. The QuickFinder enables you to index files you specify, so that when you search for a document based on words contained in the document file, the search takes fractions of a second rather than minutes.

The Kickoff program is a special utility that can be used to launch any program. Its primary purpose is to provide a means of automatically updating indexes at intervals you specify, but it can be used for other programs as well.

Refer to Chapter 28, "Advanced File Management," for information on this pair of powerful file-finding utilities.

QuickFormat

This new feature enables you to turn the mouse pointer into a style "paintbrush." For example, if you turn on QuickFormat while the cursor is inside Large, Bold text, then selecting other text with the mouse automatically applies the Large and Bold attributes to the selected text. You can continue applying attributes to selected text until you turn off Quick Format. See Chapter 4, "Formatting Text," for more details.

QuickMenus

Perhaps the most significant addition to WordPerfect for Windows is the use of the right mouse button to open context-sensitive QuickMenus. Click with the right mouse button on the Toolbar, and you get a list of available Toolbars and Toolbar options. Click on a table, and you get a QuickMenu of table-related choices. Click on the Ruler Bar to change tab stop types, format a paragraph, and so on. Click on a comment to edit or delete it. Click on the scroll bars for Go To, Bookmark, and Preferences features. In short, you can get a QuickMenu for nearly anything just by clicking that previously under used right mouse button. At first, you'll have to force yourself to remember to use QuickMenus, but soon you'll probably wonder how you ever survived without them. (For information on QuickMenus, see Chapter 1, "Getting Started.")

Repeat

WordPerfect for Windows users lost the ability to repeat a macro or keystroke in Versions 5.1 and 5.2. Now you can repeat macros or keystrokes by choosing Edit, Repeat; or pressing Shift+F10. (For information on repeating macros, see Chapter 12, "Creating Macros.")

Reveal Codes

Most WordPerfect users appreciate the ability to locate and manipulate format codes and other control codes. While Reveal Codes has a slightly new look, its best new features relate to the mouse. For example, you delete codes simply by dragging them out of the Reveal Codes window. Also, you can go directly to the dialog box for a feature by double-clicking its code. (For information on Reveal Codes, see Chapter 3, "Retrieving and Editing Documents.")

Revertible Codes

In earlier versions of WordPerfect for Windows, you could select text and choose a different font for that selection. WordPerfect would place the correct font code at the beginning of the selection, and place another code at the end of the selection to return to the earlier font. Now, however, when you select text and apply nearly any attribute or format setting, WordPerfect surrounds the selection with revertible codes. Suppose that your text is in

Courier font, and that you select some text to change to Times Roman font. Text before and after the selected text remains in Courier. Later, if you change the document font to Helvetica, the text before and after the Times Roman selection automatically changes to Helvetica. Revertible codes also work for format changes, such as margin and tab settings. (For information on revertible codes, see Chapter 3, "Retrieving and Editing Documents."

Show Codes

In addition to the capability to display a character to show the location of hard returns in your document window, you can choose to display codes for spaces, tabs, and other items that otherwise would not be visible. (For information on displaying codes, see Chapter 3, "Retrieving and Editing Documents.")

Sound

Although most WordPerfect users don't yet have sound boards or speakers attached to their computers, the day for "experiencing" memos, complete with sound clips, is not far away. WordPerfect enables you to record and attach sound clips, or to place digitized music in your documents. Imagine clicking on a sound bubble in your document and hearing your boss say, "I need this report by this afternoon!"

Speller

If you thought that there was no way to improve the Speller, WordPerfect Corporation has proven you wrong. Now you can check words, sentences, paragraphs, or pages without first selecting them. You also can define your own supplemental dictionaries, and even include suggested replacement words; for example, "post-nuptial fission" rather than "divorce." For more details, refer to Chapter 6, "Using Writing Tools."

Spreadsheet Features

WordPerfect tables now have the same kind of power formerly reserved for spreadsheet programs. With nearly 100 spreadsheet functions, you can create mini-spreadsheets within your WordPerfect documents.

For most WordPerfect users, this feature more than suffices, easily handling tasks such as reports, time sheets, and loan calculations. You even can import many spreadsheets directly into WordPerfect tables with their formulas intact.

For information on spreadsheet features in tables, see Chapter 30, "Advanced Tables." For details on importing spreadsheet information into WordPerfect, refer to Chapter 18, "Importing Data and Working with Other Programs."

Subdivide Pages

Rather than using the Labels feature to create partial page brochures, you now can use the Subdivide Page feature. Most importantly, you can print such pages in booklet format, in the proper order for camera-ready copy (for example, pages 4 and 1 on one side, and pages 2 and 3 on the other) without having to manually cut and paste to rearrange the pages. (For information on the Subdivide Page feature, see Chapter 5, "Formatting Pages and Documents.")

Templates

Templates, which were a new concept in WordPerfect 6.0 for Windows, help you to create documents that have a consistent look. More than styles, these templates serve as "boilerplates" to give you a great head start on document creation. You can embed macros or Toolbars in your templates, and add "triggers" that set off actions. For example, a document can prompt for input, and then fill in the document based on that input. WordPerfect supplies many standard templates for fax covers, reports, expense sheets, memos, and more, but you can create custom templates as well.

Refer to Chapter 11, "Using Templates," for more information on this powerful new feature.

TextArt

An exciting addition to WordPerfect for Windows is the TextArt program which enables you to fit text of your choosing into predefined graphic shapes, such as banners or circles. You then use the resulting images in your document just as you do any graphic image. To learn more about creating TextArt images, see Chapter 22, "Using WP Draw and TextArt."

Watermarks

You can use graphics or text as watermarks, which are lightly shaded backgrounds for your documents. For example, you might use a beach scene graphic as the watermark for your July calendar. (For information on watermarks, see Chapter 7, "Integrating Text and Graphics.")

WP Characters

Although WordPerfect's special characters have been easily viewable and accessible since the 5.1 Windows version, the number of characters and special character sets has increased to include phonetic symbols, two types of Arabic characters, and many new iconic symbols.

WP Draw

No longer do you need a separate graphics program to create or edit WordPerfect graphics images. WP Draw is a scaled-back version of WordPerfect Presentations, including powerful drawing, editing, and charting tools. When you select a graphic image to edit, you now can do much more than rotate or size it; you can actually modify the graphic image. For information on creating charts in WP Draw, refer to Chapter 17, "Creating and Modifying Charts with WP Draw." To learn more about editing graphic images, see Chapter 22, "Using WP Draw and TextArt."

If I Didn't Upgrade to WordPerfect 5.2 for Windows, What Did I Miss?

Several new features appeared in WordPerfect for Windows, versions 5.1 and 5.2, and recently found their way to WordPerfect 6.0 for DOS. If you haven't used WordPerfect for Windows before, these are some of the features, in addition to those described in the preceding sections, that you've been missing.

Auto Code Placement (and Replacement)

Under normal circumstances, you want certain format codes to take effect at the beginning of a page or a paragraph. For example, if you change a tab setting, or the left and right margins, you usually don't want that change to take place in the middle of a paragraph. WordPerfect for Windows automatically places such codes at the beginning of the current paragraph, or, if the codes are page-related, at the beginning of the current page.

Also, when you change a format setting, rather than placing multiple codes for the same format feature in your document, WordPerfect for Windows automatically updates the existing code.

Document Conversion

Converting files from other word processing formats is automatic when you open such files in WordPerfect. As of this writing, WordPerfect recognizes and converts some 50 file formats, making it one of the most "compatible" word processing applications on the market.

Dynamic Data Exchange (DDE) Links

With WordPerfect for Windows, you can use Dynamic Data Exchange (DDE) links not only to transfer data from one file to another, but to update the data automatically whenever the source file is changed. For example, you can link a fiscal year report to data in a spreadsheet—as the spreadsheet changes, the data in the report also changes. The feature only works, however, in Windows applications that support DDE.

Fonts

WordPerfect 5.2 shipped with several Adobe Type 1 fonts that could be added to those you already use with Windows. Many of these fonts, such as Broadway, Hobo, or Murray Hill, had been in WordPerfect products such as DrawPerfect for several years. See "Fonts" in the preceding section for information on the fonts that now ship with WordPerfect for Windows.

Grammatik

See "Grammatik" in the preceding sections.

Graphics

Being able to see and easily manipulate graphic images is one of the major reasons for switching to WordPerfect for Windows. No longer do you have to guess where graphics and lines are located, or what they will look like when they print.

Macro Language

WordPerfect for Windows macro language changed completely from that of WordPerfect 5.1 for DOS. Macro commands (in both the DOS and Windows versions of WordPerfect 6.x) now are based on the results of your actions (for example, "Set the margins to 1.5 inches at such-and-such location") rather than the specific keystrokes to accomplish the task. This makes it possible to include any action in a macro, regardless of whether you use function keys, menus, or mouse actions to accomplish that action.

In addition, WordPerfect has powerful macro dialog commands that enable you to create custom dialog boxes. To make macros as easy as possible to run, you can add them to your menus or Toolbars.

Multiple Documents

You can open up to nine documents simultaneously in WordPerfect for Windows. This gives you the flexibility of working with several different documents, without having to close one in order to use another.

Object Linking and Embedding (OLE)

OLE is a sophisticated method of sharing data with other OLE-capable Windows programs. In addition to transferring data, as you do using DDE, you can embed actual objects (a spreadsheet, a paintbrush picture, and so on) in your document. When you edit an embedded object, you are taken directly to the program that was used originally to create the object.

Quick List

The Quick List feature enables you to create descriptions of file locations in plain English (*Pretty Pictures* could refer to C:\OFFICE\WPWIN\GRAPHICS, for example). In any Open File dialog box, you can quickly find an actual file location by clicking on the appropriate Quick List entry.

QuickFinder

See "QuickFinder" in the preceding section.

Undo

In addition to being able to undelete text, WordPerfect for Windows enables you to reverse an action (such as changing a margin setting) by choosing **E**dit, **U**ndo; or pressing Ctrl+Z.

WP Characters

Character sets in WordPerfect for Windows are easily viewable and accessible. Ctrl+W displays any of the 14 character sets and enables you to choose a character directly from the set to be inserted into your text.

Zoom

One problem with document handling in WordPerfect for DOS is that wide documents cannot fit on-screen, forcing you to scroll horizontally to see the entire document. With the Zoom feature, you can increase or decrease the size of the text display from 50% to 200% (or to a specific percentage you choose), or you can force WordPerfect to fit the text between the margins of your display.

Where Do I Find It in WordPerfect for Windows?

Even for veteran WordPerfect for Windows users, finding features in WordPerfect 6.1 for Windows may present some challenges. Not only do certain features have new names, but also the keystrokes used to access many features have changed. The following table is a brief, but certainly not comprehensive, comparison of features and locations that have changed.

WordPerfect 5.1/5.2 for Windows (Old Feature Name)	WordPerfect 6.1 for Windows (New Feature Name)	New Menu or Key Location (If Changed)
	Grammatik	Alt+Shift+F1
Search	Find/Replace	F2 or Ctrl+F2
	Show ¶	Ctrl+Shift+F3
Print Preview	Page mode	(No longer needed)
Merge	Merge	Shift+F9
Sort	Sort	Alt+F9
	Repeat	Shift+F10
	Feature Bar Menu	Alt+Shift+F10
	Table: Data/Fill	Ctrl+Shift+F12
	Abbreviation Expand	Ctrl+A
Date Text	Date Text	Ctrl+D
	Case Toggle	Ctrl+K
	QuickMark Find	Ctrl+Q
	QuickMark Set	Ctrl+Shift+Q
	Template	Ctrl+T
	Send (WPMail)	File Menu
QuickFinder	QuickFinder	Open dialog
Printer Select	Select Printer	Print dialog
Preferences	Preferences	Edit Menu

WordPerfect 5.1/5.2 for Windows (Old Feature Name)	WordPerfect 6.1 for Windows (New Feature Name)	New Menu or Key Location (If Changed)
Retrieve File	Insert File	Insert Menu
Footnote/Endnote	Footnote/Endnote	Insert Menu
Spreadsheet Import	Spreadsheet/Database	Insert Menu
Layout	Format	Format Menu
Font	Font	Format Menu
Macro	Macro	Tools Menu
Figure	Image	Graphics Menu
Figure Editor	Draw	Graphics Menu
	Chart	Graphics Menu
	Text Art	Graphics Menu
Tables	Table	Table Menu
	Table Formulas	Table Menu
	Coaches	Help Menu
	Upgrade Advisor	Help Menu

Summary

Whether you come to WordPerfect 6.1 for Windows from another word processing program, WordPerfect for DOS, or an earlier version of WordPerfect for Windows, many new and powerful features await you. Take time early to familiarize yourself with these features. As you do, your skill level will increase and you will find that WordPerfect makes your work much easier.

Appendix C

Index of Common Problems

Writing and Editing	
If you have this problem...	**You'll find help here...**
Alt key does not activate button on the Feature Bar.	p. 33
Bullet automatically added every time Enter key is pressed.	p. 498
Buttons not added to the Power Bar.	p. 464
Help window disappears when writing in WordPerfect.	p. 54
Insertion point returns to original spot when scrolling.	p. 33
Mouse buttons difficult to use for left-handed users.	p. 107
Sorting does not always work on tabular list.	p. 665
Sorting order is incorrect with multi-word names.	p. 665
Typographical ("curly") smart quotes do not appear when the quote key is pressed.	p. 690

Footnotes and Endnotes

If you have this problem...	You'll find help here...
Endnote appears at insertion point rather than at end of document.	p. 874
Endnote reference number remains in text after deleting endnote.	p. 874
Footnote numbering restarts at *1* on new page.	p. 870
Footnote reference number remains in text after deleting footnote.	p. 871
Separator line between text and footnote cannot be edited by clicking on it.	p. 870

Tables

If you have this problem...	You'll find help here...
Cell format is not updated after changing the cell format.	p. 551
Contents of cells move to other cells when selecting text inside table.	p. 535
Custom line overlaps the text of a cell.	p. 1038
Decimal portion of dollar amount wraps to next line in cell.	p. 1064-1065
Error message appears when opening spreadsheet file.	p. 1030
Graphic image not positioned properly in table cell.	p. 558
Lines do not appear in the table.	p. 558
QuickMenu appears only briefly when clicking the right mouse button.	p. 1029
Results of calculation not correct.	p. 1064
Table column appears left-aligned after changing to decimal-aligned.	p. 551
Table too large/too small when defining table with the Power Bar.	p. 535
Text not legible after changing fill for a row of cells.	p. 1039

Outlines	
If you have this problem...	**You'll find help here...**
Changing bullet styles in an outline changes all outline levels.	p. 514
One or more levels in the outline not shown.	p. 514
Outline numbers and symbols don't appear on the left side of the document window.	p. 514
Paragraph number level cannot be specified in the Bullets & Numbers dialog box.	p. 498

Graphics and Equations	
If you have this problem...	**You'll find help here...**
Bold attribute does not appear when pressing Ctrl+B in Equation Editor.	p. 849-850
Equation font doesn't match document font.	p. 849-850
Graphic image not positioned properly in table cell.	p. 558
Graphic not selected when clicking on it with the mouse.	p. 285
Graphics do not appear when document is printed.	p. 806
Graphics line not deleted by pressing Delete or Backspace.	p. 275
Half space does not appear when using the Equation Editor.	p. 829
Inline Equations command not shown in the Graphics menu.	p. 829
Lines border style places lines between all columns.	p. 483
Out of memory or application error occurs when running WP Draw.	p. 746
Paragraph border does not appear when the paragraph border format is turned off.	p. 275
Paragraph fill pattern covers printed text.	p. 275
Shadow does not appear behind TextArt graphic.	p. 771

If you have this problem...	You'll find help here...
Spaces in equation definition do not appear in the document.	p. 829
Text of function name appears rather than the function symbol in Equation Editor.	p. 849
WP Draw does not start, or takes a long time to start.	p. 572

Templates

If you have this problem...	You'll find help here...
One or more Letter Expert letters that come with WordPerfect can't be found.	p. 414
One or more templates that come with WordPerfect can't be found.	p. 398
Templates appear together in the New Document dialog box instead of in groups.	p. 398
Templates don't appear when choosing the File, New command.	p. 398
Text does not appear when inserting a Letter Expert letter.	p. 414
Two macros cannot be associated with the same template trigger.	p. 414
WordPerfect inserts someone else's personal information when automatically filling out template.	p. 398

Document References and Master Documents

If you have this problem...	You'll find help here...
"?" appears when generating document with cross-references.	p. 913
All headings in table of contents are the same level.	p. 892
Error message `No def codes` appears when generating index.	p. 913

(continues)

If you have this problem...	You'll find help here...
Error occurs when playing macros created with WordPerfect 6.0 for Windows.	p. 1019
Error message `Bookmark not found` appears when clicking a Hypertext link.	p. 1082
Error message `Macro not found` appears when clicking a Hypertext link.	p. 1082
Macro doesn't record exiting WordPerfect.	p. 441
Macro doesn't record switching to another Windows program.	p. 441
Nothing happens when clicking on a Hypertext link.	p. 1081
One or more macros that come with WordPerfect cannot be found.	p. 434
Previously working macro now ending with an error message.	p. 441
Recorded macro cannot be found on disk.	p. 433
Saving macro file stopped by syntax errors.	p. 995
Spacing and order of addresses not correct in merged mailing label.	p. 654
Text doesn't appear in document as the macro types it.	p. 1020

File Management

If you have this problem...	You'll find help here...
File accidentally deleted.	p. 961
File accidentally saved under the wrong name.	p. 78
File cannot be found after changing its attributes.	p. 961
File cannot be found after moving or renaming it.	p. 961
File viewer shows `No Viewer available`.	p. 88
Files increase in size after inserting sound clips.	p. 1086
Only one file at a time can be selected in file list.	p. 961

(continues)

File Management Continued	
If you have this problem...	**You'll find help here...**
QuickFinder search fails to locate files.	p. 977
Results of wrong search query displayed when selecting Last Search Results option.	p. 977

Printing	
If you have this problem...	**You'll find help here...**
Choosing the Print command has no effect.	p. 295
Document prints with the wrong letters and fonts.	p. 295
Documents won't print after forgetting to turn on printer.	p. 72
Graphics do not appear when document is printed.	p. 806
Graphics look inferior when printing document.	p. 303
Printer displays an error message when printing envelopes.	p. 303
Printing doesn't resume after a printing error.	p. 72

Index

Symbols

A

D

E

F

G

H

I

J

K

L

M

Q

T

U

X–Y–Z